TAXATION OF ESTATES, GIFTS AND TRUSTS
Twenty-Sixth Edition

■ ■ ■

Vada Waters Lindsey
Professor of Law
Marquette University Law School

Regis W. Campfield
Late Professor Emeritus of Law and Marilyn Jeanne Johnson
Distinguished Law Faculty Fellow Emeritus,
Southern Methodist University

Martin B. Dickinson
Late Robert A. Schroeder Distinguished Professor Emeritus of Law,
University of Kansas

William J. Turnier
Willie Person Mangum Professor of Law Emeritus,
University of North Carolina

AMERICAN CASEBOOK SERIES®

WEST
ACADEMIC
PUBLISHING

American Casebook Series is a trademark registered in the U.S. Patent and Trademark Office.

COPYRIGHT a 1997 WEST PUBLISHING CO.
© West, at Thomson business, 1999, 2002, 2006
© 2012 Thomson Reuters
© 2020 LEG, Inc. d/b/a West Academic
© 2023 LEG, Inc. d/b/a West Academic
      860 Blue Gentian Road, Suite 350
      Eagan, MN 55121
      1-877-888-1330

West, West Academic Publishing, and West Academic are trademarks of West Publishing Corporation, used under license.

Printed in the United States of America

ISBN: 978-1-68561-231-3

This edition is dedicated to my parents Joe L. Waters and the late Margaret M. Waters and my aunt, Mildred Robinson. Thank you for the inspiration.

V.W.L.

PREFACE

This is the preface that was written by Professors Campfield, Dickinson, and Turnier in the 24th edition of this casebook:

This volume has its roots in the Study of Federal Tax Law series first published under the leadership of Professors Willard Pedrick and Vance Kirby almost thirty years ago. Publication of annual new editions then assured that it was the most up to date set of teaching materials available. In 1997 the West Group took over publication of the series with a commitment that users would always be provided with up to date materials. This is the fifth edition to be published by West.

This volume provides the materials essential for a basic course in federal estate and gift taxation. It also provides the materials required for the study of the closely related topic of the income taxation of trusts and estates. The materials begin with the taxation of lifetime gifts, proceed on to the principles of valuation for gift and estate tax purposes and move on to cover the estate tax and the generation skipping transfer tax. Finally the materials explore the principles involved in the income taxation of estates and trusts as well as related matters such as the taxation of income in respect of a decedent.

We recognize that teachers vary widely in the sequence of coverage of the topics in this volume. Therefore, each major portion of the text has been written so as to stand alone, and it is entirely feasible to begin with income taxation of estates and trusts, then move to the estate tax, or adopt some other order. In fact, we vary in our own coverage of the material.

Consistent with our practice in former editions we have included a significant number of problems to assist students in checking their understanding of materials covered in each of the chapters. We have also included materials that employ a planning perspective so that students attain some degree of understanding of how estate planners deal with the issues as they cope with their clients' estate planning goals.

We have continued most previous editing practices. Most footnotes are omitted from edited materials without indication. Those that appear bear their original numbers. Asterisks have been used to show major deletions. Minor deletions, such as dropping "of the Code" following a reference to a section of the Internal Revenue Code, have been made without indication.

Where multiple authorities within a sentence are given in support of a statement or series of statements, we have chosen not to indicate each deleted authority and have indicated the presence of such deletions with only one set of asterisks within or at the end of a sentence. Back to back deletions from different paragraphs are shown with only one set of asterisks, and deletions of dissenting or concurring opinions are not always indicated. Editorial additions to opinions are placed within brackets. With the exception of these minor editorial liberties, the edited materials are as close as possible to the officially reported versions. For example, we have italicized no materials which were not italicized in the original, and have left parenthetical comments in the form chosen by the authors of the original materials.

We have continued to use paragraph numbers to separate materials in the book. We believe that this serves several purposes. First, it facilitates the preparation of a professor's assignment without including materials that he or she would prefer neither to assign nor to discuss. Second, it facilitates cross references. Finally, because we intend to continue the practice of publishing updated supplements and editions whenever developments warrant, the use of paragraph numbers facilitates integration of new materials.

Over the years we have benefited from the assistance of many fine editors, research assistants, secretaries and other support staff. In completing this edition we were fortunate to have the assistance of a number of extremely able individuals. Roxanne Birkel of West provided cheerful and able editorial assistance. Lori Farmer and Michele Rutledge of the University of Kansas and Debbie Edge of the University of North Carolina all provided exceptional word processing assistance in the preparation of this manuscript. Jennie Chacon, Drew Cummings, Adam Dees, Hilary Meckel and Meghan Walsh provided Professor Dickinson with important research assistance. Tara Smith, Seth Glazer and Elliot Franklin provided valued research and editorial assistance to Professor Turnier. Gregory Ivy, Associate Director of the Southern Methodist University Law Library provided Professor Campfield with important research and technical support. Professor Campfield also acknowledges the technical and administrative support of Carolyn Yates of Southern Methodist University.

Although this volume represents a true collaborative effort, each of us assumed primary editorial responsibility for various individual chapters. Professor Campfield assumed primary responsibility for chapters 22, 27, 30, 31 and 32. Professor Dickinson assumed primary responsibility for chapters 2 through 14, 21, 25, 28 and 29, and Professor Turnier assumed primary responsibility for chapters 1, 15 through 20, 23, 24 and 26. This and prior editions have benefited from the comments of users, both teachers and students, and we invite the reactions of those who use these materials.

REGIS W. CAMPFIELD
MARTIN B. DICKINSON
WILLIAM J. TURNIER

October 2011

The 25th edition of this casebook is a long-awaited update to the 24th edition which was published in 2011. Many important changes have transpired since that time. Two changes, unrelated directly to estate taxation, were the deaths of Professor Emeritus Regis W. Campfield in October 2017 and Professor Emeritus Martin B. Dickinson in January 2020. In addition, my other co-author, William J. Turnier, is now Professor of Law Emeritus. Their contributions to legal academia and those of us who teach estate taxation will be greatly missed, and their voices will forever remain a big part of this casebook.

The other changes relate more directly to estate and gift taxation. Since the 24th edition was published in 2011, the Supreme Court determined that the Defense of Marriage Act was unconstitutional. As a result, same-sex marriages are now recognized for purposes of federal taxation, including estate and gift taxation. During 2013, Congress enacted the American Taxpayer Relief Act of 2012 which increased the basic exclusion amount and generation-skipping transfer tax rates to $5 million adjusted for inflation, made portability of the basic exclusion amount permanent, and increased the tax rates for the estate, gift, and generation-skipping transfer taxes to a flat 40%. The Tax Cuts and Jobs Act of 2017 made another significant change to estate and gift taxation when it temporarily doubled the basic exclusion amount and the generation-skipping transfer tax exemption to $10 million from 2018–2025. These changes are reflected in this edition. In addition, numerous cases, statutory provisions, regulations and IRS ruling have been added to the book. Finally, the cost of living increases for 2020, including the basic exclusion amount, have been added to this edition. The examples and problems in this edition incorporate these increases.

I could not have completed the work on this edition without the tremendous contributions of my three talented and dedicated research assistants, Brett Erdmann, Andrew Martzahl, and Emily Selner. While these three students provided research assistance on this edition, the names noted above of the numerous other editors, research assistants, secretaries and other support staff noted above who made contributions on prior editions will continue to be recognized in future editions.

VADA WATERS LINDSEY

March, 2020

A lot of things have occurred since the publication of the 25th edition of this casebook. The COVID-19 pandemic impacted all aspects of our lives. Sadly, many lives were lost, and businesses shuttered. My estate planning workshop moved to a virtual platform midway through the semester. Estate planners were busy writing wills and advance healthcare directives. Congress enacted the Coronavirus Aid, Relief, and Economic Security Act (CARES Act) to provide economic assistance to individuals and businesses affected by the pandemic. Under the CARES Act, nonitemizers were able to claim charitable deductions up to $300 during 2020 and 2021 to encourage charitable giving.

Another significant change was that the annual exclusion under section 2503(b) increased twice since 2020. It increased to $16,000 in 2022 after it had been $15,000 for many years, and a mere year later it increased to $17,000. There was also a substantial increase in the basic exclusion amount from $11,580,000 for 2020 to $12,920,000 for 2023. The 26th edition of this casebook discusses these changes and many more.

Finally, I'd like to thank Alana Sawall for her research assistance on this edition.

VADA WATERS LINDSEY

June, 2023

SUMMARY OF CONTENTS

PART 1. INTRODUCTION TO FEDERAL TRANSFER TAX SYSTEM

PART 2. GIFT TAX (CHAPTER 12 OF THE INTERNAL REVENUE CODE)

PART 3. VALUATION

PART 4. ESTATE TAX (CHAPTER 11 OF THE INTERNAL REVENUE CODE)

TABLE OF CONTENTS

PART 1. INTRODUCTION TO FEDERAL TRANSFER TAX SYSTEM

PART 2. GIFT TAX (CHAPTER 12 OF THE INTERNAL REVENUE CODE)

PART 4. ESTATE TAX (CHAPTER 11 OF THE INTERNAL REVENUE CODE)

PART 5. GENERATION-SKIPPING TAX (CHAPTER 13 OF THE INTERNAL REVENUE CODE)

PART 6. TRUST AND ESTATE INCOME AND INCOME FROM DECEDENTS (SUBCHAPTER J OF THE INTERNAL REVENUE CODE)

TABLE OF CASES

The principal cases are in bold type.

TABLE OF STATUTES

TABLE OF TREASURY REGULATIONS

TABLE OF TECHNICAL ADVICE MEMORANDA

TABLE OF PRIVATE LETTER RULINGS

TABLE OF REVENUE RULINGS

TABLE OF REVENUE PROCEDURES

———

TABLE OF INTERNAL REVENUE SERVICE NOTICES

TAXATION OF ESTATES, GIFTS AND TRUSTS

Twenty-Sixth Edition

PART 1

INTRODUCTION TO FEDERAL TRANSFER TAX SYSTEM

■ ■ ■

CHAPTER 1

ORIENTATION

■ ■ ■

A. CONSTITUTIONAL ISSUES

1. NOT A DIRECT TAX

The transfer of wealth at death has long been a favorite taxable event. Such a levy prevailed in ancient Rome. In the United States a federal stamp tax on legacies and shares in intestate estates was first adopted in 1797 although it was repealed in 1802. The Civil War federal inheritance tax was repealed in 1870. It is notable that the federal income tax of 1894, which provided that property acquired by gift or inheritance should be taxed as income, was held unconstitutional in Pollock v. Farmers' Loan and Trust Co.[1] A federal graduated inheritance tax adopted in 1898 was repealed in 1902, but its validity was sustained in Knowlton v. Moore.[2] In *Knowlton*, the Supreme Court held that an inheritance tax is an excise imposed on the act of passing property at death, and not a direct tax. Therefore, an inheritance tax is not subject to the requirements of Sections 2 and 9 of Article I that direct taxes be apportioned according to population.

2. THE MODERN ESTATE AND GIFT TAXES

The modern federal estate tax, in its earliest form, dates back to 1916, and that revenue measure was sustained against constitutional challenge in New York Trust Co. v. Eisner,[3] in which Justice Holmes, relying on the earlier decision in *Knowlton*, observed that "a page of history is worth a volume of logic."[4] As will be seen from some of the older cases in this course book, other constitutional attacks were launched against the federal estate tax with absolutely no success.

Congress, concerned about the erosion of the estate tax base presented by inter vivos gifts, adopted the first gift tax in 1924. Only two years later, a different Congress repealed the nation's first gift tax. Several taxpayers who were unfortunate enough to have had their gifts taxed in this two-year period challenged the constitutionality of the 1924 gift tax. In Bromley v.

---

[1] 157 U.S. 429 (1895).
[2] 178 U.S. 41 (1900).
[3] 256 U.S. 345 (1921).
[4] Id. at 349.

3

McCaughn,[5] the Supreme Court upheld the constitutionality of a gift tax. Thus, when Congress enacted the present gift tax in 1932, it did so confident of its constitutionality.

B. LEGISLATIVE HISTORY

1. FEDERAL ESTATE AND GIFT TAXATION BEFORE 1976

Prior to the Tax Reform Act of 1976, the trend of the estate and gift tax rates had been upward, so much so that in 1970 Professor Willard Pedrick used the term "fierce" to describe the estate tax rate schedule.[6] At the time, the estate tax rates went up to a maximum of 77 percent for taxable estates over $10 million, and the exemption from estate taxes was only $60,000. The gift tax rates were 75 percent of the estate tax rates, each donor was entitled to a $30,000 lifetime gift tax exemption, and a donor could give $3,000 to each person in the world each year without gift tax cost and without using any of his or her $30,000 gift tax lifetime exemption.

However, Congress, after embracing rates which as Professor Pedrick indicated would "strike terror into the heart of the clients, conveniently provided a number of toll free roads open to those with accredited guides."[7] The combination of dramatically progressive rates with a less than comprehensive gift and estate tax base and a number of generous deductions typically resulted in the imposition of transfer tax burdens which were at marked variance with those "fierce" statutory marginal rates.

In a 1977 law review article, Professor George Cooper demonstrated how, with the assistance of competent counsel, those stated rates could be dramatically at variance with actual effective rates on gratuitous transfers.[8] Cooper noted that with respect to the DuPont fortune, "[t]he combined effective tax rate will be only 5%."[9] In the article, Professor Cooper catalogued many of the devices then in use to minimize the burden of the estate tax.[10]

In the hearings on the Tax Reform Act of 1976, Professor James Casner before the House Ways and Means Committee exclaimed: "In fact we haven't got an estate tax, what we have, you pay an estate tax if you

---

[5]   280 U.S. 124 (1929).

[6]   Pedrick, Extra Sensory Perception and Estate Planning—Change and the Estate Planner's Art, 4th INST. EST. PLAN. ¶ 203,300 (1970).

[7]   Id.

[8]   See George Cooper, *A Voluntary Tax? New Perspectives on Estate Tax Avoidance,"* 77 COLUM. L. REV. 161 (1977).

[9]   Id. at 162.

[10]   Id. at 170.

want to; if you don't want to, you don't have to." In a similar vein, economist Professor Lester Thurow observed that:

> In practice, loopholes have become so large that inheritance taxes have virtually ceased to exist: collections amount to an annual wealth tax of less than 0.2 percent. For all practical purposes, gift and inheritance taxes do not exist in the United States. They do not stop wealth from being transferred from generation to generation.[11]

Professor Thurow then asked, "Are effective inheritance taxes zero because a democratic society decides they should be zero? Or are zero inheritance taxes merely the best example of the political power that wealth can buy?"[12]

The movement for reform was almost glacially slow. In 1942, Erwin Griswold, then Professor of Law at the Harvard Law School, published an article in the Harvard Law Review calling for correlation of the federal estate and gift taxes.[13] In 1947, an Advisory Committee to the Treasury Department called for integration of the gift and estate taxes. A project of the American Law Institute developed proposals for structural reform of the federal estate and gift taxes in 1969—after more than five years of intensive study. That same year the Federal Treasury published its recommended revision of the two levies—with no action then forthcoming.

2. RESTRUCTURING BEGINNING IN 1976

a. The 1976 Changes

In 1976, proposals to revise the federal estate and gift levies were incorporated into the Tax Reform Act of 1976. The structural changes made by this legislation were truly sweeping. The prime structural change was the effective consolidation of the estate tax and the gift tax into one. Though the two names continue, and nominally there is both an estate tax and a gift tax, in substance there is now one levy on the transfer of capital by gift or by inheritance. The British accomplished much the same reform in 1975. Their system is accurately labeled as the "Capital Transfer Tax." That, too, in principle, is the United States system—in all but name. The importance of recognizing that the United States has one integrated, unitized levy on the transfer of capital by gift and inheritance cannot be overemphasized.

The prime structural changes effected by the Tax Reform Act of 1976, applicable generally to events transpiring after January 1, 1977, were: (1) establishment of one unitary tax table with cumulation of lifetime and

---

[11] Lester Thurow, Generating Inequality 197 (1975).

[12] Id. at 198.

[13] See Erwin N. Griswold, *A Plan for the Coordination of the Income, Estate, and Gift Tax Provisions with Respect to Trusts and Other Transfers*, 56 HARV. L. REV. 337 (1942).

death transfers for transfer tax computation; (2) establishment of one unitary credit (which in a phasing-in process was designed to shelter by 1981 a total of $175,625 from the estate and gift taxes combined) in lieu of the separate exemptions of $30,000 and $60,000, respectively, for the old gift and estate taxes; and (3) provision of a new chapter taxing "terminations" or "distributions" from "generation-skipping trusts."

The explanatory report on the Tax Reform Act of 1976, Estate and Gift Tax Provisions, prepared by the Staff of the Joint Committee on Taxation provides the following explanation of the reasons for the changes:

> Two features of prior law which give rise to considerable variations in estate and gift tax burdens for people who transfer the same amount of wealth were the separate rate schedule and exemption provision for estates and gifts. There were several tax advantages to lifetime gifts. The gift tax rates were 75 percent of estate tax rates; and, unlike the estate tax, the amount of the gift tax itself was not included in the tax base. Also, someone who split his total transfers between gifts and bequests achieved the advantage of "rate splitting," since the first dollar of taxable bequests was taxed at the bottom estate tax rate even where there had been substantial lifetime gifts. These opportunities for reducing the overall burden by lifetime giving were inequitable, especially since many people are not wealthy enough to make lifetime gifts. The Act unified the estate and gift taxes—both the exemptions (which have been converted into a credit) and the rates—to deal with these inequities.
>
> Another cause of unequal treatment of taxpayers with the same amount of wealth transfers had been the ability to use "generation-skipping" trusts. When wealth is bequeathed from the parent to his child, then from the child to a grandchild and finally from the grandchild to a great-grandchild, the estate tax is imposed three times. However, if the parent places the wealth in a trust in which the child and then the grandchild has the right to the income from the trust, with the principal going to the great-grandchild, the parent will achieve virtually the same result and, in effect, skip two generations of estate tax. In these cases, the estate tax could be avoided for 100 years or more under prior law. Since such trust arrangements have been used largely by wealthier people, this failure to tax generation-skipping trusts has undermined the progressivity of the estate and gift taxes. The Act significantly limited estate tax avoidance through generation-skipping trusts by imposing a tax at the time of the death of the

child or grandchild. . . [subject to a limited exemption available in specified circumstances].[14]

b.   Economic Recovery Tax Act of 1981 (ERTA)

President Ronald Reagan's discomfort with the federal estate and gift tax system, often expressed during the presidential campaign of 1980, bore fruit in the Economic Recovery Tax Act of 1981. The principal instruments for dramatic reduction in the ranks of prospective estate taxpayers were: (1) an increase in the unified credit, scheduled in a gradual phasing-in process, to reach a level of $192,800 in 1987 (the equivalent of an exemption then of $600,000); (2) an increase in the annual exclusion from $3,000 to $10,000; (3) an unlimited marital deduction so that property, without monetary limits, can pass from one spouse to the other without being subjected to any federal transfer tax at all; and (4) also as noted earlier, a reduction in the top rate from 70 percent to 50 percent by 1985. Subsequent legislation froze the top rate at 55 percent through 1992 and in 1993 the top rate was permanently set at 55 percent.

c.   Revenue Act of 1987 and Revenue Reconciliation Act of 1993

The Tax Reform Act of 1986, bringing about the Internal Revenue Code of 1986, did not affect major changes in federal estate and gift taxes. But the Revenue Act of 1987 did bring some changes: notably the continuation of the top rate of 55 percent through 1992 and a phaseout of the benefits of graduated rates and unified credit in estates over $10 million. The phaseout was accomplished by imposing a supplementary tax of 5 percent on estates valued between $10 million and $21,040,000. The Revenue Reconciliation Act of 1993 permanently reinstated the top rate of 55 percent but, otherwise, did little to affect estate and gift taxation.

d.   Taxpayer Relief Act of 1997

The Taxpayer Relief Act of 1997 made several significant changes. The amount excludible from estate and gift tax over one's lifetime by the unified credit was increased from $600,000 (which had prevailed since 1987) to $625,000 in 1998 with phased-in additional increases scheduled. The 1997 Act also provided an inflation adjustment mechanism for the $10,000 per donee per annum gift tax exclusion and for the $1,000,000 generation-skipping transfer tax exclusion.

Moreover, the Act also provided that the 5% supplementary tax no longer applied when the average aggregate tax rate equals 55%, thereby restoring to the super rich the benefit of the unified credit although still depriving them of the advantage of the progressive rate structure. The

---

[14] Joint Committee on Taxation, General Explanation of the Tax Reform Act of 1976, JCS–33–76, at 13 (1976).

result was that the 5% supplementary tax would no longer be imposed on estates in excess of $17,184,000.

3. THE DEATH AND RESURRECTION OF THE ESTATE TAX

Central to former President George W. Bush's 2000 presidential campaign was the promise of substantial tax cuts and central to his tax cut program was elimination of the gift tax and the estate tax. Consequently, the Economic Growth and Tax Relief Reconciliation Act of 2001 provided for repeal of the estate tax and the generation skipping transfer tax after December 31, 2009. The Act also contained a number of other significant changes: (1) the 5 percent supplementary tax that applied to estates between $10 million and $17,184,000 was repealed and the maximum marginal rates of the estate, gift and generation skipping taxes were to be reduced to 50 percent and phased down over the remaining life of the estate tax; (2) the lifetime exclusions for the estate and generation skipping transfer taxes were raised to $1,000,000 and over those taxes remaining lives were to be phased up reaching $3,500,000 by 2009; and (3) credit for state death taxes against federal estate tax liability was to be phased out by 2005 to be replaced by a deduction for such taxes.

Awareness that the gift tax performed a critical role in backstopping the income tax against massive revenue losses led to a decision that its retention was necessary even after the estate tax saw its last days. Consequently, the Act retained the gift tax and provided for no increase in its lifetime exclusion amount beyond $1,000,000.

As the price for repeal of the estate tax, under the 2001 Act property passing at death during 2010 would not be entitled to a stepped-up basis. Instead, such property would have a basis in the hands of the estate's heirs equal to the lesser of its basis in the hands of the decedent or its date of death fair market value. However, the executor was allowed to increase (but not above fair market) basis of appreciated property passing to anyone other than a surviving spouse by up to $1,300,000 plus any unused capital loss carry forward and the amount of all reductions in basis effected in the case of property where the date of death value of such property was less than its adjusted basis in decedent's hands. The basis of property passing to a surviving spouse could have been increased by an additional $3,000,000.

Because the 2001 legislation was not made permanent, decedents dying after 2010 would be subject to the estate tax. Late in 2010, Congress was confronted with the reality that the sunset of the 2001 Act would also completely undo all the changes wrought by the Act. As a result, in mid-December a series of compromises were hastily arranged. Under this legislation, the exemption for the estate and gift taxes was unified again at the level of $5 million with a flat tax rate of 35% for any gratuitous transfers in excess of this amount. In addition, a married individual could make an election on his or her estate tax return to allow a surviving spouse to use an unused exemption amount for gratuitous transfers. This privilege of being able to pass on a deceased spouse's unused exemption amount to the surviving spouse is referred to as "portability." While the exemption for the generation-skipping transfer tax was also set at $5 million, any unused generation skipping transfer tax exemption was not transferable to a surviving spouse. Further, the 2010 legislation provided an opportunity for taxpayers to elect to file an estate tax return. If so elected, they were able to take advantage of the conventional stepped up basis rules for all assets held by the estate, have their estates subject to the 35% rate, and be subject to the $5 million unified exemption amount that was to prevail in 2011.

With the exception of the available elections for taxpayers who died during 2010, all of the other changes in the estate and gift taxes made by the 2001 and 2010 Acts were set to expire at the end of 2012. However, on January 2, 2013, former President Barack Obama signed the American Taxpayer Relief Act of 2012. That Act enacted a flat 40% rate for both the estate and gift taxes, set the basic exclusion amount at $5 million adjusted annually for inflation, and made the portability election permanent.

4. THE TAX CUTS AND JOBS ACT

Throughout his 2016 presidential campaign, former President Donald Trump reiterated his commitment to repeal the estate tax. While Congress did not pass legislation that completely repealed the estate tax, it did pass the Tax Cuts and Jobs Act of 2017[15] that reduced the number of individuals subject to the estate tax and gift tax. Under the Act, for testamentary transfers and inter vivos gifts made after December 31, 2017, the basic exclusion amount was doubled to $10,000,000 and indexed for inflation. However, this increase is only applicable through December 31, 2025, when it will sunset unless Congress enacts additional legislation. The basic exclusion amount for 2023 is $12,920,000. If the sunset is not repealed, the basic exclusion amount will revert to $5,000,000 (indexed for inflation) in 2026.

Because of the Act's sunset after December 31, 2025, there was the possibility that a decedent dying after 2025 who made taxable gifts between January 1, 2018 and December 31, 2025 totaling, for example, $8,000,000, would be liable for estate taxes if the basic exclusion amount reverted to $5,000,000 at the time of the decedent's death. Congress enacted I.R.C. § 2001(g)(2) to allow the Treasury Department to prescribe regulations to prevent a "clawback" of the tax benefits for the increase of the basic exclusion amount for decedents who died after December 31, 2025

---

[15] Pub. Law No. 115–97, 115th Cong., 1st Sess. (2017).

but who made taxable gifts between January 1, 2018 and December 31, 2025. Under the final regulations issued by the Treasury Department, a decedent is entitled to use the higher of the basic exclusion amount that was applicable for gifts made during 2018 through 2025 or the basic exclusion amount applicable on the date of the decedent's death after 2025. See Treas. Reg. § 20.2010–1.

C. FEDERAL TAXES ON TRANSFERS OF WEALTH

1. ESTATE TAX (SECTIONS 2001–2058)

The personal representative must file an estate tax return within nine months after death for a decedent whose estate tax base exceeds "the basic exclusion amount" (which is $12,920,000 in 2023). See I.R.C. §§ 6018(a) and 6075(a). The estate tax base consists of several elements, principally the decedent's gross estate and the taxable gifts made by the decedent after 1976. See I.R.C. § 6018(a)(3). Property is included (1) generally at its fair market value on the date of death as to property included in the gross estate and (2) at its fair market value as of the date of the gift in the case of taxable gifts made after 1976. See I.R.C. §§ 2031(a) & 2512(a).

The estate tax is calculated after deducting the decedent's debts and mortgages, expenses of administering the decedent's estate, the decedent's funeral expenses, losses incurred during administration, gifts to the decedent's spouse (if made in a qualifying way), and gifts to charities and certain interests in closely held family businesses.

The estate tax was originally a progressive tax, but currently a flat rate of 40% is applied to all taxed property.

2. GIFT TAX (SECTIONS 2501–2524)

Gift tax returns must be filed annually. See I.R.C. § 6075(b)(1). A gift tax return must be filed whenever total gifts to the same donee in the same year exceed the annual exclusion of $10,000 (adjusted for inflation with the figure adjusted to $17,000 as of 2023). See I.R.C. § 6019(1). A donor could thus give each person in Ohio, for example, $17,000 each year without filing a gift tax return, paying any gift tax, or using any portion of the applicable exclusion amount. While a gift tax return is required whenever gifts to a single donee in the same year exceed the annual exclusion, the donor now will not owe a gift tax until the donor's lifetime total of gifts (in excess of the annual exclusion) exceeds $12,920,000 plus any unused exemption amount available from a deceased spouse. A donor is not required to file gift tax returns for certain gifts to the donor's spouse that qualify for the marital deduction and qualifying gifts to charitable organizations. See I.R.C. § 6019(2) & (3).

3. OTHER FEATURES OF THE TAXES

a. Relationship of Estate and Gift Taxes

Although the estate and gift taxes are separate and distinct taxes, they employ the same rate schedule to determine tax liability and the same $12,920,000 basic exclusion amount.

The estate and gift taxes are imposed upon the exercise of the privilege of gratuitously transferring property. See I.R.C. §§ 2001 and 2501. In that sense, both taxes are classified as excise taxes. However, not only must there be a gratuitous transfer of property for the estate or gift tax to apply, but the tax does not apply until the gift is "complete." While "transfer" is the operative term and appears in the portion of the statute imposing the tax, the term "complete" was created under common law.

Example: Bill made a gift of Blackacre, worth $1,000,000, to his son Andrew reserving the right to revoke the gift at any time. Because Bill can revoke the gift at any time, the transfer is not complete for gift tax purposes and has no gift tax consequences.

Sometimes the estate tax and gift tax appear to overlap and, in some of those cases, the overlap is reconciled to avoid double taxation by crediting the gift tax paid against the estate tax liability. See I.R.C. § 2013.

Example: Maria deeded a farm to her nephew, Pedro, expressly reserving to herself "the right to all of the income from the farm during my life and the right to occupy" the farm for life. For gift tax purposes, Maria has made a transfer to Pedro of a future interest, namely the right to possession and enjoyment of the farm after Maria dies. This transfer is complete for gift tax purposes at the time Maria delivered the deed to Pedro. The gift to Pedro will be valued actuarially, taking into account the prevailing interest rate and Maria's age at the time of the gift. For example, if Maria made the gift on June 4, 2004 and that the fair market value of the farm was $1M. Assume also that the gift tax on the actuarial value of Pedro's future interest was fully offset by the gift tax.

While Pedro has neither the possession nor the enjoyment of the farm during Maria's life, his interest in the farm is a valuable property right—so valuable in fact that, if Pedro predeceases Maria, Pedro's future interest in the farm will be subject to estate tax at his death (and passes under his will or under the intestate laws if Pedro dies intestate).

At Maria's death—assuming she died in 2023 when the farm had a value of $14,000,000—the farm will also be included in Maria's estate for estate tax purposes at its then fair market value. See I.R.C. § 2036(a)(1). The reason for this inclusion is that: (1) Maria retained for her life the use and enjoyment of the farm; and (2) the estate tax would be eviscerated if the estate tax could be avoided by lifetime transfers such as the one Maria has made. Including the farm in Maria's estate would mean an estate tax liability of $5,545,800 (determined by reference to the tax rate table under section 2001) reduced by the applicable credit amount of $5,113,800 for 2023 under section 2010. This means that Maria's estate would pay $432,000 in estate taxes. Had any gift taxes been paid by Maria on the gift to Pedro of the future interest, she would have received a credit against her estate tax liability for that payment.

b. Unified Credit (Sections 2010 and 2505)

From 1987 through 1997, each taxpayer was provided with a so called "unified credit" of $192,800 which could be used first against any gift tax otherwise due and to the extent not so used would be available for use against the taxpayer's estate tax liability. This $192,800 translated into an aggregate $600,000 exclusion that was available for use against the gift tax and, to the extent not so used, against the estate tax.

As noted above, in 1997 Congress increased the amount excludible under the unified credit. In 2001, it revisited the issue and further increased the amount excludible from tax. In the case of the gift tax for gifts made in years between 2002 and 2011 the unified credit was frozen at $345,800, which was the equivalent of a $1,000,000 exclusion. In the case of the estate tax, the 2001 Act provided that the exclusion and its unified credit equivalent was to be increased for individuals dying during a given year accordingly:

Year	Exclusion	Unified Credit
2002–2003	$1,000,000	$ 345,800
2004–2005	$1,500,000	$ 555,800
2006–2008	$2,000,000	$ 780,800
2009	$3,500,000	$1,455,800
2010–2011	$5,000,000	$1,730,800

For tax years after 2011, the unified credit (now called the applicable credit amount) and applicable exclusion amount for the both the estate and gift taxes for each year were as follows:

Year	Exclusion	Unified Credit
2012	$ 5,120,000	$1,772,800
2013	$ 5,250,000	$2,045,800

2014	$ 5,340,000	$2,081,800
2015	$ 5,430,000	$2,117,800
2016	$ 5,450,000	$2,125,800
2017	$ 5,490,000	$2,141,800
2018	$11,180,000	$4,417,800
2019	$11,400,000	$4,505,800
2020	$11,580,000	$4,577,800
2021	$11,700,000	$4,625,800
2022	$12,060,000	$4,769,800
2023	$12,920,000	$5,113,800

It must be kept in mind that the $12,920,000 applicable exclusion amount applies first to the gift tax and then, to the extent the excluded amount does not exceed $12,920,000, to the estate tax. For example, assume, for simplicity, that the annual exclusion is not available, and that Lindsay made no gifts other than a taxable gift of $1,000,000 in 2017 and died in 2023 with an estate of $16,920,000. In 2017, Lindsay's entire $1,000,000 gift would have been offset by the unified credit. In 2023, her estate would be left with the equivalent of a $11,920,000 basic exclusion amount which could shelter from estate taxation all but $5,000,000 of her $16,920,000 estate. The mechanics of computing the estate and gift taxes are described in Chapters 2 and 15.

c. Annual Exclusion (Section 2503(b))

The gift tax—but not the estate tax—allows a $10,000 annual exclusion that is adjusted for inflation. For 2022, Congress increased the annual exclusion to $16,000. Surprisingly, Congress Increased the annual exclusion to $17,000 the following year (for gifts made beginning in 2023). That means that an individual can make a gift of the annual exclusion amount each year to every person in the country without gift tax consequences and without having to file a gift tax return.

d. Adjusted Taxable Gifts (Section 2001(b))

As part of the integration of the estate and gift taxes, gifts made after December 31, 1976, are included in the base used for determining the tax rate applicable to transfers made at death by an individual. These post-1976 gifts are referred to as adjusted taxable gifts and are distinguished from earlier gifts (which are not taken into account for estate tax computation purposes).

Example: Mario made a gift of $100,000 to his son, Jasper, in 1975 and another gift of $1,010,000 to Jasper in 1983. Mario died in

2023. He devised all his property to Jasper. At his death in 2023, Mario's estate was valued at $15,000,000, but the base used in computing his estate tax liability was grossed up to $16,000,000 by including the $1,000,000 of post-1976 gifts. (Note that the gift tax exclusion allowed $10,000 to escape classification as an adjusted taxable gift.) Using the rate tables given in section 2001, Mario's tax liability before the $5,113,800 unified credit allowable for 2023 is $6,345,800, and, after the credit is taken off, his estate tax liability is $1,232,000. Importantly, although Mario did not have to pay a gift tax in 1983 because his $1,010,000 transfer to Jasper was sheltered by the gift tax exclusion and the applicable credit amount, he was obligated to file a gift tax return.

D. GENERATION-SKIPPING TAX (SECTIONS 2601–2663)

The generation-skipping transfer tax (GST) is a flat-rate tax that generally applies to transfers by individuals or distributions from trusts that skip generations. Its purpose is to backstop the estate tax. Congress believed that it was appropriate to impose a wealth transfer tax each generation and where very wealthy families managed to avoid imposition of a transfer tax every generation by arranging for transfers that skipped generations, Congress decided to impose a special supplementary generation-skipping tax to compensate for the revenues which were thereby otherwise lost. In general, the tax is imposed at a rate equal to the maximum estate tax rate. Transferors who are subject to the GST are entitled to a lifetime exemption equal to the estate tax exclusion for the year in question.

Example: In 2023, Madeline transferred $5,920,000 to an irrevocable trust for the benefit of her grandson Alexander and his issue and allocated $5,920,000 of her then available $12,920,000 GST exemption to the trust. Because the amount placed in the trust is completely sheltered by the GST exemption allocated to the trust, distributions from the trust to anyone will be forever free of the GST. After making the transfer and allocating $5,920,000 of her GST exemption, Madeline will have $7,000,000 remaining of the GST exemption. Further, the GST is independent of federal estate and gift taxes, which means that Madeline may still have incurred gift tax liability when she placed $5,920,000 in the trust.

Example: In 2023, Austin transferred $17,225,000 to an irrevocable trust for the benefit of his daughter Betsy and his grandson Corey and allocated all his then available $12,920,000 GST exemption to the trust. The GST will apply to distributions from the trust to Corey (but not to distributions to Betsy). Because the amount of the GST exemption allocated to the trust was equal to three-quarters of the amount transferred to the trust ($12,920,000/$17,225,000) three-quarters of all distributions from the trust to Corey will effectively be forever exempt from the GST. Because the GST is independent of federal estate and gift taxes, Austin incurred gift tax liability when the $17,225,000 was placed in the trust.

E. BASIC COMPUTATIONAL MODEL

1. INTEGRATION OF ESTATE AND GIFT TAXES

The estate and gift tax computational scheme is quite complex, in part because the two separate taxes are to be integrated to limit each taxpayer to the equivalent of a coordinated single lifetime exemption. Additional complication results from the need to integrate the tax rules applicable to gifts made before 1977 with those made after 1976. In sum, the complication results from the fact that gifts made any time by a taxpayer are aggregated to determine the tax due on the most recent gift. However, in determining the tax due on property subject to the estate tax, only gifts made after 1976 are aggregated with the property from the taxpayer at death. These post-1976 gifts are referred to as "adjusted taxable gifts," a term that is important only for estate tax purposes.

2. THE TAX-EXCLUSIVE GIFT TAX AND THE TAX-INCLUSIVE ESTATE TAX

Although the same nominal rate applies under the gift tax as applies under the estate tax, there is an important difference in computing each of the taxes which results in a lower effective tax burden being imposed on gifts than on estates. The estate tax is computed on a tax-inclusive basis. In other words, the tax is imposed on all that one transfers at death, including the estate tax itself. The gift tax, on the other hand, is calculated on a tax-exclusive basis, which means that only the gift going to donees and not the gift tax paid with respect to it forms the base of the tax. This difference in the method of calculating the two taxes dates back to the first days of the gift tax. It means that in the right circumstances there may be significant tax advantages in making gifts. This critical difference between the two taxes will be dealt with in greater detail in Chapter 2.

3. DEDUCTION FOR STATE DEATH TAXES PAID (SECTION 2058)

In early 20th century America, death taxes had traditionally been a major source of revenue for the states. To reassure the states that the federal government did not intend to elbow them out of this important source of revenue, Congress in 1924 provided a statutory credit mechanism whereby a portion of the federal estate tax could be offset by state death taxes paid.

In 2001, Congress decided to break with tradition and provided that the amount that qualified for the credit had to be reduced by 25 percent each year commencing in 2002, resulting in complete repeal of the credit for taxpayers dying after December 31, 2004. Today, under section 2058, in determining their federal estate tax, decedents are allowed to deduct from their gross estate the amount of estate and inheritance taxes actually paid to a state or the District of Columbia.

F. STATE DEATH TAX SYSTEMS

Not to be ignored are the death tax systems that exist in the various states. The death tax systems in some of the states are patterned after the federal estate tax, while other states have another form of death tax commonly referred to as an inheritance tax. An inheritance tax differs from an estate tax in that the available exemption and the applicable tax rates are determined by the relationship of the decedent and the beneficiaries of the decedent's estate. That is, property passing to a surviving spouse or child will be subject to lower rates and enjoy a higher exemption than property passing from the decedent to a nonrelative. In the past, many states had what could be called a "soak up" or a "sponge" tax. These states had imposed a tax exactly equal to the maximum federal credit that had been available when computing the estate tax liability of the decedent for state death taxes paid by that decedent. Depending on the wording of state "sponge" or "soak up" tax legislation, repeal of the credit for state death taxes resulted in de facto repeal of state death taxes in many states that imposed only "soak up" or "sponge" taxes. Hence, some states no longer have an estate tax after repeal of the federal credit.[16] However, some of the states that imposed only a "soak up" or "sponge" tax have decoupled their estate tax scheme from the now repealed federal credit by providing that their estate tax is equal to the maximum amount allowed as a credit under federal law as it then prevailed on some date prior to the phaseout of the federal credit.[17]

In an era in which most states face significant budgetary problems, several states impose either an estate tax or an inheritance tax with exemptions far below those allowed by the federal estate tax. The District of Columbia and 11 states, Connecticut, Hawaii, Illinois, Maine,

---

[16] See, e.g., Ala. Code § 40–15–2 (2022); Cal. Rev. & Tax. Code § 13302 (2022); Fla. Stat. Ann. § 198.02 (2022); Mo. Rev. Stat. § 145.011 (2022); Wis. Stat. § 72.02 (2022).

[17] See, e.g., Mass. Gen. Laws ch. 65C, § 2A (2022) (computing its tax based on the credit in effect on December 31, 2000); R.I. Gen. Laws § 44–22–1.1(a)(4) (2022) (imposing a tax equal to the maximum credit in effect on January 1, 2001 reduced by a stated credit).

Massachusetts, Minnesota, New York, Oregon, Rhode Island, Vermont, and Washington, impose an estate tax only.[18] Most of these states have exemptions lower than the federal basic exclusion amount.[19] However, Connecticut's exemption equals the federal basic exclusion amount.[20] In addition, rather than imposing an estate tax, Iowa, Kentucky, Nebraska, New Jersey, and Pennsylvania impose an inheritance tax.[21] Maryland imposes both an estate tax and an inheritance tax with any amount of tax paid under the inheritance tax being available as a credit against the state estate tax.[22]

It is not uncommon for states to impose an estate tax with rates that are equal to the rates that were once used to determine the credit for state death taxes that were allowed against federal estate tax liability. These rates escalated upward to a maximum of 16%. The states that impose an estate tax are not barred from imposing a tax at a rate in excess of 16% and in fact Washington imposes a tax at a maximum rate of 20%. States that have decided to stick with their inheritance taxes impose taxes at rates that are determined based on the degree of kindred of the beneficiaries. The failure of all states to either reject imposing an estate tax or to embrace the federal exemption means that, in a number of states, estates with values far below the amount of the federal exemption may face significant tax liability under either a state inheritance tax or estate tax. This book is limited to dealing with three federal transfer taxes, the gift, estate, and generation-skipping transfer taxes as well as the income taxation of trusts and estates. Nonetheless, the transfer tax concepts which are dealt with in

[18] See Conn. Gen. Stat. § 12–391(g)(9) (2022) (imposing a flat 12% rate of tax for decedents dying after January 1, 2023); D.C. Code Ann. § 47–3702(a-1)(a) (2022) (providing a maximum estate tax rate of 16%); Haw. Rev. Stat. § 236E–8 (2022) (providing a progressive rate schedule with a top rate of 20% on taxable estates that exceed $10,000,000); 35 Ill. Comp. Stat. 405/3 (2022) (providing an exclusion amount of $4,000,000); Mass. Ann. Laws ch. 65C, § 2 (2022) (providing a progressive rate schedule with a top rate of 16% on taxable estates that exceed $4,000,000); Minn. Stat. § 291.03 (2022) (imposing a top progressive rate of 16% on taxable estates over $10,100,000); Me. Rev. Stat. Ann. 36 § 4103 (2022) (imposing a maximum rate of 12%); N.Y. Tax Law § 952 (2022) (providing a maximum estate tax rate of 16%); Or. Rev. Stat. § 118.010 (2022) (providing a progressive rate schedule with a top rate of 16% on taxable estates that exceed $9,500,000); R.I. Gen. Laws § 44–22–1.1(a)(4) (2022) (imposing a tax equal to the maximum credit in effect on January 1, 2001 reduced by a stated credit); Vt. Stat. Ann. tit.32, § 7442a(a) (2022) (providing a progressive rate schedule with a top rate of 16% on taxable estates that exceed $5,000,000); Wash. Rev. Code § 83.100.040(2)(a) (2022) (imposing a top rate of 20% on taxable estates that exceed $9,000,000).

[19] See, e.g., Me. Rev. Stat. Ann. 36 § 4102(5) (2022) (providing an exemption of $5,600,000 for decedents dying after December 31, 2017); N.Y. Tax Law § 952(c)(2)(A) (2022) (exempting $5,000,000 adjusted for inflation for decedents dying after December 31, 2019); Or. Rev. Stat. § 118.010(4) (2022) (exempting estates valued at less than $1,000,000); Vt. Stat. Ann. tit.32, § 7442a(b) (2022) (providing exemption for estates under $5,000,000).

[20] See Conn. Gen. Stat. § 12–391(g)(9).

[21] See Iowa Code Ann. § 450.10 (2022); Ky. Rev. Stat. Ann. § 140.070 (2022); Neb. Rev. Stat. 77–2001 (2022); N.J. Stat. Ann. § 54:34–1 (2022); Pa. Stat. Ann. tit.72, § 9116 (2022).

[22] See Md. Code Ann. Tax-Gen. §§ 7–202, 7–302, & 7-304 (2023). Maryland also allows for the portability of the deceased spouse unused exclusion amount. See Md. Code Ann. Tax-Gen. § 7–302(b)(3)(i)(6) (2020).

the chapters that follow are typically also found in state estate and inheritance taxes. In states which still impose an estate or an inheritance tax, mastery of those concepts may prove helpful even in the case of many smaller estates that are exempt from taxation under the $12,920,000 exclusion of the federal estate tax.

It is important to note that just because the decedent is domiciled in a particular jurisdiction does not mean that the decedent will not owe state estate taxes in other jurisdictions. If the decedent owned assets that acquired a tax situs in another state, he can also be subject to taxation in such other state. For example, an individual who is domiciled in Florida and who owns real estate in New York will likely find himself subject to estate taxes in New York despite the individual not having set foot in that state for a dozen years. The Supreme Court has held that assets may acquire a situs in a state if, in the case of tangible assets, the assets are located in the state. In the case of intangible assets, they are normally deemed to have acquired a situs in the state of the decedent's domicile. The Supreme Court, however, has held that a state may tax intangible assets if a basic legal protective relationship existed with respect to the assets in question. Such a relationship can be found in the case of stock based on the fact that a state served as the state of incorporation, although actual use of this as a basis for taxation is rare. Similarly, a state may assert jurisdiction to impose a death tax on trust assets if a trustee is domiciled in a jurisdiction and a state may impose a death tax on certain intangible assets such as receivables which have business situs in a jurisdiction in which a business was operated.[23]

Many states avoid this problem of ancillary tax jurisdiction by providing that they will not assert jurisdiction with respect to such property if the state of domicile accords reciprocal treatment to domiciliaries of their state. Unfortunately, most such reciprocal statutes deal only with intangible assets and not all states have adopted them. Where ancillary tax jurisdiction exists, some states impose an estate tax based on a proportionate basis. That would mean that if the decedent died domiciled in State A which has no estate tax while possessed of $10,000,000 in assets consisting of $9,000,000 with a tax situs in state A and $1,000,000 of assets with a tax situs in State B which imposed an estate tax at the rate of 15% on a proportionate basis but provided an exemption of $1,000,000, a tax of $135,000 would be due State B. This result would be reached by State B imposing a tax at the rate of 15% on $900,000 (one tenth of $10,000,000–$1,000,000). Similarly, if the decedent died while domiciled in State A with an estate worth $4,000,000 consisting of $3,000,000 worth of assets with a tax situs in State A and $1,000,000 of assets with a tax situs

---

[23] See, e.g., Frick v. Pennsylvania, 268 U.S. 473 (1925), Curry v. McCanless, 307 U.S. 357 (1939), and State Tax Comm'n v. Aldrich, 316 U.S. 174 (1942). See also Reed J. In Newark Fire Ins. Co. v. State Board, 307 U.S. 313 (1939) and Wheeling Steel Corp. v. Fox, 298 U.S. 193 (1936).

in State B, the decedent's estate would owe State B an estate tax of $112,500. This would be produced by imposing a tax at the rate of 15% on $750,000 (one quarter of $4,000,000–$1,000,000).

Clearly, even in the case of estates well below the $12,920,000 threshold or those above this amount which were not subject to federal estate tax due to portability, the possibility that the estate may be subject to state estate or inheritance tax cannot be overlooked.

G. DETERMINING TRANSFERS AND OWNERSHIP OF PROPERTY—THE APPLICABILITY OF STATE LAW

In Morgan v. Commissioner, 309 U.S. 78 (1940), the Supreme Court stated that, "State law creates legal interests and rights. The federal revenue acts designate what interests or rights, so created, shall be taxed." Id. at 80. Accordingly, the federal estate tax statute must normally turn to the state law to determine the existence of the interests in property that may be held by the decedent at the time of death. For example, the life beneficiary of a trust may die, and the question arises whether certain property, such as crops and livestock on the farm held in the trust, belongs to the life beneficiary or to the trust (and, in turn, the remainderman). The answer to such issues would depend on state law. If the issue of ownership is directly presented to the state court and decided conclusively as far as the contending parties are concerned, should such a decision bind the IRS for tax purposes? Pursuing the situation of the life beneficiary of the farm held in trust: if the issue of ownership of the crops and livestock had been brought to the probate court for resolution and if the probate court had held that the life beneficiary did not own such property, must the IRS accept the court's decision as determining the inclusion of such property in the life beneficiary's gross estate? The IRS might have serious doubts about the propriety of its being bound by state court litigation in which it was not represented and in which the ownership issue was not actively contested. In our example, if the life beneficiary's heir was also the remainderman of the trust, the ownership issue tried before the probate court would not be important except for estate tax purposes, and the contest between the estate of the life beneficiary and the remainderman in probate court would be unreal.

For some time, the test for determining which state decisions were conclusive for the Internal Revenue Service had not been wholly clear; however, the Supreme Court resolved the issue in Commissioner v. Estate of Bosch, 387 U.S. 456 (1967).

COMMISSIONER V. ESTATE OF BOSCH

Supreme Court of the United States, 1967.
387 U.S. 456.

MR. JUSTICE CLARK delivered the opinion of the Court.

[In 1930, the decedent conveyed property to a revocable trust from which his wife was to be paid income for her life. Under the terms of the trust wife had a general power of appointment. Provision was made for disposition of trust assets to the extent that at termination wife had failed to appoint property from the trust. In 1951, the wife executed an instrument purporting to release the general power and convert it into a special power. The decedent died in 1957. Under section 2056(b)(5) of the Code, the entire trust corpus would have been excluded from taxation if the wife had held a general, rather than a special, power of appointment at the decedent's death. The decedent's executor brought an action in state court seeking to have the wife's 1951 release of the general power declared invalid, hoping thereby to in essence exclude trust corpus from taxation. All parties at the proceeding argued that the wife's 1951 release was invalid, and the trial court judge made a finding that the release was invalid. The issue before the United States Supreme Court was the degree of deference, if any, which should be accorded to state court determinations in such situations. The following explanation was offered for the Court's disposition of the case.]

First, the Commissioner was not made a party to either of the same proceedings here and neither had the effect of *res judicata*, nor did the principle of collateral estoppel apply. It can hardly be denied that both state proceedings were brought for the purpose of directly affecting federal estate tax liability. Next, it must be remembered that it was a federal taxing statute that the Congress enacted and upon which we are here passing. Therefore, in construing it, we must look to the legislative history surrounding it. We find that the report of the Senate Finance Committee recommending enactment of the marital deduction used very guarded language in referring to the very question involved here. It said that "proper regard," not finality, "should be given to interpretations of the will" by state courts and then only when entered by a court "in a bona fide adversary proceeding." * * * These restrictive limitations clearly indicate the great care that Congress exercised in the drawing of the Act and indicate also a definite concern with the elimination of loopholes and escape hatches that might jeopardize the federal revenue. This also is in keeping with the long-established policy of the Congress, as expressed in the Rules of Decision Act, 28 U.S.C. § 1652. There it is provided that in the absence of federal requirements such as the Constitution or Acts of Congress, the "laws of the several states . . . shall be regarded as rules of decision in civil actions in the courts of the United States, in cases where they apply." This Court has held that judicial decisions are "laws of the . . . state" within the section. Erie R. Co. v. Tompkins, [304 U.S. 64 (1938)]; Cohen v. Beneficial Loan Corp., 337 U.S. 541 (1949); King v. Order of Travelers, 333 U.S. 153 (1948).

Moreover, even in diversity cases this Court has further held that while the decree of "lower state courts" should be "attributed some weight . . . the decision [is] not controlling . . ." where the highest court of the State has not spoken on the point. King v. Order of Travelers, supra, at 160–161. And in West v. A.T. & T. Co., 311 U.S. 223 (1940), this Court further held that "an intermediate appellate state court . . . is a datum for ascertaining state law which is not to be disregarded by a federal court *unless it is convinced by other persuasive data that the highest court of the state would decide otherwise.*" At 237. (Emphasis supplied.) Thus, under some conditions, federal authority may not be bound even by an intermediate state appellate court ruling. It follows here then, that when the application of a federal statute is involved, the decision of a state trial court as to an underlying issue of state law should *a fortiori* not be controlling. This is but an application of the rule of Erie R. Co. v. Tompkins, supra, where state law as announced by the highest court of the State is to be followed. This is not a diversity case but the same principle may be applied for the same reasons, *viz.*, the underlying substantive rule involved is based on state law and the State's highest court is the best authority on its own law. If there be no decision by that court then federal authorities must apply what they find to be the state law after giving "proper regard" to relevant rulings of other courts of the State. In this respect, it may be said to be, in effect, sitting as a state court. Bernhardt v. Polygraphic Co., 350 U.S. 198 (1956).

We believe that this would avoid much of the uncertainty that would result from the "non-adversary" approach and at the same time would be fair to the taxpayer and protect the federal revenue as well.

* * *

Note

Mary E. Scott v. Commissioner, 226 F.3d 871 (7th Cir. 2000), provides a good example of the need for federal courts to be vested with the power to disregard lower state court decisions. Lucille Horstmeier and Mary Scott had lived together for 19 years. During that time Horstmeier had earned almost all of the couple's income while Scott tended to their household maintenance and financial management. A home in Glenview, Illinois was purchased by Horstmeier and placed in her name. She effected the purchase by putting $50,000 down and taking out a mortgage of $55,000 in her name alone. No evidence was provided to indicate that Scott ever provided any consideration for the home. Shortly thereafter, the couple fully displayed that they knew how to create a co-tenancy when they intended to do so by purchasing a second home in Skokie which was titled in both names and for which Scott made financial contributions. After Horstmeier's death in 1993, Scott, who was the executor of Horstmeier's estate (and her sole beneficiary under a revocable trust), sought and obtained an uncontested determination in Illinois probate court that Scott actually owned one-half of the Glenview home under a resulting trust theory. On the basis of the probate court's finding of a resulting trust, Scott only included one-half of the value of the Glenview home in Horstmeier's estate. Both the Tax Court (T.C. Memo. 1999–145, 77 T.C.M. (CCH) 1940 (1999)) and the Eleventh Circuit Court of Appeals disregarded the Illinois probate court's determination in finding that the full value of the Glenview home should be included in Horstmeier's estate.

H. SOME STATISTICAL INFORMATION ON THE REACH OF THE TRANSFER TAXES

1. ESTATE AND GIFT TAXES

In 2021, the federal estate and gift taxes combined raised about $27 billion.[24] While this is a considerable sum, it is relatively unimportant when compared to the $1.24 trillion in federal individual income tax and the $367 billion in corporate income tax raised in that year.[25]

However, the relative importance to the legal establishment and the Treasury of the gift and estate taxes cannot be gauged by comparing the revenue raised by the two income taxes and the estate and gift tax. The individual whose death results in the collection of estate or gift tax typically represents an important client for a law firm; only a very small minority of income taxpayers are in this category. Further, given the relative ease with which competent estate planners and determined taxpayers can significantly reduce gift and estate taxes which would otherwise be due, the relative amounts of tax raised by the individual and corporate income taxes and the estate and gift taxes are far from indicative of the career opportunities for lawyers represented by these various taxes. Finally, portability and the temporary nature of the Tax Cuts and Jobs Act of 2017 have complicated the task of estate planners and require clients to "check-in" with their attorneys on a periodic basis.

2. PERSONAL WEALTH

According to a recent study by Edward Wolff with the National Bureau of Economic Research, the economic wealth in the United States is concentrated in the wealthiest one percent of Americans.[26] Statistics show that the top one percent of Americans held 38.2% of the wealth in the United States and the top twenty percent held 88.9% of economic wealth

---

[24] Internal Revenue Service 2021 Data Book, Pub. No. 55B, at 3 tbl. 1 (2022).

[25] Id.

[26] Edward N. Wolff, *Household Wealth Trends in the United States, 1962 To 2019: Median Wealth Rebounds...But Not Enough*, NAT'L BUREAU OF ECON. RES., at 48 tbl. 2 (2021), https://www.nber.org/system/files/working_papers/w28383/w28383.pdf.

during 2019.[27] According to Wolff, from 1983 to 2019, the average wealth for the top one percent and the top twenty percent grew by 157.2 percent and 148.8 percent, respectively.[28] Conversely, the average wealth of the bottom 40% fell by $14,200 to -$7,200.[29] The bottom 80% accounted for about only five percent of the total growth in wealth from 1983 to 2019.[30] Moreover, recent data indicates that as of 2019, in the United States there were just over 9,266,000 millionaire households, roughly 1,819,600 penta-millionaire ($5 million or more) households, and 692,800,000 deca-millionaire ($10 million or more) households.[31]

"The very rich are different from you and me," wrote Ernest Hemingway in The Snows of Kilimanjaro, "they have more money."[32] The very rich are different not merely in terms of having more but are also different in the type of assets that they own. The division of assets in the United States continues to show a large discrepancy between the top 10% of households and the bottom 90%. Consider that in 2019 the top 10% of all households owned 93.6% of all stocks and mutual fund assets, 92.7% of other financial securities, 85.9% of assets held in trust, and 94% of all other business equity.[33] The top 10% of all households also owned 79.5% of non-home real estate, 41.2% of all principal residence assets, 64.1% of all money on deposit, 63% of the value of all life insurance, and 66.6% of all pension assets.[34] Significantly, the bottom 90% owned 72.7% of total debt.[35]

I. THE CASE FOR AND AGAINST ESTATE AND GIFT TAXATION

1. COMPARATIVE DATA

There are 38 OECD countries. These countries are Australia, Austria, Belgium, Canada, Chile, Colombia, Costa Rica, Czech Republic, Denmark, Estonia, Finland, France, Germany, Greece, Hungary, Iceland, Ireland, Israel, Italy, Japan, Korea, Latvia, Lithuania, Luxembourg, Mexico, Netherlands, New Zealand, Norway, Poland, Portugal, Slovak Republic, Slovenia, Spain, Sweden, Switzerland, Turkey, United Kingdom, and the United States. Despite much political rhetoric to the contrary, the American citizen is not, at least from a relative standpoint, dramatically overtaxed. During 2020, the United States ranked 30th out of the 36 OECD

---

[27] Id.

[28] Id. at 13.

[29] Id. at 13.

[30] Id. at 14.

[31] Id. at 49 tbl.3.

[32] Ernest Hemingway, The Snows of Kilimanjaro and Other Stories 24 (Schribner 2003).

[33] Wolff, supra note 26, at 56 tbl. 10.

[34] Id.

[35] Id.

member nations reporting data (Australia and Japan did not report data) in respect to total (federal, state, and local) tax revenue as a percentage of gross domestic product. [36] Taxes amounted to 26.6% of GDP for the United States compared to 46.9% in Denmark (ranked first), 33.2% in Canada (ranked 24th), and 16.7% for Mexico (ranked last).[37] The average for all OECD countries was 34.1% in 2021.[38]

2.   TO TAX OR NOT TO TAX

The very notion of a tax on the transfer of wealth has drawn its fair share of strong support and criticism. No less a capitalist than Andrew Carnegie called for the enactment of a federal estate tax on the ground that:

> Of all forms of taxation this seems the wisest. Men who continue hoarding great sums all their lives, the proper use of which for public ends would work good to the community from which it chiefly came, should not be made to feel that the community, in the form of the State, cannot thus be deprived of its proper share. By taxing estates heavily at death the State marks its condemnation of the selfish millionaire's unworthy life.

Carnegie, "The Gospel of Wealth," reprinted in The Gospel of Wealth and Other Timely Essays, 14, at 22 (Kirkland ed. 1965).

Andrew Mellon who served as Secretary of the Treasury from 1921 to 1932 and like Carnegie was one of the wealthiest men of his generation, on the other hand, saw transfer taxes as inevitably leading to the "destruction of the total capital of the country" which would "destroy the very source from which revenue is to flow." Mellon, Taxation: The People's Business, 114, at 122 (1924).

In recent years there has been renewed interest in debating the role, if any, that a tax on gratuitous transfers should play in our federal tax system. The debate has ranged from proposals to do away completely with all transfer taxes and to replace them and the present income tax with one form or another of a tax on consumption to a proposal to, after providing for certain exclusions, confiscate all wealth at death.

Professor Edward McCaffrey in The Uneasy Case for Wealth Transfer Taxation, 104 Yale L.J. 283 (1994), urged repeal of both the income, estate and gift taxes and replacement of all three with a progressive tax on consumption. Under such a tax, individuals would presumably be taxed on income but would be given a deduction for all savings and investments.

---

[36] Organization for Economic Cooperation and Development, Tax Levels and Tax Structures, 1965–2021, Revenue Statistics 2022:The Initial Impact of COVID-19 on OECD Tax Revenues, tbl. 3.1, OECD iLibrary (oecd-ilibrary.org).

[37] Id.

[38] Id.

Taxpayers would also be taxed on withdrawals from savings when spent on consumption. This would be true whether the savings which were withdrawn to finance consumption were the fruit of the consumer's past efforts or represented wealth that had been given to or inherited by the consumer. McCaffrey opposes wealth transfer taxes on the ground that they punish behavior (principally work and saving) that a liberal society ought to encourage and encourage behavior (principally leisure and consumption) which such a society ought to discourage. The values that McCaffrey identifies with a liberal society as they impact on the issue of tax structure design are efficiency, fairness, rewarding productivity, discouragement of private, and especially large-scale, preclusive use of resources and encouragement of use of resources for productive purposes in the economy of the larger society. Professor McCaffrey summarizes his arguments in favor of terminating all wealth transfer taxes (along with the income tax) and replacing them with a progressive consumption tax as follows:

> The five arguments can now be summarized and related as follows. (1) The current estate tax is porous, ineffective, and counterproductive on purely liberal grounds. (2) No stronger version is popular or practical, in part because (3) the liberal theory supporting an estate tax does not fit in a nonideal world where individual earnings lack presumptive, decisive moral weight, and in part because (4) our objective, political values, even under ideal conditions, lead liberal society to approve of work and savings and only or at least especially to disapprove of the wanton private use of resources, and any wealth tax is perverse on these scores. (5) Therefore, our practices have been moving, at least inchoately, toward a progressive consumption-without-estate tax. If we more consciously and consistently implemented what our practices suggest, we would have a better liberal egalitarian system than any featuring a wealth transfer tax. By meeting our objective values and changing the very meaning and hence the dangers of the private possession of wealth, we achieve in the end a happy convergence between liberal egalitarian theory and our actual practices.

Id. at 297.

On the other extreme is Professor Mark Ascher advocates for something that closely resembles confiscation of wealth at death:

> My proposal views inheritance as something we should tolerate only when necessary—not something we should always protect. My major premise is that all property owned at death, after payment of debts and administration expenses, should be sold and the proceeds paid to the United States government.

There would be six exceptions. A marital exemption, potentially unlimited, would accrue over the life of a marriage. Thus, spouses could continue to provide for each other after death. Decedents would also be allowed to provide for dependent lineal descendants. The amount available to any given descendant would, however, depend on the descendant's age and would drop to zero at an age of presumed independence. A separate exemption would allow generous provision for disabled lineal descendants of any age. Inheritance by lineal ascendants (parents, grandparents, etc.) would be unlimited. A universal exemption [$250,000] would allow a moderate amount of property either to pass outside the exemptions or to augment amounts passing under them. Thus, every decedent would be able to leave something to persons of his or her choice, regardless whether another exemption was available. Up to a fixed fraction of an estate could pass to charity. In addition, to prevent circumvention by lifetime giving, the gift tax would increase substantially.

My proposal strikes directly at inheritance by healthy, adult children. And for good reason. We cannot control differences in native ability. Even worse, so long as we believe in the family, we can achieve only the most rudimentary successes in evening out many types of opportunities. And we certainly cannot control many types of luck. But we can—and ought to—curb one form of luck. Children lucky enough to have been raised, acculturated, and educated by wealthy parents need not be allowed the additional good fortune of inheriting their parents' property. In this respect, we can do much better than we ever have before at equalizing opportunity. This proposal would leave "widows and orphans" essentially untouched. The disabled, grandparents, and charity would probably fare better than ever before. But inheritance by healthy, adult children would cease immediately, except to the extent of the universal exemption.[39]

Professors Charles Davenport, Jay Soled, and Willard Pedrick have provided good examples of the conventional case which can be made for retention of a gratuitous transfer tax.[40] Traditional defenders typically make the following case for retention of taxes on gratuitous transfers.

First, the estate and gift taxes have the potential to make a significant contribution to the Treasury. However, the enactment of the Tax Cuts and

---

[39] Mark Ascher, *Curtailing Inherited Wealth*, 89 MICH. L. REV. 69, 73–75 (1990).

[40] See Charles Davenport and Jay A. Soled, *Enlivening the Death-Tax Death-Talk*, 84 Tax Notes 591 (1999); Willard Pedrick, Through the Glass Darkly: Transfer Taxes Tomorrow, 19 Inst. Est. Plan. ¶ 1902 (1985). See also Paul L. Caron, *One-Hundredth Anniversary of the Federal Estate Tax: It's Time to Renew Our Vows*, 57 B.C. LAW REV. 823 (2016) (reviewing the importance of the estate tax in raising revenue, enhancing the progressivity of the tax system, and curbing the concentration of wealth).

Jobs Act significantly reduced the estate and gift tax revenue. The increase in the exemption amount under the Tax Cuts and Jobs Act is estimated to reduce revenue by $83 billion from 2018 through 2025.[41]

Second, proponents of transfer taxes note that they enhance the overall progressivity of our federal tax system. For example, Professor Michael Graetz noted that the estate and gift taxes have accounted for as much as one-third of the progressivity in the federal tax system. To appreciate this point consider that the Social Security Tax is a moderately regressive tax, imposed only on wage and self-employment income, the Medicare tax is a proportional tax imposed only on wage and self-employment income, and the federal income tax ranks only as a moderately progressive tax after one makes allowance for capital gains preferences and deferral of taxation on many such gains due to the realization principle (the increase in the value of property is not taxed until disposition of appreciated property).

Third, transfer taxes contribute to the breakup of large concentrations of personal wealth that provide wealthy families and individuals with disproportionate influence on political, cultural and social affairs at both the national and local levels. Leading political proponents of this argument Republican Theodore Roosevelt and his Democratic cousin Franklin. It is argued that transfer taxes have thereby made our society and economy more dynamic.

Fourth, the transfer tax concentrates the attention of the wealthy on the need to engage in estate planning. Absent the tax, most households would defer confronting the issue of disposition of wealth until death was imminent. In a good number of cases it is likely that, absent the tax, the issue might never be addressed leaving the family without a well-developed plan for the devolution of property at death.

Fifth, the alleged need to liquidate assets to pay the federal estate tax has the economic benefit of forcing assets to the market where they will presumably pass to those who can make the economically most efficient use of those assets. For example, an estate strapped for cash to pay the estate tax will sell those assets which produce the lowest return for it. The marketplace will ensure that the property so sold passes to those who can make the most efficient use of it.

Sixth, the presence of the estate tax and its deduction for bequests to charities provides substantial incentive for wealthy decedents to bestow some significant portion of their wealth on philanthropic institutions. A repeal of the estate tax would result in a major reduction in charitable donations by individuals. Data suggests that the estate tax is an important factor for individuals when determining whether to give charitable gifts.

---

[41] Jane G. Gravelle, Recent Changes in the Estate and Gift Tax Provisions, Congressional Research Service 4 (Jan. 11, 2018), *available at* https://fas.org/sgp/crs/misc/R42959.pdf.

Studies on the impact of the repeal of the estate tax vary. Some studies suggest the impact could be as low as 12% while other studies claim the impact could be around 37%.[42]

Seventh, the tax satisfies the moral imperative that the affluent come to the aid of the poor. It guarantees that even miserly multi-millionaires embrace this obligation, albeit entirely unwillingly.

NOTE

To the foregoing litany of justifications for a wealth transfer tax we might add a consideration provided by multi-billionaire Warren Buffett, one of America's wealthiest individuals. Buffett finds it curious that while many of the rich worry about the debilitating effects of food stamps and welfare on the work ethic of the poor, they themselves live off a boundless supply of "privately funded food stamps" and fret about an estate tax which stands in the way of providing the same opportunity for their descendants. Buffett's version of an ideal tax system is a markedly progressive tax on personal consumption and an enormous wealth transfer tax, with the latter presumably intended to spare the children of the wealthy from the corruption of their work ethic. Buffett says that when he dies, he intends to leave his children enough so that they can do anything but not do nothing. Roger Lowenstein, Buffett, 334–350 (1995).

J. TRUST AND ESTATE INCOME (SECTIONS 641–678)

The taxation of the income of trusts and estates is not much different from the taxation of the income of individuals. One of the differences is the distribution deduction available to trusts and estates. That is, trusts and estates, unlike corporations, enjoy a deduction for certain distributions made to the beneficiary of the trust or estate. Much of the discussion of trust and estate income taxation relates to implementation of this scheme. Furthermore, rules have been developed to discourage, if not eliminate, the use of the trust and the estate as tax shelters, i.e., entities to be used for warehousing income: (1) to avoid or postpone taxing that income to the beneficiaries who might be in higher income tax brackets; or (2) to keep that warehoused income out of the estates of the beneficiaries for federal estate tax purposes. These rules relate to distributions of accumulated income, multiple trusts for the same beneficiary, etc. Also, the income tax rates applicable to trusts and estates are "compressed" relative to the income tax rates applicable to individuals, e.g., the maximum income tax rate of 37% applied to trust and estate income that exceeded $14,450 in 2023 while, in the case of married individuals filing joint income tax returns, the top tax bracket began at $693,750. The materials in this course

---

[42] See David Joulfaian, *Behavioral Effects on the Estate Tax*, 57 B.C. L. REV. 843, 855 (2016).

book develop these and other issues related to the income taxation of estates and trusts.

K. INCOME FROM DECEDENTS (SECTION 691)

Income from decedents, technically referred to as "income in respect of a decedent" (IRD) presents several issues. Examples of IRD include commissions paid a salesman after his death which are attributable to sales made before death. Such commissions are subject to both the federal estate tax and the federal income tax when received. Reconciling this and other issues presented by IRD is considered in this course book.

L. TAX COMPLIANCE AND CONTROVERSIES

The federal estate tax and the federal gift tax are plainly rather small potatoes in the garden patch of federal taxation. Nevertheless, they do affect the course of living and dying, do yield significant revenue and do, as well, generate some tax controversies. Compliance with the requirements of the estate tax and gift tax rules is the subject of later chapters.

The procedural setting for resolving controversies arising out of federal estate and gift tax cases is essentially the same as for the federal income tax. When the audit of the estate tax or gift tax return results in a claim for additional tax by the Treasury, essentially the same administrative and judicial remedies are available for resolving the dispute. Treasury regulations and rulings in the estate and gift tax field are subject to challenge and sometimes come off the loser in court.

M. ON TO SUBSTANCE

The materials in this course book are intended to start the student in an acquaintance with the substantive provisions of the federal transfer tax system, together with some of the most significant interpretations by the courts and the Treasury. A beginning acquaintance with the federal transfer tax is enough in most to kindle a relatively keen interest in planning, i.e., arrangements to minimize the federal levies on intergenerational transfers of property. The many options provided by the system in its present configuration mean that there are planning opportunities. The matter of planning to minimize exposure to federal transfer taxes, moreover, is a challenging activity. This course book is not designed as a planning book as such, but recognition is given from time to time to the planning possibilities offered by particular features of the system.

N. REFERENCE MATERIAL

There are a number of sources of varying length to assist the beginning student in understanding the federal transfer tax system. A great supplement is McNulty and McCouch, Federal Estate and Gift Taxation in a Nutshell (West 9th ed. 2020). Lindsey, Gilbert Law Summary on Estate and Gift Taxation (17th ed. 2022) is also a good resource for students. In addition, U.S. Master Estate and Gift Tax Guide (CCH 2022 ed.) is a helpful resource. Finally, for an overview of the major provisions in the tax code addressing estate and gift taxation and the generation-skipping transfer tax, see John A. Miller & Jeffrey A. Maine, *Wealth Transfer Tax Planning for 2013 and Beyond*, 2013 B.Y.U.L. REV. 879 (2013).

PART 2

GIFT TAX

(Chapter 12 of the Internal Revenue Code)

■ ■ ■

CHAPTER 2

INTRODUCTION

■ ■ ■

A. EVOLUTION OF THE GIFT TAX

Our present gift tax dates back only to 1932 and is now incorporated in Chapter 12 of sections 2501 through 2524. An earlier gift tax was enacted in 1924, but it proved so ineffective that it was repealed in 1926.

In concept the gift tax is simple enough. Section 2501(a) imposes a tax "on the transfer of property by gift . . . by any individual." At the time of its enactment, the gift tax was designed to plug the principal loophole in the estate tax system. Without the gift tax, an individual could simply make lifetime transfers of property to donees. If the individual retained no strings or powers over the property, the federal estate tax could be avoided altogether.

Despite the enactment of the gift tax in 1932, important advantages of lifetime gifts over death transfers remained in effect until 1976. The gift tax rates were only 75 percent of the estate tax rates, and in all cases a lifetime gift removed from the donor's gross estate not only the property given, but also the funds used to pay the gift tax imposed on the transfer.

Enactment of the unified transfer tax system in 1976 eliminated much of the advantages of lifetime giving as compared to death transfers. After the enactment of the unified transfer tax system in 1976, in most cases the total transfer tax burden would be about the same whether the decedent's property was transferred during the decedent's lifetime, at the decedent's death, or some combination of the two.

During the period 2002 through 2010 the gift tax and estate were decoupled to some degree. While the estate tax unified credit provided an exemption that rose to $5,000,000 in 2010, the gift tax unified credit exemption remained fixed at $1,000,000.

Effective for years after 2010, the gift tax and estate tax were once again fully unified, and the basic exclusion amount was the same under both taxes. A single set of rate brackets, with a maximum rate of 40%, now applies to both taxes. In 2011, the basic exclusion amount was $5,000,000 indexed for inflation. For gifts made after December 31, 2017, the basic exclusion amount was doubled to $10,000,000 indexed for inflation. This increase is only applicable through December 31, 2025, when it will sunset. If the sunset is not repealed, the basic exclusion amount will revert to

$5,000,000 (indexed for inflation) in 2026. I.R.C. §§ 2010(c)(3) and 2505(a)(1). The basic exclusion amount for 2023 is $12,920,000.

B. EXCLUSIONS

Some gifts are entirely excluded from application of the gift tax. These gifts do not become part of taxable gifts and do not absorb any portion of the unified credit. Therefore, a donor may make countless excluded gifts without consuming any of the unified credit.

The most important exclusion for gifts is the annual exclusion. I.R.C. § 2503(b). The allowable amount is indexed in $1,000 increments and is currently $17,000 for gifts as of 2023. The exclusion is "annual" because it is available anew each year. It is "per donee" because the exclusion can be applied to as many separate donees as one wishes. For example, if a grandmother gives $17,000 to each of her 10 grandchildren in 2023 and then gives another $17,000 to each of them in 2024, all of these gifts totaling $340,000 are excluded.

There is also an exclusion for direct payments of tuition and medical expenses. I.R.C. § 2503(e). There is no limit on the number or dollar amounts of such transfers, provided the transfers consist entirely of payment of tuition or medical expenses paid directly to the educational institution on behalf of a donee.

These exclusions are examined more fully in Chapter 7.

C. DEDUCTIONS

Certain gifts to charities and to the donor's spouse are deductible. See I.R.C. §§ 2522 and 2523. In other words, the value of these gifts is offset by deductions of the same amount. These deductions are explored in Chapter 7.

D. MECHANICS OF THE GIFT AND ESTATE TAXES

Determination of the gift tax—and the estate tax as well—involves the following procedure:

1. After the donor's total gifts during the calendar year are determined, exclusions and deductions are applied to produce the total of "taxable gifts."

2. The gift tax imposed on the donor's taxable gifts is determined as follows:

    (a) First, a tentative gift tax is determined under the section 2001(c) rate table. This is the tax that would be imposed on the total of all taxable gifts made by the donor at any time after June 6, 1932, *including the calendar year in question*. I.R.C. § 2502(a)(1) & (b).

(b) From the tentative tax determined in paragraph (a) there is subtracted another tentative tax computed under the section 2001(c) rate table on the total of all gifts made after June 6, 1932, *and prior to the year in question*. I.R.C. § 2502(a)(2).

(c) The excess of the paragraph (a) tentative tax (the tax on all gifts) over the paragraph (b) tentative tax (the tax on all gifts prior to the year in question) is the gift tax imposed on the taxable gifts made during the year. I.R.C. § 2502(a).

(d) The applicable credit amount specified in section 2505(a)(1), less the amount of credit allocable to gifts in prior years (section 2505(a)(2)) is applied to offset the gift tax determined in paragraph (c). The tax payable is the excess of the gift tax determined under paragraph (c) over the available credit determined by the preceding sentence. In determining the credit allocable to prior years, the current tax rate structure, rather than the rate structure in effect in prior years, is used. I.R.C. § 2505(a).

3. With respect to gifts in later years, the computations described in paragraph 2 are repeated each year a gift is made, with the effect that the available applicable credit amount will decline as the credit is used to shelter gifts in earlier years.

4. The last step in the unified tax system is determination of the individual's estate tax under Chapter 11 of the Code (sections 2001–2010). The starting point is determination of the decedent's "taxable estate." The taxable estate consists of the gross estate (which includes all property owned at death as well as certain transfers that are considered testamentary in character), less various deductions. I.R.C. § 2051.

(a) All taxable gifts made by the decedent after 1976 (other than gifts that are already included in the gross estate because of their testamentary character) are added to the taxable estate. Then a tentative tax is computed for the total of the taxable estate and the taxable gifts, using the section 2001(c) rate table. I.R.C. § 2001(b)(1).

(b) From the tentative tax determined in paragraph (a) there is subtracted the total gift taxes payable, after application of the unified credit, with respect to gifts after 1976. I.R.C. § 2001(b)(2). The amount deducted is not the gift tax actually paid, but the hypothetical amount that would have been paid if the gift tax rate structure for the year of death, rather than the year of gift, were used. I.R.C. § 2001(b)(2) and (g)(1). The excess of the tentative estate tax (paragraph (a)) over the gift taxes payable is the estate tax before credits.

(c)   The unified credit amount specified in section 2010(c) is allowed against the estate tax computed in (b).

The last step described above—application of the full unified credit amount specified in section 2010(c)—sometimes causes confusion. The credit is meant to be truly "unified" (i.e., a single credit amount that can be used against both lifetime and death transfers). Therefore, it may seem incongruous to allow the full credit amount at death if the decedent used a portion of the credit to shelter lifetime gifts from tax.

The answer to this conundrum lies in the arithmetic required by section 2001(b)(2), the effect of which is to reduce the estate tax payable by the gift tax that was payable by the decedent. To the extent the decedent used a portion of her unified credit to eliminate payment of gift tax, the gift tax payable is thereby decreased, resulting in a concomitant *decrease* in the section 2001(b)(2) deduction for gift tax payable. This produces a concomitant *increase* in the estate tax payable under section 2001(b). The net effect is to increase the estate tax payable by the amount of the unified credit used to shelter lifetime gifts. Therefore, the estate tax due is increased on a dollar-for-dollar basis in the amount of the credit used to reduce gift tax liability. The result is that the benefits of the gift tax credit are eliminated when the estate tax is computed, and it is appropriate to allow the full estate tax unified credit at death, regardless of the amount of gift tax credit used during life.

For example, assume that the decedent made a lifetime taxable gift of $100,000, thereby creating a gift tax liability, before the unified credit, of $23,800. Thus, $23,800 of her unified credit would be applied to offset the gift tax otherwise due, so that she would actually pay no gift tax. The taxable gift of $100,000 will be added to the decedent's taxable estate for purposes of determining the tax due at her death under section 2001(b)(1)(B). If the decedent had actually paid the $23,800 in gift tax during her life, this would have reduced the estate tax due under section 2001(b) by $23,800. I.R.C. § 2001(b)(2). Because the decedent used $23,800 of her unified credit to avoid payment of tax, however, the section 2001(b)(2) reduction is zero. As a result, the decedent's estate tax is $23,800 higher than it would have been had $23,800 of credit not been used to shelter lifetime gifts. In effect, section 2001(b)(2) eliminates the benefit of the gift tax credit, and it is therefore appropriate to allow the full unified credit at death.

PROBLEMS

1. Alice Jones made no gifts prior to 2014. In 2014, Alice gave her daughter, Emily, a cash gift of $514,000. Assume that the annual exclusion was $14,000 and the basic exclusion amount was $5,340,000 in 2014. How much gift tax, if any, does Alice owe?

2. Assume the same facts as in problem one. In 2015, Alice gave Emily a cash gift of $6,014,000. Assume that the annual exclusion was $14,000 and the basic exclusion amount was $5,430,000 in 2015. How much gift tax, if any, does Alice owe?

3. Assume the same facts as in problem two. Alice dies in 2023 with a taxable estate of $8,000,000. Assume that in 2023 the basic exclusion amount is $12,920,000 and the section 2001(c) rate structure that was in effect in 2014 remains in effect in 2023. How much estate tax, if any, is owed by reason of Alice's death?

E. GIFTS BY EXPATRIATES

Section 2801 imposes a tax on gifts made by certain expatriates to a United States citizen or resident. The entire gift, to the extent it exceeds the section 2503(b) annual exclusion, is taxed at the highest rate provided by section 2001(c). I.R.C. § 2801(a) and (c). The unified credit is not applicable, but the tax is reduced to the extent of any gift tax imposed by a foreign country. I.R.C. § 2801(d). The tax is paid by the donee rather than the donor. I.R.C. § 2801(b).

The purpose of the section 2801 tax is to prevent the avoidance of the gift tax that would otherwise be possible where the donor moves away from the United States and relinquishes citizenship. The donor then makes gifts to United State citizens. Without section 2801 the donor's gifts would entirely escape the United States transfer taxes.

The tax applies only to a gift by a "covered expatriate." I.R.C. § 2801(e)(1)(A) and (f). The "covered expatriate" term is defined in section 877A. A "covered expatriate" is a person who relinquished his or her United State citizenship within the ten-year period ending with the year of the gift, and whose United States income tax liability or net worth exceeds either of the levels specified in section 877(a)(2). I.R.C. §§ 877A(g)(1) and 877(a)(1). The income tax liability floor is an average annual income tax liability of $190,000 (the inflationary amount for 2023) for the five taxable years preceding relinquishment of United State citizenship. I.R.C. § 877(a)(2)(A). The net worth floor is $2,000,000 at the time of relinquishment of citizenship. I.R.C. § 877(a)(2)(B).

The section 2801 tax does not apply to a gift reported on a United States gift tax return. I.R.C. § 2801(e)(2). Also, it does not apply to a gift that would be eligible for the gift tax marital or charitable deduction. I.R.C. § 2801(e)(3). Special rules apply to gifts to trusts. See I.R.C. § 2801(e)(4).

F. BASIS IN GIFT TRANSFERS

The general rule applicable to gift transfers is that the donee takes the donor's basis for income tax purposes. I.R.C. § 1015(a). For example, assume that a donor buys stock for $6,000. The stock appreciates to a value of $10,000, at which point the donor transfers the stock to a donee by gift. The donee's basis for the stock is $6,000. If the donee later sells the stock for $11,000, the donee will have a taxable gain of $5,000.

A special rule applies to gift transfers if the value of the gift is lower than the donor's basis at the time of the gift. In this case, for purposes of determining loss, but not gain, the basis to the donee is the value on the date of the gift. I.R.C. § 1015(a). Assume that a donor buys stock for $20,000. The stock drops in value to $13,000, at which point the donor gives the stock to a donee. If the stock value declines further, and the donee sells the stock for $10,000, the donee will have a deductible loss of only $3,000. If the donee sells the stock for a price between $13,000 and $20,000, there is neither gain nor loss. Treas. Reg. § 1.1015–1(a)(2). The purpose of the special rule is to prevent a donor from transferring a loss to a family member who is in a higher tax bracket or otherwise better positioned to use the loss. The donor may have no capital gains against which to offset the loss, while the donee may have substantial capital gains. Alternatively, if the stock appreciates to $25,000 and the donee then sells the stock, the carryover basis rule applies, and the donee will have taxable gain of $5,000.

If the gift is between spouses or former spouses incident to divorce, the donee spouse takes the donor spouse's basis in all cases, even if the donor spouse's basis is higher than the value of the property at the time of the gift. I.R.C. § 1041(b) & Treas. Reg. § 1.1041–1T(d), Q & A 11.

The donee can increase the donee's basis by a portion of any gift tax paid by the donor with respect to the transfer. I.R.C. § 1015(d). For example, assume that a donor gives land worth $100,000 to a donee at a time when the annual exclusion is $17,000. Assume further that the donor's basis for the land is $58,500, and the donor pays $20,000 of gift tax with respect to the transfer. The general rule of section 1015(a) is that the donee takes the donor's basis of $58,500. Section 1015(d), however, permits the donee to increase the basis by the portion of the $20,000 gift tax that is allocable to the portion of the taxable value of the gift that constitutes unrealized appreciation. I.R.C. § 1015(d)(6). In this case, the unrealized appreciation portion is $100,000 less $58,500, or $41,500. The taxable amount, after deducting the annual exclusion, is $100,000 less $17,000, or

$83,000. The appreciation portion is therefore $41,500/$83,000, or 50%. The donee can therefore increase the basis for the property by 50% of $20,000, or $10,000. The donee's basis for the land is $58,500 plus $10,000, or $68,500. This "carryover basis" rule is dramatically different from the "stepped-up basis" rule that applies to transfers at death. If the donee later sells the stock for $118,000, the donee will have a taxable gain of $59,500 ($118,000 less $68,500).

In the above example, assume that the donor, rather than transferring the stock by gift, holds the stock until death and bequeaths the stock, then worth $100,000, to the donee (technically, a devisee). The donee has a basis for the stock equal its fair market value on the date of the donor's death—$100,000. I.R.C. § 1014(a). If the donee later sells the stock for $118,000, the donee will have a taxable gain of only $18,000 ($118,000 less $100,000). The $41,500 appreciation that occurred before the donor's death escapes taxation entirely. If the alternate valuation date provided by section 2032 and explained in Chapter 9 is elected for the donor's estate, the donee's basis will be the fair market value of the stock on the alternate valuation date. I.R.C. § 1014(a)(2). Section 1014(a) can also produce a "stepped-down basis" if the value of the stock at the donor's death is lower than the donor's basis for the stock.

CHAPTER 3

WHAT CONSTITUTES A GIFT

■ ■ ■

It is well established that Congress intended an expansive definition of what constitutes a "gift" so as to be subject to the gift tax. Section 2511(a) provides that the gift tax is to apply "whether the transfer is in trust or otherwise, whether the gift is direct or indirect, and whether the property is real or personal, tangible or intangible . . ." Treas. Reg. § 25.2511–1(c)(1) states that "any transaction in which an interest in property is gratuitously passed or conferred upon another, regardless of the means or device employed, constitutes a gift subject to tax." In Commissioner v. Wemyss,[1] the Supreme Court described Congress as intending "to hit all the protean arrangements which the wit of man can devise that are not business transactions within the meaning of ordinary speech. . ."[2]

A. IS DONATIVE INTENT NECESSARY?

One might assume that Congress intended the term "gift" to connote the common-law concept of a transfer made gratuitously and with donative intent. The Regulations, however, take a very expansive view, refusing to follow the path of the common law: "Donative intent on the part of the transferor is not an essential element in the application of the gift tax to the transfer." Treas. Reg. § 25.2511–1(g)(1). Even more explicitly, Treas. Reg. § 25.2512–8 states:

> Transfers reached by the gift tax are not confined to those only which, being without a valuable consideration, accord with the common law concept of gifts, but embrace as well sales, exchanges, and other dispositions of property for a consideration to the extent that the value of the property transferred by the donor exceeds the value in money or money's worth of the consideration given therefor. However, a sale, exchange, or other transfer of property made in the ordinary course of business (a transaction which is bona fide, at arm's length, and free from any donative intent), will be considered as made for an adequate and full consideration in money or money's worth.

---

[1]   324 U.S. 303 (1945).

[2]   Id. at 306.

COMMISSIONER V. WEMYSS

Supreme Court of the United States, 1945.
324 U.S. 303.

FRANKFURTER, J.: In 1939 taxpayer proposed marriage to Mrs. More, a widow with one child. Her deceased husband had set up two trusts, one half the income of which was for the benefit of Mrs. More and the other half for that of the child with provision that, in the event of Mrs. More's remarriage, her part of the income ceased and went to the child. The corpus of the two trusts consisted of stock which brought to Mrs. More from the death of her first husband to her remarriage, about five years later, an average income of $5,484 a year. On Mrs. More's unwillingness to suffer loss of her trust income through remarriage the parties on May 24, 1939, entered upon an agreement whereby taxpayer transferred to Mrs. More a block of shares of stock. Within a month they married. The Commissioner ruled that the transfer of this stock, the value of which, $149,456.13, taxpayer does not controvert, was subject to the Federal Gift Tax, §§ 501 and 503 of the Revenue Act of 1932. Accordingly, he assessed a deficiency which the Tax Court upheld, 2 T.C. 876, but the Circuit Court of Appeals reversed the Tax Court, 144 F.2d 78. We granted certiorari to settle uncertainties in tax administration engendered by seemingly conflicting decisions. 324 U.S. 308.

The answer to our problem turns on the proper application of §§ 501(a) [1986 Code § 2501(a)(1)] and 503 [1986 Code § 2512(b)] supra to the immediate facts. These provisions are as follows:

Sec. 501. Imposition of Tax.

(a) For the calendar year 1932 and each calendar year thereafter a tax, computed as provided in section 502, shall be imposed upon the transfer during such calendar year by any individual . . . of property by gift.

Sec. 503. Transfers for less than adequate and full consideration.

Where property is transferred for less than an adequate and full consideration in money or money's worth, then the amount by which the value of the property exceeded the value of the consideration shall, for the purpose of the tax imposed by this title, be deemed a gift, and shall be included in computing the amount of gifts made during the calendar year.

In view of the major role which the Tax Court plays in federal tax litigation, it becomes important to consider how that court dealt with this problem. Fusing, as it were, §§ 501 and 503, the Tax Court read them as not being limited by any common law technical notions about "consideration." And so, while recognizing that marriage was of course a valuable consideration to support a contract, the Tax Court did not deem marriage to satisfy the requirement of § 503 in that it was not a consideration reducible to money value. Accordingly, the Court found the whole value of the stock transferred to Mrs. More taxable under the statute and the relevant Treas. Reg. 79 (1936 ed.) Art. 8: "A consideration not reducible to a money value, as love and affection, promise of marriage, etc., is to be wholly disregarded, and the entire value of the property transferred constitutes the amount of the gift." In the alternative, the Tax Court was of the view that if Mrs. More's loss of her trust income rather than the marriage was consideration for the taxpayer's transfer of his stock to her, he is not relieved from the tax because he did not receive any money's worth from Mrs. More's relinquishment of her trust income, and, in any event, the actual value of her interest in the trust, subject to fluctuations of its stock earnings, was not proved. One member of the Tax Court dissented, deeming that the gift tax legislation invoked ordinary contract conceptions of "consideration."

The Circuit Court of Appeals rejected this line of reasoning. It found in the marriage agreement an arm's length bargain and an absence of "donative intent" which it deemed essential: "A donative intent followed by a donative act is essential to constitute a gift; and no strained and artificial construction of a supplementary statute should be indulged to tax as a gift a transfer actually lacking donative intent." 144 F.2d 78, 82.

Sections 501 and 503 are not disparate provisions. Congress directed them to the same purpose, and they should not be separated in application. Had Congress taxed "gifts" simpliciter, it would be appropriate to assume that the term was used in its colloquial sense, and a search for "donative intent" would be indicated. But Congress intended to use the term "gifts" in its broadest and most comprehensive sense. H. Rep. No. 708, 72d Cong., 1st Sess., p. 27; Rep. No. 665, 72d Cong., 1st Sess., p. 39 * * * Congress chose not to require an ascertainment of what too often is an elusive state of mind. For purposes of the gift tax it not only dispensed with the test of "donative intent." It formulated a much more workable external test, that where "property is transferred for less than an adequate and full consideration in money or money's worth," the excess in such money value "shall, for the purpose of the tax imposed by this title, be deemed a gift. . . ." And Treasury Regulations have emphasized that common law considerations were not embodied in the gift tax.

To reinforce the evident desire of Congress to hit all the protean arrangements which the wit of man can devise that are not business transactions within the meaning of ordinary speech, the Treasury Regulations make clear that no genuine business transaction comes within the purport of the gift tax by excluding "a sale, exchange, or other transfer of property made in the ordinary course of business (a transaction which is bona fide, at arm's length, and free from any donative intent)." Treas. Reg. 79 (1936 ed.) Art. 8. [Treas. Reg. § 25.2512–8.] Thus on finding that a transfer in the circumstances of a particular case is not made in the ordinary course of business, the transfer becomes subject to the gift tax to the extent that it is not made "for an adequate and full consideration in money or money's worth." See 2 Paul, Federal Estate and Gift Taxation (1942) p. 1113.

The Tax Court in effect found the transfer of the stock to Mrs. More was not made at arm's length in the ordinary course of business. It noted that the inducement was marriage, took account of the discrepancy between what she got and what she gave up, and also of the benefit that her marriage settlement brought to her son. These were considerations the Tax Court could justifiably heed, and heeding, decide as it did. * * *

If we are to isolate as an independently reviewable question of law the view of the Tax Court that money consideration must benefit the donor to relieve a transfer by him from being a gift, we think the Tax Court was correct. * * * To be sure, the Revenue Act of 1932 does not spell out a requirement of benefit to the transferor to afford relief from the gift tax. Its forerunner, § 320 of the 1924 Act, 43 Stat. 253, 314, was more explicit in that it provided that the excess of the transfer over "the consideration received shall . . . be deemed a gift." It will hardly be suggested, however, that in reimposing the gift tax in 1932 Congress meant to exclude transfers that would have been taxed under the 1924 Act. The section taxing as gifts transfers that are not made for "adequate and full [money] consideration" aims to reach those transfers which are withdrawn from the donor's estate. To allow detriment to the donee to satisfy the requirement of "adequate and full consideration" would violate the purpose of the statute and open wide the door for evasion of the gift tax. See 2 Paul, supra, at 1114.

Reversed.

B. INTEREST-FREE AND LOW-INTEREST LOANS

1. JUDICIAL RESPONSE

DICKMAN V. COMMISSIONER
Supreme Court of the United States, 1984.
465 U.S. 330.

CHIEF JUSTICE BURGER delivered the opinion of the Court:

We granted certiorari to resolve a conflict among the Circuits as to whether intrafamily, interest-free demand loans result in taxable gifts of the value of the use of the money lent.

I

A

Paul and Esther Dickman were husband and wife; Lyle Dickman was their son. Paul, Esther, Lyle, and Lyle's wife and children were the owners of Artesian Farm, Inc. (Artesian), a closely-held Florida corporation. Between 1971 and 1976, Paul and Esther loaned substantial sums to Lyle and Artesian. Over this five-year interval, the outstanding balances for the loans from Paul to Lyle varied from $144,715 to $342,915; with regard to Paul's loans to Artesian, the outstanding balances ranged from $207,875 to $669,733. During the same period, Esther loaned $226,130 to Lyle and $68,651 to Artesian. With two exceptions, all the loans were evidenced by demand notes bearing no interest.

Paul Dickman died in 1976, leaving a gross estate for federal estate tax purposes of $3,464,011. The Commissioner of Internal Revenue audited Paul Dickman's estate and determined that the loans to Lyle and Artesian resulted in taxable gifts to the extent of the value of the use of the loaned funds.[2] The Commissioner then issued statutory notices of gift tax deficiency both to Paul Dickman's estate and to Esther Dickman.[3]

Esther Dickman and the estate, petitioners here, sought redetermination of the deficiencies in the Tax Court. Reaffirming its earlier decision in Crown v. Commissioner, 67 T.C. 1060 (1977), aff'd, 585 F.2d 234 (C.A.7 1978), the Tax Court concluded that intrafamily, interest-free demand loans do not result in taxable gifts. 41 TCM 620, 623 (1980). Because the Tax Court determined that all the loans to Lyle and Artesian were made payable on demand, it held that the loans were not subject to the federal gift tax. Id., at 624.

B

The United States Court of Appeals for the Eleventh Circuit reversed, holding that gratuitous interest-free demand loans give rise to gift tax liability. 690 F.2d 812, 819 (1982). Reviewing the language and history of the gift tax provisions of the Internal Revenue Code of 1954 (Code), 26 U.S.C. § 2501 et seq., the Court of Appeals concluded that Congress intended the gift tax to have the broadest and most comprehensive coverage possible. The court reasoned that the making of an interest-free demand loan constitutes a "transfer of property by gift" within the meaning of 26 U.S.C. § 2501(a)(1), and accordingly is subject to the gift tax provisions of the Code. In so holding, the Court of Appeals squarely rejected

---

[2] In valuing the gifts, the Commissioner multiplied the loan balances outstanding at the end of each taxable quarter by interest rates ranging from six percent to nine percent per annum. These interest rates were taken from § 6621 of the Internal Revenue Code of 1954, 26 U.S.C. § 6621, made applicable by Code § 6601 to under payments of tax.

[3] The Commissioner asserted a $42,212.91 deficiency against Paul Dickman's estate and a $41,109.78 deficiency against Esther Dickman.

the contrary position adopted by the United States Court of Appeals for the Seventh Circuit in Crown v. Commissioner, 585 F.2d 234 (1978). We granted certiorari to resolve this conflict * * *; we affirm.

II

A

The statutory language of the federal gift tax provisions purports to reach any gratuitous transfer of any interest in property. Section 2501(a)(1) of the Code imposes a tax upon "the transfer of property by gift." 26 U.S.C. § 2501(a)(1). Section 2511(a) highlights the broad sweep of the tax imposed by § 2501, providing in pertinent part:

> Subject to the limitations contained in this chapter, the tax imposed by section 2501 shall apply whether the transfer is in trust or otherwise, whether the gift is direct or indirect, and whether the property is real or personal, tangible or intangible. . . .

Id., at § 2511(a). The language of these statutes is clear and admits of but one reasonable interpretation: transfers of property by gift, by whatever means effected, are subject to the federal gift tax.

The committee reports accompanying the Revenue Act of 1932, 47 Stat. 169, which established the present scheme of federal gift taxation, make plain that Congress intended the gift tax statute to reach all gratuitous transfers of any valuable interest in property. Among other things, these reports state:

> The terms "property," "transfer," "gift," and "indirectly" are used in the broadest and most comprehensive sense; the term "property" reaching every species of right or interest protected by law and having an exchangeable value.

> The words "transfer . . . by gift" and "whether . . . direct or indirect" are designed to cover and comprehend all transactions . . . whereby, and to the extent . . . that, property or a property right is donatively passed to or conferred upon another, regardless of the means or the device employed in its accomplishment.

H.R. Rep. No. 708, 72d Cong., 1st Sess., 27–28 (1932); S. Rep. No. 665, 72d Cong., 1st Sess., 39 (1932). The plain language of the statute reflects this legislative history; the gift tax was designed to encompass all transfers of property and property rights having significant value.

On several prior occasions, this Court has acknowledged the expansive sweep of the gift tax provisions. In Commissioner v. Wemyss, 324 U.S. 303, 306 (1945), the Court explained that:

> Congress intended to use the term "gifts" in its broadest and most comprehensive sense. . . . [in order] to hit all the protean

arrangements which the wit of man can devise that are not business transactions within the meaning of ordinary speech.

The Court has also noted that the language of the gift tax statute "is broad enough to include property, however conceptual or contingent," Smith v. Shaughnessy, 318 U.S. 176, 180 (1943), so as "to reach every kind and type of transfer by gift," Robinette v. Helvering, 318 U.S. 184, 187 (1943). Thus, the decisions of this Court reinforce the view that the gift tax should be applied broadly to effectuate the clear intent of Congress.

B

In asserting that interest-free demand loans give rise to taxable gifts, the Commissioner does not seek to impose the gift tax upon the principal amount of the loan, but only upon the reasonable value of the use of the money lent. The taxable gift that assertedly results from an interest-free demand loan is the value of receiving and using the money without incurring a corresponding obligation to pay interest along with the loan's repayment.[5] Is such a gratuitous transfer of the right to use money a "transfer of property" within the intendment of § 2501(a)(1)?

We have little difficulty accepting the theory that the use of valuable property—in this case money—is itself a legally protectible property interest. Of the aggregate rights associated with any property interest, the right of use of property is perhaps of the highest order. One court put it succinctly:

> "Property" is more than just the physical thing—the land, the bricks, the mortar—it is also the sum of all the rights and powers incident to ownership of the physical thing. Property is composed of constituent elements and of these elements the right to use the physical thing to the exclusion of others is the most essential and beneficial. Without this right all other elements would be of little value. . . . Passailaigue v. United States, 224 F.Supp. 682, 686 (M.D.Ga.1963).

What was transferred here was the use of a substantial amount of cash for an indefinite period of time. An analogous interest in real property, the use under a tenancy at will, has long been recognized as a property right. E.g., Restatement (Second) of Property § 1.6 (1977); G. Thompson, Commentaries on the Modern Law of Real Property § 1020 (J. Grimes ed. 1980). For example, a parent who grants to a child the rent-free, indefinite use of commercial property having a reasonable rental value of $8000 a month has clearly transferred a valuable property right. The transfer of

---

[5] The Commissioner's tax treatment of interest-free demand loans may perhaps be best understood as a two-step approach to such transactions. Under this theory, such a loan has two basic economic components: an arm's length loan from the lender to the borrower, on which the borrower pays the lender a fair rate of interest, followed by a gift from the lender to the borrower in the amount of that interest. See Crown v. Commissioner, 585 F.2d 234, 240 (C.A.7 1978).

$100,000 in cash, interest-free and repayable on demand, is similarly a grant of the use of valuable property. Its uncertain tenure may reduce its value, but it does not undermine its status as property. In either instance, when the property owner transfers to another the right to use the object, an identifiable property interest has clearly changed hands.

The right to the use of $100,000 without charge is a valuable interest in the money lent, as much so as the rent-free use of property consisting of land and buildings. In either case, there is a measurable economic value associated with the use of the property transferred. The value of the use of money is found in what it can produce; the measure of that value is interest—"rent" for the use of the funds. We can assume that an interest-free loan for a fixed period, especially for a prolonged period, may have greater value than such a loan made payable on demand, but it would defy common human experience to say that an intrafamily loan payable on demand is not subject to accommodation; its value may be reduced by virtue of its demand status, but that value is surely not eliminated.

* * *

Against this background, the gift tax statutes clearly encompass within their broad sweep the gratuitous transfer of the use of money. Just as a tenancy at will in real property is an estate or interest in land, so also is the right to use money a cognizable interest in personal property. The right to use money is plainly a valuable right, readily measurable by reference to current interest rates; the vast banking industry is positive evidence of this reality. Accordingly, we conclude that the interest-free loan of funds is a "transfer of property by gift" within the contemplation of the federal gift tax statutes.

C

Our holding that an interest-free demand loan results in a taxable gift of the use of the transferred funds is fully consistent with one of the major purposes of the federal gift tax statute: protection of the estate tax and the income tax. The legislative history of the gift tax provisions reflects that Congress enacted a tax on gifts to supplement existing estate and income tax laws. H.R. Rep. No. 708, supra, at 28; S. Rep. No. 665, supra, at 40; see also 65 Cong. Rec. 3119–3120, 8095–8096 (1924); Harriss, Legislative History of Federal Gift Taxation, 18 Taxes 531, 536 (1940). Failure to impose the gift tax on interest-free loans would seriously undermine this estate and income tax protection goal.

A substantial no-interest loan from parent to child creates significant tax benefits for the lender quite apart from the economic advantages to the borrower. This is especially so when an individual in a high income tax bracket transfers income-producing property to an individual in a lower income tax bracket, thereby reducing the taxable income of the high-bracket taxpayer at the expense, ultimately, of all other taxpayers and the government. Subjecting interest-free loans to gift taxation minimizes the potential loss to the federal fisc generated by the use of such loans as an income tax avoidance mechanism for the transferor. Gift taxation of interest-free loans also effectuates Congress' desire to supplement the estate tax provisions. A gratuitous transfer of income-producing property may enable the transferor to avoid the future estate tax liability that would result if the earnings generated by the property—rent, interest, or dividends—became a part of the transferor's estate. Imposing the gift tax upon interest-free loans bolsters the estate tax by preventing the diminution of the transferor's estate in this fashion.

III

Petitioners contend that administrative and equitable considerations require a holding that no gift tax consequences result from the making of interest-free demand loans. In support of this position, petitioners advance several policy arguments; none withstands studied analysis.

A

Petitioners first advance an argument accepted by the Tax Court in Crown v. Commissioner, supra:

> [O]ur income tax system does not recognize unrealized earnings or accumulations of wealth and no taxpayer is under any obligation to continuously invest his money for a profit. The opportunity cost of either letting one's money remain idle or suffering a loss from an unwise investment is not taxable merely because a profit *could have been made* from a wise investment. 67 T.C., at 1063–1064.

Thus, petitioners argue, an interest-free loan should not be made subject to the gift tax simply because of the possibility that the money lent might have enhanced the transferor's taxable income or gross estate had the loan never been made.

This contention misses the mark. It is certainly true that no law requires an individual to invest his property in an income-producing fashion, just as no law demands that a transferor charge interest or rent for the use of money or other property. An individual may, without incurring the gift tax, squander money, conceal it under a mattress, or otherwise waste its use value by failing to invest it. Such acts of consumption have nothing to do with lending money at no interest. The gift tax is an excise tax on transfers of property; allowing dollars to lie idle involves no transfer. If the taxpayer chooses not to waste the use value of money, however, but instead transfers the use to someone else, a taxable event has occurred. That the transferor himself could have consumed or wasted the use value of the money without incurring the gift tax does not change this result. Contrary to petitioners' assertion, a holding in favor of the taxability of interest-free loans does not impose upon the transferor a duty profitably to invest; rather, it merely recognizes that certain tax consequences inevitably flow from a decision to make a "transfer of property by gift." 26 U.S.C. § 2501(a)(1).

B

Petitioners next attack the breadth of the Commissioner's view that interest-free demand loans give rise to taxable gifts. Carried to its logical extreme, petitioners argue, the Commissioner's rationale would elevate to the status of taxable gifts such commonplace transactions as a loan of the proverbial cup of sugar to a neighbor or a loan of lunch money to a colleague. Petitioners urge that such a result is an untenable intrusion by the government into cherished zones of privacy, particularly where intrafamily transactions are involved.

Our laws require parents to provide their minor offspring with the necessities and conveniences of life; questions under the tax law often arise, however, when parents provide more than the necessities, and in quantities significant enough to attract the attention of the taxing authorities. Generally, the legal obligation of support terminates when the offspring reach majority. Nonetheless, it is not uncommon for parents to provide their adult children with such things as the use of cars or vacation cottages, simply on the basis of the family relationship. We assume that the focus of the Internal Revenue Service is not on such traditional familial matters. When the government levies a gift tax on routine neighborly or familial gifts, there will be time enough to deal with such a case.

Moreover, the tax law provides liberally for gifts to both family members and others; within the limits of the prescribed statutory exemptions, even substantial gifts may be entirely tax free. First, under § 2503(e) of the Code, 26 U.S.C. § 2503(e), amounts paid on behalf of an individual for tuition at a qualified educational institution or for medical care are not considered "transfer[s] of property by gift" for purposes of the gift tax statutes. More significantly, section 2503(b) of the Code provides an annual exclusion from the computation of taxable gifts of $10,000 per year, per donee; this provision allows a taxpayer to give up to $10,000 annually to each of any number of persons, without incurring any gift tax liability. The "split gift" provision of Code § 2513(a), which effectively enables a husband and wife to give each object of their bounty $20,000 per year without liability for gift tax, further enhances the ability to transfer significant amounts of money and property free of gift tax consequences. Finally, should a taxpayer make gifts during one year that exceed the § 2503(b) annual gift tax exclusion, no gift tax liability will result until the unified credit of Code § 2505 has been exhausted. These generous exclusions, exceptions, and credits clearly absorb the sorts of de minimis gifts petitioners envision and render illusory the administrative problems that petitioners perceive in their "parade of horribles."

* * *

IV

As we have noted, * * * Congress has provided generous exclusions and credits designed to reduce the gift tax liability of the great majority of taxpayers. Congress clearly has the power to provide a similar exclusion for the gifts that result from interest-free demand loans. Any change in the gift tax consequences of such loans, however, is a legislative responsibility, not a judicial one. Until such a change occurs, we are bound to effectuate Congress' intent to protect the estate and income tax systems with a broad and comprehensive tax upon all "transfer[s] of property by gift." Cf. Diedrich v. Commissioner, 457 U.S. 191, 199 (1982).

We hold, therefore, that the interest-free demand loans shown by this record resulted in taxable gifts of the reasonable value of the use of the money lent. Accordingly, the judgment of the United States Court of Appeals for the Eleventh Circuit is

Affirmed.

[JUSTICE POWELL, joined by JUSTICE REHNQUIST, dissented.]

2. STATUTORY RESPONSE

Although *Dickman* eliminated the advantageous gift tax treatment of interest-free loans, the IRS continued to view interest-free or low-interest loans as significant income tax avoidance devices, and especially so in times of high interest rates. For example, a parent in a high-income tax bracket could make an interest-free loan to a child who could then invest the funds—perhaps in the very same investment the parent would have chosen. The income from the investment would be taxed at the child's low-income tax bracket rather than the parent's high bracket. IRS attempts to impute income to the recipient of such an interest-free loan were consistently rebuffed. See, e.g., Martin v. Commissioner, 649 F.2d 1133 (5th Cir. 1981); Beaton v. Commissioner, 664 F.2d 315 (1st Cir. 1981); Baker v. Commissioner, 677 F.2d 11 (2d Cir. 1982); Suttle v. Commissioner, 625 F.2d 1127 (4th Cir. 1980); Parks v. Commissioner, 686 F.2d 408 (6th Cir. 1982); Hardee v. United States, 708 F.2d 661 (Fed. Cir. 1983).

Interest-free or low-interest loans grew rapidly in popularity in the early 1980s, encouraged by the unprecedented high interest rates during that time. Such loans became a favorite device for intra-family income shifting, principally to children. An interest-free loan could effectively shift the burden of taxation on income for any period the parent might choose—whether months or years—an approach that proved especially popular for accumulation of college expense funds.

Confronted with a growing tax avoidance threat, Congress responded aggressively, incorporating in the Tax Reform Act of 1984 a very broad provision—section 7872—that forcefully addresses both the gift and income tax aspects of interest-free or low-interest loans.

A simple example using current income tax rates will illustrate the application of section 7872. Assume that a mother, whose marginal income tax bracket is 35 percent, wishes to finance an adult child's college education in part with earnings from funds invested in United States Treasury Bills. The mother lends $50,000 to the child on January 1, receiving in return a no-interest note, payable on demand. The loan is outstanding throughout the year. The child invests the $50,000 in Treasury Bills and earns interest on the $50,000 at 6 percent—totaling $3,000. The results before and after section 7872 are as follows:

1. Prior to enactment of section 7872, the results were very favorable for the mother and child. Although use of the $50,000 constituted a gift under *Dickman*, the use value of the $50,000 was well within the annual exclusion, with the result that no gift tax return was required. The $3,000 in Treasury Bill income was taxed entirely to the child, at a total tax cost that would probably not exceed 10 percent, even if the child had income from other sources as well. Therefore, the earnings available for the child's college education after income taxes were $3,000 less income taxes of $300, or $2,700. By contrast, if the mother had earned the same income herself and paid income tax at a 35 percent rate, only $1,950 would be available for college expenses.

2. Section 7872 radically changes the treatment of the transaction. First, section 7872 assigns a definite value to use of the $50,000 for both gift and income tax purposes. This is determined by the "applicable Federal rate," which is typically higher than the rate obtainable on Treasury Bills. If the applicable Federal rate throughout the year is 7 percent, the value of the loan for both gift and income tax purposes is $3,500. The $3,500 amount is treated for all tax purposes as an imputed gift from the mother to the child, followed by an imputed interest payment from the child to the mother, with these results:

    (a) The mother is treated as making a $3,500 gift to the child. This amount is excluded from the child's gross income by section 102(a). However, there is a $3,500 gift by the mother for gift tax purposes. If the mother has exhausted the section 2503(b) annual exclusion for other gifts to the child, the $3,500 is a taxable gift; and

(b) The mother is treated as receiving $3,500 in interest from the child, and the mother must pay income tax on this amount. Therefore, the mother pays more in income tax than she invests the funds herself invested in 6% Treasury Bills, yielding interest income of $3,000.

The "kiddie tax," currently embodied in section 1(g), reduces the avoidance potential inherent in unearned income of children below the age of 18 and, in most cases, children under age 24 who are full-time students. It effectively negates much of the benefit of interest-free or low-interest loans. Under the Tax Cuts and Jobs Act of 2017, the unearned income, including interest, will be taxed using the rates for trusts and estates from 2018 through 2025. When the Act sunsets, the unearned income will be taxed at the marginal rate of the child's parents. Section 1(g) was not enacted until 1986—two years after enactment of section 7872.

Although the application of section 7872 to the transaction described above is relatively simple, the complexities involved in applying the same principles more broadly are formidable. A few of the more important aspects of section 7872 are described below:

1. The section applies to any "gift loan," which is defined as a loan as to which "the forgoing of interest is in the nature of a gift." I.R.C. § 7872(c)(1)(A) and (f)(3).

2. The section also applies to a loan that in fact constitutes compensation to an employee or a dividend to a shareholder or that has a tax avoidance purpose. I.R.C. § 7872(c)(1)(B) & (C). If the loan falls in the compensation or dividend category, the imputed transfer of $3,500 from lender to borrower is treated as payment of salary or a dividend rather than a gift.

3. The section applies to both demand and term loans and provides complex rules for valuation of term loans. I.R.C. § 7872(a) and (b).

4. The section applies not just to interest-free loans, but to any loan that bears interest at a rate below the applicable Federal rate. In the case of a low-interest gift loan, the amount of the gift (and imputed interest) is the difference between the Applicable Federal Rate and the interest actually paid. I.R.C. § 7872(e)(2).

5. The crucially important minimum required interest rate— the Applicable Federal Rate—is determined by reference to the average yield on United States government obligations. I.R.C. §§ 7872(f)(2) and 1274(d)(1)(C). For demand instruments the rate is the federal short-term rate—the average market interest rate on government obligations

having a maturity of three years or less. I.R.C. §§ 7872(f)(2)(B) and 1274(d)(1)(A). For term loans of more than three years, the market interest rates for longer-term government obligations are used, depending on the term of the loan. The Applicable Federal Rates are redetermined each month. I.R.C. § 1274(d)(1)(B). In the case of a term loan, the applicable Federal rate for the entire period of the loan is determined by the rate for the month in which the loan is made. I.R.C. § 7872(f)(2)(A). In the case of a demand loan, the rate varies from month to month as the federal rates are redetermined. I.R.C. § 7872(f)(2)(B).

Because loans between family members may have legitimate purposes other than tax avoidance, Congress has provided exceptions for circumstances in which tax avoidance is not present. However, the exceptions are narrow:

1. A general de minimis exception is provided for gift loans between individuals not exceeding $10,000 outstanding at any one time. I.R.C. § 7872(c)(2)(A). This exception, however, is not available if the loan is "directly attributable to the purchase or carrying of income-producing assets." I.R.C. § 7872(c)(2)(B). Therefore, if the borrower directly or indirectly invests the borrowed funds in an asset that produces income, (such as Treasury Bills or a certificate of deposit) the $10,000 exception will not apply. As a result, the de minimis exception will not be available for the typical income-shifting interest-free loan. However, the de minimis exception will apply if the borrower does not invest the borrowed funds but rather expends them immediately, e.g., for tuition and other college expenses. It is uncertain how the de minimis rule would be applied to circumstances in which the borrower temporarily invests a portion of the borrowed funds in income-producing assets before expending them.

2. A more important exception applies to loans up to $100,000. I.R.C. § 7872(d)(1). This exception is designed for circumstances such as a loan by a parent to a child to enable the child to make a down payment on a personal residence. If the loan arrangements do not "have as 1 of their principal purposes the avoidance of any federal tax" (I.R.C. § 7872(d)(1)(B)), the amount of interest imputed is limited to the borrower's net investment income from all sources—not just the earnings investment of the borrowed funds. I.R.C. § 7872(d)(1)(A). Note that this exception eliminates only the imputed interest—not the imputed gift. Note also that any investment income earned by the borrower will automatically

be imputed to the lender if the borrower's net investment income exceeds $1,000. I.R.C. § 7872(d)(1)(E)(ii). This produces the strange result that in years when the loan is outstanding, interest earned by a borrower child from a bank account or other investment is immediately attributed to the lender parent, so that the parent in effect pays tax on income that is earned by the child. "Tax avoidance" is defined so broadly in the proposed regulations that it may be difficult for many taxpayers to qualify for the I.R.C. § 7872(d) exception. Prop. Treas. Reg. § 1.7872–4(e).

The practical effect of section 7872 is to largely eliminate the tax advantages of interest-free or low-interest loans, making such loans attractive only under limited circumstances. One such case is a family that has investment alternatives producing a yield substantially greater than the Applicable Federal Rate. If an investment available to the family yields 10 percent and the Applicable Federal Rate is 4 percent, a loan at 4 percent permits shifting of the income tax burden on the additional 6 percent to the child. Another possible application involves the child's investment of demand loan funds in a long-term investment that produces a yield higher than the Applicable Federal Rate for demand instruments. Again, the income tax on the difference between the long-term rate and the Applicable Federal Rate for demand instruments is shifted to the child. Finally, interest-free loans to eliminate or reduce the child's need to borrow for purchase of a residence may be attractive, at least until the child begins to have significant investment income. For example, if the parent would earn an after-tax rate of only 4 percent on the invested funds and the child would have to pay interest on mortgage debt at 8 percent, with little offsetting tax benefit because of the child's low tax bracket, the parent's provision of an interest-free loan to reduce the need for borrowing by the child may be attractive. However, once the child's net investment income exceeds $1,000, the entirety of the investment income will be imputed to the parent, and the advantages of the loan will be diminished.

From a planning perspective, section 7872 can be entirely avoided if interest is charged at, or higher than, the Applicable Federal Rate. For that reason, low interest loans are especially attractive when the federal rates are low.

PROBLEMS

1.　Nicole entered law school at State University in the fall of Year 1. Nicole's age is 24, with the result that the section 1(g) "kiddie tax" is not applicable. Her mother, Renae, paid a total of $20,000 toward tuition and other expenses for the fall of Year 1. Late in Year 1 Renae, who has high income from a retail business as well as from various investments, was advised that she could save a substantial amount of income tax by making an interest-free loan to Nicole, so that Nicole could use the earnings to pay her college expenses directly.

On January 1 of Year 2, Renae lent $500,000 in cash to Nicole, without interest, to be repaid upon Renae's demand. Nicole invested the $500,000 in United States Treasury bills throughout Year 2 at an average yield of 4 percent, producing $20,000 of income, which Nicole used to pay her college expenses for the spring of Year 2. Renae did not demand repayment of the loan during Year 2. Assume that throughout Year 2 the applicable Federal rate for demand instruments under section 1274(d), compounded semiannually, was 5 percent.

How should Renae and Nicole treat this transaction for gift and income tax purposes in Year 2?

2.   Would the result in Problem 1 be changed if the amount that Renae lent to Nicole were only $10,000?

3.   Assume the same facts as in Problem 1. Nicole repaid the entire $500,000 to Renae on December 31 of Year 3.

Nicole graduated from law school in Year 4 and moved to another city, where she wished to purchase a residence. On July 1 of Year 4, Renae lent $50,000 in cash, without interest, to Nicole to be repaid on Renae's demand. Nicole used the entirety of the funds to make a down payment on a home on July 1 of Year 4. During Year 4 Nicole had no investment income.

During Year 5 Nicole's salary increased, and she began to put some money aside in a money market account. During Year 5 she received interest of $1,800 on the money market account, and all of this constituted investment income as defined in section 163(d)(3).

Renae did not demand repayment of the loan at any time during Year 4 or Year 5. Assume that throughout Year 4 and Year 5 the applicable Federal rate for demand instruments under section 1274(d), compounded semiannually, was 6 percent.

How should Renae and Nicole treat these transactions for gift and income tax purposes in Year 4 and Year 5?

4.   George, a first-year medical student, was so exhausted by his studies that his parents became worried about his health. Thinking that George needed rest and recreation, George's parents arranged for George and his friends to use the parents' condominium at Vail, Colorado, during the week of George's spring vacation.

George and his friends used the condominium without charge. The usage occurred at a popular time for skiing, and George's parents could have readily rented the condominium to others for $3,000 for the week.

Did George's parents make a taxable gift to him? If so, what is the amount of the gift?

C. GIFTS OF SERVICES

1. IN GENERAL

Section 2501 states that the gift tax is to be imposed on the "transfer of property by gift." Does the word "property" include personal services? The Commissioner has not, in fact, pressed for an expansive interpretation of the word "property" to include personal services. A gift of a right to income, however, is clearly taxable as a gift, making the timing of a gift of services crucial. If the taxpayer waits until after the services have been performed to manifest donative intent, the services may have already earned him a right to income, and a transfer of that right will be subject to the gift tax.

The issue arises often in the context of decedents' estates. An executor who is a family member may prefer to forego a fee in order to maximize the amount that will go to the beneficiaries of the estate. Alternatively, the executor could claim his fee as executor. In that event, the fee would be taxable to the executor as income, and the amount the beneficiaries receive would be reduced accordingly.

An executor who decides that it is preferable to forego the fee must be sure to avoid being treated as having made a gift to the beneficiaries in the amount of the executor's entitlement to compensation. The following ruling provides the Commissioner's guidance as to how that can be accomplished.

REVENUE RULING 66–167
1966–1 C.B. 20.

* * *

In the instant case, the taxpayer served as the sole executor of his deceased wife's estate pursuant to the terms of a will under which he and his adult son were each given a half interest in the net proceeds thereof. The laws of the state in which the will was executed and probated impose no limitation on the use of either principal or income for the payment of compensation to an executor and do not purport to deal with whether a failure to withdraw any particular fee or commission may properly be considered as a waiver thereof.

The taxpayer's administration of his wife's estate continued for a period of approximately three full years during which time he filed two annual accountings as well as the usual final accounting with the probate court, all of which reported the collection and disposition of a substantial amount of estate assets.

At some point within a reasonable time after first entering upon the performance of his duties as executor, the taxpayer decided to make no charge for serving in such capacity, and each of the aforesaid accountings accordingly omitted any claim for statutory commissions and was so filed with the intention to waive the same. The taxpayer-executor likewise took no other action which was inconsistent with a fixed and continuing intention to serve on a gratuitous basis.

The specific questions presented are whether the amounts which the taxpayer-executor could have received as fees or commissions are includible in his gross income for Federal income tax purposes and whether his waiver of the right to receive these amounts results in a gift for Federal gift tax purposes.

In Revenue Ruling 56–472, the executor of an estate entered into an agreement to serve in such capacity for substantially less than all of the statutory commissions otherwise allowable to him and also formally waived his right to receive the remaining portion thereof. The basic agreement with respect to his acceptance of a reduced amount of compensation antedated the performance of any services and the related waiver of the disclaimed commissions was signed before he would otherwise have become entitled to receive them. Under these circumstances, the ruling held that the difference between the commissions which such executor could have otherwise acquired an unrestricted right to obtain and the lesser amount which he actually received was not includible in his income and that his disclaimer did not effect any gift thereof.

In Revenue Ruling 64–225, the trustees of a testamentary trust in the State of New York waived their rights to receive one particular class of statutory commissions. This waiver was effected by means of certain formal instruments that were not executed until long after the close of most of the years to which such commissions related. This circumstance, along with all the other facts described therein, indicated that such trustees had not intended to render their services on a gratuitous basis. The Revenue Ruling accordingly held that such commissions were includible in the trustees' gross income for the taxable year when so waived and that their execution of the waivers also effected a taxable gift of these commissions.

The crucial test of whether the executor of an estate or any other fiduciary in a similar situation may waive his right to receive statutory commissions without thereby incurring any income or gift tax liability is whether the waiver involved will at least primarily constitute evidence of an intent to render a gratuitous service. If the timing, purpose, and effect of the waiver make it serve any other important objective, it may then be proper to conclude that the fiduciary has thereby enjoyed a realization of income by means of controlling the disposition thereof and, at the same time, has also effected a taxable gift by means of any resulting transfer to a third party of his contingent beneficial interest in a part of the assets under his fiduciary control. See the above cited Revenue Rulings and the authorities therein cited, as well as section 25.2511–1(c) of the Gift Tax Regulations.

The requisite intention to serve on a gratuitous basis will ordinarily be deemed to have been adequately manifested if the executor or administrator of an estate supplies one or more of the decedent's principal legatees or devisees, or of those principally entitled to distribution of decedent's intestate estate, within six months after his initial appointment as such fiduciary, with a formal waiver of any right to compensation for his services. Such an intention to serve on a gratuitous basis may also be adequately manifested through an implied waiver if the fiduciary fails to claim fees or commissions at the time of filing the usual accountings and if all the other attendant facts and circumstances are consistent with a fixed and continuing intention to serve gratuitously. If the executor or administrator of an estate claims his statutory fees or commissions as a deduction on one or more of the estate, inheritance, or income tax returns which are filed on behalf of the estate, such action will ordinarily be considered inconsistent with any fixed or definite intention to serve on a gratuitous basis. No such claim was made in the instant case.

Accordingly, the amounts which the present taxpayer-executor would have otherwise become entitled to receive as fees or commissions are not includible in his gross income for Federal income tax purposes and are not gifts for Federal gift tax purposes.

2. INVESTMENT COUNSEL, BUSINESS OPPORTUNITIES, AND LOAN GUARANTEES

A parent with expertise, contacts, and substantial resources may be in a position to provide valuable assistance to a son or daughter undertaking business or investment activities. For example, the parent can provide expertise that would cost the child a great deal if obtained through a compensated consultant, or the parent can refer promising business opportunities to the child. The IRS has shown little inclination to tax such transfers as gifts and has generally been unsuccessful when it has tried.

In Commissioner v. Hogle, 165 F.2d 352 (10th Cir.1947), the IRS sought to tax as a gift the value of a parent's investment counsel, which provided substantial profits and income for his children. The Tenth Circuit declined to treat this as a taxable transfer. In Estate of Blass v. Commissioner, 11 T.C.M. (CCH) 622 (1952), the taxpayer identified business opportunities, brought those opportunities to the attention of trusts benefitting other family members, and provided services and expertise making possible the trusts' profitable purchase and sale of property. The Tax Court, following *Hogle*, held that there was no taxable gift.

Another mechanism a prosperous parent can employ is to guarantee loans to her children, thereby making available to the children sources of credit the children could not otherwise obtain. In Priv. Ltr. Rul. 9113009 the IRS asserted that a parent's guarantee of a loan made by a bank to a child of the parent would be treated as a taxable gift to the extent of the market value of the guarantee. In Priv. Ltr. Rul. 9409108, however, the IRS withdrew Priv. Ltr. Rul. 9113009 because of a change in the IRS position on another issue and stated the IRS "express[es] no opinion at this time" on the other issues involved in Priv. Ltr. Rul. 9113009, presumably including treatment of a loan guarantee as a gift. There remains the possibility that the IRS might someday reassert the principle that a loan guarantee can be taxed as a gift. However, the difficulty of valuing the parent's guarantee may prove an insurmountable obstacle.

D. GIFTS BY AGENTS

Because inter vivos gifts can produce important estate tax savings, arrangements are often made to empower an agent to make gifts on behalf of an incapacitated principal. This can be especially important in facilitating annual exclusion gifts under section 2503(b).

As explained in Chapter 7, there are important advantages to a donor who makes gifts that qualify for the section 2503(b) annual exclusion because the donor can entirely avoid gift and estate tax. For example, if the donor has three children and seven grandchildren, and the section 2503(b) annual exclusion is $17,000, $17,000 can be transferred entirely tax-free to each descendant—a total of $170,000. In light of the 40% estate tax rate, the donor can save $68,000 in a future estate tax liability. Moreover, this can be repeated each year while the donor is alive.

A donor who is still competent can make such transfers directly. However, if the donor's capacity is in doubt, there will arise the question whether an agent under a power of attorney is authorized to make such gifts for the donor. If transfers by the agent are binding on the principal under local law, the gifts will be treated as complete prior to the principal's death, and the $170,000 will not be included in the principal's gross estate. On the other hand, if the transfers are not binding on the principal, with the result that the principal's executor has legal power to void the gifts and reclaim the funds, the gifts are not treated as complete prior to death, and the $170,000 will be included in the principal's gross estate, fully subject to estate tax. The same rule would be applied to each year in which gifts are made by an agent.

Two separate issues are involved. The first is whether the principal has executed a power of attorney that authorizes the agent to act after the principal loses legal capacity. Under the traditional common-law rule, the principal's incapacity terminated the agency. However, after the increased use of durable powers of attorney, states began to seek out statutory solutions to address increased litigation. The majority of states have adopted the Uniform Power of Attorney Act or similar statutes to provide a statutory framework for power of attorney duties, effect, liability, and authority. Under the Act, a power of attorney is "durable" unless the power expressly states that it is terminated by the incapacity of the principal. Hence, the agent will have authority to act despite the principal's legal incapacity. The Uniform Power of Attorney Act replaced the Uniform Durable Power of Attorney Act. Under the Uniform Durable Power of Attorney Act, failure to include specific language to assure "durability" made the power nondurable, and the principal—or successor—had power to void the agent's actions. In that event, gifts by the agent would not be treated as completed during the principal's life, and the transferred property would be included and taxed in the principal's gross estate.

The second issue is whether the power of attorney—even if valid despite the principal's incapacity—confers authority for the agent to make gifts on behalf of the principal. A typical case is Estate of Casey v. Commissioner, 948 F.2d 895 (4th Cir. 1991). The agent made gifts under a power of attorney that authorized the agent:

> to do, execute and perform all and every other act or acts, thing or things as fully and to all intents and purposes as I myself might or could do if acting personally, it being my intention by this instrument to give my attorney hereby appointed, full and complete power to handle any of my business or to deal with any and all of my property of every kind and description, real, personal, or mixed, wheresoever located and howsoever held in his full and absolute discretion.

Id. at 897. Despite the breadth of this language, the Fourth Circuit, applying Virginia law, held that the absence of an express reference to power to make gifts deprived the agent of that power. Therefore, the gifts were voidable by the principal's executor, and the gifted property was included in the principal's gross estate. Virginia, like many other states, has since enacted specific statutory provisions regarding the power of an agent to make gifts. The agent has no power to make a gift of the principal's property unless that power is expressly granted.[3] If the power of attorney includes only a general power to make gifts, the agent cannot make a gift to any donee in an amount greater than the currently effective section 2503(b) annual exclusion. The principal can permit larger gifts by the agent, but only if that power is expressly granted.[4]

Typically, the principal will not be comfortable granting an unfettered power to make gifts. Usually, the primary tax objectives can be obtained by

---

[3] Va. Code Ann. § 64.2–1622 (2022).

[4] Va. Code Ann. § 64.2–1638 (2022).

authorizing gifts not exceeding the annual exclusion for each donee each year within certain categories of family members, such as descendants. If the principal is willing, it may be desirable in some cases to go further and authorize more substantial transfers, e.g., up to the applicable exclusion amount under the gift tax unified credit.

Additional decisions reaching the same result as *Casey*, as well as cases reaching the contrary result, are cited in connection with taxation of powers to alter or revoke for estate tax purposes under section 2038.

PROBLEMS

Jennifer, a widow, has a substantial estate that will be subjected to an estate tax rate of 40% at her death. Jennifer has four children and eight grandchildren, and in recent years she has made annual gifts to each of these descendants each year in the amount of the maximum section 2503(b) annual exclusion.

One month ago, Jennifer suffered a stroke. She is now in a coma, not expected to be revived, and will probably die within a month. Jennifer has not yet made any gifts during the current year. The maximum section 2503(b) annual exclusion is $17,000.

Jennifer's children have consulted her estate planner to inquire about the possibility that an agent, acting on behalf of Jennifer, could make an additional $17,000 transfer to each of the 12 descendants prior to Jennifer's death, thereby potentially $81,600 in estate taxes.

How would you respond to the children's query under each of the following alternative circumstances?

1. Jennifer has not executed a power of attorney.

2. Jennifer has executed a power of attorney, but it is not "durable," i.e., it does not survive incapacity of the principal.

3. Jennifer has executed a durable power of attorney that does not expressly provide that it is terminated upon the incapacity of the principal. The power of attorney does not expressly authorize the attorney-in-fact to make gifts. However, it does state that it grants to the attorney-in-fact "general power" to act for Jennifer "with respect to all lawful subjects and purposes."

4. Jennifer has executed a durable power of attorney that authorizes the attorney-in-fact to make the power survive incapacity of the principal. In addition to the language set forth in Problem 3, the power authorizes the attorney-in-fact "to make gifts to any one or more of my descendants as determined by my attorney-in-fact in his absolute discretion, provided that the total value of the gifts to any donee during any calendar year shall not exceed the maximum amount that can be excluded from taxable gifts for purposes of the United States Gift Tax pursuant

to section 2503(b) of the Internal Revenue Code, as in effect at the time of the gift."

E. INDIRECT GIFTS

A gift can occur without a direct transaction between donor and donee. Typically, this occurs in the context of a closely held business.

For example, if a mother provides all the capital for a newly formed corporation but takes only part of the stock herself and causes the remainder of the stock to be issued to her daughter, there will be a taxable gift by the mother to the daughter. For both income and gift tax purposes, the transaction will be treated as if the entirety of the stock had first been issued to the mother, followed by a gratuitous transfer of part of the stock by the mother to the daughter. See Treas. Reg. § 1.351–1(b); D'Angelo Associates, Inc. v. Commissioner, 70 T.C. 121 (1978).

There may be a gift even if the daughter contributes property as well, provided the value received by the mother is less than the value she contributes. A good example is Estate of Trenchard, 1995–121 T.C. Memo., 169 T.C.M. (CCH) 2164 (1995). Here both parents and children contributed property to capitalize a newly formed corporation. The parents received preferred stock, the children received common stock, and both parents and children received debentures. The court determined that the value of the property contributed by the parents was greater than the value of the preferred stock and debentures received by them, with the result that the parents were treated as making a gift of the difference to their children.

Similarly, a recapitalization of a corporation that changes the relative values of the ownership interests among family members without consideration can constitute a taxable gift. I.R.C. § 356(g)(1); Rev. Ruls. 86–39, 1986–1 C.B. 301 and 89–3, 1989–1 C.B. 278.

Typically, the crucial issue in indirect gift cases is valuation. A good example is Estate of Maggos, T.C. Memo. 2000–129, 79 T.C.M. (CCH) 1861 (2000). Here a mother and her son owned all the stock of a corporation. In 1987 the mother's 567 shares were redeemed for $3,000,000. The Tax Court undertook a thorough analysis of the value of the corporation, employing the various valuation techniques and discounts discussed in Chapter 11. The court concluded that the 567 shares were in fact worth $4,900,000 at the time of the redemption. Therefore, the mother had made a gift of $1,900,000 in 1987. The Tax Court determination occurred in 2000, with the result that interest on the unpaid gift tax had presumably accrued for more than 12 years. As explained in Chapter 8, filing a gift tax return with the necessary disclosures and appraisals can initiate the three-year statute of limitations under section 6501(a), with the result that such a transaction could not be questioned for either gift or estate tax purposes after three years. The *Maggos* circumstances demonstrate the wisdom of filing such gift tax returns for any substantial transaction that might conceivably be viewed as incorporating a value disparity.

If a contribution, redemption, recapitalization, or other change in the capital structure of a corporation or partnership has the effect of giving one family member liquidation or distribution rights different from those held by other family members, the transaction may be treated as a gift. I.R.C. § 2701(e)(5). Furthermore, the strict valuation rules of section 2701(a) may be applied, with the result that the magnitude of the gift may be greatly expanded.

Indirect gifts can occur by inaction. If one shareholder gratuitously waives or fails to exercise legal rights in such a way as to benefit other shareholders, a gift may occur. For example, if a shareholder controlling a closely held corporation foregoes the opportunity to require the corporation to pay noncumulative dividends on preferred stock held by the controlling shareholder, there is a taxable gift to the common shareholders whose interests are thereby enhanced. Tech. Adv. Mem. 8723007. Likewise, if a shareholder fails to exercise a right to convert preferred stock to common, thereby causing the fruits of growth in the value of the corporation to accrue entirely to the benefit of the existing holders of common stock, a taxable gift to the common shareholders may occur. Tech. Adv. Mem. 8726005.

In Snyder v. Commissioner, 93 T.C. 529 (1989), stock in a closely held corporation was held primarily by a mother and her children. The mother held Class A preferred, which had a noncumulative seven percent dividend right. The Class A preferred could be converted at any time to Class B preferred, which had a cumulative seven percent dividend right. Several years passed when dividends were not paid on the Class A preferred, yet the mother did not convert to Class B, which would have assured her of entitlement to cumulative dividend payments. The Tax Court held that the mother made a gift each year in the amount of the missed dividend by failing to exercise her conversion right.

The IRS, relying on Snyder, carried the gift-by-inaction doctrine to an even more sophisticated level in Tech. Adv. Mem. 9301001. Here, a father held 55 percent of the corporation voting rights and under local law could dictate any corporate action he wished, including liquidation. The father arranged for issuance to himself of preferred stock that paid a dividend of only 0.38 percent of the liquidation value of the stock, at a time when the going market yield for preferred dividends was 11.55 percent. Common stock was issued to the children. The father acquiesced in continuation of this arrangement over the years as the corporation grew in value, thereby enhancing the value of the common. The IRS concluded that the father had made an indirect gift to the children each year because the father could have liquidated the corporation at any time and invested the liquidation proceeds in other assets that would have produced a return much greater than 0.38 percent. Apparently, the IRS viewed the value of the annual gift as being the reasonable preferred dividend the father should have received, less the tiny amount actually paid.

Where a corporation is involved in a gift, the gift tax is generally applied by looking through the corporation and treating the shareholders as the real parties in interest. If a corporation makes a gift, the gift is treated as if made by the shareholders. Treas. Reg. § 25.2511–1(h)(1). Likewise, if a gift is made to a corporation, the gift is treated as if made to the shareholders, and the gift will be treated as a future interest for purposes of the section 2503(b) annual exclusion. CTUW Hollingsworth v. Commissioner, 86 T.C. 91 (1986).

A special rule, however, is applied to gifts to charitable and other entities in which members do not have traditional economic interests. Treas. Reg. § 25.2511–1(h)(1). In these cases, the entity is treated as the donee. In Priv. Ltr. Rul. 200533001, for example, a gift was made to a social club exempt from income tax under section 501(c)(7). The IRS ruled that the social club was not formed for the economic benefit of the members. Therefore, the gift was treated as made to the entity, not the members. Because the gift was available for immediate expenditure, it was treated as a present interest qualifying for the section 2503(b) annual exclusion.

As with direct transfers, an indirect transfer will not constitute a gift unless the transferor receives less than adequate and full consideration in money or money's worth from the person receiving the benefit. I.R.C. § 2512(b). In United States v. Marshall, 798 F.3d. 296 (5th Cir. 2015), a donor sold stock back to a corporation for below market value. At the time of the sale, there were five other stockholders. The fifth stockholder was a Grantor Retained Income Trust ("GRIT") that the donor created for the benefit of his ex-wife per their divorce settlement. The GRIT paid the income to the ex-wife and after 10 years, the trust would terminate and the remainder would go to the donor's son. In a stipulation in a previous action involving the then deceased donor, the IRS and the donor's estate agreed that there was an indirect gift to the shareholders because the donor sold the stock for below market value. The ex-wife argued that the ordinary course of business exception applied; hence, she argued that the transfer was made for an adequate and full consideration in money or money's worth. According to the ex-wife, the ordinary course of business exception applied because she and the donor were divorced for more than 35 years, they had remarried other people, and there was no close family relationship. However, the court rejected the ex-wife's argument and held that the exception did not apply based on the donor's stipulation. Because there was a gift, the ex-wife was liable for the donor's unpaid gift taxes per section 6324(b). Under section 6324(b), a donee is secondarily liable for the payment of gift taxes if the donor does not pay them.

F. PAYMENT OF TAXES ON TRUST INCOME

The IRS has ruled that the grantor's payment of income taxes imposed on the income of a "grantor trust" does not constitute a gift to the trust or to the beneficiaries who receive the trust income.

The "grantor trust" concept is explored in Chapter 31. Under the grantor trust rules set forth in sections 671–677, the grantor is taxed on the income of a trust if the grantor retains certain powers or benefits with respect to the trust. Such a trust is called a "grantor trust" because the grantor is taxed on the income. For example, a mother might create a trust the income of which would be paid to her son. If the mother retained any of certain powers described in sections 671–677, she would be required to pay the tax on the trust income, despite the son's receipt of the income. This leads to the question whether the mother's payment of taxes on the income might be treated as a gift from the mother to the son. The son receives all the benefits, while the mother bears the tax burden.

The IRS has ruled unequivocally that there is no gift of the income tax paid by the grantor. Rev. Rul. 2004–64, 2004–27 I.R.B. 7. The IRS recognizes that the gratuitous payment of tax for which another person is liable constitutes a gift by the payor. Doerr v. United States, 819 F.2d 162 (7th Cir. 1987). The IRS distinguished the *Doerr* rule, however, because, in the case of a grantor trust, neither the trustee nor the beneficiary has any obligation to pay tax on trust income. Hence the grantor's payment of tax does not relieve either the trustee or the beneficiary of a legal obligation.

Rev. Rul. 2004–64 provides a significant opportunity for untaxed transfers. The grantor can give the beneficiary the benefit of entirely untaxed income, while the grantor's prospective gross estate is diminished to the extent of the tax payments.

G. GIFTS BY TRUSTEES

Trustees make "gratuitous" transfers every day, in the sense that the beneficiary receiving the transfer gives no consideration. For example, if the Tenth National Bank is trustee of a trust that gives the Bank discretion to distribute property to Sam or Alice, the Bank's decision to distribute property to Sam rather than Alice is certainly "gratuitous," and might be viewed as a "gift" in the sense that Sam is enriched, while the Bank receives nothing in return.

It is important to remember, though, that the gift tax is not a tax on property, but an excise imposed on the transferor for the privilege of transferring the transferor's property to another person. The gift tax cannot apply unless the transferor makes herself poorer while making the transferee richer. In the example above, the Tenth National Bank has no beneficial interest in the property. Hence it gives up nothing when it transfers property to Sam, and the gift tax has no application. This principle is stated explicitly in the Regulations: "A transfer by a trustee of trust property in which he has no beneficial interest does not constitute a gift. . . ." Treas. Reg. § 25.2511–1(g)(1).

There are two important exceptions to the rule that a distribution by a trustee is not treated as a gift for gift tax purposes. First, if the trustee was the grantor of the trust, the transfer may constitute a gift because the transfer to the beneficiary *completes* a gift that was initiated when the grantor transferred property to the trust. Under principles that will be explored in Chapter 4, a transfer to a trust is not a completed gift if the transferor retains the power to direct the beneficial enjoyment of the property transferred. Treas. Reg. § 25.2511–2(b). When the grantor, acting as trustee, exercises that power by transferring property to a beneficiary of her choice, the gift is complete, and therefore taxable at that time (rather than when the original transfer was made to the trust).

Second, if the trustee has a beneficial interest in the property, the general rule is that a distribution that diminishes the trustee's beneficial interest but benefits the distributee constitutes a gift by the trustee to the beneficiary. For example, if the trustee is herself a permissible beneficiary, her decision as trustee to distribute property to another beneficiary is clearly a gift. There is an exception, however, if the trustee, although holding a beneficial interest, makes the distribution pursuant to a power "the exercise or nonexercise of which is limited by a reasonably fixed or ascertainable standard which is set forth in the trust instrument." Treas. Reg. § 25.2511–1(g)(2). For example, if the instrument directs the trustee to distribute to the beneficiary amounts "necessary for medical care," this would constitute a "fixed or ascertainable standard," with the result that a distribution for medical care would not be a gift. By contrast, a power to distribute for the beneficiary's "pleasure, desire, or happiness" would not be viewed as subject to a fixed or ascertainable standard. Treas. Reg. § 25.2511–1(g)(2).

H. LAPSING RIGHTS

A gift may occur by operation of law where certain rights in a partnership or corporation lapse, in effect producing a transfer of value between partners or stockholders.

For example, assume that a father owns all the stock of a corporation. Only voting common stock is outstanding. The father gives one-third of the stock to his daughter. For gift tax purposes, the transfer to the daughter will be valued taking into account the father's retention of two-thirds of the voting power, thereby reducing the value assigned to the gift of a minority interest to the daughter. Assume further that at the time of the gift the corporation's articles of incorporation are changed to provide that on November 1, 2023. The father's stock will cease to have voting rights.

Section 2704(a)(1) requires that the lapse of voting rights on November 1, 2023, be treated as a gift by the father to the daughter on that date. The gift consists of the difference between the value of the father's stock with voting rights and the value of the father's stock without voting rights. I.R.C. § 2704(a)(2).

If the rule of section 2704(a)(1) were not imposed, the father and daughter could accomplish a transfer of the controlling voting rights, which may have very substantial value, without imposition of gift or estate tax. This would occur because, after the lapse of voting rights, the value of the father's stock would be discounted to reflect the lack of voting rights. This was the result prior to adoption of section 2704 in 1990. See Estate of Harrison v. Commissioner, T.C. Memo. 1987–8, 52 T.C.M. (CCH) 1306 (1987).

Section 2704 is effective only as to lapses of rights or restrictions created after October 8, 1990. In other words, the rule of section 2704 would not apply to the above example if the change in the articles of incorporation were made prior to October 9, 1990. Revenue Reconciliation Act of 1990, section 11602(e)(1)(A)(iii). The Conference Committee Report on the 1990 Act states the Committee's intention that "no inference be drawn regarding the transfer tax effect of restrictions and lapsing rights under present law." H.R. Conf. Rep. No. 964, 101st Cong., 2d Sess. at 157 (1990).

Section 2704 applies to lapsing rights in both corporations and partnerships and to voting, liquidation, and similar rights. I.R.C. § 2704(a)(1) and (3). Section 2704 applies only if the family of the person holding the lapsing right controls the corporation or partnership. I.R.C. § 2704(a)(1) and (c).

I. FAMILY SETTLEMENT AGREEMENTS

Unfortunately, disputes among family members regarding disposition of the property of a decedent parent or grandparent are common. If there is genuinely adversarial litigation, there is no settlement agreement between the parties, and the litigation culminates in a court judgment directing disposition of the assets, then there is little possibility that the ultimate disposition of assets could be treated as a gift between the family members involved.

Often, however, such a dispute is resolved through a "family settlement agreement" whereby family members agree to a disposition that compromises the claims of the parties. Typically, certain family members receive more than might have been dictated by the will or trust, while others receive less. Because this result is produced by a voluntary agreement, it could be argued that there is a gift from those receiving less than expected to those receiving more than expected. The IRS response to these situations has varied depending on the circumstances.

In Priv. Ltr. Rul. 200707158 one family member claimed that another family member had abused his power as agent under the decedent's power of attorney, thereby disrupting the dispositive plan the decedent had intended. A suit was filed, but the dispute was ultimately settled, producing a reduced amount for the family member who acted as agent and an increased amount for the complaining family member. The IRS ruled that there was no gift because there was a genuine dispute, and the final result was consistent with the decedent's dispositive plan.

In Priv. Ltr. Rul. 200618003 the grantor created a trust that was to distribute principal and income to the "trustor's children." The trust instrument, however, appeared to define "trustor's children" as including only the grantor's sons, and not his daughters. The daughters claimed that the grantor has intended the daughters to be included among his "children" for this purpose. The parties entered into a "construction agreement" interpreting "children" as including the daughters. The agreement was submitted to and approved by a court, with the result that the trust was construed in accord with the agreement. The IRS ruled that the "construction agreement" did not constitute a gift from the sons to the daughters. The IRS noted that there was a genuine controversy and that the result was supported by applicable local law as it would have been construed by the highest court of the state.

In Priv. Ltr. Rul. 200917004, however, the IRS ruled that a family settlement agreement did constitute a gift. Here the beneficiaries of the trust were the "descendants" or "issue" of the grantor, and the trust instrument made no provision for inclusion of adopted descendants in the class of beneficiaries. The trustee, with consent of the natural descendants, petitioned a court for reformation of the trust instrument to provide for inclusion of adopted descendants. The court granted the trustee's request. The IRS concluded that this constituted a taxable gift from the natural descendants to the adopted descendants in the amount by which the natural descendants' rights were reduced and the adopted descendants' rights enhanced.

As these three rulings indicate, it may be difficult to predict whether a family settlement agreement will be treated as a gift. It appears that gift treatment can be avoided only if two factors are present. First, there must be genuine controversy in which the position of each side is at least arguable. Second, the final result must be within the range of arguable interpretations of the instrument under local law. As indicated by Private Letter Ruling 200917004, however, even with both these elements satisfied, the IRS may contend that a gift has occurred.

J. CONSIDERATION

Because the principal function of the gift tax is to backstop the estate tax by levying a toll on lifetime transfers that would not otherwise be taxed, the concept of "consideration" naturally plays an important role in the gift tax. If the transfer is made for full consideration, the transferor is not making herself poorer by the transfer; no tax is being avoided, because the transferor's estate, by reason of the consideration received, is just as large as before the transfer. Thus, lack of full consideration becomes the acid test in determining whether a "gift" is present for gift tax purposes. The consideration test is stated succinctly in section 2512(b): "Where property is transferred for less than an adequate and full consideration in money or money's worth, then the amount by which the value of the property exceeded the value of the consideration shall be deemed a gift. . ."

This statement of the consideration rule introduces two central concepts. First, only consideration in "money or money's worth" counts. This reflects a hard-headed, even cynical, approach that, in the interest of certainty and administrative convenience, disregards nonmonetary items, such as a promise to marry, despite the great value the parties might actually assign to such a promise.

The second concept involves the requirement of "adequate and full consideration." There will be a gift to the extent the monetary value of the consideration received is less than the monetary value of the consideration given. A mother who gives a parcel of land worth $100,000 to her son in exchange for $25,000 in cash is treated as making a $75,000 gift to her son. Of course, this principle could be carried to great extremes if the IRS sought to tax the gift implicit in any "bad bargain," e.g., where the buyer has through ignorance paid too much, or the seller has for some reason accepted too little. The IRS has disavowed any such intent, stating in its Regulations that "a sale, exchange, or other transfer of property made in the ordinary course of business (a transaction which is bona fide, at arm's length, and free from any donative intent), will be considered as made for an adequate and full consideration in money or money's worth." Treas. Reg. § 25.2512–8.

1. WHAT CONSTITUTES CONSIDERATION?

The gift tax provisions of the Code provide little assistance in determining what might constitute "money or money's worth" consideration for purposes of section 2512(b). At an early date, the courts were required to interpret section 2512(b) in the context of the typical antenuptial agreement providing that one spouse will surrender future marital rights in return for an immediate transfer of cash or property.

In the case that follows, the Supreme Court resolved the issue by looking to the estate tax law, which from 1932 forward had expressly addressed this issue in section 2043(b). Section 2043(b)(1) expressly denies marital rights the status of consideration for purposes of determining whether a death transfer is made for consideration.

MERRILL V. FAHS

Supreme Court of the United States, 1945.
324 U.S. 308.

FRANKFURTER, J.:

This is a companion case to Commissioner v. Wemyss, No. 629, just decided.

On March 7, 1939, taxpayer, the petitioner, made an antenuptial agreement with Kinta Desmare. Taxpayer, a resident of Florida, had been twice married and had three children and two grandchildren. He was a man of large resources, with cash and securities worth more than $5,000,000, and Florida real estate valued at $135,000. Miss Desmare's assets were negligible. By the arrangement entered into the day before their marriage, taxpayer agreed to set up within ninety days after marriage an irrevocable trust for $300,000, the provisions of which were to conform to Miss Desmare's wishes. The taxpayer was also to provide in his will for two additional trusts, one, likewise in the amount of $300,000, to contain the same limitations as the inter vivos trust, and the other, also in the amount of $300,000, for the benefit of their surviving children. In return Miss Desmare released all rights that she might acquire as wife or widow in taxpayer's property, both real and personal, excepting the right to maintenance and support. The inducements for this agreement were stated to be the contemplated marriage, desire to make fair requital for the release of marital rights, freedom for the taxpayer to make appropriate provisions for his children and other dependents, the uncertainty surrounding his financial future and marital tranquility. That such an antenuptial agreement is enforceable in Florida is not disputed, North v. Ringling, 149 Fla. 739, nor that Florida gives a wife an inchoate interest in all the husband's property, contingent during his life but absolute upon death. Florida Statutes (1941) § 731.34 [Under section 731.11, dower and curtesy have been abolished]; Smith v. Hines, 10 Fla. 258; Henderson v. Usher, 125 Fla. 709. The parties married, and the agreement was fully carried out.

On their gift tax return for 1939, both reported the creation of the trust but claimed that no tax was due. The Commissioner, however, determined a deficiency of $99,000 in taxpayer's return in relation to the transfer of the $300,000. Upon the Commissioner's rejection of the taxpayer's claim for refund of the assessment paid by him, the present suit against the Collector was filed. The District Court sustained the taxpayer, 51 F. Supp. 120, but was reversed by the Circuit Court of Appeals for the Fifth Circuit, one judge dissenting. 142 F.2d 651. We granted certiorari in connection with Commissioner v. Wemyss and heard the two cases together. 323 U.S. 703.

* * * [L]ike the *Wemyss* case, this case turns on the proper application of § 503 of the Revenue Act of 1932 [1986 Code § 2512(b)]. In the interest of clarity we reprint it here: "Where property is transferred for less than an adequate and full consideration in money or money's worth, then the amount by which the value of the property exceeded the value of the consideration shall, for the purpose of the tax imposed by this title, be deemed a gift, and shall be included in computing the amount of gifts made during the calendar year." Taxpayer claims that Miss Desmare's relinquishment of her marital rights constituted "adequate and full consideration in money or money's worth." The Collector, relying on the construction of a like phrase in the estate tax, contends that release of marital rights does not furnish such "adequate and full consideration."

We put to one side the argument that in any event Miss Desmare's contingent interest in her husband's property had too many variables to be reducible to dollars and cents, and that any attempt to translate it into "money's worth" was "mere speculation bearing the delusive appearance of accuracy." Humes v. United States, 276 U.S. 487, 494. We shall go at once to the main issue.

The guiding light is what was said in Estate of Sanford v. Commissioner, 308 U.S. 39: "The gift tax was supplementary to the estate tax. The two are in pari materia and must be construed together." The phrase on the meaning of which decision must largely turn—that is, transfers for other than "an adequate and full consideration in money or money's worth"—came into the gift tax by way of estate tax provisions. It first appeared in the Revenue Act of 1926. Section 303(a)(1) of that Act, 44 Stat. 9, 72, allowed deductions from the value of the gross estate of claims against the estate to the extent that they were bona fide and incurred "for an adequate and full consideration in money or money's worth." It is important to note that the language of previous Acts which made the test "fair consideration" was thus changed after courts had given "fair consideration" an expansive construction.

The first modern estate tax law had included in the gross estate transfers in contemplation of, or intended to take effect in possession or enjoyment at, death, except "a bona fide sale for a fair consideration in money or money's worth." Section 202(b), Revenue Act of 1916 [1986 Code § 2053(c)(1)(A)]. Dower rights and other marital property rights were intended to be included in the gross estate, since they were considered merely an expectation, and in 1918 Congress specifically included them. Section 402(b), 40 Stat. 1057, 1097 [1986 Code § 2034]. This provision was for the purpose of clarifying the existing law. H. Rep. No. 767, 65th Cong., 2d Sess., p. 21. In 1924 Congress limited deductible claims against an estate to those supported by "a fair consideration in money or money's worth", § 303(a)(1), 43 Stat. 253, 305, employing the same standard applied to transfers in contemplation of death, H. Rep. No. 179, 68th Cong. 1st Sess., pp. 28, 66. Similar language was used in the gift tax, first imposed by the 1924 Act, by providing, "Where property is sold or exchanged for less than a fair consideration in money or money's worth" the excess shall be deemed a gift. Section 320, 43 Stat. 253, 314.

The two types of tax thus followed a similar course, like problems and purposes being expressed in like language. In this situation, courts held that "fair consideration" included relinquishment of dower rights. * * * Congress was thus led, as we have indicated, to substitute in the 1926 Revenue Act, the words "adequate and full consideration" in order to narrow the scope of tax exemptions. When the gift tax was reenacted in the 1932 Revenue Act, the restrictive phrase "adequate and full consideration" as found in the estate tax was taken over by the draftsman.

To be sure, in the 1932 Act Congress specifically provided that relinquishment of marital rights for purposes of the estate tax shall not constitute "consideration in money or money's worth." The Committees of Congress reported that if the value of relinquished marital interests "may, in whole or in part, constitute a consideration for an otherwise taxable transfer (as has been held so), or an otherwise unallowable deduction from the gross estate, the effect produced amounts to a subversion of the legislative intent. * * * " H. Rep. No. 708, 72d Cong., 1st Sess., p. 47; S. Rep. No. 665, 72d Cong., 1st Sess., p. 50. Plainly, the explicitness was one of cautious redundancy to prevent "subversion of the legislative intent." Without this specific provision, Congress undoubtedly intended the requirement of "adequate and fair consideration" to exclude relinquishment of dower and other marital rights with respects to the estate tax.

We believe that there is every reason for giving the same words in the gift tax the same reading. Correlation of the gift tax and the estate tax still requires legislative intervention. * * * But to interpret the same phrases in the two taxes concerning the same subject matter in different ways where obvious reasons do not compel divergent treatment is to introduce another and needless complexity into this already irksome situation. Here strong reasons urge identical construction. To hold otherwise would encourage tax avoidance. Commissioner v. Bristol, supra at 136; 2 Paul, Estate and Gift Taxation (1942) p. 1118. And it would not fulfill the purpose of the gift tax in discouraging family settlements so as to avoid high income surtaxes. H. Rep. No. 708, 72d Cong., 1st Sess., p. 28; S. Rep. No. 665, 72d Cong., 1st Sess., p. 40. There is thus every reason in this case to construe the provisions of both taxes harmoniously. * * *

Affirmed.

2. DIVORCE TRANSFERS

Application of the consideration rule to divorce transfers is controlled by section 2516. This section is founded on the premise that property transfers incident to divorce are fundamentally arm's-length transactions in which consideration of equal monetary value flows to each party. Therefore, the gift tax should not apply.

Section 2516 requires both a written agreement and a divorce decree. The divorce decree must occur during the three-year period beginning one year before the date of the agreement and ending two years after the agreement. If this test is met, all transfers pursuant to the agreement, whenever made, that are intended to either settle property rights or provide reasonable support for minority issue of the marriage, are treated as made for full and adequate consideration. Therefore, none of the qualifying payments will be treated as gifts for gift tax purposes.

If section 2516 is not satisfied (e.g., the divorce occurs outside the 3-year window), treatment of the transfers for gift tax purposes is less certain. Under language and reasoning adopted from the estate tax, there will not be full and adequate consideration if the payments are founded solely on a "promise or agreement." I.R.C. §§ 2043(b) and 2053(c)(1)(A). In the typical case, however, the property settlement agreement will be incorporated in the divorce decree, with the result that the payments will be viewed as founded not only on a "promise or agreement," but also on the decree. In that event sections 2043(b) and 2053(c)(1)(A) will be inapplicable, and the transfers will generally be treated as made for full and adequate consideration. As a result, the transfers will not constitute gifts. See Harris v. Commissioner, 340 U.S. 106 (1950). This rule, however, applies only if the divorce court has power to modify the divorcing parties' settlement agreement. See Estate of Barrett v. Commissioner, 56 T.C. 1312 (1971).

The correlative estate tax provision—section 2043(b)(2)—likewise treats transfers that satisfy section 2516(1) as made for adequate and full consideration. Therefore, an amount owed to a former spouse pursuant to a divorce decree is deductible from the decedent's gross estate pursuant to section 2053(a)(3) if the requirements of section 2516 are satisfied.

3. DISCHARGE OF SUPPORT OBLIGATIONS

When a parent provides food and shelter for a minor child, is there a gift? The answer is "no" on the ground that the parent receives full and adequate consideration in the form of discharge of a support obligation[5] that could otherwise be enforced against the parent. If the transfers go beyond the parent's obligation of support, however, there is a gift from the

---

[5] The issue of what constitutes support necessarily arises under sections 677(b) and 678(c), involving the grantor trust rules. Resolution of the issue in that context is explored in Chapter 31.

parent to the child in the amount of the portion that exceeds the support obligation. Converse v. Commissioner, 5 T.C. 1014 (1945), *aff'd*, 163 F.2d 131 (2d Cir. 1947).

The rule becomes less clear when the payments move beyond support to discretionary expenditures that might or might not be considered a part of the parent's support obligation (e.g., automobiles, recreational travel, and private school expenses). Because the extent of the support obligation is a matter of state law, the result could vary widely across the country.

Similarly unclear is the extent to which there is a support obligation after a child attains the age of majority, typically at age 18. The traditional view is that there is no such obligation if the child is competent. That would produce the result that any transfer to or for the benefit of a child age 18 or over would constitute a gift. In many states, however, divorce courts have power to order divorcing parents to provide support, especially education, after majority. This responsibility is explored in Braun v. Commissioner[6] in Chapter 31. If there is such a potential obligation after the age of majority, at least some transfers for the benefit of adult children might not constitute gifts.

With the age of majority typically at eighteen and college tuition at high levels in many cases, parents funding higher education for their children could be viewed as making substantial taxable gifts. Two exclusions, however, tend to prevent this. The first is the annual exclusion, which permits husband and wife collectively to make substantial transfers entirely free of the gift tax. The other is the section 2503(e) exclusion for tuition and medical expenses, which permits tax-free direct payment of tuition, over and above the annual exclusion, without limit as to amount.

4. ADEQUACY OF CONSIDERATION

Under section 2512, the presence of consideration for purposes of contract law does not assure that the transfer will escape the gift tax. The value of the consideration must equal the value of the property transferred. If the consideration received has less value than the consideration given, the difference will be taxable as a gift. Treas. Reg. § 25.2512–8 adds that the consideration must be reducible to money or money's worth. For example, the value of living expenses furnished for the family of a taxpayer's adult son was a taxable gift because the son's family returned nothing but love and affection. Rev. Rul. 54–343, 1954–2 C.B. 318.

Regulation § 25.2512–8 softens this rule by stating that even if the consideration is not objectively equal in value to the property transferred, the IRS will not assert gift tax liability if the transfer was made in the ordinary course of business. This alleviates the possibility of imposing the

---

[6] T.C. Memo. 1984–284, 48 T.C.M. (CCH) 210 (1984).

gift tax on a seller who, in a bad bargain, has not received the full value of the property sold, a result that would only compound the seller's misfortune.

5.   PAYMENT OF GIFT TAX AS CONSIDERATION

Sometimes a donor is willing to make a gift on the condition that the donee pays the gift tax. For example, a donor parent may wish to transfer stock in a closely held family corporation to a son or daughter but may not wish to give up the cash necessary to pay the gift tax on such a transfer. In that event, the son or daughter may agree to pay the tax.

Because the primary obligation to pay the gift tax is imposed on the donor by section 2502(c), the donee's payment of the tax must be viewed as an offsetting benefit to the donor. Therefore, the "net gift" that is taxable is the difference between the value of the property transferred and the amount of the donor's gift tax obligation discharged by the donee. The net gift rule is fully developed in Rev. Rul. 75–72, 1975–1 C.B. 310. This ruling describes the algebraic formula that may be necessary to determine both the amount of the gift and the gift tax due. Such a formula is necessary because the donee's commitment to pay the tax reduces the amount of the gift, which in turn reduces the tax due, and so on.

A net gift may have income tax consequences as well. The income tax issue arises if the amount of gift tax discharged by the donee exceeds the donor's basis for the property transferred. The Supreme Court addressed this issue in Diedrich v. Commissioner, 457 U.S. 191 (1982). In one of the two cases addressed in *Diedrich*, the donor's basis for the stock transferred was only $8,742, and the gift tax liability discharged by the donee was $232,630. The Supreme Court, relying on Old Colony Trust Co. v. Commissioner, 279 U.S. 716 (1929), concluded that for income tax purposes there was a sale, and the amount realized by the donor was the amount of the donor's tax obligation discharged by the donee, or $232,630. Therefore, the donor realized a taxable gain of $232,630 less $8,742, or $223,888.

In McCord v. Commissioner, 461 F.3d 614 (5th Cir. 2006), the net gift concept was significantly expanded. In *McCord*, the donees agreed to pay not just the gift tax, but all federal and state transfer taxes imposed by reason of the transfer. There was no question that the gift tax liability should be subtracted in determining the amount of the net gift. The donees, however, argued that the prospective estate tax liability triggered by the gift should be subtracted as well. If a decedent dies within three years after making a gift, section 2035(b) requires that any gift tax imposed on the gift be included in the decedent's gross estate, thereby increasing the estate tax liability. Any addition to the estate tax liability would reduce the amount received by the donees at death, with the result that the donees would in effect bear the cost of the additional estate tax. In *McCord*, the Tax Court concluded that determination of possible liability pursuant to section 2035(b) was too speculative to be taken into account as consideration provided by the donees. The Fifth Circuit disagreed. It concluded that the possibility of the donor's death within three years could be reliability estimated, and that reasonable assumptions could be made as to the applicable estate tax rate in effect at the donor's death. The result was that the net gift amount was determined by taking into account both the gift tax liability and the potential estate tax liability triggered by section 2035(b).

6. GIFTS OF ENCUMBERED PROPERTY

The possibility that a gift may cause imposition of income tax liability on the donor seems a strange result. Nevertheless, it is an important principle that must be borne in mind as a donor chooses the property to be given to the objects of her bounty.

Although *Diedrich* directly addresses only the circumstance in which the benefit to the donor is the donee's payment of gift tax, there is equivalent benefit to the donor if the transfer has the effect of relieving the donor of any other liability with respect to the property transferred. This result is founded on the Supreme Court's holding in Crane v. Commissioner, 331 U.S. 1 (1947), that a party who conveys property subject to a liability must be treated as receiving consideration in the amount of the liability because the transferee can be expected to discharge the debt.

For example, assume that a mother owns farmland with a fair market value of $350,000 and a basis to her of $120,000, but encumbered by a mortgage securing an indebtedness of $170,000. If the mother transfers the land to her son as an inter vivos gift, the annual exclusion and unified credit may prevent the imposition of any gift tax. The transfer, however, will cause a realized taxable gain to the mother of $50,000—the amount by which the $170,000 mortgage exceeds the mother's $120,000 basis for the property. Estate of Levine v. Commissioner, 634 F.2d 12 (2d Cir.1980).

Sometimes gain can be avoided by selecting for the transfer property that is not encumbered by a mortgage in excess of the donor's basis. Alternatively, it may be possible to shift the encumbrance to other property that is not to be transferred.

Note that the "mortgage over basis" problem has no application to transfers between spouses or pursuant to divorce. Section 1041 provides nonrecognition treatment for all such transfers except those in trust. I.R.C. § 1041(e); Treas. Reg. § 1.1041–1T(d), Q–12.

7. POLITICAL CONTRIBUTIONS

Application of the consideration test to contributions to political parties and candidates could raise interesting questions. That inquiry, however, is largely obviated by section 2501(a)(4), which provides that any transfer to a "political organization" is excluded from taxable gifts. Section 2501(a)(4) refers to section 527(e)(1), which defines "political organization" as any party, committee, association, fund, or organization organized and operated primarily for the nomination, election, or appointment of an individual to a federal, state, or local office. There is no limitation on the amount excluded by section 2501(a)(4).

Many contributions intended to affect political campaigns now flow through section 501(c)(4) organizations, some of which may have a primary purpose other than direct political activity. Such an organization might not be within the section 527(e)(1) definition of "political organization." In that event, a contribution to the section 501(c)(4) organization could possibly be treated as a gift for gift tax purposes. See Rev. Rul. 82–216, 1982–2 C.B. 220.

CHAPTER 4

WHEN A GIFT OCCURS

■ ■ ■

A. INTRODUCTION

Usually, it is easy to determine when a gift occurs. A mother hands $100 in cash to her daughter. A father delivers to his son an executed deed conveying real estate to the son.

In other cases, the timing of the gift is less clear. If the donor retains control over the property—either directly or indirectly—completion of the gift may be prevented because the donor has the power to recall the property. More difficult questions arise if the donor retains not the power to revoke the gift, but only a power to modify the terms of the gift.

Timing questions also arise when multiple steps are necessary to place full ownership in the donee. In the case of a gift by check, for example, does the gift occur when the check is delivered to the donee, when the donee deposits the check in his or her account, or when the check is ultimately paid by the drawee bank?

Timing questions have obvious importance in determining when—or if—the gift tax applies. Often such questions arise at death, in circumstances in which the decedent made an arguably incomplete transfer prior to death. If the transfer did not constitute a completed gift during the decedent's life, the asset purportedly transferred during life will generally remain a part of the decedent's gross estate for estate tax purposes and will therefore be subject to the estate tax. On the other hand, if the transfer was a completed gift during life, the usual result is that the estate tax does not apply to the asset.

The timing of a gift can be important even if death does not intervene. For example, assume that in both Year 1 and Year 2 the section 2503(b) annual exclusion is $17,000. Further assume that Grandmother transfers a check for $17,000 to Grandson in December of Year 1, following by another $17,000 check in January of Year 2. If Grandson retains the Year 1 check and does not deposit it until Year 2, should the Year 1 check be treated as a gift in Year 1 or Year 2? If the Year 1 check is treated as a Year 1 gift, the section 2503(b) exclusions for Year 1 and Year 2 fully shelter both transfers, and Grandmother has made no taxable gifts. By contrast, if the Year 1 check is treated as a Year 2 gift, Grandmother will have lost the availability of the $17,000 annual exclusion for Year 1, and her Year 2 gifts will total $34,000. Only $17,000 of this amount can be sheltered by the Year 2 annual exclusion, and Grandmother will have made a taxable gift of $17,000 in Year 2.

The time of completion of the gift also has valuation ramifications. Assume that the donor purports to transfer real estate by gift in Year 1, when the real estate is worth $200,000. Assume further, however, that the gift is treated as incomplete because the donor has retained control over the real estate, and the donor does not surrender control until Year 4, when the real estate is worth $500,000. The gift is not complete until Year 4, and the value of the gift is determined at that time. For gift tax purposes there is a gift of $500,000—not $200,000.

B. RETAINED CONTROL

The most difficult questions involving timing of the gift arise when the donor retains control of some kind over the gift. If the donor retains an unlimited power to revoke the gift, it is clear that no gift has occurred. If the retained power is less extensive, however, the timing question becomes more difficult.

1. THE CONTROL CONCEPT

ESTATE OF SANFORD V. COMMISSIONER
Supreme Court of the United States, 1939.
308 U.S. 39.

MR. JUSTICE STONE delivered the opinion of the Court:

This and its companion case, No. 37, Rasquin v. Humphreys, present the single question of statutory construction whether in the case of an inter vivos transfer of property in trust, by a donor reserving to himself the power to designate new beneficiaries other than himself, the gift becomes complete and subject to the gift tax imposed by the federal revenue laws at the time of the relinquishment of the power. Co-relative questions, important only if a negative answer is given to the first one, are whether the gift becomes complete and taxable when the trust is created or, in the case where the donor has reserved a power of revocation for his own benefit and has relinquished it before relinquishing the power to change beneficiaries, whether the gift first becomes complete and taxable at the time of relinquishing the power of revocation.

In 1913, before the enactment of the first gift tax statute of 1924, decedent created a trust of personal property for the benefit of named beneficiaries, reserving to himself the power to terminate the trust in whole or in part, or to modify it. In 1919 he surrendered the power to revoke the trust by an appropriate writing in which he reserved "the right to modify any or all of the trusts" but provided that this right "shall in no way be deemed or construed to include any right or privilege" in the donor "to withdraw principal or income from any trust." In August, 1924, after the effective date of the gift tax statute, decedent renounced his remaining power to modify the trust. After his death in 1928, the Commissioner following the decision in Hesslein v. Hoey, 91 F. (2d) 954, in 1937, ruled that the gift became complete and taxable only upon decedent's final renunciation of his power to modify the trusts and gave notice of a tax deficiency accordingly.

The order of the Board of Tax Appeals sustaining the tax was affirmed by the Court of Appeals for the Third Circuit, 103 F.2d 81, which followed the decision of the Court of Appeals for the second circuit in Hesslein v. Hoey, supra, in which we had denied certiorari, 302 U.S. 756. In the *Hesslein* case, as in the *Humphreys* case now before us, a gift in trust with the reservation of a power in the donor to alter the disposition of the property in any way not beneficial to himself, was held to be incomplete and not subject to the gift tax under the 1932 Act so long as the donor retained that power.

We granted certiorari in this case May 15, 1939, and in the *Humphreys* case May 22, 1939, upon the representation of the Government that it has taken inconsistent positions with respect to the question involved in the two cases and that because of this fact and of the doubt of the correctness of the decision in the *Hesslein* case decision of the question by this Court is desirable in order to remove the resultant confusion in the administration of the revenue laws.

It has continued to take these inconsistent positions here, stating that it is unable to determine which construction of the statute will be most advantageous to the Government in point of revenue collected. It argues in this case that the gift did not become complete and taxable until surrender by the donor of his reserved power to designate new beneficiaries of the trusts. In the *Humphreys* case it argues that the gift upon trust with power reserved to the donor, not afterward relinquished, to change the beneficiaries was complete and taxable when the trust was created. It concedes by its brief that "a decision favorable to the government in either case will necessarily preclude a favorable decision in the other."

In ascertaining the correct construction of the statutes taxing gifts, it is necessary to read them in the light of the closely related provisions of the revenue laws taxing transfers at death, as they have been interpreted by our decisions. Section 319 of the Revenue Act of 1924, 43 Stat. 253, reenacted as Sec. 501 of the 1932 Act, 47 Stat. 169, imposed a graduated tax upon gifts. It supplemented that laid on transfers at death, which had long been a feature of the revenue laws. When the gift tax was enacted Congress was aware that the essence of a transfer is the passage of control over the economic benefits of property rather than any technical changes in its title. Following the enactment of the gift tax statute, this Court in Reinecke v. Northern Trust Company, 278 U.S. 339 (1929) held that the relinquishment at death of a power of revocation of a trust for the benefit of its donor was a taxable transfer. * * * and * * * the relinquishment by a donor at death of a reserved power to modify the trust except in his own favor is likewise a transfer of the property which could constitutionally be taxed under the provisions of § 302(d) of the 1926 Revenue Act (reenacting in substance 302(d) of the 1924 Act) [1986 Code § 2036(a)] although enacted after the creation of the trust. * * *

The rationale of decision in both cases is that "taxation is not so much concerned with the refinements of title as it is with the actual command over the property taxed" * * * and that a retention of control over the disposition of the trust property, whether for the benefit of the donor or others, renders the gift incomplete until the power is relinquished whether in life or at death. The rule was thus established, and has ever since been consistently followed by the Court, that a transfer of property upon trust, with power reserved to the donor either to revoke it and recapture the trust property or to modify its terms so as to designate new beneficiaries other than himself is incomplete, and becomes complete so as to subject the transfer to death taxes only on relinquishment of the power at death.

There is nothing in the language of the statute, and our attention has not been directed to anything in its legislative history to suggest that Congress had any purpose to tax gifts before the donor had fully parted with his interest in the property given, or that the test of the completeness of the taxed gift was to be any different from that to be applied in determining whether the donor has retained an interest such that it becomes subject to the estate tax upon its extinguishment at death. The gift tax was supplementary to the estate tax. The two are in *pari materia* and must be construed together. * * * An important, if not the main, purpose of the gift tax was to prevent or compensate for avoidance of death taxes by taxing the gifts of property inter vivos which, but for the gifts, would be subject in its original or converted form to the tax laid upon transfers at death.

Section 322 of the 1924 Act provides that when a tax has been imposed by § 319 upon a gift, the value of which is required by any provision of the statute taxing the estate to be included in the gross estate, the gift tax is to be credited on the estate tax. The two taxes are thus not always mutually exclusive as in the case of gifts made in contemplation of death which are complete and taxable when made, and are also required to be included in the gross estate for purposes of the death tax. But § 322 is without application unless there is a gift inter vivos which is taxable independently of any requirement that it shall be included in the gross estate. Property transferred in trust subject to a power of control over its disposition reserved to the donor is likewise required by § 302(d) to be included in the gross estate. But it does not follow that the transfer in trust is also taxable as a gift. The point was decided in the *Guggenheim* case where it was held that a gift upon trust, with power in the donor to revoke it is not taxable as a gift because the transfer is incomplete, and that the transfer whether inter vivos or at death becomes complete and taxable only when the power of control is relinquished. We think, as was pointed out in the Guggenheim case, supra, 285, that the gift tax statute does not contemplate two taxes upon gifts not made in contemplation of death, one upon the gift when a trust is created or when the power of revocation, if any, is relinquished, and another on the transfer of the same property at death because the gift previously made was incomplete.

It is plain that the contention of the taxpayer in this case that the gift becomes complete and taxable upon the relinquishment of the donor's power to revoke the trust cannot be sustained unless we are to hold, contrary to the policy of the statute and the reasoning in the *Guggenheim* case, that a second tax will be incurred upon the donor's relinquishment at death of his power to select new beneficiaries, or unless as an alternative we are to abandon our ruling in the *Porter* case. The Government does not suggest, even in its argument in the *Humphreys* case, that we should depart from our earlier rulings, and we think it clear that we should not do so both because we are satisfied with the reasoning upon which they rest and because departure from either would produce inconsistencies in the law as serious and confusing as the inconsistencies in administrative practice from which the Government now seeks relief.

There are other persuasive reasons why the taxpayer's contention cannot be sustained. By §§ 315(b), 324 and more specifically by § 510 of the 1932 Act [1986 Code § 6324(b)], the donee of any gift is made personally liable for the tax to the extent of the value of the gift if the tax is not paid by the donor. It can hardly be supposed that Congress intended to impose personal liability upon the donee of a gift of property, so incomplete that he might be deprived of it by the donor the day after he had paid the tax. Further, § 321(b)(1) [1986 Code § 2522(a)] exempts from the tax, gifts to religious, charitable, and educational corporations and the like. A gift would seem not to be complete, for purposes of the tax, where the donor has reserved the power to determine whether the donees ultimately entitled to receive and enjoy the property are of such a class as to exempt the gift from taxation. Apart from other considerations we should hesitate to accept as correct a construction under which it could plausibly be maintained that a gift in trust for the benefit of charitable corporations is then complete so that the taxing statute becomes operative and the gift escapes the tax even though the donor should later change the beneficiaries to the non-exempt class through exercise of a power to modify the trust in any way not beneficial to himself.

The argument of petitioner that the construction which the Government supports here, but assails in the *Humphreys* case, affords a ready means of evasion of the gift tax is not impressive. It is true, of course, that under it gift taxes will not be imposed on transactions which fall short of being completed gifts. But if for that reason they are not taxed as gifts they remain subject to death taxes assessed at higher rates, and the Government gets its due, which was precisely the end sought by the enactment of the gift tax.

* * *

Affirmed.

NOTE

The *Sanford* result is now codified in Treas. Reg. § 25.2511–2(c).

In *Sanford*, the Court implied that the test of completeness for gift tax purposes is the same as that applied under the estate tax. If that were the case, the gift tax and estate tax would always be mutually exclusive. In other words, a gift treated as complete for gift tax purposes would never be included in the gross estate for estate tax purposes, and an incomplete gift would never be subject to the gift tax but would be included in the gross estate. Four years after *Sanford*, however, the Supreme Court retreated from this position and squarely held that the gross estate may include an asset that was taxed as a completed gift during life. See Smith v. Shaughnessy, 318 U.S. 176 (1943).

For example, assume that a mother transfers property to a trust for her son and daughter. The trust instrument provides that the daughter is to receive the trust income until she attains age 25, at which time the son is to receive the principal. The mother reserves the power, with the consent of the son and daughter, to pay income or principal to the mother's sister. As discussed in the next section, this would be treated as a completed gift of the entire trust property for gift tax purposes because the son and daughter have interests adverse to the mother's exercise of her retained power. Treas. Reg. § 25.2511–2(e). Nevertheless, if the mother dies prior to the daughter's attainment of age 25, the entire value of the trust property at the time of the mother's death will be included in the mother's gross estate for estate tax purposes. See I.R.C. §§ 2036(a)(2) and 2038(a)(1) and Treas. Regs. §§ 20.2036–1(b)(3) and 20.2038–1(a), discussed in Chapters 18 and 19.

This scenario appears to impose double taxation on the same trust property—once under the gift tax and a second time under the estate tax. That is not the actual result, however, because two provisions prevent double taxation. First, the last sentence of section 2001(b) prohibits the inclusion in "adjusted taxable gifts" of property that is includible in the decedent's gross estate. In other words, at the mother's death only the current value of the trust property is taxed, and there is no double inclusion. Second, section 2001(b)(2) permits the mother's executor to deduct from the estate tax due at death any gift tax allocable to the inter vivos transfer. In other words, to the extent the mother paid gift tax on the original transfer in trust, she will be fully credited with that payment.

2. THE SUBSTANTIAL ADVERSE INTEREST CONCEPT

If a donor learns that her retention of control over a trust will have the effect of including the trust in her gross estate, she might seek to avoid this rule by requiring that another person acquiesce in the donor's exercise of control. Naturally, the donor is likely to confer such a power on a friend or a bank that the grantor expects to be compliant. The result is that the requirement of acquiescence by a third party may have little or no practical effect on the donor's retained control.

Avoidance of estate tax in these circumstances is prevented by sections 2036(a)(2) and 2038(a)(1), which, under certain circumstances, require inclusion of an asset in the decedent's gross estate if, at the date of death, the asset is subject to a power of disposition exercisable by the decedent either alone or in conjunction with any other person. See Chapters 18 and 19.

A corollary is applied to gifts: the general rule is that a gift is neither complete nor taxable if the donor has retained a power over the property, either alone or in conjunction with any other person. Under the gift tax, however, there is an important exception not found in the estate tax. The gift will be considered complete and therefore taxable if the person holding power jointly with the donor has a "substantial adverse interest in the disposition of the transferred property or the income therefrom." Treas. Reg. § 25.2511–2(e). The issue that arises is what constitutes a "substantial adverse interest."

COMMISSIONER V. PROUTY
United States Court of Appeals, First Circuit, 1940.
115 F.2d 331.

MAGRUDER, J.:

In 1923 Olive H. Prouty, the taxpayer herein, set up three trusts. Between 1923 and 1931 the grantor, by virtue of power reserved to her, made various amendments to the trust instruments. The Commissioner ruled that the gifts were not complete in 1931; that under Section 501 of the Revenue Act of 1932 (47 Stat. 245), as amended by Section 511 of the Revenue Act of 1934 (48 Stat. 758) [1986 Code I.R.C. § 2501(a)(1)], gift taxes became due upon amendment of each of the trusts on January 2, 1935, whereby the grantor finally relinquished all reserved power to revoke or amend the trust instruments. Upon petition for redetermination of the deficiency, the Board of Tax Appeals held with the taxpayer that the gifts had been completed prior to the enactment of the gift tax in 1932, and decided that there was no deficiency in gift taxes for the year 1935. The correctness of this decision by the Board is now before us on petition for review.

After the amendments in 1931 each of the three trust instruments contained a provision reserving to the grantor a power to revoke or amend, with the written consent of her husband, Lewis I. Prouty, during his lifetime, and thereafter, alone. As a condition precedent to the exercise of this power in a given calendar year, the grantor had to serve upon the trustee, during the preceding year, a formal notification of intention to revoke or amend.

* * *

If, therefore, Lewis Prouty is determined to be a person not having a substantial adverse interest in the disposition of the trust corpus or income therefrom, the gifts were not complete in 1931 and gift taxes accrued in 1935 upon the grantor's unqualified relinquishment of her power to revoke or amend.

We shall refer first to Trusts Nos. 2 and 3, because in them we think it clear that Lewis did not have a substantial adverse interest as of 1931.

In Trust No. 2 the grantor declared herself trustee of certain securities, with direction to the trustee to pay out of the net income the sum of $2,500 a year to Lewis I. Prouty during his lifetime, "and to add the balance of the net income to the principal and invest it as a part thereof during the lifetime of Lewis I. Prouty, with full power and authority in the sole and uncontrolled discretion of said Olive Higgins Prouty as long as she shall be the Trustee hereunder from time to time to pay to said Lewis I. Prouty and said Jane Prouty [a daughter], or either of them, in such proportions as the said Trustee may see fit the whole or any part of the principal of the trust fund if said Trustee deems it necessary or advisable for the maintenance, support and welfare of said Lewis I. Prouty and said Jane Prouty or either of them. . . ." It was provided that Lewis would succeed as trustee if he outlived the grantor; but in that event Lewis as trustee would not be empowered to make any payments to himself, other than the annuity, though he could in his "sole and uncontrolled discretion" make payments of the whole or any part of the principal to Jane Prouty if he deemed it advisable for her maintenance, support and welfare. At Lewis' death the property was to pass to Jane, with various remainders over. The power in the grantor to amend or revoke the trust, with the consent of Lewis, has already been mentioned.

Trust No. 3 was the same as Trust No. 2, except that Richard Prouty, a son, was substituted for Jane.

So far as the annuity is concerned, the Commissioner conceded that an effective gift thereof in each trust had been made prior to the passage of the Revenue Act of 1932. Accordingly, in determining the deficiency, he

subtracted the value of the annuities, calculated on the basis of Lewis' life expectancy, and subjected the remaining value of the corpus of each trust to the gift tax. This method of apportionment might be objected to on the ground that if the annuity constituted a substantial adverse interest, it was an interest in the whole of the corpus out of the net income of which the annuity was payable, so that the gift should be treated as having been completed in 1931 as to all the trust res. But such an interpretation would afford an obvious facility for tax evasion, particularly with respect to the grantor's income tax in the application of the comparable provisions of Section 166 dealing with revocable trusts. To the extent that a proposed partial revocation would leave Lewis' annuity intact, he would have no substantial countervailing interest tending to induce him to withstand the grantor's wishes. We think that the Commissioner was justified in deducting the capital value of the annuity and in treating the transfer in 1935 upon relinquishment of the power as being a gift merely of the remainder of the corpus after such deduction. Therefore, in considering whether Lewis had a substantial adverse interest in Trusts Nos. 2 and 3, we may leave out of account the annuities to him provided in these trusts.
* * *

The only other interest which Lewis had in the corpus of Trusts Nos. 2 and 3 was the possibility that, under the provision previously quoted, his wife, as trustee, might in her "sole and uncontrolled discretion" pay over to him such portions of the principal as she might deem advisable for his maintenance, support and welfare. But the main purpose of the trust was to accumulate the income during Lewis' lifetime, and the record does not suggest the existence of circumstances indicating any likelihood that Lewis would ever receive anything by virtue of this provision. Certainly Lewis, while receiving aggregate annuities of $7,500 from the three trusts, could never obtain a court decree compelling the trustee to give him something under this discretionary power. That such a remote and speculative possibility of gain does not constitute a "substantial adverse interest" was ruled by this court on quite similar facts in Fulham v. Commissioner, 110 F. (2d) 916, 918.

Another point was stressed by the Board in connection with Trusts Nos. 2 and 3, namely, that in each case the corpus at the death of Lewis was to go to his children. "It is natural to assume," said the Board, "that his desire and concern for the support, maintenance, and welfare of his children after his death would prompt him to resist any effort on the part of the grantor of the trust to alter, amend or revoke that part of the trust so as to revest in her title to such property." No doubt this is an interest of a sort. But we think the phrase "substantial adverse interest," as it was used in Section 501 (c) of the Revenue Act of 1932 and as it is used in Sections 166 and 167, means a direct legal or equitable interest in the trust property, and not merely a sentimental or parental interest in seeing the trust fulfilled for the advantage of other beneficiaries. Loeb v. Commissioner, 113 F. (2d) 664, 666.

Trust No. 1 presents a different situation. We may lay to one side the annuity of $2,500 payable to Lewis; and also the possibility that Lewis might receive something through the exercise by the grantor as trustee of her discretion to pay to Lewis such part of the principal as she might deem advisable for his maintenance, support and welfare. Under this trust instrument Lewis had, in addition, two important interests affecting the whole of the corpus, interests which were lacking in the other two trusts. (1) If he should outlive the grantor, the corpus was to pass at his death as he should by his last will direct and appoint. The prospect of acquiring this power of disposition certainly would furnish a pecuniary motive, far from negligible, tending to induce Lewis to stand out against any desire of the grantor to revoke the trust. Cf. Curry v. McCanless, 307 U.S. 357, 371. (2) If he should outlive the grantor, he would succeed as trustee and, as such trustee, would have full discretion to pay to himself the whole or any part of the principal should he deem it advisable for his own maintenance, support and welfare. In Cox v. Commissioner, 110 F. (2d) 934, such a power held by a grantor-trustee was held to be so substantial as to amount in effect to a power in the grantor to revest in himself the corpus of the trust estate and hence to subject the grantor to an income tax under Section 166; this despite the fact that the power may have been technically a fiduciary one.

Examining these intimate family trusts, one must recognize an element of unreality in the inquiry whether a beneficiary's interest is substantially adverse to the grantor. The supposition is that, given a sufficient stake in the trust, the beneficiary is not likely to yield to a wish of the grantor to revoke the trust. In many cases the grantor may have full confidence in the compliant disposition of the member of the family he selects to share his power of revocation, even though such member is named as beneficiary of a handsome interest in the trust. The very fact that the grantor reserved a power to revoke indicates a mental reservation on his part as to the finality of the gift; and if the grantor wishes to hold on to a power of recapture, * * * it stands to reason he will vest the veto power in someone whose acquiescence he can count on. However, we cannot read into the gift tax, any more than into Sections 166 and 167, the proposition that a member of the grantor's immediate family can never be deemed to have "a substantial adverse interest." So far as the gift tax is concerned, it is fair enough to take the grantor at his word. As to the income tax, it might be rational for Congress to tax all family income as a unit. But as the law now stands—both gift tax and income tax—we must give weight to the formal rights conferred in the trust instrument in determining whether a given beneficiary has a substantial adverse interest, bearing in mind the admonition of Helvering v. Clifford, 309 U.S. 331, 335, that "where the grantor is the trustee and the beneficiaries are members of his family group, special scrutiny of the arrangement is necessary. * * * "

The present case is on the border line, but considering the aggregate of Lewis' interests under the terms of Trust No. 1, we are not persuaded that the Board was in error in its conclusion that Lewis had a "substantial adverse interest." It is true that Lewis will have to outlive the grantor to reap the benefits, but in the normal vicissitudes of life the chance of his survival is substantial. Lewis has a contingent interest in the whole of the current income, for if the trustee does not pay it to him under her discretionary power, it must be added to the corpus and thus becomes subject to Lewis' testamentary power of appointment. A substantial chance of coming into a good thing may constitute a "substantial adverse interest"; especially where, as here, it is a chance to control the disposition of the entire corpus of a large estate. It is a chance one would not lightly relinquish. The interest need not be presently vested in possession and enjoyment. See Jane B. Shiverick, 37 B. T. A. 454.

The Commissioner further contends, however, that a gift is not complete even where the grantor's reserved power to revoke is subject to the veto of a person who does have a substantial adverse interest; and that therefore a gift tax became payable in 1935 when the grantor relinquished this power. * * * It is pointed out that when such a power so restricted is extinguished by death of the grantor, the corpus is treated as part of the gross estate of the grantor for purposes of the estate tax. * * * And in Estate of Sanford v. Commissioner, 308 U.S. 39, the court said that the gift tax is supplementary to the estate tax; that the two are in pari materia and must be construed together; that "There is nothing in the language of the statute, and our attention has not been directed to anything in its legislative history to suggest that Congress had any purpose to tax gifts before the donor had fully parted with his interest in the property given, or that the test of the completeness of the taxed gift was to be any different from that to be applied in determining whether the donor has retained an interest such that it becomes subject to the estate tax upon its extinguishment at death." Nevertheless, as the court pointed out (308 U.S. at 45), the two taxes * * * are not always mutually exclusive.

[W]e conclude that since Lewis had a substantial adverse interest in Trust No. 1 as of 1931, the gift was complete at that time, despite the power of revocation reserved to the grantor in conjunction with Lewis. As a result, Trust No. 1 escapes both the gift tax and the estate tax. However, our decision is not a precedent endangering the revenue. The tax is avoided here only because the gift was made before the gift tax was enacted. These family trusts, created since 1932, will inevitably be subject to the gift tax, or the estate tax, or in some instances, both. The Commissioner's argument, advanced to meet the exigencies of the case at bar, if accepted and applied in future cases, would only result in postponing the incidence of the tax.

We have not overlooked an additional argument advanced by the Commissioner. Leaving aside the question whether Lewis had a substantial adverse interest in Trust No. 1, the Commissioner contends that the "bundle of rights and powers" retained by Mrs. Prouty as of 1931 was such that she remained in substance the owner of the corpus, and that the income of the trust was then taxable to her under Section 22(a) by the doctrine of Helvering v. Clifford, 309 U.S. 331; that the gift being regarded as incomplete for purposes of the income tax should be similarly regarded for purposes of the gift tax. The answer is twofold. In the first place, it is far from clear that the premise is correct as to the applicability of Helvering v. Clifford. Cf. Commissioner v. Branch, decided by this court October 23, 1940. Second, the gift tax does not seem to be so closely integrated with the income tax that decisions like the Clifford case extending the applicability of Section 22(a) to the grantor of a trust, must necessarily be read as holding that no gift tax was payable upon the creation of the trust. It may be frankly recognized, however, that the interrelation of the income, estate, and gift taxes presents many puzzling problems which deserve the attention of Congress.

The decision of the Board of Tax Appeals is affirmed as to Trust No. 1 and reversed as to Trusts Nos. 2 and 3; and the case is remanded to the Board for further proceedings not inconsistent with this opinion.

NOTE

Regulation § 25.2511–2(e) does not entirely solve the problem of collusion. A beneficiary with a substantial adverse interest could make a secret bargain with the donor to agree to any exercise of power the donor might desire. Such arrangements, however, would be stricken down as shams. See, e.g., Camp v. Commissioner, 195 F.2d 999 (1st Cir. 1952). Further explication of the "substantial adverse interest" concept for gift tax purposes is found in *Camp*, where the following observations are offered:

1. If the trust instrument gives a designated beneficiary any interest in the corpus of the trust property or of the income therefrom, which is capable of monetary valuation, and the donor reserves no power to withdraw that interest, in whole or in part, except with the consent of such designated beneficiary, then the gift of that particular interest will be deemed to be complete, for the purposes of the gift tax. See accord, our discussion in Commissioner v. Prouty, 115 F.2d 331, 334 (1940), with reference to the annuities to the husband in Trusts 2 and 3. * * *

2. If the only power reserved by the donor is a power to revoke the entire trust instrument (not a power to modify the trust in any

particular), and this power may be exercised only in conjunction with a designated beneficiary who is given a substantial adverse interest in the disposition of the trust property or the income therefrom, then the transfer in trust will be deemed to be a present gift of the entire corpus of the trust, for purposes of the gift tax. In such cases, the gift of the entire corpus will be deemed to have been "put beyond recall" by the donor himself.

3.　If the trust instrument reserves to the donor a general power to alter, amend or revoke, in whole or in part, and this power is to be exercised only in conjunction with a designated beneficiary who has received an interest in the corpus or income capable of monetary valuation, then the transfer in trust will be deemed to be a completed gift, for purposes of the gift tax, only as to the interest of such designated beneficiary having a veto over the exercise of the power. As to the interests of the other beneficiaries, the gifts will be deemed to be incomplete, for as to such interests the donor reserves the power to take them away in conjunction with a person who has no interest in the trust adverse to such withdrawal. * * *

195 F.2d at 1004.

3.　INFORMAL RESERVATIONS

In most cases, whether a gift is complete is determined by the documents executed by the parties. However, if the actual disposition of the property is in fact controlled by oral understandings or other directions contrary to the documents, the facts—not the documents—will determine taxability.

In Warner v. Commissioner, 49 T.C.M. (CCH) 5 (1984), the donor, seeking to shelter his assets from his wife's divorce claims, transferred property to a bank as trustee of an ostensibly irrevocable trust. However, the responsible bank officer orally agreed to dispose of the trust assets as dictated by the donor and agreed to return the assets to the donor upon the donor's request. The bank did in fact honor the donor's directions. The Tax Court held that the donor had not in fact relinquished control; hence there was no completed gift.

4.　RETENTION OF POWER TO CHANGE THE TRUSTEE

The donor may transfer property to a trustee (other than himself) who has power to modify beneficial enjoyment. If the donor can replace the trustee with himself, it seems clear that the trustee's powers must be imputed to the donor, necessarily making the gift incomplete. A similar doctrine is applied to include the trust property in the decedent's gross estate under sections 2036 and 2038. See Chapters 18 and 19.

At one time the IRS sought to expand this rule to circumstances in which the donor retains a power to replace the trustee, not with the donor, but with another person or entity of the donor's choosing. The IRS reasoned that the donor could search among trustee candidates and ultimately find one willing to do the donor's bidding, thereby giving the donor effective control over the trustee's exercise of discretion. Under this rationale, the transfer in trust would not be a completed gift, and the trust property would be included in the donor's gross estate for estate tax purposes. The IRS view was rejected for purposes of both the gift tax in Estate of Vak v. Commissioner, 973 F.2d 1409 (8th Cir.1992) and the estate tax in Estate of Wall, 101 T.C. 300 (1993). Ultimately, the IRS conceded defeat and acknowledged that, if the donor retains power to replace the trustee with a person who is neither the donor nor a person related or subordinate to the donor, the retention of such a power will neither cause the transfer in trust to be an incomplete gift nor require inclusion of the trust property in the donor's gross estate. Rev. Rul. 95–58, 1995–36 I.R.B. 16. This issue is further explored in Chapter 18.

PROBLEMS

The problems below provide an opportunity to apply the tests for a completed gift set forth in Treas. Reg. § 25.2511–2. In each case, assume that the donor is not the trustee unless otherwise indicated. Further assume that the donor has not retained any power over the trust unless otherwise indicated.

In each case, determine (1) whether and when there is a completed gift, and (2) the interest that has been transferred by gift.

1. Donor places $100,000 in trust for 11 years with income to be paid to A, remainder to Donor.

2. Donor places $100,000 in trust for 11 years with income to be paid to A and B in such proportions as the trustee designates, remainder to Donor.

3. Donor places $100,000 in trust for 11 years with Donor named as trustee, and with income to be paid to A, remainder to C. As trustee, Donor has only fiduciary powers, which impose a fixed and ascertainable standard relating to allocation of trust receipts between income and principal.

4. Donor places $100,000 in trust for 11 years with Donor named as trustee, and with income to be paid to A and B in such proportions as the trustee in her uncontrolled discretion designates, remainder to C.

5. Donor places $100,000 in trust for 11 years with Donor's husband named as trustee, and with income to be paid to A and B in such proportions as the trustee in his uncontrolled discretion designates, remainder to C.

6. Donor places $100,000 in trust for 11 years, with Donor named as trustee, and with income to be paid to A and/or B "as necessary for medical care," remainder to C.

7. Donor places $100,000 in trust for 11 years, with Donor and E named as trustees, and with income to be paid to A and B in such proportions as the trustees in their uncontrolled discretion designate, remainder to C. E has no beneficial interest in the trust.

8. Donor places $100,000 in trust for 11 years, income to be paid to A, remainder to C. Donor reserves the right to revoke the trust during the first five years.

9. Donor places $100,000 in trust for 11 years, income is to be paid to A, who is to receive the remainder as well. However, Donor reserves the power to require that the income be accumulated and added to principal during the 11 years of the trust.

C. PROMISSORY NOTES

REVENUE RULING 84–25
1984–1 C.B. 191.

ISSUE

What are the gift and estate tax consequences if a donor/decedent gratuitously transfers a legally binding promissory note that has not been satisfied at the decedent's death?

FACTS

On August 1, 1977, D gratuitously transferred to A a promissory note in which D promised to pay A a sum of money on December 31, 1982. The note was legally enforceable under state law.

On May 30, 1982, D died. The note had not been satisfied at D's death.

LAW AND ANALYSIS

In the case of a legally enforceable promise for less than an adequate and full consideration in money or money's worth, the promisor makes a completed gift under section 2511 of the Internal Revenue Code on the date when the promise is binding and determinable in value rather than when the promised payment is actually made. In such a case, the amount of the gift is the fair market value of the contractual promise on the date it is binding. Section 25.2512–4 of the Gift Tax Regulations.

Section 2053(a)(3) of the Code provides for an estate tax deduction for the amount of claims against the estate as are allowable by the laws of the state under which the estate is being administered. These deductions, when founded on a promise or agreement, are limited by section 2053(c)(1) to the extent that the obligations are contracted bona fide and for an adequate and full consideration in money or money's worth.

Under section 2001(b) of the Code, the estate tax is computed by determining a tentative tax on the sum of the taxable estate and the adjusted taxable gifts (section 2001(b)(1)) and subtracting from that amount the tax payable, calculated as provided in section 2001(b)(2), with respect to gifts made after 1976. The adjusted taxable gifts include only the value of the taxable gifts made by the decedent after 1976 that are not includible in the decedent's gross estate.

In this case, D made a completed gift under section 2511 of the Code on August 1, 1977, the date on which D's promise was legally binding and determinable in value. Compare, Rev. Rul. 67–396, 1967–2 C.B. 351, which provides that the transfer of a promissory note that is unenforceable under state law is not a completed gift.

No deduction is allowable under section 2053 of the Code for A's claim as promisee on D's note, because the note was not contracted for an adequate and full consideration in money or money's worth. Section 2053(c)(1).

Since the note has not been paid, the assets that are to be used to satisfy D's promissory note are a part of D's gross estate. Therefore, D's 1977 gift to A is deemed to be includible in D's gross estate for purposes of section 2001 of the Code. Thus, D's 1977 gift is not an adjusted taxable gift as defined in section 2001(b) of the Code. Consequently, the value of D's 1977 gift is not added under section 2001(b)(1)(B) to D's adjusted taxable gifts in computing the tentative estate tax under section 2001(b)(1).

Of course, a different situation would be presented had the note been partially satisfied prior to D's death. To the extent that the note had been paid, the assets used to satisfy the note would not be included in D's estate and hence there would be no reason not to treat the satisfied portion of the note as an adjusted taxable gift. Therefore, the holding of this ruling applies only to the extent the promissory note remains unsatisfied at D's death.

HOLDING

The gratuitous transfer of a legally binding promissory note is a completed gift under section 2511 of the Code. If the note has not been satisfied at the promisor's death, no deduction is allowable under section 2053(a)(3) for the promisee's claim with respect to the note. The completed gift is not treated as an adjusted taxable gift in computing the tentative estate tax under section 2001(b)(1).

* * *

D. CHECKS

A gift by check raises especially difficult questions in determining when the gift is complete. Under typical state law the donor has power to stop payment of the check at any time until the check is actually accepted and paid by the drawee bank. Treasury Regulation § 25.2511–2(b) provides that a gift is complete only when the donor has put the property beyond the donor's "dominion and control." It would seem that that does not occur until the check is actually accepted and paid by the drawee bank. Nevertheless, there are some circumstances in which the gift may be treated as complete when the check is transferred to the donee, depending on the nature of the gift and the reason for determining the time of completion.

If the check is transferred to a charity, the gift is treated as relating back to the time the charity receives the check, even though the check may not be accepted and paid until after the donor's death. This conclusion is based on the premise that the giving of the check evidences a binding commitment to a charitable subscription that could be enforced against the donor even if payment is stopped on the check. Estate of Spiegel v. Commissioner, 12 T.C. 524 (1949).

If the check is transferred to a noncharitable donee, however, the time of completion depends on several factors.

If the donor remains alive until the check is paid by the drawee bank, the time of the gift may relate back to the transfer of the check to the donee if certain conditions are met. In Estate of Metzger v. Commissioner, 100 T.C. 204 (1993), aff'd, 38 F.3d 118 (4th Cir. 1994), the Tax Court held that the gift relates back to the delivery of the check to the donee if (1) there is an unconditional delivery to the donee, (2) the check is deposited in the donee's bank account within a reasonable time, (3) the donor's account has a sufficient balance to permit payment when the check is delivered to the donee, and (4) the check is ultimately paid by the drawee bank.

In Rev. Rul. 96–56, 1996–2 C.B. 161, the IRS acquiesced in *Metzger,* but imposed more stringent conditions. The IRS stated that delivery of a check to a noncharitable donee will be deemed a completed gift "on the earlier of (i) the date on which the donor has so parted with dominion and control under local law as to leave in the donor no power to change its disposition, or (ii) the date on which the donee deposits the check (or cashes the check against available funds of the donee) or presents the check for payment, if it is established that: (1) the check was paid by the drawee bank when first presented to the drawee bank for payment; (2) the donor was alive when the check was paid by the drawee bank; (3) the donor intended to make a gift; (4) delivery of the check by the donor was unconditional; and (5) the check was deposited, cashed, or presented in the calendar year for which completed gift treatment is sought and within a reasonable time of issuance." Note that requirement (2) has the effect of denying the benefit of Rev. Rul. 96–56 if the donor dies before the check is paid by the drawee bank. More significantly, requirement (5) grants relation back treatment only if the check is deposited or cashed within the calendar year in which the donee received the check.

In cases where the donor dies before presentment of the check to the drawee bank, the courts support the IRS position stated in requirement (2) of Rev. Rul. 96–56. The relation back treatment is not allowed if the donee is not a charity and the check is not paid by the drawee bank until after the donee's death. McCarthy v. United States, 806 F.2d 129 (7th Cir. 1986); Estate of Dillingham v. Commissioner, 903 F.2d 760 (10th Cir. 1990); Rosano v. United States, 245 F.3d 212 (2d Cir. 2001); Estate of Newman v. Commissioner, 203 F.3d 53 (D.C. Cir. 1999). In Demuth v. Commissioner, T.C. Memo. 2022-72, 2022 WL 2679050 (July 12, 2022), the decedent executed a power of attorney that authorized his son to make gifts to the decedent's descendants up to the amount of the annual exclusion. The son wrote 11 checks on September 6, 2015 totaling $464,000. The decedent died on September 11, but only one check had been paid by that date. The Tax Court looked to the relevant state law of Pennsylvania to determine whether the decedent had parted with dominion and control of the funds. Under Pennsylvania law, the gift of a check is incomplete or revocable if the drawer "can make a stop-payment order on the check." Based on this standard, the 10 checks paid after the decedent's death would be includible in his gross estate under section 2033. Ironically, the Tax Court determined that three of these checks (totaling $70,000) would not be included in the decedent's gross estate because the IRS had made a concession in its brief that those checks had been credited by the banks before the decedent's death. In *Demuth*, because most of the checks (totaling $366,000) were included in the decedent's gross estate, the decedent was deprived of the benefit of the annual exclusion for these checks that were transferred (but unpaid) prior to death.

PLANNING NOTE

Donors making year-end gifts or gifts during a serious illness should be alert to the ramifications of the above rules. Where a serious illness is not present, and the objective is optimum utilization of the annual exclusion each year, donors should bear in mind the requirement of Rev. Rul. 96–56 that the check be deposited within a reasonable time and in any event within the year for which an exclusion is to be claimed. Recipients of traditional holiday gifts made late in December should be instructed as to the importance of prompt deposit. Where a serious illness is present, the rule is even stricter, and actual payment by the drawee bank must be achieved before death. In this situation prompt deposit is even more important.

E. CO-OWNERSHIP

If title to property is conveyed to the donor and another person as co-owners, treatment of the transfer under the gift tax depends on both the nature of the ownership and the type of property involved.

If the transfer is to another person as tenant in common with the donor, there is a completed gift of one-half of the property. The donee co-owner has an immediate right to dispose of one-half of the property as she wishes. Therefore, the donor has surrendered all dominion and control over that one-half of the property, and treatment as a completed gift is consistent with the "dominion and control" test expressed in Treas. Reg. § 25.2511–2(b).

The result is the same for a transfer to joint tenancy with right of survivorship if the property is something other than a bank account or a United States savings bond. For example, if the property transferred to joint tenancy is real estate, most states give the donee joint tenant an immediate right to sever the property and dispose of one-half as the donee wishes. Therefore, there is a completed gift as to one-half of the property. Treas. Reg. § 25.2511–1(h)(5).

If the property transferred to joint tenancy is a bank account (or any similar property that could be retrieved in its entirety by the donor), there is not a completed gift. This is so because the entirety of the funds could be withdrawn from the account by the donor, thereby restoring the entire property to the donor. A completed gift occurs only when and if the donee actually withdraws funds from the account. The same principle is applied to United States savings bonds registered to "A or B" (Treas. Reg. § 25.2511–1(h)(4)) and to joint brokerage accounts. See Rev. Rul. 69–148, 1969–1 C.B. 226.

Although the gift tax rules relating to co-ownership are simple, the estate tax rules are more complex. As explained below in Chapter 16, special estate tax rules are applied so as to recognize the survival aspect of joint tenancy, with the result that part or all of joint tenancy property may be included in the decedent joint tenant's gross estate, depending on the circumstances. In the case of a tenancy in common, the inclusion is always the decedent's proportionate share of the property.

F. GIFTS BY CONTRACT

REVENUE RULING 79–384
1979–2 C.B. 344.

ISSUE

What are the federal gift tax consequences of the payment of $10,000 as a result of a judgment against the payer, who promised to make the payment if the payee graduated from college?

FACTS

In 1972, A promised in writing to pay B, A's child, $10,000 if B graduated from college. At that time B was 16 years old. B graduated from college on June 1, 1977. B promptly demanded payment of the $10,000 in accordance with A's promise. A refused to pay the money and B brought suit in the local courts. On September 25, 1978, a judgment was issued by the local court against A on the contract with B in the amount of $10,000. A paid the money to B on the same day.

LAW AND ANALYSIS

* * *

In Estate of Copley v. Commissioner, 15 T.C. 17 (1950), affirmed, 194 F.2d 364 (7th Cir.1952), acq., 1965–2 C.B. 4, the petitioner entered into an antenuptial agreement in which the petitioner promised to give the future spouse a sum of money in consideration of the marriage and in lieu of all of the spouse's marital rights in the petitioner's property. The agreement became legally enforceable under state law on the date of the marriage in 1931. The petitioner transferred part of the sum in 1936 and the remainder in 1944. The court concluded that a gift tax would have been due in 1931 if there had been a gift tax law in effect at that time.

In Harris v. Commissioner, 178 F.2d 861 (2d Cir.1949), reversed on other grounds, 340 U.S. 106 (1950), 1950–2 C.B. 77, the Court of Appeals held that a promise to make a gift becomes taxable in the year in which the obligation becomes binding and not when the discharging payments are made. See, also, Rosenthal v. Commissioner, 205 F.2d 505 (2d Cir.1953); Rev. Rul. 69–347, 1969–1 C.B. 227.

Therefore, where one promises to transfer property in the future, the gift tax consequences of the promise are judged as of the first date on which it is possible to determine that the transfer must be made and that the transfer will be of a determinable amount. See also Rev. Rul. 69–347, 1969–1 C.B. 227.

In the present case, the fact that B graduated from college is not consideration, in money or money's worth, received by A. Even if A had received some benefit from B's graduation from college, it is not possible to place a monetary value on that benefit. Therefore, under section 25.2512–8 of the regulations, discussed above, A received no consideration, for federal gift tax purposes, in exchange for A's promise to pay $10,000 even though B's graduating from college may have been "consideration" under state law. See Hamer v. Sidway, 27 N.E. 256 (Ct.App.1891); Restatement of Contracts § 76 (1932); 1 A. L. Corbin, Corbin on Contracts 132 (1963).

In the present case, as in the Copley case, discussed above, A's promise to pay became binding on A before the subject of the promise was transferred. As in Rev. Rul. 69–346, discussed above, it was not possible to determine, as of the date when the donor's promise was made, whether a gift would actually result.

Such a determination could be made only when B graduated from college. Since B properly fulfilled the condition of A's obligation, A became bound to make the payment on B's graduation. It is thus on that date that A's gift was made, for federal gift tax purposes.

The fact that B found it necessary to obtain the assistance of the local courts in order to compel A to comply with the terms of the agreement and that A did not actually transfer the $10,000 until more than a year after B reached age 21 does not alter the conclusion in the present case. In Copley, discussed above, the donor's promise became binding in 1931, although payment was not made until 1936 and 1944. It was held that the gift was made in 1931 when the promise became enforceable.

HOLDING

The donor, A, made a gift of $10,000 on the day B graduated from college, the date when A's promise became enforceable and determinable in value, notwithstanding the fact that A did not actually make the payment of $10,000 until a later date when judgment was rendered against A.

G. JOINT AND MUTUAL WILLS

Under the law of many states, two or more persons (typically spouses) may make "joint and mutual" wills[1] that become binding and irrevocable

---

[1] "Joint wills" and "mutual wills" are defined as:

A joint will is a single testamentary instrument signed by all the makers. The joint will actually creates two testamentary schemes and must be independently probated on the death of each of the joint testators.

A mutual will is one executed pursuant to an agreement between the parties (usually a husband and wife) who are making the will. The term "mutual" is essentially synonymous with "contractual," although the dispositive provisions of the will are not the contract. The will itself may, however, contain provisions of the contract or refer to an independent contract. The mutual will goes further than a joint will in that revocation or alteration by the surviving party is generally not allowed.

15 Powell on Real Property § 85.16 (citations omitted).

upon the death of the first person to die.[2] For example, assume that Husband and Wife execute identical wills that are stated to be joint and mutual. Each will provides that the property is to go outright to the couple's children upon the death of the second spouse to die. Wife dies first, bequeathing a life estate in her property to Husband, remainder to the children. The IRS takes the position that at the moment of Wife's death there is a completed gift by Husband of a remainder interest (after Husband's life) in his property to the children. This is founded on local law, which makes Husband's bequest of his property to the children binding and irrevocable immediately upon Wife's death. In Grimes v. Commissioner, 851 F.2d 1005 (7th Cir.1988), the Seventh Circuit upheld the IRS position, reasoning that this was like any other gift by contract, i.e., completion of performance by Mother makes the contract—and hence the Husband's transfer to the children—binding and irrevocable. The taxpayer sought to prevent this result by arguing that local law (Illinois) permitted the surviving spouse to consume the property subject to the joint and mutual wills, but the court construed Illinois law as prohibiting such consumption.

H. INSTALLMENT TRANSFERS

Timing issues often arise because of the dollar limit on the annual exclusion provided by section 2503(b). Because the exclusion is available for gifts to each donee in each separate calendar year, it is often important that a gift be treated as occurring in the calendar year or years that will provide optimum benefit from the exclusion.

This may be especially difficult if the property to be transferred is a single asset having a value greater than the annual exclusion. For example, assume that a grandparent wishes to transfer to a grandchild a parcel of land worth $85,000. Assume further that the annual exclusion is $17,000. In order to assure full availability of the annual exclusion, the gift must somehow be divided into five separate gifts of $17,000 in each of five years. Such a division may be cumbersome because of changes in value of the

---

[2] See, e.g., Davis v. Parris, 710 S.E.2d 757 (Ga. 2011) (affirming trial court's judgment that will was joint and mutual, and unable to be revoked by wife's later will); In re Schwebel, 479 N.E.2d 500 (Ill. App. Ct. 1985) (affirming lower court's finding that a will was inoperative due to a prior joint and mutual will executed by the deceased and deceased's brother); In re Estate of Graham, 690 N.W.2d 66 (Iowa 2004) (reversing lower court and holding that clear and convincing evidence of the testators' intent to form a contractual will existed in the joint will such that the surviving spouse broke her contractual obligations through a subsequent codicil); Fisher v. Capp, 597 S.W.2d 393 (Tex. App. 1980) (determining that will was both joint and mutual, and thus contractual, and prohibited the surviving spouse from altering the terms after the decedent's death); In re Estate of Cikanek, 2003 WI App 111, 264 Wis. 2d 893, 664 N.W.2d 126 (affirming trial court's finding that sufficient evidence was presented to establish that a contract not to revoke existed). But see In re Estate of Signore, 501 N.E.2d 282 (Ill. App. Ct. 1986) (affirming trial court's judgment that will was not joint and mutual, and allowed petitioner to renounce the decedent's will and receive half of the estate); In re Estate of Diefenbach, 282 N.W.2d 636 (Wis. Ct. App. 1979) (affirming lower court's judgment that joint will was not inherently contractual and sufficient evidence was not presented to establish that a contract not to revoke existed).

land, necessitating annual appraisals. Also, gifts of partial interests create an awkward divided ownership situation.

The case and rulings below illustrate some of the mechanisms used to address this problem, as well as the IRS responses. These authorities relate to an earlier time when the annual exclusion was only $3,000.

HAYGOOD V. COMMISSIONER

Tax Court of the United States, 1964.
42 T.C. 936.

SCOTT, JUDGE:

[The taxpayer transferred properties to each of her two sons and in return took a vendor's lien note from each for the full value of the properties, payable $3,000 per year, the first payments being due the day after the deeds were executed. Each vendor's lien note was secured by a deed of trust on the properties transferred. In accordance with her intention when she transferred the properties, the taxpayer canceled the $3,000 payments due the day after the execution of the deeds and in subsequent years canceled the other $3,000 payments.]

OPINION

It is respondent's position that in addition to the property of a value of $28,180 given by petitioner to her sons in December 1961 with respect to which no issue is here involved, petitioner made total gifts in the year 1961 of property to her sons of $32,500. Respondent takes the position that since the value of the pieces of city property which petitioner deeded to her sons, taking back a non-interest-bearing vendor's lien note in the amount of $16,500 from one son and a similar note in the amount of $16,000 from the other, was $32,500, this represents the amount of petitioner's gifts to her sons since the notes executed by her sons and the liens given as security therefor were without substance. It is respondent's position that petitioner's sons owed her nothing for the property in 1961 and were vested with ownership thereof and that such gifts constituted transfers subject to tax.

It is petitioner's position that she gave the rural property valued at $28,180 to her sons in 1961, and in addition gave them $6,000 of the value of the city property in that year. It is eminently clear from the testimony that it was petitioner's intent to give only a $3,000 interest to each of her sons in the city property deeded to them in the year 1961. Had petitioner in 1961 deeded only a 3/16.5 interest to C. Gerald Haygood in the portion of the city property which she intended to give to him and only a 3/16 interest to F. Donald Haygood in the portion of the city property she intended to give to him, which was apparently the procedure her accountant intended for her to follow, and in subsequent years deeded similar interests until the entire property was transferred, respondent apparently would not question the transaction as being a gift of a value of only $3,000 to each son in the year 1961. In fact respondent's regulations specifically provide for such a transfer.

It is respondent's position that petitioner transferred all of her interest in the property and in return therefor received nothing of value. Respondent does not consider there to be any substance to the notes and deeds of trust signed by petitioner's sons. Respondent states that his position is supported by the provisions of section 2501 of the Internal Revenue Code of 1954 imposing a tax for years after 1954 on the transfer of property by gift, section 2511 providing that the tax shall apply whether the transfer is in trust or otherwise and whether the gift is direct or indirect, and section 2512 providing that where the gift is made in property the value of the property at the date of the gift and when property is transferred for less than an adequate and full consideration in money or money's worth, that the amount by which the value of the property exceeds the value of the consideration shall be deemed a gift. Respondent contends that it is immaterial whether petitioner intended to give the entire value of the property in 1961 since she in that year actually did part with dominion and control over the property without receiving any valuable consideration in return therefor, relying on his regulations which he contends so state.

Respondent cites in support of his position the case of Minnie E. Deal, 29 T.C. 730 (1958). *Minnie E. Deal* involved a conveyance by the taxpayer there involved of real property to a trust for the benefit of her four daughters. The property was conveyed to the trust unencumbered. On the same date that the real property was conveyed by the taxpayer in *Minnie E. Deal*, supra, to the trust, each of her four daughters gave her a non-interest-bearing note which they would have been, with one exception, financially able to pay. The taxpayer forgave a $3,000 portion of each note to each daughter in the year of the transfer of the property, and a similar portion of each note in the 2 subsequent years, and the remaining balance of the note in the following year. In *Minnie E. Deal*, supra, we stated at page 736:

> After carefully considering the record, we think that the notes executed by the daughters were not intended to be enforced and were not intended as consideration for the transfer by the petitioner, and that, in substance, the transfer of the property was by gift. * * *

In conclusion we stated:

> * * * We have found, and held, that these notes were not given as a part of the purchase price of the property which petitioner conveyed to the trust and did not serve to reduce the amount of

the gift. Therefore, even if we assume, as petitioner argues, that the daughters were legally liable on the notes to petitioner, that fact has no effect on the question we have here to decide. The Commissioner has not included as part of the gifts made by petitioner in 1952 the cancellation of the 4 notes for $3,000 each [of] which had been executed by the daughters to petitioner. Since no such gifts were included by respondent in his determination of the deficiency, the cancellation cannot be made the basis for the exclusions in the amount of $12,000 which petitioner claimed on her return and which she still contends should be granted.

The *Minnie E. Deal* case is clearly distinguishable on its facts from the instant case. Here the notes were vendor's lien notes given for the property. Clearly as a matter of law, they would have been enforceable and respondent does not contend otherwise. Respondent's position is, and the record shows, that it was not petitioner's intention to enforce payment of the notes. Respondent points out that petitioner's sons were not able to pay the $3,000 payments on the notes due on December 31, 1961, on that date since they did not have the funds with which to make the payments. There is a stipulated fact that the sons were not financially able to make the $3,000 payments due on December 31, 1961. This stipulation must imply without considering the rural property given to petitioner's sons the preceding day since this property had a value of $28,180. However, the ability of the sons to pay $3,000 on December 31, 1961, is academic since it was petitioner's intention to and she did forgive the payment due on that day. It is stipulated that at the time these notes were given, the fair market value of the properties conveyed was $16,000 and $16,500, respectively. In view of the agreed value of the properties, the deeds of trust to the properties further securing the vendor's lien notes would obviously have some value.

* * *

We hold that the value of the property transferred by petitioner did not exceed the value of the vendor's lien notes and deeds of trust received in return therefor by more than the $3,000 in the case of each son, which amounts petitioner has reported as gifts in the year 1961.

Decision will be entered for petitioner.

REVENUE RULING 77–299
1977–2 C.B. 343.

Advice has been requested with respect to the Federal gift tax consequences of a transfer of property under the circumstances described below.

G had given A and B, G's grandchildren, $3,000 per year at Christmas since each grandchild was 10 years old. When A and B were, respectively, 21 and 22 years old and enrolled in graduate school, G proposed to give Blackacre, with a fair market value of $27,000, to A and Whiteacre, with a fair market value of $24,000, to B. Both Blackacre and Whiteacre were unimproved tracts of nonincome-producing real property. A and B had spent the money previously given them by G, did not have any other funds, and did not have an independent source of income. When informed of G's intent, G's attorney, in order to minimize G's Federal gift tax on the transfer, suggested a sale of the property to each grandchild in return for installment notes that would be payable in yearly amounts equal to the annual gift tax exclusion.

The plan was implemented in July 1972, at which time A and B each received a package of instruments in the mail from G's attorney. A's package contained a check from G for $50, a deed to Blackacre, a mortgage on the property, one note with a face amount of $2,950 and eight notes each in the amount of $3,000. B's package contained a check from G for $50, a deed to Whiteacre, a mortgage on the property, one note with a face amount of $2,950 and seven notes each in the amount of $3,000. A letter also accompanied each package explaining the transaction to A and B and indicating that G did not intend to collect on the notes, but intended to forgive each payment as it became due. A and B did not have prior knowledge of the transaction. There were no negotiations concerning the transaction, and G's attorney represented all of the parties to the transaction.

The notes were noninterest-bearing and nonnegotiable. The notes provided that A owed $26,950 on Blackacre and B owed $23,950 on Whiteacre. The first note of each grandchild in the amount of $2,950 matured on January 1, 1973, and each additional note in the amount of $3,000 matured on January 1 of each succeeding year. Each of the deeds recited that it was given in consideration of a cash payment of $50 and the notes. Additionally, each deed described the notes and recited that the mortgages on the property were taken to secure the payment of the notes. The deeds, mortgage, and notes were executed on July 15, 1972, and at the same time A and B each transferred $50 to G. Thereafter, the deeds (but not the mortgages) were recorded with the proper county authorities.

On December 25, 1972, G forgave the $2,950 due from A and B on January 1, 1973. On December 25 of 1973 and 1974, G forgave the $3,000 due from A and B on January 1 of the following years.

The specific question presented is whether the transfer of the property in return for the notes secured by a purchase money mortgage was a bona fide sale between the parties or whether the transaction was in substance a gift of the transferor's entire interest in the property structured to avoid the Federal gift tax.

Section 2501 of the Internal Revenue Code of 1954 imposes a tax on the transfer of property by gift. The gift tax applies, under the provisions of section 2511 of the Code and section 25.2511–1(a) of the Gift Tax Regulations, whether the transfer is in trust or otherwise and whether the gift is direct or indirect. Thus, the gift tax applies to all transactions whereby property or property rights or interests are gratuitously passed or conferred upon another, regardless of the means or device employed. See section 25.2511–1(c) of the regulations.

In the case of present interests, section 2503 of the Code excludes $3,000 of gifts per calendar year for each donee from gifts subject to the gift tax.

Section 2512 of the Code provides that when property is transferred for less than an adequate and full consideration in money or money's worth, the amount by which the value of the property exceeds the value of the consideration shall be deemed a gift and shall be included in computing the amount of gift made during the calendar year.

Section 25.2512–8 of the regulations states:

Transfers reached by the gift tax are not confined to those only which, being without a valuable consideration, accord with the common law concept of gifts, but embrace as well sales, exchanges, and other dispositions of property for a consideration to the extent that the value of the property transferred by the donor exceeds the value in money or money's worth of the consideration given therefor. However, a sale, exchange, or other transfer of property made in the ordinary course of business (a transaction which is bona fide, at arm's length, and free from any donative intent), will be considered as made for an adequate and full consideration in money or money's worth.

In Minnie E. Deal, 29 T.C. 730 (1958), the taxpayer transferred in trust a remainder interest in unimproved, nonincome-producing property to the taxpayer's children in return for noninterest-bearing, unsecured demand notes. The taxpayer canceled $3,000 of each child's indebtedness each year until the balance due was completely canceled. The Tax Court held the notes executed by the children were not intended as consideration for the transfer and, rather than a bona fide sale, the taxpayer made a gift of the remainder interest to the children. * * *

Thus, in the instant case, whether the transfer of property was a sale or a gift depends upon whether, as part of a pre-arranged plan, G intended to forgive the notes that were received when G transferred the property.

It should be noted that the intent to forgive notes is to be distinguished from donative intent, which, as indicated by section 25.2511–1(g)(1) of the regulations, is not relevant. A finding of an intent to forgive the note relates to whether valuable consideration was received and, thus, to whether the transaction was in reality a bona fide sale or a disguised gift. Therefore, such an inquiry is necessary in situations such as the one described here. "Nothing can be treated as consideration that is not intended as such by the parties." Fire Insurance Association v. Wickham, 141 U.S. [564,] 579 (1891). Donative intent, on the other hand, rather than relating to whether a transaction was actually a sale or a gift, relates to whether the donor intended the transaction to be a sale or a gift. Although the same facts would be used in determining either type of intent, they relate to two entirely different inquiries.

In the instant case, the facts clearly indicate that G, as part of a prearranged plan, intended to forgive the notes that were received in return for the transfer of G's land. Therefore, the transaction was merely a disguised gift rather than a bona fide sale.

The Service will not follow the decisions in Selsor R. Haygood, 42 T.C. 936 (1964), acq. in result, 1965–1 C.B. 4, nonacq., 1977–32 I.R.B. 5, and J.W. Kelley, 63 T.C. 321 (1974), nonacq., 1977–32 I.R.B. 5, that held that forgiveness of notes constituted a gift of a present interest, under circumstances similar to the present ruling.

Accordingly, for Federal gift tax purposes, G made a transfer by gift to A in 1972 in the amount of $27,000. In addition, G made a transfer by gift to B in 1972 in the amount of $24,000.

REVENUE RULING 83–180
1983–2 C.B. 169.

ISSUE

What are the gift tax consequences where, under the circumstances described below, the donor transfers specified portions of real property equal in value to the annual gift tax exclusion allowable under section 2503 of the Internal Revenue Code in effect for the years of the transfers?

FACTS

In 1980, A owned 10 acres of income producing real estate and transferred 3 of those acres to B. At that time the land was correctly appraised at $1,000 per acre. In 1981, A transferred 2 of A's remaining 7 acres to D. The land was correctly valued at $1,500 per acre. In 1982, A transferred to B the remaining 5 acres which were appraised at $2,000 per acre. Because the value of each transfer was equal to the annual exclusion available in the respective years of transfer, A did not file federal gift tax returns for the transfers, and consequently paid no gift tax.

LAW AND ANALYSIS

Section 2501 of the Code imposes a tax on the transfer of property by gift. Section 25.2511–2(b) of the Gift Tax Regulations provides that the gift is complete to the extent that the donor has parted with dominion and control over the property. Section 25.2511–2(a) of the regulations states that the gift tax is not imposed upon the receipt of the property by the donee but rather is an excise upon the donor's act of transfer.

Section 2503(b) of the Code as in effect for 1980 and 1981 provided that the first $3,000 may be excluded from the value of gifts of present interests in property made by a donor to any donee during the calendar year. For gifts of present interests made after December 31, 1981, section 2503(b) now provides that the annual exclusion is $10,000. Under section 25.2503–3 of the regulations, a "present interest" in property is defined as an unrestricted right to the immediate use, possession, or enjoyment of property or the income from property.

In Rev. Rul. 77–299, 1977–2 C.B. 343, in a purported sale transaction, G deeded nonincome producing land to G's grandchildren in exchange for a series of noninterest bearing notes that were payable annually, each note maturing in a succeeding year. Each note was equal in amount to the annual gift tax exclusion. In a letter to the transferees G stated that each note would be forgiven as the payment became due. Rev. Rul. 77–299 holds that in view of G's intent to forgive the notes as they matured, the notes received were not valuable consideration for the transfer. Rev. Rul. 77–299 concludes that the transaction was a disguised gift of the donor's entire interest in the property. In view of the fact that G deeded G's entire interest in the property to the grandchildren, and received less than adequate consideration for the transfer, a single gift of G's entire interest in the property occurred at the time of the "sales" transaction.

In the present case, unlike the situation presented in Rev. Rul. 77–299, A made separate completed gifts to B in separate taxable years. Each annual gift consisted of a portion of A's interest in the real property. A retained ownership and control of the remaining portions. Because A made a completed gift of only a portion of the property each year, only that portion transferred to B each year is subject to the gift tax. Each of the gifts qualifies for the annual exclusion under section 2503 of the Code because under the terms of the transfers, B received the present unrestricted right to the immediate use, possession, and enjoyment of an ascertainable interest in the real property. Because separate annual gifts are involved, and the value of each gift equals the annual gift tax exclusion in effect for the year of transfer, A, unlike the donor in Rev. Rul. 77–299, can use the exclusion for each annual gift.

HOLDING

Where a donor transfers, on an annual basis, a specified portion of real property, the donor has made a completed gift each year of the portion transferred, and each gift qualifies for the annual exclusion under section 2503 of the Code. It is not relevant that the value of each portion transferred equals the annual gift tax exclusion in effect for the year of the transfer.

PLANNING NOTE

As explained above, a donor is often confronted with the need to make a series of gifts of portions of a single larger property. Typically, this occurs because the donor wishes to keep the value of each gift within the section 2503(b) annual exclusion. Several alternatives are available to the donor. Each has its advantages and disadvantages.

The simplest approach is to transfer a portion of the property itself each year. For example, the donor might transfer by deed a specific number of acres of land, as was done in Rev. Rul. 83–180. Alternatively, the donor might give a percentage tenancy in common interest. Either approach assures qualification for the annual exclusion if the value of the property given does not exceed the section 2503(b) limit, but these methods have significant disadvantages. The most troublesome is uncertainty as to value. If the transferred acreage is later determined to have a value greater than the section 2503(b) limit, a portion of the donor's applicable credit amount (i.e., unified credit) will have been consumed. This danger can be minimized by obtaining an appraisal, but the appraisal would have to be repeated each year as subsequent gifts are made.

The second disadvantage of a gift of a portion of the property is the divided ownership that necessarily results. The donor and donee become co-owners (either as tenants in common or as owners of separate parcels) of a single tract as to which unified management may be desirable. The donor will thereby surrender some of his control over the property, and conflict between the donor and donee may result.

Another approach is the installment sale technique that was used in *Haygood*. This has the advantage of requiring only one appraisal. It also provides assurance that each year's transfer will not exceed the section 2503(b) limit, and it assures unified ownership and control of the land by the purchaser-donee. A major disadvantage is the possibility of a contention by the IRS, in accord with Rev. Rul. 77–299, that the donor did not intend to enforce the notes given by the buyer, with the result that the entire gift is treated as occurring in the year of the alleged sale. The installment sale approach also triggers taxable gain to the seller and brings into play complex income tax issues related to installment reporting under sections 453 and 453B, as well as the time value of money rules imposed by sections 483 and 1272. If the sale contract provides that the remaining installments due are to be canceled in the event of the donor's death, there are immediate income tax consequences when the donor dies. The income inherent in the canceled installments is taxed to the donor's estate as if it were realized immediately upon the donor's death. See Rev. Rul. 86–72, 1986–1 C.B. 253.

A third approach is contribution of the property to an entity such as a corporation, partnership, or limited liability company. The donor can transfer the property to a newly formed corporation, partnership, or limited liability company without recognition of gain pursuant to section 351 or section 721. The donor can then give shares of stock or interests in the partnership or limited liability company to the donee each year. The need for annual appraisals is not avoided, but the entity approach permits the donor to keep control of the property as long as the donor retains ownership of a majority of the interests in the entity. In addition, gifts of interests in the entity may qualify for minority discounts, as explained below in Chapter 11.

PROBLEMS

Beth Jenkins, age 76, is a widow. She is in good health but is worried about estate tax exposure because the value of her property is well in excess of the amount that can be sheltered by the applicable credit amount. She has few liquid assets, and her property consists almost entirely of land she actively farms. She wants to continue to farm this land, but is willing to give one parcel, the "Back 80," worth $150,000, to her son, Dan. Beth believes the Back 80 may appreciate substantially in value in the years ahead. Beth's basis for the Back 80 is $60,000.

1, What methods could you offer to Beth for transferring the Back 80 to Dan at minimum tax cost? What would be the advantages or disadvantages of each?

2. How would your advice be changed if Beth expressed strong interest in keeping control of farming on the Back 80 for as long as possible despite the transfer to Dan?

I. EFFECT OF A REVERSION

The gift tax can be imposed only on the property actually transferred by the donor. If the donor gives only a life estate to the donee, and the remainder is to revert to the donor, the taxable gift consists only of the life estate.

In the life estate example, the value of the gift can be readily computed by reference to the life expectancy of the donee. See Chapter 10. The issue becomes more complex, however, if there is uncertainty as to whether the reversion will in fact return to the donor. For example, assume that the reversion to the donor is to be effective only if the donor is married at the time of the donee's death. This cannot be predicted with actuarial certainty, and the value of the reversion is not determinable. In that event, the reversion is assigned a zero value for gift tax purposes, and the donor is treated as having made a completed gift of all interests in the property at the time of the transfer. Robinette v. Helvering, 318 U.S. 184 (1943), which appears in Chapter 14.

CHAPTER 5

POWERS OF APPOINTMENT

(SECTION 2514)

■ ■ ■

The history of the tax treatment of powers of appointment and the current complexities are fully explored in Chapter 22 in the context of the estate tax. Therefore, this chapter provides only a general description of the major principles applicable to powers of appointment for purposes of the gift tax.

Both the gift tax and the estate tax distinguish sharply between general and nongeneral powers. The term "general power" is carefully defined in section 2514(c) and (subject to certain exceptions) includes any power that permits the property to be appointed to *any one or more* of the following: the powerholder, the powerholder's creditors, the powerholder's estate, or creditors of the powerholder's estate. A powerholder who holds a general power is viewed as having rights essentially equivalent to full ownership. Therefore, if the powerholder exercises such a power by appointing the property to another, the exercise is taxable to the same extent as if the powerholder had transferred property owned outright. I.R.C. § 2514(a) and (b).

For example, assume that a husband creates a trust, granting a life estate to his spouse, remainder to the couple's children. The husband gives the spouse a power to appoint the principal of the trust to the spouse or to anyone else at any time within the first ten years after the trust is created. The spouse holds a general power, and the exercise of that power to appoint trust property to a person other than the spouse constitutes a taxable gift.

But the law goes further. If a powerholder holds such a general power but releases it or permits it to lapse, a taxable transfer occurs, subject to certain exceptions. I.R.C. § 2514(b) and (e). The powerholder is viewed as having effectively dictated the disposition of the property by releasing the power or by permitting it to lapse. By voluntarily forgoing exercise of the power, the powerholder has caused the property to go to others. It should be noted that this extension of the rule, i.e., taxing releases and lapses in the same way as exercises, applies only to powers created after October 21, 1942. Powers created on or before October 21, 1942, are taxed only if actually exercised. I.R.C. § 2514(a).

If the power described in the example above was created after October 21, 1942, and the spouse voluntarily releases the power, the spouse is treated as making a taxable gift of the remainder to the children at the time of the release. Similarly, if the spouse lets the ten years expire without exercising the power, so that the power lapses at the end of that period, the spouse is treated as making a taxable gift of the remainder to the children on the date of the lapse, subject to the exception noted below. In either case, because the children will receive the property if the power is not exercised, the children are referred to as the "takers in default of appointment."

If the power is exercised or released, the amount of the gift is the value of the property subject to the power. In the case of the spouse's release described above, the gift would consist of the actuarial value, at the time of the release, of the remainder after the spouse's life estate.

A special rule applies to lapses, however. A lapse is treated as a taxable transfer only to the extent that the value of the property subject to the lapse exceeds the greater of $5,000 or five percent of the aggregate value of the property out of which the power could have been satisfied. I.R.C. § 2514(e). For example, if the powerholder has a general power to appoint $35,000 out of a trust that has a total value of $200,000, and the powerholder permits the power to lapse, the powerholder is treated as having made a transfer in the amount of $25,000—the excess of $35,000 over $10,000 (five percent of the $200,000 value of the trust). There is a taxable gift of $25,000 if the powerholder has no other beneficial interest in the trust.

A power designed to take maximum advantage of this rule is called a "5 and 5 power." Typically, such a power permits the powerholder to withdraw the greater of $5,000 or 5 percent of the trust fund each year, and the power lapses at the end of each year if not exercised. Each annual lapse of such a power is fully covered by the $5,000 or 5 percent exception expressed in section 2514(e), and no taxable gifts will occur unless the powerholder actually exercises the power.

The $5,000 limit applies to the total of all powers held by the powerholder, regardless of the number of trusts involved. The limit cannot be multiplied by giving the powerholder a "5 and 5 power" in each of multiple trusts. Rev. Rul. 85–88, 1985–2 C.B. 202.

By contrast, nongeneral powers escape taxation entirely—even if exercised. For example, assume that in the circumstances above, the spouse has power to appoint the principal only to the husband's descendants. This is not a general power, and the spouse's exercise or release of the power—or its lapse—is not a taxable transfer. The following case addresses whether the holder of a nongeneral power of appointment makes a gift after relinquishing an income interest upon the appointment of a portion of trust property.

SELF V. UNITED STATES
United States Court of Claims, 1956.
142 F. Supp. 939.

LITTLETON, JUDGE:

This is a suit to recover gift taxes paid by plaintiff for the year 1951, in the amount of $918.23. The facts have been stipulated and may be summarized as follows:

On November 23, 1948, plaintiff's father transferred a block of common stock of a corporation called Greenwood Mills in trust, with the income from the trust fund to be paid to plaintiff for life, with remainders to plaintiff's descendants, if any, and if none, to a charitable foundation. By this trust instrument plaintiff was given the right at any time during his life to appoint by deed all or part of the trust property to or among his descendants. The plaintiff's father paid a gift tax upon the entire value of the property transferred in trust on November 23, 1948.

On October 2, 1951, plaintiff exercised the limited power of appointment given him under the trust instrument by executing 2 deeds appointing 100 shares of the Greenwood Mills common stock to a trust for his son and 100 shares of the same stock to a trust for his daughter. The 200 shares were, pursuant to the terms of the trust, separated and transferred to the 2 trusts for the benefit of plaintiff's children. The plaintiff filed a gift tax return for 1951, and paid, inter alia, a gift tax on the value of the right to receive the income for life from the 200 shares of Greenwood Mills common stock. The plaintiff filed a timely claim for refund. No action has been taken on the claim and this suit was timely filed.

The issue before the court is whether in exercising his limited power of appointment the plaintiff made a taxable gift equal to the value of the right to receive the income for life from the trust property transferred.

* * *

At common law, the transfer of property under a power of appointment was considered to have been made directly from the donor to the appointee. The donor's instrument effected the transfer and the property did not belong to the donee. Prior to 1942, the common law concept of powers of appointment was followed by the courts in gift tax cases and it was held that the appointment by the donee of the power did not constitute a taxable gift on the part of the donee. Section 452 of the Revenue Act of 1942, 56 Stat. 798, and section 3(a) of the Powers of Appointment Act of 1951, 65 Stat. 91, amended section 1000 of the 1939 Internal Revenue Code to provide that the exercise or release of a general power of appointment is taxable, with certain limitations relative to effective dates.

The defendant concedes that the transfer of an interest in property pursuant to the exercise of a limited or special power of appointment is not subject to the gift tax. It is defendant's position that the plaintiff's power related only to the trust corpus, not to the trust income, and that the transfer of the income interest was not made pursuant to a limited power and is therefore subject to the gift tax. The defendant argues that plaintiff transferred two separate interests when he exercised his limited power of appointment. First, he transferred 200 shares of stock in which he had no interest or vested right. Second, he transferred his vested right to the income from those 200 shares for his life. The plaintiff contends that because of the inherent nature of the income-producing property, such as the stock, it was impossible to transfer the property pursuant to the power of appointment without transferring the fruits from the property.

We believe that when the donee exercises a power of appointment over a corpus consisting of income-producing property by transferring part of the income-producing property to the appointee, the income to be earned from the property thus transferred automatically and necessarily goes with the legal title to the property, unless provision is specifically made for the contrary. In fact, the terms of the provision granting the power of appointment to plaintiff indicate that plaintiff's right to the income from the part of the corpus transferred pursuant to the power was to terminate upon the exercise of the power. The first sentence of this article provides that the "entire net income of the trust fund" should be paid to plaintiff during his life. The second sentence provides that, nevertheless, plaintiff should have the power by deed to appoint any or all of the corpus to his descendants. The third sentence provides that upon the exercise of the power the "trustees shall separate from the trust fund the portion or portions appointed and pay over such portions" as instructed by plaintiff.

The defendant admits that the right to the income to be earned from the shares was transferred automatically pursuant to the exercise of the power of appointment by the imposition of a gift tax on the value of the income when the power was exercised. The plaintiff did not purport to make an independent gift of the right to the income and the deeds of appointment by their terms related only to the shares of stock.

The defendant makes a general argument, the essence of which is that a gift tax should be imposed on the donee of a limited power of appointment upon the exercise of the power when the donee has a beneficial interest in the property transferred pursuant to the power. This argument is based on the theory that such a donee is giving up an economic interest when he exercises the power. This same argument and precise question were presented to the court in Commissioner v. Walston, 4 Cir. 168 F.2d 211. In that case, the taxpayer's father left a share of his estate in trust with the income to the taxpayer for life with remainders over. The taxpayer was also given the power to appoint the principal or income of the trust to or among her father's descendants by deed during her lifetime and/or to appoint the property to anyone by will at her death. In 1938, the taxpayer appointed by deed to her brother one-half of the trust corpus and the income for his life from the remaining half of the trust corpus. The Commissioner of Internal Revenue contended that the taxpayer made a taxable gift of her right to the income from the trust for her life. The Tax Court and the Court of Appeals held that the right to the income was transferred under the power of appointment and not by the taxpayer in her independent capacity and therefore the transfer was not taxable. Each court pointed out that where the income beneficiary had a life estate subject to a power of appointment, the income beneficiary had a temporary interest which might last for life, but which was subject to termination if and when the power of appointment was exercised. Consequently, to the extent the power is exercised, the income beneficiary's estate is terminated by reason of the power and not by a desire on the part of the income beneficiary to give up the life estate irrespective of the power.

The donor of the power of appointment is considered the transferor of the gift and the donee merely acts as his agent and gives direction to the gift pursuant to the donor's wishes. Unless the power of appointment concept is ignored, there is no difference between making the income beneficiary the donee of the special or limited power of appointment and making a third person who has no beneficial interest in the income or corpus the donee of the power. In the latter event no one would suggest that a gift tax should be imposed when the life estate of the income beneficiary is terminated by the transfer of the corpus pursuant to the exercise of the power.

The Congress has chosen to ignore this concept insofar as general powers of appointment are concerned and therefore has specifically subjected them to tax under section 1000(e) [1986 Code § 2514]. However, as defendant concedes, this concept is still applicable to property or interest that is transferred under a special or limited power of appointment.

The defendant refers us to Treasury Regulations 108, sec. 86.2(b)(2) (as amended by T.D. 6077, 1954–2 C.B. 308) as authority for its position. Congress has chosen not to impose a gift tax on property transferred under a special or limited power of appointment and if the property was transferred under a special or limited power of appointment, as it was in this case, it is not taxable. We do not deem this portion of the regulation necessarily inconsistent with our decision because the plaintiff in the instant case did not have, in addition to his special power, a general power to appoint by will, as is the case in the example given in the regulation. However, to the extent that the example given in the regulation implies that a donee, who has only the right to the income from the corpus subject to a special or limited power of appointment, is subject to a gift tax on the exercise of the special or limited power of appointment, we disagree with it.

Plaintiff is entitled to recover and judgment will be entered in the amount of $918.23, with interest as provided by law.

It is so ordered.

NOTE

The IRS is unwilling to follow the *Self* decision. See Rev. Rul. 79–327, 1979–2 C.B. 342. The IRS's position is also embodied in the regulations: Treas. Regs. §§ 25.2514–1(b)(2) and 25.2514–3(e) Example (3). Accord Estate of Regester v. Commissioner, 83 T.C. 1 (1984) (concluding that the taxpayer made a taxable gift of her income interest when the trust corpus was transferred to a beneficiary when she exercised a nongeneral power of appointment).

The IRS's opposition to the *Self* result was implemented in Tech. Adv. Mem. 9419007. Here the taxpayer, under age 30, was entitled to the income from a trust until attaining age 30, at which time the entire trust principal was to be paid to the taxpayer if the taxpayer was then living. The instrument also granted the taxpayer a power to appoint her interest in the trust to certain family members. The taxpayer, before attaining age 30, exercised the power by appointing both her remaining income interest and the remainder to one of the designated family members. Clearly, the taxpayer's power was nongeneral for purposes of section 2514(c), and the taxpayer argued that section 2514 prevented taxation of the exercise. The IRS, however, ruled that the taxpayer had made a taxable gift of the remaining income interest as well as the remainder. In the IRS's view, the taxpayer had full ownership and enjoyment of the property transferred (i.e., the income interest and the remainder). Had the taxpayer so chosen, she could have continued to receive the income and ultimately receive the remainder upon attaining age 30. Therefore, the taxpayer transferred property in which she had full ownership, not just a power of appointment, and the section 2514 power of appointment rules did not control.

PROBLEMS

1. In January of Year 1, Tamara Rodriguez died. She bequeathed $400,000 of her estate to the Rodriguez Trust, naming the Seventh National Bank as trustee. Tamara's son, Diego, is to receive all income from the trust throughout his life. Until January 10 of Year 10, Diego has a power to appoint part or all of the trust property to anyone, including himself. Upon Diego's death the remaining trust property goes outright to Diego's then living grandchildren.

    (a) As to each alternative event described below, state whether there is a gift and the value of the gift, assuming the value of the trust property is $700,000 on the date when each event occurs.

     (i)   On March 10 of Year 2, Diego appoints the entire trust property to his son, Luis.

     (ii)   On November 10 of Year 8, Diego irrevocably releases the power of appointment. On November 10 of Year 8, the actuarial value of the remainder after Diego's life estate is $500,000.

     (iii) Diego does not exercise the power. At midnight on January 10 of Year 10, the power lapses. On January 10 of Year 10, the actuarial value of the remainder after Diego's life estate is $550,000.

(b)   Assume the same facts, except that Diego's power of appointment permits him to appoint the property only to his wife and children. How would this change the results in part (a)?

2.   Alan Brown died in Year 1. He bequeathed most of his estate to the Tenth National Bank as trustee of the Brown Trust, which was created by Alan's will. The will provides that the income of the Brown Trust is to be paid to Alan's wife, Sydney, throughout her life. Upon Sydney's death the trust principal is to be distributed to the children of Alan and Sydney.

The will also provides that Sydney has power to appoint a maximum of $40,000 of principal each calendar year to herself or to her children, all adults. If the power is not exercised, it lapses at the end of each calendar year. The value of the property transferred to the Brown Trust was $1,000,000, and the value of the trust property has increased since then.

The trust was funded in Year 1. Sydney did not exercise her invasion power during Year 1, Year 2, or Year 3. Did Sydney make taxable gifts during Year 1, Year 2, or Year 3? If so, what was the value of each gift?

3.   Assume the same facts as in Problem 2, except that Sydney has power each year to appoint "the greater of $5,000 or 5% of the value of the trust property at the time the power is exercised." Answer the same questions as in Problem 2.

CHAPTER 6

DISCLAIMERS

(SECTION 2518)

■ ■ ■

In considering the transfer tax treatment of disclaimers or renunciations of property that otherwise would have been received by the person disclaiming, one starting place is the traditional rule that is applied to intestate property absent enactment of state or federal disclaimer legislation. At common law, an intestate taker was prohibited from disclaiming. An heir who renounced her interest was treated as having received the property immediately upon her ancestor's death and as having then made a gift to the person who took the property as a result of the heir's relinquishment of her interest. Today, all states have enacted a provision in their state statutes that allow beneficiaries to disclaim property received through intestate succession.[1]

Similarly, the common law rule allows a legatee or devisee under a will to disclaim an interest. The decedent is viewed as having gratuitously transferred property to the legatee or devisee, who should be entitled to reject the transfer. Therefore, a legatee or devisee is generally entitled under local law to refuse a testamentary gift.[2] In most states the common law rules have been supplanted by statutes that expressly authorize disclaimer of a wide variety of property interests.[3]

Because of the diversity of local statutory and case law, there was an extended period of uncertainty as to the efficacy of a disclaimer for United States estate and gift tax purposes. Relief came in the form of section 2518, adopted in 1976. This provision provides definitive and uniform national rules dictating the effect of disclaimers for purposes of the gift tax, estate tax, and tax on generation-skipping transfers.

---

[1] See, e.g., 755 Ill. Comp. Stat. 5/2–7(a) (2022) (providing that a person may disclaim property that passes to that person "by whatever means"); Mass. Gen Laws ch. 190B § 2–801(b)(1) (2022) (stating that beneficiaries may disclaim an interest passing by intestate succession); Ohio Rev. Code Ann. § 5815.36(A)(1)(a) (West 2022) (including heirs who receive property by intestate succession as eligible disclaimants); Wis. Stat. § 852.13 (2022) (allowing a person who receives property under intestate succession laws to disclaim).

[2] Brown v. Routzahn, 63 F.2d 914 (6th Cir.1933), cert. denied, 290 U.S. 641 (1933).

[3] See, e.g., Conn. Gen. Stat. § 45a–579(a) (2022); Okla. Stat. tit. 60 § 751 (2022); Utah Code Ann. § 75–2–801 (2022); Vt. Stat. Ann. tit. 14, § 1951 (2022); Wash. Rev. Code § 11.86.011(6) (2022).

If a disclaimer qualifies under the section 2518 rules, the interest disclaimed is treated as though it had never been transferred to the individual making the disclaimer. Therefore, the transfer of property that occurs by virtue of the disclaimer is not treated as a gift for purposes of the gift tax. Similarly, the disclaimer is not treated as a transfer for purposes of the estate tax or the tax on generation-skipping transfers. I.R.C. § 2518(a); Treas. Reg. § 25.2518–1(b). For example, if a child of the decedent disclaims a bequest, with the result that under local law the property goes to the decedent's surviving spouse, the bequest will be treated as a transfer directly from the decedent spouse to the surviving spouse; therefore, it will qualify for the marital deduction with respect to the decedent's estate. Treas. Reg. § 20.2056(d)–2(b).

To qualify under section 2518, the disclaimer must be irrevocable and unconditional. In addition, the following requirements must be met:

1.   The disclaimer must be in writing;

2.   The disclaimer must be received by the transferor or the holder of title to the property not later than nine months after the transfer that creates the interest in the disclaimant. However, if the disclaimant is under age 21 when the interest is created, the period for making the disclaimer is extended until nine months after the disclaimant has reached age 21;

3.   The disclaimant must not have accepted any interest or benefit with respect to the property disclaimed; and

4.   The interest disclaimed must pass to another person without any direction or control by the disclaimant.

The Treasury's regulations on disclaimers construe the requirements of section 2518 very strictly. For example, any "affirmative act which is consistent with ownership of the property," such as acceptance of dividends, interest, or rent, can be treated as a disqualifying acceptance of benefits. Treas. Reg. § 25.2518–2(d)(1). Similarly, if the disclaimer causes property to pass to a trust over which the disclaimant has discretionary power to determine beneficial enjoyment by others, the property may be treated as having passed with direction by the disclaimant. In that event the disclaimer will not meet the test of section 2518(b)(4) and will be treated as a taxable gift by the disclaimant. See Treas. Reg. § 25.2518–2(e). The idea is that the disclaimant must truly renounce any and all dominion over the property. The one exception to this rule involves the decedent's surviving spouse. A disclaimer by the surviving spouse qualifies even though the result of the disclaimer is to give the benefits of the property to the surviving spouse in another form. I.R.C. § 2518(b)(4)(A); Treas. Reg. § 25.2518–2(e)(2).

As noted in the preceding paragraph, and as specifically provided in section 2518(b)(3), a disclaimer is not qualified under section 2518 if, as of the time of the disclaimer, the disclaimant has "accepted the interest or any of its benefits." This rule creates a special problem with IRAs and qualified retirement plan interests because the relevant income tax rules require that certain minimum distributions be made in each calendar year. I.R.C. § 401(a)(9). If the decedent dies before the distribution for the calendar year of death has been made, the distribution must be made in that calendar year to the named beneficiary. Depending on the date of death, the distribution may be made shortly after the date of death, and long before the expiration of the 9-month period section 2518 provides for disclaimers. This raises the question whether the beneficiary's receipt of such a required distribution violates section 2518(b)(3), thereby barring the beneficiary from disclaiming his or her remaining interest in the IRA or qualified plan. The IRS resolved this problem in Rev. Rul. 2005–36, 2005–26 I.R.B. 1368. The IRS ruled that receipt of a required distribution would not prevent the beneficiary from disclaiming the remaining value of the IRA. Although the ruling literally applies only to IRA's, the rationale should apply with equal force to qualified plans in general.

Special rules are applied to disclaimers of joint tenancy interests. As to property other than bank accounts and brokerage and investment accounts, application of section 2518 is premised on the concept that a two-step transfer is involved. First, one-half of the property is deemed to be transferred when the transferor creates the joint tenancy. Second, the other one-half of the property is deemed to be transferred when the decedent joint tenant dies. In the typical case the decedent joint tenant dies more than nine months after the creation of the joint tenancy, so that a disclaimer of the first one-half after the decedent joint tenant's death would not be timely. But the surviving joint tenant can disclaim the second one-half within nine months after the death of the decedent joint tenant. This rule applies regardless of which joint tenant originally contributed the property, and regardless of whether local law permits each tenant to unilaterally sever the joint tenancy. Treas. Reg. § 25.2518–2(c)(4)(i). This rule, as stated in the Regulations, confirms and follows several court decisions.[4]

A different rule is applied to joint bank, brokerage, and investment accounts. If under local law a transferor may unilaterally regain her contributions without the consent of the other joint tenant, with the result that under Treasury Regulation § 25.2511–1(h)(4) the transfer into joint tenancy is not a completed gift, the entire transfer to the surviving joint tenant is viewed as occurring upon the death of the first joint tenant to die.

---

[4]   Kennedy v. Comm'r, 804 F.2d 1332 (7th Cir.1986); Estate of Dancy v. Comm'r, 872 F.2d 84 (4th Cir.1989); McDonald v. Comm'r, 853 F.2d 1494 (8th Cir.1988), cert. denied, 490 U.S. 1005 (1989).

Therefore, the surviving joint tenant may disclaim the entirety of the joint tenancy property until nine months after the death of the decedent joint tenant. The surviving joint tenant, however, cannot disclaim any portion of the account attributable to consideration furnished by her. Treas. Reg. § 25.2518–2(c)(4)(iii). For example, if Alice contributed 70% of the property and Betty contributed 30%, a disclaimer of the entire account by Betty within nine months after Alice's death would be treated as follows: There would be a valid disclaimer as to 70%, and this amount would be treated as going directly from Alice to the persons entitled to the property under local law in the event Betty predeceased Alice. The remaining 30%, however, would not be treated as having been validly disclaimed for purposes of the estate tax. Betty would be treated as making a gift of 30% of the property to the persons receiving that 30%.

Disclaimers can be dangerous. A disclaimer that is valid for purposes of local property law may nevertheless be invalid for federal gift, estate, and generation-skipping tax purposes. Imagine, for example, a circumstance in which Father bequeaths property to Son. Son disclaims the property, with the result that the property goes to Father's widow. Although the disclaimer might be invalid for federal tax purposes because it violates one of the requirements of section 2518, it would nevertheless be valid for local property law purposes. As a result, the property would go to the widow, with two unfortunate results. First, the property would be treated as transferred from Son to the widow as a taxable gift. Second, Son would no longer have any interest in the property and therefore might not have funds for payment of the gift tax.

Section 2518 is applicable only where the transfer creating an interest in the person disclaiming is made after 1976. In the case of transfers made before 1977, the rules relating to disclaimers in effect prior to 1977 remain applicable. In that event, under Treas. Reg. § 25.2511–1(c)(2), the disclaimer will be treated as a taxable gift unless it is made "within a reasonable time after knowledge of existence of the transfer." This rule applies to all pre-1977 transfers, including those that took place before the gift tax was adopted. United States v. Irvine, 511 U.S. 224 (1994).

PLANNING NOTE

Disclaimers play an important role in tax-oriented estate planning. Three factors contribute to this phenomenon. First, the presence of section 2518 and of disclaimer statutes in most states permits certainty as to the property law and tax law results of a disclaimer. Second, the unlimited estate tax marital deduction, discussed in Chapter 27, makes it attractive to transfer all of the decedent spouse's property to the surviving spouse, giving the surviving spouse the opportunity to reduce the transfer by disclaimer if desired. Third, the substantial and growing size of the estate tax unified credit makes optimum use of the credit an important objective, and a disclaimer may be vital in achieving that goal.

The typical plan relying on a disclaimer involves a bequest of most or all of the decedent spouse's property outright to the surviving spouse. This transfer qualifies for the unlimited estate tax marital deduction under section 2056. However, the decedent's will also creates a "bypass trust" that provides substantial economic benefits for the surviving spouse without causing inclusion of any of the bypass trust assets in the surviving spouse's gross estate. For example, the bypass trust may provide life income and limited principal invasion rights for the surviving spouse. The will may provide only a modest bequest or perhaps no bequest at all to the bypass trust.

The will further provides that, should the surviving spouse disclaim any of the property bequeathed to the surviving spouse, the property disclaimed will go to the bypass trust. This permits the surviving spouse to evaluate the family's financial circumstances during the nine months after the decedent spouse's death and then determine the best allocation of assets between the surviving spouse and the bypass trust. The optimum division is then achieved by a partial or total disclaimer by the surviving spouse.

For example, assume that a wife dies with a gross estate of $20,000,000 when the estate tax basic exclusion amount is $12,920,000. She bequeaths $1,000,000 outright to each of her three children and bequeaths the remaining $17,000,000 outright to her spouse. The wife's will, however, also creates a bypass trust and provides that any property that the spouse disclaims will go to the bypass trust. This arrangement permits the spouse to evaluate the family's circumstances after the wife's death and decide how best to divide the estate. In most cases, it will be best for the spouse to disclaim $9,920,000 to the bypass trust. This amount, together with the $3,000,000 bequest to the children, will fully utilize the $12,920,000 basic exclusion amount available at the wife's death.

An alternative, of course, is to rely on the portability of the basic exclusion amount provided by section 2010(c) so that the spouse can use any of the basic exclusion amount not used at the wife's death.

The advantage of the disclaimer arrangement is great flexibility in adjusting the family's tax planning after the wife's death, providing an important opportunity for postmortem tax planning. This opportunity is especially important in times of uncertainty as to the time when one of the spouses might die, or as to the law that may be in effect at that time.

PROBLEMS

1. Kelly Wilson signed her last will in 1994. At that time, she owned 100 shares of Tech Corp. stock, which were then worth $1,000,000. In her will she bequeathed all shares of Tech Corp. stock she would own at her death to her daughter, Maddie. Kelly's will provided that, in the event Maddie did not survive Kelly, the Tech Corp. stock would go to Kelly's husband,

Alan. Kelly bequeathed all the rest of her estate to Alan. Under section 2056(a), the general rule is that any property that goes outright to the spouse of a decedent qualifies for the marital deduction, with the result that the marital deduction property is excluded from the decedent's taxable estate.

Kelly died on February 2 of this year. Tech Corp. had prospered greatly in the 15 years prior to Kelly's death. By the time of Kelly's death, after numerous stock splits, the original 100 shares had grown to 3000 shares, with a total value of $16,920,000. The remainder of Kelly's assets had a value of only $1,000,000. Kelly had failed to change her will to reflect the dramatically increased value of the Tech Corp. stock.

By the time of Kelly's death, Maddie had become prosperous. Also, she was concerned about Alan's resources. Alan owned few assets. Finally, she was concerned about the estate taxes that would be imposed on Kelly's estate if Maddie received the Tech Corp. stock.

As a result, on October 20 of this year Maddie disclaimed all rights to 1500 shares of the Tech Corp. stock. The disclaimer was delivered to Kelly's executor, a bank. Under local law the disclaimer is valid, with the result that 1500 shares of the Tech Corp. stock are to be disposed of as if Maddie had predeceased Kelly. On December 2 of this year the executor distributed 1500 shares to Alan and 1500 shares to Maddie.

The executor received dividends from Tech Corp. in March, June, and September and deposited each dividend in the estate bank account.

How much estate tax is owned at Kelly's death? Does Maddie owe any gift tax? If so, how much?

2.   Assume the same facts as in Part 1, except that in each of March, June, and September the executor of Kelly's estate received a dividend of $100,000 from Tech Corp. and immediately endorsed the check to Maddie. Maddie deposited each dividend check in her own bank account.

How much estate tax is owed at Kelly's death? Does Maddie owe any gift tax? If so, how much?

CHAPTER 7

UNIFIED CREDIT, EXCLUSIONS AND DEDUCTIONS

■ ■ ■

A. UNIFIED CREDIT

1. IN GENERAL

As explained in Chapter 2, section 2505 provides a credit against the gift tax that would otherwise be due. Under the Tax Cuts and Jobs Act of 2017, the "basic exclusion amount" is $10,000,000 from January 1, 2018 through December 31, 2025. See I.R.C. § 2001(a)(3)(C). Pursuant to section 2010(c)(3)(B), the basic exclusion amount is indexed for inflation. The credit amount is determined by a complex statutory route. Section 2505(a)(1) provides that the credit is equivalent to the "applicable credit amount" that would be applicable under section 2010(c) if the decedent died during the calendar year of the gift. The "applicable credit amount" is the tax that would be imposed on a transfer of the "applicable exclusion amount." I.R.C. § 2010(c)(1). The "applicable exclusion amount" consists of the "basic exclusion amount" and the "deceased spousal unused exclusion amount." I.R.C. § 2010(c)(2). The "deceased spousal unused exclusion amount" is ignored at this point and is addressed in the following section.

In 2023, the basic exclusion amount after the inflationary adjustment is $12,920,000. The gift tax on an $12,920,000 gift computed under section 2001(c) is $5,113,800 ($345,800 + (11,920,000 × .40)). Hence, the credit for 2023 is $5,113,800. The $12,920,000 sheltered amount is often described as the "exemption equivalent" of the $5,113,800 credit.

The credit is referred to as "unified" because it is available only once to each taxpayer and applies to both inter vivos transfers and transfers at death. To the extent the gift tax credit is used to shelter lifetime transfers, the benefit of the credit against the estate tax will be concomitantly reduced. This is not achieved by reducing the estate tax credit as such, but through the section 2001(b) estate tax computation process. Although the statutory provisions incorporating the unified credit appear to permit double use of the credit, once during life and again at death, the mechanics of the tax computation under section 2001(b) are such that each individual can obtain the benefit of only a single unified credit, the maximum credit being the estate tax credit applicable in the year of the individual's death.

The credit available in any year is reduced by the credit used in prior years. I.R.C. § 2505(a)(2). For purposes of determining the credit used in prior years, the rates applicable in the current year are applied in lieu of the rates applicable in the earlier year. I.R.C. § 2505(a). For example, assume that the donor made taxable gifts of $8,000,000 in 2022 and $12,000,000 in 2023. Under the section 2001(c) rate structure in effect for 2022, the tax on taxable gift of $8,000,000 would be $3,145,800, and a credit of $3,145,800 would eliminate any tax liability. Therefore, $3,145,800 is subtracted from the maximum unified credit of $5,113,800 available in 2023, producing a net credit available in 2023 of $1,968,000. The 2023 gift tax is computed by considering the cumulative taxable gifts for 2022 and 2023. The tax before credits on the cumulative taxable gifts of $20,000,000 is $7,945,800. Subtracting the tax on the 2022 gift of $3,145,800 produces a tentative gift tax of $4,800,000. Subtracting the available unified credit of $1,968,000 produces a gift tax due of $2,832,000 for the 2023 gift. As noted, the donor's transfers for both years total $20,000,000. The tax due of $2,832,000 on the total taxable gifts of $20,000,000 represents the tax at the flat tax rate of 40% on $7,080,000, the amount by which the $20,000,000 total gifts exceed the $12,920,000 basic exclusion amount for 2023.

The section 2010 credit is termed "unified" because it applies to both lifetime gifts and death transfers. Under section 2001(b)(1)(B) the decedent's taxable gifts after 1976 are added to the decedent's taxable estate to determine the tax due. Therefore, the credit is consumed by both gifts and death transfers. For example, assume that the basic exclusion amount is $12,920,000 at the decedent's death. If the decedent made taxable gifts of $3,000,000 (but paid no gift tax) and died with a taxable estate of $16,920,000, the section 2001(b) tax would be determined by the total of all transfers—$19,920,000. The tax on $19,920,000 is $7,913,800. Subtracting the unified credit of $5,113,800 produces a tax due of $2,800,000. In effect the first $12,920,000 of all transfers is exempt, and the remaining $7,000,000 is taxed at a 40% rate totaling $2,800,000.

As noted above, the $10,000,000 basic exclusion amount (adjusted for inflation) is subject to a sunset post-2025 when the basic exclusion amount will revert to $5,000,000. A significant issue is whether a decedent will be subject to estate tax if the decedent makes taxable gifts of $10,000,000 during 2018 through 2025 that are exempt from gift taxation, but the decedent dies after 2025 and the basic exclusion amount reverts to $5,000,000. Under section 2001(g)(2), Congress delegated to the Treasury Department the authority to issue necessary or appropriate regulations to address the difference between the basic exclusion amount at the time of a decedent's death and the basic exclusion amount at the time of a decedent's gifts. In November 2019, the Treasury Department issued final regulations (the so-called "clawback regulations") to prevent the decedent from being unfairly subject to an estate tax resulting from this disparity. Under the regulations, to the extent the basic exclusion amount exceeds the allowable amount at the time of the decedent's death, the basic exclusion amount in computing the estate tax equals the sum of the allowable basic exclusion amount on the decedent's post-1976 gifts. Treas. Reg. § 20.2010–1(c). As a result, if a decedent makes taxable gifts totaling $12,920,000 in 2023 equal to the basic exclusion amount in 2023 and the decedent dies in 2026 when the basic exclusion amount totals $5,000,000, the decedent's basis exclusion amount will equal $12,920,000. The regulations apply to decedents dying after November 26, 2019.

Significantly, the Treasury Department issued proposed regulations in 2022 to distinguish between lifetime transfers that are included in the computation of the estate tax as "adjusted taxable gifts" per section 2001(b)(1)(B) and transfers that are included in the gross estate for estate tax purposes. See Prop. Reg. § 20.2010–1(c)(3). The proposed regulations contain an example where a decedent makes a lifetime gift of an enforceable promissory note resulting in a completed gift. Upon the decedent's death, the note remains unpaid and is satisfied with assets from the decedent's estate. The proposed regulations apply to other types of transfers included in the gross estate (e.g., property included under section 2036). Under these proposed regulations, the clawback regulations will not apply to property included in the gross estate to satisfy the promissory note or "transfers with strings," such as section 2036 transfers. The proposed regulations will apply to decedents dying on or after April 27, 2022.

Finally, the 2010 Act added a new concept: portability of the unified credit between spouses for both gift and estate tax purposes. In essence, portability permits a surviving spouse to utilize any portion of the unified credit of a previously deceased spouse that went unused. This result is achieved by adding to the "basic exclusion amount" ($12,920,000 in 2023), the "deceased spousal unused exclusion amount." I.R.C. § 2010(c)(2)(B). The Treasury's final regulations issued in November 2019 provide that, if an executor elects portability for a spouse who dies during the time of the increased basic exclusion amount, the surviving spouse's applicable exclusion amount includes the full amount of the deceased spousal unused exclusion that is based on the deceased spouse's increased basic exclusion amount. See Treas. Regs. §§ 20.2010–1(c)(2)(iii) and 20.2010–1(c)(2)(iv), Examples 3 and 4. When the surviving spouse makes a gift, the deceased spousal unused amount is applied to the gift before the surviving spouse's basic exclusion amount. The portability rule is more fully examined in Chapter 28.

B. ANNUAL EXCLUSION

1. IN GENERAL

A provision of central importance to the gift tax is section 2503(b), which provides an annual exclusion. The exclusion is "annual" because the specified amount is available anew each year. Gifts of the specified amount to each and every donee, without limitation as to number of donees, may be excluded by a single donor. The exclusion is not limited to donees who are family members.

The exclusion was originally set at $5,000 in 1932 and then reduced to $4,000 in 1939 and $3,000 in 1943. Several of the cases referred to in this chapter were decided when the exclusion amount was only $3,000. The annual exclusion remained at $3,000 until 1982, when it was raised to $10,000 for gifts after 1981. The exclusion remained fixed at $10,000 through 1998 but was indexed for inflation thereafter. Under the indexing regime set forth in section 2503(b)(2), the annual exclusion is not increased until indexation requires an additional amount of at least $1,000. Therefore, the annual exclusion is not usually increased annually. The annual exclusion was $15,000 from 2018 through 2021. It was increased to $16,000 for 2022. Surprisingly, the annual exclusion was increased one year later to $17,000 beginning in 2023.

The annual exclusion occupies an important position in gift and estate planning. Continued and carefully planned use of the exclusion provides a ready vehicle for transfer of substantial amounts to younger generations without a tax burden of any kind.

For example, assume that parents with substantial wealth have three children and seven grandchildren, and that the annual exclusion is $17,000. Ten donees are available, and the husband and wife together may give $34,000 to each donee each year tax free. As a result, $340,000 can be transferred entirely tax free to the children and grandchildren each year. Continuation of this pattern over a ten-year period would permit tax-free transfer of $3,400,000.

This method of avoiding transfer taxes is especially convenient and attractive if each spouse makes one-half of the gifts from his or her own funds, so that section 2513 gift-splitting (see Chapter 8) need not be used. In that event no gift tax return will be required for any of the gifts. I.R.C. § 6019(a)(1). The same no-return result can be achieved even if only one spouse will provide the gift property. If the spouse from whose assets the gifts are to be made transfers one-half of the intended gift property outright to the other spouse, followed by independent gifts of that amount by the transferee spouse, no return is necessary. The transfer between spouses is covered by the section 2523 gift tax marital deduction, and no return need be filed with respect to transfers that qualify for the deduction. I.R.C. § 6019(a)(2).

If only one spouse is to make the gifts, and that spouse is unwilling to make an outright transfer to the other spouse as described in the preceding paragraph, the full benefit of the annual exclusion is nevertheless available through gift-splitting under section 2513. As explained in Chapter 8, if both spouses agree to treat the gifts of either spouse as if made one-half by each spouse, each gift is treated as split between the spouses for all purposes of the gift tax. If a wife gives $34,000 to her son, and the wife's spouse agrees to split gifts, the wife and spouse are each treated as giving $17,000 to the son. Gift splitting is available only if a gift tax return is filed. I.R.C. § 2513(b); Treas. Reg. § 25.2513–2.

A further attraction of annual exclusion gifts is the zero inclusion ratio assigned to most such gifts for purposes of the tax on generation-skipping transfers. I.R.C. § 2642(c). As a result, such gifts may entirely escape the generation-skipping tax, regardless of the number of generations skipped. See Chapter 29.

2. PRESENT INTEREST REQUIREMENT

a. Limitation on Annual Exclusion

The most important limitation on the annual exclusion is that it does not apply to gifts of future interests. A gift of a future interest is fully subject to tax except to the extent sheltered by deductions or the unified credit. Treas. Reg. § 25.2503–3(a) states:

> "Future interests" is a legal term, and includes reversions, remainders, and other interests or estates, whether vested or contingent, and whether or not supported by a particular interest or estate, which are limited to commence in use, possession, or enjoyment at some future date or time. The term has no reference to such contractual rights as exist in a bond, note (though bearing no interest until maturity), or in a policy of life insurance, the obligations of which are to be discharged by payments in the future.

By contrast, the Regulations define a present interest as "an unrestricted right to the immediate use, possession, or enjoyment of property or the income from property (such as a life estate or term certain)." Treas. Reg. § 25.2503–3(b). Thus, an unrestricted gift of an immediate income interest in a trust is a gift of a present interest for which an exclusion is available to the extent of the actuarial value of the income interest.

If an income interest is given, the exclusion is available only if the donor transfers the unrestricted right to receive all or some identifiable part of the income, beginning immediately. If the donor transfers the right to a fixed percentage of the income the gift constitutes a present interest in the amount of that percentage multiplied by the actuarial value of the entire income interest.

If the beneficiary's right to income is restricted or deferred in any way, the income right is a future interest and does not qualify for the exclusion. For example, if the trustee is to distribute to the beneficiary only such income as the trustee determines to be desirable, there is no present interest. Similarly, if the beneficiary has an unrestricted right to income but will not begin receiving income until the end of a significant period of time after the transfer, there is no present interest. Treas. Reg. § 25.2503–3. The deferral rule is applied strictly. For example, in Estate of Jardell v. Commissioner, 24 T.C. 652 (1955), the donor transferred on October 2, 1949, the right to receive royalties from mineral production occurring after December 31, 1949. The Tax Court held that the delay of less than three months prevented the transfer from qualifying as a present interest.

Whether the gift is a present or future interest is determined when the gift becomes "complete" under the tests described in Chapter 4. For example, assume that the donor transfers property to a trust, and the trust instrument permits the donor to determine who among several beneficiaries is to receive the income each year. The gift is not complete when the transfer is made to the trust because the donor has retained control over disposition of the income. When income is actually distributed each year there is a completed gift of the income to the recipient. At that point the recipient has a present interest in the amount received, and the distribution of income therefore qualifies for the annual exclusion.

The result is different if the gift is complete at the outset. For example, assume that the donor names a bank as trustee and the trust instrument permits the trustee to distribute income among three individuals as the trustee determines is best. This is a completed gift because the donor has put the property beyond his control. But there is no present interest because no individual beneficiary has an assured right to income. See Treas. Reg. § 25.2503–3(c), Ex. 3. The actual distribution of income to a beneficiary is not a further gift for gift tax purposes. The entire value of the contribution to the trust has already been taxed at the outset.

An indirect gift may or may not constitute a present interest. If the donor transfers property to a corporation, thereby gratuitously benefitting its shareholders, an indirect gift to the shareholders has occurred. The gift, however, is not a present interest because the shareholders have no immediate right to the benefits of the gift. Estate of Stinson v. United States, 214 F.3d 846 (7th Cir. 2000); CTUV Hollingsworth v. Commissioner, 86 T.C. 91 (1986); Rev. Rul. 71–443, 1971–2 C.B. 337. By contrast, if the donor gratuitously transfers property to a general partnership, thereby making a gift to the partners, the result is different. Under the Uniform Partnership Act, the partners have an immediate right to withdraw the amounts in their respective capital accounts. Therefore, a gift that increases a partner's capital account constitutes a present interest. Wooley v. United States, 736 F. Supp. 1506 (S.D. Ind. 1990).

A gift to a limited partnership, or a gift consisting of a limited partnership interest, may or may not qualify as a present interest. In Tech. Adv. Mem. 9751003, the IRS concluded that gifts of limited partnership interests did not constitute present interests. The donee limited partners had no certain entitlement to an income stream but would receive only such distributions as the general partner thought appropriate. Furthermore, the donee limited partners could not freely sell their interests but were subject to significant restrictions.

If a gift is made to an entity that is charitable, public, or political, with the result that the members or owners have no economic interest in the entity, the gift is treated as made to the entity rather than the members. Treas. Reg. § 25.2511–1(h)(1). For example, in Priv. Ltr. Rul. 9818042, the taxpayer made a gift to a social club exempt from income taxation under § 501(c)(7). The IRS concluded that no individual member had an economic interest in the gift, with the result that the gift was treated as made to the club, not the members. Because the club had the right to immediate and unrestricted use of the gift, the gift qualified for the section 2503(b) exclusion.

It is important to remember that the present interest question is secondary to, and entirely apart from, the question of whether a gift is complete. One first determines whether a gift is complete, using the principles explored in Chapter 4. Only if the gift is complete does one then ask whether the gift constitutes a present interest. A conclusion that the gift is not a present interest has no effect whatever on the prior conclusion that the gift is complete.

PROBLEMS

Ryan is very generous. During the current year he made gifts as described below. In the case of each gift, state whether any portion of the gift constitutes a present interest for purposes of section 2503(b), thereby qualifying for the annual exclusion.

1.   Ryan gave $17,000 in cash to Emily.

2.   Ryan gave an insurance policy to Kelsey on Ryan's life. The amount payable upon Ryan's death is $500,000. Kelsey has an insurable interest in Ryan's life, and at the time of the gift the policy had a market value of $10,000.

3.   Ryan paid the annual premium of $3,000 under a $100,000 insurance policy on Ryan's life owned by Michael, who has an insurable interest in Ryan's life.

4.   Ryan contributed $51,000 to Powell Corporation, a manufacturing business. The stock of Powell Corporation is owned in equal one-third amounts by David, Donald, and Debbie. Ryan has no interest in the corporation.

5.   Ryan transferred $40,000 to an irrevocable trust. A bank is the trustee, and the trust is to last for 12 years. The trust instrument provides that one-half of the trust income must be paid to Alexandra each year. The trustee has discretion to distribute to Alexandra the other one-half of the income, as well as any or all of the principal. Upon termination of the trust, the principal and accumulated income are to be paid to Joshua.

6.   Ryan transferred $500,000 to the Fargo Trust. A bank serves as trustee, and the trust is to last for 12 years. The income for the first year of the trust is to be accumulated and added to principal. The trustee is to pay all trust income earned after the first year to Frank on an annual basis. Upon termination of the trust all trust property is to be paid to Andrea.

7.   Ryan transferred $300,000 to an irrevocable trust. A bank serves as trustee, and the trust is to last for 12 years. Each year the entirety of the income is to be paid to the three named beneficiaries in such shares as the trustee in its discretion determines.

8.   Ryan transferred $200,000 to an irrevocable trust. A bank serves as trustee, and the trust is to last for 12 years. Jordan is to receive all income of the trust annually, and upon termination of the trust the trust property is to be paid to Jayrd. The trustee has power to distribute principal to Jennifer at any time.

b. Trusts: Requirement of Income-Producing Property

If property is transferred outright, and the donee is free to sell or otherwise dispose of the property, the transfer constitutes a present interest whether the property produces income. For example, an outright gift of unproductive land is a present interest because the donee could sell the land and realize an immediate cash benefit.

If property is transferred into a trust, however, the income producing capacity of the property has a direct bearing on availability of the annual exclusion for an income interest. Although the donee may be entitled to any income produced by the property, the right to income is meaningless if there is no realistic expectation that income will in fact be produced. As evidenced by the following case, the IRS, with considerable success, has taken the position that the annual exclusion is not available for a gift of closely held stock to a trust if the stock cannot realistically be expected to produce dividend income.

STARK V. UNITED STATES
United States Court of Appeals, Eighth Circuit, 1973.
477 F.2d 131, cert. denied, 414 U.S. 975 (1973).

PER CURIAM:

We are presented with the question whether, in order to claim the $3,000 gift tax exclusion pursuant to 26 U.S.C. § 2503(b), a taxpayer might satisfy his burden of proving that an income interest in a trust has "ascertainable value,"[1] by reference to the actuarial tables found in Treas. Reg. 26 CFR § 25.2512–5(c).

The taxpayer made gifts of the stock of a closely held corporation to three trusts, for the benefit of each of the taxpayers' three minor grandchildren. The beneficiaries were to receive the net income from the trusts until each reached the age of 30, at which time the beneficiaries could terminate the trusts and receive the trust corpus. The parties agree that the gifts of the shares of stock to the trusts constitute gifts of future interests and thus are not subject to the annual exclusion, but the taxpayers claim that their making the gifts of the income from the stock entitles each to the annual exclusion of $3,000 for each beneficiary of the trusts pursuant to § 2503(b). The taxpayers based their asserted right to the exclusions on the argument that the right of the beneficiaries to the net income of the trusts was a present interest and was capable of valuation by the use of the actuarial tables prepared by the Commissioner in Treas. Reg. § 25.2512–5(c). The Government argued that since the stock of the corporation had never publicly traded and since no dividends had been paid on the stock since 1950, the taxpayers had not established an "ascertainable value" for the right to the income from the stock held in trust.

The undisputed evidence indicates, and the district court specifically found, that there was little possibility that any income would be forthcoming to the beneficiaries from the trusts in question. Under these circumstances, we hold that the income interest had no ascertainable value, and that the taxpayers cannot be allowed to assert a value for the income interest simply by using the actuarial tables of Treas. Reg. § 25.2512–5(c). * * *

---

[1] In order for a gift to be subject to the § 2503(b) exclusion, two requirements must be satisfied. First, the gift must not be a gift of a future interest, as that term is defined in Treas. Reg. 26 C.F.R. § 25.2503–3(a). Second, the gift must have an "ascertainable value." This requirement of ascertainable value is one judicially imposed. * * *

NOTE

The requirement of income production in the case of trust interests has been applied to assets other than closely held stock. In Calder v. Commissioner, 85 T.C. 713 (1985), the donor transferred Alexander Calder paintings to trusts that required payment to the beneficiaries of any income earned by the trust. In addition, the trust instruments permitted the trustees to convert the paintings to income-producing property. The Tax Court nevertheless denied annual exclusions for the gifts because there was no showing that the paintings were likely to produce income.

The rule enunciated in *Stark* applies only to gifts in trust. If the property is given outright, and the donee is free to sell or otherwise transfer the property, its income-producing capacity is irrelevant because the donee could sell the property for its fair market value and reinvest the proceeds. Also, the *Stark* rule does not apply "to such contractual rights as exist in a bond, note (though bearing no interest until maturity), or in a policy of life insurance, the obligations of which are to be discharged by payments in the future." Treas. Reg. § 25.2503–3(a). Presumably this exception is based on the assumption that bonds, notes, and the like are readily marketable for cash, thereby giving the donee immediate access to cash if desired. It could be argued that similar interests in trusts should likewise be treated as present interests, at least if readily marketable. But the IRS has consistently and successfully rejected this argument in the case of trust interests.

c. Restrictions on Transfer

HACKL V. COMMISSIONER
United States Court of Appeals, Seventh Circuit, 2003.
335 F.3d 664.

TERENCE T. EVANS, CIRCUIT JUDGE.

Most post-retirement hobbies don't involve multi-million dollar companies or land retirees in hot water with the IRS, but those are the circumstances in this case. Albert J. (A.J.) and Christine M. Hackl began a tree-farming business after A.J.'s retirement and gave shares in the company to family members. The Hackls believed the transfers were excludable from the gift tax, but the IRS thought otherwise. The Tax Court agreed with the IRS, *Hackl v. Comm'r,* 118 T.C. 279, 2002 WL 467117 (2002), resulting in a gift tax deficiency of roughly $400,000 for the couple. The Hackls appeal.

Our story begins with A.J. Hackl's retirement and subsequent search for a hobby that would allow him to keep his hand in the business world, diversify his investments, and provide a long-term investment for his family. Tree-farming fit the bill and, in 1995, A.J. purchased two tree farms (worth around $4.5 million) and contributed them, as well as about $8 million in cash and securities, to Treeco, LLC, a limited liability company that he set up in Indiana * * *

A.J. and his wife, Christine, initially owned all of Treeco's stock (which included voting and nonvoting shares), with A.J. serving as the company's manager. Under Treeco's operating agreement, the manager served for life (or until resignation, removal, or incapacity), had the power to appoint a successor, and could also dissolve the company. In addition, the manager controlled any financial distributions, and members needed his approval to withdraw from the company or sell shares. If a member transferred his or her shares without consent, the transferee would receive the shares' economic rights but not any membership or voting rights. Voting members could run Treeco during any interim period between managers, approve any salaries or bonuses paid by the company, and remove a manager and elect a successor. With an 80-percent majority, voting members could amend the Articles of Organization and operating agreement and dissolve the company after A.J.'s tenure as manager. Both the voting and the nonvoting members had the right to access Treeco's books and records and to decide whether to continue Treeco following an event of dissolution (such as the death, resignation, removal, retirement, bankruptcy, or insanity of the manager). During A.J.'s watch, Treeco has operated at a loss and not made any distributions to its stockholders. While Treeco has yet to turn a profit, A.J. was named "Tree Farmer of the Year" in Putnam County, Florida, in 1999.

Shortly after Treeco's creation, A.J. and Christine began annual transfers of Treeco voting and nonvoting shares to their children, their children's spouses, and a trust set up for the couple's grandchildren. After January 1998, 51 percent of the company's voting shares were in the hands of the couple's children and their spouses. The Hackls attempted to shield the transfers from taxation by treating them as excludable gifts on their gift tax returns. While the Internal Revenue Code imposes a tax on gifts, 26 U.S.C. § 2501(a), a donor does not pay the tax on the first $10,000 of gifts, "other than gifts of future interests in property," made to any person during the calendar year, 26 U.S.C. § 2503(b)(1). Unfortunately for the Hackls, the IRS thought that the transfers were future interests and ineligible for the gift tax exclusion. The Hackls took the dispute to the Tax Court which, as we said, sided with the IRS.

* * *

The crux of the Hackls' appeal is that the gift tax doesn't apply to a transfer if the donors give up all of their legal rights. In other words, the future interest exception to the gift tax exclusion only comes into play if the donee has gotten something less than the full bundle of legal property rights. Because the Hackls gave up all of their property rights to the shares, they think that the shares were excludable gifts within the plain meaning of § 2503(b)(1). The government, on the other hand, interprets the gift tax exclusion more narrowly. It argues that any transfer without a substantial present economic benefit is a future interest and ineligible for the gift tax exclusion.

The Hackls' initial argument is that § 2503(b)(1) automatically allows the gift tax exclusion for their transfers. The Hackls argue that their position reflects the plain—and only—meaning of "future interest" as used in the statute, and that the Tax Court's reliance on materials outside the statute (such as the Treasury regulation definition of future interest and case law) was not only unnecessary, it was wrong. We disagree. Calling any tax law "plain" is a hard row to hoe, and a number of cases (including our decision in *Stinson Estate v. United States,* 214 F.3d 846 (7th Cir.2000)) have looked beyond the language of § 2503(b)(1) for guidance. *See, e.g., United States v. Pelzer,* 312 U.S. 399, 403–04, 61 S. Ct. 659, 85 L. Ed. 913 (1941), and *Comm'r v. Disston,* 325 U.S. 442, 446, 65 S. Ct. 1328, 89 L. Ed. 1720 (1945) (stating that regulatory definition of future interest has been approved repeatedly). The Hackls do not cite any cases that actually characterize § 2503(b)(1) as plain, and the term "future interest" is not defined in the statute itself. Furthermore, the fact that both the government and the Hackls have proposed different—yet reasonable— interpretations of the statute shows that it is ambiguous. Under these circumstances, it was appropriate for the Tax Court to look to the Treasury regulation and case law for guidance.

Hedging their bet, the Hackls say that the applicable Treasury regulation supports the conclusion that giving up all legal rights to a gift automatically makes it a present interest. The applicable Treasury regulation states that a "future interest" is a legal term that applies to interests "which are limited to commence in use, possession, or enjoyment at some future date or time," Treas. Reg. § 25.2503–3. The regulation also provides that a present interest in property is "[a]n unrestricted right to the immediate use, possession, or enjoyment of property or the income from property (such as a life estate or term certain)." We don't think that this language automatically excludes all outright transfers from the gift tax. *See also Hamilton v. United States,* 553 F.2d 1216, 1218 (9th Cir.1977).

We previously addressed the issue of future interests for purposes of the gift tax exclusion in *Stinson Estate.* In that case, forgiveness of a corporation's indebtedness was a future interest outside the gift tax exclusion because shareholders could not individually realize the gift without liquidating the corporation or declaring a dividend—events that could not occur upon the actions of any one individual under the corporation's bylaws. *See* 214 F.3d at 848. We said that the "sole statutory distinction between present and future interests lies in the question of whether there is postponement of enjoyment of specific rights, powers or privileges which would be forthwith existent if the interest were present."

Id. at 848–49 (quoting *Howe v. United States*, 142 F.2d 310, 312 (7th Cir.1944)). In other words, the phrase "present interest" connotes the right to substantial present economic benefit. *See Fondren v. Comm'r*, 324 U.S. 18, 20, 65 S. Ct. 499, 89 L. Ed. 668 (1945).

In this case, Treeco's operating agreement clearly foreclosed the donees' ability to realize any substantial present economic benefit. Although the voting shares that the Hackls gave away had the same legal rights as those that they retained, Treeco's restrictions on the transferability of the shares meant that they were essentially without immediate value to the donees. Granted, Treeco's operating agreement did address the possibility that a shareholder might violate the agreement and sell his or her shares without the manager's approval. But, as the Tax Court found, the possibility that a shareholder might violate the operating agreement and sell his or her shares to a transferee who would then not have any membership or voting rights can hardly be called a substantial economic benefit. Thus, the Hackls' gifts—while outright—were not gifts of present interests.

The Hackls protest that Treeco is set up like any other limited liability corporation and that its restrictions on the alienability of its shares are common in closely held companies. While that may be true, the fact that other companies operate this way does not mean that shares in such companies should automatically be considered present interests for purposes of the gift tax exclusion. As we have previously said, Internal Revenue Code provisions dealing with exclusions are matters of legislative grace that must be narrowly construed. *See Stinson Estate*, 214 F.3d at 848. The onus is on the taxpayers to show that their transfers qualify for the gift tax exclusion, a burden the Hackls have not met.

The decision of the Tax Court is AFFIRMED.

3.   GIFTS TO MINORS

As explained above, the annual exclusion is not available unless the donee receives either outright ownership or an unrestricted and immediate right to income from the property. This requirement impairs the practical utility of the exclusion if the gift is to be made to a minor.

For example, assume that a grandmother, who has a substantial estate, wishes to make gifts to each of several grandchildren. The grandchildren vary in age from 4 to 16, and the grandmother intends that the gifts be used to fund college education for the grandchildren. The grandmother fears that outright gifts would not accomplish this purpose because the grandchildren might use the property for other purposes. For the same reason, she is uncomfortable with gifts to trusts that would require distribution of income to the grandchildren.

The situation is frustrating for the grandmother because the annual exclusion offers such an attractive opportunity to transfer substantial amounts to her descendants without any tax burden. Planners have responded to such circumstances with efforts to devise vehicles that will accomplish the grandmother's purposes. As demonstrated below, Congress has done its part through enactment of sections 529 and 2503(c), and creative lawyering has played an important role as well.

a. Outright Gifts

REVENUE RULING 54–400
1954–2 C.B. 319.

Advice is requested whether a gift of shares of stock to a minor is a gift of a present or a future interest where the shares are issued in the name of minor (1) before the appointment of a legal guardian, (2) after the appointment of a legal guardian, or (3) if no legal guardian is appointed.

Section 86.11 of Regulation 108 provides that no part of the value of a gift of a future interest may be excluded in determining the total amount of gifts made during the calendar year. "Future interests" is a legal term, and includes reversions, remainders, and other interests or estates, whether vested or contingent, and whether or not supported by a particular interest or estate, which are limited to commence in use, possession, or enjoyment at some future date or time.

An unqualified and unrestricted gift to a minor, with or without the appointment of a legal guardian, is a gift of a present interest; and disabilities placed upon minors by State statutes should not be considered decisive in determining whether such donees have the immediate enjoyment of the property or the income therefrom within the purport of the Federal gift tax law. See John E. Daniels v. Commissioner, Tax Court Memorandum Opinion entered February 13, 1951. In the case of an outright and unrestricted gift to a minor, the mere existence or nonexistence of a legal guardianship does not of itself raise the question whether the gift is of a future interest. Cf. Rev. Rul. 54–91, C. B. 1954–1, 207 involving a gift in trust for the benefit of a minor. It is only where delivery of the property to the guardian of a minor is accompanied by limitations upon the present use and enjoyment of the property by the donee, by way of a trust or otherwise, that the question of a future interest arises. See Kathryn Schuhmacher, 8 T.C. 453.

In view of the foregoing, it is held that a gift of the type involved herein to a minor is a gift of a present interest unless the use and enjoyment of the property is in some manner limited or restricted by the terms of the donor's conveyance. The exclusion authorized by section 1003(b) of the

Internal Revenue Code of 1939 [1986 Code § 2503(b)] may be applied against such gift.

b.   Trust Gifts in General

At an early date the Supreme Court confronted the issue of trust gifts benefitting minors. See Fondren v. Commissioner, 324 U.S. 18 (1945); Commissioner v. Disston, 325 U.S. 442 (1945). In each case, the donor created a trust for the benefit of a minor. In *Fondren*, the trustee had discretionary power to distribute principal and income for the support, maintenance, and education of the minor. In *Disston*, the trustee was specifically directed to apply for the minor's benefit such income "as may be necessary for the education, comfort, and support" of the minor. In both cases the Supreme Court concluded that the minor had no entitlement to a specific and identifiable income stream. Therefore, there was no present interest. This was true despite the "education, comfort, and support" mandate in *Disston* because it was not possible to identify a specific amount of income that would be distributed for those purposes. Hence, the annual exclusion was denied in both cases.

Planners then turned to another approach. As already explained, an outright gift always constitutes a present interest. Planners reasoned that if the minor (or the minor's guardian) is given an unfettered right to demand the trust property, the minor should be viewed as having the equivalent of outright ownership; that should certainly constitute a present interest. The result was creation of trusts for the benefit of minors, with provision for discretionary distributions of principal and income to the minor, and with the added element that the minor or the minor's guardian could demand and receive the trust property at any time.

This "right of withdrawal" approach was successful in the Seventh Circuit, which concluded that the minor, regardless of age, regardless of the extent of need for funds, and regardless of whether a guardian had in fact been appointed, must be viewed as possessing a withdrawal right tantamount to outright ownership. Hence the annual exclusion was allowed for the entire transfer in trust. See Kieckhefer v. Commissioner, 189 F.2d 118 (7th Cir.1951).

The Second Circuit was less hospitable. It concluded that under *Fondren* the minor's access to the property must be evaluated in realistic terms, taking into account the probability that the minor would in fact need funds and whether a guardian had in fact been appointed. See Stifel v. Commissioner, 197 F.2d 107 (2d Cir.1952). The practical effect of the Second Circuit view was to deny or severely limit the exclusion in most cases.

c. Crummey Trusts: General Rule

The split between *Kieckhefer* and *Stifel* regarding withdrawal rights left the estate planning community uncertain as to whether providing a withdrawal right could assure availability of the annual exclusion. Even if the *Kieckhefer* view should prevail, there remained the problem that the withdrawal right remained extant indefinitely, posing the threat that the minor might actually exercise the right and thereby thwart the donor's intent.

Both issues were resolved in the case that follows, which has given its name to a widely used technique that can now assure availability of the annual exclusion while minimizing the minor's access to the funds.

CRUMMEY V. COMMISSIONER

United States Court of Appeals, Ninth Circuit, 1968.
397 F.2d 82.

BYRNE, DISTRICT JUDGE:

* * *

On February 12, 1962, the petitioners executed, as grantors, an irrevocable living trust for the benefit of their four children. The beneficiaries and their ages at relevant times are as follows:

	Age 12/31/62	Age 12/31/63
John Knowles Crummey	22	23
Janet Sheldon Crummey	20	21
David Clarke Crummey	15	16
Mark Clifford Crummey	11	12

Originally the sum of $50 was contributed to the trust. Thereafter, additional contributions were made by each of the petitioners in the following amounts and on the following dates:

$4,267.77	6/20/62
49,550.00	12/15/62
12,797.81	12/19/63

The dispute revolves around the tax years of 1962 and 1963. Each of the petitioners filed a gift tax return for each year. Each petitioner claimed a $3,000 per beneficiary tax exclusion under the provisions of 26 U.S.C. 2503(b). The total claimed exclusions were as follows:

D.C. Crummey ....1962—$12,000 1963—$12,000

E.E. Crummey ....1962—$12,000 1963—$12,000

The Commissioner of Internal Revenue determined that each of the petitioners was entitled to only one $3,000 exclusion for each year. This determination was based upon the Commissioner's belief that the portion of the gifts in trust for the children under the age of 21 were "future interests" which are disallowed under § 2503(b). The taxpayers contested the determination of a deficiency in the Tax Court. The Commissioner conceded by stipulation in that proceeding that each petitioner was entitled to an additional $3,000 exclusion for the year 1963 by reason of Janet Crummey having reached the age of 21.

The Tax Court followed the Commissioner's interpretation as to gifts in trust to David and Mark, but determined that the 1962 gift in trust to Janet qualified as a gift of a present interest because of certain additional rights accorded to persons 18 and over by California law. Thus, the Tax Court held that each petitioner was entitled to an additional $3,000 exclusion for the year 1962.

The key provision of the trust agreement is the "demand" provision which states:

> THREE *Additions*. The Trustee may receive any other real or personal property from the Trustors (or either of them) or from any other person or persons, by lifetime gift, under a Will or Trust or from any other source. Such property will be held by the Trustee subject to the terms of this Agreement. A donor may designate or allocate all of his gift to one or more Trusts, or in stated amounts to different Trusts. If the donor does not specifically designate what amount of his gift is to augment each Trust, the Trustee shall divide such gift equally between the Trust then existing, established by this Agreement. The Trustee agrees, if he accepts such additions, to hold and manage such additions in trust for the uses and in the manner set forth herein. *With respect to such additions, each child of the Trustors may demand at any time (up to and including December 31 of the year in which a transfer to his or her Trust has been made) the sum of Four Thousand Dollars ($4,000) or the amount of the transfer from each donor, whichever is less, payable in cash immediately upon receipt by the Trustee of the demand in writing and in any event, not later than December 31 in the year in which such transfer was made. Such payment shall be made from the gift of that donor for that year. If a child is a minor at the time of such gift of that donor for that year, or fails in legal capacity for any reason, the child's guardian may make such demand on behalf of the child. The*

property received pursuant to the demand shall be held by the guardian for the benefit and use of the child. (Emphasis supplied.)

The whole question on this appeal is whether or not a present interest was given by the petitioners to their minor children so as to qualify as an exclusion under § 2503(b). The petitioners on appeal contend that each minor beneficiary has the right under California law to demand partial distribution from the Trustee. In the alternative they urge that a parent as natural guardian of the person of his minor children could make such a demand. As a third alternative, they assert that under California law a minor over the age of 14 has the right to have a legal guardian appointed who can make the necessary demand. The Commissioner, as cross petitioner, alleges as error the Tax Court's ruling that the 1962 gifts in trust to Janet (then age 20) were present interests.

It was stipulated before the Tax Court in regard to the trust and the parties thereto that at all times relevant all the minor children lived with the petitioners and no legal guardian had been appointed for them. In addition, it was agreed that all the children were supported by petitioners and none of them had made a demand against the trust funds or received any distribution from them.

The tax regulations define a "future interest" for the purposes of § 2503(b) as follows:

"Future interests" is a legal term, and includes reversions, remainder, and other interests or estates, whether vested or contingent, and whether or not supported by a particular interest or estate, which are limited to commence in use, possession or enjoyment at some future date or time. Treasury Regulations of Gift Tax, § 25.2503–3.

This definition has been adopted by the Supreme Court. Fondren v. Commissioner, 324 U.S. 18 (1945); Commissioner v. Disston, 325 U.S. 442 (1945). In *Fondren* the court stated that the important question is when enjoyment begins. There the court held that gifts to an irrevocable trust for the grantor's minor grandchildren were "future interests" where income was to be accumulated and the corpus and the accumulations were not to be paid until designated times commencing with each grandchild's 25th birthday. The trustee was authorized to spend the income or invade the corpus during the minority of the beneficiaries only if need were shown. The facts demonstrated that need had not occurred and was not likely to occur.

Neither of the parties nor the Tax Court has any disagreement with the above summarization of the basic tests. The dispute comes in attempting to narrow the definition of a future interest down to a more specific and useful form.

The Commissioner and the Tax Court both placed primary reliance on the case of Stifel v. Commissioner, 197 F.2d 107 (2d Cir.1952). In that case an irrevocable trust was involved which provided that the beneficiary, a minor, could demand any part of the funds not expended by the Trustee and, subject to such demand, the Trustee was to accumulate. The trust also provided that it could be terminated by the beneficiary or by her guardian during minority. The court held that gifts to this trust were gifts of "future interests." They relied upon Fondren for the proposition that they could look at circumstances as well as the trust agreement and under such circumstances it was clear that the minor could not make the demand and that no guardian had ever been appointed who could make such a demand.

The leading case relied upon by the petitioners is Kieckhefer v. Commissioner, 189 F.2d 118 (7th Cir.1951). In that case the donor set up a trust with his newly born grandson as the beneficiary. The trustee was to hold the funds unless the beneficiary or his legally appointed guardian demanded that the trust be terminated. The Commissioner urged that the grandson could not effectively make such a demand and that no guardian had been appointed. The court disregarded these factors and held that where any restrictions on use were caused by disabilities of a minor rather than by the terms of the trust, the gift was a "present interest." The court further stated that the important thing was the right to enjoy rather than the actual enjoyment of the property.

The *Kieckhefer* case has been followed in several decisions. In Gilmore v. Commissioner, 213 F.2d 520 (6th Cir.1954) there was an irrevocable trust for minors. It provided that all principal and accumulated income would be paid on demand of the beneficiary. The trust was to terminate on the beneficiary's death. Anything remaining in the trust at the time of death would go to the beneficiary's estate.

The Tax Court stated that the demand provision would have made the advancements "present interests" but for spendthrift provisions and the authority of the Trustee to invest in nonincome producing properties. The Circuit agreed that the demand provision made the advancements "present interests" and further held that the other provisions did not change that character. Reliance was placed on the "right to enjoy" language of *Kieckhefer*.

* * *

Although there are certainly factual distinctions between the *Stifel* and *Kieckhefer* cases, it seems clear that the two courts took opposing positions on the way the problem of defining "future interests" should be resolved. As we read the *Stifel* case, it says that the court should look at the trust instrument, the law as to minors, and the financial and other circumstances of the parties. From this examination it is up to the court to determine whether it is likely that the minor beneficiary is to receive any present enjoyment of the property. If it is not likely, then the gift is a "future interest." At the other extreme is the holding in *Kieckhefer* which says that a gift to a minor is not a "future interest" if the only reason for a delay in enjoyment is the minority status of the donee and his consequent disabilities. The *Kieckhefer* court noted that under the terms there present, a gift to an adult would have qualified for the exclusion and they refused to discriminate against a minor. The court equated a present interest with a present right to possess, use or enjoy. The facts of the case and the court's reasoning, however, indicate that it was really equating a present interest with a present right to possess, use or enjoy except for the fact that the beneficiary was a minor. In between these two positions there is a third possibility. That possibility is that the court should determine whether the donee is legally and technically capable of immediately enjoying the property. Basically this is the test relied on by the petitioners. Under this theory, the question would be whether the donee could possibly gain immediate enjoyment and the emphasis would be on the trust instrument and the laws of the jurisdiction as to minors. It was primarily on this basis that the Tax Court decided the present case, although some examination of surrounding circumstances was apparently made. This theory appears to be the basis of the decision in George W. Perkins, 27 T.C. 601 (1956). There the Tax Court stated that where the parents were capable of making the demand and there was no showing that the demand could be resisted, the gift was of a present interest. This approach also seems to be the basis of the "right to enjoy" language in both *Kieckhefer* and *Gilmore*.

Under the provisions of this trust the income is to be accumulated and added to the corpus until each minor reaches the age of 21, unless the trustee feels in his discretion that distributions should be made to a needy beneficiary. From 21 to 35 all income is distributed to the beneficiary. After 35 the trustee again has discretion as to both income and corpus, and may distribute whatever is necessary up to the whole thereof. Aside from the actions of the trustee, the only way any beneficiary may get at the property is through the "demand" provision, quoted above.

One question raised in these proceedings is whether or not the trust prohibits a minor child from making a demand on the yearly additions to the trust. The key language from paragraph three is as follows:

If a child is a minor at the time of such gift of that donor for that year, or fails in legal capacity for any reason, the child's guardian may make such demand on behalf of the child.

The Tax Court interpreted this provision in favor of the taxpayers by saying that "may" is permissive and thus that the minor child can make the demand if allowed by law, or, if not permitted by law, the guardian may do it. Although, as the Commissioner suggests, this strains the language somewhat, it does seem consistent with the obvious intent in drafting this provision. Surely, this provision was intended to give the minor beneficiary the broadest demand power available so that the gift tax exclusion would be applicable.

There is very little dispute between the parties as to the rights and disabilities of a minor accorded by the California statutes and cases. The problem comes in attempting to ascertain from these rights and disabilities the answer to the question of whether a minor may make a demand upon the trustee for a portion of the trust as provided in the trust instrument.

It is agreed that a minor in California may own property. Estate of Yano, 188 Cal. 645, 206 Pac. 995 (1922). He may receive a gift. De Levillain v. Evans, 39 Cal. 120. A minor may demand his own funds from a bank (Cal. Fin. Code §§ 850 & 853), a savings institution (Cal. Fin. Code §§ 7600 & 7606), or a corporation (Cal. Corp. Code §§ 2221 & 2413). A minor of the age of 14 or over has the right to secure the appointment of a guardian and one will be appointed if the court finds it "necessary or convenient." Cal. Prob. Code § 1406; Guardianship of Kentera, 41 Cal.2d 639, 262 P.2d 317 (1953).

It is further agreed that a minor cannot sue in his own name (Cal. Civ. Code § 42) and cannot appoint an agent. (Cal. Civ. Code § 33). With certain exceptions a minor can disaffirm contracts made by him during his minority. Cal. Civ. Code § 35. A minor under the age of 18 cannot make contracts relating to real property or personal property not in his possession or control. Cal. Civ. Code § 33.

The parent of a child may be its natural guardian, but such a guardianship is of the person of the child and not of his estate. Kendall v. Miller, 9 Cal. 591; Cal. Civ. Code § 202.

After examining the same rights and disabilities, the petitioners, the Commissioner, and the Tax Court each arrived at a different solution to our problem. The Tax Court concentrated on the disabilities and concluded that David and Mark could not make an effective demand because they could not sue in their own name, nor appoint an agent and could disaffirm contracts. The court, however, concluded that Janet could make an effective demand because Cal. Civ. Code § 33 indirectly states that she could make contracts with regard to real and personal property.

The Commissioner concentrated on the inability to sue or appoint an agent and concluded that none of the minors had anything more than paper rights because he or she lacked the capacity to enforce the demand.

The petitioners urge that the right to acquire and hold property is the key. In the alternative they argue that the parent as a natural guardian could make the demand although it would be necessary to appoint a legal guardian to receive the property. Finally, they urge that all the minors over

14 could make a demand since they could request the appointment of a legal guardian.

The position taken by the Tax Court seems clearly untenable. The distinction drawn between David and Mark on the one hand, and Janet on the other, makes no sense. The mere fact that Janet can make certain additional contracts does not have any relevance to the question of whether she is capable of making an effective demand upon the trustee. We cannot agree with the position of the Commissioner because we do not feel that a lawsuit or the appointment of an agent is a necessary prelude to the making of a demand upon the trustee. As we visualize the hypothetical situation, the child would inform the trustee that he demanded his share of the additions up to $4,000. The trustee would petition the court for the appointment of a legal guardian and then turn the funds over to the guardian. It would also seem possible for the parent to make the demand as natural guardian. This would involve the acquisition of property for the child rather than the management of the property. It would then be necessary for a legal guardian to be appointed to take charge of the funds. The only time when the disability to sue would come into play, would be if the trustee disregarded the demand and committed a breach of trust. That would not, however, vitiate the demand.

All this is admittedly speculative since it is highly unlikely that a demand will ever be made or that if one is made, it would be made in this fashion. However, as a technical matter, we think a minor could make the demand.

Given the trust, the California law, and the circumstances in our case, it can be seen that very different results may well be achieved, depending upon the test used. Under a strict interpretation of the *Stifel* test of examining everything and determining whether there is any likelihood of present enjoyment, the gifts to minors in our case would seem to be "future interests." Although under our interpretation neither the trust nor the law technically forbid a demand by the minor, the practical difficulties of a child going through the procedures seem substantial. In addition, the surrounding facts indicate the children were well cared for and the obvious intention of the trustors was to create a long term trust. No guardian had been appointed and, except for the tax difficulties, probably never would be appointed. As a practical matter, it is likely that some, if not all, of the beneficiaries did not even know that they had any right to demand funds from the trust. They probably did not know when contributions were made to the trust or in what amounts. Even had they known, the substantial contributions were made toward the end of the year so that the time to make a demand was severely limited. Nobody had made a demand under the provision, and no distributions had been made. We think it unlikely that any demand ever would have been made.

All exclusions should be allowed under the *Perkins* test or the "right to enjoy" test in *Gilmore*. Under *Perkins*, all that is necessary is to find that the demand could not be resisted. We interpret that to mean legally resisted and, going on that basis, we do not think the trustee would have any choice but to have a guardian appointed to take the property demanded.

Under the general language of *Kieckhefer* which talked of the "right to enjoy", all exclusions in our case would seem to be allowable. The broader *Kieckhefer* rule which we have discussed is inapplicable on the facts of this case. That rule, as we interpret it, is that postponed enjoyment is not equivalent to a "future interest" if the postponement is solely caused by the minority of the beneficiary. In *Kieckhefer*, the income was accumulated and added to the corpus until the beneficiary reached the age of 21. At that time everything was to be turned over to him. This is all that happened unless a demand was made. In our case, on the contrary, if no demand is made in any particular year, the additions are forever removed from the uncontrolled reach of the beneficiary since, with the exception of the yearly demand provision, the only way the corpus can ever be tapped by a beneficiary, is through a distribution at the discretion of the trustee.

We decline to follow a strict reading of the *Stifel* case in our situation because we feel that the solution suggested by that case is inconsistent and unfair. It becomes arbitrary for the I.R.S. to step in and decide who is likely to make an effective demand. Under the circumstances suggested in our case, it is doubtful that any demands will be made against the trust—yet the Commissioner always allowed the exclusion as to adult beneficiaries. There is nothing to indicate that it is any more likely that John will demand funds than that any other beneficiary will do so. The only distinction is that it might be easier for him to make such a demand. Since we conclude that the demand can be made by the others, it follows that the exclusion should also apply to them. In another case we might follow the broader *Kieckhefer* rule, since it seems least arbitrary and establishes a clear standard. However, if the minors have no way of making the demand in our case, then there is more than just a postponement involved, since John could demand his share of yearly additions while the others would never have the opportunity at their shares of those additions but would be limited to taking part of any additions added subsequent to their 21st birthdays.

We conclude that the result under the *Perkins* or "right to enjoy" tests is preferable in our case. The petitioners should be allowed all of the exclusions claimed for the two year period.

The decision of the Tax Court denying the taxpayers' exclusions on the gifts to David and Mark Crummey is reversed. The decision of the Tax Court allowing the taxpayers' exclusions on the 1962 gift to Janet Crummey is affirmed.

MIKEL V. COMMISSIONER

United States Tax Court, 2015.
T.C. Memo. 2015–64, 109 T.C.M. (CCH) 1355.

MEMORANDUM OPINION

Petitioners in these consolidated cases, Israel and Erna Mikel, are husband and wife. With respect to their Federal gift tax liabilities for 2007, the Internal Revenue Service (IRS or respondent) determined against each petitioner a tax deficiency of $268,950 and a late-filing addition to tax under section 6651(a)(1) of $67,238.

During 2007 each petitioner made to a family trust a gift with an asserted value of $1,631,000. In December 2011 petitioners filed separate gift tax returns reporting these gifts; each petitioner claimed under section 2503(b) an annual exclusion of $720,000. The claimed annual exclusions of $720,000 were based on the contention that each petitioner's gift included a $12,000 gift of a present interest to each of the trust's 60 beneficiaries.

* * *The IRS disallowed the claimed exclusions, determining that the beneficiaries lacked legally enforceable rights to withdraw funds from the trust and hence that petitioners had made gifts of future, not present, interests.

I.   * * *

On June 7, 2007, petitioners as grantors and Salomon Mikel as trustee executed a declaration of trust (declaration) establishing the IEM Family Trust (trust), an irrevocable inter vivos trust. The trust's beneficiaries were petitioners' children and lineal descendants and their respective spouses. On June 15, 2007, petitioners jointly transferred to the trust property with an asserted value of $3,262,000. The trust at the time allegedly had 60 beneficiaries, many of whom were under 18 years of age.

Article V of the declaration, captioned "Right of Beneficiaries to Withdraw Principal," granted each beneficiary the power, during the year in which the trust was created and during any subsequent year when property was added, "to withdraw property from the Trust including the property transferred." * * *

Within a reasonable time after the contribution of property to the trust, the trustees were required to notify all beneficiaries, and the guardians for all minor beneficiaries, that the trust had received property "as to which the beneficiary has a demand right." The demand right was required to be exercised in writing by the beneficiary or the beneficiary's guardian and generally lapsed if not exercised within 30 days of such notice. The declaration states that the trustees, upon receipt of a timely withdrawal demand, "shall immediately distribute to such beneficiary or Guardian the properties allocable to them, free of trust." * * *

Apart from directing mandatory distributions in response to withdrawal demands, the trust empowered the trustees, "in their sole and absolute discretion," to make discretionary distributions during the term of the trust. Such distributions could be made for the health, education, maintenance, or support of any beneficiary or family member. Such distributions could also be made, in the trustees' "absolute and unreviewable discretion," to assist a beneficiary in defraying "reasonable wedding costs, * * * purchasing a primary residence, or * * * entering a trade or profession." In exercising this discretion the trustees were empowered to distribute "at any time and from time to time, any amount of income or principal (even to the extent of all)." The declaration specifies that "[t]he judgment of the Trustees as to the amounts of such payments and the advisability thereof shall be final and conclusive" upon all beneficiaries and other persons interested in the trust. Declaration art. VI(b)(3).

If any dispute arises concerning the proper interpretation of the declaration, article XXVI provides that the dispute "shall be submitted to arbitration before a panel consisting of three persons of the Orthodox Jewish faith." * * *

Article XXVI contains an in terrorem provision designed to discourage beneficiaries from challenging discretionary acts of the trustees. It provides:

In the event a beneficiary of the Trust shall directly or indirectly institute, conduct or in any manner whatever take part in or aid in any proceeding to oppose the distribution of the Trust Estate, or files any action in a court of law, or challenges any distribution set forth in this Trust in any court, arbitration panel or any other manner, then in such event the provision herein made for such beneficiary shall thereupon be revoked and such beneficiary shall be excluded from any participation in the Trust Estate * * *.

On October 9, 2007, an attorney acting for the trust mailed to each beneficiary, in his or her capacity as such and as the guardian of any minor children, a written notice captioned "Notice of Right of Withdrawal." Each letter informed its respective recipient that a contribution had been made to the trust and that "you and each of your children under the age of 18 years as beneficiaries of the Trust have a right to withdraw property or funds up to $24,000.00 each from the Trust." This letter advised that withdrawal rights had to be exercised within 30 days from its receipt. The record does not indicate whether any beneficiary has ever exercised withdrawal rights, whether the trustees have ever made discretionary distributions, or whether a dispute has ever arisen concerning either. There is no evidence of any prearranged plan or understanding among petitioners and the beneficiaries that would prevent the latter from exercising their withdrawal rights.

II. * * *

Neither petitioner timely filed Form 709, United States Gift (and Generation-Skipping Transfer) Tax Return, for 2007. On December 15, 2011, after being contacted by the IRS, each petitioner submitted a separate Form 709 reporting gifts to the trust during 2007 of assets valued at $1,631,000. These assets consisted of petitioners' residence in Brooklyn, New York, two other properties in Brooklyn (held directly or through a limited liability company), and a condominium in Florida.* * *

The annual exclusion is available only for gifts of a "present interest in property." Sec. 2503(a)(1). A "present interest in property" is defined as "[a]n unrestricted right to the immediate use, possession, or enjoyment of property or the income from property." Sec. 25.2503–3(b) Gift Tax Regs. "No part of the value of a gift of a future interest may be excluded" from taxable gifts. *Id.* para. (a).

On its face the declaration gave each trust beneficiary an unrestricted right to withdraw, during 2007, an amount equal to "[t]he maximum federal gift tax exclusion under section 2503(b) of the Code in effect at the time of [the] transfer." Because petitioners elected to split their gifts, each beneficiary was thus empowered to withdraw $24,000. Each beneficiary received (directly or through his or her parent) timely and effective notice of the right to withdraw this sum. The declaration states unequivocally that, upon receipt of a timely withdrawal demand, "the Trustees shall immediately distribute to such beneficiary or guardian the properties allocable to them, free of trust."

Respondent concedes that the declaration affords each beneficiary an unconditional right of withdrawal and suggests no colorable basis on which the trustees could properly refuse to honor a timely withdrawal demand. Respondent nevertheless contends that the beneficiaries did not receive a "present interest in property" because their rights of withdrawal were not "legally enforceable" in practical terms. According to respondent, a right of withdrawal is "legally enforceable" only if the beneficiary can "go before a state court to enforce that right." This is something that respondent believes a beneficiary of the trust would be very reluctant to do.

Respondent starts by hypothesizing that the trustees might refuse, without legal basis, to honor a timely withdrawal demand. In that event, article XXVI of the declaration would require the beneficiary to submit the dispute to [the arbitration panel]. If the [arbitration panel], again without legal basis, sustained the trustees' refusal to honor the demand, respondent agrees that the beneficiary could seek redress in a New York court despite the State's general reluctance to disturb arbitral decisions. But a beneficiary would be extremely reluctant to go to court, respondent insists, because he would thereupon forfeit all his rights under the trust by virtue of article XXVI's in terrorem clause. Practically speaking, therefore, respondent contends that the beneficiaries' withdrawal rights are "illusory" and do not constitute a "present interest in property."

III. * * *

A little background may help in evaluating respondent's chain of reasoning. The trust at issue here is a "demand trust," often called a "*Crummey* trust" because of the favorable treatment accorded such a trust by the Court of Appeals for the Ninth Circuit in Crummey v. Commissioner, 397 F.2d 82 (9th Cir. 1968), *rev'g in part* T.C. Memo. 1966–144. The court there "approved an ingenious device to obtain an [annual gift tax] exclusion for a discretionary accumulation trust by giving beneficiaries the right to demand immediate distribution of particular amounts." * * *

The demand clause in *Crummey*, substantially similar to that here, provided that whenever an addition was made to the trust, a beneficiary or guardian acting for a minor beneficiary could demand immediate withdrawal of an amount keyed to the maximum annual exclusion under section 2503(b). The court held this demand right to be a "present interest in property" even though no guardian for the minor beneficiaries had been appointed. Under the test it adopted, "all that is necessary is to find that the demand could not be resisted," which the court understood to mean "legally resisted." * * *

IV. * * *

We discern two flaws in respondent's argument. First, if we adopt his premise that a withdrawal right must not only be "legally irresistible" under the trust instrument, but also be "legally enforceable" in an extrinsic sense, it is not obvious why the beneficiary must be able to "go before a state court to enforce that right." Here, if the trustees were to breach their fiduciary duties by refusing a timely withdrawal demand, the beneficiary could seek justice from [the panel], which is directed to "enforce the provisions of this Declaration * * * and give any party the rights he is entitled to under New York law." A beneficiary would suffer no adverse consequences from submitting his claim. * * *

Second, if we assume arguendo that our hypothetically-frustrated beneficiary must have an enforcement remedy in State court, respondent concedes that the beneficiaries of the trust have such a remedy. Respondent's argument is not that judicial enforcement is unavailable, but that this remedy is "illusory" because the in terrorem provision would deter beneficiaries from pursuing it. We think respondent has misapprehended this provision's meaning.

Article XXVI of the declaration provides that a beneficiary shall forfeit his rights under the trust if he "directly or indirectly institute[s] * * * any proceeding to oppose the distribution of the Trust Estate, or files any action in a court of law, or challenges any distribution set forth in this Trust in any court, arbitration panel or any other manner." While not a paragon of draftsmanship, this provision is evidently designed to discourage legal challenges to decisions by the trustees to make discretionary distributions of trust property, e.g., to help beneficiary A finish college, help beneficiary B enter a business, or enable beneficiary C to have a nice wedding. Article VI(b)(3) gives the trustees "absolute and unreviewable discretion" in such matters and states that their judgment "as to the amounts of such payments and the advisability thereof shall be final and conclusive."

The evident purpose of the in terrorem provision is to backstop article VI by discouraging legal actions seeking to challenge the trustees' "absolute and unreviewable discretion" concerning discretionary distributions from the trust. The first and third clauses of the in terrorem provision explicitly track this purpose, providing that a beneficiary will forfeit his rights if he institutes a proceeding "to oppose the distribution of the Trust Estate" or "challenges any distribution * * * in any court." A beneficiary who filed suit to compel the trustees to honor a timely withdrawal demand would not be "opposing or challenging" any distribution (discretionary or otherwise) from the trust. Because the beneficiary's action would not be covered by the in terrorem provision, that provision logically would not dissuade him from seeking judicial enforcement of his rights.

In urging a broader construction of the in terrorem provision, respondent focuses on its second clause, "or files any action in a court of law." But this clause cannot be read literally; otherwise, it would bar beneficiaries from participating in the trust if they filed suit to recover for mischievous behavior by their neighbor's dog. The second clause must be given a limiting construction. We think the most sensible limiting construction is to interpret this clause in pari materia with the two clauses that surround it. The second clause thus bars a beneficiary from enjoying benefits under the trust if he files suit in any court to oppose or challenge a decision by the trustees to distribute trust property to another beneficiary. This interpretation gives the in terrorem provision a coherent meaning that is consistent with the provisions of article VI affording the trustees "absolute and unreviewable discretion" concerning such matters.

In sum, we conclude that the beneficiaries of the trust possessed a "present interest in property" because they had, during 2007, an unconditional right to withdraw property from the trust and their withdrawal demands could not be "legally resisted" by the trustees. [citations omitted]. Assuming arguendo that the beneficiaries' withdrawal rights must be enforceable in State court, we conclude that this remedy, which respondent concedes was literally available, was also practically available because the in terrorem provision, properly construed, would not deter beneficiaries from pursuing judicial relief. * * *

NOTE

The *Mikel* case is significant because the court allowed annual exclusions totaling $1,440,000 for *Crummey* rights given to trust beneficiaries even though the trust contained a mandatory arbitration clause and an *in terrorem* provision that discouraged the beneficiaries from challenging the trustees' discretionary powers.

PRIVATE LETTER RULING 8004172
November 5, 1979.

This is in response to your letter of * * * in which you request rulings on the gift tax consequences of a proposed inter-vivos trust, under sections 2503 and 2514 of the Internal Revenue Code of 1954.

According to your letter, A intends to establish an irrevocable trust for the benefit of his minor grandchildren.

By the terms of the trust agreement, the income and principal are payable to the grandchildren at the trustee's discretion. When B's oldest child reaches age 21, a separate trust will be created for each of B's children (A's grandchildren). The income and principal of these separate trusts will be payable to the grandchildren in the trustee's discretion. The principal will be distributed (or held in further trust) as each grandchild reaches the age of 35.

The proposed trust agreement provides in part as follows:

Item IV

Dispositive Provisions

Section 1. Withdrawal Rights. Within seven (7) days of receipt of any and all property placed in this trust as a gift, the Trustee shall notify each of the living children of the Settlor's son, * * * (hereinafter referred to as the "Settlor's grandchildren"), of the nature and value of the property received. From the time of the transfer to the trust, each such grandchild shall have the unrestricted right until thirty (30) days after the date of notification to demand and immediately receive from the trust a share of the additional contribution equal to one (1) divided by the number of such grandchildren living at the time of the transfer to the trust. The maximum value of property that may be received by a grandchild at any time shall be an amount which when added to all other amounts received by such grandchild during the calendar year pursuant to this provision shall not exceed the greater of Five Thousand Dollars ($5,000.00) or five percent (5%) of the value of the additional contribution. Should any of the Settlor's grandchildren be a minor, this power of withdrawal may be exercised by his or her natural or legal guardian.

* * *

Analysis

Item IV, section 1, of the trust agreement provides that the grandchild has 30 days from the date of notification to demand the additional contributions to the trust (subject to the $5,000 or 5 percent limit). The grandchild can compel immediate distribution of those additional contributions. Accordingly, provided that there is no impediment under the trust or local law to the appointment of a guardian, annual exclusions under section 2503(b) of the Code will be allowable for additional contributions to the original trust. Crummey v. Commissioner, 397 F.2d 82 (9th Cir.1968). Such annual exclusions are available to the grantor or to any other donor who makes a completed gift in accordance with the terms of the trust agreement.

* * *

NOTE

In Rev. Rul. 73–405, 1973–2 C.B. 321, the Commissioner acquiesced in the *Crummey* decision. Priv. Ltr. Rul. 8004172 sets forth language that became typical for "Crummey withdrawal rights." When the 30-day withdrawal period expires, the holder of the withdrawal right has no further access to the trust property and will receive only such income or principal as may be provided pursuant to the trust instrument.

There are limits on the extent to which the withdrawal right can be restricted. The Commissioner has taken the position that the beneficiary must be given a realistic and meaningful right to withdraw. For example, in Rev. Rul. 81–7, 1981–1 C.B. 474, the Service denied the annual exclusion because the beneficiary had only two days in which to exercise the right to withdraw and, furthermore, was not informed of the withdrawal right. Another effort to restrict the withdrawal right failed in Tech. Adv. Mem. 9532001. There the donor included the customary withdrawal language, but when the trust was created, he obtained from each beneficiary a document whereby the beneficiary irrevocably waived any right to withdraw subsequent contributions and also waived any right to be informed of subsequent contributions. The IRS ruled that no exclusion would be allowed as to any contribution after the initial transfer. The IRS reasoned that there is a present interest only if the beneficiary has an immediate right to possession at the time of each gift—a right that was prospectively destroyed by the waiver.

In practice, of course, few Crummey withdrawal rights are ever exercised. When a donor contributes funds to an education trust for a beneficiary, and the beneficiary has power to withdraw the contribution, everyone involved understands that beneficiary is not expected to exercise the withdrawal right. In fact, the donor may make it clear to the beneficiary that if the withdrawal right is exercised, there will be no further contributions to the trust.

d. Crummey Trusts: Contingent Beneficiaries

Once the *Crummey* withdrawal right became established, it occurred to planners that the number of donees holding such rights, and therefore the number of section 2503(b) exclusions allowed, could be expanded indefinitely by giving such withdrawal rights to numerous contingent beneficiaries. Although the donor would not expect any of the contingent beneficiaries to exercise their withdrawal rights, and although the interests of the contingent beneficiaries might be quite remote, the rationale of the *Crummey* opinion suggested that each beneficiary's withdrawal right could qualify for an additional exclusion.

The IRS addressed this issue in Tech. Adv. Mem. 8727003, in which the donor created a trust that provided a life estate and general power of appointment for the donor's son. The son's wife and six descendants were to receive the trust property in default of appointment by the son, but they had no other interests in the trust. The donor gave *Crummey* withdrawal rights to the wife and each of the six descendants as well as the son, thereby generating a total of eight annual exclusions. The IRS ruled that no exclusion would be allowed for the withdrawal rights held by the wife and the descendants, who had only "remote contingent interests." The IRS reasoned that Congress intended the annual exclusion to be allowed only as to donees having a "continuing interest" in the trust.

Subsequently, the Tax Court addressed the issue in the case that follows.

ESTATE OF CRISTOFANI V. COMMISSIONER

United States Tax Court, 1991.
97 T.C. 74, acq., 1992–1 C.B. 1.

RUWE, JUDGE:

Respondent determined a deficiency in petitioner's Federal estate tax in the amount of $49,486. The sole issue for decision is whether transfers of property to a trust, where the beneficiaries possessed the right to withdraw an amount not in excess of the section 2503(b) exclusion within 15 days of such transfers, constitute gifts of a present interest in property within the meaning of section 2503(b).

FINDINGS OF FACT

Petitioner is the Estate of Maria Cristofani, deceased, Frank Cristofani, executor. Maria Cristofani (decedent) died testate on December 16, 1985. * * *

Decedent has two children, Frank Cristofani and Lillian Dawson. Decedent's children were both born on July 9, 1948. They were in good health during the years 1984 and 1985.

Decedent has five grandchildren. Two of decedent's five grandchildren are Frank Cristofani's children. They are Anthony Cristofani, born July 16, 1975, and Loris Cristofani, born November 30, 1978. Decedent's three remaining grandchildren are Lillian Dawson's children. They are Justin Dawson, born December 1, 1972, Daniel Dawson, born August 9, 1974, and Luke Dawson, born November 14, 1981. During 1984 and 1985, the parents of decedent's grandchildren were the legal guardians of the person of their respective minor children. There were no independently appointed guardians of decedent's grandchildren's property.

* * *

On June 12, 1984, decedent executed an irrevocable trust entitled the Maria Cristofani Children's Trust I (children's trust). Frank Cristofani and Lillian Dawson were named the trustees of the children's trust.

In general, Frank Cristofani and Lillian Dawson possessed the following rights and interests in the children's trust corpus and income. Under Article Twelfth, following a contribution to the children's trust, Frank Cristofani and Lillian Dawson could each withdraw an amount not to exceed the amount specified for the gift tax exclusion under section 2503(b). Such withdrawal period would begin on the date of the contribution and end on the 15th day following such contribution. Under Article Third, Frank Cristofani and Lillian Dawson were to receive equally the entire net income of the trust quarter-annually, or at more frequent intervals. After decedent's death, under Article Third, the trust estate was to be divided into as many equal shares as there were children of decedent then living or children of decedent then deceased but leaving issue. Both Frank Cristofani and Lillian Dawson survived decedent, and thus the children's trust was divided into two equal trusts. Under Article Third, if a child of decedent survived decedent by 120 days, that child's trust would be distributed to the child. Both Frank Cristofani and Lillian Dawson survived decedent by 120 days, and their respective trusts were distributed upon the expiration of the 120-day waiting period. During the waiting period, Frank Cristofani and Lillian Dawson received the entire net income of the separate trusts as provided for in Article Third.

In general, decedent's five grandchildren possessed the following rights and interests in the children's trust. Under Article Twelfth, during a 15-day period following a contribution to the children's trust, each of the grandchildren possessed the same right of withdrawal as described above regarding the withdrawal rights of Frank Cristofani, and Lillian Dawson. Under Article Twelfth, the trustee of the children's trust was required to notify the beneficiaries of the trust each time a contribution was received. Under Article Third, had either Frank Cristofani or Lillian Dawson predeceased decedent or failed to survive decedent by 120 days, his or her equal portion of decedent's children's trust would have passed in trust to his or her children (decedent's grandchildren).

Under Article Third, the trustees, in their discretion, could apply as much of the principal of the children's trust as necessary for the proper support, health, maintenance, and education of decedent's children. In exercising their discretion, the trustees were to take into account several factors, including "The settlor's desire to consider the settlor's children as primary beneficiaries and the other beneficiaries of secondary importance."

* * *

[In each of the taxable years 1984 and 1985 the decedent transferred property worth $70,000 to the trust.]

Decedent did not report the two $70,000 transfers on Federal gift tax returns. Rather, decedent claimed seven annual exclusions of $10,000 each under section 2503(b) for each year 1984 and 1985. These annual exclusions were claimed with respect to decedent's two children and decedent's five grandchildren.

There was no agreement or understanding between decedent, the trustees, and the beneficiaries that decedent's grandchildren would not exercise their withdrawal rights following a contribution to the children's trust. None of decedent's five grandchildren exercised their rights to withdraw under Article Twelfth of the children's trust during either 1984 or 1985. None of decedent's five grandchildren received a distribution from the children's trust during either 1984 or 1985.

Respondent allowed petitioner to claim the annual exclusions with respect to decedent's two children. However, respondent disallowed the $10,000 annual exclusions claimed with respect to each of decedent's grandchildren claimed for the years 1984 and 1985. Respondent determined that the annual exclusions that decedent claimed with respect to her five grandchildren for the 1984 and 1985 transfers ... were not transfers of present interests in property. Accordingly, respondent increased petitioner's adjusted taxable gifts in the amount of $100,000.

Opinion

* * *

In the instant case, petitioner argues that the right of decedent's grandchildren to withdraw an amount equal to the annual exclusion within 15 days after decedent's contribution of property to the children's trust constitutes a gift of a present interest in property, thus qualifying for a $10,000 annual exclusion for each grandchild for the years 1984 and 1985. Petitioner relies upon Crummey v. Commissioner, 397 F.2d 82 (9th Cir.1968), revg. on this issue T.C. Memo. 1966–144.

* * *

In deciding whether the minor beneficiaries received a present interest, the Ninth Circuit specifically rejected any test based upon the likelihood that the minor beneficiaries would actually receive present enjoyment of the property. Instead, the court focused on the legal right of the minor beneficiaries to demand payment from the trustee. The Ninth Circuit, relying on Perkins v. Commissioner, 27 T.C. 601 (1956), and Gilmore v. Commissioner, 213 F.2d 520 (6th Cir.1954), revg. 20 T.C. 579 (1953), stated:

All exclusions should be allowed under the Perkins test or the "right to enjoy" test in *Gilmore*. Under *Perkins*, all that is necessary is to find that the demand could not be resisted. We interpret that to mean legally resisted, and going on that basis, we do not think the trustee would have any choice but to have a guardian appointed to take the property demanded. [Crummey v. Commissioner, 397 F.2d at 88.]

The court found that the minor beneficiaries had a legal right to make a demand upon the trustee, and allowed the settlors to claim annual exclusions, under section 2503(b), with respect to the minor trust beneficiaries.

The Ninth Circuit recognized that there was language in a prior case, Stifel v. Commissioner, 197 F.2d 107 (2d Cir.1952), affg. 17 T.C. 647 (1951), that seemed to support a different test.

As we read the *Stifel* case, it says that the court should look at the trust instrument, the law as to minors, and the financial and other circumstances of the parties. From this examination it is up to the court to determine whether it is likely that the minor beneficiary is to receive any present enjoyment of the property. If it is not likely, then the gift is a "future interest." [Crummey v. Commissioner, supra at 85.]

As previously stated, the Ninth Circuit rejected a test based on the likelihood that an actual demand would be made. Respondent does not rely on or cite *Stifel* in his brief. We believe that the test set forth in Crummey v. Commissioner, supra, is the correct test.

Subsequent to the opinion in *Crummey*, respondent's revenue rulings have recognized that when a trust instrument gives a beneficiary the legal power to demand immediate possession of corpus, that power qualifies as a present interest in property. * * *

In the instant case, respondent has not argued that decedent's grandchildren did not possess a legal right to withdraw corpus from the children's trust within 15 days following any contribution, or that such demand could have been legally resisted by the trustees. In fact, the parties have stipulated that "following a contribution to the children's trust, each of the grandchildren possessed the *same right of withdrawal* as * * * the withdrawal rights of Frank Cristofani and Lillian Dawson." (Emphasis added.) The legal right of decedent's grandchildren to withdraw specified amounts from the trust corpus within 15 days following any contribution of property constitutes a gift of a present interest. Crummey v. Commissioner, *supra*.

On brief, respondent attempts to distinguish *Crummey* from the instant case. Respondent argues that in *Crummey* the trust beneficiaries not only possessed an immediate right of withdrawal, but also possessed "substantial, future economic benefits" in the trust corpus and income. Respondent emphasizes that the children's trust identified decedent's children as "primary beneficiaries," and that decedent's grandchildren were to be considered as "beneficiaries of secondary importance."

Generally, the beneficiaries of the trust in *Crummey* were entitled to distributions of income. Trust corpus was to be distributed to the issue of each beneficiary sometime following the beneficiary's death. See Crummey v. Commissioner, T.C. Memo. 1966–144. Aside from the discretionary actions of the trustee, the only way any beneficiary in *Crummey* could receive trust corpus was through the demand provision which allowed each beneficiary to demand up to $4,000 in the year in which a transfer to the trust was made. The Ninth Circuit observed:

In our case * * * if no demand is made in any particular year, the additions are forever removed from the uncontrolled reach of the beneficiary since, with exception of the yearly demand provision, the only way the corpus can ever be tapped by a beneficiary, is through a distribution at the discretion of the trustee. [Crummey v. Commissioner, 397 F.2d at 88.]

In the instant case, the primary beneficiaries of the children's trust were decedent's children. Decedent's grandchildren held contingent remainder interests in the children's trust. Decedent's grandchildren's interests vested only in the event that their respective parent (decedent's child) predeceased decedent or failed to survive decedent by more than 120 days. We do not believe, however, that *Crummey* requires that the beneficiaries of a trust must have a vested present interest or vested remainder interest in the trust corpus or income, in order to qualify for the section 2503(b) exclusion.

As discussed in *Crummey*, the likelihood that the beneficiary will actually receive present enjoyment of the property is not the test for determining whether a present interest was received. Rather, we must examine the ability of the beneficiaries, in a legal sense, to exercise their right to withdraw trust corpus, and the trustee's right to legally resist a beneficiary's demand for payment. Crummey v. Commissioner, 397 F.2d at 88. Based upon the language of the trust instrument and stipulations of the parties, we believe that each grandchild possessed the legal right to withdraw trust corpus and that the trustees would be unable to legally resist a grandchild's withdrawal demand. We note that there was no agreement or understanding between decedent, the trustees, and the beneficiaries that the grandchildren would not exercise their withdrawal rights following a contribution to the children's trust.

Respondent also argues that since the grandchildren possessed only a contingent remainder interest in the children's trust, decedent never intended to benefit her grandchildren. Respondent contends that the only reason decedent gave her grandchildren the right to withdraw trust corpus was to obtain the benefit of the annual exclusion.

We disagree. Based upon the provisions of the children's trust, we believe that decedent intended to benefit her grandchildren. Their benefits, as remaindermen, were contingent upon a child of decedent's dying before decedent or failing to survive decedent by more than 120 days. We recognize that at the time decedent executed the children's trust, decedent's children were in good health, but this does not remove the possibility that decedent's children could have predeceased decedent.

In addition, decedent's grandchildren possessed the power to withdraw up to an amount equal to the amount allowable for the 2503(b) exclusion. Although decedent's grandchildren never exercised their respective withdrawal rights, this does not vitiate the fact that they had the legal right to do so, within 15 days following a contribution to the children's trust. Events might have occurred to prompt decedent's children and grandchildren (through their guardians) to exercise their withdrawal rights. For example, either or both of decedent's children and their respective families might have suddenly and unexpectedly been faced with economic hardship; or, in the event of the insolvency of one of decedent's children, the rights of the grandchildren might have been exercised to safeguard their interest in the trust assets from their parents' creditors. In light of the provisions in decedent's trust, we fail to see how respondent can argue that decedent did not intend to benefit her grandchildren.

Finally, the fact that the trust provisions were intended to obtain the benefit of the annual gift tax exclusion does not change the result. As we stated in Perkins v. Commissioner, supra,

regardless of the petitioners' motives, or why they did what they in fact did, the legal rights in question were created by the trust instruments and could at any time thereafter be exercised. Petitioners having done what they purported to do, their tax-saving motive is irrelevant. [Perkins v. Commissioner, 27 T.C. at 606.]

Based upon the foregoing, we find that the grandchildren's right to withdraw an amount not to exceed the section 2503(b) exclusion, represents a present interest for purposes of section 2503(b). Accordingly, petitioner is entitled to claim annual exclusions with respect to decedent's grandchildren as a result of decedent's transfers of property to the children's trust in 1984 and 1985.

NOTE

The Commissioner acquiesced in *Cristofani*, but only "in result." 1992–1 C.B. 1. The Commissioner's position on withdrawal rights held by contingent beneficiaries is illustrated by the following ruling.

TECHNICAL ADVICE MEMORANDUM 9731004
April 21, 1997.

ISSUE:

Whether transfers of property to trusts granting each of 16, or in some cases 17, named individuals the right to withdraw a specified portion of the trust corpus at any time during the year following the transfer constitute gifts of present interests in property and therefore qualify for 16, or 17, annual exclusions under § 2503(b) of the Internal Revenue Code.

FACTS:

* * * In 1981, 1982, 1983, 1984, 1985, 1986, and 1992, Donor established a total of eight irrevocable trusts and transferred to each trust a portion of her tenancy in common interest in the real estate and cash.

* * *

The term of each trust was for the life of the Donor. Article III of each trust provides that any income realized by the trust during the Donor's lifetime shall (subject to the withdrawal provisions of the trust) be distributed annually to the son or daughter of Donor who is the primary beneficiary of that trust. In the event the Donor's child (the primary beneficiary) is deceased with children surviving, then such income is to pass equally to his or her children, *per stirpes*. In the event the Donor's son or daughter is deceased without children surviving him or her, then the income is to pass to the Donor's remaining children, *per stirpes*.

Article III of each trust also provides that during the Donor's lifetime each beneficiary named in Exhibit B of each trust has a non-cumulative power to withdraw a specified amount at all times during a one year period commencing on the date of a contribution made on the beneficiary's behalf during the calendar year. If the withdrawal right has not been exercised by the end of such year, it shall lapse. If the withdrawal right is not fully exercised, the amount subject to the power and not withdrawn is to be held in further trust and administered in accordance with the terms of the trust. * * *

The individuals named in Exhibit B of each trust are the Donor's four children, the spouses of those children, and all of the Donor's grandchildren. A total of 16 individuals are named in each Exhibit B of the trusts created in 1981–1986. A total of 17 individuals are named in Exhibit B of the 1991 and 1992 trusts.

* * *

The total value of Donor's transfers to these trusts was \$835,950. No gift tax returns were filed with respect to any transfers made to these trusts.

LAW AND ANALYSIS:

* * *

The Service generally does not contest gift tax annual exclusions for transfers subject to withdrawal powers that are held by current income beneficiaries and persons with vested remainder interests. These individuals have current or long term economic interest in the trust and in the value of the corpus. It is understandable that in weighing these interests, they decide not to exercise their withdrawal rights. However, where nominal beneficiaries enjoy only discretionary income interests, contingent rights to the remainder, or no rights whatsoever in the income or remainder, their non-exercise of the withdrawal rights indicates that there was some kind of prearranged understanding with the donor that these rights were not meant to be exercised or that their exercise would result in undesirable consequences, or both.

The facts and circumstances of the instant case indicate that Donor was attempting to obtain multiple exclusions to eliminate the gift tax on the transfers to the trusts. In substance, however, the Donor did not make *bona fide* gifts of present interests when she granted withdrawal rights in Trusts #1–#6 and Trusts #7 and #8 to 15 or 16 individuals other than the primary beneficiary.

We do not dispute that, with respect to transfers initially funding each trust and the subsequent transfer in 1993 to Trust #7, each donee of a withdrawal right received timely notice of the existence of the right and had adequate time in which to exercise the right. (There is no indication, however, that notice was received by the donees of the withdrawal rights with respect to the transfer to Trust #6 that occurred on January 6, 1987.)

However, only the primary beneficiary of each trust had a vested income or vested remainder interest in that trust. This fact is evident upon an examination of the terms of Trust #1, which is similar to the other seven trusts except for the identity of the primary beneficiary and the contingent beneficiaries.

Trust #1 was established on December 28, 1981, with a transfer of an interest in real property. Under the terms of Trust #1, *B*, the primary beneficiary and daughter of the Donor, was to receive the income realized by the trust on an annual basis during the life of Donor. In the event that B died during the Donor's life, the income of the trust was to pass equally to B's surviving children, *per stirpes*, if any, or if none to Donor's remaining children, *per stirpes*.

Each of the 16 individuals named in Exhibit B (a group consisting of the Donor's children and their spouses, and the Donor's grandchildren) had the non-cumulative power to withdraw an amount specified at all times during a one-year period commencing on the date of a contribution to the trust.

Upon Donor's death, subject to the withdrawal powers, the trustee was to distribute the trust property to B. In the event [B] predeceased D, the trust property was to pass equally to B's surviving children, *per stirpes*. In the event B had no children surviving her, the trust property was to pass equally to the Donor's remaining children, *per stirpes*.

Because B's sons were entitled to income of Trust #1 only in the event that they survived B while the Donor lived they had a contingent income interest in Trust #1. Because B's sons were entitled to receive the corpus of Trust #1 only in the event that the Donor died, predeceased by B, the sons had a contingent remainder interest in Trust #1.

Donor's other children, A, C, and D, had only remote contingent remainder interests in Trust #1. In the event that B and all B's children died, while the Donor survived, the Donor's children were entitled to the income from Trust #1. In the event that at the time the Donor died neither [B] nor any of B's children survived, the trust corpus would pass to the Donor's remaining children.

The children of A, C, and D had even more remote contingent income and remainder interests in Trust #1 because they would receive income or corpus only if B, all of B's children, and their own parent died before the Donor. For example, A's children would receive income from the trust only if B, all of B's children, and A died before the Donor. Similarly, the trust corpus would pass to A's children only if at the time Donor died B, all of B's children, and A were deceased.

Neither the spouse of B nor the spouses of B's siblings, (A, C, and D) had any interest in Trust #1 aside from his or her withdrawal right.

Each of the other seven trusts had substantially similar dispository terms.

* * *

The substantive effect of all these trusts and all these transfers was to carry out the Donor['s] intention that upon her death the farm property comprising the corpus of the eight trusts would be transferred outright in four approximately equal shares to the Donor's four children. Such a purpose could not be accomplished if any of the 15 or 16 individuals (other than the primary beneficiary) had exercised his or her withdrawal right to remove property from the trust.

In fact, none of the individuals ever exercised a withdrawal right with respect to any of the ten transfers to the trusts. The individuals (other than the primary beneficiary of the trust) had only a contingent interest, a remotely contingent interest, or no possible interest in any property left in the trust upon the expiration of the withdrawal rights. The children of the primary beneficiary would receive trust property only if their parent died before their grandmother. The siblings of the primary beneficiary would receive trust property only if the primary beneficiary and all the primary beneficiary's children died before the siblings' mother. The grandchildren of the Donor, other than those who are children of the primary beneficiary, would receive trust property only if the primary beneficiary, and the grandchildren's parent died before their grandmother. The spouses of the donor's children would never receive any interest in the trust property.

The fact that none of the withdrawal rights was ever exercised, even by those who had no other interests in the trusts, leads to the conclusion that as part of a prearranged understanding, all of the individuals (other than the primary beneficiary) knew that their rights were paper rights only, or that exercising them would result in unfavorable consequences. There is no other logical reason why these individuals would choose not to withdraw the amount specified in each trust as a gift which would neither be includible in their income nor subject the Donor to the gift tax.

Having considered the facts and circumstances surrounding the creation, funding, and purpose of each trust, we conclude that Donor did not [intend] to make *bona fide* gifts of present interests to any of the trusts' beneficiaries other than the primary beneficiary of each trust.

NOTE

In Estate of Kohlsaat v. Comm'r, 73 T.C.M. (CCH) 2732 (1997), sixteen descendants of the trust grantor, all contingent beneficiaries of the trust, were given *Crummey* withdrawal rights. The IRS argued that there were "understandings" between the grantor and the beneficiaries that the withdrawal rights would not be exercised. Although the opinion does not describe the evidence presented, the Tax Court concluded that the evidence did not establish the existence of such understandings. Also, the Tax Court noted that several credible reasons were offered by the trust beneficiaries as to why they did not exercise the withdrawal rights. The court refused to infer the existence of "understandings" simply because there were no withdrawals, and section 2503(b) exclusions were allowed as to all contingent beneficiaries.

e. Crummey Trusts: Planning

The *"Crummey* withdrawal right" has become an accepted and frequently used method of making gifts to minors in such a way as to qualify for the annual exclusion. This approach permits greater flexibility than is provided by use of either a section 2503(c) trust or a gift to a custodian under the Uniform Transfers to Minors Act, both discussed below. Care must be exercised, however, to assure adequate notice to the donee as well as a reasonable time for exercise of the withdrawal right, as explained above.

Many taxpayers are tempted to use *Crummey* withdrawal rights to shelter the maximum amount excludable under section 2503(b). It should be recognized, however, that hidden dangers lie in granting any right to withdraw more than $5,000 per year per donee. If the donee fails to exercise such a withdrawal right, it is clear that the donee has thereby made a transfer to the beneficiaries of the trust (if other than herself) in the amount that could have been withdrawn. This is so because the donee has permitted a general power of appointment to lapse. See I.R.C. § 2514(e) discussed in Chapter 5. Section 2514(e) further provides that such a lapse is considered a transfer only to the extent that the amount as to which lapse occurs exceeds the greater of $5,000 or five percent of the amount subject to the power.

If a donor transfers $15,000 to a trust and grants withdrawal rights to a powerholder and the assets of the trust do not exceed $100,000, the "$5,000 or 5 percent" rule of section 2514(e) will apply only to the first $5,000 subject to the withdrawal right. Lapse of the withdrawal right as to the amount in excess of $5,000 will constitute a taxable gift to the extent the beneficiaries of the trust are persons other than the powerholder. Because this will be a gift in trust, it will ordinarily not qualify as a present interest gift and thus will not be sheltered by the annual exclusion. In that event a taxable gift will result, a portion of the unified credit of the powerholder will be consumed, and a gift tax return will be required.

The result is that a *Crummey* gift greater than $5,000 (or five percent) per donee may cause an unintended "secondary" gift by the holder of the *Crummey* power, requiring a gift tax return and use of a portion of the donee's unified credit. The problem is exacerbated because all of the powerholder's withdrawal rights are aggregated for purposes of the section 2514(e) $5,000 or five percent rule. In other words, the powerholder of a withdrawal right can annually apply only one $5,000 or five percent exclusion against all the withdrawal rights held by powerholder, even if the withdrawal rights relate to separate trusts and separate donors. Rev. Rul. 85–88, 1985–2 C.B. 202.

The secondary gift problem can be avoided—regardless of the amount subject to withdrawal—if the holder of the withdrawal right holds all beneficial interests in the trust. In that event the lapse of the power constitutes a transfer by the power holder for his or her own benefit, and there is no gift.

Another way to avoid the secondary gift problem is through use of "hanging powers." Under this approach, the trust instrument provides that failure to exercise the withdrawal power causes a lapse of the power only to the extent of the greater of $5,000 or 5% of the fund subject to withdrawal. The remaining portion of the power "hangs" in suspense to be used in later years—or to lapse in subsequent years if the donor ceases or diminishes contributions to the trust. For example, assume that the donor transfers $8,000 to such a trust, and the donee has the power to withdraw the entirety of this amount within 30 days. The donor can use the annual exclusion to shelter the entire transfer from tax. When the 30 days pass without exercise, the power lapses only as to $5,000, and the donee retains a power to withdraw $3,000 in later years. Because the lapse falls within the "5 and 5" exception provided by section 2514(e), there is no gift by the donee. If the donor transfers $2,000 or less to the trust during the subsequent year and no withdrawal rights are exercised in that year, both the current $2,000 withdrawal right and the "hanging" withdrawal right of $3,000 will lapse at the end of the subsequent year. Because the total lapse is not in excess of $5,000, there is no secondary gift. The only catch is that, if the donee dies while holding the "hanging" power to withdraw $3,000, that amount will be included in the donee's gross estate. See I.R.C. § 2041(a)(2).

Even if the amount subject to the withdrawal right is limited to $5,000 per donee, so that the gift tax problems described above are avoided, income tax complications remain. A holder of the *Crummey* power who does not exercise the power may be taxed on the income from the property subject to the power, at least during the period the property is subject to the power, and perhaps afterwards as well, all pursuant to section 678, explored in Chapter 31.

PROBLEMS

1. At the beginning of Year 1 Tyler, who is not married, transferred $20,000 in cash to a trust that gives Sara, Tyler's daughter, the right to withdraw within 30 days any amount transferred to the trust. The $20,000 is the only trust asset. Sara does not exercise her withdrawal right. The trust provides that one-half of the income of the trust is to be paid each year to Sara or her estate, and the other one-half is to be paid to Sara's brother, Brady, or his estate. The trust is to terminate at the end of Year 12, when the entire corpus is to be transferred to Brady's daughter, Amanda. Assume for purposes of this problem that the value of the income interest of a 12-year term certain is .503031 and that the value of the remainder

after a 12-year certain is .496969 of the principal. Further assume that the annual exclusion is $17,000.

Has Tyler or Sara made a taxable gift? If so, what is the amount of each taxable gift?

2.   Assume the same facts as in *Cristofani*, with these additions: The trust provides that if no descendant of Maria is living 120 days after Maria's death, the trust property is to be distributed to Eloise Gantry and Nancy Nearing, friends of Maria. The trust also provides that Eloise and Nancy are to have immediate withdrawal rights of the same kind Maria's descendants possess. Eloise and Nancy, good friends of Maria, are both prosperous, and Maria feels sure neither will exercise her withdrawal right. Each year Maria contributes $153,000 to the trust. Assume that the annual exclusion is $17,000.

To what extent are exclusions available under section 2503(b)?

3.   Assume the same facts as in *Cristofani*, with these additions: The trust provides that each of Janet Wilson, Ruth Neville, Sally Branson, Alice Newt, Helen Gutbohl, and Irma Wilson is to have withdrawal rights of the same kind Maria's descendants possess. However, none of them have any other interest in the trust. All of them are prosperous and good friends of Maria, who feels sure that none will exercise the withdrawal right. Each year Maria contributes $221,000 to the trust. Assume that the annual exclusion is $17,000.

To what extent are exclusions available under section 2503(b)?

f.   Section 2503(c) Trusts

The confusion that resulted from the early conflict between the Seventh Circuit in *Kieckhefer* and the Second Circuit in *Stifel*, referred to in *Crummey*, caused Congress, in its enactment of the 1954 Code, to include a new provision granting a "safe harbor" for donors who wanted to use a trust vehicle without providing for withdrawal privileges by the minor (whether through a guardian or not). For those donors who do not choose the *Crummey* approach, an assured, although less flexible, alternative is available under section 2503(c).

The premise of section 2503(c) is that the annual exclusion should be allowed if all beneficial interests in the trust are held by the minor, even if the minor's actual enjoyment of those interests may be deferred. A trust qualifies only if (1) the trustee has unrestricted power to expend the trust property for the benefit of the minor, and (2) the trust property will pass to the minor upon attainment of age twenty-one. If the minor dies before attaining age twenty-one the trust property must be distributed to the minor's estate or in accord with the exercise of a general power by the minor.

Section 2503(c) is strictly construed, and any "substantial restriction" limiting the trustee's discretion in making distributions to the minor will disqualify the trust. See Treas. Reg. § 25.2503–4(b)(1).

Although the title of section 2503(c) refers to a trust for the benefit of a "minor," the text of the section refers only to attainment of age 21. Therefore, the operation of section 2503(c) is not affected by state laws granting majority at age 18.

A section 2503(c) trust is inflexible and requires preparation of a trust instrument as well as annual income tax returns. If the purpose of the trust is to accumulate funds for the minor's college education, a section 529 Plan, described later in this chapter, is usually a better choice. Nevertheless, a section 2503(c) trust may be preferable if (1) the purpose of the trust is not to fund education, or (2) it is important for the donor to retain control over investment of the trust funds.

Another disadvantage of a section 2503(c) trust is the requirement that the entirety of the trust assets be made available to the beneficiary when the beneficiary attains age 21. Under a *Crummey* trust, the beneficiary's ultimate access to the trust property (after the initial withdrawal period) can be deferred as long as the donor desires.

The availability of section 2503(e) further diminishes the attraction of a section 2503(c) trust. As explained below in Part C, section 2503(e) permits an unlimited exclusion for direct payment for medical expenses or payment of tuition to an educational institution, including elementary and secondary schools as well as colleges and universities.

g. Uniform Gifts to Minors Act and Uniform Transfers to Minors Act

REVENUE RULING 59–357
1959–2 C.B. 212.

The Internal Revenue Service has been requested to clarify its position in regard to the income, gift, and estate tax consequences of gifts to minors under both the Uniform Gifts to Minors Act and the Model Gifts of Securities to Minors Act.

Uniform laws have been adopted in many states to facilitate gifts to minors. Generally, these laws eliminate the usual requirement that a guardian be appointed or a trust set up when a minor is to be the donee of a gift. Under the Model Gifts of Securities to Minors Act, a donor may appoint either himself or a member of the minor's family as custodian to manage a gift of securities. The Uniform Gifts to Minors Act provides that money as well as securities may be the subject of a gift to a minor and that a bank, trust company, or any adult may act as custodian. When a gift is made pursuant to the model or uniform act the property vests absolutely in the minor. The custodian is authorized to apply as much of the income or principal held by him for the benefit of the minor as he may deem advisable in his sole discretion. Income and principal not so applied are to be delivered to the donee when he reaches the age of 21 or, in event of his prior death, to his estate.

Revenue Ruling 56–86, C.B. 1956–1, 449, holds that a transfer of securities to a minor donee, pursuant to a statute similar to the Model Gifts of Securities to Minors Act, constitutes a completed gift for Federal gift tax purposes at the time the transfer was made. Such a gift qualifies for the annual gift tax exclusion authorized by section 2503(b) of the Internal Revenue Code of 1954.

Revenue Ruling 56–484, C.B. 1956–2, 23, holds that income, which is derived from property transferred under the Model Gifts of Securities to Minors Act and which is used in the discharge or satisfaction, in whole or in part, of a legal obligation of any person to support or maintain a minor, is taxable to such person to the extent so used, but is otherwise taxable to the minor donee.

Revenue Ruling 57–366, C.B. 1957–2, 618, holds that the value of property transferred to a minor donee under the Model Gifts of Securities to Minors Act is includible in the gross estate of the donor for Federal estate tax purposes if the donor appoints himself custodian and dies while serving in that capacity and before the donee attains the age of 21 years.

The provision of the Uniform Gifts to Minors Act regarding the powers of the custodian as to distributions differs from the comparable provision of the Model Gifts of Securities to Minors Act in only three respects. First, the "model" act authorizes the custodian to apply so much of the income from the securities "as he may deem advisable for the support, maintenance, general use and benefit of the minor in such manner, at such time or times, and to such extent as the custodian in his absolute discretion may deem suitable and proper, without court order, without regard to the duty of any person to support the minor and without regard to any funds which may be applicable or available for the purposes." The "uniform" act does not use the term "absolute discretion," but this provision is otherwise virtually identical.

Second, the "uniform" act differs from the "model" act in that, in lieu of the latter part of the language quoted above, it provides that the income can be applied by the custodian for the minor's support without regard to the duty of himself or of any other person to support the minor or his ability to do so. Thus, the custodian, who may be legally obligated to support the minor, has power to use custodianship income for such support even though he may have adequate funds for this purpose.

Third, the "uniform" act contains a provision not found in the "model" act which gives a parent or guardian of the minor, or the minor himself after he reaches the age of 14, the right to petition the court to order the custodian to spend custodial property for the minor's support, maintenance or education. This provision, coupled with the "uniform" act's omission of the term "absolute" with reference to the discretion vested in the custodian, suggests the existence of a limitation on the custodian's otherwise uncontrolled power to withhold enjoyment of the custodial property from the minor, at least as to a portion of such property. Nevertheless, the custodian's power to withhold enjoyment is not substantially affected by such limitation.

In view of the foregoing, it is the opinion of the Internal Revenue Service that neither these nor other variations between the "model" act and the "uniform" act warrant any departure from the position previously published in Revenue Ruling 56–86, supra, Revenue Ruling 56–484, supra, and Revenue Ruling 57–366, supra, in regard to gifts made under the "model" act.

Therefore, any transfer of property to a minor under statutes patterned after either the Model Gifts of Securities to Minors Act or the Uniform Gifts to Minors Act constitutes a completed gift for Federal gift tax purposes to the extent of the full fair market value of the property transferred. Such a gift qualifies for the annual gift tax exclusion authorized by section 2503(b) of the Code. See Rev. Rul. 56–86, C.B. 1956–1, 449; and section 25.2511–2(d) of the Gift Tax Regulations. No taxable gift occurs for Federal gift tax purposes by reason of a subsequent resignation of the custodian or termination of the custodianship.

Income derived from property so transferred which is used in the discharge or satisfaction, in whole or in part, of a legal obligation of any person to support or maintain a minor is taxable to such person to the extent so used but is otherwise taxable to the minor donee. See Rev. Rul. 56–484, C.B. 1956–2, 23.

The value of property so transferred is includible in the gross estate of the donor for Federal estate tax purposes if * * * (2) the donor appoints himself custodian and dies while serving in that capacity. See Rev. Rul. 57–366, C.B. 1957–2, 618; and section 20.2038–1(a) of the Estate Tax Regulations. In all other circumstances custodial property is includible only in the gross estate of the donee.

NOTE

During the late 1960s and early 1970s many states lowered the age of majority to 18 and simultaneously lowered to 18 the age for full possession by the donee of property held under the Uniform Gifts to Minors Act. This raised the question whether a Uniform Act transfer would continue to comply with section 2503(c). The Commissioner so ruled on the ground that section 2503(c) sets forth the "maximum restrictions that may be attached to minors and still have such gifts considered as present interests . . ." Rev. Rul. 73–287, 1973–2 C.B. 321, 322.

Although Rev. Rul. 59–357 addresses only the Uniform Gifts to Minors Act and the Model Gifts of Securities to Minors Act, the ruling's conclusions should apply with equal force to the Uniform Transfers to Minors Act, promulgated by the National Conference of Commissioners on Uniform State Laws in 1986, and now adopted in most states.

As explained below, Congress adopted section 529 in 1996, thereby creating a vehicle that has important advantages over Uniform Transfers to Minors Act gifts in terms of both tax benefits and flexibility, assuming the purpose is to fund education expenses.

4.   QUALIFIED TUITION PROGRAMS

Qualified tuition programs are authorized by section 529 and are often referred to as "529 Plans." Although section 529 is included in Subtitle A of the Internal Revenue Code, relating to income taxes, section 529 includes provisions that have important gift and estate tax effects as well.

Since enactment of section 529 in 1996, 529 Plans have become a popular vehicle for accumulation of college expenses. These plans offer a combination of multiple tax benefits and flexibility that often make 529 Plans superior to both section 2503(c) trusts and Uniform Transfers to Minors Act gifts as a means of providing financing future higher education.

The benefits of section 529 Plans can be illustrated by describing the circumstances of a grandmother who wishes to establish a fund that will provide the cost of future college education for a recently born grandchild, Samuel. It is assumed that the section 2503(b) annual exclusion is $17,000.

1.   The grandmother transfers $17,000 to a 529 Plan sponsored by any state, naming Samuel as the beneficiary.

2.   The $17,000 transfer qualifies for the annual exclusion and therefore is not subject to gift tax. I.R.C. § 529(c)(2)(A)(i). No gift tax return is required. I.R.C. § 6019(1).

3.   In many states, the grandmother's contribution to the 529 Plan sponsored by her state is partially or wholly deductible for purposes of that state's income tax.[1] In some states, part

---

[1]   See, e.g., Ark. Code Ann. § 26–51–403(17) (2022) (allowing deduction from adjusted gross income up to $5,000 for contributions to the Arkansas Brighter Future Fund Plan); N.D. Cent. Code § 57–38–30.3(2)(n) (2021) (allowing a subtraction from income up to $5,000 or $10,000 if a joint return is filed); S.C. Code Ann. § 59–2–80(D) (2022) (providing a deduction to state plan up to the maximum contribution allowed under I.R.C. § 529, including funds rolled over from another qualified plan); Va. Code Ann. § 58.1–322.03(7)(a) (2022) (allowing a deduction up to $4,000 and amounts in excess of $4,000 can be carried forward to future years until the entire contribution

or all of a contribution to any state's 529 Plan is deductible for state income tax purposes.[2]

4. If the grandmother dies while the 529 Plan is in effect, none of the plan assets are included in her gross estate for estate tax purposes. I.R.C. § 529(c)(4)(A).

5. Neither the grandmother nor Samuel is taxed on the earnings within the 529 Plan. I.R.C. § 529(c)(1). Nor is the plan itself subject to income tax. I.R.C. § 529(a).

6. The grandmother determines the timing, amount, and purpose of any distribution from the 529 Plan.

7. If a distribution is used for Samuel's "qualified higher education expenses," the distribution is not taxed to either Samuel or the grandmother. For this purpose, "qualified higher education expenses" include expenditures for tuition, fees, books, supplies, and equipment. The term "qualified higher education expenses" also includes room and board costs up to the standard room and board allowance fixed by the educational institution Samuel attends if he is at least a half-time student. I.R.C. § 529(e)(3)(B).

8. The grandmother's contribution to a 529 Plan does not impair her ability to make direct tuition payments excludable for gift tax purposes under section 2503(e), whether in the year of contribution or in years when distributions are made from the 529 Plan. I.R.C. § 529(c)(2)(A)(ii). Also, in years in which 529 Plan contributions are not made (or deemed made, under section 529(c)(2)(B)), the grandmother can make annual exclusion gifts to Samuel.

9. At any time, the grandmother can, without gift tax cost, change the beneficiary from Samuel to another member of Samuel's family, as broadly defined in section 529(e)(2), provided the new beneficiary is not in a generation below Samuel. I.R.C. §§ 529(c)(3)(C)(ii) and 529(c)(5)(B).

10. If the grandmother falls into financial difficulty, she can withdraw funds from the 529 Plan for her own use. The grandmother will be taxed on the portion of the distribution allocable to the earnings of the plan, and the grandmother must pay a 10% penalty on this portion. I.R.C. §§ 529(c)(3)(A) and 529(c)(6).

---

has been deducted); Wis. Stat. Ann. § 71.05(6)(b)(32) (2022) (providing a subtraction up to $3,000 annually per beneficiary for contributions).

[2] See, e.g., Ariz. Rev. Stat. § 43–1022(19) (2022); Kan. Stat. Ann. § 79–32,117(c)(xv) (2022); Minn. Stat. § 290.0132(23)(a) (2022); Mont. Code Ann. § 15–30–2110(11) (2021).

11. Without tax consequences, the grandmother can transfer the funds in the existing 529 Plan to another 529 Plan if the funds are transferred within 60 days of a distribution. I.R.C. § 529(c)(3)(C)(i)(I).

12. Under virtually all 529 Plans, expenditures from the 529 Plan are not limited to educational institutions in the grandmother's state or to educational institutions in the state sponsoring the plan.[3]

13. Beginning in January 1, 2018, the grandmother may contribute up to $10,000 annually in connection with Samuel's attendance at a public, private, or religious elementary or secondary school. I.R.C. §§ 529(c)(7) & (e)(3)(A). The IRS issued Notice 2018–58, 2018–33 I.R.B. 305, which states that the Treasury Department and IRS intend to issue regulations that "elementary or secondary" will be defined as "kindergarten through grade 12" and will have the same definition that exists for the section 530(b)(3)(B) Coverdell savings accounts.[4]

14. Under the Secure Act 2 of 2022,[5] beginning after December 31, 2023, amounts in a 529 account that had been maintained for at least 15 years may be rolled over directly into a Roth IRA. The maximum amount that can be rolled over is $35,000, and it cannot exceed the maximum eligible annual contribution to the Roth IRA. Contributions to a 529 account made within five years and the earnings from these contributions cannot be rolled over to the Roth IRA.

The allowance of the annual exclusion for contributions to a 529 Plan is further expanded by a rule that permits spreading of a larger transfer over as many as five years for purposes of the annual exclusion. For example, assume that the grandmother transfers $85,000 to the 529 Plan in one year. Assuming the annual exclusion is $17,000, she can elect to treat the contribution as spread over five years for gift tax purposes, using the five $17,000 exclusions to shelter the entire gift. I.R.C. § 529(c)(2)(B). If the grandmother dies within five years, however, the portion of the transfer allocable to the post-death period will be included in her gross estate. I.R.C. § 529(c)(4)(C).

Although each 529 plan is nominally offered by a state, typically the funds are actually invested with a financial institution (often a family of

---

[3] See, e.g., Ark. Code Ann. § 6–84–111(a)(1) (2022); Minn. Stat. § 136G.13(1)(a) (2022); Mo. Ann. Stat. § 166.410(4) (2022).

[4] As of the publication of the 26th edition of this book, the IRS has yet to issue these regulations.

[5] Pub. Law No. 117-328, Sec. 126, H.R. 2617, 118th Cong. (2023–2024).

mutual funds) that has contracted with the state. The costs and investment results vary widely. A helpful comparison of all 529 plans is available at www.savingforcollege.com and other Internet sites.

5. QUALIFIED ABLE PROGRAMS

Congress enacted the Achieving a Better Life Experience (ABLE) Act of 2014. ABLE permits states to create tax-favored savings accounts to help designated disabled or blind beneficiaries pay for qualified disability expenses. See I.R.C. § 529A. Under section 529A(e), the individual's blindness or disability must occur before reaching age 26. However, under the Secure Act 2 of 2022, the disability must occur before the individual reaches age 46 beginning after December 25, 2025.[6] The purpose of the Act is to encourage individuals to save in order to support people with disabilities and to "provide secure funding for disability related expenses on behalf of designated beneficiaries with disabilities that will supplement, but not supplant benefits" that might be otherwise available through other government, employment, or private programs.[7] Individuals can contribute to an ABLE account for the benefit of a designated beneficiary and receive both immediate and future tax benefits. The maximum amount that can be contributed annually is the annual gift tax section 2503(b) exclusion (currently $17,000). Under the original statutory provision, designated beneficiaries were not permitted to contribute to the ABLE accounts. However, under the Tax Cuts and Jobs Act, from 2018 through 2025, designated beneficiaries who work can make the additional contributions from their wages to their own ABLE accounts as limited by the lesser of the designated beneficiary's compensation poverty line for a one-person household.[8] See I.R.C. § 529A(b)(2)(B)(ii). For gift tax purposes, contributions to an ABLE program are treated as completed gifts of present interests. I.R.C. § 529A(c)(2)(A).

Distributions from ABLE accounts are tax free if they are used for "qualified disability expenses." I.R.C. § 529A(c)(1)(B). Section 529A(e)(5) defines "qualified disability expenses" as:

any expenses related to the eligible individual's blindness or disability which are made for the benefit of an eligible individual who is the designated beneficiary, including the following expenses: education, housing, transportation, employment training and support, assistive technology and personal support services, health, prevention and wellness, financial management and administrative services, legal fees, expenses for oversight and monitoring, funeral and burial expenses, and other expenses,

---

[6]   Pub. Law No. 117-328, Sec. 124, H.R. 2617, 118th Cong. (2023–2024).

[7]   Pub. Law No. 113–295, Sec. 101, H.R. 5771, 113th Cong. (2013–2014).

[8]   For 2022, the additional contribution limit is $12,880 in the continental United States, $14,820 in Hawaii, and $16,090 in Alaska. Dept. of Treas., Publication 907, Tax Highlights for Persons with Disabilities 8 (2022).

which are approved by the Secretary under regulations and consistent with the purposes of this section.

Under the Tax Cuts and Jobs Act of 2017, after December 22, 2017 and before January 1, 2026, taxpayers can rollover funds from a beneficiary's 529 plan or an eligible family member's 529 plan to an ABLE account. See I.R.C. § 529(c)(3)(C)(i)(III).

6. RECIPROCAL AND SHAM TRANSFERS

Many taxpayers find the annual exclusion frustrating. Section 2503(b) transfers provide a "free ride" in the sense that none of the donor's unified credit is used, and section 2503(b) transfers can be made to the same individuals year after year. There is great allure in finding additional donees, so that the benefits of section 2503(b) can be multiplied. The Commissioner is alert to circumstances in which taxpayers have succumbed to the temptation to multiply donees through artificial transfers.

SATHER V. COMMISSIONER
United States Court of Appeals, Eighth Circuit, 2001.
251 F.3d 1168.

HANSEN, CIRCUIT JUDGE.

The Internal Revenue Service (IRS) imposed gift tax deficiencies and accuracy-related penalties on Larry Sather, Kathy Sather, John Sather, Sandra Sather, Duane Sather, and Diane Sather related to gifts made by each of them in 1993, * * * [T]he tax court found that the transactions at issue involved cross-gifts, denied claimed annual exclusions, and upheld the tax deficiencies and a portion of the penalties. We affirm the imposition of gift tax deficiencies but reverse the accuracy-related penalties.

I.

This case involves the transfer of stock in a closely-held family business from one generation to the next. The Sather brothers, Larry, John, Duane, and Rodney (collectively the "brothers"), along with Larry's, John's, and Duane's wives, Kathy, Sandra, and Diane, respectively (collectively the "wives"), owned 100% of the stock in Sather, Inc., which they previously received from the brothers' parents. At the time of the transfers at issue, Rodney was unmarried and had no children. Larry, John, and Duane each had three children. In an effort to transfer the stock of Sather, Inc., to the next generation of Sathers, the brothers consulted their accountant for advice on structuring the transfer. Upon their accountant's advice, Larry, John, and Duane and each of their respective wives transferred $9,997 worth of stock to each of their children and to each of their nieces and nephews on December 31, 1992. Larry, John, and Duane also transferred additional shares to their own children to effect the full transfer of Sather, Inc., stock to the next generation of Sathers. On January 5, 1993, Larry, John, and Duane each transferred $19,994 worth of stock to each of their nieces and nephews and approximately $15,000 worth of stock to each of their own children. The wives each transferred $3,283 worth of stock to each of their own children.[2] The transfers were made to irrevocable trusts for each set of children (Larry's, John's, and Duane's).

Each donor filed a separate gift tax return for 1992, claiming nine $10,000 gift tax exclusions, one for each donee (each individual's own three children and six nieces and nephews, or nine nieces and nephews in Rodney's case). Each donor likewise filed a gift tax return for 1993, again claiming nine $10,000 gift tax exclusions and electing to have each gift treated as made one-half by each spouse, as allowed under the Internal Revenue Code (I.R.C.) § 2513, 26 U.S.C. § 2513 (1994). * * * The IRS allowed only three $10,000 exclusions per year for each of the donors— Larry, Kathy, John, Sandra, Duane, and Diane—and assessed gift taxes and penalties based on the remaining transfers. The IRS reasoned that the gifts to each of the donors' own children were valid gifts, but that the gifts to each niece and nephew were constructive gifts to the donors' own children.

* * *

II.   RECIPROCAL GIFTS

The Internal Revenue Code imposes a tax "on the transfer of property by gift," I.R.C. § 2501(a), "whether the gift is direct or indirect," I.R.C. § 2511(a). The first $10,000 worth of gifts of a present interest made to any person in a calendar year is excluded from the definition of a taxable gift. I.R.C. § 2503(b). Thus, it is not uncommon for taxpayers to avoid the gift tax by structuring gifts just below the $10,000 exclusion limit. This case requires us to determine whether the gifts in this case, similar gifts made by the donors to each other's children, are really cross-gifts, that is, indirect gifts to their own children.

The tax court found that the cumulative transfers at issue lacked economic substance, relying on the reciprocal trust doctrine. The Sathers argue that there is economic substance to the transactions as a whole when Rodney's gifts to the nieces and nephews are considered, as is required by the step-transaction doctrine. Whether a transaction lacks economic substance, and whether several transactions should be considered

---

[2]   Rodney also made transfers of approximately $10,000 worth of stock to each of his nieces and nephews on both dates and made transfers to the other brothers, but those transfers are not at issue here. Rodney was not assessed any additional tax as the transfers to his nieces, nephews, and brothers were all bona fide transfers; neither he nor his immediate family (he had none) received anything in exchange.

integrated steps of a single transaction, are both fact questions which we review for clear error. * * *

The reciprocal trust doctrine, a variation of the substance over form concept, * * * was developed in the context of trusts to prevent taxpayers from transferring similar property in trust to each other as life tenants, thus removing the property from the settlor's estate and avoiding estate taxes, while receiving identical property for their lifetime enjoyment that would likewise not be included in their estate. *See* United States v. Grace's Estate, 395 U.S. 316, 320, 89 S.Ct. 1730, 23 L.Ed.2d 332 (1969). The Supreme Court held that the reciprocal trust doctrine applies to multiple transactions when the transactions are interrelated and, "to the extent of mutual value, leave the settlors in approximately the same economic position as they would have been in had they created trusts naming themselves as life beneficiaries." Id. at 324, 89 S.Ct. 1730. The doctrine seeks to discern the reality of the transaction; " 'the fact that the trusts are reciprocated or 'crossed' is a trifle, quite lacking in practical or legal significance.' " * * *

Substance over form analysis applies equally to gift tax cases. * * * It is impliedly included in the gift tax statute itself—including indirect transfers within the definition of a taxable gift. *See* I.R.C. § 2511(a). "The terms 'property,' 'transfer,' 'gift,' and 'indirectly' are used in the broadest and most comprehensive sense; . . . . The words 'transfer . . . by gift' and 'whether . . . direct or indirect' are designed to cover and comprehend all transactions . . . whereby . . . property or a property right is donatively passed. . . .' " Dickman v. Comm'r, 465 U.S. 330, 334, 104 S.Ct. 1086, 79 L.Ed.2d 343 (1984) (quoting H.R.Rep. No. 708, 72nd Cong., 1st Sess., 27–28 (1932) and S.Rep. No. 665, 72nd Cong., 1st Sess., 39 (1932)) (some alterations in original). Application of the reciprocal trust doctrine[5] is likewise appropriate in the gift tax context as a method for discerning the substance of gift transfers. " 'The purpose of the doctrine is merely to identify the transferor of property.' " Exchange Bank, 694 F.2d at 1267 (quoting Bischoff v. Comm'r, 69 T.C. 32, 45–46, 1977 WL 3667 (1977)). Once the transferor is identified, the tax code determines whether the transfer is subject to tax. Id.

Applying the reciprocal trust doctrine to this case, there can be no doubt that the gifts were interrelated. The Sather brothers together sought advice on how to transfer the stock to the next generation of Sathers. The transfers to all the children were made on the same days and were for the same amounts of stock. We cannot say that the tax court erred—clearly or otherwise—in determining that the transfers were interrelated.

---

[5]   The tax court has taken to calling it the "reciprocal transaction doctrine" in the context of reciprocal indirect transfers outside the trust arena. * * *

The second prong of the Grace's Estate analysis requires that "the settlors [be left] in approximately the same economic position as they would have been in had they created trusts naming themselves as life beneficiaries." Grace's Estate, 395 U.S. at 324, 89 S. Ct. 1730. We do not believe that the Supreme Court meant to limit the doctrine to cases involving life estate trusts, or even to cases where the donor retains an economic interest, but used that language in the context of the specific facts of the case. * * * In this case, the parents transferred stock to their nieces and nephews in exchange for transfers to their own children by the nieces' and nephews' parents. Though the Sathers received no direct economic value in the exchange, they did receive an economic benefit by indirectly benefitting their own children. The donors were in the same economic position—the position of passing their assets to their children—by entering the cross-transactions as if they had made direct gifts of all of their stock to their own children.

Applying the analysis of the reciprocal trust doctrine, we hold that these interrelated gifts were reciprocal transactions that must be uncrossed to reach the substance of the transactions. * * *

* * *

The purpose of the second Grace's Estate prong is to discern the taxability of the transactions as uncrossed in the context of a particular set of facts. * * * Uncrossing the gifts in the present case, the tax court made the factual finding that each immediate family was in the same position as if each donor had made gifts only to the donor's own children. Thus, using the reciprocal trust doctrine to identify the actual transferor, each donor made transfers to each of his or her own children but no gifts to any of the nieces and nephews. * * * We cannot say that the tax court clearly erred in making this factual finding. Under I.R.C. § 2503(b), each transferor— Larry, Kathy, John, Sandra, Duane, and Diane—was entitled to one $10,000 exclusion for gifts made to each uncrossed donee, their own children, for each year in which gifts were made. Because each transferor has only three children but claimed nine exclusions, the IRS correctly determined that the transferors understated their gift tax liabilities.

The Sathers argue that the step-transaction doctrine requires us to consider the gifts made by Rodney to each of his nieces and nephews, and that in so doing, we will find economic substance in the whole transaction. Each of Larry's, John's, and Duane's immediate families had a net increase in economic value, while Rodney's immediate family (consisting only of himself) had a net decrease in economic value. True as this may be, it does not change the fact that uncrossing the reciprocal gifts leaves each of the transferors in the same position as if he or she had transferred stock only to his or her own children. The purpose of the reciprocal trust doctrine is to discern the actual transferor—Rodney's transfers do not affect the reality of the other transferors' gifts, which amounted to a transfer of their own stock to their own children.

* * *

V. Conclusion

The transfers of stock to each donor's nieces and nephews were reciprocal transfers, or cross-gifts, made in exchange for identical transfers from the nieces and nephew's parents to the donor's own children. As such, the transfers must be uncrossed and the tax code applied to the substance of the transactions. The IRS correctly determined that each donor was entitled to three $10,000 exclusions. The signed returns prepared by the accountant, found by the tax court to be a reliable advisor, provide sufficient evidence of Kathy's, Sandra's, and Diane's reliance and afford them the protection of the reasonable cause exception to the accuracy-related penalties. We therefore affirm in part and reverse in part the tax court's decision.

NOTE

The opinion in *Estate of Grace*, on which the *Sather* opinion relies, is set forth in Chapter 18.

The attractions of the annual exclusion have proved too tempting to other taxpayers as well. In Heyen v. United States, 945 F.2d 359 (10th Cir. 1991), the donor transferred a $10,000 block of stock in a closely held corporation to each of 27 friends unrelated to the donor. At the donor's behest, each friend then transferred her stock to a member of the donor's family, and the amount ultimately received by each family member far exceeded $10,000. The donor nevertheless claimed a $10,000 exclusion for each of the 27 transfers. The Tenth Circuit concluded that the retransfer to the family members had been prearranged by the donor, and that the gifts were actually made to the family members. No exclusions were allowed for the transfers to friends.

7. TAX-SAVINGS OR ADJUSTMENT CLAUSES

REVENUE RULING 86–41
1986–1 C.B. 300.

ISSUE

What are the federal gift tax consequences in the two situations described below where a donor transfers a specified portion of real property under terms that provide for an adjustment to the portion transferred depending on the determination by the Internal Revenue Service of the value of the property for federal gift tax purposes?

FACTS

Situation 1. In 1982, A transferred an interest in a tract of income producing real property to B. Under the deed of transfer, B received a one-half undivided interest in the tract. However, the deed further provided that if the one-half interest received by B were ever determined by the Internal Revenue Service to have a value for federal gift tax purposes in excess of $10,000, then B's fractional interest would be reduced so that its value equaled $10,000. Under local law the adjustment clause operated as a condition subsequent. Thus, if the Service determined that a gift was made in excess of $10,000, the adjustment clause would effectively reconvey to A a fractional share of the tract of real property sufficient to reduce the value of B's interest to $10,000 as of the date of the gift.

On A's federal gift tax return, A reported that the fair market value of the one-half interest transferred by gift to B was $10,000 (one-half the value of the entire tract), and applied the annual exclusion against the gift. On examination of A's 1982 federal gift tax return, it was determined that the fair market value of a one-half interest in the tract subject to the transfer to B was $15,000 rather than $10,000.

Situation 2. The facts are the same as in *Situation 1*, except that B was not required to reconvey any property to A. Rather, the transfer contained the condition that if the Internal Revenue Service determined that B received a gift in excess of $10,000, B would transfer to A consideration equal to the amount of the excess.

LAW AND ANALYSIS

Section 2501 of the Internal Revenue Code imposes a tax on the transfer of property by gift. Section 2511(a) provides that the gift tax applies whether the transfer is in trust or otherwise, whether the gift is direct or indirect, and whether the property is real or personal, tangible, or intangible. Section 25.2511–2(a) of the Gift Tax Regulations states that the gift tax is not imposed upon the receipt of the property by the donee but rather is an excise upon the donor's act of transfer.

Section 2503(b) of the Code provides that a donor may exclude from his or her taxable gifts the first $10,000 of gifts of present interest in property made to each donee during the calendar year. Under § 25.2503 of the regulations, a "present interest" in property is defined as an unrestricted right to the immediate use, possession, or enjoyment of property or the income from property.

Rev. Rul. 65–144, 1965–1 C.B. 442, holds that if the terms of a trust provide that the trust terms will be substantially modified to the extent necessary to qualify the transfer in trust for the gift tax charitable deduction under section 2522 of the Code, those terms providing for modification are considered ineffective for federal gift tax purposes. Gifts subject to conditions subsequent of the kind considered in Rev. Rul. 65–144 tend to discourage the enforcement of federal gift tax provisions, because operation of the provisions would either defeat the gift or otherwise render examination of the return ineffective. See also Commissioner v. Procter, 142 F.2d 824 (4th Cir.1944), cert. denied, 323 U.S. 756 (1944). The Service, accordingly, will not give effect to such clauses and will consider the terms of the gift as unmodified for federal tax purposes.

In *Situations 1* and *2*, the facts demonstrate that A intended to make a gift to B of a present one-half interest in the property. In both cases, the purpose of the adjustment clause was not to preserve or implement the original, bona fide intent of the parties, as in the case of a clause requiring a purchase price adjustment based on an appraisal by an independent third party retained for that purpose. Rather, the purpose of the clause was to recharacterize the nature of the transaction in the event of a future adjustment to A's gift tax return by the Service. As in Rev. Rul. 65–144, the terms of the deed of transfer to B providing for the reduction of the portion transferred would tend to discourage the examination of returns and the collections of tax and therefore are ineffective for federal gift tax purposes. Because the reduction provision is ineffective for federal gift tax purposes, A has made a gift of a present one-half interest in the property, the first $10,000 of which qualifies for the annual exclusion under section 2503 of the Code. The value of the gift is $15,000, the fair market value of a one-half interest in the tract as determined on examination. The fact that, in *Situation 2*, the adjustment of the gift was to be made by recharacterizing the transfer as a part-gift/part-sale is irrelevant.

HOLDING

In both *Situations 1* and *2*, if the donor transfers a specified portion of real property under terms that provide for a recharacterization of the transaction depending on the Service's valuation of the property for federal gift tax purposes, the adjustment clause will be disregarded for federal tax purposes. Consequently, in both cases the value of the gift will be determined without regard to the adjustment clause and the first $10,000 in the value of the gift, as so determined, will qualify for the annual exclusion from gift tax.

NOTE

The Tax Court upheld the Commissioner's position on adjustment clauses in Ward v. Commissioner, 87 T.C. 78 (1986), where the donor provided for revocation of the gift to the extent the stock transferred was determined to have a value greater than $2,000 per share.

The invalidity of "condition subsequent" adjustment clauses has a long history, beginning with Commissioner v. Procter, 142 F.2d 824 (4th Cir.), cert. denied, 323 U.S. 756 (1944). In *Procter*, the instrument of gift purported to revoke the transfer to the extent it was determined to be subject to the gift tax, and this clause was held invalid for tax purposes. Therefore, the gift tax was imposed on the entire gift, without regard to whether there was an actual transfer for local property law purposes.

More recently, some taxpayers have succeeded in avoiding the *Procter* rule through use of a "defined value" clause. In Estate of Christiansen v. Commissioner, 586 F.3d 1061 (8th Cir. 2009), the estate consisted largely of family limited partnership interests. The executor reported a gross estate value of $6.5 million. The legatee entitled to the partnership interests disclaimed any portion of those interests in excess of $6.35 million as finally determined for estate tax purposes. The decedent's will provided that any disclaimed property would go to certain charities. After audit, it was finally determined that the gross estate value was $9.5 million. The estate then claimed a charitable deduction of $3.15 million—the disclaimed amount.

The IRS, relying on the *Procter* rule, disallowed $3 million of the charitable deduction, claiming that the defined value disclaimer operated as a condition subsequent—changing the disclaimer transfer after the fact. The Eighth Circuit rejected the IRS view and allowed the deduction, fundamentally rejecting the public policy argument on which *Procter* and Revenue Ruling 86–41, are based. The Tax Court later reached a similar result in Estate of Petter v. Commissioner, T.C. Memo. 2009–280, 98 T.C.M. (CCH) 534 (2009). In *Petter*, like *Christiansen*, the ultimate beneficiary of the IRS audit was a charity. This may have played some role in the willingness of these courts to reject the *Procter* doctrine.

For a good discussion of tax-savings clauses, see Jay A. Soled & Mitchell Gans, *The Public Policy Doctrine: Drawing the Line Between Permissible and Impermissible Tax-Savings Clauses*, 80 Tenn. L. Rev. 655 (2013).

C. EXCLUSION FOR EDUCATIONAL AND MEDICAL EXPENSES

An exclusion is provided for direct payment of certain educational and medical expenses. I.R.C. § 2503(e).

This exclusion is unlimited in amount and is available over and above the annual exclusion provided by section 2503(b). The section 2503(e) exclusion, however, is subject to important limitations. In the case of educational expenses, the exclusion is available only for tuition. Hence, the exclusion does not apply to other expenses, including room and board and books. See Treas. Reg. § 25.2503–6. The section 2503(e) exclusion is available for tuition at elementary and secondary schools as well as colleges and other educational institutions. See I.R.C. §§ 2503(e)(2)(a) and 170(b)(1)(A)(ii).

In the case of both educational and medical expenses, the exclusion is available only for payments made directly by the donor to the educational institution or medical care provider. A transfer to the donee, who then remits the funds to the educational institution or medical care provider, is not excluded. See Treas. Reg. § 25.2503–6.

The section 2503(e) exclusion does not apply to contributions to qualified tuition programs or to qualified ABLE programs. See I.R.C. §§ 529(c)(2)(A)(ii) and 529A(c)(2)(A)(ii). However, the exclusion applies to nonrefundable prepaid tuition expenses. In Priv. Ltr. Rul. 200602002 a grandparent paid the private school tuition through Grade 12 for each of six grandchildren. There was a separate tuition agreement for each grandchild. The tuition payments were nonrefundable and, once paid, became the sole property of the school. The IRS ruled that section 2503(e) applied to the entirety of the payments. This had the effect of permanently removing the funds from the grandparent's estate, even if the grandparent died before a grandchild completed education through Grade 12. The IRS distinguished the circumstances described in Treas. Reg. § 25.2503–6(c) Example 2. There the donor transferred to the school a pool of funds to pay tuition for the donor's grandchildren collectively. Because there was not a specific payment for a specific individual, the section 2503(e) exclusion did not apply.

Another advantage of section 2503(e) gifts is the zero inclusion ratio applied to such gifts for purposes of the tax on generation-skipping transfers. See I.R.C. § 2642(c)(3)(B). The result is that such gifts entirely escape the tax on generation-skipping transfers. See Chapter 29.

PROBLEM

Your client is Meghan Irving, an 80-year-old widow who owns property worth $15 million. Meghan is growing increasingly concerned about estate taxes and wishes to reduce the tax that would be imposed in the event of her death.

Meghan believes strongly in education, and she would like to provide funding to ensure that all her grandchildren will have access to higher education. Also, Meghan believes that private elementary and secondary schooling may be best for some of the grandchildren. She is willing to make gifts for the benefit of her grandchildren for this purpose. Meghan has seven grandchildren, ranging in age from two to 22 years.

What alternatives would you recommend to Meghan for accomplishing her purposes?

D. MARITAL DEDUCTION

The gift tax marital deduction, embodied in section 2523(a), provides an unlimited deduction for transfers between spouses during their lives. This reflects a policy judgment that spouses should be free to transfer their property between themselves as they think best, without unnecessary tax obstacles. In fact, so long as the transfer is between spouses, they need not even file a gift tax return. See I.R.C. § 6019(a)(2). Only when the property moves outside the marriage partners—typically to the children—is it subject to gift taxation.

The unlimited marital deduction is of relatively recent vintage, having been adopted in 1981. From 1948 through 1981 the marital deduction was in general limited to one-half of the property transferred. This arrangement was originally adopted in 1948, when the similar estate tax marital deduction and the income tax joint return for married couples were adopted. The common purpose of all three measures was to provide a rough kind of equality between married couples in common-law states and married couples in community property states.

In community property states, property covered by the community property law is treated as owned one-half by each spouse.[9] Therefore, community property spouses have a built-in tax benefit in that their estates (at least to the extent of their community property) are split equally between the spouses by operation of law.[10] The result of such a splitting of assets or income is a lower overall tax burden than if only one spouse had all the income or owned all the assets. The purpose of the marital deductions adopted in 1948 was to permit spouses in common law states to enjoy similar tax benefits.

The adoption of the unlimited marital deduction in 1981, however, reflected a purpose entirely different from that of the 1948 enactment. In 1981 Congress fully embraced the idea that no tax should be imposed until the property leaves the spouses.

Even after 1981, however, not every transfer between spouses qualifies for the marital deduction. Although a transfer in fee will always qualify, many transfers of less than a fee interest will not qualify because of violation of the terminable interest rule that is embodied in section 2523(b) and discussed in greater detail in Chapter 27 in the context of the estate tax.

The terminable interest rule reflects the fear that some transfers between spouses could be used to evade the estate tax. For example, assume that a wife gives her spouse a life estate in certain property, with remainder to the children. Assume further that the spouse's life estate has a current actuarial value equal to 90 percent of the full value of the property. If the transfer of the life estate to the spouse qualifies for the marital deduction, only 10 percent of the property is subject to tax at the

---

[9]   See, e.g., La. Civ. Code Ann. art. 2336 (2022); Nev. Rev. Stat. § 123.225(1) (2021); Wis. Stat. Ann. § 766.31 (West 2022).

[10]   See, e.g., Cal. Prob. Code § 100 (West 2022); N.M. Stat. Ann. § 45–2–807 (2022).

time of the gift; however, none of the property will be subject to tax at the spouse's death, because the spouse's ownership will cease at death.

To prevent such avoidance, section 2523(b) treats the spouse's life estate as a "terminable interest" that does not qualify for the marital deduction. Hence, the entire property transferred by the wife is subject to tax. The spouse's interest is nondeductible because it meets the tests stated in section 2523(b): (1) the spouse's interest will fail upon the occurrence of a contingency (death); (2) the wife has transferred an interest in the property (the remainder) to persons other than the spouse (the children); and (3) the persons other than the spouse (the children) will receive the property upon the occurrence of the contingency described in (1) (the spouse's death).

A major exception to the nondeductibility rule is the life estate with power of appointment, which has its counterpart in section 2056(b)(5) of the estate tax provisions. The estate tax rules are discussed in Chapter 27. The gift tax exception permits property to be placed in trust (or a similar arrangement) for the benefit of the donor's spouse, provided the donee spouse has an income interest for life and a power to appoint the property to the donee spouse or donee spouse's estate exercisable by will or during donee spouse's life, and under all conditions and events. I.R.C. § 2523(e).

Another exception to the terminable interest rule is available on an elective basis. If the donee spouse is entitled to all the income from the property throughout the donee spouse's life (payable no less frequently than annually) and no one has power to appoint any part of the property to a person other than the donee spouse, the donor may elect to treat the transfer as "qualified terminable interest property" (QTIP) that will qualify for the marital deduction. I.R.C. § 2523(f). If such an election is made, the property will be included in the donee spouse's gross estate at death pursuant to section 2044 unless the donee spouse gives away an interest in the property during the donee spouse's lifetime, in which case there will be a taxable gift under section 2519. The QTIP provision is important for an individual who may want his or her spouse to have the income benefits of the property without the right to determine the disposition of the property upon the donee spouse's death. This is especially useful in successive marriage situations. For example, a woman might wish to give the income from property to her second spouse for life while assuring that upon the second spouse's death the corpus would go to the children of her first marriage. The QTIP rules are examined more fully in Chapter 27 in the context of the estate tax.

The gift tax statute also provides an exception to the terminable interest rule for gifts made between spouses in joint tenancy or in tenancy by the entirety. I.R.C. § 2523(d). For example, a husband may get the benefit of the deduction when he buys stock and places it in joint tenancy with his spouse; the fact that he retains the right of severance or survivorship does not deprive the gift of the marital deduction.

In general, the gift tax marital deduction is not available if the transfer is to a spouse who is not a citizen of the United States. I.R.C. § 2523(i)(1). The annual exclusion, however, is raised to $100,000 (indexed) if the donee spouse is not a citizen. I.R.C. § 2523(i)(2). The indexed exclusion amount for 2023 is $175,000. Rev. Proc. 2022–38, 2022–45 I.R.B. 445.

Historically, the term "spouse" did not include a person married to an individual of the same sex pursuant to the Defense of Marriage Act which barred recognition of same-sex marriages for all purposes of federal law, including federal taxes. 1 U.S.C. Chap. 1, § 7. Therefore, a gift from one member of a same-sex couple to the other member did not qualify for the marital deduction. However, the constitutionality of the Defense of Marriage Act was resolved in United States v. Windsor.[11]

UNITED STATES V. WINDSOR
Supreme Court of the United States, 2013.
570 U.S. 744.

JUSTICE KENNEDY delivered the opinion of the Court.

Two women then resident in New York were married in a lawful ceremony in Ontario, Canada, in 2007. Edith Windsor and Thea Spyer returned to their home in New York City. When Spyer died in 2009, she left her entire estate to Windsor. Windsor sought to claim the estate tax exemption for surviving spouses. She was barred from doing so, however, by a federal law, the Defense of Marriage Act, which excludes a same-sex partner from the definition of "spouse" as that term is used in federal statutes. Windsor paid the taxes but filed suit to challenge the constitutionality of this provision. The United States District Court and the Court of Appeals ruled that this portion of the statute is unconstitutional and ordered the United States to pay Windsor a refund. This Court granted certiorari and now affirms the judgment in Windsor's favor.

I

In 1996, as some States were beginning to consider the concept of same-sex marriage, see, e.g., Baehr v. Lewin, 74 Haw. 530, 852 P. 2d 44 (1993), and before any State had acted to permit it, Congress enacted the Defense of Marriage Act (DOMA), 110 Stat. 2419. DOMA contains two operative sections: Section 2, which has not been challenged here, allows States to refuse to recognize same-sex marriages performed under the laws of other States. See 28 U. S. C. § 1738C.

---

[11] 570 U.S. 744, 133 S. Ct. 2675 (2013).

Section 3 is at issue here. It amends the Dictionary Act in Title 1, § 7, of the United States Code to provide a federal definition of "marriage" and "spouse." Section 3 of DOMA provides as follows:

"In determining the meaning of any Act of Congress, or of any ruling, regulation, or interpretation of the various administrative bureaus and agencies of the United States, the word 'marriage' means only a legal union between one man and one woman as husband and wife, and the word 'spouse' refers only to a person of the opposite sex who is a husband or a wife." 1 U. S. C. § 7.

The definitional provision does not by its terms forbid States from enacting laws permitting same-sex marriages or civil unions or providing state benefits to residents in that status. The enactment's comprehensive definition of marriage for purposes of all federal statutes and other regulations or directives covered by its terms, however, does control over 1,000 federal laws in which marital or spousal status is addressed as a matter of federal law. See GAO, D. Shah, Defense of Marriage Act: Update to Prior Report 1 (GAO–04–353R, 2004).

Edith Windsor and Thea Spyer met in New York City in 1963 and began a long-term relationship. Windsor and Spyer registered as domestic partners when New York City gave that right to same-sex couples in 1993. Concerned about Spyer's health, the couple made the 2007 trip to Canada for their marriage, but they continued to reside in New York City. The State of New York deems their Ontario marriage to be a valid one. See 699 F. 3d 169, 177–178 (CA2 2012).

Spyer died in February 2009, and left her entire estate to Windsor. Because DOMA denies federal recognition to same-sex spouses, Windsor did not qualify for the marital exemption from the federal estate tax, which excludes from taxation "any interest in property which passes or has passed from the decedent to his surviving spouse." 26 U. S. C. § 2056(a). Windsor paid $363,053 in estate taxes and sought a refund. The Internal Revenue Service denied the refund, concluding that, under DOMA, Windsor was not a "surviving spouse." Windsor commenced this refund suit in the United States District Court for the Southern District of New York. She contended that DOMA violates the guarantee of equal protection, as applied to the Federal Government through the Fifth Amendment.

* * *

III

When at first Windsor and Spyer longed to marry, neither New York nor any other State granted them that right. After waiting some years, in 2007 they traveled to Ontario to be married there. It seems fair to conclude that, until recent years, many citizens had not even considered the possibility that two persons of the same sex might aspire to occupy the same status and dignity as that of a man and woman in lawful marriage. For marriage between a man and a woman no doubt had been thought of by most people as essential to the very definition of that term and to its role and function throughout the history of civilization. That belief, for many who long have held it, became even more urgent, more cherished when challenged. For others, however, came the beginnings of a new perspective, a new insight. Accordingly some States concluded that same-sex marriage ought to be given recognition and validity in the law for those same-sex couples who wish to define themselves by their commitment to each other. The limitation of lawful marriage to heterosexual couples, which for centuries had been deemed both necessary and fundamental, came to be seen in New York and certain other States as an unjust exclusion.

* * *

* * * State laws defining and regulating marriage, of course, must respect the constitutional rights of persons, see, e.g., Loving v. Virginia, 388 U. S. 1 (1967); but, subject to those guarantees, "regulation of domestic relations" is "an area that has long been regarded as a virtually exclusive province of the States." Sosna v. Iowa, 419 U. S. 393, 404 (1975).

* * *

Consistent with this allocation of authority, the Federal Government, through our history, has deferred to state-law policy decisions with respect to domestic relations. In De Sylva v. Ballentine, 351 U. S. 570 (1956), for example, the Court held that, "[t]o decide who is the widow or widower of a deceased author, or who are his executors or next of kin," under the Copyright Act "requires a reference to the law of the State which created those legal relationships" because "there is no federal law of domestic relations." Id., at 580. In order to respect this principle, the federal courts, as a general rule, do not adjudicate issues of marital status even when there might otherwise be a basis for federal jurisdiction. See Ankenbrandt v. Richards, 504 U. S. 689, 703 (1992). Federal courts will not hear divorce and custody cases even if they arise in diversity because of "the virtually exclusive primacy . . . of the in the regulation of domestic relations." Id., at 714 (Blackmun, J., concurring in judgment).

The significance of state responsibilities for the definition and regulation of marriage dates to the Nation's beginning; for "when the Constitution was adopted the common understanding was that the domestic relations of husband and wife and parent and child were matters reserved to the States." Ohio ex rel. Popovici v. Agler, 280 U. S. 379, 383–384 (1930). Marriage laws vary in some respects from State to State. For example, the required minimum age is 16 in Vermont, but only 13 in New Hampshire. Compare Vt. Stat. Ann., Tit. 18, § 5142 (2012), with N. H. Rev. Stat. Ann. § 457:4 (West Supp. 2012). Likewise the permissible degree of consanguinity can vary (most States permit first cousins to marry, but a handful—such as Iowa and Washington, see Iowa Code § 595.19 (2009); Wash. Rev. Code § 26.04.020 (2012)—prohibit the practice). But these rules are in every event consistent within each State.

The Federal Government uses this state-defined class for the opposite purpose—to impose restrictions and disabilities. That result requires this Court now to address whether the resulting injury and indignity is a deprivation of an essential part of the liberty protected by the Fifth Amendment. What the State of New York treats as alike the federal law deems unlike by a law designed to injure the same class the State seeks to protect.

* * *

IV

* * * The responsibility of the States for the regulation of domestic relations is an important indicator of the substantial societal impact the State's classifications have in the daily lives and customs of its people. DOMA's unusual deviation from the usual tradition of recognizing and accepting state definitions of marriage here operates to deprive same-sex couples of the benefits and responsibilities that come with the federal recognition of their marriages. This is strong evidence of a law having the purpose and effect of disapproval of that class. The avowed purpose and practical effect of the law here in question are to impose a disadvantage, a separate status, and so a stigma upon all who enter into same-sex marriages made lawful by the unquestioned authority of the States.

* * *

DOMA's operation in practice confirms this purpose. When New York adopted a law to permit same-sex marriage, it sought to eliminate inequality; but DOMA frustrates that objective through a system-wide enactment with no identified connection to any particular area of federal law. DOMA writes inequality into the entire United States Code. The particular case at hand concerns the estate tax, but DOMA is more than a simple determination of what should or should not be allowed as an estate tax refund. Among the over 1,000 statutes and numerous federal regulations that DOMA controls are laws pertaining to Social Security, housing, taxes, criminal sanctions, copyright, and veterans' benefits.

DOMA's principal effect is to identify a subset of state-sanctioned marriages and make them unequal. The principal purpose is to impose inequality, not for other reasons like governmental efficiency. Responsibilities, as well as rights, enhance the dignity and integrity of the person. And DOMA contrives to deprive some couples married under the laws of their State, but not other couples, of both rights and responsibilities. By creating two contradictory marriage regimes within the same State, DOMA forces same-sex couples to live as married for the purpose of state law but unmarried for the purpose of federal law, thus diminishing the stability and predictability of basic personal relations the State has found it proper to acknowledge and protect. By this dynamic DOMA undermines both the public and private significance of state-sanctioned same-sex marriages; for it tells those couples, and all the world, that their otherwise valid marriages are unworthy of federal recognition. This places same-sex couples in an unstable position of being in a second-tier marriage. The differentiation demeans the couple, whose moral and sexual choices the Constitution protects, see Lawrence, 539 U. S. 558, and whose relationship the State has sought to dignify. And it humiliates tens of thousands of children now being raised by same-sex couples. The law in question makes it even more difficult for the children to understand the integrity and closeness of their own family and its concord with other families in their community and in their daily lives.

* * *

The power the Constitution grants it also restrains. And though Congress has great authority to design laws to fit its own conception of sound national policy, it cannot deny the liberty protected by the Due Process Clause of the Fifth Amendment.

What has been explained to this point should more than suffice to establish that the principal purpose and the necessary effect of this law are to demean those persons who are in a lawful same-sex marriage. This requires the Court to hold, as it now does, that DOMA is unconstitutional as a deprivation of the liberty of the person protected by the Fifth Amendment of the Constitution.

The liberty protected by the Fifth Amendment's Due Process Clause contains within it the prohibition against denying to any person the equal protection of the laws. [citations omitted]. While the Fifth Amendment itself withdraws from Government the power to degrade or demean in the way this law does, the equal protection guarantee of the Fourteenth Amendment makes that Fifth Amendment right all the more specific and all the better understood and preserved.

The class to which DOMA directs its restrictions and restraints are those persons who are joined in same-sex marriages made lawful by the State. DOMA singles out a class of persons deemed by a State entitled to recognition and protection to enhance their own liberty. It imposes a disability on the class by refusing to acknowledge a status the State finds to be dignified and proper. DOMA instructs all federal officials, and indeed all persons with whom same-sex couples interact, including their own children, that their marriage is less worthy than the marriages of others. The federal statute is invalid, for no legitimate purpose overcomes the purpose and effect to disparage and to injure those whom the State, by its marriage laws, sought to protect in personhood and dignity. By seeking to displace this protection and treating those persons as living in marriages less respected than others, the federal statute is in violation of the Fifth Amendment. This opinion and its holding are confined to those lawful marriages.

The judgment of the Court of Appeals for the Second Circuit is affirmed.

It is so ordered.

NOTE

1.   In Revenue Ruling 2013–17 C.B. 201, the IRS confirmed its position that the validity of a couple's marriage is determined by the state in which it was entered rather than the domicile of the couple. In the ruling, the IRS noted that significant administrative inconvenience would arise if the domicile of the couple controlled because "the attribution of property interests could change when a same-sex couple move[d] from one state to another with different marriage recognition rules." The IRS noted that a same-sex couple that entered into a registered domestic partnership or civil union is not treated as a marriage for federal tax purposes. However, as noted in the ruling, a common law marriage is recognized for federal tax purposes if it was entered into a jurisdiction that recognized common law marriages. See Rev. Rul. 58–66, 1958–1 C.B. 60.

2.   The IRS issued Notice 2017–15, 2017–6 I.R.B. 83, to permit a same-sex individual to file an amended gift or estate tax return to claim the marital deduction for a gift or bequest that the individual made to a same-sex spouse and recalculate the applicable exclusion amount that had been applied to the transfer. However, the individual is not entitled to claim a refund based on the recalculated applicable exclusion amount if the statute of limitations has already expired.

E. CHARITABLE DEDUCTION

Like the income tax and the estate tax, the gift tax has a generous deduction for contributions to charity. See I.R.C. § 2522(a). The deductions for gifts to charity under the estate and gift taxes are unlimited, whereas the charitable deduction for income taxes under section 170 has specific percentage limitations correlated to adjusted gross income. Nevertheless, all three taxes define the eligible charitable recipients in virtually identical language. I.R.C. §§ 170(c)(2), 2055(a)(2), and 2522(a)(2).

If property is given outright to charity, the gift tax charitable deduction is allowed for the entire value of the property. However, if less than all interests in the property are given to charity, the deduction will be limited to the value of the charity's interest and in some cases may be entirely disallowed.

Partial interest gifts provide a fruitful opportunity for tax avoidance. For example, assume that the donor gives a life estate in certain property to his son while giving the remainder interest in the same property to charity. Under ordinary valuation principles the donor would be permitted to deduct the current actuarial value of the charitable remainder. However, the property may be a wasting asset, such as a mineral property. In that event, the son may receive substantially all the value of the property as income during his lifetime, leaving little or nothing for the charity.

The remedy is a very tightly defined set of requirements that must be met to obtain a gift tax deduction for a gift of a partial interest gift to charity; no deduction is allowed unless one of the specified arrangements is used. I.R.C. § 2522(c). These rules are designed to assure that the charity will in fact receive value equivalent to the deduction allowed to the donor. These limitations are more fully explored in Chapter 26, which addresses the similar limitation on charitable deductions for estate tax purposes.

Special rules apply to charitable gifts of fractional interests in tangible personal property, such as art works. See I.R.C. § 2522(e).

CHAPTER 8

GIFT TAX RETURNS AND ADMINISTRATIVE REQUIREMENTS

■ ■ ■

A. RETURN REQUIREMENTS

The gift tax is imposed on a calendar-year basis. The gift tax return must be filed by April 15 of the calendar year after the year in which a gift occurs, and the tax must be paid in full with the return. I.R.C. §§ 6075(b)(1) and 6151(a). During the period 1971–1981, gift tax returns were required to be filed quarterly. Prior to 1971 returns were filed annually.

The general rule is that a return must be filed if any "transfer by gift" is made during the calendar year. However, there are four broad exceptions. I.R.C. § 6019. No return is required if all transfers fall within one or more of the following categories:

1. Annual exclusion allowed under I.R.C. § 2503(b).

2. Educational and medical expenses allowed under I.R.C. § 2503(e).

3. Transfers for which the I.R.C. § 2523 marital deduction is allowed (unless a QTIP election is made).

4. Certain transfers for which the I.R.C. § 2522 charitable deduction is allowed.

The donor has primary liability for payment of the gift tax. I.R.C. § 2502(c). The donee, however, is secondarily liable if the donor does not pay. I.R.C. §§ 6324(b) and 6901(a)(1)(A)(iii).

Form 709, United States Gift (and Generation-Skipping Transfer) Tax Return, must be used to report gifts. Form 709 is available at the IRS website: https://www.irs.gov/.

B. SPOUSAL GIFT SPLITTING

Section 2513 permits spouses to treat gifts by one spouse as if made one-half by each spouse. This permits spouses to take full advantage of the exclusions and unified credits available to both of them, although only one spouse actually makes gifts. For example, assume that the section 2503(b) annual exclusion is $17,000, a wife has substantial property, and her spouse has little property. The wife gives $34,000 to her daughter, but her spouse gives nothing to the daughter. The wife and spouse can elect to treat the transfer as a $17,000 gift by each of them for purposes of the gift tax. This qualifies the transfer for the annual exclusion available to each spouse and eliminates any consumption of the wife's unified credit. Gifts cannot be split unless a return is filed. I.R.C. § 2513(b); Treas. Reg. § 25.2513–2. Therefore, a return must be filed even if the annual exclusion will cover all gifts after splitting.

Gift splitting and filing of a return may be avoided if a donor spouse makes an outright transfer of money or property to the donee spouse, followed by the donee spouse's transfer of the money or property to a third party. If the donee spouse has unrestricted dominion over the property and the donee spouse's transfer to a third party is in fact independent of the transfer from the donor spouse, each spouse can use his or her annual exclusion to shelter the transfer. As a result, no return is required. The unlimited gift tax marital deduction prevents any tax liability with respect to the gift between the spouses. I.R.C. § 2523(a).

Gift splitting is available only if each spouse is a citizen or resident of the United States. I.R.C. § 2513(a)(1).

The benefits of gift splitting are not limited to the annual exclusion. Gifts that are split under section 2513 are treated as split for all purposes of the gift tax. I.R.C. § 2513(a)(1). For example, gift splitting can be used to take advantage of the nontransferring spouse's section 2505 unified credit. In addition, gift splitting under section 2513 is honored for purposes of the tax on generation-skipping transfers, discussed in Chapter 29. I.R.C. § 2652(a)(2). Therefore, gift splitting can be used to take full advantage of the generation-skipping tax exemption available to each spouse. I.R.C. § 2631(a).

Gift splitting is not without cost. A nontransferring spouse who consents to split gifts undertakes joint and several liability for the entire gift tax liability of the donor spouse for the year in which gifts are split. I.R.C. § 2513(d).

C. STATUTE OF LIMITATIONS

As with other taxes, the general statute of limitations requires that the United States assess additional gift tax within three years after the return is filed. I.R.C. § 6501(a). Likewise, the tax may be assessed at any time if the return is false or fraudulent with intent to evade tax, there is a willful attempt to defeat or evade the tax, or no return is filed. I.R.C. § 6501(c)(1), (2), and (3).

A stricter and special rule, however, applies only to the gift tax. If a gift required to be shown on a return is not so shown, gift tax may be imposed at any time. This special rule, however, does not apply to any item that is disclosed on the return or an attachment "in a manner adequate to apprise the Secretary of the nature of such item." I.R.C. § 6501(c)(9). This rule gives great importance to full disclosure of gifts. First, if there is adequate disclosure, the three-year statute of limitations *will* apply, and the IRS cannot seek to impose additional tax after that time. Second, if there is adequate disclosure, with the result that the three-year statute applies, the IRS cannot after three years increase the value of the gift for purposes of increasing the tax on later transfers. For example, assume that the basic exclusion amount is $12,920,000 and that the donor files a gift tax return showing a gift of property valued at $10,920,000. If the donor later makes a gift of $2,000,000, the IRS might seek to raise the value of the earlier gift above $10,920,000, thereby raising total gifts above $12,920,000, resulting in taxation of the excess. If there was adequate disclosure on the return reporting the first gift and three years have passed, the IRS cannot raise the $10,920,000 valuation of the first gift. The same principle applies to the estate tax. Assume again a gift of $10,920,000 and that the donor later dies with a taxable estate of $2,000,000. The IRS might seek to raise the value of the $10,920,000 gift, producing a taxable amount in excess of $12,920,000 for purposes of section 2001(b)(1), thereby producing an estate tax liability. If there was adequate disclosure of the gift and three years have passed since the return was filed, the IRS is barred from raising the value of the gift for purposes of the estate tax. I.R.C. §§ 2001(f), 2504(c), and 6501(c)(9).

Because adequate disclosure is necessary to assure the benefit of the three-year statute of limitations, the required level of disclosure is a crucial issue. The Treasury expectations in this regard are set forth in Treas. Reg. § 301.6501(c)–1(f). Typically, the central issue is that of valuation. If an independent appraisal is not provided, the donor must provide extensive information on the method used to value the asset transferred, including a full explanation of any discounts taken. Treas. Reg. § 301.6501(c)–1(f)(2)(iv). If an independent appraisal is provided, there will be adequate disclosure if the appraisal provides the extensive valuation data described in Treas. Reg. § 301.6501(c)–1(f)(3)(ii).

As explained in Chapter 3, the IRS may seek to treat as a gift any transaction in which a disparity of value is present. For example, if a parent's stock is redeemed by a corporation in which a child has substantial ownership, the IRS may argue that the redemption price is lower than the true value of the stock redeemed, creating an indirect gift from parent to child. The regulations state that in the case of a transaction "in the ordinary course of operating a business," such as payment of salary to a family member, adequate disclosure is provided through simple reporting of the transaction on the *income* tax return. As to other transactions, however, fuller disclosure is required. Treas. Reg. § 301.6501(c)–1(f)(4). It seems likely that the redemption described above would not be regarded as being "in the ordinary course of business." Therefore, although the redemption could be reported on the income tax (rather than gift tax) return, full disclosure should be made at the level that would be required on a gift tax return, as described above.

D. GIFT TAX PROBLEM

This year Margaret Brown made the following transfers:

1. She gave publicly traded securities worth $6,017,000 to her daughter, Alexis.

2. She gave $10,000 in cash to her son, Brian, who was a full-time student at a university. Brian used the $10,000 for books, automobile expenses, and entertainment. In addition, she paid directly to the university $30,000 for Brian's tuition and $14,000 for his room and board in a university dormitory.

3. She gave a painting to an art museum that was a qualified section 501(c)(3) organization. She obtained an appraisal valuing the painting at $60,000. Margaret's basis for the painting was $40,000.

4. She transferred $5,000,000 in cash to the Ninth National Bank of Nashville, Tennessee, as trustee of the Georgia Smith Trust. The instrument creating the Georgia Smith Trust provides that Georgia Smith is to receive all income from the trust until Georgia's death, at which time the principal is to be returned to Margaret or her estate. Georgia, who is not related to Margaret, was age 51 at the time of the gift. Assume that the I.R.C. § 7520 rate at the time of the transfer is 4%, with the result that the value of Georgia's life income interest in the $5,000,000 gift made this year is .64404 of the principal of $5,000,000, or $3,320,200, pursuant to Table S (the life estate factor is based on Treasury's proposed actuarial tables issued on May 5, 2022).

5. Margaret gave a parcel of real estate to her spouse, Imani. Margaret and Imani entered into a same-sex marriage in 2015. They were married in a lawful ceremony. Margaret had bought the land in 1995 for $600,000, and its value at the time of the gift was $900,000.

6. Margaret transferred $1,000,000 to a trust with all income to be distributed to her sister, Rebecca, for 10 years. At the end of the 10-year term, the trust would terminate, and the corpus would be distributed to Rebecca. Margaret was

designated as the trustee and retained the right to accumulate income and add it to the corpus.

7. Margaret transferred an office building worth $2,000,000 to a trust with her brother, Andrew, named as the income beneficiary. Under the trust, income was payable to Andrew for life and upon his death, the trust would terminate, and the corpus would be distributed to Margaret's children, equally. Margaret was designated as the trustee. The trustee had the power with Andrew's consent to accumulate the income and add it to the corpus. With Andrew's consent, Margaret decided to accumulate the income during the current year.

8. Margaret owned a baseball that Mickey Mantle had autographed. It was a ball from Mantle's last game as a member of the New York Yankees, and it was worth $2,000,000. Because her brother, Tom, was a huge fan of the Yankees, she knew that he would cherish the baseball forever. She adored her brother, but when she attempted to give the baseball to him, Tom stated that he felt uncomfortable accepting it without paying her something for it. After much resistance, Margaret finally accepted $500,000 for the baseball.

9. Last year, Margaret gave her daughter, Denise, an apartment building worth $3,034,000. No gift tax was paid. Imani agreed to split this gift with Margaret. Neither Margaret nor Imani made any additional gifts during that year.

Determine Margaret's gift tax liability, if any, for this year. Assume that Imani will not split this year's gifts with Margaret. Assume that both Imani and Margaret are United States citizens. Assume also that the section 2503(b) annual exclusion is $17,000 for each tax year.

PART 3

VALUATION

■ ■ ■

CHAPTER 9

GENERAL PRINCIPLES OF VALUATION

■ ■ ■

A. GENERAL RULES

The valuation process is crucial to determination of the estate, gift, and generation-skipping taxes. It is the value of the property (or the interest in the property) transferred (or deemed to be transferred) that is subjected to the tax rates imposed by the three taxes, i.e., section 2001 for the estate tax, section 2501 for the gift tax, and section 2601 for the generation-skipping tax. Surprisingly, the statute itself is not helpful in addressing the valuation issue; the statute appears to be written on the assumption that the term "value" is self-defining. See, for example, how the term "value" is used in section 2031(a) for the estate tax, section 2512(a) for the gift tax, and sections 2621, 2622, and 2623 for the generation-skipping tax.

Fortunately, the Regulations are much more specific. The estate tax regulations equate "value" to "fair market value," which in turn is defined as "the price at which the property would change hands between a willing buyer and a willing seller, neither being under any compulsion to buy or to sell and both having reasonable knowledge of relevant facts." Treas. Reg. § 20.2031–1(b). There is a similar definition under the gift tax regulations. See Treas. Reg. § 25.2512–1. The Regulations then present special rules for the valuation of certain types of property; for example, stocks and bonds (Treas. Regs. §§ 20.2031–2 and 25.2512–2), interests in businesses (Treas. Regs. §§ 20.2031–3 and 25.2512–3), household effects (Treas. Reg. § 20.2031–6), annuities, life estates, terms for years, remainders and reversions (Treas. Regs. §§ 20.2031–7 and 25.2512–5), and life insurance contracts (Treas. Regs. §§ 20.2031–8 and 25.2512–6). If the special rules of valuation are not applicable, the general principles of valuation set forth in Treas. Regs. §§ 20.2031–1 and 25.2512–1 govern.

The valuation principles under the generation-skipping tax are the same as those employed under the gift and estate taxes. The generation-skipping tax regulations incorporate the gift and estate tax valuation principles by reference. See Treas. Reg. § 26.2642–2(a).

Valuation principles and techniques developed for purposes other than the gift and estate tax are often employed. For example, the concept of valuation based on "highest and best use" is applied. Although land may be used exclusively for agricultural purposes at the time of the decedent's death, the presence of residential development potential requires that the land be valued at its residential development price rather than the lower agricultural value (unless the special valuation method described in Chapter 13 is available). Estate of Pattison v. Commissioner, T.C. Memo. 1990–428, 60 T.C.M. (CCH) 471 (1990). However, in Estate of Pulling v. Commissioner, T.C. Memo. 2015–134, 110 T.C.M. (CCH) 93 (2015), the decedent owned three parcels of land and a 28% interest in the trust that owned two additional parcels. The parcels of land were contiguous. The land was used for agricultural purposes. The court refused to value the land as a residential development, its highest and best use. The court determined that the land owned outright by the decedent should be valued separately from the land owned by trust. Expert witnesses agreed that if the decedent's separately owned parcels and the trust parcels could be consolidated, the highest and best use would be residential development. Without consolidation, residential development of the decedent's land would not have been economically feasible. The court reasoned that it could consolidate the land for purposes of valuation if it was reasonably likely that the land would be consolidated in the reasonably near future. As a question of fact, the court concluded that consolidation was unlikely even though the decedent owned a large minority interest in the trust. Therefore, the court valued the land owned by the decedent as separate property and determined that residential development was not the highest and best use of the decedent's land.

The "willing buyer-willing seller" concept forms the foundation for all transfer tax valuation. Although numerous special rules have been developed for application to specific types of property, all are necessarily founded on a free market approach: how would independent actors value the property for purposes of purchase or sale? As more fully explained in Chapter 11, this inevitably leads to their conclusion that the hypothetical buyer and seller are anonymous, i.e., entirely unrelated to the transferor and transferee. The characteristics of the actual buyer and seller may not reflect those of the hypothetical buyer and seller.

The hypothetical "willing buyer" is assumed to have full knowledge of the relevant facts, which may increase or decrease the fair market value. In Estate of Crossmore v. Commissioner, T.C. Memo. 1988–494, 56 T.C.M. (CCH) 483 (1988), a major asset of the decedent's estate was a legacy from the decedent's aunt, whose will had not yet been admitted to probate when the decedent died. Because the aunt bequeathed her entire residuary estate to the decedent and the decedent had acted as a close personal adviser to the aunt during the aunt's declining years, it appeared likely that the aunt's will and the legacy to the decedent would be contested. The Tax Court concluded that the value of the legacy to the decedent should be discounted accordingly.

The "willing buyer-willing seller" rule has the effect of giving value for gift or estate tax purposes to rights that have accrued but are not yet realized. In this sense, the gift and estate taxes apply an accrual accounting approach, without regard to whether the donor or decedent is a cash or accrual taxpayer for income tax purposes. For example, if the decedent owns a bond, the estate tax value of the bond at the date of death includes interest accrued to the date of death because that is how the marketplace would value the bond if it were sold on that date. The accrued interest is added to the principal value of the bond although the interest may not be payable until after the decedent's death. Priv. Ltr. Rul. 9047062.

The same accrual principle applies to compensation for services. Assume that the decedent receives a monthly salary of $5,000 paid at the end of each month, and that the decedent dies after one-half of a month has elapsed. The accrued right to $2,500 is included as an asset of the decedent's gross estate for estate tax purposes. This is so without regard to the accounting method the decedent used for income tax purpose. The treatment of the accrued salary for income tax purposes, however, is entirely different. If the decedent is a cash basis taxpayer, none of the accrued salary is includible in the decedent's income for the period ending with his death; this is so because the decedent did not actually receive the salary prior to his death. Instead, the $2,500 will constitute income to the decedent's estate when actually received by the estate. Under section 691 the $2,500 will constitute "income in respect of a decedent" and will be treated as salary income when received by the estate. This rule is explored in Chapter 32.

The gift and estate taxes reach far, and the courts have supported the IRS in taxing any asset to which the real world would attach economic value. The degree to which this principle has been carried is illustrated by Estate of Andrews v. United States, 850 F. Supp. 1279 (E.D.Va.1994), in which the decedent's very name was taxed. The decedent's name was Virginia Andrews, and she was an internationally known, best-selling author. Andrews' publisher proposed to continue publication of books that would be attributed to Andrews, while in fact ghostwritten by others. This required that Andrews' executor and legatees consent to use of Andrews' name. The executor had not treated Andrews' name as an asset of the estate for estate tax purposes, but the IRS did so. The court agreed with the IRS, finding that the amount to be received under a book contract signed by Andrews several weeks before her death could be used as evidence of the amount a publisher would pay for the right to use Andrews' name. The IRS argued that Andrews' name had a value of $1,244,910, but the court concluded that the realistic value was only $703,500—the amount on which the estate was ultimately taxed. See the further discussion of *Andrews* in Chapter 15 related to property included in a decedent's gross estate.

B. VALUATION DATE

For gift tax purposes, the valuation date is the date of transfer without any exceptions; this rule is set forth in the statute. I.R.C. § 2512(a). For estate tax purposes, all property is valued at the date of death, pursuant to section 2031(a), unless the alternate valuation date is elected as discussed in the next section.

The date of death valuation rule applies not only to property owned outright by the decedent but also to property that is included in the decedent's gross estate but not in fact owned by the decedent at death. For example, assume that ten years prior to her death the decedent transferred property to a trust as to which she retained a right to control beneficial enjoyment, thereby causing inclusion of the trust assets in her gross estate under section 2036, discussed in Chapter 18. The trust assets will be included in the decedent's gross estate at their value on the date of the decedent's death—not the value at the time the assets were originally transferred to the trust. Treas. Reg. § 20.2031–1(b).

Although it is clear that valuation is to be determined as of the date of gift (for purposes of the gift tax) or the date of death (for purposes of the estate tax), the statute does not state whether subsequent events can be considered. The Supreme Court addressed this issue at an early date in Ithaca Trust Co. v. United States, 279 U.S. 151 (1929). The decedent husband had granted a life estate to his wife, followed by a remainder to charity. The wife died before the estate tax return for the husband's estate was filed, and the executor of the husband's estate sought to value the charitable remainder in light of the wife's premature death—rather than according to the Treasury's actuarial tables, which forecast a longer life for the wife. Justice Holmes, writing for the Court, resoundingly repudiated consideration of subsequent events:

> [T]he value of the thing to be taxed must be estimated as of the time when the act is done. But the value of property at a given time depends upon the relative intensity of the social desire for it at that time, expressed in the money that it would bring in the market. . . .Like all values, as the word is used by the law, it depends largely on more or less certain prophecies of the future, and the value is no less real at that time if later the prophecy turns out false than when it comes out true. . . .Tempting as it is to correct uncertain probabilities by the now certain fact, we are of the opinion that it cannot be done, but that the value of the wife's life interest must be estimated by the mortality tables.[1]

The *Ithaca Trust* rule, however, does not prevent consideration of all subsequent events. For example, in Morrissey v. Commissioner, 243 F.3d

---

[1]   279 U.S. at 155.

1145 (9th Cir. 2001), the decedent's stock was sold one and two months after the alternate valuation date, which the estate had elected. The Ninth Circuit viewed these sales as credible evidence of the value on the alternate valuation date. In Estate of Scull v. Commissioner, T.C. Memo. 1994–211, 67 T.C.M. (CCH) 2953 (1994), the decedent owned artwork that was auctioned nearly 11 months after death. The court concluded that the auction prices provided the best evidence of value, but the court reduced the auction prices by 15%, representing appreciation that had occurred in the art market during the 11 months after death. Finally, in Gettysburg National Bank v. United States, 92–2 USTC ¶ 60,108 (M.D. Pa. 1992), the property in question was sold 16 months after death. The court held that the sale price was relevant in proving fair market value on the date of death because there had been no material change in the property or the market during the sixteen months after the death.

The distinction between *Ithaca Trust* on the one hand, and *Morrissey, Scull,* and *Gettysburg* on the other, is crucial. In *Ithaca Trust* an independent and unforeseen event—the wife's death—had occurred to change the value of the life estate after the death of the decedent. In *Morrisey, Scull,* and *Gettysburg,* by contrast, the post-death sales were not events that changed the value of the assets. The sales were, instead, simply *evidence* of value. Such evidence must of course be considered in the light of events that occur after the date of death and before the date of sale. For example, if the general market for similar assets rises significantly between the date of death and the sale, the value indicated by the sale price will be too high and should be adjusted downward. This is exactly what the court did in *Scull,* taking into account an independent event—the 15% percent appreciation in the art market between the date of death and the sale.

Significantly, the Ninth Circuit in Dieringer v. Commissioner, 917 F.3d 1135 (2019), stated that deductions were valued separately from the valuation of the gross estate. Id. at 1142. It also stated that *Ithaca Trust* did not "set in stone" the date of death as the date of valuing assets for purposes of a deduction and prohibited developing an estate plan that would "game the system and guarantee a charitable deduction that [was] larger than the amount actually given to charity." Id. at 1143–1144. Hence, in order to prevent abuse caused by the executor's manipulation of the charitable deduction amount, the court concluded that the date of death value did not apply where the estate had claimed an $18,205,476 charitable deduction based on the date of death value of assets, but the charity received assets worth only $6,434,578. Id. at 1145.

C. ALTERNATE VALUATION DATE

In the case of the estate tax, section 2032 permits election of an alternate valuation date. This provision permits the executor to elect on the original estate tax return to value the gross estate assets as of the date exactly six months after the date of death. The purpose of this section when originally enacted in 1935 was to permit estates that had shrunk in value during the Great Depression to use the lower values that might prevail one year after the date of death. With the 1970 revenue legislation, which accelerated the payment of the estate and gift taxes, the optional date was changed to six months from the date of death.

Although the alternate valuation date was designed to prevent imposition of an excessively high estate tax, some taxpayers sought to use it instead to reduce income taxes. If the alternate valuation date is elected, the estate's basis for the assets is the value on that date, not the date of death. I.R.C. § 1014(a)(2). An executor might well wish to elect the alternate valuation date because of *higher* values on that date if the income tax advantages of a higher basis more than offset the increase in estate tax caused by the election. For example, if the election of the alternate valuation date raises the estate tax payable by only $50,000, but the result is an increase in the basis of estate assets by $400,000, the prospective income tax saving might be greater than the estate tax cost of the election. Such a strategy is especially attractive if the executor expects the major estate assets to be sold soon and if the estate tax liability will be low in any event.

Because Congress viewed this tactic as a perversion of the purpose of section 2032, it adopted a rule limiting the alternate valuation date election to circumstances in which the election produces both a decrease in the value of the gross estate and a decrease in the sum of the estate tax and the generation-skipping tax that will be imposed with respect to the decedent's estate. I.R.C. § 2032(c). Although this change restricts the election to circumstances in which estate values decline, the executor should nevertheless continue to weigh both the income and estate tax effects of the election. While electing the alternate valuation date may lower the estate tax liability, the estate tax saving may be less than the additional income tax liability caused by the resulting lower basis.

The alternate valuation date election, if made, applies to all assets of the estate; one cannot "pick and choose" the assets to be valued on the alternate date. Nor does the election provide an opportunity to redetermine what property is includible in the gross estate; inclusion of property in the gross estate is invariably made as of the date of death and is unaffected by subsequent events, whether or not the optional date has been elected. The election of the alternate date merely allows a different time for valuation of the property that is a part of the gross estate as determined at the date of death.

If the election is made, property sold, distributed, or otherwise disposed of prior to the alternate valuation date is valued as of the date of sale, distribution, or other disposition. I.R.C. § 2032(a)(1).

The alternate valuation date election is intended to permit reflection of declining market values during the six months after death. For example, a stock selling for $80 per share on the date of death might be selling at $45 per share six months later. If the alternate valuation date election is made, the $45 per share price is used.

There is a special rule, however, for assets that decline in value, not by reason of changes in the market, but because of the inherent character of the asset. This rule applies to assets that decline in value because of "mere lapse of time." I.R.C. § 2032(a)(3). An example of such property is a patent, which by its nature has a limited life under patent law. A term for years is a further example. Valuing such items on the alternate date without adjustment would allow the natural and inevitable decline in value of such properties to reduce the estate tax even though there is no general decline in market valuation of the underlying property. Accordingly, § 2032(a)(3) requires that such property be valued as of the date of death, with adjustment for any difference in value on the alternate date not attributable to mere lapse of time. Treas. Reg. § 20.2032–1(f) provides illustrations of the treatment of such property, such as life estates, remainders, and patents, under the "mere lapse of time" rule. But there remain difficult valuation issues, as illustrated by the following authority.

REVENUE RULING 63–52
1963–1 C.B. 173.

Advice has been requested whether the increase in the value of certain life insurance policies, by reason of the death of the insured during the alternate valuation period, would constitute "included property" for purposes of valuing the gross estate of the deceased beneficiary under the alternate valuation provisions of section 2032 of the Internal Revenue Code of 1954.

Among the assets of a decedent, at the time of his death, were several insurance policies on the life of another person. The decedent was the owner and beneficiary of these policies. Within one year after the decedent's death, the insured also died. The estate of the decedent, to which his interest in these policies had passed, became entitled to and thereafter collected the death proceeds of the policies. The value of the policies following the death of the insured substantially exceeded their value at the date of the decedent's death.

* * *

Section 20.2032–1(d) of the Estate Tax Regulations provides that all property interests existing at the date of a decedent's death which form a part of his gross estate are "included property" for the purpose of valuing the gross estate under the alternate valuation method. Such property remains "included property" for the purpose of valuing the gross estate even though the property interests change in form during the alternate valuation period by being actually received, or disposed of, in whole or in part, by the estate. On the other hand, the regulations provide that property earned or accrued (whether received or not) after the date of the decedent's death and during the alternate valuation period with respect to any property interest existing at the date of the decedent's death, which does not represent a form of "included property" itself or the receipt of "included property," is excluded in valuing the gross estate under the alternate valuation method.

In Herbert H. Maass v. Higgins, 312 U.S. 443 (1941), Ct. D. 1494, C.B. 1941–1, 434, the Supreme Court of the United States held that ordinary rents, dividends, and interest received during the year following the decedent's death are not to be included in the value of the gross estate, if such estate is valued under the optional (alternate) valuation provisions of section 302(j) of the Revenue Act of 1926, as amended (corresponding to section 2032(a) of the 1954 Code). The Court stated as follows:

It is not denied that, in common understanding, rents, interest, and dividends are income. Under the Revenue Acts, if such items are collected by a decedent's estate, the executors are bound to return them and pay tax upon them as income.

The decision of the Supreme Court as to rents, dividends, and interest, however, does not preclude the inclusion in the gross estate of the appreciation in the value of an insurance policy resulting from the death of the insured within the alternate valuation period.

In the instant case, the death of the insured was the precise event which caused the increase in the value of the insurance policies as of the alternate valuation date. The increase in value occasioned by the death of the insured was not due to "mere lapse of time," within the meaning of section 2032(a)(3) of the Code. See Estate of John A. Hance v. Commissioner, 18 T.C. 499 (1952), acquiescence, C.B. 1953–1, 4. The increase in value of the policies cannot, therefore, be attributed to a "mere lapse of time."

An insurance policy is not, in common understanding, income producing property, and the appreciation in value of an insurance policy by reason of the death of the insured is not income in the statutory sense. Accordingly, the appreciation in value of the life insurance policies in the instant case, which occurred when the insured died is not "property earned or accrued" as in the case of ordinary interest, rents and dividends. Rather, the termination of the insurance contracts, brought about by the death of the insured, constitutes a disposition of the property interest in the contracts, within the meaning of section 2032(a)(1) of the Code.

The increase in value of the insurance contracts is, therefore, "included property," for purposes of valuing the gross estate under the alternate valuation method.

This interpretation is supported by H.R. Report No. 1885, on the Revenue Act of 1935, 74th Cong., 1st Sess., C.B. 1939–1 (Part 2), 660, at 664, which gives an example showing how the calculation of the value of property included in the gross estate should be made during the one-year period following the decedent's death. In this example, the appreciation and depreciation in the value of stocks and bonds and other assets, occurring during the year after death, are shown in the values of those assets as of one year after the date of the decedent's death or as of the date of sale, distribution, or other disposition of such assets (maturity in the case of foreign bonds). This example negatives a construction that the appreciation in value of the insurance policies, resulting from the death of the insured during the alternate valuation period, was "property earned or accrued" within the meaning of the Estate Tax Regulations.

Accordingly, it is held that for Federal estate tax purposes, the appreciation in value of the life insurance policies which matured by reason of the death of the insured during the alternate valuation period is not property earned or accrued. Therefore, no part of the proceeds of the insurance is excluded property, but is "included property," within the meaning of the Estate Tax Regulations, so that the entire value of the proceeds of the policies is includible in the gross estate.

Compare Revenue Ruling 55–379, C.B. 1959–1, 449, which holds that the increase in value of a policy of insurance, such as one owned by a decedent who was not the insured, which increase is attributable to the payment of premiums, or any interest earned, during the year following date of death, is deemed to be "excluded property." Note, however, that ruling involved the valuation of a policy in the estate of a person other than the insured where the policy did not mature during the alternate valuation period by reason of the death of the insured.

PROBLEMS

1. Mike Page died on February 10. At his death Mike owned the right to receive income from the Webster Trust until the death of Sam Webster. If Mike should die prior to the death of Sam, Mike's estate would become entitled to the income until Sam's death. Upon the death of Sam Webster the trust property was to be paid to Sam's children, Drew and Erica.

   On February 10, the Webster Trust had a value of $1,000,000 and was invested largely in technology stocks. On May 5, Sam Webster died in an automobile accident. On May 5, the value of the Webster Trust was only $700,000.

Mike's executor filed the United States estate tax return for Mike's estate on November 3. Mike's executor elected use of the alternate valuation date (August 10) under section 2032(a).

How should the right to income from the Webster Trust be valued for purposes of determining Mike's gross estate?

2.   Emily Lewis died on March 4 of Year 1. At her death she owned a patent on an industrial chemical process. The patent was to expire on March 4 of Year 2. On March 4 of Year 1 the patent was worth $500,000. On September 4 of Year 1 the patent was worth only $250,000. Emily's executor elected the alternate valuation date (September 4 of Year 1).

How should the patent be valued in Emily's gross estate?

3.   Henry and Anne Bennett had been married for 15 years. Henry had two adult children from a previous marriage. Eight months ago, Henry died. By his duly probated will, he transferred an apartment building that he owned individually to a trust. At the time of his death, the building was valued at $1,000,000. Under the trust, income was payable to Anne quarterly for life, and upon her death, the corpus would be distributed to Henry's children. Before the executor filed Henry's estate tax return, Anne was killed in a car accident. If elected, Anne's life estate qualified for the marital deduction as a QTIP under section 2056(b)(7). Under actuarial tables, the marital deduction would be valued at $600,000. However, based on the actual value of Anne's life estate after her sudden death, the marital deduction would total $15,000.

What is the amount of the marital deduction that the executor can report on Henry's estate tax return?

CHAPTER 10

ACTUARIAL VALUATION

■ ■ ■

A. GENERAL PRINCIPLES

Many property rights must be valued by use of actuarial principles. For example, if a donor transfers a remainder that will become possessory upon the death of a person whose age is 74, the value of the remainder depends on the probable longevity of the life tenant. As explained below, the general rule is that the probable longevity of the life tenant is determined actuarially (i.e., by reference to the average longevity of all persons age 74, rather than by reference to the health or circumstances of the life tenant individually). Currently the Treasury uses Life Table 2000CM, set forth at the end of Treas. Reg. § 20.2031–7(d)(7), to determine life expectancy. The Life Table 2000CM expectancy figures are used to determine the remainder values set forth in Treas. Reg. § 20.2031–7(d)(7) Table S.

Once the probable longevity of the life tenant is determined, discounting principles must be used to determine the value of the remainder interest, as provided in Treas. Regs. §§ 20.2031–7 and 25.2512–5. For example, if the age of the life tenant is 74 and a discount rate (prevailing interest rate) of 8% per annum is assumed, the present value of the remainder interest is determined by using a remainder factor of .46235 of the fair market value of the entire property. If the entire property is worth $100,000, the remainder interest is assigned a present value of $46,235. Treas. Reg. § 20.2031–7(d)(7) Table S.

A similar approach is used if the interest to be valued is a right to income rather than a remainder interest. For example, if a donor gives to a donee age 74 the right to receive the income from property until the donee's death, and a discount rate of 8% is assumed, the present value of the income interest is determined by using an income factor of .53765. If the entire property is worth $100,000, the income interest is assigned a value of $53,765. As explained in Treas. Reg. § 20.2031–7(d)(2)(iii), the value of the income interest is derived by subtracting the value of the remainder interest (.46235) from the value of the entire property (1.00000), producing a .53765 value for the income interest.

The $46,235 value for the remainder and the $53,765 value for the income interest are the "present values" of those interests (i.e., what a buyer would theoretically pay right now for each interest). In a market where the prevailing interest rate is 8%, a buyer would theoretically pay $46,235 for the remainder, which represents the right to receive $100,000 at the death of person currently age 74. The present value is far below the prospective $100,000. This is so because until the death occurs, the buyer will be deprived of the opportunity to invest and earn income from the $100,000. When interest rates are high, the lost use value is greater, with the result that the present value of the remainder is a smaller portion of the $100,000. Conversely, when interest rates are low, the lost use value is lower, with the result that the present value of the remainder is a larger portion of the $100,000.

A similar approach underlies valuation of the income interest. In a market where the prevailing interest rate is 8%, a buyer will theoretically pay $53,765 for the right to receive the income from $100,000 until the death of a person who is age 74. Under normal economic circumstances, when interest rates are high the income right will have a greater value relative to the principal of $100,000, and when interest rates are low, the income right will have a smaller value relative to the principal of $100,000.

Note that under this approach, the total of the present value of the income interest ($53,765) and the present value of the remainder ($46,235) is $100,000, the exact present value of the entire property. The regulations are based on the assumption that the total value for partial interests will be 100% of the current value of the entire property. This is a logical result, based on the premise that "the whole must equal the sum of its parts." In the real world, however, the marketplace may evaluate the remainder and income interests differently, producing a cumulative value less or more than 100%. In the interest of administrability, however, the regulations ignore this possibility.

Section 7520 establishes the guidelines for actuarial valuation, delegating to the Treasury the authority to promulgate specific formulas and tables. Section 7520 authorizes the Treasury to issue tables that incorporate current actuarial data, and the tables must be updated at least every 10 years. Currently, the Treasury has implemented this mandate as to the estate tax through tables set forth in Treas. Regs. §§ 20.2031–7(d)(6) and 20.2031–7(d)(7). The estate tax tables are applied as well to lifetime gifts pursuant to Treas. Reg. § 25.2512–5(d). The current tables apply to gifts and deaths after April 30, 2009. On May 5, 2022, Treasury issued proposed regulations based on actuarial data around 2010 (the current regulations are based on actuarial data around 2000). From January 1, 2021 to the effective date of final regulations, under the proposed regulations, taxpayers may use either the current regulations or the proposed regulations to determine life expectancy. If the proposed regulations are used in the above example, the income factor is .56935, and the remainder factor is .43065. As a result, the income interest will be valued at $56,935, and the remainder will be valued at $43,065. Because of increasing life expectancy, the proposed regulations have established lower values for remainders following life terms.

The interest rate to be applied is 120 percent of the section 1274(d)(1) federal midterm rate as determined and published by the Treasury each month. I.R.C. § 7520(a). This rate—commonly referred to as the "section 7520 rate"—determines the discount rate to be applied under the current regulations §§ 20.2031–7 and 25.2512–5. For example, if the section 7520 rate for the month in which the gift occurs is 8%, the donor transfers a remainder interest that becomes possessory after the life of a person age 70, and the property involved is worth $100,000, Table S of Reg. § 20.2031–7(d)(7) indicates that the value of the remainder is .39443 of the total value, or $39,443. The life estate value is therefore $100,000 less $39,443, or $60,557.

If a term certain (i.e., a specific time period) is involved, Table B of Regulation § 20.2031–7(d)(6) is used. Treas. Reg. § 20.2031–7(d)(2)(iii). For example, if the section 7520 rate is 8% and the interest to be valued consists of the right to receive income from property for 20 years, Table B indicates that the remainder after the income interest is worth .214548 of the total value. Therefore, the term certain value is 1.0 less .214548, or .785452. If the entire property is worth $100,000, the 20-year term certain is worth $78,545. Note that the factor for a remainder after a fixed number of years is found in Table B of Regulation § 20.2031–7, while the factor for a remainder after the death of a person is found in Table S of Treas. Regulation § 20.2031–7.

The value of an annuity must be interpolated from the tables using the method explained in Regulation § 20.2031–7(d)(2)(iv). For example, assume that a donor transfers $200,000 to a trust. The trust instrument provides that Alice (or her estate) is to receive payments totaling $15,000 from the trust each year for 12 years. Payments are to be made at the end of each quarter. After 12 years the entire trust principal is to be paid to Edward. Assume that the section 7520 rate is 8%. Table B of Regulation § 20.2031–7(d)(6) indicates that the value of the remainder after a 12-year term certain at 7% is .397114. Therefore, the value of the income interest is 1.0 less .397114, or .602886. The "annuity factor" is then computed by dividing the income interest value of .602886 by the section 7520 rate (8% in this case), producing an annuity factor of 7.53607. The tentative value of the 12-year annuity interest is therefore $15,000 × 7.53607, or $113,041. Because payments are to be made quarterly rather than annually, the tentative value of the annuity must be multiplied by 1.0259 to produce a final value for Alice's annuity of $115,969. Regulation §§ 20.2031–7(d)(2)(iv)(B) and 20.2031–7(d)(6) Table K. The value of the remainder is the amount that remains after subtracting the value of the annuity from the value of the entire property. Therefore, Edward's remainder is worth $200,000 less $115,969, or $84,031.

In the above example the payments are to be made at the *end* of each quarter. Therefore, Regulation § 20.2031–7(d)(6) Table K is used. If the payments are to be made at the *beginning* of each quarter, each payment will be received earlier and will therefore have a slightly higher value. Table J provides the values for payments to be made at the beginning of each period.

In the case of term certain interests, the Regulation § 20.2031–7(d)(6) tables provide values for section 7520 rates from 4.2% to 14.0%. In the case of interests involving longevity, the Regulation § 20.2031–7(d)(7) tables provide values for section 7520 rates from 0.2% to 14.0%. Values for higher and lower rates are provided in IRS Publication 1457.

B. EXCEPTIONS

Valuation under section 7520 and the Treasury's tables is based on the assumption of average mortality and an average income return from the property. It is of course understood that individual cases may vary widely from these assumptions and incorporate a shorter or longer actual life expectancy or a lower or higher actual income return. In the vast majority of cases, such variances are ignored, and the tables are applied to derive the actuarial value.

In extreme cases, however, the real-world facts may be so different from the assumptions incorporated in the tables that reliance on the tables becomes inappropriate. The regulations specify circumstances in which the tables are to be disregarded for this reason. Treas. Regs. §§ 20.7520–3 and 25.7520–3. The breadth of these regulations may stretch the bounds of statutory authority. Section 7520(a) decrees that the section 7520 rate and the tables "shall" be used for valuation of "any annuity, any interest for life or a term of years, or any remainder or reversionary interest." The only exception to this mandate is section 7520(b), which specifies that section 7520 rate is not to be applied to qualified retirement plans (Part I of Subchapter D of Chapter 1 of the Code), or to "any other provision specified in regulations." This exception seems designed to permit the Commissioner to exempt designated areas of the tax law from the operation of section 7520. It does not seem to encompass the Treasury's exclusion of certain types of property interests, as is done in Regulations §§ 20.7520–3 and 25.7520–3.

Nevertheless, the regulations delineate several circumstances in which the tables are not to be applied. If the tables are not applied, the value of the interest "is based on all of the facts and circumstances." Treas. Regs. §§ 20.7520–3(b)(1)(iii) and 25.7520–3(b)(1)(iii).

One issue addressed in these regulations is longevity. The tables are conclusive despite the health or probable longevity of the specific individual involved, unless the individual is "terminally ill" at the time of the transfer. For this purpose, an individual is considered terminally ill if he or she has "an incurable illness or other deteriorating physical condition" and "there is at least a 50 percent probability that the individual will die within 1 year." Treas. Regs. §§ 20.7520–3(b)(3)(i) and 25.7520–3(b)(3). If there is a terminal illness, the "actual life expectancy" must be used in valuing the transfer. Treas. Regs. §§ 20.7520–3(b)(4), Ex. 1 and 25.7520–3(b)(4).

The Treasury also takes the position that section 7520 and the tables are not applicable if the value of the interest may be impaired. For example, if the trustee or another party has discretion to invade principal without the income beneficiary's consent, thereby reducing the amount producing income for the holder of an income interest, the income interest is considered impaired, and the tables are not to be used. Treas. Regs. §§ 20.7520–3(b)(2)(ii)(B) and 25.7520–3(b)(2)(ii)(B). The regulations further assert the broader rule that the tables are not to be used unless the governing instrument provides for the income beneficiary "that degree of beneficial enjoyment of the property during the term of the income interest that the principles of the law of trusts accord to a person who is unqualifiedly designated as the income beneficiary of a trust for a similar period of time." Treas. Regs. §§ 20.7520–3(b)(2)(ii)(A) and 25.7520–3(b)(2)(ii)(A). This rule is specifically applied to unproductive property. If the principal of the trust consists of closely held stock on which no dividends have been paid for a number of years, there is no expectation that dividends will be paid, and the income beneficiary has no right to demand that the trust property be made productive, the income beneficiary is not viewed as having the full beneficial rights of a trust income beneficiary; hence the tables are not applicable. However, if the beneficiary has a right to require that the trust property be made productive, the income interest will be valued under the tables without regard to the historic or prospective productivity of the property. Treas. Reg. § 20.7520–3(b)(2)(v), Examples 1 and 2; Treas. Reg. § 25.7520–3(b)(2)(v), Examples 1 and 2.

Application of the section 7520 rate in the context of the tables raises more difficult questions if the income from the property transferred is far above or below the rate mandated by section 7520. The result of using the section 7520 rate may be a dramatically unrealistic valuation of either the income interest or the remainder interest. The regulations appear to accept this possibility, provided the income beneficiary has the right to require the trustee to make the property productive (i.e., invest in assets producing a reasonable yield). The regulations expressly allow use of the tables even though the minimum rate of income that the beneficiary can require under local law is below the section 7520 rate. Treas. Regs. §§ 20.7520–3(b)(2)(v),

Ex. 2 and 25.7520–3(b)(2)(v), Ex. 2. However, if the beneficiary has no right to demand productivity and the property is unlikely to produce income, the income and remainder interests will be valued in light of the probable actual return rather than the section 7520 rate. Treas. Regs. §§ 20.7520–3(b)(2)(v), Ex. 1 and 25.7520–3(b)(2)(v), Ex. 1.

Even if the beneficiary has the right to require that the property be made productive, there remains the possibility of tax avoidance through use of the tables. For example, a donor parent may transfer a remainder interest to a child while retaining an income interest in circumstances in which the actual income is likely to be very low. In this circumstance use of the section 7520 rate may dramatically overstate the value of the income interest and understate the value of the remainder, effectively permitting the parent to transfer the property to the donee child at a substantially discounted value for gift tax purposes.

Exploitation of the tables in intra-family transfers is effectively prevented by section 2702, discussed in Chapter 12. In transfers between family members, section 2702 assigns a zero value to the retained interest unless there is a required payment, at least annually, of a fixed dollar amount or a fixed percentage of the value of the trust. I.R.C. §§ 2702(a)(2)(A) and 2702(b). For example, if a parent transfers a remainder interest to a child, and the parent retains a right to the "income" from the property, the income interest is treated as valueless. As a result, the entire value of the property is assigned to the remainder, and the parent is treated as making a gift to the child of the entire value of the property. This prevents exploitation of the tables by transferring property that will produce income far below the level assumed in the tables.

By contrast, if the parent retains a right to receive a fixed dollar payment from the property each year, or a right to a payment equal to the value of a fixed percentage of the property, the tables are used to value the remainder that is given to the child. I.R.C. § 2702(b)(1) and (2). In this case the payment to the parent is fixed and cannot be manipulated.

SHACKLEFORD V. UNITED STATES

United States Court of Appeals, Ninth Circuit, 2001.
262 F.3d 1028.

THOMAS, CIRCUIT JUDGE:

This appeal presents the question of whether a statutory anti-assignment restriction on lottery payments justifies departure from the Department of Treasury's annuity tables when determining the asset's present value in calculating estate tax. Under the circumstances of this case, we conclude that it does and affirm the judgment of the district court.

I

***

Like most lottery winners, retired Air Force officer Thomas J. Shackleford probably wasn't thinking of tax consequences when he hit the $10 million California Lotto in 1987. Nor were his heirs. However, the estate tax problem became abundantly clear upon Shackleford's untimely death after receiving only three of twenty $508,000 annual payments. At that time, California law prohibited any assignment of lottery payments. Cal. Gov't Code § 8880.32(g). On death, future payments were to be made to a deceased winner's estate according to the annuity terms. Id. However, the payment of federal estate tax is not similarly structured. Thus, although the estate was limited to receiving annual installments, the estate tax was calculated based on the present value of the income stream, due on a much shorter schedule. Under the present value annuity tables in the Treasury regulations, 26 C.F.R. § 20.2031–7, the present value of the remaining payments was calculated to be $4,023,903. This meant that the estate owed $1,543,397 in federal estate taxes without any concomitant source of revenue to fund the payment.

The estate initially filed a return that reported the federal estate tax liability in accordance with the Treasury regulation tables and paid a total federal estate tax liability in the amount of $1,543,397. After auditing the return, the Internal Revenue Service ("IRS") found no error in the reported tax. Subsequently, the estate filed both amended tax returns and claims for refund, asserting that the value of the future payments was improperly reported. The last of the claims for refund argued that the proper value of the lottery payments was zero. In the alternative, the estate argued that use of the annuity tables to value the payments resulted in an unrealistic and unreasonable value because it did not reflect the fair market value of the asset. The IRS rejected the final refund claim, and the estate filed its claim for refund in district court.

The government filed a motion for summary judgment arguing that the estate was not entitled to a refund because the payments were an annuity for a term of years, the value of which was properly determined under the tables in 26 C.F.R. § 20.2031–7. The district court denied the motion, holding that if the estate could prove that the true value of the interest was substantially below the value attributed by the tables then departure would be warranted. *Shackleford v. United States*, No. 98–105580, 1998 WL 723161 (E.D. Cal. July 29, 1998). After a bench trial, the district court found that the lack of a market must be considered in determining a fair valuation of property for estate tax purposes and that because marketability is not a factor considered by the tables, using them would result in "a substantially unrealistic and unreasonable result." *Shackleford v. United States*, No. Civ. S–96–1370, 1999 WL 744121

(E.D.Cal. August 6, 1999). The court thereupon departed from the tables and valued the payments at $2,012,500. Id. Based on this valuation, the parties stipulated to a judgment for the estate in the amount of $1,622,674.86 ($1,104,156.27 in tax and $518,518.59 in interest).

II

* * *

The "value" of property to be included in the gross estate is the fair market value of the item at the time of the decedent's death. 26 C.F.R. § 20.2031–1(b). The fair market value is the price at which the property would change hands between a willing buyer and a willing seller, neither being under any compulsion to buy or sell and both having reasonable knowledge of relevant facts. The fair market value of a particular item of property includible in the decedent's gross estate is not to be determined by a forced sale price. Nor is the fair market value of an item of property to be determined by the sale price of the item in a market other than that in which such item is most commonly sold to the public, taking into account the location of the item wherever appropriate. . . . All relevant facts and elements of value as of the applicable valuation date shall be considered in every case. 26 C.F.R. § 20.2031–1(b).

Non-commercial annuities, such as the lottery payments at issue, are valued pursuant to tables promulgated by the Secretary of the Treasury, except when another regulatory provision applies. 26 U.S.C. § 7520. The general "fair market value" regulation quoted above, 26 C.F.R. § 20.2031–1(b), is such a provision, allowing departure from the tables "where they do not produce a value that reasonably approximates the fair market value. . . ." *O'Reilly v. Comm'r,* 973 F.2d 1403, 1407 (8th Cir.1992).

The IRS has explained that the "[v]aluation factors for determining the present value of interests measured by a term certain are based on two components: a term of years component and an interest rate component." Notice 89–24, 1989–1 C.B. 660. Although the tables provide the presumptive valuation of non-commercial annuities, courts have long recognized that a table-produced valuation is not applicable when the result is unrealistic and unreasonable. *See, e.g., Weller v. Comm'r,* 38 T.C. 790, 803, 1962 WL 1155 (1962). In such cases, a modification to the valuation or a complete departure from the tables may be justified.

As the Eighth Circuit explained:

> When use of the tables produces a substantially unrealistic and unreasonable result *and* when a more reasonable and realistic valuation technique is available, faith that the tables will "average out" in the long run will not suffice. Compliance with the statute and fairness in the particular case require that the

reviewing court use that alternative method to determine the fair market value of the gifted property.

O'Reilly, 973 F.2d at 1409. *See also Estate of Christ v. Comm'r,* 480 F.2d 171, 172 (9th Cir.1973) (approving of tax court's adoption of *Hanley v. United States,* 105 Ct. Cl. 638, 63 F. Supp. 73, 81 (1945), which held that the tables are to apply unless the result would be "substantially at variance with the facts"); *Froh v. Comm'r,* 100 T.C. 1, 3–4, 1993 WL 1869 (1993) ("use of the actuarial tables is presumptively correct unless it is shown that such use is 'unrealistic and unreasonable' ").

For these reasons, although the general rule requires that the tables be used because they provide both certainty and convenience when applied in large numbers of cases, *see Bank of California v. United States,* 672 F.2d 758, 759–60 (9th Cir.1982), exceptions have been made when the tables do not reasonably approximate the fair market value of the asset. However, because the table-produced valuation is presumed correct, the party who desires to use an alternative method to value an estate's interest bears the "considerable burden of proving that the tables produce such an unrealistic and unreasonable result that they should not be used." *O'Reilly,* 973 F.2d at 1408.

III

In this case, the district court concluded that the discount tables did not reasonably approximate the fair market value of the lottery payments because California's statutory anti-assignment restriction reduced the fair market value. The district court's conclusion is consistent with tax theory. Indeed, the reality of a decedent's economic interest in any particular property right is a major factor in determining valuation for estate tax purposes.* * * Each of the characteristics of a property interest must be considered in determining its value for taxing purposes. * * * The right to transfer is "one of the most essential sticks in the bundle of rights that are commonly characterized as property[.]" * * * It is axiomatic that if an asset's marketability is restricted, it is less valuable than an identical marketable asset. * * * We have long recognized that restrictions on alienability reduce value. *See e.g., Bayley v. Comm'r,* 624 F.2d 884, 885 (9th Cir.1980) (holding that stock transfer restrictions affect valuation); *Trust Services of Am., Inc. v. United States,* 885 F.2d 561, 569 (9th Cir.1989) ("[I]f stock is subject to resale restrictions under the federal securities laws which prevent it from being sold freely in the public market, a discount from the mean may be necessary to measure the stock's value accurately." (citation omitted)). *Estate of Jung v. Comm'r,* 101 T.C. 412, 434, 1993 WL 460544 (1993) (because stock of closely held corporations is not publicly traded, minority shares ordinarily receive "[a] marketability discount [to reflect] the hypothetical buyer's concern that there will not be a ready market when that buyer decides to sell the stock"); *see also Theophilos v.*

Comm'r, 85 F.3d 440 (9th Cir.1996) (minority shareholders in close corporations generally receive a discount to reflect lack of control).

In this case, there is little doubt that the statutory restrictions on transfer reduced the fair market value of the right to receive future lottery payments. The district court, after considering expert testimony on the point, reached the same conclusion in finding that the "[u]se of the annuity tables produces a substantially unrealistic and unreasonable result because the table does not reflect the discount which must be taken by virtue of the non-liquidity of the prize." * * *

Contrary to the government's argument, the lack of a market due to the anti-assignment restriction does not mean that the asset cannot be valued except by the tables. Where a willing seller and willing buyer do not exist, we will presume both their presence and a hypothetical sale.* * * Thus, given the expert testimony presented, the district court did not err in analyzing fair market value by assuming a hypothetical market.

The government also contends that allowing consideration of alienability in determining fair market value would undercut the bright line regulatory rule established by employment of the tables. Of course, this "bright line rule" has not deterred the IRS from seeking exceptions when it is the disadvantaged party. In fact, the IRS has often taken advantage of the economic reality rationale for departure from the tables, urging that the table-produced result under-values the particular asset at issue. * * *

More importantly, consideration of transfer restrictions in a fair market analysis does not alter the presumption that the value provided by the tables is correct and subject to revision only if the party seeking departure shows that the tables produce an unrealistic and unreasonable value. In such a case, if the taxpayer proves that a more realistic and reasonable valuation method exists that more closely approximates fair market value, courts are free to employ it. In this case, on the basis of the evidence presented, the district court concluded that strict application of the discount tables did not accurately reflect economic reality and reached an alternate determination of fair market value. We cannot say that the district court erred in this assessment.

As to the floodgates that the government believes to be opened by the injection of economic reality, one must only note the improbability of the confluence of government intervention, untimely death, and the lotto. * * *

AFFIRMED.

NOTE

In a case with virtually identical facts, including a state law (Connecticut) prohibition on assignment of the lottery prize, the Second Circuit reached the same result. Estate of Gribauskas v. Commissioner, 342 F.3d 85 (2d Cir. 2003).

In a split decision, however, the Fifth Circuit reached the opposite conclusion on essentially identical facts involving a nontransferable Texas lottery prize. Cook v. Commissioner, 349 F.3d 850 (5th Cir. 2003). The majority observed that the actuarial tables are routinely applied to other nonmarketable annuities, such as survivor annuities under ERISA, and that "non-marketability of a private annuity is an assumption underlying the annuity tables." The majority also argued that all the nonlottery cases in which application of the tables had been found unreasonable involved circumstances in which the assumptions underlying the tables were in question, e.g., the reliability of the rate of return. Finally, the majority reasoned that there is no rational basis for applying a discount for nonmarketability to a certain, fixed, and secure income stream. The Fifth Circuit therefore affirmed the Tax Court's application of the Treasury tables to determine the value of the lottery prize.

The reference in *Cook* to the inalienability of survivor annuities under ERISA raises interesting possibilities. In *Shackleford*, the court notes that "it is axiomatic that if an asset's marketability is restricted, it is less valuable than an identical marketable asset." If the lottery payments involved in *Shackleford* were appropriately discounted because of inalienability, could not an inalienable survivor annuity under ERISA be similarly discounted? The answer is "no," for reasons explained in Chapter 11.

The Sixth Circuit concurred with the Fifth, likewise concluding that the Treasury tables do not produce an unrealistic and unreasonable value when applied to inalienable lottery payments. Therefore, the Treasury tables must be used to determine the prospective value of the payments. Negron v. United States, 553 F.3d 1013 (6th Cir. 2009). The *Negron* result is especially striking because Negron, as the executor of two estates entitled to lottery payments, elected for each estate to receive a lump sum in lieu of the continuing payments, and under state law the lump sum was valued by applying a 9% discount rate, whereas the Treasury tables called for a discount rate of 5.0% in one estate and 5.6% in another. As a result, each estate received less from the state than the value on which they were taxed. The court reasoned that the lump sum settlement computation was irrelevant because at the time of death the decedents owned a continuing right to payments, and the Treasury tables are specifically designed to value such a continuing stream of payments.

The Fifth Circuit has applied the same rationale to a structured settlement under which the decedent had a right to receive periodic payments for injuries sustained in an automobile accident. Anthony v. United States, 520 F.3d 374 (5th Cir. 2008). Although the payments were nontransferable, the court held that the Treasury tables controlled.

The usual rules of actuarial valuation are clearly inappropriate for wasting assets, i.e., assets that will necessarily be consumed over time. A good example is Froh v. Commissioner, 100 T.C. 1 (1993), aff'd by unpublished opinion, 46 F.3d 1141 (9th Cir. 1995). In *Froh*, the donor created trusts that provided 10-year income interests for the donees, with remainders reserved to the donor. The donor then transferred interests in natural gas reserves to the trusts. The donor contended that the 10-year income interests should be assigned a value of only .614457 of the full value of the reserves, pursuant to the usual rules for valuing term interests, now embodied in Treas. Reg. § 25.2512–5(d)(2)(iii). The Commissioner, however, presented evidence that the gas properties were wasting assets and would probably be exhausted within ten years. The Tax Court agreed, concluding that in these circumstances use of the regulations would be "unrealistic and unreasonable." The result was assignment to the gifted income interests of 100 percent of the value of the gas properties.

PROBLEMS

Assume in each case that that the section 7520 rate at the time of each transfer is 6% per annum. Assume further that in each case the donee of the interest is not a family member as defined in section 2704(c)(2); therefore, the special valuation principles of section 2702 do not apply.

1. On November 1 of Year 1 Eric Williams transferred $100,000 to an irrevocable trust. The trust provides that for 12 years the income from the trust is to be paid to Maria Jones or her estate. At the end of the 12 years the trust is to terminate and the corpus is to be returned to Eric. How should the gift to Maria be valued for gift tax purposes?

2. Assume the same facts as in Problem 1. Eric dies on November 1 of Year 3. At what value would the reversion be included in Eric's estate for estate tax purposes, assuming that the trust value on November 1 of Year 3 is $120,000?

3. Carrie Wilson transferred $100,000 to an irrevocable trust. The trust provides that the income is to be paid to Amelia Cooper, age 60, until Amelia's death. At that time the trust is to terminate, and the corpus is to be transferred to Greg Harris, or Greg's estate. How should the gifts to Amelia and Greg, respectively, be valued for gift tax purposes?

4. Jane Porter transferred $300,000 to a trust. The trust instrument requires that the trustee pay $1,500 to Alan Porter on the last day of each month in each year until Alan's death. Alan was 55 years at the time of Jane's transfer. Upon Alan's death the remaining trust funds are to be paid to Jane. What is the value of the gift to Alan?

CHAPTER 11

CLOSELY HELD BUSINESSES AND OTHER ASSETS

■ ■ ■

A. GENERAL PRINCIPLES

Closely held businesses raise difficult valuation issues because interests in such businesses are not regularly traded. Although willing buyers and willing sellers determine prices every day for actively traded business interests (such as stock listed on an exchange), the willing buyer-willing seller analysis is essentially hypothetical in its application to nontraded business interests.

The starting point in valuing closely held businesses is section 2031(b), which dictates that nontraded stock and securities be valued by reference to the actual market valuation of similar enterprises, the stock or securities of which are actively traded. The regulations somewhat expand this mandate by specifying the aspects of a closely held business that are to be given the greatest weight for purposes of comparison with actively traded securities. Treas. Regs. §§ 20.2031–2(f) and 20.2031–3.

The regulations on valuation of closely held businesses are very brief. The general principles set forth in the regulations are amplified by Rev. Rul. 59–60, which follows and remains the landmark IRS pronouncement on valuation of closely held businesses.

REVENUE RULING 59–60
1959–1 C.B. 237.

SEC. 1. PURPOSE

The purpose of this Revenue Ruling is to outline and review in general the approach, methods and factors to be considered in valuing shares of the capital stock of closely held corporations for estate tax and gift tax purposes. The methods discussed herein will apply likewise to the valuation of corporate stock on which market quotations are either unavailable or are of such scarcity that they do not reflect the fair market value.

SEC. 2. BACKGROUND AND DEFINITIONS

.01 All valuations must be made in accordance with the applicable provisions of the Internal Revenue Code of 1954 and the Federal Estate Tax and Gift Tax Regulations. Sections 2031(a), 2032 and 2512(a) of the 1954 Code (sections 811 and 1005 of the 1939 Code) require that the property to be included in the gross estate, or made the subject of a gift, shall be taxed on the basis of the value of the property at the time of death of the decedent, the alternate date if so elected, or the date of gift.

.02 Section 20.2031–1(b) of the Estate Tax Regulations (section 81.10 of the Estate Tax Regulations 105) and section 25.2512–1, of the Gift Tax Regulations (section 86.19 of Gift Tax Regulations 108) define fair market value, in effect, as the price at which the property would change hands between a willing buyer and a willing seller when the former is not under any compulsion to buy and the latter is not under any compulsion to sell, both parties having reasonable knowledge of relevant facts. Court decisions frequently state in addition that the hypothetical buyer and seller are assumed to be able, as well as willing, to trade and to be well informed about the property and concerning the market for such property.

.03 Closely held corporations are those corporations the shares of which are owned by a relatively limited number of stockholders. Often the entire stock issue is held by one family. The result of this situation is that little, if any, trading in the shares takes place. There is, therefore, no established market for the stock and such sales as occur at irregular intervals seldom reflect all of the elements of a representative transaction as defined by the term "fair market value."

SEC. 3. APPROACH TO VALUATION

.01 A determination of fair market value, being a question of fact, will depend upon the circumstances in each case. No formula can be devised that will be generally applicable to the multitude of different valuation issues arising in estate and gift tax cases. Often, an appraiser will find wide differences of opinion as to the fair market value of a particular stock. In resolving such differences, he should maintain a reasonable attitude in recognition of the fact that valuation is not an exact science. A sound valuation will be based upon all the relevant facts, but the elements of common sense, informed judgment and reasonableness must enter into the process of weighing those facts and determining their aggregate significance.

.02 The fair market value of specific shares of stock will vary as general economic conditions change from "normal" to "boom" or "depression," that is, according to the degree of optimism or pessimism with which the investing public regards the future at the required date of appraisal. Uncertainty as to the stability or continuity of the future income from a property decreases its value by increasing the risk of loss of earnings and value in the future. The value of shares of stock of a company with very uncertain future prospects is highly speculative. The appraiser must exercise his judgment as to the degree of risk attaching to the business of the corporation which issued the stock, but that judgment must be related to all of the other factors affecting value.

.03 Valuation of securities is, in essence, a prophecy as to the future and must be based on facts available at the required date of appraisal. As a generalization, the prices of stocks which are traded in volume in a free and active market by informed persons best reflect the consensus of the investing public as to what the future holds for the corporations and industries represented. When a stock is closely held, is traded infrequently, or is traded in an erratic market, some other measure of value must be used. In many instances, the next best measure may be found in the prices at which the stocks of companies engaged in the same or a similar line of business are selling in a free and open market.

SEC. 4.   FACTORS TO CONSIDER

.01 It is advisable to emphasize that in the valuation of the stock of closely held corporations or the stock of corporations where market quotations are either lacking or too scarce to be recognized, all available financial data, as well as all relevant factors affecting the fair market value, should be considered. The following factors, although not all-inclusive, are fundamental and require careful analysis in each case:

(a)   The nature of the business and the history of the enterprise from its inception.

(b)   The economic outlook in general and the condition and outlook of the specific industry in particular.

(c)   The book value of the stock and the financial condition of the business.

(d)   The earning capacity of the company.

(e)   The dividend-paying capacity.

(f)   Whether or not the enterprise has goodwill or other intangible value.

(g)   Sales of the stock and the size of the block of stock to be valued.

(h)   The market price of stocks of corporations engaged in the same or a similar line of business having their stocks actively traded in a free and open market, either on an exchange or over-the-counter.

.02 The following is a brief discussion of each of the foregoing factors:

(a)   The history of a corporate enterprise will show its past stability or instability, its growth or lack of growth, the diversity or lack of diversity of its operations, and other facts needed to form an opinion of the degree of risk involved in the business. For an enterprise which changed its form of organization but carried on the same or closely similar operations of its predecessor, the history of the former enterprise should be considered. The detail to be considered should increase with approach to the required date of appraisal, since recent events are of greatest help in predicting the future; but a study of gross and net income, and of dividends covering a long prior period, is highly desirable. The history to be studied should include, but need not be limited to, the nature of the business, its products or services, its operating and investment assets, capital structure, plant facilities, sales records and management, all of which should be considered as of the date of the appraisal, with due regard for recent significant changes. Events of the past that are unlikely to recur in the future should be discounted, since value has a close relation to future expectancy.

(b) A sound appraisal of a closely held stock must consider current and prospective economic conditions as of the date of appraisal, both in the national economy and in the industry or industries with which the corporation is allied. It is important to know that the company is more or less successful than its competitors in the same industry, or that it is maintaining a stable position with respect to competitors. Equal or even greater significance may attach to the ability of the industry with which the company is allied to compete with other industries. Prospective competition which has not been a factor in prior years should be given careful attention. For example, high profits due to the novelty of its product and the lack of competition often lead to increasing competition. The public's appraisal of the future prospects of competitive industries or of competitors within an industry may be indicated by price trends in the markets for commodities and for securities. The loss of the manager of a so-called "one-man" business may have a depressing effect upon the value of the stock of such business, particularly if there is a lack of trained personnel capable of succeeding to the management of the enterprise. In valuing the stock of this type of business, therefore, the effect of the loss of the manager on the future expectancy of the business and the absence of management-succession potentialities are pertinent factors to be taken into consideration. On the other hand, there may be factors which offset, in whole or in part, the loss of the manager's services. For instance, the nature of the business and of its assets may be such that they will not be impaired by the loss of the manager. Furthermore, the loss may be adequately covered by life insurance, or competent management might be employed on the basis of the consideration paid for the former manager's services. These, or other offsetting factors, if found to exist, should be carefully weighed against the loss of the manager's services in valuing the stock of the enterprise.

(c) Balance sheets should be obtained, preferably in the form of comparative annual statements for two or more years immediately preceding the date of appraisal, together with a balance sheet at the end of the month preceding that date, if corporate accounting will permit. Any balance sheet descriptions that are not self-explanatory, and balance sheet items comprehending diverse assets or liabilities, should be clarified in essential detail by supporting supplemental schedules. These statements usually will disclose to the appraiser (1) liquid position (ratio of current assets to current liabilities); (2) gross and net book value of principal classes of fixed assets; (3) working capital; (4) long-term indebtedness; (5) capital structure; and (6) net worth. Consideration also should be given to any assets not essential to the operation of the business, such as investments in securities, real estate, etc. In general, such nonoperating assets will command a lower rate of return than do the operating assets, although in exceptional cases the reverse may be true. In computing the book value per share of stock, assets of the investment type should be revalued on the basis of their market price and the book value adjusted accordingly. Comparison of the company's balance sheets over several years may reveal, among other facts, such developments as the acquisition of additional production facilities or subsidiary companies, improvement in financial position, and details as to recapitalizations and other changes in the capital structure of the corporation. If the corporation has more than one class of stock outstanding, the charter or certificate of incorporation should be examined to ascertain the explicit rights and privileges of the various stock issues including: (1) voting powers, (2) preference as to dividends, and (3) preference as to assets in the event of liquidation.

(d) Detailed profit-and-loss statements should be obtained and considered for a representative period immediately prior to the required date of appraisal, preferably five or more years. Such statements should show (1) gross income by principal items; (2) principal deductions from gross income including major prior items of operating expenses, interest and other expense on each item of long-term debt, depreciation and depletion if such deductions are made, officers' salaries, in total if they appear to be reasonable or in detail if they seem to be excessive, contributions (whether or not deductible for tax purposes) that the nature of its business and its community position require the corporation to make, and taxes by principal items, including income and excess profits taxes; (3) net income available for dividends; (4) rates and amounts of dividends paid on each class of stock; (5) remaining amount carried to surplus; and (6) adjustments to, and reconciliation with, surplus as stated on the balance sheet. With profit and loss statements of this character available, the appraiser should be able to separate recurrent from nonrecurrent items of income and expense, to distinguish between operating income and investment income, and to ascertain whether or not any line of business in which the company is engaged is operated consistently at a loss and might be abandoned with benefit to the company. The percentage of earnings retained for business expansion should be noted when dividend-paying capacity is considered. Potential future income is a major factor in many valuations of closely-held stocks, and all information concerning past income which will be helpful in predicting the future should be secured. Prior earnings records usually are the most reliable guide as to the future expectancy, but resort to arbitrary five-or-ten-year averages without regard to current trends or future prospects will not produce a realistic valuation. If, for instance, a record of progressively increasing or decreasing net income is found, then greater weight may be accorded the most recent years' profits in estimating earning power. It will be helpful, in judging risk and the extent to which a business is a marginal operator, to consider deductions from income and net income in terms of percentage of sales. Major categories of cost and expense to be so analyzed include the consumption of raw materials and supplies in the case of manufacturers, processors and fabricators; the cost of purchased merchandise in the case of merchants; utility services; insurance; taxes; depletion or depreciation; and interest.

(e)   Primary consideration should be given to the dividend-paying capacity of the company rather than to dividends actually paid in the past. Recognition must be given to the necessity of retaining a reasonable portion of profits in a company to meet competition. Dividend-paying capacity is a factor that must be considered in an appraisal, but dividends actually paid in the past may not have any relation to dividend-paying capacity. Specifically, the dividends paid by a closely held family company may be measured by the income needs of the stockholders or by their desire to avoid taxes on dividend receipts, instead of by the ability of the company to pay dividends. Where an actual or effective controlling interest in a corporation is to be valued, the dividend factor is not a material element, since the payment of such dividends is discretionary with the controlling stockholders. The individual or group in control can substitute salaries and bonuses for dividends, thus reducing net income and understating the dividend-paying capacity of the company. It follows, therefore, that dividends are less reliable criteria of fair market value than other applicable factors.

(f)   In the final analysis, goodwill is based upon earning capacity. The presence of goodwill and its value, therefore, rests upon the excess of net earnings over and above a fair return on the net tangible assets. While the element of goodwill may be based primarily on earnings, such factors as the prestige and renown of the business, the ownership of a trade or brand name, and a record of successful operation over a prolonged period in a particular locality, also may furnish support for the inclusion of intangible value. In some instances it may not be possible to make a separate appraisal of the tangible and intangible assets of the business. The enterprise has a value as an entity. Whatever intangible value there is, which is supportable by the facts, may be measured by the amount by which the appraised value of the tangible assets exceeds the net book value of such assets.

(g) Sales of stock of a closely held corporation should be carefully investigated to determine whether they represent transactions at arm's length. Forced or distress sales do not ordinarily reflect fair market value nor do isolated sales in small amounts necessarily control as the measure of value. This is especially true in the valuation of a controlling interest in a corporation. Since, in the case of closely held stocks, no prevailing market prices are available, there is no basis for making an adjustment for blockage. It follows, therefore, that such stocks should be valued upon a consideration of all the evidence affecting the fair market value. The size of the block of stock itself is a relevant factor to be considered. Although it is true that a minority interest in an unlisted corporation's stock is more difficult to sell than a similar block of listed stock, it is equally true that control of a corporation, either actual or in effect, representing as it does an added element of value, may justify a higher value for a specific block of stock.

(h) Section 2031(b) of the Code states, in effect, that in valuing unlisted securities the value of stock or securities of corporations engaged in the same or a similar line of business which are listed on an exchange should be taken into consideration along with all other factors. An important consideration is that the corporations to be used for comparisons have capital stocks which are actively traded by the public. In accordance with section 2031(b) of the Code, stocks listed on an exchange are to be considered first. However, if sufficient comparable companies whose stocks are listed on an exchange cannot be found, other comparable companies which have stocks actively traded in on the over-the-counter market also may be used. The essential factor is that whether the stocks are sold on an exchange or over-the-counter there is evidence of an active, free public market for the stock as of the valuation date. In selecting corporations for comparative purposes, care should be taken to use only comparable companies. Although the only restrictive requirement as to comparable corporations specified in the statute is that their lines of business be the same or similar, yet it is obvious that consideration must be given to other relevant factors in order that the most valid comparison possible will be obtained. For illustration, a corporation having one or more issues of preferred stock, bonds or debentures in addition to its common stock should not be considered to be directly comparable to one having only common stock outstanding. In like manner, a company with a declining business and decreasing markets is not comparable to one with a record of current progress and market expansion.

SEC. 5. WEIGHT TO BE ACCORDED VARIOUS FACTORS

The valuation of closely held corporate stock entails the consideration of all relevant factors as stated in section 4. Depending upon the circumstances in each case, certain factors may carry more weight than others because of the nature of the company's business. To illustrate:

(a) Earnings may be the most important criterion of value in some cases whereas asset value will receive primary consideration in others. In general, the appraiser will accord primary consideration to earnings when valuing stocks of companies which sell products or services to the public; conversely, in the investment or holding type of company, the appraiser may accord the greatest weight to the assets underlying the security to be valued.

(b) The value of the stock of a closely held investment or real estate holding company, whether or not family owned, is closely related to the value of the assets underlying the stock. For companies of this type the appraiser should determine the fair market values of the assets of the company. Operating expenses of such a company and the cost of liquidating it, if any, merit consideration when appraising the relative values of the stock and the underlying assets. The market values of the underlying assets give due weight to potential earnings and dividends of the particular items of property underlying the stock, capitalized at rates deemed proper by the investing public at the date of appraisal. A current appraisal by the investing public should be superior to the retrospective opinion of an individual. For these reasons, adjusted net worth should be accorded greater weight in valuing the stock of a closely held investment or real estate holding company, whether or not family owned, than any of the other customary yardsticks of appraisal, such as earnings and dividend paying capacity.

SEC. 6. CAPITALIZATION RATES

In the application of certain fundamental valuation factors, such as earnings and dividends, it is necessary to capitalize the average or current results at some appropriate rate. A determination of the proper capitalization rate presents one of the most difficult problems in valuation. That there is no ready or simple solution will become apparent by a cursory check of the rates of return and dividend yields in terms of the selling prices of corporate shares listed on the major exchanges of the country. Wide variations will be found even for companies in the same industry. Moreover, the ratio will fluctuate from year to year depending upon economic conditions. Thus, no standard tables of capitalization rates applicable to closely held corporations can be formulated. Among the more important factors to be taken into consideration in deciding upon a capitalization rate in a particular case are: (1) the nature of the business; (2) the risk involved; and (3) the stability or irregularity of earnings.

SEC. 7.   AVERAGE OF FACTORS

Because valuations cannot be made on the basis of a prescribed formula, there is no means whereby the various applicable factors in a particular case can be assigned mathematical weights in deriving the fair market value. For this reason, no useful purpose is served by taking an average of several factors (for example, book value, capitalized earnings and capitalized dividends) and basing the valuation on the result. Such a process excludes active consideration of other pertinent factors, and the end result cannot be supported by a realistic application of the significant facts in the case except by mere chance.

* * *

REVENUE RULING 65–193
1965–2 C.B. 370.

Revenue Ruling 59–60, C.B. 1959–1, 237, is hereby modified to delete the statements, contained therein at section 4.02(f), that "In some instances it may not be possible to make a separate appraisal of the tangible and intangible assets of the business. The enterprise has a value as an entity. Whatever intangible value there is, which is supportable by the facts, may be measured by the amount by which the appraised value of the tangible assets exceeds the net book value of such assets."

The instances where it is not possible to make a separate appraisal of the tangible and intangible assets of a business are rare and each case varies from the other. No rule can be devised which will be generally applicable to such cases.

Other than this modification, Revenue Ruling 59–60 continues in full force and effect.

NOTE

The principles of Rev. Rul. 59–60 have been applied in hundreds of litigated cases involving a wide variety of businesses. An analysis or summary of those cases is far beyond the scope of this work.

B. PREMIUM FOR CONTROL

ESTATE OF CHENOWETH V. COMMISSIONER
United States Tax Court, 1987.
88 T.C. 1577.

KÖRNER, JUDGE:

Respondent determined a deficiency of Federal estate tax against petitioner in the amount of $232,227.50. The sole issue between the parties is whether, in computing the marital deduction to which it is entitled under the provisions of section 2056, petitioner may value certain stock passing to decedent's surviving spouse by taking into account an alleged additional element of value because of the control which such block of stock has over the company involved.

* * *

Petitioner herein is the Estate of Dean A. Chenoweth (hereinafter "decedent"), acting by and through Julia Jenilee Chenoweth (hereinafter "Jenny"), the duly appointed personal representative of the estate. At the time of filing of the petition herein, petitioner's residence was in Tallahassee, Florida.

Decedent died on July 31, 1982. A timely Federal estate tax return was thereafter filed for his estate by the personal representative. The principal asset of decedent's gross estate was all of the outstanding common voting stock of Chenoweth Distributing Company, Inc. (hereinafter the "company"), which was owned by decedent at the date of his death and which was valued in the Federal estate tax return at $2,834.033. For purposes of arriving at the value of the gross estate under section 2031, respondent has accepted this valuation.

Under decedent's will, duly probated, decedent left 255 shares, or 51 percent, of the company's stock to his surviving wife, Jenny, and 245 shares, or 49 percent, of the company's stock to his daughter by a prior marriage, Kelli Chenoweth. So far as the bequest to Jenny is concerned, there is no dispute between the parties that the bequest was outright and qualifies for the marital deduction provided by section 2056. The parties are likewise in agreement that under Florida law, which governs here, the 51 percent stock interest passing to Jenny gives her complete control of the company.

As filed with respondent, decedent's estate tax return claimed a marital deduction with respect to the stock interest in the company passing to Jenny in the amount of $1,445,356, which was precisely 51 percent of the date of death value of $2,834,033 for all the stock. In the petition filed herein, however, petitioner now claims that the value of the company's stock passing to Jenny for marital deduction purposes should be $1,996,038, arrived at by adding a "control premium" of 38.1 percent to the value of such stock as originally reported.

Respondent contests this claim, and, in his motion for summary judgment, takes the position that, as a matter of law, petitioner is not entitled to increase the value of the controlling interest in the company, and claimed as a marital deduction, above a strict 51 percent share of the value of all the stock of the company, as reported in the gross estate. Petitioner, opposing respondent's motion, contends that there is no such prohibition as a matter of law. * * *

The issue presented here is a novel one, and does not seem to have been directly addressed until now, at least by this Court. It requires us to consider the fundamental nature of the Federal estate tax, as a basis for how assets are to be valued for purposes of inclusion in the gross estate under section 2031. At the same time, we must also consider the nature of the marital deduction provided by section 2056, the valuation of assets qualifying for deduction under that section, and the moment in time when such assets are to be valued.

* * *

We may accept as a first step, then, that for purposes of inclusion in the decedent's gross estate under section 2031, his assets are to be valued at their worth at the moment of death. In this context, and for these purposes, respondent recognizes that a block of stock which represents the controlling interest in a company may be worth more than a block of stock in the same company which does not carry with it the control of the company. Thus, respondent's regulations provide, in part:

> On the other hand, if the block of stock to be valued represents a controlling interest, either actual or effective, in a going business, the price at which other lots change hands may have little relation to its true value. [Treas. Regs. § 20.2031–2(e).]

* * *

The courts have likewise recognized that an additional element of value may be present in a block of shares representing a controlling interest, for valuation purposes under section 2031. * * * By the same token, a block of shares in a closely held corporation which is a noncontrolling minority interest may call for a reduction of its fair market value.

In the instant case, there is no dispute between the parties as to the value of the stock of the company. It was all owned by decedent at the moment of his death, and the value of that 100 percent interest was included in decedent's gross estate at a value which respondent has accepted. Certainly ownership of 100 percent of the outstanding stock of the company constitutes control. Whether the value used in this case for purposes of section 2031 included an element of value because of the control factor is not clear from this record, but we assume that it did.

* * *

This brings us to a consideration of the marital deduction provisions of section 2056.

* * *

The regulations * * * provide:

> The value, for the purpose of the marital deduction, of any deductible interest which passed from the decedent to his surviving spouse is to be determined as of the date of the decedent's death, * * *. The marital deduction may be taken only with respect to the net value of any deductible interest which passed from the decedent to [the] surviving spouse, * * * [Treas. Regs. § 20.2056(b)–4(a).]

At this point, the focus of our inquiry has changed. For purposes of section 2031, we were concerned only with the value of the assets to be included in the decedent's gross estate as a whole, and without reference to the destination of those assets under decedent's will or through the laws of descent and distribution. Under section 2056, however, a somewhat different question is presented: What is the asset that passes to the decedent's surviving spouse, and what is the value of it? Here, for the first time, we are concerned with the destination of the asset and the nature and the value of that interest which passes.

Under decedent's will, 255 shares of the company's stock, representing a controlling interest in the company, was broken off from the total stock ownership of decedent, as reflected for gross estate purposes under section 2031, and was bequeathed to his surviving spouse Jenny. That 51 percent share of the stock of the company carried with it the element of control and the additional element of value which inheres in such a controlling interest. For the first time, then, we must consider the total stock interest of decedent as composed of two pieces: the 51 percent share passing to decedent's surviving spouse, including the control element, and the 49 percent interest representing a minority share of the company which passed to decedent's child Kelli. As we have indicated above herein, it is clear to us that these two blocks of stock have different values. As we said in Estate of Salsbury v. Commissioner, supra:

> The payment of a premium for control is based on the principle that the per share value of minority interests is less than the per share value of a controlling interest. * * * A premium for control is generally expressed as the percentage by which the amount paid for a controlling block of shares exceeds the amount which would have otherwise been paid for the shares if sold as minority interests and is not based on a percentage of the value of the stock held by all or a particular class of minority shareholders. * * *

* * * In the instant case, it is clear to us that the block of the company's stock passing under decedent's will to his surviving widow was the controlling interest in the company, and was entitled to be valued for purposes of section 2056 so as to include an additional element of value because of that control. Thus, simply valuing the 51 percent share of the

company's stock qualifying for the marital deduction at a mechanical 51 percent of the total value ascribed to the stock for purposes of inclusion in the gross estate would not give effect to the additional element of value for control which inheres in that block of stock. The amount of such control premium presents a material issue of fact which is not resolved in the present record and therefore requires that respondent's motion for summary judgment be denied.

* * * While we would tend to agree that the sum of the parts cannot equal more than the whole—that is, that the majority block together with the control premium, when added to the minority block of the company's stock with an appropriate discount for minority interest, should not equal more than the total 100 percent interest of the decedent, as reported for purposes of section 2031—it might well turn out that the sum of the parts can equal less than the whole—that is, that the control premium which is added to the majority block passing to decedent's surviving spouse might be less than the proper minority discount to be attributed to the shares passing to decedent's daughter Kelli.

In any event, this question is not before us at this time. We are not required to determine at this point whether the minority block of shares passing to Kelli requires that a discount be assigned to it, nor the amount of such discount, nor that such discount must precisely equal the amount of control premium which is properly assignable to the majority block of shares qualifying for marital deduction under section 2056. All we decide here is that such majority block may be entitled to an extra element of value because of the control over the company which such block possesses; that such additional element of value can properly be considered in computing the amount of the marital deduction; and that this presents a material question of fact which has not been resolved between the parties and as to which petitioner must have an opportunity to present its proof.

* * *

NOTE

In theory, the magnitude of the control premium should vary from case to case, depending on the nature of the business and the realistic economic advantages offered by control, such as power to determine (1) salaries and other expenditures, (2) the extent of dividend or other distributions, (3) the extent to which earnings are reinvested and the business expanded, and (4) participation in mergers, liquidations, and substantial asset sales. Although a controlling owner has a theoretical duty to deal fairly with minority owners, in the real world a majority owner has a great deal of latitude.

In Estate of Salsbury v. Commissioner, 34 T.C.M. (CCH) 1441 (1975), the Tax Court assigned a 38.1% control premium to a 51.8% ownership interest. In Estate of Trenchard v. Commissioner, 69 T.C.M. (CCH) 2164 (1995), the Tax

Court assigned a 40% control premium to a 61% ownership interest. Although the magnitude of the premium varies from case to case, these two cases, decided 20 years apart, are typical.

C. MINORITY DISCOUNTS

ESTATE OF BRIGHT V. UNITED STATES

United States Court of Appeals, Fifth Circuit, 1981.
658 F.2d 999.

ANDERSON III, CIRCUIT JUDGE:

This case presents to the en banc court an important question involving the principles of federal estate tax valuation. Mary Frances Smith Bright died on April 3, 1971. During her lifetime, she and her husband, Mr. Bright, owned 55% of the common stock of East Texas Motor Freight Lines, Inc., 55% of the common stock of twenty-seven affiliated corporations, and 55% of the common and preferred stock of Southern Trust and Mortgage Company (the stock of all such corporations is hereinafter referred to collectively as the "stock").

During her lifetime, Mr. and Mrs. Bright held the 55% block of stock as their community property under the laws of the State of Texas. The remaining forty-five percent is owned by parties unrelated to the Brights; a thirty percent block of stock is owned by H.G. Schiff, and the remaining fifteen percent is owned by two or three other individuals. None of the stock was publicly traded and no market existed for any of the stock on the date of Mrs. Bright's death. Mr. Bright is executor under the will of his wife. The will devised Mrs. Bright's interest in the stock to Mr. Bright as trustee of a trust for the primary benefit of Mrs. Bright's four children.

After audit of the estate tax return, the government assessed a deficiency, which was paid by the estate, and the instant suit for a refund of over $3 million in federal estate taxes and assessed interest was brought in the district court. The sole issue before the district court was the value of the estate's stock. Before the bench trial on the fair market value issue, the district judge ruled as a matter of law that "no element of control can be attributed to the decedent in determining the value of the decedent's interest in the stock . . . for estate tax purposes. The parties are hereby ordered to proceed with preparation for trial and trial of this case on that basis." At the trial the district court found that the value of the stock was consistent with the testimony of the estate's expert witnesses, and entered judgment for the estate. The government filed a timely notice of appeal. A panel of this court vacated the judgment of the district court and remanded with instructions, holding that the district court erred in entering the pretrial order relating to the element of control. 619 F.2d 407 (June 18, 1980). The estate's petition for rehearing en banc was granted, and the panel opinion was vacated. 628 F.2d 307 (Oct. 2, 1980). We now affirm the judgment of the district court.

The only issue facing the en banc court is whether the district court erred in entering the above quoted pretrial order relating to the element of control. We reject the heart of the government's arguments, and also reject a secondary government argument because it was raised for the first time on appeal.

Two principal arguments constitute the heart of the government's case, the first based on its description of the property transferred as an undivided one-half interest in the control block of 55% of the stock, and the second based on family attribution between the estate's stock interest and the stock interest held individually by Mr. Bright.[1]

First, the government argues that the property to be valued for estate tax purposes is an undivided one-half interest in the control block of 55% of the stock, and that the proper method of valuation would be to value the 55% control block, including a control premium, and then take one-half thereof. Both parties agree that the estate tax is an excise tax on the transfer of property at death, and that the property to be valued is the property which is actually transferred, as contrasted with the interest held by the decedent before death or the interest held by the legatee after death. * * * Both also agree that state law, Texas in this case, determines precisely what property is transferred. * * * Both parties agree that, under Texas law, the stock at issue was the community property of Mr. and Mrs. Bright during her life, that Mrs. Bright's death dissolved the community, that upon death the community is divided equally, that each spouse can exercise testamentary disposition over only his or her own half of the community, and that "only the decedent's half is includable in his gross estate for federal tax purposes." Commissioner v. Chase Manhattan Bank, 259 F.2d at 239. Under Texas law, upon the division of the community at death, each spouse owns an undivided one-half interest in each item of community property. Caddell v. Lufkin Land & Lumber Co., 255 S.W. 397 (Tex.Com.App., 1923).

In its brief the government argued that, because the interest to be valued was an undivided one-half interest in the full 55% control block, the proper method would be to value the whole, including its control premium, and then take one-half thereof to establish the value of the estate's undivided one-half interest. The estate points out that the government's

---

[1] The government also argued in the court below, and argues on appeal, that the district court's pre-trial order held as a matter of law that a minority discount should be applied. The government argues that a minority discount should be allowed only if evidence supporting a discount is adduced. We do not disagree with the government's statement of the law, but we reject the government's characterization of the district court's pretrial order. The order did not mandate a minority discount: it held only that the interest to be valued was in fact a 27 1/2% interest, which of course left open for proof at trial whether or not the taxpayer would in fact adduce proof to support a minority discount. Accordingly, there is no merit in the government's argument.

argument overlooks the fact that the block of stock is subject to the right of partition under Texas law at the instance of either the surviving spouse or the estate of the deceased spouse. Tex. Prob. Code Ann. § 385 (Vernon 1980). The government has not argued that partition would not be freely granted in a case involving fungible shares, such as this case. Thus, the estate has no means to prevent the conversion of its interest into shares representing a 27 ½% block, and we conclude that the estate's interest is the equivalent of a 27 ½% block of the stock. Accordingly, we reject the government's approach of valuing the 55% control block, with its control premium, and then taking one-half thereof. Accord Estate of Lee v. Commissioner, 69 T.C. 860 (1978).

Having determined that the property which is to be valued for estate tax purposes is the 27 ½% block of stock owned by the estate, we turn to the government's second argument, which is based on the doctrine of family attribution[2] between the successive holders of interest to be taxed, the decedent, the executor, and the legatee, on the one hand, and the related party, Mr. Bright, on the other. The government argues that the following facts are relevant and should have been considered by the district court in valuing the 27 ½% block: the fact that Mr. and Mrs. Bright were husband and wife and held their stock during her lifetime as a control block of 55%; the fact that Mr. Bright held the estate's 27 ½% block after her death as executor and subsequently as trustee of the testamentary trust for their children, while he simultaneously held another 27 ½% block in his individual capacity, thus continuing the control block after death; and the fact that the government might be able to adduce evidence that Mr. Bright, as executor or trustee, would not be willing to sell the estate's 27 ½% block as a minority interest, but would be willing to sell it only as part of the block of 55% including his individually-owned stock so that a substantial control premium could be realized.[3] Such facts and evidence, the government argues, would have formed the basis of expert testimony that the value of the estate's stock includes some control premium. For several reasons, we reject the government's attempt to import into this area of the estate tax law this kind of family attribution, and we hold that the

---

[2]   At several points, the government's brief seems to disavow any attempt to import family attribution into this area. A close reading of the government's brief reveals, however, that the government shuns only the argument that family attribution requires or mandates that the stock of related parties be valued as a unit. The government's position is that the relationship between the decedent, executor or legatee, on the one hand, and another stockholder, on the other hand, is a fact relevant to value. When we refer in this opinion to family attribution, we refer to this non-mandatory version. Similarly, our opinion deals only with family attribution based on the identity of the decedent, the executor or the legatee. It is this identity which is irrelevant under the case law and reasoning which this opinion will develop.

[3]   This opinion will show that all three facts are irrelevant to the proper valuation formula because they depend upon the family relationship between the decedent, the executor or the legatee, on the one hand, and another stockholder, i.e., Mr. Bright in his capacity as an individual stockholder, on the other hand. The third factor is inadmissible also because it assumes an unwillingness to sell in direct contradiction to the established valuation formula which assumes a willing seller.

foregoing evidence proffered by the government is not admissible to prove the value of the stock at issue.

First, we reject any family attribution to the estate's stock because established case law requires this result. A recent case directly in point is Estate of Lee v. Commissioner, supra. There Mr. and Mrs. Lee held as community property 4,000 of the 5,000 outstanding shares of the common stock of a closely held corporation. They also held all 50,000 shares of the preferred stock. Upon the death of Mrs. Lee, the community was dissolved, leaving Mr. Lee and the estate of Mrs. Lee each with an undivided one-half interest in each item of the community property. 69 T.C. at 873. The Tax Court held that this was the equivalent of 2,000 shares of common stock and 25,000 shares of preferred stock, and that the estate's interest was a minority interest. 69 T.C. at 874.

In United States v. Land, supra, this court held that a restrictive agreement, which depressed the value of a partnership interest but which by its terms expired at decedent's death, did not affect value for estate tax purposes because the estate tax is an excise tax on the transfer of property at death and accordingly valuation is to be made at the time of the transfer, i.e., at death, and the valuation is to be measured by the interest that actually passes. 303 F.2d at 172. It follows necessarily from our *Land* holding that the fact that Mr. and Mrs. Bright held their stock during her lifetime as a control block of 55% is an irrelevant fact. It is a fact which antedates her death, and no longer exists at the time of her death. Dictum in *Land* also suggests that the post-death fact—that the estate's 27 ½% will pass to Mr. Bright as trustee of the testamentary trust—is also irrelevant:

> Brief as is the instant of death, the court must pinpoint its valuation at this instant—the moment of truth, when the ownership of the decedent ends and the ownership of the successors begins. It is a fallacy there, therefore, to argue value before—or—after death on the notion that valuation must be determined by the value either of the *interest that ceases or of the interest that begins*. Instead, the valuation is determined by the interest that passes, and the value of the interest before or after death is pertinent only as it serves to indicate the value at death.

303 F.2d at 172. (Emphasis added.)

Beginning at least as early as 1940, the Tax Court has uniformly valued a decedent's stock for estate tax purposes as a minority interest when the decedent himself owned less than 50%, and despite the fact that control of the corporation was within the decedent's family. * * * Similarly, many district courts have either expressly or impliedly rejected the application of family attribution to an estate's stock in the valuation process for estate tax purposes. * * * Our research has uncovered no cases, and the government has cited none, which have attributed family-owned stock to the estate's stock in determining the value thereof for estate tax purposes.

* * *

We conclude that the case law reflects long established precedent that family attribution should not apply to lump a decedent's stock with that of related parties for estate tax valuation purposes. This constitutes our first reason for rejecting family attribution in the instant context.

Our second reason for rejecting this kind of family attribution is our conclusion that the doctrine is logically inconsistent with the willing buyer-seller rule set out in the regulations. Reg. § 20.2031–1(b) provides in pertinent part:

> The fair market value is the price at which the property would change hands between a willing buyer and a willing seller, neither being under any compulsion to buy or to sell and both having reasonable knowledge of relevant facts.

> This cardinal rule for determining value has been universally applied, both by the Internal Revenue Service and the courts.

It is apparent from the language of the regulation that the "willing seller" is not the estate itself, but is a hypothetical seller. In Revenue Ruling 59–60, the Internal Revenue Service has so held:

> Court decisions frequently state in addition that the hypothetical buyer and seller are assumed to be able, as well as willing, to trade and to be well informed about the property and concerning the market for such property.

1959–1 C.B. at 237 (emphasis added). Courts also have so held. In United States v. Simmons 346 F.2d 213, 217 (5th Cir.1965), this court said that "the 'willing buyer and seller' are a hypothetical buyer and seller having a reasonable knowledge of relevant facts." In Rothgery v. United States 475 F.2d 591 (Ct.Cl.1973), the Court of Claims said:

> [I]t is necessary to begin the resolution of any valuation problem by presupposing a "willing seller." In the present case, therefore, we must begin with the assumption that the decedent's 125 shares of stock in the corporation were not bequeathed by the decedent to his son, the plaintiff, and that such shares were available for sale by the decedent's estate as a "willing seller."

475 F.2d at 594.

The notion of the "willing seller" as being hypothetical is also supported by the theory that the estate tax is an excise tax on the transfer of property at death and accordingly that the valuation is to be made as of the moment of death and is to be measured by the interest that passes, as contrasted with the interest held by the decedent before death or the interest held by the legatee after death. Earlier in this opinion, we noticed that our United States v. Land, supra, decision logically requires a holding that the relationship between Mr. and Mrs. Bright and their stock is an irrelevant, before death fact. Thus, it is clear that the "willing seller" cannot be identified with Mrs. Bright, and therefore there can be no family attribution with respect to those related to Mrs. Bright. Similarly the dictum in *Land*—that valuation is not determined by the value of the interest in the hands of the legatee—means that the "willing seller" cannot be identified with Mr. Bright as executor or as trustee of the testamentary trust. Therefore, there can be no family attribution based on identity of the executor and trustee, Mr. Bright. The *Land* dictum is established law. Edwards v. Slocum, 264 U.S. at 62, 44 S.Ct. at 293 (Holmes, J. saying, "It [the tax] comes into existence before, and is independent of, the receipt of the property by the legatee."); Ithaca Trust Co. v. United States, 279 U.S. at 155, 49 S.Ct. at 292 (Holmes, J. saying, "The tax is on the act of the testator, not on the receipt of the property by the legatees."); Walter v. United States, 341 F.2d 182, 185 (6th Cir.1965) ("[T]he estate tax is imposed upon the *transfer* of property by a decedent, and not the *receipt* of property by a beneficiary. . . ." (emphasis in original)). The *Land* dictum also comports with common sense. It would be strange indeed if the estate tax value of a block of stock would vary depending upon the legatee to whom it was devised.

* * *

Accordingly, we affirm the district court's ruling to the extent that it defined the interest to be valued as equivalent to 27 ½% of the stock, to the extent that it excluded as evidence of value the fact that the estate's stock had, prior to decedent's death, been held jointly with Mr. Bright's interest as community property, and the fact that, after death, the particular executor (Mr. Bright) and legatee (Mr. Bright as trustee) was related to another stock holder (Mr. Bright individually), and to the extent that it excluded any evidence that Mr. Bright, as executor or trustee, would have refused to sell the estate's 27 ½% block except in conjunction with his own stock and as part of a 55% control block. We hold that family attribution cannot be applied to lump the estate's stock to that of any related party, but rather that the stock is deemed to be held by a hypothetical seller who is related to no one.

* * *

For the foregoing reasons, we AFFIRM.

DISSENTING OPINION

ALVIN B. RUBIN, CIRCUIT JUDGE, with whom VANCE, FRANK M. JOHNSON, JR., POLITZ and HATCHETT, CIRCUIT JUDGES, join, dissenting:

It requires my brethren twenty pages of manuscript to explain why they affirm the valuation for estate tax purposes of stock at an amount that is but 27% of the value that the taxpayer's own experts placed on that stock's pro rata share of the corporation's "public value." Thus, stock that, according to the bearish view of the taxpayer's appraisers, would have a "public value" of $4.4 million is valued at $1.2 million for tax purposes. The estate tax law imposes a tax based on fair market value and the majority affirms a tax refund on the basis of a record from which evidence relevant to the determination of that value was excluded. I, therefore, respectfully dissent from the result reached. I would remand the case so that all of the admissible evidence can be weighed.

Like the majority, I reject many of the government's contentions. The time for evaluation of donated stock is the moment of transfer. Whether stock transferred either inter vivos or upon death was, before its transfer, held in community with the owner's spouse is, of course, irrelevant to its value at the moment of transfer. So, too, is the kinship of the decedent with other stockholders.

While my colleagues discuss at length why the value of the 27.5% interest should not be enhanced because it is part of a majority block and thus controls the corporation, they do not discuss why it should be discounted to one-half its public value because it is a minority interest. An appraisal based on "public value" of $4.4 million might be increased if control-value is considered. It does not necessarily follow that, because the control-value premium cannot be added, a subtraction because the stock represents a minority interest is correct.

The value that must be determined is the "price at which the property would change hands between a willing buyer and a willing seller, neither being under any compulsion to buy or to sell and both having reasonable knowledge of relevant facts." Reg. § 20.2031–1(b). This classic formulation assumes shrewd traders on both sides. Such traders would know that Mr. Bright owned 27.5% of the stock, Mr. Schiff owned 30%, and that the 27.5% available from the willing seller would give control to Bright or to Schiff or could be used to maneuver a course between them. My colleagues agree that these facts would be admissible evidence and that the facts at least "might" affect the fair market value of the 27.5% interest.

* * *

Insofar as the pre-trial order ruled that the stock should not be valued as part of the community, it was correct. Insofar as it went further, it was premature and it foreclosed evidence plainly admissible. Because this barrier excluded light that might have revealed the fair market value of the stock and, indeed, the possible gross injustice of valuing it at 27% of its "public value," I respectfully dissent.

Revenue Ruling 93–12
1993–1 C.B. 202.

Issue

If a donor transfers shares in a corporation to each of the donor's children, is the factor of corporate control in the family to be considered in valuing each transferred interest, for purposes of section 2512 of the Internal Revenue Code?

Facts

P owned all of the single outstanding class of stock of X corporation. P transferred all of P's shares by making simultaneous gifts of 20 percent of the shares to each of P's five children, A, B, C, D, and E.

Law and Analysis

* * *

Section 25.2512–2(a) of the regulations provides that the value of stocks and bonds is the fair market value per share or bond on the date of the gift. Section 25.2512–2(f) provides that the degree of control of the business represented by the block of stock to be valued is among the factors to be considered in valuing stock where there are no sales prices or bona fide bid or asked prices.

Rev. Rul. 81–253, 1981–1 C.B. 187, holds that, ordinarily, no minority shareholder discount is allowed with respect to transfers of shares of stock between family members if, based upon a composite of the family members' interests at the time of the transfer, control (either majority voting control or de facto control through family relationships) of the corporation exists in the family unit. The ruling also states that the Service will not follow the decision of the Fifth Circuit in Estate of Bright v. United States, 658 F.2d 999 (5th Cir.1981).

In *Bright*, the decedent's undivided community property interest in shares of stock, together with the corresponding undivided community property interest of the decedent's surviving spouse, constituted a control block of 55 percent of the shares of a corporation. The court held that, because the community-held shares were subject to a right of partition, the decedent's own interest was equivalent to 27.5 percent of the outstanding shares and, therefore, should be valued as a minority interest, even though the shares were to be held by the decedent's surviving spouse as trustee of a testamentary trust. See also, Propstra v. United States, 680 F.2d 1248 (9th Cir.1982). In addition, Estate of Andrews v. Commissioner, 79 T.C.

938 (1982), and Estate of Lee v. Commissioner, 69 T.C. 860 (1978), nonacq., 1980–2 C.B. 2, held that the corporation shares owned by other family members cannot be attributed to an individual family member for determining whether the individual family member's shares should be valued as the controlling interest of the corporation.

After further consideration of the position taken in Rev. Rul. 81–253, and in light of the cases noted above, the Service has concluded that, in the case of a corporation with a single class of stock, notwithstanding the family relationship of the donor, the donee, and other shareholders, the shares of other family members will not be aggregated with the transferred shares to determine whether the transferred shares should be valued as part of a controlling interest.

In the present case, the minority interests transferred to A, B, C, D, and E should be valued for gift tax purposes without regard to the family relationship of the parties.

HOLDING

If a donor transfers shares in a corporation to each of the donor's children, the factor of corporate control in the family is not considered in valuing each transferred interest for purposes of section 2512 of the Code. For estate and gift tax valuation purposes, the Service will follow *Bright, Propstra, Andrews,* and *Lee* in not assuming that all voting power held by family members may be aggregated for purposes of determining whether the transferred shares should be valued as part of a controlling interest. Consequently, a minority discount will not be disallowed solely because a transferred interest, when aggregated with interests held by family members, would be a part of a controlling interest. This would be the case whether the donor held 100 percent or some lesser percentage of the stock immediately before the gift.

* * *

NOTE

As indicated by *Bright*, a central issue is that of aggregation—whether minority interests can be combined for valuation purposes. In *Bright*, the court declined to aggregate the respective 27.5% interests of the husband and wife, with the result that the decedent wife's 27.5% interest was treated separately, and therefore qualified for a minority discount. Had the two interests been aggregated to total 55%, not only would a minority discount have been denied, but a control premium would have been added. Thus, the *Bright* rule negating aggregation among family members can be crucially important.

In Estate of Bonner v. United States, 84 F.3d 196 (5th Cir.1996), the *Bright* rule was extended to deny aggregation in the case of separate interests included in the same decedent's gross estate. The principle is best illustrated by the court's treatment of what it refers to as the "New Mexico property." The wife died first, bequeathing to a trust benefitting her husband a 50% interest in the New Mexico property. The husband was entitled to all income from the trust throughout his life. The wife's executor made the election described in section 2056(b)(7) as to the trust, thereby qualifying the trust's 50% interest for the marital deduction in the wife's estate but requiring inclusion of the trust's 50% interest in the husband's gross estate at his death pursuant to section 2044. At his death the husband owned the other 50% of the New Mexico property outright, and this was included in his gross estate under section 2033. Although 100% of the New Mexico property was therefore included in the husband's gross estate, the court nevertheless concluded that each 50% must be viewed separately, and each qualified for a fractional interest discount, discussed later in this chapter.

In Estate of Mellinger v. Commissioner, 112 T.C. 26 (1999), the Tax Court reached the same result—again declining to combine the decedent's own stock with stock held in a QTIP trust for his benefit (and therefore included in the decedent's gross estate under section 2044). The Commissioner acquiesced in this decision. See IRS Announcement 99–116, 1999–2 C.B. 763. Further analysis of *Mellinger* is provided in Chapter 27 in the context of the marital deduction.

In Estate of Fontana v. Commissioner, 118 T.C. 318 (2002), however, the Tax Court reached the contrary result in the case of a section 2056(b)(5) life estate power of appointment trust. Here the wife had predeceased the husband, transferring 44% of the stock to a trust that provided a life estate for the husband and giving him a general power to appoint the stock to anyone (including himself) at his death. Upon the husband's later death, he owned 50% of the stock outright. The Tax Court concluded that the two blocks should be treated as combined to produce 94% ownership in the husband, thereby denying any minority discount. The court observed that a general power of appointment is viewed as "essentially identical to outright ownership." Therefore, the husband could dispose of the entire 94% collectively, and aggregation was appropriate. The court distinguished the *Bonner* and *Mellinger* cases on the ground that in those cases the surviving spouse did not have power to dictate the disposition of the trust property after the surviving spouse's death.

Like control premiums, minority discounts can vary widely, depending on the circumstances, such as the nature of the business and the pattern of ownership. Nevertheless, many planners have come to expect a minority discount of 30% or more in routine situations. This view is based on such cases as Carr v. Commissioner, 49 T.C.M. (CCH) 507 (1985), in which a 25% discount was allowed, and Ward v. Commissioner, 87 T.C. 78 (1986), in which a 50% discount was allowed. Both the IRS and the courts, however, take the position that a substantial minority discount will be allowed only if the taxpayer can offer persuasive evidence in support of the discount. For example, in Knight v. Commissioner, 115 T.C. 506 (2000), the Tax Court reduced the claimed total discounts of 44% to only 15%. The court viewed the evidence offered in support of the discounts as insufficient to support the higher levels claimed. Still, the converse is equally valid. If the taxpayer can effectively document the reasons why a prospective buyer would discount the purchase price substantially, a large discount should be achieved.

A minority discount has been allowed for a 50% interest on the ground that a 50% owner cannot control corporate action. Wheeler v. United States, 96–1 U.S.T.C. ¶ 60,226, 77 A.F.T.R.2d 96–1411 (W.D. Tex. 1996). For that reason, the minority discount is sometimes referred to as the "lack of control" discount.

D. MARKETABILITY DISCOUNTS

Discounts are often allowed in order to reflect the lack of marketability of an asset. The willing buyer-willing seller approach can produce unrealistically high values if the market is thin, buyers are few, or the asset has unusual infirmities.

Such discounts, which can be as high as 35 percent, are often applied to interests in closely held businesses, even if a minority discount is not available. The valuation initially assigned to the business under Rev. Rul. 59–60 is derived by analogy from publicly traded interests. Buyers will not pay as much for investments for which there is no ready market. The IRS often resists or seeks to reduce marketability discounts, especially in circumstances in which the assets held by the entity are readily marketable.

Historically, there was some confusion between minority discounts and marketability discounts. Courts often granted a single discount percentage, such as 40%, without segregating the discount between that attributable to minority status and that attributable to lack of marketability. The distinction between the two is important because even a controlling interest can qualify for a marketability discount if interests in the entity are not regularly traded. In recent years, the courts have properly tended to segregate the minority, marketability, and other discounts described below, specifying a percentage for each discount.

As indicated above, a modest marketability discount is routinely allowed if the stock is not listed on an exchange. If the marketability of the stock is subject to specific restrictions on sale, the marketability discount may be substantially greater. For example, in Estate of McClatchy v. Commissioner, 147 F.3d 1089 (9th Cir. 1998), the Ninth Circuit faced the difficult issue of determining value where the securities laws restricted sale of the decedent's stock. In *McClatchy*, the decedent owned two million shares of a publicly traded stock. Because the decedent was an "affiliate" of the corporation for securities law purposes, sale of the shares by him would have been importantly restricted. For that reason, the executor contended that the shares should be valued at only $25 million, as compared to the $36 million value that would be applied (according to the IRS) if no such restrictions were present. The executor of the decedent's estate, however, was not an "affiliate." Therefore, the executor was free to sell the stock without securities law restrictions. The IRS argued that because the decedent's death had the effect of eliminating the securities law restrictions, the stock should be valued for estate tax purposes at $36 million.

A divided Ninth Circuit rejected the IRS position and held that the proper valuation was $25 million. The court reasoned that the securities law restrictions were eliminated, not by the death of the owner, but by the ownership of stock by a nonaffiliate (i.e., the executor). The court cited well established law, including *Bright*, to the effect that for estate tax purposes assets must be valued without regard to the identity of the recipient. The majority proved its point by observing that if the executor were an affiliate, the restrictions would remain in place, and the stock would then be worth only $25 million. Therefore, the increase in value to $36 million was not attributable to the death of the decedent, but to the nonaffiliate status of the executor. Permitting the nonaffiliate status of the executor to control would directly violate the rule that, for estate tax purposes, the identity of the recipient of the property is irrelevant to valuation.

E. DISCOUNTS FOR PROSPECTIVE INCOME TAX LIABILITY

If the asset to be valued is corporation stock, and the corporation owns appreciated assets, a buyer of the stock might well take into account the prospective tax that would have to be paid upon the corporation's sale of the appreciated assets, or upon distribution of the corporate assets to the buyer (as shareholder). Hence it is arguable that the value of the stock should be discounted to take into account the prospective tax liability that would be incurred on such a sale or distribution.

Under current corporation tax rules, it is generally not possible for a corporation to get appreciated corporation assets into the hands of shareholders without paying tax on the appreciation. The gain will be taxed to the corporation whether the transfer of the asset to the shareholders occurs in the form of a distribution, redemption of stock, or liquidation. I.R.C. §§ 311(b)(1) & 336(a). If the corporation has elected to be taxed under Subchapter S, however, it may be possible to effectively avoid taxation of the gain embodied in the corporation's appreciated property.

The following case addresses the availability of a valuation discount where there may be prospective income tax liability of this kind.

ESTATE OF JELKE V. COMMISSIONER

United States Court of Appeals, Eleventh Circuit, 2007.
507 F.3d 1317.

HILL, CIRCUIT JUDGE:

This estate tax case presents on appeal an issue of first impression in this circuit. It involves the proper valuation for estate tax purposes of a 6.44% stock interest, or 3,000 shares, owned by the decedent, Frazier Jelke III (Jelke or decedent or estate), in a closely-held, investment holding company, Commercial Chemical Company (CCC), owning appreciated, marketable securities.

The issue is whether or not the Tax Court used the appropriate valuation methodology in computing the net asset value of CCC to determine the value of Jelke's interest in CCC for estate tax purposes on the date of death. The Tax Court, adopting the Commissioner's expert witness appraiser's approach, allowed the estate only a partial $21 million discount for CCC's built-in capital gains tax liability, indexed to reflect present value on the date of Jelke's death, using projections based upon the court's findings as to when the assets would likely be sold and when the tax liability would likely be incurred, i.e., in this case, over a sixteen-year period. Using what could be termed an economic market reality theory, the estate argued, under the rationale set forth by the Fifth Circuit Court of Appeals in *Estate of Dunn v. Comm'r,* 301 F.3d 339 (5th Cir.2002), that a 100% dollar-for-dollar discount was mandated for CCC's entire contingent $51 million capital gains tax liability. Under this theory, it is assumed that CCC is liquidated on the date of Jelke's death, the valuation date, and all assets of CCC are sold, regardless of the parties' intent to liquidate or not, or restrictions on CCC's liquidation in general.

Based upon the following historical overview, discussion, and precedential authority, we are in accord with the simple yet logical analysis of the tax discount valuation issue set forth by the Fifth Circuit in *Estate of Dunn,* 301 F.3d at 350–55, providing practical certainty to tax practitioners, appraisers and financial planners alike. Under a *de novo* review, as a matter of law, we vacate the judgment of the Tax Court and remand with instructions that it recalculate the net asset value of CCC on the date of Jelke's death, and his 6.44% interest therein, using a dollar-for-dollar reduction of the entire $51 million built-in capital gains tax liability of CCC, under the arbitrary assumption that CCC is liquidated on the date of death and all assets sold.

I. FACTUAL BACKGROUND

Jelke died testate on March 4, 1999, in Miami, Florida. On the date of his death, CCC's marketable securities had a fair market value of $178 million, plus a built-in contingent capital gains tax liability of $51 million on those securities. Combined with $10 million in other CCC assets, without regard to the tax liability, CCC's net asset value totaled $188 million.

On the estate's federal estate tax return filed December 6, 1999, Jelke's 6.44% interest in CCC, held through his revocable trust, was included in his gross estate under Section 2031 at a value of $4,588,155. I.R.C. § 2031. The estate calculated this figure by reducing CCC's $188 million net asset value by $51 million, or 100% of the built-in capital gains tax liability. It then applied a 20% discount for lack of control and a 35% discount for lack of marketability.

In his December 2, 2002, notice of deficiency issued to the estate, the Commissioner determined that Jelke's estate owed a deficiency in estate tax of $2,564,772, resulting from an undervaluation of Jelke's 6.44% interest in CCC. The Commissioner determined that the value of Jelke's 6.44% interest in CCC was $9,111,000, not the $4,588,155, claimed by the estate. Unlike the estate's 100% discount, he calculated the $9,111,000 using a zero discount for built-in capital gains taxes, and what he described as "reasonable" discounts for lack of control and lack of marketability.

II.   PROCEDURAL BACKGROUND

The estate filed a petition in Tax Court in March 2003, contesting the Commissioner's $9,111,000 fair market value of Jelke's 6.44% interest in CCC stock on the date of death. It claimed that the Commissioner had based his value on an incorrect net asset value of CCC, by declining to discount CCC's net asset value of $188 million, by the $51 million in contingent built-in capital gains tax liability, accrued as of the date of death. The estate also claimed that the Commissioner undervalued the two additional discounts available to the estate, one for lack of marketability and one for lack of control.

After a two-day bench trial, the Tax Court rejected the estate's position that CCC's net asset value must be reduced dollar-for-dollar by the entire amount of the built-in capital gains tax liability under *Estate of Dunn*, 301 F.3d at 351–53, as the *Estate of Dunn* was a Fifth Circuit, not an Eleventh Circuit, case. It determined that a discount was available, but not one for 100%.

The Tax Court noted that a hypothetical buyer of 6.44% of CCC stock single-handedly would be unable to cause or force a liquidation of CCC. It stated that CCC's long-term history of dividends and appreciation, with no immediate plans to liquidate (one trust continues until 2019), together with its low annual turnover of securities in the portfolio, belied the *Estate of Dunn's* threshold, arbitrary assumption of complete liquidation on the valuation date. Further, the Tax Court distinguished *Estate of Dunn* on the fact that the Fifth Circuit in *Estate of Dunn* was valuing a majority, not a minority, shareholder interest as was present here. Also the company valued in the *Estate of Dunn* was primarily (85%) an operating company, unlike CCC, a 100% investment holding company.

Under the net asset valuation approach, the Tax Court adopted the Commissioner's argument that the capital gains tax discount should be reduced to present value, as computed on an annualized, indexed basis, over the sixteen-year period it was expected to be incurred as the assets turned over. Instead of a $51 million reduction, the Tax Court's present value application to net asset value resulted in a $21 million tax discount reduction, and a net deficiency in estate tax of $1 million.

This appeal follows.

* * *

IV. DISCUSSION

A. Introduction

The issue in this case is, for estate tax purposes, the proper calculation of the magnitude of the discount for built-in capital gains taxes in valuing stock in a closely-held corporation on the date of death. A general overview of the applicable tax statutes, regulations and revenue rulings is appropriate.

* * *

B. Historical Overview of the Issue Presented on Appeal

1. The Law Prior to the Tax Reform Act of 1986

In *General Utilities & Operating Co. v. Helvering,* 296 U.S. 200, 56 S.Ct. 185, 80 L. Ed. 154 (1935), the Supreme Court held that a C corporation did not recognized taxable income at the corporate level on a distribution of appreciated property to its shareholders. Id. at 206, 56 S.Ct. 185. Congress responded to this holding, later to become known as "the *General Utilities* doctrine," by enacting § 311(a). From 1935 to 1986, the fair market value of the distributed corporate property became the shareholders' adjusted stepped-up basis for the property received. It was therefore possible for a corporation to distribute its appreciated assets to its shareholders without incurring any income tax liability at the corporate level. Id.; *see also* I.R.C. § 301(d).

With one exception during this fifty-one year period, case law did not allow a discount for built-in capital gains tax liability when a sale or liquidation was neither planned nor imminent, as it was deemed by the courts to be too uncertain, remote or speculative. *See Estate of Andrews v. Comm'r*, 79 T.C. 938, 942 (1982) (projected capital gains taxes do not reduce the value of closely-held stock when liquidation is only speculative as it is unlikely taxes will ever be incurred); *Estate of Piper v. Comm'r*, 72 T.C. 1062, 1086–87 (1979) (in gift tax case, capital gains discount unwarranted under net asset value method where there is no evidence that a liquidation of the investment companies was planned); *Estate of Cruikshank v. Comm'r*, 9 T.C. 162, 165 (1947) (no sale of portfolio securities projected in closely-held family investment corporation).

* * *

2.   The Tax Reform Act of 1986

The Tax Reform Act of 1986 (TRA 1986) made dramatic tax law changes. New rules were enacted to require the recognition of corporate-level gains on the distributions of appreciated property under Section § 311(b), thereby repealing the *General Utilities* doctrine and I.R.C. §§ 336 and 337. *See* I.R.C. § 311(b).

Prior to the repeal of the *General Utilities* doctrine by TRA 1986, no corporate tax would have been required to be paid and no discount would have been allowed. TRA 1986 required recognition of corporate-level gains and losses on liquidating sales and on distributions of corporate property.

With the repeal of the doctrine, courts began to recognize the possibility that a discount related to the capital gains taxes incurred should be allowable. Due to the taxpayer's inability to receive a step-up in basis to fair market value on the valuation date after TRA 1986, it now became more important than ever for a taxpayer to be able to quantify his or her loss in value of the stock due to inherent capital gains tax liability in the corporation.

* * *

C.   Historical Evolution of Precedential Case Law on the Issue on Appeal

* * *

In *Estate of Eisenberg v. Comm'r*, 74 T.C.M (CCH) 1046 (1997), the donor gave away shares of stock in her closely-held corporation. She owned all 1,000 shares in a corporation whose only asset was a commercial office building. The corporation's only activity was renting office space in the building to clients. There were no plans to sell the building or liquidate the corporation.

Nevertheless, the donor sought to reduce the value of the gifted shares of the closely-held corporation to account for the fact that, if its asset was sold, the sale would trigger a tax gain to the corporation. *Estate of Eisenberg*, 74 T.C.M. at 2. The Tax Court, notwithstanding the repeal of the *General Utilities* doctrine, and still citing its pre-1986 cases, declined to allow the tax discount to the donor on the basis that it was unlikely that a hypothetical buyer would want to liquidate the corporation or sell its underlying assets on the transfer date. "[T]he primary reason for disallowing a discount for capital gains taxes in this situation is that the tax liability itself is deemed to be speculative," therefore, its discount value should be zero.

The Second Circuit Court of Appeals disagreed. *Eisenberg v. Comm'r,* 155 F.3d 50, 57 (2d Cir.1998). Buoyed by the Tax Court's own recent decision in *Estate of Davis,* the Second Circuit concluded that, although no liquidation of the corporation or sale of corporate assets was imminent or contemplated at the time of the gift, the requirement of an imminent sale was unnecessary. Id. It was the opinion of the court that a willing buyer would demand a discount to take account of the fact that, sooner or later, the tax would have to be paid.

For the first time since the enactment of TRA 1986, the mandate by the Commissioner and the Tax Court of an imminent sale or liquidation, *notwithstanding* the revocation of the *General Utilities* doctrine, was addressed directly by a circuit court of appeal:

> The issue is not what a hypothetical willing buyer plans to do with the property, but what considerations affect the fair market value of the property he considers buying. While prior to the [TRA 1986] any buyer of a corporation's stock could avoid potential built-in capital gains tax, there is simply no evidence to dispute that a hypothetical willing buyer today would likely pay less for the shares of a corporation because of a buyer's inability to eliminate the contingent tax liability.

Eisenberg, 155 F.3d at 57.

"Further, we believe, contrary to the opinion of the Tax Court, since the *General Utilities* doctrine has been revoked by statute, a tax liability upon liquidation or sale for built-in gains is not too speculative in this case." Id. at 58. The Second Circuit vacated and remanded the Tax Court decision for recalculation.

* * *

There is dicta in *Eisenberg* to suggest, however, that it would be incorrect to conclude that the full amount of the potential capital gains tax should be used. After the *Estate of Eisenberg,* disputes between the taxpayers and the Commissioner focused upon the magnitude of the discount allowable, not the legal right of the taxpayers to claim them.

* * *

A year later, the Fifth Circuit went one step further in *Estate of Dunn v. Comm'r,* 301 F.3d 339 (5th Cir. 2002). At the time of her death, Mrs. Dunn owned a majority 62.96% of the stock of a family-owned corporation engaged in the rental of heavy equipment. The family company also managed certain commercial property as an investment.

As Texas corporate law required a 66.66% interest in the voting shares to affect a liquidation, with 62.9%, Mrs. Dunn did not own a "supermajority," or 66.6%, that could force a liquidation. The facts further indicated that the family company planned to remain viable and in operation for some time.

Using a willing buyer-willing seller fair market value test, the Tax Court in the *Estate of Dunn,* while agreeing with the Commissioner's argument that the tax was certainly speculative, still agreed to discount the stock price by 5% of the built-in capital gains as a matter of law. This holding was in response to the existence of a very small possibility that a hypothetical buyer would liquidate the company. The 5% discount was in lieu of the 34% reduction sought by the taxpayers. The Tax Court concluded that it was much more likely that a hypothetical buyer would continue to operate the company.

The Fifth Circuit disagreed emphatically with the Tax Court. In the *Estate of Dunn,* under a net asset valuation approach, the Fifth Circuit determined value by totaling the corporation's assets and subtracting its liabilities. It held that a hypothetical willing buyer-willing seller *must always be assumed* to immediately liquidate the corporation, triggering a tax on the built-in gains. Thereby substantially altering the Tax Court's fair market value test, the Fifth Circuit held, as a matter of law, that, *as a threshold assumption,* liquidation must always be assumed when calculating an asset under the net asset value approach. The Fifth Circuit labeled as a "red herring" the fact that no liquidation was imminent or even likely.

Turning to the proper amount of the discount, the Fifth Circuit concluded that the value of the assets must be reduced by a discount equal to 100% of the capital gains liability, dollar for dollar. The court relied upon the assumption that, in a net asset valuation context, the hypothetical buyer is predisposed to buy stock to gain control of the company for the sole purpose of acquiring its underlying assets. Id. This, in turn, triggers a tax on the built-in gains. Hence, the discount should be 100%, dollar-for-dollar. An era of valuation certainty had begun.

* * *

D. Applying the Fifth Circuit *Estate of Dunn* Rationale to the Present Appeal

Juxtaposed against the backdrop of this emerging case law, the question before the Tax Court in this case, and now before us, is what was the value of Jelke's 6.44% interest in CCC on March 4, 1999? Which dollar figure do we use to discount the fair market value of CCC's securities for built-in capital gains on March 4, 1999? Is it dollar-for-dollar, as the estate contends, under the rationale set forth in 2002 by the Fifth Circuit in the

Estate of Dunn, or $51 million? Or is it the present value of the capital gains indexed over a sixteen-year period, as the Commissioner contends, or $21 million?

* * *

In our case, why would a hypothetical willing buyer of CCC shares *not* adjust his or her purchase price to reflect the entire $51 million amount of CCC's built-in capital gains tax liability? The buyer could just as easily venture into the open marketplace and acquire an identical portfolio of blue chip domestic and international securities as those held by CCC. Yet the buyer could accomplish this without any risk exposure to the underlying tax liability lurking within CCC due to its low cost basis in the securities.

* * *

The Fifth Circuit in the *Estate of Dunn* is the first court to emerge with a precise valuation approach as to the amount of the reduction and how to calculate it. As a threshold matter, the court creates the arbitrary assumption that all assets are sold in liquidation on the valuation date, and 100% of the built-in capital gains tax liability is offset against the fair market value of the stock, dollar-for-dollar. *Estate of Dunn,* 301 F.3d at 352–54.

Cases prior to the *Estate of Dunn,* prophesying as to when the assets will be sold and reducing the tax liability to present value, depending upon the length of time discerned by the court over which these taxes shall be paid, require a crystal ball. The longer the time, the lower the discount. The shorter the time, the higher the discount.

* * *

We think the approach set forth by the Fifth Circuit in the *Estate of Dunn* is the better of the two. The estate tax owed is calculated based upon a "snap shot of valuation" frozen on the date of Jelke's death, taking into account only those facts known on that date. It is more logical and appropriate to value the shares of CCC stock on the date of death based upon an assumption that a liquidation has occurred, without resort to present values or prophesies.

* * *

The *Estate of Dunn* dollar-for-dollar approach also bypasses the unnecessary expenditure of judicial resources being used to wade through a myriad of divergent expert witness testimony, based upon subjective conjecture, and divergent opinions. The *Estate of Dunn* has the virtue of simplicity and its methodology provides a practical and theoretically sound foundation as to how to address the discount issue.

* * *

This 100% approach settles the issue as a matter of law, and provides certainty that is typically missing in the valuation arena. We thereby follow the rationale of the Fifth Circuit in the *Estate of Dunn,* that allows a dollar-for-dollar, $51 million discount for contingent capital gains taxes in valuing CCC on the date of Jelke's death, and his 6.44% interest therein. This result prevents grossly inequitable results from occurring and also prevents us, the federal judiciary, from assuming the role of arbitrary business consultants.

V.   CONCLUSION

Based upon the foregoing discussion, as a matter of law, under a *de novo* review, we vacate the judgment of the Tax Court and remand with instructions that the Tax Court recalculate the net asset value of CCC on the date of Jelke's death, and his 6.44% interest therein, using a dollar-for-dollar reduction of the entire $51 million in built-in capital gains tax liability, under the assumption that CCC is liquidated on the date of death and all assets sold.

VACATED and REMANDED with INSTRUCTIONS.

CARNES, CIRCUIT JUDGE, dissenting:

* * *

By adopting and extending the arbitrary assumption rule of least effort from *Estate of Dunn v. Comm'r,* 301 F.3d 339 (5th Cir.2002), the majority gives in to the judicial equivalent of the doctrine of ignoble ease. To avoid the effort, labor, and toil that is required for a more accurate calculation of the estate tax due, the majority simply assumes a result that we all know is wrong. We can do better than that. The Tax Court did.

* * *

The Tax Court summarized the IRS's contention, put forward by its expert, Mr. Shaked, as follows:

> Respondent's expert, Mr. Shaked, started with the same market value of CCC's securities. Mr. Shaked then reduced the assets by liabilities, but he used a different approach from Mr. Frazier's in arriving at a reduction for the built-in capital gain tax liability. First, he computed CCC's average securities turnover by reference to the most recent data (1994–98). Using that data, Mr. Shaked computed a 5.95-percent average annual turnover derived from the parties' stipulated asset turnover rates for 1994–98. Mr. Shaked believed that the 5.95-percent rate was conservative, because the turnover trend was generally decreasing. The use of the 5.95-percent turnover rate results in the capital gain tax's being incurred over a 16.8-year period (100 percent divided by 5.95 percent).

Mr. Shaked then divided the $51,626,884 tax liability by 16 years to arrive at the average annual capital gain tax liability that would have been incurred each year over this 16-year period—$3,226,680.25 ($51,626,884 divided by 16). Next, he selected a 13.2-percent discount rate based on the average annual rate of return for large-cap stocks in the period from 1926 to 1998, as described in Ibbotson Associates Stocks, Bonds, Bills & Inflation, 1999 Yearbook (Ibbotson 1999). He then computed the present value of the $3,226,680.25 annual tax liability discounted over 16 years using a 13.2-percent interest rate to arrive at a present value for the total capital gain tax liability of $21,082,226. By reducing the $188,635,833 net asset value by the $21,082,226 future tax liability, Mr. Shaked arrived at a $167,553,607 value for CCC. Finally, Mr. Shaked concluded that the undiscounted value for decedent's 6.44-percent interest in CCC was $10,789,164 in contrast to Mr. Frazier's undiscounted value of $8,823,062. This difference reflects numerically the parties' differing approaches to the amount of capital gain tax that should be used to reduce the net asset value of CCC.

The Tax Court adopted the IRS's real value approach, even though it is more complicated than the estate's simple but arbitrary assumption that all of the assets were sold at the time of death. The court chose the real value approach because it produces a result closer to the actual value of the company's assets, which in turn leads to a more accurate determination of the sales price a willing buyer and seller would agree on for the shares of the holding company that Jelke owned on the date of his death.

* * *

The majority's approach assumes that the holding company was liquidated on the date of Jelke's death, and therefore all of its built-in capital gains were incurred (and therefore passed on to its shareholders) immediately. The majority makes that assumption despite the fact that: historically the company has sold only 5.95 percent of its investments and therefore precipitated only that small portion of the total built-in capital gains liability per year, the company is earning an annual return of more than 23 percent on its portfolio investments, and, "[a]s of the date of decedent's death, CCC's board of directors had no plans to liquidate an appreciable portion of CCC's portfolio, and they intended to operate CCC as a going concern." Under these circumstances, the notion that the company would suddenly dispose of its highly profitable portfolio, ending the enviable earnings stream, and inflicting a substantial capital gains tax on its shareholders is preposterous. The fact that Jelke died does not make it any less so.

* * *

Any rational being would prefer to pay $51 million in taxes spread out over the next 16.8 years, which is how long it would take for the embedded tax liability to come fully due under the company's historical rate of liquidation, instead of paying the entire $51 million immediately. Ask yourself: If you had the choice would you prefer to pay the taxes you are going to owe over the next 16 or so years in advance, right now, or would you choose to pay those taxes only when they come due in the future? The majority would assume, because it makes the calculations easier, that you would choose to pay all of your future taxes now.

* * *

To its credit, the majority concedes that its approach is arbitrary. The majority describes its operating premise that a holding company would instantly liquidate its entire investment portfolio on the date of a minority shareholder's death as an "arbitrary assumption." Seeking to justify its approach, the majority argues that being arbitrary "provides certainty and finality" and "bypasses the unnecessary expenditure of judicial resources" that is required to make a more realistic calculation. Indeed, it does. Of course, the same could be said about any arbitrary assumption, including one that the securities had no value at all or that the capital gains tax liability would never actually be paid for some unknown reason. Either of those arbitrary assumptions would also avoid the unnecessary expenditure of judicial resources while providing certainty and finality. Once the doctrine of ignoble ease and seductive simplicity is allowed to reign, there is no end to the shortcuts that can be taken.

* * *

NOTE

The discount for prospective tax liability is sometimes referred to as the "BIG discount," with BIG referring to "built in gain."

Efforts to expand the BIG discount beyond C corporation stock have been unsuccessful. In Estate of Smith v. Commissioner, 391 F.3d 621 (5th Cir. 2004), the executor argued that retirement accounts owned by the decedent should be discounted to reflect the tax liability that distributees would incur upon distribution of the account funds to them. Such distributions would be fully taxable to the distributees because the distribution would constitute income in respect of a decedent (IRD). (IRD is discussed in Chapter 32.) The court denied any discount, reasoning that a hypothetical buyer of the accounts would not be one of the beneficiaries and hence would not be concerned with tax liability. The court's more convincing rationale, however, was that Congress has already granted relief against double taxation (both estate and income) in these circumstances through the special IRD deduction allowed by section 691(c).

The Tax Court applied the same rationale in denying a discount for the prospective tax liability inherent in an IRA owned by the decedent. Estate of Kahn v. Commissioner, 125 T.C. 227 (2005). Similarly, the IRS denied a discount for the prospective tax liability that would be imposed upon any distribution of accrued interest under Series E United States Savings Bonds. Tech. Adv. Mem. 200303010.

F. DISCOUNTS FOR PROSPECTIVE ESTATE TAX LIABILITY

In Succession of McCord v. Commissioner, 461 F.3d 614 (5th Cir. 2006), the taxpayer achieved a substantial discount for prospective estate tax liability.

The octogenarian donor transferred limited partnership interests to his children. As a condition of the transfers, the children agreed to pay any gift tax that might be imposed on the transfers. As discussed in Chapter 3, the value of a gift for gift tax purposes must be reduced to the extent the donee commits to pay the attendant gift tax. The donor is personally liable for payment of the gift tax. I.R.C. § 2502(c). The donee's payment of gift tax therefore constitutes consideration to the donor, with the result that the "net gift" consists of the full value of the property transferred less the attendant gift tax liability.

In *McCord*, the parties went a step further, and the donee children agreed to pay any estate tax liability that might be caused by the gift. The estate tax liability referred to is imposed by section 2035(b), which requires that the gross estate be "grossed up" to the extent of any gift tax liability caused by a gift within three years prior to death.

For example, assume that Tad makes a gift of $1,000,000 in 2019. Because Tad had made large prior gifts, the $1,000,000 gift creates a gift tax liability of $400,000, which is paid by Tad. If Tad dies in 2020, which is within three years after the gift, the $400,000 is added to Tad's gross estate per section 2035(b). The result is an additional tax of 40% of $400,000, or $160,000.

Because the donor in *McCord* was in his eighties, there was a substantial possibility that he would die within three years after the gift. Therefore, the donor argued that the value of the gift should be discounted not just by the gift tax liability undertaken by the donees, but also by the additional tax liability that would accrue under section 2035(b) if the donor should die within three years after the gift. The prospective tax liability would be analogous to the $160,000 described in the preceding paragraph.

The donor provided expert appraisal testimony that took into account the actuarial probability of the donor's death within three years and further discounted the possible future tax liability back to a present value at the time of the gift. This amount was then subtracted from the value of the gift—in addition to the certain gift tax liability.

A majority of the Tax Court found the prospective section 2035(b) liability too speculative. McCord v. Commissioner, 120 T.C. 358 (2003). The majority reasoned that allowance of a discount would require a series of uncertain assumptions involving the longevity of the donor, the continued existence of the estate tax and of section 2035(b), and the rate at which estate tax would be imposed in a later year.

In a unanimous decision, the Fifth Circuit reversed the Tax Court, finding that the process of determining probable liability under section 2035(b) was no more speculative than many other valuation procedures necessarily employed under the estate tax law. Therefore, a discount should be allowed.

G. FRACTIONAL INTEREST DISCOUNTS

A discount may be available if the decedent owns a fractional interest in an asset—especially real estate—even if the decedent's interest is greater than 50 percent. The theory is that the full value may be obtainable only with integrated disposition and development of the entire property. At the very least, a buyer unwilling to acquiesce in the desires of co-owners would have to bear the cost of a partition action. Even if partition could be achieved inexpensively, the potential development value of a fractional portion might be diminished when separated from the remainder of the property.

For these reasons, significant discounts have been allowed where there is convincing evidence that a severed partial interest would have a value less than its proportionate share of the entire property value.[1] In Estate of Williams v. Commissioner, 75 T.C.M (CCH) 1758 (1998), the taxpayer achieved a total discount of 44%. The taxpayer transferred undivided one-half interests in timberland as a gift. The taxpayer's experts were persuasive, and the court accepted their valuation approach: first a 20% discount for marketability, lowering the net value to 80%. Then a 30% discount from this figure for lack of control, lowering the value by an additional 24% to 56% of the original, undiscounted value.

H. RESTRICTIVE AGREEMENTS

If sale of a security is restricted, its value may be dramatically affected. For example, if a shareholder cannot sell the security to an outsider without first offering it to other shareholders or the issuing corporation for $100 per share, it is difficult to view the value of the security as exceeding $100 per share. Certainly, if a buyer were subject to the same restriction, no prospective buyer would pay more than $100 per share. Hence the

---

[1] See, e.g., Propstra v. United States, 680 F.2d 1248 (9th Cir.1982) (permitting a 15 percent discount on real estate); Estate of Pillsbury v. Commissioner, 64 T.C.M. (CCH) 284 (1992) (permitting a 15 percent discount on commercial real estate); Estate of Youle v. Commissioner, 56 T.C.M. (CCH) 1594 (1989) (allowing a 20–25 percent discount on farmland).

"willing buyer-willing seller" analysis produces a value equivalent to the restriction price.

Although the principle is sound, it has sometimes been exploited to produce unrealistically low valuations in circumstances in which the restriction had little purpose other than tax avoidance. The Treasury and the courts long sought to differentiate between restrictions that legitimately fix values for nontax reasons and those that should be disregarded as tax motivated.

Because of continuing litigation involving restrictive agreements, Congress in 1990 adopted legislation aimed squarely at the use of restrictive agreements to fix valuation for transfer tax purposes. Section 2703(a) states the general rule that all such restrictions are to be disregarded in determining valuation of the restricted property.

Nevertheless, the restriction will be given effect for valuation purposes if the restriction meets the following requirements enumerated in section 2703(b):

1. The restriction must be a "bona fide business arrangement."

2. The restriction must not be "a device to transfer such property to members of the decedent's family for less than full and adequate consideration in money or money's worth."

3. The terms of the restriction must be "comparable to similar arrangements entered into by persons in an arms' length transaction."

Requirements 1 and 2 were already well established prior to adoption of section 2703 and are expressly stated in Regulation § 20.2031–2(h). However, the Senate Committee Report states that section 2703 is designed to strengthen requirement 2:

> [Section 2703] clarifies that the business arrangement and device requirements are independent tests. The mere showing that the agreement is a bona fide business arrangement would not give the agreement estate tax effect if other facts indicated that the agreement is a device to transfer property to members of the decedent's family for less than full and adequate consideration. In making this clarification, it adopts the reasoning of St. Louis County Bank v. United States, 674 F.2d 1207 (8th Cir.1982), and rejects the suggestions of other cases that the maintenance of family control standing alone assures the absence of a device to transfer wealth.

S. Rep. No. 3209, 101st Cong., 2d Sess. 67–68 (1990).

Requirement 3 was new with section 2703 and imposes the additional requirement that the agreement must conform to industry valuation practices that would be applied if unrelated parties were involved.

Section 2703 is effective as to restrictions or agreements entered into or "substantially modified" after October 8, 1990. Revenue Reconciliation Act of 1990, section 11602(e)(1)(A)(ii). The Treasury has taken a very expansive view of what might constitute a "substantial modification" of a pre-October 9, 1990, agreement. Under the Treasury interpretation, even minor changes or the addition of new parties could be treated as "substantial modifications," triggering application of section 2703 rather than the more liberal case law rules that controlled prior to adoption of section 2703. Treas. Reg. § 25.2703–1(c). Therefore, caution should be exercised in amending or adding parties to any pre-October 9, 1990, agreement.

I. LAPSING RIGHTS

Special valuation rules are applied to lapsing rights involving closely held businesses. The lapse of certain rights is treated as a gift if the lapse occurs during the lifetime of the person holding the rights. If the lapse occurs at the death of the person holding the rights, that person's gross estate is increased by the value of the lapsing rights. I.R.C. § 2704(a).

For example, assume that Mother and Daughter control a corporation, and that Mother's stock has voting rights that lapse upon Mother's death. Under section 2704, when Mother dies, her gross estate will include the value of the lapsed voting rights. Similarly, if Mother's voting rights lapsed prior to her death, Mother would be treated as making a taxable gift, on the date of lapse, in the amount of the value of the lapsed voting rights. I.R.C. § 2704(a)(1).

Section 2704 is intended to overrule Estate of Harrison v. Commissioner, 52 T.C.M. (CCH) 1306 (1987), in which the Tax Court held that liquidation rights lapsing at death are not included in the gross estate of the decedent. H.R. Conf. Rep. No. 964, 101st Cong., 2d Sess. 157 (1990).

Treatment of a lapse as a taxable transfer applies only to voting or liquidation rights in a corporation or partnership, and only if the family of the person holding the lapsing right controls the entity. I.R.C. § 2704(a)(1). The value of the transfer consists of the difference between the value of the interests held by the person whose right has lapsed, including the lapsed right, and the value of those interests without the lapsed right. I.R.C. § 2704(a)(2).

J. RESTRICTIONS ON LIQUIDATION

As explained above in connection with minority discounts and fractional interest discounts, the power of the owner of an interest in an entity to force liquidation of the entity may be important in determining the value of the interest. If the owner of the interest is "locked in," in the sense that she cannot force liquidation, then she may not be able to gain the full benefits of her interest without the cooperation of her fellow owners. This is especially damaging to owners of minority interests. A buyer of the interest would be similarly limited; therefore, the value of the interest should be discounted accordingly.

By contrast, if the owner of the interest has legal power to force liquidation, she can thereby obtain her pro rata share of the underlying assets. She would then become the sole owner of those assets and could dispose of them as she wishes. Under these circumstances, a minority discount would not be appropriate, although a fractional interest discount might be available.

Many taxpayers have tried to take advantage of these rules by creating artificial restrictions limiting liquidation of the entity involved. A substantial discount is then claimed on the ground that a buyer of the interest could not compel liquidation.

Section 2704(b) addresses this problem. It applies only in circumstances in which the transferor (the decedent or donor) and her family control the entity. I.R.C. § 2704(b)(1)(B). In the case of a corporation, control means ownership of at least 50% (by vote or value) of the stock. In the case of a partnership, control means ownership of at least 50% of the capital or profits interest, or, in the case of a limited partnership, ownership of any general partner interest. I.R.C. §§ 2704(c)(1) and 2701(b)(2).

Section 2704 applies only if there is a transfer (by gift or at death) of an interest to a member of the transferor's family, as defined in section 2704(c)(2). I.R.C. § 2704(b)(1)(A).

Finally, Section 2704 applies only to an "applicable restriction." I.R.C. § 2704(b)(1). A restriction is an "applicable restriction" only if it limits the ability of the entity to liquidate and (1) the restriction lapses after the transfer described in the prior paragraph or (2) the family has power to remove the restriction after the transfer. I.R.C. § 2704(b)(2)(B).

The practical effect of these rules is that virtually any restriction on liquidation is disregarded in valuing an intra-family transfer because the family controlling the entity has power to eliminate the restriction. Congress, however, thought this result too extreme. Therefore, it provided an exception honoring restrictions imposed by federal or state law. I.R.C. § 2704(b)(3)(B). The regulations implementing this exception state that a restriction imposed by the documents governing the entity will be disregarded for purposes of section 2704(b) only if the restriction is "more restrictive than the limitations that would apply under the State law general applicable to the entity in the absence of the restrictions." Treas. Reg. § 25.2704–2(b).

An example will illustrate this principle. Assume that the Wilson family owns all interests in Wilson LLC, a limited liability company. Wilson LLC owns investment real estate. Dad Wilson dies owning 60% of the membership interests. The operating agreement of Wilson LLC requires that owners of 75% of the membership interests must concur in a liquidation and that owners of 75% of the membership interests must concur in any major business decision. If this restriction is considered in valuing Dad's interest, his interest might be significantly reduced in value because of Dad's inability to liquidate the LLC and obtain 60% of the assets. Without liquidation, Dad must obtain the consent of owners of an additional 15% of the membership interests in order to control the operations of the business. A hypothetical buyer would take these limitations into account and discount the price he would offer for Dad's 60% interest.

Further assume that the limited liability company statute governing Wilson LLC requires that 51% of the owners concur in any liquidation but permits limited liability companies to impose a higher percentage. Because the 75% requirement imposed by the operating agreement of Wilson LLC is more restrictive that the general state law, section 2704(b) applies, and the 75% liquidation requirement is ignored in valuing Dad's interest. For estate and gift tax valuation purposes; therefore, Dad is treated as having power to liquidate the entity whenever he wishes and thereby obtain direct ownership of the entity's assets. As a result, no discount should be allowed for Dad's 60% interest. Treas. Reg. § 25.2704–2(d), Ex. 1.

By contrast, assume that state law requires that owners of 80% of the membership interests in any limited liability company concur in a liquidation. In that event, the Wilson LLC 75% requirement would not be more restrictive than general state law, and the restriction on liquidation would not be disregarded for purposes of valuation. In other words, section 2704(b) would not apply, and the restriction on liquidation would be considered in valuing Dad's interest. As a result, Dad's interest should be substantially discounted because of his inability to compel liquidation and thereby obtain direct ownership of the entity's assets.

K. FAMILY LIMITED PARTNERSHIPS

As discussed above, in Rev. Rul. 93–12, the IRS acquiesced in the holding in *Bright*, to the effect that there is no attribution among family members for purposes of determining whether a minority discount will be allowed. This was a crucial turning point because it was now possible to obtain minority and other discounts while maintaining family ownership and control. The key lies in creation of an entity to hold the assets, because the principal discounts are available only as to interests in an entity, such as a corporation or partnership.

A limited partner is a frequent entity of choice for a family business. Where members of a family are the sole or principal owners, such an entity is referred to as a "family limited partnership" or "FLP." Limited liability companies and S corporations are sometimes used as well.

The strategy is elegantly simple. Mom and Dad Wilson transfer substantial assets to Wilson Limited Partnership. Mom and Dad later transfer minority interests in the partnership to their children, leaving each of Mom and Dad with minority interests. Furthermore, the partnership agreement provides for restrictions that prevent Mom and Dad from forcing liquidation. Although Mom and Dad may not have a legal right to control the operation of Wilson Limited Partnership, in practice the children permit Mom and Dad to make the important management decisions.

The minority interests initially transferred to the children qualify for substantial discounts, and Mom and Dad can make gifts of additional discounted minority interests in later years. At the death of Mom and Dad, each owns a minority interest that likewise qualifies for substantial discounts. The result is that all the interests in Wilson Limited Partnership are discounted for gift and estate tax purposes. For example, although the Wilson Limited Partnership might hold assets worth $20,000,000, the aggregate value of the partnership interests for gift and estate tax purposes might be only $16,000,000, producing a dramatic reduction in gift and estate tax liability.

Ultimately, after the death of Mom and Dad, all interests in Wilson Limited Partnership are held by the children. At that point the children, if they so wish, can liquidate Wilson Limited Partnership and distribute the assets outright among themselves. The overall result is passage of Mom and Dad's assets to their children, but the interim creation of a partnership "wrapper" permits passage of the assets at substantial discounts for gift and estate tax purposes.

The IRS views such arrangements as artificial tax avoidance devices, and especially so in cases in which the FLP holds passive investment assets that could just as well be held outright. IRS acceptance of the principle that ownership by different family members cannot be aggregated, however, has made it difficult for the IRS to attack FLPs. Over the years the IRS made strenuous efforts to defeat FLPs, but with only limited success.

The IRS has achieved some success through application of the "step transaction doctrine," a principle developed primarily in the context of corporate taxation. Under the step transaction doctrine, multiple steps are telescoped into one, and intermediate steps are ignored. Tax principles are then applied to the substance of the transaction.

A good example is Senda v. Commissioner, 433 F.3d 1044 (8th Cir. 2006). Here the parents created limited partnerships. The parents transferred to the partnerships stock worth approximately $3,500,000. At about the same time the parents transferred the majority of their partnership interests to trusts for their children. The parents contended that they had transferred to their children minority partnership interests that qualified for discounts. The IRS argued that in substance the parents had simply transferred interests in the underlying stock to the children, with the result that no discount should be available.

The court held for the IRS on two grounds. First, the court concluded that the parents could not prove that the transfers of stock preceded the transfers of the partnership interests. If the transfer of partnership interests occurred first, the transfer of stock to the partnership constituted an indirect gift of the stock. Second, the court concluded that even if the transfer of stock occurred first, the step transaction doctrine should be applied. The result was that the transfer of stock to the partnership was ignored, and the parents were treated as having transferred the stock directly to the trusts for children. Therefore, no discounts were available.

Although the IRS prevailed in *Senda*, the taxpayer prevailed in a case with similar facts involving a limited liability company (LLC). Linton v. United States, 630 F.3d 1211 (9th Cir. 2011). In *Linton*, the court determined that the traditional step transaction tests were not satisfied, despite the fact that the transfers of property to the LLC and the transfers of LLC interests to trusts for the children occurred on the same day.

The IRS has also achieved significant success by applying section 2036 to FLPs. Section 2036, the subject of Chapter 18 of this book, is an estate tax provision that includes in the decedent's gross estate (and therefore subjects to estate tax) any asset as to which the decedent retained until his death a right to the income from the property or a right to control disposition of the income. If it is determined that the decedent in fact retained such rights in an FLP, the result is to include the underlying FLP assets in the decedent's gross estate, as if the decedent owned those assets directly. In effect, the partnership "wrapper" is ignored, and no discounts are available.

In Estate of Thompson v. Commissioner, 382 F.3d 367 (3d Cir. 2004), the IRS achieved exactly this result. In *Thompson*, the FLP was formed only two years before the decedent's death and consisted largely of marketable securities. There was no business purpose (other than tax avoidance) for creation of the FLP. The decedent retained only modest assets in his own hands and necessarily relied on income distributions from the FLP for his support. Finally, the transfers to the FLP occurred when the prospective decedent was 95 years old, giving a testamentary feel to the transaction. These circumstances led the court to conclude that there was a de facto understanding that the decedent would continue to benefit from the FLP assets throughout his life.

In Strangi v. Commissioner, 417 F.3d 468 (5th Cir. 2005), the Fifth Circuit reached the same result on facts similar to those in *Thompson*. In *Strangi* the transfers were made only two months before the decedent's death. The decedent transferred $10 million of assets, primarily cash and securities. There was no realistic business purpose for the transfer, and the transfer left the decedent with insufficient funds for his needs, necessitating distributions from the FLP for his support. The court therefore concluded that there was an implied agreement that the decedent would retain the enjoyment of the FLP property.

In another case, however, the Fifth Circuit reached the contrary result. Estate of Kimbell v. United States, 371 F.3d 257 (5th Cir. 2004). As in *Thompson* and *Strangi*, the decedent had transferred property to a newly created FLP not long before his death. But there were good business reasons for placing the assets (which included oil and gas working interests) in a partnership, and the decedent retained ample property to provide for his own support. Hence the court concluded that the decedent should not be viewed as having retained the benefits of the transferred property. The court reached this result despite the fact that the decedent was 96 years old.

Future developments will undoubtedly provide more chapters in this saga. For the present, though, it is possible to identify factors that will tend to protect an FLP against IRS attack and thereby preserve substantial discounts. The prospects for success will be greater to the extent most or all of these elements are present: (1) the assets are transferred to the FLP before the FLP interests are transferred to the children; (2) there is a considerable time period between transfer of the assets to the FLP and transfer of interests in the FLP to the children; (3) the FLP is not created shortly before the death of the decedent, (4) there is a business purpose (other than tax avoidance) for creation of the FLP, (5) the assets transferred to the FLP are operating assets requiring management, rather than passive investment assets, such as marketable securities, (6) the decedent retains adequate assets to support himself without receiving income from the FLP; (7) there is not a pattern of distributions from the FLP to the decedent for his support; (8) all the formalities of partnership existence and operation are carefully observed.

PROBLEMS

1. At his death Luis Ortega owned 1000 shares of General Motors stock. On the date of his death, the high price for the stock on the New York Stock Exchange was 40, and the low was 39. How will the stock be valued in Luis' gross estate?

2. At his death Arnold Porter owned all 10,000 shares of stock of Porter, Inc. Porter, Inc. is engaged in manufacturing paint. None of the stock has ever been traded. A comparison of Porter, Inc. with similar paint companies the shares of which are listed on exchanges, using the approach described in Rev. Rul. 59–60, produces a fair market value of $60 per share. How will the stock be valued in Arnold's estate?

3. Assume the same facts as in Problem 2, except that Arnold owned 60% of the Porter, Inc. stock, and the remaining 40% was owned by an unrelated party. What principles should be applied in valuing the stock in Arnold's gross estate?

4. Assume the same facts as in Problem 2, except that Arnold owned only 40% of the Porter, Inc. stock, and the remaining 60% was owned by a single unrelated party.

5. Assume the same facts as in Problem 4, except that the remaining 60% of stock was spread among five other owners.

6. Assume the same facts as in Problem 3, except that Arnold does not die, but instead during his life gives all his stock to his three children—20% to each. How will the stock be valued for gift tax purposes?

7. Elana, Tom, and Sallie purchased a large parcel of real estate outside a major city, hoping to develop the real estate for both residential and commercial purposes. Each has a one-third tenancy in common interest. After the purchase was made but before development, Elana died and bequeathed his interest to her daughter, Alicia. How should Elana's interest be valued for estate tax purposes?

8. At her death Renee Feltner owned all the stock of Feltner, Inc., a C corporation. The only asset of Feltner, Inc. is a commercial office building valued at $10,000,000. The basis of Feltner, Inc. for the building at Renee's death was $2,000,000. If Feltner, Inc. sold the building at the time of Renee's death, there would be a recognized gain of $8,000,000, and Feltner, Inc. would owe United States income tax of $1,680,000. How should the stock of Feltner, Inc. be valued for estate tax purposes?

CHAPTER 12

RETAINED INTERESTS
AND VALUE FREEZES

(SECTIONS 2701 AND 2702)

■ ■ ■

A. INTRODUCTION

Special valuation problems are created if a donor transfers to a donee only a portion of the donor's interest in an asset. Both Congress and the Commissioner have taken steps to assure that the transferred interest and the retained interest, respectively, are realistically valued for gift and estate tax purposes.

Historically, transfers of partial interests were often exploited for tax avoidance purposes. A parent might transfer a partial interest in property to a child while retaining an interest in the same property. For gift tax purposes, the parent might treat the retained interest as having a value equal to a large portion of the value of the entire property. That would imply a modest value for the transferred interest and little gift tax liability. It often turned out later that the true value of the transferred interest was much higher than the value originally determined by the parent, with the result that the parent had successfully transferred a large part of the value of the property at little or no gift tax cost.

The most dramatic example of this technique is "value freeze." A typical value freeze would be undertaken in circumstances such as these: Dad owns all the common stock issued by a corporation through which Dad operates his business. The common stock (the only class outstanding) is worth $1,000,000. Dad believes the enterprise will grow in value. Dad has other substantial assets and is concerned about future estate tax exposure. He would like to involve Daughter in management and wants to give her a stake in the business, while retaining for himself much of the income produced by the enterprise.

Dad effects a value freeze as follows. First, Dad completes an income tax-free recapitalization of the corporation whereby his $1,000,000 of common stock is exchanged for $980,000 of preferred stock and $20,000 of common stock. The preferred stock has voting rights that assure Dad of continued control. The preferred stock pays a cumulative dividend at a market rate and is entitled to the first $980,000 of assets if the corporation is liquidated. Dad gives the $20,000 of common stock to Daughter. If Dad splits the gift with Mom under section 2513, the entire gift can be sheltered by the annual exclusion.

Dad dies 10 years later, when the value of the corporation has risen to $3,000,000. Assuming no change in interest rates or creditworthiness of the corporation, the value of Dad's preferred stock is "frozen" at $980,000, and only this amount—perhaps augmented by a modest premium for control—is included in Dad's gross estate. No estate tax is imposed at Dad's death on Daughter's common stock, which is now worth $3,000,000 less $980,000, or $2,020,000. In effect, $2,020,000 of enterprise value has passed to Daughter entirely tax free. The key to this result lies in the "freezing" of Dad's interest. The value of Dad's preferred stock is determined by the dividend and liquidation preference. The growth in value of the corporation has little or no effect on the value of Dad's preferred stock.

Value freezes of this kind represent only one type of tax avoidance made possible by use of retained interests. However, because corporation value freezes present the most dramatic and readily understood avoidance opportunity, the "Dad-Daughter" value freeze described above will be used as a universal example throughout the discussions in this chapter, which explore the efforts of the Commissioner and Congress to prevent such avoidance in the context of corporations and partnerships. Similar principles have been applied to retained interest transactions involving trusts and other assets.

B. RESPONSES BY COMMISSIONER AND CONGRESS

1. HISTORICAL RESPONSE

The Commissioner's initial efforts to combat value freezes proved unsuccessful. The Commissioner argued that the value of Dad's retained preferred stock at his death should include most of the enterprise value because Dad retained control of the corporation. The Commissioner was singularly unsuccessful in this effort and typically achieved only the addition of a modest control premium to the preferred stock value, as in Estate of Salsbury v. Commissioner, T.C. Memo. 1975–333, 34 T.C.M. (CCH) 1441 (1975).

The Commissioner then shifted to an effort to assure proper valuation of the common when it was transferred to Daughter. This approach was embodied in Rev. Rul. 83–120, 1983–2 C.B. 170. Rev. Rul. 83–120 established valuation rules designed to assure that the preferred and common, respectively, are properly valued when Dad gives the common to

Daughter. For example, Rev. Rul. 83–120 dictated that if the preferred dividend is at a level below market or is not cumulative, the value of the preferred must be reduced accordingly, causing a concomitant increase in the value of the common for gift tax purposes. However, Rev. Rul. 83–120 proved difficult to enforce and generally ineffective in preventing widespread value-freezing transactions spawned by the highly inflationary early 1980s. It became clear that the Commissioner could not defeat value freezes through administrative action alone, and that legislation would be necessary. The result was adoption in 1987 of section 2036(c). Section 2036(c) attacked value freezes aggressively by requiring inclusion in Dad's gross estate of the full value ($2,020,000) of Daughter's common stock at Dad's death despite Dad's completed transfer of the common stock ten years earlier. This result was achieved by treating Dad as having retained "enjoyment" of the common stock until his death for purposes of section 2036(a).

Ultimately, Congress retroactively repealed section 2036(c) because it was extremely complex and appeared to endanger a wide variety of otherwise innocuous transactions involving closely held businesses and property. In addition, section 2036(c) imposed prospective liability that was unlimited in both duration and amount. Under section 2036(c), Dad's gross estate would include the full value of Daughter's common stock regardless of whether the common stock had been transferred one year or 40 years before Dad's death, provided the transfer occurred after the effective date of section 2036(c). Furthermore, Dad's estate would include the entire value of Daughter's common stock whether that value was $2,020,000 or $100,000,000. For these reasons, section 2036(c) was vigorously attacked by small business advocates and by many lawyers and accountants involved in estate planning.

2. SECTIONS 2701 AND 2702

Congress enacted sections 2701 and 2702 in 1990, part of a new Chapter 14 of the Code. Chapter 14 also includes section 2703, relating to restrictive agreements, and section 2704, relating to certain lapsing rights. Chapter 14 represents an attempt to defeat a wide variety of gift and estate tax avoidance devices involving valuation of closely held businesses and other property. Sections 2701 and 2702 are aimed squarely at value-freezing strategies involving retained interests.

Section 2701 focuses on proper valuation of the common stock for gift tax purposes at the time the common stock is transferred by Dad to Daughter. Section 2702 applies similar principles to transfers involving trusts and other property.

Section 2701 applies stringent rules to valuation of Dad's preferred stock for gift tax purposes at the time Dad transfers the common stock to

Daughter. These rules may dramatically decrease the value assigned to Dad's preferred stock, necessarily increasing the value of the common stock transferred to Daughter. However, the section 2701 valuation rules do not apply unless specific circumstances are present, as explained below. If section 2701 is not applicable, the general principles of valuation (including Rev. Rul. 83–120) will be applied to value the common. S. Rep. No. 3209, 101st Cong., 2d Sess. at 63 (1990). If section 2701 is applicable, the common stock may be assigned a value much higher than $20,000. In certain instances, the entire $1,000,000 enterprise value will be assigned to the common stock for gift tax purposes.

The remainder of Chapter 12 describes the valuation rules imposed by sections 2701 and 2702. Section 2701 applies to interests in corporations and partnerships. Section 2702 applies to interests in trusts and other property.

C. SECTION 2701 VALUATION RULES

Section 2701 mandates application of special valuation rules to transfers of interests in corporations or partnerships. The starting point is the general rule that any interest transferred will be valued according to the usual fair market value standard (i.e., willing buyer-willing seller). This approach includes all the valuation principles applicable to closely held businesses, including marketability, minority, and other discounts. S. Rep. No. 3209, 101st Cong., 2d Sess. at 61 (1990). The special valuation rules of section 2701 apply only if (1) the transferor transfers an interest in a corporation or partnership to a member of his family (as defined in section 2701(e)(1)); and (2) the transferor or an applicable family member (as defined in section 2701(e)(2)) retains an interest in the same corporation or partnership. I.R.C. § 2701(a)(1). If section 2701 applies, one or both of two special valuation rules, described below, must be used to value the transfer for gift tax purposes.

1. MINIMUM VALUE RULE FOR TRANSFERRED INTERESTS

If common stock is transferred, all issued common stock, including that transferred, must be assigned a value equal to at least 10 percent of the total enterprise value. I.R.C. § 2701(a)(4)(A). For this purpose, the enterprise value includes not only all equity interests, but also the amount of any debt owed by the corporation to the transferor or a family member. I.R.C. § 2701(a)(4)(A)(ii). However, certain short-term debt is excluded. Treas. Reg. § 25.2701–3(c)(3)(i)(A).

In the example of Dad and Daughter, the common stock transferred to Daughter would be assigned a minimum value of $100,000—10 percent of the $1,000,000 enterprise value. This minimum value rule "is intended to reflect the 'option value' of the right of the [common stock] to future appreciation." S. Rep. No. 3209, 101st Cong., 2d Sess. at 65 (1990). If Dad transferred only one-half of the issued common stock to Daughter, the transferred common stock would be assigned a minimum value of $50,000. The 10% minimum value is assigned collectively to all common stock, not just the stock transferred to Daughter. Note that this rule sets only a minimum value, which may be raised by application of the usual valuation principles or by operation of the zero-value rule described in the next section.

2.   ZERO-VALUE RULE FOR RETAINED INTERESTS

The second rule mandates a zero value for the transferor's retained interest if certain conditions are present. I.R.C. § 2701(a)(3)(A). A "subtraction" method is then used in valuing the transferred interest. Treas. Reg. § 25.2701–3(a)(1). If the transferor owns all interests in the corporation before the transfer, the value of the retained interest is subtracted from the entire enterprise value to produce the value of the transferred interest. If the retained interest is valued at zero, the entire enterprise value will necessarily be assigned to the transferred interest. If persons other than the transferor and the transferee hold interests in the enterprise, determination of the value of the interest becomes more complex. See Treas. Reg. § 25.2701–3(b) and (d).

In the Dad-Daughter example, the result of assigning a zero value to Dad's preferred stock would be to assign the entire enterprise value of $1,000,000 to Daughter's common stock, so that Dad would be treated as making a taxable gift of $1,000,000 when he transfers the common stock to Daughter.

The zero-value rule may be applied to two types of rights:

1.   Any liquidation, put, call, or conversion right retained by the transferor is assigned a zero value unless that right must be exercised at a specific time and at a specific amount. I.R.C. § 2701(a)(3)(A), (b)(1)(B), (c)(2)(A), and (c)(2)(B)(i). Therefore, the typical preferred stock entitlement to a set dollar amount upon liquidation of the corporation is treated as worthless because there is no fixed time for liquidation. The rationale for assigning a zero value to such rights is that if the family controls the business, and there is no requirement that the liquidation or conversion right be exercised at a specified date and time, the family will, in its own best interest, arrange for the right never to be exercised. In the example above, Dad should not be permitted to subtract the value of his preferred stock liquidation entitlement in determining the value of the common stock transferred to Daughter because, as a practical

matter, it is unlikely that the family will ever liquidate the corporation.

2.   The general rule is that a right to receive distributions (such as dividends) from a corporation is assigned a zero value if the transferor and the transferor's family control the corporation. I.R.C. § 2701(a)(3)(A) and (b)(1)(A). However, the zero-value rule does not apply if a dividend of a fixed amount must be paid at stated intervals and the dividend is cumulative. A dividend of this kind, i.e., a dividend that escapes the zero-value rule, is called a "qualified payment." I.R.C. § 2701(a)(3)(A) and (c)(3)(A). For this purpose, a dividend is regarded as fixed in amount if it bears a fixed relationship to a specified market interest rate. I.R.C. § 2701(c)(3)(B). In the Dad-Daughter example, if the dividend on the preferred stock is fixed in amount, payable periodically, and cumulative, the dividend right will not be assigned a zero value. However, if the dividend is not cumulative, does not have fixed dates, or does not have a fixed payment amount, the dividend right will be assigned a zero value. The rationale for this distinction again derives from family control of the corporation. If there is no requirement that dividends be paid regularly, the family is unlikely to cause payment of dividends that would simply increase the assets to be taxed in Dad's estate at his death. For that reason, the dividend right should be regarded as essentially valueless. On the other hand, if dividends are required to be paid, Dad's estate will necessarily be enhanced by the dividend payments, and the right to dividends should be valued accordingly.

A zero value will typically be assigned to the liquidation preference embodied in preferred stock because there is no requirement that liquidation occur at a specific time. A zero value will be assigned to the distribution (dividend) right if the dividend is not cumulative. The resulting zero value for the preferred stock in such circumstances is appropriate because the preferred has only an illusory value—a value that can be entirely controlled by the family. Liquidation may never occur, with the result that the liquidation right may have no practical value. Furthermore, the family may choose to forgo payment of preferred stock dividends. If the dividends are not cumulative, the dividend right will be rendered meaningless. As a result, the family can effectively shift all the future growth in enterprise value to the holders of the common stock. Under these circumstances, section 2701 produces the right result: Dad's transfer of common stock to Daughter is tantamount to transfer of all meaningful economic interests in the business.

In some cases, the preferred will be assigned a zero value, but the distribution (dividend) right will escape the zero-value rule because the dividend is fixed in amount and cumulative. This triggers a special valuation rule. First, the fair market value of the distribution right is determined without regard to section 2701. Under Rev. Rul. 83–120, 1983–2 C.B. 170, this would include such factors as the dividend yield relative to that of comparable publicly traded preferred stock and the extent to which corporation earnings provide adequate funding to pay the dividend. Once the dividend value is determined, a special "lower of" rule is applied to value the dividend and liquidation right in conjunction with one another. I.R.C. § 2701(a)(3)(B); Treas. Reg. § 25.2701–2(a)(3). Under this rule the value of the entire interest, i.e., the preferred stock, is the "lower of" the value of the distribution right or the value of the liquidation right, assuming exercise of the liquidation right in such a way as to produce the lowest possible value.

For example, assume that preferred stock has a par value of $1,000,000, but that the holder has the right to require the corporation to redeem the stock at any time for $900,000. Further assume that the preferred stock pays a fixed, cumulative dividend, and that the market value of the right to receive the dividend is $1,000,000. In determining the value of the preferred stock, it is assumed that the liquidation right will be exercised so as to produce the lowest possible value (i.e., redemption for $900,000). Because this is lower than the $1,000,000 value of the distribution right, the value of the preferred stock is $900,000 for purposes of section 2701. If the value of the distribution right were only $850,000, that value would be lower and would prevail. Treas. Reg. § 25.2701–2(a)(5).

If the retained interest consists only of a qualified payment right, without any liquidation right, the qualified payment is valued without regard to section 2701. I.R.C. § 2701(a)(3)(C). In other words, the usual valuation rules, including those enunciated in Rev. Rul. 83–120, are applied.

D. OTHER ASPECTS OF THE SECTION 2701 VALUATION RULES

If, in the Dad-Daughter example, both the liquidation preference and the dividend right are assigned a zero value, the result is that the entire $1,000,000 enterprise value is assigned to the common stock given to Daughter. There remains the question of how Dad's preferred stock should be valued at Dad's later death. Double taxation would result if Dad's preferred stock were valued at $980,000 at Dad's death. This result is avoided by section 2701(e)(6), which requires that "appropriate adjustments" be made at Dad's death "to reflect the increase in the amount of any prior taxable gift" the valuation of which was affected by section

2701. The purpose of the adjustment is "to prevent the double taxation of rights that were given a zero value" under Section 2701. S. Rep. No. 3209, 101st Cong., 2d Sess. at 65 (1990).

For example, if section 2701 was applied to increase the gift tax value of the common stock given to Daughter by $980,000, the value assigned to Dad's retained preferred stock would be reduced by $980,000 at Dad's death or upon a subsequent gift of the preferred stock by Dad. Treas. Reg. § 25.2701–5. This adjustment, however, is subject to a number of limitations specified in the Regulation.

On the other hand, section 2701 can increase the value included in Dad's gross estate if the dividend right is a qualified payment and the corporation fails to timely pay the required dividends on the preferred stock. In that event, any dividend not paid is added back to Dad's gross estate at his death, together with an increment representing imputed earnings that would have accrued from investment of timely paid dividends. A similar increase in value applies for gift tax purposes if Dad gives the preferred stock away during his life. I.R.C. § 2701(d)(1).

Application of the section 2701 valuation rules can transform a sale into a gift, and section 2701 expressly provides that the rules of the section are used not just to determine valuation but to determine whether a gift has occurred. I.R.C. § 2701(a)(1). Assume, for example, that Dad's preferred stock has a fixed, cumulative dividend supporting a market value of $980,000, and that Dad sells the common stock to Daughter for $20,000 rather than simply giving the common stock to Daughter as a gift. The valuation rules discussed in the previous section would produce a value of $980,000 for the preferred stock and therefore $20,000 for the common stock, but the minimum value rule of section 2701(a)(4) would dictate a value of $100,000 for the common stock. Therefore, Dad would be viewed as having transferred $100,000 of value to Daughter in exchange for $20,000 of cash, resulting in a $80,000 gift from Dad to Daughter.

Section 2701 can transform other transactions into gifts. Any transaction that has the effect of giving one type of interest to Dad and another type of interest to Daughter can have this effect. Obvious examples are contributions to capital, redemptions, and recapitalizations. I.R.C. § 2701(e)(5). For example, if Dad and Daughter together capitalize a new corporation, with Dad contributing $980,000 and receiving preferred stock, while Daughter contributes $20,000 and receives common stock, the transaction may be treated as a section 2701 transfer. Treas. Reg. § 25.2701–1(b)(2)(i). It appears that, under section 2701(e)(5), Dad would be treated as purchasing all interests in the corporation, followed by a sale of all the common stock to Daughter for $20,000. If the common stock is valued at $1,000,000 because section 2701 assigns a zero value to the preferred stock, the result is a net gift by Dad of $980,000. S. Rep. No. 3209, 101st Cong., 2d Sess. at 64, Ex. 6 (1990).

E. PRACTICAL EFFECTS OF THE SECTION 2701 VALUATION RULES

The practical effects of the section 2701 valuation rules may be illustrated in the context of the Dad-Daughter example. Because Dad has transferred common stock to Daughter, the minimum value for transferred interest rule will apply, resulting in assignment of a minimum value of $100,000 to the common stock. This will raise the minimum value of Dad's gift of common stock from $20,000 to $100,000.

Whether or not the zero value for retained interest rule will apply depends on the nature of the preferred stock Dad retains. If the preferred stock is not required to be redeemed at a fixed date, and the dividend is either not cumulative or not fixed in amount, the preferred stock is assigned a zero value. The full enterprise value will be assigned to the common stock, and Dad will be treated as having made a gift of $1,000,000.

Dad and Daughter will likely seek to avoid this result by making the dividend cumulative and fixed in amount—therefore a qualified payment. § 2701(c)(3). If the dividend supports valuation of the dividend right at $980,000 pursuant to Rev. Rul. 83–120, the "lesser of" rule will produce a value of $980,000 for the preferred, leaving a value of only $20,000 for the common. Because this is less than the $100,000 dictated by the minimum value rule, the $100,000 value will apply, and Dad will be treated as making a gift of $100,000.

Assuming no change in interest rates or creditworthiness, at Dad's death his preferred stock will be valued at $980,000, presumably less a $80,000 adjustment pursuant to section 2701(e)(6), representing the amount by which section 2701 increased the value of Dad's gift. If the preferred stock dividends are paid timely, there will be no addition to Dad's gross estate pursuant to section 2701(d).

The bottom line is that Dad and Daughter can escape the most damaging effects of section 2701 and achieve the most important benefits of traditional value freezing. If the preferred stock dividend is cumulative and can support a valuation of $980,000, the only effect of section 2701 will be to raise the value of the gift of common stock from $20,000 to $100,000. Dad's preferred stock will be included in his gross estate at $980,000, less a reduction under section 2701(e)(6) in the amount of $80,000. The result is that $2,000,000 of value will have been transferred to Daughter at the cost of the gift tax on a gift of $100,000 and a gross estate inclusion of $900,000. In effect, $2,000,000 of the $3,000,000 enterprise value will have passed to Daughter tax free.

Nevertheless, section 2701 creates significant impediments to value freezes. In order to avoid section 2701, Dad will have to make the preferred stock dividend cumulative and assure that the dividend rate and coverage support a $980,000 valuation. If the value of the dividend right is below $980,000, this will lower the value of the preferred and raise the value of the common. If the dividend is cumulative but the corporation fails to actually pay the dividend, Dad's gross estate will be increased accordingly.

The practical result is that the value-freezing objective will be fully achieved only if the preferred stock carries an adequate cumulative dividend that is actually paid. The dividends will not be deductible by the corporation for income tax purposes, will be taxed as income to Dad, (albeit at a favorable rate of 15%), and may constitute such a corporation cash drain that Dad will find it difficult to achieve the growth in corporation value that he anticipates. The net result is to limit the benefits of value freezing to enterprises that can achieve a growth in enterprise value more rapid than the requisite preferred stock dividend rate.

Consequently, Congress has achieved part but not all of its objectives in combating value freezes. Taxpayers can no longer "play games" by creating illusory retained interests, such as noncumulative dividends and redemption rights that might or might not be exercised. If the retained interest is to be assigned any value, it must be a real preferred or a similar interest with finite and certain economic rights. However, if the taxpayer can meet those tests and the enterprise can afford to pay an adequate dividend, much of the benefit of value freezing can still be achieved.

F. TRANSACTIONS NOT SUBJECT TO THE SECTION 2701 VALUATION RULES

The general rule is that any transfer of an interest in a corporation or partnership to a family member is subject to the section 2701 valuation rules if the donor (or a member of the donor's family) retains an interest in the same corporation. However, there are exceptions that exclude many transactions from application of section 2701.

The "minimum value for transferred interests" rule applies only to transfers of common stock. I.R.C. § 2701(a)(4)(A) and (B)(i). Also, it does not apply if market quotations for the common stock are readily available on an established securities market. I.R.C. § 2701(a)(1).

The "zero value-rule for retained interests" does not apply if any one of the following circumstances is present:

1. The corporation has issued only one class of stock. I.R.C. § 2701(a)(2)(B).

2. The corporation has issued more than one class of stock, but the only difference between the classes relates to voting rights. I.R.C. § 2701(a)(2)(C).

3. The corporation has issued more than one class of stock, but all interests transferred by the donor are in the same proportion as the donor's retained interest. I.R.C. § 2701(a)(2)(C). For example, if the donor owns both preferred stock and common stock and transfers one-third of his holding of each to the donee, the zero-value rule does not apply. Treas. Reg. § 25.2701–1(c)(4). Similarly, if the transferor owns only one class of stock, the zero-value rule will not apply to a gift of a portion of that stock to a family member.

4. Market quotations are readily available for the retained interest on an established securities market. I.R.C. § 2701(a)(2)(A).

5. Market quotations are readily available for the transferred interest on an established securities market. I.R.C. § 2701(a)(1).

These exceptions have great practical importance and permit a variety of typical stock dispositions among family members without triggering section 2701. If only one class of stock is outstanding, Exception 1 permits any and all transfers of stock among family members without application of the zero-value rule. Parents in these circumstances can continue a regular program of annual exclusion gifts of stock to children or other descendants but still maintain control of the corporation. Although the "minimum value for transferred interests" will technically apply, it will have no practical effect. The minimum value rule requires that all issued common stock be assigned a minimum value of 10 percent of the enterprise value. If only common stock is outstanding, the common will have a value equal to 100 percent of enterprise value (less appropriate discounts) even without application of the minimum value rule.

Exception 2 allows even greater flexibility because it permits creation of voting and nonvoting stock without triggering application of section 2701. Thus, parents may transfer to descendants rights to future appreciation, in the form of non-voting common stock, while retaining full voting control. Exception 2 is especially significant because it has the practical effect of excluding S corporations from the operation of section 2701. An S corporation is permitted to have only one class of stock, but differences in voting rights are permissible. I.R.C. § 1361(b)(1)(D) and (c)(4).

Exception 3 is important because it permits multiple classes of stock without application of the zero-value rule, provided all transfers are proportionate. This is sometimes called the "vertical slice" rule. However, the minimum value rule for common stock remains operative even if all transfers are proportionate.

G. PARTNERSHIPS

If the transfer involves a partnership, principles similar to those applicable to corporations are applied. I.R.C. § 2701(a)(1) and (4). Several definitions and rules specifically applicable to partnerships are provided. I.R.C. §§ 2701(a)(2), (a)(4)(B)(i), (b)(2)(B) and (c)(1)(A)(ii).

PROBLEMS

1. Mom has worked hard to build the manufacturing business she operates through Dynamic Corporation. The business now has a fair market value of $2,000,000. Mom owns all the stock—100 shares of common stock. Dynamic Corporation has no indebtedness to Mom. Mom wants to bring Son into the business and is concerned about the estate tax liability that her death would cause. Mom has proposed to you a number of alternative dispositions of stock described below. As to each proposed disposition, Mom wants to know whether the transaction would be treated as a gift for gift tax purposes and, if so, the principles that would be applied to value the interest transferred.

   (a) Mom transfers 20 shares of common stock to Son.

   (b) Dynamic Corporation is recapitalized, with the result that Mom holds 50 shares of Class A common stock and 50 shares of Class B common stock. The only difference between the classes is that Class A common stock shares have voting rights, while Class B common stock shares do not. Mom transfers 20 shares of Class B common stock to Son.

   (c) Dynamic Corp. is recapitalized, with the result that Mom owns 80 shares of preferred stock and 20 shares of common stock. The preferred has a preference right of $20,000 per share in the event of liquidation, and a cumulative dividend of $2,000 per share must be paid on the preferred stock annually. Mom gives all 20 shares of common stock to Son. The 10 percent dividend on the preferred stock is consistent with current yields on preferred stock. As a result, the dividend right has a market value of $20,000 per share. The earnings are fully adequate to cover the preferred stock dividend.

   (d) The facts are the same as in (c), except that the preferred stock dividend is not cumulative.

2. Dad and Daughter decide to pool their resources and create Synergistic Corporation for the development of computer software. Dad contributes $800,000 and receives 80 shares of preferred stock. Each share of preferred stock has a $10,000 preference on liquidation and a 14 percent ($1,400) annual noncumulative dividend. Daughter contributes $200,000

and receives common stock. Does this transaction have gift tax consequences?

H. TRUSTS

1. GENERAL PRINCIPLES: GRITs, GRATs, AND GRUTs

Trusts offer opportunities for overvaluation of retained interests, resulting in artificially reduced valuation of transferred interests. For this reason, if an interest in a trust is transferred, section 2702 imposes certain rules for valuation of retained interests similar to those that are applicable to retained interests in corporations and partnerships under section 2701.

An example will illustrate the kind of tax avoidance section 2702 is intended to prevent. Assume that Mom transfers to a trust a parcel of investment real estate worth $100,000 that produces an annual income of only $2,000. Mom retains the right to receive the income from the trust for 15 years. At that time, the trust is to terminate, and the real estate is to be distributed outright to Son.

In the absence of section 2702, the actuarial valuation principles described in Chapter 10 would be used to value Son's remainder for gift tax purposes. If the section 7520 rate at the time the trust is created were 10 percent, the remainder would be assigned a value of .239392, or $23,939. Treas. Regs. §§ 25.2512–5(d)(2) and 20.2031–7(d)(6), Table B. Therefore, the remaining value of .760608, or $76,061 would be assigned to Mom's retained income interest. Mom would be treated as making a taxable gift of only $23,939. Mom, however, will in fact receive far less than $76,061 over the life of the trust because the actual income yield is only 2 percent, or $2,000 per year.

If Mom lives longer than 15 years, the trust will terminate, Son will receive the real estate outright, and nothing will be included in Mom's gross estate at her death. As a result, $100,000 will have been transferred to Son at the cost of a gift tax on only $23,939, and the 15 years of income will augment Mom's gross estate very little. Furthermore, Son may in fact receive property that is worth much more than $100,000 if the property appreciates substantially during the 15-year period. This avoidance technique, known as a "grantor retained income trust," or "GRIT," was frequently employed prior to adoption of section 2702.

The Commissioner could attack Mom's valuation of the remainder by arguing that use of the 10 percent interest rate is "unrealistic and unreasonable" in light of the actual 2 percent return, relying on the principle discussed in *Shackleford* in Chapter 10. However, it is by no means clear when the actual return becomes so low that use of the section 7520 rate is "unrealistic and unreasonable." Furthermore, this approach requires the Commissioner to litigate the issue on a case-by-case basis. As a result, section 2702 was adopted to provide a clear, definitive, and easily administered solution.

Section 2702 prevents tax avoidance of this kind by applying strict valuation rules to both the retained interest and the transferred interest if the transfer is between members of the same family. Section 2702(a)(2)(A) requires that any trust interest retained by the grantor be valued at zero unless it constitutes a "qualified interest." An interest is a qualified interest only if annual payments are required and those payments consist of (1) a fixed dollar amount or (2) an amount equal to a fixed percentage of the trust value, determined annually. I.R.C. § 2702(b)(1) and (2). In the above example, Mom is entitled merely to the "income," not a fixed dollar amount or a percentage of trust assets. Therefore, her retained income right is not a "qualified interest." As a result, Mom's income right is assigned a zero value, and the entire $100,000 value of the trust is assigned to Son's remainder. Mom is treated as making a taxable gift of $100,000 when she transfers the remainder to Son.

If the retained right is a "qualified interest," i.e., a right to annual payments of a fixed dollar amount or a fixed percentage of trust value, section 2702 does not apply, and the retained interest is valued according to the usual rules of section 7520. Because the payments are fixed in amount or percentage, they will be made without regard to the income actually produced. Under these circumstances the usual section 7520 rules will necessarily produce an accurate valuation of the retained income interest.

For example, if the trust described above provides for payment to Mom of $2,000 at the end of each year (rather than payment of the "income") and the section 7520 rate at the time the trust is created is 10 percent, Mom's right to the $2,000 annual payments is valued at only $15,212 under the method described in Chapter 10A. Therefore, the remainder given to Son is valued at $100,000 less $15,212, or $84,788. Mom is treated as making a taxable gift of $84,788. This should be compared with the taxable gift value of $23,939 that obtained under the pre-section 2702 valuation of the remainder, assuming Mom retained the right to "income." In this manner, section 2702 requires that the remainder interest be realistically valued, preventing a greatly undertaxed transfer of value to Son.

The regulations impose strict requirements as to what constitutes a "qualified interest," including specific provisions that must be included in the granting instrument. Treas. Reg. § 25.2702–3.

Trust interests providing "qualified interests" that meet the requirements of section 2702 have commonly accepted names. A "grantor retained annuity trust," or "GRAT," is a trust that provides for the grantor a retained right to annual payments of a specific dollar amount. A "grantor retained unitrust," or "GRUT," is a trust that provides for the grantor a retained right to annual payments equal to a fixed percentage of the total value of the trust assets, determined annually.

Although section 2702 is aimed primarily at transfers of remainder interests, it also applies to a transfer of an income interest if the transferor retains a remainder interest. Such transactions provide similar opportunities for tax avoidance if the return from the property exceeds the yield assumed under section 7520. A similar valuation approach is therefore applied to transfers of income interests. If the transferor retains a remainder, that remainder is treated as having a zero value unless the transferred interest is a right to annual payments of a fixed dollar amount or a fixed percentage of trust assets. I.R.C. § 2702(a)(1) and (b)(3). If the transferred interest is a right merely to "income," the remainder will be treated as valueless, and the entire value of the trust property will be assigned to the transferred income interest.

Section 2702 does not apply to every transfer of a trust remainder interest. Section 2702 applies only if the transfer is to a member of the transferor's family (as defined in section 2704(c)(2)), and the retained interest is held by the transferor or a member of the transferor's family as defined in section 2701(e)(2). I.R.C. § 2702(a)(1). Also, section 2702 does not apply to a transfer that is not yet complete for gift tax purposes. I.R.C. § 2702(a)(3)(A)(i).

2. QUALIFIED PERSONAL RESIDENCE TRUSTS

An important exception to the rules of section 2702 is that for personal residences. Section 2702(a)(3)(A)(ii) provides that section 2702 does not apply to a trust if the sole trust property is an interest in a personal residence that is occupied by the holder of a term interest in the trust. This gives rise to a frequently used vehicle—the qualified personal residence trust, or QPRT.

A typical QPRT operates as follows. Mom, a 70-year old widow, owns a home worth $400,000. She wants to continue to reside in the home but is concerned about estate tax exposure because she expects the home to appreciate substantially in the years ahead. The solution is a QPRT. Mom transfers the home to a trust. The trust instrument provides that Mom is entitled to occupy the home for 10 years. After 10 years the home will pass outright to Son, but Mom will continue to occupy the home upon payment of market level rent. Because the sole trust asset is a personal residence, section 2702 does not apply. I.R.C. § 2702(a)(3)(A)(ii). The remainder given to Son is therefore valued under Treas. Regs. §§ 25.2512–5(d)(2) and 20.2031–7(d)(6) Table B. If the section 7520 rate at the time of the transfer is 9%, the value of the remainder is .422411 of the $400,000 total value, or $168,964. This is the value of Mom's gift to Son for gift tax purposes. In practice, the trust instrument often includes a provision requiring reversion of the entire property to Mom if she dies within 10 years. This reversion possibility has an actuarial value that substantially reduces the value of the remainder below $168,964, further lowering the amount of the taxable gift.

If Mom dies within 10 years, the entire value of the home at the time of Mom's death is included in her gross estate under section 2036(a)(1), explored in Chapter 18. Under section 2001(b), last sentence, the $168,964 gift is not treated as an adjusted taxable gift and is not added to the amount taxed at Mom's death. Hence the value of the home is not subject to double taxation.

If Mom survives for 10 years, nothing is included in her gross estate, and the home passes tax free to Son. In addition, Mom's gross estate will be reduced by her rental payments to Son after 10 years. If, for example, the home has appreciated in value to $700,000 by the time of Mom's death, the family will have succeeded in passing a $700,000 asset to Son at the cost of gift tax on only $168,964. A crucial element in assuring this result is payment by Mom to Son of rent at a market level after 10 years. If Mom pays less than market rent, she could be viewed as having retained enjoyment of the home for purposes of section 2036(a)(1), thereby causing inclusion of the home in her estate, under principles discussed in Chapter 18.

A QPRT may be used for two personal residences, so that a vacation home may be transferred in this way as well. Treas. Reg. § 25.2702–5(b)(2). The regulations include many specific requirements for a QPRT. See Treas. Reg. § 25.2702–5.

3. PRACTICAL EFFECTS OF SECTION 2702

Section 2702 effectively prevents donors from using the customary rules of actuarial valuation to achieve tax avoidance in intrafamily transfers. In the case of transfers of remainder interests, the retained income right must be "tied down" to a specific dollar figure or a specific percentage of trust value—without regard to the actual income to be generated. This assures realistic valuation of both the retained income right and the transferred remainder.

Still, retained income transfers can offer significant tax savings, especially when viewed as value-freezing devices. Assume, for example, that Mom creates a grantor retained annuity trust, or GRAT, retaining a right to payments of $10,000 annually for 10 years, with remainder outright to Son. If the value of the trust property is $100,000 and the Section 7520 rate is 10 percent, the retained right will be valued at $61,446, and the transferred remainder will be valued at only $38,554.

If Mom survives beyond 10 years the property goes to Son without further payment of tax, and the property will not be included in Mom's gross estate. If the property appreciates in value at a rate faster than 10 percent, the family will achieve substantial tax savings because Mom's estate will be augmented only by the annual $10,000 payments. If the property is worth $300,000 at Mom's death, that amount will have passed to Son at the cost of only (1) the gift tax on transfer of the $38,554 remainder to Son and (2) estate tax on any of the $10,000 income payments Mom still holds at her death.

A more extreme use of a GRAT or GRUT to achieve a value-freezing objective is explained in the following material.

4. ZEROED-OUT GRATs AND GRUTs

In a GRAT, if the retained right to payments is set at a high enough level, the actuarial value of the gifted remainder can be reduced essentially to zero. This is referred to as a "zeroed-out GRAT." The same strategy can be employed with a GRUT. The purpose of such an arrangement is to "freeze" the value of the property transferred, so that much of the appreciation during the period of the GRAT or GRUT benefits the remainderman rather than the transferor who has retained a right to periodic payments.

A dramatic example of this technique was involved in Walton v. Commissioner, 115 T.C. 589 (2000), acq., Notice 2003–72, 2003–2 C.B. 964. The donor was Audrey Walton, and the donees were Audrey's two daughters. On April 7, 1993, Audrey transferred 7.2 million shares of Wal-Mart Stores, Inc. stock to trusts for her daughters. The value of the stock transferred to each trust was $100,000,000. The trusts were to terminate in two years, at which time the remaining principal was to be transferred to Audrey's daughters. The trusts provided that during the first year Audrey would receive a payment equal to 49.35% of the initial trust value, and that during the second year Audrey would receive a payment equal to 59.22% of the value of the trust at the beginning of the second year. The payments could be made in kind using Wal-Mart stock, and in fact most of the payments did consist of Wal-Mart stock. Under the section 7520 rate in effect for April of 1993, the actuarial value of each daughter's remainder was $6,195. Audrey filed a gift tax return reporting a taxable gift of $6,195 to each daughter.

As of the inception of the trust, the total of the payments to be made to Audrey from each trust was $109,000,000. Any amount in excess of this value at the termination of the trust would go tax-free to the daughter. If, for example, the Wal-Mart stock in each trust rose in value to $129,000,000 by the time the trust terminated, each daughter would receive $129,000,000 less $109,000,000 or $20,000,000. In that event Audrey would have succeeded in transferring $20,000,000 of Wal-Mart stock to each daughter at the cost of the gift tax on a transfer of only $6,195.

As it turned out, the price of Wal-Mart stock declined, with the result that the payments to Audrey exhausted all the Wal-Mart stock, and the daughters received nothing. Although nothing was accomplished, the cost to Audrey was only the gift tax on two remainder transfers of $6,195 each, plus the modest cost of creating and administering the trusts. If Wal-Mart stock had risen in value, however, a great deal of value might have been passed at minimal tax cost.

In order to achieve the very low remainder value of $6,195, it was necessary to provide that, in the event of Audrey's death prior to termination of the trust, her estate would receive the remaining payments. The IRS argued that under this approach, the retained interest should be valued as an annuity payable for the shorter of two years or the period ending with Audrey's death. This analysis would reduce the value of the retained interest and therefore increase the value of the remainder. The result would be value for the gifted remainder interest in each trust of $1.9 million, rather than the $6,195 value reported by Audrey. The IRS position on valuation was based on Regulation § 25.2702–3(e) Example 5. The Tax Court, examining the legislative history of section 2702 and concluded that Regulation § 25.2702–3(e) Example 5 was an "unreasonable interpretation and invalid extension" of section 2702. *Walton*, 115 T.C. at 604. Therefore, the correct value of each remainder interest was $6,195, as asserted by Audrey.

The Commissioner has since acquiesced in *Walton* and has modified the regulations to confirm the *Walton* result. See Notice 2003–72, 2003–2 C.B. 964; Treas. Reg. § 25.2702–3(e) Ex. 5.

The short-term "zeroed-out GRAT" has become a popular estate planning device, as demonstrated by the *Walton* case. Although it turned out that Audrey Walton gained no tax advantage from the two-year GRATs addressed in the case, she could create other two-year GRATs immediately upon expiration of the original GRATs. If Wal-Mart stock should appreciate substantially during those two years, the appreciation in excess of the annuity payments would pass tax-free to the daughters. Ms. Walton could do this over and over again, thereby standing ready to achieve a tax-free transfer of wealth whenever Wal-Mart stock appreciated substantially.

The Obama Administration proposed that such GRATs be limited to a minimum ten-year term. See Dept. of the Treasury, General Explanations of the Administration's Fiscal Year 2010 Revenue Proposals, at 123 (May 2009). This would have subjected a taxpayer like Audrey Walton to a greater danger that she would die during the term of the GRAT. If that occurred, the value of the GRAT assets necessary to produce the required annuity would be included in Audrey's gross estate pursuant to section

2036. See Treas. Reg. § 20.2036–1(c)(2)(i). This would substantially diminish the perceived benefits of a zeroed-out GRAT. Congress never acted on this proposal.

Throughout the years, the 2010 proposal was enhanced to include multiple changes to GRATs. In the last proposal, the Treasury Department advocated for the following:

1. A maximum term of the life expectancy of the annuitant plus 10 years.

2. The remainder interest in the GRAT must have a minimum value equal to the greater of 25% of the value of the assets in the GRAT or $500,000.

3. A decrease in the annuity during the GRAT term would be prohibited.

4. The grantor would be prohibited from engaging in a tax-free exchange of assets in the GRAT.

5. If an owner of the GRAT engages in a sale or exchange transaction with the trust, then the property subject to the transaction would be subject to estate tax and any applicable gift tax.

6. The total taxable amount of the trust would be reduced by the property already subject to a prior gift tax.[1]

The proposals were not put forward by the Trump Administration during the drafting of the Tax Cuts and Jobs Act of 2017. The proposals were given new life when Senator Bernie Sanders introduced the "For the 99.8 Percent Act" in the Senate on January 31, 2019.[2] This plan specifically addressed the same GRAT proposals pushed by the Obama Administration and added additional provisions to increase estate taxes on the wealthy.[3] However, the proposal was not enacted. Given the current composition of Congress, it is unlikely that any similar proposals will be enacted.

I.   INTERESTS IN OTHER PROPERTY

Retained interests in property other than corporations, partnerships, and trusts offer similar tax avoidance possibilities. For example, assume that Dad transfers a parcel of real estate to Son, while retaining a right to income from the real estate for 15 years. The usual rules for valuation of income interests might greatly overstate the value of the income interest,

---

[1] Dept. of the Treasury, General Explanations of the Administration's Fiscal Year 2017 Revenue Proposals, at 180 (February 2016).

[2] For the 99.8 Percent Act, S. 309, 116th Cong. (2019).

[3] Id.

thereby unjustifiably reducing the value assigned to the remainder for gift tax purposes.

Section 2702(c)(1) addresses this problem by treating any transfer of an interest in property as if it were a transfer of a trust interest. This triggers the valuation rules of section 2702(a), and the interest retained by the transferor will be valued at zero unless it is a "qualified interest" as defined in section 2702(b). If the retained interest is expressed as an annual payment of a fixed dollar amount or a fixed percentage of the value of the property, determined annually, the usual rules of valuation under section 7520 will apply. If the retained interest is not so expressed, however, the retained interest will be assigned a zero value, and the entire value of the property will be assigned to the remainder.

It might appear that section 2702 could be readily avoided by a joint purchase of property, so that no "transfer" is present. For example, Dad and Son might jointly purchase a parcel of real estate. Dad would buy an income interest, and Son would buy the remainder interest. Technically, there would be no "transfer" triggering application of section 2702(c).

This loophole is closed by section 2702(c)(2), which treats any joint purchase by two members of the same family as if the person acquiring the income interest had first acquired the entire property and then transferred the remainder to the other family member in exchange for the consideration provided by the other family member. This triggers the section 2702(c)(1) rule calling for treatment of the transaction as if it were a transfer of an interest in a trust. If the retained income interest is not a qualified interest, the retained interest will be valued at zero. Therefore, the transferor will be treated as having transferred the entire property to the holder of the remainder interest in exchange for the consideration provided by the transferee. The difference in value will be a taxable gift. Treas. Reg. § 25.2702–4(d), Ex. 1.

PROBLEMS

1. Dad, age 60, transfers $2,000,000 to an irrevocable trust. The trust provides that Dad (or his estate) is to receive at the end of each year a payment of $50,000 from the trust, regardless of the amount of income. The trust is to terminate in 20 years, at which time all principal and accumulated income, if any, is to be distributed to Daughter. At the time the trust is created the section 7520 rate is 10 percent. How should Dad treat this transfer for gift tax purposes?

2. Assume the same facts as in Problem 1, except that the trust provides that Dad is to receive all "income" from the trust each year for 20 years. How should Dad treat this transfer for gift tax purposes?

3. Mom and Daughter decide to pool their resources and purchase an office building. Mom contributes $400,000 and Daughter contributes $100,000.

Mom purchases the right to receive the income from the property for 15 years, and Daughter purchases all other interests in the property. How should Mom treat the purchase for gift tax purposes?

CHAPTER 13

SPECIAL USE VALUATION

(SECTION 2032A)

■ ■ ■

As explained in Chapter 9, the general rule is that fair market value is determined by the "willing buyer—willing seller" rule set forth in Treas. Regs. §§ 20.2031–1(b) and 25.2512–1. This approach requires that property be valued at the "highest and best use" to which the property could be put, rather than the actual use at the time of valuation. Furthermore, in the case of real estate, fair market value is typically derived from prices actually paid for comparable properties in recent sales. If agricultural land near a city is valued at its urban development potential, the estate tax burden may make continuation of farm use impossible. The economic return from farm use may be far below the level necessary to pay the high estate tax based on urban development valuation.

Estate tax valuation based on comparable sales may have dramatic consequences even if no urban development potential is present. Since the Nineteenth Century there has been a consistent reduction in the number of farms, and a concomitant rise in the acreage per farm. Economies of scale require ever larger assemblages of land. As a result, when parcels become available, there is often strong demand from neighboring farm owners who can benefit from spreading high fixed costs of equipment over a larger enterprise. Often the result is artificially high prices for parcels that are actually sold.

Even without this aggregation phenomenon, the general valuation rules could result in especially onerous estate tax liabilities for farm families. Since World War II farmland has consistently sold at prices that incorporate a lower return from invested capital than is customary in other industries. There is disagreement as to the reason for this phenomenon. It probably relates to both the bidding up of prices for available acreage in a time of aggregation, as explained above, and the strong desire of farm families to retain the lifestyle implicit in farm ownership.

The result is that many farm families tend to be "land poor." Their land may have very substantial value, but the actual income produced tends to be relatively low. This can result in heavy estate tax liability without income sufficient to pay the tax, even if payment of the tax is deferred. As a result, many farm families fear that they may have no choice but to sell substantial acreage in order to pay estate taxes. This may lower the farm size below an economically sustainable level and ultimately force the family out of farming.

Congress responded to this concern in 1976, adopting section 2032A. Section 2032A is designed to alleviate the problem by permitting valuation of farmland by reference to its income producing potential rather than its hypothetical sale value. In other words, under section 2032A the value for estate tax purposes is a reasonable multiple of hypothetical farm earnings, not the higher price the farmland might actually bring on the market. Although section 2032A can apply to any real estate used in a trade or business, its practical use is limited almost entirely to farming. The total reduction in value for any individual's estate was limited to $750,000 through 1998, but it is indexed in subsequent years. I.R.C. § 2032A(a)(2) and (3). In 2023, for example, the maximum value reduction permissible under section 2032A was $1,310,000. Rev. Proc. 2022–38, 2022–45 I.R.B. 445.

Section 2032A is intended to benefit only families that retain the land in the family and continue to use it for farming purposes. Therefore, the availability of section 2032A is tightly restricted, and estate planners who seek to use section 2032A must give careful attention to the eligibility requirements before, at, and after death.

The first requirement for section 2032A qualification is that farm assets must constitute a substantial portion of the decedent's estate. The real and personal property of the farm or other closely held business included in the decedent's gross estate must have an aggregate value equal to 50 percent or more of the decedent's gross estate, and the real property must have an aggregate value equal to 25 percent or more of the decedent's gross estate. I.R.C. § 2032A(b)(1)(A) and (B). These computations are made using the "adjusted value" of each asset, i.e., the fair market value less debt encumbering the asset. I.R.C. § 2032A(b)(3).

The farm or other business must pass from the decedent to a "qualified heir," defined as (1) an ancestor or spouse of the decedent, (2) a lineal descendant of the decedent, the decedent's spouse, or a parent of the decedent, or (3) a spouse of such lineal descendant. I.R.C. § 2032A(b)(1) and (e)(1) and (2). In addition, during five of the eight years preceding the decedent's death, the decedent or a member of his family must have owned the land and used it for a qualified use, and the decedent or a member of his family must have materially participated in the operation of the farm or other closely held business. I.R.C.§ 2032A(b)(1)(C). The material participation issue is crucial in many cases in which farm ownership is relatively passive. Treas. Reg. § 20.2032A–3(e)(2) states the following general rules: "No single factor is determinative of the presence of material participation, but physical work and participation in management decisions are the principal factors to be considered. As a minimum, the decedent and/or a family member must regularly advise or consult with the other managing party on the operation of the business."

The five-of-eight-year material participation test period may end prior to the death of the decedent if he became disabled or began receiving and continued to receive Social Security retirement benefits until his death. I.R.C. § 2032A(b)(4). This important provision permits an older person to retire and receive Social Security benefits without endangering I.R.C. § 2032A qualification.

The five-of-eight-year "qualified use" requirement is even more rigorous than the material participation requirement because qualified use must exist at the date of the decedent's death as well as during the five-of-eight-year period preceding death. I.R.C. § 2032A(b)(1). "Qualified use" means an "equity interest" in the operation. The decedent or a member of his family must, both at the time of death and during five of the eight years preceding death, receive a return from the land that is dependent on the economic productivity of the farm or business. Treas. Reg. § 20.2032A-3(b)(1). For example, if the decedent (or a family member) receives rent that consists of an agreed percentage of the crop production less expenses, this is regarded as an equity interest that constitutes qualified use. However, if the decedent (or a family member) receives a fixed rent of an agreed number of dollars per acre, regardless of production, qualified use is not present. Estate of Abell v. Commissioner, 83 T.C. 696 (1984).

The election to make use of section 2032A must be made no later than the time for filing the estate tax return (including any extensions) and must be joined with an agreement, signed by each person who has an interest in the property, consenting to the recovery by the United States of any tax that was saved by the election if, within a period of 10 years after death, the qualified heir disposes of the property or ceases to use it for the qualified purpose. I.R.C. § 2032A(d)(1) and (2).

The recapture provision (I.R.C. § 2032A(c)), which is referred to in the above described agreement, is directed at the estate tax saving attributable to the election. If the qualified heir, within 10 years after the decedent's death but before the death of the qualified heir, disposes of the property to a nonfamily member or ceases to use the property for a qualified purpose, he must repay all or a portion of the tax savings obtained by virtue of the reduced valuation under the section 2032A election. In the case of a disposition of the farmland, the amount of the recapture tax imposed is the lesser of (1) the tax benefit attributable to the special use valuation or (2) the excess of the amount realized upon the disposition of the property over the value of the property as determined under special use valuation. If the disqualification occurs other than by a disposition (e.g., a change to nonfarming use), the amount of the recapture tax is the lesser of (1) the tax benefit attributable to the special use valuation; or (2) the excess of the fair market value of the land over the value determined under special use. I.R.C. § 2032A(c)(2)(A). If the qualified heir dies without having disposed of the farmland or ceasing the qualified use, recapture is no longer applicable to the farmland owned by the qualified heir. I.R.C. § 2032A(c)(1).

The qualified heir is expressly liable for the recapture amount, and a special lien is imposed upon the land to support the possible recapture. I.R.C. §§ 2032A(c)(5) and 6324B.

There are two valuation methods available under a section 2032A election:

1.   The farm method. This method involves capitalization of the average annual cash rent for comparable land used for farming in the same locality (reduced by state and local real estate taxes). The capitalization rate is the average interest rate for all new Federal Land Bank (now Farm Credit System) loans in the Farm Credit System district in which the land is located. I.R.C. § 2032A(e)(7); Treas. Reg. § 20.2032A–4(e)(1). Each number used is the average amount for the five most recent calendar years preceding the decedent's death. In the case of decedents dying in 2022, the capitalization rate varied by district from 4.47% to 5.14%. Rev. Rul. 2022–16, 2022–35 I.R.B. 171.

2.   The multiple factor method. For those farms where no comparable cash rent may be determined, or where the executor elects not to use the farm method, and for other closely held businesses, the section 2032A(e)(8) provides for use of the following factors in arriving at the value of the qualified land:

   (a)   Capitalization of the income reasonably expected to be derived from the property;

   (b)   Capitalization of the fair rental value of the property;

   (c)   Assessed land values in a state that provides a differential or use value assessment law for farmland or closely held business;

   (d)   Comparable sales in the same geographical area sufficiently removed from an urban or resort area that a nonqualified use would not be a significant factor in the price; and

   (e)   Any other factor that fairly values the qualified use of the property.

Section 2032A can have a dramatic impact on valuation of property for estate tax purposes, especially in circumstances where sale prices greatly exceed the value justified by the income produced by the property. For example, assume the case of a ranch consisting of 1,000 acres of grassland suitable for grazing cattle. Because of the financial structure of agriculture, such land might be selling at $800 per acre at a time when, for the preceding five years, the average market rental value was only $30 per acre, the property taxes averaged $4 per acre, and the applicable Farm Credit System loan rate averaged 5 percent. In the absence of section 2032A, the Commissioner might well be successful in fixing the estate tax value of the land at a figure near the price it could command in the market—$800 per acre. However, under section 2032A(e)(7) a much lower value would be produced: the rental value ($30) less the property taxes ($4), or $26, would be divided by the Farm Credit System loan rate of 5 percent to produce a value of only $520 per acre. Thus, the total value of the 1,000 acres for estate tax purposes would be lowered from $800,000 to $520,000.

A section 2032A election has an important downside: the post-death basis of the property will be the reduced value under section 2032A, not the full fair market value. I.R.C. § 1014(a)(3). If the land is later sold, the lower basis will increase the amount of gain—and consequently the income tax due—on the sale. Many families, however, have no expectation of selling, with the result that the basis is viewed as having little importance. In any event, the prospect of certain and immediate estate tax savings will likely be viewed as outweighing a speculative and perhaps long-delayed income tax cost.

If the executor transfers the section 2032A land to a qualified heir in satisfaction of a pecuniary bequest, a sale or exchange occurs for income tax purposes. Because the basis of the land to the executor will be artificially lowered by section 1014(a)(3), there would ordinarily be taxable gain to the executor in the amount of the difference between the true fair market value and the section 2032A valuation. This result is ameliorated by section 1040(a), which limits recognition of the gain to the difference between the true value on the date of transfer and the true value on the death of death (or alternative valuation date). For example, assume that the fair market value of the property at death was $1,000,000 and that section 2032A lowered the valuation for estate tax purposes to $800,000. After the decedent's death the value of the property rises to $1,100,000, and the executor transfers the property to a beneficiary in satisfaction of a $1,100,000 pecuniary bequest. Because of the special rule of section 1040(a), the taxable gain to the executor will be only $100,000, not $300,000. The basis of the property to the beneficiary is only $900,000, not $1,100,000, per section 1040(c).

PROBLEM

John Nelson's wife, Tracy, died 15 years ago. John has only one child, Tom. John farmed until his death and hoped that Tom might continue the farm enterprise. John bequeathed his entire estate to Tom.

John dies in the year 2023. The state of his domicile, where all the land is located, does not impose a death tax. John's estate consists of six assets: four parcels of farmland, a collection of equipment used in farming, and a substantial holding of Microsoft stock. At the date of his death and at the alternate valuation date the six assets have fair market values as follows:

Asset	Date of Death	Alternate Valuation Date
Microsoft Stock	$ 3,900,000	$ 4,500,000
Equipment	3,100,000	2,900,000
Land parcel A	1,400,000	1,400,000
Land parcel B	2,000,000	2,000,000
Land parcel C	1,000,000	1,000,000
Land parcel D	1,600,000	1,600,000
Total	$13,000,000	$13,400,000

Each land parcel consists of 600 acres. There are no encumbrances on any of the assets at the time of John's death.

During the years 2010 through 2022 and during 2023 until his death, John leased Parcel A to Carrie Fox, who is the daughter of John's sister, Ronda. The lease to Carrie Fox required a fixed cash rental payment of $103 per acre per year. Carrie Fox used the land in her own farming enterprise, in which she materially participated.

During the years 2014 through 2023 John leased Parcel B to Mike Gregg, who was not related to John. Under the lease, John was to receive a fixed rent of $70 per acre per year. The lease provided that John would materially participate in farming decisions as to Parcel B, and John did so throughout the period 2014 through 2023.

During the years 2014 through 2023 John leased Parcel C to Maria Urban, who is not related to John. The lease provided that John was to receive rent consisting of one-half of the gross proceeds from crop production, less one-half of fertilizer and seed costs. The lease provided that John was to participate fully in farm management decisions, and John did so throughout the period 2014 through 2023.

John used Parcel D for his own farming operations from 2002 through 2023. He used the equipment described above for this purpose as well.

For the five calendar years preceding John's death the average annual gross cash rental rates per acre for farmland in the vicinity of John's land and of the same quality as John's parcels, were as follows:

Parcel A	$103
Parcel B	$70
Parcel C	$83
Parcel D	$151

Property taxes for all the parcels averaged $3 per acre during the five years preceding John's death. For the five years preceding John's death, the average annual Farm Credit System interest rate for new loans for John's region was 6 percent.

Assume that the maximum § 2032A value reduction permitted in 2023 is $1,310,000.

Could the value of John's gross estate be reduced by an election under Section 2032A? If so, what would be the amount of the reduction?

CHAPTER 14

OTHER VALUATION MATTERS

■ ■ ■

A. BLOCKAGE

In the case of listed securities, the quoted trading price may not accurately represent the price the decedent could have obtained for the securities at the time of death. This will often be the case if the decedent's holdings were large relative to the usual trading volume in the security. For example, if the decedent held 300,000 shares of a security with an average daily trading volume of only 20,000 shares, it is obvious that the market would be depressed if the decedent put all his stock on the market at the same time.

This phenomenon is called "blockage," and the Treasury has recognized that blockage may dictate a lower price for the stock than the quoted trading price on the date of death. Treas. Reg. §§ 20.2031–2(e) and 25.2512–2(e). Under these circumstances the value for estate tax purposes is the price at which the decedent's stock could hypothetically be sold as one block outside the usual market, e.g., through an underwriter.

The blockage concept has been applied to property other than securities. The estate of Alexander Calder included 1292 gouache (opaque watercolor) paintings executed by Calder. At the time of his death, the average number of gouaches sold each year did not exceed 61. Therefore, the Commissioner permitted a blockage discount of 60 percent, lowering the value of the gross estate by almost $2 million. Shortly after the artist's death, his widow, to whom he bequeathed the gouaches, transferred almost all of the paintings to six separate trusts for family members, so that each trust had from 153 to 306 gouaches. The widow took the position that the 60-percent blockage discount permitted for estate tax purposes should likewise be allowed for gift tax purposes. The Commissioner took issue with this, arguing that each trust should be viewed separately, so that the determining factor would be the number of years each trust would require to liquidate its gouaches without taking into account sales by other trusts. The court accepted this argument, and also took into account the actual rate of sales of the gouaches by the trusts. The result for gift tax purposes was a smaller discount than that employed for estate tax purposes. Calder v. Commissioner, 85 T.C. 713 (1985).

Substantial discounts were likewise allowed as to works of art still held by sculptor David Smith and artist Georgia O'Keeffe at their deaths. Estate of O'Keeffe v. Commissioner, 63 T.C.M. (CCH) 2699 (1992); Estate of Smith v. Commissioner, 57 T.C. 650 (1972), aff'd, 510 F.2d 479 (2d Cir.1975), cert. denied, 423 U.S. 827 (1975).

The blockage concept has been further extended to other assets, especially real estate, and sometimes characterized as an "absorption discount."

B. UNASCERTAINABLE VALUE

ROBINETTE V. HELVERING
Supreme Court of the United States, 1943.
318 U.S. 184.

MR. JUSTICE BLACK delivered the opinion of the Court.

This is another case under the gift tax provisions of the Revenue Act of 1932, §§ 501, 506 [1986 Code §§ 2501(a)(1), 2512(a)], which, while presenting certain variants on the questions decided today in Smith v. Shaughnessy, No. 429, is in other respects analogous to and controlled by that case.

In 1936, the petitioner, Elise Biddle Robinson, was thirty years of age and was contemplating marriage; her mother, Meta Biddle Robinette, was 55 years of age and was married to the stepfather of Miss Robinson. The three, daughter, mother and stepfather, had a conference with the family attorney, with a view to keeping the daughter's fortune within the family. An agreement was made that the daughter should place her property in trust, receiving a life estate in the income for herself, and creating a second life estate in the income for her mother and stepfather if she should predecease them. The remainder was to go to her issue upon their reaching the age of 21, with the further arrangement for the distribution of the property by the will of the last surviving life tenant if no issue existed. Her mother created a similar trust, reserving a life estate to herself and her husband and a second or contingent life estate to her daughter. She also assigned the remainder to the daughter's issue. The stepfather made a similar arrangement by will. The mother placed $193,000 worth of property in the trust she created, and the daughter did likewise with $680,000 worth of property.

The parties agree that the secondary life estates in the income are taxable gifts, and this tax has been paid. The issue is whether there has also been a taxable gift of the remainders of the two trusts. The Commissioner determined that the remainders were taxable, the Board of Tax Appeals reversed the Commissioner, and the Circuit Court of Appeals reversed the Board of Tax Appeals. 129 F.2d 832.

The petitioner argues that the grantors have not relinquished economic control and that this transaction should not be subject both to the estate and to the gift tax. What we have said in the Smith case determines these questions adversely to the petitioner. However, the petitioners emphasize certain other special considerations.

First. Petitioner argues that since there were no donees in existence on the date of the creation of the trust who could accept the remainders, the transfers cannot be completed gifts. The gift tax law itself has no such qualifications. It imposes a tax "upon the transfer . . . of property by gift." And Treasury Regulations provide that "The tax is a primary and personal liability of the donor, is an exercise upon his act of making the transfer, is measured by the value of the property passing from the donor, and attaches regardless of the fact that the identity of the donee may not then be known or ascertainable." We are asked to strike down this regulation as being invalid because inconsistent with the statute. We do not think it is. As pointed out in the *Smith* case, the effort of Congress was to reach every kind and type of transfer by gift. The statute "is aimed at transfers of the title that have the quality of a gift." Burnet v. Guggenheim, 288 U.S. 280, 286. The instruments created by these grantors purported on their face wholly to divest the grantors of all dominion over the property; it could not be returned to them except because of contingencies beyond their control. Gifts of future interests are taxable under the Act, § 504(b), and they do not lose this quality merely because of the indefiniteness of the eventual recipient. The petitioners purported to give the property to someone whose identity could be later ascertained and this was enough.

Second. It is argued that the transfers were not gifts but were supported by "full consideration in money or money's worth." This contention rests on the assumption that an agreement between the parties to execute these trusts was sufficient consideration to support the transfers. We need not consider or attempt to decide what were the rights of these parties as among themselves. Petitioners think that their transaction comes within the permissive scope of Article 8 of Regulation 79 (1936 edition) which provides that "a sale, exchange or other transfer of property made in the ordinary course of business (a transaction which is bona fide at arm's length and free from any donative intent) will be considered as made for an adequate and full consideration in money or money's worth." The basic premise of petitioner's argument is that the moving impulse for the trust transaction was a desire to pass the family fortune on to others. It is impossible to conceive of this as even approaching a transaction "in the ordinary course of business."

Third. The last argument is that "in any event, in computing the value of the remainders herein, allowance should be made for the value of the grantor's reversionary interest." Here unlike the Smith case the government does not concede that the reversionary interest of the petitioner should be deducted from the total value. In the Smith case, the grantor had a reversionary interest which depended only upon his surviving his wife, and the government conceded that the value was therefore capable of ascertainment by recognized actuarial methods. In this case, however, the reversionary interest of the grantor depends not alone upon the possibility of survivorship but also upon the death of the daughter without issue who should reach the age of 21 years. The petitioner does not refer us to any recognized method by which it would be possible to determine the value of such a contingent reversionary remainder. It may be true as the petitioner argues that trust instruments such as these before us frequently create "a complex aggregate of rights, privileges, powers and immunities and that in certain instances all these rights, privileges, powers and immunities are not transferred or released simultaneously." But before one who gives this property away by this method is entitled to deduction from his gift tax on the basis that he had retained some of these complex strands it is necessary that he at least establish the possibility of approximating what value he holds. Factors to be considered in fixing the value of this contingent reservation as of the date of whether or not the daughter would marry; whether she would have children; whether they would reach the age of 21; etc. Actuarial science may have made great strides in appraising the value of that which seems to be unappraisable, but we have no reason to believe from this record that even the actuarial art could do more than guess at the value here in question. Humes v. United States, 276 U.S. 487, 494.

The judgment of the Circuit Court of Appeals is *affirmed*.

LOCKARD V. COMMISSIONER

United States Court of Appeals, First Circuit, 1948.
166 F.2d 409.

MAGRUDER, CIRCUIT JUDGE.

Barbara M. Lockard petitions for review of a decision of the Tax Court of the United States determining that there is a deficiency in gift tax of $5,517.39 for the year 1941. (7 T.C. 1151.)

* * *

We come now to the remaining question in the case, as to the valuation of the gift made by petitioner in 1941.

On December 31, 1941, petitioner, having meanwhile resigned as cotrustee, executed an instrument in which she undertook to assign to the remaining trustee all her reversionary interest in the trust and directed the trustee to continue from and after April 1, 1944, if Mr. Lockard should then be living, to hold the trust property in trust for the following purposes:

2.   Until the death of my said husband, Derwood W. Lockard, to pay the entire net income thereof to him, and to pay to him such amounts from principal, not in excess of $3,000 in any calendar year, as the trustee in his uncontrolled discretion shall think necessary for the comfortable maintenance and support of the said Derwood W. Lockard.

3.   Upon the death of said Derwood W. Lockard to transfer the principal then held to me if I shall then be living, and if I shall not then be living, to my executors, administrators or assigns free of trust.

Since petitioner had reserved no power to amend the terms of the original trust, this instrument of December 31, 1941, was perhaps technically the creation of a new trust rather than an extension of the term of the old one. In any case, the instrument constituted a new taxable gift to Mr. Lockard. Since he already had the irrevocable right to receive the income up to March 31, 1944, the new gift was of the right to receive the income from and after April 1, 1944, for the remainder of his life, plus the right to receive such amounts from principal, not in excess of $3,000 in any calendar year, as the trustee might in his uncontrolled discretion think necessary for the life beneficiary's comfortable maintenance and support.

In her gift tax return for 1941, petitioner valued this new gift to Mr. Lockard at $55,000. The Commissioner ruled that this valuation should be increased to the amount of $99,459.37, which amount, according to the stipulation, is the "value as of December 31, 1941, of the right of the beneficiary to receive each year after March 30, 1944, the amount of $3,000 from the principal of the trust together with the income of the diminishing trust fund, for the remainder of his life." Part of the deficiency determined by the Commissioner was attributable to this increase in the valuation of the gift. The Tax Court upheld the Commissioner.

Petitioner challenges this ruling on the ground that it treats the discretionary power in the trustee to make payments out of principal up to a maximum of $3,000 a year as a completed gift to the beneficiary of the absolute right to receive such payments, disregarding the limitations imposed on the trustee's power to invade the principal. It is argued that, since the corpus may never be invaded, the gift in 1941 should be valued at the sum of $84,535.90, which is the stipulated "value as of December 31, 1941, of the right of the beneficiary to receive the trust income after March 30, 1944, for the remainder of his life"; and that, if and when invasion of the corpus may become necessary, gifts of principal will then become complete and subject to the gift tax in the years in which principal is actually distributed. This argument of petitioner, as the Tax Court conceded, "is an impressive one and has a strong practical appeal." Nevertheless, we feel obliged to sustain the Tax Court in rejecting it.

By the transfer in 1941, there was a gift of something more than a right to future income; there was also a gift of another intangible interest of a contingent nature, a right to receive payments out of principal, to a maximum of $3,000 in any calendar year, to the extent that the trustee should deem such payments necessary for the comfortable maintenance and support of the beneficiary.[2] This interest, which will be protected by a court of equity, is certainly worth something, despite its contingent nature; in fact the donee could hardly fail to regard its existence as a valuable assurance against future adversity, and it certainly is a property interest within the broad terms of the gift tax law. The gift in its entirety must be valued as of the date of the gift. I.R.C. § 1005 [1986 Code § 2512(a)]. If it be objected that the valuation fixed by the Commissioner ignores the limitations upon the trustee's power to invade corpus, it is equally true that petitioner's suggested valuation of the 1941 gift ignores the beneficiary's contingent interest in the principal conferred upon him by the transfer in trust executed by petitioner on December 31, 1941.

The government argues that, by the transfer of December 31, 1941, "the taxpayer relinquished completely her right to have the corpus to the extent of $3,000 annually returned to her"; that she "parted completely with the reversion to, and dominion over corpus to this extent"; and that, since so much of the corpus as will be necessary to pay such annuity of $3,000 per year for the remainder of the beneficiary's life "cannot be returned to her except because of contingencies beyond her control," she must be deemed to have made a taxable gift of corpus to this extent under the authority of Robinette v. Helvering, 318 U.S. 184 (1943), and Smith v. Shaughnessy, 318 U.S. 176 (1943). We would not put the matter quite this way. The taxpayer did not relinquish completely the right to have the corpus returned to her intact at the termination of the trust. She retained the right to have the corpus so return to her, except in so far as the trustee might find it necessary, within the limits of his discretionary power, to invade the corpus. It is true, as the government says, that the corpus cannot be returned to her intact "except because of contingencies beyond her control"; but that is not the test of her taxability for a gift in 1941 of an interest in corpus. This is apparent from Smith v. Shaughnessy, supra, where there was an irrevocable transfer of property in trust, the income to be paid to the settlor's wife for life, and upon her death the corpus to go to the settlor if living, or if not, to the wife's heirs. The government conceded "that the right of reversion to the donor in case he outlives his wife is an

---

[2] It might be suggested that the gift of this contingent interest in corpus should be regarded as not "complete" for gift tax purposes, because it is subject to the discretionary power of the trustee, a person who has no interest in the trust estate adverse to the settlor. But this suggestion, however intrinsically reasonable, is inadmissible in view of the legislative history of the gift tax with reference to the closely analogous power of revocation, for it there clearly appears "that Congress intended the gift tax to fall on transfers in trust where the power to revoke is held solely by others, regardless of their complete lack of interest." 2 Paul, Federal Estate and Gift Taxation, § 17.11 (1942), and id. 1946 Supplement. * * *

interest having value which can be calculated by an actuarial device, and that it is immune from the gift tax" (318 U.S. at 178). This concession was made notwithstanding the fact that the corpus could not be returned to the donor except upon a contingency beyond the donor's control, namely, the predecease of the donor's wife.

The real difficulty with the petitioner's case here is that the Commissioner's determination is presumptively correct; and petitioner has not suggested, and cannot suggest, any reliable actuarial method of computing the value of her reserved right to receive the corpus back intact in case the trustee should not find it necessary to invade the corpus, to the extent permitted, for the comfortable maintenance and support of Mr. Lockard during the remainder of his life. Robinette v. Helvering, supra. * * * Indeed, the stipulation of facts does not even furnish a sufficient basis for an informed guess, as of December 31, 1941; with respect to the likelihood of an invasion of corpus. No facts appear as to Mr. Lockard's accustomed scale of living, nor as to his other sources of income, if any. Considering Mr. Lockard's age (thirty-four, in 1941), the trust might well last for twenty or thirty years; and on the facts of record it could not be assumed to be unlikely that the trustee would find it necessary to invade the corpus for the beneficiary's "comfortable maintenance and support", in view of the modest income that might be expected from a trust estate of not over $140,000. It appears from the stipulation that, up to October 1, 1945, the trustee had in fact not made any payment to Mr. Lockard from the principal of the trust. But events subsequent to the date of the transfer have no bearing on the value of the gift as of the date it was made. Cf. Ithaca Trust Co. v. United States, 279 U.S. 151 (1929).

A judgment will be entered affirming the decision of the Tax Court.

NOTE

The Seventh Circuit adopted a different approach to the valuation of an interest subject to trustee discretion in Estate of Gokey v. Commissioner, 735 F.2d 1367 (7th Cir.1984) (unpublished opinion). In *Gokey* the issue was the valuation for estate tax purposes of a remainder after a life estate under a trust instrument that permitted the trustee to make corpus distributions to the life tenant if the trustee "deems such use necessary for her care, comfort, support or welfare." In its original opinion, the Tax Court held that the remainder should be valued in accord with the ordinary actuarial principles for remainder interests as set forth in the regulations under section 2031, ignoring the possible reduction of the remainder value that would be caused by invasion to benefit the life tenant. 72 T.C. 721 (1979). The Seventh Circuit reversed, holding that "the expected value of the remainder interest must reflect the probability" that the trustee will in fact invade corpus. On remand, the Tax Court examined the resources and needs of the life tenant and concluded that the probability of invasion of corpus was such that the remainder should be valued at only 25 percent of its actuarial value without consideration of the invasion possibility. 49 T.C.M. (CCH) 368 (1984). See further discussion of Gokey in Chapter 18.

C. DISCOVERY OF COMMISSIONER'S VALUATION METHOD

The rapid inflation of the 1970s, especially in real estate, gave greater importance to the valuation issue and produced even wider disparities between the values determined by taxpayers and those determined by the Commissioner. The problem was compounded because many taxpayers experienced difficulty in obtaining information as to the Commissioner's valuation method. Congress responded to this problem in 1976 by enacting section 7517, which permits the taxpayer to obtain information from the Commissioner as to the basis for any value determination made for estate or gift tax purposes. The Commissioner must respond within 45 days, must explain the basis for the value determination, including computations, and must provide a copy of any expert appraisal obtained by the Commissioner. I.R.C. § 7517(a) & (b).

D. BURDEN OF PROOF

The general rule in Tax Court cases is that the taxpayer has the burden to prove the Commissioner's asserted deficiency to be invalid. If the taxpayer proves that the Commissioner's deficiency is invalid, the burden shifts to the Commissioner to prove that there is a deficiency. Cohen v. Commissioner, 266 F.2d 5, 11 (9th Cir. 1959).

Under certain circumstances, however, section 7491, added to the Code in 1998, imposes the initial burden of proof on the IRS. This provision applies only to factual issues. A taxpayer seeking to take advantage of section 7491 must satisfy all of several requirements: (1) the taxpayer must present credible evidence for the taxpayer's position, (2) the taxpayer must comply with all substantiation requirements, and (3) the taxpayer must comply with all "reasonable" IRS requests for documents, witnesses, and other information. I.R.C. § 7491(a).

Section 7491 has its greatest impact in cases in which the court must choose between two conflicting positions and cannot split the difference. If the issue is valuation, however, the court can adopt a value between those proposed by the IRS and the taxpayer, respectively, with the result that the burden of proof may have limited importance. In Estate of Adell v, Commissioner, T.C. Memo. 2014–155, 108 T.C.M. 107 (2014), the decedent had created a trust and transferred his 100% interest in a closely-held business for the benefit of his wife and three children. It was undisputed that the value of the trust was included in the decedent's gross estate. The primary issue that the Tax Court considered was the valuation of the closely-held stock, On the estate tax return, an expert valued the stock at $9.3 million. Five years later, the same expert and another expert for the estate claimed that it was valued at approximately $4.3 million. Conversely, the IRS's expert witness found the value to be approximately $26 million.

The impact of section 7491 on valuation issues was addressed in Estate of Thompson v. Commissioner, 499 F.3d 129 (2d Cir. 2007), vacating and remanding 88 T.C.M. (CCH) 48. The parties agreed that the taxpayer had satisfied the requirements of section 7491, thereby shifting the burden of proof to the Commissioner. Because the Tax Court rejected the Commissioner's valuation, the taxpayer argued that the Commissioner had failed to carry its burden of proof, requiring the court to adopt the taxpayer's valuation. The Tax Court rejected this argument and proceeded to make its own determination of value, taking into account arguments presented by both the Commissioner and the taxpayer. The Second Circuit affirmed the Tax Court's reasoning that determination of value is not an "either/or" process, but an evaluation of complex facts.

E. DECLARATORY JUDGMENT BY THE TAX COURT

Section 7477 permits a donor to obtain a declaratory judgment from the Tax Court as to the value of a gift, provided the donor has exhausted all available administrative remedies within the IRS. Without section 7477, Tax Court jurisdiction would not be available in many cases. Ordinarily, the Tax Court has jurisdiction only if a deficiency in tax has been asserted by the IRS. If the IRS seeks to raise the value to be assigned to a gift, but the available unified credit fully shelters the IRS-asserted value from tax, there would be no deficiency and hence no Tax Court jurisdiction without section 7477. Yet assigning a higher value to the gift would consume more of the donor's unified credit and accelerate the point at which later transfers become taxable. Section 7477 permits the taxpayer to petition the Tax Court to determine the valuation.

F. PENALTY FOR UNDERVALUATION

Often it appears that a taxpayer has little to lose and much to gain from a substantial understatement of value on a gift or estate tax return. If the return should escape careful audit and the value is not questioned, the taxpayer will have gained a saving in tax. If the valuation should be questioned by the IRS and adjusted upward, the only loss to the taxpayer from the understatement of value would appear to be the interest imposed on the late payment of tax.

Section 6662 deters such an approach by imposing a penalty of 20 percent of the underpayment if the understatement of value is substantial.

I.R.C. § 6662(a) and (b)(5). The penalty does not apply unless the value stated on the return is 65 percent or less of the value finally determined. I.R.C. § 6662(g)(1). If the reported value is 40 percent or less of the finally determined value, the penalty is 40 percent of the tax deficiency attributable to the undervaluation. I.R.C. § 6662(h)(2)(C).

Interest on the underpayment accrues from the original return due date. I.R.C. § 6601(a). In addition, interest must be paid on the section 6662 penalty, and this interest likewise accrues from the original return due date. I.R.C. § 6601(e)(2)(B).

The undervaluation penalty can be avoided if the taxpayer can show that there was "reasonable cause" for the reported value and the taxpayer acted in good faith. I.R.C. § 6664(c)(1). In Estate of Thompson v. Commissioner, 499 F.3d 129 (2d Cir. 2007), vacating and remanding 88 T.C.M. (CCH) 48 (2004), the Second Circuit rejected the Tax Court's conclusion that the taxpayer's reliance on counsel for the determination of value permitted application of the "reasonable cause" exception. The Second Circuit concluded that the taxpayer had selected counsel who did not have adequate experience in valuation of assets of this complexity, and the Second Circuit directed the Tax Court to determine whether the taxpayer acted reasonably and in good faith in relying on the counsel who was selected.

PROBLEMS

1. Lois Olson died on January 10 of Year 1, when the basic exclusion amount under section 2010(c) was $12,920,000. Her estate consisted entirely of closely held stock that was difficult to value. Because the Olson family wished to hold estate tax liability to the lowest amount possible, the family persuaded the executor to value the stock at only $12,920,000, with the result that no estate tax was payable. The executor filed a return on the October 10 due date, reporting no tax due.

    More than two years later, the Internal Revenue Service questioned the value assigned to the stock. After extended negotiations, an agreement was reached whereby the stock would be valued at $30,000,000 for estate tax purposes. This resulted in an estate tax liability of $6,832,000. The executor paid the additional $6,832,000 to the United States on October 10 of Year 4.

    What penalties and interest would be payable on October 10 of Year 4? Assume that the section 6621(a)(2) rate was 6 percent per annum throughout Years 1 through 4, and ignore compounding, including section 6622.

2. Assume the same facts, except that on the original return the stock was valued at $20,000,000, with the result that $2,832,000 of estate tax was payable. The executor paid the $2,832,000 with the return, which was

filed on the return due date of October 10 of Year 1. Answer the same question as in Problem 1.

G. PENALTY FOR OVERVALUATION

There are circumstances in which overvaluation on the federal estate tax return may lead to imposition of the section 6662(e) penalty for overstatement of value with respect to the income tax. The Commissioner takes the position that adoption by a legatee of the value used for federal estate tax purposes as the basis for property received at death, pursuant to section 1014, is not a defense to imposition of the section 6662(e) penalty if the estate tax value is unreasonably high. Rev. Rul. 85–75, 1985–1 C.B. 376.

Typically, overvaluation poses such a problem in circumstances in which most or all of the estate is sheltered from tax by the marital deduction and unified credit, so that the legatees have an incentive to assign high values to estate property. In these circumstances, the high valuation may trigger little or no estate tax liability, but the high valuation will increase the section 1014 basis for the property, thereby decreasing the amount of gain on a later sale.

PART 4

ESTATE TAX

(Chapter 11 of the Internal Revenue Code)

■ ■ ■

CHAPTER 15

PROPERTY OWNED

(SECTIONS 2033)

■ ■ ■

A. BASIC ISSUES

Under section 2033, a decedent's gross estate includes the value of all property that the decedent had an interest at death. The nature of section 2033 is intended to include in the gross estate property owned by the decedent in the probate sense, i.e., property reachable by the decedent's creditors in the probate proceeding, and that was set out in the statute itself for many years. Thus from 1916 to 1926 the section prescribed that property should be included in the gross estate "to the extent of the interest therein of the decedent at the time of his death which after his death is subject to the payment of the charges against his estate and the expenses of its administration and is subject to distribution as part of his estate." Under this language the Supreme Court, in United States v. Field, 255 U.S. 257 (1921), held that exercise of a general power of appointment did not subject the appointive property to the estate tax under this section because the donee did not own the property in the conventional sense.

In its original form section 2033, thus, was certainly limited to property owned by the decedent in the conventional sense, i.e., property owned within the meaning of the state law of property and estate administration. There are arrangements such as employee pension and death benefit plans that leave the grantor feeling no poorer than if the fund were in the grantor's bank account, yet it may be difficult in the extreme to claim that under the local law of property the decedent died owning an interest in the property. Is there a prospect that section 2033 can burst the bonds of its antecedents? Could section 2033 reach interests that might be deemed sufficiently significant to be taxable for federal estate tax purposes even though not considered interests in property within the meaning of the local law of property? The cases and rulings in this chapter will shed some light on this question.

Before examining those authorities, it might be worthwhile noting that federal courts have considerable discretion in determining the precise nature of an individual taxpayer's interest in property under state property law. The need for such flexibility is apparent when one considers that,

313

without this power, cooperating, unethical heirs could attain favorable tax results by, in essence, redefining the nature and extent of the deceased's property interests at a proceeding in a local probate court at which no truly adverse parties were present.

HELVERING V. SAFE DEPOSIT AND TRUST CO. OF BALTIMORE

Supreme Court of the United States, 1942.
316 U.S. 56.

MR. JUSTICE BLACK:

* * *

Zachary Smith Reynolds, age 20, died on July 6, 1932. At the time, he was beneficiary of three trusts: one created by his father's will in 1918, one by deed executed by his mother in 1923, and one created by his mother's will in 1924. From his father's trust, the decedent was to receive only a portion of the income prior to his twenty-eighth birthday, at which time, if living, he was to become the outright owner of the trust property and all accumulated income. His mother's trusts directed that he enjoy the income for life, subject to certain restrictions before he reached the age of 28. Each of the trusts gave the decedent a general testamentary power of appointment over the trust property; in default of exercise of the power the properties were to go to his descendants, or if he had none, to his brother and sisters and their issue *per stirpes*.

The Commissioner included all the trust property within the decedent's gross estate for the purpose of computing the Federal Estate Tax. The Board of Tax Appeals and the Circuit Court of Appeals, however, held that no part of the trust property should have been included.

The case presents two questions, the first of which is whether the decedent at the time of his death had by virtue of his general powers of appointment, even if never exercised, such an interest in the trust property as to require its inclusion in his gross estate under [§ 2033]. * * *

The Government argues that at the time of his death the decedent had an "interest" in the trust properties that should have been included in his gross estate, because he, to the exclusion of all other persons, could enjoy the income from them; would have received the corpus of one trust upon reaching the age of 28; and could alone decide to whom the benefits of all the trusts would pass at his death. These rights, it is said, were attributes of ownership substantially equivalent to a fee simple title, subject only to specified restrictions on alienation and the use of income. The respondents deny that the rights of the decedent with respect to any of the three trusts were substantially equivalent to ownership in fee, emphasizing the practical importance of the restrictions on alienation and the use of income, and arguing further that the decedent never actually had the capacity to make an effective testamentary disposition of the property because he died before reaching his majority.

We find it unnecessary to decide between these conflicting contentions on the economic equivalence of the decedent's rights and complete ownership.[1] For even if we assume with the Government that the restrictions upon the decedent's use and enjoyment of the trust properties may be dismissed as negligible and that he had the capacity to exercise a testamentary power of appointment, the question still remains: Did the decedent have "at the time of his death" such an "interest" as Congress intended to be included in a decedent's gross estate under § 302(a) of the Revenue Act of 1926 [now § 2033]? It is not contended that the benefits during life which the trusts provided for the decedent, terminating as they did at his death, made the trust properties part of his gross estate under the statute. And viewing § 302(a) in its background of legislative, judicial, and administrative history, we cannot reach the conclusion that the words "interest . . . of the decedent at the time of his death" were intended by Congress to include property subject to a general testamentary power of appointment unexercised by the decedent.

The forerunner of § 302(a) of the Revenue Act of 1926 [now § 2033] was § 202(a) of the Revenue Act of 1916, 39 Stat. 777. In United States v. Field, 255 U.S. 257, this Court held that property passing under a general power of appointment *exercised* by a decedent was not such an "interest" of the decedent as the 1916 Act brought within the decedent's gross estate. While the holding was limited to *exercised* powers of appointment, the approach of the Court, the authorities cited, and certain explicit statements in the opinion left little doubt that the Court regarded property subject to *unexercised* general powers of appointment as similarly beyond the scope of the statutory phrase "interest of the decedent."

* * *

When it was held in the *Field* case that property subject to an *exercised* general testamentary power of appointment was not to be included in the decedent's gross estate under the Revenue Act of 1916, this Court referred to an amendment passed in 1919 which specifically declared property passing under an *exercised* general testamentary power to be part of the decedent's gross estate. The passage of this amendment, said the Court, "indicates that Congress was at least doubtful whether the previous act included property passing by appointment." In the face of such doubts,

---

[1]   In declining to pass upon this issue, we do not reject the principle we have often recognized that the realities of the taxpayer's economic interest, rather than the niceties of the conveyancer's art, should determine the power to tax. See Curry v. McCanless, 307 U.S. 357, 371, and cases there cited. Nor do we deny the relevance of this principle as a guide to statutory interpretation where, unlike here, the language of a statute and its statutory history do not afford more specific indications of legislative intent. Helvering v. Clifford, 309 U.S. 331.

which cannot reasonably be supposed to have been less than doubts with respect to *unexercised* powers, Congress nevertheless specified only that property subject to exercised powers should be included. From this deliberate singling out of *exercised* powers alone, without the corroboration of the other matters we have discussed, a Congressional intent to treat *unexercised* powers otherwise can be deduced. At the least, § 302(f) of the 1926 Act,[7] the counterpart of the 1919 amendment referred to in the *Field* case, represents a course of action followed by Congress, since 1919, entirely consistent with a purpose to exclude from decedents' gross estates property subject to unexercised general testamentary powers of appointment.

In no judicial opinion brought to our attention has it been held that the gross estate of a decedent includes, for purposes of the Federal Estate Tax, property subject to an unexercised general power. On the contrary, as the court below points out, "the courts have been at pains to consider whether property passed under a general power or not so as to be taxable under Section 302(f), a consideration which would have been absolutely unnecessary if the estate were taxable under 302(a) [now § 2033] because of the mere existence of a general power whether exercised or not." 121 F.2d 307, 312. In addition, the uniform administrative practice until this case arose appears to have placed an interpretation upon the Federal Estate Tax contrary to that the Government now urges. No regulations issued under the several revenue acts, including those in effect at the time this suit was initiated, prescribe that property subject to an unexercised general testamentary power of appointment should be included in a decedent's gross estate. Because of the combined effect of all of these circumstances, we believe that a departure from the long-standing, generally accepted construction of § 302 (a), now contested for the first time by the Government, would override the best indications we have of Congressional intent.

[The portion of the opinion relating to a second issue has been omitted.]

NOTE

Because of the narrow reading given to section 2033 in *Safe Deposit and Trust Co.* and other similar cases, it became necessary for Congress to pass a number of special provisions including in the taxable estate several items that might have been included under section 2033 had the courts given it a broader

---

7   "The value of the gross estate of the decedent shall be determined by including the value at the time of his death of all property, real or personal, tangible or intangible, wherever situated—

* * *

"(f) To the extent of any property passing under a general power of appointment exercised by the decedent (1) by will, or (2) by deed executed in contemplation of, or intended to take effect in possession or enjoyment at or after, his death, except in case of a bona fide sale for an adequate and full consideration in money or money's worth;" 44 Stat. 9, 70–71.

reach. These provisions will be treated extensively in a number of subsequent chapters. The narrow reading given to section 2033 might profitably be contrasted with the broad reading given to section 61, which under the income tax constitutes the basic starting point for defining income. Much of the study of the estate tax in subsequent chapters will involve statutory provisions that sweep into the gross estate items excluded under the narrow readings given to section 2033, the basic starting point for a study of the estate tax. By contrast, much of the study of income tax typically involves an examination of provisions that narrow the scope of section 61, the basic starting point for a study of that tax. The Supreme Court's restrictive reading of section 2033 in the above case should be contrasted with the Fifth Circuit's more liberal reading of that section in the case that follows.

FIRST VICTORIA NATIONAL BANK V. UNITED STATES

United States Court of Appeals, Fifth Circuit, 1980.
620 F.2d 1096.

GOLDBERG, CIRCUIT JUDGE:

[Under the rice allotment program as it operated in Texas (decedent's domicile), the Secretary of Agriculture, with help of local officials, assigns to producers acreage on which rice may be grown under the Agricultural Assistance Act of 1938. Allotments that may be of significant value and are sold in local markets, are annually assigned to producers based on their history of rice production. Under certain circumstances, production history can be transferred to others. Since this history can carry with it the right to rice allotments, it, in itself, may be viewed as a thing of value. By federal law, the rice history of a producer can be transferred to the producer's heirs or devisees under limited circumstances and subject to certain requirements. This favorable history can then be used by the transferee to qualify for allotments in a given year. At issue in the case was whether the rice history of the decedent could be included in the estate.]

* * * The decedent, T. J. Babb, died on July 4, 1973. He had been engaged for many years in the production of rice, and had annually been granted rice allotments under the Act since at least 1958. By notices dated December 1, 1972, and May 1, 1973, Babb was issued producer rice allotments of 1208.3 acres. Prior to the deadline of May 1, 1973, in compliance with the applicable regulations, Babb allocated his 1973 allotment to farms on which he intended to produce rice for the crop year 1973.

At the time of his death, no producer rice allotment for 1974 had been determined for or issued to Babb. After Babb's death, by notice dated March 28, 1974, a producer rice allotment of 1142.6 acres was issued to his estate.

The estate tax return filed by the First Victoria National Bank, appellee here, as executor included no amount for either the value of decedent's interests in the rice allotment program or the value of the rice crop growing on July 4, 1973. After examination of the return by an agent of the Internal Revenue Service, the Service determined that items of $50,000, representing the value of crops growing on July 4, 1973, and $285,600, representing the value of decedent's rice producer allotment and rice production history, were includable in the gross estate.

* * *

The trial court granted appellee's motion, ruling that (1) on July 4, 1973, decedent's 1973 rice allotment was "used up" and its value merged with the growing crops (which were valued at $50,000), (2) decedent's history of rice production did not constitute property for estate tax purposes, and (3) there was no transfer of rice history upon Babb's death because any transfer was conditional upon subsequent events; to wit, that the transferees continue the rice farming operations. * * *

Is the value of "rice history acreage" includable in decedent's estate?

The proper resolution of this appeal turns on whether "rice history acreage" is "property" within the contemplation of I.R.C. §§ 2031 and 2033, n.1 supra. * * *

The attempt to define "property" is an elusive task. There is no cosmic synoptic definiens that can encompass its range. The word is at times more cognizable than recognizable. It is not capable of anatomical or lexicographical definition or proof. It devolves upon the court to fill in the definitional vacuum with the substance of the economics of our time.

* * *

The precise question before us is whether "rice acreage history" is "property" for purposes of the estate tax laws. In deciding this question, we start with the basic principle that "unless there is some special reason intrinsic to the particular provision [under consideration] . . ., the general word 'property' has a broad reach in tax law." Du Pont de Nemours & Co. v. United States, 471 F.2d 1211, 1218, 200 Ct. Cl. 391 (1973). * * *

We find the analogy to the good will of a business to be * * * apt. No one can seriously doubt that good will is an asset whose value is includable in its owner's estate. Yet good will is an intangible asset which, like "rice history acreage," has value only because it carries the expectancy of receiving future assets of more concrete value. Like "rice history acreage," good will is an asset whose value may evaporate overnight. Like "rice history acreage" good will can be sold or devised. Like "rice history acreage," good will is ordinarily transferred along with other assets (in the case of good will, a business; in the case of rice acreage history, a rice farm).

Moreover, such expectancies as a right to compensation under a contingent fee contract, and a promise to return property to an estate if other property is insufficient to meet the estate's tax obligations, have been held to be "property" includable in a decedent's estate. "Rice history acreage" is no less certain an interest than these.

* * *

We also fail to find convincing appellee's strained attempt to analogize "rice history acreage" to an interest created after death, like a cause of action for wrongful death * * *. We note the crucial distinction that neither a cause of action for wrongful death nor Social Security survivors' benefits can ever be transferred by a decedent prior to his death. Each of these interests is "created" only upon a decedent's death, whereas Babb possessed rice acreage history prior to this death.

"Rice acreage history" is not only devisable and descendible, but also transferable *inter vivos*. Those heirs who inherited Babb's rice farming operations, by filing the requisite document with the county commission, were able to retain possession of the "rice history acreage" possessed by Babb the moment before his death. They could have converted the value of the rice acreage history into cash by selling it to others by early 1974, if not earlier. When an interest possesses these attributes, there can be no doubt that its value must be included in the owner's estate, for the focus of the estate tax is on the passage of an interest at death.

* * *

NOTES

1. Under Treas. Reg. § 20.2033–1(a), for a resident or citizen of the United States, a decedent's gross estate includes "the value of all property, whether real or personal, tangible or intangible, and wherever situated" that the decedent owned at death. Examples include accrued interest and rents before the decedent's death, dividends declared before the decedent's death, notes (i.e., loans), and claims. Treas. Reg. § 20.2033–1(b). In Bolles v. Commissioner, 119 T.C.M. (CCH) 1502 (2020), the decedent had given her son loans totaling a little over $1.06 million from 1985 to 2007. They remained outstanding at her death. In determining whether the payments to the son were loans includible in the decedent's gross estate under section 2033 (increased by interest) or gifts included in the computation of "adjusted taxable gifts" of about $1 million under section 2001(b), the Tax Court considered several factors, including whether:

    > (1) there was a promissory note or other evidence of indebtedness, (2) interest was charged, (3) there was security or collateral, (4) there was a fixed maturity date, (5) a demand for repayment was made, (6) actual repayment was made, (7) the transferee had the ability to repay, (8) records maintained by the

transferor and/or the transferee reflect the transaction as a loan, and (9) the manner in which the transaction was reported for Federal tax purposes is consistent with a loan.

The IRS conceded that the payments were not included in the decedent's gross estate under section 2033. After applying the factors, the court determined that the payments were loans that could not be repaid through 1989, and the payments after that time were gifts because the decedent knew that the son was unable to repay the "loans." The $1.06 million payments were considered to be advances of the son's inheritance and were included in the "adjusted taxable gifts" under section 2001(b). While that figure was included in the computation of the estate tax as adjusted taxable gifts, the IRS was unable to include any imputed interest in the tax base, which would have been allowed if section 2033 applied.

2.   In Estate of Andrews v. United States, 850 F. Supp. 1279 (E.D.Va.1994), (also discussed in Chapter 9) the court included the value of the name of a well-known author in her taxable estate. Virginia Andrews was the predominant author in the "children in jeopardy" genre. At her death, Andrews' publisher proposed that her estate permit it to obtain ghostwriters for future works which would bear her name. The estate agreed, and several highly successful books were figuratively, if not literally, ghostwritten. The decedent's executor had failed to include the value of Andrews' name on the estate tax return. The IRS assessed a deficiency and the court agreed with the IRS that, under these circumstances, the decedent's name was a valuable commercial asset, the value of which should be included in her taxable estate.

3.   The right to exploit the persona of dead celebrities can be very valuable. Such rights are created by state law under what are sometimes described as "Dead Celebrity Laws." The value of these rights should be taxed under the estate tax as valuable property rights. Each year Forbes magazine runs a list of the top dead celebrity earners.[1] Several of these celebrities have been dead for decades. Up until a few years ago, Albert Einstein routinely made the list due to the "Baby Einstein" line of products. Assuredly, Einstein, as clever as he was, would never have imagined that his name would be featured a line of baby toys that would earn millions of dollars a year for his heirs decades after his death in 1955. During 2022, the top 13 dead celebrities earned $1.6 billion, and the top five each earned at least $100 million. According to the Forbes article, the top five earners in order of rank were J.R.R. Tolkien, Kobe Bryant, David Bowie, Elvis Presley, and James Brown. Tolkien earned $500 million after his estate sold a business enterprise that handles various interests, such as intellectual property rights in movies and video games. Kobe Bryant earned $400 million from his estate's sale of a sports drink business to

---

[1]   See The Highest Paid Dead Celebrities of 2022—A Writer Earns Half-A-Billion from the Great Beyond, Lisette Voytko FORBES, (Oct. 31, 2022), https://www.forbes.com/sites/lisettevoytko/ 2022/10/31/the-highest-paid-dead-celebrities-of-2022-a-writer-earns-half-a-billion-from-the-great-beyond//?sh=1be175f52bb3.

Coca Cola. David Bowie earned $250 million after his estate sold his musical publishing catalogue and masters. Elvis Presley's estate earned $110 million, primarily from tours and merchandise sales at Graceland. Finally, the Forbes article noted that James Brown earned $100 million after his estate sold various items, including Brown's music rights, likeness, and name. Given that some celebrities can be worth more dead than alive, this could create serious problems for estates of celebrities who die with other assets whose value is eclipsed by the commercial potential of their persona. Significantly, estimating the value of such rights in many cases can be little short of guess work.

4.　　In the following Technical Advice Memorandum, the IRS considers whether a decedent must include stolen property in the decedent's gross estate under section 2033.

TECHNICAL ADVICE MEMORANDUM 9152005
August 30, 1991.

[In this Technical Advice Memorandum, the IRS was called upon to indicate the proper tax treatment for stolen property held by the decedent, a resident of Texas, who had stolen valuable works of art during 1945 while serving with the US Army in Europe. At his death in 1980, the decedent bequeathed these items to his sister and brother and some of their children, who retained them for six years before attempting to sell them first in the legitimate art market and then in the illegal art market. Under the law of Texas, a holder of stolen property has title to such property which is superior to that of all potential claimants other than that of the person from whom the property was stolen. Borrowing from the line of income tax cases which holds that thieves and other criminals are taxable on the income from their criminal ventures, the IRS reached the following conclusion.]

Similarly, for federal estate tax purposes, no distinction should be drawn between a decedent's property that has been obtained by theft and decedent's property that has been lawfully obtained. If the decedent, at death, possessed the use and economic benefits of the stolen property that are equivalent to ownership, the decedent's lack of title to the stolen property does not affect its inclusion in the decedent's gross estate under § 2033 when the decedent can successfully transfer the property to his heirs. See also Burnet v. Wells, 289 U.S. at 678; Sanford's Estate v. Commissioner, 308 U.S. at 43.

Estate of Bluestein, 15 T.C. 770 (1950), a case cited by the taxpayer's representative in support of his contentions, is distinguishable from the present case because, in *Estate of Bluestein*, the property that had been converted was restored to its rightful owner immediately after the decedent's death during the course of the administration of the decedent's estate. In contrast, in the present case, the art objects were distributed to the Decedent's heirs, who held the property under their complete dominion and control for more than a decade.

* * *

The art objects that the Decedent stole during and immediately after World War II, and that he possessed at his death, are includible in his gross estate under § 2033 of the Code. [The IRS also held that since most stolen art is sold in the illicit market, that market should be employed in assigning a value to decedent's art for estate tax purposes.]

NOTES

1. Under Texas law, after the one-year period for making claims against the estate has expired, the true owners can recover possession of stolen property in an action brought against the heirs. The potential result in this situation is to leave the thief's heirs without the stolen property and his estate with a substantial tax bill.

2. In Tech. Adv. Mem. 9207004, the IRS further pursued the estate tax treatment of the proceeds of crime, this time in the case of a drug dealer whose marijuana-laden plane crashed, killing the drug dealer pilot. The IRS, consistent with its analysis in Tech. Adv. Mem. 9152005, held that the seized illegal drugs were includible in the decedent's estate at their street value in the locus of the crash. Moreover, despite the fact that the drugs were seized by Florida officials, the IRS held that to allow a deduction under either section 2053 (claims against the estate) or section 2054 (casualty losses by the estate) to reflect this fact "would violate the sharply defined public policy against drug trafficking."

3. Similar in result to Tech. Adv. Mem. 9152005 is Estate of Hester v. United States 2007–1 USTC (CCH) ¶ 60,537 (W.D. Va. 2007), aff'd 2008–2 USTC (CCH) ¶ 60,568 (4th Cir. 2008), cert. denied sub nom. Bishop v. United States, 556 U.S. 1222 (2009). In this case the decedent had inherited from his spouse a life estate in a trust, with his children as remainerpersons. Several years later decedent who was also trustee of the trust, which then had $3.2 million in assets, misappropriated the trust assets and co-mingled them with his own assets in his brokerage account which at the time contained almost $4 million of his own funds. He then engaged in a wild bout of day trading using his funds and the misappropriated funds, lost almost $2 million and died shortly thereafter. His estate followed normal procedures in the state calling upon all those with debts and demands to come forward. The children did not advance any claims against their father's estate. His estate tax return listed all the funds remaining in the brokerage account as assets of the decedent's estate and the return did not list the children's deductible claims against the estate under section 2053(a)(3). The court held that because the decedent had "exercised dominion and control over the assets as though they were his

own without an expressed recognition of an obligation to repay and without restriction as to their disposition" they were to be included in his estate. Moreover, the failure of the children to step forward and make a claim at the appropriate time proved fatal to any claim that a deduction should be allowed for claims against the estate under section 2053.

B. INTERESTS AT DEATH

1. GENERATION SKIPPING

Even a careless reading of section 2033 would lead to the conclusion that one who dies holding only a life estate would not be subjected to estate tax under these sections. This is so because the decedent died possessing no interest which he could transfer. On this principle rested much of the tax-minimization estate planning of bygone years. A life estate to a child with remainder to the grandchildren, embroidered perhaps with a nontaxable power of appointment, which is discussed more fully in Chapter 22, gave the child much of the substance of ownership without requiring the child to pay the rate that would have been exacted had the property been left to the child outright. But the old order has changed. Generation-skipping transfers are now subject (after allowance of a generous exclusion) to special supplementary tax, imposed under Chapter 13 of the Code. That subject is discussed in Chapter 29.

2. EFFECT OF DEATH ON INTERESTS HELD

At death, interests in property that are potentially includible in the estate are often affected in a fashion that may have significant tax consequences. For example, on some occasions such interests have their values dramatically enhanced and on others they are terminated or voided—all with dramatic results for the estate of the decedent.

In Estate of Riegelman v. Commissioner, 253 F.2d 315 (2d Cir.1958), the court included in the gross estate of a deceased attorney amounts to which his estate was entitled pursuant to the firm's partnership agreement. The agreement called for the estate of the taxpayer to be paid an amount which reflected the value of: (1) the deceased's partner's share of undistributed profits realized and collected by the partnership prior to death; (2) the deceased's share of profits realized and collected after his death attributable to work performed before his death; and (3) a share, for a limited period of time, of post death fees and profits attributable to work completed after the deceased's death on matters in process in the firm at his death as well as certain matters upon which work was commenced and completed by the firm after death. While the decedent's executor conceded that items (1) and (2) were properly includible in his gross estate, the executor objected to including in decedent's gross estate item (3) payments received for work done subsequent to decedent's death. The court in including this item in decedent's gross estate noted:

> The right of Riegelman's estate to share in the profits of the partnership for the stipulated period after his death was a chose in action, in lieu of that to which it would have succeeded in the absence of an agreement, which passed from Riegelman to his estate as a part of his wealth and hence was properly includible in his gross estate for the purpose of computing an estate tax.[2]

While death can create or fix the value of items of wealth that are includible in decedent's gross estate, as was done in *Riegelman,* it can also, as the case which follows demonstrates, extinguish wealth possessed during life.

ESTATE OF MOSS V. COMMISSIONER
United States Tax Court, 1980.
74 T.C. 1239.

IRWIN, JUDGE:

[John A. Moss, prior to his death, sold his interest in a mortuary and related realty to his employees under a contract that provided for monthly installment payments which were characterized by the court as "adequate and full consideration," and which were spread out over nine years and seven months. The note for the stock was referred to in the contract as Note B and the note for the related realty was referred to as Note C. The contract provided that: "Unless sooner paid, all sums, whether principal or interest, shall be deemed canceled and extinguished as though paid upon death of J.A. Moss." When the parties entered into the contract, Moss, who was 72 years old, was of good health and there was no indication that he would die prior to his collecting all payments under the contract. Monthly payments were made under the contract until Moss unexpectedly died about 16 months later. Pursuant to the contract, no further payments were made.

The principal issue presented for consideration by the court was whether the remaining payments under Notes B and C, which were extinguished at his death, are includible in Moss's gross estate.]

In *Estate of Buckwalter,* decedent's son was indebted to a bank on a 20-year note due in 1971 bearing 4 1/2 percent interest. Decedent proposed that he and his son enter into an arrangement whereby decedent would pay off the unamortized principal of his son's note on December 31, 1954. The son would pay him the identical monthly amounts which would have been due the bank, except that interest would be computed at 2 1/2 percent so that the entire loan would be repaid in 1968 rather than in 1971. The son was instructed to keep the transaction secret, the payments were to be

---

[2]　*Riegelman,* 253 F.2d at 317.

a "matter of honor" and the decedent stated that it was [his] intention not to show "in any way that [the son was] in any way indebted to me, otherwise [decedent] would be required to pay in Penna. a personal property tax each year." Decedent recognized that he probably would not be alive at the end of the amortization period, and stated that his son was to be entirely free of any obligation to his estate. He added a long postscript to the letter setting forth a summary schedule of 30-day payments, showing components of interest and principal in each such payment in December of each year as well as "balance of amortized principal" until final payment in 1968. He also stated that his son might "cut away" the schedule and "destroy the rest of the letter after all details are consummated."

In a second letter to his son about a week later, after the proposal had been accepted, decedent stated that he was sending his son a schedule for payments and credits for the period January 1, 1955, to May 23, 1962, and that for the period thereafter he had "a schedule made up to show complete amortization of an honor loan," which he intended to seal and enclose in his lock box with a legend on the envelope in his son's handwriting reading "Personal Property of Abraham L. Buckwalter, Jr." In a single sentence, decedent informed his son that he could "consider the proposition on my part as a form of annuity at 2 and 1/2%."

We held that decedent had an interest in a debt owed to him by his son at the time of his death and that the unpaid principal was includable in his gross estate under section 2033. The taxpayer there argued that in substance, decedent merely had purchased an annuity from his son which terminated with his death, and therefore, nothing should be included in his gross estate. We disagreed with the contention that the substance of the transaction was an annuity and held that decedent had an interest in the loan at the time of his death.

Respondent contends that decedent, in this case, simply chose to pass the funeral home business to his employees under the guise of the notes which were canceled upon death rather than through his will as he had planned prior to 1972 and, therefore, this case is no different than the situation in *Buckwalter*.

Petitioner argues that the case at bar is factually distinguishable. We agree. In *Buckwalter*, the decedent retained control of the entire debt until his death. The son was not relieved of the debt until he removed the evidence of the loan after the decedent's death. Therefore, at any time prior to his death, decedent could have revoked his decision to cancel the debt at his death and required the son to be obligated to his estate. The decedent sought to achieve the same result as a bequest in a will by keeping the details of the loan contained in a sealed envelope in his own lock box and permitting the son to cancel the debt at his death.

This is not the case here. The parties have stipulated that decedent's sale of stock for which the notes were issued was a bona fide sale for adequate and full consideration. The cancellation provision was part of the bargained for consideration provided by decedent for the purchase price of the stock. As such, it was an integral provision of the note. We do not have a situation, therefore, where the payee provided in his will or endorses or attaches a statement to a note stating that the payor is to be given a gift by the cancellation of his obligation on the payee's death.

We believe there are significant differences between the situation in which a note contains a cancellation provision as part of the terms agreed upon for its issue and where a debt is canceled in a will. The most significant difference for purposes of the estate tax is, as petitioner points out, that a person can unilaterally revoke a will during his lifetime, and, therefore, direct the transfer of his property, at his death. All interest that decedent had in the notes lapsed at his death.

Respondent next contends that the cancellation provision can be considered an assignment of the notes by the decedent to his employees to become effective upon his death. We believe that this is simply a variation of his argument that the cancellation provision is similar to a bequest in a will, and we reject it for the same reasons that we rejected that argument.

* * * [T]he situation here is analogous to that of an annuity or an interest or estate limited for decedent's life. Since there is not [an] interest remaining in decedent at his death, we hold that the notes are not includable in his gross estate.

* * *

Even should we consider the payments to decedent as an "annuity" the value of the notes would still not be includable in his gross estate. In Estate of Bergan v. Commissioner, 1 T.C. 543 (1943), the decedent had made an inter vivos transfer to her sister of her interest in an estate in exchange for her sister's promise to care for and support the decedent for the remainder of the decedent's life. We held therein that the decedent did not retain a life interest in the income from the transferred property under the predecessor of section 2036 because no trust was created to secure the "annuity" nor did the decedent reserve to herself the right to the income from the transferred property. The decedent merely contracted with her sister for her support and her share of the estate was transferred as the consideration for such contract. Similarly, in the present case, decedent transferred his stock and the * * * property as full consideration for Note B and Note C. While the notes were secured by a stock pledge agreement, this fact, alone, is insufficient to include the value of the notes in decedent's gross estate. * * *

PLANNING NOTE

Lest visions of sugar plums dance in your head as a result of the *Moss* case, you should understand that it is uniformly agreed that, if a self-cancelling installment note (SCIN) is employed, the purchasers must pay a premium that reflects the economic advantage to them which results from the cancellation privilege. Failure to provide for a premium would result in the vendor being deemed to have made a taxable gift to the vendee equal to the fair market value of the premium which should have been created. The premium must be in the form of either a purchase price premium, an interest rate premium or a combination of the two. Given this premium consideration, in the law of large numbers, the Treasury should lose no revenue because of the use of such devices. For every taxpayer who, like Moss, dies earlier than expected, there should be a sufficient number of taxpayers who use a SCIN to sell a business and collect in full on their SCIN and who, because of the use of premiums, die with estates which are larger than they would have been had a SCIN not been employed.

In addition to being required to develop the value of the premium component based on actuarial factors, the authorities also agree that the taxpayer must then adjust the premium to reflect added considerations regarding the vendor's projected life span. For example, a 70 year old vendor with a history of heart disease would be expected to employ a SCIN with a premium significantly in excess of the premium which a septuagenarian of normal health might be expected to employ.

Taking some of the bloom off the SCIN rose is Estate of Frane v. Commissioner, 998 F.2d 567 (8th Cir.1993) (discussed in Chapter 32), in which the court held that, under sections 453B and 691, where the vendor and vendee are related, cancellation, at death, of the installment notes should give rise to income in respect of a decedent equal to the thus far unrecognized gain despite the fact that it reflects sales proceeds that will never be received. Should this negative tax result be considered in assigning a lower premium to a SCIN with related parties?

A SCIN involving sale of a family restaurant by a father to a son passed judicial scrutiny in Estate of Costanza v. Commissioner, 320 F.3d 595 (6th Cir. 2003). The Court of Appeals did note that a SCIN involving family members is presumed to be a gift, with the presumption rebuttable by an affirmative showing which it found present.

3. LAPSING RIGHTS IN FAMILY CONTROLLED BUSINESSES (SECTION 2704)

Suppose that a parent seeks to affect the value of property that the parent owns with a child by providing that some of the parent's rights lapse at death, thereby enhancing the value of the child's rights in the property. Because the parent has not formally transferred property to the child, the parent hopes to escape the reach of section 2033. Congress has added section 2704 to the Code to cope with such ploys in a limited context. That section deals with the estate and gift tax ramifications of lapsing rights involving closely held businesses. If death triggers a lapse of voting or liquidation rights in a corporation or partnership, the lapse is deemed to result in a transfer of the lapsed rights for estate tax purposes if the individual holding the lapsing rights and that person's family, both before and after death, hold control of the business. For these purposes, control is defined as 50 percent of voting rights in a corporation or 50 percent of the capital or profits in a partnership. See I.R.C. §§ 2704(c)(1) & 2701(b)(2).

Under section 2704(a)(2) the value included in the estate of the holder of the lapsing rights is the value of all interests in the business entity owned by the holder before lapse over the value of all such interests immediately after the lapse. Where restrictions to liquidate a corporation or partnership are present and are either the product of an arm's-length commercial arrangement with a lender or are imposed by law, they are to be ignored in determining the value of the transferred interest. In addition to the value determined under section 2704(a)(2), there is also included in the estate of the deceased under section 2033 or other relevant sections the value of the property owned by the deceased with respect to which lapsing rights existed.

For example, assume that Father owned all 100 shares of class A common stock of Ajax Inc., that Daughter owned all 900 shares of class B common stock of Ajax and that no other class of Ajax stock existed. The class A and class B stock are identical except that class A stock is entitled to 10 votes per share and the class B stock is entitled to one vote per share. Moreover, in the event that Ajax is liquidated, the holders of class A stock are entitled to receive, on a per share basis, nine times the amount of property that the holders of class B stock are entitled to receive. Both the super voting rights of the class A stock and its liquidation preference lapse at Father's death. Assume further that before Father's death the Ajax common stock, held by him was worth $1.2 million and that after his death it was worth $200,000. Under section 2704(a)(2) there is to be included in Father's estate the $1 million decline in the value of his stock attributable to the lapse. Furthermore, the $200,000 value assigned to the Ajax common stock held by Father's estate after lapse is to be included in his taxable estate under section 2033.

C. CONTINGENT INTERESTS

Under section 6163 the executor may elect to postpone the portion of the estate tax generated by inclusion in the gross estate of "a reversionary or remainder interest" until six months after the termination of the prior interests. If undue hardship will result, the Commissioner can extend the date for payment for an additional period of up to three years. Section 6163 plainly contemplates that remainder and reversionary interests are includable in the gross estate under section 2033. But what if the future interest is contingent—one that may fail upon an event distant in time, such as the death of a named person without issue? Are such contingent interests subject to estate taxation, and, if so, at what valuation? What are the competing considerations and how are they to be reconciled?

IN RE ESTATE OF HILL

United States Court of Appeals, Second Circuit, 1952.
193 F.2d 724.

SWAN, CHIEF JUDGE.

[Walter J. Hill, the decedent, at the time of his death possessed three distinct contingent interests under an inter vivos trust that he had established. The issue before the court was the degree to which, in each of those three cases, contingent interests should give rise to includible property.]

The taxpayer contends that each of the decedent's three interests in the trust property is so speculative as to be incapable of valuation and therefore nothing whatever should have been included in the gross estate because of the trust. This contention, however, is not seriously pressed with respect to the right to receive annually excess net income during the life of the trust, and obviously could not be supported if it were. During the years 1919 to 1943 inclusive the settlor had received from this source an aggregate of more than $228,000; and for the years 1944 to 1947 inclusive he or his estate received $42,000 additional. At the date of his death the annual income requirements of the trust were $5,000 to the wife and $12,000 to the daughter, while the net income of the trust for 1944 and the three succeeding years has averaged better than $27,000. Actuarially the trust might be expected to continue for about 32 years after the settlor's death. The annual payments are known, the earnings of the trust can be estimated, and the difference will be the surplus returnable to the settlor's estate. Discounted to present worth, that surplus should be included in the taxable estate. The taxpayer estimates that on the assumption that excess income maintains the previous average rate over the remainder of the trust, the value on March 4, 1944 of the right to receive it would be $176,000, using a discount factor of 4 per cent. We do not pass upon the validity of the taxpayer's assumption or discount factor, for the case must be remanded for reasons hereafter explained and the valuation of the right to excess income is for the Tax Court's determination in the first instance. Appellant further argues that in terms of what this right would sell for in the market, a prospective purchaser would require the actuarial value of so uncertain a right to be drastically discounted. This is also a matter for the Tax Court's consideration upon which we express no opinion.

Next to be considered is the decedent's right during the continuance of the trust to have returned to him or his estate upon the happening of certain contingencies such portions of the trust corpus as the trustees in their discretion should determine to be not needed for the subsequent administration of the trust. * * * [C]ontingencies upon which portions of the corpus may be returned to the settlor or his estate are the death of the wife or the daughter during the life of the trust. If the wife dies before the daughter the trustees are to select such portion of the trust property "as shall in their judgment, which shall be final in the premises, be sufficient in amount and character safely to produce such amount of income as shall be reasonably necessary for the subsequent administration of the trust." This portion they shall retain as trust property and the balance they shall deliver to the settlor or his estate. If the daughter dies before the wife the portion retained as trust property must be sufficient in the judgment of the trustees, "which shall be final in the premises" safely to produce "a net income, after the payment of taxes thereon," of $12,000 per year. The taxpayer argues that because the decedent's expectancy of having returned to him or his estate some part of the corpus during the life of the trust depended upon the exercise of discretionary powers conferred upon the trustees, it was not a judicially enforceable right and therefore was not an "interest" in property within the meaning of section 811(a) [now section 2033]. In this the taxpayer is in error. The case upon which he particularly relies, Commissioner v. Irving Trust Co., 147 F.2d 946 (2d Cir.1945), is distinguishable. There the trustees had absolute discretion in the return of corpus, without any standard having been set up to guide them. Here the settlor has directed that they return so much of the corpus as they determine not "reasonably necessary for the subsequent administration of the trust." At the date of death the trust property was worth $786,569.60 and produced an annual income $10,000 in excess of the amount needed to pay the wife and daughter. If the wife shall die before the daughter, as is actuarially probable, the trustees will be relieved of the annual $5,000 payment to her and it seems likely that they would exercise their discretion to return some part of the corpus as they had previously done when her share of the income was reduced by her remarriage. If they refused to do so we cannot doubt, even though the trustees' judgment is declared "final in the premises," that a court of equity would intervene to enforce the settlor's mandate that they retain only so much as is reasonably necessary safely to produce the income needed for their subsequent administration. The amount of corpus returnable to the decedent's estate under these provisions of the trust is somewhat speculative and admits of no accurate determination, but we cannot doubt that the right had value at the date of the settlor's death. As this court said in Bankers Trust Co. v. Higgins, 136 F.2d 477, 479, " * * * we should not demand certainty; better a fair guess than the one answer sure to be wrong."

The decedent's other interest in the corpus was a contingent reversion upon termination of the trust. This was conditional upon the complete failure of the daughter's issue. Actuarially it is most unlikely that the estate will receive anything under this provision. At the settlor's death there was alive an infant granddaughter who might marry and have children before the trust terminated. Also the daughter aged 35 survived; she was married and the prospect that she might have additional children was not improbable. We agree with the taxpayer's contention that the possibility of enjoyment by the decedent's estate of this contingent reversion was so remote at the date of death that the reversion had no ascertainable value. Commissioner v. Cardeza's Estate, 173 F.2d 19, 23; see also Robinette v. Helvering, 318 U.S. 184, 189 (1943).

* * *

We agree with the taxpayer that under section 811(a) [now § 2033] the proper method of computation in the case of a trust is to determine as of the date of death the values of the decedent's rights in the trust property and to include in the gross estate the sum of such values.

The case is remanded for further proceedings consistent with this opinion.

NOTES

1. The Treasury adopts a realistic attitude on the subject of fertility. Thus, in Rev. Rul. 61–88, 1961–1 C.B. 417, where the life tenant was a married woman aged 44 at the time of the decedent's death and the decedent's remainder was conditioned on the death without issue of the life tenant, the ruling takes the position that the remainder is one of substantial value—to be valued by the usual principles unless it is shown by medical evidence that birth of issue is impossible. An earlier ruling dealing with the problem of the deductibility of a charitable remainder contingent on death without issue of two childless women of 55 and 59 years of age generously ruled that the contingent bequest to charity was sufficiently assured to warrant allowance of the deduction. Rev. Rul. 59–143, 1959–1 C.B. 247.

2. Though not to be classified as a contingent interest in the property sense, what of a deceased attorney's claim for a contingent fee? Suppose the attorney dies in midstream; should the executor include something in the attorney's gross estate with respect to this item, and, if so, how is a value to be placed on the property right? The Treasury's position on the question should not occasion surprise. Consider this extract from Rev. Rul. 55–123, 1955–1 C.B. 443:

> In the instant case, the decedent's right to receive payment for services rendered in cases completed in his lifetime, was fixed by contract. After the decedent's death, his personal

representatives had a right to recover on a *quantum meruit* basis the reasonable value of the services rendered by him on a contingent fee basis in the cases in which settlements or judgments were obtained after his death. This right of the personal representatives is a chose in action, a species of personal property.

A determination of the fair market value as of the date of decedent's death or other applicable valuation date, of the right of the personal representatives of a deceased attorney to recover for services rendered on a contingent fee basis in cases remaining unsettled as of such date may present a difficult problem, but it is possible to fairly appraise or estimate the value of such right. * * *

In the instant case, the executor elected to have the property of the estate valued in accordance with Section 811(j) [now section 2032 which now provides an alternate valuation date of six months] of the Internal Revenue Code of 1939; that is, one year after the date of death or as of the date of sale, exchange, or other disposition in the interim. The amount realized by the estate during the year following the decedent's death for his services constitutes a disposition of the claim for compensation and the amount received therefor represents the fair market value of the property as of the date of such disposition. In view of the foregoing, it is held that the fair market value as of the applicable valuation date of the right of the executor to receive compensation for legal services performed by the decedent on a contingent fee basis is includible in his gross estate as an interest in property within the purview of [section 2033].

3.   If the contingency is resolved within six months after the decedent's death, the option under section 2032 to value the property as of six months after the date of death (or the disposition date if that is earlier) averts the horrible prospect of paying an estate tax on a value that later evaporates. But what if the event that saps all value from the contingent interest takes place six months and a day after the decedent's death? Why not tax at full value when the interest falls in—and wholly exempt from tax when the interest fails?

D. EMPLOYEE DEATH BENEFITS

Death benefits that an employer pays to the estate or survivors of an employee can often be of significant value. Typically, these benefits are paid to individuals designated by the employee, but on occasion they are payable to persons designated by the employer. Two principal issues arise in this area. First, under what circumstances are such benefits included in the estate and, second, when so included, what is the proper amount to be included?

1. ISSUE OF INCLUSION

Employee death benefits payable to the decedent's estate under an existing plan that had granted these rights to the employee before his or her death, or which rather than being payable to his or her estate are payable to individuals designated by the employee, are includible in the decedent's taxable estate of the deceased. See Rev. Rul. 65–217, 1965–2 C.B. 214, and authorities cited therein. Benefits provided at the discretion of the employer, after death, to individuals designated by the employer are treated differently. Revenue Ruling 65–217 indicates that such benefits are to be excluded from the estate on the ground that, because no right to such property existed at death, the benefits may not be deemed to be passing from the decedent. A similar result prevails where, although the benefits were not discretionary at death, they were, under the terms of the employer's plan, payable to a class of individuals designated by the employer, such as the surviving spouse or lineal issue. Since tax consequences of vast magnitude revolve around whether designation of the class of beneficiaries has been made by the employer or the employee, it is not surprising to discover that the IRS occasionally takes the position that, for purposes of section 2033, designations of beneficiaries by employers should be imputed to the employee. The case below addresses the inclusion of death benefits in the decedent's gross estate.

ESTATE OF TULLY

United States Court of Claims, 1976.
528 F.2d 1401.

KUNZIG, JUDGE.

The single issue presented in this estate tax case is the includability in decedent Edward A. Tully, Sr.'s gross estate of death benefits paid directly to Tully's widow by his employer. Plaintiffs (coexecutors) move for partial summary judgment claiming that no estate tax provision compels such treatment. Defendant's cross-motion counters that the death benefits must be added to the gross estate as required either by section 2038(a)(1) or section 2033 of the Internal Revenue Code of 1954. We agree with plaintiffs and hold the sum at issue not includable in Tully's gross estate.

The facts in this case are uncontested. Before his death, Tully was employed by Tully and DiNapoli, Inc. (T & D), a company owned 50% by decedent and 50% by Vincent P. DiNapoli. On July 1, 1959, Tully, DiNapoli and T & D entered into a contract whereby T & D promised to pay death benefits to the Tully and DiNapoli widows. Later, in October 1963, the same parties amended the 1959 agreement to limit the maximum amount of death payments to $104,000. On March 7, 1964, Tully died. T & D paid his widow the $104,000 called for in the contract.

Because the death benefits were paid directly by T & D to the widow, plaintiffs did not include this sum in Tully's gross estate when they filed the estate tax return. On audit, the Internal Revenue Service (IRS) concluded that the $104,000 was part of Tully's gross estate and assessed an estate tax deficiency. Plaintiffs paid the deficiency, filed a refund claim and by timely petition filed in this court, brought the present action after the IRS disallowed their claim.

* * *

The Government relies only on sections 2038(a)(1) and 2033, and no others, in its argument that the death benefits at issue here are includable in Tully's gross estate.

Defendant's contentions, specifically its argument that sections 2038(a)(1) and 2033 must be treated as virtually identical, suggest at the outset that we consider the basic philosophy of estate tax law. As enacted by Congress, the primary purpose of the estate tax is to tax "the transfer of property at death." C. Lowndes & R. Kramer, Federal Estate and Gift Taxes § 2.2 (3d Ed. 1974). If sufficient incidents of ownership in an item of property are given away before death, no tax will be imposed. Since all estate tax statutes are direct[ed] at taxing property transferred at death, it can become easy to confuse their operation or to apply them in an overlapping fashion.

Within this context, the two estate tax sections involved in the instant case, 2038(a)(1) and 2033, both impose a tax on property transferred at death. However, they are directed at two different situations. Section 2038(a)(1) is specific in its terms. It taxes property which an individual has given away while retaining enough "strings" to change or revoke the gift. Section 2033 is more general in its approach, and taxes property which has never really been given away at all.

Certain of defendant's arguments misconstrue this basic difference between section 2038(a)(1) and section 2033. By suggesting that the same "controls" over property which might represent a section 2038(a)(1) "power" can also be viewed as a section 2033 "interest," the Government attempts to turn section 2033 into an estate tax "catch all." This was not the intent of Congress in enacting section 2033. Congress has provided a "catch all" in the income tax statutes. It has not done so in the estate tax area. Therefore, defendant's efforts to treat the two sections as virtually identical by the "catch all" method are misplaced.

In accordance with this analysis, our inquiry takes two avenues. First, did Tully transfer the death benefits but keep a power to change or revoke them until the time of his death? If so, section 2038(a)(1) applies. Second, did Tully have an "interest" in the benefits at his death? If he had an "interest," section 2033 applies.

[The Court's explanation as to why section 2038 is not applicable is reproduced in Chapter 19.]

Nor does section 2033 require addition of the benefits to Tully's gross estate. The Government argues that corporate control, "pegging" the benefits to Tully's salary, and naming "widow" as beneficiary constituted section 2033 "interests" kept by Tully until his death. We found above that these facts did not give rise to a section 2038(a)(1) "power." We also determine that they did not create a section 2033 "interest."

Having found that Tully transferred the death benefits to his wife and that he could not reach them for his own use, he could not have kept a section 2033 "interest." The *de minimis* associations Tully may have still had with the benefits are not strong enough to force a conclusion that decedent never transferred his interests in the benefits to his wife.

* * *

Defendant would use section 2033 as a "catch all." The simple answer to this is that section 2033 is not a "catch all," but applies to situations where decedent kept so much control over an item of property that in substance he still owns the property. "Interest" as used in section 2033 connotes a stronger control than "power" as used in section 2038(a)(1). If controls over property cannot rise to the dignity of section 2038(a)(1) "powers" they equally cannot create section 2033 "interests." In the instant case, having failed to establish that corporate stock ownership, "pegging" the benefits to Tully's salary and naming the "widow" as beneficiary created section 2038(a)(1) "powers," defendant equally fails to demonstrate that the same facts create section 2033 "interests."

In summary, we have considered an employee plan in which the employee transferred death benefits to his wife, but kept until his death certain tangential associations with the plan. These *de minimis* associations did not rise to the level of section 2038(a)(1) "powers" to "alter, amend, revoke or terminate" the transfer, and did not constitute "interests" sufficient to force the conclusion that section 2033 applies. Therefore, the death benefits at issue here were not includable in Tully's gross estate.

NOTE

In Rev. Rul. 55–87, 1955–1 C.B. 112, the IRS ruled that there is no inclusion in the estate with respect to social security lump-sum death benefits, which under social security rules are payable to a surviving spouse, because the decedent has no control over the designation of the beneficiary. To the same effect is Rev. Rul. 67–277, 1967–2 C.B. 322 and Rev. Rul. 75–145, 1975–1 C.B. 298, which deals with the tax treatment of uncashed benefit checks.

PLANNING NOTE

Since, in the absence of a showing of employee control of the employer, we do not include employee death benefits in the taxable estate unless such benefits are paid to the estate of the employee or to individuals designated by the employee, corporate counsel might often be expected to advise against establishment of plans under which benefits are payable to beneficiaries designated by the employee or are payable to the employee's estate.

In structuring a death benefit plan, care must also be exercised to consider nontax factors such as the impact of the different types of plans on employee morale. The employer might quite possibly decide that the benefit, in terms of employee morale, derived with respect to most employees from a taxable plan that allows the employee to designate beneficiaries, outweighs the detriment that the employer suffers with respect to a few wealthy employees as a result of establishing a plan that has a negative tax impact on a handful of highly compensated employees. By creating a plan that pays death benefits for lowly compensated individuals to their estates and pays death benefits for highly compensated individuals to an employer-designated class of individuals, the employer might be able to maximize its credits with each group of employees.

2. AMOUNT INCLUDIBLE

Where an inclusion is appropriate with respect to a death benefit because, for example, the benefit was payable to the employee's estate or the employee had the right to designate beneficiaries, there is still an issue as to the amount properly includible. Is the value included in the estate the estimated fair market value of the benefit before death or is it the fair market value of the benefit transferred? For example, presume that under a death benefit plan $1,000,000 is to be transferred to the estate of a 52-year-old male employee if he is employed at death. The employee and his insurance agent, moments before the employee's fatal heart attack at the eighteenth hole at the country club, might consider the right to be worth only $50,000 and the employer's actuary might have asked him to set aside only that amount to meet the employer's responsibilities to this employee under the plan. At death, do we include this value in the employee's estate on the ground that it is the value of what he owned, or do we include the fair market value of the rights transferred to the estate (i.e., $1,000,000)? The following case addresses that issue.

GOODMAN V. GRANGER
United States Court of Appeals, Third Circuit, 1957.
243 F.2d 264, cert. denied, 355 U.S. 835 (1957).

KALODNER, CIRCUIT JUDGE.

When does the federal estate tax attach?

More specifically stated, when does such tax attach to a decedent-employee's contractual right to annual deferred compensation payments from his employer, payable to his estate after his death?

That problem, of first impression, is presented by this appeal by the government from a judgment in favor of the taxpayer, Eleanor D. Goodman, administratrix of the estate of Jacques Blum, deceased, in a suit brought by her in the District Court for the Western District of Pennsylvania to recover estate taxes and interest alleged to have been erroneously assessed and collected.

The District Court, subscribing to the taxpayer's contention, concluded as a matter of law that the decedent's contractual right was to be " * * * valued during decedent's lifetime and *at the moment before death* * * * " and made the factual finding that at such moment the contractual right was "valueless", for reasons which will subsequently be discussed. In its opinion the District Court stated "It must be admitted that if the value in the contracts is to be fixed *the moment after death*, then the Government is correct in its contention in this case." [Emphasis in original.]

* * *

The decedent, Jacques Blum, for several years prior to his sudden death of a heart attack at the age of 52 on May 2, 1947, was executive vice-president of Gimbel Brothers, Inc. ("Gimbels") in charge of its Pittsburgh store.

On October 19, 1944, June 1, 1945 and May 26, 1946, decedent entered into identical contracts of employment with Gimbel Brothers covering the years ending January 31, 1945, January 31, 1946 and January 31, 1947, respectively. Each contract provided for a basic salary of $50,000 per year, and for additional "contingent benefits" of $2,000 per year for fifteen years "after the employee ceases to be employed by the employer" by reason of death or otherwise. The post-employment "contingent payments" were to be made only if the employee duly performed the services agreed upon and did not engage in a competing business within a specified period after termination of his employment; and they were to be reduced if his post-employment earnings from a non-competing business plus the contingent payments exceeded seventy-five percent of his yearly average compensation under the contracts. Any of the fifteen annual contingent payments which fell due after the employee's death were to be paid to his estate, or to a nominee designated in his will.

The third contract for the period of employment ending January 31, 1947 was, by its terms, renewed on a month-to-month basis and was in effect at the time of decedent's death. At the latter time there was every prospect that he would continue to advance in his highly successful career in retailing.

After the decedent's death Gimbels paid the $6,000 annual installments provided by the three separate contracts ($2,000 each) to the taxpayer in her capacity as administratrix as they became due. She filed with the Collector a timely federal estate tax return and included the three contracts at a value of $15,000. Upon audit of the return the Internal Revenue Agent in Charge, Pittsburgh, increased the value of the three contracts from $15,000 to $66,710.34, the present worth of $90,000, payable in equal annual installments of $6,000 a year over a period of fifteen years. The increase in the value of the contracts resulted in a deficiency of $15,958.18, including interest, which was assessed against and paid by the taxpayer, and for the recovery of which she brought the suit here involved.

* * *

The sum of the taxpayer's position is (1) what is taxed is "the value" of the decedent's interest in his contract that "ceased by reason of death," not the value of what is received by the recipient (the administratrix); otherwise stated, "the value" of the decedent's interest in his contract was to be determined as "of the moment before death."

The government's position may be summarized as follows: (1) the estate tax is measured by the value of property transferred by death and here an absolute right to the fifteen deferred compensation payments passed by decedent's death to the taxpayer inasmuch as the possibility of forfeiture was extinguished by decedent's death; (2) the government properly valued the right to the deferred compensation payments in the same manner as an annuity for a term certain, i.e. at the commuted value in accordance with the applicable Treasury Regulations.

As earlier noted, the District Court agreed with the taxpayer's view. In doing so it stated:

> "It seems clear under the authorities and the statute and the regulations that the value of the contract rights *is limited to the interest of the decedent during his lifetime.* That interest * * * is valueless. There was no fair market value on which to base a deficiency assessment." [Emphasis in original.]

It may be noted parenthetically that the taxpayer's testimony as to lack of value, adverted to by the District Court, was premised on the circumstance that the employment contracts specified four contingencies which, if any of them had occurred, would have forfeited the decedent's right to the deferred compensation payments.

It is clear that the decedent's interest in the employment contracts was "property" includible in his gross estate under Section 811(a) of the Internal Revenue Code of 1939 [now section 2033]. Determination of the time when that interest is to be valued is the crux of the dispute.

We have had the benefit of thorough discussions by both the government and the taxpayer of the nature of the federal estate tax. Both parties cited Knowlton v. Moore, 178 U.S. 41 (1900); Young Men's Christian Association v. Davis, 264 U.S. 47 (1924); and Edwards v. Slocum, 264 U.S. 61 (1924). The government cited them for the proposition that the subject of the tax is neither the property of the decedent, nor the property of the legatee, but rather the transfer of assets affected by death. The taxpayer emphasizes the language in these cases which supports the theory that what is taxed is the value of the interest that ceased by reason of death, not the value of what is received by the recipient. We are in accord with both of these general axioms which aid in clarifying the nature of the federal estate tax. However, the cases cited and the principles drawn therefrom are not decisive of the question posed by this case. While the nature of the tax has been discussed in numerous Supreme Court cases, the question of the proper time to determine the nature of a decedent's interest and the value thereof requires a more particularized analysis.

The taxpayer has ignored the very nature of the tax which it is urged is dispositive of this case. True, the tax reaches the " ' * * * interest which ceased by reason of the death' ", Knowlton v. Moore, supra at 49, but the reference there was to the distinction between an estate tax and an inheritance tax. The inheritance tax is levied upon the individual shares of the decedent's estate after distribution to the legatees; the estate tax is imposed upon the total estate of the decedent which is transferred to the legatees. The estate tax has been characterized as "an excise imposed upon the transfer of or shifting in relationships to property at death." United States Trust Co. v. Helvering, 307 U.S. 57, 60 (1939). The estate and inheritance taxes have the common element of being based upon the transmission of property from the dead to the living. In Knowlton v. Moore, supra, the Supreme Court recognized this basic principle when it said:

> " * * * tax laws of this nature in all countries rest in their essence upon the principle that death is the generating source from which the particular taxing power takes its being, and that it is the power to transmit, or the transmission from the dead to the living, on which such taxes are more immediately rested."

Since death is the propelling force for the imposition of the tax, it is death which determines the interests to be includible in the gross estate. Interests which terminate on or before death are not a proper subject of the tax. Assets may be acquired or disposed of before death, possibilities of the loss of an asset may become actualities or may disappear. Upon the same principle underlying the inclusion of interests in a decedent's gross estate, valuation of an interest is neither logically made nor feasibly administered until death has occurred. The taxpayer's theory of valuing property before death disregards the fact that generally the estate tax is neither concerned with changes in property interests nor values prior to death. The tax is measured by the value of assets transferred by reason of death, the critical value being that which is determined as of the time of death.

As was so succinctly stated by Judge Hartshorne in Christiernin v. Manning, 138 F.Supp. 923, 925 (D.N.J.1956):

"There cannot be a decedent, till death has occurred. A decedent's estate is not transferred either by his will or by intestacy, till death has occurred. * * * And the decedent's interest in the property taxable is to be such interest 'at the time of his death' * * *."

Here the employment contracts provided for additional "contingent" compensation of $6,000 per year for fifteen years to be paid to Blum or his estate after the termination of his employment by reason of death or otherwise. True, the right to these payments was forfeitable upon the occurrence of any of the specified contingencies. However, forfeiture as a result of the contingencies never occurred during Blum's lifetime, and any possibility of their occurrence was extinguished by his death. Gimbels has been making and the estate has been collecting the payments provided by the contracts. Valuation of the right to these payments must be determined as of the time of Blum's death when the limiting factor of the contingencies would no longer be considered. Death ripened the interest in the deferred payments into an absolute one, and death permitted the imposition of the tax measured by the value of that absolute interest in property.

In Mearkle's Estate v. Commissioner, 129 F.2d 386 (3d Cir.1942), we considered the proper method of valuing an annuity upon the death of the decedent which by its terms was payable to the decedent during his life and to his wife for her life. The criterion adopted was the purchase price of an annuity contract upon the life of the wife measured by her life expectancy on the date of her husband's death. There is no reference in this test to the husband's life expectancy upon the date of his death or to the joint expectancies of the decedent and his wife. See Christiernin v. Manning, supra. The value of decedent's interest in the annuity up to the time of his death is not considered, and, as in the situation here involved, death cuts off prior limiting factors.

For the reasons stated the judgment of the District Court will be reversed with directions to proceed in accordance with this opinion.

E. CLAIMS UNDER WRONGFUL DEATH AND SURVIVAL STATUTES

In this country, when death results from intentional or negligent action, damages are awarded in most cases under two different statutory theories of recovery. Under the pure wrongful death statute, a right to sue is created in a class of beneficiaries who have a statutorily defined familial relationship with the decedent. These parties are allowed a recovery for their economic losses resulting from death. Under the survival type statute, the executor or administrator of the estate sues as the representative of the decedent and is awarded damages based on the economic loss and pain and suffering inflicted on the decedent. In recent years, states have been creating wrongful death statutes that draw on both types of statutes.

In Rev. Rul. 54–19, 1954–1 C.B. 179, the IRS indicated that damages under a pure wrongful death statute were not includible in the estate of the decedent. Since under the wrongful death statute the decedent never possessed any interest in property transferred at death, the IRS indicated that there was no basis for including any awarded damages in the decedent's estate.

An action under a survival-type statute presents a situation that offers the potential to produce a different result. The following case deals with the taxability of damages under a survival-type statute.

CONNECTICUT BANK AND TRUST CO. v. UNITED STATES

United States Court of Appeals, Second Circuit, 1972.
465 F.2d 760.

ROBERT P. ANDERSON, CIRCUIT JUDGE:

[Warren and Virginia Horton, as well as a passenger in their automobile, were killed when the car was struck by a tractor trailer on the Chesapeake Bay Bridge Tunnel. Since plaintiffs were domiciled in Connecticut, suit was brought under that state's survival-type statute. Prior to trial, the suits were settled for $320,000 with nothing paid with respect to antemortem pain and suffering.]

The crucial issue to be decided under § 2033 is whether or not the value of an action for wrongful death is "property . . . of the decedent at the time of his death." Much of the Government's argument and the opinion of the court below rest on the differences between the Connecticut statutory scheme for wrongful death recovery and the more common pattern of recovery in the majority of the states based upon "Lord Campbell's Act," which provides for a direct right of action on behalf of designated beneficiaries of the decedent to recover for his wrongful death, with damages to be measured by the loss to the survivors. The Connecticut statutes, on the other hand, provide for a right of action in the executor or administrator, with damages to be measured on the basis of the loss of the decedent's ability to carry on life's activities. In addition, by recent amendments, the wrongful death proceeds in Connecticut are distributed according to the terms of the decedent's will, if there is one, and are subject to the general claims of the estate. The differences in results under the two types of statutes may be more theoretical than real, but in any event, these differences have little relevance concerning the question of whether or not the right of action for wrongful death was *property owned at death.*

Simple logic mandates the conclusion that an action for wrongful death cannot exist until a decedent has died, at which point, he is no longer a person capable of owning any property interests. The Government's reply to this is that at the very instant of death the right of action arose which the decedent was then capable of owning at death. The only authorities cited for this position, however, are cases where *preexisting* property interests were *valued* as of the instant of death, but valuation at time of death of prior existing interests is a far different concern from that in this case where the property interest itself has sprung from the fact that the death has taken place.

While it is true that Congress may constitutionally place an excise tax on property created by death, as well as upon property transferred by death, § 2033 does not read so broadly. In a discussion of the estate tax the Supreme Court described the scope of § 2033: "What this law taxes is not the interest to which the legatees and devisees succeeded on death, but the interest which ceased by reason of death," Y.M.C.A. v. Davis, 264 U.S. 47, 50 (1924); see also, Nichols v. Coolidge, 274 U.S. 531, 537 (1927). Where, as here, there was no property interest in the decedent which passed by virtue of his death, but rather one which arose after his death, such an interest is not property owned at death and not part of the gross estate under § 2033 * * *.

The Treasury Department has issued three Revenue Rulings concerning the inclusion of wrongful death proceeds under § 2033, all of which hold that the proceeds are not part of the gross estate. In this case, the Government tries to distinguish them because they concerned rights of action arising under New Jersey and Virginia state law and the federal Death on the High Seas Act; however, the rationale of those rulings is fully applicable here. In Rev. Rul. 54–19, 1954–1 Cum.Bull. 179, 180, the Department stated: "Inasmuch as the decedent had no right of action or interest in the proceeds at the time of his death, nothing 'passed' from the decedent to the beneficiaries. Accordingly, the amounts recovered by the beneficiaries would not be includible in the decedent's gross estate for Federal estate tax purposes." It held that such proceeds were not part of the gross estate in Rev. Rul. 68–88, 1968–1 Cum.Bull. 397, 398, because "[t]he right of action for wrongful death does not accrue until death occurs," and in Rev. Rul. 69–8, 1969–1 Cum.Bull. 219, because "[t]he decedent in his lifetime never had an interest in either the right of action or the proceeds." See also Rev. Rul. 55–581, 1955–2 Cum.Bull. 381, holding that an allotment paid by the armed services to designated beneficiaries of servicemen who die in active duty is not part of the gross estate; and Rev. Rul. 55–87, 1955–1 Cum.Bull. 112, holding that a lump sum payment for funeral expenses to social security recipients is not taxable under § 2033.

[The portion of the opinion on a second point relating to section 2041, power of appointment, has been reprinted in Chapter 22.]

NOTE

In Rev. Rul. 75–127, 1975–1 C.B. 297, the IRS indicated that it would, in general, abide by the result of *Connecticut Bank and Trust Co.*; however, where the damages awarded represent damages to which the decedent had become entitled during his or her life (such as pain and suffering and medical expenses), the IRS indicated that it would persist in attempting to include these amounts in the decedent's. What does this suggest to you regarding the allocation of damages in settlement of a tort claim? Woe be to malpractice insurance carriers of those trial attorneys who feel that they can remain ignorant of the tax laws. It might be helpful to reread the summary of facts in *Connecticut Bank and Trust* to observe how the attorney in that case settled the claims so that no part of the damage award was ultimately made subject to estate taxation.

F. COMMUNITY PROPERTY IN GROSS ESTATE

REVENUE RULING 54–89
1954–1 C.B. 181.

Advice is requested relative to the extent real property acquired in the manner set forth below is to be included in the decedent's gross estate for Federal estate tax purposes.

A married man, a resident of Texas, a community property State, purchased with the community funds of himself and his wife real property situated in New Mexico [a community property state] and Kansas [a common law property state]. The husband took title to the purchased property in his own name. He died survived by his wife.

The respective rights of the husband and wife in real property are governed by the law of the place where such property is situated rather than by the law of the domicile of the parties.

The law of descent and distribution contained in chapter 31 of the New Mexico Statutes, annotated, 1941, provides that upon the death of the husband one-half of the community estate goes to the wife and the other half is subject to the testamentary disposition of the husband. (Sec. 31–109.) Accordingly, it is held that the value of only one-half of the New Mexico real estate is includible in the deceased husband's gross estate.

The general rule in a community property State is that where a husband, as manager and business agent of the community, purchases real property in a common law State with community funds and takes title thereto in his own name, he holds a one-half interest in the property as trustee for his wife.

Section 67–406 of General Statutes of Kansas, Annotated, reads as follows:

> Conveyance to one person when consideration paid by another. When a conveyance for a valuable consideration is made to one person and the consideration therefor is paid by another, no use or trust shall result in favor of the latter; but the title shall vest in the former, subject to the provisions of the next two sections.

Section 67–407 provides that every such conveyance shall be presumed fraudulent as against the creditors of the person paying the consideration.

Section 67–408 provides as follows:

> The provisions of the section next before the last shall not extend to cases where the alienee shall have taken any absolute conveyance in his own name without the consent of the person with whose money the consideration was paid; or where such alienee in violation of some trust shall have purchased the land with moneys not his own; or where it shall be made to appear that by agreement and without any fraudulent intent the party to whom the conveyance was made, or in whom the title shall vest, was to hold the land or some interest therein in trust for the party paying the purchase money or some part thereof.

In construing the provisions of sections 67–406 and 408 of the General Statutes of Kansas, the Supreme Court of Kansas has consistently held that where the husband purchases land in Kansas in part or in whole with his wife's money, a trust is impressed on the land in favor of the wife to the extent the purchase price was paid with her funds, unless the wife intended to make a gift to her husband. Accordingly, it is held that the value of only one-half of the Kansas real property is includible in the deceased husband's gross estate.

NOTE

In Rev. Rul. 72–443, 1972–2 C.B. 531, the decedent, a resident of Norway, a community property jurisdiction, purchased realty in a U.S. common law property state using community assets. The Treasury indicated that the general rule in such situations is that the property rules of the state or country where the realty is located determine its character as separate or community property, whereas in the case of movable property, the law of domicile of the owners will be used to determine its character. The common law property state in which the purchased realty was located provided that when a domiciliary of a community property jurisdiction uses community funds to purchase realty in the state in question, the party holding title to the property will be deemed to hold it as trustee for the other spouse to the extent that the other spouse's assets were used to effect the purchase. The ruling concluded with the observation that: "In light of the above, the decedent is considered, under the laws of the state in which that property is located, to own one-half the property as trustee for his wife. Accordingly, it is held that only one-half the value of the real property is includible in his gross estate under section 2033 of the Code."

PROBLEMS

1. Anne transfers Blackacre to Justin for life, remainder to Justin's issue. If Justin dies without issue, Blackacre will be gifted to the American Red Cross. When Justin dies, how much will be included in his taxable estate?

2. Andrew transfers Blackacre to Christine for life, remainder to Taylor in fee simple. Taylor dies while Christine is living. At his death, what is includible in Taylor's taxable estate?

3. Paul gave his 53-year-old, childless daughter, Alyssa, a term of years for 20 years in income of a trust, with remainder to Alyssa's issue. Alyssa died intestate five years after establishment of the trust. At her death, what is includible in her estate?

4. In the prior problem, assume that Paul, rather than Alyssa had died. At his death, is anything includible in his estate?

5. In an arm's-length transaction, Mary sold her business to her employees for $4 million, to be paid in 10 annual payments of $400,000 bearing interest at a fair market rate. Under the terms of the contract of sale, Mary's death will result in cancellation of all remaining payments. The interest rate on the notes contained premium to reflect the potential loss to Mary's estate due to the cancellation provision. At her death two years after the sale, will anything be included in her estate?

6. Nancy is a vice president at Apex, Inc. Under the company's death benefit plan, one full year's salary is to be paid to "the surviving spouse of any deceased employee and in absence of a surviving spouse to the surviving issue of such employee." At Nancy's death, $750,000 was paid to her husband Paul. What, if anything, is includible in Nancy's estate?

7. John died in a plane crash and at his death $4 million was paid by the airline's insurer in settlement of all claims. The $4 million consisted of $3.5 million paid to John's dependents under the state wrongful death statute to compensate them for their economic losses and $500,000 paid to compensate for pain and suffering inflicted on John. What, if anything, is includible in John's estate?

8. At Jordyn's death she owned Blackacre, worth $500,000, and Whiteacre, worth $800,000. Jordyn was married to Chris for 20 years, and they spent their entire lives as residents of a community property state. Jordyn inherited Blackacre from her father two years earlier when it was worth $300,000. Whiteacre was purchased eight years prior to her death for

$200,000, which came from savings from her job accumulated over the six years prior to the purchase. What amount, if any, is includible in Jordyn's estate?

CHAPTER 16

JOINT TENANCIES

(SECTION 2040)

■ ■ ■

A. INTRODUCTION

At the outset, the student must distinguish joint tenancies and tenancies by the entirety from tenancies in common. Tenancies in common are merely the co-ownership of property, with the usual incidents that accompany property interests held outright. A tenant in common has a separate, undivided interest in the property, which is devisable and descendible at death and transferable by deed. Accordingly, tenancies in common are fully covered by the provisions of section 2033, which is directed generally at interests in property held by the decedent at death.

Joint tenancies and tenancies by the entirety have as their distinguishing feature the right of survivorship. Upon the death of a joint tenant or a tenant by the entirety, that co-tenant's right to share in the possession and enjoyment of the property terminates and passes by operation of law to the surviving co-tenants. Nothing passes to the heirs or devisees of the joint tenant or tenant by the entirety. The last survivor winds up with the full possession and ownership in the entire property.

Traditionally, joint tenancies have required at their creation the co-existence of the mystical four unities of time, title, interest, and possession; hence, without all these unities existing for the tenants, a joint tenancy with its survivorship rights cannot arise. Rather, a tenancy in common is created with no survivorship rights.

A joint tenancy is easily destroyed or severed and converted to a tenancy in common by an act of one of the joint tenants. For example, a sale of a joint tenant's interest destroys the unity of title and results in a tenancy in common between the purchaser and the other joint tenants. The joint tenancy is severed for that joint tenant even if he or she sells the property without the consent of the other joint tenants. The remains co-tenants continue to hold their interests as joint tenants with each other.

While the tenancy by the entirety also requires the four unities and has the right of survivorship as its characteristic feature, it differs from the joint tenancy in that it can arise only where the tenants are spouses and only for the duration of their marriage. Moreover, it cannot be destroyed, as in the case of a joint tenancy, merely by the unilateral act of one of the tenants; it terminates only upon divorce, death or mutual agreement.

B. STATUTORY PROVISIONS OF SECTION 2040

Without a special provision designed to deal with the peculiar common law estates of joint tenancy and tenancy by the entirety, it is not at all clear how a decedent's interest in such property would be treated for estate tax purposes. This is because the joint tenancy property passes by operation of law to the survivor; hence, the decedent does not have an interest in the property at the time of the decedent's death within the meaning of section 2033. However, under the general rule of section 2040(a), the value of the gross estate includes property held by the decedent as a joint tenancy with any other person and as a tenant by the entirety with a spouse.

There are three exceptions to the general rule. First, where the property has been acquired by the deceased tenant and the other tenant or tenants by gift, bequest, devise, or inheritance, the value of the property will be includible in the deceased tenant's gross estate to the extent of the deceased's fractional share. See I.R.C. § 2040(a). Second, in all other cases, except joint tenancies between spouses, the entire value of the tenancy property will be includible in the deceased tenant's gross estate except such portion thereof as is allocable to the part of the consideration furnished by the other tenant or tenants for the acquisition of the property. See I.R.C. § 2040(a). For example, when two co-tenants purchase property in joint tenancy and each pays a portion of the purchase price, the fraction which each tenant pays determines the fraction of the value of the property at the date of death which is includible in the gross estate of the first to die. It is to be particularly noted that the statute, in this type of transaction, requires the inclusion of the entire joint tenancy property except such portion thereof "as may be shown" to have originated with the surviving tenant; thus, this has the effect of a presumption of inclusion no matter which tenant may die first, leaving the burden of rebuttal to the estate. Finally, with respect to a "qualified joint interest" held by a deceased spouse and the surviving spouse, one-half of the value of the property is includible in the estate of the deceased spouse. See I.R.C. § 2040(b)(1). A qualified joint interest is property held by the deceased spouse and the surviving spouse as either tenants by the entirety or joint tenants but only if they are the only joint tenants. See I.R.C. § 2040(b)(2). The result of this is that the value of one-half of the spousal joint tenancy is includible in the estate of the first spouse who dies but that value, because it passes to a surviving spouse, then qualifies for the marital deduction in computing the taxable estate. See Chapter 28.

This rule of half includability of section 2040(b) supersedes the consideration furnished rule of section 2040(a) and in some cases will give a more favorable result and in other cases a less favorable result. In any event, the rule for spousal joint tenancies is now simple. Moreover, as pointed out earlier, the includability of half a spousal joint tenancy in the estate of the deceased spouse exacts no estate tax price because joint tenancy property qualifies for the marital deduction which, by virtue of the 1981 Act, is now an unlimited marital deduction in respect to amount. Consequently, spousal joint tenancy property will not be subject to estate tax in the estate of the first spouse to die.

One significant consequence of the spousal joint tenancy rule is that only one-half such joint tenancy property will qualify for a stepped-up (or stepped-down) basis presently prescribed by section 1014. By contrast and as something of an anomaly, community property under the terms of section 1014(b)(6) qualifies for a stepped-up basis at date of death for both halves of the community property. Accordingly, while the law remains in this curious posture, community property spouses are well advised to stick with community property as against conversion to joint tenancies in light of the income tax basis rules.

There are situations involving spouses that do not result in inclusion of one-half of the property in the deceased spouse's gross estate. For example, in Gallenstein v. United States, 975 F.2d 286 (6th Cir.1992), the court held that because of statutory language about the effective dates of several changes in section 2040, the one-half inclusion rule of section 2040(b) with respect to spousal joint tenancies did not apply to spousal joint tenancies created before 1977. These joint tenancies would follow the old rule—in the absence of proof that the surviving joint tenant had provided any of the consideration used to purchase the joint tenancy there would be a full inclusion of the joint tenancy in the estate of the first to die. Given the unlimited marital deduction which was added in 1981, this full inclusion, for joint tenancies purchased prior to 1977, is without adverse estate tax consequences and results in the surviving spouse taking a stepped-up (or stepped-down) basis in the entire joint tenancy. It is important to remember that *Gallenstein* applies only to spousal joint tenancies created before 1977.

In addition, section 2056(d)(1)(B) provides that the one-half includability rule of section 2040(b) with respect to spousal joint tenancies shall not apply in certain cases where the surviving spouse is not a US citizen. In such cases the spousal joint tenancy is treated as a non-spousal joint tenancy. Assuming that the surviving non-citizen spouse cannot establish that he or she provided consideration for the purchase of the joint tenancy, full includability is the proper result, thereby, avoiding the possibility that property which constituted the joint tenancy will never be taxed, even at the death of the surviving non-citizen who may not be subject to US estate taxation at his or her death. The special treatment accorded to property passing from one spouse to a non-citizen spouse is discussed at length in Chapter 27.

Significantly, in Private Letter Ruling 201216005, the spouses owned property as a tenancy by the entirety, but they were considering executing an agreement where on the death of the first spouse to die, one-half of the property would be held in a trust until the death of the surviving spouse, and the other half would be owned outright by the surviving spouse. Under the proposed agreement, the surviving spouse was entitled to receive trust income subject to certain contingencies and could exchange his or her separate property with the property held in trust. Upon the surviving spouse's death, the trust property would be distributed to designated remaindermen. The IRS concluded that the agreement was a binding contract that created rights that superseded those of the tenancy by the entirety and that the property was nontestamentary and passed in accordance with state law. Therefore, the IRS declined to address the tax consequences under section 2040. The IRS distinguished the agreement from a situation involving a testamentary joint and mutual will. See Rev. Rul. 71–51, 1971–1 C.B. 274.

C. SECTION 2040(a)

1. SERVICES AS CONSIDERATION

Survivors, who succeed in establishing that their labor constituted consideration for the purchase of jointly held assets, find themselves having to establish the existence of a business partnership for the operation of the jointly owned enterprise. See, e.g., United States v. Neel, 235 F.2d 395 (10th Cir.1956) (court found partnership based on course of conduct and pattern of behavior); Singer v. Shaughnessy, 198 F.2d 178 (2d Cir.1952) (formal understanding later supplemented by written agreement). Less fortunate are those survivors who are not able to establish the presence of a business partnership and find their dedicated services characterized as the product of love and affection. See, e.g., Estate of Kjorvestad v. United States, 81–1 USTC ¶ 13,401, 47 AFTR 2d 81–1635 (D.N.D.1981); Loveland's Estate v. Commissioner, 13 T.C. 5 (1949).

Often joint tenants work with each other in the operation of a jointly held farm or business. If they labored together on the understanding that some or all of the fruits of the labor of the survivor were to be invested in the jointly held property, this provides the survivor with the opportunity to claim that the survivor provided a portion of the consideration for purchase of at least some of the jointly held assets.

Many of the cases, such as *Neel*, involve spouses. After the addition of section 2040(b) to the Code in 1981, which makes the whole issue of the relative value of consideration provided by spousal joint tenants irrelevant, there has been a marked decrease of cases in which the issue of services as consideration has been raised under section 2040. In the future one will typically encounter the issue in the context of a parent and child, or unmarried couples, who operate a jointly held business or farm together. For example, in Estate of Anderson v. Commissioner, 58 T.C. Memo. 1989–643, T.C.M. (CCH) 840 (1989), the Tax Court found that in one mother-son joint enterprise the son, through his performance of substantial uncompensated services, had provided full and adequate consideration so that only one-half of a joint tenancy with rights of survivorship was to be included in his mother's estate at her death. In a second venture, where the son performed no services, full inclusion resulted. Similarly, in Fratini v. Commissioner, T.C. Memo. 1998–308, 76 T.C.M. (CCH) 342 (1998), in the case of joint tenancies involving life partners, the court determined the value of managerial, maintenance and janitorial services provided by the surviving joint tenant.

2. INCOME AND PROFITS ON GIFT PROPERTY

ESTATE OF GOLDSBOROUGH v. COMMISSIONER
United States Tax Court, 1978.
70 T.C. 1077, aff'd, 673 F.2d 1310 (4th Cir.1982).

FEATHERSTON, JUDGE.

* * *

Section 2040 provides in general that the decedent's gross estate includes the entire value of jointly held property but that section "except[s] such part thereof as may be shown to have originally belonged to * * * [the surviving joint tenant(s)] and never to have been received or acquired by the latter from the decedent for less than an adequate and full consideration in money or money's worth." Section 2040 further provides that if the decedent owned property jointly with another, the amount to be excluded from the decedent's gross estate is "only such part of the value of such property as is proportionate to the consideration furnished by * * * [the surviving joint tenant(s)]." Mathematically this "consideration furnished" exclusion can be expressed as follows:

$$\text{Amount excluded} = \text{Entire value of property (on the date of death or alternate valuation date)} \times \frac{\text{Survivor's consideration}}{\text{Entire consideration paid}}$$

In the instant case, the decedent (Goldsborough) acquired on May 12, 1937, real property (St. Dunstans) in her individual name. On April 4, 1946, decedent transferred St. Dunstans, valued at $25,000 on that date, to her two daughters (Eppler and O'Donoghue) as a gift. On July 17, 1949, the daughters sold St. Dunstans to H.W. Ford and his wife for $32,500.

Sometime in that same year, each daughter invested her share of the proceeds from the sale of St. Dunstans in various stocks and securities; each daughter took title to her respective stocks and securities in joint tenancy with decedent. These stocks and securities remained in joint tenancy until December 21, 1972, the date of decedent's death, and during the period of joint tenancy the stocks and securities appreciated in value to $160,383.19, the value on the alternate valuation date.

Thus, the section 2040 exclusion depends on the amount, if any, of the consideration Eppler and O'Donoghue, the surviving joint tenants, furnished toward the $32,500 purchase price of the jointly held stocks and securities.

Respondent contends that all the funds used to purchase the stocks and securities in question were derived from decedent and thus the entire value of the jointly held property ($160,383.19) is includable in her gross estate.

Petitioners Buppert and Eppler argue that only the value of St. Dunstans at the time the gift was made to decedent's two daughters (i.e., $25,000) is includable in decedent's gross estate. In the alternative, petitioner Eppler contends that the gain of $7,500, measured by the appreciation in value from the time St. Dunstans was given to the two daughters in 1946 until that property was sold by them in 1949, constitutes consideration furnished by the daughters toward the $32,500 purchase price of the jointly held stocks and securities. Thus Eppler argues that $37,011.50 ($7,500/$32,500 of $160,383.19), the value of the jointly held property on the alternate valuation date, should be excluded from decedent's gross estate. We agree with this alternative argument.

To be sure, section 2040 is not a paragon of clarity, and the courts and Internal Revenue Service have wrestled with the question of whether a contribution made out of gain representing appreciation in value of property received gratuitously from decedent is attributable to the decedent or, instead, is to be treated as income from the property and thus separate funds of the surviving tenant.[5] The law, as we perceive it, recognizes two distinct situations and treats the two differently. In one situation, the surviving joint tenant receives property gratuitously from the decedent; the property thereafter appreciates, and the property itself is contributed in an exchange for jointly held property. In this circumstance section 20.2040–1(c)(4),[6] Estate Tax Regs., treats all the property as having

---

[5]   It is clear that income from property acquired gratuitously from the decedent constitutes a contribution from a surviving joint tenant's separate funds. Sec. 20.2040–1(c)(5), Estate Tax Regs.

[6]   Sec. 20.2040–1(c)(4), Estate Tax Regs., provides as follows:

"If the decedent, before the acquisition of the property by himself and the other joint owner, gave the latter a sum of money or other property which thereafter became the other joint owner's entire contribution to the purchase price, then the value of the entire property is so included, notwithstanding the fact that the other property may have been paid for by the decedent, and the entire value of the property is included in the decedent's gross estate. See Estate of Kelley v. Commissioner, 22 B.T.A. 421, 425 (1931).

In the second situation, the surviving joint tenant receives property gratuitously from the decedent; the property thereafter appreciates or produces income and is sold, and the income or the sales proceeds are used as consideration for the acquisition of the jointly held property. In this situation, the income or the gain, measured by the appreciation from the time of receipt of the gift to the time of sale, has been held to be the surviving joint tenant's income and a part of that joint tenant's contribution to the purchase price. Harvey v. United States, 185 F.2d 463, 467 (7th Cir.1950); First National Bank of Kansas City v. United States, 223 F. Supp. 963, 967 (W.D.Mo.1963); Swartz v. United States, 182 F.Supp. 540, 542 (D.Mass.1960). Thus, in the words of the statute, "such part of the value of such property as is proportionate to the consideration furnished by [the surviving joint tenant]" is excluded.

The facts of the instant case fall precisely within this second situation. In Harvey v. United States, supra at 465, the court characterized the facts and framed the issue as follows:

> The jointly held property is not the gift property itself, in either its original or transmuted form, but property traceable to (1) the profits made through sales of the original gift property and successive reinvestments of the proceeds of such sales or (2) the rents, interest and dividends produced by such property in its original or converted form, while title thereto was in the wife. The question presented by this appeal, then, is whether such profits and income, realized from property originally received by the wife as a gift from her husband and traceable into property which was held by them as joint tenants at the time of the husband's death, came within the exception to the requirement of Section 811(e) [predecessor to sec. 2040] that the entire value of property held in joint tenancy shall be included in the decedent's gross estate.

The Government in *Harvey* argued that the full value of the jointly held property should be included in the decedent's gross estate, and the court dealt with that argument in the following manner (185 F.2d at 467):

> It seems clear that none of the cases cited contains any support for the novel proposition that income produced by gift property, after the gift has been completed, belongs to the donor and is property received or acquired from him by the donee; nor is there, in these cases, anything to impeach the conclusion of the trial

---

appreciated in value due to market conditions between the time of the gift and the time of the acquisition of the jointly held property."

court, or that of the Tax Court in the *Howard* case,[7] that the income produced by property of any kind belongs to the person who owns the property at the time it produces such income and does not originate with a donor who has made a completed gift of that property prior to its production of the income. * * *

* * * Moreover, no reason is suggested for holding that one form of income, i.e., "profit gained through a sale or conversion of capital assets," * * * is outside the exception, whereas other forms of income, such as dividends, rentals and interest, fall within its terms. It follows that the government's contention that the full value of the property held in joint tenancy by decedent and his wife at the time of his death should have been included in decedent's gross estate must be rejected. [Citations omitted.]

Thus we conclude that Eppler and O'Donoghue furnished $7,500 toward the $32,500 purchase price paid for the stocks and securities they held in joint tenancy with decedent until her death on December 21, 1972. Under the terms of the statute, such part of the value of the property, i.e., $160,383.19 on the alternate valuation date, as is proportionate to the $7,500 of consideration Eppler and O'Donoghue furnished is excluded from decedent's gross estate. Under the mathematical formula, set out above, the amount of the exclusion is $37,011.50.

* * *

NOTE

In English v. United States, 270 F.2d 876 (7th Cir.1959), the court was confronted with how it should treat stock dividends received with respect to stock held by joint tenants with rights of survivorship where the decedent joint tenant had provided all the consideration for the purchase of the original jointly held stock. The court concluded that such dividends were not to be considered income from jointly held property that could qualify as adequate consideration under the line of cases referred to in *Goldsborough*. The court viewed the stock dividends as representing the same interest as the original jointly held stock, with the result that both were included in the decedent's estate at his death.

D. CONTRIBUTIONS AND CHANGING VALUES

Section 2040(a) permits exclusion from the gross estate of such part of the value of the joint tenancy property "as is proportionate to the consideration furnished" by the surviving joint tenant. This exclusion contemplates the determination of a ratio or fraction by reference to the total consideration furnished and the portions thereof contributed by the

---

7   Estate of Howard v. Commissioner, 9 T.C. 1192, 1202–1203 (1947).

joint tenants, all at values at the time of acquisition. The fraction representing the surviving tenant's contribution so ascertained is then applied to the value of the property at the date of death for the purpose of excluding the portion of the joint tenancy attributable to the surviving tenant. However, suppose that the contributions towards the acquisition of the joint tenancy were made at separate times when the property may have changed substantially in value. For example, in 1970, F purchased a lot for $10,000 of his own funds, taking title in joint tenancy with daughter D; in 1975, when the lot had increased in value to $20,000, D built on the lot a house costing $40,000, which D paid out of her own funds. Upon F's death in 2006, when the house and lot were worth $180,000, what portion is to be treated as originating with F and what portion should be excluded from his estate as being allocable to D?

There is scant authority on what the answer should be. There are three possible results. First, we could tax the full $180,000 minus only the $40,000 consideration paid by D. This should be rejected as inconsistent with the proportionate consideration language of section 2040. Second, we could ignore the fact that the property had increased in value by the time the improvement had been made and allow D to exclude 4/5 of the value of the house and lot, since her $40,000 investment reflected 4/5 of the total of $50,000 invested by F and D. This result should be rejected since it would theoretically allow a party who made a modest investment in improvements in vastly appreciated joint property dramatically to alter tax results. For example, assume that no improvement had been made in the land which shortly before F's death had appreciated to $90,000. A $10,000 investment by D in modest improvements should not be allowed to exclude $50,000 from taxation at F's death. Third, at each new investment in improvements, we could recalculate the relative value of each holder's contribution. For example, until 1975 F could be deemed to have provided all the consideration for the lot. In 1975, after D's $40,000 investment in the joint tenancy, F could be deemed to have provided 1/3 of the consideration and D to have provided 2/3 of the consideration for the tenancy. Estate of Peters v. Commissioner, 386 F.2d 404 (4th Cir.1967), provides some authority for concluding that this is the proper result.

Although the third approach is probably the correct one to follow, it does not take much imagination to realize how difficult it would be to apply this rule in an environment where little is typically known of the value of the property each time one of the joint tenants makes an improvement.

E. MORTGAGES AND CONTRIBUTIONS

An interesting problem arises in connection with purchase money mortgages. Where the property is acquired in joint tenancy partially for cash and partially for mortgaged indebtedness in which the tenants are jointly and severally liable, with either joint tenant being entitled to contribution from the other in the event that he or she is compelled to satisfy more than one-half of the debt, each tenant is treated as contributing toward the purchase price his or her share of the debt, as well as the cash which each contributes. See Bremer v. Luff, 7 F. Supp. 148 (N.D.N.Y.1933).

Assume that A and B purchased a joint tenancy in Whiteacre for $100,000 with A and B each contributing $10,000 in cash toward the purchase price and the balance funded with an $80,000 mortgage on which A and B were jointly and severally liable. No payments on the principal of the mortgage were made and at A's death Whiteacre was worth $120,000. This will result in one-half of the value of Whiteacre, or $60,000, being included in A's estate at A's death.

Whenever one of the joint tenants makes payment on the principal of the mortgage debt, this operates to increase that party's contribution to the purchase price and reduce the contribution of the other joint tenant. For example, assume that A had retired $20,000 of the mortgage debt, A's contribution toward the purchase price of Whiteacre would be $60,000. That sum would be comprised of: (1) $10,000 cash payment; (2) $20,000 of retired debt; and (3) $30,000, one-half of the remaining $60,000 mortgage. B would be treated as having provided $40,000 toward the purchase of Whiteacre consisting of: (1) $10,000 cash payment; and (2) $30,000, one-half of the remaining mortgage debt. Assuming Whiteacre was worth $120,000 on A's death, this would result in 60 percent of its value, $72,000, being included in A's estate. See Rev. Rul. 79–302, 1979–2 C.B. 328. For additional refinements of the law in this area, see Rev. Ruls. 81–183, 1981–2 C.B. 180, and 81–184, 1981–2 C.B. 181, which deal with the consequences of second mortgages and refinancings.

F. SIMULTANEOUS DEATHS OF JOINT TENANTS

In Rev. Rul. 76–303, 1976–2 C.B. 266, the IRS indicated how jointly held property was to be taxed where one of the joint tenants (X) provided all the consideration, and the parties (X and Y) died in a common accident in a jurisdiction which had adopted the Uniform Simultaneous Death Act, which provides that "[w]here there is no sufficient evidence that two joint tenants or tenants by the entirety have died otherwise than simultaneously the property so held shall be distributed one-half as if one had survived and one-half as if the other had survived." The IRS indicated that in such circumstance, since there is no evidence to indicate that Y had provided any consideration for purchase of the property, the value of the one-half with respect to which Y is considered to have survived X is includible in X's estate under section 2040. Since X provided all the consideration, none of the one-half of the property with respect to which X is considered to have survived Y is includible in Y's estate. Moreover, since X and Y are each deemed to have survived as to one-half of the property, each is considered to have acquired absolute ownership in one-half of the property, which will be included in their gross estates under section 2033. The net result is that the entire value of the jointly held property will be taxed in X's estate and one-half of its value will be taxed in Y's estate.

If X and Y are married, the marital deduction will effectively exclude from X's estate the one-half which passes to Y. However, if they are not, the only relief will come from section 2013 which provides a decedent's estate with a credit for all or some of the estate tax paid on property transferred to the decedent by the estate of another within 10 years before or 2 years after the decedent's death. Since the credit is not necessarily total, this presents special challenges for estate planners who represent unmarried couples that desire to hold property as joint tenants with rights of survivorship.

G. UNSCRAMBLING THE JOINT TENANCY OMELET

In nonspousal situations, section 2040 provides the IRS with a "heads I win, tails I still may win" rule. It does that by basically including all joint property with survivorship rights in the estate of the first to die unless the survivor can shoulder the burden of establishing the portion of the purchase price provided by the survivor, in which case, based on the relative amount of consideration provided by the survivor, some or all of the property will be excluded from the decedent's estate. When one adds to this taxpayer disadvantage the complexity of dealing with simultaneous deaths, improvements, mortgages and rules regarding the source of consideration, it readily becomes apparent that, from a tax standpoint, nonspouses typically should not establish joint tenancies with rights of survivorship and should terminate most such estates which already exist. Moreover, due to the limited availability of the "stepped-up" basis under section 1014, spouses also may wish to minimize the creation of such estates or to terminate some or all which do exist. Fortunately, it is not at all difficult to transmute a joint tenancy into another form of property ownership beyond the reach of section 2040. By simply severing a joint interest with rights of survivorship or by transforming it into a tenancy in common, property can be removed from the clutches of section 2040. When studying section 2035 (Chapter 23), it may be desirable to reread this section and notice that section 2035(a) does not deal with jointly held property, the result being that a deathbed transformation of a joint tenancy with rights of survivorship into a tenancy in common or severance of the joint interest could remove vast amounts from the estate where the soon-to-die individual provided all consideration for purchase of the original joint tenancy.

In United States v. Chandler, 410 U.S. 257 (1973), the Supreme Court considered whether a registered owner of a US Savings Bond, Series E, who made physical delivery to a donee has thereby eliminated the joint bond from the donor's estate. The Treasury regulations provided that the only way to convey ownership of the bond was to have it reissued; the Court held that the regulations were valid and, accordingly, the property was still in the estate of the deceased bond owner.

H. COMMUNITY PROPERTY

Prior to 1942, community property, which exists in nine states, was taxed only under the predecessor provision of section 2033 (then section 811(a)). This type of ownership is quite distinct from joint tenancies and tenancies by the entirety, and the courts had held, without specific legislation, that the interest of each spouse in community property was includible in each spouse's gross estate for estate tax purposes to the extent that the interest was vested in the spouse under state law. See Greenwood v. Commissioner, 134 F.2d 915 (9th Cir.1943).

In an attempt to equalize the estate tax treatment of married couples in community property states with that of married couples residing in the common-law states, Congress enacted in 1942, over the heated opposition of representatives of the community property states, legislation designed to bring all the community property within the gross estate of the spouse whose personal services or investments earned it. The constitutionality of this legislation was questioned in due course, but was sustained in Fernandez v. Wiener, 326 U.S. 340 (1945). The Court concluded:

> This redistribution of powers and restrictions upon power is brought about by death notwithstanding that the rights in the property subject to these powers and restrictions were in every sense "vested" from the moment the community began. It is enough that death brings about changes in the legal and economic relationships to the property taxed, and the earlier certainty that those changes would occur does not impair the legislative power to recognize them, and to levy a tax on the happening of the event which was their generating source.

Id. at 356–57.

By 1948, the pressure of the community property states was combined with tax counsel and others from the common-law states to push through compromise legislation that would restore to the community property couples their former tax advantage of dividing their estates automatically and would accord to couples in the common-law states a comparable privilege in the form of a marital deduction under section 2056, which will be fully considered in Chapter 28.

As already noted, one aspect of the favoritism shown to community property is found in the income tax basis provision of section 1014(b)(6), which prescribes that, on death of one of the spouses in a community property jurisdiction, both halves of the community property acquire a "stepped-up" new income tax basis equivalent to the value of both halves of the community property as of the date of the death of one of the community property spouses. This sharp differential in favor of community property as compared to joint tenancy property is difficult to rationalize as a matter of policy.

PROBLEMS

1. Five years ago, Brad and his wife, Maria, purchased a lot as tenants by the entireties with rights of survivorship, with Brad providing the full $500,000 purchase price. At his death four years later, the lot was worth $800,000. What value is included in Brad's estate, and what is Maria's adjusted basis in the lot after Brad's death?

2. What would your answer be in the prior problem if Brad and Maria were not married but were sister and brother and the property was held by them as a joint tenancy with rights of survivorship?

3. Jordan purchased 1,000 shares of stock for $20 per share, with Jordan providing the full $20,000 consideration. He took title in joint tenancy with rights of survivorship with himself, his wife, Alicia, and their daughter, Gabriella. Two years later when the stock was worth $30,000, Jordan died. What amount is includible in his estate?

4. Jackson provided the full $50,000 purchase price for ABC stock to which he and his son, Angelo, took title as joint tenants with rights of survivorship. The stock was sold several years later for $100,000. Jackson and Angelo placed their shares of the sale proceeds in separate bank accounts. They subsequently used their full share of the sale proceeds to purchase, as joint tenants with rights of survivorship, an unimproved lot. At Jackson's death the lot was worth $160,000. What is the value of the property includible in Jackson's estate at his death?

5. Carly and her son, Alex, purchased Sunny Valley Farm as joint tenants with rights of survivorship for $1,000,000. Carly provided $200,000 in cash as a down payment on the property, and both Carly and Alex assumed personal liability for an $800,000 mortgage taken out on the property. No payments other than interest were made on the mortgage, and, at Carly's death, Sunny Valley was worth $2,000,000. What are the estate tax consequences?

6. Would the analysis in the prior problem change if it were discovered that, while the farm was operated during Carly's lifetime, $100,000 in payments on the principal of the mortgage had been made from income

produced by the operation of Sunny Valley? What if, rather than coming from income of the joint enterprise, the full $100,000 in payments on principal had been provided by Carly?

CHAPTER 17

LIFE INSURANCE

(SECTION 2042)

■ ■ ■

A. INTRODUCTION

Insurance is a device whereby a group of individuals or enterprises, typically with the aid of a corporate intermediary referred to as the insurer, share or spread a risk of loss.

Although there are hundreds of different types of life insurance products available, there are two basic categories, term and whole or cash value. Under term insurance, the holder or owner of the policy pays a premium to the insurer sufficient to enable the insurer, in the event of death of the insured, to pay to the policy's beneficiaries the face amount of the policy. Term insurance is sometimes described as "pure" insurance in that the premium charged reflects only the risk of death for the insured, the cost of administering the insurance program and profit for the insurer. As the insured increases in age, the premium increases or the coverage (face amount) of the policy declines.

Under whole or cash value life insurance, the holder of the policy in essence acquires two separate interests, an insurance policy and a savings account. The annual premium paid for such a policy is typically several times that charged for a term policy but unlike term insurance, the premium for this form of life insurance normally does not increase (nor does coverage decline) with the age of the insured. The surplusage in premiums over that needed to cover risk of death, administration expenses and profits for the insurer forms the basis for creation of a savings component in the policy. The value of this savings component is often referred to as the cash surrender value because the owner of the policy can surrender her rights in the policy to the insurer, in exchange for this sum. Typically, the owner of such a policy can "borrow" the cash value of the policy from the insurer, in which case, in the event of death of the insured, the amount so withdrawn will not be available for distribution to the policy's beneficiaries. Earnings on cash value typically are used to: (1) pay all or part of the higher premium necessitated by increasing mortality risk as the insured ages; (2)

add coverage to keep up with inflation; or (3) enhance the cash value through reinvestment.[1]

Under state law, for a party to be able to acquire a life insurance policy that party must have what is defined by statute or judicial decision as an "insurable interest" in the life of the insured. In general, for a party to have an insurable interest in the life of another he must have an economic interest in the continued existence of the insured. The reason for this is understandable once we step back into history. Prior to the development of the insurable interest doctrine in eighteenth century England, it was common for people to wager on the outcomes of trials involving capital offenses by purchasing insurance on the life of the accused. It was also fashionable to use insurance to place wagers on the lives of prominent personages, such as the King or the Duke of Norfolk. Not unexpectedly, this led to lively coverage in the financial press of every detail of the state of health of those favored by individuals who fancied gambling in this fashion.[2]

It was to eliminate this unsavory form of gambling, as well as to foil plots for enrichment based on schemes to insure and then murder strangers that the insurable interest doctrine was developed. In addition to being able to insure one's own life, the insurable interest rule permits insurance of the lives of close relatives, key employees and business associates. The actual parties covered will vary from state to state.[3] Occasionally the insurable interest rule will impact tax planning involving life insurance.

The estate tax as originally enacted in 1916 contained no specific provision for the inclusion of life insurance in the gross estate, with the result that only insurance payable to the estate was subject to taxation. In 1918, Congress reacted by passing a specific provision which included in the decedent's estate the proceeds of policies on the life of the deceased payable: (1) to the decedent's executor; or (2) to "all other beneficiaries as

---

[1] For a more thorough discussion of these and other life insurance products, see ROBERT H. JERRY, II & DOUGLAS RICHMOND, UNDERSTANDING INSURANCE LAW § 13A (Carolina Academic Press 6th ed. 2018).

[2] See Jerry, supra note 1, at § 40.

[3] See, e.g., Cal. Ins. Code § 10110.1 (Deering 2022) (stating that those with an insurable interest includes the individuals closely related to the insured by blood or law, employers, the individual, and certain trusts); Fla. Stat. ch. 627.404(2)(b) (2022) (providing that individuals with insurable interests include those who are parties to a contract for the purchase or sale of an interest in any business entity in the life of other parties to the contract but only for purposes of the contract and business entities in the life of any of the owners, directors, officers, partners, managers or key employees); Wyo. Stat. Ann. § 26–15–102(C)(ii) & (iii) (2022) (stating that individuals with insurable interests include those with "a lawful and substantial economic interest" in the life of the insured and parties to a contract or option for the purchase or sale of an interest in a business partnership or shares of a closed corporation).

insurance under policies taken out by the decedent."[4] The provision is similar to the language used in the current statutory language.[5]

Few serious problems ever arose with respect to the taxation of the first category, insurance payable to the executor, although the courts and the IRS have made clear that encompassed by that language is life insurance which, while not designated as payable to the estate, financially benefits the estate.[6] For example, a life insurance policy payable to a decedent's creditor as collateral for a loan to the decedent is considered to be payable to the decedent's estate.[7] Given its uncontroversial history, it is not surprising that section 2042(1), which includes in the estate life insurance payable to the decedent's executor, has remained in the Code virtually unchanged since 1918.

With respect to the second category of insurance—that payable to "all other beneficiaries"—the statute has gone through a number of changes. In 1942, Congress decided to tax the proceeds of such insurance on the life of the decedent if the decedent: (1) directly or indirectly paid the premiums; or (2) possessed any of the incidents of ownership with respect to the policy.[8]

In 1954, Congress, doubtless not without some prompting from the life insurance industry, decided to drop the premiums payment test on the ground that no other property which is owned by others is included in the estate of the deceased because the deceased purchased it for others. In 1954 the statute was also amended to indicate that possession by a decedent of a reversionary interest in a policy on his or her life would give rise to inclusion of policy proceeds in his or her estate if the value of the reversionary interest exceeds five percent of the value of the policy immediately before death.[9]

Since 1954 there has been no change of substance to section 2042 and proceeds of a policy are now includible in the estate of the insured decedent if: (1) payable to the decedent's executor; or (2) payable to others if the decedent retained with respect to the policy "any of the incidents of ownership, exercisable either alone or in conjunction with any other person."[10]

[4] See Revenue Act of 1918, 40 Stat. 1057 § 402(f) (1919).

[5] See I.R.C. § 2042(1) & (2) (2022).

[6] See Treas. Reg. § 20.2042–1(b); Bintliff v. United States, 462 F.2d 403 (5th Cir.1972).

[7] Id.

[8] Revenue Act of 1942, 52 Stat. 798 § 404 (1942).

[9] See Merle H. Miller & H. G. Emery, Estate Planning and the Internal Revenue Code of 1954, 30 NOTRE DAME L. REV. 3, 6 (1954).

[10] See I.R.C. § 2042(1) & (2) (2022).

1. INCIDENTS OF OWNERSHIP

The report of the House Ways and Means Committee that accompanied the 1942 legislation, which added the "incidents of ownership" language to the Code, contains the following statement on the meaning of the phrase:

> There is no specific enumeration of incidents of ownership, the possession of which at death forms the basis for inclusion of insurance proceeds in the gross estate as it is impossible to include an exhaustive list. Examples of such incidents are the right of the insured or his estate to the economic benefits of the insurance, the power to change the beneficiary, the power to surrender or cancel the policy, the power to assign it, the power to revoke an assignment, the power to pledge a policy for a loan, or the power to obtain from the insurer a loan against the surrender value of the policy. Incidents of ownership are not confined to those possessed by the decedent in a technical legal sense. For example, a power to change the beneficiary reserved to a corporation of which the decedent is the sole stockholder is an incident of ownership in the decedent. * * *[11]

Regulation § 20.2042–1(c)(2) contains forms of incidents of ownership which are fundamentally the same as those provided in the legislative history of the 1942 legislation.

2. APPLICATION OF OTHER CODE SECTIONS

While section 2042 sets forth the principal rules for taxation of life insurance on the decedent's life, other sections may also cause an inclusion of policy proceeds in the estate of the insured. For example, under section 2035, which covers transfers within three years of death, if the decedent transferred the incidents of ownership in a policy on his life to other parties and died within three years of the transfer, there would be an inclusion, under section 2035, in the decedent's estate of the amount paid to beneficiaries under the policy. See Chapter 23.

Also, note that section 2042 applies only to policies on the life of the decedent. Section 2042 does not apply where the decedent owned a policy of insurance on the life of another person and that other person, the insured, survives the deceased owner of the policy. Instead, the policy is included in the deceased policy owner's estate (rather than that of the insured) under section 2033. Generally speaking, the value of the policy thereby included is its interpolated terminal reserve, i.e., roughly its cash value plus unearned premium. The basic valuation rules are provided in Treas. Reg. § 20.2031–8(a)(1) and (2).

---

[11]   H.R. Rep. No. 2333, 77th Cong., 2d Sess. 57, at 163.

3. LIABILITY FOR TAX ON LIFE INSURANCE

If, as form wills commonly do, the will directs that all taxes and debts be borne by the probate residue, this could result in little or nothing of value passing to the residual legatee, especially in a case where there is a large non-probate estate. Aware of this potential for unintended injustices, Congress has selectively attempted to deal with this issue for a number of non-probate assets which are included in the taxable estate. In the case of life insurance, unless the decedent clearly directs otherwise in his will, under section 2206, the executor is entitled to collect from the beneficiaries of taxable life insurance on the life of decedent "such portion of the total tax paid as the proceeds of such policies bear to the taxable estate."

B. LIFE INSURANCE BROADLY DEFINED

In order for benefits paid at death to be taxable as life insurance under section 2042 there must be a spreading of a risk of loss of life among a larger group. It is unimportant precisely what label is placed on the contract or arrangement. For example, death benefits paid by fraternal beneficial societies, flight insurance, accidental death insurance, and double indemnity riders on conventional life insurance policies all constitute life insurance for purposes of section 2042. See Commissioner v. Estate of Noel, 380 U.S. 678 (1965); Estate of Ackerman v. Commissioner, 15 B.T.A. 635 (1929); Reg. § 20.2042–1(a)(1); & Rev. Rul. 65–222, 1965–2 C.B. 374. In Commissioner v. Treganowan, 183 F.2d 288 (2d Cir.1950), the court, perhaps operating at the outer limits of the law, ruled that death benefits paid to designated beneficiaries of deceased members of the New York Stock Exchange constituted life insurance since the fund from which such benefits were paid had its origins in levies on the 1,374 members of the Exchange.

The following ruling demonstrates not only how less than garden variety life insurance can be subject to tax under section 2042 but also demonstrates a situation in which sections 2042(1) and 2033 could be applied in the context of an accidental death.

REVENUE RULING 83–44
1983–1 C.B. 228.

ISSUE

Is the value of death benefits receivable under a policy issued pursuant to State Y's no-fault insurance statute by the executor of D, the operator of the insured vehicle, and C, a passenger in the vehicle, includible in the respective gross estates of D and C under section 2042 of the Internal Revenue Code?

FACTS

D, a resident of State *Y*, died as a result of an injury incurred when the automobile that *D* owned and was driving was involved in a collision. *C*, a passenger in the automobile, died in the collision. Under State *Y*'s no-fault motor vehicle insurance statute, an owner of a motor vehicle registered in State *Y* must carry no-fault insurance or maintain another form of financial security, such as a cash bond, for the payment of benefits specified in the statute. * * *

D carried the required no-fault insurance policy. The policy provided for the payment of up to $50x$ dollars as a "basic economic loss benefit" covering *D*'s medical expenses and loss of income arising from *D*'s injury while operating the insured vehicle. In addition, in the event of *D*'s accidental death while operating the insured vehicle, a $10x$ dollar "death benefit" was paid to *D*'s estate. The policy also provided that a "death benefit" of $10x$ dollars was to be paid to the estate of any passenger killed in the insured vehicle. Payment of the death benefit did not preclude the recipient estates, or heirs of the decedents, from pursuing any right of action for additional damages arising on account of the accident. *D*'s estate and *C*'s estate each received a $10x$ dollar death benefit payment under the policy, and $20x$ dollars was paid to *D*'s estate as a basic economic loss benefit covering *D*'s medical expenses incurred as a result of the accident.

LAW AND ANALYSIS

Section 2042(1) of the Code provides that the gross estate includes the proceeds of insurance receivable by the executor under policies on the life of the decedent. Section 20.2042–1(a)(1) of the Estate Tax Regulations provides that the term "insurance" refers to life insurance of every description, including death benefits paid by fraternal beneficial societies operating under the lodge system.

In Helvering v. LeGierse, 312 U.S. 531 (1941), 1941–1 C.B. 430, the Court, in defining what constitutes life insurance for purposes of the predecessor of section 2042 of the Code, stated that the essential elements of life insurance are risk-shifting and risk-distributing in the event of loss because of death.

In Rev. Rul. 57–54, 1957–1 C.B. 298, an airplane owner carried insurance which provided for payments to passengers or their representatives in the event of accidental death. The ruling holds that the payments made to a decedent's estate are not life insurance proceeds under section 2042 of the Code even though they are paid without regard to the legal liability of the insured because, under the facts of the ruling, the proceeds were payable only if the insured were released from liability by those persons having a cause of action arising out of the accident. The ruling holds that payments are includible under section 2042 if an insurer unconditionally agrees to make payments in the event of the insured's death and the executor accepts the payments.

In Rev. Rul. 68–88, 1968–1 C.B. 397, amounts were payable under an uninsured motorists endorsement in an automobile liability policy. This endorsement provided that the insurer would pay to a deceased insured's estate all amounts which the insured's estate would have been legally entitled to recover as damages from the operator of an uninsured automobile in an action for wrongful death. The ruling holds that the payments originated under the state's wrongful death statute since, after payment of the claim, the decedent's executor was foreclosed from instituting a wrongful death action and the insurer became subrogated to the rights of the insured against the uninsured motorist. Thus, in that situation, the payments were not life insurance proceeds for purposes of section 2042 of the Code.

In this case, the no-fault insurance policy purchased by D is a contract under which D shifted the risk of deaths to the insurer, and the insurer distributed the risk of loss among those participating in the no-fault insurance program. The payment of a death benefit to D's executors is conditioned only upon D's loss of life and is not a substitute for a wrongful death suit. The death benefit, which is payable regardless of the existence of a wrongful death claim, flows from the insurance policy and is similar to the unconditional payment discussed in Rev. Rul. 57–54, cited above. Consequently, the death benefit payable under the policy to D's executor is proceeds of insurance on the life of D. Since the proceeds are payable to the executor, the proceeds are includible in D's gross estate under section 2042(1) of the Code.

Similarly, the death benefit payable to C's executor also represents the proceeds of insurance on the life of C, includible in C's gross estate under section 2042(1) of the Code. See Rev. Rul. 57–54, cited above.

The basic economic loss benefit of $20x$ dollars was paid to D's estate to cover medical expenses incurred by D, and not on account of D's loss of life. Consequently, the $20x$ dollars is not includible in D's gross estate under section 2042(1) of the Code. However, the benefit is includible under section 2033 of the Code. See Rev. Rul. 75–127, 1975–1 C.B. 297.

HOLDING

The value of death benefits receivable under a policy issued pursuant to State Y's no-fault insurance statute by the executors of D, the operator of the insured vehicle, and C, a passenger in the vehicle, is includible in the respective gross estates of D and C under section 2042(1) of the Code.

C. POSSESSION OF THE INCIDENTS OF OWNERSHIP

UNITED STATES V. RHODE ISLAND HOSPITAL TRUST CO.

United States Court of Appeals, First Circuit, 1966.
355 F.2d 7.

COFFIN, CIRCUIT JUDGE.

This appeal presents the question whether the proceeds of a life insurance policy on decedent's life are properly includable in the gross estate of the decedent by reason of the alleged possession at his death of "any of the incidents of ownership, exercisable either alone or in conjunction with any other person," under Section 2042 of the Internal Revenue Code of 1954, 26 U.S.C. § 2042.

* * *

The facts, undisputed, are of two kinds: "intent facts"—those relating to the conduct and understanding of the insured and his father, who was the instigator, premium payer, and primary beneficiary of the policy; and the "policy facts"—those revealed by the insurance contract itself.

Decedent's father, Charles A. Horton, was a textile executive, a prominent businessman in his community, and, according to the testimony, "a man with strong convictions and vigorous action." Charles and his wife, Louise, had two sons, decedent and A. Trowbridge Horton. In 1924, when decedent was 18 and Trowbridge 19, their father purchased an insurance policy on the life of each boy from Massachusetts Mutual Life Insurance Company. The policies were identical, each having the face amount of $50,000, the proceeds being payable to Charles and Louise, equally, or to the survivor.

Charles Horton's purpose was to assure that funds would be available for his wife, should he and either son die. Charles kept the policies in his safe deposit box and paid all premiums throughout his life. Under the policies, however, the right to change beneficiaries had been reserved to the sons. In January, 1952, the boys' mother, Louise, died. In March, 1952, Charles told each of his sons to go to the insurance company's office and sign a change of beneficiary form. The amendment executed by decedent named his father as primary beneficiary, with decedent's wife, brother, and the executors or administrators of the last survivor being the successive beneficiaries. After this amendment, decedent continued to retain the right to make further changes, but none was made. Decedent died on April 1, 1958, survived by his wife and father. His father died on October 2, 1961.

The father, Charles, regarded the policies as belonging to him, saying at one point that it would be "out of the question" for the sons to claim them. Decedent's brother never discussed the policies with his father, never asked for a loan based on the policies, obediently signed the change of beneficiary form at his father's request, and considered the policy on his life as the property of his father. Decedent's widow recalled only that decedent had once told her that his father had a policy on himself and his brother but that "in no way did it mean anything to us or would it ever. It was completely his." She added that her husband, the decedent, had wanted more insurance of his own, but was not able to obtain it.

Coming to what we call "policy facts", a careful reading of the policy, captioned "Ordinary Life Policy—Convertible", reveals the following rights, privileges, or powers accorded to the decedent.

—Right to change beneficiary. In the application, an unrestricted change of beneficiary provision was elected by striking out two alternative and more limited provisions. The policy itself indicated reservation of "the right successively to change the beneficiary" by the insertion of typewritten dashes where, otherwise, the word "not" would have been inserted.

—Assignment. No assignment would be recognized until the original assignment, a duplicate, or a certified copy was filed with the company. The company did not assume responsibility for the validity of an assignment.

—Dividends. The insured had the option to have dividends paid in cash, used to reduce premiums, used to purchase paid-up additions, or accumulate subject to withdrawal on demand.

—Loans. On condition that the unlimited right to change the beneficiary was reserved, as in this case, the company would "loan on the signature of the insured alone".

—Survival. Should no beneficiary survive the insured, the proceeds were payable to his executors and administrators.

—Alteration. The policy could be altered only on the written request of the insured and of "other parties in interest".

—Discharge of company's obligations. The company would not be responsible for the conduct of any trustee or for the determination of the identity or rights of beneficiaries. Payment at the direction of a trustee or in good faith to a beneficiary would discharge the company of its contractual obligations. Beneficiaries were advised by the policy that they need hire no firm or person to collect the amount payable under the policy, but that they would save time and expense by writing to the company directly.

The plaintiffs contend that the district court properly held that decedent possessed no incidents of ownership in the policy; that the term "incidents of ownership" refers to the rights of insured or his estate to the economic benefits of the policy; that the question of possession of such incidents is one of fact; that such possession depends upon all relevant facts and circumstances, including the intention of the parties; and that these facts and circumstances clearly establish that decedent's father was the real owner of the policy, while decedent was merely the nominal owner, having no real economic interest in it.

The government asserts that, as a matter of law, the facts bring this case squarely within the reach of Section 2042, as applied by the cases, notwithstanding the evidence as to the intentions and extra-policy circumstances of the parties, and the lack of economic benefit to decedent.

* * *

Taking the subsidiary facts as presented to the district court, we differ with its conclusion that "the decedent's father was actually the real owner of the various incidents of ownership in said policy." But in differing we recognize that early holdings and occasional dicta, early and late, have invited litigation. This is the kind of case where the government enters, appearing to seek its pound of flesh on the basis of petty technicality, while the taxpayer's decedent generally appears as a person who had very little to do with the insurance policy which is causing so much trouble to his estate. If such hard cases have not made bad law, they have at least made bad dicta. * * * [W]e think it appropriate to set forth the considerations of fact, law, and policy which have persuaded us.

To begin, the statute which bears on this case has a reason for being, is part of a general rationale and tax law pattern, and is deliberately precise. Before the Revenue Act of 1942, the tax criterion governing cases in this area was "policies taken out" by the decedent on his own life. Section 302(g), Revenue Act of 1926, ch. 27, 44 Stat. 9. This led to difficult problems of interpretation, which the courts resolved by creating two criteria: "payment of premiums" and possession of "incidents of ownership." The Revenue Act of 1942, ch. 619, 56 Stat. 798, Section 404, eliminated the "policies taken out" language, and sanctified the judicial gloss, with Congress, in its committee reports, including an illustrative list of the kinds of rights included under "incidents of ownership." These included decedent's right to change beneficiaries, to borrow, to assign, to revoke an assignment, and to surrender or cancel. H.Rep.No.2333, 77th Cong., 2d Sess., p. 164, 1942–2 Cum.Bull. 372, 491.

In acting this way, Congress was, we think, trying to introduce some certitude in a landscape of shifting sands. In the provision which was the predecessor of Section 2042, it was not trying to tax the *extent* of the interest of the decedent. That it knew how to do this is evident, for example, from a reading of Section 2033 * * * which includes in the gross estate of the decedent "the value of all property * * * to the extent of the interest therein * * *." What it was attempting to reach in Section 2042 and some other sections was the *power* to dispose of property * * *. Power can be and is exercised by one possessed of less than complete legal and equitable title. The very phrase "incidents of ownership" connotes something partial, minor, or even fractional in its scope. It speaks more of possibility than of probability.

Plaintiffs seize on Section 20.2042–1(c)(2) of the Treasury Regulations on Estate Tax, which says " * * * the term 'incidents of ownership' is not limited in its meaning to ownership of the policy in the technical legal sense. Generally speaking, the term has reference to the right of the insured or his estate to the economic benefits of the policy." Plaintiffs urge that there must be "a real control over the economic benefits." To this there are two answers. First, it is clear that the reference to ownership in the "technical legal sense" is not abandoned and supplanted by reference to "economic benefits." Second, the regulation goes on to list illustrative powers referred to by Congress in its reports. All of these are powers which may or may not enrich decedents' estate, but which can affect the transfer of the policy proceeds.

Viewed against this background, what power did decedent possess? This is the relevant question—not how did he feel or act. Did he have a capacity to do something to affect the disposition of the policy if he had wanted to? Without gaining possession of the policy itself, he could have borrowed on the policy. He could have changed the method of using dividends. He could have assigned the policy. He could have revoked the assignment. Should he have gained possession of the policy by trick (as by filing an affidavit that the policy was lost), force, or chance, he could have changed the beneficiary, and made the change of record irrevocable. Other such possibilities might be imagined. We cite these only to evidence the existence of some power in decedent to affect the disposition of the policy proceeds. In addition, he always possessed a negative power. His signature was necessary to a change in beneficiary, to a surrender for cash value, to an alteration in the policy, to a change in dividend options. Even with this most limited power, he would be exercising an incident of ownership "in conjunction with" another person.

The existence of such powers in the decedent is to be distinguished from such rights as may have existed in decedent's father or duties owed the father by decedent. It is, therefore, no answer that decedent's father might have proceeded against him at law or in equity. The company made it clear in the contract that it bore no responsibility for the validity of an assignment, that it could pay a beneficiary without recourse, and that it was under no obligation to see to the carrying out of any trust. It even made clear that a beneficiary need only write to the home office to receive payment. Should a third party—for example, an innocent creditor who had given valuable consideration to decedent—receive the proceeds of the policy, the proceeds of a loan on the policy, or the cash value, it could not be said that the transaction between decedent and such third person would in all such cases be nugatory. For decedent had some powers—perhaps not rights, but powers—which could, if exercised alone or in conjunction with another, affect the disposition of some or all of the proceeds of the policy.

Nor is it a compelling argument that decedent lacked physical possession of the policy. Moreover, as we have noted, some rights could be exercised without physical possession of the policy.

* * *

To the principle of heavy predominance of the "policy facts" over the "intent facts" there must be added the caveat that, where the insurance contract itself does not reflect the instructions of the parties, as where an agent, on his own initiative, inserts a reservation of right to change a beneficiary contrary to the intentions which had been expressed to him, no incidents of ownership are thereby created. The case before us presents no such issue, for the right in decedent to change beneficiaries was recognized on the one occasion when it was exercised and this right continued thereafter.

* * *

In any event, the statute has been on the books since the Revenue Act of 1942. This is only one of a number of cases applying it in the face of considerable external evidence of intent. Charles Horton, who caused the policy to be taken out, saw fit to vest decedent with rights in the policy and to allow such rights to continue for thirty-four years. Charles was a successful businessman and with as much incentive, opportunity, and capacity to be aware of the laws of the land as most people. It is difficult to speculate what purpose he thought was being served by his son's retention of rights in the policy. Had he wished to deprive his son of all incidents of ownership in the policy, this result could easily have been accomplished. But the step was not taken. We find that the decedent died, possessing at least an incident of ownership in the policy on his life.

* * *

MORTON v. UNITED STATES
United States Court of Appeals, Fourth Circuit, 1972.
457 F.2d 750.

CRAVEN, CIRCUIT JUDGE:

* * * The district judge concluded * * * the Commissioner erroneously included in the gross estate the proceeds of a policy of life insurance. We affirm. We think that the decedent did not possess any of the incidents of ownership of this insurance policy at the time of his death so as to require

inclusion of the proceeds in the decedent's gross estate under Section 2042(2) of the Internal Revenue Code of 1954.

* * * [T]he policy was taken out in 1932 by the decedent at the instigation of his father-in-law, who wanted to provide financial security for his daughter. The decedent paid none of the premiums on this insurance policy and it is clear that he never considered that he "owned" it. The premiums were paid by his father-in-law, then by a corporation owned by the decedent's wife and her sister, and finally by the decedent's wife until the decedent's death in 1963. The policy was kept in the office safe of another corporation owned by the decedent's wife and her sister.

The provisions of the policy which have a bearing on whether or not the proceeds should be included in the decedent's gross estate have been summarized correctly by the district court as follows:

1. *Assignments.* No assignment of the policy would be binding upon the Company until filed at its home office, and the Company assumed no responsibility as to the validity or effect of any assignment.

2. *Premium loans.* The insured and assignees, if any, could request the insurer for a premium loan provided the request was made prior to default and the cash surrender value was sufficient to cover the premium then due.

3. *Cash surrender value.* Upon receipt of the policy and a full and valid surrender of all claims thereunder, and "without the consent or participation of any Beneficiary not irrevocably designated or any Contingent Beneficiary" the Company would pay the cash surrender value of the policy.

4. *Policy loans.* At any time after premiums for two full years had been paid and while the policy was in force except as extended-term insurance, without the consent or participation of any beneficiary not irrevocably designated or any contingent beneficiary, a policy loan could be obtained by properly assigning the policy and forwarding it to the Company at its home office. The amount of the policy loans was limited to the amount secured by the cash surrender value of the policy.

5. *Dividend options.* At the option of the insured, dividends could be (a) withdrawn in cash; (b) applied toward the payment of premiums; (c) applied toward the purchase of a participating paid-up addition to the policy; (d) left to accumulate with interest. Dividends were subject to withdrawal in cash at any time or could be paid with the proceeds of the policy.

6. *Endowment option.* Whenever the reserve on the policy at the end of a policy year, together with the reserve on the existing dividend additions, should be equal to or in excess of the face amount of the policy, the insured could upon surrender of the policy, as well as a full and valid

surrender of all claims thereunder, without consent or participation of any beneficiary not irrevocably designated or any contingent beneficiary, obtain the face amount of the policy.

7. *Full paid participating insurance.* The insured could obtain full paid participating insurance provided certain specified conditions were met.

8. *Paid-up insurance.* The insured and assigns, if any, upon written request to the Company, could obtain participating paid-up life insurance instead of automatic extended-term insurance, if such request was made prior to default in premium payment or within the grace period.

9. *Beneficiaries.* The insured could (1) designate one or more beneficiaries either with or without reservation of the right to revoke such designation; (2) designate one or more contingent beneficiaries; (3) change any beneficiary not irrevocably designated; and (4) change any contingent beneficiary.

10. *Method of payment.* The insured could designate the method by which the proceeds of the policy would be paid to the beneficiaries.

11. *Reinstatement.* The insured could have the policy reinstated at any time within five years after default in payment of premiums by paying all premium arrears, with interest, and any indebtedness which might exist, with interest, upon evidence satisfactory to the Company of his insurability.

In 1938 the decedent executed an endorsement of the policy effecting an irrevocable designation of beneficiaries and mode of settlement. It is the effect of this endorsement upon the other terms of the policy which is determinative of the issue raised.

* * *

It is clear that before the execution of the irrevocable designation of beneficiaries and mode of settlement the policy conferred upon the decedent, as the insured, many, if not all of the powers which Congress had in mind as being incidents of ownership sufficient to cause the proceeds to be included in his gross estate. Ordinarily the possession by the insured of the power to cash the policy in, to elect the endowment option, to get a loan on the policy or to change the beneficiary is sufficient to cause the proceeds to be included in his gross estate. However, we think that the irrevocable designation of beneficiaries and mode of settlement, coupled with payment of premiums by persons other than the insured, made it legally impossible for the decedent to exercise other powers purportedly given him as insured by the policy in such a way that any economic benefit would accrue to him or his estate or so that he could subsequently control the transfer of the proceeds of the policy.

The government concedes that the endorsement of April 7, 1938, divested the decedent of the right to change beneficiaries and to select another method of payment. However, it maintains that other provisions of the policy were left unaffected and there remained in the decedent some incidents of ownership.

It is well established that if the insured retains no right to change the beneficiary of a life insurance policy or, as here, gives up that right, the beneficiary stands in the position of a third party beneficiary to the insurance contract with indefeasibly vested rights in the proceeds. * * * Most authorities are also in agreement that the insured cannot deal with the policy in such a way as to defeat the irrevocably designated third party beneficiaries' interest in the proceeds, by, for example, surrendering the policy for its cash surrender value, without the consent of the beneficiaries, and we think the district court was clearly correct that this result would obtain in [the state of decedent's domicile].

The inquiry is not ended here, however. The district court rejected the government's secondary contention that even if the insured had no independent power he nevertheless had the power to act "in conjunction with" the beneficiaries in exercising incidents of ownership and thus the proceeds of the policy would be includable in the decedent's gross estate under the express language of Section 2042(2) of the Code. We agree that the decisive factor is the existence of the *power* to exercise incidents of ownership either alone or in conjunction with any other person. If both the decedent and the beneficiaries were legally required to act in conjunction in order to affect any of the options of the policy which could be called incidents of ownership, and even if these options could only be exercised in the best financial interest of the beneficiaries and with the approval of a court, the decedent nevertheless possessed the power to exercise the incidents of ownership "in conjunction with any other person." That would suffice under Section 2042(2) to bring the proceeds of the policy within the gross estate. But we are convinced the beneficiaries could effectively act alone to exercise the incidents of ownership. Participation by the decedent "in conjunction with" the beneficiaries was not required, we think, on the facts of this case.

The law of [the state of decedent's domicile] with regard to the right of irrevocably designated beneficiaries to exercise options of a life insurance policy without the consent of the insured is unclear at best. Other courts which have considered analogous insurance problems have done so in light of earlier revenue acts which did not make the proceeds taxable if any incident of ownership was exercisable in conjunction with another person, and hence did not fully consider whether the consent of the insured would be a prerequisite to the exercise of a particular power by an irrevocably designated beneficiary. We think that whether or not an irrevocably designated beneficiary would have the right to obtain a loan on the policy, cash it in, or elect the endowment option when the *insured* had paid the premiums is doubtful. The indefeasibly vested right to the proceeds by the beneficiary probably would not extend to the right to the use of the premiums which these options represent when the premiums were contributed by another. However, when the irrevocably designated beneficiary has also paid the premiums, we think that he has the legal power to exercise the options in the insurance contract which pertain to the use of these premiums without participation of the insured.

Full paid participating insurance, dividends, paid-up insurance, cash surrender value, premium loans and the endowment option all represent use of the premiums with the consent of the insurance company. We think that general principles of equity and contract law strongly suggest that exercise of such premium payment derived rights properly belong to the irrevocably designated beneficiary who has paid the premiums to the exclusion of the insured who contributed nothing. It is not necessary to ignore the policy facts in order to recognize that with respect to premium derived options it is clear that the decedent never considered the policy his, and had the question come up, that all parties would have doubtless agreed that the decedent's wife should be entitled to exercise these options.

The options for premium loans and reinstatement provide for methods of keeping the policy alive in the event of nonpayment of premiums, and the insured's participation would not be necessary where the beneficiary has a vested right to the proceeds. To hold otherwise would allow the insured to indirectly defeat this vested interest. We hold that where an insured has never paid a premium and has never for any purpose treated the policy as his own that his irrevocable designation of beneficiaries and mode of payment of proceeds is an effective assignment of all of his incidents of ownership in the policy.

The judgment of the district court will be

Affirmed.

NOTE

How do you reconcile *Rhode Island Hospital Trust* and *Morton*? Could the attorney in *Rhode Island Hospital Trust* have attempted to save the day by establishing that under state law the insured decedent held the policy as a nominee or agent for the benefit of his father whom the court characterized as "the instigator, premium payer, and primary beneficiary of the policy?"

D. AVOIDING POSSESSION OF THE INCIDENTS OF OWNERSHIP

An insured who wishes to avoid having proceeds of a policy on her life included in her estate has two fundamental options. First, she can avoid purchasing a policy on her life and leave that task to others making sure that the policy so acquired vests her with no incidents of ownership. Second, she can assign to others all incidents of ownership held by her in policies on her life and can then hope to live at least three additional years thereafter.[12] The materials below deal with these alternatives in a variety of contexts.

1. INTRODUCTION

Obviously, one of the best ways of avoiding inclusion of life insurance proceeds in the estate of the insured, in addition to not making it payable to the executor, is avoiding the insured's ever possessing any incidents of ownership by having others with an insurable interest purchase the policy on the life of the insured and make sure that the policy vests no incidents of ownership in the insured. Often the beneficiary of a policy will be a spouse or child, and it is simple enough for that party to take out the policy. Moreover, since there is no longer a premium payment test, it matters little if the insured financially assists the holder of the policy. Where this strategy is employed, care must be taken in planning the estate of the holder of the policy so that an unanticipated sequence of deaths and failure to draft carefully the will of the holder of the policy do not combine to produce undesirable tax consequences. For example, assume that a wife acquires a policy on the life of her husband payable to their children and predeceases her husband with a will which leaves her entire estate to the husband, thereby transferring to him the incidents of ownership on a policy on his life. The husband's only means of avoiding possession of the incidents of ownership on the policy would seem to be a timely disclaimer of all interest in the policy under section 2518.

Where the intended beneficiary is a party without an insurable interest, for example a son-in-law, a niece, or a companion, there are two alternatives. First, the insured could apply for and acquire a policy on her life and assign the policy to the intended beneficiary. This strategy has several problems: (1) the insurable interest rules of a minority of states will allow insurers to void such policies; and (2) under section 2035 unless the insured lives three years after assignment of the policy, the policy proceeds will be included in her estate. A second strategy which works in some cases and which avoids the section 2035 problem is to arrange to have a party (other than the insured) who has an insurable interest acquire the policy on the life of the insured. For example, if a woman, as part of her estate plan, wished to have a policy payable to her niece or son-in-law, it would be simple enough to arrange for the woman's husband or daughter to acquire the policy, naming the niece or son-in-law as beneficiary. If state insurable interest rules permit, the policy could then be assigned to the

---

[12] See Chapter 23C which addresses life insurance transfers within three years of death.

beneficiary although this step is not essential to exclude the policy from the estate of the insured.

There can be unexpected and costly gift tax consequences where someone other than the insured or the beneficiary of a policy purchases a policy from an insurer and continues to hold the incidents of ownership with designation of the beneficiary remaining revocable until death of the insured. In such a circumstance the holder of the revocable power to designate beneficiaries may be deemed to have made an incomplete or revocable gift of the policy which becomes complete at the death of the insured. At this moment there will be a completed gift by the holder to the beneficiary of the value of the proceeds of the policy.

For example, were a mother to acquire from an insurer a policy on her husband's life payable to a child as a revocable beneficiary and were she not to designate irrevocably the child as the beneficiary prior to her husband's death, at the moment of her husband's death the mother would be deemed to be making a gift of the policy proceeds to the child. See Goodman v. Commissioner, 156 F.2d 218 (2d Cir.1946). What was saved from the estate tax could be lost to the gift tax. To guard against such losses, it is wise to consider designating irrevocably both beneficiaries and contingent beneficiaries when policies are acquired and then held by other than the beneficiary.

Where spouses seek to avoid the impact of the incidents of ownership test by acquiring policies on each other's life from an insurer, at least two potential problems are present. First, as previously mentioned, unless the first to die transfers to a person other than the surviving spouse all ownership of the policy on the life of the survivor, or by will bequeaths all interest in this policy to someone other than the surviving spouse, the survivor will find himself or herself with an unintended estate planning problem which can be solved with a timely disclaimer of all interest in the policy. Second, it is possible that the IRS could employ the reciprocal trust doctrine, which you will study in Chapter 18, to include all or some of the insurance proceeds on the life of the first to die in that party's estate.[13]

2. POSSESSION OF UNRETAINED INCIDENTS HELD AS A FIDUCIARY

In Estate of Skifter v. Commissioner, 468 F.2d 699 (2d Cir.1972), the decedent who owned a policy on his life, more than three years prior to his death, assigned all incidents of ownership in the policy to his wife who predeceased her husband and left the policy in question to a trust for the benefit of third parties with her husband as trustee. When the husband subsequently died, the IRS sought to include the policy proceeds in his

---

[13] But see Rev. Rul. 56–397, 1056–2 C.B. 599 (reciprocal trust doctrine does not apply where partners insure each other to fund buy-sell agreement).

estate on the ground that he possessed the incidents of ownership in the policy in question. The Second Circuit refused to include the policy proceeds in husband's estate on the ground that based on analogy to sections 2036 and 2038 (Chapters 18 and 19) he had not *retained* the incidents of ownership which after their reconveyance to him he only held in a fiduciary capacity with no possibility of self-benefit. Three years later in Terriberry v. United States, 517 F.2d 286 (5th Cir.1975), cert. denied, 424 U.S. 977 (1976) the IRS was able to get the Fifth Circuit to reach a contrary result on virtually identical facts. Moreover, shortly before deciding *Terriberry* the Fifth Circuit had repudiated the Second Circuit's *Skifter* analysis in Rose v. United States, 511 F.2d 259 (5th Cir.1975). In *Rose*, the decedent's brother had created three separate trusts for each of the decedent's children funding each with $100 and naming the decedent as trustee. As the trustee of each trust, the decedent applied for three separate policies on his life. At his death twelve years later, the decedent still held the policies as a trustee under each of the trusts. The Fifth Circuit rejected the reasoning of the Second Circuit in *Skifter* that section 2042(2) applied only to *retained* incidents of ownership noting that the statute specifically referred only to "possessed" incidents and included the proceeds from each of the policies in the decedent's taxable estate.

Nine years after its resounding victories in *Rose* and *Terriberry*, the IRS indicated in the ruling which follows that, on rethinking the issue, it had come to agree with the Second Circuit's opinion in *Skifter*.

REVENUE RULING 84–179
1984–2 C.B. 195.

ISSUE

For purposes of section 2042(2) of the Internal Revenue Code, does an insured decedent possess incidents of ownership in an insurance policy if the decedent transferred all incidents of ownership to another person who, in an unrelated transaction, transferred all incidents of ownership to another person who, in an unrelated transaction, transferred the policy in trust and, at death, the decedent was a trustee with discretionary powers which, although broad, could not be exercised for *D*'s personal benefit?

FACTS

In 1960, *D*, the decedent, purchased an insurance policy on *D*'s life and transferred all incidents of ownership to *D*'s spouse. The spouse designated their adult child as the policy beneficiary.

The spouse died in 1978 and, by will, established a residuary trust for the benefit of the child. *D* was designated as trustee. The insurance policy on *D*'s life was included in the spouse's residuary estate and was transferred to the testamentary trust. The drafting of the spouse's will to provide for the residuary trust and the appointment of D as trustee were unrelated to D's transfer of the policy to the spouse.

As trustee, D had broad discretionary powers in the management of the trust property and the power to distribute or accumulate income. Under the terms of the policy, the owner could elect to have the proceeds made payable according to various plans, use the loan value to pay the premiums, borrow on the policy, assign or pledge the policy, and elect to receive annual dividends. The terms of the old will did not preclude D from exercising these rights, although D could not do so for D's own benefit. D paid the premiums on the policy out of other trust property.

D was still serving as trustee when D died in 1984.

LAW AND ANALYSIS

Section 2042(2) provides that the value of the gross estate includes the value of all property to the extent of the amount receivable as insurance under policies on the life of the decedent by beneficiaries (other than the executor), with respect to which the decedent possessed at date of death any of the incidents of ownership in the policies, exercisable either alone or in conjunction with any other person.

Section 20.2042–1(c)(2) of the Estate Tax Regulations provides that the meaning of the term "incidents of ownership" is not confined to ownership of the policy in the technical legal sense. The term includes the power to change the beneficiary, to surrender or cancel the policy for a loan, or to obtain from the insurer a loan against the surrender value of the policy, etc.

Section 20.2042–1(c)(4) of the regulations provides that a decedent is considered to have an incident of ownership in a policy held in trust if under the terms of the policy the decedent (either alone or in conjunction with another person) has the power (as trustee or otherwise) to change the beneficial ownership in the policy or its proceeds, or the time or manner of enjoyment thereof, even though the decedent has no beneficial interest in the trust.

The legislative history of section 2042 indicates that Congress intended section 2042 to parallel the statutory scheme governing those powers that would cause other types of property to be included in a decedent's gross estate under other Code sections, particularly sections 2036 and 2038. S. Rep. No. 1622, 83rd Cong., 2d Sess. 124 (1954). See Estate of Skifter v. Commissioner, 468 F.2d 699 (2d Cir.1972).

Sections 2036(a)(2) and 2038(a)(1) concern lifetime transfers made by the decedent. Under these sections, it is the decedent's power to affect the beneficial interests in, or enjoyment of, the transferred property that required inclusion of the property in the gross estate. Section 2036 is directed at those powers retained by the decedent in connection with the transfer. See, for example, United States v. O'Malley, 383 U.S. 627 (1966), 1966–2 C.B. 526. Section 2038(a)(1) is directed at situations where the transferor-decedent sets the machinery in motion that purposefully allows fiduciary powers over the property interest to subsequently return to the transferor-decedent, such as by an incomplete transfer. See Estate of Reed v. United States, Civil No. 74–543 (M.D. Fla., May 7, 1975); Estate of Skifter v. Commissioner, above cited, at 703–05.

In accordance with the legislative history of section 2042(2), a decedent will not be deemed to have incidents of ownership over an insurance policy on decedent's life where decedent's powers are held in a fiduciary capacity, and are not exercisable for decedent's personal benefit, where the decedent did not transfer the policy or any of the consideration for purchasing or maintaining the policy to the trust from personal assets, and the devolution of the powers on decedent was not part of a prearranged plan involving the participation of decedent. This position is consistent with decisions by several courts of appeal. See *Estate of Skifter*; Estate of Fruehauf v. Commissioner, 427 F.2d 80 (6th Cir.1970); Hunter v. United States, 624 F.2d 833 (8th Cir.1980). But see Terriberry v. United States, 517 F.2d 286 (5th Cir.1975), cert. denied, 424 U.S. 977 (1976); Rose v. United States, 511 F.2d 259 (5th Cir.1975), which are to the contrary. Section 20.2042–1(c)(4) will be read in accordance with the position adopted herein.

The decedent will be deemed to have incidents of ownership over an insurance policy on the decedent's life where decedent's powers are held in a fiduciary capacity and the decedent has transferred the policy or any of the consideration for purchasing and maintaining the policy to the trust. Also, where the decedent's powers could have been exercised for decedent's benefit, they will constitute incidents of ownership in the policy, without regard to how those powers were acquired and without consideration of whether the decedent transferred property to the trust. *Estate of Fruehauf*; *Estate of Skifter*, above cited at 703. Thus, if the decedent reacquires powers over insurance policies in an individual capacity, the powers will constitute incidents of ownership even though the decedent is a transferee.

In the present situation, *D* completely relinquished all interest in the insurance policy on *D*'s life. The powers over the policy devolved on *D* as a fiduciary, through an independent transaction, and were not exercisable for *D*'s own benefit. Also, *D* did not transfer property to the trust. Thus, *D* did not possess incidents of ownership over the policy for purposes of section 2042(2) of the Code.

HOLDING

An insured decedent who transferred all incidents of ownership in a policy to another person, who in an unrelated transaction transferred powers over the policy in trust to the decedent, will not be considered to possess incidents of ownership in the policy for purposes of section 2042(2) of the Code, provided that the decedent did not furnish consideration for maintaining the policy and could not exercise the powers for personal benefit. The result is the same where the decedent, as trustee, purchased the policy with trust assets, did not contribute assets to the trust or maintain the policy with personal assets, and could not exercise the powers for personal benefit.

NOTE

Given Congressional rejection of the premium payment test in 1954, it is curious to see non-payment of premiums mentioned by the IRS as a critical factor in Rev. Rul. 84–179.

3.   IRREVOCABLE LIFE INSURANCE TRUSTS

Often because of unforeseeable changes in family situations, such as the birth of additional children or a shift in economic status among dependents, irrevocably assigning a policy to an individual or group of individuals or having such parties purchase and hold such a policy prove to be less than optimal solutions to accommodating both tax minimization and changing family financial needs.

An individual who holds, or is about to purchase, life insurance on her life and who wishes to avoid inclusion of the policy proceeds in her estate at death, but at the same time wishes to ensure the insurance will be available to benefit the insured's family in a flexible fashion, frequently seeks to attain these goals by effecting a transfer of the policy to an irrevocable trust or by arranging for the trustee to purchase the policy. Although with the demise of the premium payment test it is unnecessary, the trust is sometimes funded with property, the income from which will be used to pay policy premiums. A trusted family friend, attorney, or financial institution is often appointed as trustee to provide for responsive treatment of the family. Since, at his or her death, the insured will not possess any of the incidents of ownership, the policy proceeds will typically be excluded from the estate of the insured. In establishing the trust, care must be taken so that the insured does not retain any rights or powers with respect to the trust that could result in its inclusion in the estate under not only section 2042, but also sections 2036, 2037, or 2038.

Moreover, if an existing policy on which the insured holds the incidents of ownership is transferred into the trust, unless the insured lives for at least three years after effecting the transfer, the proceeds of the policy will be included in the taxable estate of the insured decedent under section 2035. See Salyer v. United States, 98–2 USTC ¶ 60,326, 82 AFTR 2d ¶ 98,5967 (E.D. Ky.1998).

The following ruling, while impliedly indicating IRS acceptance of the principle of the irrevocable life insurance trust as an effective estate planning device, also indicates the need for the estate planner to pay attention to detail when employing such a device.

REVENUE RULING 79–129
1979–1 C.B. 306.

ISSUE

To what extent are the proceeds of a life insurance policy on a decedent's life includible in the decedent's gross estate under section 2042 of the Internal Revenue Code of 1954, in the circumstances described below?

FACTS

In 1973, *D* obtained an ordinary life insurance policy on *D*'s life. The policy had a face amount of $150,000. Simultaneously, *D* created an irrevocable funded insurance trust and named the *X* Trust Company as trustee.

The insurance policy designated the trustee of the insurance trust as owner of the policy. Under the terms of the policy, *D* possessed the right to borrow against the cash surrender value in an amount not to exceed the total amount of the policy premiums paid by *D*. However, the policy had no cash surrender value during the first year.

The policy designated *D*'s estate as the beneficiary of the policy proceeds to the extent of an amount equal to the cash surrender value of the policy immediately prior to *D*'s death, less any outstanding indebtedness against the policy. The policy designated the *X* Trust Company, as trustee of the insurance trust, as the beneficiary of the balance of the proceeds.

With the exception of *D*'s right to borrow against the cash surrender value, noted above, all other contract rights with respect to the policy were exercisable by the trustee of the insurance trust, as owner of the policy. These contract rights included the right to assign and surrender the policy, to elect paid up insurance, and to change the beneficiary of the policy proceeds to the extent they exceeded the cash surrender value, which was payable to *D*'s estate.

The terms of the trust provide that, on *D*'s death, the trustee is to hold the insurance proceeds for the benefit of *D*'s spouse and children. The trust agreement further provides that *D* would be responsible for payment of the portion of the annual premium that is equal to the increase in the cash surrender value of the policy during the year. The trustee would be responsible for the payment of the balance of the annual premium.

D died in 1977, more than three years after *D* obtained the insurance policy and created the insurance trust. Between 1973 and 1977, *D* paid a total of $12,000 in premiums on the policy, in accordance with *D*'s obligations under the terms of the trust agreement. During the period, *D* did not exercise the power to borrow against the cash surrender value. At the time of *D*'s death, the cash surrender value of the policy was $12,000. Consequently, $12,000 of the policy proceeds was paid to *D*'s estate. The balance of the proceeds, $138,000, was paid to the *X* Trust Company in accordance with the terms of the policy.

On the Federal estate tax return filed for *D*'s estate, the executor included the $12,000 in policy proceeds payable to the decedent's estate under section 2042(1). The executor excluded the $138,000 balance of the proceeds, which was payable to a beneficiary other than the decedent's estate, on the ground that this portion of the proceeds was not includible under section 2042(2), because the incidents of ownership in the policy possessed by *D* could not be exercised to affect this portion of the policy proceeds.

LAW AND ANALYSIS

Section 2042(1) provides for the inclusion in the gross estate of the proceeds of insurance on the decedent's life receivable by the decedent's estate. Section 2042(2) of the Code includes in the gross estate proceeds of insurance on the decedent's life receivable by beneficiaries other than the decedent's estate under policies with respect to which the decedent possessed at his death any incidents of ownership, exercisable either alone or in conjunction with any other person.

Section 20.2042–1(c)(2) of the Estate Tax Regulations describes "incidents of ownership" as follows:

"For purposes of this paragraph, the term 'incidents of ownership' is not limited in its meaning to ownership of the policy in the technical legal sense. Generally speaking, the term has reference to the right of the insured or his estate to the economic benefits of the policy. Thus, it includes the power to change the beneficiary, to surrender or cancel the policy, to assign the policy, to revoke an assignment, to pledge the policy for a loan, or to obtain from the insurer a loan against the surrender value of the policy, etc. . . ."

The right of an insured to obtain a loan against the surrender value of the policy is specified in the regulations as an incident of ownership. The courts have recognized that this power furnishes grounds for including the entire policy proceeds in the gross estate, even in situations where the decedent's power to borrow is limited to the amount of the policy premiums.

In the situation presented in the instant case, $12,000 in policy proceeds were paid to *D*'s estate, under the terms of the policy. Since this $12,000 in proceeds is payable to *D*'s estate, this amount is includible in *D*'s gross estate pursuant to section 2042(1).

The balance of the proceeds, $138,000, was paid to the X Trust Company, a beneficiary other than the decedent's estate. Consequently, the estate taxation of these proceeds is governed by section 2042(2).

Under the terms of the insurance contract, D possessed the right to borrow against the cash surrender value of the policy to the extent of the premiums paid by D and not recovered. In accordance with section 20.2042–1(c)(2) of the regulations, and [reported cases], this power qualifies as an incident of ownership for purposes of section 2042(2), even though the amount D could borrow against the surrender value was limited. If the decedent possessed an incident of ownership in the policy, then the entire policy proceeds payable to a beneficiary other than the decedent's estate are includible in the decedent's gross estate regardless of the fact that a portion of the proceeds subject to inclusion could not be affected by the exercise of the incident of ownership.

HOLDING

1) Pursuant to section 2042(1), $12,000 of the policy proceeds are includible in D's gross estate.

2) The balance of the proceeds, $138,000, is includible in D's gross estate pursuant to section 2042(2).

The same Federal estate tax consequences would obtain regardless of the source of premium payments, or the portion of proceeds payable to the trustee and the decedent's estate.

Further, if D had died within the first year after the policy was issued, then the policy would have had no cash surrender value at the time of D's death. Under the terms of the policy the entire policy proceeds, $150,000, would have been paid to the trustee. Under these circumstances, $150,000 would be includible in D's gross estate under section 2042(2) of the Code, representing the proceeds payable to a beneficiary other than the decedent's estate under an insurance policy with respect to which the decedent possessed incidents of ownership. No amount of the proceeds would be includible under section 2042(1), since no portion of the proceeds would be payable to D's estate.

NOTES

1. The Internal Revenue Service has given its blessing to the following. A married couple purchased a joint policy payable on the death of the survivor, commonly called a "last to die" policy. The policy was held by an irrevocable life insurance trust which, by its terms, did not require the trust to use the policy proceeds to pay the estate tax due on the death of the survivor (or any other debts of the parties) but merely authorized the trust to do so. Because the trust was not obligated, but was merely authorized, to satisfy the estate tax debts of the estate of the survivor with the policy proceeds, the IRS ruled that the proceeds were not to be

included in the estate of the survivor under section 2042(1) as proceeds payable to the estate of the survivor. Priv. Ltr. Rul. 200147039 (Aug. 21, 2001).

2. There has been some interest in using split dollar life insurance in conjunction with irrevocable life insurance trusts for the purpose of minimizing payment of gratuitous transfer taxes. Split dollar life insurance is a means whereby parties share the cost of paying premiums and the benefits of life insurance. Under one devised strategy, married couples establish an irrevocable life insurance trust and then either cause the trust to acquire a whole life last-to-die insurance policy on the lives of the couple or assign an existing such policy to the trust which typically will designate the couple's issue as beneficiaries who are to receive policy proceeds. The couple will have no interest in the trust, will possess none of the incidents of ownership on the policy and neither will serve as trustee. The couple, which intends to pay all of the policy premiums, will then enter into an agreement which will provide that at the death of the survivor when the proceeds are paid to the trust, the survivor's estate will be paid the greater of the cash surrender value of the policy or the premiums paid. In several private letter rulings, the IRS has indicated that such an arrangement results in a taxable gift only of a small portion of the premium (roughly the amount necessary to pay for the pure insurance component of the arrangement) with the balance untaxed as a gift based on income tax rules for determining the ownership of split dollar policies. One of the critical factors in applying these income tax rules is that the survivor will be paid the greater of the cash surrender value or the premiums paid. Moreover, at the death of the last to die, as long as the trust was properly set up and administered, the policy proceeds paid to the trust will not be included in the estate of the survivor under section 2042(2). However, the amount repaid to the survivor's estate under the agreement will be taxed in his or her estate under section 2042(1). See Priv. Ltr. Rul. 200910002 (Sept. 30, 2008) and Priv. Ltr. Rul. 200825011 (Feb. 5, 2008). See also Priv. Ltr. Rul. 200848002 (Aug. 19, 2008) and Priv. Ltr. Rul. 200822003 (Jan. 28, 2008). The principal advantage of such arrangements seems to be to provide the couple's offspring with assets (policy proceeds) not subject to estate taxes that can be used to absorb the blow of estate taxes or otherwise benefit these individuals. Moreover, this is done at the cost of either no, or very little, gift tax on the premiums paid by the couple whose lives are insured although at the cost of the inclusion of the repaid amount in the estate of the last to die spouse under section 2042(1).

4. ASSIGNING GROUP TERM LIFE INSURANCE

Employment, or membership in a professional association, union, or alumni association often brings with it an opportunity to participate in a group term life insurance program. Typically, after coverage is extended under the group policy, as long as the insured remains a member of the group and premiums are paid, the policy remains in effect. To remove the proceeds of such policies from their estates, insureds will often assign all interests in the group policy to family members or an irrevocable life insurance trust if this is permitted under the group contract.

The IRS had initially contended that because of the ability of the insured to terminate membership in the organization which entitled the insured to continued coverage, the insured, even after assignment of all interest in the policy, had effectively retained a key incident of ownership, ability to cancel the policy. See Rev. Rul. 69–54, 1969–1 C.B. 221 (Situation 1) (termination of employment). While this might make considerable sense in the case of an alumni association or American Bar Association group policy, it makes considerably less sense where the insured could only terminate the group policy by resigning from employment or from membership in a union or an integrated bar association where termination of membership might mean loss of a means of livelihood. In Rev. Rul. 72–307, 1972–1 C.B. 307, the IRS abandoned the position taken in Rev. Rul. 69–54 that the power to terminate a group policy by resigning one's employment constituted possession of an incident of ownership with respect to an assigned employment-based group life insurance policy. The IRS observed that the significant collateral consequence of termination of employment had caused the Commissioner to reverse the position taken in Rev. Rul. 69–54 on this issue.

Occasionally, employment-based group term policies, in order to avoid leaving retired or terminated employees uninsured or underinsured, provide that on termination of employment the insured can convert the group policy into an individual policy. In Rev. Rul. 69–54, 1969–1 C.B. 221 (Situation 2), the IRS initially indicated that where an employee insured had assigned all interests in a group policy but had retained such a conversion privilege, the proceeds of the policy were includible in the employee's taxable estate on the ground that the employee had retained an incident of ownership.

In the following ruling the IRS indicated that it had also reconsidered and changed its opinion on this issue.

REVENUE RULING 84–130

1984–2 C.B. 194.

ISSUE

If a decedent transferred all the incidents of ownership in a noncontributory group-term life insurance policy on decedent's life, but retained the right to convert the policy to an individual policy should the decedent cease employment, are the proceeds includible in the decedent's gross estate under section 2042(2) of the Internal Revenue Code?

FACTS

D died in March 1982. At the time of death, *D* was employed by *Y* Corporation which made all the payments on a group term life insurance policy on *D*'s life. Under the terms of the policy, *D* owned all the incidents of ownership. In 1977, *D* transferred all the ownership rights to *A*. However, *D* retained the right to convert the policy to an individual policy in the event *D*'s employment with *Y* was terminated.

LAW AND ANALYSIS

Section 2042(2) provides that the value of the gross estate includes the value of proceeds from insurance policies on the life of the decedent receivable by beneficiaries other than the executor where the decedent possessed incidents of ownership in the policy exercisable either alone or in conjunction with any other person.

Section 20.2042–1(c)(2) of the Estate Tax Regulations provides that the term "incidents of ownership," in general, means the right of the insured or the insured's estate to the economic benefits of the policy. Examples of incidents of ownership include the power to change the beneficiary, to surrender or cancel the policy, to assign the policy, to revoke an assignment, to pledge the policy for a loan, and to obtain from the insurer a loan against the surrender value of the policy.

These examples contained in section 20.2042–1(c)(2) of the regulations concern powers that directly affect the insurance policy rather than powers that are collateral consequences of potentially costly related actions of the decedent. An example of a power exercisable only as a result of potentially costly related action, and thus not an incident of ownership for purposes of section 2042(2), is the power to cancel a group-term policy by termination of employment. The power of cancellation is considered a collateral consequence of the power that every employee has to terminate employment. Similarly, a power to convert a group-term policy that is exercisable only by the voluntary termination of employment is a collateral consequence of a potentially costly action. That is, * * * the power to convert is a collateral consequence of the power that every employee has to terminate employment.

Although termination of employment may occur either at the complete discretion of the employer or by the decedent's voluntary action, for purposes of section 2042(2) of the Code, the Service will not distinguish between conversion rights exercisable upon voluntary termination of employment and such rights exercisable upon involuntary termination.

Accordingly, the insurance proceeds payable to *A* under the group insurance policy are not includible in *D*'s gross estate because *D*'s retained conversion privilege is not an incident of ownership for purposes of section 2042(2). * * *

HOLDING

If a decedent transferred all the incidents of ownership in a noncontributory group-term life insurance policy on the decedent's life, but retained the right to convert the policy to an individual policy should the decedent's employment be terminated, the proceeds are not includible in the decedent's gross estate under section 2042(2).

* * *

NOTES

1. Why does the IRS limit its ruling to a noncontributory life insurance policy? Is this appropriate in a post-premiums payment test world? Could the IRS be concerned about the fact that many employee group policies are contributory, with the employee signing up for the desired level of coverage which is to be paid for by salary deduction, and the employee by revoking salary deduction authorization could effectively revoke an assigned group life insurance policy? What if the group policy provided for payment by a means other than salary deduction; would there then be any need to bar an insured from effectively removing the policy from his or her estate through assignment on the ground that the policy is contributory?

2. Occasionally, employers will have death benefit plans which provide benefits payable to a designated group of individuals such as a surviving spouse and issue. Since the employee has no right to designate beneficiaries, benefits paid under the plan are not included in the employee's estate under section 2033. If the employee has any other right with respect to the death benefit, the IRS may attempt to assert that the right constitutes an incident of ownership with respect to employer provided life insurance, the proceeds of which are includible in the employee's estate at death. For example, in Estate of Lumpkin, 474 F.2d 1092 (5th Cir.1973), the Fifth Circuit included in the estate of a deceased employee under section 2042(2) death benefits paid to an employer (Humble Oil Co., now Exxon) designated class of beneficiaries under a plan which gave the employee only the right to designate whether benefits were to be paid out in a lump sum or in installments over a period of years. The Third Circuit in Estate of Connelly v. United States, 551 F.2d 545 (3d Cir.1977), reached a contrary result on the identical plan with the identical employer on the ground that a right which was so ethereal could not constitute an incident of ownership. Since the IRS in Rev. Rul. 81–128, 1981–1 C.B. 469, has indicated that, in all Circuits other than the Third, it will not follow *Connelly*, estate planners should make sure that employee insureds who wish to remove death benefits from their estates assign even ethereal rights in such benefits.

E. THE UNIFORM SIMULTANEOUS DEATH ACT

Under the general rule of the 1993 version of the Uniform Simultaneous Death Act (which prevails in a clear majority of states), absent clear evidence that two parties died other than simultaneously, each party's property is distributed as if he or she survived the other. The Act contains a special rule where the insured and the primary beneficiary under a life insurance policy die simultaneously. The insured is deemed to have survived the beneficiary. Consequently, in such a situation benefits under the policy will be paid to the policy's contingent beneficiary. The impact of the Act in a classic life insurance cross ownership situation is illustrated by the following ruling.

REVENUE RULING 77–181
1977–1 C.B. 272.

Advice has been requested whether the full value of certain life insurance policies is includible in the gross estates of the decedents under the circumstances described below. If the full value of the insurance policies is not includible, advice has been further requested as to how they should be valued.

A and *B*, residents of State *Y*, each owned insurance policies on the other's life with the proceeds payable to the owner or the owner's estate. In 1973, *A* and *B* were killed under circumstances that led a court to decree that no order of death could be estimated, thus bringing into operation State *Y*'s Uniform Simultaneous Death Act in the administration of their property. The State *Y* statute provides the presumption that for purposes of life or accident insurance policy proceeds, the insured will be presumed to have survived the beneficiary. Accordingly, the proceeds of each policy were paid to the contingent beneficiary, which in each case was the estate of the owner. Thus, the proceeds of life insurance on the life of *A* were paid to the estate of *B*, and the proceeds on the life of *B* were paid to the estate of *A*.

Section 2033 provides that "The value of the gross estate shall include the value of all property to the extent of the interest therein of the decedent at the time of his death."

Section 20.2033–1(a) of the Estate Tax Regulations provides:

In general. The gross estate of a decedent who was a citizen or resident of the United States at the time of his death includes under section 2033 the value of all property, whether real or personal, tangible or intangible, and wherever situated, beneficially owned by the decedent at the time of his death. * * *

Section 20.2031–8(a)(2) of the Estate Tax Regulations provides:

As valuation of an insurance policy through sale of comparable contracts is not readily ascertainable when, at the date of the decedent's death, the contract has been in force for some time and further premium payments are to be made, the value may be approximated by adding to the interpolated terminal reserve at the date of the decedent's death the proportionate part of the gross premium last paid before the date of the decedent's death which covers the period extending beyond that date. If, however, because of the unusual nature of the contract such an approximation is not reasonably close to the full value of the contract, this method may not be used.

State law governs what the decedent owns for purposes of estate taxation. The Federal taxing statutes merely determine how that interest shall be taxed. Rogers v. Helvering, 320 U.S. 410 (1943); Morgan v. Commissioner, 309 U.S. 78 (1940). Federal estate tax liability attaches to the value of the property at the instant of the decedent's death. United States v. Land, 303 F.2d 170 (5th Cir.1962), cert. denied, 371 U.S. 862. At the moment of death in the instant case, both *A* and *B* possessed valuable ownership rights in the life insurance policies they owned, properly includible in their respective gross estates under section 2033. Chown v. Commissioner, 428 F.2d 1395 (9th Cir.1970); Old Kent Bank & Trust Co. v. United States, 430 F.2d 392 (6th Cir.1970); Meltzer v. Commissioner, 439 F.2d 798 (4th Cir.1971); Wien v. Commissioner, 441 F.2d 32 (5th Cir.1971). Hence the instant problem is solely one of valuation.

In *Chown* and the related cases cited above, which also involved the taxability of life insurance proceeds in a simultaneous death situation, the courts held that the full value of policy proceeds was improperly included in the decedent-beneficiary's gross estate. However, since in the instant case, the policy proceeds were in fact paid to each decedent-beneficiary's estate as contingent beneficiary, whereas in *Chown* and the related cases the proceeds did not flow to the estate of the decedent-beneficiary but instead passed directly to the decedent's children as secondary beneficiaries, the question arises whether the Federal estate tax is properly due and owing on the full value of the proceeds since *A* and *B* each had a transmittable interest in the insurance proceeds paid to their estates.

To tax the decedent's estate on the full value of the policy proceeds when at the moment of the decedent's death, the decedent, by law, retains only the ownership interest in a yet unmatured policy negates the effect of the simultaneous death statutes, as well as the fundamental estate taxation concept, that estate tax liability attaches to the value of the property at the *instant* of the deceased's death. The fact that the decedent-beneficiary's estate has, subsequent to the decedent's death, received the policy proceeds is without legal significance for estate tax purposes since estate tax liability is fixed as of the instant of death.

Chown and the related cases have decided that in a simultaneous death situation only the interpolated terminal reserve value of a life insurance policy is to be included in the estate of the owner. As set forth in section 20.2031–8(a)(2) of the regulations, the interpolated reserve value provides a stable method of estimating the value of an ordinary life insurance policy. "To allow either the taxpayers' or the government's method to prevail would destroy this certainty and replace it with fluctuating individual imponderables with which no court could cope and which the Supreme Court rejected in [Commissioner v. Noel, 380 U.S. 678 (1965) (1965–2 C.B. 371)]." Wien v. Commissioner, 441 F.2d 32, 41 (1971).

Accordingly, in a simultaneous death and cross-owned insurance situation where the local law establishes the presumption that the insured survived the beneficiary, the value of the proceeds to be included in the gross estate of each of the owners is the sum of the interpolated terminal reserve of the policy at the date of the insured decedent's death and the proportionate part of the gross premium last paid before the date of the insured's death which covers the period extending beyond that date.

NOTE

There are two versions of the Uniform Simultaneous Death Act. The first version, which was adopted in 1940 and amended in 1953, is the version of the Act referred to in Rev. Rul. 77–181. It is commonly called the Uniform Simultaneous Death Act. A second version of the Act which was adopted in 1991 and amended in 1993 is officially referred to as the Uniform Simultaneous Death Act (1993). The revised Act adopted a 120-hour survival rule under which a person is considered to have survived a decedent if it is not established that the person survived the decedent by 120 hours. Similarly, the decedent is considered to have survived the other person for purposes of determining the decedent's estate. The 120-hour rule has been adopted in most states. Unlike the original Act, the 1993 Act does not specifically refer to life insurance, but the reporter's comments indicate that no change in treatment of life insurance was intended by this change in language. Given appropriate facts the IRS could therefore be expected to reach the same conclusion under the 1993 Act as it reached under the original Act in Rev. Rul. 77–181.

F. ATTRIBUTION OF INCIDENTS OF OWNERSHIP TO SHAREHOLDERS AND PARTNERS

The question sometimes arises whether incidents of ownership are to be attributed to the principal shareholder of a closely held corporation which has taken out a policy on the life of the shareholder. Regulation § 20.2042–1(c)(6) meets this issue head-on by specifically providing that, with respect to proceeds of corporate-owned life insurance payable to either the corporation or a third party for a valid business purpose, incidents of ownership held by the corporation will not be attributed to the decedent (insured) through his stock ownership, whether or not the decedent is the sole or controlling stockholder. However, to the extent that the corporate-owned life insurance is not payable to the corporation or to a third party for a valid business purpose, the incidents of ownership will be attributed to the insured decedent who is a sole or controlling shareholder. Generally, a decedent will not be deemed a controlling shareholder unless "he owned stock possessing more than 50 percent of the total combined voting power of the corporation."

The proper treatment of insurance held by a partnership in which the insured is a partner is somewhat murkier, although it, in general, is similar to the treatment of insurance held by a corporation. In Estate of Knipp v. Commissioner, 25 T.C. 153 (1955), acq. 1959–1 C.B. 4, aff'd on another issue, 244 F.2d 436 (4th Cir.1957), cert. denied, 355 U.S. 827 (1957), the Tax Court refused to find that a 40 percent partner possessed incidents of ownership in a policy on his life held by the partnership. The Tax Court reasoned that it would result in unfair double taxation to conclude otherwise since the proceeds of the policy were to be considered in valuing the decedent's partnership interest. In Rev. Rul. 83–147, 1983–2 C.B. 158, the IRS indicated that it agrees with the result in *Knipp* as long as the policy proceeds are payable to or for the benefit of the partnership. Where, as in Rev. Rul. 83–147, the policy held by a partnership in which the decedent insured was a one-third general partner was payable to a third party (the decedent's child) for a purpose unrelated to partnership activities, the IRS indicated the incidents of ownership on the policy would be attributed to the deceased partner. In Rev. Rul. 83–148, 1983–2 C.B. 153, the IRS ruled on a situation involving a partner in a large law firm who assigned to a trust all the partner's interest in a group term life insurance policy on the partner's life held by the partnership. The IRS held that in this case the proceeds of the assigned policy were not includible in decedent's estate despite the fact that decedent's partnership, even after the assignment, retained the right to cancel the group policy and section 2042(2) indicates that possession by the insured at death of incidents of ownership "exercisable either alone or in conjunction with any other person" warrants inclusion of policy proceeds in the estate of the insured.

G. BUY-SELL AGREEMENTS FUNDED WITH LIFE INSURANCE

When one co-owner in a business dies, the survivors commonly wish to carry on the business by themselves, without the decedent's heirs who often know nothing of the enterprise. Similarly, the decedent's surviving spouses and issue often would rather not participate in the business enterprise and would rather sell their newly inherited interests for a fair price.

To meet these concerns co-owners often enter into two types of arrangements whereby the interest of the deceased co-owner is purchased at her or his death for its fair market value: (1) the cross purchase; and (2) the entity purchase. On occasion, the purchase is structured as a combination of cross purchase and entity purchase.

Under a cross purchase, the co-owners agree that the surviving co-owners shall purchase the decedent's interest for its fair market value, whereas under the entity purchase arrangement they agree that the business enterprise itself shall effect such a purchase. Where the co-owners, or the enterprise, anticipate that they will lack sufficient assets to enable them to comply with the buy-sell agreement, they commonly use life insurance to enable them to satisfy their contractual obligations.

Under the cross purchase arrangement, as properly structured, each co-owner will obtain life insurance on the life of the other co-owners payable to the co-owner taking out the policy, and on the death of one of his partners or fellow shareholders will use the policy proceeds to help him satisfy his obligation to purchase the deceased partner's interest in the business enterprise. Since, under the arrangement as outlined, the surviving co-owner holds all the incidents of ownership on the life insurance policy on the deceased co-owner payable to the surviving co-owner, there will be no inclusion of the policy proceeds in the estate of the deceased co-owner. Occasionally, co-owners who attempt to structure cross purchases without the aid of estate planners make the error of each co-owner taking out a policy on his life payable to fellow co-owners to enable them to carry out their purchase obligations. This has the disastrous result of the policy proceeds being included in the deceased co-owner's estate since he died possessed of the incidents of ownership on the policy on his life. In addition, there will be included in the deceased co-owner's estate the value of the business interest purchased by his surviving co-owners with the policy proceeds, thereby in essence resulting in a double inclusion under the defectively structured arrangement.

Under the entity purchase arrangement, the business enterprise, to enable it to purchase the decedent's interest, will take out and hold a life insurance policy, frequently a so-called renewable first-to-die policy, under which the insurer pays the policy proceeds to the entity as soon as any one of the entity co-owners dies. As in the case of the cross-purchase arrangement, all the incidents of ownership rules previously discussed in this chapter apply in determining whether the policy proceeds, or any portion thereof, will be included in the estate of the deceased co-owner under section 2042.

Although the entity purchase seems preferable to a cross purchase, especially in the case of a business with a number of co-owners where a stupefying number of policies might have to be issued to provide for a cross purchase, it is not without its problems. For example, in the case of a partnership which holds a life insurance policy, as required under *Knipp*, there will be an increase (modest for a small minority partner) in the value of the partnership interest of the deceased partner when the policy proceeds are included in valuing her partnership interest to avoid the incidents of ownership on the policy from being attributed to her. In the case of C corporations, there may be alternative minimum tax problems, with the annual internal build up in value of the policy and the excess of death benefits over basis in the policy both considered to be part of the corporation's alternative minimum tax base. See I.R.C. § 56(g)(4)(B)(ii) and Treas. Reg. § 1.56(g)–1(c)(5)(v). Moreover, while surviving co-owners who purchase interests from the decedent under a cross purchase acquire basis in the interest thus acquired, a purchase of a deceased shareholder's stock by the corporation or a deceased partner's interest by the partnership provides the surviving co-owners with no additional basis in their ownership interests in the enterprise, a not inconsequential consideration if they are considering selling out in the not too distant future.

H. INSURANCE PURCHASED WITH COMMUNITY FUNDS

The regulations provide fairly basic guidance as to the estate tax treatment of life insurance in community property or marital property states.[14] If proceeds of a life insurance policy which is community property are payable to the deceased spouse's estate and under local community property law one-half of the proceeds belongs to the decedent's spouse, only one-half will be considered receivable for the benefit of the decedent's estate and subject to tax under section 2042(1). See Treas. Reg. § 20.2042–1(b)(2). In Wisconsin, the state statute sets forth a formula to determine which portion of the proceeds is marital property versus separate property by computing the ratio of the period that premiums are paid from marital property and the entire period that the life insurance policy is in effect.[15]

Where the policy calls for payment at decedent's death not to the decedent's estate but to a third party such as a child, and the decedent has retained incidents of ownership as agent for the other spouse or as manager of the community assets, the decedent is deemed to possess incidents of ownership only with respect to one-half of the policy on his life and consequently only one-half of the policy proceeds will be included in his estate at his death under section 2042(2). See Treas. Reg. § 20.2042–1(c)(5).

---

[14]   There are nine community or marital property states in the United States. See Ariz. Rev. Stat. § 25–211 (2022); Cal. Prob. Code § 100 (2022); Idaho Code § 32–906 (2022); La. Civ. Code Ann. art. 2336 (West 2022) Nev. Rev. Stat. § 123.250 (2021); N.M. Stat. Ann. § 40–3–12 (2022); Tex. Fam. Code Ann. § 3.002 (2021); Wash. Rev. Code Ann. § 26.16.030 (2022); Wis. Stat. Ann. § 766.31 (2022) (stating that property acquired during marriage is presumed to be "marital" property).

[15]   See Wis. Stat. Ann. § 766.61 (2022).

Assuming that the policy remained revocable as to designation of the beneficiary, at decedent's death the surviving spouse will be deemed to have made a gift to the beneficiary equal to the other one-half of the proceeds. See Treas. Reg. § 25.2511–1(h)(9). If the uninsured spouse were to die first only one-half of the interpolated terminal reserve value of the policy would be included in her estate under section 2033. See Treas. Reg. § 20.2042–1(c)(5); Rev. Rul. 75–100, 1975–1 C.B. 303.

PROBLEMS

1. Six years ago, Anna purchased from an insurance company a $300,000 policy on her life payable to her son, Jaden, who her will also designated as the executor of her estate. One month after taking out the policy Anna irrevocably assigned all incidents of ownership in the policy to Jaden. Anna annually gave $17,000 to Jaden who, after the first year paid the $3,000 annual premium on the policy. At Anna's death $300,000 was paid to Jaden by the insurance company. What are the estate tax consequences?

2. Molly last year acquired a $500,000 policy on the life of her husband, Charles, payable to their son, Scott. Until Charles death last month, Molly continued to hold all incidents of ownership in the policy which included the ability to change beneficiaries. What are the estate and gift tax consequences of the above to Molly, Scott, and Charles' estate?

3. In the prior problem assume that two months after acquiring the policy Molly assigned all incidents of ownership in the policy to Scott.

4. In problem (2) assume that Scott rather than Molly had acquired the policy on his father's life.

5. Ten years ago, David purchased a $500,000 life insurance policy on his life, and irrevocably designated his children, Rebecca and Erica, as the beneficiaries. David retained the right to take out loans against the cash surrender value of the policy. The insurance policy had a $100,000 cash surrender value. Three years ago, David was injured in a car accident. He had several medical bills not covered by health insurance. Since David did not have enough savings to cover the medical costs, he took out a $75,000 loan against the insurance policy. Last month, David died unexpectedly. David had repaid the loan before his death. The insurance company paid the $500,000 insurance proceeds to Rebecca and Erica. What are the estate tax consequences?

6. Michael was appointed guardian of the property of his four-year old daughter, Samantha, and acting in his capacity as guardian purchased a $750,000 policy on his life payable to Samantha. Michael, as guardian of the property, continued to hold all incidents of ownership in the policy until his death five years later. What are the estate tax consequences for Michael's estate?

7.　Patricia had held all incidents of ownership on a $500,000 policy on her life payable to her daughter, Maria. On advice from her attorney, Patricia, six years ago, assigned all incidents of ownership on the policy to an irrevocable trust for the benefit of Maria with her attorney serving as trustee. On Patricia's death earlier this month $500,000 was paid to Maria. What are the estate tax consequences?

8.　Steve and Emma, who are married, each took out a $300,000 policy on the other's life payable equally to their children, Andrew and Gabriella. Until Steve's death six weeks ago they each had retained all incidents of ownership in the policies acquired by them, including the ability to change beneficiaries. What are the gift and estate tax consequences of the above?

9.　Alex and his son Brian were equal partners in a construction company which was worth $12 million. Alex's interest in the partnership was the principal asset which he owned and Alex, who was a widower, wished at his death to benefit equally Brian and Brian's sister, Libby, who is a successful doctor and has no interest in being a partner in a construction company. Brian and Alex are considering solving this problem with a buy-sell arrangement but Brian does not have much by way of liquid assets available to him. What suggestions do you have?

CHAPTER 18

RETAINED LIFE ESTATES

(SECTION 2036)

■ ■ ■

A. BACKGROUND AND GENERAL APPLICATION

As originally enacted in 1916, the Internal Revenue Code contained a provision including in the estate all transfers "intended to take effect in possession or enjoyment at or after death." It was originally thought that the types of transfers presently taxed under sections 2036, 2037, and 2038 would be taxed under this provision. Due to several Supreme Court decisions of questionable quality, which dramatically limited the scope of the old "possession or enjoyment" provision, Congress found it necessary to pass sections 2036, 2037, and 2038 in much their present form for the purpose of unequivocally indicating the proper tax treatment of the types of transactions that it intended to tax under the "possession or enjoyment" standard. This little bit of legislative history will explain why, on occasion, this older language is employed in state death tax statutes and why state courts occasionally construe the language in these statutes by resorting to federal court decisions under sections 2036, 2037, and 2038. This history also explains why all three of these sections have some reference to either "possession" or "enjoyment" and why the courts will occasionally stress these terms in their decisions.

Section 2036, in general, includes within the estate two types of transfers: (1) those under which the transferor retains income from property for life; and (2) those under which the transferor retains the right for life to designate the persons who are to enjoy the transferred property or the income from it. Section 2036 is applicable where the decedent made a transfer for life, for a period that does not end before the decedent's death, or for a period that is not ascertainable without reference to the decedent's death. It does not apply if the decedent's transfer was a bona fide sale for an adequate and full consideration in money or money's worth. Needless to say, the statute is not so simple, and, as this chapter will reveal, section 2036, like much of the Code, has grown in complexity.

Two observations are in order before proceeding to learn more about this section. First, were it not for section 2036, avoidance of estate taxes would be child's play for all but a handful of the nation's wealthiest. For example, assume that an individual, upon reaching adulthood, established a trust under which she retained income for life with remainder to a class such as surviving issue per stirpes or heirs under a state intestate statute. Because of the donor's age, enormous discounts would be employed in determining the value of the taxable gift, the remainder interest transferred to the trust. A gift tax would then be imposed only on this amount. Moreover, the unified credit would certainly bar taxation of such gifts in all but a few cases. Furthermore, all subsequent appreciation of trust corpus would escape taxation and, absent section 2036, at death no estate tax would be due since section 2033, in the prevailing judicial environment, could hardly be expected to reach such property. Thus, it is apparent that the Treasury needs section 2036 if the estate tax is to be expected to be more than a leaky sieve for the legally sophisticated.

Second, the inclusion within the sweep of section 2036 of not only situations involving retained possession or enjoyment but also of the right to designate possession or enjoyment of property or income is indicative of the fact that Congress deems retention of this incident of ownership sufficient to warrant taxation. For the dynastically wealthy, riches provide more than mere personal pleasure. Vast material wealth, for example, brings with it the power to control the lives of others by granting or withholding the opportunity to participate in the enjoyment of that wealth.

B. SECTION 2036(a)(1)—RETAINED LIFE ESTATES

1. INFORMAL RESERVATIONS

It should come as no surprise that a donor will attempt to avoid the reach of section 2036 by making conveyances absolute on their face but with understandings that the donor will still reap some benefit, such as retaining rental income from or use of the property in question. For example, in Estate of McNichol v. Commissioner, 265 F.2d 667 (3d Cir.1959), a father conveyed rental property to his children pursuant to an oral understanding that he would continue to receive rents from the property during his life. Understandably, the court allowed the oral agreement to characterize the nature of the father's interest in the conveyed property and included the property in his estate under section 2036(a)(1). See also Estate of Stewart v. Commissioner, 617 F.3d 148 (2d Cir. 2010) (mother conveyed a co-ownership in rental units to son but continued to receive all rent). Where the donor transfers property to a limited partnership and makes gifts of interests in the partnership to family members but still collects income from the transferred property as if the donor was the sole owner or lives rent free in a residence contributed to the partnership, courts are able to infer the presence of an informal reservation of income and include the value of the transferred property in the donor's estate.

In addition, taxpayers attempt to structure transfers as bona fide sales for an adequate and full consideration. The following case addresses such an attempt.

ESTATE OF MAXWELL V. COMMISSIONER

United States Court of Appeals, Second Circuit, 1993.
3 F.3d 591.

LASKER, SENIOR DISTRICT JUDGE:

This appeal presents challenges to the tax court's interpretation of section 2036(a) of the Internal Revenue Code, relating to "Transfers with retained life estate." The petitioner, the Estate of Lydia G. Maxwell, contends that the tax court erred in holding that the transaction at issue (a) was a transfer with a retained life estate within the meaning of 26 U.S.C. § 2036 and (b) was not a bona fide sale for adequate and full consideration under that statute.

The decision of the tax court is affirmed.

I.

On March 14, 1984, Lydia G. Maxwell (the "decedent") conveyed her personal residence, which she had lived in since 1957, to her son Winslow Maxwell, her only heir, and his wife Margaret Jane Maxwell (the "Maxwells"). Following the transfer, the decedent continued to reside in the house until her death on July 30, 1986. At the time of the transfer, she was eighty-two years old and was suffering from cancer.

The transaction was structured as follows:

(1) The residence was sold by the decedent to the Maxwells for $270,000;[1]

(2) Simultaneously with the sale, the decedent forgave $20,000 of the purchase price (which was equal in amount to the annual gift tax exclusion to which she was entitled);

(3) The Maxwells executed a $250,000 mortgage note in favor of decedent;

(4) The Maxwells leased the premises to her for five years at the monthly rental of $1800; and

(5) The Maxwells were obligated to pay and did pay certain expenses associated with the property following the transfer, including property taxes, insurance costs, and unspecified "other expenses."

While the decedent paid the Maxwells rent totaling $16,200 in 1984, $22,183 in 1985 and $12,600 in 1986, the Maxwells paid the decedent

---

[1] The parties have stipulated that the fair market value of the property on the date of the purported sale was $280,000.

interest on the mortgage totaling $16,875 in 1984, $21,150 in 1985, and $11,475 in 1986. As can be observed, the rent paid by the decedent to the Maxwells came remarkably close to matching the mortgage interest which they paid to her. In 1984, she paid the Maxwells only $675 less than they paid her; in 1985, she paid them only $1,033 more than they paid her, and in 1986 she paid the Maxwells only $1,125 more than they paid her.

Not only did the rent functionally cancel out the interest payments made by the Maxwells, but the Maxwells were at no time called upon to pay any of the principal on the $250,000 mortgage debt; it was forgiven in its entirety. As petitioner's counsel admitted at oral argument, although the Maxwells had executed the mortgage note, "there was an intention by and large that it not be paid." Pursuant to this intention, in each of the following years preceding her death, the decedent forgave $20,000 of the mortgage principal, and, by a provision of her will executed on March 16, 1984 (that is, just two days after the transfer), she forgave the remaining indebtedness.

The decedent reported the sale of her residence on her 1984 federal income tax return but did not pay any tax on the sale because she elected to use the once-in-a-lifetime exclusion on the sale or exchange of a principal residence provided for by 26 U.S.C. § 121.

She continued to occupy the house by herself until her death. At no time during her occupancy did the Maxwells attempt to sell the house to anyone else, but, on September 22, 1986, shortly after the decedent's death, they did sell the house for $550,000.

Under I.R.C. § 2036(a), where property is disposed of by a decedent during her lifetime but the decedent retains "possession or enjoyment" of it until her death, that property is taxable as part of the decedent's gross estate, unless the transfer was a bona fide sale for an "adequate and full" consideration. 26 U.S.C. § 2036.

* * *

There are two questions before us: Did the decedent retain possession or enjoyment of the property following the transfer. And if she did, was the transfer a bona fide sale for an adequate and full consideration in money or money's worth.

II.

Section 2036(a) provides in pertinent part:

The value of the gross estate shall include the value of all property to the extent of any interest therein of which the decedent has at any time made a transfer (except in case of a bona fide sale for an adequate and full consideration in money or money's worth), by trust or otherwise, under which he has retained for his life or for any period not ascertainable without reference to his death or for any period which does not in fact end before his death—

(1)   the possession or enjoyment of, or the right to the income from, the property, . . .

26 U.S.C. § 2036(a). In the case of real property, the terms "possession" and "enjoyment" have been interpreted to mean "the lifetime use of the property." United States v. Byrum, 408 U.S. 125, 147 (1972).

In numerous cases, the tax court has held, where an aged family member transferred her home to a relative and continued to reside there until her death, that the decedent-transferor had retained "possession or enjoyment" of the property within the meaning of § 2036. * * *

[T]he tax court found as a fact that the decedent had transferred her home to the Maxwells "with the understanding, at least implied, that she would continue to reside in her home until her death." This finding was based upon the decedent's advanced age, her medical condition, and the overall result of the sale and lease. The lease was, in the tax court's words, "merely window dressing"—it had no substance.

* * *

[The tax] court held, on the basis of all the facts described above, that the decedent's use of the house following the transfer depended not on the lease but rather on an implied agreement between the parties that the decedent could and would continue to reside in the house until her death, as she actually did. It found that the lease "represented nothing more than an attempt to add color to the characterization of the transaction as a bona fide sale." The tax court did not rely on the tenancy alone to establish "possession or enjoyment."

Just as petitioner argues that the decedent's tenancy alone does not justify inclusion of the residence in her estate, so it argues that the decedent's payment of rent sanctifies the transaction and renders it legitimate. Both arguments ignore the realities of the rent being offset by mortgage interest, the forgiveness of the entire mortgage debt either by gift or testamentary disposition, and the fact that the decedent was eighty-two at the time of the transfer and actually continued to live in the residence until her death which, at the time of the transfer, she had reason to believe would occur soon in view of her poor health.

The Estate relies primarily on Barlow v. Commissioner, 55 T.C. 666 (1971). In that case, the father transferred a farm to his children and simultaneously leased the right to continue to farm the property. The tax court held that the father did not retain "possession or enjoyment," stating that "one of the most valuable incidents of income-producing real estate is the rent which it yields. He who receives the rent in fact enjoys the property."

Barlow, 55 T.C. at 671 (quoting McNichol's v. Commissioner, 265 F.2d 667, 671 (3d Cir.), cert. denied, 361 U.S. 829 (1959)). However, *Barlow* is clearly distinguishable on its facts: In that case, there was evidence that the rent paid was fair and customary and, equally importantly, the rent paid was not offset by the decedent's receipt of interest from the family lessor.

* * *

For the reasons stated above, we conclude that the decedent did retain possession or enjoyment of the property for life and turn to the question of whether the transfer constituted "a bona fide sale for adequate and full consideration in money or money's worth."

III.

Section 2036(a) provides that even if possession or enjoyment of transferred property is retained by the decedent until her death, if the transfer was a bona fide sale for adequate and full consideration in money or money's worth, the property is not includible in the estate. Petitioner contends that the Maxwells paid an "adequate and full consideration" for the decedent's residence, $270,000 total, consisting of the $250,000 mortgage note given by the Maxwells to the decedent, and the $20,000 the decedent forgave simultaneously with the conveyance.[3]

The tax court held that neither the Maxwells' mortgage note nor the decedent's $20,000 forgiveness constituted consideration within the meaning of the statute.

$250,000 Mortgage Note

As to the $250,000 mortgage note, the tax court held that:

Regardless of whether the $250,000 mortgage note might otherwise qualify as "adequate and full consideration in money or money's worth" for a $270,000 or $280,000 house, the mortgage note here had no value at all if there was no intention that it would ever be paid.

The conduct of decedent and the Maxwells strongly suggest that neither party intended the Maxwells to pay any part of the principal of either the original note or any successor note.

---

[3] As noted above, the parties have stipulated that the fair market value of the property on the date of the purported sale was $280,000. The Estate contends that $270,000 was full and adequate consideration for the sale, with a broker, for a house appraised at $280,000. We assume this fact to be true for purposes of determining whether the transaction was one for "an adequate and full consideration in money or money's worth."

There is no question that the mortgage note here is a fully secured, legally enforceable obligation on its face. The question is whether it is actually what it purports to be—a bona fide instrument of indebtedness—or whether it is a facade. The petitioner argues not only that an allegedly unenforceable intention to forgive indebtedness does not deprive the indebtedness of its status as "consideration in money or money's worth" but also that "[t]his is true even if there was an implied agreement exactly as found by the Tax Court." (Petitioner's Memorandum of Law at 3).

We agree with the tax court that where, as here, there is an implied agreement between the parties that the grantee would never be called upon to make any payment to the grantor, as, in fact, actually occurred, the note given by the grantee had "no value at all." We emphatically disagree with the petitioner's view of the law as it applies to the facts of this case. As the Supreme Court has remarked,

> the family relationship often makes it possible for one to shift tax incidence by surface changes of ownership without disturbing in the least his dominion and control over the subject of the gift or the purposes for which the income from the property is used.

Commissioner v. Culbertson, 337 U.S. 733, 746 (1949). There can be no doubt that intent is a relevant inquiry in determining whether a transaction is "bona fide." As another panel of this Court held recently, construing a parallel provision of the Internal Revenue Code, in a case involving an intrafamily transfer:

> when the bona fides of promissory notes is at issue, the taxpayer must demonstrate affirmatively that "there existed at the time of the transaction a real expectation of repayment and an intent to enforce the collection of the indebtedness." Estate of Van Anda v. Commissioner, 12 T.C. 1158, 1162 (1949), aff'd per curiam, 192 F.2d 391 (2d Cir.1951). See also Estate of Labombarde v. Commissioner, 58 T.C. 745, 754–55 (1972), aff'd, 502 F.2d 1158 (1st Cir.1973).

Flandreau v. Commissioner, [994 F.2d 91, 93 (2d Cir.1993)] (case involving I.R.C. § 2053(c)(1)). In language strikingly apposite to the situation here, the court stated:

> it is appropriate to look beyond the form of the transactions and to determine, as the tax court did here, that the gifts and loans back to decedent were "component parts of single transactions."

Id. (citation omitted).

The tax court concluded that the evidence "viewed as a whole" left the "unmistakable impression" that regardless of how long decedent lived following the transfer of her house, the entire principal balance of the mortgage note would be forgiven, and the Maxwells would not be required to pay any of such principal.

Id.

The petitioner's reliance on Haygood v. Commissioner, 42 T.C. 936 (1964), not followed by Rev. Rul. 77–299, 1977–2 CB 343 (1977), Kelley v. Commissioner, 63 T.C. 321 (1974), not followed by Rev. Rul. 77–299, 1977–2 C.B. 343 (1977), and Wilson v. Commissioner, 64 T.C.M. (CCH) 583 (1992),[4] is misplaced. Those cases held only that intent to forgive notes in the future does not *per se* disqualify such notes from constituting valid consideration. In contrast, in the case at hand, the decedent did far more than merely "indicate[ ] an intent to forgive the indebtedness in the future." *Wilson*, 64 T.C.M. (CCH) 583, 584 (1992).

In *Haygood*, *Kelley*, and *Wilson*, the question was whether transfers of property by petitioners to their children or grandchildren in exchange for notes were completed gifts within the meaning of the Internal Revenue Code. None of the notes was actually paid by the grantees; instead the notes were either forgiven by petitioners at or about the time they became due (*Haygood* and *Kelley*) or the petitioner died prior to the date when the note was due (*Wilson*). In those circumstances, the tax court held that the notes received by petitioners, secured by valid vendor's liens or by deeds of trust on the property, constituted valuable consideration for the transfer of the property.

The *Kelley* court made no finding as to intent to forgive the notes. In *Haygood*, although the court did find that the "petitioner had no intention of collecting the debts but did intend to forgive each payment as it became due," it also found that the transfer of the property to the children had been a mistake.[5] And, the *Wilson* court found that:

> The uncontradicted testimony in this case establishes that petitioner and her children intended that the children would sell the property and pay the note with the proceeds.

Wilson, 64 T.C.M. (CCH) at 584.

By contrast, in the case at hand, the tax court found that, at the time the note was executed, there was "an understanding" between the Maxwells and the decedent that the note would be forgiven.

---

[4] Apart from all of the other distinctions outlined below, *Wilson* is not a tax court opinion but a tax court memorandum; moreover, the decision in *Wilson* succeeded the Tax Court decision in this case.

[5] The court stated that it was "eminently clear from the testimony that it was petitioner's intent to give only a $3,000 interest [in the property] to each of her sons" that year but her lawyer accidentally structured the transaction to give the entire property to the petitioner's sons. Haygood v. Commissioner, 42 T.C. 936, 942 (1964).

In our judgment, the conduct of decedent and the Maxwells with respect to the principal balance of the note, when viewed in connection with the initial "forgiveness" of $20,000 of the purported purchase price, strongly suggests the existence of an understanding between decedent and the Maxwells that decedent would forgive $20,000 each year thereafter until her death, when the balance would be forgiven by decedent's will.

If *Haygood* is read as holding that the intent to forgive notes has no effect on the question of whether the notes constitute valid consideration, it appears to be inconsistent with controlling tax principles and tax court decisions. For example, in Deal v. Commissioner, 29 T.C. 730 (1958),[6] the tax court held that the notes executed by the children were not intended as consideration for the transfer, holding that:

> After carefully considering the record, we think that the notes executed by the daughters were not intended to be enforced and were not intended as consideration for the transfer by the petitioner, and that, in substance, the transfer of the property was by gift.

29 T.C. at 746, quoted by *Haygood*. See also Rev. Rul. 77–299, 1977–2 C.B. 343 (1977). Even *Kelley* stated that notes "in proper legal form and regular on their face" are only "prima facie" what they purport to be. *Kelley*, 63 T.C. at 324–25.

$20,000 Initial Forgiveness

We also agree with the tax court that, as to the $20,000 which was forgiven simultaneously with the conveyance,

> In the absence of any clear and direct evidence that there existed an obligation or indebtedness capable of being forgiven . . .

the $20,000 item had "no economic substance."

To conclude, we hold that the conveyance was not a bona fide sale for an adequate and full consideration in money or money's worth.

* * *

Section 2043

The petitioner argues finally that the tax court should be reversed because, under 26 U.S.C. § 2043, if there was any consideration in money

---

[6]   *Deal* involved a conveyance by the taxpayer of a remainder interest in real property to a trust for the benefit of her four daughters. The taxpayer forgave a $3,000 portion of each note to each daughter in the year of the transfer of the property, and a similar portion of each note in the two subsequent years, and the remaining balance of the note in the following year. The tax court held that the taxpayer had made a gift of the remainder interest to the children.

The petitioner claims that *Deal* "may have been wrongly decided." However, *Deal* is still good law. Although *Haygood* reached a different conclusion, the court was careful not to overrule *Deal* but to distinguish it on its facts. Haygood v. Commissioner, 42 T.C. 936, 944 (1964).

or money's worth paid to the decedent, even if the payment was inadequate, the Estate is at least entitled to an exclusion pro tanto. The argument has no merit in the circumstances of this case. The tax court held, and we do also, that the transfer was without *any* consideration. Section 2043 applies only where the court finds that some consideration was given.

The decision of the tax court is affirmed.

NOTES

1. For years the Treasury attacked informal arrangements by which an individual conveyed legal title but continued to enjoy the property in fact. Thus, a husband may deed the house to his wife without any assurance that he will not be thrown out into the cold but without any expectation that it will happen. Is the house still includible in his gross estate? Should only a half be includible, even on the government's theory? The question has thus far produced several district court and Tax Court decisions— almost all rejecting the government's theory. See, e.g., Estate of Gutchess v. Commissioner, 46 T.C. 554 (1966), acq. 1967–1 C.B. 2. But, the Commissioner's acquiescence in *Gutchess* does not reach a parent's gift of the home to the children—at least where they do not move in with the parent. See Estate of Honigman v. Commissioner, 66 T.C. 1080 (1976) (where mother remained in the house after transfer, section 2036 applies by its terms); Rev. Rul. 78–409, 1978–2 C.B. 234 (where decedent lived in the house, it is taxable under section 2036 despite an absolute deed); Estate of Trotter, 82 T.C.M. (CCH) 633 (2001) (taxpayer deeded condo to trust for benefit of children and continued to live there paying only occupancy expenses, taxable under section 2036). But see Estate of Roemer v. Commissioner, 46 T.C.M. (CCH) 1176 (1983) (reviewing the "live together" cases and dealing the IRS a defeat in a situation in which a mother gave her house to her daughter who had lived with her for five years prior to the gift and the two remained together in the house after the gift).

    Somewhat related is Estate of Wyly v. Commissioner, 610 F.2d 1282 (5th Cir.1980). A gift by husband to wife of his community property does not result in the inclusion of one-half the gift in his taxable estate under section 2036 though Texas law treats income from separate property during marriage as community property. The fact that husband did not reserve any interest was of controlling importance. It was the local law that provided half ownership of income from the transferred interest.

2. In Rev. Rul. 79–109, 1979–1 C.B. 297, the IRS ruled that, where a parent conveyed a vacation home to children, expressly reserving the right to use the home for one month, only that portion of the value of the home represented by the retained use need be included in the estate. Although this might have been deemed an overly generous concession in another era, the result is hardly shocking to a Bar familiar with the concept of interval ownership. Although Rev. Rul. 79–109 involved an express

reservation, its embrace of segmented ownership has potential application in the area of informal reservations.

In Estate of Stewart v. Commissioner, 617 F.3d 148 (2d Cir. 2010), the court accepted the rationale of Rev. Rul. 79–109 to find divided ownership where a parent made a gift of a portion of a dwelling that she shared with her adult son, with the result that only her portion of the dwelling was included in her estate.

3.   In Estate of du Pont v. Commissioner, 63 T.C. 746 (1975), the Tax Court saw through a rather complicated manipulation involving formation of a corporation and transfer to the corporation of residential property with a leaseback at a substantially less than fair market value rent. The Tax Court found this to be a reserved life estate under section 2036.

2.   CONTINGENT RETAINED LIFE ESTATES

When a donor transfers the property to pay the income for life to the beneficiary and then to pay the income back to the donor if he is still living at the beneficiary's death, is such a transfer within the reach of the language of section 2036?

Consider the following extract from Commissioner v. Estate of Nathan, 159 F.2d 546 (7th Cir.1947), cert. denied, 334 U.S. 843 (1948):

> The doubt, if any exists in this case, is over the question, was the property which was transferred and in which deceased retained a contingent life interest, terminable by his death or by that of his sister? Stated differently, was the period during which his contingent estate therein existed ascertainable without reference to his death or did the period of the contingent estate which decedent retained in the trust he created have a possible ending before his death?

> Notwithstanding some doubt (in view of the discussion in the *Curie* case) we hold the language of the statute must be so construed as to impose an estate tax on the property covered by this trust less the value of the life estate of the sister. Our decision is not predicated on the Regulation [Treas. Reg. § 20.2036–1(a)]. It is made necessary by the statute which, without the Regulation, imposes the tax.

> The Commissioner could not have found or held otherwise. The transfer in which the deceased retained a contingent estate was held by him for a period which did not in fact end before his death. It was his death, not his sister's death, which terminated his contingent interest.

* * *

The factual difference between the instant case and the usual trust agreement which may be called testamentary has not been ignored. The decedent here retained only a contingent estate which became effective in case he survived his sister. Notwithstanding this rather important fact so far as enjoyment is concerned, it did not take the transfer out of the reach of the language of Section 811(c) [now section 2036] which controls our decision. We cannot lessen the effect or the meaning of the words because the settlor's interest was less certain or the enjoyment of the estate reserved more remote. We feel we must give the words used their fair, rightful meaning and we can not make them depend on the size or nature of the settlor's reservation appearing in his transfer. The vital test of said reservation in settlor's favor necessitates an answer to the query—was the transfer one which was for a period not ascertainable without reference to his death?

Id. at 548–49.

Further support for the view expressed in *Estate of Nathan* is found in the Report of the Conference Committee on the Revenue Act of 1949 (H.R. Report No. 1412, 81st Cong., 1st Sess., reported in 49–2 C.B. 300):

The expression "not ascertainable without reference to his death" as used in section 811(c)(1)(B) [now section 2036(a)] and elsewhere in the conference amendments includes the right to receive the income from transferred property after the death of another person who in fact survived the transferor; but in such a case the amount to be included under section 811(c)(1)(B) in the transferor's gross estate does not include the value of the outstanding income interest in such other person.

Consistent with the foregoing authorities is Regulation § 20.2036–1(a), which indicates that, where a donor has retained a contingent life estate in property, the estate is to include the full value of the property in question minus only the value of an income interest which precedes that of the donor and which is actually being enjoyed. A question arises as to whether this might not, on occasion, result in the inclusion in the estate of more value than is called for by section 2036. For example, assume that the donor had established a trust with income to his wife for her life, then to his son for the son's life, and then to himself for his life, with remainder to a granddaughter (or her estate). Under the regulations, at the donor's death only the value of the wife's life estate is subtracted from the value of the trust in determining the amount includible. Since the donor's death does not transfer anything of value to the son, it seems inappropriate also not to exclude the value of the son's contingent life estate. That result, however, is inconsistent with the regulations.

3. RECIPROCAL TRUSTS

Section 2036 includes within the estate only property that was the object of a "retained" life estate or power and does not include life estates given to the taxpayer by third parties. Consequently, taxpayers may attempt, with varying degrees of success, to avoid the reach of section 2036 by arranging for others to create or hold the critical interests.

Taxpayers and their counsel are inventive and often seem to underrate the IRS's capability for recognizing the substance of a transaction. Over the years a variety of unsuccessful attempts to disguise retained life estate transfers have perished in court. In a "reciprocal trust" device each of the parties (commonly spouses), creates a trust for the other with income for life to the other and remainder to third parties (typically children) subject perhaps to a power of appointment of some sort. The substance is that the result is precisely the same as though each grantor had created his or her own trust, which plainly would then be subject to section 2036. In the following case, the Supreme Court decided that such devices offered the taxpayer little salvation.

UNITED STATES v. ESTATE OF GRACE

Supreme Court of the United States, 1969.
395 U.S. 316.

MR. JUSTICE MARSHALL delivered the opinion of the Court.

This case involves the application of § 811(c)(1)(B) of the Internal Revenue Code of 1939 [1986 Code § 2036] to a so-called "reciprocal trust" situation. After Joseph P. Grace's death in 1950, the Commissioner of Internal Revenue determined that the value of a trust created by his wife was includible in his gross estate. A deficiency was assessed and paid, and, after denial of a claim for a refund, this refund suit was brought. The Court of Claims, with two judges dissenting, ruled that the value of the trust was not includible in decedent's estate under § 811(c)(1)(B) and entered judgment for respondent. * * *

Decedent was a very wealthy man at the time of his marriage to the late Janet Grace in 1908. Janet Grace had no wealth or property of her own, but, between 1908 and 1931, decedent transferred to her a large amount of personal and real property, including the family's Long Island estate. Decedent retained effective control over the family's business affairs, including the property transferred to his wife. She took no interest and no part in business affairs and relied upon her husband's judgment. Whenever some formal action was required regarding property in her name, decedent would have the appropriate instrument prepared and she would execute it.

On December 15, 1931, decedent executed a trust instrument, hereinafter called the Joseph Grace trust. Named as trustees were decedent, his nephew, and a third party. The trustees were directed to pay the income of the trust to Janet Grace during her lifetime, and to pay to her any part of the principal which a majority of the trustees might deem advisable. Janet was given the power to designate, by will or deed, the manner in which the trust estate remaining at her death was to be distributed among decedent and their children. The trust properties included securities and real estate interests.

On December 30, 1931, Janet Grace executed a trust instrument, hereinafter called the Janet Grace trust, which was virtually identical to the Joseph Grace trust. The trust properties included the family estate and corporate securities, all of which had been transferred to her by decedent in preceding years.

The trust instruments were prepared by one of decedent's employees in accordance with a plan devised by decedent to create additional trusts before the advent of a new gift tax expected to be enacted the next year. Decedent selected the properties to be included in each trust. Janet Grace, acting in accordance with this plan, executed her trust instrument at decedent's request.

Janet Grace died in 1937. The Joseph Grace trust terminated at her death. Her estate's federal estate tax return disclosed the Janet Grace trust and reported it as a nontaxable transfer by Janet Grace. The Commissioner asserted that the Janet and Joseph Grace trusts were "reciprocal" and asserted a deficiency to the extent of mutual value. Compromises on unrelated issues resulted in 55% of the smaller of the two trusts, the Janet Grace trust, being included in her gross estate.

Joseph Grace died in 1950. The federal estate tax return disclosed both trusts. The Joseph Grace trust was reported as a nontaxable transfer and the Janet Grace trust was reported as a trust under which decedent held a limited power of appointment. Neither trust was included in decedent's gross estate.

The Commissioner determined that the Joseph and Janet Grace trusts were "reciprocal" and included the amount of the Janet Grace trust in decedent's gross estate. A deficiency in the amount of $363,500.97, plus interest, was assessed and paid.

* * *

The doctrine of reciprocal trusts was formulated in response to attempts to draft instruments which seemingly avoid the literal terms of § 811(c)(1)(B) [now § 2036], while still leaving the decedent the lifetime enjoyment of his property. The doctrine dates from Lehman v. Commissioner, 109 F.2d 99 (C.A. 2d Cir.), cert. denied, 310 U.S. 637 (1940).

In *Lehman*, decedent and his brother owned equal shares in certain stocks and bonds. Each brother placed his interest in trust for the other's benefit for life, with remainder to the life tenant's issue. Each brother also gave the other the right to withdraw $150,000 of the principal. If the brothers had each reserved the right to withdraw $150,000 from the trust that each had created, the trusts would have been includible in their gross estates as interests of which each had made a transfer with a power to revoke. When one of the brothers died, his estate argued that neither trust was includible because the decedent did not have a power over a trust which he had created.

The Second Circuit disagreed. That court ruled that the effect of the transfers was the same as if the decedent had transferred his stock in trust for himself, remainder to his issue, and had reserved the right to withdraw $150,000. The court reasoned:

> "The fact that the trusts were reciprocated or 'crossed' is a trifle, quite lacking in practical or legal significance. . . . The law searches out the reality and is not concerned with the form." 109 F.2d, at 100.

The court ruled that the decisive point was that each brother caused the other to make a transfer by establishing his own trust.

The doctrine of reciprocal trusts has been applied numerous times since the *Lehman* decision. It received congressional approval in § 6 of the Technical Changes Act of 1949, 63 Stat. 893. The present case is, however, this Court's first examination of the doctrine.

The Court of Claims was divided over the requirements for application of the doctrine to the situation of this case. Relying on some language in *Lehman* and certain other courts of appeals' decisions, the majority held that the crucial factor was whether the decedent had established his trust as consideration for the establishment of the trust of which he was a beneficiary. The court ruled that decedent had not established his trust as a *quid pro quo* for the Janet Grace trust, and that Janet Grace had not established her trust in exchange for the Joseph Grace trust. Rather, the trusts were found to be part of an established pattern of family giving, with neither party desiring to obtain property from the other. Indeed, the court found that Janet Grace had created her trust because decedent requested that she do so. It therefore found the reciprocal trust doctrine inapplicable.

The court recognized that certain cases had established a slightly different test for reciprocity. Those cases inferred consideration from the establishment of two similar trusts at about the same time. The court held that any inference of consideration was rebutted by the evidence in the case, particularly the lack of any evidence of an estate tax avoidance motive on the part of the Graces. In contrast, the dissent felt that the majority's approach placed entirely too much weight on subjective intent. Once it was established that the trusts were interrelated, the dissent felt that the subjective intent of the parties in establishing the trusts should become irrelevant. The relevant factor was whether the trusts created by the settlors placed each other in approximately the same objective economic position as they would have been in if each had created his own trust with himself, rather than the other, as life beneficiary.

We agree with the dissent that the approach of the Court of Claims majority places too much emphasis on the subjective intent of the parties in creating the trusts and for that reason hinders proper application of the federal estate tax laws. It is true that there is language in *Lehman* and other cases that would seem to support the majority's approach. It is also true that the results in some of those cases arguably support the decision below. Nevertheless, we think that these cases are not in accord with this Court's prior decisions interpreting related provisions of the federal estate tax laws.

Emphasis on the subjective intent of the parties in creating the trusts, particularly when those parties are members of the same family unit, creates substantial obstacles to the proper application of the federal estate tax laws. As this Court said in Estate of Spiegel v. Commissioner, 335 U.S. 701, 705–706 (1949):

> "Any requirement . . . [of] a post-death attempt to probe the settlor's thoughts in regard to the transfer, would partially impair the effectiveness of . . . [section 811(c)] as an instrument to frustrate estate tax evasions."

We agree that "the taxability of a trust corpus . . . does not hinge on a settlor's motives, but depends on the nature and operative effect of the trust transfer." Id., at 705.

We think these observations have particular weight when applied to the reciprocal trust situation. First, inquiries into subjective intent, especially in intrafamily transfers, are particularly perilous. The present case illustrates that it is, practically speaking, impossible to determine after the death of the parties what they had in mind in creating trusts over 30 years earlier. Second, there is a high probability that such a trust arrangement was indeed created for tax-avoidance purposes. And, even if there was no estate-tax-avoidance motive, the settlor in a very real and objective sense did retain an economic interest while purporting to give away his property. Finally, it is unrealistic to assume that the settlors of the trusts, usually members of one family unit, will have created their trusts as a bargained-for exchange for the other trust. "Consideration," in the traditional legal sense, simply does not normally enter into such intrafamily transfers.

For these reasons, we hold that application of the reciprocal trust doctrine is not dependent upon a finding that each trust was created as a *quid pro quo* for the other. Such a "consideration" requirement necessarily involves a difficult inquiry into the subjective intent of the settlors. Nor do we think it necessary to prove the existence of a tax-avoidance motive. As we have said above, standards of this sort, which rely on subjective factors, are rarely workable under the federal estate tax laws. Rather, we hold that application of the reciprocal trust doctrine requires only that the trusts be interrelated, and that the arrangement, to the extent of mutual value, leaves the settlors in approximately the same economic position as they would have been in had they created trusts naming themselves as life beneficiaries.

Applying this test to the present case, we think it clear that the value of the Janet Grace trust fund must be included in decedent's estate for federal estate tax purposes. It is undisputed that the two trusts are interrelated. They are substantially identical in terms and were created at approximately the same time. Indeed, they were part of a single transaction designed and carried out by decedent. It is also clear that the transfers in trust left each party, to the extent of mutual value, in the same objective economic position as before. Indeed, it appears, as would be expected in transfers between husband and wife, that the effective position of each party *vis-a-vis* the property did not change at all. It is no answer that the transferred properties were different in character. For purposes of the estate tax, we think that economic value is the only workable criterion. Joseph Grace's estate remained undiminished to the extent of the value of his wife's trust and the value of his estate must accordingly be increased by the value of that trust.

The judgment of the Court of Claims is reversed and the case is remanded for further proceedings consistent with this opinion.

It is so ordered.

NOTES

1. In Estate of Levy v. Commissioner, 46 T.C.M. (CCH) 910 (1983), the Tax Court declined to apply the "reciprocal trust" doctrine on the ground that a special power to appoint either the income or the corpus of the trust established by the husband for the wife with no such power in the wife's trust for the husband meant that the trusts were so substantially different as to preclude the operation of the doctrine. Consistent with this approach is Private Letter Ruling 9643013 in which the IRS ruled that the reciprocal trust doctrine did not apply to a situation in which a husband and wife each established trusts which were not mirror images of the other. Each of the trusts named the couple's children as beneficiaries, but one of the trusts also named the donor's spouse as a beneficiary. Moreover, the two trusts varied somewhat in vesting special powers of appointment in different parties with the holder in one case being an independent party. See also Priv. Ltr. Rul. 200426008.

2. In Revenue Ruling 74–533, 1974–2 C.B. 293, the IRS confronted the issue of the proper amount to be included in the estate where parties establish reciprocal trusts of different value. A husband transferred $400,000 to a trust with income to his wife for her life, remainder to their issue. The wife, on the same day, contributed $300,000 to a trust with income to her husband for his life, remainder to their issue. At the husband's death more than 10 years later, the principal of the trust established by the wife had grown from $300,000 to $500,000 and was paid over to the children at that moment. The value of the trust established by the husband had grown from $400,000 to $600,000 by the time the wife died six months after her husband. The IRS indicated that, since it deemed the trusts to be reciprocal trusts, at the husband's death it was appropriate to include in his estate the full value of the $500,000 principal of the trust established by his wife. However, since only three-quarters of the $400,000 trust that the husband established for the wife's benefit could be deemed to have been established in exchange for the $300,000 trust that wife established for her husband, only three-quarters of its value at the wife's death, or $450,000, should be included in the wife's estate at her death.

4. SUPPORT OF DEPENDENTS AND OTHER BENEFICIAL RETENTIONS

a. Basic Parameters of the Problem

As the regulations make clear, the retention of income in a form that assures that it will be used to meet the legal obligations of the transferor, such as to pay the transferor's taxes or grocery bills, is surely a retention of the income by the transferor. Suppose the relation between the prescribed use of the income and the legal obligation of the transferor is not so clear? In Hays' Estate v. Commissioner, 181 F.2d 169 (5th Cir. 1950), the decedent transferred mortgaged property in trust and provided that the trust income should be used to retire the mortgage on which the decedent was personally liable. To the government's claim that this amounted to a retention of the income by the decedent, the court responded in part as follows:

> The indebtedness secured by liens on the land conveyed by decedent to the trust, although originally incurred by her, constituted no charge upon her capital assets after the conveyance. Thereafter, the decedent's liability for said indebtedness was contingent, not only upon the failure of the trust to pay the same, but upon the existence of a deficiency after a foreclosure sale of the land and the application of the proceeds of the sale to the payment of the indebtedness. The possibility of decedent's liability for said debts was so remote that her direction that the trust pay the same did not constitute a reservation of income by her from the land conveyed in trust. Such possibility of

liability was too remote to come within the meaning of the statute. 26 U.S.C.A. § 811(d)(1) [now I.R.C. § 2036(a)].

* * *

It is not a general or indefinite benefit but a pecuniary benefit that is necessary for a transaction to constitute a reservation of income, and in this case no pecuniary benefit resulted to the decedent by the trustee's payment of the mortgage notes. A pecuniary benefit means an increase in one's net worth by the receipt of money or property. The payment of the mortgage notes did not and could not increase the decedent's net worth; she received no money; she received no property; none of her property was thereby enhanced in value or released from liens or encumbrances. The payment of the mortgage debts resulted in pecuniary benefit to the trust alone, in that the net worth of its land was increased to the extent of the payments made. There was no legal obligation upon the decedent to discharge this debt except in case of a deficiency being due after there had been a sale of the land upon foreclosure of the mortgage.[1]

b. Support of Dependents

Regulation § 20.2036–1(b)(2) states that a decedent is considered to have retained use, possession, right to the income, or other enjoyment of transferred property to the extent that it is used to discharge the decedent's legal obligation. Since state law imposes an obligation on parents to support their minor children, it should come as no surprise that the IRS views trusts established by parents to support their minor children includible under section 2036(a)(1).

ESTATE OF CHRYSLER V. COMMISSIONER

Tax Court of the United States, 1965.
44 T.C. 55.

ARUNDELL, JUDGE:

* * *

By trust indenture dated June 16, 1945, under which Nicholas Kelley, John W. Drye, Jr., and Harry C. Davis were trustees, decedent created an irrevocable trust for the benefit for life of his daughter, Helen F. Chrysler, who was born on February 2, 1944.

By trust indenture dated December 6, 1946, under which Nicholas Kelley, John W. Drye, Jr., and Harry C. Davis were trustees, decedent

---

[1] Id. at 171.

created an irrevocable trust for the benefit for life of his son Jack F. Chrysler, Jr., who was born on May 31, 1946.

The provisions of each trust were identical in all material respects except for the language necessary to make one trust pertain to the decedent's infant daughter and the other trust to his infant son. The corpus of each trust was $115,000 in cash. The trust for the daughter provided in part:

> 1. A. The Trustees shall hold, manage, invest and from time to time reinvest the trust estate and shall collect the income therefrom and shall pay over the net annual income therefrom to Helen Forker Chrysler, daughter of the Grantor, during her life; provided, however, that as long as Helen Forker Chrysler shall be a minor, the Trustees shall use and apply so much of the net annual income and any accumulated income of the trust estate as the Trustees shall deem advisable for the maintenance, education and support of said Helen Forker Chrysler; or instead of making personal application of such income, the Trustees may transfer, assign and pay over so much of such income as they deem advisable to either parent or the guardian of the person or property of said Helen Forker Chrysler, or the person with whom she resides, to be by such parent, guardian or person so used and applied (and the receipt of such parent, guardian or person shall be full acquittance and discharge to the Trustees in respect of any such sum or sums so paid over, and the Trustees shall have no duty or responsibility in supervising the application of any such income) and the Trustees shall accumulate the balance of such income during the minority of said Helen Forker Chrysler, and upon her attaining the age of twenty-one years, the Trustees shall transfer, assign and pay over to her all accumulations of income on the trust estate; or if said Helen Forker Chrysler shall die before attaining the age of twenty-one years, all accumulations of income on the trust estate shall be transferred, assigned and paid over to the executor or administrator of the estate of said Helen Forker Chrysler.

> In the management, administration and investment of any accumulated income, the Trustees shall have all the powers, authority and discretion given to them with respect to the trust estate by any provisions of this trust indenture.

Each trust provided for the complete disposition of the remainder after the termination of the respective life estate.

The fair market value on November 7, 1958, of the principal of each of the two trusts was $534,920.37 and $698,120.83, respectively, which amounts were included in the decedent's gross estate as items 2 and 3, respectively.

Decedent was never a trustee under either trust. None of the income of either trust collected by the trustees was used for the maintenance, education or support of the respective beneficiary during decedent's lifetime and all such income of both trusts was taxed to the trustees and the net income of both trusts was accumulated by them.

* * *

Respondent contends that the values of the corpora of the two trusts (items 2 and 3) created by decedent on June 16, 1945, and December 6, 1946, are includable in the decedent's gross estate under the provisions of section 2036(a), I.R.C. 1954. In so contending, the respondent, in effect *assumes* that the two trusts were created for the maintenance, education and support of his two minor children. In his brief he argues thus:

> Decedent established each of the trusts shortly after the respective births of his two children. The purpose for which the trusts were created was for the maintenance, education and support of his children. These trusts were an effective instrumentality through which the decedent could discharge his legal obligation to support his children. Since both of decedent's children were minors at the date of decedent's death, decedent was under a duty imposed by law to support them (Sec. 32, Domestic Relations Law of New York). Decedent could have availed himself at any time until his death to have the income applied for the support of his children.

The above argument, except for the part that decedent was under a duty imposed by law to support his minor children, is not supported by the facts. Decedent could *not* have availed himself at any time until his death of having the income applied for the support of his children. This could only be done in the discretion of the three trustees. Decedent was not one of the trustees. The trusts were irrevocable. They created life estates with remainders over. When decedent created the trusts he parted forever with all right to the income or principal of the trusts, or the right, either alone or in conjunction with any person, to designate the persons who shall possess or enjoy the property or the income therefrom.

The facts in the cases principally relied upon by the respondent involve facts entirely different from the facts in the instant case. In the first case cited in the footnote the decedent there created a trust, the income of which was payable to his wife with the provision that she should use it for their family and joint living expenses and for her own maintenance and support. In Commissioner v. Dwight's Estate, 205 F.2d 298 (C.A.2, 1953), reversing and remanding 17 T.C. 1317, the husband decedent had created two trusts to pay the income to his wife and children for their "support and maintenance." And in Estate of William H. Lee, 33 T.C. 1064, our syllabus is as follows:

> *Held*: Decedent, in making transfers of property in trust with income to be paid to his wife "for her maintenance and support," retained the right to have the income used to fulfill his legal obligation of support, and the trust corpus is to be included in the valuation of his gross estate. Commissioner v. Dwight's Estate, 205 F.2d 298 (C.A.2), followed.

In the instant case, the decedent could not direct the trustees to apply any of the income for the maintenance, education and support of the minor beneficiaries. Sole discretion as to whether any income of the trusts was to be so applied rested and remained in the trustees. The trust instruments specifically provided that only "so much" of such income "as the Trustees shall deem advisable" shall be so used, and the balance accumulated.

We think the facts in the instant case are more like those in Commissioner v. Douglass' Estate, 143 F.2d 961 (C.A.3, 1944), affirming 2 T.C. 487, cited and relied upon by petitioner. The decedent in that case created a trust for the benefit of his four children. Neither decedent nor any of the beneficiaries was among the three trustees named. Decedent died in 1938. In the trust instrument decedent gave the trustees permission to apply the income of the minor's share to the extent that the trustees "may deem necessary for the education, support and maintenance of said minor." In denying the Commissioner's claim that one-fourth of the value of the principal of the trust was to be included in the decedent's gross estate, the court said in part:

> In addition to the theory thus advanced the Commissioner's argument cites Helvering v. Mercantile-Commerce Bank & Trust Co. et al., 8 Cir., 111 F.2d 224, certiorari denied, 1940, 310 U.S. 654. This involved a trust for a wife created by a husband in his lifetime. The income was to be paid to her for family expenses and her own maintenance and support. The Eighth Circuit held that the corpus of the trust was to be included as part of his estate for estate tax purposes. The decision is, obviously, not an authority on the question before us in this litigation. *There is certainly an important difference of fact between the trust set up for the very purpose of providing for the settlor's legal obligation to his wife and the one in which disinterested trustees have an option to apply a portion of the income for the support of the settlor's minor child.*

Under the section of the estate tax law already quoted, the settlor's estate is subject to the tax if he retained the possession or enjoyment of the income from the property or the right to designate the persons who should enjoy it. But he did neither. *He granted the property to trustees, retaining nothing.* The Commissioner's argument that these trustees would be likely to do what he asked of them about assigning income for the support of a minor child departs from the "practical" and "realistic" approach we are asked, in the same argument, to take. We have no notion what the trustees would have done had such a request been made. *It is apparent, from the terms of the instrument, that the settlor could not direct or control the matter, once the trust settlement had become effective.* [Emphasis supplied.]

We hold that the respondent erred in including items 2 and 3 in the decedent's gross estate.

PLANNING NOTE

If a donor establishes a trust like the trust in *Chrysler* and makes herself or himself the trustee with discretionary disbursement powers, such trust will, of course, be included in the donor's estate under section 2036. The key to *Chrysler* rests in granting discretion to a third party.

The trust in *Chrysler* was prepared by what, at the time, were some of the nation's best estate planners. If a responsive third-party trustee is selected, the granting of discretion to that trustee to make disbursements to income beneficiaries who are minor issue of the settlor and whom the settlor is obliged to support provides an excellent means whereby the corpus of the trust can be put beyond the reaches of section 2036. Care must be taken, however, to avoid the reciprocal trust doctrine. The dynastically wealthy should have little interest in this device since, in such families, settlors seldom would wish, or need, to have trust resources used to satisfy their support obligations. Among the "marginal millionaire" crowd, the device used in *Chrysler* should have strong appeal.

The case that follows demonstrates the degree to which care must be exercised when trying to squeeze through the opening given to the taxpayer by *Chrysler.*

ESTATE OF GOKEY v. COMMISSIONER

Tax Court of the United States, 1979.
72 T.C. 721, aff'd in part and rev'd in part, 735 F.2d 1367 (7th Cir.1984).

WILES, JUDGE:

[The deceased, Joseph Gokey, on October 1, 1961, established three trusts, one each for the benefit of his then minor children, Bridget, Gretchen and Patrick. He then also created a trust for the benefit of his wife, Mildred. Under the terms of her trust she was to receive income for her life and the trustee was vested with discretion to invade corpus for her care, comfort, support or welfare. On her death, the corpus of that trust was to be distributed equally to the three trusts established for the benefit of the children. The trusts for benefit of the children each contained the following provision:]

Section 2: Until each beneficiary becomes twenty-one (21) years of age, the Trustee shall use such part or all of the net income of his or her trust for the support, care, welfare, and education of the beneficiary thereof, payments from such net income to be made to such beneficiary or in such other manner as the Trustee deems to be in the best interest of the beneficiary, and any unused income shall be accumulated and added to the principal of such beneficiary's trust. After each beneficiary becomes twenty-one (21) years of age, the Trustee shall pay to him or her, in convenient installments, the entire net income of his or her trust. In the Trustee's discretion, said income payments may be supplemented at any time with payments of principal from a beneficiary's share whenever the Trustee deems any such payments necessary for the support, care, welfare, or education of the beneficiary thereof.

[The decedent died on October 20, 1969. Bridget had reached majority so no effort was made to effect an inclusion under her trust. Gretchen and Patrick were then 15 and 13 years old, respectively. The Commissioner sought to include the full value of their trusts, $797,583.66. On the theory that if Gretchen's and Patrick's trusts were deemed to satisfy Joseph's support obligation with respect to them, the Commissioner sought to include in Joseph's taxable estate the value of their remainder interests in their mother's trust. His theory for doing so was that Joseph, through Gretchen's and Patrick's trusts, had retained a contingent life estate (satisfaction of his support obligation with respect to Gretchen and Patrick) in this trust subject to Mildred's life estate which was presently being enjoyed.]

The first issue is whether decedent retained the possession or enjoyment of, or the right to the income from, property transferred by him to irrevocable trusts for the benefit of Gretchen and Patrick. If so, the value of the property in those trusts is properly includable in decedent's gross estate under section 2036. The resolution of this issue depends upon whether, within the meaning of section 20.2036–1(b)(2), Estate Tax Regs., the income or property of the trusts was to be applied toward the discharge of the decedent's legal obligation to support Gretchen and Patrick during his lifetime.

Respondent contends that under Illinois law, decedent was under a legal duty to support his minor children, Gretchen and Patrick; that the terms of the children's trusts clearly require the trustees to use the trusts' income and property for their support; and that, therefore, the value of the trust property is includable in decedent's gross estate.

Petitioners do not dispute decedent's obligation to support Gretchen and Patrick under Illinois law; however, they contend that the use of the property or income therefrom for the children's support was within the unrestricted discretion of the trustees; that even if trusts did not give the trustees any discretion in this matter, the decedent nevertheless intended to grant them this discretion; that the use of the term "welfare" in the trusts creates an unascertainable standard which, even if ascertainable, is much broader than the standard for support; and that, therefore, the value of the trust property is not includable in decedent's gross estate. We agree with respondent on this issue.

Respondent relies upon section 20.2036–1(b)(2), Estate Tax Regs., which states that the use, possession, right to the income, or other enjoyment of the transferred property is considered as having been retained by or reserved to the decedent within the meaning of section 2036(a)(1) to the extent that the use, possession, right to the income, or other enjoyment *is to be applied* toward the discharge of a legal obligation of decedent which includes an obligation to support a dependent. "Is to be applied" is not to be read as "may be applied," which exists where an independent trustee is vested with discretion over distributions. Estate of Mitchell v. Commissioner, 55 T.C. 576, 580 (1970). This creates a factual question as to whether the income from the trust property must be restricted or confined to fulfilling the settlor's obligation to support his dependents. Estate of Lee v. Commissioner, 33 T.C. 1064, 1067 (1960).

We believe the language of the children's trusts found in section 2 of the 1961 trust agreement which relates "shall use such part or all of the net income * * * for the support, care, welfare, and education of the beneficiary" clearly manifests decedent's intent to require the trustees to apply the income for the stated purpose. In our view, it is impossible to construe the instrument as one which gives the trustees discretion as to whether or not income shall be used for "support, care, welfare, and education." That standard completely controls the application of the trusts' funds. If those needs exceed the trusts' income, principal may be utilized. If those needs do not absorb all the trusts' income, the remaining income is accumulated and added to principal. Moreover, the section 2 phrase "payments from such net income to be made to such beneficiary or in such other manner as the Trustee deems to be in the best interest of the beneficiary" does not alter our interpretation. Clearly, this phrase only grants the trustee discretion in the method of payment adopted. Since we find decedent's intent clearly expressed in the trust instrument, we need not look beyond the four corners of the instrument to determine intent.

Petitioners next argue that the use of the word "welfare" within the phrase "the Trustee shall use such part or all of the net income of his or her trust for the support, care, welfare, and education of the beneficiary thereof" in section 2 of the 1961 trust instrument, gives the trustee authority to make nonsupport expenditures which, in turn, violates the "is to be applied" language of section 20.2036–1(b)(2), Estate Tax Regs. They support this theory by arguing that the standard "support, care, welfare, and education" is not ascertainable under, among others, sections 2036(a)(2) and 2041; and even if ascertainable, "welfare" is broader than "support" under Illinois law.

In determining whether "support, care, welfare, and education" is subject to an ascertainable external standard, we must rely upon Illinois law. In Estate of Wood v. Commissioner, 39 T.C. 919, 923–924 (1963), we held that the phrase "support, maintenance, welfare, and comfort" was subject to an ascertainable standard:

> We think that these four somewhat overlapping nouns were intended in the aggregate to describe the life beneficiary's standard of living in all its aspects * * *
>
> Admittedly, the words "support," and "maintenance" are regarded as referable to a standard of living, and the addition of the naked words "comfort" and "welfare" in the context of the instrument before us merely rounds out the standard of living concept.

In Estate of Bell v. Commissioner, 66 T.C. 729, 734–735 (1976), we found that the phrase "well being and maintenance in health and comfort" was subject to an ascertainable standard in Illinois:

> Although providing a modicum of discretion to the trustees, this language created a standard enforceable in a court of equity. Under Illinois law, a court of equity would look to the beneficiary's accustomed living standard in compelling compliance by the trustees, either to require income distributions for the stated purposes or to restrain distributions for unauthorized purposes. In re Whitman, 22 Ill. 511 (1859) ("support, education, and maintenance"); French v. Northern Trust Co., 197 Ill. 30, 64 N.E. 105, 106 (1902) ("properly maintained and comfortably provided for out of such property"); Burke v. Burke, 259 Ill. 262, 102 N.E. 293, 294 (1913) ("the comforts and necessities of life").

We similarly believe that under Illinois law, a court of equity would look to Gretchen's and Patrick's accustomed living standard in compelling compliance by the trustee to require income distributions for the stated purposes. As a result, we find that the terms "support, care, welfare, and education," when viewed in the aggregate, were intended to describe the children's standard of living and are, therefore, subject to an external ascertainable standard. Having found that the phrase in the aggregate created an ascertainable standard requiring the trustee to make expenditures for the children's accustomed living standard, we must reject petitioners' argument that the term "welfare" in the phrase allows the trustee to make nonsupport payments because "welfare" is broader than "support" under Illinois law.

* * * [After further examining Illinois law, the Court concluded] that, under Illinois law, support is equivalent to accustomed standard of living. We are satisfied that the instrument before us provides an ascertainable standard under Illinois law. Accordingly, we find that decedent's gross estate includes the value of Gretchen's and Patrick's trusts since we find them to be support trusts within the meaning of section 2036(a)(1) and section 20.2036–1(b)(2), Estate Tax Regs.

[Having thus included in Joseph's estate the aggregate value of the assets in Gretchen's and Patrick's trusts, the Court then turned its attention to the values of the remainders which both Gretchen's and Patrick's trusts were entitled to be paid under the terms of Mildred's trust upon the expiration of her life estate.]

Having determined that the value of the assets in the children's trusts is includable in decedent's gross estate, we must now determine the value of the assets in each trust; specifically, what is the value of the children's trusts' one-third remainder interests in a trust decedent created for the benefit of Mrs. Gokey in the October 1, 1961, trust agreement. Article I, sections 1 and 2 of that trust, grants Mrs. Gokey a life estate with remainder over equally to decedent's three children. Relying upon section 20.2031–7, Estate Tax Regs., respondent values Mrs. Gokey's life estate at $215,040.17 with a resulting remainder interest of $66,245.78 to each of the children. He then included $66,245.78, separately, in the value of assets held in Gretchen's and Patrick's trusts. Petitioners do not dispute the existence of the remainder interests, but, nevertheless, value them at zero because of the trustee's power of invasion in favor of Mrs. Gokey's life estate and the spendthrift clause prohibiting the children from alienating their remainder interests. Petitioners agree that if we hold for respondent on this issue, the proper value of each remainder interest is $66,245.78. Thus, we must only decide whether the value of each remainder interest is zero or $66,245.78. We find the value of each to be $66,245.78.

Petitioners' argument essentially suggests that under the "willing buyer and seller test" of section 20.2031–1(b), Estate Tax Regs., the remainder interests have no value since no one would buy a remainder interest that could not be alienated because of a spendthrift provision or a remainder interest subject to a power of invasion of principal in favor of the life tenant. This argument is without merit.

Valuation questions are primarily factual and although alienability and powers of invasion affect value, we do not believe they destroy it as a matter of law. In United States v. Simmons, 346 F.2d 213, 216–217 (5th Cir.1965), the court found that even a tax refund claim which could not be lawfully sold or assigned because of a Federal anti-assignment statute, had some value: "The 'willing buyer and seller' are a *hypothetical* buyer and seller having a reasonable knowledge of relevant facts." (Emphasis added.)

With regard to petitioners' second point, we do not question the difficulties associated with valuing an interest subject to a power of invasion. However, life estates coupled with a power to invade have been valued in the past. Moreover, the fact that this power of invasion is limited by the ascertainable standard "care, comfort, support or welfare" relating to Mrs. Gokey's accustomed standard of living assists in determining a value for her life estate interest. Since we have already found that the phrase "support, care, welfare, and education" constituted an ascertainable standard under Illinois law, we believe this standard is similarly ascertainable, since only "comfort" is substituted for "education" and Rock Island Bank & Trust Co. v. Rhoads, [353 Ill. 131, 187 N.E. 139 (1933)], held that comfort means support. Of course, if the life estate may be valued, so may the remainder interests. Accordingly, we find that, under the record before us, the remainder interests have some value. As a result, pursuant to the agreement of the parties and petitioners' burden of proof to overcome the correctness of respondent's determined value, we find the value of Gretchen's and Patrick's remainder interests to be $66,245.78 each.

We have considered the parties' other arguments and find them unpersuasive.

To reflect the foregoing,

Decisions will be entered under Rule 155.

NOTES

1. On appeal, the Seventh Circuit affirmed most parts of the decision of the Tax Court but reversed with respect to the value of the remainder interests in Mildred's trust that were to be included in Joseph's estate. See *Estate of Gokey*, 735 F.2d at 1367. The Seventh Circuit determined that the actuarially determined value of the includible remainder interests in Mildred's trust should be discounted by the value of the probability that an invasion of corpus for Mildred's benefit, as permitted by the terms of the trust, would take place. On remand, the Tax Court allowed a discount of 75 percent due to consideration of this element. Estate of Gokey v. Commissioner, 49 T.C.M. (CCH) 368 (1984).

2. Most of the decided cases, like *Gokey*, involve families that were intact up until the moment of death. In such circumstances, establishment by the settlor of a trust under which income is to be used to satisfy the settlor's legal support obligation with respect to a minor child results in the finding that a retained life estate is present if the settlor dies prior to the child's legal emancipation.

3. Where a support trust for the child of a broken marriage is present, a new wrinkle is added. In these circumstances, if the settlor retains custody of the minor, the courts have been willing to find the presence of a retained life estate if the settlor dies prior to legal emancipation. See National

Bank of Commerce v. Henslee, 179 F. Supp. 346 (M.D. Tenn. 1959). A different result is obtained where the settlor does not have legal custody of the minor and pursuant to a separation agreement with the spouse agrees to establish, in satisfaction of the support obligation to spouse and child, a trust with income to both. In such circumstances, discharge of the support obligation is deemed to provide the consideration that places the trust beyond the reach of section 2036. See Estate of McKeon v. Commissioner, 25 T.C. 697 (1956). For a case involving a support trust entered into during days of marital bliss and subsequently referred to in a divorce decree, see Estate of Pardee v. Commissioner, 49 T.C. 140 (1967).

4.   In Rev. Rul. 59–357, 1959–2 C.B. 212, the IRS ruled that where a parent, who has a legal support obligation with respect to a minor child, makes a gift to his child under the Uniform Gifts to Minors Act (UGMA), appointing himself as custodian for the gift, and dies while the child is still a minor, the property which is the subject of the gift shall be included in the parent's estate. The ruling bases its rationale on the fact that the donor parent under the UGMA has the right to use income from the gifted property to support the minor. The ruling goes on to state that "[i]n all other circumstances custodial property is includible only in the gross estate of the donee." This has been interpreted as indicating that a parent can avoid the reach of section 2036(a)(1) on gifts to minor children by simply appointing a spouse as custodian. Exchange Bank and Trust Co. of Florida v. United States, 694 F.2d 1261 (Fed. Cir. 1982) (dictum).

Parents who have support obligations with respect to minor children and who appoint each other as custodians with respect to gifts under the UGMA or the Uniform Transfers to Minors Act (UTMA) will find the IRS asserting that application of the reciprocal trust doctrine results in an inclusion in the estate if one of the parents dies while a child is still in minority.

c.   **Support of Spouse**

Where a donor establishes a trust for support of a spouse, the same basic issues arise since each spouse has a legal obligation to support the other. Critical to a determination of whether an inclusion is present are: (1) whether the trust requires, or as in *Chrysler* merely permits, income to be used for support and maintenance; and (2) whether the beneficiary spouse is given discretion as to how the income is to be used. Where income must be used to meet a legal support obligation with respect to a spouse, inclusion in the estate is required. See, e.g., Richards v. Commissioner, 375 F.2d 997 (10th Cir. 1967) (inclusion despite fact that the decedent supported a spouse and trust income was never so used). Where, as in *Chrysler*, the trustee is given discretion as to use of the income, no inclusion results under section 2036. See, e.g., Estate of Mitchell v. Commissioner, 55 T.C. 576 (1970). Where the beneficiary spouse has discretion to use income as he or she wishes, no inclusion results. See, e.g., Estate of

Sessoms v. Commissioner, 8 T.C.M. (CCH) 1056 (1949); Estate of Sherman v. Commissioner, 9 T.C. 594 (1947).

In Estate of Sullivan v. Commissioner, 66 T.C.M. (CCH) 1329 (1993), the court held that, where the donor of a trust effectively reserved the right to distribute corpus for support and maintenance of his wife, an inclusion in the donor's estate should be made of an amount equal to a portion of the trust which, given the couple's standard of living, would be needed to support donor's widow.

Where a donor establishes a trust incident to a divorce to support an ex-spouse or soon to be ex-spouse, a special rule prevails. In 1984, section 2043(b)(2) was added to the Code providing that a transfer incident to a divorce, which meets the requirements of section 2516, shall be considered made for full and adequate consideration. The impact of section 2043(b)(2) on alimony trusts is illustrated by the following private letter ruling.

Private Letter Ruling 9235032
May 29, 1992.

[A and B entered into a settlement agreement pursuant to their obtaining a divorce. Under paragraph 10 of the agreement, B was obliged monthly to pay A a fixed sum of money as alimony. The agreement authorized B to meet this obligation by making direct payments to A, purchasing an annuity, or establishing an alimony trust. Sometime later B chose the latter course of action and the IRS ruled that at B's death, the alimony trust was to be taxed in the following manner.]

Section 2036(a) provides that the value of the gross estate shall include the value of all property to the extent of any interest therein of which the decedent has at any time made a transfer (except in a case of a bona fide sale for adequate and full consideration in money or money's worth), by trust or otherwise, under which he has retained for his life or for any period not ascertainable without reference to his death or for any period that does not in fact end before his death (1) the possession or enjoyment of, or the right to the income from, the property, or (2) the right, either alone or in conjunction with any person, to designate the persons who shall possess or enjoy the property or the income therefrom.

Section 20.2036–1(b)(2) of the Estate Tax Regulations provides that the term "use, possession, right to income, or other enjoyment of the transferred property" is considered to have been retained by or reserved to the decedent to the extent that the use, possession, right to income, or other enjoyment is to be applied toward the discharge of a legal obligation of the decedent, or otherwise for his pecuniary benefit. The term "legal obligation" includes a legal obligation to support a dependent during the decedent's lifetime.

Section 2053(a) provides for a deduction in determining the amount of the taxable estate for amounts that are paid in satisfaction of claims against the estate. Under section 2053(c), the deduction for claims against the estate is allowed only to the extent that the claim is contracted bona fide for an adequate consideration in money or money's worth.

Section 2043(b)(2) provides that for purposes of section 2053, a transfer of property which satisfies the requirements of section 2516(1) is considered as made for an adequate and full consideration in money or money's worth.

In the instant case, under the terms of Paragraph 10 of the agreement, a personal obligation is imposed on the taxpayer to pay A the monthly amount. The taxpayer's transfer to the trust does not relieve the taxpayer, or his estate, of this personal obligation because, under the terms of the agreement, the taxpayer, or his estate, is required to discharge the maintenance obligation, in the event the trust does not generate sufficient funds. Rather, the taxpayers transfer to the trust enabled the taxpayer to satisfy that obligation if and to the extent that each payment is in fact made from the trust. If any trust payment were to fall short of the obligation, then the taxpayer would be required to pay the difference from other funds. Accordingly, in the instant case, the taxpayer has retained the use, possession, enjoyment or right to income from the property under section 2036(a)(1) of the Code and section 20.2036–1(b)(2) of the regulations, since the trust income and corpus is to be applied to discharge the taxpayer's continuing legal obligation under the agreement. Accordingly, the value of the trust corpus on the date of the taxpayer's death will be includible in his gross estate under section 2036(a)(1). In this regard, we note that section 2516(1) does not apply to satisfy the full and adequate consideration exception contained in section 2036. Estate of Nelson v. Commissioner, 47 T.C. 279, 287 (1966), rev'd. on other grounds, 396 F.2d 519 (2d Cir.1968).

However, the value of A's remaining maintenance right on the date of the taxpayer's death would be treated as a claim contracted for adequate consideration under section 2043(b)(2) and therefore, would be deductible under section 2053(a)(3). Cf. Rev. Rul. 76–113, 1976–1 C.B. 276.

NOTES

1. Presumably, under the IRS position as set forth in Private Letter Ruling 9235032, the amount deductible under section 2053(a)(3) will not equal the amount included under section 2036(a)(1). For example, assume that an alimony trust contains $800,000 and requires that all income is to be paid to an ex-spouse who at decedent's death is age 67. If we assume that the value of the ex-spouse's income interest is $480,000, under the theory of the ruling, this will result in a net inclusion of $320,000 ($800,000 − $480,000). Do you agree with this result?

2.　Suppose that rather than the donor designating who shall enjoy the remainder interest, the recipient of alimony, as part of the divorce proceedings, was allowed to designate the remainder person. What should then follow?

C.　RETENTION OF BENEFICIAL ENJOYMENT— SECTION 2036(a)(2)

Clearly, section 2036(a)(2) requires that a donor's estate include property with respect to which the donor retained the right to designate which one of several beneficiaries is to enjoy the use of, or the income from, property. Occasionally, the donor, by retaining a power that under certain circumstances effectively retains this privilege, finds that an interest has been retained that will make the property subject to inclusion in the estate. Also, at issue under section 2036(a)(2) is whether inclusion in the donor's estate is appropriate when the donor has retained not the right to determine who is to enjoy the income from property but rather the right to determine when, or under what circumstances, the beneficiary will enjoy the income from the property.

1.　CONTROL OVER TIMING OF ENJOYMENT

STRUTHERS V. KELM

United States Court of Appeals, Eighth Circuit, 1955.
218 F.2d 810.

COLLET, CIRCUIT JUDGE:

The question for determination is whether the creator of three trusts, Mrs. Mary Case Barney, reserved the right, in conjunction with other persons, to designate the persons who should possess or enjoy the property constituting the trusts or the income therefrom. If she did so, the property constituting the trusts was subject to estate tax on her estate under [1939 Code] § 811(c)(1)(B)(ii), 26 U.S.C.A. § 811(c)(1)(B)(ii), 1953 Supp. [The 1939 Code section involved in this case is the same in all material respects as § 2036 of the 1986 Code.] * * *

The facts are not in dispute. The trust indenture was executed February 18, 1937. By it Mrs. Barney created three separate [irrevocable] trusts in favor of her three children, Hadwen C. Barney, Mary B. Struthers, and Elizabeth B. Wesbrook. With the exception of the named beneficiary, the terms of the three trusts were for present purposes identical. In each Mrs. Barney was designated as one of the three trustees.

The trust instrument in which Mary B. Struthers is the beneficiary is typical of the three trust agreements. The pertinent portions thereof are as follows:

* * *

"3. The Trustees shall collect and receive all interest, income and profits earned by said Trust Fund. The net income from said Trust Fund, or so much thereof as the Trustees shall deem advisable, may be accumulated by said Trustees and invested for the benefit of Mary B. Struthers, daughter of said Mary Case Barney, or the Trustees may in their discretion pay the net income or so much thereof as they deem advisable to the said Mary B. Struthers at such times and in such amounts as in their sole judgment they deem advisable. In addition thereto the Trustees may use such amounts out of the principal from time to time as in their judgment and discretion they may deem necessary and advisable for the care, comfort, support and maintenance of said Mary B. Struthers.

"4. Upon the death of the said Mary Case Barney, the Trust hereby created shall cease and terminate and the entire Trust Fund and all accumulated or unpaid net income shall be paid over and distributed to the said Mary B. Struthers.

* * *

"7. The Trustor declares that she has been fully advised as to the legal effect of the execution of this agreement and informed as to the character and amount of the property hereby transferred and conveyed; and further that she has given consideration to the question whether the trust hereby created shall be revocable or irrevocable, and she now declares that it shall be irrevocable and that she shall hereafter be without power at any time, either alone or in conjunction with any other person, or persons, to revoke, change, amend, alter, annul, or terminate the trust hereby created or any of the provisions herein contained."

* * *

The Government's position is that the value of the three trusts should be included in Mrs. Barney's estate and taxed as a part of her estate because she retained the right, in conjunction with the other trustees, to designate the persons who should possess or enjoy the property or the income therefrom. That position is based upon the wording of the trust instruments which provide that the net income of the trust, or so much thereof as the trustees shall deem advisable, may be accumulated and invested for the benefit of the named beneficiary, or the net income, or such portion of it as the trustees deem advisable, may be paid to the beneficiary, or that the trustees may use such amount of the principal from time to time for the care, support and maintenance of the beneficiary as they in their judgment and discretion may determine.

At the time the case was heard the trial court, applying the law of Minnesota as declared in First & American National Bank of Duluth v. Higgins, 208 Minn. 295, 293 N.W. 585, concluded that Mrs. Barney retained no possibility of a reverter; that since the trust instruments made no provision as to the disposition of the trust income or the trust fund in the event the beneficiary predeceased Mrs. Barney, and since the beneficiary's interest in the estate was vested in the manner declared by the law of Minnesota and not susceptible to change by Mrs. Barney or by her and the trustees acting jointly or severally, as trustees, that no control of the remainder was retained by or was vested in Mrs. Barney and that the mere control of the time when the beneficiary or the beneficiary's possible devisees might enjoy the fund did not constitute such a substantial control over the trusts contemplated by the statute as would require the treatment of the trusts as part of Mrs. Barney's estate. Reliance for that conclusion was placed upon Hays' Estate v. Commissioner, 181 F.2d 169. Taking cognizance, however, of Lober v. United States, 108 F.Supp. 731, 124 Ct. Cl. 44, and the pendency of that case before the Supreme Court on certiorari, the trial court reserved formal judgment pending final disposition of the *Lober* case. When the latter was decided by the Supreme Court, Lober v. United States, 346 U.S. 335, the trial court, being convinced that this case was controlled by the *Lober* case, entered judgment for the Government, dismissing the complaint. We are convinced that the *Lober* case is determinative of this.

Appellant undertakes to distinguish this from the *Lober* case upon two grounds. First, that in this case the right of control over the disposition of the trusts vested entirely in the beneficiaries at the time the trusts were established, that the beneficiary might have subjected the entire trust to the payment of the beneficiary's debts or by devise designated another as the recipient in event the beneficiary predeceased Mrs. Barney, or, in the event neither occurred, that the law of descents and distribution of the State of Minnesota fixed with certainty the recipient of the trust fund beyond the power of any person to change. For that reason it is said that Mrs. Barney could not have had the power, acting alone or in conjunction with the other trustees, to designate the persons who should possess or enjoy the trusts or the income therefrom. The further argument is advanced that the facts in this case distinguish it from the *Lober* case because of paragraph 7 of the trust instrument, heretofore quoted, wherein Mrs. Barney stated that—"She shall hereafter be without power at any time, either alone or in conjunction with any other person or persons, to revoke, change, amend, or terminate the trust hereby created or any of the provisions herein contained."

The *Lober* case was decided under [1939 Code] § 811(d)(1), 26 U.S.C.A. § 811(d)(2) [substantially the same as § 2038 of the 1986 Code], which made trusts taxable as part of the donor's estate " 'where the enjoyment thereof was subject at the date of his death to any change through the exercise of a power * * * to alter, amend, or revoke * * *.' " Lober v. United States, 346 U.S. 335, 336. But the gravamen of both [1939 Code] § 811(d)(2) and § 811(c)(1)(B)(ii) is the same. Both deal, in regard to the question before us, with the "enjoyment" or "possession" of the trust. Both sections adopt as the factor determinative of whether the trust shall be treated as a part of the donor's estate the existence or nonexistence of the power of the donor to "alter, amend or revoke", [1939 Code] § 811(d)(2), or, to designate the person who shall "possess or enjoy" the property or its income (§ 811(c)(1)(B)(ii)). The *Lober* opinion, quoting from Commissioner v. Holmes' Estate, 326 U.S. 480, states that [1939 Code] § 811(d)(2) "was more concerned with 'present economic benefit' than with 'technical vesting of title or estates.' " In the *Lober* case the fact relied on as distinguishing this case from the *Lober* case was assumed, i.e., that the trust instrument gave Lober's children a vested interest under state law so that if they had died after creation of the trusts their interests would have passed to their estates. But that fact was held undeterminative and Lober's estate was charged with the estate tax because Lober's children, as beneficiaries of the trust, were granted no "present right to immediate enjoyment of either income or principal" without Lober's consent. In this case the beneficiary under Mrs. Barney's trust instrument was not granted the present right to immediate enjoyment of the income or principal without Mrs. Barney's permission, acting "in conjunction with" the other trustees. Since the *Holmes' Estate* case and the *Lober* case give controlling emphasis and effect to the present right of enjoyment of the trust by the beneficiary, rather that [sic] when the title to the trust property technically vested under state law, or the absence of power on the part of the donor to alter or amend that title, this case may not be distinguished from Lober v. United States and Commissioner v. Holmes' Estate, supra. It must follow that the judgment is correct and is affirmed.

NOTES

1. In Estate of Alexander v. Commissioner, 81 T.C. 757 (1983), the doctrine of *Struthers* was applied in uncompromising fashion to a trust where the grantor-decedent could only distribute or accumulate income for eventual distribution to the beneficiary or her estate and even that would have required that he exercise his authority to remove the trustee and name himself, which he had not done. Still, the application of the *Struthers* doctrine does seem indicated on such facts.

   Other cases reaching the conclusion that retention by the donor of control over merely the timing of a designated beneficiary's enjoyment of income results in an inclusion in the donor's gross estate under section 2036(a)(2) are Estate of Sulovich v. Commissioner, 587 F.2d 845 (6th Cir. 1978); Rott v. United States, 321 F. Supp. 654 (E.D. Mo. 1971) and Deaktor v. Commissioner, 25 T.C.M. (CCH) 992 (1966). Both *Rott* and *Deaktor* involved a version of the spendthrift trust in which the donor had retained the right to withhold from the income beneficiary annual income which was added to corpus. In both cases the income beneficiary, her estate or designees were the remaindermen of the trusts. Had the donor in these cases or in *Struthers* been willing to vest control over timing of enjoyment in an independent party, estate taxation could have been easily avoided.

2.   Some commentators have objected to the holding of *Struthers* and its progeny on the ground that since section 2036(a)(2) speaks in terms of a retained right to designate the "persons" who shall enjoy income, section 2036(a)(2) should not apply in a situation such as that involved in *Struthers* where the beneficiary could, at her death, by will finally obtain enjoyment of the income by conveying her interest in it to others. This they believe is a sufficient guarantee of the beneficiary being assured that she alone will enjoy the income and since the decedent could not pick and choose among various beneficiaries, section 2036(a)(2) by its terms does not apply. This argument, to date, has had little appeal to the judiciary or to the IRS and perhaps also to beneficiaries who, deprived of enjoyment of income during their life, find the power to control its enjoyment at their death by will to be a poor substitute.

3.   In Regulation § 20.2036–1(b)(3), the Treasury indicates that the "right . . . to designate the person or persons who shall possess or enjoy the transferred property or the income therefrom" does not include a power over the transferred property itself that does not affect the enjoyment of the income received or earned during the decedent's life. As a result of this language, there is no inclusion under section 2036 in the decedent's estate in the following circumstance. Assume that X established a trust under which income goes to A for 10 years, after which corpus of the trust is to be distributed to A. Assume that X also retained the right to terminate the trust at any moment and vest A in complete immediate ownership of the corpus. Since X's actions can never deprive A of the income, there is no inclusion in X's estate under section 2036, even if X dies possessed of the power to terminate. Although retention of such a power does not result in taxation under section 2036, it can result in taxation under section 2038, which is discussed below. For present purposes, consideration should be confined to how this language in the regulations relates to the result in *Struthers*. Regulation § 20.2036–1(b)(3) also states that it is immaterial whether the decedent's right to affect beneficial enjoyment is exercisable only in conjunction with a person who has an adverse interest.

PLANNING NOTE

Gifts to minors under either the Uniform Gifts to Minors Act (UGMA) or the Uniform Transfers to Minors Act (UTMA) may result in inclusion under section 2036 or section 2038 if the donor appoints himself or herself as custodian and dies before the donee reaches the age at which the custodianship ends. See, e.g., Prudowsky's Estate v. Commissioner, 55 T.C. 890 (1971), aff'd, 465 F.2d 62 (7th Cir.1972) (gift with donor-parent as custodian taxable under sections 2036(a)(1) and 2038); see also Rev. Rul. 59–357, 1959–2 C.B. 212 (holding that gifts under UGMA with donor as custodian are taxable under section 2038).

The favored way of avoiding this problem is for the donor to designate a trusted third party as the custodian under the UGMA or the UTMA. Married couples who wish to make gifts to their minor children might instinctively be tempted to designate each other as the custodian for their gifts. However, the estate planner must be concerned with the possibility that the IRS might seek to resort to the reciprocal trust doctrine to effect an inclusion in the estate of the first such spouse to die.

2. CONTINGENT RETAINED POWERS TO DETERMINE ENJOYMENT

As discussed above, a retained contingent life estate will give rise to an inclusion in the estate under section 2036(a)(1). The principal issue here under consideration is whether anything is to be included within the estate under section 2036(a)(2) where the donor-decedent had, under certain circumstances, retained the right to determine the conditions of enjoyment for other beneficiaries.

ESTATE OF FARREL v. UNITED STATES
United States Court of Claims, 1977.
553 F.2d 637.

DAVIS, JUDGE.

[In 1961 Marian Farrel established an irrevocable trust with her grandchildren (and their issue) as beneficiaries. Two independent individuals were named as trustees and were given discretionary power to pay income and principal out among the trust beneficiaries. At some time in the future, trust assets were to be divided among the beneficiaries or contributed to a new trust over which the trustees were to have discretionary powers. No provision was made for any distribution to Mrs. Farrel.

The trust called for two trustees at all times and gave Mrs. Farrel the power to fill any vacancy. Mrs. Farrel did not have the power, either under the deed of trust or Connecticut law, to remove a trustee. The instrument was silent as to whether Mrs. Farrel could appoint herself to fill a vacancy, but this would be permitted under state law. On two separate occasions when vacancies occurred Mrs. Farrel appointed independent third parties as successor trustees.

After Mrs. Farrel died in 1969, the IRS sought to include trust corpus in her estate under section 2036(a)(2)]

Both parties agree that (a) the trustees had "the right, either alone or in conjunction with any person, to designate the persons who shall possess or enjoy the property or the income therefrom" within the meaning of Section 2036(a)(2); (b) Mrs. Farrel, the decedent settlor, could lawfully designate herself (under the trust and Connecticut law) as successor trustee if a vacancy occurred during her life; (c) the occurrence of a vacancy in the office of trustee was a condition which Mrs. Farrel could not create and which was beyond her control; and (d) Mrs. Farrel had the opportunity, before her 1969 death, to appoint a successor trustee only during the two periods in 1964 and 1965 mentioned above. The legal conflict is whether the right of the trustees (as to who should enjoy or possess the property or income) should in these circumstances be attributed to the decedent under § 2036(a) for any of the three periods designated in that statutory provision—her life; any period not ascertainable without reference to her death; any period which does not in fact end before her death. The Government's answer is yes and the plaintiff of course says no.

Only Section 2036(a) is now before us but, since taxpayer's presentation emphasizes a comparison of that provision with Section 2038 (a cognate but separate part of the estate tax), it is important to set out, at the beginning, the relevant aspects of the latter, as we do in the margin. Plaintiff's primary point is that (i) it is now and has long been settled that Section 2038 does not cover a power or right subject to a conditional event which has not occurred prior to and does not exist at the decedent's death, such as a discretionary power to distribute income or principal under specified conditions which have not occurred before the death, and (ii) the same rule has been and is applicable to Section 2036(a).

There is no question that taxpayer is correct as to the construction of Section 2038. That slant was given by the courts to the provision's predecessor under the 1939 Code * * * and the Treasury has itself adopted the same interpretation for the 1954 Code as well. Treasury Regulations on Estate Tax (1954 Code), Section 20.2038–1(a) and (b).

The initial and fundamental question we have to face is whether this settled understanding of Section 2038 necessarily governs Section 2036(a), as it now stands. We think not for two reasons which we shall consider in turn: first, that the critical points-of-view of the two provisions differ, and, second, that the regulations governing the two sections take diametrically opposed positions on the narrow issue of contingent rights and powers of the kind involved here.

The two separate provisions appear to diverge sharply in their perspective—the point from which the pertinent powers and rights are to be seen. Section 2038(a) looks at the problem from the decedent's death— what he can and cannot do at that specific moment. Excluded are contingent rights and powers (beyond the decedent's control) which are not exercisable at that moment because the designated contingency does not exist at that time. Section 2036(a), on the other hand, looks forward from the time the decedent made the transfer to see whether he has retained any of the specified rights "for his life or for any period not ascertainable without reference to his death or for any period which does not in fact end before his death." This language makes the transferor's death one pole of the specified time-span but the whole of the time-span is also significant. Because of the statute's reference to the time-span, differences of interpretation are quite conceivable. It is possible for instance, to hold the words to mean that the retained right has to exist at all times throughout one of the periods, but it is also possible to see the language as covering contingencies which could realistically occur at some separate point or points during the designated periods—always including the moment of decedent's death. We take it (from the argument's insistence on the parallel to 2038) that taxpayer would not stand on the former ("at all times") interpretation if a vacancy in the trusteeship existed and had not been filled at Mrs. Farrel's death. But under the language of 2036(a) there is no compelling reason why the moment of death has to be exclusively important. Unlike Section 2038, this provision seems to look forward from the time of transfer to the date of the transferor's death, and can be said to concentrate on the significant rights with respect to the transferred property the transferor retains, not at every moment during that period, but whenever the specified contingency happens to arise during that period (so long as the contingency can still occur at the end of the period).

There is nothing unreasonable about this latter construction, which accords with Congress' over-all purpose to gather into the estate tax all transfers which remain significantly incomplete—on which the transferor still holds a string—during his lifetime. It is hard to believe, for instance that, whatever may be true of 2038, 2036(a) would have to be seen as failing to cover a trust where the trustee, with discretionary powers, could be removed by the settlor, and the settlor substituted as trustee, whenever economic conditions fell below a stated level (e.g., a designated level on a certain stock exchange index or a level of earnings of the trust) even though fortuitously that condition did not happen to exist at the time of death. In a case like that, the lifetime link between the decedent and the trust property (and income) would be so strong as plainly to measure up to both the letter and the spirit of 2036(a) if the Treasury chose to see it that way. This case, though perhaps less clear, falls into the same class of a continuing substantial tie.

The other element which leads us to reject plaintiff's attempt to equate 2036(a) with 2038, for this case, is that the Treasury has affirmatively chosen to separate the two sections—there is a Treasury regulation under the former § 20.2036–1 which, to our mind, clearly covers this decedent's situation (in contrast to the regulation under 2038 which excludes it).

Taxpayer urges us to read the regulation otherwise, and if we cannot to hold it invalid.

The regulation says flatly * * * that it is immaterial "(iii) whether the exercise of the power was subject to a contingency beyond the decedent's control which did not occur before his death (e.g., the death of another person during the decedent's lifetime)." This would seem on its surface to blanket this decedent's position under her trust, but plaintiff would read it very literally and narrowly to apply only where the contingency relates to the "exercise" of an already existing power, and conversely, to be inapplicable where the power only springs into existence when a trustee vacancy occurs. Similarly, taxpayer sees in the broad sweep of the last sentence of § 20.2036–1(b)(3) * * * the implied negative pregnant that a restricted power in the decedent to appoint herself a substitute trustee only in the event of a vacancy lies outside 2036(a). We cannot accept these strained (if not casuistic) analyses of the regulation because they go directly counter to its apparent purpose to cover just such contingencies as we have here. If proof of that objective is needed it is fully supplied by the companion regulation under 2038 (Treasury Regulation on Estate Tax (1954 Code), § 20.2038–1(b)) which declares in coordinate terms that "section 2038 is not applicable to a power the exercise of which was subject to a contingency beyond the decedent's control which did not occur before his death (e.g., the death of another person during the decedent's life). *See, however Section 2036(a)(2) for the inclusion of property in the decedent's gross estate on account of such a power*" (emphasis added).

We are required, then, to consider whether § 20.2036–1(b)(3) should be overturned as invalid. Recognizing the deference due Treasury Regulations * * *, we cannot take that step. We have pointed out that 2036 is not the same as 2038 in its wording or in the viewpoint from which it appraises the decedent's link to the transferred property. We have also said that it is not unreasonable to regard 2036(a), in the way the Treasury does, as a blanket overall sweeping-in of property over which the decedent still has at death some significant, though contingent, power to choose those who shall have possession or enjoyment.

To this, plaintiff's ultimate response is double-barreled: (i) the regulation was not contemporaneous with the adoption of the predecessor of 2036 but came years later, and (ii) for taxable years before the regulation was adopted courts applied the same rule to the predecessors of 2036 as they have to 2038 and its predecessors. Both points may be technically correct. The relevant regulation was promulgated in 1958 many years after the first predecessor of 2036 was enacted. And in 1947 Jennings v. Smith, supra, seemed to use, as an alternative holding, the same rule for the forerunner of 2036 that it applied to the predecessor of 2038. To the same effect was Estate of Kasch v. Commissioner, supra (1958) (predecessor section). Nevertheless the Treasury was not foreclosed, in our view, from taking the position it did in 1958. As we have stressed, neither the text nor the purpose of 2036 demands that it be treated the same as 2038. The judicial observations lumping the two predecessor provisions responded to Government arguments treating the two sections as fully parallel on this point. Moreover, *Jennings v. Smith* was the only appellate decision on the point which was outstanding when the 1958 regulations were promulgated, and its statement was, at best, a rather summary alternative holding not truly necessary to the ultimate decision. Thus, the judicial interpretation of Section 2036's predecessor was neither so strong nor so encrusted that Congress may be thought to have embodied it in Section 2036 when it adopted the 1954 Code. On the contrary, we think the Treasury was free to take a new look under that new Code, as it evidently did. In sum, the current regulation under 2036 is a reasonable reading of the text and objective of the statute and the previous contrary judicial interpretation was not such that the Treasury was forced to bow to it despite the *prima facie* acceptability of the administrative stance.

We end by noting that the contingent right of Mrs. Farrel to make herself a trustee in the event of a vacancy—unlike the *de facto* "powers" involved in United States v. Byrum, 408 U.S. 125 (1972) and in Estate of Tully v. United States, 208 Ct. Cl. 596, 528 F.2d 1401 (1976)—was a legally enforceable right, in effect imbedded in the trust instrument, which bore directly on the designation of the persons to possess or enjoy the trust property or income. That the exercise of this right was foreseeable when the trust was created—that it was a real right, neither insignificant nor illusory—is shown by the fact that Mrs. Farrel had two opportunities to exercise it in eight years and, if she had lived, may well have had more.

For these reasons we hold that plaintiff is not entitled to recover and the petition is dismissed.

3. POWER TO REMOVE TRUSTEES

It is desirable to retain the power to remove and replace a trustee for several reasons. A trustee may be surcharged for any disbursements or other losses not in accord with the deed of trust. As a consequence, most trustees, but in particular corporate trustees, err on the side of caution when discretionary disbursements are called for both by circumstances and by the terms of the trust. Trustees often seek court approval for all but pedestrian matters, and the cost of such legal action is typically charged to the trust as an expense. Appointment of a stranger or a corporation as trustee can thus result in expensive unresponsiveness. Since most trustees enjoy their fees, it is rare for a trustee, even one with a dreadful record for investments, ever to step down voluntarily. Spending trust corpus to defend their position and reputation, trustees can take on all challengers who seek to have them removed by judicial action. Consequently, settlors have traditionally been advised by their attorneys to retain some control over trustees by, if allowed by state law, retaining the right to remove the trustee and appoint a new trustee in order to insure their responsiveness and to guard against years of poor investment strategy.

In Rev. Rul. 79–353, 1979–2 C.B. 325, the IRS dealt with a situation where a settlor vested a corporate trustee with powers that, had they been retained by the settlor, would have resulted in inclusion of the trust corpus in settlor's estate at settlor's death. Since the settlor had retained the right to remove the corporate trustee and replace it with another corporate trustee, the IRS held that the corpus of the trust was to be included, under section 2036(a)(2), in the settlor's estate at death. The decision of the IRS appears to have been based on the theory that the settlor, by threatening the trustee with removal or by finding a compliant replacement, could have caused the trustee to do exactly as the settlor wished in exercising discretion regarding distribution of trust income. Fourteen years after its issuance Rev. Rul. 79–353 received judicial scrutiny in the case which follows.

ESTATE OF WALL v. COMMISSIONER
United States Tax Court, 1993.
101 T.C. 300.

NIMS, JUDGE:

* * *

* * * Mrs. Wall, the grantor, retained the right in each trust indenture to remove the corporate sole trustee and replace it with another corporate trustee which had to be "independent" from the grantor. In each case the trustee was given the authority to distribute principal and income to a beneficiary essentially unrestrained by an ascertainable standard. Did the right to replace the corporate trustee in turn encompass the right to exercise the powers of the trustee? For the following reasons, we think not.

The underlying assumption of Rev. Rul. 79–353 and respondent's argument is that even a corporate trustee will be compelled to follow the bidding of a settlor who has the power to remove the trustee; otherwise the settlor will be able to find another corporate trustee which will act as the settlor wishes. In other words, says respondent, under these circumstances the settlor has the de facto power to exercise the powers vested in the trustee. But the Supreme Court has said in *Byrum* that the section 2036(a)(2) right connotes an ascertainable and legally enforceable power, as exemplified by the facts in United States v. O'Malley, 383 U.S. 627 (1966). As the Supreme Court states in *Byrum*, *"O'Malley* was covered precisely by the statute [§ 2036(a)(2)] for two reasons: (1) there the settlor had reserved a legal right, set forth in the trust instrument; and (2) this right expressly authorized the settlor, 'in conjunction' with others, to accumulate income and thereby 'to designate' the persons to enjoy it." United States v. Byrum, 408 U.S. at 136.

In the case before us respondent simply speculates that Mrs. Wall, by merely threatening First Wisconsin to replace it, could indirectly have exercised powers of the trustee similar to, though broader than, those in *O'Malley*. In Estate of Beckwith v. Commissioner, 55 T.C. 242 (1970), the trust indenture explicitly provided for the periodic distribution of trust income to a named beneficiary. Under the terms of the trust indenture the settlor retained no power or right to control the amounts or the timing of the distributions. The Commissioner, however, relied upon certain "practical considerations" which, he contended, enabled the decedent to control the flow of the income. The so-called practical considerations included the authority for the trust to retain stock in the settlor's closely held corporation; the power given the trustee to vote the stock; the settlor's retained right to remove a trustee and appoint a successor other than himself; and the close business relationships between the settlor and the individual trustees. We held that none of the so-called practical considerations nor all of them combined provided a basis for an inference that the settlor, by prearrangement or informal understanding or otherwise, reserved the right to cause the trustees to retain the closely held stock or to give the settlor proxies with respect thereto. Estate of Beckwith v. Commissioner, 55 T.C. at 248–249.

While it is true that First Wisconsin's power to distribute income and principal is not restricted to the extent existing in *Estate of Beckwith*, it is also true that, under established principles of the law governing trusts, a trustee would violate its fiduciary duty if it acquiesced in the wishes of the settlor by taking action that the trustee would not otherwise take regarding the beneficial enjoyment of any interest in the trust, or agreed with the settlor, prior to appointment, as to how fiduciary powers should be exercised over the distribution of income and principal. The trustee has a duty to administer the trust in the sole interest of the beneficiary, to act impartially if there are multiple beneficiaries, and to exercise powers exclusively for the benefit of the beneficiaries. See, e.g., Bogert, Law of Trusts and Trustees, sec. 543, at 217 (2d ed. 1993) ("Perhaps the most fundamental duty of a trustee is that he must display throughout the administration of the trust complete loyalty to the interests of the beneficiary and must exclude all selfish interest and all consideration of the interests of third persons."). While the parties and amicus have not briefed the Wisconsin law on this virtually universal rule, it would seem highly unlikely that there is a variance between Wisconsin and other jurisdictions.

In irrevocable trusts such as those under scrutiny, the trustee is accountable only to the beneficiaries, not to the settlor, and any right of action for breach of fiduciary duty lies in the beneficiaries, not in the settlor. Bogert, supra, sec. 42, at 431–433. It also seems incontrovertible that the trustee's duty of sole fidelity to the beneficiary remains the same regardless of whether or not distributions are discretionary and whether or not limited by a standard such as one related to health, education, support in reasonable comfort, and the like.

In the absence of some compelling reason to do so, which respondent has not shown, we are not inclined to infer any kind of fraudulent side agreement between Mrs. Wall and First Wisconsin as to how the administration of these trusts would be manipulated by Mrs. Wall. Instead, since the language of the trust indentures provides maximum flexibility as to distributions of income and principal, the trustee would be expected to look to the circumstances of the beneficiaries to whom sole allegiance is owed, and not to Mrs. Wall, in order to determine the timing and amount of discretionary distributions.

It seems also likely that Mrs. Wall might have conceived that a beneficiary might move to a distant location, making the beneficiary's personal contact with the trust department impractical, or that First Wisconsin might merge with an out-of-state bank in a way that would change the character of its trust department. These motives, if they indeed existed, are not the equivalent of a retained right contemplated by section 2036(a)(2). Nor do they imply arrangements, not previously contemplated, made after a transfer has been completed to permit the transferor to enjoy the benefits of the property. See Estate of Barlow v. Commissioner, 55 T.C. 666, 670 (1971). We therefore apply the Supreme Court's definition of a section 2036(a)(2) retained right; namely, that it must be an ascertainable and legally enforceable power. United States v. Byrum, 408 U.S. at 136. We hold that Mrs. Wall did not retain such an ascertainable and enforceable power to affect the beneficial enjoyment of the trust property.

On brief respondent points out that sections 2036(a)(2) and 2038(a)(1) frequently overlap and urges that in this case both are equally applicable. We agree that these sections frequently overlap, but for reasons stated above we hold that neither is applicable. We have focused essentially on section 2036(a)(2), but for the reasons given, Mrs. Wall's retained power to substitute another independent corporate trustee for First Wisconsin is not the type of power which would affect the "enjoyment" of the trust property contemplated by section 2036(a)(2) or section 2038(a)(1).

To reflect the foregoing.

Decision will be entered for petitioner.

PLANNING NOTE

In Rev. Rul. 95–58, 1995–36 I.R.B. 16, the IRS accepted the results in *Wall*. The IRS stated that it would no longer claim that a retained power to remove and replace a trustee possessed of discretionary powers results in an inclusion under section 2036(a)(2) so long as the grantor's power to remove and appoint a new trustee does not permit the grantor to appoint as a replacement trustee: (1) the grantor; or (2) "an individual or corporate successor trustee * * * related or subordinate to the decedent (within the meaning of section 672(c))." Under the IRS's approach, this would preclude appointment of a spouse, parent, issue, sibling, employee, or a corporation or employee of a corporation with respect to which the grantor and trust, either alone or combined, have significant voting control. The IRS's focus on section 672(c) is interesting because there is no statutory justification to be found in section 2036 for so restricting the category of potential replacement trustees.

4.   RETENTION OF VOTING CONTROL

UNITED STATES V. BYRUM

Supreme Court of the United States, 1972.
408 U.S. 125.

MR. JUSTICE POWELL delivered the opinion of the Court.

[The decedent, Milliken Byrum, created an irrevocable trust, for the benefit of his children and their issue, to which he transferred stock in three Ohio corporations in which he owned at least 71 percent of the stock prior to the transfers. After the transfers and at his death four years later Byrum owned less than 50 percent of the stock in two corporations and 59 percent of the stock in the third corporation. Under the deed of trust, Byrum retained the right to vote the transferred stock (thus giving him voting control), to veto its transfer, to approve all new investments and to remove the corporate trustee. At Byrum's death, the Commissioner sought to effect an inclusion of trust corpus on the theory that Byrum's retained voting privileges and control over retention by the trust of the stock in question allowed him not only to retain the enjoyment of income from the property but also to determine the flow of income from the trust and thereby to designate the persons who will enjoy the income.]

* * *

The Government relies primarily on its claim, made under § 2036(a)(2), that Byrum retained the right to designate the persons who shall enjoy the income from the transferred property. The argument is a complicated one. By retaining voting control over the corporations whose stock was transferred, Byrum was in a position to select the corporate directors. He could retain this position by not selling the shares he owned and by vetoing any sale by the trustee of the transferred shares. These rights, it is said, gave him control over corporate dividend policy. By increasing, decreasing, or stopping dividends completely, it is argued that Byrum could "regulate the flow of income to the trust" and thereby shift or defer the beneficial enjoyment of trust income between the present beneficiaries and the remaindermen. The sum of this retained power is said to be tantamount to a grantor-trustee's power to accumulate income in the trust, which this Court has recognized constitutes the power to designate the persons who shall enjoy the income from transferred property.

At the outset we observe that this Court has never held that trust property must be included in a settlor's gross estate solely because the settlor retained the power to manage trust assets. On the contrary, since our decision in Reinecke v. Northern Trust Co., 278 U.S. 339 (1929), it has been recognized that a settlor's retention of broad powers of management does not necessarily subject an *inter vivos* trust to the federal estate tax. Although there was no statutory analogue to § 2036(a)(2) when *Northern Trust* was decided, several lower court decisions decided after the enactment of the predecessor of § 2036(a)(2) have upheld the settlor's right to exercise managerial powers without incurring estate-tax liability. * * *

[The Court noted that *Northern Trust*, while it was of some value, was not controlling since it was not decided under § 2036(a)(2) or its predecessor. It then went on to discuss the case.] The holding of *Northern Trust*, that the settlor of a trust may retain broad powers of management without adverse estate-tax consequences, may have been relied upon in the drafting of hundreds of *inter vivos* trusts. The modification of this principle now sought by the Government could have a seriously adverse impact, especially upon settlors (and their estates) who happen to have been "controlling" stockholders of a closely held corporation. Courts properly have been reluctant to depart from an interpretation of tax law which has been generally accepted when the departure could have potentially far-reaching consequences. When a principle of taxation requires reexamination, Congress is better equipped than a court to define precisely the type of conduct which results in tax consequences. When courts readily undertake such tasks, taxpayers may not rely with assurance on what appear to be established rules lest they be subsequently overturned. Legislative enactments, on the other hand, although not always free from ambiguity, at least afford the taxpayers advance warning.

* * *

[The Court next addressed the IRS contention that United States v. O'Malley compelled inclusion of the donated stock in Byrum's estate under § 2036(a)(2). It noted *O'Malley* was covered by § 2036(a)(2) because in that case the settlor, in the deed of trust, had expressly reserved the legal right, in conjunction with two other parties, to accumulate income and thereby designate the condition of its enjoyment by others.]

It must be conceded that Byrum reserved no such "right" in the trust instrument or otherwise. The term "right," certainly when used in a tax statute, must be given its normal and customary meaning. It connotes an ascertainable and legally enforceable power, such as that involved in

O'Malley. Here, the right ascribed to Byrum was the power to use his majority position and influence over the corporate directors to "regulate the flow of dividends" to the trust. That "right" was neither ascertainable nor legally enforceable and hence was not a right in any normal sense of that term.

Byrum did retain the legal right to vote shares held by the trust and to veto investments and reinvestments. But the corporate trustee alone, not Byrum, had the right to pay out or withhold income and thereby to designate who among the beneficiaries enjoyed such income. Whatever power Byrum may have possessed with respect to the flow of income into the trust was derived not from an enforceable legal right specified in the trust instrument, but from the fact that he could elect a majority of the directors of the three corporations. The power to elect the directors conferred no legal right to command them to pay or not to pay dividends. A majority shareholder has a fiduciary duty not to misuse his power by promoting his personal interests at the expense of corporate interests. Moreover, the directors also have a fiduciary duty to promote the interests of the corporation. * * *

The Government seeks to equate the *de facto* position of a controlling stockholder with the legally enforceable "right" specified by the statute. Retention of corporate control (through the right to vote the shares) is said to be "tantamount to the power to accumulate income" in the trust which resulted in estate tax consequences in *O'Malley*. The Government goes on to assert that "[t]hrough exercise of that retained power, [Byrum] could increase or decrease corporate dividends . . . and thereby shift or defer the beneficial enjoyment of trust income." This approach seems to us not only to depart from the specific statutory language, but also to misconceive the realities of corporate life.

* * * In making decisions with respect to dividends, the board must consider a number of factors. It must balance the expectation of stockholders to reasonable dividends when earned against corporate needs for retention of earnings. The first responsibility of the board is to safeguard corporate financial viability for the long term. This means, among other things, the retention of sufficient earnings to assure adequate working capital as well as resources for retirement of debt, for replacement and modernization of plant and equipment, and for growth and expansion. The nature of a corporation's business, as well as the policies and long-range plans of management, are also relevant to dividend payment decisions. Directors of a closely held, small corporation must bear in mind the relatively limited access of such an enterprise to capital markets. This may require a more conservative policy with respect to dividends than would be expected of an established corporation with securities listed on national exchanges.

Nor do small corporations have the flexibility or the opportunity available to national concerns in the utilization of retained earnings. When earnings are substantial, a decision not to pay dividends may result only in the accumulation of surplus rather than growth through internal or external expansion. The accumulated earnings may result in the imposition of a penalty tax.

These various economic considerations are ignored at the directors' peril. Although vested with broad discretion in determining whether, when, and what amount of dividends shall be paid, that discretion is subject to legal restraints. If, in obedience to the will of the majority stockholder, corporate directors disregard the interests of shareholders by accumulating earnings to an unreasonable extent, they are vulnerable to a derivative suit. They are similarly vulnerable if they make an unlawful payment of dividends in the absence of net earnings or available surplus, or if they fail to exercise the requisite degree of care in discharging their duty to act only in the best interest of the corporation and its stockholders.

Byrum was similarly inhibited by a fiduciary duty from abusing his position as majority shareholder for personal or family advantage to the detriment of the corporation or other stockholders. There were a substantial number of minority stockholders in these corporations who were unrelated to Byrum. Had Byrum and the directors violated their duties, the minority shareholders would have had a cause of action under Ohio law. * * *

We conclude that Byrum did not have an unconstrained *de facto* power to regulate the flow of dividends to the trust, much less the "right" to designate who was to enjoy the income from trust property. His ability to affect, but not control, trust income, was a qualitatively different power from that of the settlor in *O'Malley*, who had a specific and enforceable right to control the income paid to the beneficiaries. Even had Byrum managed to flood the trust with income, he had no way of compelling the trustee to pay it out rather than accumulate it. Nor could he prevent the trustee from making payments from other trust assets, although admittedly there were few of these at the time of Byrum's death. We cannot assume, however, that no other assets would come into the trust from reinvestments or other gifts.

We find no merit to the Government's contention that Byrum's *de facto* "control," subject as it was to the economic and legal constraints set forth above, was tantamount to the right to designate the persons who shall enjoy trust income, specified by § 2036(a)(2).

The Government asserts an alternative ground for including the shares transferred to the trust within Byrum's gross estate. It argues that by retaining control, Byrum guaranteed himself continued employment and remuneration, as well as the right to determine whether and when the corporations would be liquidated or merged. Byrum is thus said to have retained "the . . . enjoyment of . . . the property" making it includable within his gross estate under § 2036(a)(1). The Government concedes that the retention of the voting rights of an "unimportant minority interest" would not require inclusion of the transferred shares under § 2036(a)(1). It argues, however, "where the cumulative effect of the retained powers and the rights flowing from the shares not placed in trust leaves the grantor in control of a close corporation and assures that control for his lifetime, he has retained the 'enjoyment' of the transferred stock."

It is well settled that the terms "enjoy" and "enjoyment," as used in various estate tax statutes, "are not terms of art, but connote substantial present economic benefit rather than technical vesting of title or estates." For example, in Reinecke v. Northern Trust Co., 278 U.S. 339 (1929), in which the critical inquiry was whether the decedent had created a trust "intended . . . 'to take effect in possession or enjoyment at or after his death,'" the Court held that reserved powers of management of trust assets, similar to Byrum's power over the three corporations, did not subject an *inter vivos* trust to the federal estate tax. In determining whether the settlor had retained the enjoyment of the transferred property, the Court said:

> "Nor did the reserved powers of management of the trusts save to decedent any control over the economic benefits or the enjoyment of the property. He would equally have reserved all these powers and others had he made himself the trustee, but the transfer would not for that reason have been incomplete. The shifting of the economic interest in the trust property which was the subject of the tax was thus complete as soon as the trust was made. His power to recall the property and of control over it for his own benefit then ceased and as the trusts were not made in contemplation of death, the reserved powers do not serve to distinguish them from any other gift *inter vivos* not subject to the tax." 278 U.S., at 346–347.

* * *

As the Government concedes, the mere retention of the right-to-vote shares does not constitute the type of "enjoyment" in the property itself contemplated by § 2036(a)(1). In addition to being against the weight of precedent, the Government's argument that Byrum *retained* "enjoyment" within the meaning of § 2036(a)(1) is conceptually unsound. This argument implies, as it must under the express language of § 2036(a), that Byrum "retained for his life . . . (1) the possession or enjoyment" of the *"property"* transferred to the trust or the *"income"* therefrom. The only property he transferred was corporate stock. He did not transfer "control" (in the sense used by the Government) as the trust never owned as much as 50% of the stock of any corporation. Byrum never divested himself of control, as he was able to vote a majority of the shares by virtue of what he owned and the right to vote those placed in the trust. Indeed, at the time of his death he still owned a majority of the shares in the largest of the corporations and probably would have exercised control of the other two by virtue of being a large stockholder in each. The statutory language plainly contemplates retention of an attribute of the property transferred—such as a right to income, use of the property itself, or a power of appointment with respect either to income or principal.[34]

Even if Byrum had transferred a majority of the stock, but had retained voting control, he would not have retained "substantial present economic benefit." The Government points to the retention of two "benefits." The first of these, the power to liquidate or merge, is not a *present* benefit; rather, it is a speculative and contingent benefit which may or may not be realized. Nor is the probability of continued employment and compensation the substantial "enjoyment of . . . [the transferred] property" within the meaning of the statute. The dominant stockholder in a closely held corporation, if he is active and productive, is likely to hold a senior position and to enjoy the advantage of a significant voice in his own compensation. These are inevitable facts of the free enterprise system, but the influence and capability of a controlling stockholder to favor himself are not without constraints. Where there are minority stockholders, as in this case, directors may be held accountable if their employment, compensation and retention of officers violate their duty to act reasonably in the best interest of the corporation and all of its stockholders. Moreover, this duty is policed, albeit indirectly, by the Internal Revenue Service, which disallows the deduction of unreasonable compensation paid to a corporate executive as a business expense. We conclude that Byrum's retention of voting control was not the retention of the enjoyment of the transferred property within the meaning of the statute.

* * *

NOTES

1. A case applying the *Byrum* doctrine to dramatic facts was Estate of Gilman v. Commissioner, 547 F.2d 32 (2d Cir.1976). There the decedent set up a voting trust with six shares representing control of a paper company. Though the government claimed that the decedent continued to "enjoy" the six shares, which were valued at $24,500,000 by the Commissioner, the court held the case was governed by *Byrum*.

---

[34] The interpretation given § 2036(a) by the Government * * * would seriously disadvantage settlors in a control posture. If the settlor remained a controlling stockholder, any transfer of stock would be taxable to his estate. * * *

2.   The Tax Reform Act of 1976 added a so-called anti-*Byrum* provision that, refined by the Revenue Act of 1978, now appears as section 2036(b). In general, under this section the retention of the right to vote stock of a controlled corporation is deemed to be retention of the enjoyment of the transferred property with the potential for inclusion in the estate under section 2036(a)(1). A corporation is treated as a controlled corporation if, at any time within the three years preceding the decedent's death or after the transfer of its stock, the decedent owned or had the right (either alone or in conjunction with another) to vote stock possessing at least 20 percent of the combined voting power of all classes of stock.

Within a few years after the passage of section 2036(b), its limited potential was amply demonstrated by Revenue Ruling 81–15, 1981–1 C.B. 457. In that ruling, the IRS indicated that section 2036(b) would not apply to a situation in which an individual contributed assets to a newly formed corporation in exchange for 10 shares of voting common stock and 990 shares of nonvoting common stock and then proceeded to retain the voting stock and to transfer the nonvoting stock to a trust for the benefit of his children. Since the donor could not vote the transferred stock and since it never was endowed with voting rights, he could not be viewed as having retained voting rights with respect to it. Several private letter rulings have subsequently been issued, which are in accord with Revenue Ruling 81–15. See, e.g., Priv. Ltr. Ruls. 9004017 and 9004009.

In addition, the IRS ruled on a situation in which two brothers each transferred an identical amount of stock possessing more than 20% of the voting control in a family corporation to a family limited partnership in which each brother would be a 50% general partner. The partnership agreement provided that in the event the brothers could not agree to how the stock was to be voted, each could vote a proportionate share (50%) of the stock held by the partnership. On the occasion of the death of one brother, the IRS ruled that the shares that he contributed to the partnership were to be included in his estate under section 2036(b) because under the agreement he would be allowed to vote those shares without the agreement of his brother. Moreover, the IRS noted that even if acquiescence of the other brother had been required for the stock to be voted, the "either alone or in conjunction with any person" language of section 2036 (b)(2) would have required inclusion of the stock in the decedent's estate. Tech. Adv. Mem. 199938005.

Typical corporations first confront an income tax on their profits and then must pay their dividends, which are taxable as income to their shareholders from after-tax earnings. Moreover, compensation paid to a corporation's employees, although taxable to them as income, is deductible by the corporation in calculating its income for tax purposes. The result of this is that most owners of small businesses arrange to draw their profits from the enterprise in the form of tax-deductible salaries. Consequently, they typically tend to view corporate offices and employment, and not ownership of stock on which dividends might be paid, as the principal means whereby they are to be provided with a stream of income from the corporate enterprise. They are concerned with maintaining voting control with respect to the corporation for two reasons: (1) to insure their continued employment in the enterprise; and (2) to control the economic future of the enterprise. Revenue Ruling 81–15 provides them with a splendid means whereby they can realize these goals and yet remove from their estates much of the economic value of their companies.

5.   RETAINED POWER SUBJECT TO STANDARD

Where the decedent retains a power subject to a standard, the issue occasionally arises as to whether the standard in essence has deprived the decedent of discretion so that we may safely conclude that the decedent in fact does not possess a "power" (as contrasted with a mere ministerial obligation) described in section 2036(a)(2).

OLD COLONY TRUST CO. v. UNITED STATES
United States Court of Appeals, First Circuit, 1970.
423 F.2d 601.

ALDRICH, CHIEF JUDGE.

The sole question in this case is whether the estate of a settlor of an inter vivos trust, who was a trustee until the date of his death, is to be charged with the value of the principal he contributed by virtue of reserved powers in the trust. The executor paid the tax and sued for its recovery in the district court. All facts were stipulated. The court ruled for the government, 300 F.Supp. 1032, and the executor appeals.

The initial life beneficiary of the trust was the settlor's adult son. Eighty per cent of the income was normally to be payable to him, and the balance added to principal. Subsequent beneficiaries were the son's widow and his issue. The powers upon which the government relies to cause the corpus to be includible in the settlor-trustee's estate are contained in two articles. A third article, purporting to limit the personal liability of the trustees for acts of mismanagement, although relied on by the government, has no bearing on the questions in this case because it does not affect the meaning, extent or nature of the trustees' duties and powers. Briggs v. Crowley, 1967, 352 Mass. 194. We will not consider it further.

Article 4 permitted the trustees to increase the percentage of income payable to the son beyond the eighty per cent,

> "in their absolute discretion * * * when in their opinion such increase is needed in case of sickness, or desirable in view of changed circumstances."

In addition, under Article 4 the trustees were given the discretion to cease paying income to the son, and add it all to principal, "during such period as the Trustees may decide that the stoppage of such payments is for his best interests."

Article 7 gave broad administrative or management powers to the trustees, with discretion to acquire investments not normally held by trustees, and the right to determine, what was to be charged or credited to income or principal, including stock dividends or deductions for amortization. It further provided that all divisions and decisions made by the trustees in good faith should be conclusive on all parties, and in summary, stated that the trustees were empowered, "generally to do all things in relation to the Trust Fund which the Donor could do if living and this Trust had not been executed."

The government claims that each of these two articles meant that the settlor-trustee had "the right * * * to designate the persons who shall possess or enjoy the [trust] property or the income therefrom" within the meaning of section 2036(a)(2) of the Internal Revenue Code of 1954, 26 U.S.C. § 2036(a)(2), and that the settlor-trustee at the date of his death possessed a power "to alter, amend, revoke, or terminate" within the meaning of section 2038(a)(1) (26 U.S.C. § 2038(a)(1)).

If State Street Trust Co. v. United States, 1 Cir., 1959, 263 F.2d 635, was correctly decided in this aspect, the government must prevail because of the Article 7 powers. There this court, Chief Judge Magruder dissenting, held against the taxpayer because broad powers similar to those in Article 7 meant that the trustees "could very substantially shift the economic benefits of the trusts between the life tenants and the remaindermen," so that the settlor "as long as he lived, in substance and effect and in a very real sense * * * 'retained for his life * * * the right * * * to designate the persons who shall possess or enjoy the property or the income therefrom; * * *.'" 263 F.2d at 639–40, quoting 26 U.S.C. § 2036(a)(2). We accept the taxpayer's invitation to reconsider this ruling.

It is common ground that a settlor will not find the corpus of the trust included in his estate merely because he named himself a trustee. Jennings v. Smith, 2 Cir., 1947, 161 F.2d 74. He must have reserved a power to himself[2] that is inconsistent with the full termination of ownership. The government's brief defines this as "sufficient dominion and control until his death." Trustee powers given for the administration or management of the trust must be equitably exercised, however, for the benefit of the trust as a whole. The court in *State Street* conceded that the powers at issue were all such powers, but reached the conclusion that, cumulatively, they gave the settlor dominion sufficiently unfettered to be in the nature of ownership. With all respect to the majority of the then court, we find it difficult to see

---

[2] The number of other trustees who must join in the exercise of that power, unless the others have antagonistic interests of a substantial nature is, of course, immaterial. Treas. Reg. § 20.2036–1(a)(ii), (b)(3)(i)(1958); § 20.2038–1(a)(1958).

how a power can be subject to control by the probate court, and exercisable only in what the trustee fairly concludes is in the interests of the trust and its beneficiaries as a whole, and at the same time be an ownership power.

The government's position, to be sound, must be that the trustee's powers are beyond the court's control. Under Massachusetts law, however, no amount of administrative discretion prevents judicial supervision of the trustee. Thus in Appeal of Davis, 1903, 183 Mass. 499, a trustee was given "full power to make purchases, investments and exchanges * * * in such manner as to them shall seem expedient; it being my intention to give my trustees * * * the same dominion and control over said trust property as I now have." In spite of this language, and in spite of their good faith, the court charged the trustees for failing sufficiently to diversify their investment portfolio.

The Massachusetts court has never varied from this broad rule of accountability, and has twice criticized *State Street* for its seeming departure. Boston Safe Deposit & Trust Co. v. Stone, 1965, 348 Mass. 345, 351, n. 8; Old Colony Trust Co. v. Silliman, 1967, 352 Mass. 6, 8–9. See also, Estate of McGillicuddy, 54 T.C. 315 (1970). We make a further observation, which the court in *State Street* failed to note, that the provision in that trust (as in the case at bar) that the trustees could "do all things in relation to the Trust Fund which I, the Donor, could do if * * * the Trust had not been executed," is almost precisely the provision which did not protect the trustees from accountability in *Appeal of Davis,* supra.

We do not believe that trustee powers are to be more broadly construed for tax purposes than the probate court would construe them for administrative purposes. More basically, we agree with Judge Magruder's observation that nothing is "gained by lumping them together." State Street Trust Co. v. United States, supra, at 642. We hold that no aggregation of purely administrative powers can meet the government's amorphous test of "sufficient dominion and control" so as to be equated with ownership.

This does not resolve taxpayer's difficulties under Article 4. Quite different considerations apply to distribution powers. Under them the trustee can, expressly, prefer one beneficiary over another. Furthermore, his freedom of choice may vary greatly, depending upon the terms of the individual trust. If there is an ascertainable standard, the trustee can be compelled to follow it. If there is not, even though he is a fiduciary, it is not unreasonable to say that his retention of an unmeasurable freedom of choice is equivalent to retaining some of the incidents of ownership. Hence, under the cases, if there is an ascertainable standard the settlor-trustee's estate is not taxed, but if there is not, it is taxed.

The trust provision which is uniformly held to provide an ascertainable standard is one which, though variously expressed, authorizes such distributions as may be needed to continue the beneficiary's accustomed way of life. On the other hand, if the trustee may go further, and has power to provide for the beneficiary's "happiness," or "pleasure," or "use and benefit," or "reasonable requirement[s]," the standard is so loose that the trustee is in effect uncontrolled.

In the case at bar the trustees could increase the life tenant's income "in case of sickness, or [if] desirable in view of changed circumstances." Alternatively, they could reduce it "for his best interests." "Sickness" presents no problem. Conceivably, providing for "changed circumstances" is roughly equivalent to maintaining the son's present standard of living. The unavoidable stumbling block is the trustees' right to accumulate income and add it to capital (which the son would never receive) when it is to the "best interests" of the son to do so. Additional payments to a beneficiary whenever in his "best interests" might seem to be too broad a standard in any event. * * * [S]ee Estate of Yawkey, 1949, 12 T.C. 1164, where the court said, at p. 1170,

> "We can not regard the language involved ['best interest'] as limiting the usual scope of a trustee's discretion. It must always be anticipated that trustees will act for the best interests of a trust beneficiary, and an exhortation to act 'in the interests and for the welfare' of the beneficiary does not establish an external standard."

Power, however, to decrease or cut off a beneficiary's income when in his "best interests," is even more troublesome. When the beneficiary is the son, and the trustee the father, a particular purpose comes to mind, parental control through holding the purse strings. The father decides what conduct is to the "best interests" of the son, and if the son does not agree, he loses his allowance. Such a power has the plain indicia of ownership control. The alternative, that the son, because of other means, might not need this income, and would prefer to have it accumulate for his widow and children after his death, is no better. If the trustee has power to confer "happiness" on the son by generosity to someone else, this seems clearly an unascertainable standard. Cf. Merchants Nat'l Bank v. Com'r, supra, at 261–263.

The case of Hays' Estate v. Com'r, 5 Cir., 1950, 181 F.2d 169, is contrary to our decision. The opinion is unsupported by either reasoning or authority, and we will not follow it. With the present settlor-trustee free to determine the standard himself, a finding of ownership control was warranted. To put it another way, the cost of holding onto the strings may prove to be a rope burn. State Street Bank & Trust Co. v. United States, supra.

Affirmed.

PLANNING NOTE

Where the settlor of a trust does not wish to retain the right to income from a trust but rather wishes to retain some flexibility with respect to the degree of enjoyment of property or designation of the ultimate beneficiaries, it is often possible to strike some balance that goes a long way toward realizing the settlor's goals. By not personally retaining the section 2036(a)(2) right, but by placing that right in a trusted individual who shares the settlor's values, the planning goals of the settlor can often be accommodated. Siblings of the settlor, a spouse, close friends, or even a trusted attorney often prove to be adequate alter egos for settlors who can let go at least to this degree. When selecting such individuals three principal concerns exist. First, the settlor should be sure that potential beneficiaries of the power possessed by these individuals are neither the individuals themselves nor the natural objects of the bounty of these individuals. Here, however, an exception may be tolerated if the designated individual is a spouse without issue from a prior marriage who are potential beneficiaries along with the settlor's own issue. For example, to allow one's brother to designate who among the issue of the settlor's parents will enjoy income from a trust is only asking for trouble. Problems might also be expected to arise if a previously married spouse with issue from both marriages is allowed to designate who among her issue will enjoy income from a trust. Second, care should be taken that the designated individual does not have similar plans for the settlor with the result that reciprocal trusts may be found to be present. Third, care should be taken that the trustee has and functions with sufficient independence from the settlor so as to preclude the IRS from asserting that, based on the trustee's lack of independence, the settlor has retained the powers invested in the trustee. Recall that in Rev. Rul. 95–58, the IRS embraced section 672(c) as a standard. Given the accepted use of relatives as trustees in numerous cases and rulings, section 672(c) is unlikely to become a judicial standard. Nonetheless, care should be taken that, at a minimum, the designated individual functions independently.

From the settlor's standpoint, appointment of a trusted attorney as a trustee who possesses discretionary powers may provide a solution to the settlor's tax problems. However, because of significant potential legal liability, it may be wise for the attorney to decline the honor and fee unless the attorney's firm and liability insurance policies are well equipped to cope with all eventualities.

D. AMOUNT INCLUDIBLE

Significant questions occasionally arise as to the amount of property that is required to be included in the decedent's gross estate when section 2036 applies. Generally, the entire corpus of a trust subject to a retained life interest is to be included in the gross estate at its date of death value (or at its alternate valuation date value). The regulations indicate that several exceptions to this general rule are worthy of consideration. First, Regulation § 20.2036–1(a) indicates that, where the decedent retained an income interest in only a portion of an asset (e.g., a one-third interest), just that portion of the trust corpus will be included in the decedent's estate. Moreover, as noted previously, if the decedent retained only a contingent life estate following upon the life estate of another, which life estate was presently being enjoyed, the estate would include the full value of the trust, minus the value of the life estate that was being enjoyed at the decedent's death. See Treas. Reg. § 20.2036–1(b)(1)(ii).

Another issue of interest involves situations in which income from a trust, with respect to which decedent retained a prohibited interest or power, is retained by the trust and added to corpus. At the decedent's death should the entire trust corpus be included or, as is done under section 2035, should the value represented by the retained income be excluded?

In United States v. O'Malley, 383 U.S. 627 (1966), the Supreme Court decided that in such a situation the entire trust corpus, consisting of the original corpus as well as retained income, should be included in the estate of the decedent, Edward Fabrice. The following excerpt from its opinion explains why the Court reached this conclusion:

> At the time Fabrice established these trusts, he owned all of the rights to the property transferred, a major aspect of which was his right to the present and future income produced by that property. With the creation of the trusts, he relinquished all of his rights to income except the power to distribute that income to the income beneficiaries or to accumulate it and hold it for the remaindermen of the trusts. He no longer had, for example, the right to income for his own benefit or to have it distributed to any other than the trust beneficiaries. Moreover, with respect to the very additions to principal now at issue, he exercised his retained power to distribute or accumulate income, choosing to do the latter and thereby adding to the principal of the trusts. All income increments to trust principal are therefore traceable to Fabrice himself, by virtue of the original transfer and the exercise of the power to accumulate. Before the creation of the trusts, Fabrice owned all rights to the property and to its income. By the time of his death he had divested himself of all power and control over accumulated income which had been added to the principal, except the power to deal with the income from such additions. With respect to each addition to trust principal from accumulated income, Fabrice had clearly made a "transfer" as required by § 811(c)(1)(B)(ii) [now § 2036(a)(2)]. Under that section, the power over income retained by Fabrice is sufficient to require the inclusion of the original corpus of the trust in his gross estate. The accumulated income added to principal is subject to the same power and is likewise includable.

Id. at 432–33.

E. FAMILY LIMITED PARTNERSHIPS

In brief, members of the senior generation, typically a mother and father, will contribute assets to a partnership, receiving partnership interests in exchange for the contributed assets. The parents will then give each of the children an interest in the partnership, claiming a large valuation discount based on the interposition of an entity (the partnership) between the underlying assets and the ownership interest transferred and will also claim a discount based on the transfer of a minority interest to each of their children. On death, each of the parents will also claim a significant discount (typically in the range of 50%) based on their ownership of a minority interest in an entity that owns the underlying assets. If the parents prefer, they can dispense with the lifetime gifts and merely seek a more modest discount based solely on interposition of an entity.

In addition to addressing the legitimacy of the discounts, the Internal Revenue Service has also sought to attack such transfers under section 2036 on the ground that the taxpayer has retained either: (1) the enjoyment of the income from property held by the partnership; or (2) the right to control enjoyment of such property. Taxpayers may encounter difficulties under section 2036(a)(1) or section 2036(a)(2). Taxpayers typically encounter problems under section 2036(a)(1) by transferring all, or virtually all, their assets to the family limited partnership (FLP) and leaving themselves reliant on the FLP for housing and funds for their support and maintenance. Relying on either explicit agreement to provide for the taxpayer's support or implicit understandings, the courts may include the transferred assets in the taxpayer's gross estate. Taxpayers can likely avoid the reach of section 2036(a)(1) by retaining housing and sufficient assets to provide for their support and maintenance and other anticipated needs and pleasures and transferring to the partnership assets employed in the conduct of a business or assets requiring active management. See, e.g., Estate of Kimbell v. United States, 371 F.3d 257 (5th Cir. 2004).

FLP cases in which the taxpayer's loss hinges on section 2036(a)(2) are less common. The theory of any such holding would center on the fact that the taxpayer retained the right to control enjoyment by others of income from transferred property based on his control over the distribution of income and assets from the FLP. In Kimbell v. United States, 244 F. Supp. 2d 700 (N.D. Texas 2003), the district court held that the property was included in the taxpayer's gross estate under section 2036(a)(2), based on taxpayer's ability to control entity decisions with a 50% ownership interest, only to be reversed by the court of appeals, which noted that more than 50% ownership by the taxpayer would be essential to find a controlling interest. More importantly, the court of appeals also found that, because the taxpayer, pursuant to arrangements set in place as part of establishment of the entity, had obtained the benefit of participation in the management by his son of properties contributed to the FLP, adequate and full consideration (in the form of management services) was present and it was actually irrelevant whether the taxpayer retained any control over transferred assets. See Kimbell v. United States, 371 F.3d 257 (5th Cir. 2004). In Estate of Strangi v. Commissioner, 85 T.C.M. (CCH) 1331 (2003), the Tax Court found that that property was included in the taxpayer's gross estate under both sections 2036(a)(1) and 2036(a)(2). The court's section 2036(a)(1) finding was based on the fact that the taxpayer had placed ninety-eight percent of his wealth, including his residence, in the FLP. The section 2036(a)(2) finding was based on the fact that, pursuant to the arrangement that the taxpayer had put in place, through his son-in-law/attorney-in-fact, the taxpayer held the power to determine distributions of income and other partnership assets. The Tax Court's decision in *Strangi* was affirmed by the court of appeals. See Estate of Strangi v. Commissioner, 417 F.3d 468 (5th Cir. 2005). Because the Tax Court found a deficiency based on both sections 2036(a)(1) and 2036(a)(2), it is uncertain whether the court of appeals fully bought into the Tax Court's section 2036(a)(2) finding or it should be characterized as mere dictum.

One of the most important cases dealing with FLPs since *Strangi* is the reviewed Tax Court decision in Estate of Powell, 148 T.C. 392 (2017). In *Powell*, the decedent's son as power of attorney contributed about $10 million in money and securities from the decedent's revocable trust to a FLP in return for a 99% limited partnership interest. The son was the general partner. On the same day and within seven days of the decedent's death, the son as power of attorney transferred the decedent's interest to a charitable lead annuity trust (CLAT). The court determined that section 2036(a)(2) applied because the limited partnership in conjunction with the other partners could have dissolved the partnership at any time. The *Powell* case is excerpted in Chapter 24 that extensively discusses FLPs and whether these types of transfers are "bona fide for an adequate and full consideration in money or money's worth." Even if a transfer falls within the scope of either section 2036(a)(1) or section 2036(a)(2), the taxpayer still has the opportunity to demonstrate that the property was transferred for adequate and full consideration.

A taxpayer who seeks to form a FLP and thereby obtain a significant valuation discount, as well as keeping a good distance from the reaches of section 2036, should be sure that her estate planner has consulted the most recent cases and has paid special attention to the line of cases that will be determinative of the result in her legal forum.

PROBLEMS

1. A mother gave a beach cottage to her son Paul, but as a result of an understanding with Paul she continued to use the cottage free of any rent for the month of September until her death eight years after the gift. What, if anything, is includible in the mother's estate?

2. Nick established a trust for the benefit of his grandchildren. Under the terms of the trust, the income was annually distributed to the grandchildren in equal amounts, with the corpus to be divided equally among them when the youngest reached 25 years. Nick, who died while the trust was in effect, retained the right to remove the corporate trustee and to replace it with an independent corporate trustee. Does this result in an inclusion in Nick's estate?

3. Would your answer be any different in the prior problem if the corporate trustee had discretion to distribute income among the grandchildren in unequal shares and to withhold income, adding it to corpus?

4. Alan made a gift of $50,000 of stock to his minor son, Zack, under the Uniform Transfers to Minors Act, naming himself as custodian. Alan died when Zack was still a minor and the stock was worth $80,000. What, if anything, is includible in Alan's estate?

5. In the prior problem, assume that rather than appointing himself as guardian, Alan had appointed his wife, Carolyn. What is the tax result?

6. In the prior problem, assume that Carolyn had also made a gift of $50,000 of stock to Zack and that, just as Alan decided to appoint her as custodian for his gift, she also decided to appoint Alan as custodian for her gift. What is the tax result?

7. Marsha and John divorced. John was given custody of their minor son, Chase, and Marsha was given custody of their minor daughter, Brittany. As part of the divorce settlement, John, to satisfy his support obligation, placed $1,200,000 in trust with income to Marsha for her life and remainder over to a trust for the children. In addition, as part of the settlement, in satisfaction of his obligation to support Brittany, he placed $400,000 in trust with income to Brittany for her support until she reaches age 25, at which time corpus is to be distributed to Brittany. In order to protect Chase's feelings, John established a similar support trust for him, funding it with $400,000. At John's death last month, the children were still in their minority and the trusts had not increased in value. What are the estate tax consequences of the above arrangements?

8. Sally established a trust for the benefit of her three adult children, appointing herself as trustee. Under the terms of the trust, the income was to be divided equally among them, except that Sally retained the right to vary distribution to provide for "medical emergencies, professional education and inability of any beneficiary to support himself or herself." What are the tax consequences of this trust at Sally's death?

9. In the prior problem, assume that the trust also gave Sally the right to vary distributions "for any other valid reason." What are the tax consequences?

10. Brianna created an irrevocable trust and transferred stock to it. Under the terms of the trust, all income was to be paid to her daughter, Shelby, for life, and upon Shelby's death, the corpus was to be distributed to Shelby's son, Jeff. Brianna retained the right to terminate the trust at any time with Shelby's consent and give the stock outright to Jeff. When Brianna died, Shelby and Jeff were alive, and the trust had not been terminated. Is the stock included in Brianna's gross estate?

11. Adam established an irrevocable trust under which he was entitled to income for 10 years and transferred an apartment building into the trust. The apartment building was worth $800,000 at the time of the transfer. At the end of the 10-year period, the trust would terminate, and the corpus would be distributed to his daughter, Jordyn. Adam died eight years after he had created the trust. The apartment building was worth $1 million at the time of Adam's death. What, if anything, is included in Adam's gross estate?

12. Garrett created an irrevocable trust and transferred stock to it. Under the terms of the trust, all income was to be paid to his daughter, Candace, for life, and upon Candace's death, the corpus was to be distributed to Candace's son, Anthony. Garrett retained the right to terminate the trust at any time and give the property outright to Candace. When Garrett died, Candace and Anthony were alive, and Garrett had not terminated the trust. Is the stock included in Garrett's gross estate?

CHAPTER 19

POWERS TO ALTER, AMEND, REVOKE, OR TERMINATE

(SECTION 2038)

■ ■ ■

A. HISTORICAL INTRODUCTION

As mentioned in the introduction of Chapter 18, the Internal Revenue Code as originally enacted in 1916 contained a provision that included in the gross estate all transfers "intended to take effect at or after death." The Supreme Court gave a very limited interpretation to this provision, in effect rendering this language impotent. Congress responded by passing several specific sections, among them section 2038, which were intended to sweep within the gross estate those property interests that an unenthusiastic Supreme Court allowed to escape.

Clearly, a taxpayer who once owned property and transferred it while retaining the right to revoke the transfer should be deemed to be the owner of the property at death. It is the death of the taxpayer holding such a right to revoke that effectively transfers the taxpayer's right to the property. Section 2038 insures that all such property will be included in the taxpayer's gross estate. It goes somewhat further and, in general, sweeps into the gross estate property transferred by a taxpayer who retained the power, acting alone or in conjunction with others, to alter, amend, revoke or terminate enjoyment of the property transferred. It does not apply if the transfer was a bona fide sale for an adequate and full consideration in money or money's worth.

In the cases that follow some light is shed on the kinds of powers regarded as taxable under section 2038. The student should be able to achieve some feeling of confidence concerning the taxable status of powers not exercisable in favor of the transferor, narrow powers permitting only a shift as between two beneficiaries, powers to simply speed up distribution to a beneficiary, and perhaps as to the taxability of powers subject to standards as well as the significance for purposes of section 2038 of retained administrative powers.

As you read section 2038 and the materials that follow, consider how the section partially overlaps with section 2036(a)(2). The extent of the overlap will be addressed elsewhere in this chapter.

B. BREADTH OF POWER

Many of the issues that were confronted under section 2036(a)(2) are also issues under section 2038. For example, in defining the breadth of section 2038, it is necessary to consider whether that section encompasses within its sweep retentions of the right to alter enjoyment of property in a personally nonbeneficial manner or the right to determine not who will enjoy the property but merely when the designated beneficiary will enjoy it.

In Porter v. Commissioner, 288 U.S. 436 (1933), the Supreme Court was asked to pass on a situation in which the grantor of a trust for benefit of his issue retained to himself the power to alter or modify the terms of the trust indenture "in any manner but expressly excepting any change in favor of himself or his estate." Id. at 439. The executor of his estate argued, to no avail, that, since the retained power could not be exercised in a fashion that would benefit the holder, it should not be included in his estate under section 2038. In finding that inclusion under section 2038 [subdivision (d) of I.R.C. § 302 of the 1926 Revenue Act] requires far less than reservation of the right to revoke enjoyment and revest it in the donor, the Court observed:

> The net estate upon the transfer of which the tax is imposed, is not limited to property that passes from decedent at death. Subdivision (d) [now § 2038] requires to be included in the calculation all property previously transferred by decedent, the enjoyment of which remains at the time of his death subject to any change by the exertion of a power by himself alone or in conjunction with another. Petitioner argues that, as decedent was without power to revoke the transfers or to alter or modify the trusts in favor of himself or his estate, the property is not covered by subdivision (d). But the disjunctive use of the words "alter," "modify" and "amend" negatives that contention. We find nothing in the context or in the policy evidenced by this and prior estate tax laws or in the legislative history of subdivision (d) to suggest that conjunctive use of these words was intended, or that "alter" and "modify" were used as equivalents of "revoke" or are to be understood in other than their usual meanings. We need not consider whether every change, however slight or trivial, would be within the meaning of the clause. Here the donor retained until his death power enough to enable him to make a complete revision of all that he had done in respect of the creation of the trusts even to the extent of taking the property from the trustees and

beneficiaries named and transferring it absolutely or in trust for the benefit of others. So far as concerns the tax here involved, there is no difference in principle between a transfer subject to such changes and one that is revocable. The transfers under consideration are undoubtedly covered by subdivision (d).

Id. at 439.

Porter definitively established that property is to be included within the donor's estate where the donor retains the right to determine the identity of the individual who is to enjoy property or to choose among a class of potential beneficiaries. An issue not decided in *Porter* was whether section 2038 encompassed within its sweep transfers in which only the right to determine the timing of enjoyment is retained by the donor. The case that follows addresses this issue.

LOBER V. UNITED STATES
Supreme Court of the United States, 1953.
346 U.S. 335.

MR. JUSTICE BLACK delivered the opinion of the Court.

This is an action for an estate tax refund brought by the executors of the estate of Morris Lober. In 1924 he signed an instrument conveying to himself as trustee money and stocks for the benefit of his young son. In 1929 he executed two other instruments, one for the benefit of a daughter, the other for a second son. The terms of these three instruments were the same. Lober was to handle the funds, invest and reinvest them as he deemed proper. He could accumulate and reinvest the income with the same freedom until his children reached twenty-one years of age. When twenty-one they were to be paid the accumulated income. Lober could hold the principal of each trust until the beneficiary reached twenty-five. In case he died his wife was to be trustee with the same broad powers Lober had conveyed to himself. The trusts were declared to be irrevocable, and as the case reaches us we may assume that the trust instruments gave Lober's children a "vested interest" under state law, so that if they had died after creation of the trusts their interests would have passed to their estates. A crucial term of the trust instruments was that Lober could at any time he saw fit turn all or any part of the principal of the trusts over to his children. Thus he could at will reduce the principal or pay it all to the beneficiaries, thereby terminating any trusteeship over it.

Lober died in 1942. By that time the trust property was valued at more than $125,000. The Internal Revenue Commissioner treated this as Lober's property and included it in his gross estate. That inclusion brought this lawsuit. The Commissioner relied on § 811(d)(2) [this section is the predecessor of § 2038 of the 1986 Code] of the Internal Revenue Code, 26 U.S.C. § 811 (1946 ed.). That section, so far as material here, required inclusion in a decedent's gross estate of the value of all property that the decedent had previously transferred by trust "where the enjoyment thereof was subject at the date of his death to any change through the exercise of a power . . . to alter, amend, or revoke. . . ." In Commissioner v. Holmes, 326 U.S. 480, we held that power to terminate was the equivalent of power to "alter, amend, or revoke" it, and we approved taxation of the Holmes estate on that basis. Relying on the *Holmes* case, the Court of Claims upheld inclusion of these trust properties in Lober's estate. 108 F.Supp. 731. This was done despite the assumption that the trust conveyances gave the Lober children an indefeasible "vested interest" in the properties conveyed. The Fifth Circuit Court of Appeals had reached a contrary result where the circumstances were substantially the same, in Hays' Estate v. Commissioner, 181 F.2d 169, 172–174. Because of this conflict, we granted certiorari. 345 U.S. 969.

Petitioners stress a factual difference between this and the *Holmes* case. The *Holmes* trust instrument provided that if a beneficiary died before expiration of the trust his children succeeded to his interest, but if he died without children, his interest would pass to his brothers or their children. Thus the trustee had power to eliminate a contingency that might have prevented passage of a beneficiary's interest to his heirs. Here we assume that upon death of the Lober beneficiaries their part in the trust estate would, under New York law, pass to their heirs. But we cannot agree that this difference should change the *Holmes* result.

We pointed out in the *Holmes* case that § 811(d)(2) was more concerned with "present economic benefit" than with "technical vesting of title or estates." And the Lober beneficiaries, like the *Holmes* beneficiaries, were granted no "present right to immediate enjoyment of either income or principal." The trust instrument here gave none of Lober's children full "enjoyment" of the trust property, whether it "vested" in them or not. To get this full enjoyment they had to wait until they reached the age of twenty-five unless their father sooner gave them the money and stocks by terminating the trust under the power of change he kept to the very date of his death. This father could have given property to his children without reserving in himself any power to change the terms as to the date his gift would be wholly effective, but he did not. What we said in the *Holmes* case fits this situation too: "A donor who keeps so strong a hold over the actual and immediate enjoyment of what he puts beyond his own power to retake has not divested himself of that degree of control which § 811(d)(2) requires in order to avoid the tax." Commissioner v. Holmes, supra, at 487.

Affirmed.

NOTES

1. The *Lober* decision, holding that a power to alter or amend does not require that there be any power to shift benefits between beneficiaries but that a mere acceleration or postponement is enough, has far-reaching implications. There may, for example, be disguised powers to advance corpus. In Walter v. United States, 341 F.2d 182 (6th Cir.1965), a power to remove and replace the trustee subjected the trust to the estate tax where the trustee had power to advance principal and the donor could theoretically have removed the trustee and replaced him with herself. Compare Estate of Wall v. Commissioner, 101 T.C. 300 (1993) and Rev. Rul. 95–58 discussed in Chapter 18.

2. Retention or reacquisition by the donor of an overly broad power to divide income and principal can also result in inclusion under section 2038. See Commissioner v. Estate of Hager, 173 F.2d 613 (3d Cir.1949). Clearly, a settlor of a trust who retained the right to designate, as he wished, all accretions to the trust as either income or principal, has reserved to himself the power to determine the timing of enjoyment of property and in many circumstances the identification of the beneficiary. Where the settlor retains merely ordinary fiduciary powers to divide income and principal, a contrary result is clearly in order. In *Hager*, the trust was funded equally by a husband and wife and the retained power was held only by the husband. Since the wife had funded one-half of the trust, the Commissioner successfully sought to include only the one-half of the trust funded by the decedent who had retained the power in question.

PLANNING NOTE

As in the case of section 2036(a)(2), where the settlor of a trust wishes to retain some degree of flexibility with respect to the enjoyment of property and yet desires to escape the reach of the estate tax, this goal can be accomplished by vesting the otherwise troublesome powers in a trusted third party.

C. JOINT POWERS

Section 2038 clearly states that, even if the prohibited power is exercisable by the decedent in conjunction with another person, an inclusion in the estate will, nonetheless, result. Although clear on its face, there are several issues that could be raised about the section. For example, is it relevant that the co-holder of the power has a financial interest that is adversely affected by exercise of the power? Moreover, since common-law trust doctrine allows a trust to be revoked by the settlor and all beneficiaries acting together, are all settlors thereby deemed to be holders of a prohibited joint power? In the case of employee death benefits, is it possible to view a shareholder-employee who has voting control of the corporate employer as a co-holder of the power to alter employee death benefit plans that would otherwise not be taxable? These are the sorts of issues that will be addressed by the cases that follow.

1. BASIC PARAMETERS OF THE PROBLEM

Helvering v. City Bank Farmers Trust Co.

Supreme Court of the United States, 1935.
296 U.S. 85.

Mr. Justice Roberts delivered the opinion of the Court.

* * *

The questions for decision are whether [§ 302(d) of the Revenue Act of 1926; now § 2038] requires inclusion in the gross estate of the value of the corpus of a trust established in 1930 where the creator reserved a power to revoke or modify, to be exercised jointly with a beneficiary and the trustee * * *.

By a writing dated February 21, 1930, Gertrude Feldman James, a non-resident citizen, transferred securities to the respondent as trustee, the trust to last during the lives of her two daughters or the survivor of them. The income was to be paid to her until her death, or until the termination of the trust, whichever should first occur. After her death, her husband surviving, the income was to be paid to him. If he did not outlive her, or upon his death, the income was to be distributed amongst their issue per stirpes. At the termination of the trust the corpus was to be delivered to the husband, if he were alive; if not, to the settlor, if living, or, if she were dead, to the beneficiaries at that time entitled to receive the income; if there were none such, to the heirs at law of the husband. The trust was irrevocable save that the settlor reserved the right to modify, alter or revoke it, in whole or in part, or to change any beneficial interest, any such revocation or alteration to be effected with the written consent of the trustee and her husband or, if the husband were dead, of the trustee and her husband's brother. If they could not agree the decision of the husband or of the brother, as the case might be, was to be final. Samuel James, the husband, survived the grantor, whose death occurred before the termination of the trust, and he is in receipt of the income.

The petitioner included the value of the corpus of the trust in Mrs. James' gross estate and determined a deficiency of tax. The Board of Tax Appeals reversed, holding that § 302(d) [now § 2038] did not apply. The Circuit Court of Appeals affirmed the Board's decision. We granted the writ of certiorari because the decision below conflicts with that in another circuit. We hold that the section covers this case and as so applied is valid.

* * *

The respondent insists that a power to recall an absolute and complete gift only with the consent of the donee is in truth no power at all; that in such case the so-called exercise of the power is equivalent to a new gift from the donee to the donor. And so it is claimed that the statute arbitrarily declares that to exist which in fact and law is nonexistent. The position is untenable. The purpose of Congress in adding clause (d) to the section as it stood in an earlier act was to prevent avoidance of the tax by the device of joining with the grantor in the exercise of the power of revocation someone who he believed would comply with his wishes. Congress may well have thought that a beneficiary who was of the grantor's immediate family might be amenable to persuasion or be induced to consent to a revocation in consideration of other expected benefits from the grantor's estate. Congress may adopt a measure reasonably calculated to prevent avoidance of a tax. * * *

In view of the evident purpose of Congress we find nothing unreasonable or arbitrary in the provisions of § 302(d) of the Revenue Act of 1926 [now § 2038] as applied in the circumstances of this case. It was appropriate for Congress to prescribe that if, subsequently to the passage of that Act, the creator of a trust estate saw fit to reserve to himself jointly with any other person the power of revocation or alteration, the transaction should be deemed to be testamentary in character, that is, treated for the purposes of the law as intended to take effect in possession or enjoyment at the death of the settlor.

The judgment is

Reversed.

NOTE

Is it critical to the Court's analysis that a settlor could modify, revoke, or terminate the trust with consent of only one of the beneficiaries? Should the result be different if the deed of trust required the settlor to obtain the consent of all beneficiaries to undertake such action? The answers are provided by a companion case, *Helvering v. Helmholz*, 296 U.S. 93 (1935), in which the Supreme Court confronted a situation where the settlor, who was also a beneficiary of the trust which she established, merely retained the right to terminate the trust acting together with all beneficiaries. The Court noted that, under common law, all beneficiaries acting with the consent of the settlor could terminate a trust. Consequently, since the settlor had retained no power beyond that provided her by the common law, the Court concluded that Congress cannot tax such transfers under section 2038.

Note that Treas. Reg. § 20.2038–1(a) now incorporates the holdings of the *City Bank Farmers Trust Co.* and *Helmholz* cases.

2. EMPLOYEE DEATH BENEFITS

As we have seen in Chapter 15, if employee death benefits are paid to individuals designated by the employer, rather than by the employee, these benefits are not included in the deceased employee's estate under section 2033. Unhappy with defeats in the section 2033 arena, the Commissioner has sought victory in the section 2038 arena. These efforts have been predicated on the theory that, where the decedent employee is also a shareholder, director or officer of the employer, he or she, acting in conjunction with others of similar stature, could alter the death benefit plan, thereby resulting in inclusion under the joint holder language of section 2038.

ESTATE OF TULLY
United States Court of Claims, 1976.
528 F.2d 1401.

KUNZIG, JUDGE.

[The facts and one issue considered by the court, relating to the application of section 2033, appear in Chapter 15E wherein the court concluded that the employee death benefits provided by the decedent's employer were not includible, under section 2033, in his gross estate. The court here addresses itself to the possibility that section 2038 might make the benefits taxable.]

Defendant argues that Tully transferred an interest in the death benefits at some point prior to his death and kept a section 2038(a)(1) power to "alter, amend, revoke or terminate" the enjoyment of the benefits after the transfer until his death. Plaintiffs counter that there was no "transfer" in the 1959 contract or thereafter because decedent never had any interest in the benefits which he could transfer. Even if a transfer is found, plaintiffs claim Tully did not keep a section 2038(a)(1) "power" after such transfer.

Contrary to plaintiffs' position, Tully did transfer an interest in the death benefits to his wife by executing the 1959 contract. In one of the three death benefit plans at issue in Estate of Bogley v. United States, 514 F.2d 1027, 206 Ct. Cl. 695 (1975), the decedent (an employee, officer, director and 34% shareholder) entered into an enforceable contract with his employer. In consideration of decedent's past and future services, the employer promised to pay decedent's *widow* or the estate two years' salary after his death. We found that where decedent was married at the time of the execution of the contract he " * * * did make a transfer of his interest to his wife during his lifetime by making the contract with [the employer]." Bogley, supra, 514 F.2d at 1039, 206 Ct. Cl. at 715. In the instant case, the basic facts are nearly identical. The 1959 agreement looked to Tully's past and future services to T & D for consideration. The benefits here were also payable to the "widow" and decedent was married at the time of the 1959 contract. Tully in substance, if not in form, made a gift of a part of his future earnings to his wife.

However, within the meaning of section 2038(a)(1), Tully did not keep a power to "alter, amend, revoke or terminate" the death benefit transfer after the 1959 contract. There was no express reservation of such power in either the 1959 or 1963 contracts and no indication in the record of any other express agreements in which Tully obtained a section 2038(a)(1) power.

The Government implies that Tully's 50% stock ownership of T & D gave him unfettered power to change the death benefit plan to suit his own tastes. The facts do not bear this out. To the contrary, Tully's every movement could have been blocked by the other 50% shareholder. Tully did not have individual control of T & D and could not by himself, alter the terms of the death benefit, agreement. As stated by the court in Harris v. United States, 29 Am.Fed.Tax R.2d 1558 (C.D.Cal.1972), section 2038(a)(1) powers must be *demonstrable, real, apparent* and *evident,* not speculative. See also Hinze v. United States, 29 Am.Fed.Tax R.2d 1553 (C.D.Cal.1972). We agree with this test and find Tully did not have a section 2038(a)(1) power to "alter, amend, revoke or terminate" through his 50% stock ownership in T & D at the time of his death.

Moreover, the death benefits are not includable in Tully's gross estate despite the fact that Tully *might* have altered, amended, revoked or terminated them in conjunction with T & D and DiNapoli. A power to "alter, amend, revoke or terminate" expressly exercisable in conjunction with others falls within section 2038(a)(1), but "power" as used in this section does not extend to *powers of persuasion.* If section 2038(a)(1) reached the possibility that Tully might convince T & D and DiNapoli to change the death benefit plan, it would apply to *speculative powers.* Section 2038(a)(1) cannot be so construed. *Harris,* supra; *Hinze,* supra. In addition, if section 2038(a)(1) applies to situations where an employee *might* convince an employer to change a death benefit program, it would sweep all employee death benefit plans into the gross estates of employees. It would always be at least possible for an employee to convince the employer that it would be to their mutual benefit to modify the death benefit plan. In light of the numerous cases where employee death benefit plans similar to the instant plan were held not includable in the employee's gross estate, we find that Congress did not intend the "in conjunction" language of section 2038(a)(1) to extend to the mere possibility of bilateral contract modification. Therefore, merely because Tully might have changed the benefit plan "in conjunction" with T & D and DiNapoli, the death benefits are not forced into Tully's gross estate.

Tully also did not obtain a section 2038(a)(1) "power" from the remote possibility that he could have altered the amount of death benefits payable to his widow by changing his compensation scheme. The death benefits here were to be paid based on decedent's annual salary. From this, defendant reasons that up until the time of his death, Tully could have accepted lesser compensation or terminated his employment in order to alter or revoke the death benefits. In practical terms, we reject this *possibility*. This is not a factor which rises to the level of a section 2038(a)(1) "power." An employee might accept lesser compensation or terminate his employment for a myriad of reasons, but to conclude that a motive for such action would be the death benefit plan itself is not only speculative but ridiculous. And we have already made clear that a section 2038(a)(1) "power" cannot be speculative, but must be *demonstrable, real, apparent* and *evident*. *Harris*, supra; *Hinze*, supra. In addition, modification of Tully's employment contract would have required the cooperation of T & D or a breach by Tully. Neither of these two events constitutes a section 2038(a)(1) "power." Further, it is a common practice to "peg" employee death benefit plans to the employee's salary. To our knowledge, no court has ever held that such practice subjects death benefits to inclusion in the employee's gross estate. On the contrary, in Estate of Whitworth v. Commissioner, 22 CCH Tax Ct. Mem. 177 (1963), the court concluded that although the decedent could have terminated his widow's benefits by leaving his employ or by breaching his employment contract, the death benefits at issue were *not* includable in his estate as a section 2038(a)(1) revocable transfer. Due to the practicalities of death benefit contracts and using the rationale of the *Whitworth* case, we hold that no section 2038(a)(1) power was created by the remote possibility that Tully might have changed the amount of death benefits prior to his death.

Finally, Tully did not retain a section 2038(a)(1) "power" to revoke or terminate the transfer to his wife by virtue of the *possibility* that he could have divorced her. The contract called for T & D to make the death benefit payments to Tully's *widow*. It might be argued that Tully could have divorced his wife to terminate her interest in the death benefits, but again such an argument ignores practicalities, reduces the term "power" to the speculative realm, and is not in accord with prior cases. In reality, a man might divorce his wife, but to assume that he would fight through an entire divorce process merely to alter employee death benefits approaches the absurd. Further, in various cases, death benefits payable to the "widow" * * * were not thereby held includable in the gross estate. The possibility of divorce in the instant situation is so *de minimis* and so speculative rather than *demonstrative, real, apparent,* and *evident* that it cannot rise to the level of a section 2038(a)(1) "power." *Harris*, supra; *Hinze*, supra. Thus the use of "widow" in the death benefit contract did not give Tully a real power to revoke or terminate the death benefit transfer to his wife.

In short, in the 1959 contract Tully transferred certain interests to his wife by obtaining T & D's promise to pay death benefits. While it may be argued that Tully kept a certain *de minimis* association with the death benefit plan, such association never rose to the dignity of a power to "alter, amend, revoke, or terminate" the transfer. In *Kramer*, supra, we held that a substantially similar plan did not create section 2038(a)(1) powers. The facts here are not significantly different. Therefore, section 2038(a)(1) does not operate to compel inclusion of the death benefits in decedent's gross estate.

* * *

NOTES

1. In Estate of Levin v. Commissioner, 90 T.C. 723 (1988), aff'd, 891 F.2d 281 (3d Cir.1989), the court confronted death benefits which were payable under the company plan to a company designated beneficiary, the spouse of the employee. The decedent was Chairman of the Board of Directors of the employer corporation and owned stock possessing more than 80 percent of the corporation's voting power. Based on the decedent's control of the corporate employer both as shareholder and officer, the court found the death benefits includible in decedent's estate under section 2038.

2. In Rev. Rul. 76–304, 1976–2 C.B. 269, the IRS indicated that where an executive had power to change beneficiaries, the death benefit paid by the employer under the employer's plan was includible in the employee's estate under section 2038.

D. RECIPROCAL TRUSTS

The reciprocal trust issue that was studied with respect to section 2036 is also of significance with respect to section 2038. The leading reciprocal trust cases in the section 2038 context are Estate of Green v. United States, 68 F.3d 151 (6th Cir.1995) and Estate of Bischoff v. Commissioner, 69 T.C. 32 (1977). In *Bischoff*, a husband and wife had separately created trusts appointing each other as the trustee of the trusts that each had established. The trusts were of equal value and were created one day apart. Husband's and wife's trust each designated the same parties as beneficiaries and vested the trustee with the discretion to accumulate trust income or distribute it and corpus to the beneficiaries. The Tax Court applied the reciprocal trust principles articulated by the Supreme Court in *Estate of Grace* (discussed in Chapter 18) to tax the trust created by wife in husband's estate and that created by husband in wife's estate. As previously noted in Chapter 18, the Sixth Circuit in *Estate of Green* surprisingly took the position that *Bischoff* was wrongly decided and that the reciprocal trust doctrine could not be applied to either section 2036(a)(2) or section 2038. However, the Court of Appeals for the Federal Circuit had previously indicated that it was of the opinion the doctrine applied to sections 2036 and 2038 equally well. See Exchange Bank and Trust Co. of Fla. v. United States, 694 F.2d 1261 (Fed.Cir.1982).

PLANNING NOTE

The strategy disclosed under Planning Note in Chapter 18 with respect to section 2036(a)(2) is also worthy of consideration with respect to section 2038.

E. INCOMPETENCY

Unfortunately, a fair percentage of all elderly will confront incompetency. Its impact on the tax treatment of powers held by the incompetent can be significant. For example, assume that an individual, who established a trust under which she retained a power to revoke the trust, becomes incompetent and under state law may not during incompetency exercise the power to revoke. What are the estate tax consequences if she dies while incompetent, unable to exercise the power?

ROUND V. COMMISSIONER
United States Court of Appeals, First Circuit, 1964.
332 F.2d 590.

HARTIGAN, CIRCUIT JUDGE.

* * *

The decedent [John J. Round] died on April 4, 1958 at the age of eighty-six. In 1934 and 1935 the decedent established three "spendthrift" trusts under which his five minor children were the principal beneficiaries. The first trust (hereinafter called the September trust) was established on September 14, 1934 by a trust agreement entered into between decedent and Old Colony Trust Company. The second trust (hereinafter called the August trust) was established by a trust agreement entered into between decedent and State Street Trust Company of Boston on August 21, 1935. On December 31, 1935, the third trust (hereinafter called the December trust) was established by a trust agreement entered into between decedent and State Street Trust Company.

The August trust provided for the children to receive all of the income from their respective shares "so long as they shall live." It also allowed the trustees to advance or pay over portions of the principal held for the income beneficiary "if at any time in their sole discretion they shall deem such a distribution desirable." The September and December trusts gave the trustees the power to invade and advance principal "in case of emergency, from time to time and upon such conditions as in their sole discretion they shall determine to be for the best interests of said children."

[The August and September trusts gave the trustees power to accumulate income in their discretion. There was no such power with respect to the December trust.] John R. Round, the decedent and various financial institutions were appointed as co-trustees of the various trusts.

* * * All of the trusts provided that upon the decease, resignation or incapacity of decedent, the corporate trustee should act as the sole trustee of the particular trust.

In the latter part of 1955 or the early part of 1956 the decedent was unable to handle the details of his affairs. On April 6, 1956, he gave his son, John J. Round, Jr., a general power of attorney, and thereafter the son handled most of the decedent's affairs.

* * *

The decree of the Middlesex County Probate Court dated October 28, 1957, recited that "After a hearing of the matter of said petition, it appears to the Court that said John J. Round is incapable of caring properly for his property" and decreed that the Boston Safe Deposit and Trust Company be appointed conservator of the property of the decedent.

* * *

* * * Shortly after its appointment as conservator Boston forwarded to Old Colony Trust Company and to State Street Trust Company certified copies of its appointment. Both trust companies thereupon halted all compensation payments to decedent and took over sole responsibility for the trusts. There is no evidence that decedent took any action in regard to the trusts following the appointment of the conservator.

The trust property was not included in decedent's gross estate on the estate-tax return. The fair market value as of the date of decedent's death of the property held in the three trusts was $493,445.92. Included in this value was undistributed income totaling $131,109.21 which had been accumulated and added to the principal. The respondent included the value of the three trusts at $493,445.92 in the decedent's gross estate and determined a deficiency in the Federal estate tax of $162,072.88.

The Tax Court sustained the action of respondent. It held that decedent in establishing the trusts, retained sufficient powers as co-trustee to accumulate or distribute income and to invade and distribute corpus to make the trusts includible in his estate by reason of section 2036(a) and section 2038(a)(2) of the Internal Revenue Code of 1954. Petitioners do not here question this holding (except as to the income accumulations which will be discussed later) and, in any event, it is supported by well-established authority. E.g., Lober v. United States, 346 U.S. 335 (1953).

Petitioners' argument is that at the date of decedent's death, decedent no longer retained his powers as co-trustee; that under the terms of the trust decedent was removed as trustee upon his becoming incapacitated; further, the appointment of a conservator for decedent's property was a definitive act which extinguished all of the right, power and authority of decedent to act as co-trustee under the three instruments. The Tax Court held that decedent was not permanently removed from his trusteeship position and the appointment of a conservator was not the definitive act called for by Hurd v. Commissioner of Internal Revenue, 160 F.2d 610 (1st Cir.1947), affirming Estate of Edward L. Hurd, 6 T.C. 819 (1946).

The three trust instruments contained the following provision:

> "Upon the decease, resignation or incapacity of * * * [decedent, the corporate trustee] shall act as sole Trustee hereunder, and shall exercise all of the rights, privileges, immunities, discretions and duties hereunder."

Petitioners read this provision to provide that upon any of the three described contingencies, the corporate trustee would *become* sole trustee. It is reasoned that since upon resignation or death the corporate trustee would, in fact, become sole trustee rather than merely *act* as such, a harmonious construction of the provision requires the finding that upon incapacity as well, the corporate trustee would become sole trustee, extinguishing any powers decedent had over the trust.

While it is true that regardless of the words used in the trust instruments, the corporate trustee would, in fact, become sole trustee upon death or resignation of decedent, this fact is the necessary result of the permanent removal caused by those two events. Such a permanent removal does not necessarily follow from incapacity, which is often a temporary condition. Only an unusually strict construction of the provision could lead to the conclusion that upon the incapacity of a co-trustee his powers over the trust would be forever terminated. "Incapacity" is not defined in the trust instruments and if the word is given its common meaning, a two week hospital stay following an automobile accident would find a trustee sufficiently incapacitated and subject to removal within the contended-for meaning of the trust provision. It could not have been the intention of decedent, who as co-trustee maintained a large share of control over the trust, that he could be so easily ousted. Rather, it is more likely that the provision was drawn with the intention of decedent resuming his duties as co-trustee when the incapacity was at an end.

In Hurd v. Commissioner, supra, at 613, this court said "The statute is not concerned with the *manner* in which the power is exercised, but rather with the existence of the power." So long as the powers retained by decedent *still existed in his behalf* the trust property was includible in his estate. What is required, this court said, is "some definitive act correlating the decedent's actual incompetence with his incapacity to serve as trustee." The court suggested that besides resignation and removal, an adjudication of mental incompetency might be sufficient to extinguish a trustee's interest in the trust, undoubtedly following the belief that under the circumstances of that case a legal determination of insanity was the least that was necessary if the purpose of the statute was not to be defeated. The Tax Court, however, has gone even further and has held that a judicial declaration of a trustee's incompetence was insufficient to terminate for tax purposes a power held under a trust where the New York law "specifically grants the Supreme Court of New York jurisdiction over the care of the person and property of an insane person." Estate of Charles S. Inman, 18 T.C. 522, 526 (1952), rev'd on other grounds, 203 F.2d 679 (2d Cir.1953).

We do not need to go that far here. Suffice [it] to say that decedent was never declared mentally incompetent. The appointment of a conservator did not remove the possibility that decedent could have recovered and resumed his position as co-trustee. Mass. Laws Ann. ch. 201 § 18 (1955). A conservatorship "raises * * * no [conclusive] presumption of continued incapacity." Chase v. Chase, 216 Mass. 394, 396, 103 N.E. 857, 858 (1914). The trust instruments provided that upon incapacity the corporate trustee shall act as sole trustee, thus leaving decedent free to resume his duties as trustee upon the recovery of capacity. The definitive act required before a trustee's powers can be said to have been extinguished must certainly be more than an act which contains within it the possibility of a temporary incapacity. To this, it may be added, as the Tax Court noted, that the Probate Court's adjudication of decedent's capacity to file the petition for conservatorship makes clear that he "would have had capacity to resign at that time had it been his intention to abandon the trusteeship." 40 T.C. at 979. See Simons v. United States, 135 F. Supp. 461, 463 (E.D.N.Y.), aff'd per curiam, 227 F.2d 168 (2d Cir.1955), cert. denied, 350 U.S. 949 (1956).

[The discussion of the second issue in this case has been omitted; it related to the includibility in the gross estate of the accumulated income in the trusts. On this second issue, the First Circuit took the same position as was later confirmed by the Supreme Court in *O'Malley* discussed in Chapter 18.]

* * *

Judgment will be entered affirming the decision of the Tax Court.

NOTES

1.   Should a distinction have been made between the December trust with no power to accumulate income and the August and September trusts which did contain such a power? Remember that contingent life estates and contingent powers are subject to section 2036, whereas section 2038 reaches only those powers exercisable at the time of death. Whether *Round* is an appropriate interpretation of section 2038 with respects to incapacity at the time of death of a grantor-powerholder is still something of a question.

2.   Where a holder of a durable power of attorney uses the power to make gifts, unless the grantor of the power explicitly authorizes the holder to do so, the IRS has consistently challenged the authority of the holder to make gifts arguing that the holder in making gifts is acting ultra vires. The IRS asserts that gifts so made are revocable transfers, taxable in the estate of the grantor of the power at his or her death under section 2038. See, e.g., Priv. Ltr. Ruls. 8635007 and 9634004. The judiciary has often upheld the IRS position on this issue. See, e.g., Estate of Casey v. Commissioner, 948 F.2d 895 (4th Cir. 1991); Wilkinson v. Commissioner, T.C. Memo. 1993–336, 66 T.C.M. (CCH) 270 (1993); Estate of Swanson v. United States, 46 Fed. Cl. 388 (2000), aff'd 10 Fed. Appx. 833, 2001–1 USTC ¶ 60,408, 87 A.F.T.R. 2d (RIA) 2345 (2001); Estate of Gaynor, T.C. Memo. 2001–206, 82 T.C.M. (CCH) 379 (2001); Barnett v. United States, 2009–2 USTC ¶ 60,576 (W.D. Pa. 2009). However, where state law and the facts of the case are favorable, the courts have found authority for the holder of the power to make the gifts and have rejected the IRS position that such gifts are taxable under section 2038, or section 2036. See, e.g., Estate of Gagliardi v. Commissioner, 89 T.C. 1207 (1987); Estate of Bronston v. Commissioner, T.C. Memo. 1988–510, 56 T.C.M. (CCH) 550 (1988). Estate of Pruitt v. Commissioner, T.C. Memo, 2000–287, 80 T.C.M. (CCH) 348 (2000).

3.   Historically, to protect grantors of powers of attorney, state law has typically insisted on an explicit grant of a power to make gifts before finding such power present. In recent years, to accommodate those seeking tax minimization, several states have liberalized their standards allowing gift giving by a holder of a power of attorney. See, e.g., Ala. Code § 26–1–2.1 (2022) (affording attorney in fact authority to make gifts of principal's property within limits of the annual exclusion); Tenn. Code Ann. § 34–6–110 (2022) (grants authority to attorney-in-fact or other agent to make gifts, in any amount, of principal's property where the power of attorney or other writing evidences the principal's intent to grant full power to handle the principal's affairs or grant the power to execute or perform any act that the principal could perform); Va. Code Ann. § 64.2–1638 (2022) (grant of general authority to gift in power of attorney allows gifts up to the amount of the gift tax annual exclusion and additional gifts consistent with the principal's best interests).

PLANNING NOTE

Given the approach taken by the court in *Round* and the very real possibility of incompetence due to maladies such as strokes, dementia, and Alzheimer's disease, estate planners who draft deeds of trust for taxpayers who wish to retain revocable powers now have something added to think about. It might be possible to avoid the problem produced in *Round* by providing that a power lapses at incompetence. Another way of dealing with the problem is by creating a durable power of attorney and granting the holder of the power the right to terminate a revocable power in the event of incompetency. In the cases where a durable power is employed to avoid inclusion under *Round*, it is likely that, due to either section 2035(a) or the three-year rule of section 2038(a)(1), the former holder of the power would have to live for three years after the durable power was exercised to terminate the revocable power. In the case of lapse triggered by incompetence, as contrasted with the durable power, since the incompetent, or the incompetent's attorney, could claim that they neither "transferred" nor "relinquished" a revocable power, as required by statute, it does not appear that in order to avoid inclusion it is necessary that the former holder live three years after lapse. See Priv. Ltr. Rul. 9032002.

F. POWER SUBJECT TO STANDARD

As in the case of section 2036(a)(2), inclusion in the gross estate does not result where the donor did not retain a discretionary power with respect to transferred property but merely retained a power subject to a fiduciary standard capable of being administered by a court of equity.

JENNINGS V. SMITH
United States Court of Appeals, Second Circuit, 1947.
161 F.2d 74.

SWAN, CIRCUIT JUDGE.

This is an action by the executors of the will of Oliver Gould Jennings, a resident of Connecticut whose death occurred on October 13, 1936, to recover such part of the estate tax paid by them to the defendant collector as had been illegally collected.

[Decedent established identical trusts for the benefit of the families of each of his sons. Decedent and his two sons, B. Brewster and Lawrence K. Jennings, were named co-trustees with a majority vote required for all trustee actions. Under the terms of each trust, annual income was to be accumulated but the trustees were given power to distribute it for the benefit of each son and his family, provided "the trustees shall determine that such disbursement is reasonably necessary to enable the beneficiary in question to maintain himself and his family, if any, in comfort and in accordance with the station in life to which he belongs." Because of the financial situation of Lawrence, distributions of income were being made to him at decedent's death. The trustees also had the power to invade corpus for extraordinary medical or financial emergencies.]

Section 811(d)(2) [now I.R.C. § 2038] of the Code, which is applicable to transfers made before June 22, 1936, provides for inclusion in the gross estate of all property "To the extent of any interest therein of which the decedent has at any time made a transfer, by trust or otherwise, where the enjoyment thereof was subject at the date of his death to any change through the exercise of a power, either by the decedent alone or in conjunction with any person, to alter, amend, or revoke, * * *."

[The Court rejected taxpayer's argument that I.R.C. § 811(d)(2), now I.R.C. § 2038, did not reach situations where the settlor retained a power to alter, amend or revoke where held by settlor in a fiduciary capacity.]

The next question is whether the powers conferred upon the trustees in the case at bar are powers of the character described in section 811(d)(2) [now I.R.C. § 2038], which requires that enjoyment of the trust property must be subject at the date of the decedent's death to change through the exercise of a power. The trustees' power to invade the capital of the trust property was exercisable only if the son or his issue "should suffer prolonged illness or be overtaken by financial misfortune which the trustees deem extraordinary." Neither of these contingencies had occurred before the decedent's death; hence enjoyment of the capital was not "subject at the date of his death to any change through the exercise of a power." In Commissioner v. Flanders, 111 F.2d 117, although decision was rested on another ground, this court expressed the opinion that a power conditioned upon an event which had not occurred before the settlor's death was not within the section. * * * The question has recently been explored by the Tax Court in Estate of Budlong v. Commissioner, 7 T.C. 756. There it was held in a convincing opinion that the power of trustees to invade corpus in case of "sickness or other emergency," which had not occurred before the decedent's death, was not a power to "alter, amend or revoke" within the meaning of the statute. The court reasoned that the trustees had not unlimited discretion to act or withhold action under the power, since the trust instrument provided an external standard which a court of equity would apply to compel compliance by the trustees on the happening of the specified contingency or to restrain threatened action if the condition were not fulfilled. In the case at bar the district judge was of opinion that even if the trustees found that the stated conditions had been fulfilled, "their finding created no enforceable rights in any of the beneficiaries." 63 F.Supp. 834 at 837. In this view we are unable to concur. The condition upon which the power to invade capital might arise is sufficiently definite to be capable of determination by a court of equity. As Judge L. Hand said in Stix v. Commissioner, 152 F.2d 562, 563 (2d Cir.), "no language, however strong, will entirely remove any power held in trust from the reach of a court of equity." Since the trustees were not free to exercise untrammeled discretion but were to be governed by determinable standards, their power to invade capital, conditioned on contingencies which had not happened, did not in our opinion bring the trust property within the reach of section 811(d)(2).

Similar reasoning leads to the same conclusion with respect to the trustees' power over net income. At the end of each calendar year they were to accumulate the net income of that year unless prior to its amalgamation into capital they exercised their power to disburse it to, or for the benefit of, the son or his issue. The power the trustees had with respect to disbursing income was exercisable year by year; and at the date of the decedent's death the only income of which the enjoyment was subject to change through exercise of a power was the income of the B. Brewster Jennings trust for the year 1936. But the exercise of this power was conditioned on the trustees' determination that disbursement of the income was necessary to enable the beneficiary to whom it might be allotted to maintain himself and his family "in comfort and in accordance with the station in life to which he belongs." The contingency which would justify exercise of the power had not happened before the decedent's death; consequently the 1936 net income of the B. Brewster Jennings trust was not subject at the date of the decedent's death "to any change through the exercise of a power." Hence it was not includible in the gross estate of the decedent under § 811(d). This conclusion is not inconsistent with Commissioner v. Newbold's Estate, 158 F.2d 694 (2d. Cir.), for there the trustees had unlimited discretion, the trust instrument expressly providing that no beneficiary should have any vested right to receive any payment from income.

There remains for consideration the question whether the value of the trust property is includible in the decedent's estate under § 811(c) [now I.R.C. § 2036] upon which the appellee also relies. This section, * * * provides for inclusion within the gross estate of all property "To the extent of any interest therein of which the decedent has at any time made a transfer by trust or otherwise, in contemplation of or intended to take effect in possession or enjoyment at or after his death, or of which he has at any time made a transfer, by trust or otherwise, under which he has retained for his life or for any period not ascertainable without reference to his death or for any period which does not in fact end before his death (1) the possession or enjoyment of, or the right to the income from, the property, or (2) the right, either alone or in conjunction with any person, to designate the persons who shall possess or enjoy the property or the income therefrom; * * *."

* * * The "right," referred to in clause (2), to designate the persons who shall possess or enjoy the property or the income therefrom, is not so limited and apparently overlaps the powers mentioned in § 302(d) as amended, § 811(d) [now § 2038] of the Code. See Art. 19, Treas. Reg. 80. At first glance it might seem that clause (2) covers the present case, because the decedent, for a period that did not in fact end before his death, "retained the right," in conjunction with another of the trustees, to designate the persons who should enjoy the trust property or the income therefrom. But for the reasons that moved us when considering the applicability of § 811(d) we think the decedent effectively put that "right" beyond his own control or retention by imposing conditions upon the exercise of it. A "right" so qualified that it becomes a duty enforcible in a court of equity on petition by the beneficiaries does not circumvent the obvious purpose of § 811(c) to

prevent transfers akin to testamentary dispositions from escaping taxation. * * * In the Jennings trusts the rights of the beneficiaries were no more affected by the settlor's death in October 1936 than they would have been had he resigned as a trustee in January 1936. In either event the contingent power of the trustees to invade corpus or to disburse the net income of 1936 or any subsequent year would remain the same as before his death or resignation. Only when the interest of some beneficiary is enlarged or matured by the decedent's death, is § 811(c) applicable, in our opinion. In the case at bar the decedent's death had no such effect.

The judgment is reversed and the cause remanded with directions to enter judgment for the plaintiffs.

NOTE

In Rev. Rul. 2008–22, 2008–1 C.B. 796, a grantor had established an irrevocable trust for the benefit of his descendants and prohibited himself from serving as trustee. The grantor had reserved the power, exercisable at any time, to substitute property of equal value for trust property. The trust document did not indicate that this power was exercisable by the grantor only in a fiduciary capacity and did not indicate that a trust fiduciary must approve of any such transfer. However, under local law, the trustee had a fiduciary obligation to ensure that the properties exchanged were of equal value. Moreover, under local law the trustee had the power to sell or otherwise exchange trust assets and substitute other assets of equal value. The IRS ruled that in such a situation, the grantor lacked the power that was described in either section 2038 or section 2036(a)(2). Important in reaching this result was the fact that the trustee's powers provided under local law, prevented the grantor from diminishing or otherwise impacting the value the beneficiaries' interests. This result is consistent with the result in Estate of Jordahl v. Commissioner, 65 T.C. 92 (1975), acq. 1977–2 C.B. 1, in which the settlor decedent had retained the power to substitute assets of equal, or greater, value for trust assets. In rejecting IRS attempts to include the trust corpus under section 2038, the court noted that, because, in this case, the decedent's actions were constrained by a fiduciary standard, there could be no shifting of benefits among beneficiaries nor could there be any diminishment in the value of those interest and consequently, there could be no inclusion under section 2038. Revenue Ruling 2008–22 and *Jordahl* indicate that to properly assess whether the settlor decedent is possessed of a power which would create a problem under either section 2038 or section 2036(a)(2), one must carefully examine the trust governing documents as well as state law.

PLANNING NOTE

As in the case of section 2036(a)(2), the donor who wishes to make a gift that escapes under the "power subject to a standard" exception must be careful that the standard chosen is one that is enforceable by a court of equity. Moreover, it is wise to stay quite close to the most commonly chosen standards so as to minimize potential problems. Consequently, standards should be expressed in terms of support, maintenance, health and education while general language such as "best interests" or "as trustee deems advisable" should be avoided.

G. UNIFORM TRANSFERS TO MINORS ACT

Where gifts are made to a minor under the Uniform Transfers to Minors Act (UTMA) or the Uniform Gifts to Minors Act (UGMA) and the donor appoints himself custodian and dies while the donee is under the age at which the custodianship terminates (typically 21), the IRS has two distinctly different theories whereby it can seek inclusion of the gifted property in the donor's gross estate. First, if the donor is also the parent of the donee and is appointed as custodian under UGMA or UTMA, since the donor has the obligation to support the donee and as custodian has retained the power to use income from the gifted property to fulfill that obligation, inclusion in the taxable estate follows under I.R.C. § 2036(a)(1). See, e.g., Estate of Prudowsky v. Commissioner, 55 T.C. 890 (1971), aff'd 465 F.2d 62 (7th Cir.1972); Eichstedt v. United States, 354 F. Supp. 484 (N.D.Cal.1972). Second, regardless of whether the donor is a parent, if the donor is appointed as custodian under UGMA or UTMA and dies prior to termination of the custodianship, because the donor, as custodian, has the power to bestow upon or withhold from the donee enjoyment of the income from the property (as well as this property itself), inclusion in the donor's taxable estate follows under either section 2036(a)(2) or section 2038. See, e.g., Stuit v. Commissioner, 452 F.2d 190 (7th Cir.1971), Rev. Rul. 59–357, 1959–2 C.B. 212 and Rev. Rul. 57–366, 1957–2 C.B. 618. The same rule applies where the donor held the property was a successor custodian at the time of the donor's death.

Where two donors seek to avoid section 2036 or section 2038 problems by appointing each as custodian for the other's gift under UTMA or UGMA, they may run afoul of the reciprocal trust doctrine. The IRS decreed in Rev. Rul. 74–556, 1974–2 C.B. 300, that, where an individual appoints a spouse as custodian for a gift under UGMA and that spouse joins in making a split gift, in the event of death of the custodian during minority there will not be an inclusion of one-half of the property in the gross estate of the deceased custodian spouse.

In Rev. Rul. 70–348, 1970–2 C.B. 193, a donor made a gift to minor children under UGMA, appointing his wife as custodian. At her death he was appointed successor custodian. At the donor's death the children were still in minority. No inclusion could be made under section 2036 since the donor merely possessed, but had not retained, a section 2036(a)(2) power. Since section 2038 requires that the donor merely possess, not retain, the power to alter, amend, revoke, or terminate, the gift was included in the donor-custodian's gross estate under that section.

Rather than using the UTMA or UGMA to make gifts to minors, donors occasionally create "Totten Trust" bank accounts.[1] Whether done for benefit of a minor or an adult, where the donor remains as trustee of a classic "Totten Trust" account, the value of such an account will be included in the estate of the donor. In Estate of Sulovich v. Commissioner, 587 F.2d 845 (6th Cir.1978), the taxpayer established savings bank accounts with himself as trustee for his niece and her children. Although he gave the passbooks to his niece, under the signature card contracts, withdrawals could be made only by him or with his approval. Based on this fact, the court found that the contents of the accounts were to be included in the estate of the settlor-trustee under both sections 2036(a)(2) and 2038.

H. POWER TO SUBSTITUTE TRUSTEE

Suppose that the settlor of a trust grants the trustee powers that, if retained by the settlor, would result in inclusion of trust corpus in the settlor's gross estate. Further suppose that the settlor retained the right to remove the trustee and replace him with the settlor or a trustee of the settlor's own choosing. Would inclusion result here, as it would under section 2036(a)(2)? Treasury Regulation § 20.2038–1(a)(3) indicates that inclusion results under section 2038 where the decedent settlor had the unrestricted power to remove a trustee and replace the trustee with the decedent, and the trustee is invested with discretionary powers which if retained by the decedent would have resulted in inclusion under section 2038. See also Mathey v. United States, 491 F.2d 481, 486–487 (3d Cir.1974) (rejecting the decedent's argument that age, lack of financial knowledge, and lack of interest made section 2038 inapplicable because it was not relevant whether the power was exercised or likely to be exercised). However, where the power of the decedent settlor to appoint herself is limited to conditions not present at the time of death (e.g., death or resignation of the trustee) there is no inclusion under section 2038. See Treas. Reg. § 20.2038–1(a)(3) & (b). This is a critical distinction between section 2036(a)(2), which applies to contingent retained powers and section 2038, which applies only to powers that are exercisable at death. See Estate of Farrel v. United States, 553 F.2d 637 (1977) (discussed in Chapter 18).

---

[1]   A good definition of a "Totten Trust" is:

Totten trusts are named for trusts first approved in In re Totten. A "Totten" trust is a purported trust whereby an owner of a bank account provides a written declaration to the bank that he or she is the trustee of the account for another person. However, the owner of the account reserves the right to withdraw or otherwise revoke the trust during his or her lifetime. Id. A Totten trust works in the same way as a "payable on death" (POD) and "transfer on death" (TOD) designations. That is, a Totten trust is a means of leaving an account to another upon death without the need for a will and without the disadvantages of a joint tenancy (i.e., requiring a present gift of property thereby losing the right to revoke).

Daniel W. Matthews, *Trusts and Estates*, 55 WAYNE L. REV. 645, 655 n. 102 (2009).

Except for this critical distinction, the contingent power issue should be resolved similarly under sections 2036(a)(2) and 2038.

If the settlor has the power to remove and replace a trustee with someone who is not related or subordinate to the settlor, the IRS has concluded that trust corpus will not be included in the estate under section 2038. See Priv. Ltr. Rul. 201647001 (Aug. 8, 2016). According to the IRS, the "retained removal and replacement powers" are insufficient to warrant inclusion under section 2038.

I.   OVERLAP OF SECTIONS 2038 AND 2036(a)(2)

There is substantial overlap of sections 2036(a)(2) and 2038. In most cases involving overlap, the Internal Revenue Service will prefer to employ section 2036 since it typically results in the inclusion of a greater amount in the gross estate. This is so for several reasons. When property is included in a decedent's gross estate under section 2036, Regulation § 20.2036–1(c) indicates that the estate should include "the value of the entire property less only the value of any income interest which is not subject to the decedent's interest or right and which is actually being enjoyed by another person at the time of the decedent's death." In the case of section 2038, Regulation § 20.2038–1(a) states that "only the value of an interest in property subject to a power to which section 2038 applies is included in the decedent's gross estate under section 2038." The impact of these two rules and the Commissioner's preference for section 2036(a)(2) can be demonstrated as follows: Assume that X established a trust under which income was to be divided among X's children as X designated until the youngest child reached age 25, at which time the corpus was to be divided equally among the children. Assume that X died long before X's youngest child had reached 25 and that at X's death the trust was worth $400,000, with the income interest worth $150,000 and the remainder interest worth $250,000. Under Regulation § 20.2038–1(a) only the value of the income interest ($150,000) would be included in X's estate, whereas under Regulation § 20.2036–1(c) the entire $400,000 value of the trust would be included in X's estate.

Much of the time a decedent who possesses a section 2036(a)(2) power will also possess a section 2038 power and vice versa. However, there are several circumstances where the two sections are not coextensive. For example, as discussed in Chapter 18, *Estate of Farrel* indicates that, under section 2036, even a retained contingent power to designate enjoyment that is not presently exercisable will result in inclusion in the estate. Regulation § 20.2038–1(a)(3) and (b) indicates that unless such a power is presently exercisable at death, there will be no inclusion under section 2038.

There are other situations in which the two sections are inconsistent. Section 2036 taxes only "retained" powers to designate enjoyment whereas under section 2038, if the decedent settlor holds at death a power to designate enjoyment, taxation follows regardless of "when or from what source the decedent acquired such power." Thus, most commentators are of the opinion that if a settlor establishes a trust, vests powers to designate enjoyment of income in an independent trustee who dies and the settlor is appointed as successor trustee, an inclusion will be effected under section 2038. However, since the power to designate was not retained by the settlor, no inclusion results under section 2036. Recall, however, that in Rev. Rul. 84–179 (discussed in Chapter 17) the IRS based its acceptance of the result and rationale in Skifter v. Commissioner,[2] and its rejection of Rose v. United States[3] and Terriberry v. United States[4] on a belief that the "when and from what source" language of section 2038 was limited to essentially contrived situations where, for example, to avoid the technical application of section 2038 a power was temporarily vested in a third party before being "returned" to the settlor. This limited reading of the "when and from what source" language of section 2038 would, in the absence of collusive tax avoidance, make that section basically coextensive with section 2036 on the issue of non-retained powers.

There is an extremely significant situation in which section 2038 and not section 2036 will be the operative section where a power to designate enjoyment is present. This situation involves circumstances where the settlor holds a power which, while it affects the enjoyment of wealth, does not affect the enjoyment of income during the settlor's life. Section 2036(a)(2) is a parallel provision to section 2036(a)(1), including in the estate property with respect to which the decedent decided that, rather than enjoying "income" or the "use" of property during life (which would be taxed under section 2036(a)(1)), the decedent would prefer to determine who, or under what circumstances individuals should enjoy income or the use of property during the decedent's life. Consequently, where the settlor has retained a power that affects wealth that the settlor has transferred but does not affect its enjoyment during the donor's life, section 2038 and not section 2036 will be the operative section. For example, assume that X conveys property in trust with income to A for her life and the remainder to her estate and retains the power to terminate the trust, paying all of the corpus to A. Treas. Reg. § 20.2036–1(b)(3) (sentence 3 and the parenthetical) indicates that this property will not be includible in X's estate under section 2036 although it will be includible under section 2038. Having gone this far, it might be helpful to look back to *Struthers* (discussed in Chapter 18) and ask how that case is distinguishable. What added power did the settlor in that case retain with respect to the right of the beneficiary to enjoy income?

---

[2]   468 F.2d 699 (2d Cir. 1972).

[3]   511 F.2d 259 (5th Cir. 1975).

[4]   517 F.2d 286 (5th Cir. 1975), cert. denied, 424 U.S. 977 (1976).

For a good discussion of the overlap of these two sections see Matthew A. Reiber, *Untangling the Strings: Transfer Taxation of Retained Interests and Powers*, 48 Akron L. Rev. 455, 472–75 (2015) and Michael R. Houston, Comment, *Estate of Wall v. Commissioner: An Answer to the Problem of Settlor Standing in Trust Law?*, 99 Nw. U. L. Rev. 1723, 1746–50 (2005).

J. REVOCABLE TRUSTS

In recent years revocable trusts which make provision for distribution of trust assets at the death of the settlor-beneficiary have been increasingly used as will substitutes or supplements in modest to medium sized estates. A few examples of the advantages of revocable trusts will illustrate why they have been gaining increasing popularity. Wills are public documents, open to all as are other documents such as asset inventories filed by the estate in probate. Revocable trusts remain private even when used to dispose of property at death. Real property located out of state will result in expensive ancillary probate if disposed of by will or intestacy. Contribution of such realty to a revocable trust provides a means of avoiding ancillary probate. Revocable trusts also provide acceptable means of: (1) guarding against the glare of public proceedings regarding incompetency; and (2) avoiding probate fees and related expenses. In keeping with its descriptive title, the trust remains revocable by the settlor, thereby giving her the same flexibility that a will would provide. Add to this the fact that a revocable trust is at least as, if not more, easy to change as is a conventional will and it is easy to see why revocable trusts have been gaining popularity among estate planners and their clients.

Clearly, if a settlor places her wealth in a simple revocable trust, the corpus of the trust will be treated as part of her taxable estate at her death under section 2038. Accordingly, at death of the settlor the corpus of a revocable trust will qualify for a stepped-up basis.

K. POWER RELEASED WITHIN THREE YEARS OF DEATH

Section 2038 specifically provides that, where the decedent relinquishes a retained power "to alter, amend, revoke or terminate" within three years of the decedent's death, the property subject to this power is to be included in the decedent's estate. Given the general rule of section 2035 and the specific provision of section 2035(a)(2), which refers to property that "would have been included in the decedent's gross estate under" section 2038, the specific inclusionary language in section 2038 for gifts made within three years of death can be viewed as a bit of legislative overkill.

A donor who has made a gift, retains a power "to alter, amend, revoke or terminate," and subsequently wishes to exclude such property from the gross estate should consequently be doubly mindful of the need to sever the taxable strings long before the "golden years."

L. COMMUNITY PROPERTY AND POWERS

KATZ V. UNITED STATES

United States Court of Appeals, Ninth Circuit, 1967.
382 F.2d 723.

DUNIWAY, CIRCUIT JUDGE:

Appellant [Sadie Katz] is the widow of Leroy Joseph Katz, who died a resident of California on February 27, 1960. * * *

On August 29, 1956, Title Insurance and Trust Company executed a Declaration of Trust, in which "Leroy Joseph Katz, a married man," was named Trustor. This paper acknowledged receipt by the Trust Company, without consideration, of real and personal property from Leroy, and that the property was to be held in trust for the benefit of Sadie and of Leroy's children, their surviving spouses and surviving issue. Sections One, Two and Three give the trustee the usual powers to manage the properties, collect income, and invest the trust's funds. * * *

Sadie claims that all of the assets conveyed to the trust were the community property of herself and Leroy. The government denies this, but the trial court, for the purpose of its decision, assumed that Sadie is right. * * *

Clearly, if Leroy placed his separate property in the trust, sections 2036 and 2038 would apply. But each section is limited by its express terms; property is to be included only "to the extent of any interest therein of which the decedent [Leroy] has at any time made a transfer." Here, assuming that the property conveyed to the trustee was community, acquired after 1927, Sadie and Leroy each had a "present, existing and equal" interest in it (Cal. Civ. C. § 161a). Leroy had certain powers of management and disposition (Cal. Civ. C. § 172), but he could not, without Sadie's written consent, "make a gift of such community personal property, or dispose of the same without a valuable consideration" (Cal. Civ. C. § 172) or convey community real property without her joinder (Cal. Civ. C. § 172a).

It seems clear to us that the interest in the property of which Leroy, the decedent, made a transfer was his one-half interest in the property. If he can be said at all to have made a transfer of Sadie's one-half interest, he did so only as managing agent for the two of them. What he did, being done without consideration required by Civil Code § 172, was voidable by her. Sadie's written approval, if it was a transfer at all, was in substance a transfer by her to the trustee, not to Leroy, of her one-half interest. This is even more clear, as to the real property. Leroy could not convey it. Both joined in the deeds; each transferred his or her one-half interest. Thus, the extent of the interest in the property that Leroy transferred is one-half, and that is the extent to which, under sections 2036 and 2038, the property is includible in his estate.

Nor can we accept the trial court's conclusion that by virtue of the execution of the Declaration of Trust, all of the property conveyed to the trustee became the separate property of Leroy. It is well settled in California that property acquired with community funds or property is also community property. We know of no case that holds that the equitable interests of a husband and wife in an inter vivos trust, created by them by conveyance of their community property to the trustee, cannot also be community property. We would not expect the California courts to so hold.

There is a statutory presumption that property acquired by the spouses during marriage is community property (Cal. Civ. C. § 164). The presumption is a strong one, which the California Supreme Court has characterized as fundamental to the community property system. It can be overcome only by clear and satisfactory proof. It is even stronger when the property was acquired with community property. It extends to every conceivable type of property, including insurance policies and their proceeds, Scott v. C.I.R., supra; United States v. Stewart, supra; a cause of action for the wrongful death of or injury to a minor child; a cause of action for injury to either spouse; * * * the interest of a spouse in a partnership; good will of a business; borrowed money; and leasehold interests; Why not to a retained equitable interest in a trust?

We find at least three California decisions that hold that such an interest can be community property. * * *

It is, however, well established that the spouses can, by agreement, change separate property to community, and vice versa. And the form of conveyance by which property is acquired may be inconsistent with its being community property, as in joint tenancies. Even in such a case, however, the spouses can agree that the property is community property. Here, there is, as the trial court found, no such collateral agreement as to the spouses' interest in the trust.

The trial court was of the opinion that the terms of the Declaration of Trust itself were inconsistent with there being community property. It treated the execution of the Declaration as, in substance, a conveyance by Sadie to Leroy. It said that the property became his separate property "since, under the terms of the trust, he was accorded the right solely to enjoy the income from the trust and was given the power to revoke, terminate or amend the trust. These rights and powers vested in the said decedent control of, and the beneficial enjoyment of, all of the trust property." 255 F. Supp. at 643.

We do not agree. In the first place, nothing that Sadie signed contains any express language whereby she conveyed anything to Leroy. In the second place, if she had conveyed all her rights when the Declaration was executed, why was her further approval of each amendment required? The Declaration does not require her approval of amendments. But if the property remained community, then Civil Code §§ 172 and 172a do require her consent or joinder, if the amendment would deprive her of any of her community interest. Absent such consent or joinder, she could have, at Leroy's death, set aside the trust as to her one-half of the community property. The fact that her consent was sought, each time, is some indication that the parties believed that she had a community property interest in the trust. In the third place, we do not find that the powers given to Leroy to "collect, receive, and disburse, without accounting to the trustee or any other person, all income" from the trust property (Section Four) and to "revoke, terminate or amend this trust" (Section Thirteen) are so inconsistent with the continued community character of the trust property as to overcome the presumptions to which we have referred.

* * *

We think that, whatever powers Leroy had under Section Four and Section Thirteen, they were held by him as manager of or agent for the community property and subject to his obligations as such manager. In this respect, we agree * * * [that] the trust was not created by Leroy with his property; it was created by Leroy and Sadie with their property.

Our views are reinforced by the peculiar nature of this trust. If ever a trust came close to being a "dry" trust, a mere agency, during Leroy's lifetime, and testamentary in character, this one does. See our discussion of this problem in Dessar v. Bank of America, 1965, 353 F.2d 468. There is far less substance to this trust than there was to the *Dessar* trust. We do not pass on the validity of this trust; we assume that it is valid. (The question was not argued in the trial court). We note its nature as a further aid to determining, from the instrument itself, the probable intent of the parties and the legal effect of what they did. In substance, and for all practical purposes, it left the management and control of the community property, during Leroy's life, exactly where it was before the trust was created, in Leroy. If it enlarged his managerial powers at all, it did so in but one respect—it permitted him to give away the community income. Its principal purpose is not to change, in any substantial way, the property rights of the parties during their joint lives, but to govern the disposition of those properties at death. We cannot find in it any intent on the part of either spouse to transmute their community property into Leroy's separate property. * * *

Alternatively, the government argues that the Declaration of Trust conferred upon Leroy a general power of appointment over Sadie's community interest, and that therefore that interest is includible under Int. Rev. Code of 1954 § 2041. See also Treasury Regulations on Estate Tax (1954 Code), 26 C.F.R. § 20.2041–1. The government relies on both Section Four and Section Thirteen of the Declaration. Section Four merely reserves to Leroy general powers of management, sale and investment of the trust property within the trust, and the right to collect, receive and disburse income. It is not a general power of appointment. Section Thirteen reserves to Leroy the power to revoke, terminate or amend. This, we have held, is a power as agent for the community. It is no more a general power of appointment than the powers that he had over the community property before the trust was created. It has never been held that those powers amount to a general power of appointment over the wife's interest.

As we have indicated, there remains a factual question as to whether the properties conveyed to the trustee were community property. That question remains to be tried. The judgment is therefore reversed, with instructions that the trial court take such further proceedings as are consistent with this opinion.

PROBLEMS

1. David established a trust for the benefit of his daughter, Candace. Under the terms of the trust, income was to be distributed to Candace as Valley Trust Co. determined to be "in her best interests" until Candace was 25 years old, at which time all accumulated income and corpus were to be distributed to Candace. David retained the right to remove the trustee and substitute for it another trustee, including himself. David died when Candace was 22 years old and the trust corpus was worth $800,000. What are the tax consequences for David's estate?

2. Rashaad created and funded a trust for the benefit of his nephew, Marcel. Rashaad was named the trustee. The trust income was to be paid to Rashaad for life, with the corpus to Marcel upon Rashaad's death. The trust documents provided that the trustee, in conjunction with Marcel, had the power to change the recipient of the corpus.

3. Patricia owns 75 percent of the stock of Acme, Inc. Patricia is the president of Acme, which has an employee death benefit under which "two times annual compensation is to be paid to the spouse of each employee who dies while employed by Acme." At Patricia's death, $800,000 was paid to her husband, Jerry. What are the tax consequences? Would your answer be any different if Patricia owned only 10 percent of the stock of Acme?

4. Morris established a trust for the benefit of his grandchildren, naming himself as trustee. Under the terms of the trust, income, in most circumstances, is to be distributed equally among the beneficiaries until the youngest reaches age 25, at which time the corpus is to be divided per stirpes among all grandchildren or their issue. The sole circumstance in which income is not to be divided equally arises when there is "a severe

medical or other financial emergency." In such cases, the trustee is required to distribute income among beneficiaries so as to provide for the "support and maintenance of the individual experiencing the emergency." What are the tax consequences of this arrangement if Morris dies while the trust is still in operation?

5. Sara made a gift of stock to her 10-year-old son, Ben, under the Uniform Transfers to Minors Act, appointing herself as custodian. She died four years later when the stock was worth $100,000. What are the tax consequences to Sara's estate?

6. Kevin established a trust under which income was to be paid to his grandson, Anthony, until Anthony reached age 35, at which time the corpus of the trust was to be distributed to Anthony. Kevin reserved to himself, acting in conjunction with Anthony's mother, Lisa, the right to terminate the trust and accelerate Anthony's enjoyment of the remainder. What are the tax consequences if Kevin dies while the trust is still in operation?

CHAPTER 20

TRANSFERS GEARED TO GRANTOR'S LIFE

(SECTION 2037)

■ ■ ■

A. INTRODUCTION

The original antecedent of section 2037 was section 202(b) of the Revenue Act of 1916, which brought into the gross estate transfers "intended to take effect in possession or enjoyment at or after" the grantor's death. Due to a series of Supreme Court decisions that gave this language an exceedingly narrow construction, section 202(b) did not reach the types of transfers that many believed a fair-minded reading of the statute would treat as subject to taxation under the section.

Congress responded to the situation with the passage of several pieces of legislation that were intended to compensate for the narrow readings given to section 202(b) by the Supreme Court. Section 2037 is one such addition to the Code. In its present form, it is the product of legislation passed by Congress in 1949, 1951 and 1954.

Under section 2037, except for a bona fide sale for adequate and full consideration in money or money's worth, property transferred during the decedent's life will be included in his or her estate if: (1) possession or enjoyment of the property, through ownership, can be obtained by an individual only by that individual or another party surviving the decedent; and (2) the decedent has retained a reversionary interest in the property, which immediately before the decedent's death, exceeds five percent of the value of such property.[1] It is important to remember that, for inclusion to result under section 2037, both requirements must be satisfied. Moreover, in situations where a reversion is present, but one or both tests under section 2037 have not been met, taxation of the reversion in the decedent's estate under section 2033 should not be overlooked.

---

[1] For a good discussion of section 2037 and the other the other estate tax provisions addressing transfers with strings, see Matthew A. Reiber, *Untangling the Strings: Transfer Taxation of Retained Interests and Powers*, 48 AKRON L. REV. 455 (2015). Professor Reiber advocates modifying the string provisions by enacting a "single, stand-alone provision" for several reasons, including eliminating complexity. Id. at 459–460.

B. REMOTE AND UNINTENDED REVERSIONS

Since section 2037 requires both a reversion in the grantor and an interest that may pass to another only by surviving the grantor, an estate planner who wishes to put his client's transfer beyond its reach merely need insure that one of these two requirements of section 2037 is not present. This is often easier said than done.

Problems sometimes arise where the deed of conveyance contains no express reversion, but one arises by operation of law because the deed did not effect a complete conveyance. For example, in Estate of Spiegel v. Commissioner, 335 U.S. 701 (1949), the taxpayer established a trust that provided that income was to be divided among his three children for his life, and if they did not survive him, the income was to be distributed among his grandchildren. On the taxpayer's death, the same pattern of distribution was to be employed to dispose of the corpus. The deed of trust failed to specify how the property was to be distributed if the taxpayer's children and grandchildren had all predeceased him. The Court found that, under Illinois law, the taxpayer's incomplete conveyance resulted in a reversion, albeit a remote one. Moreover, since the taxpayer's children and grandchildren could inherit the corpus that was transferred at his death only by surviving him, the Court found that, at the taxpayer's death, the corpus was to be included in his estate under the predecessor of section 2037.

Subsequent to the Supreme Court's decision in *Spiegel*, the Code was amended to provide that an inclusion under section 2037 results only where the value of the reversion exceeds five percent of the value of the property subject to the reversion. Occasionally, this amendment serves to bail out taxpayers who, like the taxpayer in *Spiegel*, employed an estate planner with an inadequate understanding of state property law. As the materials in this chapter will illustrate, inclusions under section 2037 are often the result of sloppy or unskilled drafting of deeds of trust. The five-percent provision is a potential escape hatch for the unfortunate taxpayer and the estate planner who otherwise might be anxiously checking the limits on a malpractice policy. *Spiegel* and other cases like it are excellent illustrations of the fact that the able estate planner must be well versed in both tax and property law.

A classic example of a situation in which an unintended reversion was found to exist is Commissioner v. Estate of Marshall, 203 F.2d 534 (3d Cir.1953). In *Marshall*, the decedent established a trust with income to his wife for life. At her death the corpus was to be paid as she had by will designated and, in default of such designation, to her then-heirs under Pennsylvania's intestate laws. After establishing the trust, Mrs. Marshall surrendered her right to designate by will the identification of the takers of the corpus at her death. The court decided that, as Mrs. Marshall's spouse at his death, Mr. Marshall, under Pennsylvania's intestacy laws which were incorporated by reference, had a potential reversion in a one-third share of the corpus on her death. The court then addressed the issue of whether the remaining requirement of section 2037 was satisfied, namely if it was possible for the Marshall children to take the reversionary interest of their father other than by surviving the decedent. The Third Circuit stated:

> Undoubtedly then, in determining whether a transferred interest which might revert back to the settlor-decedent was intended to take effect in possession or enjoyment at or after his death, we must inquire whether it was possible, immediately prior thereto for some person who need not have survived him to take that interest. Or, otherwise stated, we must determine whether there was any other contingency, besides the settlor-decedent's death, upon the happening of which his reverter interest would be entirely cut off. If there was, and that contingency was 'real', then the transfer was not intended to take effect in possession and enjoyment at or after his death.

> At the moment preceding Marshall's death it was possible for beneficiaries to take the one-third interest without surviving him. This could have resulted (1) by a change in the intestate laws of Pennsylvania, mitigating or eliminating the surviving spouse's share; (2) under the present intestate laws if Marshall had divorced his wife or she had divorced him; (3) if Marshall either wilfully neglected or refused to provide for Mrs. Marshall for one year previous to her death, or if he wilfully and maliciously had deserted her for that period. Had any one of those things occurred, the one-third interest which decedent would otherwise have gotten, would have gone to persons (the children, if they survived their mother) who would not have had to survive the decedent.

> Nor can these contingencies be disregarded on the ground that they are 'unreal.' They cannot be regarded as 'sham', for, as the Tax Court said:

> 'The indications are that the decedent was not thinking of himself or intending to provide that a part of the trust property was to revert to him and was not to pass to others save upon the condition that he predeceased his wife. * * * [I]t seems unlikely that he had it in mind.'

> The possible contingencies taken together under which beneficiaries could have taken the interest without surviving Marshall cannot be regarded as so remote as to be 'unreal.'

> Thus, there being another event (or events) upon which the beneficiaries could have taken the one-third interest without

surviving the decedent, the transfer * * * is therefore not includible in Marshall's gross estate.

Id. at 538–541 (citations omitted).

Assume that the beneficiary of the trust in *Estate of Marshall*, rather than being decedent's spouse, had been a child. Since the status of parent is not as legally fragile as that of spouse in an era in which divorce is commonplace, one should ponder if the same result would follow.

The injection of real conditions other than survivorship, whereby parties whose interests are otherwise conditioned on survivorship may take possession or enjoyment of the property, often provides a means by which an estate planner can snatch an interest from the jaws of section 2037.

As is the case under sections 2036 and 2038, severance of a taxable string, if done earlier than three years prior to death, is a strategy to be considered in cases where the estate planner was not able to avoid inclusion in the first place.

C. VALUING THE REVERSION

1. ACTUARIAL VALUES AND CONDITION OF HEALTH

Regulation § 20.2037–1(c)(3) tells us that when determining if, immediately prior to death, the value of the decedent's reversion exceeds five percent, we are to ascertain the value of the reversion using recognized valuation principles for determining the value of conditional and future interests. Moreover, the regulation also indicates that the valuation shall be made without regard to whether the decedent's executor had elected the alternative valuation method under section 2032.

Congress delegated to the Treasury the authority under section 7520, using a few legislatively mandated standards, to prescribe tables for determining the actuarial value of annuities, life estates, terms of years, remainders and reversions. Regulation § 20.2037–1(c)(3) indicates that in determining if, immediately prior to death, the value of the decedent's reversion exceeds five percent, one should employ the recognized valuation principles prescribed by Regulations §§ 20.2031–1, 20.2031–7 and 20.2031–9. The process of actuarial valuation required by the regulations is well explained in considerable detail in Chapter 10 of this book, and it now might be helpful to review those materials paying special attention to the section entitled "Exceptions." Under the valuation techniques required by the regulations, the tables provided in Regulation § 20.2031–7, in general, provide conclusive guidance for determining whether the value of decedent's reversion at the time of her death exceeds five percent.

Occasionally the question arises whether, in valuing decedent's reversion, it is appropriate to consider that the decedent suffers from a terminal disease. Although Regulation § 20.7520–3(b)(3)(i) allows some modest wiggle room for consideration of the impact of the presence of a terminal condition on most actuarial calculations, Regulation § 20.7520–3(b)(3)(ii) specifically provides that "[t]he value of a decedent's reversionary interest under section 2037(b) * * * shall be determined without regard to the physical condition, immediately before decedent's death, of the individual who is the measuring life." Were the regulations not to so provide, section 2037 would be almost exclusively restricted to situations involving sudden and unexpected deaths such as those which follow from accidents or coronaries in seemingly healthy individuals. In many other situations (such as death by cancer, stroke or, for that matter, most heart attacks) in the closing moments of the decedent's life few, if any, such individuals, regardless of their age, would have their reversionary interests valued in excess of five percent if one were to consider the medical condition of the decedent. For example, assume that A, while in good health, established a trust with income for life to husband B, and that at B's death, the corpus of the trust was to revert to A if she did not predecease B. If A predeceased B, the corpus was to be paid to their child C or her estate. Assume that A, survived by B and C, died in a plane crash six years after establishing this trust and that at the time of her death her reversionary interest was actuarially valued at 9.5% of the corpus of the trust, thereby, resulting in an inclusion in her estate of the value of the trust corpus minus the value of B's life estate. Next, assume that rather than dying in a plane crash, A had been diagnosed with advanced systemic esophageal cancer, had been given weeks to live and died several weeks after detection of her disease. Were we to consider the condition of A's health immediately prior to her death, the value of her reversion would be considerably less than five percent and there would be no inclusion under section 2037. Several courts which, prior to Congressional delegation under section 7520 to the Treasury of the power to issue "legislative" regulations and the Treasury's issuance of Treas. Reg. § 20.7520–3(b)(3)(ii), had considered the issue had concluded that to preclude section 2037 from being limited in application to totally unexpected deaths, it was necessary to disregard the status of decedent's health immediately prior to her death in determining the value of that party's reversionary interest.[2]

Although it may be inappropriate to consider the health of the decedent immediately prior to her death for the purpose of determining whether the value of the decedent's reversion exceeds five percent, what of the health of other parties? Assume that, in the case of the previous example involving A, B and C, use of actuarial tables alone would result in

---

[2]   See Robinson v. United States, 632 F.2d 822 (9th Cir.1980); Estate of Allen v. United States, 558 F.2d 14 (Ct. Cl.1977); Estate of Roy v. Commissioner, 54 T.C. 1317 (1970). But see Hall v. United States, 353 F.2d 500 (7th Cir. 1965).

A's reversion being assigned a value of 4.5% immediately prior to her death in the plane crash. If this were all that was to be considered, nothing would be included in her estate under section 2037. However, what result should prevail if B weeks earlier had been diagnosed as suffering from a terminal disease which would likely claim his life within six months and if this had been considered in valuing A's reversion, it would have been assigned a value of ninety percent? Strict adherence to the language of Treas. Reg. § 20.2037–3(b)(3)(ii) would seem to indicate that the condition of B's health, as well as that of A, should be ignored.[3]

2. OTHER FACTORS

Suppose that factors other than those dealing with death will impact on the value of the decedent's reversion. Should they be considered in determining if the value of the decedent's reversionary interest exceeds five percent? Moreover, if they are to be considered, how is one to determine their relative weight? The issue of the impact of other factors is addressed by the case which follows.

ESTATE OF CARDEZA v. UNITED STATES

United States District Court, Eastern District of Pennsylvania, 1957.
57–1 USTC ¶ 11,681, 52 AFTR 1911, aff'd, 261 F.2d 423 (3d Cir.1958).

KIRKPATRICK, CH. JUDGE:

The Technical Changes Act, 26 U.S. C., 1952 ed., Section 811(c)(2) [now § 2037], provides that inter vivos transfers made on or before October 7, 1949, and intended to take effect in possession or enjoyment at or after death need not be included in the gross estate unless the decedent had retained a reversionary interest of a value of more than 5% of the transferred property. In this estate, the decedent during her lifetime transferred property to a trust set up by her father's will, the terms of which provided that, in the event that the decedent survived all of her children and their issue, she would then become entitled to receive the income for life and to dispose of the principal by testamentary power of appointment. At the time of her death the decedent was 85 years old. She had one son then living who was 64 and married to a wife who was 59. The son had no children but was physically able to procreate. The decedent had no other children or lineal descendants.

The question for the Court is whether immediately before her death the decedent's reversionary interest had a value in excess of 5% of the value of the corpus or, stated in another way, whether it can be established that a woman 85 years old has a less than 5% chance of surviving a man of 64

---

[3]   It is worth noting that the court in the *Hall*, whose opinion is inconsistent with Treas. Reg. § 20.2037–3(b)(3)(ii), and which represents a distinct minority position, in reaching its conclusion had considered the pre-death health of all parties concerned.

married to a woman of 59 and also any child or children whom he may have in the future.

The taxpayer has the burden of proof, but that does not mean that he must come forward with evidence to prove the negative on which his case depends. The burden of proof in a case like this is the burden of convincing the Court, and the taxpayer has the risk of non-persuasion.

In this case statutory provisions govern the means of proof and define the issue. The Act provides that the value should be determined "by usual methods of valuation, including the use of tables of mortality and actuarial principles." The Conference Committee Report states that "The rule of Robinette v. Helvering (318 U.S. 184), under which a reversionary interest not having an ascertainable value under recognized valuation principles is considered to have a value of zero, is to apply." (1949–2 Cum. Bull. 295, 297) and a regulation issued under the Act by the Commissioner of Internal Revenue provides, "If a reversionary interest does not have an ascertainable value under the applicable valuation principles, it is considered to have a value of zero." (Reg. 105, Sec. 81.17(c).)

In the *Robinette* case, supra, the Court had before it a situation like the present one (except that the ages of the parties involved were different), namely, a deed of trust which provided for a life estate in a woman, remainder to her issue upon their reaching the age of 21 and, in default of issue, then to whomever she should appoint by will. The Court's ruling upon the point in which we are here interested is embodied in the following sentences: "Factors to be considered in fixing the value of this contingent reservation as of the date of the gift would have included consideration of whether or not the daughter would marry; whether she would have children; whether they would reach the age of 21; etc. Actuarial science may have made great strides in appraising the value of that which seems to be unappraisable, but we have no reason to believe from this record that even the actuarial art could do more than guess at the value here in question." Thus the taxpayer must demonstrate to the Court's satisfaction that the best that the actuarial art can do toward establishing the value of the reversion is no more than a guess, but if he can do that by the admitted facts and the defendant's evidence, he need not produce evidence and is entitled to judgment.

In Commissioner of Internal Revenue v. Cardeza's Estate, 173 F.2d 19, (another phase of the tax question arising in this estate, decided in 1949) the Court of Appeals for the Third Circuit followed the *Robinette* case, supra, and in Commissioner v. Sternberger's Estate, 348 U.S. 187, decided as late as January 1955, the Supreme Court had before it a case involving the same general scheme of devolution—an estate in trust during the joint lives of the decedent's wife and daughter, the principal payable to the then living descendants of the daughter upon the death of the survivor and, in default of such descendants, then over to designated relatives and charities. The question was the value of the part of the remainder bequeathed to charities. The Court had before it considerable [sic] more in the way of actuarial statistics than in the *Robinette* case, supra, and the data were more complete and up-to-date. The Court recognized that there had been advances in the actuarial art since the *Robinette* decision and that actuarial estimates are employed more widely than formerly. Nonetheless, the Court held that the amount of the bequest to the charity was incapable of ascertainment and disallowed the claim for a pro tanto deduction.

The Government relies upon several decisions including Brotherhood v. Pinkston, 293 U.S. 96, Commissioner of Internal Rev. v. State Street T. Co., 128 F.2d 618, and Commissioner of Internal Revenue v. Maresi, 156 F.2d 929, in all of which the possibility of ascertaining the likelihood of remarriage was accepted as a basis for the Court's decision. The distinction between these cases and the *Sternberger*, *Cardeza* and *Robinette* cases becomes clear when one considers the reasoning of the *Sternberger* opinion. The key is to be found in the following sentence: "The bequest, in fact, offers to the daughter an inducement . . . to remarry and leave a descendant." All the cases relied upon by the Government involved an interest in the life tenant which would cease upon her remarriage—a pension, a divorce settlement and payments to a widow during widowhood. In such cases the figures supporting the probability of remarriage in the whole population would naturally show a higher probability of remarriage than in a case in which remarriage would lead to the loss of income, and any error in the actuarial result would be on the safe side. On the other hand, in the cases cited by the taxpayer, as well as in the present case, there was a decided inducement to remarry so that the life tenant could leave a descendant. This would tend to make the actuarial figures too low to apply to any case where such inducement existed, but no statistics can possibly even approximate how much too low. If the actuarial estimates of the probability of remarriage are too low, then the estimate of the value of the reversion must be too high, but again there is no possibility of saying how much too high.

Granted that the mere fact that an act is voluntary does not defeat the possibility of determining statistically the probability of its occurrence, yet, where inducements of widely varying potency and rewards of widely varying attractiveness are offered to people of widely varying personalities, it is manifestly impossible to arrive at a statistical analysis sufficiently accurate to permit of any intelligent valuation of reversion. Nor, in the nature of things, is any advance in the actuarial art conceivable, which would meet the difficulty.

My conclusion is that the reversionary interest in the present case does not have any ascertainable value under the applicable valuation principles and it, therefore, must be considered to have a valuation of zero.

I have carefully considered the argument of the Government that the conclusion of its actuary contained in his affidavit is an opinion as to a fact and that the taxpayer must offer evidence to show that it is unsound, thus creating a factual issue and preventing summary judgment. The actuary's valuation of the reversion was based on the assumption that the marriage between the son and his wife would not be dissolved except by death. Even accepting such assumption as a fact, the question is still whether the probability of the husband's remarriage can be ascertained [by] actuarial procedure in a case where the devolution of a large estate depends upon it and the birth of progeny offers substantial inducements to remarry. In such case, it seems to me, no results obtained by any kind of actuarial procedure can reach a higher level than a guess.

Judgment may be entered for the plaintiff.

AFFIRMED.

NOTES

1.   Are the court in *Cardeza* and the Conference Committee Report on which the court based its opinion misreading the Supreme Court in *Robinette*?[4] In that case, the Court confronted a situation where three donors had contributed property to a trust and retained life estates for themselves with the remainder payable to the unborn issue of one of the donors, an unmarried young woman, when the unborn issue reach age 21. In the event of failure of this event, the corpus of the trust was to be distributed as designated by the will of the last survivor of the three donors. In determining the amount that was subject to the gift tax, the parties sought to have the gift tax imposed on the value that each transferred to the trust, less the value of their retained life estates and the value of their reversions. In a less than clear opinion, the Court refused to fix a value for the reversions and allowed no exclusion from the gift tax for a value attributable to them. If *Robinette* is viewed as a burden of proof case, with the taxpayer having the burden of proof as the law then stood, then a different result should be obtained in *Cardeza*. It is possible to read *Robinette* as holding that, in computing the amount of the gift, no discount should be allowed for the value of potential reversionary interests because of the inability of the taxpayer to establish actuarially the value of the likelihood that the young unmarried female beneficiary would produce an issue who would survive until the age of 21. So construed, *Robinette* thus becomes a burden of proof case, that is to say, since the taxpayer could not meet his burden of proof in valuing a reversion, no discount was allowed with respect to it. Seemingly, the Court in *Robinette* would allow the taxpayer to meet his burden of proof in seeking a discount only by providing evidence that could be actuarially determined. This is far

---

[4]   For a good discussion of this issue, see Wendy C. Gerzog, *Contingencies and the Estate Tax*, 5 FLA. TAX REV. 49, 72–73 (2001).

different from reading the case as holding, as the Conference Committee did, that in all cases where a reversionary interest does not have an ascertainable value, its value will be deemed to equal zero. Indeed, if *Robinette* is merely viewed as a burden of proof case, Cardeza's estate should have been deemed not to have met its burden of proof in establishing actuarially that the value of the decedent's reversion was less than five percent. Perhaps this reading of the authorities is what prompted the Senate Finance Committee in its report on section 2037 under the 1954 Code to comment:

> Where it is apparent from the facts that property could have reverted to the decedent under contingencies that were not remote, the reversionary interest is not to be regarded as having no value merely because the value thereof cannot be measured precisely.

S. Rep. No. 1622, 83d Cong., 2d Sess. at 469.

It might be beneficial here to review and reconsider the materials dealing with contingent interests in Chapter 15.

2. Would it not have been appropriate for the court in *Cardeza* to have merely valued decedent's reversion using normal actuarial techniques and ignoring the possibility that her 59-year old daughter-in-law would produce a child or that taxpayer's 64-year old son might take up with another woman and that issue would result? If the court in *Cardeza* is correct, the five percent reversion requirement can always be defeated by injecting into the mix a non-actuarial wild card which is highly unlikely to disrupt the real-world likelihood of decedent enjoying her reversion.

3. Even if valuation of a reversionary interest is to be based entirely on actuarially determinable factors (i.e., life expectancies), opportunities for dispute as to what that value should be still exist. For example, in Manufacturers Hanover Trust Co. v. United States, 775 F.2d 459 (2d Cir.1985), the court agreed that the IRS could use "gender based" mortality tables in calculating the value of retained reversionary interests under section 2037. The result in that case was to render taxable a reversionary interest retained by the female transferor—an interest that would have been nontaxable had a unisex mortality table been used. The Treasury, meanwhile, had nevertheless issued "gender neutral" tables based on a higher interest rate applicable to decedents dying after November 30, 1983. See Treas. Reg. § 20.2031–7.

D. DETERMINATION OF AMOUNT INCLUDIBLE

Bear in mind that the value of the reversionary interest of the decedent-donor is calculated only to determine if we have met one of the two statutory requirements for inclusion under section 2037. If that requirement and the other requirement of section 2037 (an interest which is to be transferred only by surviving) have been met, inclusion results and the value included bears no relationship to the value of the decedent's reversionary interest. Under section 2037, the value included is the value of those interests which pass to parties by virtue of their surviving the decedent. Illustration of the operation of this principle is provided by Treas. Reg. § 20.2037–1(e), Examples 3 and 4, and the ruling which follows.

REVENUE RULING 76–178
1976–1 C.B. 273.

Advice has been requested whether, under the circumstances described below, the interests transferred in trust are to be included in a decedent's gross estate under section 2037 of the Internal Revenue Code of 1954.

Pursuant to the terms of a trust agreement executed in 1961, the decedent (a male) gave A (a female) a life interest in Blackacre, a parcel of income-producing real property. The trust agreement provided that Blackacre would revert to the decedent if the decedent survived A; but, if A survived the decedent, then upon A's death Blackacre should pass to the decedent's child or to the child's estate.

The decedent died on July 1, 1973, survived by A and decedent's child. At the date of decedent's death both the decedent and A were aged 88. The fair market value of Blackacre on such date was $100,000.

Section 2037(a) provides that the gross estate includes the value of a property interest that a decedent transferred by trust or otherwise, if (1) possession or enjoyment of the property can, through ownership of such interest, be obtained only by surviving the decedent, and (2) the decedent has retained a reversionary interest in the property, and the value of such reversionary interest immediately before the decedent's death exceeds 5 percent of the value of such property.

Section 2037(b) provides that the term "reversionary interest" includes a possibility that property transferred by the decedent (1) may return to the decedent or the decedent's estate, or (2) may be subject to a power of disposition by the decedent, but such term does not include a possibility that the income alone from such property may return to the decedent or become subject to a power of disposition by the decedent.

Section 20.2037–1(c)(3) of the Estate Tax Regulations provides that the value of the decedent's reversionary interest is computed without regard to whether or not the executor elects the alternate valuation method under section 2032 and without regard to the fact of the decedent's death. The value is ascertained in accordance with recognized valuation principles for determining the value, for estate tax purposes, of future or conditional interests in property under sections 20.2031–1, and 20.2031–10 of the regulations.

Section 20.2037–1(c)(4) of the regulations provides that in order to determine the value of the decedent's reversionary interest the value of the reversionary interest is compared with the value of the transferred property, including interests therein that are not dependent upon survivorship of the decedent.

Upon creation of the trust, *A* had immediate, absolute, and unconditional enjoyment of a life interest in Blackacre, which would be unaffected by the decedent's subsequent death. Consequently, the transfer of the life interest, does not come within the purview of section 2037. Compare Frank W. Thacher, 20 T.C. 474 (1953), acq., 1954–1 C. B. 7, which reached a contrary conclusion when a spouse's life interest was subject to divestment upon divorce and the property would revert to the decedent.

On the other hand, the vesting of the decedent's child's remainder interest in Blackacre is postponed until the decedent's death. Thus, with respect to the remainder interest the survivorship requirement of section 2037 is satisfied. Under the express terms of the trust agreement, the decedent retained a reversionary interest and includibility of the transferred property depends on whether the value of this reversionary interest meets the percentage requirement of section 2037.

The decedent's reversionary interest is described as the present worth of the right of the decedent (a male aged 88) to receive $100,000 upon the death of *A* (a female aged 88), provided the decedent survives. The actuarial factor representing this described reversionary interest is 0.43194. (This factor cannot be found in the tables contained in section 20.2031–10(f) of the regulations. Rather, it is a special factor that will be computed by the National Office upon submission of the information specified in section 20.2031–10(f) of the regulations.)

Using the factor of 0.43194 applicable in the present case the value of the decedent's reversionary interest is $43,194 ($100,000 × 0.43194). In determining whether the value of the decedent's reversionary interest exceeds 5 percent of the value of the transferred property, *A*'s life estate is not excluded from such value for purposes of making this determination under section 20.2037–1(c)(4) of the regulations. Since the value of the decedent's reversionary interest exceeds 5 percent of the value of Blackacre, the percentage requirement of section 2037 is satisfied.

The value of the reversionary interest determines the applicability of section 2037, but this is not the interest includible in the decedent's gross estate. Since the decedent's child's possession or enjoyment of the underlying property, through ownership of the remainder interest, is dependent on surviving the decedent, the value of such property less the value of the outstanding life estate in *A* is includible in the decedent's gross estate. Klein v. United States, 283 U.S. 231 (1931), X–1 C.B. 462.

Accordingly, section 2037 requires the inclusion of the entire trust corpus at its date of death value of $100,000 less the value of A's life estate; or using the remainder factor applicable to a female aged 88, as specified in Table A(2) of section 20.2031–10(f) of the regulations, the includible interest is the present worth of the right to receive $100,000 upon the death of a female aged 88 or $81,569 ($100,000 × 0.81569).

PROBLEMS

Note: For purposes of these problems, assume that all reversions in the decedent exceed five percent in value and that all transfers were made after October 8, 1949.

1. Brian established a trust under which income was to be paid to his wife, Sally, for her life and the remainder was to be distributed to their son, Nick. In the event that Nick dies first and Sally predeceased Brian, the corpus is then to revert to Brian. Brian was survived by both Sally and Nick and, at his death, the trust corpus was worth $750,000. What are the estate tax consequences?

2. John established a trust under which income was to go to a local charity for his life with the remainder to go to his daughter Brittany or her estate. John died four years later and was survived by Brittany. At his death, trust corpus was worth $400,000. What are the estate tax consequences?

3. Anne established a trust under which income was to go to a local charity for her life with the remainder to go to her brother, Cody, if living. Anne died eight years later, survived by Cody, when the value of the trust corpus was $1,200,000. What are the estate tax consequences?

4. Nicole established a trust under which income was to be paid to her husband Eric for his life with the remainder to be distributed to Nicole or if she predeceased Eric to their son Paul or his estate. Nicole died and was survived by Eric and Paul. At her death, the trust corpus was worth $1,300,000 and Eric's life estate was worth $500,000. What are the estate tax consequences?

5. Emily established a trust with $400,000 of corpus. Under the terms of the trust all income was to be accumulated until there was only one child of her father surviving, at which point the corpus and accumulated income were to be distributed to that child. Emily died and was survived by her brother Macon and her sister Rose. At Emily's death the trust corpus and accumulated income were worth $900,000. What are the estate tax consequences?

6. Kendall established a trust under which income was to go to her husband, Nathan, for his life with remainder to their daughter, Barbara, or her estate. In the event Nathan divorced Kendall, the trust was to terminate and the corpus was to be distributed to Kendall. At Kendall's death, she and Nathan were still happily married, and the trust corpus was worth $2,400,000. What are the estate tax consequences?

7. Aaron established a trust with income to his wife, Patrice, for her life, remainder to their son, Dan, or his estate. If Patrice divorced or predeceased Aaron, the trust was to terminate, and the corpus was to be distributed to Aaron. At Aaron's death the entire trust corpus was worth $1,000,000 and Patrice's life estate was actuarially determined to be worth $400,000. What are the estate tax consequences?

8. Martin established a trust under which income was to be distributed to his wife, Lisa, for her life with remainder to Lisa's heirs under the state's intestate law in effect at her death. Martin died and was survived by Lisa and their daughter, Nancy. At Martin's death the entire corpus of the trust was worth $900,000 and the actuarially computed value of Lisa's life estate was $300,000. Under the state's intestate succession statute, the property of an individual who dies without a will and who is survived by a spouse and issue is to be divided accordingly, one-third to the surviving spouse and the balance equally among issue. Where there is no surviving spouse and only issue, the property is to be divided equally among the issue. Where there is a surviving spouse and no surviving issue, the surviving spouse will take all property. Where a child dies and is survived only by parents, that child's property is to be divided equally between the parents and, if the child is survived by only one parent, that parent will inherit all the child's property. What are the estate tax consequences?

9. Martin also established a second trust under which income was to go to his daughter, Nancy, for her life with remainder to go to her heirs under the state's intestate laws. As in the preceding problem, Martin died and was survived by both Lisa and Nancy. At Martin's death, the entire corpus of his trust was worth $1,200,000 and the actuarially computed value of Nancy's life estate was worth $800,000. What are the estate tax consequences?

CHAPTER 21

ANNUITIES AND RETIREMENT BENEFITS

(SECTION 2039)

■ ■ ■

A. THE NATURE AND IMPORTANCE OF ANNUITIES

The term "annuity" is derived from the Latin *annus*, for "year." The year reference is appropriate because the purchase of a traditional annuity involves the conversion of a lump sum into periodic (such as annual) payments. The purchaser of an annuity transfers a lump sum to an annuity or insurance company; in return, the company agrees to pay to the beneficiary a designated amount each year for an agreed period of years. The purchaser is said to "annuitize" the lump sum, and the beneficiary of the annual payments is called the "annuitant." Although the year reference remains incorporated in these terms, in modern practice payments are more likely to be made monthly or quarterly.

Annuities can offer unique advantages in appropriate circumstances. Assume, for example, that a childless 76-year old widow has finite resources of $200,000 to support her for the rest of her life. She could invest the $200,000 and live on the earnings—perhaps $10,000 per year. But this amount may be inadequate, and especially so if she encounters health problems. Furthermore, this approach essentially "wastes" the principal, which will not itself be used for the widow's benefit, but instead may go to a distant relative, friend, or charity at the widow's death. Alternatively, the widow could consume a portion of the principal each year, but this would decrease future income. Worse still, if the widow lives longer than expected, she may consume the entire principal and find herself destitute.

The solution is an annuity. The widow transfers $200,000 to an annuity or insurance company in exchange for the company's commitment to pay an agreed amount to the widow each year for as long as she lives. The company knows that the average life expectancy of a 76-year old is approximately 10 years. Therefore, the company is willing to commit to pay 10% of the principal, or $20,000, to the widow each year. In addition, the company will have the principal (beginning at $200,000 and gradually declining) to invest, yielding perhaps $60,000 over the expected 10-year

505

period. After subtracting $10,000 for its profit, the company can commit to pay $50,000 in earnings to the widow—providing an additional $5,000 per year. Therefore, the company will commit to pay $25,000 to the widow each year for as long as she lives.

This is a perfect solution from the widow's viewpoint. She has raised her annual expendable resources from $10,000 to $25,000. She gets full benefit from the principal, and she is assured of the $25,000 annual amount regardless of how long she lives. The company may or may not make a profit, depending on whether the widow lives for fewer or more than 10 years. However, because the company will have entered into similar contracts with many other 76-year old individuals, the company can rely on the high probability that the average longevity of this group will be 10 years. Therefore, the company is likely to achieve the expected results for the group as a whole.

While traditional annuities of this kind remain important, the market has spawned numerous modifications and additional features designed to meet specific needs and objectives.

One of these is the "variable" annuity. Here the company does not guarantee a specific annual payment amount, but invests the principal in an agreed vehicle, such as a common stock fund. The return to the annuitant depends on the investment experience of the fund, including appreciation or depreciation as well as dividends. Hence the payment to the annuitant will vary over the years—a risk assumed by the annuitant.

A popular modification is the "refund" annuity. A parent purchasing an annuity for life may not want to take the risk that the parent might die shortly after the purchase, which would create a windfall for the annuity company and deprive the parent's children of assets they would have received had the annuity not been purchased. In response to this concern, the company will guarantee a refund to designated beneficiaries if the total payout to the parent does not reach a certain level. For example, the contract might provide that if the parent dies before receiving an amount equal to the original investment, the difference between the original investment and the amount actually received will be paid to a designated beneficiary, such as a child. Of course, this refund feature has a cost, and insertion of the refund feature will require a reduction in the periodic payments to be made during the life of the parent.

Another version of the refund feature is a contract guaranteeing payments for a minimum number of years, such as ten. If the annuitant dies before expiration of the ten-year period, his designated beneficiaries will continue to receive payments through the tenth year. Again, such a guaranteed term feature has a cost, and inclusion of this feature will require that the periodic payment amount be reduced.

An often used variant is the "survivor" annuity, whereby an annuity is paid to a survivor after the death of the original annuitant. For example, a wife might purchase an annuity providing $2,000 per month for herself during her life, and $1,500 per month for her husband throughout his life after the wife's death, should the husband survive.

By far the most important development is the adoption of the annuity as the preferred method for payment of retirement benefits. As retirement benefits have expanded dramatically since World War II, employers have typically chosen to make those benefits available in the form of periodic payments, rather than as lump sums. Retirement benefits provided by the employer in this way are referred to as "defined benefit" plans because the plan specifies the amount and nature of the benefits to be received by the employee upon retirement. In more recent years such defined benefit plans have been increasingly replaced by "defined contribution" plans. Under a defined contribution plan the employer contributes a specified amount to the retirement account of the employee. Each employee's account is separately invested—typically as directed by the employee—and the employee's benefits upon retirement depend upon the amount in the account at retirement. Often the account is funded by tax-free contributions from both the employer and the employee.

Typically, a defined contribution plan permits the employee to designate the method of payout and the disposition of the funds remaining in the account at the employee's death, subject to certain limitations. Usually the employee simply designates a beneficiary who will receive the remaining funds in the account upon the employee's death, and that beneficiary can elect the form of payout, ranging from a lump sum to a periodic or annuity payment.

B. GENERAL TAXATION PRINCIPLES

The taxation of annuities is governed by section 2039. An annuity is included in the gross estate if both of two tests (greatly simplified here) are met:

1. The decedent must have had an entitlement to payments—either current or prospective—during his life.

2. Another person must receive benefits by reason of surviving the decedent.

The application of these two rules produces results entirely consistent with the estate tax principles developed earlier, as is demonstrated by these examples:

1. Assume that the decedent was receiving a monthly payment of $1,000 at the time of his death. Under the annuity contract, the payments terminate at the decedent's death, and no one

is entitled to payments after the decedent's death. Here the second test is not satisfied, and nothing will be included in the decedent's gross estate. There is no asset remaining after the decedent's death; hence there is no transfer and nothing to tax. This is consistent with the principle developed in Chapter 15: the estate tax has no application to assets that terminate or disappear by reason of the decedent's death.

2. Assume that the decedent was not entitled to payments during his life. The annuity contract provides that beginning upon the decedent's death, and continuing for ten years thereafter, payments of $1,000 per month are to be made to a child of the decedent. Here the first test is not satisfied, and section 2039 is not applicable. The reason is that, at least on the facts given, there is no indication that the decedent retained an interest in the property until his death. Provisions other than section 2039, however, might cause the annuity to be subjected to gift or estate tax. If the decedent purchased the annuity prior to his death and retained no power to change the beneficiary, the purchase would have constituted a completed gift to the child, and a taxable gift would have occurred when the annuity was purchased. If, on the other hand, the decedent purchased the annuity prior to his death but reserved a power to control beneficial enjoyment (such as changing the beneficiary), the purchase would not have been a completed taxable gift, but the annuity would be included in the decedent's gross estate because of the decedent's retained power, pursuant to sections 2036 and 2038.

3. Assume that the decedent was receiving payments of $1,000 per month at the time of death, and that the contract provides that beginning at the decedent's death and continuing for ten years thereafter, the decedent's daughter is to receive payments of $750 per month. Here both section 2039 tests are met, and the annuity will be included in the decedent's gross estate pursuant to section 2039. The amount included is the value of the annuity immediately after the decedent's death. As explained below, that value is the cost of an annuity of $750 per month for 10 years, under interest rates prevailing at the decedent's death.

The two tests described above state only the core of section 2039. Although section 2039 is mercifully short, it is packed with additional rules and qualifications, the most important of which are these:

1.   The annuity is included in the decedent's gross estate only to the extent the decedent contributed the funds to purchase the annuity. I.R.C. § 2039(b). This rule is appropriate because there has been no transfer that can legitimately be taxed if the annuity does not ultimately derive from the decedent's resources. For example, if a mother purchases an annuity providing for payments for her daughter during the daughter's life, followed by payments to a son during his life, there would be no inclusion of the annuity in the daughter's gross estate at the daughter's death because the daughter did not purchase the annuity. If the daughter provided a part of the consideration for the annuity, that proportionate part of the total annuity value would be included in her gross estate. For example, if the daughter provided 40% of the total purchase cost, 40% of the total value would be included in the daughter's gross estate.

2.   For purposes of the rule stated in the preceding paragraph, any contribution to the annuity by the decedent's employer or former employer is treated as if the employee herself made the contribution, provided the contribution is made by reason of the decedent's employment. I.R.C. § 2039(b). The rationale is that the contribution in essence constitutes additional compensation to the employee and should be viewed as first distributed to the employee, followed by contribution of that amount by the employee toward the annuity. This rule has immense importance because it subjects to estate tax the many noncontributory retirement plans, i.e., those purchased entirely with funds provided by the employer. It also causes inclusion in the gross estate of the entirety of retirement plans purchased jointly by the employer and employee.

3.   The annuity is included in the decedent's gross estate if the survivor's entitlement to payments is based on "any form of contract or agreement . . . other than as insurance under policies on the life of the decedent." I.R.C. § 2039(a). This rule makes it clear that the nature of the contract or agreement makes no difference. Any arrangement for payments (other than life insurance) is covered, whether or not denominated as an annuity. Life insurance is entirely excluded from section 2039, leaving section 2033 and section 2042 to determine inclusion in the gross estate, as explained in Chapter 17.

4.   The first core requirement—that the decedent be currently or prospectively entitled to payments—can be satisfied in either of two ways. One is current receipt of payments by the

decedent at the time of his death. The other is entitlement to payments at a later date, such as subsequent to retirement. For example, assume that an employee dies while still employed, and that the employer has provided a plan that would have made payments to the employee after his retirement had he lived, with continuing payments to the employee's designated beneficiary upon the employee's death. The prospective entitlement to payments satisfies the first test, and the annuity will be included in the employee's gross estate. The issue becomes more complex, however, where there are conditions imposed on the employee's prospective entitlement, and those conditions might or might not be met at a later date. The regulations resolve this issue by providing that the decedent will be treated as having satisfied the required conditions if he satisfies those conditions as of the date of death. Treas. Reg. § 20.2039–1(b)(1).

5. The fact that the decedent received payments at some point during his life is not sufficient to satisfy the first test. The annuity is included in the decedent's gross estate only if the decedent's entitlement is to payments "for his life or for any period not ascertainable without reference to his death or for any period which does not in fact end before his death." I.R.C. § 2039(a). This language replicates the retained life estate language of section 2036(a) and confirms that the annuity should be included in the decedent's gross estate only if the passage of the annuity to the survivor beneficiary has a testamentary or death-related character. That is the case in the typical situation, where the annuity payments are to continue until the decedent's death. If, however, the annuity payments are to be made for a specific period, such as ten years, and the last payment is made prior to the decedent's death, the first test is not satisfied, and there is no inclusion by reason of section 2039. There might, however, be inclusion under another provision, such as section 2036 or section 2038, if the decedent had retained until his death the power to designate the recipient of the payments after his death.

6. The requirement that the decedent be entitled to payments during his life is satisfied even if he had only the right to receive payment jointly with another person. I.R.C. § 2039(a).

In many cases imposition of estate tax on annuities is prevented by the marital deduction, covered in Chapter 27. A typical example is the joint and survivor annuity, providing for payments to one spouse throughout that spouse's life, followed by payments to the surviving spouse. If no payments are to be made after the death of both spouses, the entire annuity will qualify for the marital deduction upon the death of the first spouse to die, and there will be nothing to tax at the death of the surviving spouse.

The following committee report that accompanied enactment of section 2039 provides a helpful summary of the section 2039 rules. Under current estate tax law there is no special exclusion for tax qualified plans or IRAs.

EXCERPTS FROM SENATE COMMITTEE REPORT ON THE REVENUE ACT OF 1954

Senate Report No. 1622, 83d Cong. 2d sess. at p. 470.

§ 2039. Annuities. * * * With certain limitations, this section requires the inclusion in the decedent's gross estate of the value of an annuity or other payments receivable by any beneficiary by reason of surviving the decedent under any form of contract or agreement (other than as insurance under policies on the life of the decedent) * * * if under the contract or agreement an annuity or other payment was payable to the decedent, or the decedent possessed the right to receive such annuity or payment, either alone or in conjunction with another for his life or for any period not ascertainable without reference to his death or for any period which does not in fact end before his death. * * * [T]he provisions of this section apply not only to cases where an annuity was payable to a decedent but also to contracts or agreements under which a lump-sum payment was payable to the decedent or the decedent possessed the right to receive such a lump-sum payment in lieu of an annuity. For purposes of this section, the term "annuity" includes periodic payments for a specified period of time. The following are examples of contracts, but are not necessarily the only forms of contracts to which this section applies:

(1) A contract under which the decedent immediately before his death was receiving or was entitled to receive for the duration of his life an annuity, or other stipulated payment, with payments thereunder to continue after his death to a designated beneficiary if surviving the decedent.

(2) A contract under which the decedent immediately before his death was receiving or was entitled to receive, together with another person, an annuity, or other stipulated payment payable to the decedent and such other person for their joint lives, with payments thereunder to continue to the survivor following the death of either.

(3) A contract or agreement entered into by the decedent and his employer under which the decedent immediately before his death and following retirement was receiving or was entitled to receive an annuity or other stipulated payment, payable to the decedent for the duration of his life and thereafter to a designated beneficiary, if surviving the decedent, whether the

payments after the decedent's death are fixed by the contract, or subject to an option or election exercised or exercisable by the decedent.

(4) A contract or agreement entered into by the decedent and his employer under which at decedent's death, prior to retirement or prior to the expiration of a stated period of time, an annuity or other payment was payable to a designated beneficiary if surviving the decedent.

(5) A contract or agreement under which the decedent immediately before his death was receiving or was entitled to receive an annuity for a stated period of time, with the annuity or other payment to continue to a designated beneficiary, upon the decedent's death prior to the expiration of such period, if surviving the decedent.

The amount to be included in the gross estate is the value at the decedent's death of the annuity or other payment receivable by the survivor of the decedent, and it is immaterial whether the payments to the survivor are payable in a lump sum, in installments, in the same, or in a greater or lesser amount than the annuity or payment to the decedent.

This section applies only to that part of the value of the annuity or other payment receivable by the surviving beneficiary which the decedent's contribution to the purchase price of the contract or agreement bears to the total purchase price thereof. For example, assume that the value of the annuity to the beneficiary at decedent's death is $20,000 and that the decedent contributed one half of the purchase price of the contract. In such case, $10,000 would be includible in the decedent's gross estate.

In determining the amount of the decedent's contribution to the purchase price of the contract, there shall be taken into account contributions made by his employer, if made by reason of decedent's employment * * *.

* * *

The provisions of this section shall not prevent the application of any other provision of law relating to the estate tax. For example, if a contract provides for a refund of a portion of the cost thereof, in the event of the decedent's premature death, payable to the decedent's estate the amount thereof shall be treated as any other property of the decedent. This section does not, however, apply to insurance under policies on the life of the decedent to which § 2042 is applicable.

The provisions of this section are applicable only to annuities or other payments payable to the decedent, or which the decedent possessed the right to receive, either alone or in conjunction with another for his life or for any period not ascertainable without reference to his death or for any period which does not in fact end before his death. The rules applicable under § 2036 in determining whether the annuity or other payment was payable to the decedent, or whether he possessed the right thereto, for his life or such periods shall be applicable under this section.

NOTE

The reach of section 2039(b) was tested in Estate of Shackleford v. United States, 98–2 USTC ¶ 60,320, 82 AFTR2d 98–5538 (E.D.Cal.1998), aff'd, 262 F.3d 1028 (9th Cir. 2001). In *Shackleford*, the decedent had won a California lottery prize entitling him to twenty annual payments of $508,000 each. The decedent had received only three payments prior to his death. The executor contended that the right to receive seventeen additional payments constituted an annuity and was therefore controlled by section 2039. The executor further argued that section 2039(b) limited inclusion in the gross estate to the amount of the decedent's contribution—the one dollar the decedent had paid for the ticket. Nevertheless, the court concluded that section 2039(b) should not be applied because "the lottery payments represent the accumulated wealth of the decedent," with the result that the prospective payments should be included as property owned under section 2033. Therefore, the entire present value of the prospective payments was included in the decedent's estate.

C. VALUATION

Valuation of an annuity that is included in a decedent's gross estate is entirely prospective. The age of the decedent and the payments to which the decedent was entitled prior to death are irrelevant. All that matters is the value to be received by the person or persons who become entitled to payments by reason of the decedent's death.

The general rule is that an annuity is valued using the Treasury tables under section 2031, applying the current section 7520 rate, as explained in Chapter 10. If, however, the annuity is issued by a company regularly engaged in the sale of annuities, the annuity is valued under Regulations §§ 20.2031–8 and 25.2512–6. See Treas. Regs. §§ 20.2031–7(b) and 25.2512–5(b). Under these provisions, the value of such a "commercial annuity" is determined by the cost charged by the company for comparable contracts. Treas. Regs. §§ 20.2031–8(a)(1) and 25.2512–6(a).

D. APPLICATION TO TAX QUALIFIED PLANS AND IRAs

If the decedent is the beneficiary of a defined benefit plan, the terms of the plan will determine whether there is inclusion under section 2039. If the defined benefit plan provides an annuity only for the retired employee, with no benefits for survivors, there will be no inclusion under section 2039. Nothing passes to anyone else upon the retired employee's death.

If the defined benefit plan provides for annuity payments to a survivor after the retired employee's death, section 2039 will apply if the retired employee was entitled to payments during her life. Typically, however, survivor payments are made only to the retired employee's spouse. In that event the survivor payments will qualify for the marital deduction, and the marital deduction will effectively shelter the survivor's payments from estate tax.

Section 2039 is less likely to apply to a defined contribution plan. If the retired employee has irrevocably elected an annuity payout for both herself and the person she has named as the beneficiary after her death, section 2039 will apply. Typically, however, the retired employee will not have irrevocably elected a payout method for the beneficiary after the employee's death. In other words, the beneficiary becomes entitled to whatever amount is in the account at the employee's death, and the beneficiary's election of payout method has no effect on that value. The amount in the account can be viewed as an asset owned by the decedent at death, includable in the decedent employee's gross estate under section 2033. Alternatively, the amount in the account can be viewed as an asset as to which the decedent retained possession and enjoyment until the decedent's death; therefore, the account is includable in the decedent's gross estate under section 2036. The beneficiary's election of payout method—whether annuity or lump sum—has no effect on this value.

The same approach is applied to an IRA. A decedent owning an IRA will have named a beneficiary to receive the IRA upon the decedent's death. The value of the IRA at the decedent's death is included in the decedent's gross estate, and the named beneficiary's election as to payout method has no effect on that value.

PROBLEMS

Jane died at the age of 60, survived by her son, William, age 40. At the time of her death Jane was employed by Corbin, Inc., a manufacturer of hardware. Jane supervised the accounting department of Corbin, Inc.

Jane was a strong believer in annuities as an investment and estate planning device. For that reason, she had invested a substantial amount of her savings in certain annuities, and Corbin, Inc. had joined her in the purchase of one annuity. These annuity contracts are described below.

In the case of each annuity contract, indicate whether the annuity should be included in Jane's gross estate, whether under section 2039 or another section.

1. Jane purchased Annuity 1 with her own funds five years prior to her death, irrevocably naming William as the beneficiary. This annuity provides $10,000 per year for William throughout his

life, beginning at Jane's death. Jane was not entitled to any payments during her life.

2. Jane purchased Annuity 2 with her own funds. It provides $10,000 per year for Jane throughout her life, beginning at age 55, and after Jane's death to William throughout his life. Jane was receiving annuity payments at the time of her death.

3. Jane purchased Annuity 3 with her own funds. It provides $10,000 per year for Jane throughout her life, beginning at age 70, and then throughout William's life as well. If Jane should die before attaining age 70, the annuity to William is to start immediately.

4. Jane purchased Annuity 4 with her own funds. It provides $10,000 per year for Jane throughout her life, beginning at age 55. The payments end at Jane's death. Jane was receiving the annuity at the time of her death.

5. Annuity 5 was purchased one-half with funds furnished by Jane and one-half with funds furnished by Corbin, Inc. It provides $10,000 per year for Jane throughout her life, beginning at age 65, and then throughout William's life as well. Jane and William would become entitled to the annuity only if, at the earlier of Jane's death or attainment of age 65, Jane was employed by Corbin, Inc. If Jane should die while employed by Corbin, Inc. and before attaining age 65, the annuity to William would begin immediately.

6. In addition, Corbin Inc. established a tax qualified defined contribution plan, and both Corbin Inc. and Jane had made contributions to this plan over the years. Jane did not receive any payments from the plan prior to her death. Jane had designated her daughter, Alice, as the beneficiary of the plan upon Jane's death. On the date of Jane's death, the value of the assets in the plan was $207,000. After Jane's death, Alice elected to receive the $207,000 gradually through annuity distributions over her lifetime. To what extent should the assets in the defined contribution plan be included in Jane's gross estate?

E. COMBINING ANNUITIES WITH OTHER BENEFITS

ESTATE OF BAHEN V. UNITED STATES

Court of Claims of the United States, 1962.
305 F.2d 827.

DAVIS, JUDGE:

The estate of a former high-ranking officer of The Chesapeake and Ohio Railway Company claims that sums paid by the C. & O. to his widow on his death in 1955, under benefit plans unilaterally adopted by the railroad in 1952 and 1953, were improperly included in his gross estate for tax purposes.

* * *

After Mr. Bahen's death, the C. & O. made payments to his widow under two plans which it had earlier established for its employees. The first was the Death Benefit Plan, adopted in January 1952, which provided that, if a covered employee with more than 10 years' service died while in the company's employ and before becoming eligible for retirement, the C. & O. would pay, "in recognition of the services rendered by him", a sum equal to three months' salary to his widow or (if she died prior to payment) to the guardian of any of his minor children.

The more significant arrangement was the Deferred Compensation Plan adopted by the company in February 1953 for forty of its officers and executives. For a designated officer who was under 60 at that time, like Mr. Bahen, the C. & O. would pay a stated maximum sum ($100,000 in Mr. Bahen's case), at his death either before or after retirement, to his widow and to those of his surviving children under 21 the officer might specify (and in the proportions he designated), in 60 equal monthly installments. These payments were to be made only if a wife or minor child survived the officer and would continue only so long as there was a surviving wife or child under 21. However, if prior to retirement the officer became totally incapacitated, mentally or physically, for further performance of duty, the payments would be made to him in 60 equal monthly installments so long as he survived, any unpaid installment going to his widow or minor children. The president of the company was to notify each officer covered by the Plan of the benefits payable to him and was also "to represent that the Plan is irrevocable, not subject to later withdrawal by this Board [of Directors], and represents a firm commitment on the part of the company to extend benefits in accordance with the terms and conditions herein set forth." Mr. Bahen was immediately notified of this Deferred Compensation Plan and its irrevocability.

* * *

Section 2039 was a development of the earlier provisions of the estate tax which spoke of the decedent's "property" and of "transfers" by the decedent in contemplation of or taking effect at death. See § 811 of the Internal Revenue Code of 1939. The new section does not use that phraseology but frames its operative requirements more directly in terms of particular types of transactions or arrangements involving the decedent. This change is significant. We must pay heed to the precise new form in which Congress cast its net and not become entangled in the older meshes.

A. *The Deferred Compensation Plan*: We first consider the application of § 2039 (and the Regulations) to the C. & O's major plan, the Deferred Compensation Plan (of 1953) under which $100,000 was paid to Mrs. Bahen in a five-year span. As we read the section and the Regulations, they demand inclusion in the estate of the proceeds of this Plan. Every requirement is squarely met, not only in literal terms but in harmony with the legislative aim.

1. There is, initially, no doubt that the Plan, though adopted by the company unilaterally and without negotiation with the officers and employees, was a "form of contract or agreement" under the statute. This phrase is defined by § 20.2039–1(b)(1)(ii) of the Treasury Regulations on Estate Tax to include "any arrangement, understanding or plan, or any combination of arrangements, understandings, or plans arising by reason of the decedent's employment." A compensation plan unilaterally adopted by the employer, but made irrevocable and communicated to the employee, falls directly within this definition, at least where the employee continues in the company's service after the adoption of the plan.

2. There is likewise no doubt that Mrs. Bahen, the beneficiary, received "an annuity or other payment" under the statute when she was paid the $100,000 in sixty equal installments. The Regulations (Sec. 20.2039–1(b)(1)(ii)) appropriately say that this double term in § 2039, as used with respect to both the beneficiary and the decedent, "has reference to one or more payments extending over any period of time", and that the payments may "be equal or unequal, conditional or unconditional, periodic or sporadic." * * *

3. The next problem is whether at Mr. Bahen's death there was payable to him or he possessed the right to receive "*an annuity or other payment*." The Deferred Compensation Plan provided that, if Mr. Bahen became totally incapacitated for further performance of duty before retirement, the C. & O.

would pay him the $100,000 in 60 equal monthly installments. Under both the normal understanding of the statutory words "annuity or other payment" and the broad definition given them by the Regulations (referred to above), these sums must be characterized as at least an "other payment." Stressing Congress's use of the singular ("payment") and a reference in the Senate Committee Report to a lump-sum payment in lieu of an annuity, plaintiff appears to urge that the *only* "payment" to a decedent covered by § 2039 is a lump sum paid or payable in the place of a strict lifetime annuity (i.e., an annuity paid in the form of a lump sum). But we cannot confine the general language of § 2039, as interpreted by the Regulations, within the limits of one illustration given by the Committee as a reason for adding the all-inclusive words "other payment" to "annuity." As we point out more in detail below, the history and pattern of § 2039 fail to indicate that it deals only with true lifetime annuities (in installment form or in a commuted lump sum). The statute covers—as an "other payment", at least— disability compensation benefits of the type involved here.

4. Were these benefit payments—assuming, as we have just decided, that they constituted an "annuity or other payment" within § 2039—"payable to" Mr. Bahen at his death or did he "possess the right to receive such annuity or payment"? The Regulations (Sec. 20.2039–1(1)(ii)) establish that amounts are "payable" to a decedent "if, at the time of his death, the decedent was in fact receiving an annuity or other payments, whether or not he had an enforceable right to have payments continue." Since Mr. Bahen was not receiving disability benefits when he died, this term of the statute is not satisfied.

We hold, however, that at his death Mr. Bahen did "possess the right" to receive the disability payments in the future if certain conditions were fulfilled, and therefore that the alternative requirement of § 2039 is met. The intentional juxtaposition in the statute of amounts "payable" and those the decedent "possessed the right to receive" indicates that the former relates to the present (i.e. at time of death) and the latter to the future. The Regulations make clear that, in circumstances like these, the decedent's interest in future benefits, even if contingent, is sufficient. Where the employer has offered a plan of this kind, the employee's compliance with his obligations to the company gives him "an enforceable right to receive payments in the future, whether or not, at the time of his death, he had a present right to receive payments." This provision of the Regulations both governs the Deferred Compensation Plan and faithfully reflects its essential characteristics. The arrangement may have been unilateral in inception but it was also irrevocable, and its irrevocability was deliberately communicated to the individuals covered. It thus became an integral article of Mr. Bahen's terms of employment by the C. & O. * * * There can be no doubt that he and the others relied upon the Plan, as they were expected to do. * * * The right they possessed may have been contingent but it was not at the whim of the employer. * * *

In answer, the plaintiff insists that the decedent cannot be considered to have "possessed the right to receive" these disability payments because they were contingent on his becoming totally disabled before retirement, and would never have been received had he lived healthily to retirement age. Only future payments which are sure to be paid if the decedent lives to a designated time are covered by § 2039, plaintiff says. However, as we have pointed out, in specifically covering amounts not payable to the decedent at the time of his death but which he then had merely the "right to receive", the statute and the Regulations obviously cover sums becoming due in the future; and there is no support in the statute's language for the distinction plaintiff makes between the different types of such future payments (at least if they are not forfeitable at the will of another). Both classes of payment are contingent and neither is sure. A benefit payable only if a man lives to a certain age is conditioned upon his living that long, just as a benefit payable only if he becomes disabled is conditional on his future disability. Any distinction between the types seems rejected by the Regulations which include "conditional" payments without qualification. * * * Moreover, the comparable term "right to income" in related earlier provisions of the estate tax (such as present § 2036, former § 811(c)(1)(B)) has been in effect read as including a contingent right to receive income. * * * The legislative history of § 2039 suggests that the rules applicable under § 2036, in this connection, should likewise control under the new provision. S. Rept. No. 1622, 83d Cong., 2d Sess., at p. 472; H. Rept. No. 1337, 83d Cong., 2d Sess., at p. A316. * * *

5. Another requirement of § 2039 is that the decedent's right to receive payments must be possessed "for his life or for any period not ascertainable without reference to his death or for any period which does not in fact end before his death." For the period from February 1953, when the Deferred Compensation Plan was adopted, to his death in November 1955, Mr. Bahen had the right to receive, under this Plan, $100,000 in 60 installments upon his total disability prior to retirement. He thus possessed the right to receive this "annuity or other payment" for a period which did not in fact end before his death—and, accordingly, this element of § 2039 is also present. The correctness of this conclusion is shown by the Regulations (Sec. 20.2039–1(b)(2)), Example (5) of which concerns a plan under which an employer-contributed fund is

to be divided, on retirement at age 60, one-half in a lump sum to the employee and one-half to his beneficiary, the entire amount going to the beneficiary if the employee died before retiring. The Regulations state that if the employee dies before retirement the payment to the beneficiary is includible in gross estate under § 2039 because "the decedent possessed the right to receive a lump sum payment [at retirement] for a period which did not in fact end before his death [before retirement]." This regulation is consistent with the holdings, under older provisions of the estate tax, relating to the meaning of the phrase "for any period which does not in fact end before his death" * * *—rulings which Congress has indicated should be applied under § 2039. S. Rept. No. 1622, 83d Cong., 2d Sess., at p. 472; H. Rept. No. 1337, 83d Cong., 2d Sess., at p. A316.

6. The last element necessary for coverage by § 2039 is that Mr. Bahen must have "contributed" the "purchase price" of the "annuity or other payment" received by Mrs. Bahen which is to be included in the taxable estate. Subsection (b), which adds this requirement, provides:

"(b) *Amount includible.*—Subsection (a) shall apply to only such part of the value of the annuity or other payment receivable under such contract or agreement as is proportionate to that part of the purchase price therefor contributed by the decedent. For purposes of this section, any contribution by the decedent's employer or former employer to the purchase price of such contract or agreement (whether or not to an employee's trust or fund forming part of a pension, annuity, retirement, bonus or profit sharing plan) shall be considered to be contributed by the decedent if made by reason of his employment."

The second sentence of this subsection automatically attributes the employer's contribution to the employee "if made by reason of his employment." This phrase is given broad scope by the Senate Committee Report (S. Rept. No. 1622, 83d Cong., 2d Sess., at p. 471) which holds that it applies "if, for example, the annuity or other payment is offered by the employer as an inducement to employment, or a continuance thereof, or if the contributions are made by the employer in lieu of additional compensation or other rights, if so understood by employer and employee, whether or not expressly stated in the contract of employment or otherwise." The Deferred Compensation Plan, we have already noted, plainly meets this standard; it was an inducement to continued service with the C. & O. It is immaterial, we think, that the company did not formally make "contributions" to a separate fund, or actually purchase annuity or like contracts. Section 2039(b) does not use the words "contribution", "contributed", or "purchase price" in a narrow literal sense, any more than subsection (a) uses "contract or agreement" in that rigid fashion. The section deals, for the area it covers, with the substance of transactions, not with the mechanical way they happen to be formulated. The C. & O.'s undertaking to make payment under the Plan was its "contribution," made by reason of the decedent's employment. Congress did not demand that the company create a tangible fund as a condition to coverage of its employees under this new estate tax provision, and so far as we can see there would be no reason to impose that requirement in a taxing statute such as this.

7.　To all of this the plaintiff—in addition to challenging the existence in this case of some individual elements of coverage—protests that despite its literal language § 2039 is applicable only where there is a true lifetime annuity payable to the decedent for life. Plaintiff correctly points out that the main impetus for the new section was the doubt in 1954 that the former estate tax provisions covered conventional joint and survivor annuities purchased wholly or partly *by the decedent's employer* (as distinguished from those purchased by the decedent himself). S. Rept. No. 1622, 83d Cong., 2d Sess., at p. 123; H. Rept. No. 1337, 83d Cong., 2d Sess., at p. 90. But the Committee Reports do not indicate that Congress, although using language in § 2039 which goes well beyond the precise situation which initially impelled the change, restricted the scope of the new provision to those very circumstances alone. We find nothing to show that Congress desired the broader words it carefully used in § 2039 not to have their normal significance and application; indeed some of the examples and words Congress used in the Committee Reports show that wider coverage was plainly intended. And the Treasury Regulations, as our prior discussion explains, cover annuities and payments to a decedent other than a full lifetime annuity.

8.　Finally, we note briefly that § 2039, as we construe it, is harmonious with the general objective of the federal estate tax to include in the decedent's estate (with designated exceptions) the valuable interests belonging to, accumulated by, or created by or for him, which pass to others at his death. Many such benefits promised, given, and paid for by an employer were specifically brought within this framework by the new section in 1954. In subsection (b), quoted above, Congress provides that contributions by the employer "shall be considered to be contributed by the decedent if made by reason of his employment." Phrased in terms of the earlier concepts of a decedent's "property" "transferred" at his death, Section 2039 declares that annuities or other payments payable by an employer to his employee, and on his death to a beneficiary, constitute his property—created by him through his employer as part of the employment arrangement and in consideration of his continued services—which is transferred to another at his death. * * * A new provision of the estate tax which attempts to apply these fundamental concepts to a fairly well understood set of concrete situations should not be grudgingly read so as to chip away at the specific rule and to continue (as in the past) to leave as much as possible to the ambiguities of the general sections.

* * *

B.   *The Death Benefit Plan*: It is a more difficult question whether the Death Benefit Plan—under which the C. & O. paid Mrs. Bahen a sum equal to Mr. Bahen's salary for three months—is covered by § 2039. Under that arrangement no benefits were payable to the decedent during his life, and if the Plan were to be judged by itself it would fall outside the ambit of the section for lack of "an annuity or other payment" to the decedent. The defendant contends that this factor is present because the words "or other payment" can include the decedent-employee's regular salary; the Death Benefit Plan must be taken, defendant says, together with Mr. Bahen's entire employment arrangement including his ordinary compensation. We cannot agree. Since employees normally receive salary or wages, defendant's interpretation would effectively obliterate, for almost all employees, the express requirement in § 2039 of "an annuity or other payment" to the decedent. If Congress had intended that strange result, it would certainly have mentioned or referred to it. The Government's argument also runs counter to the theory and examples of the Regulations (Sec. 20.2039–1) which impliedly exclude ordinary salary from consideration.

But the Government makes another point which we do accept as bringing the Death Benefit Plan under § 2039. The suggestion is that this Plan should not be viewed in isolation but must be considered together with the Deferred Compensation Plan—as if both arrangements were combined into one plan, providing two types of benefits for beneficiaries after the employee's death but only one type of benefit (disability compensation) to the employee himself. There is some factual support, if that be necessary, for looking at the two plans together, since the Death Benefit Plan was adopted in January 1952 and the Deferred Compensation Plan only a year later in February 1953. There appears to be a common genesis and a unifying thread.

The firmer legal basis is provided by the Regulations (Sec. 20.2039–1(b)(2), Example (6)) which provide: "All rights and benefits accruing to an employee and to others by reason of the employment (except rights and benefits accruing under certain plans meeting the requirements of section 401(a) (see § 20.2039–2)) are considered together in determining whether or not section 2039(a) and (b) applies. The scope of § 2039(a) and (b) cannot be limited by indirection." Effect must be given to this declaration, adopted pursuant to the Treasury's recognized power to issue regulations and not challenged by plaintiff, since it does not violate the terms or the spirit of § 2039. In view of the general purpose of the statute to cover a large share of employer-contributed payments to an employee's survivors, it is not unreasonable to lump together all of the employer's various benefit plans taking account of the employee's death (except those qualified under § 401(a), which are excepted by the statute, see footnotes 2 and 3, supra) in order to decide whether and to what extent § 2039 applies to his estate. There is no immutable requirement in the legislation that each plan separately adopted by a company must be considered alone. One good ground for rejecting that position is to prevent attempts to avoid the reach of the statute by a series of contrived plans none of which, in itself, would fall under the section.

This directive in the Regulations that all rights and benefits "are to be considered together"—read with another part of the same Regulation which defines "contract or agreement" under § 2039 to cover "any combination of arrangements, understandings, or plans arising by reason of the decedent's employment"—requires the two plans of the C. & O. to be deemed a coordinated whole for the purposes of § 2039. On that view the payments under the Death Benefit Plan were includible in the decedent's gross estate for the reasons given above with respect to the Deferred Compensation Plan. If the two Plans are integrated into one, each element required for coverage of all payments is present.

* * *

ESTATE OF SCHELBERG V. COMMISSIONER

United States Court of Appeals, Second Circuit, 1979.
612 F.2d 25.

FRIENDLY, CIRCUIT JUDGE:

This appeal by a taxpayer from a decision of the Tax Court, 70 T.C. 690 (1978), raises a serious question with respect to the interpretation of § 2039, which was added to the Internal Revenue Code in 1954.

I.

Decedent William V. Schelberg was born on March 14, 1914 and died on January 6, 1974 from lung cancer after a week's illness. He was survived by his wife, Sarah, and two daughters, one aged 23 and the other 19. He had been employed by International Business Machines Corp. (IBM) since 1952. At his death he was serving as assistant director of international patent operations at a salary of $4,250 per month.

IBM maintained a variety of employee benefit plans, each adopted at a different time and separately administered. Those here relevant are the Group Life Insurance Plan, the Retirement Plan, the Sickness and Accident Income Plan, and the Total and Permanent Disability Plan. Schelberg was entitled to participate in each.

The Group Life Insurance Plan provided two basic benefits—a group term life insurance, which is not here at issue, and an uninsured and unfunded survivors income benefit, which is. This benefit, determined on the basis of the employee's compensation at the time of death and the amount of the aforementioned life insurance, was payable to a decedent's "eligible" survivors in an order of preference stated in the plan. Payment was to be made monthly, at the rate of one-quarter of the decedent's regular monthly compensation, until the total benefit was exhausted. Payments continued only so long as at least one eligible survivor remained.

The Retirement Plan was a qualified pension plan under I.R.C. § 401. Under IBM's general employment policy, Schelberg would have been required to retire at age 65 and would have been entitled to the retirement benefits provided in the plan.

Under the Sickness and Accident Plan all regular IBM employees were entitled to receive full salary (reduced by any workmen's compensation payments) while absent from work on account of sickness or accident for up to 52 weeks in any 24-month period. Benefits could be continued for more than 52 weeks at IBM's discretion in individual cases; these were known as "individual consideration" benefits.

The Disability Plan covered all IBM employees with more than five years' service. Eligibility was based on determination of "total and permanent disability" by a corporate panel on the basis of medical evidence. The quoted phrase was defined to mean that the employee was unable to perform any employment for pay or profit and had no reasonable expectation of becoming able to do so. Benefits were calculated on the basis of the employee's regular compensation prior to disability, taking account of eligibility for Social Security payments and workmen's compensation. They began on the expiration of the 52-week period of Sickness and Accident benefits plus any period of individual consideration benefits and continued until normal retirement date, at which time the employee became eligible for benefits under the Retirement Plan. During the period of disability an employee remained covered by a variety of other IBM employee plans and could, under certain conditions, accrue further credits under the Retirement Plan. If, contrary to expectation, the employee became able to work again, he was entitled to return, but few did so. As of January 1, 1974, a total of 393 IBM employees out of 150,000 were receiving benefits under the Disability Plan.

At the time of his death Schelberg was not receiving benefits under any of these plans. By virtue of his decease his widow became entitled under the Group Life Insurance Plan to a death benefit of $23,666.67 under the group life insurance policy, and to a survivor's benefit of $1,062.50 per month. The value of the latter amount was not included in decedent's gross estate in his federal tax return, although its existence was reported. The Commissioner of Internal Revenue entered a notice of deficiency on the sole ground that the present value of the survivors annuity, which is stipulated to have been $94,708.83, was includible in the estate pursuant to I.R.C. § 2039. The Tax Court upheld the Commissioner * * *.

II.

The estate does not dispute that the survivors benefit constituted "an annuity or other payment receivable by any beneficiary by reason of surviving the decedent under any form of contract or agreement entered into after March 3, 1931 (other than as insurance under policies on the life of the decedent)" within the opening clause of § 2039(a). It is likewise indisputable that this alone would not suffice to make the survivors benefit includible in the gross estate. The Commissioner must also satisfy the condition that "under such contract or agreement, an annuity or other payment was payable to the decedent, or the decedent possessed the right to receive such annuity or payment, either alone or in conjunction with another for his life or for any period not ascertainable without reference to his death or for any period which does not in fact end before his death."

Not contending that he can satisfy this requirement within the four corners of the Group Life Insurance Plan, the Commissioner asserts that, as provided by the Treasury Regulations, 26 C.F.R. § 20.2039–1(b), he is entitled to consider "any arrangement, understanding or plan, or any combination of arrangements or plans arising by reason of the decedent's employment." Although this is a rather sharp departure from the letter of the statute, . . . we accept it with the caveat that while the Commissioner is entitled to "consider" such arrangements, this does not mean that the mere possibility of an employee's receiving some benefit under an arrangement other than that giving rise to the survivors benefit necessarily satisfies the condition of § 2039(a). The Commissioner does not rely on either the Retirement Plan or the Sickness and Accident Plan to satisfy the condition that "an annuity or other payment" was payable to Schelberg. Apart from other considerations, any such reliance is precluded by previous revenue rulings. Revenue Ruling 76–380, 1976–2 C.B. 270, concluded that qualified plans, like the Retirement Plan, and non-qualified plans, like the Survivors Income Benefit Plan, were not to be considered together in determining the applicability of § 2039(a) and (b). [This ruling is based on the rationale that because § 2039 then excluded from the gross estate payments under qualified plans, payments from qualified plans could not be considered as one of the elements constituting "a combination of arrangements or plans" that satisfied the statutory conditions for taxation of other benefits under § 2039.] * * * Revenue Ruling 77–183, 1977–1 C.B. 274, held that benefits such as those Schelberg might have been entitled to under the Sickness and Accident Plan had he lived longer "were in the nature of compensation" and thus no more meet the test set out in the condition than would compensation payments themselves, * * *. This left as the Commissioner's sole reed the fact that, at the time of his death, Schelberg possessed the right that after 52 weeks (or more, if he qualified for "individual consideration") under the Sickness and Accident Plan, he might become entitled to payments under the Disability Plan. The estate contends that Schelberg's rights under the Disability Plan were too dissimilar in nature from an "annuity or other payment" and too contingent to meet the condition of § 2039(a). We agree.

It is worth repeating that the Commissioner's position here would apply to every IBM employee having more than five years' service who dies before attaining age 64 (or taking early retirement) although he neither received nor had any reasonable expectation of receiving anything under the Disability Plan. On the other hand, if he died after attaining age 64 but before taking retirement, the survivors benefit would not be includible since the first twelve months away from work would be covered by the Sickness and Accident Plan and he could never become eligible for the Disability Plan. And, of course, if he died after actually taking retirement, the most common case, the survivors benefit would not be includible by virtue of Revenue Ruling 76–380, 1976–2 C.B. 270. We find nothing in the language of § 2039, in its legislative history, or in the Treasury Regulations sufficient to justify a conclusion that the action of an employer in creating a plan whereby a handful of employees can receive disability benefits because of a rare health or accident syndrome should bring the survivors of all within § 2039.

As recognized by a learned commentator shortly after § 2039 was enacted, the statute was aimed at "annuity contracts under which the purchaser (alone or with a joint annuitant) was entitled to payments for his life, with payments to continue after his death at either the same or a reduced rate, to a survivor." Bittker, Estate and Gift Taxation under the 1954 Code: The Principal Changes, 29 Tul. L. Rev. 453, 469 (1955). While inclusion of the survivor's rights in the estate had been generally sustained, courts had differed as to the reason. Some courts had proceeded on the theory that purchase of the contract was in effect a transfer of property with the reservation of a life estate and thus taxable under the predecessors of I.R.C. § 2036. Others had proceeded on the theory that the transfer was intended to take effect at death. Id. A fundamental purpose of § 2039 was to supply an affirmative answer to the question of inclusion in such cases without further need to debate the theory.

A further purpose, as revealed by the relevant House and Senate Committee reports on what became § 2039 of the revised I.R.C. of 1954, H.R. Rep. No. 1337, 83d Cong. 2d Sess. 90–91, A 314–6 (1954); S. Rep. No. 1622, 83d Cong. 2d Sess. 123–24, 469–72 (1954); H.R. Rep. No. 2543 (Conference Report), 83d Cong. 2d Sess. 74 (1954), was to settle the question of includibility of a joint and survivor annuity where the annuity was purchased by the decedent's employer or both the decedent and the employer made contributions. Congress decided that such an annuity should be included except when the employer's contributions were made pursuant to "an approved trust, pension or retirement plan."

Both text and context show that § 2039 was conceived as dealing only with the problem of what in substance was a joint annuity, although to be sure in all its various ramifications, not with the whole gamut of arrangements under which an employee, his employer or both may create benefits for the employee's survivors. The new section applied only "if, under such contract or agreement, an annuity or other payment was payable to the decedent, or the decedent possessed the right to receive such annuity or payment, either alone or in conjunction with another for his life or for any period not ascertainable without reference to his death or for any period which does not in fact end before his death." If Congress had wished to legislate more broadly, it would have eliminated this clause or chosen more general language for it. The intended sphere of application is made quite clear by the illustrations given in the House and Senate reports "as examples of contracts, but . . . not necessarily the only forms of contracts to which this section applies." Under all of these the decedent was receiving or entitled to receive at death what anyone would consider an "annuity or other payment" for the duration of his life or for a stipulated term. Furthermore, in each case the beneficiary succeeded to the interest of the decedent, as in the classic instance of a joint and survivor annuity, quite unlike the present case. Although the term "other payment" is literally broad, Congress was clearly thinking of payments in the nature of annuities—the same types of payments which, if made to the survivor, would be includible in the estate. * * * None of the examples is even close to payments receivable only if the deceased employee might have become totally and permanently disabled had he lived.

We do not consider the case to be altered in the Government's favor by the Treasury Regulations. While these contain some broad language, there is nothing to indicate that their framers addressed the problem here presented. The closest of the illustrations is example (6). While we have no quarrel with this, it is inapposite since the payments both to the employee and to the beneficiary were life annuities. Without endeavoring to be too precise, we deem it plain that, in framing the condition on § 2039(a), Congress was not going beyond benefits the employee was sure to get as a result of his prior employment if he lived long enough. Even more plainly Congress was not thinking of disability payments which an employee would have had only a remote chance of ever collecting had he lived. Not only are the disability payments in this case extremely hypothetical, they are also far from the "annuity or other payment" contemplated by Congress. Courts have, consistent with basic principles of statutory construction, recognized that "annuity or other payment" does not mean "annuity or any payment," but that the phrase is qualitatively limited by the context in which it appears. See Estate of Fusz, supra, 46 T.C. at 217–18. The Service itself has acquiesced in and furthered this view. See Rev. Rul. 77–183, supra. Thus, it seems clear to us that Congress did not intend the phrase to embrace wages, * * *; possible sickness and accident payments, which were a substitute for wages, * * *; or the disability payments involved in this case, which likewise were a partial continuation of wages when an employee's physical health deteriorated even further. The disability payments theoretically achievable here by the decedent in his lifetime are closer to the sickness benefits which he would have received at an early stage of his illness than they are to post-retirement benefits. The Tax Court's treatment of possible disability benefits as presupposing a post-retirement status linked to the widow's ultimate succession thereto seems to us to be unsupported in fact. * * *

III.

The final paragraph of the Tax Court's opinion, 70 T.C. at 705, * * * gives us some reason to think the able judge might have reached the same conclusion as we have if he had not deemed himself bound by authority. Of the cases cited by him, only one, All v. McCobb, 321 F.2d 633 (2 Cir.1963), is binding upon us. We think that he and others have given that decision a significance on the type of issues here presented that is unwarranted, and that most of the other cases are also distinguishable.

In *All* the decedent had been receiving annuities under a non-contributory non-qualified annuity plan and a partially contributory, non-qualified supplemental annuity plan of the Standard Oil Company of New Jersey. His widow received twelve monthly payments under a death benefit for such annuitants. The case for application of § 2039 would seem almost too clear for argument. The sole claim advanced against this by the taxpayer was that the payments were within the exception for insurance—a claim to which this court gave the short shrift that it deserved. The case thus has simply no bearing on the issue here before us.

The most influential decision on what the decedent must receive or be entitled to receive in order to trigger application of § 2039 is Estate of Bahen v. United States, 305 F.2d 827 (Ct.Cl.1962) (Davis, J.). The opinion is indeed a virtuoso performance which has tended to dominate the field to the extent that . . . courts seem to look to the *Bahen* opinion rather than to the statute and the committee reports as indicative of the legislative intent. Beyond all this it is of peculiar importance here since it involved a sum payable only in the event of disability, and the Commissioner quite properly relies heavily upon it.

* * *

While * * * [*Bahen*] bears some resemblance to ours, there is a different flavor about it, at least so far as concerns the payments under the Deferred Compensation Plan. There was in fact a unitary right to receive deferred compensation of $100,000 in 60 equal monthly payments, this to be paid to Mrs. Bahen if Bahen died or to him if he became totally disabled prior to retirement. There was no question of grouping separate plans together, since both Mr. and Mrs. Bahen's rights were pursuant to the same Deferred Compensation Plan. Even more to the point, if payments were being made to Mr. Bahen due to his disability and he died prior to exhausting the fund, the remaining payments would be made to Mrs. Bahen. In this respect the Deferred Compensation Plan was much like the joint and survivor annuity at which § 2039 was aimed. Here, of course, Mrs. Schelberg had no rights to any payments under the Disability Plan. The possible payments to Mr. Bahen were not, as under IBM's Disability Plan, true disability payments intended to cover a portion of previous salary; they were deferred compensation, as the plan's title indicates, payable by the railway in any event, to be made available to Mr. Bahen at a date earlier than death if his needs so required. They thus met the test * * * as IBM's disability benefits do not, of being of the same nature as the payments to the beneficiary. We are not sure that the distinction is sufficient or—what is more or less the same thing—that we would have decided *Bahen* as the Court of Claims did. For the moment we shall leave the matter that way.

* * *

We here decide only that to consider a deceased employee's potential ability to have qualified at some future time for payments under a plan protecting against total and permanent disability—a disagreeable feat that had been accomplished as of January 1, 1974, by only a quarter of one percent of IBM's employees—as meeting the condition in § 2039(a) that there must be a contract or agreement under which the decedent received or be entitled to receive "an annuity or other payment", is such a departure from the language used by Congress, read in the light of the problem with which it was intending to deal, as to be at war with common sense. The only decision by which we are bound, All v. McCobb, supra, 321 F.2d 633, does not come near to the problem here presented. Of the other decisions cited to us, there are clear grounds of distinguishing all with the possible exception of the leading one, Estate of Bahen, supra, 305 F.2d 827, and the certain exception of Gaffney [v. United States, 200 Ct. Cls. 744 (1972)]. Although we have been able to distinguish the cases other than Gaffney and possibly Bahen on grounds that seem to us sufficient, we would not wish to be understood as necessarily agreeing with all of them or with the general approach taken in Bahen, see 305 F.2d at 833. Some other case may require complete rethinking whether courts, under the influence of the Bahen opinion, have not unduly eroded the condition in § 2039(a), as is pointedly suggested by Judge Aldisert's dissent in Gray v. United States, [410 F.2d 1094, at 1112–14 (3d Cir.1969)]; on the other hand, Congress might decide to cast its net more widely and eliminate or broaden the condition, as it could have done in 1954. We simply decline to carry the erosion of the condition to the extent here urged by the Commissioner.

The judgment is reversed and the cause remanded with instructions to annul the determination of a deficiency.

NOTES

1. The Sixth Circuit in Van Wye's Estate v. United States, 686 F.2d 425 (6th Cir.1982), fully accepted the rationale of the Second Circuit in *Schelberg* in disposing of a case involving comparable facts with a different employer. A district court, addressing facts virtually identical to those in *Schelberg*, reached the opposite conclusion. See Looney v. United States, 569 F. Supp. 1569 (M.D.Ga.1983).

2. Regulation § 20.2039–1(b)(1) indicates that the decedent will be deemed to have " 'possessed the right to receive' an annuity or other payment if, immediately before his death, the decedent had an enforceable right to receive payments at some time in the future, whether or not, at the time of his death, he had a present right to receive payments." Although Schelberg was entitled to receive pension benefits from IBM at age 65, the court, acting pursuant to the direction of Rev. Rul. 76–380 refused to consider Schelberg's future retirement benefits for the purpose of being able to tax the survivors' income benefits payable under the Group Life Insurance Plan. The IRS, in Rev. Rul. 76–380, reasoned that to consider rights to retirement benefits under a qualified plan for the purpose of exposing other benefits to taxation would be inconsistent with the grant of tax-exempt status to qualified plan benefits then granted to qualified plans. After qualified plans were stripped of their exemption under section 2039 in 1984, the IRS in Rev. Rul. 88–85, 1988–2 C.B. 333 declared Rev. Rul. 76–380 obsolete.

Thus, it would appear that under present law, if an employee is presently receiving either qualified or unqualified pension benefits, or as indicated by Regulation § 20.2039–1(b)(1) has "an enforceable right to receive" such benefits in the future, these benefits may be considered for the purpose of subjecting to taxation other payments, whether periodic or lump sum, made to survivors under other employer provided benefit plans.

3. The IRS was unsuccessful in its attempt to tax the life insurance portion of an annuity-life insurance combination in Fidelity-Philadelphia Trust Co. v. Smith (F.R.), 356 U.S. 274 (1958), under the predecessor provisions to section 2036, as if a life estate had been reserved by the insured-decedent. However, since the advent of section 2039 in 1954, the IRS has often been successful in looking to section 2039 as a basis for including the proceeds of annuity-life insurance packages in the annuitant's gross estate. See, e.g., Estate of Montgomery v. Commissioner, 458 F.2d 616 (5th Cir.1972).

F. INCOME TAXATION OF TAX QUALIFIED RETIREMENT PLANS AND IRAs

Tax qualified retirement plans and Individual Retirement Accounts enjoy broad protection from income taxation until distribution to the beneficiary, as is fulsomely provided in sections 401–420. Most contributions are made with pretax dollars; hence, no income tax is imposed on the funds contributed to the plan. Similarly, earnings on such plans are typically exempt from income tax. The price the beneficiary pays for the privilege of tax-free contribution and compounding is that all payments from the plan to the beneficiary are taxed as income to the beneficiary, except to the extent nondeductible contributions were made. Typically, there are no nondeductible contributions, with the result that all payments to the beneficiary are fully taxable.

Often the payments to the beneficiary are enhanced by appreciation of plan assets. Furthermore, as explained above, the entire plan will usually be included in the gross estate of the deceased owner. For that reason, it would seem that upon the death of the owner the surviving beneficiaries should get the benefit of the stepped-up basis at death pursuant section 1014. Hence, the beneficiaries should have a basis for the plan equal to its value at the date of death or alternate valuation date, if elected. If that were the case, immediate distribution of the plan assets to the beneficiaries would produce no taxable gain to the beneficiaries, who would receive the assets entirely free of income tax.

Congress and the Treasury thought that result a bit much, reasoning that, in return for the immense advantages of the shelter from income taxes, *someone* should pay tax on the plan assets, which typically represent either untaxed compensation or untaxed earnings on those funds. Assurance of taxation of qualified plan and IRA proceeds is provided by treating such assets as "income in respect of a decedent," or "IRD." As more fully explained in Chapter 32, IRD is income "not properly includible in respect of the taxable period in which falls the date of [the decedent's] death or a prior period. . ." I.R.C. § 691(a)(1). Qualified plan and IRA assets meet this definition because sections 401–420 have the effect of deferring, but not forgiving, taxation on both contributions and earnings. Under section 691(a)(1), IRD, such as a qualified plan distribution, is taxed to the surviving plan beneficiary in the same manner and to the same extent as if the decedent had received the funds during her life. Any argument that the basis of the plan assets should be stepped-up at death is prevented by section 1014(c), which expressly denies a stepped-up basis to IRD assets.

The ultimate result is that qualified plan and IRA assets, to the extent attributable to untaxed contributions and earnings, are fully subject to income tax when distributed to plan beneficiaries, including beneficiaries who receive payments by reason of surviving the original owner. Because most plans consist entirely of untaxed assets, the usual result is that all plan distributions will be taxed to the ultimate recipients—whoever the recipients may be and whenever the distributions are made.

Because of the heavy tax burden that might result from imposition of both estate tax and income tax on IRD items such as qualified plans and IRAs, some relief is provided by section 691(c). This subsection grants an income tax deduction for estate tax imposed on an IRD item. As a result, a portion of the qualified plan or IRA corresponding to the estate tax imposed can be received free of income tax, as more fully explained in Chapter 32.

Much of the value of a qualified plan or IRA lies in the "tax shelter" because of the ability to defer taxation of the plan earnings until distribution to the beneficiary. This permits tax-free compounding of earnings as long as the assets are in the plan. Because Congress intended qualified plans and IRAs to serve primarily as funding vehicles for retirement, and not as perpetual tax shelters, Congress has imposed minimum distribution rules that require the beneficiary to begin withdrawals at a certain age and to continue the withdrawals at a required level. In specified circumstances, the withdrawal period can extend beyond the original beneficiary's life and well into the lives of other beneficiaries. The result can be perpetuation of the tax shelter benefits for many years. The minimum distribution rules do not apply to a Roth IRA during the life of the participant. I.R.C. § 408A(c)(5).

Because of the importance of perpetuating the income tax shelter, the selection of beneficiaries entitled to receive the qualified plan or IRA after the death of the original beneficiary typically involves both income tax and estate tax issues. Specifically, the designation of beneficiaries should be designed so as to produce the longest perpetuation of the tax shelter consistent with the minimum distribution rules, estate tax minimization, and the decedent's nontax objectives.

CHAPTER 22

POWERS OF APPOINTMENT

(SECTION 2041)

■ ■ ■

A. INTRODUCTION

The property law concept of a power of appointment is a power of disposition over property that, typically, is given to a third person by deed or will by the owner of the property.[1] The owner of the property who creates the power of appointment is usually called the donor, and the person who is given the power to designate the one who is to take the property or its enjoyment, i.e., the holder of the power, is called the donee. The person who receives the property or interest upon the exercise of the power is the appointee, and the person who would take the property in default of the exercise of the power is called the taker in default.

Powers of appointment are variously classified for property law purposes. However, for estate and gift tax purposes, powers are classified as either general powers or special (nongeneral) powers. Special powers are those exercisable in favor of a limited group of people. Generally, neither exercise nor nonexercise of a special power of appointment has estate or gift tax consequences. Consider the following illustration:

Example: Abby is trustee of a trust established by her father for the benefit of her three sons. The trust provides that Abby is to receive all the income from the trust for her life and, at her death, the trust is to terminate and the trust property is to be distributed in equal shares to Abby's three sons. However, the trust provides that Abby is authorized to include a provision in her will changing the shares her sons are to receive. In fact, Abby has included such a provision in her will and, as a result, Abby's oldest son is to receive 70 percent of the trust and the two younger sons are to receive only 15 percent each. Abby's power to vary the share each of her sons is to receive in the trust at her death is referred to as

---

[1] For a good discussion of powers of appointment, see John G. Steinkamp, *Estate and Gift Taxation of Powers of Appointment Limited By Ascertainable Standards*, 79 MARQ. L. REV. 195 (1995) and Amy Morris Hess, *The Federal Taxation of Nongeneral Powers of Appointment*, 52 TENN. L. REV. 395 (1985).

a special power. Despite the power vested in Abby, no part of the trust property will be subject to estate tax at Abby's death.

General powers are different. General powers are those powers that may be exercised in favor of the powerholder, the powerholder's estate, the powerholder's creditors, or the creditors of the powerholder's estate. I.R.C. § 2041(b)(1). Because the holder of a general power can benefit directly from the power, the powerholder's exercise of such a power will result in the property subject to the power being included in the powerholder's estate if the power is exercised at death (or being subject to gift tax if the power is exercised during life). Similarly, failure to exercise a power will also generally have either estate or gift tax consequences, the reasoning being that forbearance to exercise is a decision committed to the powerholder and is truly effective control of the power property that ends only when the power can no longer be exercised.

> *Example*: Bert is trustee of a trust established for his benefit by his father. As trustee, Bert has the discretion by the terms of the trust to distribute to himself "all or some of the income and principal of the trust for any purpose." In this case, Bert will be deemed to have a general power of appointment—and even if he never takes a distribution from the trust, the trust property will be included in his estate at his death. See I.R.C. § 2041(a)(2).

In the early stages of the estate tax, unexercised general powers of appointment had no estate tax consequences, as was seen in the *Safe Deposit and Trust*[2] case discussed in Chapter 15. However, since 1918, there have been several developmental legislative revisions aimed at general powers of appointment.

Section 2041 is the current provision that sets forth the complex set of rules governing the taxation of property subject to a general power of appointment. This section has remained virtually unchanged since 1951. The present approach of section 2041 is to classify all general powers in accordance with their date of creation, between those existing on or before October 21, 1942 (the date of an interim revenue act dealing with powers), and those created thereafter. See I.R.C. § 2041(a).

Such pre-existing powers—"pre-October 21, 1942, powers"—are to be taxed only if the power is exercised (1) by will, or (2) by a disposition that would have made the property includible if the disposition had been a transfer of property owned by the decedent. Accordingly, the nonexercise of such a power results in no estate tax; moreover, the release of such a power is permitted wholly tax free.

For the purpose of this division between pre-1942 and post-1942 powers, the regulations point out that the date the power is created is

---

[2] 316 U.S. 56 (1942).

controlled by the date when the instrument creating the power takes effect. Treas. Reg. § 20.2041–1(e).

As for post-1942 powers, under the statute, mere possession of such a power at death will cause inclusion of the property in the holder's gross estate. Also, the inter vivos exercise or release of the post-1942 power will result in estate taxation, provided that the transaction occurs under such circumstances as would have required the inclusion of the property in the gross estate if it had been a transfer of property owned by the holder of the power at death. See I.R.C. § 2041(a)(2).

The foregoing guidelines for pre-1942 and post-1942 powers assume that the power falls within the definition of a general power. Any power that is not a general power (no matter when created) will not result in the inclusion in the gross estate of the property subject to the power. However, while the property subject to a nongeneral power of appointment is not included in the holder's gross estate under section 2041, it may be included under a different estate tax provision.

> *Example*: Klalid is the trustee of an irrevocable trust that he created for his three children. While Klalid cannot make distributions to himself, he can make distributions of income or corpus to his children—and he can be selective in amount and distribution, meaning that he can favor one of the children to the exclusion of the others. In this case, the trust property will be included in Klalid's estate at his death because he has transferred property and, at his death, he has the power to control the enjoyment of that property by the trust beneficiaries. See I.R.C. §§ 2036(a)(2) & 2038.

An explicit definition of a general power was developed for the purpose of determining what powers should be treated as taxable. While the term "general power" is used for this purpose, the definition is really more closely allied to a beneficial power, i.e., a power that can be used to the economic advantage of the holder. See I.R.C. § 2041(b)(1). Thus, a general power is any power that is exercisable in favor of (1) the powerholder, or (2) the powerholder's creditors, or (3) the powerholder's estate, or (4) creditors of the powerholder's estate. Whether any other possible appointees are included within the group is immaterial if at least one of the foregoing can be an appointee.

There are two major exclusions from the definition of a general power. First, a power to "consume, invade, or appropriate" the property for the benefit of the donee is exempt if its exercise is subject to "an ascertainable standard relating to the health, education, support, or maintenance" of the donee. I.R.C. § 2041(b)(1)(A). The fact that the power is subject to a fixed standard deprives it of the broad discretion inherent in a general or taxable power.

The second exception to general powers relates to jointly held powers. I.R.C. § 2041(b)(1)(C). Any jointly held power created on or before October 21, 1942, is not a general power. With respect to joint powers created thereafter, they are classed as general powers only if the other holder of the power is not the donor or if the other holder has no substantial adverse interest in the property which would be adverse to the exercise of the power in favor of the donee.

It is useful to note, too, that estate taxes attributable to the inclusion of power property in the power holder's gross estate can be recovered from the power property except in cases where the power holder's will otherwise directs. I.R.C. § 2207. This relief opportunity is intended to prevent burdening the powerholder's other beneficiaries with the taxes on the power property where estate tax inclusion of the power property was not anticipated by the powerholder.

Sometimes the holder of a general power is viewed as having the practical equivalent of a fee simple interest in the power property. For example, a lifetime exercise or release of a post-1942 general power will result in inclusion of the power property in the powerholder's estate at death in those cases where a similar transfer by a decedent of nonpower property would be recaptured under sections 2035 to 2038. I.R.C. § 2041(a)(2). As an illustration, suppose the trust created in Mom's will provided Dad with all trust income for life and also gave Dad a general power of appointment over the remainder. During life, Dad exercised the power in favor of Goddaughter. Under one analysis, the value of the power property at Dad's later death would be included in his gross estate because he made a transfer subject to a retained life estate. See I.R.C. § 2036(a)(1). Under another analysis, it is said to be arguable that section 2041(a)(2) does not reach the power property (so long as Dad lives three years after exercise) because Mom, rather than Dad, created the life estate enjoyed by Dad. If the latter position were to prevail, would Dad (or Goddaughter) be tax advantaged by his lifetime exercise of the power?

B. WHAT IS A POWER OF APPOINTMENT?

KEETER V. UNITED STATES
United States Court of Appeals, Fifth Circuit, 1972.
461 F.2d 714.

GOLDBERG, CIRCUIT JUDGE:

* * *

The decedent's husband, Daniel A. Shaw, died in 1930, the owner of an insurance policy on his own life in the amount of $100,000, which he had purchased in 1919. In 1926 Mr. Shaw (the "insured" or the "settlor") elected a settlement option which provided that the insurance proceeds should be held under four identical supplementary contracts, issued to the decedent, Mrs. Bessie Love Shaw, and their daughters in equal shares. By the terms of this settlement option decedent was to receive interest on her share of the proceeds for her life, and a supplementary contract in the amount of $25,000 was accordingly issued to the decedent. The settlement option also expressly provided that the principal and accrued interest from the proceeds were to be paid to "the executors or administrators" of the decedent at her death. Mrs. Shaw, domiciled in Florida, died in 1964, leaving a will, duly probated, that read in part:

> All the rest, residue and remainder of my property of every kind and description and wherever located, and any property over which I may hold the power of appointment or distribution, I give, devise, and bequeath in three equal portions for [her daughters].

Pursuant to the 1926 settlement election, the insurance company paid the $25,000 to the decedent's executor. The executor did not include that sum in the decedent's gross estate when he filed the estate tax return, and the Commissioner assessed a deficiency. * * *

General powers of appointment created on or before October 21, 1942, are includable in the gross estate of a decedent only if they are "exercised," * * * § 2041(a)(1). * * * The issue in this case is whether or not the settlor's election of annuities-cum-payments to the decedent's executor constitutes such a power of appointment for purposes of the estate tax. It is acknowledged by all parties that if the settlement option elected by the decedent's husband constituted a general power of appointment, the power was "created," for tax purposes, prior to 1942. * * * And it is also conceded by all that the power of appointment, if that is what it really was, was "exercised," for tax purposes, by a specific provision in the decedent's will that distributed any of her property held under power of appointment to her three daughters in equal shares.

We will look to applicable state law to determine whether the substance of the property interests created by the settlor fits within the federal tax law's definition of a power of appointment, but we emphasize that it is the substance of the state law that is relevant and not any labels that a state or the parties might attach to that substance. * * * see also Morgan v. Commissioner, 1940, 309 U.S. 78, 60 S. Ct. 424, 84 L.Ed. 585:

> State law creates legal interests and rights. The federal revenue acts designate what interests or rights, so created, shall be taxed.

The law in this case is as clear as the Internal Revenue Code and attendant regulations are ever wont to be. A general power of appointment is defined by the Code as "a power which is exercisable in favor of the decedent, *his estate*, his creditors, or the creditors of his estate," * * * § 2041(b)(1) [emphasis added]. The Code definition is cast in the disjunctive, so that the donee is in possession of a general power of appointment if he or she is able to exercise that power in favor of any one of the four groups of beneficiaries specified in the statute. * * * A donee possesses a general power of appointment when he or she holds

> . . . such a power of control as to be able to apply it to his own benefit, or the benefit of his creditors, to dispose of it by will, or to appoint it to his estate or the creditors of his estate, or to consume it without restriction. Security-Peoples Trust Co. v. United States, W.D.Pa.1965, 238 F. Supp. 40 at 45. * * *

Mrs. Shaw's executor argues that the settlement option elected by Mrs. Shaw's husband was not a general power of appointment, resting his argument principally upon the assertion that Mrs. Shaw did not receive solely from that settlement option, and at the moment of the death of the insured, the unrestricted power to dispose of the insurance proceeds. Mrs. Shaw's power to distribute the funds came, the executor concludes, from the laws of Florida which empowered her to make a will and not from her husband's settlement option. In sum, the executor's argument is that because the proceeds would have to receive their direction under the will and not directly under the insurance clause, the option could not be called a power of appointment at the time of the insured's death. The executor's argument is unrealistic at best, conclusory at worst. We conclude that the making of a will was merely a conduit, not a rheostat, in the legal authority that ran between the decedent and the insurance option.

* * *

It appears to this court that Mrs. Shaw was granted at her husband's death an absolute power of appointment over the insurance proceeds, the power to be exercisable by her will at her death. We are aware of the fact that the Seventh Circuit was presented with a set of circumstances substantially similar to those we face, and that the court held for the taxpayer. Second National Bank of Danville v. Dallman, 7 Cir.1954, 209 F.2d 321. In *Dallman* the insured (the decedent's father) selected an insurance settlement option that required the insurance company to pay interest to the decedent for life and then gave to the decedent the right to designate a contingent beneficiary to take the proceeds at the decedent's death. If the decedent failed to designate her beneficiary expressly, the insurance company was to pay the proceeds to the decedent's "executors, administrators, or assigns." The decedent never designated a beneficiary. Her will provided that her entire residuary estate should be held in trust but did not mention specifically the insurance proceeds. In accordance with the contract with the decedent's father, the insurance company paid the funds to the decedent's testamentary trustee, and the government included the proceeds in the decedent's gross estate for estate tax purposes. The

Seventh Circuit, reversing the district court, held that the proceeds were not includable in the decedent's gross estate:

> [T]he proceeds were payable at decedent's death *not by her direction but by that of her father as contained in the contract.*

209 F.2d at 324 [emphasis added]. We are unable to distinguish the *Dallman* case on its facts, and we are thus compelled to disagree with that case on the law. In essence, we hold that there is no substantive difference between directly granting the power to dispose of property and placing that same property in such a position that the donee is able to dispose of it to her benefit by means of some power that existed prior to or separate from the settlor's grant.

It appears to this court that the settlors in *Dallman* and in our case granted absolute powers of appointment to their respective donees subject only to the proviso that the donees were to exercise their powers of appointment by means of a will. * * * Therefore, the substance of the settlement option was to grant an absolute power of appointment of the insurance principal and interest to Mrs. Shaw, exercisable at her death by her will. It is quite true that Mrs. Shaw could not dispose of the insurance proceeds to her own benefit immediately after the death of her husband. But a power of appointment need not be exercisable only immediately or only in favor of the donee. The power is also taxable if it is exercisable at some point in favor of the grantee's estate. * * *

In brief, Mrs. Shaw's husband directed the funds to Mrs. Shaw's executor, and Mrs. Shaw directed the executor. In practical terms, Mr. Shaw simply put the insurance proceeds into a receptacle from which his wife could appoint them, but it is Mrs. Shaw who substantively directed the funds to the ultimate recipients. And the fact that Mrs. Shaw spoke through her executor does not make her voice any less her own. For estate tax purposes, the critical question is whether the decedent directed her property after her death, not how that property got into the position from which she could direct it. In terms of the actual authority of direction over the insurance proceeds that was conferred and exercised, we see no substantive differences among an express grant of a general power of appointment, a grant utilizing a previously-existing trust with the donee as the sole trustee, an express grant of a general power of appointment exercisable only by will, and a grant employing a previously-existing law that allows the donee to distribute property freely by will. In each instance the power realistically conferred and exercised is the power to direct the fund as the donee sees fit at the point of her death, or in legalese the power to appoint. Abrasive as it may seem to the donees of the power, ". . . that is precisely what the federal estate tax hits—an exercise of the privilege of directing the course of property after . . . death." Estate of Rogers v. Helvering, 1943, 320 U.S. 410, 413 * * *. Mrs. Shaw exercised her general power of appointment by specifically directing her executors in her will, and her estate is therefore taxable on the value of the exercise.

NOTE

At one level, it is appropriate to note that *Keeter* highlights the fact that no special words need be used to create a power of appointment. Regulation § 20.2041–1(b)(1) provides that the term includes "all powers which are in substance and effect powers of appointment regardless of the nomenclature used in creating the power and regardless of local property law connotations."

At another level, however, it is useful to compare *Keeter* with Estate of Margrave v. Commissioner, 618 F.2d 34 (8th Cir.1980), a case with an odd set of facts. A wife owned a policy of life insurance on her husband (Margrave) and had used her own property to pay the premiums. A bank, as trustee of a revocable trust created by the husband, was designated beneficiary of the policy proceeds—and the bank received those proceeds at the husband's death. The court concluded that the policy proceeds were not included in the husband's estate at his death despite the IRS contention that the husband's unrestricted right to revoke or amend the trust constituted a general power of appointment taxable under section 2041. The court explained its decision in these terms:

> In order for such a power to result in the inclusion of an item in decedent's gross estate under § 2041, the decedent must at least (1) possess a power within this definition of "a general power of appointment," and (2) there must be a property interest to which this "general power of appointment" attaches.

> While it is clear that the decedent possessed a "general power of appointment" by virtue of his ability to modify or revoke the trust, we do not believe that any property interest attached to that power. [citations omitted].

> * * * Prior to his death, Margrave possessed only a power over an expectancy because the rights of the trustee to the proceeds were subject to Mrs. Margrave's power to change the designation of the trustee as beneficiary. Although the death of Mr. Margrave caused the trustee's right to the proceeds to vest and create a property interest to which Mr. Margrave's power of appointment might attach, Mr. Margrave's death simultaneously terminated his ability to modify or revoke the trust. Thus, Mr. Margrave's "general power of appointment" was at all times merely a power over an expectancy. In such circumstances, we do not believe the proceeds of the life insurance policy can be included in decedent's gross estate under 26 U.S.C. § 2041.[3]

---

[3]   Id. at 38–39.

Subsequently, the IRS acquiesced in *Margrave* in Rev. Rul. 81–166, 1981 C.B. 477. The ruling also expressed that the wife made a taxable gift of the insurance proceeds when the insurance proceeds were paid to the trust.

The court in *Margrave* noted approvingly the result reached in *Connecticut Bank and Trust Co.*, which follows. Part of the decision in *Connecticut Bank and Trust Co.* appears in Chapter 15 on the issue of what constitutes "property" for estate tax purposes. In that portion of the case, the government lost its argument that proceeds received from the settlement of a wrongful death action were "property owned at death" and thus includible in the decedent's taxable estate. The second part of the opinion follows, and the government fared no better on its argument that the proceeds were includible under section 2041.

CONNECTICUT BANK AND TRUST CO. V. UNITED STATES

United States Court of Appeals, Second Circuit, 1972.
465 F.2d 760.

ROBERT P. ANDERSON, CIRCUIT JUDGE:

* * *

As a second point on appeal, the Government argues that the wrongful death proceeds must also be included in the gross estate under § 2041, as "property with respect to which the decedent has at the time of his death a general power of appointment." This argument must actually assume that the wrongful death proceeds were not property owned by the decedent at death under § 2033, because § 2041 is concerned with the power to deal with property belonging to someone else, cf. Reg. § 20.2041–1(b)(2) (1972).

The Government claims that the wrongful death proceeds are subject to a § 2041 power of appointment because they are to be distributed under the terms of the decedents' wills as authorized by Connecticut General Statutes § 45–280. This, in effect, asserts that any property which is distributed according to a testamentary disposition is taxable as part of the gross estate, a view which enlarges the statute far beyond the purposes intended for it by Congress. A sufficient answer to the Government's position is that, at the very least, property subject to a § 2041 power of appointment must be in existence prior to the time of the decedent's death. * * *

Section 2041 was never intended to encompass within the gross estate what the Government now claims. If the Government were correct, then income earned during the administration of an estate and later distributed according to the terms of the will would be included in the value of the gross estate under § 2041, but it is abundantly clear that such income is not subject to the estate tax * * *.

Moreover § 2041(a)(2) provides that "[a] disclaimer or renunciation of such a power of appointment shall not be deemed a release of such power." "If a decedent exercises this right [to disclaim], the value of property as to which he has renounced the power will not be included in his gross estate," Jenkins v. United States, 428 F.2d 538, 550 (5 Cir.), cert. denied, 400 U.S. 829 (1970); see also, Reg. § 20.2041–3(d)(6). Under the Government's theory, however, it would be impossible for the decedent to renounce his "general power of appointment" over the wrongful death proceeds, because they did not exist prior to his death.

NOTE

In Tech. Adv. Mem. 9722001, the IRS concluded that the decedent did not have a general power of appointment. An aunt's trust provided the decedent with all the trust income and access to principal on the following terms:

> I am desirous that the corpus hereof be liberally invaded in favor of my niece, [the decedent], to the fullest extent necessary or advisable to provide her with a secure and comfortable living and to provide her with ample funds for investment or business purposes. In the absence of potential tax savings in favor of her beneficiaries, I should prefer and, therefore, would have mandated that distribution be made to her upon my demise, but in view of potential benefits to her and to her estate and beneficiaries, I leave the matter on a discretionary basis with the trustee, but I am desirous that the same be paid and distributed to her in accord with her wishes.

The IRS said that contrasting the aunt's use of precatory language ("I am desirous") when speaking of the decedent's access to the trust principal with her use of the language of imperative elsewhere in the will ("I hereby give and bequeath") made it clear that the decedent had not been given a general power of appointment over the trust principal.

C. DISTINGUISHING GENERAL AND SPECIAL POWERS

PRIVATE LETTER RULING 7903055
October 18, 1978.

* * * [Y]ou ask about the includibility in the gross estate [of B] of a power of appointment created by [H's] trust.

* * * The trustees are to pay;

> [T]he net dividends and income to [B] for and during the term of her natural life. Upon her death the principal is given either outright or upon further trust, to her heirs-at-law and next of kin, in such manner, interests and proportions as she shall in and by

her Last Will and Testament in that behalf direct, limit and appoint and in default of such appointment or insofar as the same shall fail effectually to dispose of said fund then unto the issue of [B] per stirpes.

* * * In exercising the power of appointment, [B, in her] will provided that the principal of the trust was to pass outright to her four children in equal shares.

Section 2041(a)(2) provides that the value of the gross estate shall include the value of all property with respect to which the decedent had, at the time of her death, a general power of appointment. Section 2041(b)(1) defines general power of appointment as a power which is exercisable in favor of the decedent, her estate, her creditors or the creditors of her estate.

[B] possessed the testamentary power to appoint the principal of the trust only to her heirs-at-law or next of kin. She could not exercise the power in favor of herself, her estate, her creditors, or the creditors of her estate. Thus, at death, [B] did not have a general power of appointment over the principal * * *. The principal will not be includible in her gross estate under section 2041.

REVENUE RULING 69–342
1969–1 C.B. 221.

* * *

The decedent's husband, who died in 1950, devised and bequeathed the residue of his estate to his wife for her life "with power to mortgage, sell, assign, and convey the same, and use and dispose of the proceeds thereof to all intents and purposes as if she were the absolute owner thereof." Upon her death, the unconsumed portion of the husband's estate, if any, was to be distributed in fee to their daughter. The decedent died in 1968. Under the laws of the state in which the decedent's husband's will was probated the quoted language is not construed to include a power to dispose of the property by gift.

Under the state law applicable to the administration of the deceased wife's estate, an absolute power of disposition given to the owner of a particular estate for life creates a life estate absolute in respect to the rights of creditors and purchasers, but subject to any future estate provided by the grantor.

Section 2041(a)(2) provides that the value of the gross estate shall include the value of all property with respect to which the decedent has at the time of his death a general power of appointment created after October 21, 1942. A power of appointment created by will is, except as provided by section 2041(b)(3), considered to have been created on the date of testator's death.

Section 2041(b) defines the term "general power of appointment" as a power that is exercisable in favor of the decedent, his estate, his creditors, or the creditors of his estate. An exception is provided where a power to consume, invade, or appropriate property for the benefit of the decedent is limited by an ascertainable standard relating to the health, education, support, or maintenance of the decedent.

Section 20.2041–1(b) provides that the term "power of appointment" includes all powers which are in substance and effect powers of appointment regardless of the nomenclature used in creating the powers and regardless of local property law connotations.

The language of the husband's will giving his wife the power to mortgage, sell, assign, and convey the property and use and dispose of the proceeds as if she were the absolute owner thereof clearly manifests his intention that his wife was to have the unlimited right to consume and dispose of the estate (except by gift) without reference to her needs or to any other standard. The interests of the remainderman are entirely subordinate to the desires of the wife, the husband having provided only that the remainderman receive the balance of the estate, if any, at his wife's death.

A power possessed by a lifetime beneficiary to consume, invade, or appropriate the estate for his own benefit, which power is not limited by an ascertainable standard, is within the statutory definition of a general power of appointment for purposes of the estate tax, notwithstanding the beneficiary's lack of power to exercise testamentary control over any unconsumed portion of the estate. * * *

Accordingly, it is held that the deceased wife possessed a general power of appointment, notwithstanding her lack of power to exercise testamentary control over the unconsumed portion of her predeceased husband's estate and notwithstanding that she did not possess the power during her lifetime to dispose of the property by gift. The value of the remaining property of her husband's estate is includible in her gross estate under section 2041.

NOTE

In Gaskill v. United States, 561 F. Supp. 73 (D.Kan.1983), aff'd per curiam, 787 F.2d 1446 (10th Cir.1986), on facts relatively identical to those found in Rev. Rul. 69–342, the district court found that the surviving spouse did not have a general power of appointment. In reaching its conclusion in favor of the taxpayer, the court distinguished a number of cases reaching contrary results on the ground that the Gaskill will stipulated that "all of the remainder of my estate" was to be distributed to the decedent's children after the death of the surviving spouse, whereas the dispositive provisions found in the cases reaching contrary results indicated that the respective decedents:

explicitly recognized the possibility that the property held by the life tenants would diminish in quantity and value before that property found its way into the hands of the remaindermen by the use of language such as "the remainder of such residue remaining," "such of my estate as shall remain," and "whatever of my said property, if any . . ." The Gaskill will, in strong contrast, unambiguously directs that all of the life estate property shall go to the remaindermen at the life tenant's death.[4]

Contrast the use of the word "all" in *Gaskill* and the conclusion reached by the court with the operative words described in Rev. Rul. 69–342. Note that in Rev. Rul. 69–342, the IRS concludes that the "interests of the remainderman are entirely subordinate to the desires of the wife." The court in *Gaskill*, on the other hand, says that while the surviving spouse "had unlimited powers to dispose of the life estate property," state law "imposed a correlative duty on her to make any such dispositions for full consideration and to hold the proceeds as a quasi-trustee for the remaindermen."

In Tech. Adv. Mem. 9431004, the IRS concluded that a power to mortgage was a power of appointment when held by the holder of a life estate. In this case, husband mortgaged the ranch in which he held a life estate (provided him in the joint will he and his deceased first wife had executed). He then gifted the proceeds of the loan to his new spouse. Rejected was the argument that the power to mortgage enjoyed by the husband was administrative only. In the opinion of the IRS, the husband's ability to "encumber or mortgage all or any part of" the ranch if he deemed it "necessary to essential for any purpose" was a power to consume or dispose of the property in favor of himself because the mortgage was "binding upon the remaindermen"—and was, in fact, subsequently assumed. Also, the loan secured by the mortgage was repaid by the remaindermen. Even if the husband could not have consumed the property or disposed of it in favor of himself, the IRS concluded that the husband could exercise the power in favor of his creditors—and that was sufficient taint.

D. ASCERTAINABLE STANDARD

Under section 2041(b)(1)(A), a decedent does not hold a general power of appointment if the decedent's power to invade or consume the property is limited by an ascertainable standard relating to the decedent's "health, education, support, or maintenance." The volume of reported cases and rulings suggest that a claim that an otherwise general power is tax sheltered because it meets the conditions of the ascertainable standard exception provided in section 2041(b) will often be disputed by the IRS. New ground is continually being plowed because few, if any, situations are identical. As an illustration consider the ruling and case set forth below. See also Treas. Reg. § 20.2041–1(c)(2).

---

[4]   Id. at 77.

REVENUE RULING 77–60
1977–1 C.B. 282.

Under the will of decedent's spouse, who died in 1970, the decedent was granted a life estate in certain properties, with the power to invade corpus as desired "to continue the donee's accustomed standard of living." Upon the death of the decedent, the corpus was to be distributed to other named beneficiaries. The decedent died in 1975. Under the state law applicable to the administration of the estate of decedent's spouse, the quoted language is not construed to impose an objective limitation on the exercise of the power of invasion granted by the donor, other than one of good faith.

* * *

The ascertainable standard set forth in section 2041(b)(1)(A) spells out the limited degree of economic control over property that Congress chose to exempt from the estate tax. The language of the Code is detailed, i.e., if the exercise of the power is restricted by definite bounds relating to the health, education, support, or maintenance of the donee, it is not a general power of appointment with the resulting tax consequence. Further, section 20.2041–1(c)(2) provides that the power must be limited to the donee's "needs for health, education, or support (or any combination of them)." While this ascertainable standard is not restricted to the bare necessities of life, the power must be exercisable only for the designated statutory purposes.

In determining whether property subject to a power is limited by an ascertainable standard within the meaning of section 2041, the test is the "measure of control" over the property by virtue of the grant of the power, i.e., whether the exercise of the power is restricted by definite bounds. That the amount of property that could be consumed for the benefit of the donee is not measurable or predictable is of no consequence. * * *

A power to use property to enable the donee to continue an accustomed mode of living, without further limitation, although predictable and measurable on the basis of past expenditures, does not come within the ascertainable standard prescribed in section 2041(b)(1)(A) since the standard of living may include customary travel, entertainment, luxury items, or other expenditures not required for meeting the donee's "needs for health, education or support." Nor does the requirement of a good faith exercise of a power create an ascertainable standard. Good faith exercise of a power is not determinative of its breadth.

Accordingly, the power possessed by the decedent to invade trust principal as desired to continue an accustomed standard of living was not limited by an ascertainable standard relating to health, education, support or maintenance. Therefore, the decedent possessed at death a general power of appointment requiring inclusion of the value of the trust property in the decedent's gross estate under section 2041.

ESTATE OF SOWELL V. COMMISSIONER
United States Court of Appeals, Tenth Circuit, 1983.
708 F.2d 1564.

WILLIAM E. DOYLE, CIRCUIT JUDGE.

* * *

The issue is whether the Tax Court erred in holding that the power to invade the trust corpus, "in case of emergency or illness," constitutes a general power of appointment and therefore the entire corpus should have been included in the gross estate of appellant's decedent pursuant to Section 2041. The appellant's argument states that in determining whether this invasion meets the requirements of section 2041(b)(1)(A) for exclusion from treatment as a power of appointment requires a two-step analysis. *First,* the standard of invasion must be ascertainable, that is, capable of being readily interpreted and applied by a court of law. Secondly, the standard of invasion must be related to or reasonably measurable in terms of the decedent's needs for health, support, or maintenance. Appellant urges that Mrs. Sowell's power of invasion is ascertainable and in addition is reasonably measurable in terms of her need for health and support. Accordingly, it does not constitute a general power of appointment within the meaning of the code.

* * *

Ida Maude Sowell was the surviving spouse of Thomas R. Sowell, who died in November of 1967. She was named Trustee of a testamentary trust established by her husband's will. By the terms of the trust the net income was payable to Mrs. Sowell during her natural life, and upon her death, the corpus of the trust and all accumulations were to be distributed to Mr. Sowell's sons and daughter-in-law. The Trustee was also given "the right to invade the corpus of said trust in cases of emergency or illness."

* * *

Appellee's contention boils down to the question whether the phrase "in cases of emergency or illness" is an ascertainable standard related to Mrs. Sowell's health, education and support or maintenance. The taxability of an interest or power possessed by the decedent is determined under federal law, according to appellee, and the extent of the decedent's interest is governed by state law. A more precise question then is whether the courts of New Mexico, the jurisdiction in which decedent's will was probated, would hold that the phrase "in cases of emergency or illness" constitutes an ascertainable standard relating solely to decedent's health, education, support or maintenance. New Mexico law provides that the intent and meaning of the testator must be ascertained from the will itself, according to appellee. In determining the testator's intention, the purpose is to ascertain not what he meant to express apart from the language used, but what the words used actually express. Certainly the New Mexico court could readily ascertain the meaning of the governing words here.

* * *

The appellee maintains that the term "emergency" is not one that is clearly limited in its exercise to matters relating to decedent's health, education, support or maintenance. As used, the term "emergency" is clear and unambiguous, they say. The use of such a general term creates a broad power that can be utilized for any purpose so long as an emergency exists. To relate the word "emergency" to decedent's health, education, support or maintenance would require the addition of words that would contradict the plain meaning of the will.

* * *

Our conclusion is that an emergency is an emergency, and it is not susceptible to the expansive application suggested.

In the case of Funk v. Commissioner of Internal Revenue, 185 F.2d 127, 130–32 (3d Cir.1950), * * * [the] court reviewed a decision of the Tax Court of the United States to determine whether the income of four trusts, of which the petitioner was the sole trustee, was taxable to the petitioner. The Court of Appeals held that the petitioner was not endowed in the trust instruments with such unfettered command that the income from the trusts was her own money. She was only entitled, therefore, to receive income in accordance with her "needs." The Court there said:

> The term "needs" is not, of course, one the content of which can be defined precisely. * * * If, as the Tax Court observed, the trusts are unambiguous and specific it can only be said of the term "needs" that it must [be] construed according to its ordinary meaning. While obviously it must include the essentials of life, it has been construed in New Jersey to mean that which is reasonably necessary to maintain a beneficiary's station in life. It is not indicative of an unqualified gift, nor is it dependent upon the fancy of the administrator. Thus, its use confined the trustee to limits objectively determinable, and any conduct on her part beyond those limits would be unreasonable and breach of trust; certainly it did not countenance extravagance, whim, or caprice. * * *

The case of Pittsfield National Bank v. United States, 181 F. Supp. 851, 854 (D.Mass.1960) involved the power to invade corpus on basis of "need" and it was held not to be a general power of appointment within the meaning of § 2041. In *Pittsfield,* the Court said:

> The word "need" according to its dictionary definition and the cases interpreting it, has an even narrower and explicit meaning than the words discussed above, i.e., "want to the means of subsistence, necessity." The principal case explaining the word . . . requires a showing of "actual financial or physical necessity" before the life tenant could exercise a power to sell "if she should need to during her lifetime." * * *

The Court further said:

> * * * The grant of the power must be read in its entirety, and so read I (*sic*) rule that it was a grant of power to invade corpus only in the event the donee was in financial or physical need.

* * *

We have exhaustively researched this issue and have not discovered a case which broadly construes the term "emergency" so as to allow a general power of appointment, sufficient to render a fund taxable to an estate.

Our conclusion is that no such case exists; that the term "emergency" is a restricted term which would tolerate obtaining the money from the trust only if the situation was extraordinary.

Accordingly, the judgment of the Tax Court must be reversed, and the cause must be remanded for further proceedings.

It is so ordered.

NOTE

1. Has the court in *Sowell* expanded the meaning of "health, education, maintenance and support" to include "emergency" or has it restricted the meaning of "emergency" as it relates to "health, education, support, or maintenance"? If the latter is correct, does that mean that the outcome of similar cases will depend on the interpretation placed on "emergency" by applicable state law, i.e., that the outcome in similar cases will vary from state to state and case to case depending on what a court finds to be the decedent's intention in using the word "emergency," or by applicable state-supplied rules of construction in those cases where the decedent's intention cannot be determined?

2. In Hyde v. United States, 950 F. Supp. 418 (D.N.H.1996), the court concluded that the decedent had a general power of appointment where she was authorized to use the income and principal of a trust "as in her sole discretion shall be necessary or desirable." By way of contrast, though, in Best v. United States, 902 F. Supp. 1023 (D. Neb.1995), the decedent's power of appointment was found to have satisfied the

ascertainable standard exception even though, by its plain terms, it would seem to have flunked the test. In *Best*, the court concluded that the words "sole and absolute discretion" to make distributions of principal as may be "reasonably necessary for her comfort, support and maintenance" protected the trust from inclusion in the decedent's estate because "the Supreme Court of the state of Nebraska, if presented with this case at hand, would hold" these words to "create an invasionary power 'limited by an ascertainable standard relating to the health, education, support or maintenance'" of the decedent "consistent with" section 2041(b)(1)(A).

An interesting aspect of *Best* is the court's failure to be especially troubled by the presence of the word "comfort" in the trust. Most practitioners avoid the word "comfort" (as well as words such as "welfare" and "happiness") out of fear that its presence might jeopardize the protection of the ascertainable standard exception. Thus, the *Best* court's analysis is useful:

> Courts have held that use of the word "comfort," when used conjunctively with the other specified purposes permitting excludability from a decedent's gross estate, does not destroy an invasionary power limited by an ascertainable standard in reference to "health, education, support, or maintenance of the decedent" pursuant to 26 U.S.C. § 2041(b)(1)(A). For instance, in Vissering v. Commissioner of Internal Revenue, 990 F.2d 578 (10th Cir.1993), the court examined the testamentary language in a trust which allowed an invasion "required for the continued comfort, support, maintenance, or education of said beneficiary." The trust assets, according to a decision by the United States Tax Court that was under review, were includable in the Estate of Norman Vissering, the deceased beneficiary of the trust. As observed by the Circuit Court in Vissering: "The appeal turns on whether decedent held powers permitting him to invade the principal of the trust for his own benefit unrestrained by an ascertainable standard relating to health, education, support, or maintenance." 990 F.2d at 578. In Vissering, the court also stated:
>
> > "The Internal Revenue Service (IRS) and the Tax Court focused on portions of the invasion provision providing that the trust principal could be expended for the 'comfort' of decedent, declaring that this statement rendered the power of invasion incapable of limitation by the courts."
> >
> > . . . The instant language states that invasion of principal is permitted to the extent "required for the continued comfort" of the decedent, and is part of a clause referencing the support, maintenance and education of the beneficiary. Invasion of the corpus is not permitted to the extent "determined" or "desired" for the beneficiary's comfort but only to the extent that it is "required." Furthermore, the

invasion must be for the beneficiary's "continued" comfort, implying, we believe, more than the minimum necessary for survival, but nevertheless reasonably necessary to maintain the beneficiary in his accustomed manner of living. These words in context state a standard essentially no different from the examples in the Treasury Regulation, in which phrases such as "support in reasonable comfort," "maintenance in health and reasonable comfort," and "support in his accustomed manner of living" are deemed to be limited by an ascertainable standard. Treas. Reg. § 20.2041–1(c)(2).[5]

PROBLEMS

Sun is both trustee and beneficiary of a trust established by her father. Distributions from the income and principal of the trust are to be made to Sun. Which, if any, of the following dispositive provisions will result in the trust property's being included in Sun's estate for estate tax purposes at her death? See Treas. Reg. § 20.2041–1(c)(2).

1. The trustee shall distribute so much or all of the income and principal of the trust estate as shall be needed by Sun for her health, education, maintenance and support.

2. The trustee shall distribute so much or all of the income and principal of the trust estate as shall be needed by Sun for her health, education, maintenance and support in her accustomed manner of living.

3. The trustee shall distribute so much or all of the income and principal of the trust estate as shall be needed by Sun for her welfare and happiness.

4. The trustee shall distribute so much or all of the income and principal of the trust estate as shall be needed by Sun for her health, education, maintenance, support, welfare and happiness in her accustomed manner of living.

E. COMPETENCY OF HOLDER OF POWER

ESTATE OF ALPERSTEIN V. COMMISSIONER
United States Court of Appeals, Second Circuit, 1979.
613 F.2d 1213.

FRIENDLY, CIRCUIT JUDGE:

* * * Fannie Alperstein died intestate on December 3, 1972, after surviving her husband, Harry, who had died more than five years earlier on July 6, 1967. His will established a trust for the benefit of the decedent.

---

[5] *Best*, 902 F. Supp. at 1027–1028.

* * * Fannie Alperstein was to receive all the net income from the trust payable at frequent intervals for the duration of her life, and was granted a testamentary power to appoint the principal of the trust free of any restrictions. If the decedent failed to exercise her testamentary power of appointment, Mr. Alperstein's children or their issue would take in default.

On January 16, some six months before Harry Alperstein's death, Fannie Alperstein had entered a nursing home where she remained until shortly before her death. On December 27, 1967, a New York court declared Fannie to be incompetent * * *. Although the judicial determination of the decedent's incompetence followed the death of Mr. Alperstein by almost six months, the parties have stipulated that from her husband's death until her own death, the decedent lacked the capacity to execute a will under New York law, did not purport to exercise the power of appointment granted by her husband's will, and was legally incapable of exercising that power.

Rosalind A. Greenberg, the decedent's executrix, filed a federal estate tax return that did not include in the decedent's gross estate the value of the property over which the decedent had been granted testamentary power of appointment by her husband's will. The Commissioner asserted a deficiency based on his determination that the decedent possessed at death a general power of appointment within the meaning of I.R.C. § 2041(a)(2), which required the inclusion of the entire value of the property subject to that power within her gross estate. The parties have stipulated that if the property subject to the power created by Mr. Alperstein's will is included in the decedent's gross estate, that property is to be valued at $242,167.17.

* * *

Appellant does not question that, so far as language is concerned, the power of appointment conferred by Article Fourth of Harry Alperstein's will met the statutory test. The claim is that, despite this § 2041(a)(2) is inapplicable because, under the stipulated facts, Fannie Alperstein was never able to exercise the power vested in her by her husband's will—a situation allegedly not present in any of the cases that have sustained the taxability of powers against attacks of the same general sort as that mounted here.

I.

We start, as always, with the words of the statute * * *. The operative verb in § 2041(a)(2) is "has." Beyond cavil Mrs. Alperstein "had" a general power of appointment at the time of her death. This had been granted by her husband's will and nothing done by the New York courts purported to take it away. Even if we assume that the judgment of Fannie Alperstein's incompetency conclusively established her inability to exercise this power, that judgment was subject to being vacated if her mental condition changed for the better. The argument is rather that although Mrs. Alperstein "had" such a power, it was not "exercisable" at the time of her death since she had long since been declared incompetent and in fact had been so ever since her husband had died. However, the word "exercisable" is found not in the operative portion of the statute but in a section addressed to how broad a power must be in order to be "general." The natural meaning of the words is that "exercisable" is shorthand for "which by its terms may be exercised," and does not mean that § 2041(a)(2) is limited to cases where the decedent could in fact exercise the power at the moment of death—something which, in the absence of a will or similar instrument could rarely occur.

* * *

III.

We find no basis for a contrary view in the Service's rulings and regulations.

The Service first addressed the relationship between incompetency and § 2041(a)(2) in Rev. Rul. 55–518, 1955–2 Cum. Bul. 384 (1955), which ruled on the estate of a surviving spouse who had enjoyed an unrestricted lifetime power of appointment over a testamentary trust created by her husband. In a dual holding, the Service determined that the husband's estate qualified for a marital deduction and the wife's estate was taxable for her power even though the wife was incompetent from the date of her husband's death until the time of her own death. Id. 385. The Service reasoned that the wife could have exercised her power with the aid of a local court and, therefore, "possessed" the power at the time of her death even if she could not have freely exercised it at any time. Id.

* * *

[The gift tax regulations relating to the circumstances under which transfers to minors of a future interest would qualify for the gift tax annual exclusion as provided in § 2503(c) are consistent. Reg.] § 25.2503–4(b) stated:

> if the minor is given a power of appointment . . . the fact that under local law a minor is under a disability to exercise an inter vivos power or to execute a will does not cause the transfer to fail to satisfy the conditions of section 2502(c) [2503(c)].

* * * Rev. Rul. 74–350, 1975–2 Cum. Bull. 367, the Service's most recent pronouncement on the relationship between incompetency and the possession of a general power within the meaning of § 2041, extends the Service's original determination of taxability to a legally incompetent holder of a testamentary power who is indistinguishable from Mrs. Alperstein in all relevant respects. This ruling abandons any reliance on the possibility that a legally incompetent holder of a power might be able to exercise his power with the aid of a court or anyone else. Instead, it concludes:

> [j]ust as incapacity or incompetency does not render property owned outright by a decedent exempt from estate taxation, neither is property subject to a general power of appointment exempt in such circumstances, unless *by the terms of the grant of the power* such circumstances have caused the existence of the power itself to cease prior to the decedent's death. [Emphasis original.]

Id. at 368.

IV.

Although appellant may be right in contending that no decision upholding the estate taxation of property subject to a general power of appointment has presented facts quite so humanly appealing in favor of the donee as this, the general thrust of the case law in appellate courts is decidedly unfavorable to her.

While the Supreme Court has not had occasion to rule on the effect of incompetency of the holder of a general power on taxability under § 2041, C.I.R. v. Estate of Noel, 380 U.S. 678 (1965), strongly indicated the Court's probable approach. Noel required a construction of I.R.C. § 2042, which provides inter alia that a decedent's estate is taxable for the proceeds of insurance policies on the life of the decedent "with respect to which the decedent possessed at his death any of the incidents of ownership, exercisable alone or in conjunction with any other person." Immediately before boarding a plane doomed to a fatal crash, the decedent in *Noel* purchased several flight insurance policies which he left with his wife on the ground. The decedent's estate contended that on these facts there had been no exercisable incidents of ownership within the meaning of the statute. While acknowledging that "there was no practical opportunity" to exercise ownership power, the Court concluded:

> It would stretch the imagination to think that Congress intended to measure estate tax liability by an individual's fluctuating, day-to-day, hour-by-hour capacity to dispose of property which he owns. We hold that estate tax liability for policies "with respect to which the decedent possessed at his death any of the incidents of ownership" depends on a general, legal power to exercise ownership, without regard to the owner's ability to exercise it at a particular moment.

Id. at 684.

Three courts of appeals have considered the effect upon taxability under § 2041 of the inability of the holder of a power to exercise it; all have ruled in favor of the Government. [Discussion and citations omitted.] * * *

In sum we hold, on the basis of statutory language, legislative history (particularly the interaction of § 2041(a)(1) with the marital deduction, § 2056(b)(5)), administrative interpretation and case law, that when an instrument has conferred a testamentary power which by its terms can be exercised in favor of the donee's estate, the property subject to the power is part of the donee's gross estate even though the donee, by virtue of incompetency was unable to make a valid will at any time after the power was granted.

Affirmed.

NOTE

At death, Lillian Halpern held a testamentary general power of appointment over a certain trust and as a result the trust property was included in her estate for estate tax purposes. Estate of Halpern v. Commissioner, T.C. Memo. 1995–352, 70 T.C.M. (CCH) 229 (1995). All trust income was to be paid to Lillian. Principal could be invaded for her benefit at the discretion of the trustees in the event of illness or other emergency. While she lived, trust property was given to Lillian's loved ones by the trustees even though the trust authorized distributions only to Lillian. Gift tax returns were filed by Lillian reflecting these gifts. The transfers to Lillian's loved ones were made over a period of years, beginning in 1982 and ending in 1988, the year of Lillian's death. Lillian suffered a stroke in 1986 and was incompetent at all times thereafter. Lillian had consented in writing to the transfers made from the trust before she became incompetent. Other family members joined in the consents. The IRS claimed that all of the gifts should be included in Lillian's estate for estate tax purposes. It reasoned that the trustees could recover the transfers made from the trust because they were improper and, therefore, that property was included in Lillian's gross estate because it was subject to her general power of appointment. The court agreed as to the transfers made after Lillian became incompetent but concluded that the pre-incompetence transfers were not included in Lillian's estate. The IRS expressed concern that excluding the lifetime transfers from Lillian's estate "would undermine the federal transfer tax system." The court rejected the IRS's argument reasoning that Lillian reported these transfers for gift tax purposes. So far as impropriety is concerned, Lillian's consent to the transfers made prior to her incompetence would be considered effective family agreements under state law. The post-competency transfers were included in Lillian's estate because, under local law, Lillian had not effectively consented to those transfers and, as a result, either Lillian or her successors in interest could revoke them and recapture the transferred property either before or after her death.

F. RELEASE AND DISCLAIMER

A release of a post-1942 general power is considered an inter vivos exercise of the power. I.R.C. § 2514(b). Moreover, the property subject to the power will be included in the powerholder's gross estate if the power is released in such a way that the property would have been included in the powerholder's gross estate if it had been owned and so transferred by the powerholder, i.e., if the provisions of sections 2035–2038 would apply to the transaction if nonpower property had been transferred. I.R.C. § 2041(a)(2). For example, if the life income beneficiary of a trust also had a general testamentary power of appointment over the trust property and this power was released by the life income beneficiary by an inter vivos conveyance, the release would likely bring the trust property into the life income beneficiary's gross estate at death because the release was the equivalent of a transfer of the trust property by the donee subject to a retained life estate under section 2036(a)(1).

Section 2518(c)(2) allows disclaimer of a power of appointment. Satisfying the statutorily imposed disclaimer requirements means that what would otherwise be a taxable release will have no transfer tax consequences.

G. LAPSE

1. INTRODUCTION

Section 2041(b)(2) equates a lapse of a power created after 1942 with a release of a power—and a release of a power triggers gift tax. However, section 2041(b)(2) carves out an exception whereby the lapse of certain powers of appointment will not be treated as a taxable release. This exception, commonly referred to as the "five-and-five power," provides that a lapse is not to be considered a taxable release to the extent that the property subject to the lapsing power, at the time of the lapse, did not exceed in value the greater of $5,000 or 5 percent of the value of the property out of which the exercise of the lapsed power could be satisfied. The plain meaning of this exception is to create, practically speaking, an exemption from tax for estate and gift tax purposes.

2. FIVE-AND-FIVE POWERS

The lapse exemption, or five-and-five power as it is more commonly referred to, is regularly used as a basis of a plan which gives trust beneficiaries the right to make annual withdrawals from the trust without adverse estate or gift tax consequences. Pure and simple, a right of withdrawal is a general power of appointment by another name—and property subject to a general power is included in the estate of the powerholder at death for estate tax purposes (or is subject to gift tax if the power is exercised during the lifetime of the powerholder). However, in cases where the trust is drafted to take advantage of the five-and-five lapse exemption, the trust beneficiary (or beneficiaries) can benefit from the trust without having the trust property included in the estate of the beneficiary at his or her subsequent death. In the typical case, the beneficiary may be given all of the trust income along with the right to withdraw from the trust on an annual noncumulative basis, for example, "the greater of $5,000 or 5 percent of the value of the property constituting the trust estate, the trust to be valued for these purposes as of the last calendar day of the year." The purpose of such a provision is to give the trust beneficiary the unfettered right to withdraw a limited amount from the trust, the goal being, perhaps, to give the beneficiary some discretionary funds, or a source of funds for some unanticipated needs.

The exercise or nonexercise of a five-and-five right of withdrawal power is generally estate and gift tax neutral. That is, neither estate nor gift taxes are triggered by the exercise or nonexercise of a five-and-five right of withdrawal power. One exception to this general proposition may be noted. In the year of death, the powerholder's estate will be deemed to include the amount eligible for withdrawal by the powerholder at the moment of death. Treas. Reg. § 20.2041–3(d)(3). In addition, as discussed in Chapter 31, the powerholder will be taxed under the income tax on the portion of the trust income attributable to the portion of the property that he or she could have withdrawn each year. This latter point relates to the possibility that with each lapse or nonexercise of the powerholder's annual right of withdrawal, the powerholder will be treated as owner of an ever increasing share of the trust—and will be taxed on the trust income attributable to that portion in those cases where the powerholder does not receive that income or is not otherwise taxed on it.

Suppose, however, that a generous settlor provides that the income beneficiary of a trust may withdraw $20,000 per annum from the trust "with the right of withdrawal to lapse to the extent not exercised at the end of each calendar year during the continuance of the trust." In those years when the trust property has a value of less than $400,000, the failure of the beneficiary to exercise his or her right of withdrawal will result in a taxable transfer being made by the powerholder. I.R.C. § 2514(e). Furthermore, the failure to exercise the right of withdrawal will have estate tax consequences. For example, assume the trust consists of property having a value of $300,000 and the trust beneficiary is to receive all of the trust income quarterly. Failure to withdraw the $20,000 means that the beneficiary will have made a transfer of $5,000 ($20,000 minus $15,000 (5 percent of $300,000)), the lapse exclusion shielding $15,000 from gift tax. Technically, the value of the $5,000 transfer, for gift tax purposes, would be reduced by the value of the beneficiary's retained right to the income from the transferred $5,000. But that is not all. At the death of the powerholder, a portion of the trust property will be included in the estate of the powerholder. For estate tax purposes, the powerholder will be deemed to have made a transfer to the trust of the $5,000 that was not sheltered by the five-and-five lapse exclusion—and to have retained the right to the income from the transferred $5,000 for life. Section 2036(a)(1), relating to retained life estates, is then invoked to cause a fraction of the trust property, valued at the time of the death of the powerholder, to be included in the estate of the powerholder for estate tax purposes. In addition, the $20,000 eligible for withdrawal by the powerholder at death will be included in the powerholder's estate for estate tax purposes. Treas. Reg. § 20.2041–3(d)(3).

3. TAX SHELTER

Not only does the five-and-five lapse exception have positive planning possibilities, but it can also have utility in sheltering property subject to a general power from estate taxation. Consider the case where a trust beneficiary has the right to withdraw from the trust all trust income annually but, to the extent that the trust income is not withdrawn at year-end, the portion of the income remaining in the trust is to be added to principal. Obviously, the power of withdrawal lapsed at year-end, meaning that the five-and-five lapse exemption is available to shelter the amount not withdrawn from the gift tax—and the estate tax. However, the question arises as to the application of the five-and-five lapse exception. That is, is the exempt amount five percent of the value of the trust corpus or is it five percent of the value of the trust income (inasmuch as it is only the income that can be withdrawn)? While the issue may appear to be esoteric, its resolution can have significant financial consequences and is presented all too frequently when it comes time for preparation of the estate tax return of the powerholder. The following case considers this issue.

FISH v. UNITED STATES
United States Court of Appeals, Ninth Circuit, 1970.
432 F.2d 1278.

TAYLOR, DISTRICT JUDGE:

* * * Clarence G. Blagen, the husband of Minnie C. Blagen, died on May 28, 1951. The residuary clause of his will established a trust, the terms of which provided that Minnie C. Blagen should have, during her lifetime, the right in any calendar year to demand payment to her of all or part of the net income of the trust for that year, but that any income not so claimed by her would be added to the corpus of the trust. Upon the death of Minnie C. Blagen, the trust corpus, including such accumulated income added to the corpus, was to be distributed to the grandchildren of Clarence G. Blagen.

Minnie C. Blagen (decedent) never exercised or released her power over the income of the trust in any year from the inception of the trust until her death on July 13, 1960, except insofar as the annual lapse of the power, if any such lapse occurred, constituted a release of the power as a matter of law under Section 2041(b)(2) * * *. The Commissioner, in assessing the tax deficiency, included in the decedent's gross estate the net income of the trust, less allowable exemptions, for the years 1955, 1956, 1957, 1958 and 1959. The inclusion of accumulated income which had been added to the trust in those years resulted in an increase in the decedent's gross estate of $116,045.36. The taxpayer had not included this amount in the estate tax return which he had filed for the estate.

The Commissioner determined that the decedent possessed a general power of appointment over the trust income and that the failure of the decedent to exercise this power constituted a lapse of the power in each year in which it was not exercised. The Commissioner contends that the lapse constitutes a release of the power under Section 2041(b)(2) in such a way that, if it were a transfer of property owned by the decedent, the property would have been includible in the decedent's gross estate as a transfer with a retained life estate under Section 2036(a)(1). [The court explained in a footnote that "As income was added to the trust each year as a result of the decedent's inaction, that income generated additional income in following years which was subject to the decedent's lifetime power of appointment, and thus the 'transfer' each year by the decedent was one which left her with a lifetime interest in the property. Such a transfer, resulting from the exercise or release of a power of appointment, becomes includible in the gross estate of the decedent under the provisions of Section 2041(a)(2)."]

The taxpayer agrees that the decedent possessed a general power of appointment, and that the "transfer" each year, had the property been owned by the decedent, would be a transfer with a retained life estate. The taxpayer contends, however, that * * * the Commissioner and the District Court erred in computing the allowable exemption under Section 2041(b)(2) on the basis of five per cent of the net income of the trust instead of * * * five per cent of the total trust assets.

* * * [§ 2041(b)(2)] allows as an exemption to the amount includible in the taxable estate an amount equal to five per cent of "the aggregate value of the assets out of which, or the proceeds out of which, the exercise of the lapsed powers could be satisfied," or the sum of $5,000, whichever is the greater. The District Court, in determining the amount of the exemption, computed the exemption on the basis of five per cent of the trust income. Since for each year in question, the sum of $5,000 was greater than five per cent of the trust income, the District Court allowed an exemption of $5,000 for each year, as the Commissioner had done. The taxpayer argues that the exemption should be $5,000 or five per cent of the total trust assets, and since five per cent of the total assets would exceed the net income for three of the five years in question and would nearly equal the net income in the other two years, the end result should be that the amount includible in the decedent's estate should be reduced to $15,858.47. The taxpayer argues that since the income payable to the decedent, had she demanded it, would

have been payable either from corpus or income, the entire trust represents "assets out of which, or the proceeds out of which, the exercise of lapsed powers could be satisfied," and thus the entire trust assets should serve as the basis for the five per cent computation. We do not agree. Even if the trustee could have satisfied a demand for income out of either corpus assets or income funds, a point which we do not here decide, the distribution would necessarily have been a distribution of income as a matter of federal tax law or as a matter of trust accounting, since the decedent had no power whatever to invade the corpus of the trust.

While the language of Section 2041(b)(2)(B), like much of the statutory tax law, is hardly a model of precision and clarity on the point, we are satisfied from a reading of the statute together with its legislative history that the applicable basis for computation on the allowable exemption is the trust or fund in which the lapsed power existed. The District Court correctly determined that the power of appointment in the instant case existed only with respect to the trust income, and properly allowed an exemption of $5,000 for each year in question.

* * *

NOTE

While the court in *Fish* states that the Commissioner has included all of the net income of the trust in the decedent's estate as a result of the decedent's power to withdraw that income, the regulations suggest that, in a case like *Fish,* the correct amount to be included in the estate of the deceased powerholder is the sum of a series of fractions of the trust rather than the dollar amount that could have been withdrawn by the deceased powerholder. Treas. Reg. § 20.2041–3(d)(4). The numerator of each such fraction will be equal to the amount that could have been withdrawn by the powerholder in each year less the amount of the lapse exemption available to the powerholder that year. The denominator will be equal to the value of the fund out of which the right of withdrawal could have been satisfied, the fund being valued on the date that the right of withdrawal lapsed. Using the example given in the regulations, where the value of the trust is $800,000 and the powerholder had the right to withdraw $50,000, a taxable release of 1/80th of the total value of the trust resulted from the failure of the powerholder to exercise his or her right of withdrawal. The numerator of the fraction is determined by subtracting five percent of the value of the trust corpus ($800,000), or $40,000, from the amount that could have been withdrawn ($50,000). The denominator is the value of the corpus ($800,000). In the case where the trust beneficiary has an annual right of withdrawal of $50,000 that is not exercised and that lapses at year-end and the value of the trust corpus is a constant $800,000 over a seven-year period, 7/80ths of the value of the trust at the time of the death of the powerholder will be included in the powerholder's estate for estate tax purposes—provided, of course, that the powerholder retains or possesses a sections 2036–2038 power over the trust, such as a right to receive all of the trust income during the seven-year period.

Problems

1. Review the facts in the *Fish* case and consider the following:

    (a) Could the controversy in *Fish* have been avoided if the powerholder had exercised her right of withdrawal each year?

    (b) Should the drafter of the will have anticipated the controversy that arose in *Fish* and suggested to the client that the will contain a provision requiring the trustee to distribute the trust income at least annually?

2. Suppose Mary has the power to withdraw $40,000 annually from a trust, the right of withdrawal to be exercised on or before year-end, and, to the extent not exercised, the $40,000 will be added to the principal of the trust. At the time of her death, Mary had not exercised the power for that year. Is it appropriate to conclude that the full $40,000 will be included in Mary's estate for estate tax purposes? See Treas. Reg. § 20.2041–3(d)(3).

H. STATE LEGISLATION TO LIMIT GENERAL POWER

State legislators routinely add default rules to the state's probate code or equivalent so as to effect a "best results" or "most likely results" outcome in cases where the text appearing in the governing instrument is susceptible of more than one meaning. Typically, the statutory interpretation is intended to prevail unless, in the specified instances, the governing instrument is found to otherwise provide.[6] In more recent times, legislatures have taken to "fixing" instruments that might be construed to have a "bad result." For example, Virginia has a "tax savings" provision that provides unless expressly stated in the trust, a beneficiary and trustee (other than the grantor) who has the right to make "discretionary distributions" for his or her own benefit may exercise the power pursuant to an ascertainable standard.[7] Many other states, including California, Iowa, and New Hampshire have similar statutes.[8] Because the trustee/beneficiary is prohibited from making discretionary distributions

---

[6] See, e.g., N.C. Gen. Stat. § 31D–2–203 (2022) (providing that a power of appointment is presumed to be a general power of appointment unless the contrary intent of the donor is manifested in the creating instrument).

[7] Va. Code Ann. § 64.2–776 (2022).

[8] Cal. Pro. Code § 16081(c) (2022); Iowa Code § 633A.4214 (2022); N.H. Rev. Stat. Ann. § 564–A:3 (2022); N.C. Gen. Stat. § 36C–8–814(b)(2) (2022). The New Hampshire statute expressly states that the purpose of the provision is construed in this manner to prevent the "inherent conflict of interest" and applies unless the express terms of the trust provides a contrary interpretation.

for their own benefit, the trust property will not be included in trustee/beneficiary's gross estate under section 2041(b)(2).

An example follows in Private Letter Ruling 200530020. Should the likely presence of such legislation in the jurisdiction whose law governs embolden the inexperienced draftsperson, strong in resolve (to take the assignment) but weak in fundamentals? Would it be helpful to recite, in the governing instrument, the desired tax benefit? What about the case where the draftsperson was not even aware of the peril and/or benefit that might result from certain choices? Suppose the document included text stating that the maker wanted "the best tax outcome possible and the instrument should be so construed or modified?" Is it possible that some instruments would contain text that, perhaps unintentionally, precluded application of a state statute aimed at providing the best tax outcome?

PRIVATE LETTER RULING 200530020
April 6, 2005.

Decedent died testate on Date 1, a date prior to September 25, 1985. At his death, Decedent was a resident of State and was survived by Spouse and three children.

Article 6 of Decedent's Will created Trust. Under the terms of Trust, until the death of Spouse, the trustees may accumulate the net income of the trust or pay to or apply so much thereof to the use of such one or more of Spouse, Decedent's children, and the then living issue of Decedent's children, in such amounts and proportions as the trustees in their sole and absolute discretion deem advisable from time to time without regard to equality of distribution. There is no power to distribute the principal of Trust during the lifetime of Spouse. At Spouse's death, Trust provides for distributions to Decedent's descendants.

In Article 7 of Decedent's Will, Decedent designated his father, his brother, and Spouse as original co-trustees of Trust. Spouse and sister of Spouse are the current trustees and have been serving as co-trustees since Year 6 of Trust.

Trust was irrevocable on September 25, 1985. * * *

In 1995, Statute was added to the State Code that provides, in part, that unless the terms of a trust refer specifically to this provision and provide to the contrary, a trustee shall not, on behalf of or for the benefit of a beneficiary who is also a trustee, make discretionary distributions of either principal or income for the benefit of the trustee, except to provide for the health, education, maintenance, or support of the trustee as described under §§ 2041 and 2514 of the Internal Revenue Code (Code). The Statute also provides that a trustee shall not, on behalf of or for the benefit of a beneficiary who is also a trustee, make discretionary distributions of either principal or income to satisfy any legal or support obligations of the trustee. This provision applies to all irrevocable trusts existing on July 7, 1995, unless all parties in interest elect affirmatively not to be subject to the application of this section.

It is represented that the parties in interest with respect to Trust have not elected affirmatively for Trust to be excluded from the application of Statute.

You have asked us to rule, as follows:

1.   That, upon her death, no portion of trust income will be included in Spouse's gross estate under § 2041(b)(2).

2.   That, during Spouse's lifetime, no distributions of trust income from Trust after the effective date of Statute will be subject to gift tax under § 2514(c)(1).

* * *

LAW AND ANALYSIS

* * *

While federal law controls what rights or interests shall be taxed after they are created, creation of legal rights and interests in property (such as the breadth and scope of a power of appointment over the corpus of a testamentary trust) is a matter of state law. United States v. Pelzer, 312 U.S. 399 (1941), 1941–1 C.B. 441; Morgan v. Commissioner, 309 U.S. 78 (1940), 1940–1 C.B. 229.

As referred to above, Statute provides that unless the terms of a trust refer specifically to the provision and provide to the contrary, a trustee shall not perform any of the following on behalf of or for the benefit of a beneficiary who is also a trustee: (1) make discretionary distributions of either principal or income for the benefit of the trustee, except to provide for the health, education, maintenance, or support of the trustee as described under §§ 2041 and 2514 of the Internal Revenue Code, as amended; (2) make discretionary allocations of receipts or expenses as between principal and income, unless the trustee has no power to enlarge or shift any beneficial interest except as an incidental consequence of the discharge of the fiduciary duties of the trustee; and (3) make discretionary distributions of either principal or income to satisfy any legal or support obligations of the trustee.

Statute provides, in part, that it applies to all irrevocable trusts existing on July 7, 1995, unless all parties in interest elect affirmatively not to be subject to the application of this section.

Rev. Proc. 94–44, 1994–2 C.B. 683, sets forth the Service's position regarding the transfer tax consequences of the enactment of Florida

Statutes Annotated (F.S.A.) § 737.402(4)(a)(1). Under this statute, any fiduciary power conferred upon a trustee to make discretionary distributions of either principal or income to or for the trustee's own benefit cannot be exercised by the trustee, except to provide for that trustee's health, education, maintenance, or support, as described in §§ 2041 and 2514. The statute was effective with respect to trusts that were irrevocable on or after July 1, 1991. Pursuant to the revenue procedure, the Service will not treat the statute as causing the lapse of a general power of appointment for purposes of §§ 2041 and 2514, where the scope of a fiduciary power held by a beneficiary was restricted as a result of the statute.

In the present case, prior to the effective date of Statute, Spouse's unlimited power to distribute income to herself as a trustee-beneficiary constituted a general power of appointment over the income of Trust under §§ 2041(b)(1)(A) and 2514(c)(1). See § 20.2041–1(b)(1) and (3) and § 25.2514–1(b)(1) and (3). Consistent with the principles of Rev. Proc. § 94–44, the enactment of Statute will not be treated as causing a lapse of Spouse's general power of appointment over Trust income for transfer tax purposes. The statute will be treated as effective with respect to Trust on the effective date of Statute. Therefore, as of the effective date, Spouse, as trustee-beneficiary of Trust, will not have the power to appoint trust income for her own benefit except in satisfaction of any needs she may have for health, education, maintenance, and support. Since Spouse's power to distribute income to herself is limited to an ascertainable standard as described in §§ 2041(b)(1)(A) and 2514(c)(1), Spouse will not possess a general power of appointment over the trust income for transfer tax purposes by virtue of any fiduciary power to distribute income. Accordingly, we conclude that no portion of trust income will be included in Spouse's gross estate under § 2041(b)(2) upon her death and that distributions of trust income to the trust beneficiaries after the effective date of Statute will not be subject to gift tax under § 2514(c)(1).

I. JOINT POWERS

A major exception to the rule that general powers of appointment held or exercised at death are included in the decedent's taxable estate relates to jointly held powers. As to powers created on or before October 21, 1942, any power that the decedent holds jointly with another party is not a general power and thus not subject to the estate tax. Jointly held powers created thereafter will escape taxation as general powers if: (1) the other holder of the power is the donor; or (2) the other holder has a substantial interest in the property adverse to that of the donee. As the following case illustrates, the other holder does not have a "substantial adverse interest" unless that holder somehow has a personal stake in seeing that the power is not exercised by the donee in the donee's own favor.

ESTATE OF TOWLE V. COMMISSIONER

United States Tax Court, 1970.
54 T.C. 368.

TANNENWALD, JUDGE: * * *

[At the death of Janet McNear Towle in 1964, she was the income beneficiary of three post-1942 settlement contracts of insurance on her deceased father's life. The contracts gave her two further rights: (1) a noncumulative privilege to withdraw $13,500 annually from principal and (2) the privilege (unexercised at her death) of withdrawing at any time all of the principal with the consent of the First National Bank, as trustee under the will of her father, Charles W. McNear. Upon the decedent's death, undistributed funds remaining with the insurance company were to be paid to the bank as trustee of a residuary trust set up in her father's will. The residuary trust provided that the income was to be paid to the decedent for life with the remainder to her son. The bank as trustee under the will was authorized to invade principal for the decedent if the net income from the residuary trust was insufficient for her support and maintenance.]

* * *

Petitioner makes a two-pronged argument to support its contention that the power of withdrawal by the decedent of the entire proceeds of the insurance settlement contracts was not a general power of appointment within the meaning of section 2041(b)(1) and that therefore the amount of those proceeds, in excess of that subject to the noncumulative annual right of withdrawal, is not includable in the decedent's gross estate under section 2041(a).

The first prong is developed along the following lines: (1) First National, albeit concededly as a trustee, held a direct remainder interest under the insurance settlement contracts and consequently had an "interest in the property, subject to the power"; (2) because of the fiduciary duty imposed upon First National to protect the interests of the remaindermen of the residuary trust under the will of Charles W. McNear, its "interest" was "substantial" and "adverse" within the meaning of subsection (C)(ii) of section 2041(b)(1); and (3) First National was simply an agent of the grandson remainderman whose interest was undeniably substantial and adverse to that of the decedent. We disagree.

As a general rule, the interest of a nonbeneficiary trustee is neither substantial nor adverse. Reinecke v. Smith, 289 U.S. 172 (1933), so holds with respect to the income tax and its principles are fully applicable to the estate tax. * * * This conclusion is further supported by the following statement in the committee reports which accompanied the original enactment of the pertinent portion of section 2041, as an amendment to section 811(f) of the 1939 Code, by the Powers of Appointment Act of 1951, 65 Stat. 91:

> a future joint power is totally exempt if it is not exercisable by the decedent except with the consent or joinder of a person having a substantial interest. In the property subject to the power, which is adverse to the exercise of the power in favor of the decedent, his estate, his creditors, or the creditors of his estate, a taker in default of appointment has an interest which is adverse to such an exercise. Principles developed under the income and gift taxes will be applicable in determining whether an interest is substantial and the amount of property in which the adversity exists. A coholder of the power has no adverse interest merely because of his joint possession of the power nor merely because he is a permissible appointee under a power, since neither the power nor the expectancy as appointee is an 'interest' in the property. * * * [See H. Rept. No. 327, to accompany H.R. 2084 (Pub. L. 58), 82d Cong., 1st Sess., pp. 5–6 (1951); S. Rept. No. 382 to accompany H.R. 2084 (Pub. L. 591), 82d Cong., 1st Sess., p. 5 (1951).]

In Reinecke v. Smith, supra, the Supreme Court stated:

> In approaching the decision of the question before us it is to be borne in mind that the trustee is not a trustee of the power of revocation and owes no duty to the beneficiary to resist alteration or revocation of the trust. Of course he owes a duty to the beneficiary to protect the trust res, faithfully to administer it, and to distribute the income; but the very fact that he participates in the right of alteration or revocation negatives any fiduciary duty to the beneficiary to refrain from exercising the power. * * * [See 289 U.S. at pp. 176–177.]

Petitioner seeks to avoid the application of the principles announced in Reinecke v. Smith, supra, by claiming that First National had a direct remainder interest in the insurance proceeds and that its fiduciary obligations arose only under the will of Charles W. McNear after it had collected the insurance proceeds. In essence, petitioner asserts that First National was a beneficiary of those proceeds in its own right. But a beneficiary is one who has a beneficial interest of his own and not one who administers property for the benefit of others. * * * Clearly, First National fits the latter category. We do not think its status as the remainderman of the insurance proceeds so enlarged its interest as to place it outside the rationale of Reinecke v. Smith, supra. * * * Nor does petitioner's recital of numerous authorities under state law with respect to the requirement of good faith imposed upon the exercise of discretionary powers by a trustee or the ability of a beneficiary to enforce that requirement by injunction, surcharge, or otherwise have any bearing on the issue before us.

Petitioner admits that, "No provision in the Will of Charles W. McNear in express terms directs or controls the exercise of the Trustee's power to permit the withdrawal of the retained funds by Janice McNear Towle." Petitioner argues that the testamentary objective of Charles W. McNear was to assure that the principal of his estate would pass to his grandson or his heirs and that the trustee had a special duty to see that such objective was accomplished. But on this record it is at least equally, if not more, plausible to conclude that Charles W. McNear considered the insurance settlements to be separate from the residuary trust in order that the decedent would have funds adequate to meet her reasonable desires during her lifetime, as she saw them, and that the corporate trustee had merely the usual fiduciary responsibility to guard against the capricious exhaustion of the insurance principal.

We think that the phrase "substantial interest in the property, subject to the power, which is adverse to exercise of the power in favor of the decedent," as used in section 2041(b)(1)(C)(ii), was intended at the very least to require that the third person have a present or future chance to obtain a personal benefit from the property itself. * * * Compare also the provisions of section 2041(b)(1)(C)(iii), which exclude, on an allocable basis, a portion of property subject to a power which would otherwise be a general power of appointment, but which is exercisable "in favor of" a person whose consent is required.

As the final element in the first prong of its argument, petitioner asserts that First National was simply the agent of the grandson remainderman under the will of Charles W. McNear in granting or withholding its consent to the invasion of the insurance principal by decedent. We can find nothing in the record herein to support such an assertion. Clearly, First National's relationship to the grandson was simply that of a trustee to a beneficiary and, in this context, our previous analysis refutes petitioner's contention.

* * *

Decision will be entered for the respondent.

PROBLEMS

1. In 1940, Austin's father died leaving the residue of his estate (valued at $100,000) to a trust company "to pay the income to Austin for life and upon his death the trust corpus is to be distributed among Austin's then living children in equal shares." Under the terms of the testamentary trust, Austin was given the power to alter or amend the trust provisions.

   By will, Austin exercised his power of amendment over his father's trust by prescribing that the trust corpus was to be held in trust for 20 years after his death, with the income being divided among his then living children, and at the end of that period, the corpus to be divided among his then living children in equal shares. At Austin's death, the trust corpus was valued at $1,000,000.

Was Austin well advised to exercise the power of amendment? What are the tax consequences? What were his alternatives?

2.   Austin's mother died in 1964, leaving a will by which she directed that her 70-percent stock interest in Rumble Motors be placed in trust with Austin as sole trustee. Under the terms of the trust, the income was to be divided equally among Austin's children, with the remainder upon the death of the last survivor of such children to go to their issue then living. If such children died without issue, then the trust corpus was to be distributed to Austin or his estate. In addition, the trust provided that Austin was authorized to withdraw $10,000 per year from trust corpus "if his needs so required."

At the time of Austin's death last year, the corpus of the trust was valued at $150,000, and the value of Austin's remainder interest was $5,000; Austin left two children surviving him.

What are the estate tax consequences of Austin's powers?

3.   A decedent's will created a trust with her spouse and sons, Brian, Mike, and Luke as trustees. The trust's income and principal were to be distributed among the spouse and sons "as needed" by each of them for "health, education, maintenance and support in his accustomed manner of living taking into consideration any other property available" for these purposes. In addition, distributions could be made to any or more of the sons "to assist him in purchasing a home or starting a business." Undistributed income is to be added to principal. The trust is to terminate at the spouse's death. Mike has died, survived by the spouse, Brian, and Luke. Is any part of the trust included in Mike's estate for estate tax purposes?

CHAPTER 23

TRANSFERS WITHIN THREE
YEARS OF DEATH

■ ■ ■

A. INTRODUCTION

1. SECTION 2035 BEFORE 1976

Since the beginning of the federal estate tax in 1916, it has been recognized that the tax base had to be protected against lifetime transfers motivated by thoughts of death, estate taxes, or both. "Transfers in contemplation of death" were accordingly swept back into the estate tax base by what is now section 2035. But the question of whether the transfer was or was not in "contemplation of death" provided a field day for lawyers who litigated that issue, often in federal district court with juries, to the frequent advantage of estates, beneficiaries and those same lawyers.

Illustrative of the bizarre nature of evidence deemed relevant and germane to the question of a decedent's motives in making a transfer shortly prior to death is the case of Kniskern v. United States, 232 F. Supp. 7 (S.D. Fla. 1964), involving a decedent who made substantial gifts at age 99 and died one year later at age 100. The IRS's attempt to include the transferred property, valued at date of death at $157,800, failed. Included in the findings of facts supportive of the court's conclusion that the patriarch was not contemplating death when he made his substantial gifts were the following: (1) he repaired the sprinkler system in his yard; (2) he worked with a sledgehammer to help support fruit trees; (3) he took frequent automobile rides with the maid; (4) he bounced his great-grandchildren on his knees; (5) he frequently attended church and smoked his pipe before services; (6) he was very interested in radio and television; (7) he was proud of his age and condition and boasted of having the physique of a man 25 to 30 years his junior; (8) he had asserted that he was going to make the centennial mark and live even longer; and (9) his minister had testified that "HE WAS FULL OF THE JOY OF LIVING." Id. at 13–17.

It has long been recognized that litigation of the contemplation of death issue was not very sensible or rewarding in a larger social sense. In 1926 Congress attempted to solve the problem with an irrebuttable presumption that gifts made in the last two years of life were in contemplation of death. However, the Supreme Court held that irrebuttable presumption to be unconstitutional in Heiner v. Donnan, 285 U.S. 312 (1932).

As a result, the feeble "contemplation of death" standard was often the lone legal defenseman that stood between octogenarians and the tax advantages of inter vivos gifts. Juries, which passed on the factual issue of whether a gift was in contemplation of death, seemed regularly to show their approval of the spunk of cocky oldsters, who thought they would go on forever, by rarely finding against those who lost the foot race with the grim reaper.

2.   THE 1976 ACT CHANGES

The Tax Reform Act of 1976 changed all of this. Section 2035 was amended to provide that all transfers within the last three years of the decedent's life should be swept into the taxable estate as death-related transfers—along with the gift taxes paid on the gifts. This process of including the gift taxes paid, known as "grossing up," accomplishes the result of treating transfers during the last three years in the same way as the rest of the taxable estate, in the sense that the transfer tax money is included in the tax base. The old and bizarre practice of making gifts in contemplation of death to take the gift tax money out of the taxable estate, while retaining its use as a down payment on the estate tax through the credit for gift tax paid under section 2012, has thus been brought to a complete and deserved end.

3.   THE 1981 ACT AND THE 1997 ACT CHANGES

Gradually, there was awareness that the federal gift tax had truly been integrated by the 1976 Act into a unified transfer tax so that lifetime gifts enter into the computation of the tax payable on the final transfer at death. Thus, there was little need for a provision sweeping deathbed transfers into the taxable estate, since all post-1976 transfers are reflected in the final estate tax return in any case. The Economic Recovery Tax Act of 1981 accepted the view that section 2035 could be largely disarmed without adverse impact on the system. The Taxpayer Relief Act of 1997, with one exception mentioned later, reenacted the changes made to the substance of section 2035 by the 1981 Act and rearranged the various subsections of the statute to produce a sensibly ordered, more user-friendly provision.

The general rule of section 2035, which under the Tax Reform Act of 1976 was a rule of automatic inclusion in the taxable estate, has been drastically altered. The statute now provides that except in certain limited situations there is no special rule of inclusion in the gross estate for deathbed transfers. All such transfers are subject to the gift tax and will, in addition, be reflected in the final estate tax return as lifetime transfers, affecting the tax rate to be applied to the property in the taxable estate. But the valuation of transfers within three years of death will occur at the date of the gift and not, as under former section 2035, at the date of death. Thus, there may be some leakage in terms of escape from transfer tax of the appreciation of the donated property between the date of gift and the date of the donor's death.

The three-year rule is preserved for certain gift tax inclusion transfers described by the language of section 2035(a) as transfers of property with respect to which "the value of such property (or an interest therein) would have been included in the decedent's gross estate under section 2036, 2037, 2038 or 2042 if such transferred interest or relinquished power had been retained by the decedent on the date of his death." In all such cases, the statute calls for inclusion in the decedent's gross estate of the value which would have been included, had the transfer within three years of death not been made.

Since a decedent can now make a large outright gift in the final year, the final month, or the final day of life, and the gift will not be subject to the old rule requiring inclusion of that transfer in the gross estate, one might wonder whether it is sensible to require inclusion in the gross estate when the original transfer was made, perhaps years earlier, and it is only in the final days of life that the retained taxable string is cut. The answer must be that Congress thought the opportunity to enjoy what amounts to constructive ownership of the property for an extended period should not also enable the decedent to avoid transfer tax on appreciation in value enjoyed, in a sense, by the decedent in the final years or days of life. Thus, the target seems to be appreciation of transferred property with respect to which the decedent retained, to within three years of death, enjoyment in some fashion.

It should be noted, as well, that the "grossing-up" rule that calls for putting the gift tax on transfers within three years of death back into the gross estate continues, under section 2035(b), to be operational. In addition, the three-year rule is retained to de-emphasize manipulations of property ownership during the final years of life to achieve certain income or transfer tax advantages under sections 303, 2032A and 6166. A brief explanation of the revision of section 2035, as effected by the Economic Recovery Tax Act of 1981, appears in the House Committee Report on P.L. 97–34, as follows:

> In general, the bill provides that . . . gifts made within 3 years of death will not be included in the decedent's gross estate, and the post-gift appreciation will not be subject to transfer taxes. Accordingly, such property will not be considered to pass from the decedent and the step-up basis rules of section 1014 will not apply.

The committee bill contains exceptions which continue the application of [the old rule] to (1) gifts of life insurance and (2) interests in property otherwise included in the value of the gross estate pursuant to sections 2036, 2037, 2038, * * * or 2042 (or those which would have been included under any of such sections if the interest had been retained by the decedent).

In addition, [under what is now section 2035(c)] all transfers within 3 years of death (other than gifts eligible for the annual gift tax exclusion) will be included for purposes of determining the estate's qualification for special redemption, valuation, and deferral purposes (under secs. 303, 2032A, and 6166) and for purposes of determining property subject to the estate tax liens (under subchapter C of Chapter 64).

Section 2035(c) [now section 2035(b)], requiring the inclusion of all gift taxes paid by the decedent or his estate on any gift made by the decedent or his spouse after December 31, 1976, and within 3 years of death, will continue to apply to all estates.

Effective Date—This provision applies to the estates of decedents dying after December 31, 1981.

As previously mentioned, the 1997 Act rearranged the various subsections of sections 2035 and provided clearer wording of the provision. While extremely helpful, this revision also means that considerable care must be exercised in referring to primary materials, such as cases, and to secondary materials, such as treatises, which may be referring to section 2035 subsections under the pre-1997 version of the law. The 1997 Act added section 2035(e); making a substantive change to the law which impacts transfers from revocable trusts.

B. "GROSSING UP"

As noted above, under section 2035(b) gift taxes paid on gifts made during the last three years of the decedent's life are to be added to the gross estate of the decedent. This process of including the gift taxes paid in the gross estate is known as "grossing up" and has the effect of including the tax money, i.e., the money used to pay the transfer tax, in the tax base. That is the system as respects the estate tax. In contrast, the gift tax, even under the single uniform rate schedule that has prevailed since 1976, is imposed against the amount passing to the donee only, a very different (and favorable to the taxpayer) way of calculating the tax base. Under section 2035(b) the decedent who fails to live three years after the lifetime gift loses the advantage of excluding the transfer tax from the tax base. In other words, the decedent who makes a gift, pays a gift tax and lives three years pays no additional estate tax due to the gift. Were the decedent not to survive for three years after making the gift, however, pursuant to section

2035(b), the amount of any gift tax paid would be included in that decedent's gross estate. In T.A.M. 200432016, the IRS has ruled that where a decedent dies precisely on the same date as a gift made three years previously his gift will not be deemed to have been made "during the 3-year period ending on the date of the decedent's death" as required by section 2035(b), with the result that "grossing up" is not called for in such situation.

The language of section 2035(b) provides for "grossing up" the amount of gift tax paid with respect to a gift within the last three years of life by the "decedent or his estate." In Estate of Sachs v. Commissioner, 88 T.C. 769 (1987), the court was faced with a "net gift," whereby, under the terms of the gift, the gift tax was to be paid by the donee, and was, in fact, so paid. To the estate's argument that it did not have to include the gift tax paid by the donee, the Tax Court turned an unsympathetic ear. The court was of the view that it was entitled to stretch the literal language of section 2035(b) to cover the gift tax payment by the donee to make the system work as Congress intended. A concurring opinion took the view that the donee's payment of the gift tax was really a payment on behalf of the donor who otherwise would have had to make the payment. Surely, the result is in accordance with congressional intent.

Consistent with the rationale of *Estate of Sachs* is Estate of Morgens, 133 T.C. 402 (2009). This case involved a bequest to a spouse that qualified for the marital deduction as a QTIP transfer under section 2056(b)(7) which allows an estate to obtain a marital deduction where one spouse makes a bequest to a surviving spouse under which the survivor is entitled at least annually to all income for life with the remainder bequeathed to parties designated by the deceased spouse. If an election is made to claim the marital deduction in such cases, then the estate of the surviving spouse must include the property in the estate of the surviving spouse for estate tax purposes unless the survivor elects to gift his or her life income interest in the property. Under section 2519, if such a gift is made, there will be a taxable gift by the donor surviving spouse. Although the donor is liable for any such gift tax, he or she is entitled to seek reimbursement for the tax from the persons receiving the property. See I.R.C. 2207A. In *Estate of Morgens*, the surviving spouse made gifts of her income interests in several qualifying trusts and the trusts paid the resulting gift tax. The surviving spouse died within three years of making the gifts and her estate sought to avoid grossing up her estate by the amount of the gift tax paid on the theory that she had not paid the tax. The Tax Court noted that, because the statute imposed the burden of paying the gift tax on the donor, her estate should be grossed up by the amount of the gift tax paid. In so holding the court noted that the situation before it was analogous to that in *Estate of Sachs*.

In Priv. Ltr. Rul. 9128009, the IRS dealt with a situation where a wife joined with her husband in effectively splitting a gift under section 2513, with the wife's one-half of the gift tax paid by the husband. The husband died within three years. The IRS ruled that the gross-up amount includible in the husband's estate consists of both the gift tax directly paid by the husband on his one-half and the gift tax indirectly paid by him on the wife's one-half of the gift. The same result was produced where an aged wealthy husband transferred to his wife money to fund a life insurance trust and sufficient funds to pay the resulting gift tax, with the couple electing to treat the gift of the policy as a split gift under section 2513 and the husband died within three years of making the transfer. The court held that despite the fact that the tax was technically paid by the wife, the step transaction doctrine dictated that the gift tax formally paid by the wife (but indirectly and practically speaking by the husband) be swept back into husband's estate. See Brown v. United States, 329 F.3d 664 (9th Cir. 2003).

Where the estate is unable to pay estate tax because it has insufficient assets on hand, section 6324(a)(2) imposes liability for the tax on the transferees of property included in the gross estate. Frank Armstrong, Jr. transferred most of his substantial wealth by gift to his issue, retaining little more than the $4.7 million needed to pay the federal gift tax. When Armstrong died near penniless within two years of his gift giving binge, his issue took the position that, because estate tax resulted under section 2035 from inclusion in Armstrong's estate of the gift tax paid to the government and not the $9–$10 million in gifts made by Armstrong to them, they, as donees, should not be liable for unpaid estate tax under section 6324(a)(2). The Tax Court rejected this contention in Frank Armstrong III, 114 T.C. 94 (2000), holding that, in such circumstances, donees whose gifts generate estate tax liability under the gross up provisions of section 2035 are to be deemed transferees under section 6324(a)(2). The court also held that the grossing up feature of section 2035(c) violated neither the due process nor the equal protection requirements of the Fifth Amendment of the Constitution.

In the following case, the donees agreed to pay any taxes imposed under section 2035(b) if the decedent passed away within three years of the transfers. These types of gifts are known as "net gifts."

STEINBERG V. COMMISSIONER

United States Tax Court, 2015.
145 T.C. 184.

KERRIGAN, JUDGE:

* * *

The issues for consideration are (1) whether a donee's promise to pay any Federal or State estate tax liability that may arise under section 2035(b) if the donor dies within three years of the gift should be considered in determining the fair market value of the gift, and (2) if so, the amount, if any, that the promise to pay reduces the fair market value of the gift.

* * *

The fair market value of the properties transferred by petitioner to her daughters before consideration of the gift tax liability and section 2035(b) estate tax liability assumed by the daughters was $109,449,307.

* * *

[The petitioner and her daughters entered into a net gift agreement.] To determine the fair market value of the property rights petitioner transferred pursuant to the net gift agreement, petitioner hired William H. Frazier, a qualified appraiser. Mr. Frazier concluded that the aggregate value of the net gift on the date it was made, April 17, 2007, was $71,598,056. He determined that the present value of the net gifts was the fair market value of assets conveyed by transfer from the donor less the liabilities (tax or otherwise) assumed by the donees. According to the valuation, the payment by the donees of their share of the estate taxes is a contingent liability and the probability of this liability can be calculated.

* * *

On July 25, 2011, respondent mailed the notice of deficiency, which increased the aggregate value of petitioner's net gifts to her daughters from $71,598,056 to $75,608,963, for a total gift tax increase of $1,804,908. Respondent disallowed the discount petitioner made for her daughters' assumption of the section 2035(b) estate tax liability. The parties agree that the net gift agreement resulted in a net gift.

* * *

II.   Statutory Framework

A.   Gift Tax Generally

Section 2501(a) imposes a tax on the transfer of property by gift. The donor is primarily responsible for paying the gift tax. *See* Sec. 2502(c); *see also* sec. 25.2502–2, Gift Tax Regs. The gift tax is imposed upon the donor's act of making the transfer, rather than upon receipt by the donee, and it is measured by the value of the property passing from the donor, rather than the value of enrichment resulting to the donee. Sec. 25.2511–2(a), Gift Tax Regs. Donative intent on the part of the donor is not an essential element for gift tax purposes; the application of gift tax is based on the objective facts and circumstances of the transfer rather than the subjective motives of the donor. Sec. 25.2511–1(g)(1), Gift Tax Regs.

The amount of gift tax is based on the aggregate value of taxable gifts made during the year, among other things. * * * The value of the property is the price at which it would change hands between a willing buyer and a willing seller, neither being under any compulsion to buy or to sell and both having reasonable knowledge of the relevant facts. Sec. 25.2512–1, Gift Tax Regs.

* * *

The amount of the gift is the amount by which the value of the property transferred exceeds the value of consideration received in money or money's worth. *See* sec. 2512(b); secs. 25.2511–1(g)(1), 25.2512–8, Gift Tax Regs.; *see also Commissioner v. Wemyss*, 324 U.S. 303, 306–307, 65 S. Ct. 652, 89 L. Ed. 958, 1945 C.B. 416 (1945). Thus, if a donor makes a gift subject to the condition that the donee pay the resulting gift tax, the amount of the gift is reduced by the amount of the gift tax. *See Harrison v. Commissioner*, 17 T.C. 1350, 1357 (1952).

* * *

B.   Section 2035(b) "Gross-Up" Provision

Under section 2035(b) (formerly section 2035(c), amended by the Taxpayer Relief Act of 1997, Pub. L. No. 105–34, sec. 1310(a), 111 Stat. at 1043) a decedent's gross estate is increased by the amount of any gift tax paid by the decedent or the decedent's estate on any gift made by the decedent during the three-year period preceding the decedent's death. For purposes of this "gross-up" provision, we have decided that the phrase "gift tax paid by the decedent or the decedent's estate" during the relevant three-year period includes gift tax attributable to a net gift the decedent made during that period (despite the fact that the donee is responsible for paying the gift tax in that situation). * * *

Congress enacted what is now section 2035(b) as part of an effort to mitigate the disparity of treatment between the taxation of lifetime transfers and transfers at death. [citation omitted] Congress imposed the gross-up provision on gift tax paid within three years of death because "the gift tax paid on a lifetime transfer which is included in a decedent's gross estate is taken into account both as a credit against the estate tax and also as a reduction in the estate tax base, [so] substantial tax savings can be derived under present law by making so-called 'deathbed gifts' even though the transfer is subject to both taxes." [citation omitted] Congress intended the gross-up rule to "eliminate any incentive to make deathbed transfers to remove an amount equal to the gift taxes from the transfer tax base." * * *

C.   Net Gifts

The net gift rationale flows from the basic premise that the gift tax applies to transfers of property only to the extent that the value of the property transferred exceeds the value in money or money's worth of any consideration received in exchange therefor. See sec. 2512(b); sec. 25.2512–8, Gift Tax Regs. When a net gift occurs, the donor calculates his or her gift tax liability by reducing the amount of the gift by the amount of the gift tax. Estate of Morgens v. Commissioner, 133 T.C. 402, 417 (2009), aff'd, 678 F.3d 769 (9th Cir. 2012). The rationale is that "because the donee incurred the obligation to pay the tax as a condition of the gift, 'the donor did not have the intent to make other than a net gift.' " Id.* * * In other words the donor reduces the value of the gift by the amount of the tax because the donor has received consideration for a part of the gift equal to the amount of the applicable gift tax. Id.

* * *

III. Steinberg I

Respondent contends that the daughters' assumption of petitioner's section 2035(b) estate tax liability does not constitute consideration in money or money's worth under section 2512(b). We earlier denied respondent's motion for summary judgment on this point, concluding that the "estate depletion" theory involved material facts that were the subject of genuine dispute. See Steinberg v. Commissioner (Steinberg I), 141 T.C. 258 (2013). In Steinberg I we held that the daughters' assumption of the section 2035(b) estate tax liability might be quantifiable and reducible to monetary value and that a willing buyer and a willing seller, in arriving at a sale price, might take the daughters' assumption of this liability into account in appropriate circumstances. * * *

IV. Consideration of the Promise To Pay

A. A Willing Buyer and a Willing Seller

The fundamental question posed by this case is the fair market value of the property rights transferred under the net gift agreement. Pursuant to section 25.2512–1, Gift Tax Regs., fair market value is the price at which such property would change hands between a willing buyer and a willing seller, neither being under any compulsion to buy or to sell and both having reasonable knowledge of relevant facts. All relevant facts and elements of value as of the time of the gift must be considered. Id. The "willing buyer/willing seller" test is the bedrock of transfer tax valuation. It requires us to determine what property rights are being transferred and on what price a hypothetical willing buyer and willing seller would agree for those property rights.

Pursuant to the net gift agreement (1) the daughters receive property with a fair market value of $109,449,307 and (2) the daughters' have an obligation to pay the $32,012,711 gift tax liability. In Steinberg I we held that a willing buyer and a willing seller in appropriate circumstances could consider the donee's assumption of the section 2035(b) estate tax liability when determining a sale price. 141 T.C. at 281. We now decide whether the net gift agreement is such an appropriate circumstance. An appropriate circumstance arises when the donee's assumption of the section 2035(b) estate tax liability is a detriment to the donee and is a benefit to the donor.

1.   Detriment to the Donee

A willing buyer of the property rights pursuant to the net gift agreement would recognize that to obtain the properties, he or she would also have to assume both the gift tax and the section 2035(b) estate tax liabilities associated with the transfer. The gift tax and the section 2035(b) estate tax liabilities did not exist before the net gift agreement. These liabilities arose as a result of the net gift agreement. The net gift agreement was the product of lengthy negotiations. The daughters had to agree to assume the liabilities in order to gain the benefit of the property they received under the net gift agreement. The donor would not have been willing to transfer the properties without requiring any section 2035(b) estate tax liability to be satisfied.

Any hypothetical recipient of the properties who assumed the liabilities would insist on a reduction of the purchase price to reflect his or her assumption of any section 2035(b) estate tax liability. A similar reduction for valuation purposes is made when a donor makes a gift of his or her interest in an entity with built-in capital gains. See Estate of Davis v. Commissioner, 110 T.C. 530. In Eisenberg, the taxpayer transferred stock in a C corporation to her children. Eisenberg v. Commissioner, 155 F.3d 50, 51–52 (2d Cir. 1998), vacating and remanding T.C. Memo. 1997–483. When she valued the stock for gift tax purposes, she reduced the net asset value of the corporation by the amount of the capital gains tax that she would have incurred if the corporation had liquidated, sold, or distributed its assets. Id. at 52. The Commissioner challenged that reduction and argued that as a matter of law a willing buyer would not consider the built-in capital gains tax liability in the valuation analysis. Id.

The Court of Appeals' reasoning in Eisenberg has been adopted by other Courts of Appeals. See Estate of Jelke v. Commissioner, 507 F.3d 1317 (11th Cir. 2007), vacating and remanding T.C. Memo. 2005–131; Dunn v. Commissioner, 301 F.3d 339 (5th Cir. 2002), rev'g T.C. Memo. 2000–12; Estate of Jameson v. Commissioner, 267 F.3d 366; Estate of Welch v. Commissioner, 208 F.3d 213 (6th Cir. 2000), rev'g T.C. Memo. 1998–167. The Commissioner subsequently acquiesced to the Eisenberg decision. See AOD 1999–01, 1999–1 C.B. xix (Jan. 25, 1999).

* * *

The daughters' assumption of the section 2035(b) estate tax liability is a detriment to the daughters because it might result in reductions in the values of the gifts they received if the donor died within three years of the gifts. As in Eisenberg a hypothetical willing buyer of the properties would recognize that to obtain the properties transferred, he or she would need to assume both the gift tax liability and the section 2035(b) estate tax liability and would demand that the price be reduced to account for both of the liabilities.

* * *

2.   Benefit to the Donor

[The] benefit to the donor in money or money's worth, rather than the detriment to the donee, determines the existence and amount of any consideration offset in the context of an otherwise gratuitous transfer.

* * *

Under Federal tax law the cost of any section 2035(b) estate tax liability is generally borne by the donor's estate and not the donee of the gift. See secs. 2001, 2002, 2035(b), 2501. When petitioner made the gifts to her daughters, petitioner accrued both gift tax liability and the potential section 2035(b) estate tax liability. When the daughters assumed the gift tax liability, petitioner's assets were relieved of the gift tax liability and therefore her estate was replenished. Likewise, when the daughters assumed the section 2035(b) estate tax liability, petitioner's estate was relieved of that estate tax liability. This assumption, which we held in Steinberg I may be reducible to a monetary value, has replenished petitioner's assets. Steinberg I, 141 T.C. at 280.

The daughters' assumption of the section 2035(b) estate tax liability might relieve petitioner's estate of a portion of its estate tax liability. If petitioner died within three years of the gift, her estate would have recourse against the daughters. Accordingly, the willing buyer would demand that price of the properties be reduced to account for the section 2035(b) estate tax liability.

* * *

V.   Fair Market Value of the Daughters' Promise To Pay

Since we find that the daughters' promise to pay any Federal or State estate tax liability that might arise under section 2035(b) if petitioner died within three years of the net gift agreement should be considered in determining the fair market value of the gift, we need to decide what effect the promise has on the fair market value of the gift. Petitioner submitted an expert report that calculates the value of the daughters' assumption of the section 2035(b) liability to be $5,838,540. Respondent did not submit an expert report.

* * *

[The court concluded that a hypothetical willing buyer and willing seller would take into account the daughters' assumption of section 2035(b) estate tax liability in arriving at a sale price. The court further concluded that the daughters' assumption of section 2035(b) estate tax liability reduced the value of petitioner's gift to the daughters by $5,838,540.]

C. LIFE INSURANCE TRANSFERS WITHIN THREE YEARS OF DEATH

Along with gross-up situations, the areas described in section 2035(a) and (c) are the principal areas where the Commissioner and taxpayers will remain keenly concerned about whether a donor survives for three years after making a gift. Moreover, given the importance of life insurance as an asset of significant value in many estates, much interest will focus on the treatment of this asset under section 2035.

Quite clearly, where the decedent purchases from an insurer a life insurance policy and transfers all incidents of ownership in the policy to another individual within three years of death, the proceeds of the policy, and not merely the value of the interpolated terminal reserve, will be included in the gross estate of the decedent pursuant to section 2035(a). Of more interest are situations in which an individual taxpayer, within three years of death, strongly suggested to another person that he or she purchase a policy on the taxpayer's life and then proceeded to furnish that person with the funds necessary to pay the premiums on the policy.

1. PRE-1982 DEATHS

The courts have uniformly agreed that, based on statutory language which predates the present version of section 2035, the following rule applies to decedents dying on or before December 31, 1981. If the decedent was the propelling force in the acquisition of the policy (even if acquired by another) and provided for the payment of premiums, the decedent may be deemed the transferor of the policy with the result that, if death occurred within three years of a "deemed transfer" of a life insurance policy on decedent's life, the proceeds of the policy may be included in the decedent's estate under section 2035. See, e.g., Knisley v. United States, 901 F.2d 793 (9th Cir.1990); Estate of Schnack v. Commissioner, 848 F.2d 933 (9th Cir.1988).

2. POST-1981 DEATHS

The different language employed by Congress in the 1981 Act under section 2035 with respect to transfers made by decedents who die after December 31, 1981, provided the courts with an opportunity to produce a different result.

As a result of the 1981 Act changes, the statute made explicit reference to section 2042 when dealing with the includibility of life insurance under section 2035. The judiciary was thereby given the opportunity to determine if the explicit statutory cross-reference meant that, in the case of life insurance policies, the incidents of ownership test of section 2042 would control. This would mean that, even though the decedent was the propelling force for the acquisition of a policy on her life, if she never possessed (and consequently never transferred) any of the incidents of ownership with respect to the policy within three years prior to her death, there could be no inclusion of policy proceeds in her estate under section 2035.

In a series of decisions handed down in the late 1980s and early 1990s, the judiciary served notice that the language employed by the 1981 Act with respect to decedents dying after 1981 was intended to represent a break with the "deemed transfer" rationale of the pre-1981 Act version of section 2035. See, e.g., Estate of Perry v. Commissioner, 927 F.2d 209 (5th Cir.1991); Estate of Headrick v. Commissioner, 918 F.2d 1263 (6th Cir.1990); and Estate of Leder v. Commissioner, 893 F.2d 237 (10th Cir.1989).

Most instructive of these cases is *Estate of Headrick.* In that case, the decedent, a young tax attorney who had recently obtained an LL.M. from the NYU Graduate Tax Program, had established and funded an irrevocable life insurance trust that acquired a policy on his life. The trustee of the trust held all incidents of ownership from the first moment of its issuance on January 8, 1980. The insured died in an accident on June 19, 1982, less than three years after issuance of the policy. The court held that, since the decedent had never held any of the incidents of ownership of the life insurance policy on his life, he could not and did not transfer them within three years of his death, and the proceeds of the policy were therefore not includible in his gross estate under section 2035. It asserted that the cross-reference to section 2042 in section 2035 with respect to post-1981 deaths indicates that the "incidents of ownership" test of that section is to apply in determining taxation under section 2035. In other words, only if decedent had held, and transferred within three years of his life, incidents of ownership on the policy on his life could the proceeds of the policy be included in his estate under section 2035 for post-1981 deaths. Thus, just as who is the propelling force for issuance of a policy and who provides consideration for payment of premiums is irrelevant under section 2042 (see Chapter 17), so too should it be irrelevant under section 2035. In brief, the cross-reference to section 2042 in the revised version of section 2035 provided by the 1981 Act was viewed as: (1) incorporating tests of that section for purposes of determining the tax treatment of transfers of life insurance under what is now section 2035(a); and (2) rejecting the "deemed transfer" test which applied to pre-1982 deaths. In Tech. Adv. Mem. 9323002 the IRS threw in the towel on this issue with the result that the "deemed transfer" test saw its last with those taxpayers who also saw their last day on or before December 31, 1981.

D. REMAINING ISSUES UNDER SECTION 2035(a)

It should come as no surprise that, with the exception of the previously mentioned life insurance cases, to date there has not been much litigation shedding significant light on what is now section 2035(a). Nonetheless, in addition to consulting some of the recent authorities, it is possible to look to some of the pre-1981 section 2035 cases and authorities to gain some insight into what might still be deemed significant remaining issues under section 2035(a).

1. INDIRECT TRANSFERS

Where an individual controls an entity such as a corporation and the entity makes a gratuitous transfer that, had it been made by the controlling individual, would have been deemed covered by section 2035(a), should such transfer be deemed to have been made by the controlling individual?

In Rev. Rul. 82–141, 1982–2 C.B. 209, the IRS ruled that where the decedent owned 80 percent of the stock of a corporation that transferred ownership of a policy of insurance on his life within three years of death, the transfer was to be charged to the shareholder and included in his gross estate under section 2035. The ruling indicates that the result would be the same regardless of whether the transaction was covered by what is now section 2035(a) or the pre-1981 version of section 2035. Cases consistent with Rev. Rul. 82–141 involving deaths that occurred prior to 1981 are Estate of Porter v. Commissioner, 442 F.2d 915 (1st Cir.1971), and Haneke v. United States, 548 F.2d 1138 (4th Cir.1977).

In Rev. Rul. 90–21, 1990–1 C.B. 172, the IRS amplified Rev. Rul. 82–141. Here, the IRS ruled on two situations. The first situation involved a corporation that, within three years of the death of the decedent-insured, made a gift of a life insurance policy on the life of the insured. At the time of the gift, the insured held 80 percent of the stock of the corporation. Shortly before his death, the insured gave his controlling interest in the corporation to his child. The IRS ruled that the gift of stock did not change the result produced by Rev. Rul. 82–141 and the policy proceeds were included in the donor's estate. In the second situation, the insured-decedent, who also owned 80 percent of the stock of a corporation that owned a policy on the life of the insured payable to a child of the insured, gave most of his stock in the corporation to a third party within three years of his death. Piercing through the corporate veil, the IRS included in the decedent's taxable estate the full value of the policy proceeds.

2. AMOUNT INCLUDED

Where an inclusion in the gross estate results because of the application of section 2035(a), an issue may arise as to the value of the property to be included in the estate in a situation in which the transferred property was sold after the transfer and either the transferred property, or the property purchased as a replacement, fluctuated wildly in value. For example, assume that a taxpayer who had retained a life estate with respect to Blackacre subsequently transferred her life estate to her children and failed to live the required three years. Assume also that the children, who also owned the remainder interest, sold Blackacre immediately before it doubled in value and replaced it with bonds that did not change in value. What value is to be included in the taxpayer's estate? Similarly, difficult issues are presented by income realized on transferred property, as well as stock dividends and redemptions.

ESTATE OF HUMPHREY V. COMMISSIONER
United States Court of Appeals, Fifth Circuit, 1947.
162 F.2d 1.

SIBLEY, CIRCUIT JUDGE.

The case relates to the estate taxes of Albert P. Humphrey, who died testate February 23, 1942, the reported value of his estate being $185,475. On January 18, 1941, within two years prior to his death, decedent and his wife each made cash gifts to their two sons of $40,000. The Commissioner included this $40,000 in the gross estate of decedent and taxed it. The Tax Court sustained this action * * *

The Tax Court made no finding of the value at decedent's death of the property so transferred. The evidence is that the two sons took the $80,000 given by their parents and combined it with $80,000 of their own and by their operations prior to their father's death had lost about half of the $160,000 capital. It is therefore contended that $20,000 rather than $40,000 is to be included in this estate for taxation. I.R.C. § 811, supra, says that all included property, real or personal, tangible or intangible, is to be valued at the time of decedent's death. Regulation 105, Sec. 81.15, declares more specifically that *transferred property* in the estate is to be valued at the *date of decedent's death.* The evident purpose is to make the transferred property cause the same tax result as if the decedent had kept it till he died instead of transferring it. We do not accede to the argument that if the transferee injures or makes way with it, it shall be considered that he has acted as the agent of the decedent, or that he may substitute it by other property of less value. What is to be valued at the time of decedent's death is the very property which the decedent transferred. He transferred $40,000, and its money value was the same in 1942 as in 1941. No finding to that effect was needed. That the transferees may have lost some of it does not diminish the sum that was transferred. The Commissioner's inclusion of the $40,000 value was demanded as a matter of law.

Affirmed.

NOTES

1. In a later ruling, Rev. Rul. 72–282, 1972–1 C.B. 305, the IRS dealt with the situation where a gift two years before the death of the decedent consisted of shares of stock that was sold by the donee and reinvested with spectacular results. But the IRS ruled that the value to be included in the decedent's gross estate was the value of the original shares transferred and not the value of the newly acquired stock purchased by the son with the proceeds of the sale of the original shares. The ruling states, "The value of stock acquired by subsequent independent actions of the donee is not that which is includible in the decedent's gross estate, despite the fact that the stock now owned by the donee can be attributed to the proceeds of the sale of the transferred property. Rather, what is includible is the present value of the property originally transferred by the decedent."

2. In Estate of DeWitt v. Commissioner, 68 T.C.M. (CCH) 1136 (1994), the Tax Court was called upon to determine the proper amount to be included under section 2035 where the decedent, prior to December 31, 1981, had funded a trust for the benefit of her son with $250,000 in cash and the trust had invested in assets which by decedent's death 17 months later had declined in value to $187,500. Since the decedent had transferred to her son an interest in trust, and not $250,000, the Tax Court concluded that it was the value of that interest ($187,500) which was to be included in decedent's estate under section 2035.

COMMISSIONER V. ESTATE OF GIDWITZ

United States Court of Appeals, Seventh Circuit, 1952.
196 F.2d 813.

SWAIM, CIRCUIT JUDGE.

[The Tax Court found that the transfer by the decedent was in contemplation of death. Factors supporting this conclusion were the age of the decedent at the time of transfer (72), the circumstance that he had suffered a heart attack previously, the fact that under the transfer the beneficiaries could not enjoy the property during the life of the transferor, and the fact that the transfers were made so as to equalize the holdings of his sons. On appeal the Court of Appeals affirmed the Tax Court decision that the transfer was in contemplation of death. That portion of the Circuit Court's opinion is omitted here. Another question of some importance concerned the amount of property to be hauled back into the taxable estate under § 2035. That question was dealt with as follows:]

The Commissioner insists that the Tax Court erred in not including in the decedent's gross estate the income, together with property purchased by such income, which accrued in the trust prior to the decedent's death. When Gidwitz died the total assets in the trust had a value of $341,102.02. The original shares of stock transferred to the trust had a valuation of

$140,610. The difference of $200,492.02 represented the value of accrued income and property purchased for the trust with accrued income.

The Commissioner, while admitting that the statute places in the gross estate only property *transferred* by the decedent, bases the Government's claim that the valuation of the gross estate should include all income received by the trust prior to the decedent's death on the theory that the property transferred to the trust in 1936 included not only the ownership of the 83 1/3 shares of stock but also a separate property right to receive the income on the stock. It is argued that the value of this property right to receive income is measured by the income accumulated in the trust prior to the decedent's death.

The same theory advanced by the Commissioner in this case was rejected by the Supreme Court in Maass v. Higgins, 312 U.S. 443. The *Maass* case involved two estates where the executors had elected to have the gross estates valued as of one year after the decedents' deaths, pursuant to 26 U.S.C.A. § 811(j) [now § 2032]. During the year after the decedents' deaths the executors had collected interest and dividends on bonds and stocks belonging to the estates. The Commissioner determined tax deficiencies against the estates for failures to include these collections as part of the gross estates. A Treasury regulation, then being enforced, required the return and inclusion of such income as a part of the gross estate. The Supreme Court, while recognizing that a bond embodies two promises to pay—one to pay the principal at maturity and the other to pay interest periodically—and while recognizing that the income factor affects the value of a security, said, at page 448:

> "But these elements are not separately valued in appraising the worth of the asset at any given time."

The Supreme Court there, at page 447, agreed with the taxpayer:

> " * * * that the Government's position is unreal and artificial; that it does not comport either with economic theory or business practice; and that the regulation is an unwarranted extension of the plain meaning of the statute and cannot therefore, be sustained."

In Humphrey's Estate v. Commissioner, 5 Cir. 162 F.2d 1, the donees of an *inter vivos* gift made in contemplation of death, by an improvident investment, lost one-half of the amount of the gift. It was contended that the half of the property lost should not be included in the decedent's gross estate. The Court held, however, that it was the *transferred* property which was to be valued at the time of the decedent's death. The Court said, at page 2:

> "What is to be valued at the time of decedent's death is *the very property which the decedent transferred.*" (Italics by court)

In Burns v. Commissioner, 5 Cir. 177 F.2d 739, affirming Estate of James E. Frizzell, 9 T.C. 979, a father established an irrevocable trust and, in contemplation of death, made an *inter vivos* gift of certain shares of the stock of the Coca Cola Company to the trust. The trustee invested part of the income from the trust in other stocks and bonds prior to the donor's death. The Court accepted the conclusion of the Tax Court that part of the corpus of the trust which represented income received prior to the death of the donor, or property acquired with such income, had not been *transferred* by the decedent and, therefore, should not be included in the decedent's gross estate for estate tax purposes. The Court said, at page 741:

> "The tax statute in question should be strictly construed in favor of the taxpayer, and since it does not expressly provide for the inclusion of income derived from the *transferred* property in the gross estate, it is not our prerogative, by judicial fiat, to give it that effect. Title 26 U.S.C.A., Sections 811(c), 811(j). (Citing cases.)" (Italics by court)

As against the principles announced in the above cases the Commissioner cites decisions involving other provisions of the Internal Revenue Code which admittedly deal with transfers intended to take effect in possession or enjoyment at or after death, or in which the grantor had retained until death the power to designate the persons who would enjoy the property, or in which the grantor had retained until death the power to alter, amend or revoke. The Commissioner admits that such transfers are included in the gross estate on the theory that such a transfer does not become complete and effective until death, whereas a transfer in contemplation of death is included because of the motive inducing it. The Commissioner argues that the same rules should apply in both classes of cases. Such an argument ignores the realities of the two types of transfers.

In transfers made in contemplation of death, such as in the instant case, the donor has made an actual transfer during his life. The transfer became effective at that time. The transfer was irrevocable. The terms of the trust agreement expressly prohibited any change in the provisions of the agreement which would in any manner effect a change relating to the distribution, disposition, possession or enjoyment of the trust property. Here the income was paid to the trust because it belonged to the trust, not to Gidwitz. The income was payable to the trust and belonged to the trust as an incident of the ownership by the trust of the stock transferred to the trust by Gidwitz in 1936. The Tax Court correctly held that such income and the property acquired with such income should not be included in the decedent's gross estate for estate tax purposes.

In both of these petitions for review the decision of the Tax Court is affirmed.

NOTES

1. One might ask if the result in *Gidwitz* should prevail where, under section 2035(a), a "severed string" is involved under a provision such as sections 2036 or 2038 and, had no gift been made, a different result would prevail under those sections with respect to retained income or property purchased with retained income? Should the result depend on whether the retained income was realized prior to, or after, the severance of the string? We all await judicial enlightenment on these issues.

2. In Rev. Rul. 80–336, 1980–2 C.B. 271, the IRS ruled that where a corporation, the stock of which was the object of a gift covered by section 2035, makes a one-for-two stock dividend, both the original stock and the dividend stock are included in the estate. In McGehee v. Commissioner, 260 F.2d 818 (5th Cir. 1958), the court distinguished between stock dividends representing pre-and post-gift earnings, including only those reflective of the former.

E. REVOCABLE TRUSTS

1. THE PARAMETERS OF THE PROBLEM

Nontax estate planning goals, such as avoidance of probate, protection of privacy or coping with incompetency, frequently result in individuals contributing a significant portion of their estates to revocable trusts. Often the grantors of such trusts are their sole beneficiaries. On other occasions the beneficiaries include not only the grantor but other individuals. In the past decade there was flurry of judicial decisions and administrative releases regarding how post-1981 transfers from such trusts should be treated under what is now section 2035(a). In 1997, Congress decided to weigh in on the topic with the passage of section 2035(e).

Prior to the passage of section 2035(e), decedents who had created revocable trusts designating themselves as beneficiaries, provided the IRS with the opportunity to argue that at their death, under what is now section 2035(a), all gratuitous transfers from the trust within three years of death were to be taxed as transfers described in section 2038. Had the IRS prevailed with this argument, it would have meant that decedents who had conveyed their assets to such a trust for the simple purpose of avoiding probate and then made gifts from the trust within three years of their death would have suffered adverse tax consequences when compared to decedents who had not transferred their assets to such a trust and had followed an identical pattern of gift giving in the three years prior to their death.

There would have been two important consequences for taxpayers had the IRS prevailed in including in decedent-grantor's estate (under what is now section 2035(a)) all transfers from such revocable trust under which the decedent-grantor had retained the power to revest title in herself. First, the benefit of the annual exclusion would have been lost to the taxpayer. For example, assume that Grandma had placed all her assets in such a trust to avoid probate and made gifts of $10,000 from the trust to each of four grandchildren for two years prior to her death. Had the IRS position been accepted, the full $80,000 would have been swept back into her estate. Of course, had Grandma never been concerned about using a revocable trust to avoid probate and had she merely retained direct title to her property and made the same gifts to her grandchildren, the $80,000 so gifted would not have been swept back into her estate. Second, where the value of property gifted from such a revocable trust increased by the date of death, if what is now section 2035(a) could have been used to effect an inclusion of the gifted property in decedent-grantor's estate, the principles set forth earlier in this section would indicate that the increased amount be included in decedent's estate. For example, assume that Grandma, after placing all her assets in a revocable trust, decided to give, from trust assets, 100 shares of XYZ stock worth $10,000 to Grandson and that the stock increased in value to $30,000 by the date of Grandma's death. Ignoring the presence of the annual exclusion, had the IRS prevailed in applying section 2035(a) to the transfer, the full $30,000 in value would have been included in Grandma's estate. As in the case of the previously mentioned gifts, had Grandma held the stock directly and gifted it to Grandson, nothing would have been included in her estate under section 2035.

The principal test of this IRS theory came in Estate of Jalkut v. Commissioner, 96 T.C. 675 (1991), acq. 1991–2 C.B.1. Lee Jalkut, the decedent, in 1971 conveyed most of his assets to a revocable trust designed to act as a will substitute. Jalkut was the trustee and sole beneficiary of the trust. Acting pursuant to powers he had retained, Jalkut subsequently amended the trust to provide that during his lifetime all income and so much of the principal as he requests shall be paid to him. In the event of Jalkut's incapacity, successor trustees were authorized to make distributions for Jalkut's benefit and for the benefit of his descendants and historically favored charities and private donees. In late 1984 Jalkut, after being diagnosed as having a terminal disease, made transfers from his revocable trust to various irrevocable trusts created for benefit of his issue. In early 1985, shortly after Jalkut was declared incapable of serving as trustee and several days prior to his death, Jalkut's successor trustees made additional gifts to these same irrevocable trusts.

The Tax Court refused to include in Jalkut's gross estate, under what is now section 2035(a), the transfers from the revocable trust made by Jalkut in 1984 on the theory that, because he was the sole permissible distributee from the trust, the transaction must be treated as a transfer from the trust to Jalkut followed by a transfer from him to the ultimate donees. Since the final transfer to the donees was not from a revocable trust it could not be deemed described in section 2038 and consequently escaped tax under what is now section 2035(a).

In contrast, the Tax Court held the 1985 transfers made by the successor trustees were not required to be, and in fact could not be, treated as withdrawals made by Jalkut followed by transfers by him to the ultimate donees. The court held that these transfers must be deemed transfers described in section 2038 which occurred within three years of decedent's death with the result that they were to be taxed under what is now section 2035(a).

Despite the IRS's limited loss in *Jalkut* with respect to the 1984 transfers, the Tax Court's formalistic reading of the statute and especially its treatment of the 1985 transfers provided the IRS with encouragement to argue that, in a variety of circumstances which differed slightly from the 1984 transfers, it was appropriate to include within the estate, under what is now section 2035(a), transfers from revocable trusts where the power was retained to revest title in the decedent-grantor. It could and did argue that inclusion under what is now section 2035(a) was appropriate where: (1) as in the case of the 1985 transfers, appointment could be made to beneficiaries in addition to the decedent; (2) the decedent accomplished a transfer to others merely by relinquishing a power to revoke and did not actually withdraw property from the revocable trust to effect the transfer; or (3) the decedent exercised her power of revocation to create separate irrevocable accounts within the revocable trust for the benefit of her donees. The IRS met defeat with respect to a number of such endeavors. See Kisling v. Commissioner, 32 F.3d 1222 (8th Cir. 1994); McNeely v. United States, 16 F.3d 303 (8th Cir. 1994); Estate of Barton v. Commissioner, 66 T.C.M. (CCH) 1547 (1993). Nonetheless, taxpayers were uncertain as to precisely where the line would ultimately be drawn by the judiciary.

To quiet the issue Congress, in 1997, added to the Code section 2035(e) which addresses the taxation, under both sections 2035(a) and 2038, of transfers by a decedent-grantor from revocable trusts where the right to revest the grantor in title has been retained.

2. THE STATUTORY SOLUTION

Section 2035(e) provides that, in the case of qualifying revocable trusts, a transfer from the trust to other parties shall be treated as a transfer made directly by the decedent. The revocable trusts which qualify for this benefit are those that, under section 676, are treated as owned by the decedent by reason of a power in the grantor to revest title of trust corpus in the grantor. The principal consequence of section 2035(e) is to ensure that where a decedent had placed property in a trust, retaining the power to revest herself with title to the property, and within three years of her death made gifts from such trust, neither section 2035(a) nor section 2038 shall operate to include within her estate any such gifts to the extent excluded from the gift tax by the annual exclusion. Another consequence of the addition of section 2035(e) is to repeal that portion of the *Jalkut* opinion which deals with the 1985 transfers. It is now irrelevant whether the decedent-grantor or a third party, such as a guardian or other fiduciary acting on the decedent's behalf, made the transfers from the qualifying revocable trust and whether the trust allowed transfers to be made to beneficiaries other than the decedent. In neither case shall they be included in the decedent's estate under sections 2035(a) or 2038 solely because they were made within three years of death. It is also irrelevant whether the transfers were accomplished: (1) by withdrawal; (2) by relinquishment of a power to revoke; or (3) by creation of segregated irrevocable accounts within the trust. Moreover, the legislative history indicates that Congress intended that, in addition to not effecting an inclusion of gifts or a portion of gifts excluded from gift taxation by the annual exclusion, section 2035(e) would operate to disregard post gift appreciation with respect to transfers from qualifying revocable trusts. S. Rep. No. 105–33 at 682–684 (1997). In the final analysis the principal impact of section 2035(e) is to treat property held by a revocable inter vivos trust, which is intended to function as a will substitute, as if the property were held directly by the decedent-grantor.

F. SECTION 1014(e)—AN INCOME TAX WRINKLE

Section 1014(e), which was added to the Code in 1981, is an interesting provision. Under section 1014, individuals who receive property from a decedent at death by devise, bequest or inheritance will, in general, receive a basis in the property equal to its fair market value at the decedent's death. Section 1014 is typically referred to as the "stepped-up basis" rule. It should be kept in mind that the rule also results in a stepped-down basis where property has declined in value prior to the decedent's death.

The stepped-up basis rule permits a family to escape income tax on built-in gain where a decedent transfers appreciated property to a family member on his or her deathbed. The current basic exclusion amount of $11,580,000 permits many wealthy decedents to strategically hold onto appreciated property until death without being subjected to an estate tax while enabling their beneficiaries to escape income tax liability because of the stepped-up basis on the built-in gain.

The unlimited marital gift and estate tax deductions that were brought to us by the 1981 Tax Act meant that married couples with one spouse at death's door could achieve a stepped-up basis at no gift or estate tax cost. For example, assume that a wife is on her deathbed and that her husband has $300,000 worth of stock that he purchased for $50,000. If he were assured of his wife's loyalty and cooperation and if the simple stepped-up basis rule were available to him, he could give the stock to his wife and at her death acquire a basis in the stock equal to its then-fair market value. Section 1014(e) was added to the Code to bar that result.

In general, under section 1014(e), if a donor gives appreciated property to a donee who dies within one year of the gift, no stepped-up basis is effected under section 1014 if the appreciated property is inherited by the donor or if such property is sold by the estate of the deceased and the donor is entitled to the proceeds of the sale.

Several observations are in order. First, a married couple that wishes to attempt to attain a stepped-up basis in a situation in which death is imminent has everything to win, from a tax standpoint, and nothing to lose. If the ill spouse lives for a year and a day after the gift, the couple will attain a tax-free stepped-up basis. If death comes earlier, the couple will have lost nothing from a tax standpoint. It is only under the Internal Revenue Code that an early death could be characterized as a no-loss situation.

Second, by the donee's leaving the gift property to other than the donor, section 1014(e) is easily avoided. For example, take the case of our previously mentioned couple with $300,000 of appreciated stock. Assume that the husband gives the stock to his wife and that the wife's will provides for a credit shelter trust, a relatively common estate planning device. The credit shelter trust names the couple's children as the beneficiaries of that trust. The balance of the wife's estate is then left to her husband. As its title implies, the credit shelter trust will be funded with an amount sufficient to take advantage of some, or all, of the wife's unused unified credit, which means that, in the absence of significant inter vivos gift giving by the wife, a considerable amount will be transferred to the trust for the benefit of the children. If the wife's will provides that, in the event she dies within one year of the date of the gift, her credit shelter trust is to be funded with, among other things, the $300,000 of appreciated stock that the husband gave to her, section 1014(e) will be rendered ineffectual, and the family will reap an enormous potential income tax saving at no estate or gift tax cost. The same result could, presumably, be obtained even if the wife's will contained no such direction with respect to the funding of her credit shelter trust so long as her executor decided to fund the trust with the appreciated gift property. About the only risk in all of this is that the wife, on her deathbed, might decide to disinherit the entire miserable bunch and either leave her estate to other individuals or buy her way past the pearly gates with substantial charitable gifts.

PLANNING NOTE

For some decedents, the failure of the post-1981 version of section 2035 to include within the decedent's estate all gifts made within three years of death has the unhappy result of depriving them of a windfall stepped-up basis which they otherwise would have realized under the pre-1981 statute. Prior to 1981, the automatic inclusion in the estate of all gifts made within three years of death resulted in a stepped-up basis for all such assets. The 1981 changes deprived taxpayers of this potential benefit unless inclusion in the estate results under section 2035(a). However, a clever estate planner who wishes to assist a terminally ill client in making an inter vivos gift that qualifies for the stepped-up basis can cause the transfer to be taxed under section 2035(a) by creating a revocable transfer, which will thereby be includible in the taxable estate, as a transfer described in section 2038, thus assuring the client's donee of a stepped-up basis so long as death comes within three years of any relinquishment of the power to revoke. For example, assume that an aged, ill donor wishes to make an inter vivos gift of a vastly appreciated vacation home to a child. By making a revocable gift of the house to the child, the donor can assure that the child will realize a stepped-up basis upon the donor's death so long as the power of revocation remains outstanding. Moreover, even if the power of revocation is surrendered, so long as the donor dies within three years of surrender, a stepped-up basis will be available. Care must be taken, of course, to avoid loss of a stepped-up basis through application of the step transaction doctrine to the gift and subsequent surrender of the power of revocation.

PROBLEMS

1. Christina made a gift of stock to Nora eighteen months ago. At the time of the gift, the stock was worth $500,000 and Christina paid $155,800 of gift tax on the transaction. At Christina's death six months ago, the stock was worth $600,000. What value is included in Christina 's estate.

2. Tony took out a $1,000,000 life insurance policy on his life 10 years ago. Last year, when the policy's interpolated terminal reserve was worth $400,000, Tony gave the policy to his son, Chase. Tony paid $100,000 in gift tax on the transaction. At Tony's death last month, Chase, who was both the full owner of the policy and sole beneficiary, was paid $1,000,000. What amount is included in Tony's estate.

3. Monica, the mother of Debbie, urged Debbie, in the fall of last year, to purchase a $500,000 policy on Monica's life. Debbie paid for the premiums on the policy with income from a trust that was funded by Monica. Monica died last week. Are the $500,000 in proceeds taxable in her estate?

4. Eight years ago, Charlie established a trust under which he retained income for his life with remainder to his son Ken. On finding that he had a terminal disease, Charlie transferred his life interest to Ken. The trust's sole asset then consisted of an apartment house. At the time of the transfer, Charlie's life estate was worth $450,000 and Ken's remainder interest was worth $300,000. Charlie paid $150,000 in gift tax on the transfer. At Charlie's death 15 months later, the value of the trust's assets (the same apartment house) was $1,200,000. What value, if any, is includible in Charlie's taxable estate?

5. Emma was sole shareholder of Acme, Inc., which held a $250,000 term insurance policy on Emma's life payable to her son, Alex. Two years ago, when the stock of Acme was worth $1,000,000, Emma gave the stock to Alex and paid a gift tax of $400,000 on the transfer. At Emma's death last month Acme, exclusive of the insurance policy, was worth $1,300,000. Shortly after Emma's death Blitzkrieg Insurance paid Alex $250,000 in policy proceeds. What value, if any, is includible in Emma's estate?

6. During 2015, Alan created an irrevocable trust and transferred $1,000,000 worth of stock to the trust. Alan served as trustee. Under the terms of the trust, income was payable to Alan's son for life. Upon the son's death, the corpus was to be paid to Alan's granddaughter. The trustee had the discretion at any time to distribute any or all of the corpus to the granddaughter for her best interest. During 2021, Alan resigned as the trustee, and a successor trustee was appointed. Alan died in 2023. At the time of his death, the stock was worth $2,500,000.

CHAPTER 24

CONSIDERATION IN MONEY
OR MONEY'S WORTH

■ ■ ■

A. INTRODUCTION

In addition to the property owned by the decedent at the time of death, the federal estate tax reaches a variety of lifetime transfers, as have already been explored, that may serve as substitutes for testamentary disposition—joint tenancies, life insurance, some gifts within three years of death, retained life estates, certain reversionary interest trusts geared to the grantor's life and trusts amendable by the grantor while the grantor lives. These lifetime transfers have one element in common. They deplete the probate estate while serving as testamentary substitutes—hence their taxability.

In contrast, lifetime transfers for value do not deplete the prospective estate tax base and, therefore, such transfers are not subject to estate taxation. Similarly, with respect to claims deductible by the estate, a requirement that claims be based on a valuable consideration serves to protect the estate tax base from depletion by the deduction of claims enforceable at law (under seal or with formal consideration recited) but representing estate depleting testamentary substitutes. See I.R.C. § 2053(c)(1)(A).

To perform the function of separating the nondepleting transfers and claims for value from the estate-depleting type of gratuitous transfers or claims, the estate tax prescribes a test of "consideration in money or money's worth." This concept appears in a variety of settings. See I.R.C. §§ 2036 & 2037 (taxing certain transfers "except in the case of a bona fide sale for an adequate and full consideration in money or money's worth"). Similar language appears in sections 2035 and 2038. In addition, under section 2043 the rule is prescribed for transfers falling under sections 2036, 2037 and 2038 that are only partially supported by a consideration in money or money's worth.

Finally, section 2043(b)(1) provides that "[f]or purposes of this chapter, a relinquishment or promised relinquishment of dower or curtesy, or of a statutory estate created in lieu of dower or curtesy, or of other marital rights in the decedent's property or estate, shall not be considered to any extent a consideration 'in money or money's worth'."

B. CONSIDERATION RECEIVED

Section 2043(a) provides that transfers or powers under sections 2035 through 2038 that are created, exercised, or relinquished for consideration in money or money's worth that is not a bona fide sale for an adequate and full consideration, the amount included in the decedent's gross estate is the excess of the fair market value of the property over the fair market value of the consideration received by the decedent. The following case considers whether consideration given by a decedent when a power is created is relevant under section 2043(a).

ESTATE OF FROTHINGHAM V. COMMISSIONER
United States Tax Court, 1973.
60 T.C. 211.

The Commissioner determined a $103,046.62 deficiency in the estate tax of the Estate of C(harles) Mifflin Frothingham. As part of a compromise of a will contest [involving the will of decedent's cousin, George Mifflin] the decedent acquired a general power of appointment in respect of a property interest valued at $856,330.01 as of the date of his own death. He exercised that power by will without receiving any consideration, and the property subject to it was includable in his gross estate under section 2041 of the 1954 Code, unless rendered nontaxable by section 2043(a). The principal issue is whether section 2043(a) is applicable by reason of consideration *given* by the decedent in connection with the creation of the power, or whether the consideration referred to in section 2043(a) relates only to consideration *received* by the decedent.

* * *

RAUM, JUDGE:

There is no dispute between the parties that the decedent at his death had a "general power of appointment" over an asset having a value of $856,330.01, that he exercised that power of appointment, and that section 2041 calls for the inclusion of the amount in his gross estate unless some other provision of the statute requires a different result. Petitioner contends, however, that the property passing under the decedent's power is excludable from his gross estate by reason of section 2043(a) * * *.

It is petitioner's theory that the compromise agreement through which George's will was amended to grant the decedent the power of appointment here in issue represented a "bona fide sale for an adequate and full consideration in money or money's worth," and that therefore section 2043(a) renders section 2041(a) inoperative. The requisite consideration, the argument goes, is to be found in the decedent's bargained-for relinquishment of the interest he had sought as George's heir by intestacy. The Commissioner argues that whether the decedent *paid* any consideration for the power of appointment is irrelevant, that the "adequate and full consideration" clause in section 2043(a) refers only to consideration *received* by the decedent in connection with the property passing under the power at his death, that he received no consideration in that respect, and that section 2041(a) remains operative, unaffected by section 2043(a). We hold that the Commissioner is correct.

It is important that the structure of the estate tax statute and the part played therein by the "adequate and full consideration" clause be kept clearly in mind. Sections 2035–2038 deal with various types of inter vivos transfer that are regarded as testamentary in character and are therefore included in a decedent's gross estate—e.g., transfers in contemplation of death, transfers taking effect at death, and revocable transfers. In each case the property transferred is includable in the gross estate, but in each of the sections 2035–2038 there is a parenthetical clause rendering the provisions inoperative "in case of a bona fide sale for an adequate and full consideration in money or money's worth." This clause first appeared in the estate tax law in the Revenue Act of 1926. See, e.g., sec. 302(c) of that Act.

The obvious purpose of the clause was to relieve of estate tax those transfers, etc., in respect of which the decedent-transferor had *received* an equivalent amount of consideration. Thus, where the transferred property is replaced by other property of equal value received in exchange, there is no reason to impose an estate tax in respect of the transferred property, for it is reasonable to assume that the property acquired in exchange will find its way into the decedent's gross estate at his death unless consumed or otherwise disposed of in a nontestamentary transaction in much the same manner as would the transferred property itself had the transfer not taken place. Stated differently, the aim of the "consideration" provisions in the Federal gift and estate tax laws "was to prevent the depletion of the transferor's or decedent's estate, unless a tax was paid on the transfer, by requiring that the transferor or decedent receive in exchange something of the same money value." Commissioner v. Bristol, 121 F.2d 129, 134 (1st Cir.).

In short, unless replaced by property of equal value that could be exposed to inclusion in the decedent's gross estate, the property transferred in a testamentary transaction of the type described in the statute must be included in his gross estate. The only consideration involved is the consideration *received* by the decedent. The consideration, if any, given by the decedent is of no greater consequence than the amount, if any, that he may have paid for property which he owns at his death and which is included in his gross estate at its fair market value as of that time. It is with the foregoing as background that the meaning and scope of section 2043(a) must be examined.

* * * It was plainly designed to deal with the situation where the decedent has received some, but not "adequate and full," consideration for the transfer. In providing that there shall be included in the gross estate "only the excess of the fair market value at the time of death of the property * * * over the value of the consideration *received* therefor by the decedent" (emphasis supplied), Congress was obviously attempting merely to provide a measure of relief from double taxation of the same economic interest. We have found no support whatever for petitioner's contention that Congress may have intended to relieve from estate tax property passing under a general power of appointment that was "created" for a consideration supplied by the decedent himself.

Petitioner merely isolates the word "created" in section 2043(a) and assumes that since the power of appointment in issue was "created" for an "adequate and full" consideration furnished by the decedent at the time of the dispute with respect to George's will, the property passing under that power may not be included in his gross estate. Petitioner argues that a literal reading of the statute requires that result. We disagree. The language of section 2043(a) certainly does not call for that interpretation. Section 2043(a) is concerned not only with powers of appointment but also with transfers of the character dealt with in sections 2035–2038, and it seems likely that the word "created" was intended to relate to "trusts" or "interests" involving such transfers for which the decedent received consideration, rather than to powers of appointment. The portion of section 2043(a) that more appropriately relates to "powers" is the language "exercised, or relinquished for a consideration in money or money's worth"—language that clearly contemplates the *receipt* of consideration by the decedent, not the payment of consideration by him. And finally, the last clause in section 2043(a) refers explicitly to "the consideration received therefor by the decedent."

* * *

NOTE

Courts will consider the true substance of a transfer to determine whether there is a bona fide sale for an adequate and full consideration. See, e.g., Estate of Maxwell v. Commissioner, 3 F.3d 591 (2d Cir. 1993). The *Maxwell* case is discussed in Chapter 18.

C. CHILD SUPPORT AS CONSIDERATION

As discussed in Chapter 18, courts have determined that property is not included in the gross estate under section 2036 where trusts have been established by a noncustodial parent for the support of minor issue of a dissolved marriage because the discharge of the support obligation provides the consideration necessary to put the trust beyond the reach of section 2036. Occasionally, grantors of such trusts will retain rights (e.g., a contingent life estate) or powers (e.g., a power to alter, amend, or revoke) with respect to such trusts that will result in their being included in the grantor's estate. The question that then arises is how much of the value of the support trust is to be excluded because the discharge of the support obligation provided adequate consideration for establishment of all or a portion of the trust. The following case addresses this issue.

ESTATE OF MCDONALD V. COMMISSIONER
Tax Court of the United States, 1953.
19 T.C. 672.

TIETJENS, JUDGE:

[Decedent, on separation from his wife, created a trust (Trust 924) for the purpose of first providing support and maintenance for his children during their minority. They were income beneficiaries thereafter and entitled to the corpus on reaching the age of 35. Decedent reserved the power to alter, amend and revoke the trust in conjunction with his divorced wife. The Commissioner took the position that the entire trust property should be included in the decedent's gross estate. The first issue, as to whether the trust assets had been community property and therefore not entirely owned by the decedent, was resolved against the decedent. Accordingly, the Tax Court now addresses the issue of whether the transfer in trust had been made for consideration.]

The parties are in apparent agreement that in the event we hold that decedent was the transferor of the assets to Trust 924, the value of such assets is includible in the gross estate unless the transfer of all or some part thereof was made for an adequate and full consideration in money or money's worth.

The question, then, is whether the transfer to Trust 924, or any part thereof, was made for "money's worth." In dealing with gift tax questions and questions involving claims deductible in determining gross estate where the statutory language is similar to the language used in section 811(i) [now section 2043] it has been held and recognized that transfers of property or contracts entered into for the support of children by the father are made for "money's worth." On this point both parties cite Helvering v. United States Trust Co., 111 Fed. (2d) 576 (2d Cir.1940), reversing on another issue and remanding 39 B. T. A. 783, certiorari denied 311 U.S. 678. * * *

The *United States Trust Co.* case involved the question of whether any part of a trust fund was includible in the gross estate of decedent under the then equivalent of section 811(d)(2) [now section 2038] of the Internal Revenue Code. In that case decedent had become estranged from his wife some years before he died, and in contemplation of a divorce he made an agreement with her on January 31, 1929, by which he agreed to pay her $2,500 a month during her life, out of which she was to support herself without further recourse to him, and, in addition, to support, maintain, and educate her daughter during the time the said daughter resided with her. The child was to spend half her time with her father and half with her mother, and the testator agreed to assume certain of her expenses while she was with her mother. The amount of $2,500 per month was fixed by the parties as the approximate amount reasonably required for the support of the wife and daughter in accordance with their station in life and with the decedent's ability to furnish such support. The stipulation upon which the case was tried declared that it was established and fixed by agreement of the parties that of the said sum of $2,500 it was contemplated that approximately one third thereof should be allocated and devoted to the support and maintenance of the daughter during her minority.

The agreement of 1929 also provided that the decedent might at any time commute the annuity by setting up a trust for $425,000, the income from which was to be paid to his wife for life, and which she should accept in satisfaction of any claims against him under the agreement. The parties were divorced in May 1929. In the following June the decedent exercised his option to discharge his obligations by setting up a trust, and transferred to trustees securities valued at about $414,000, the income from which was to be paid to the wife for life, she to have a power to appoint $200,000 of the principal by will. The balance of the corpus, or the entire corpus in case there was no valid exercise of the power of appointment, went to the daughter at the death of the wife or to her lawful issue, if any. If she left no issue, then the corpus went to decedent, or as he should appoint by will. Decedent reserved a joint power in himself and his wife at any time to terminate, modify, alter, or revoke the trust in whole or part. The property of the decedent in 1929 was worth more than $1,425,000. He died in May 1935. At the date of decedent's death the child was ten and one-half years of age.

The Board of Tax Appeals (now this Court) excluded the corpus from decedent's estate on the ground that the release by the wife was adequate and full consideration in money or money's worth. The Circuit Court of Appeals held that the release of the wife's marital right of support was not "money's worth," but that insofar as the trust was set up in consideration of a release of that part of the annuity for the support of the child, it was not set up in consideration of the release of a marital right, and was not includible in the gross estate.

* * *

The Circuit Court of Appeals also concluded that it was necessary to find the prospective yearly cost of the child's support when the trust was set up in 1929; then find the commuted value of the cost and what proportion it represented of the value of the trust fund when it was set up; and exclude from the gross estate that proportion of the value of the trust fund when the decedent died.

In the case before us both parties agree that the trust was for the primary benefit of the children and that no marital rights are involved. Nevertheless, in its essentials, it seems to us that the purposes and terms of the trust instrument executed by decedent here are substantially similar to those involved in Helvering v. United States Trust Co., supra, and that the question is what was the prospective value of the children's support.

Petitioners contend that the full value of the transferred assets is to be taken as "money's worth" since the settlement agreement and the terms of the trust were agreed upon at arm's length and only after bitter negotiations between decedent and Lenore and their attorneys. We cannot accept this contention. It is apparent that decedent went beyond his legal obligation to his children in creating the trust. At most, Delos was entitled to his father's support for about four years when the trust was established; Nedra for about 12 years. In 1931 the corpus of the trust was worth at least $220,000 and it produced net income ranging from some $28,000 in 1931 to $33,500 in 1943. In 1936 the income was $65,000 while in 1933 it amounted to but $8,578.90. That decedent thought this income alone was more than necessary for the support of the children is shown by the fact that provision was made for the accumulation of unused income in the event of Lenore's death before the children attained their majority. Furthermore, after majority, when decedent's obligation to support would cease, the children were still entitled to certain amounts of income and on reaching the age of 35 the trust corpus was distributable to them. Also, the recital in decedent's will in connection with bequests of $5 to each child that "my reason for such bequest is that I have previously made a settlement upon (them) from my estate," is evidence that decedent was doing more in setting up the trust then merely meeting his legal obligation of support. The arrangement had aspects of a testamentary disposition. Certainly, in these circumstances, we cannot say that the entire value of the trust assets was transferred for "money's worth." Only that portion of the value which represents the children's right to support is to be so treated. Helvering v. United States Trust Co., supra.

The question of the proper valuation of the children's support has given us pause. The evidence on this point is meager at best. Respondent argues that petitioners have failed in their burden of proof and that nothing whatever should be allowed. Nevertheless, it seems incumbent on the Court to place a reasonable prospective value on the children's support and after carefully considering the evidence, and "bearing heavily" on the petitioners "whose inexactitude" raises the problem, we have found that value to be $30,000. Cohan v. Commissioner, 39 F.2d 540, 544 Edith M. Bensel, et al., Executors, 36 B. T. A. 246, 255, affd. 100 F.2d 639.

Accordingly, pursuant to section 811 (i) [now section 2043], there should be included in the gross estate only "the excess of the fair market value at the time of death" of the assets of Trust 924 over the sum of $30,000 which we have found to be the value of the children's rights to support at the time the trust was set up.

* * *

NOTE

Should a trust set up for the support of minor children be regarded as a transfer for a valuable consideration to any extent? The taxpayer who retains property in his or her own name and supports children with the resulting income gets no deduction. Why should a formal trust arrangement make any difference? Is a trust that is classed as a retained life estate because it supports legal dependents different at all as regards "consideration?" Does the circumstance that only the income from the transfer is used for support indicate that the principal is being handed over eventually as a type of testamentary substitute to the natural objects of the grantor's bounty? The IRS fully accepts that a transfer in satisfaction of the support obligation can be consideration in money or money's worth. See, e.g., Rev. Rul. 77–314, 1977–2 C.B. 349 and Rev. Rul. 79–363, 1979–2 C.B. 346.

D. SALES OF REMAINDER INTERESTS

During the 1970s and early 1980s, the estate planning Bar became fascinated with planning devices involving sales of remainder interests. The devices employed relied on the fact that section 2036(a) excludes from taxation transfers involving bona fide sales for "adequate and full consideration." Owners of property, such as a ranch or stock in a closely held business were often advised to retain ownership of the asset for their life but to sell the remainder interest to family members. At the death of the owner (life tenant), it was thought that, because of the "adequate and full consideration" exception, all that would remain to be taxed in the life tenant's estate from such a transaction would be what remained of the consideration that the life tenant received from the remaindermen on their purchase of the remainder interest.

Another variation on the above theme was the so-called surviving spouse's election, which in tribute to women's longevity is commonly called the widow's election. This estate planning devise, which first gained favor more than a decade before the conventional sales of remainders previously described, was quite popular in community property states, and in point of fact, was basically a sale of a remainder in family garb. In the community property version of the widow's election, the will of the first spouse to die, who in our example is the husband, gives the surviving spouse either her share of the community property or, if she elects, an income interest in both the husband's interest and her interest in the community property. The will of the first spouse to die disposes of all community property in exchange for the surviving spouse receiving the extra income from deceased spouse's share of community property. Assuming that all the couple's assets are community assets and the surviving spouse makes the election, the hoped for result is that the only assets that will be taxed in the estate of the husband will be his share of the community property and that at surviving spouse's death the only assets that will be taxed in her estate will be whatever property she did not consume from the income paid to her. As in the case of the sale of a remainder interest, the avoidance of any estate tax under section 2036, at the death of the surviving spouse, is predicated on the election qualifying under the "adequate and full consideration" exception of section 2036.

Although these devices have been described by some as providing a "taxpayer's utopia," in fact, like the private annuity, if they are properly priced, which they often were not, no abuse is present. In the conventional sale of a remainder interest, if the transaction is properly priced, if the life tenant invests the sales proceeds in property which produces a rate of return equal to the modest rate of return used in the discount tables in pricing the sale and if the life tenant lives to his or her projected life expectancy, the value of the sales proceeds so invested should, at the life tenant's death, equal the fee simple value of the property sold. Moreover, although there will be some life tenants who will not reach their normal life expectancies and will die with less accumulated than was projected, they will be offset by other life tenants who will exceed their life expectancies and will die with more accumulated under the arrangement than was projected.

The two principal cases in this area are Gradow v. United States, 11 Cl. Ct. 808 (1987), aff'd 897 F.2d 516 (Fed.Cir.1990), and Estate of D'Ambrosio v. Commissioner, 101 F.3d 309 (3d Cir.1996), which reach contrary conclusions. *Gradow* is a widow's election case in which the court concluded that for the sale of a remainder to be deemed to be for adequate consideration, the purchasers of the remainder interest would have to pay the life tenant an amount equal to the amount which would be included in the life tenant's estate had the sale not taken place. This, of course, produces the troubling possibility that by doing so the purchaser might be slapped with gift tax liability if the amount transferred in excess of full and adequate consideration does not qualify for the marital deduction. Although this deficiency of the result in *Gradow* was not addressed by the court in *D'Ambrosio*, a number of the other defects of the opinion in *Gradow* are discussed in the opinion which follows.

ESTATE OF D'AMBROSIO v. COMMISSIONER

United States Court of Appeals, Third Circuit, 1996.
101 F.3d 309.

NYGAARD, CIRCUIT JUDGE.

[Decedent Rose D'Ambrosio was the owner of half the preferred stock of Vaparo, Inc. which had a fair market value of $2,350,000. In 1987, at age 80, she sold a remainder interest in her shares to a family owned corporation in exchange for an annuity of $296,039 per year and retained the income interest in her shares. The annuity had a value of $1,324,014 which the parties stipulate was the fair market value of D'Ambrosio's remainder interest in the stock. Decedent died in 1990 after having received a total of $592,078 under the annuity. Her executor included nothing in her estate with respect to the stock. The IRS issued a notice of deficiency including in decedent's estate, under § 2036(a)(1), $2,350,000 (the still then value of the stock) minus the payments received by decedent under the annuity. The executor brought suit in the Tax Court which decided that decedent's transfer of a remainder interest did not fall within the adequate consideration exception of § 2036(a)(1). Its opinion relied principally on two widow's election cases, Estate of Gregory v. Commissioner, 39 T.C. 1012 (1963) and Gradow v. United States, 11 Cl. Ct. 808 (1987), aff'd 897 F.2d 516 (Fed. Cir.1990). It, however, did allow the estate to subtract, from the $2,350,000 value of the stock, as "inadequate consideration" the $1,324,014 value of the annuity, not the amounts actually paid to decedent. Taxpayer appealed to the Court of Appeals for the Third Circuit.

The Court of Appeals in its opinion found *Estate of Gregory* to be of little assistance in resolving how the issue before it should be decided since that case did not involve adequate consideration with the widow exchanging property worth almost $66,000 for a life estate with an actuarial value of about $12,000. It then turned its attention to an analysis of the claims Court's opinion in *Gradow*.]

The facts in *Gradow* were similar to those in *Gregory*; both are "widow's election" cases. That case is particularly significant, however, because the court focused on the statutory language of § 2036.

* * *

We examine first the *Gradow* court's construction of the statute. It opined that

there is no question that the term "property" in the phrase "The gross estate shall include ... all property ... of which the decedent has at any time made a transfer" means that part of the trust corpus attributable to plaintiff. If § 2036(a) applies, all of [the electing widow's] former community property is brought into

> her gross estate. Fundamental principles of grammar dictate that the parenthetical exception which then follows—"(except in case of a bona fide sale . . .)"—refers to a transfer of that same property, i.e. the one-half of the community property she placed into the trust.

Id. (ellipses in original). We disagree; although the *Gradow* court's rationale appears plausible, we note that the court, in quoting the statute, left out significant portions of its language. Below is the text of § 2036, with the omitted words emphasized:

> The *value of the* gross estate shall include *the value* of all property *to the extent of any interest therein* of which the decedent has at any time made a transfer (except in case of a bona fide sale for an adequate and full consideration in money or money's worth), by trust or otherwise, under which he has retained for his life * * * (1) the possession or enjoyment of, or the right to the income from, the property * * *

After parsing this language, we cannot agree with the *Gradow* court's conclusions that "property" refers to the fee simple interest and that adequate consideration must be measured against that value. Rather, we believe that the clear import of the phrase "to the extent of any interest therein" is that the gross estate shall include the value of the remainder *interest*, unless it was sold for adequate and fair consideration.

In addition to § 2036, Treas. Reg. § 20.2036–1 also addresses this issue. It provides, in pertinent part (emphases added):

> (a) In general. A decedent's gross estate includes under section 2036 the value of any *interest* in property *transferred* by the decedent . . . except to the extent that the transfer was for an adequate and full consideration in money or money's worth if the decedent retained or reserved (1) for his life . . .

> (i) The use, possession, right to the income, or other enjoyment of *the transferred property*, . . .

Appellant refers us to the emphasized words "interest" and "transferred" in § 20.2036–1(a) and argues that "adequate and full consideration" must be measured against the interest transferred. The Commissioner, on the other hand, looks at the phrase "of the transferred property" in § 20.2036–1(a)(i) and concludes that, because one cannot retain any lifetime interest in a remainder, "property" must refer to the fee simple interest.

The regulation, unfortunately, is not exactingly drafted and does not parse "cleanly" under either party's interpretation. The Commissioner is of course correct that one cannot enjoy any sort of life interest in a remainder. On the other hand, appellant validly asks why, if the drafters of the regulation meant to include the full value of the property, they referred to the value of any *"interest* in property transferred." On balance, we believe that, if some words of the regulation must be construed as surplusage, it is more reasonable and faithful to the statutory text to render inoperative the word "transferred" in § 20.2036–1(a)(i) than it would be to strike "interest" in the first part of the section. We think it is likely that, although the choice of verbiage was less than precise, the drafters meant merely to refer to the "transferred" property so as to distinguish it from other property owned by the estate. It strains the judicial imagination, however, to conclude that the drafters used the term of art "interest in property" when they meant simply "property."

The *Gradow* court also believed that its construction of § 2036 was "most consistent" with its purposes. 11 Cl.Ct. at 813. The tax court in this case, although recognizing that the issue has spawned considerable legal commentary and that scholars dispute its resolution, 105 T.C. at 254, was persuaded that decedent's sale of her remainder interest was testamentary in character and designed to avoid the payment of estate tax that otherwise would have been due. *Id.* at 260. It noted particularly that the transfer was made when decedent was eighty years old and that the value of the annuity she received was over $1 million less than the fee simple value of the stock she gave up. *Id.* Again, we disagree.

We too are cognizant that techniques for attempting to reduce estate taxes are limited only by the imagination of estate planners, and that new devices appear regularly. There is, to be sure, a role for the federal courts to play in properly limiting these techniques in accordance with the expressed intent of Congress.

* * *

On the other hand, it is not our role to police the techniques of estate planning by determining, based on our own policy views and perceptions, which transfers are abusive and which are not. That is properly the role of Congress, whose statutory enactments we are bound to interpret. As stated *supra*, we think the statutory text better supports appellant's argument.

Even looking at this case in policy terms, however, it is difficult to fathom either the tax court's or the Commissioner's concerns about the "abusiveness" of this transaction. A hypothetical example will illustrate the point.

A fee simple interest is comprised of a life estate and a remainder. Returning to the widow's election cases, assume that the surviving spouse's share of the community property is valued at $2,000,000. Assuming that she decides not to accept the settlement and to keep that property, its whole value will be available for inclusion in the gross estate at death, but only as long as the widow lives entirely on the income from the property. If she invades principal and sells some of the property in order to meet living expenses or purchase luxury items, then at least some of that value will not be included in the gross estate. Tax law, of course (with the exception of the gift tax), imposes no burdens on how a person spends her money during life.

Next, assume that same widow decides to sell her remainder and keep a life estate. As long as she sells the remainder for its fair market value, it makes no difference whether she receives cash, other property, or an annuity. All can be discounted to their respective present values and quantified. If she continues to support herself from the income from her life estate, the consideration she received in exchange for the remainder, if properly invested, will still be available for inclusion in the gross estate when she dies, * * *. On the other hand, if her life estate is insufficient to meet her living expenses, the widow will have to invade the consideration she received in exchange for her remainder, but to no different an extent than she would under the previous hypothetical in which she retained the fee simple interest. In sum, there is simply no change in the date-of-death value of the final estate, regardless of which option she selects, at any given standard of living.

On the other hand, if the full, fee simple value of the property at the time of death is pulled back into the gross estate under § 2036(a), subject only to an offset for the consideration received, then the post-sale appreciation of the transferred asset will be taxed at death. Indeed, it will be double-taxed, because, all things being equal, the consideration she received will also have appreciated and will be subject to tax on its increased value. In addition, it would appear virtually impossible, under the tax court's reasoning, ever to sell a remainder interest; if the adequacy of the consideration must be measured against the fee simple value of the property at the time of the transfer, the transferor will have to find an arms-length buyer willing to pay a fee simple price for a future interest. Unless a buyer is willing to speculate that the future value of the asset will skyrocket, few if any such sales will take place.

Another potential concern, expressed by the *Gradow* court, is that, under appellant's theory, "[a] young person could sell a remainder interest for a fraction of the property's [current, fee simple] worth, enjoy the property for life, and then pass it along without estate or gift tax consequences." 11 Cl.Ct. at 815. This reasoning is problematic, however, because it ignores the time value of money. Assume that a decedent sells his son a remainder interest in that much-debated and often-sold parcel of land called Blackacre, which is worth $1 million in fee simple, for its actuarial fair market value of $100,000 (an amount which implicitly includes the market value of Blackacre's expected appreciation). Decedent then invests the proceeds of the sale. If the rates of return for both assets are equal and decedent lives exactly as long as the actuarial tables predict, the consideration that decedent received for his remainder will equal the value of Blackacre on the date of his death. The equivalent value will, accordingly, still be included in the gross estate. Moreover, decedent's son will have only a $100,000 basis in Blackacre, because that is all he paid for it. He will then be subject to capital gains taxes on its appreciated value if he decides to ever sell the property. Had Blackacre been passed by decedent's will and included in the gross estate, the son would have received a stepped-up basis at the time of his father's death or the alternate valuation date. We therefore have great difficulty understanding how this transaction could be abusive.

On this appeal, the Commissioner likewise argues for the *Gradow* rule on the rationale that "the retained life interest is in closely held stock whose dividend treatment is subject to the control of decedent and her family. In such circumstances, the amount of the dividend income that decedent was to receive from her life income interest in the Vaparo preferred stock was susceptible of manipulation[.]" Commissioner's Brief at 33. There is no evidence, however, that the Vaparo dividends *were* manipulated, and the Commissioner directs us to no authority that we should presume so. In addition, implicit in her argument is the proposition that the life estate was overvalued by the executor and the remainder correspondingly undervalued. Such a position, however, is directly contrary to the Commissioner's own stipulation regarding the values of those interests.

The Commissioner also asserts that the D'Ambrosio estate plan is "calculated to deplete decedent's estate in the event that she should not survive as long as her actuarially projected life expectancy." Commissioner's Brief at 34–35. We note first that the Commissioner does not argue that decedent transferred her remainder in contemplation of imminent death under such circumstances that the tables should not be applied. Leaving aside the untimely death of Rose D'Ambrosio, any given transferor of a remainder is equally likely to *outlive* the tables, in which case she would collect more from her annuity, the gross estate would be correspondingly larger and the Commissioner would collect more tax revenue than if the remainder had never been transferred.

Because we conclude that the tax court erred as a matter of law when it determined that the consideration received by Rose D'Ambrosio for her remainder interest was not adequate and full, we will reverse and remand for it to enter judgment in favor of the estate.

NOTES

1.   Although the court's opinion in *D'Ambrosio* is well reasoned and is correct in its economic analysis, the ultimate judicial resolution of adequacy of consideration in situations involving sales of remainder issues may require Supreme Court intervention. Support for the *Gradow* approach can be found in Pittman v. United States, 878 F. Supp. 833 (E.D. N.C. 1994), whereas the Fifth Circuit in Wheeler v. United States, 116 F.3d 749

(5th Cir. 1997) (sale of remainder interest in ranch) and the Ninth Circuit in Estate of Magnin v. Commissioner, 184 F.3d 1074 (9th Cir. 1999) are supportive of the Third Circuit analysis in *D'Amrosio* as are several older cases. See Estate of Christ v. Commissioner, 54 T.C. 493 (1970), aff'd 480 F.2d 171 (9th Cir. 1973) & Estate of Vardell v. Commissioner, 307 F.2d 688 (5th Cir. 1962).

2.   In 1990, Congress added sections 2701 and 2702 to the Code. These sections will have special meaning for parties contemplating a sale of a remainder interest. Section 2701 will impact on situations such as those involved in *D'Ambrosio* in which a remainder interest in a family corporation or partnership is transferred and an income interest is retained, whereas section 2702 will apply to transfers of other assets in trust or other transfers involving life or term interests. While these provisions, which are discussed in detail in Chapter 12, will not preclude taxpayers from engaging in sales of remainder interests for full and adequate consideration to avoid taxation under section 2036, the harshness of the zero-valuation rule for retained interests for gift tax purposes will ensure that most sales of remainder interests are structured so as to avoid the zero value rule. For example, if a taxpayer wishes to sell a remainder interest in a trust to a child, she will likely structure it as a sale of an interest in a qualified annuity or unitrust to avoid the zero-valuation rule.

E. INADEQUATE CONSIDERATION —AMOUNT INCLUDED

Assuming that the statute means what it says, and that the courts in *D'Ambrosio* and *Wheeler* are correct in their analysis and that the courts in *Gradow* and its progeny have misconstrued the law, we now turn our attention to the issue of the amount includible where inadequate consideration has been employed.

Where inadequate consideration has been used to effect the transfer of an interest, determination of the amount to be included in the estate presents an interesting issue. For example, assume that A, who owns Blackacre, which is worth $100,000, retains a life estate in Blackacre and sells the remainder to her nephew for $40,000. If the actuarially determined value of A's life estate was $60,000, at her death nothing should be included in her estate under section 2036 since she has made a transfer of the remainder interest "for an adequate consideration in money or money's worth," which is consequently excluded from taxation under the parenthetical consideration rule found in section 2036(a). Even if Blackacre doubles in value prior to A's death, there should be no inclusion since the transfer was for adequate consideration. Assume, however, that A sold the $40,000 remainder interest to the nephew for $20,000, what amount should be included in her estate? A literal reading of section 2043 indicates that, if A dies with Blackacre worth $100,000, the amount to be included would be determined by subtracting from Blackacre's $100,000 value the $20,000 paid, with the result that $80,000 in value would be included in her estate. Moreover, if Blackacre doubles in value, the same subtractional rule is applied and $180,000 in value is included in her estate. Theoretically, if she were to be a mere $1,000 short in the value assigned to the remainder interest and were to value it at $39,000, then $61,000 would be included in her estate if Blackacre did not increase in value and $161,000 would be included if it doubled in value. These results all follow from a literal reading of the subtractional nature of the cure provided by section 2043. Fortunately, courts do not expect exacting precision and are content with approximately equal valuations. In re Estate of Davis, 440 F.2d 896 (3d Cir. 1971); Estate of Carli v. Commissioner, 84 T.C. 649 (1985).

An interesting case in which a modest discrepancy in consideration cost the taxpayer mightily is Estate of Magnin v. Commissioner, 81 T.C.M. (CCH) 1126 (2001). A taxpayer, who held a life interest in a trust which would be includible in his estate under section 2036 sold his interest in the trust for $43,878. He died shortly after the sale. Absent the sale of his interest $3,833,743 would have been included in his estate because of his retained life estate. The Tax Court in an earlier proceeding applied *Gradow* and decided that since the taxpayer had not received $3,833,747 for his life interest, full and adequate consideration was lacking. The Ninth Circuit reversed the Tax Court accepting the reasoning of the Third Circuit in *Estate of D'Ambrosio*. It remanded the case to the Tax Court to determine if full and adequate consideration was present. Judge Ruwe, the same judge who had been reversed by the Ninth Circuit, found that the value of taxpayer's life estate was between $90,000 and $110,000. He indicated that while the adequate consideration rule did not require pinpoint accuracy, this more than 2 to 1 disparity in values did not measure up. The result was that he included in taxpayer's estate $3,833,747 minus the $43,878 paid to taxpayer to purchase his life interest.

A better consideration rule is provided by the proportional consideration rule of section 2040, which taxes joint property. Under that rule, where the surviving joint tenant provided a part of the consideration, the amount to be included in the estate of the deceased joint tenant is that portion of the fair market value of the property that is reflective of the portion of the total consideration provided by the deceased joint tenant. For example, if the deceased joint tenant provided three-quarters of the consideration used to purchase Blackacre and the surviving joint tenant provided the balance, only three-quarters of the value of Blackacre would be included in the deceased joint tenant's estate, regardless of how value had changed by date of death.

Should Congress consider changing the inadequate subtractional consideration rule of section 2043 into a proportional consideration rule such as is provided by section 2040? For example, where A sold the $40,000 life estate to her nephew for $20,000, under a proportional rule, one-half of the value of Blackacre would be included in her estate at death. Such an approach certainly seems to be more reflective of the economic realities. Had this been the rule in *Magnin* only a little more than one-half of the $3.8 million trust would have been included in the taxpayer's estate. As it turned out, being about $50,000 short on consideration resulted in a $3.8 million inclusion.

F. INTRAFAMILY TRANSFERS AND ENTITIES

Taxpayers in search of valuation discounts have, in recent years, made transfers to entities (typically limited partnerships) for the purpose, or at very least having the effect, of reducing the valuation of transferred assets. The IRS has seized upon the opportunity to impose estate tax on many such transfers on the grounds that they come within the scope of one of the basic inclusion sections, such as sections 2036 and 2035. Where taxpayers are unable to escape the general reach of these sections, they find themselves falling back on the argument that the transfer is not covered by the provision in question because it is a "bona fide sale for an adequate and full consideration in money or money's worth." See, e.g., I.R.C. §§ 2035(d) & 2036(a). The cases discussing the requirements of this language in such situations are legendary and final resolution of what these words mean must await further discussion and consideration by the courts. The case that follows provides a good discussion of the principles related to intrafamily transfers and family partnership situations.

ESTATE OF BONGARD V. COMMISSIONER
United States Tax Court, 2005.
124 T.C. 95.

GOEKE, JUDGE.

[Wayne C. Bongard (Bongard) was a highly successful businessman who was a founder of Empak, Inc., a very successful business. Bongard was, until his death, the sole member of the board of directors of Empak and was also its CEO. In 1986 he transferred some of his shares of Empak to a trust (ISA Trust) for the benefit of his children and one other individual. In 1995 Bongard entered into serious discussions with financial advisers as to how best to secure an additional infusion of capital for Empak. Based on their advice, in January of 1996 he formed WBC Holdings, LLC (WBC Holdings) for the purpose of eventually positioning Empak "for a corporate liquidity event" (a primary issuance of additional stock to obtain added operating capital). Bongard's financial advisers asserted that outsiders would be more willing to invest in the company if the Bongard family interests in Empak were placed in a holding company. Wayne Bongard's son Mark was made the manager of WBC Holdings and was invested with significant decision making powers, although members who possessed the majority of the voting power (Bongard) were invested with the power to overrule a number of critical decisions made by the manager and their approval must be obtained for a number of actions such as sales of stock held by WCB Holdings in excess of $10,000 per year, purchases of new investments, borrowing even modest sums and voting stock held by WCB Holdings. In addition, those with majority voting power in WCB Holdings were authorized to take any action that the manager could take and were authorized to remove him at will. On December 28, 1996, Bongard and ISA Trust each transferred all their Empak stock to WCB Holdings with each receiving in exchange both class A and class B membership units in WCB Holdings. Class A units were voting units whereas class B units were nonvoting units. Based on his holdings in Empak, Bongard was issued an 86.39 percent ownership interest in each class of ownership units, making him alone the majority owner of WCB Holdings vested with the special powers noted. On the next day, at the behest of his estate planners, The Bongard Family Limited Partnership (BFLP) was formed with ISA Trust and Bongard each transferring all their WBC Holdings class B membership units to BFLP in exchange for interests in BFLP reflective of the value of the class B units each transferred. The court found that the formation of BFLP was part of Bongard's estate plan and was not part of the planning for the "liquidity event." In December of 1997, Bongard entered into a postmarital agreement with his wife Cynthia (his second wife with whom he had no children) and transferred to her a 7.72 percent limited partnership in BFLP as part of that agreement. On November 16, 1998, Bongard unexpectedly died at age 58 on a hunting trip to Austria. The estate sought valuation discounts from the value of the Empak shares based on: (1) the interposition of WBC Holdings between the Empak shares and Bongard's ownership interest; and (2) the added interposition of BFLP between Bongard's ownership and the underlying Empak shares. The I.R.S. countered, asserting that there was an inclusion of Bongard's interests in Empak under § 2036. Prior to addressing the basic § 2036 issue, the Tax Court addressed whether it need not wade into those waters because both transfers had been made in a "bona fide sale for adequate and full consideration."]

In the context of family limited partnerships, the adequate and full consideration requirement is met where the record establishes the existence of a legitimate and significant nontax reason for creating the family limited partnership, and the transferors received partnership interests proportionate to the value of the property transferred. * * * The objective evidence must indicate that the nontax reason was a significant factor that motivated the partnerships creation. * * * A significant purpose must be an actual motivation, not a theoretical justification.

By contrast, the bona fide sale exception is not applicable where the facts fail to establish that the transaction was motivated by a legitimate and significant nontax purpose. * * * A list of facts that support such a finding includes the taxpayer standing on both sides of the transaction, the taxpayer's financial dependence on distributions from the partnership, the partners' commingling of partnership funds with their own and the taxpayer's actual failure to transfer the property to the partnership * * *.

A transaction between family members is, however, subjected to heightened scrutiny to ensure that it is not a sham or a disguised gift. * * *

C.   DECEDENT'S TRANSFER OF EMPAK STOCK TO WCB HOLDINGS

* * *

In 1995, decedent, while in good health, met with his advisers, Messers. Boyle, Bernards, and Eitel, to discuss how Empak could remain successful and competitive. These discussions determined that Empak needed to develop additional means for acquiring capital to remain successful and competitive. Mr. Bernards testified that for Empak to grow, "additional capital other than bank debt and through [reinvesting its] earnings" was needed. It was believed that positioning Empak for either a public or private offering (a corporate liquidity event) would accomplish this goal. Decedent and his advisers discussed how to facilitate a corporate liquidity event for Empak. Mr. Boyle drafted a memo and a checklist detailing the specific steps of the plan to position Empak for a corporate liquidity event.

Many of the steps in the checklist were completed. * * *

The positioning and structuring of Empak to facilitate a corporate liquidity event was also beneficial for decedent and ISA Trust. ISA Trust held a single asset, Empak stock. The value of the shares held by both decedent and ISA Trust was maximized by positioning Empak to attract potential investors. Moreover, the potential market for Empak shares was increased. These facts together support that positioning Empak for a corporate liquidity event was a legitimate and significant nontax reason that motivated the Empak shareholders to create WCBHoldings.

1.   Bona Fide Sale

* * *

Respondent appears to assert that an arm's-length transaction cannot occur between related parties. An arm's-length transaction has been defined as "A transaction between two unrelated and unaffiliated parties" or alternatively, a transaction "between two parties, however closely related they may be, conducted as if the parties were strangers, so that no conflict of interest arises." * * * The bona fide sale exception has not been limited to transactions involving unrelated parties as respondent's argument implies. * * *

It is axiomatic that intrafamily transactions are subjected to a higher level of scrutiny, but this heightened scrutiny is not tantamount to an absolute bar. In that connection, we have already concluded that decedent and ISA Trust had mutual legitimate and significant nontax reasons for forming WCB Holdings. In addition, both decedent and ISA Trust received interests in WCB Holdings proportionate to the number of shares transferred. We believe that had this transaction occurred between two unrelated parties the majority interest holder in Empak would have received similar powers to those received via WCB Holdings' member control agreement. An important purpose for creating WCB Holdings was to position Empak for a corporate liquidity event, and the record does not contain any credible evidence that unrelated parties would not have agreed to the same terms and conditions. Given these facts, we cannot hold that the terms of the transaction differed from those of two unrelated parties negotiating at arm's length.

Respondent's final argument is that the formation of WCB Holdings was not a bona fide sale because there was not a true pooling of assets. WCB Holdings' purpose was to pool the Bongard family's Empak stock within a single entity, which decedent and ISA Trust satisfied through their respective contributions. WCB Holdings' creation was part of a much grander plan, to attract potential investors or to stimulate a corporate liquidity event to facilitate Empak's growth. Moreover, when WCB Holdings was capitalized, the members' capital accounts were properly credited and maintained, WCB Holdings' funds were not commingled with decedent's, and all distributions during decedent's life were pro rata. The amalgamation of these facts evidences that this transaction resulted in a true pooling of assets.

2.   Full and Adequate Consideration

The factual circumstances of this case further establish that the decedent and ISA Trust each received an interest in WCB Holdings that represented adequate and full consideration reducible to money value. * * * Decedent and ISA Trust received interests in WCB Holdings proportionate to the number of Empak shares each contributed. Although by itself this may not be sufficient evidence to meet the adequate and full consideration requirement, two additional facts do support such a finding. We have determined that the respective assets contributed by the members were properly credited to the respective capital accounts of each contributing member, and distributions from WCB Holdings required a negative adjustment in the distributee member's capital account. Most importantly, we have found the presence of a legitimate and significant nontax business reason for engaging in this transaction.

Respondent nonetheless argues that decedent did not receive adequate and full consideration since decedent contributed 86.31 percent of Empak's outstanding stock without receiving a control premium for his contribution. Decedent did not need to receive a control premium because he retained effective control over Empak after he contributed his Empak stock to WCB Holdings. True, decedent was not the chief manager of WCB Holdings [Mark Bongard was], but the 86.31 percent interest in the class A governance units he received in the exchange provided him with the power to remove the WCB Holdings chief manager and replace him with himself as chief manager, to take any action the chief manager himself could take, and to approve any significant action the chief manager could take including selling more than $10,000 of any security in any 12-month period and the voting of any security held by WCB Holdings. * * *

3. Conclusion

We hold that decedent's transfer of Empak stock to WCB Holdings satisfies the bona fide sale exception of section 2036(a). Therefore, we need not determine whether decedent retained a section 2036(a) or (b) interest in the transferred property. * * *

D. BFLP

The estate argues that section 2036(a) is not applicable to decedent's transfer of WCB Holdings class B membership units to BFLP since the transfer was also a bona fide sale for adequate and full consideration. The estate contends that the creation of BFLP was motivated by nontax reasons. The BFLP agreement provides that BFLP was established to "acquire, own and sell from time to time stocks (including closely held stocks), bonds, options, mutual funds and other securities." At trial, Mr. Fullmer [one of Bongard's estate planners] testified that BFLP was established to provide another layer of credit protection for decedent. Additionally, the estate assets that BFLP facilitated decedent's and Cynthia Bongard's postmarital agreement. Messers. Bernards and Fullmer [Bongard's attorneys] both also testified that BFLP was established, in part, to make gifts. On December 10, 1997, decedent made a gift of a 7.72 percent interest in BFLP to Cynthia Bongard. This gift was the sole transfer of a BFLP interest by decedent during his life. BFLP also never diversified its assets during decedent's life, never had an investment plan, and never functioned as a business enterprise or otherwise engaged in any meaningful economic activity.

* * *

Estate tax savings did play an important role in motivating the transfer to BFLP. The record does not support that the nontax reasons for BFLP's existence were significant motivating factors. The formation of WCB Holdings eliminated direct stock ownership in Empak and allowed decedent to make gifts without diversifying the direct ownership of Empak. Messers. Fullmer and Bernards testified that an impetus for forming BFLP was to continue decedent's gift giving. Decedent, in fact made numerous gifts after the formation of BFLP, but not of his BFLP interest . . . except for the 7.72-percent limited partnership interest he gave to Cynthia Bongard in 1997. At the time of BFLP's formation and at the time of his death, any additional gifts decedent had contemplated were speculative and indefinite at best. There was no immediate plan for such gifts. Such intent is not sufficient to establish . . . a significant nontax reason.

* * *

The estate's credit protection argument is also unpersuasive because WCB Holdings served this function for decedent. In fact, decedent via letter stated that "by holding a majority of my assets in the limited liability company or the limited partnership, I will be providing a greater amount of protection for those assets from both creditors and lawsuits." * * * Decedent's initial transfer of his Empak shares to WCB Holdings accorded him the credit protection he sought.

* * *

Our determination that the bona fide sale exception does not apply . . . does not end our inquiry. [S]ection 2036(a) includes in a decedent's gross estate "all property to the extent of any interest therein" of which the decedent has made a transfer wherein he has "retained for his life" either "(1) the possession or enjoyment of, or the right to income from, the property, or (2) the right, either alone or in conjunction with any person, to designate the persons who shall possess or enjoy the property or the income therefrom." * * *

The decedent did not need the membership interest in WCB Holdings class B shares to continue his lifestyle. However, decedent retained ownership of more than 91 percent of his BFLP interest and did not make gifts of such interest prior to his death. More importantly, decedent controlled whether BFLP could transform its sole asset, the class B WCB Holdings membership units, into a liquid asset. Decedent as CEO and sole member of Empak's board of directors determined when Empak redeemed its stock in each of the seven instances of redemptions prior to his death, including the last redemption . . . in 1998 after WCB Holdings was formed. * * * In order for BFLP to be able to diversify or take any steps other than simply holding the class B membership units, decedent would have to cause the membership units and the underlying Empak stock to be redeemed. He chose not to do this. By not redeeming the WCB membership units held by BFLP, decedent ensured that BFLP would not engage in asset management. Thereby, decedent exercised practical control over BFLP and limited its function to simply holding title to the class B membership units. Whether decedent caused the WCB membership units held by BFLP and the underlying Empak stock to be redeemed or not, his ability to decide whether that event would occur demonstrates the understanding of the parties involved that the decedent retained the right to control the units transferred to BFLP.

The estate's argument that the general partner's fiduciary duties prevents a finding of an implied agreement is overcome by a lack of activity following BFLP's formation and BFLP's failure to perform any meaningful functions as an entity.

* * *

Under the circumstances of this case, an implied agreement existed that allowed decedent to retain the enjoyment of the property held by BFLP. Therefore, under section 2036(a)(1), decedent's estate includes the value of the WCB Holdings class B membership units held by BFLP on decedent's death that is proportionate to decedent's 91.28 percent limited partnership interest. Given this finding, it is unnecessary to determine whether the terms of the BFLP agreement provided decedent explicit rights to control the property.

* * *

[The parties had stipulated as to the discounts which would apply in the event that the court held that § 2036 did not apply to the transfer to WCB holdings and the transfer to BFLP. The court then entered a judgement consistent with its holding and the stipulation of the parties. The case also involved other issues, not relevant to our purposes.]

Laro, J., concurring in result: I concur only because I am uncomfortable with the analysis used by the majority in arriving at its result. That analysis applies a new test that the majority has created to decide whether a transfer to a family limited partnership should be respected for Federal tax purposes. The majority applies its test in lieu of deeply ingrained caselaw that conditions satisfaction of the "bona fide sale for an adequate and full consideration in money or money's worth" exception of section 2036(a) (adequate and full consideration exception) on the transferor's receipt of property equal in value to that of the property transferred by the transferor. In other words, under that caselaw, the adequate and full consideration exception may apply only where the transferor's receipt of consideration is of a sufficient value to prevent the transfer from depleting the transferor's estate.

The majority states its test as follows: "In the context of family limited partnerships, the bona fide sale for adequate and full consideration exception is met where [1] the record establishes the existence of a legitimate and significant nontax reason for creating the family limited partnership, and [2] the transferors received partnership interests proportionate to the value of the property transferred." * * * I disagree with both prongs of this test. I believe that a transferor satisfies the adequate and full consideration exception in the context of a transfer to a partnership only when: (1) The record establishes either that (i) in return for the transfer, the transferor received a partnership interest and any other property with an aggregate fair market value equal to the fair market value of the transferor's transferred property, or (ii) the transfer was an ordinary commercial transaction (in which case, the transferred property and the consideration received in return are considered to have the same fair market values), and (2) the transfer was made with a business purpose or, in other words, a "useful nontax purpose that is plausible in light of the taxpayer's [transferor's] conduct and useful in light of the taxpayer's economic situation and intentions."

* * *

Halperin, J., concurring in part and dissenting in part.

[Judge Halperin concurred with the majority's decision to allow a discount for the WCB Holdings units but dissented from the decision not to allow a discount for the BFLP holdings.]

I believe that the majority has strayed from the traditional interpretation of the bona fide sale exception by incorporating into the exception an inappropriate motive test ("a legitimate significant nontax reason"), and by concluding that a partnership interest "proportionate" to the value of the property transferred constitutes adequate and full consideration in money or money's worth.

* * *

I would approach the question of whether the value of property transferred by the decedent is included in the gross estate on account of section 2036 by, first, determining whether the decedent retained lifetime possession, enjoyment, income, or control of transferred property. Only after answering that question in the affirmative would I proceed to determine whether the bona fide sale exception applies to the transfer. In determining whether the bona fide sale exception applies, I would first determine whether the transfer was made in the ordinary course of business, as that term is used in section 25.2512–8, Gift Tax Regs. If not, I would determine whether the transfer was made for full value (i.e., whether the value of the transferred property at most equaled the cash value of the consideration received therefor). If not, I would find that the value of the transferred property was included in the value of the gross estate pursuant to section 2036. Motive would only play the limited role I have outlined above (i.e., determining donative intent for purposes of the ordinary-course-of-business test).

NOTE

Bongard is regarded by both Courts of Appeal and lower courts as having set the standards for determining whether adequate consideration is present in family partnership situations and consequently is an important and well cited authority on the subject.

The court in *Bongard* posited a two-prong test for satisfying the adequate consideration test with respect to family limited partnerships. First, the parties must receive interests in the family limited partnership (FLP) or LLC which are in proportion in value to what they contribute. For example, if a parent and child were equal co-owners in an unincorporated business and contributed that to an LLC, each would have to obtain interests in the LLC that were equal in value. Presumably, if the parent was turning over greater managerial responsibilities in the business to the child and this was reflected in the LLC's operating agreement, this requirement could be satisfied with a greater interest being conveyed to the child, although this may have income tax ramifications for the child. Second, there must be a legitimate and significant non-tax reason for creating the entity and transferring property to it.

It is this second prong of the *Bongard* test that typically causes most of the problems for members of the older transferor generation and the results reached by the courts in dealing with this issue seem to lack a general consistency producing difficulties for an attorney who wishes to provide reliable advice for a client. If an active business or assets that demand active management are involved and the transfer is motivated by changing the form of the operating entity or the entity holding enterprise and a shifting of managerial responsibilities to the younger generation or other valid business reasons such as preparing a business for a private placement or other capital infusion, as was the case in *Bongard*, the second prong of the test will generally be satisfied. More problematic are cases where it is alleged that the reason for transferring assets to a FLP or an LLC is to protect family members from claims of creditors. In such cases courts sometimes evaluate the situation by determining whether, under local law, such protection from creditors resulted from the transfer. Compare Estate of Bigelow v. Commissioner, 503 F.3d 955 (9th Cir. 2007) (test not satisfied because transferor's status as general partner preserved her exposure to creditors) and Estate of Rector v. Commissioner, 94 T.C.M. (CCH) 567 (2007) with Estate of Kimbell v. United States, 371 F.3d 257 (5th Cir. 2004) (transfer of oil and gas interests to a partnership in which transferor was a limited partner and a newly formed LLC, in which the taxpayer's interest was confined to being the beneficiary of a revocable trust which was a 50% owner of the LLC, protected transferor from claims of potential creditors).

The problems posed for the second prong of the *Bongard* test in the absence of business or assets needing active management are well illustrated by Thompson v. Commissioner, 382 F.3d 367 (3d Cir. 2004). There the court determined that there was an absence of a significant non-tax reason for a transfer to an FLP and that the decedent transferor, who was in his nineties, was motivated by tax planning considerations where all he transferred to the FLP was marketable securities and notes of family members. The *Thompson* case should be contrasted with Estate of Schutt v. Commissioner, 89 T.C.M. (CCH) 1353 (2005), in which the taxpayer, who was in his late eighties and was a member of the duPont family, transferred to a Delaware business trust (an entity taxed as a partnership) $31 million of duPont stock and transferred to another Delaware business trust $11 million of Exxon stock, allegedly so that his heirs would not be free to immediately sell the stock and must follow his "buy and hold" strategy until such time following his death when the stock would be distributed to them. Small amounts of other marketable securities were also transferred to the entities. Amazingly enough, the decedent's limited buy and hold strategy was found to be a sufficient non-tax ground to justify formation of, and transfer of the assets to, the trusts and to enable the court to find that the adequate consideration standard had been satisfied. On the other hand, a buy and hold strategy was deemed an inadequate non-tax justification in the case of the surviving spouse of an ex-colonel in the Army Air Corp. for a somewhat diversified investment portfolio of just a few million dollars. See, Estate of Jorgensen v. Commissioner, 97 T.C.M. (CCH) 1328 (2009). What could possibly justify the different results?

Estate of Mirowski v. Commissioner, 95 T.C.M. (CCH) 1277 (2008), is a case in which the taxpayer's executor was able to convince the court that the taxpayer (an aged woman lacking in business skills and financial sophistication) by transferring financial assets and intellectual property (the patent for the implantable automatic heart defibrillator developed by her deceased spouse) to an entity was obtaining the nontax motives of both protection from potential claimants and the advantage of management of the assets in question and thereby qualified for a significant valuation discount.

Perhaps one of the most questionable cases in which an extremely large discount was allowed is Keller v. United States, 2009–2 USTC ¶ 60,579, 104 AFTR 2d (RIA) 6015 (S.D. TX 2009). Mrs. Williams, a widow in her 90s with an estate worth several hundred million dollars, almost all in highly liquid assets, with the aid of her accountants and estate planners, established several FLPs for the avowed purposes of saving taxes, simplifying wealth management and making it more difficult for her heirs to lose assets in any subsequent divorce proceedings. Unfortunately, Mrs. Williams died prior to transferring the bulk of her wealth to the FLPs. Her executor prepared an estate tax return including all of the highly liquid assets at their value. He then learned of a line of Texas cases that had held that formation of a partnership in Texas was primarily governed by intent and not formalities of title and sought a discount based on the interposition of the FLPs between the deceased and the assets in question. The district court following a line of state cases found that the FLPs existed and were funded with the property that the deceased had intended to but had not as yet transferred and that a valid business purpose existed satisfying the non-tax purpose required by *Bongard*. A discount of 47.5% was allowed. Given the prevalence of divorce in our society it seems that most wealthy parents should be able to find a non-tax justification for transferring assets to a FLP if they would worry enough about the stability of their offspring's existing or possible future marriages.

The results of the adequate consideration test in the large body of FLP and LLC discount cases are impossible to reconcile and often are a product of slight (and perhaps meaningless or worse well coached) variations in the facts of the cases. Moreover, on occasion one gets the feeling that the results in the cases at times may vary based on the proclivities of the judges who presided over the initial trials or the appeals.

Significantly, the Tax Court's plurality decision in the following reviewed case adds to the uncertainty in this area. The case addresses the amount to be included in a decedent's gross estate where the decedent received some consideration, but it was not adequate and full consideration for the transfer.

ESTATE OF POWELL V. COMMISSIONER

United States Tax Court, 2017.
148 T.C. 392.

HALPERN, JUDGE.

By separate notices of deficiency, respondent determined a deficiency of $5,870,226 in the Federal estate tax of the Estate of Nancy H. Powell (decedent) and a deficiency of $2,961,366 in decedent's Federal gift tax for 2008. The estate has moved for summary judgment in its favor that there is no deficiency in either estate or gift tax. Respondent has moved for partial summary judgment in his favor that (1) the value of cash and securities transferred from decedent's revocable trust to NHP Enterprises LP (NHP), a limited partnership, in exchange for a 99% limited partner interest is includible in the value of decedent's gross estate under section 2038(a); (2) the value of those same assets is includible in the value of her gross estate under either paragraph (1) or (2) of section 2036(a); and (3) the value of the limited partner interest in NHP decedent received is includible in the value of her gross estate because her son, Jeffrey Powell, did not have the authority to transfer that interest to a charitable lead annuity trust (CLAT) before decedent's death. The estate tax notice of deficiency characterizes those three claims as alternative grounds for increasing the value of decedent's gross estate by $10,022,570, which respondent apparently determined to be the value, as of the date of decedent's death, of the cash and securities transferred to NHP. By contrast, respondent's motion does not explicitly identify the three grounds on which he seeks partial summary judgment as alternatives to each other.

* * *

* * *Decedent died on August 15, 2008 [in California]. When the petitions were filed in these cases, Mr. Powell, executor of decedent's estate, resided in California.

On August 8, 2008, cash and securities were transferred from decedent's revocable trust to NHP in exchange for a 99% limited partner interest. By stipulation, the parties agree on the date of the transfer. They also agree that, on that date, the transferred assets were worth $10,000,752 [based on a valuation by Polaris, a wealth management firm founded by Mr. Powell]. * * *

NHP had been formed two days earlier, on August 6, 2008, when Mr. Powell, as general partner, executed and filed with the Delaware secretary of state a certificate of limited partnership. NHP's limited partnership agreement gives Mr. Powell, as general partner, sole discretion to determine the amount and timing of partnership distributions. That agreement also allows for the partnership's dissolution with the written consent of all partners.

On August 8, 2008, Mr. Powell, purportedly acting on behalf of decedent under a power of attorney (POA), assigned to the CLAT decedent's 99% limited partner interest in NHP. Decedent's POA authorized Mr. Powell to take specified actions on her behalf in the event of her incapacitation. In a letter dated August 7, 2008, two doctors at Marin General Hospital expressed their opinion that decedent was incapacitated and could not act on her own behalf.

The terms of the CLAT entitled the Nancy H. Powell Foundation, a Delaware nonprofit corporation, to an annuity of a specified amount for the remainder of decedent's life. Upon decedent's death, the remaining assets in the CLAT were to be divided equally between two trusts for the benefit of Mr. Powell and his brother.

The powers granted to Mr. Powell by the POA included the ability "[t]o grant, convey, sell, transfer, mortgage deed in trust, pledge and otherwise deal in all property real and personal, which the principal may own". The POA also authorized Mr. Powell "[t]o make gifts on the principal's behalf, including, but not limited to, forgiveness of loans, to a class composed of the principal's children, any of such children's issue, or any or all to the full extent of the federal annual gift tax exclusion under Internal Revenue Code Section 2503(b) or any successor statute." A ratification provision in the POA states: "The principal hereby ratifies and confirms all that the agent shall do, or cause to be done, by virtue of this power of attorney."

Decedent's gift tax return for 2008 reported a taxable gift of $1,661,422 as a result of the purported transfer to the CLAT of her 99% limited partner interest in NHP. The amount of the taxable gift—that is, the remainder interest in the CLAT given to decedent's sons—was computed on the basis that the trust corpus (the 99% limited partner interest in NHP) was worth $7,516,773. The value assigned to the limited partner interest, in turn, was based on an appraisal conducted by Duff & Phelps, LLC. In determining the value of the limited partner interest, Duff & Phelps applied a 25%

discount for lack of control and lack of marketability. Duff & Phelps attached as an exhibit to its appraisal a statement of NHP's Polaris account as of August 8, 2008, which shows a balance of $10,022,570.

Respondent issued notices of deficiency in both estate and gift tax. In the gift tax notice, respondent determined that the 99% limited partner interest in NHP was worth $8,518,993 on August 8, 2008, and that the remainder interests in the CLAT were worth $8,363,095. Respondent determined the value of the remainder interests on the premise that decedent was terminally ill when the gift was made.

* * *

The estate tax notice increased the value of decedent's gross estate by $12,983,936. The notice explains the principal adjustment, an increase of $10,022,570 [because sections 2036(a) and 2038(a) applied.]

* * *

II. Applicability of Section 2036(a) or Section 2035(a) to Transfer to NHP

[The court granted respondent's motion for summary judgment that the transfer of cash and securities to NHP was subject to a retained right "to designate the persons who shall possess or enjoy" those assets "or the income therefrom" within the meaning of section 2036(a)(2). The court concluded that section 2036 applied if decedent retained rights in the transferred cash and securities until death. Otherwise, if she made a valid gift of her NHP interest, the assets would still be included under section 2035.]

III. The Limit Imposed by Section 2043(a) on the Amount Includible in Decedent's Gross Estate by Reason of Section 2036(a) or Section 2035(a)

* * *

The inclusion in decedent's gross estate required by section 2036(a)(2) (or, if applicable, section 2035(a)) differs in amount from the inclusion that would be required by a determination that the gift of decedent's NHP interest was either void or revocable. Neither section 2036(a)(2) nor section 2035(a) justifies the inclusion in the value of decedent's gross estate of the full date-of-death value of the cash and securities transferred to NHP in exchange for decedent's limited partner interest. Although the terms of each section, read in isolation, would require that result, those sections must be read in conjunction with section 2043(a). * * *

A. *The Purpose of Section 2043(a)*

Section 2043(a) complements the bona fide sale exception to the inclusionary rules provided in sections 2035 through 2038. The bona fide sale exception limits the reach of the inclusionary rules to transactions that deplete a decedent's estate. *E.g., Estate of Magnin v. Commissioner* [99–2 USTC ¶ 60,347], 184 F.3d 1074, 1079 (9th Cir. 1999) ("[T]he purpose underlying * * * section [2036(a)] is to prevent the depletion of the decedent's gross estate."), *rev'g* [Dec. 51,127(M)], T.C. Memo. 1996–25; *Estate of D'Ambrosio v. Commissioner* [Dec. 50,903], 105 T.C. 252, 260 (1995) ("The bona fide sale exception applies when an interest in property is transferred for sufficient consideration to prevent the depletion of the transferor's gross estate for Federal estate tax purposes."), *rev'd* [96–2 USTC ¶ 60,252], 101 F.3d 309 (3d Cir. 1996).

Section 2043(a) serves a purpose similar to that of the bona fide sale exception, limiting the scope of the various inclusionary rules so that they apply only to the extent necessary to prevent depletion of the transferor's estate. * * * [A]s we wrote in *Estate of Frothingham v. Commissioner* [Dec. 31,969], 60 T.C. 211, 216 (1973), "the purpose of section [2043(a)] is far from obscure. It was plainly designed to deal with the situation where the decedent has received some, but not 'adequate and full,' consideration for the transfer." When Congress enacted section 302(i) of the 1926 Act, it "was obviously attempting * * * to provide a measure of relief from double taxation of the same economic interest." *Id.*

Thus, if a transfer depletes a decedent's estate to any extent, the bona fide sale exception will generally not apply. But if the decedent receives *some* consideration, section 2043(a) limits the required inclusion to the amount by which the transfer depletes the decedent's estate.

B. *Applicability of Section 2043(a) in the Present Cases*

In the present cases, because of the limitation provided by section 2043(a), section 2036(a)(2), if applicable, would include in the value of decedent's gross estate only the excess of the fair market value at the time of her death of the cash and securities transferred to NHP over the value of the 99% limited partner interest in NHP issued in exchange for those assets. If, instead, section 2035(a) applies, it would require inclusion in the value of decedent's gross estate of the same amount—that is, the amount that would have been included in the value of decedent's gross estate under section 2036(a)(2) but for the transfer of her interest in NHP less than three years before her death. Section 2043(a) applies by its plain terms: We have concluded that the transfer of cash and securities to NHP was a transfer "enumerated and described" in either section 2036(a)(2) or section 2035(a). That transfer was made "for a consideration in money or money's worth," that is, a 99% limited partner interest in NHP. Because the estate does not challenge respondent's contention that Mr. Powell had no legitimate and significant nontax reason for creating NHP, the transfer of cash and securities to the partnership was "not a bona fide sale for an adequate and full consideration in money or money's worth", regardless of the value of the limited partner interest issued in exchange for those assets. *See Estate* *of Bongard v. Commissioner*, 124 T.C. at 118. Therefore, section 2043(a) limits the amount includible in the value of decedent's gross estate, by reason of section 2036(a)(2) (either alone or in conjunction with section 2035(a)), to "the excess of the fair market value at the time of death of * * * [the cash and securities], over the value of the consideration received therefor by the decedent." Put differently, section 2036(a)(2) or section 2035(a), in either case as limited by section 2043(a), includes in the value of decedent's gross estate the amount of any discounts applicable in valuing the 99% limited partner interest in NHP issued in exchange for the cash and securities (an amount that could colloquially be characterized as the "hole" in the doughnut). Only if the gift to the CLAT of decedent's limited partner interest in NHP were either void or revocable (and thus subject to section 2038(a)) would the value of her gross estate also include value of that interest (the "doughnut").

Allowing section 2043(a) to limit the amount includible in the value of a decedent's gross estate by reason of the application of section 2036(a) to a transfer to a family limited partnership carries out the purposes of those provisions. To the extent that the value of assets transferred to a family limited partnership does not exceed the value of the partnership interest received in return, the exchange does not deplete the transferor's estate or allow for the avoidance of transfer taxes. If, after formation of a family limited partnership, a decedent transfers her interest in the partnership inter vivos by gift, the value of that interest (taking into account any applicable valuation discounts) will be subject to gift tax. If the decedent instead retains her partnership interest until death, section 2033 will include the value of that interest (again, subject to applicable discounts) in the value of her gross estate. In either case, section 2036(a), as limited by section 2043(a), would bring back into the estate the amount of any discounts (that is, the doughnut holes) allowed in valuing the partnership interest. Applying section 2043(a) to limit the inclusion required by section 2036(a) simply prevents "double taxation of the same economic interest", precisely in accord with the "obvious" purpose underlying section 2043(a) and its predecessors that we discerned in *Estate of Frothingham v. Commissioner*, 60 T.C. at 216.

C.   *Estate of Harper's "Recycling of Value" Theory*

We have not previously had occasion to apply section 2043(a), in accordance with its plain terms, to limit the amount includible in the value of a decedent's gross estate by reason of the application of either section 2036(a) or section 2038(a) to a transfer to a family limited partnership. That occasion has not heretofore arisen because, in cases in which the decedent continues to own on the date of death part or all of the partnership interest she received in exchange for the transferred assets, the Commissioner customarily includes in the value of her gross estate the value of the assets transferred inter vivos to the partnership *in lieu of* the value of the partnership interest that the decedent actually owned at death (which would otherwise be includible in the value of her gross estate under section 2033). The illogic of including in the value of a decedent's gross estate *both* the assets transferred to a family limited partnership *and* the partnership interest received in return seems to have been widely recognized, but the precise legal grounds that prevent such illogical "double taxation" have gone unarticulated. The present cases—relatively unique in that respondent challenges the validity of the gift by which decedent disposed of her interest in the family limited partnership—provide us the opportunity to fill that lacuna and explain why a double inclusion in a decedent's estate is not only illogical, it is not allowed.

In the only prior case in which we considered the impact of section 2043(a) to a transfer to a family limited partnership, *Estate of Harper v. Commissioner* [Dec. 54,745(M)], T.C. Memo. 2002–121, 2002 WL 992347, at *19, we suggested that a partnership interest did not qualify as "consideration", for purposes of either section 2036(a) or section 2043(a), if the formation of the partnership did not involve a genuine pooling of assets so that the value of the partnership interest issued to the decedent "derived solely" from the assets he contributed. Such cases, we reasoned, involve "nothing but a circuitous 'recycling' of value" that does not "rise to the level of a payment of consideration." *Id.*

While the proportion of the partnership's assets contributed to a family limited partnership by a decedent-transferor, and thus the extent of pooling involved in the partnership's formation, is relevant to the applicability of the bona fide sale exception from section 2036(a), that factor is more germane to the nontax bona fides of the transaction than to the adequacy of the partnership interest as consideration for the transferred assets. That is how the Courts of Appeals that have considered *Estate of Harper's* recycling of value theory have understood it. [citations omitted,] We agree with and accept that interpretation. Thus, we conclude that the proportion of partnership assets contributed by a decedent-transferor to a family limited partnership does not affect the treatment of the partnership interest issued in return as consideration for the transferred assets for purposes of section 2036(a) or section 2043(a).

We and other courts have interpreted the bona fide sale exception to consist of two separate prongs. To satisfy the exception, an estate must establish both the nontax bona fides of the transaction and the existence of full and adequate consideration. *Estate of Bigelow v. Commissioner*, 503 F.3d at 969 (recognizing the adequacy of consideration and the bona fides of the transfer as separate, though interrelated criteria); *Kimbell*, 371 F.3d at 265 (articulating separate standards for a transaction to qualify as a bona fide sale, on the one hand, and for that sale to be for adequate and full consideration, on the other); *Estate of Bongard v. Commissioner*, 124 T.C. at 114 ("[T]he applicability of the bona fide sale exception depends on two requirements: '(1) A bona fide sale, meaning an arm's-length transaction, and (2) adequate and full consideration.' " [citation omitted]. For the reasons explained below, the extent to which the formation of a family limited partnership involves a genuine pooling of contributed assets is more germane to the first prong (the bona fides of the transaction) than to the second (adequacy of consideration).

The criterion of value equivalence on which we relied in *Estate of Harper* does not distinguish between cases in which one partner contributes essentially all of the partnership assets and those that involve a genuine "pooling" of assets contributed by different partners. Whenever a partner receives a partnership interest in exchange for property, as long as the transaction is on arm's-length terms and the value of the contributed property is credited to the transferor's capital account, the value of the partnership interest issued to the transferor will be "derived solely" from the assets the transferor contributed. *Cf. Estate of Harper v. Commissioner*, 2002 WL 992347, at *19. Of course, the more extensive the pooling of assets effected by a partnership's formation, the more significant the economic consequences of a decedent's exchange of property for a partnership interest, and the less that exchange is "only a vehicle for changing the form in which the decedent held his property". *Cf. Estate of Thompson v. Commissioner* [Dec. 54,890(M)], T.C. Memo. 2002–246, 2002 WL 31151195, at *17. Therefore, the degree of pooling is relevant to the question of the nontax bona fides of the transaction. But we see no reason why the degree of pooling should affect the extent to which a partnership interest received in exchange for transferred assets should be treated as consideration received for those assets in applying section 2036(a) or section 2043(a).

As noted above, the several Courts of Appeals that have considered *Estate of Harper's* recycling of value theory generally treat the extent that formation of a family limited partnership effects a genuine pooling of assets contributed by different partners as relevant to the nontax bona fides of transaction rather than the adequacy of the consideration provided for contributed assets. The Court of Appeals for the Fifth Circuit expressed that view most clearly in *Kimbell*, 371 F.3d at 267, stating flatly that any concern that a transaction simply recycles value "is better addressed under the 'bona fide sale' prong of th[e] exception."

In *Estate of Bigelow*, after agreeing with this Court and other courts that the application of discounts in valuing an interest in a family limited partnership does not prevent the partnership's formation from qualifying for the bona fide sale exception, the Court of Appeals for the Ninth Circuit warned that an estate cannot qualify for the exception merely by establishing the proportionality of an exchange (that is, that each partner received an interest in the partnership proportionate to the value of the assets that partner contributed). "To avoid the reach of § 2036(a)", the court cautioned, "the Estate must also show the 'genuine' pooling of assets" and a "potential [for] intangibles stemming from pooling for joint enterprise". *Estate of Bigelow v. Commissioner*, 503 F.3d at 969 (citing *Harper v. Commissioner*, 83 T.C.M. (CCH) 1641, 1654 (2002), and *Estate of Thompson v. Commissioner* [2004–2 USTC ¶ 60,489], 382 F.3d 367, 381 (3d Cir. 2004)). Because the bona fide sale and the adequate and full consideration prongs of the bona fide sale exception are "interrelated", the court reasoned, "[t]he validity of the adequate and full consideration prong cannot be gauged independently of the non-tax-related business purposes involved in making the bona fide transfer inquiry." *Id.* Thus, the court suggested, the need for an estate to show genuine pooling and the possibility of intangibles, in addition to establishing the proportionality of the exchange, arises from the interdependence between the bona fide sale and adequate consideration inquiries. The proportionality of the exchange might establish the adequacy of a partnership interest as consideration, but showing genuine pooling and the possibility of intangibles is also required to establish the transaction's nontax bona fides.

In *Estate of Thompson v. Commissioner*, 2002 WL 31151195, at *17, we applied *Estate of Harper's* recycling of value theory in concluding that "the decedent's receipt of a partnership interest in exchange for his testamentary assets is not full and adequate consideration within the meaning of section 2036." The decedent's son had made a substantial contribution to one of the two family limited partnerships we addressed in *Estate of Thompson*, having contributed a ranch property and mutual funds in exchange for a 36.72% interest in the partnership. Nonetheless, we concluded that neither partnership effected a genuine pooling of assets because each partnership arranged matters so that the income generated by a particular partnership asset went directly to the partner who had contributed it. Further, our analysis in *Estate of Thompson* did not separately apply the two requirements of the bona fide sale exception that we had identified in *Estate of Harper*. Instead, we reasoned that the transactions before us in *Estate of Thompson v. Commissioner*, 2002 WL 31151195, at *18, "were not motivated by the type of legitimate business concerns that furnish[ ] 'adequate consideration.'"

The Court of Appeals for the Third Circuit affirmed our opinion in *Estate of Thompson*, agreeing, "[f]or essentially the same reasons" on which we had relied, that the transaction at issue did not involve full and adequate consideration. *Estate of Thompson v. Commissioner*, 382 F.3d at 379. In elaborating on its conclusion, however, the Court of Appeals referred only to the absence of "any valid, functioning business enterprise" rather than on the proportion of partnership assets contributed by the decedent. *Id.* Moreover, the court distinguished *Estate of Harper* on the grounds that the decedent in that case had contributed over 99% of the total partnership assets. By contrast, the court observed, the formation of the two partnerships "involved substantial participation by decedent's family members and their respective spouses." *Estate of Thompson v. Commissioner*, 382 F.3d at 383. Thus, the court's conclusion that the formation of neither partnership was a bona fide sale for adequate and full consideration rested on the absence of business operations rather than the proportion of the assets the decedent contributed to the partnership. As the Court of Appeals for the Ninth Circuit recognized in *Estate of Bigelow*, a family limited partnership's conduct of legitimate business operations is more germane to the purposes of the entity's formation than to the adequacy of a partnership interest as consideration for contributed assets.

D. *Conclusion*

For the reasons articulated above, we conclude that, when section 2036(a) (either alone or in conjunction with section 2035(a)) requires the inclusion in the value of a decedent's gross estate of the value of assets transferred to a family limited partnership in exchange for an interest in that partnership, the amount of the required inclusion must be reduced under section 2043(a) by the value of the partnership interest received by the decedent-transferor. Consequently, when applicable, section 2036(a) (or section 2035(a)) will include in the value of a decedent's gross estate only the excess of the value of the transferred assets (as of the date of the decedent's death) over the value of the partnership interest issued in return (as of the date of the transfer). * * *

VASQUEZ, THORNTON, HOLMES, GUSTAFSON, MORRISON, BUCH, and ASHFORD, *JJ.*, agree with this opinion of the Court.

FOLEY and PARIS, *JJ.*, concur in the result only.

LAUBER, *J.*, concurring in the result only: I concur in the result that the Court reaches today. I write separately to emphasize what the Court did not decide and to highlight what the Court need not have decided.

CHAPTER 25

EXPENSES, DEBTS, CLAIMS, AND STATE DEATH TAXES

(SECTIONS 2053, 2054, AND 2058)

■ ■ ■

A. DEDUCTIONS IN GENERAL

After the gross estate is aggregated in accordance with sections 2031 through 2045, deductions are subtracted to produce the taxable estate. I.R.C. § 2051. The deductions are set forth in sections 2053 through 2058. The section 2055 deduction for charitable transfers is covered in Chapter 26, and the section 2056 deduction for marital transfers is covered in Chapter 27.

Section 2054 allows a deduction for casualty and theft losses incurred during "settlement" of the estate. The idea is that the estate tax should not be imposed on value that is destroyed by casualty or theft prior to its distribution to a beneficiary. The deduction is not allowed if the loss occurs after distribution of the asset to a beneficiary. Treas. Reg. § 20.2054–1. Casualty and theft losses may also be deductible for income tax purposes under section 165(c)(3) as limited by section 165(h), but double deductions are prohibited. The executor may elect to deduct the loss for either income or estate tax purposes, but not both. I.R.C. § 642(g); Treas. Regs. §§ 1.642(g)–1 and 20.2054–1. Significantly, for income tax purposes, from January 1, 2018 through December 31, 2025, personal casualty losses are only deductible only if attributable to a "Federally declared disaster." See I.R.C. § 165(h)(5) & (i)(5).

Section 2053 provides a deduction for four classes of expenses, debts, and claims:

1. Funeral expenses (addressed in Treas. Reg. § 20.2053–2);

2. Administration expenses;

3. Claims against the estate; and

4. Unpaid mortgages encumbering property included in the gross estate, but only if the property is included in the gross estate at its full value, without reduction for the mortgage.

Under section 2053, an estate is permitted to deduct expenses and claims only if they are allowable under the law of the jurisdiction administering the estate. Hence, no deduction in excess of the amount allowable under local law is deductible. Treas. Reg. § 20.2053–1(b)(1). Further, an estate is entitled to deductions for only amounts actually paid. Treas. Reg. § 20.2053–1(d)(1).

The requirement that the expense be "allowable" under local law would seem to limit deductions to those related to a probate estate, with the result that expenses incurred with respect to nonprobate transfers would not be deductible. This interpretation would have the effect of denying a deduction for legitimate expenses related to the numerous categories of nonprobate transfers, such as pay-on-death accounts, joint tenancies, and revocable trusts. That result, however, is avoided by section 2053(b), which allows a deduction for expenses incurred in administering property not subject to claims. Much nonprobate property often falls in this category. It is required, of course, that the expense involves property that is included in the gross estate.

A central purpose of the rules and limitations related to administration expenses and claims is to assure that the expenditure does not in fact constitute a disguised gratuitous transfer. The deduction must be bona fide and not donative in character. Payments to family members are especially suspect. Treas. Reg. § 20.2053–1(b)(2). If a local court allows an expense or claim and "actually passes upon the facts on which deductibility depends," the court's action may be relied upon to establish the bona fide nature of the expense or claim. Treas. Reg. § 20.2053–1(b)(3)(i). If there is a genuine contest, it is presumed that the court passed upon the relevant facts. A similar rule is applied to consent decrees and settlements.

Finally, with respect to unpaid mortgages, if the estate is liable for a debt secured by the mortgage, the full value of the property is included in the gross estate, and the debt is deductible under section 2053(a)(4). See Treas. Reg. § 20.2053–7. If the estate is not liable for the debt secured by the mortgage, only the equity value (full value of the property less the encumbrance) is included in the gross estate, and there is no section 2053(a)(4) deduction.

B. RULES APPLICABLE TO ADMINISTRATION EXPENSES

Fees paid to an executor or attorney are deductible if the amount is in accord with customary local practice. Treas. Reg. § 20.2053–3(b) and (c). However, an estate is not entitled to deduct a bequest or devise to an executor in lieu of a commission. Treas. Reg. § 20.2053–3(b)(2).

Under the regulations, an expense is deductible only if it is "actually and necessarily, incurred in the administration" of the estate, and it is "essential to the proper settlement of the estate." Treas. Reg. § 20.2053–3(a). Expenses of selling property, such as a broker's commission, are not deductible unless sale of the property is necessary in order to pay debts or taxes, preserve the estate, or effect distribution. Treas. Reg. § 20.2053–3(d)(2).

If the executor borrows funds to pay death taxes, the IRS is likely to question whether the interest on the loan is "essential to the proper settlement of the estate." In Rupert v. United States, 358 F. Supp. 421 (M.D. Pa. 2004), the court denied a deduction, stating that the test was whether assets could be sold to provide funds for tax payments without damage to the estate.

A question arises whether administrative expenses are deductible under section 2053 as long as the local jurisdiction allows the expense. The following case addresses whether local law is conclusive in establishing the deductibility of an expense.

HIBERNIA BANK V. UNITED STATES

United States Court of Appeals, Ninth Circuit, 1978.
581 F.2d 741.

WALLACE, CIRCUIT JUDGE:

* * * This appeal squarely presents an important issue of estate tax law which had engendered a crisp conflict among the circuits. We affirm.

I.

In May 1965, Celia Tobin Clark died testate, leaving an estate worth several million dollars. Mrs. Clark's will provided for several specific bequests of personal property. The will also directed that the residue, which included the bulk of the estate, be divided among four testamentary trusts. The income of each trust was to be paid to one of Mrs. Clark's children with the remainder to be divided equally among Mrs. Clark's grandchildren. The residue of Mrs. Clark's estate included two principal components: a mansion situated on 240 acres in Hillsborough, California, and approximately 10,000 common shares of Hibernia Bank stock.

Mrs. Clark's will named Hibernia as trustee for the four testamentary trusts. * * * Hibernia was appointed administrator with the will annexed of the Clark estate.

On June 2, 1965, Mrs. Clark's will was admitted to probate. By December 1967, all of the specific bequests and virtually all claims against the estate had been paid. Apparently, at this time, Hibernia, acting as the administrator, could have sought permission to distribute the remaining assets, including the mansion and the Hibernia stock, to the testamentary trusts and to close the estate. Rather than do so, however, Hibernia elected first to liquidate the Hillsborough mansion.

Hibernia encountered substantial difficulty in disposing of the mansion, and it was not finally sold until the spring of 1972. During this period, the administrator was required to spend some $60,000 per year in order to maintain the residence. Thus, Hibernia believed that it was necessary either to sell the estate's share of Hibernia stock or, alternatively, to borrow the funds required to maintain the mansion. Hibernia elected to borrow.

In each of the years from 1966 through 1969, Hibernia executed a substantial loan from a commercial bank. The net proceeds from these loans equaled $775,000. Hibernia itself acted as lender for two of the four loans, the proceeds of which totaled $625,000. The interest payments for the four loans totaled $196,210.

In June 1971, Hibernia filed with the Commissioner a claim for a refund of part of the estate taxes paid on the Clark estate. As part of this claim, Hibernia asserted that it was entitled to deduct from the gross estate as expenses of administration the amount it had paid in interest on the four bank loans. The Commissioner disallowed the claimed deduction for the interest and denied the corresponding refund.

* * *

II.

Hibernia's argument is straightforward. Section 2053(a)(2) provides:

> For purposes of the [estate] tax . . . the value of the taxable estate shall be determined by deducting from the value of the gross estate such amounts . . . for administration expenses . . . as are allowable by the laws of the jurisdiction, whether within or without the United States, under which the estate is being administered.

In addition, Treas. Reg. § 20.2053–1(b)(2) provides in part:

> The decision of a local court as to the amount and allowability under local law of a claim or administration expense will ordinarily be accepted if the court passes upon the facts upon which deductibility depends.

Therefore, the essence of Hibernia's argument is that the deductibility of administration expenses is exclusively a question of state law. Since in this case the California probate court expressly approved the $196,210 interest payments as administration expenses, Hibernia contends that the Commissioner was required to permit a corresponding deduction.

* * * [T]he dispute centers around whether or not the interest payments were expenses of administration within the meaning of federal estate tax law. In order to resolve this issue, the district judge focused on Treas. Reg. § 20.2053–3(a), which provides in part:

> The amounts deductible from a decedent's gross estate as "administration expenses" . . . are limited to such expenses as are actually and necessarily incurred in the administration of the decedent's estate; that is, in the collection of assets, payment of debts, and distribution of property to the persons entitled to it. The expenses contemplated in the law are such only as attend the settlement of an estate and the transfer of the property of the estate to individual beneficiaries or to a trustee. . . . Expenditures not essential to the proper settlement of the estate, but incurred for the individual benefit of the heirs, legatees, or devises, may not be taken as deductions.

Viewing the issue in this light, the district judge found that the estate had been kept open much longer than necessary, thereby rendering the loans and interest payments made during the excess period also unnecessary. Specifically, the judge found as a matter of fact that "[w]ithin fifteen months of the testator's death [Hibernia], in its capacity as administrator of the estate, had sold all the assets of the estate except the mansion with its surrounding acreage and the Hibernia Bank stock." In addition, the district judge concluded that Hibernia had failed "factually [to] demonstrate an existing necessity to keep the Clark estate open for seven years." The district judge reasoned that since it was wholly unnecessary to keep the estate open during the period of the loans, the loans and interest payments were therefore also unnecessary to the administration of the estate. The implication is that the estate was left open in order to sell the mansion not because the sale was necessary for the administration of the estate, but rather because the heirs preferred to have cash distributed to the trusts rather than an undivided interest in the mansion. Thus, the expenses were not deductible.

III.

We agree with the district judge that allowability under state law is not the sole criterion for determining the deductibility of a particular expenditure under section 2053(a)(2).

In Pitner v. United States, 388 F.2d 651 (5th Cir.1967), the Fifth Circuit held that

> [i]n the determination of deductibility under section 2053(a)(2), it is not enough that the deduction be allowable under state law. It is necessary as well that the deduction be for an "administration expense" within the meaning of that term as it is used in the statute, and that the amount sought to be deducted be

reasonable under the circumstances. These are both questions of federal law and establish the outside limits for what may be considered allowable deductions under section 2053(a)(2).

Id. at 659. * * *

We agree with the Fifth Circuit. We cannot read section 2053(a)(2) as permitting the deduction of expenditures which simply are not expenses of administration within the meaning afforded that term by federal estate tax law. Our holding is firmly supported by prior decisions as well as sound principles of policy.

* * *

Policy considerations also militate in favor of our holding. The federal estate tax is not a tax on the decedent's property, but rather a tax on the transfer of that property. * * * The mechanics of the estate tax give meaning to this distinction by permitting deductions from the decedent's gross estate for debts, administration expenses, and certain other liabilities. The resulting "taxable estate" on which the estate tax is calculated is the amount actually transferred to the heirs. Although fairness dictates that the taxable estate not include assets which will not be available for transfer to the heirs, fairness does not require the deduction of amounts which are not true liabilities of the estate. Thus, "[e]xpenditures not essential to the proper settlement of the estate, but incurred for the individual benefit of the heirs, legatees, or devises" are not expenses of administration within the meaning of section 2053. 26 C.F.R. § 20.2053–3(a).

The district judge's conclusion that the Clark estate was left open much too long is amply supported by the record. * * * Since it was unnecessary to leave the estate open during the period of the loans, it is clear that the loans were not necessary to the administration of the estate. Accordingly, the district judge was correct in disallowing an administration expense deduction for the amount of the interest payments.

AFFIRMED.

NOTE

The Second, Fourth, Fifth, Sixth, and Eleventh Circuits have concurred with the Ninth Circuit on this issue. See Estate of Grant v. Commissioner, 294 F.3d 352 (2d Cir. 2002); Estate of Milikin v. Commissioner, 125 F.3d (6th Cir. 1997); Estate of Love v. Commissioner, 923 F.2d 335 (4th Cir.1991); Marcus v. DeWitt, 704 F.2d 1227 (11th Cir. 1983); Pitner v. United States, 388 F.2d 651 (5th Cir. 1967). The Seventh Circuit, however, has held that state law controls, i.e., allowance by the probate court is conclusive. In Ballance v. Commissioner, 347 F.2d 419 (7th Cir. 1965), the Seventh Circuit stated that in determining whether an expense "constitutes an allowable expense of administration," the probate court's allowance of the expense establishes recognition by that court that it is an allowable administrative expense under the "laws of the jurisdiction." Id. at 423.

C. RULES APPLICABLE TO CLAIMS

1.   GENERAL RULES

A claim arising out of contracts or torts is deductible if it was a personal obligation of the decedent at the time of death and if the claim remains enforceable at the time of payment. Treas. Reg. § 20.2053–4(a)(1).

The Treasury takes the position that post-death events must be considered in determining the amount of the deductible claim. Under the regulations, claims may be deducted before payment (up to a collective limit of $500,000) if a qualified appraiser determines the value of the claim. Treas. Reg. § 20.2053–4(c)(1). The deduction must be adjusted up or down when the claim is actually paid. Treas. Reg. § 20.2053–4(c)(2). For example, assume that the decedent was sued for negligence in an auto accident before her death. The estimated value of the claim at the time of the decedent's death is $500,000. If the result of the litigation is a verdict in favor of the estate, with the result that the claim becomes valueless, no deduction may be taken. Treas. Reg. § 20.2053–4(a)(1) and (c)(2). The same rule is followed if the ultimate outcome is a recovery by the plaintiff of an amount greater than $500,000. If, for example, if the plaintiff ultimately recovers $800,000, the deductible claim will be $800,000.

The Treasury's position that post-death events must be considered was promulgated in the regulations in 2009. The First, Second, and Eighth Circuits had reached the same result in prior decisions. See Jacobs v. Commissioner, 34 F.2d 233 (8th Cir. 1929), cert. denied, 280 U.S. 603 (1929); Estate of Sachs v. Commissioner, 856 F.2d 1158 (8th Cir. 1988); Commissioner v. Shively's Estate, 276 F.2d 372 (2d Cir. 1960); Commissioner v. State Street Trust Co., 128 F.2d 618 (1st Cir. 1942). The Ninth, Tenth, and Eleventh Circuits, however, had reached the contrary result, holding that claims must be valued on the date of death. See Estate of Van Horne v. Commissioner, 720 F.2d 1114, cert., denied, 466 U.S. 980 (1984); Estate of McMorris v. Commissioner, 243 F.3d 1254 (10th Cir. 2001); Estate of O'Neal v. United States, 258 F.3d 1265 (11th Cir. 2001).

2.   CONSIDERATION AND DEBTS

A special rule applies to claims founded on a promise or agreement. If the claim is founded on a promise or agreement, the consideration must be "adequate and full consideration in money or money's worth" to be deductible. I.R.C. § 2053(c)(1)(A). The purpose of this rule is to assure that the gross estate is not reduced by obligations that were essentially gratuitous, i.e., obligations that reduce the decedent's assets without any offsetting receipt of value. For example, assume that a father makes a promise, under seal, to transfer $100,000 to his son at the father's death, and that under local law a promise under seal is binding despite the absence of consideration. Without the section 2053(c)(1)(A) "adequate and full consideration" rule, the $100,000 would be deductible as a claim, and $100,000 would pass to the son free of transfer tax. The following case explores an estate's attempt to circumvent the adequate and full consideration rule.

ESTATE OF FLANDREAU v. COMMISSIONER
United States Court of Appeals, Second Circuit, 1993.
994 F.2d 91.

LOKEN, CIRCUIT JUDGE:

* * * I.R.C. § 2053(a)(3) provides an estate tax deduction "for claims against the estate." A deduction "founded on a promise or agreement," however, is "limited to the extent that [the claims] were contracted bona fide and for an adequate and full consideration in money or money's worth." I.R.C. § 2053(c)(1). In this case, the Estate claims a $102,000 deduction for the face amounts of fourteen non-interest bearing, unsecured promissory notes executed by decedent in December 1970, January 1971, and January 1972 payable to her two sons and their wives.

Each note was preceded by a gift of the same amount from decedent to the purported lender. Decedent reported each of these transfers on a gift tax return but paid only $126 in federal gift taxes as all but two of the transfers were within the then-applicable gift tax exclusion. The recipients then transferred the gifted amounts back to decedent and received the notes in question. The notes were payable in 1995, when decedent would be 95 years old, or upon her death.

Mrs. Flandreau died on February 20, 1986, without having repaid any portion of the notes. The Estate claimed a deduction of $102,000 for the full amount due. The Commissioner issued a Notice of Deficiency denying the deduction on the ground that, "The debts were not bona fide debts contracted for adequate and full consideration under Section 2053 of the Internal Revenue Code." The tax court ... concluded that "these were merely circular transfers of money from decedent to her children and back to decedent." As such, the notes did not represent debts, but were rather "unenforceable gratuitous promises to make a gift, based upon neither money nor money's worth," and therefore did not qualify as deductible claims under § 2053. * * *

We have consistently rejected taxpayer's attempts to use gifts to family members followed by loans back to the taxpayer to avoid federal taxes that would otherwise be imposed.

* * * The gifts, loans, and notes were exchanged contemporaneously, and the amounts of the gifts were identical to the amounts subsequently loaned. The Estate argues that the tax court improperly considered the source of the funds that decedent's sons and daughters-in-law "loaned" to her in exchange for the notes. However, * * * it is appropriate to look beyond the form of the transactions and to determine, as the tax court did here, that the gifts and loans back to decedent were "component parts of single transactions." * * *

As the Supreme Court has observed, "the family relationship often makes it possible for one to shift tax incidence by surface changes of ownership without disturbing in the least his dominion and control over the subject of the gift or the purposes for which the income from the property is used." Commissioner v. Culbertson, 337 U.S. 733, 746 (1949). For this reason, courts examine such intrafamily transactions with heightened scrutiny; when the bona fides of promissory notes is at issue, the taxpayer must demonstrate affirmatively that "there existed at the time of the transaction a real expectation of repayment and an intent to enforce the collection of the indebtedness." Estate of Van Anda v. Commissioner, 12 T.C. 1158, 1162 (1949), aff'd per curiam, 192 F.2d 391 (2d Cir.1951). * * *Here, the tax court expressly found that the sons and daughters-in-law never expected that the money they transferred to decedent would be repaid.

Having carefully considered the entire transaction, we agree with the tax court that the Estate failed to carry its burden of showing the notes were "contracted bona fide and for an adequate and full consideration in money or money's worth."

* * * The judgment of the tax court is affirmed.

NOTE

The "adequate and full consideration" rule has special application to transfers arising from marital relationships. Section 2043(b)(1) provides that relinquishment of marital rights is not deemed to be adequate and full consideration. Assume, for example, that a wife, in consideration of her husband's agreement to surrender his right to receive a portion of the wife's property at her death, agrees to pay $200,000 to the husband at the wife's death. Section 2043(b)(1), in conjunction with section 2053(c)(1)(A), renders the husband's claim nondeductible (although the $200,000 transfer could qualify for the marital deduction if it meets the requirements of section 2056). Where the obligation arises from divorce, a special rule applies. As explained in Chapter 3, a claim arising from divorce is treated as made for full and adequate consideration if the requirements of section 2516 are met. See I.R.C. § 2043(b)(2).

Also, if any claim against the estate is founded on a promise by the decedent to make a gift to charity, the statute permits the deduction as if the promise were a bequest to charity under section 2055. See I.R.C. § 2053(c)(1)(A).

3. UNENFORCEABLE CLAIMS

REVENUE RULING 78–271
1978–2 C.B. 239.

The decedent, D, owned and operated a business as a sole proprietorship from 1945 until death. In 1956, D's spouse, A, began to actively render substantial services to the business on a full-time basis and continued to do so until D's death in 1976. D and A had no understanding, express or implied, that A would be compensated for the services. No compensation was paid to A during the time that A rendered the services.

At D's death, A submitted a claim to the executor of the estate for 200x dollars, the value of the services rendered to the business. The executor limited payment to A to 30x dollars, the value of the services rendered within the applicable time allowed by the statute of limitations for bringing an action for recovery. The decedent's federal estate tax return includes a deduction of 30x dollars with respect to the claim made by A for the value of A's services.

Applicable local law recognizes a married person's right to recover for services rendered to the spouse's business provided that the services were rendered pursuant to a contract between the spouses. Local law provides that, in the absence of a bona fide agreement to compensate the spouse, the services of the spouse are deemed to have been gratuitously rendered to the business. * * *

The specific question presented is whether A's claim for the value of services rendered to D's business qualifies as a deduction against D's estate for purposes of section 2053(a) of the Code.

The payment of a claim by an executor does not, of itself, establish the claim as being enforceable against the estate. * * * A deductible claim, within the meaning of section 2053(a), must represent a debt of the decedent that is recognized by state law. * * * A claim may be deducted from the decedent's gross estate only if the claimant had a valid right under state law to enforce the claim against the estate. * * *

In the present situation, A's claim is not enforceable under local law since there was no agreement between the spouses that A would be compensated. A is deemed, under applicable local laws, to have gratuitously rendered the services to D's business. Consequently, A's claim does not represent a personal obligation of D existing at the time of D's death.

Accordingly, A's claim for services rendered to D's business fails to meet the requirement of section 2053(a) that the claim be enforceable under local law. Therefore, the amounts paid by the executor in satisfaction of A's claim are not deductible from D's gross estate. In other cases, where there is a claim founded upon an agreement between the spouses, the claim will be allowed under section 2053(a) only if it is determined that, based on all the facts and circumstances, the agreement is bona fide and was contracted for an adequate and full consideration in money or money's worth.

PROBLEM

Nathan Brown died on March 3 of this year, survived by his daughter, Mackenzie, and his son, Samuel. Nathan's gross estate had a value of $8,000,000 on the date of his death. This included a tract of undeveloped real estate (Sunny Acres) owned entirely by Nathan. The value of Sunny Acres without taking into account any mortgage encumbering the property was $1,000,000, and this amount was included in Nathan's gross estate. Sunny Acres was encumbered by a mortgage securing a note made by Nathan and payable to the Tenth National Bank in the amount of $400,000.

Mackenzie is serving as executor and will decline any fee. She has retained Taylor Larson, a lawyer, to represent Mackenzie (as executor) in the estate proceeding. Taylor's fee will be $50,000, and Mackenzie will not make the election described in section 642(g) as to this fee.

Nathan belongs to the Bigtown Country Club, which sends bills every four weeks for Nathan's membership dues for the prior four weeks. Nathan received a bill for $800 for dues and meals through the date three weeks prior to his death, but because of his ill health he did not pay the bill prior to his death. One week after Nathan's death Mackenzie received a bill for $600 for dues for the three weeks ending at Nathan's death.

Four months before his death Nathan bought a parcel of land (Cloudy Acres) from Elinor Sheridan. The purchase price was $300,000. Nathan made a down payment of $40,000 in cash at the time of the purchase and agreed to pay the remaining $260,000 in three years. Nathan's promise is not secured by an interest in Cloudy Acres.

Five years before his death Nathan promised to pay his nephew, Austin Gordon, $20,000 if Austin completed a bachelor's degree. Austin completed the degree in January of this year, but Nathan had not yet paid the $20,000 to Austin at the time Nathan died. Nathan's promise to pay $20,000 to Austin is enforceable under local law.

Nathan was divorced from his wife, Alicia, in 2023. A divorce decree was entered on February 1, 2023, and the decree incorporated a property settlement agreement entered into between Alicia and Nathan on November 2, 2022. The decree required Nathan to transfer $500,000 to Alicia upon

Nathan's death. In return, Alicia surrendered all her marital rights relating to Nathan's property.

What is the amount of Nathan's taxable estate?

D. STATE DEATH TAXES

Any death tax imposed by a state or by the District of Columbia with regard to property included in the decedent's gross estate is deductible in determining the taxable estate. I.R.C. § 2058(a). The tax must actually be paid and the deduction claimed within a limited time period specified in section 2058(b), generally four years after the estate tax return is filed.

Because the deduction is allowed for the full amount of the state death tax paid, the amount of the state death tax must be determined before the federal estate tax can be determined. If the amount of the state death tax is determined by reference to the amount of the federal estate tax, a simultaneous equation is necessary to determine these interrelated numbers.

The section 2058 deduction first became available to estates of decedents dying on or after January 1, 2005. As to deaths prior to that date, a credit, subject to a dollar maximum that varied in proportion to the size of the taxable estate, was allowed for state death taxes paid. The section 2058 deduction was subject to a sunset provision. However, it was made permanent under the American Taxpayer Relief Act of 2012 (P.L. 112–240 § 101(a)(1) & (3)).

CHAPTER 26

CHARITABLE BEQUESTS

(SECTION 2055)

■ ■ ■

A. TRENDS IN CHARITABLE GIVING

From the outset, the federal estate tax was friendly to charitable dispositions. In sharp contrast to the income tax, where section 170 limits to a percentage of income the amount that may be claimed as an income tax deduction, the deductions provided for charitable bequests and gifts is unlimited.[1] An easy and complete escape from the federal estate tax is simply to leave all one's property to a qualified charity, and, it may be noted, the federal government itself is just such a charity.

The COVID-19 pandemic, economic and financial factors, and the advancement of racial justice impacted charitable giving. Indeed, there was an increase in charitable giving in response to these factors.[2] Charitable giving in the United States totaled $484.85 billion in 2021, representing a 4 percent increase in the United States compared to 2020.[3] The top three recipients of charitable giving during 2021 were religious organizations, educational institutions, and human services organizations.[4] According to empirical data, *inter vivos* gifts from individuals accounted for 67% ($326.87 billion) and bequests accounted for an additional 9% ($46.01 billion) of all charitable giving during 2021.[5] However, there was a 7.3 percent decline in giving by bequest from 2020 to 2021.[6]

There are several trends that impact the level of charitable giving. For example, the amount of disposable personal income impacts charitable

---

[1] See Edward A. Zelinsky, *Why the Buffet-Gates Giving Pledge Requires Limitation on the Estate Tax Charitable Deduction*, 16 FLA. TAX REV. 393 (2014) (arguing that the estate tax should be limited like the income tax deduction).

[2] Giving USA 2022, *The Annual Report on Philanthropy for the Year 2021*, Indiana University Lilly Family School of Philanthropy 14, 83 (2022) (on file with the author) [hereinafter Giving USA].

[3] Giving USA, supra note 2, at 29. While there was an increase in the dollar amount of charitable giving, the growth did not keep up with inflation. Id. at 13.

[4] Giving USA, supra note 2, at 22. Charitable giving to religious and human services organizations increased during 2021, but the level of giving to educational institutions during 2021 actually decreased from 2020. Id. at 24.

[5] Giving USA, supra note 2, at 21.

[6] Giving USA, supra note 2, at 24.

giving. Disposable personal income grew in 2021 from the 2020 level. This increase was due in part to the Coronavirus Aid, Relief, and Economic Security Act of 2020,[7] which was enacted to provide economic relief resulting from the COVID-19 pandemic.

While various trends and factors may impact the level of charitable giving, there is debate amongst scholars about the impact of the estate tax and the deduction for charitable bequests in generating such gifts. Some scholars posit that repeal of the tax would unleash a torrent of gift giving as members of the senior generation found that, due to the absence of the tax, less wealth would have to be left to offspring to provide for them thereby freeing the balance for charity. Others posit that the tax lowers the cost of giving to charity thereby propelling donors to give more than they otherwise would in its absence. The best econometric analysis seems to indicate that repeal of the estate tax would lower the dollar amount of bequests from between 12% to 37% of what it otherwise would have been, with the result depending on the model used. See David Joulfaian, On Estate Tax Repeal and Charitable Bequests, 123 Tax Notes 1221 (2009).

Based on the current composition of Congress, it is unlikely that the estate tax will be repealed. However, it will be interesting to see whether there is an increase in charitable giving after 2025 when the Tax Cuts and Jobs Act will sunset resulting in substantial drop in the basic exclusion amount.

B. CHARITABLE?

Section 2055 authorizes a deduction for transfers to three basic types of recipients: (1) the federal government, state governments or subdivisions thereof; (2) corporations operated exclusively for religious, charitable, scientific, literary, or educational purposes, which do not attempt to influence elections and are not substantially engaged in carrying on propaganda or influencing legislation; and (3) certain fraternal and veterans organizations. Court battles over the status of recipients under section 2055 are hotly waged not only by the donors and their descendants seeking deductions, but also by the recipients themselves whose contribution inflow often depends on the deductibility of the gifts.

The vast number of decisions on this issue have produced paradoxical results. The Bar Association of St. Louis is a qualified charity. See St. Louis Union Trust Co. v. United States, 374 F.2d 427 (8th Cir.1967). However, the St. Louis Medical Society is not a qualified charity. See Hammerstein v. Kelley, 349 F.2d 928 (8th Cir.1965). The self-governing Zuni Indian Tribe of Zuni, New Mexico, failed to qualify as a governmental subdivision because its political powers stemmed from "original sovereignty" rather than from an act of Congress. Rev. Rul. 74–179, 1974–1 C.B. 279. However,

---

[7]   Giving USA, supra note 2, at 74.

the Indian Tribal Government Status Act provides that Indian tribes are to be treated as state governments for federal tax purposes thereby changing that result. See I.R.C. § 7871(a)(6); Rev. Proc. 84–36, 1984–1 C.B. 10 (listing Indian tribes and approved agencies).

The types of eligible recipients enumerated in section 2055 are the only types that may receive deductible bequests—no matter how "charitable" the donor's intent. Thus, a bequest to an indigent acquaintance or to an individual orphan or invalid will not produce an estate tax deduction. Can you see what possible abuses Congress was trying to prevent?

The following case addresses whether bequests to Bar associations qualified as eligible charitable organizations.

DULLES V. JOHNSON

United States Court of Appeals, Second Circuit, 1959.
273 F.2d 362.

WATERMAN, CIRCUIT JUDGE.

[William Nelson Cromwell, a prominent New York attorney, died leaving portions of the residue of his estate to the New York County Lawyers Association, to the Association of the Bar of the City of New York and to the New York State Bar Association. His executors claimed charitable deductions for such bequests, but they were denied by the Commissioner. The executors filed a claim for refund with the District Court, but relief was denied. The executors appealed.]

In order to secure a deduction for the bequests made to the Bar Associations plaintiffs must demonstrate that these bequests come within the language of Section 812(d) [now § 2055] of the 1939 Internal Revenue Code which permits as a deduction from the value of the gross estate "[t]he amount of all bequests, legacies, devises, or transfers * * * to or for the use of any corporation organized and operated exclusively for religious, charitable, scientific, literary or educational purposes * * * and no substantial part of the activities of which is carrying on propaganda, or otherwise attempting to influence legislation * * *." The district court held that the executors failed to carry this burden, Dulles v. Johnson, 155 F.Supp. 275. That court concluded that the Associations "exist primarily to benefit members of the legal profession, and to provide a method whereby their views and recommendations as a body on legislation of various kinds is made known to the legislators." Supra, at page 279. The court appears to have based its conclusion on the following Association activities as they existed on July 19, 1948: (1) regulation of the unauthorized practice of law; (2) institution of disciplinary measures for professional misconduct of members of the bar and judiciary; (3) recommendations with respect to judicial administration and procedure and the endorsement of candidates for judicial office; and (4) activities in support of or in opposition to various legislative proposals.

The New York County Lawyers Association (sometimes referred to as "County Lawyers") was incorporated in 1908 under the New York Membership Corporations Law (Chapter 559, Laws of 1895). The Certificate of Incorporation provided:

"The purposes for which said Association is to be formed are, the cultivation of the science of jurisprudence; the promotion of reforms in the law; the facilitation of the administration of justice; the elevation of the standards of integrity, honor and courtesy in the legal profession; the cherishing of the spirit of brotherhood among the members of said Association."

County Lawyers owns its own four-story building in New York City which contains a large auditorium, a library (some 85,000 volumes as of April 1948), and a number of rooms used for conference and staff purposes. As of April 1948 there were approximately 7,000 members. The auditorium and the other facilities have been used by the Practising Law Institute for courses and lectures available to members of the bar generally. In addition, there were many other lectures and forums so available. County Lawyers publishes a magazine entitled "Bar Bulletin" which is mailed to its members and various law libraries throughout the country, and which contains articles relating to various phases of the law. Its standing and special committees comprehensively deal with a wide range of legal matters.

The Association of the Bar of the City of New York (sometimes referred to as the City Bar) was incorporated in 1871 by a Special Act of the New York Legislature (Chapter 819, Laws of 1871) (amended Chapter 134, Laws of 1924)

" * * * for the purposes of cultivating the science of jurisprudence, promoting reforms in the law, facilitating the administration of justice, elevating the standards of integrity, honor and courtesy in the legal profession, and cherishing the spirit of brotherhood among the members thereof."

The City Bar owns a four-story building in the City of New York, in which there is a large auditorium, a library of some 268,000 volumes, conference rooms, and staff and legal referral offices. The City Bar sponsors numerous lectures on a wide variety of legal subjects. The City Bar's Committee of Legal Education has sponsored a symposium on this subject at which some 45 law schools were represented. Just as in the case of the County Bar, committees are annually appointed to deal with all important phases of the law, both State and Federal. The City Bar aids in combating election frauds and actively supports legal aid work. The City Bar also publishes a magazine, entitled "The Record," which contains articles of interest both to lawyers and the public.

The New York State Bar Association (sometimes referred to as the State Bar) was incorporated in 1877 by a Special Act of the New York Legislature (Chapter 210, Laws of 1877):

> "And the said association is formed to cultivate the science of jurisprudence, to promote reform in the law, to facilitate the administration of justice, to elevate the standard of integrity, honor and courtesy in the legal profession, and to cherish the spirit of brotherhood among the members thereof."

It has offices in Albany, New York. Because of the large State Law Library located in that City, the State Bar maintains only a small library. Its committees, however, cover the same wide range as the County Lawyers and City Bar committees. State Bar publishes a magazine known as "The Bulletin." In addition, it publishes pamphlets containing summaries of recent developments in the law, legislative circulars containing analyses of important bills, and a year book.

The district court conceded that much of the activity of the Associations fulfilled the requirements of Section 812(d). However, in holding that bequests to the Associations could not be deducted from the gross estate under Section 812(d) it would appear from the stipulated facts it enumerated that the court emphasized four activities in which the Associations engage. Each activity will be considered in turn.

1. REGULATION OF THE UNAUTHORIZED PRACTICE OF LAW

The three associations maintain committees to receive and investigate complaints dealing with unauthorized practice of law. The committees also present cases for prosecution to state or federal authorities, bring actions in behalf of the organizations, and initiate and support legislation—in order to prohibit the practice of the law by persons not admitted to the bar. We cannot say that this program does not benefit the public or that it does not serve charitable and educational purposes. Recognizing the need to protect the public, New York law makes it a misdemeanor for unauthorized persons to practice or hold themselves out as authorized to practice law. And the Bar Associations are empowered to commence proceedings for the punishment and restraint of such behavior. * * * If these activities were not undertaken by the Associations, the cost of this necessary regulation would descend upon the public. Hence we conclude that as to regulation of the unauthorized practice of law the Associations must be deemed "charitable."

2. DISCIPLINING OF THE PROFESSION

The Associations maintain committees on discipline and grievance. The work of these committees has consisted of considering complaints filed against members of the bar by laymen and attorneys, of presenting to the courts charges against some of these attorneys, and of submitting requests to the Presiding Justice of the Appellate Division to appoint attorneys designated by the Bar Associations to prosecute disciplinary proceedings. Here again we think that the district court misconceived the purpose of these activities. Lawyers play a unique and important role in our society. In its dealings with lawyers the public must often act on faith. It is the function of bar associations to see that this faith is not misplaced. New York recognizes the need for this public service and confers upon bar associations statutory powers and obligations in connection therewith. While increased public esteem for lawyers may result in material advantage to members of the legal profession, the true benefit from a disciplined and socially responsive bar accrues directly to the public. Accordingly the present case is readily distinguishable from Better Business Bureau v. United States, 326 U.S. 279 (1945), cited by the Government, and relied upon by the court below. There it was "apparent beyond dispute that an important if not the primary pursuit of petitioner's organization [was] to promote not only an ethical but also a profitable business community." Supra at 283. We agree with the case of Rhode Island Hospital Trust Co. v. United States, 159 F.Supp. 204, 205 (D.R.I.1958), wherein a bequest to the Rhode Island Bar Association "to be used and employed by it for the advancement and upholding of those standards of the profession which are assumed by the members upon their admission to the Bar, and for the prosecution and punishment of those members who violate their obligations to the court and to the public," was held to be a gift to be used for charitable purposes within the meaning of Section 812(d).

3. IMPROVING COURT PROCEDURE AND ENDORSEMENT OF JUDICIAL CANDIDATES

There is no dispute but that the associations have taken an active interest in improving legal and litigation procedure and judicial administration, and have probed into the qualifications of candidates for judicial office. In the past, for example, committees of the Associations have reported to the Judicial Council on a proposed revision of the procedure to review tax assessments on real property; they have made recommendations with respect to the Appellate Division rules, they have furthered proposals to unify and consolidate certain New York courts and proposals to increase the number of judges in New York and Federal courts. Although such complaints have been happily few, committees of the Associations have investigated complaints of misconduct by judicial officers and employees. Recommendations concerning judicial candidates have been non-partisan and reflect primarily an evaluation of the professional experience and technical ability of the candidates. Here the committees perform a most valuable function, for lawyers are peculiarly well equipped to seek out and remedy flaws in the judicial machinery and to assess the performances and capabilities of judges. In today's immensely complex society they alone, perhaps, are alert to watch for and attempt correction of manifest defects prior to the time when malfunctions become apparent to everyone. These activities clearly constitute a public service, and we fail to discern that they indicate that the Associations seek to achieve a selfish professional benefit thereby.

4. INFLUENCING LEGISLATION

Finally, we must consider those activities which concern or affect legislation, a subject highlighted by the district court and upon which it would appear to have placed considerable emphasis. Through their various committees the Associations study and report on proposed and existing legislation. Often they send copies of their reports and resolutions to the legislative, executive and judicial branches of the federal and state governments. The major portion of this work is of a technical nature involving the adequacy of proposed and existing legislation in terms of its form, clarity of expression and its effect on and relation to other law. The Associations' work has been expressed in expert reports on matters uniquely within the fields of experts and has avoided questions which are outside those fields, i.e., questions which turn largely on economic or political decisions.

These activities serve no selfish purpose of the legal profession— rather they constitute an expert's effort to improve the law in technical and non-controversial areas. In our opinion these activities are scientific, educational and charitable.

The Government argues that these activities constitute propaganda and represent a substantial part of all the activities of the Associations. The cases upon which the Government relies are inapposite. Those cases involved organizations whose principal purpose was to implement legislative programs embodying broad principles of social amelioration. Here, on the other hand, approval of or opposition to proposed legislation constitutes but a small portion of the total activity of the Associations. * * * Moreover, the legislative recommendations of the Associations, insofar as these recommendations do not involve matters the responsibility for which has been entrusted to the Associations by the Legislature, are designed to improve court procedure or to clarify some technical matter of substantive law. They are not intended for the economic aggrandizement of a particular group or to promote some larger principle of governmental policy. These two factors lead us to the conclusion that the recommendations of the Associations concerning impending legislation are not such as to cause the forfeiture of charitable status under Section 812(d).

Other activities of the Associations which the district court did not refer to and yet which are substantial in nature include maintaining libraries for legal research, sponsoring lectures and forums on the law, providing free legal service through participation in legal aid, and providing low cost legal service through participation in a legal referral system. All of these activities are, in our opinion, educational and charitable. The Associations do engage in certain other incidental activities, but these activities, some social in nature, are merely auxiliary to the charitable and educational purposes we have discussed.

"Organized and operated exclusively" means only that these unconforming activities be incidental in nature. Seasongood v. C.I.R., 227 F.2d 907 (6th Cir.1955); 1 Paul, Federal Estate and Gift Taxation 668 (1946); cf. Better Business Bureau v. United States, 326 U.S. 279, 283 (1945). Such is the situation here.

Looking at the total operations of the three Bar Associations we hold that they are "charitable, scientific * * * [and] educational" within the meaning of Section 812(d) [now § 2055] and that the district court erred in disallowing deductions for the bequests to them. The judgment is reversed with respect to the disallowance of the deductions.

NOTE

In Association of Bar of City of New York v. Commissioner, 858 F.2d 876 (2d Cir. 1988), the Court of Appeals for the Second Circuit held that the Association of the Bar of the City of New York lacked exempt status. The court based its holding on the ground that the ranking of candidates for judicial office as acceptable or unacceptable constituted an impermissible attempt to influence the electoral process given the elective nature of the New York judiciary. This should be contrasted with the Second Circuit's holding in *Dulles* involving gifts to the same organization, which the Second Circuit then found to be exempt. Is this a better result?

Significantly, many Bar Associations have charitable arms to support public service. For example, the American Bar Association has the Fund for Justice and Education, American Bar Endowment, and American Bar Foundation. Illinois State Bar Association has the Illinois Bar Foundation that sponsors several charitable initiatives. The District of Columbia Bar's charitable arm, the D.C. Bar Pro Bono Center, operates the Nonprofit Legal Service Assistance Program that provides legal assistance to several community-based nonprofit organizations. None of these charitable arms have a political agenda.

Organizations with a significant base of charitable activities but with a political agenda that can result in disqualification can often have their cake and eat it too. This is frequently done by creating a second "action organization" that limits its activities to those of the impermissible political sort. The nonpolitical charitable activities are then confined to the original organization, which often has a similar name and some overlap with the board of directors of the action organization. Donors who are concerned about tax-exempt status can then focus their contributions on the exempt organization and unconcerned donors can make their gifts to the action organization.

The following case addresses whether a bequest to nonprofit cemetery associations qualified for a charitable deduction.

CHILD V. UNITED STATES
United States Court of Appeals, Second Circuit, 1976.
540 F.2d 579.

OAKES, CIRCUIT JUDGE:

[A decedent bequeathed a large portion of her estate to two nonprofit cemetery associations. Her executor claimed a deduction under § 2055(a)(2) on the ground that the associations are charitable or religious. The Commissioner rejected the claim and the executor brought an action in district court where his claim was again rejected. Appeal was then taken to the Court of Appeals which, in the following opinion, affirmed the decision of the district court.]

* * * The 1939 Internal Revenue Code did not expressly provide for either income or estate tax deductions for donations to cemetery associations. In 1954, however, the Code was amended to provide an express exemption from the *income* tax for "[c]emetery companies owned and operated exclusively for the benefit of their members or which are not operated for profit. . . ." 26 U.S.C. § 501(c)(13). [Emphasis in original.] But it is significant that this was done as a *special* exemption, wholly outside the rubric of "charitable" or "religious" status under § 501(c)(3).

* * *

No similar *estate* tax provision expanding deductibility for bequests to cemeteries either specially or as "charitable" or "religious" contributions has been made by Congress. The estate tax provision regarding such bequests in the 1939 and 1954 Codes is identical in content to the old income tax charitable contribution provision, see 26 U.S.C. § 170(c)(2), which the 1954 Congress felt did not extend to include gifts or bequests to cemetery associations. Under the congressional understanding and the prior case law, it appears that a per se rule allowing deduction for bequests to cemetery associations would be "beyond [that] allowed under present law. . . ." S.Rep. on Int.Rev.Code of 1954, supra.

In this situation, the executor is constrained to argue that the two cemetery association beneficiaries involved in this case serve in the traditional sense as charitable or religious enterprises. As was stated in Gund's Estate v. Commissioner, 113 F.2d 61, 62 (6th Cir.1940) (bequest to association not deductible where no free burial space provided or less than fair value charged for burial or upkeep), cert. denied, 311 U.S. 696 (1940), "[a] cemetery association doubtless could be so organized and operated as to be a charitable organization within the meaning of the [Internal Revenue Code]. . . ."

* * * As the district court found, however, "[t]he Cemetery Associations did not make it a practice of providing free burial to indigents, nor is it their usual custom to provide any plots at reduced prices." Here, as in Bank of Carthage v. United States, 304 F.Supp. 77, 80 (W.D.Mo.1969), "[i]t appears the rich, the poor, and the in-between are treated alike." While some of the various functions claimed to be charitable by the cemetery may in fact be so, here as in *Bank of Carthage* "the conclusion is inescapable that the [cemetery's] funds are not used *exclusively for charitable purposes*," as the statute requires. Id. (emphasis original).

We cannot accept the broad view of Dulles v. Johnson, 273 F.2d 362 (2d Cir.1959), cert. denied, 364 U.S. 834 (1960), espoused by the executor, that if the activity of burying the dead were not undertaken by these and like associations, the cost would devolve upon the public, thereby rendering the associations "charitable" in purpose. * * * In *Dulles*, however, it is clear that substantial "charitable" and "educational" activities of a more traditional sort were continuously being performed by the beneficiary associations: "maintaining libraries for legal research, sponsoring lectures and forums on the law, providing free legal service through participation in legal aid, and providing low cost legal service through participation in a legal referral system." 273 F.2d at 367–68. In our view, *Dulles* should be read for the proposition that public dedication of services by an organization may be colored by a history of that organization's performance of more traditional charitable activities to such an extent that the entire enterprise, or the "total operations" of the association, id. at 368, assume the aspect of charitable service to the community. The activities which are not charitable or educational, e.g., social or economic, must be merely "auxiliary" or "incidental in nature." Id. By concentrating solely on the factor of relieving public expense, we believe the executor has overlooked the complex of factors upon which the *Dulles* opinion was based. Relief of general tax burdens alone, in a society with some progressivity in its tax structure, cannot be deemed a single, inalienable mark of charity.

* * *

[The court below] was also correct in holding that the two cemetery associations do not qualify as "religious" entities under § 2055. Here, as in the case of "charitable" status, it must again be assumed that a cemetery could be so organized as to constitute a "religious" entity under the estate tax provisions, 26 U.S.C. § 2055(a). In fact, we have been informed on argument of this case that many cemeteries directly associated with and under the supervision of particular churches have been treated by the Commissioner as "religious" activities for purposes of § 2055, even though church or church-owned burial plots are not given free of charge except to occasional indigents. See also Estate of Elizabeth L. Audenried, 26 T.C. 120 (1956). The executor claims that Grove Cemetery and Watertown Cemetery [the object of the decedent's bounty] should be similarly treated, despite their lack of religious affiliation, because burial in general serves a religious purpose. While burial may, in many or most instances, serve a religious function, the fact remains that the cemetery associations in this case do not themselves perform that function. Accordingly, we affirm the judgment of the district court, leaving to congressional wisdom the apparent anomaly establishing different treatment of nonprofit cemetery associations for income and estate tax purposes.

Judgment affirmed.

NOTES

1. In First Nat'l Bank of Omaha v. United States, 681 F.2d 534 (8th Cir. 1982), the court rejected the approach of the *Child* decision and took the view that a bequest to a cemetery association could qualify for a charitable deduction—if the bequest was directed to a qualified charitable purpose. But the court found that, since the particular fund was first to be used for maintenance of the decedent's family plot, the bequest did not qualify for a charitable deduction under section 2055.

2. The question of whether educational institutions (and perhaps other forms of charitable institutions as well) could qualify as charities, exempt from income tax and eligible for tax deductible contributions, notwithstanding the practice of discrimination based on race, has had something of a checkered history. After a long period of nonconcern on this front, the Treasury in 1970 announced that discriminating educational institutions could not qualify as tax-exempt institutions and, thus, would not be qualified recipients for deductible contributions or bequests. IRS News Release, July 7, 1970. This followed a ruling in 1967 denying deductibility of contributions to a recreational organization that barred use of its facilities by members of a nonfavored race. See Rev. Rul. 67–325, 1967–2 C.B. 113. The ground of the ruling was the common law definition of a charity for legal purposes. In Rev. Rul. 71–447, 1971–2 C.B. 230, the IRS issued a formal public revenue ruling which was in accord with its July 7, 1970 News Release.

In Bob Jones University v. United States, 461 U.S. 574 (1983), the Supreme Court decided, in the context of an income tax question about the university's tax-exempt status, that Rev. Rul. 71–447 was valid, reinforced by unsuccessful efforts to change the rule by congressional legislation. Accordingly, the Court sustained the action of the Commissioner in revoking the university's tax-exempt status. The case is good precedent, of course, for estate and gift tax as well as income tax purposes.

The Bob Jones case involved an educational institution. What of the tax status of other types of charities? May any of them practice discrimination and still qualify for favorable tax treatment? What of institutions discriminating against women? Can McCoy v. Schultz, 73–1 USTC ¶ 12,906, 31 AFTR 2d 73–858 (D.D.C. 1973), holding that the Portland City Club denying admission to women was nevertheless tax-exempt, continue to stand? What of single sex schools?

C. VALUING THE CHARITABLE DEDUCTION

ESTATE OF DIERINGER V. COMMISSIONER

United States Court of Appeals, Ninth Circuit, 2019.
917 F.3d 1135.

PAEZ, CIRCUIT JUDGE.

In this estate tax case, the Internal Revenue Service Commissioner ("Commissioner") assessed a deficiency against the decedent's estate for overstating the amount of a charitable contribution. The estate executor and heir declared a large charitable deduction based on the value of estate property at the time of death, only to manipulate the property for personal gain, deliver assets to the charity worth substantially less than those claimed as a deduction, and receive a tax windfall in the process. The Tax Court sustained the deficiency. We affirm in light of our holding in *Ahmanson Foundation v. United States,* where we underscored "the principle that the testator may only be allowed a deduction for estate tax purposes for what is actually received by the charity." * * *

* * *

The Dieringer family owns Dieringer Properties, Inc. ("DPI"), a closely held corporation that manages commercial and residential properties in Portland, Oregon, as well as a Wendy's restaurant in Texas. After Robert passed away and before Victoria's death, Eugene was the president of DPI, Patrick was the executive vice-president and secretary, Victoria was the vice-president, and Timothy was the office manager. DPI's Board of Directors ("Board") consisted of Victoria as chairperson, and Eugene, Patrick, Timothy, and Thomas Keepes ("Keepes"), who is unrelated to the Dieringers, as directors. None of the other nine Dieringer children were involved in DPI in any capacity.

* * *

According to Victoria's will, dated November 10, 2000, upon her death all of her Estate would pass to the Victoria Evelyn Dieringer Trust ("Trust"). The Trust, as amended on April 22, 2005, provided for Victoria's children to receive some personal effects, but no other proceeds from her estate. The Trust also provided for $ 600,000 in donations to various charitable organizations. Any assets remaining in the Estate would then pass to the Bob and Evelyn Dieringer Family Foundation ("Foundation"), an I.R.C. § 501(c)(3) organization, as a charitable contribution. Under Victoria's estate plan, Eugene was appointed as the sole trustee of both the Trust and the Foundation. Patrick and Keepes served as advisory trustees of the Foundation.

* * *

When Victoria died, Eugene was appointed executor of the Estate. To determine the value of Victoria's DPI shares for Estate administration purposes, the Estate's law firm requested that Lewis Olds & Associates perform an independent appraisal of the net asset value of DPI. The appraisal determined that the value of DPI as of the date of Victoria's death was $ 17,777,626 and that Victoria's shares in DPI were worth $ 14,182,471.

* * *

The Estate filed its Form 706, United States Estate (and Generation-Skipping Transfer) Tax Return on July 12, 2010, reporting no estate tax liability. The Estate claimed a charitable contribution deduction of $ 18,812,181, based on the date-of-death value of Victoria's DPI shares.

* * *

In June 2013, the Commissioner issued a notice of deficiency to the Estate based on its July 2010 tax return (Form 706). The notice stated that there was a deficiency of $ 4,124,717* * *.

Upon receiving the notice of deficiency, the Estate filed a timely petition in the Tax Court challenging the Commissioner's deficiency notice and penalty assessment. The Estate argued that it correctly used the date-of-death appraisal to determine the value of Victoria's DPI shares for the purpose of the charitable contribution deduction. The Commissioner responded that post-death events should be considered in determining the value of the charitable contribution, as the actions by Eugene, Patrick, and Timothy reduced the value of Victoria's contribution to the Foundation.

Following trial, the Tax Court issued a decision upholding the Commissioner's reduction of the Estate's charitable deduction and the deficiency assessment. The Tax Court found that the redemption was not part of Victoria's estate plan and there were valid business reasons for many of the transactions that took place after her death. The Tax Court also concluded, however, that post-death events—primarily Eugene's decision to apply a minority interest discount to the redemption value of Victoria's DPI shares—reduced the value of the contribution to the Foundation and therefore reduced the value of the Estate's charitable deduction. But the evidence did not support the conclusion that a poor business climate caused the reported decline in share values, as the Estate argued. Further, the Tax Court affirmed the Commissioner's determination that the Estate was liable for a penalty under I.R.C. § 6662(a). After denying the Estate's motion for reconsideration, the Tax Court entered a final decision in favor of the Commissioner, which sustained an estate tax deficiency of $ 4,124,717* * *.

The Estate challenges the Tax Court's final decision on three grounds. First, it argues that the Tax Court erred by taking into account events that occurred after Victoria's death in determining the value of the charitable deduction. Instead, the Estate argues that the charitable deduction should have been valued as of Victoria's date of death. Second, the Estate argues that even if post-death events could be considered, the Tax Court erred by not accounting for a decline in value of Victoria's shares caused by economic forces. [The court rejected all of the Estate's arguments.]

At the center of the parties' dispute is whether the Estate's charitable deduction should be valued at the time of Victoria's death, or whether the post-death events that decreased value of the property delivered to charity should be considered.

The Estate Tax and Charitable Deductions

* * *Because the estate tax is a tax on the decedent's bequest of property, the valuation of the gross estate is typically done as of the date of death. *See* I.R.C. § 2031; *Tr. Servs. of Am., Inc. v. United States,* 885 F.2d 561, 568–69 (9th Cir. 1989). The pertinent statute provides that "[t]he value of the gross estate of the decedent shall be determined by including to the extent provided for in this part, the value at the time of his death of all property. . . wherever situated." I.R.C. § 2031(a); *see also* id. § 2033 (mandating that property in which the decedent had an interest be valued on the date of decedent's death); Treas. Reg. § 20.2031–1(b) (requiring the valuation of property at the "fair market value at the time of the decedent's death" unless an exception applies). Except in some limited circumstances, such as when the executor elects to use an alternative valuation under I.R.C. § 2032, post-death events are generally not considered in determining the estate's gross value for purposes of the estate tax. The parties agree that the executor did not use the alternative valuation method in this case.

A related provision allows for deductions from the value of the gross estate for transfers of assets to qualified charitable entities. I.R.C. § 2055(a). This deduction generally is allowed "for the value of property included in the decedent's gross estate and transferred by the decedent . . . by will." Treas. Reg. § 20.2055–1(a). Congress's allowance for a charitable deduction was a "liberalization[ ] of the law in the taxpayer's favor." *Helvering v. Bliss,* 293 U.S. 144, 151, 55 S.Ct. 17, 79 S.Ct. 246 (1934). Yet, as we have recognized, deductions are acts of "legislative grace." *Comm'r v.*

Shoong, 177 F.2d 131, 132 (9th Cir. 1949). "[T]he purpose of the charitable deduction [is] to encourage gifts to charity." *Ahmanson,* 674 F.2d at 772; *see also Underwood v. United States,* 407 F.2d 608, 610 (6th Cir. 1969) ("The purpose of allowing charitable deductions is to encourage testators to make charitable bequests, not to permit executors and beneficiaries to rewrite a will so as to achieve tax savings.").

Valuing the Charitable Deduction

Deductions are valued separately from the valuation of the gross estate. *See Ahmanson,* 674 F.2d at 772 ("The statute does not ordain equal valuation as between an item in the gross estate and the same item under the charitable deduction."). Separate valuations allow for the consideration of post-death events, as required by *Ahmanson* and provisions of the tax code.

We addressed valuation of a charitable deduction in *Ahmanson.* There, the decedent's estate plan provided for the voting shares in a corporation to be left to family members and the nonvoting shares to be left to a charitable foundation. Id. at 765–66. We held that when valuing the charitable deduction for the nonvoting shares, a discount should be applied to account for the fact that the shares donated to charity had been stripped of their voting power. Id. at 772. That a discount was not applied to the value of the nonvoting shares in the gross estate did not impact our holding. Id. Importantly, we recognized that a charitable deduction "is subject to the principle that the testator may only be allowed a deduction for estate tax purposes for what is actually received by the charity." Id.

In contrast, the Estate argues the charitable deduction must be valued as of the date of Victoria's death, in keeping with the date-of-death valuation of an estate. We disagree. Although the Supreme Court and our court have applied that valuation method where the remainder of an estate is donated to charity after a post-death contingency, there is no uniform rule for all circumstances. *Ithaca Trust,* 279 U.S. at 154, 49 S.Ct. 291; *Wells Fargo Bank & Union Tr. Co. v. Comm'r,* 145 F.2d 132 (9th Cir. 1944). In *Ithaca Trust,* the decedent left the remainder of his estate to his wife for her life, with any assets remaining after her death to be donated to charity. 279 U.S. at 154, 49 S.Ct. 291. The decedent's wife unexpectedly died only six months after the decedent. Id. at 155, 49 S.Ct. 291. The Court considered whether the charitable deduction should reflect the amount actually given to charity after the wife's premature death, but ultimately determined that the deduction should instead reflect a valuation based on mortality tables for the wife on the date of the decedent's death. Id.

We applied *Ithaca Trust* in *Wells Fargo,* where the decedent had created a trust with instructions that the trust's income be paid to the decedent's sister from the date of the decedent's death to the date of the sister's death, and after the sister's death that the corpus of the trust be given to charity. 145 F.2d at 133. Due to commingling of assets after the decedent's death and an unrelated tax dispute, part of the corpus of the trust was used to support the decedent's sister, which reduced the amount that went to charity upon her death. Id. The Tax Court relied on these payments to disallow part of the charitable deduction, but we reversed, concluding that the charitable deduction must be determined from data available at the time of death. Id.; *see also Estate of Van Horne v. Comm'r*, 720 F.2d 1114, 1117 (9th Cir. 1983) (relying on *Ithaca Trust* to "hold that legally enforceable claims valued by reference to an actuarial table meet the test of certainty for estate tax purposes" when valuing spousal support obligation).

Neither *Ithaca Trust* nor *Wells Fargo*, however, set in stone the date of death as the date of the valuation of assets for purposes of a deduction. *See Shedd's Estate v. Comm'r*, 320 F.2d 638, 639 (9th Cir. 1963) ("Congress did not intend to make events at the date of death invariably determinative in computing the federal estate tax obligation."). Nor could they. Certain deductions not only permit consideration of post-death events, but require them. For example, I.R.C. § 2053(a) authorizes a deduction for funeral expenses and estate administration expenses—costs that cannot accrue until after the death of the testator. Similarly, I.R.C. § 2055(c) specifies that where death taxes are payable out of a charitable bequest, any charitable deduction is limited to the value remaining in the estate after such post-death tax payment. Still another provision of the tax code, I.R.C. § 2055(d), prohibits the amount of a charitable deduction from exceeding the value of transferred property included in a gross estate—but, by negative implication, permits such a deduction to be lower than the value of donated assets at the moment of death. The Third Circuit also recognized that valuations of the gross estate and a charitable deduction are separate and may differ. *In Re Sage's Estate*, 122 F.2d 480, 484 (3d Cir. 1941) ("[W]hile a decedent's gross estate is fixed as of the date of his death, deductions claimed in determining the net estate subject to tax may not be ascertainable or even accrue until the happening of events subsequent to death.").

Indeed, "[t]he proper administration of the charitable deduction cannot ignore such differences in the value actually received by the charity." *Ahmanson*, 674 F.2d at 772; *accord Irving Tr. Co. v. United States*, 221 F.2d 303, 306 (2d Cir. 1955); *Thompson's Estate v. Comm'r*, 123 F.2d 816, 817 (2d Cir. 1941); *In Re Sage's Estate*, 122 F.2d at 484. This rule prohibits crafting an estate plan or will so as to game the system and guarantee a charitable deduction that is larger than the amount actually given to charity. *Ahmanson*, 674 F.2d at 772.

* * *

The Estate argues that any consideration of post-death events also requires finding that the decline in value of DPI stock was due, at least in part, to market forces. The Tax Court, however, found that "[t]he evidence does not support a significant decline in the economy that resulted in a large decrease in value in only seven months." The Tax Court acknowledged that the adjusted net asset value of the DPI stock decreased from $ 17,777,626 at the date of Victoria's death to $ 16,159,167 at the date used for the redemption appraisal. Still, the Tax Court found, "[t]he reported decline in per share value was primarily due to the specific instruction to value decedent's majority interest as a minority interest with a 50% discount." We find nothing in the record—nor does the Estate point to anything in the record—that suggests the Tax Court's findings were clearly erroneous.

* * *

The Estate claimed an $ 18,205,476 charitable deduction based on the value of assets earmarked for the Foundation, but the Foundation received assets worth only $ 6,434,578. The Estate, at Eugene's direction, claimed a large charitable deduction representing that such assets would be delivered to the Foundation. Eugene then revalued and delivered assets—promissory notes and DPI shares—worth far less than the claimed charitable deduction. By doing so, the Estate—and various Dieringer family entities—ended up avoiding $ 4.1 million in taxes. We agree with the Tax Court's decision upholding the Commissioner's reduction of the Estate's charitable deduction and the deficiency assessment. To hold otherwise would only "invite abuse." *Ahmanson*, 674 F.2d at 768.

AFFIRMED.

D. WHOSE CHARITABLE TRANSFER?

ESTATE OF PICKARD V. COMMISSIONER

United States Tax Court, 1973.
60 T.C. 618, aff'd, 503 F.2d 1404 (6th Cir.1974).

TANNENWALD, JUDGE:

[A decedent bequeathed her residuary estate to the Pickard Trust in which her stepfather had a vested remainder. Her stepfather, who died shortly before her, in his will left his residuary estate to the Peterson Trust, which, in its deed of trust, provided that two qualified charities were to receive the corpus upon the death of certain family members. In filing the estate tax return for the decedent, her executor claimed a charitable deduction for the amount of her estate that passed to the Pickard Trust and then to the Peterson Trust under her stepfather's will and that would in turn be received by the two charities through their remainder interests in the Peterson Trust. The Commissioner disallowed the deduction.]

Section 2055 provides, among other things, that "the value of the taxable estate shall be determined by deducting from the value of the gross estate the amount of all bequests, legacies, devises, or transfers * * * to or for the use of any corporation organized and operated exclusively for religious, charitable, scientific, literary, or educational purposes."

The parties herein are in agreement as to the exempt character of the two organizations involved and as to the amount of the deduction, if found to be allowable. Additionally, no question has been raised whether the provisions of any of the instruments involved or the possibility of claims against either the Pickard or Peterson estates or trusts might operate in such a way as to make the interests of those organizations unascertainable or subject to the so-remote-as-to-be-negligible possibility that the transfers would not become effective. See sec. 20.2055–2, Estate Tax Regs.

The sole question to be decided herein is whether the provisions of decedent's will and the Pickard Trust are operative within the framework of the above-quoted statutory language. Petitioner asserts that there are three elements contained in section 2055, all of which are satisfied in this case, namely, (1) decedent made a transfer, (2) of property includable in her gross estate, and (3), by virtue of her stepfather's death and the provisions of his will and the Peterson Trust, to or for the use of a qualified entity. Such assertion is premised upon the assumption that each of three elements is independent of each other and that section 2055 can therefore be fragmented in order to determine whether a deduction is allowable. Under petitioner's reasoning, the route of devolution is immaterial; it is enough if there is a transfer of includable property which must, because of the surrounding circumstances, inevitably find its way into the coffers of an exempt organization.

In our opinion, such separation of the three elements is improper. We believe that the first and third elements are mutually interdependent and that the "transfer * * * to or for the use of" such organization must be manifest from the provisions of the decedent's testamentary instrument.

The impact of the route of devolution has been considered in a variety of contexts. Thus, in Senft v. United States, 319 F.2d 642 (3d Cir.1963), property of the decedent, who died intestate, escheated to the Commonwealth of Pennsylvania. In denying the decedent a deduction under section 2055, the Court of Appeals emphasized decedent's failure to make the transfer, as opposed to the property passing to the qualified recipient by another force, i.e., by operation of law.

In Cox v. Commissioner, 297 F.2d 36 (2d Cir.1961), affirming a Memorandum Opinion of this Court, a deduction under the predecessor of section 2055 was denied where the testatrix, with full knowledge of all relevant facts and her express approval of the ultimate recipient of the bequest, bequeathed part of her estate to her son, a priest, who had, prior to her death but subsequent to the making of the testatrix's will, taken solemn vows of poverty and renounced all his interests in property (including donations and legacies) in favor of the Society of Jesus, a qualified entity under the statute.

Similar reasoning formed the underpinning of the Supreme Court's decision in Taft v. Commissioner, 304 U.S. 351 (1938), where the decedent died with an outstanding but unfulfilled pledge of a charitable contribution which constituted a binding contractual obligation under local law. The Supreme Court denied a deduction for estate tax purposes on the grounds that the claim was not supported by adequate and full consideration as required by then existing law and that there was no bequest, legacy, devise, or transfer within the meaning of the predecessor of section 2055.

In each of the foregoing cases, the fact that the designated portion of the decedent's estate inevitably inured to the benefit of the charity did not save the day. To be sure, they can be distinguished on their facts, but the common element which forms the foundation for decision is that the transfer to or for the use of the charity was not effectuated by a testamentary transfer on decedent's part but rather by the operation of an external force. The same is true herein, where it was the testamentary disposition of decedent's stepfather via the Peterson Trust which accomplished the transfer.

Concededly, the charities herein would not have received decedent's property if the decedent had not made the testamentary disposition to her stepfather. The lesson from the decided cases, however, is that a simple "but for" test is not, as petitioner would have us hold, sufficient. There must be something more, namely, the testamentary facts as gleaned from the decedent's own disposition must manifest the transfer to the charity. Commissioner v. Noel's Estate, 380 U.S. 678 (1965). In so stating, we do not imply that the decedent must specify the charitable recipient in so many words. But, at the very least, the instrument of testamentary disposition must sufficiently articulate, either directly or through appropriate incorporation by reference of another instrument, the manifestation of decedent's charitable bounty. See Y.M.C.A. v. Davis, 264 U.S. 47, 50 (1924). Such a situation simply does not obtain herein and, accordingly, the claimed deduction is not allowable.

* * *

NOTES

1. Regulation § 20.2055–2(c) states that a deduction is allowable for an amount that "falls into" a charitable bequest as a result of a disclaimer by a beneficiary. For example, if the residue of an estate were donated to

charity, and a legatee renounced his interest under the will, the bequest would "fall into" the charitable gift and would be deductible. To qualify, the disclaimer must be irrevocable and must be made before the estate tax return is due. The beneficiary can receive no consideration in return for a disclaimer. Can the policy behind this regulation be reconciled with the *Pickard* case and the *Senft* and *Cox* cases cited therein? It should be noted that the regulation in question was based squarely on statutory language that was contained in the first sentence of section 2055(a) prior to its deletion by the Tax Reform Act of 1976, which inserted the general provision governing disclaimers for estate and gift tax purposes. See I.R.C. § 2518. In Priv. Ltr. Rul. 201032002 the IRS held that a charitable deduction was warranted where there was a disclaimer of a bequest that then under the decedent's will was paid to the taker in default, which was a charity.

2. In Estate of Lamson v. United States, 338 F.2d 376 (Ct. Cl. 1964), it was held that a bequest to an individual, who was a member of a religious order subject to a vow of poverty, did not qualify as a charitable deduction. This was so despite the fact that the religious order might have rights under contract with the member that would insure transfer of the bequest to it. See also Estate of Barry v. Commissioner, 311 F.2d 681 (9th Cir. 1962), Rev. Rul. 55–760, 1955–2 C.B. 607, Rev, Rul. 55–759, 1955–2 C.B. 607 and Priv. Ltr. Rul. 200437032.

    In Estate of Hubert v. Commissioner, 66 T.C.M. (CCH) 1064 (1993), the Tax Court upheld the deductibility of bequests to trusts to support the missionary work of a charity through a named individual for his life, including support for the named missionary during retirement with remainder interests to be distributed to the charity.

E. SPLIT GIFTS

Taxpayers who have the opportunity to give an interest in an asset to a charity while retaining also an interest in the asset provide a special challenge to the IRS. By retaining an interest in the property, a portion of which is being conveyed to charity, these individuals create opportunities for abuse, yet it is hardly appropriate to prevent abuse by denying them a deduction of their generosity. The materials below discuss how Congress has, and has not, met this challenge.

1. THE BASIC STATUTORY SOLUTION

Prior to the passage of the Tax Reform Act of 1969, the split gift was a popular form of charitable donation. If a trust was created or property was transferred for both a private and a charitable purpose, a deduction was allowed for the value of the charitable interest. The regulations imposed two limitations on deductibility. First, the value of the charitable interest had to be "presently ascertainable," that is, subject to reasonably precise valuation. Treas. Reg. § 20.2055–2(a). Second, the charity had to be assured of eventually taking its interest. A contingent gift to charity was deductible only if the conditions imposed were "so remote as to be negligible." Treas. Reg. § 20.2055–2(b)(1).

These two tests produced a multitude of problems in their application. The courts were forced to reinterpret the valuation and contingency language under the widely varying circumstances of each case. Some taxpayers took advantage of the imprecision in the language to obtain a deduction for a larger amount than the charity actually received. The following excerpt from the House Ways and Means Committee Report on the Tax Reform Act of 1969 outlines Congress' concerns in revamping the law in this area:

> *General reasons for change*—The rules of present law for determining the amount of a charitable contribution deduction in the case of gifts of remainder interests in trust do not necessarily have any relation to the value of the benefit which the charity receives. This is because the trust assets may be invested in a manner so as to maximize the income interest with the result that there is little relation between the interest assumptions used in calculating present values and the amount received by the charity. For example, the trust corpus can be invested in high-income, high-risk assets. This enhances the value of the income interest but decreases the value of the charity's remainder interest.
>
> Your committee does not believe that a taxpayer should be allowed to obtain a charitable contribution deduction for a gift of a remainder interest in trust to a charity which is substantially in excess of the amount the charity may ultimately receive.
>
> Your committee's attention also was called to the fact that in some cases charitable contributions deductions have been allowed for gifts of charitable remainder interests in trust even though it is not probable that the gift will ultimately be received by the charity. An example of this is a situation where the charity has only a contingent remainder interest in a trust (for example, a $5,000 annuity to A for life, remainder to his children, or to charity if A has no children). Another example is the situation where a charity has a remainder interest and the trust permits invasion of the charitable share for the benefit of a noncharitable intervening interest which is incapable of reasonably certain actuarial valuation (for example, a $5,000 annuity to A for life, remainder to a charity, but the trust provides that the trustee may pay A amounts in excess of $5,000 in order to maintain his standard of living).

H. Rep. No. 91–413, 91st Cong., 1st Sess. at 58–59 (1969).

In the Tax Reform Act of 1969, Congress took its initial steps to correct these abuses. Section 2055(e), which has been amended on several occasions since, represents Congress's principal endeavor to protect the integrity of the estate tax against such abuses. Under section 2055(e), when interests in the same property pass to both a private party and a charity, no charitable deduction will be allowed unless the gift is, in general, in one of the forms prescribed below:

1. Charitable Remainder Annuity Trust—A taxpayer may establish a trust from which a private person or persons will receive a sum of money at least once a year, not less than five nor more than 50 percent of the value of the initial value of the corpus. The payments may extend for life or for a term not over 20 years. Following the termination of these payments, the remainder must be transferred to or held in trust for a charity, and it must equal or exceed 10 per cent of the initial fair market value of the property initially transferred to the trust. See I.R.C. § 664(d)(1).

2. Charitable Remainder Unitrust—This structure is similar to the annuity trust except that, instead of a fixed sum, the private beneficiaries must receive a fixed percentage (not less than five nor more than 50 percent) of the fair market value of the trust assets, valued annually. See I.R.C. § 664(d)(2).

3. Pooled Income Fund—This is a trust established by a charity to which each of several donors contributes property, retaining income interests for private beneficiaries and leaving the remainder interests to the charity. All property contributed to the trust will be commingled to form a single fund. The amount of each private beneficiary's annual payment will be determined by the rate of return on the entire fund. See I.R.C. § 642(c)(5).

4. Remainder Interest in a Farm or Personal Residence—These split interests may still be donated to charity outright and a charitable deduction allowed for the donation. See I.R.C. §§ 2055(e)(2)(A) and 170(f)(3)(B)(i).

5. Guaranteed Annuity or Fixed Percentage Income Interest— An income interest can be donated to charity in the form of a guaranteed annuity, or a fixed percentage of the assets to a trust. See I.R.C. § 2055(e)(2)(B). Although the Code does not specify that the property must be in trust, the regulations state that the donor must either establish an annuity trust or a unitrust or make the income interests payable by an organization engaged in issuing annuity contracts (e.g., an

insurance company). See Treas. Reg. § 20.2055–2(e)(2)(v) and (vi)(c).

6. Undivided Interest—A taxpayer may donate an undivided fractional interest in property to a charity and retain a fractional interest in the property. See I.R.C. §§ 2055(e)(2) and 170(f)(3)(B)(ii). Special limitations exist in the case of fractional gifts of tangible personal property such as works of art. See I.R.C. § 170(*o*).

7. Qualified Conservation Contribution—Interests, such as scenic easements, in real property conveyed to qualified charities exclusively for prescribed conservation purposes may qualify for a charitable deduction despite the fact that the donor retains rights to the property subject to the conveyed interest. See I.R.C. §§ 2055(e)(2) and 170(f)(3)(B)(iii).

The amount of the deduction allowed from the gross estate will equal the fair market value of the interest given to charity. The regulations are quite specific as to how the fair market value of the interests is to be figured. For the charitable remainder interests, the basic notion behind the rules is that the value of the stream of income payments to be received by the life beneficiary must be deducted from the fair market value of the property placed in the trust. Treas. Regs. §§ 1.664–2(c), 1.664–4 and 1.642(c)–6. The value of a charitable income interest is figured on the present value of the series of payments that the charity will receive. Treas. Reg. § 20.2031–7. The regulations leave nothing to the imagination as to how the precise calculations are to be made. A glance at the extensive formulas and tables found in the regulations should convince the student that the taxpayer has no room left for argument.

Note that Congress has solved the problems of prior law by requiring taxpayers to follow a prearranged scheme in their gift giving that simply excludes the troublesome factors altogether. The new rules do not allow any invasions of the corpus by the trustee, or any contingent gifts to charity, no matter how certain the chances of taking may be. The problem of the trustee manipulating investments and allocations to favor the individual life beneficiary is eliminated by making the individual's share dependent on total trust assets rather than trust income.

Congress replaced the uncertainties of prior law with a set of complex and inflexible rules that must be carefully followed to avoid complete loss of the charitable deduction. The intricacies of this area are now so formidable that the IRS has broken precedent and has issued forms which, if followed with religious zeal, will assure the availability of the charitable deduction for annuity trusts and unitrusts. For the road map, see, e.g., Rev. Proc. 2016–42, 2016–2 C.B. 269, Rev. Procs. 2005–52, 2005–2 C.B. 326;

2005–53, 2005–2 C.B. 339; Rev. Proc. 2005–54, 2005–2 C.B. 353, Rev. Proc. 2003–57, 2003–2 C.B. 257; 2003–55, 2003–2 C.B. 242.

A corresponding revision of the gift tax charitable deduction provision was made in section 2522(c) by the Tax Reform Act of 1969. The second important revision under the Tax Reform Act of 1969 affecting the charitable deduction for estate and gift tax purposes was the denial of the deduction for transfers to private foundations that have engaged in willful and repeated acts subjecting them to the new penalty taxes imposed by Chapter 42, relating to private foundations involved in acts of self-dealing, substantial income accumulations, excessive business holdings, improper investments, and forbidden expenditures. See I.R.C. § 508(d).

PLANNING NOTE

The charitable remainder trust is a favorite device of estate planners for two principal reasons: (1) since the corpus (as contrasted with the income interest) belongs to a tax-exempt charity, trust holdings can generally be sold without income tax liability; and (2) in the case of a gift in trust of an income interest to a private party and the remainder interest to a charity, the income from a charitable remainder trust will be taxed to the income beneficiary who may be in a low tax bracket. These advantages can be illustrated by the following examples. First, take the case of a middle-aged entrepreneur who owned a highly successful corporation who has a very low basis in that company's stock which pays little or no dividends, and who wishes to sell out and spend the rest of his life on the beach and on the ski slopes. A cash sale of his stock will leave him with only the after-tax proceeds to invest in income producing assets to fund his life of leisure. If, on the other hand, our friend were to give his stock to a charitable remainder trust, he would get the stock out of his estate, have a nice income tax deduction equal to the value of the charity's remainder interest, receive the thanks of the charity of his choice and the acclaim of his community and, since the remainder interest is held for the benefit of a tax-exempt charity, the stock could be sold by the trust with no income tax liabilities and the entire sales proceeds invested in income producing assets for the benefit of the entrepreneur, thereby leaving him with the income for his life on the full fair market value of his stock. Second, consider the case of someone like the entrepreneur, who in this instance is in a high tax bracket and is concerned about providing for a family member, such as a disabled child, who has little or no prospect of income during her or his life. If the entrepreneur were to contribute assets to a charitable remainder trust, with income to the child for life, remainder to an appropriate charity, the annual income from the trust would be taxed to the child at her or his lower rates and not those of the high bracket entrepreneur, who would also benefit from an income tax deduction equal to the value of the charitable remainder. The advantage of the first scenario, avoidance of income tax on sale of appreciated assets contributed to the trust, can also be combined with the income assignment benefits of this second scenario.

2. THE EXCLUSION FOR QUALIFIED CONSERVATION EASEMENTS

In the Taxpayer Relief Act of 1997 Congress provided an exclusion for the estates of taxpayers that hold realty subject to qualified conservation easements, which are defined broadly to include permanent environmental, recreational, educational, scenic and historic dedications of interests in property. See I.R.C. § 2031(c). Although in form an exclusion, section 2031(c) has the effect of providing an added deduction for such easements, many of which will also qualify for charitable contribution deduction under section 2055(f) noted above. This and the close coordination of section 2031(c) with many charitable contribution concepts make it appropriate to discuss this provision in this chapter.

Section 2031(c) is very technical, and the benefit provided taxpayers is of limited importance in a general estate and gift tax course, consequently the discussion which follows is restricted to the provision's most salient features.

The land which is subject to a qualifying easement must be owned by the decedent (or a member of his family or controlled entity) at all times during the three years prior to death. Moreover, if the property is debt financed, the exclusion is only available to the extent of the equity interest in the property.

The amount which qualifies for the exclusion is capped at $500,000 or 40% of the value of the land calculated without regard to the easement, reduced by the value of any charitable deduction allowed under section 2055(f) to the estate because of creation of the easement. Section 2031(c)(2) provides a phase out mechanism for the 40% exclusion for the purpose of limiting the value of the exclusion in the case of easements which, relatively speaking, effect only modest reductions in the value of the land.

One of the more interesting features of section 2031(c) is that it applies regardless of when a qualified conservation easement was donated and once land is subject to such an easement the exclusion is available to subsequent holders of the land as long as they are members of the original donor's family. Seemingly this will enable those who inherit land subject to a conservation easement to claim benefit of section 2031(c) when they die and for them to pass the benefit on to their issue or others satisfying the section 2032A(e)(2) definition of family.

Qualifying conservation easements can provide taxpayers with extraordinary tax benefits for several reasons. First, if given during life, the donor may, when calculating her income tax, obtain a charitable deduction for the reduction in value of the land that results from the easement. Second, at the donor's death her executor lists as an estate asset the value of the property reduced by the easement. Third, under section

2031(c) an estate tax exclusion will also be allowed to the donor's estate. In some cases, the value of all of the resulting tax savings can exceed the reduction in value caused by the easement. And finally, as the *pièce de résistance* the donor's heirs, if they remain as holders of the property, will also be able to claim the exclusion and list only the value of the property reduced by the easement thereby resulting in not only conservation of nature but also conservation of wealth.

F. UNASCERTAINABILITY OF IDENTITY OF CHARITY OR AMOUNT OF CHARITABLE GIFT, AND CONDITIONAL GIFTS

Decedents, with occasional unfortunate results, sometimes leave open the identification of the charitable beneficiary or the amount passing to an identified charity. The creation of conditional charitable bequests is also another potentially hazardous venture.

1. FAILURE TO IDENTIFY CHARITY

REVENUE RULING 69–285
1969–1 C.B. 222.

A, a resident of Massachusetts, died testate. Paragraph One of his will provided bequests for several persons including *B*. Paragraph Two named *B* as executrix of the estate. Paragraph Three of the will reads:

> "All the rest and residue of my estate of whatsoever kind and nature and wheresoever situated, I bequeath to said *B* to be distributed to whatever charities she may deem worthy."

Two years after *A*'s death a Massachusetts probate court issued a decree which recited that *B* had selected several organizations to receive the residue. The organizations selected were charitable within the meaning of section 2055(a).

The basic question is whether under the terms of the will the local law would (1) impose a trust upon the residuary assets and (2) require the trustee to distribute the assets to organizations that are charitable within the meaning of section 2055. If local law would not infer an intent to establish a trust relationship over the residuary estate, the property could be diverted to noncharitable uses by the voluntary act of the residuary legatee, *B*. And, even if the Commonwealth of Massachusetts would impose a trust upon the residuary estate, it must be determined whether the local law definition of "charities" is restricted to organizations that are charitable within the meaning of section 2055. No deduction is allowed if local law merely imposes a trust upon the residue but fails to restrict the trustee's choice to organizations that are deemed charitable within the meaning of section 2055.

Section 2055(a)(3) provides in part that the value of a decedent's taxable estate shall be determined by deducting from the value of the gross estate the amount of all bequests "to a trustee or trustees, * * * but only if such contributions or gifts are to be used by such trustee or trustees, * * * exclusively for religious, charitable, scientific, literary, or educational purposes * * * and no substantial part of the activities of such trustee or trustees * * * is carrying on propaganda, or otherwise attempting to influence legislation."

A state court decree is considered to be conclusive in the determination of the Federal tax liability of an estate only to the extent that it determines property rights, and if the issuing court is the highest court in the state. Commissioner v. Estate of Herman J. Bosch, et al., 387 U.S. 456 (1967), Ct. D. 1915, C.B. 1967–2, 337. Therefore, the fact that the State probate court in this case placed a stamp of approval on *B*'s appointment of the property to charity is not determinative of whether a charitable deduction is allowable.

In Delaney v. Gardner, 204 F.2d 855 (1953), the decedent bequeathed $100,000 to the executors " * * * not subject to any trust, but in the hope that they will dispose of it at their absolute discretion and according to their own judgment, but giving due weight to any memoranda I may leave or any oral expressions by me to them made during my life." The probate court admitted as part of the will a memorandum that was dated the same day as the will. The memorandum contained a list of charitable organizations to which the executors ultimately appointed the residue. The deduction was disallowed because the executors were held to have discretion under the terms of the will to withhold part or all of the bequest from charity. Amounts so withheld would have passed to noncharitable beneficiaries.

The charitable deduction was also denied in Mississippi Valley Trust v. Commissioner, 72 F.2d 197 (1934). The decedent had devised all of his property in equal shares to his wife and two sons. The will stated: "I have heretofore expressed to my sons my wishes as to certain charitable gifts, and I therefore make no such bequests herein, preferring that my sons shall make such donations within their sole discretion as shall seem to them to be best." The court held that the provision was not mandatory, but was merely an expression of desire.

Charitable deductions have been allowed where the terms of the bequest would be construed to impose a trust on the subject property by operation of local law. In Lincoln National Bank & Trust Company of Fort Wayne v. United States, 6 A.F.T.R. 2d 6142 (1960), the decedent's bequest of a portion of her estate "to such corporations, foundations, or organizations organized and operated exclusively for religious, charitable, or educational purposes, as may be selected by my said nieces, Venette Marie Sites and Mabel Margaret Sites, or the survivor of them," qualified for a charitable deduction. Charitable deductions were also allowed based on similar language in George Beggs, Executor of the Estate of Edward Farmer v. United States, 27 F.Supp. 599 (1939).

It is clear that the above-quoted provision in A's will placed a fiduciary obligation on B to distribute the residue to organizations that are charitable within the meaning of Massachusetts law. Gill v. Attorney General, 83 N.E. 676 (1908); Reilly v. McGowan, 166 N.E. 766 (1929). The intention to establish a trust may be derived from the instrument, even though the testator does not use the word "trust" or "trustee." Gordon v. Gordon, 124 N.E.2d 226 (1955), Sherwin v. Smith, 185 N.E. 17 (1933).

The fact that B might have refused to appoint the residue to charity would not have prevented the property from passing to charity. It is ordinarily to be inferred that the testator's primary purpose was that the property should be devoted to charitable uses, and the selection of those uses is a secondary matter. Scott on Trusts, section 397 (3d Ed. 1967). Scott cites Minot v. Baker, 17 N.E. 839 (1888), as "the leading case" on this point. In that case the will appointed one John Healy executor, and gave the residue to Healy, "to be disposed of by him for such charitable purposes as he shall think proper." Healy died, having disposed of only a small portion of the residuary estate in his hands for charitable purposes. In denying the claim of the first decedent's heirs the court stated at page 845:

> "The first point to be determined, therefore, is a matter of construction, whether the limitation to charities was conditional upon Healy's making an appointment, or whether it should be construed as a gift to charitable uses out and out with a super-added power to Healy to specify them if he saw fit; and on this part of the question, we are of the opinion that the gift is an unconditional gift for charitable purposes."

Section 2055(a)(3) of the Code requires that bequests to trustees must be used by the trustee for purposes that are exclusively charitable. Some jurisdictions characterize as charitable certain purposes that are not deemed charitable within the meaning of the Federal statute. * * *

Decisions by the Massachusetts Supreme Court indicate that the Massachusetts definition of "charitable" is at least as restrictive as the Federal definition of that term under section 2055. See Boston Chamber of Commerce v. Assessors, 54 N.E.2d 199 (1944); Garden Cemetery Corporation v. Baker, 105 N.E. 1070 (1914); Massachusetts Medical Society v. Assessors, 164 N.E.2d 325 (1960); Workman's Circle Educational Center v. Assessors, 51 N.E.2d 313 (1943). In these cases the court excluded from the definition of charity trade associations, nonreligious cemetery associations, professional organizations, and lobbying activities.

The executrix in this case had a fiduciary duty to use the net residuary estate for purposes which are exclusively charitable within the meaning of section 2055 of the Code. Accordingly, it is held that the charitable deduction is allowable for the value of the net amount of the residuary estate.

REVENUE RULING 78–101
1978–1 C.B. 301.

On December 30, 1976, the donor transferred property in trust under the terms of which the trustee is directed to pay a charitable lead unitrust an amount equal to 4 percent of the net fair market value of the trust property, determined annually, to such organizations described in sections 170(c) and 2522(a) of the Internal Revenue Code of 1954, as the trustee may select. The trust is to terminate at the expiration of ten years and one month, at which time the trust corpus is to revert to the donor if living; and if the donor is not living, then to the donor's estate.

Section 25.2522(c)–3(c)(2)(vi)(e) of the Gift Tax Regulations provides that, with certain exceptions not relevant here, a charitable lead unitrust interest will be considered a qualifying unitrust interest provided no amount other than the unitrust amount may be paid by the trust for a private purpose; that is, a purpose other than a charitable purpose described in section 2522(a).

Rev. Rul. 76–371, 1976–2 C.B. 305, holds that a charitable *remainder* unitrust interest will not be disallowed under section 25.2522(c)–3(c)(2)(iv) of the regulations where the trustee possessed the power to add or substitute charitable remaindermen but was required to select only organizations that qualified under section 2522(a).

Held, the failure to designate the specific charitable recipients of a charitable lead interest in the form of a unitrust interest will not disqualify the interest for the charitable deduction where the trustee is empowered to select the charitable beneficiaries and the governing instrument requires that only charitable organizations that meet the requirements of section 2522(a) can be selected.

NOTES

1.   In Private Letter Ruling 9634025 the taxpayer died with all his property held in a New York revocable trust which at his death became irrevocable. The trust provided that, with respect to certain assets, eighty percent was to pass to Catholic charities, ten percent to Protestant charities, and ten percent to Jewish charities "as shall be chosen by the trustees." As it did

in Revenue Ruling 69–285, the IRS ruled that since New York state law imposed a definition of charity which was at least as restrictive as section 2055(a), the gifts in question were valid charitable contributions under section 2055.

2.   In Rev. Rul. 71–200, 1971–1 C.B. 272, a decedent left property to be distributed by a trustee "to or for the use of those organizations to which gifts of income or principal shall qualify as tax-free under the laws relating to income, estate, inheritance, *or* gifts, of the United States, *or* of any state having jurisdiction * * *." The IRS ruled that a valid charitable estate tax deduction was not present. First, it noted that since federal income, gift, and estate tax definitions of charity are not identical, it was possible that property might be left to a valid charity under the income or gift taxes which did not qualify under section 2055. Second, there was a possibility that the trustee would distribute property to a charity that, while valid under state law, would not qualify as a charity under section 2055.

PLANNING NOTE

Careful estate planners often include language in wills and other dispositive documents, such as revocable trusts that act as wills substitutes, conditioning intended charitable bequests on an organization qualifying under section 2055(a) and providing for appropriate alternative donees in the event of failure to so qualify. For example, in Private Letter Ruling 200019011 under the decedent's will, he devised the residue of her estate to six organizations but provided that if any failed to qualify as a charity under section 2055(a) that organization shall not share in the bequest and the residue shall be divided among the remaining organizations which do qualify as charities under section 2055(a). In Private Letter Ruling 200202032, the IRS gave its blessing to a bequest of paintings to a museum conditioned on its remaining qualified under section 2055(a). The decedent's will also empowered his executors to select a substitute section 2055 charity in the event the museum declined to accept the bequest.

2.   UNASCERTAINABILITY OF AMOUNT

ESTATE OF MARINE V. COMMISSIONER

United States Court of Appeals, Fourth Circuit, 1993.
990 F.2d 136.

CHAPMAN, SENIOR CIRCUIT JUDGE:

[David N. Marine executed a will that made a number of specific bequests to designated individuals and left the residue of his estate to be divided equally between his alma maters, Princeton University and Johns Hopkins University. A little more than one year later he executed a codicil that empowered his personal representatives to compensate individuals who had contributed to his well-being or otherwise been helpful to him during his life by transferring to them such property as the representatives deemed to be a fair bequest based on the services rendered. No single person was to receive an amount in excess of one percent of Marine's gross probate estate. Marine died about two years after executing the codicil and his personal representatives, acting under the power granted by the codicil, distributed $10,000 to one individual and $15,000 to another. Marine's estate tax return reported a gross estate of about $2.6 million and a deduction of about $2.1 for the residue bequeathed to Princeton and Johns Hopkins. The IRS disallowed the claimed charitable deduction on the ground that the amount of the charitable bequest was unascertainable since the personal representatives could have used their power under the codicil to distribute the entire estate to private parties. The Tax Court upheld the Commissioner's determination and taxpayer appealed.]

Any testamentary gift to "any corporation organized and operated exclusively for . . . scientific . . . or educational purposes" may be deducted from the gross taxable estate. 26 U.S.C. § 2055(a)(2) (1988).

There is no dispute that Princeton University and the Johns Hopkins University are both legitimate recipients of § 2055(a)(2) gifts. To be deductible as a charitable gift, the value of a testamentary remainder interest must be "presently ascertainable, and hence severable from the non-charitable interest." Treas. Reg. § 20.2055–2(a) (as amended in 1986).

The Supreme Court addressed the question of ascertainability in Ithaca Trust Co. v. United States, 279 U.S. 151 (1929), and upheld a deduction for the remainder of a trust dedicated to charity even though the trustees were authorized to invade the corpus if necessary to "maintain [the widow] in as much comfort as she now enjoys."

Justice Holmes writing for the Court stated:

> The principal that could be used was only so much as might be necessary to continue the comfort then enjoyed. The standard was fixed in fact and capable of being stated in definite terms of money. It was not left to the widow's discretion. The income of the estate at the death of the testator, and even after debts and specific legacies had been paid, was more than sufficient to maintain the widow as required. There was no uncertainty appreciably greater than the general uncertainty that attends human affairs.

Id. at 154. Because there was a fixed standard, the Court found that the remainder was ascertainable at the date of death and the charitable remainder was deductible.

Ascertainability at the date of death of the amount going to charity is the test. To be "presently ascertainable" the power of the trustee to divert the corpus from the charities must be restricted by a fixed standard. In

Merchants Nat. Bank of Boston, Executor v. Commission of Internal Revenue, 320 U.S. 256 (1943), the Court was faced with a will which created a trust, with the income going to the widow for her life, and upon her death all but $100,000 of the principal was to pass to certain charities. The trustee was authorized to invade the corpus,

> at such time or times as my said trustee shall in its sole discretion deem wise and proper for the comfort, support, maintenance, and/or happiness of my said wife, and it is my wish and will that in the exercise of its discretion with reference to such payments from the principal of the trust fund to my said wife, May L. Field, my said trustee shall exercise its discretion with liberality to my said wife, and consider her welfare, comfort and happiness prior to claims of residuary beneficiaries under this trust. Id. at 257–58.

The Court held that the extent to which the principal might be used was not restricted by a fixed standard, and

> Introducing the element of the widow's happiness and instructing the trustee to exercise its discretion with liberality to make her wishes prior to the claims of residuary beneficiaries brought into the calculation elements of speculation too large to be overcome, notwithstanding the widow's previous mode of life was modest and her own resources substantial. We conclude that the Commissioner properly disallowed the deduction for estate tax purposes. 320 U.S. at 263.

There is no fixed standard that can be applied to the discretion given to Marine's personal representatives. They had "sole and absolute discretion, to compensate persons who have contributed to my well-being or who have been otherwise helpful to me during my lifetime." There is no limit as to the number of persons who may be compensated, and there are no standards for determining and measuring such imprecise elements as "contribution," "my well-being" and "have been otherwise helpful to me during my lifetime." What would be considered a "contribution" to Marine's "well-being?" How large must the contribution be, and over what period of time must it have been made? How would the personal representatives define "helpful?" Would helpfulness during his last illness be rewarded at a higher rate than helpfulness during his infancy or childhood? Dr. Marine lived 60 years and there must have been many persons "helpful" to him in different degrees throughout his life. The number of such individuals has no limit and a standard for measuring "contribution," "well-being" and "helpful" does not exist. This is similar to the problem created by the "widow's happiness" in *Merchant's Bank*, supra. These elements are uncertain and cannot be measured with any precision, and therefore they make the amount going to charity unascertainable at the time of death.

The fact that only two persons received payments under [Marine's codicil] is of no moment, because this could not be determined at the time of death so as to affect ascertainability. Henslee, Collector of Internal Revenue v. Union Planters National Bank & Trust Co., 335 U.S. 595 (1949).

* * *

We hold that the language of the codicil, giving the personal representatives "sole and absolute discretion" to reward those who had been helpful to Marine during his life, established no real standards. The personal representatives had virtually unlimited authority as to the number of gifts, although the amount of each bequest was limited to one percent of the corpus. Since the number of such bequests was unlimited and a standard for determining the amount of a bequest was uncertain, the amount of the charitable bequest could not be ascertained at the time of death and the deduction is not available. The tax court was correct in its determinations.

AFFIRMED.

NOTE

Had the decedent limited the total amount of noncharitable discretionary gifts that could be made by his personal representatives to an amount such as $200,000, seemingly, only that amount (which presumably would have been excluded from taxation by the unified credit) would have failed to qualify for charitable contribution status. Note that the real losers in *Marine* are the very charities which the decedent sought to benefit.

3. CONDITIONAL GIFTS

Under Regulation § 20.2055–2(b), if, at the decedent's death, a transfer to a qualifying charity is conditional, no charitable deduction is allowed, unless the likelihood that the charity will not receive the bequest is so remote as to be considered negligible.

REVENUE RULING 71–442
1971–2 C.B. 336.

Advice has been requested whether a deduction is allowable under section 2055 of the Internal Revenue Code of 1954 (prior to amendment by the Tax Reform Act of 1969, P.L. 91–172, C.B. 1969–3, 10) with respect to a remainder interest in a trust payable to charity under the circumstances described below.

The decedent, a resident of North Carolina, died testate in 1968. He bequeathed his entire residuary estate in trust and provided that the entire net income of the trust be paid to his son for life. At the son's death, the remainder is to be distributed to his children then living. If the son should die without children surviving him, the trust assets are to be distributed to specified charitable organizations. At the decedent's death, his son was 56 years of age and had no children.

Section 2055(a)(2) provides that a deduction from the gross estate is allowable in the amount of bequests to or for the use of any corporation organized and operated exclusively for religious, charitable, scientific, literary or educational purposes. Section 20.2055–2(b) of the Estate Tax Regulations provides that if, as of the date of a decedent's death, a transfer for charitable purposes is dependent upon the performance of some act or the happening of a precedent event in order that it might become effective, no deduction is allowable unless the possibility that the charitable transfer will not become effective is so remote as to be negligible.

Section 48–23(3) of the General Statutes of North Carolina provides:

> From and after the entry of the final order of adoption, the words "child," "grandchild," "heir," "issue," "descendant," or an equivalent, or the plural forms thereof, or any other word of like import in any deed, grant, will or other written instrument shall be held to include any adopted person, unless the contrary plainly appears by the terms thereof, whether such instrument was executed before or after the entry of the final order of adoption and whether such instrument was executed before or after the enactment of this section.

Although at the date of the decedent's death his son had no children, the possibility remained that he might be survived by children since:

1. children might be born to him at some time in the future, or

2. he might adopt a person at some future time.

In Estate of Cardeza v. Commissioner, 173 F.2d 19 (1949), it was held that men are presumed capable of fathering children until death. In City Bank Farmers' Trust Co. v. United States, 5 F.Supp. 871 (1934), the court held that the possibility of a 53-year-old, childless man having issue surviving was sufficient to require that a charitable deduction for the contingent remainder interest be disallowed. See also Revenue Ruling 68–336, C.B. 1968–1, 408.

Inasmuch as the decedent's will does not evidence a clear intent that an adopted child should not share in the class gift to his son's children, North Carolina law, as set forth in the statute cited above, would require distribution of the remainder interest, or the appropriate share thereof, to any adopted child or children surviving at the son's death, rather than to charity.

Accordingly, it is held that the bequest of a remainder interest to charitable organizations subject to defeasance by the survival at the life tenant's death of a natural-born or adopted child of such life tenant does not qualify for the deduction provided by section 2055 of the Code.

NOTES

1. In Estate of De Foucaucourt v. Commissioner, 62 T.C. 485 (1974), the Tax Court held that where a gift to a charity was contingent on the decedent's nephew dying without issue, the age (65), poor physical condition, existing lengthy marriage and unlikelihood of the nephew's adopting to create issue should all be considered to decide that there was only a remote contingency that the charity would not realize its bequest. A charitable deduction was therefore allowed. To the contrary is Priv. Ltr. Rul. 8010011 where the IRS disallowed a deduction for a charitable bequest conditioned on a decedent's 60-year-old, medically disabled, unmarried son dying without issue. The possibility of adoption alone was deemed sufficient by the IRS to bar deduction under section 2055.

2. In Rev. Rul. 59–143, 1959–1 C.B. 247, the IRS, in a sporadic display of realism, ruled that a charitable contribution deduction would stand where a bequest to a charity was contingent on the death without bodily issue of two women over 55 years of age.

G. WHEN TO GIVE: NOW, LATER OR NEVER

Estate planners frequently suggest to their clients that, if they can afford doing so, it is often preferable from a tax standpoint to make gifts to charities during the client's life. Property given during the donor's life is out of the donor's estate at death and in essence gives the donor the benefit of the estate tax deduction accorded a charitable bequest. The donor has the added advantage of an income tax deduction for the lifetime gift to the charitable organization. To be added to the tax advantages of lifetime giving are several intangible benefits.[8] The donor can enjoy public recognition of the charitable giving, if this is of importance. In addition, lifetime gifts are far less likely to be set aside by courts than are bequests, should disapproving heirs institute wills contests.

Moreover, in response to the COVID-19 pandemic, under the Coronavirus Aid, Relief and Economic Security Act (CARES Act), for taxable years 2020 and 2021, taxpayers could have claimed charitable deductions up to $300 ($600 for a married couple filing a joint return) for cash donations to qualifying tax-exempt organizations if they did not itemize their deductions.[9] In addition, for taxable years 2020 and 2021,

---

[8] See Allison Anna Tait, *The Secret Economy of Charitable Giving*, 95 B.U.L. REV. 1663, 1704–1705 (2015) (discussing the tangible benefits a donor may receive, including "naming opportunities, event invitations, social introductions, and board positions" and the intangible benefits from being a part of a particular social class).

[9] Coronavirus Aid, Relief, and Economic Security Act, Title 15, Sec. 2204, H.R. 748, Pub. L. No. 116–136.

Congress temporarily suspended the percentage limitation on qualified cash contributions under the CARES Act.[10]

PROBLEMS

1. Your client is a national charity that solicits gifts of large tracts of land to be held as wilderness and outdoor recreation areas. In recent years its board has become convinced of the need to lobby state and national elected officials to set aside surplus public lands for such purposes. The board is also interested in endorsing candidates for office who have a good track record on environmental issues. What risks are present for the organization should it follow such a strategy? What do you propose that it investigates to enable it to take steps in furtherance of its goals?

2. Martha Gibson is a wealthy widow who has three children. One of her sons is a member of a monastic order and has taken the vow of poverty. His monastery is located within close proximity to Martha. She wishes to treat all of her children equally and thinks she should divide all of her wealth equally among them at her death. She asks you if a bequest to her son who has taken a vow of poverty would qualify as a charitable bequest. She has been told by a friend that perhaps she should make the bequest to the monastery itself. What do you propose?

3. Austin wishes to leave one-third of his sizable estate to support charitable organizations active in the performing arts and intends to allow his daughter Emily to designate the appropriate charities after his death. What language do you propose be added to his will to assure that all such gifts qualify for the estate tax charitable deduction?

4. Myles has an estate well in excess of $15,000,000. He wishes to make a gift in honor of his recently deceased wife of $3,000,000 to the Center for Contemporary Opera, a highly regarded organization gifts to which qualify for a deduction under the income, gift and estate taxes. He is debating whether he should make the gift during his life or as a bequest. He seeks your advice.

---

[10] Coronavirus Aid, Relief, and Economic Security Act, Title 15, Sec. 2205, H.R. 748, Pub. L. No. 116–136.

CHAPTER 27

MARITAL DEDUCTION

(SECTION 2056)

■ ■ ■

A. INTRODUCTION

1. HISTORICAL PERSPECTIVE

One of the most significant features of the estate tax is the marital deduction, enacted in 1948. Its importance is two-fold: the large tax savings possible through the skillful use of the marital deduction and the radical effect its availability has on the drafting of wills and trusts when the goal is to maximize the inherent tax savings potential.

The marital deduction provisions initially were introduced into the estate tax as part of the overall program of Congress to equalize the burden of married couples in the common law states with those in the community property states. From the beginning of the estate tax in 1916, and of the income tax in 1913, the local community property laws of the eight western or southwestern states were accepted in determining the tax treatment of married couples residing in those states. As a result, the combined earnings of a married couple were taxed 50 percent to the husband and 50 percent to the wife, without regard to the respective contributions of each spouse to the earnings pool. This determination reflected the community property rule that each spouse is deemed to own one-half of the community—and that earnings received during marriage are community property. Also, in some states, such as Texas, income from separate property is community property, while in others income from separate property is the separate property of the spouse whose property produced the income. Extending this analysis for federal estate tax purposes resulted in a determination that only one-half of the value of community property was includible in the gross estate of the first spouse to die. For example, if a spouse in a noncommunity property state died with an estate that included accumulated earnings of $1,000,000, the entire $1,000,000 would be includible in that spouse's federal gross estate. But in a community property state, only the spouse's one-half community interest, or $500,000, would be includible in the deceased spouse's gross estate. A similar effect was applicable in the case of the gift tax; where married persons made a gift of their community property, the husband and wife were each treated as having individually made a separate gift of one-half of the property transferred.

The disparity in the impact of the federal income, gift, and estate taxes as a result of this automatic splitting of the family property for couples residing in community property states as compared with their counterparts in the common-law states was very substantial and became increasingly preferential as the tax rates were raised to meet the revenue needs of the war years. Some states, in an effort to ease the burden on their respective citizens, adopted community property laws.

2. LIMITED MARITAL DEDUCTION BEGINNING IN 1948

In 1948, Congress attempted to reconcile the differing tax consequences that resulted from ownership of community and noncommunity property and the receipt of income while resident in a community property rather than a noncommunity property jurisdiction. The income tax solution was to permit the splitting of income between husband and wife through the use of special tax tables for married couples filing joint returns. See I.R.C. § 1. The gift tax cure was accomplished at two levels: first, any gift made by a married person could be divided between husband and wife and thus be treated as a separate gift by each to the extent of one-half of the gift (I.R.C. § 2513), and, second, with respect to any gift between husband and wife, a marital deduction was allowed to the extent of one-half of the gift (I.R.C. § 2523). As to the estate tax, the correction was made through a marital deduction for property passing to the surviving spouse, the amount of the deduction being limited to the lesser of one-half of the decedent's adjusted gross estate or the amount actually passing to the surviving spouse.

While there is a tendency to believe that the effect of the marital deduction was to bring about equal tax treatment for community property and noncommunity property, the Senate Finance Committee expressly rejected any such notion in the report accompanying the 1948 changes. The Senate Finance Committee explained that the "inherent differences between community property and noncommunity property" preclude "complete equalization." However, the Committee Report concluded that the gift tax and estate tax marital deduction "will result in equality in the important situations." S. Rep. No. 1013, 88th Cong., 2d Sess., reprinted in 1948–1 C.B. 285, 305. As may be readily imagined, this lack of complete equalization occasionally has resulted in different tax consequences for community property and noncommunity property—and, in particular, frustrated taxpayers who have difficulty appreciating the subtle distinctions that are involved.

After Congress acted in 1948 to minimize the differing federal tax consequences that resulted from community property and separate property, the states that had adopted community property laws reversed course and returned to separate property systems.

3. INTERIM CHANGES TO MARITAL DEDUCTION

While no longer significant, it may sometimes be useful to bear in mind that Congress, in 1976, attempted a modification of the marital deduction that persisted until 1981. From 1977 until 1982, section 2056 allowed a marital deduction of the greater of $250,000 or one-half of the decedent's adjusted gross estate. The gift tax marital deduction allowed during this period was equal to the greater of $100,000 or one-half of the value of the transferred property. And, for the first time, both the estate tax and the gift tax marital deductions were allowed as to community property in a limited sense, i.e., to the extent of the first $250,000 and $100,000, respectively, of property transfers. Keeping in mind these special rules, which prevailed from 1977 until 1982, will sometimes be important in reading cases and rulings from that era that make reference to the marital deduction.

4. UNLIMITED MARITAL DEDUCTION AFTER 1981

In 1981, Congress eliminated completely the original 50-percent ceiling on the amount to be deducted for both the gift and the estate taxes, the result being the present-day unlimited marital deduction for transfers between spouses. I.R.C. § 2056. The 1981 marital deduction provisions were based on the policy that interspousal transfers should not be subject to taxation, rather than on the former policy that attempted to equalize the estate and gift tax treatment of noncommunity property with community property. According to the legislative history, Congress "believed that a husband and a wife should be treated as one economic unit for purposes of estate and gift taxes, as they generally are for income tax purposes. Accordingly, no tax should be imposed on transfers between a husband and wife." Senate Finance Committee, S. Rep. No. 97–144, Economic Recovery Tax Act of 1981, 97th Cong., 1st Sess. at 127 (1981). Despite the appealing simplicity of this policy, qualification for the marital deduction is subject to strict rules, the interpretation of which continues to be encrusted by considerations of an earlier time. Guiding notions include the axiom that deductions are a matter of legislative grace—that is, are to be strictly construed—and the idea that property that escapes tax at the death of the first spouse to die is to be taxed at the death of the surviving spouse.

B. REQUIREMENTS FOR MARITAL DEDUCTION—OVERVIEW

Section 2056 specifies the conditions that must be satisfied for the allowance of the marital deduction. Inasmuch as deductions are a matter of legislative grace, the marital deduction will be allowed only in cases where the taxpayer strictly complies with these conditions. However, with one notable exception to be discussed below, namely Qualified Terminable Interest Property (commonly known by the acronym "QTIP"), the marital deduction is not elective, i.e., it is mandatory in those instances where the conditions for its allowance have been satisfied.

Fundamentally, the marital deduction is available only for property passing to the decedent's surviving spouse—and passing in such a way as to be included in the surviving spouse's estate, unless the surviving spouse has disposed of the property prior to death. I.R.C. § 2056(c). As noted above, these overly simplistic premises have been implemented by stringent requirements for qualification for the marital deduction. For example, as will be seen in subsequent portions of this chapter, there are numerous cases where the marital deduction has been denied although the property for which the marital deduction had been sought was to be included in the estate of the surviving spouse, resulting in what could be simplistically referred to as double taxation.

Example: Catherine's will provided that her $10 million estate was to be placed in trust for the life of her husband, Brady. The trustee was instructed to distribute to Brady "so much or all of the income and principal of the trust as was necessary for Brady's support in his accustomed manner of living." At Brady's death, the trust was to be distributed to "those persons or institutions selected by Brady by provision in his will which makes specific reference to this provision of this trust." While Brady has a general power of appointment over Catherine's trust (which results in the inclusion of the trust property in Brady's estate at his death on the authority of section 2041), the peculiarities of section 2056 bar a marital deduction for the property Catherine placed in trust for Brady. Thus, the $10 million was taxed to Catherine at her death (with no marital deduction being allowed) and taxed again in Brady's estate at the time of his death (at its then fair market value).

As will be explained later in this chapter, Catherine's trust would have qualified for the marital deduction if the trustee had been required to distribute all the trust income to Brady at least annually. I.R.C. § 2056(b)(5).

PROBLEM

Should the person who drafted Catherine's will (described above) be subject to a claim for malpractice? Suppose Catherine's lawyer, in defense, stated that Catherine was told that the gift in trust for Brady would not qualify for the marital deduction but that Catherine insisted on the terms that were included in the trust. In such a case, what should the lawyer have done as protection against a later claim for malpractice?

1. CITIZENSHIP REQUIREMENT

The marital deduction is available only if the decedent was a citizen or resident of the United States. Moreover, except in limited circumstances, the decedent's spouse must be a U.S. citizen if the marital deduction is to be allowed for property passing from the decedent to the surviving spouse; i.e., under section 2056(d), enacted in 1988, property passing to a surviving spouse who is not a U.S. citizen does not qualify for the marital deduction. An exception is made for property passing to the noncitizen spouse in the form of a "qualified domestic trust." I.R.C. § 2056(d)(2)(A). A qualified domestic trust is defined in section 2056A(a), which requires that at least one trustee be a U.S. citizen or domestic corporation, that no distribution be made from the trust without the approval of that trustee (except in cases where the U.S. trustee has the authority to withhold estate tax generated by the distribution), that the trust meet the requirements of regulations prescribed to ensure the collection of estate tax imposed in the trust, and that an election be made by the executor of the decedent's estate. The general rule of section 2056(d)(1) does not apply if the surviving spouse becomes a citizen of the United States before the date of filing the estate tax return and the spouse was a U.S. resident at all times after the decedent's death and before becoming a U.S. citizen. I.R.C. § 2056(d)(4).

The marital deduction is denied in cases where the decedent's surviving spouse is not a citizen so as to ensure collection of the estate tax that is avoided when the marital deduction is claimed by the decedent's estate for the property passing to the surviving spouse. Congress apparently believed that there were too many instances where estate taxes were not being collected because noncitizen surviving spouses were leaving the United States—and dying elsewhere—with property for which a marital deduction had been claimed. While there was nothing illegal about the actions of such surviving spouses, the revenue opportunity lost to the United States as a result of such movements must have been too much for Congress to accept.

Example: Marie, a United States citizen and resident, died in 1987 survived by her husband, Pierre, a Canadian citizen but a resident of the United States at the time of Marie's death. As a result of Marie's will, Pierre received all Marie's $3 million estate. No estate taxes were paid at Marie's death, her executor having claimed the marital deduction for the $3 million that passed to Pierre. (Note that Marie died prior to 1988 and the advent of restrictions of the availability of the marital deduction for gifts to surviving spouses who were not citizens of the United States.) Upon receipt of the $3 million, Pierre returned to Canada on a permanent basis where he died in 2001. Since Pierre was a noncitizen nonresident of the United States at his death, no United States estate tax was ever paid on the $3 million despite the tax benefit enjoyed as a result of the marital deduction at the time of Marie's death in 1987.

The qualified domestic trust authorized in section 2056(d) provides a means by which the marital deduction may be made available if the decedent's surviving spouse is not a citizen. At the death of the surviving spouse, all the property then in the trust will be subject to estate tax as if it had been taxed to the deceased spouse at the earlier death of the deceased spouse, with the rate of tax being determined by reference to the estate of the decedent rather than to the estate of the surviving spouse. I.R.C. § 2056A(b). Furthermore, any distributions from the Qualified Domestic Trust to the surviving spouse during the lifetime of the surviving spouse in excess of the trust income (or for reasons other than hardship or reimbursement of the spouse for federal income tax on undistributed trust income) are to be subjected to the federal estate tax and taxed as if they were a part of the estate of the deceased spouse (at the marginal rate of tax applicable to the deceased spouse). The federal estate tax on such distributions is to be paid on April 15th of the year following the date of the taxable distribution. The trustee of the qualified domestic trust is personally liable for the estate tax on the qualified domestic trust and distributions from it. I.R.C. § 2056A(b)(6).

Obviously, there will be cases where property passes free of trust from a deceased citizen to a noncitizen surviving spouse with the resulting payment of estate taxes at the death of the citizen spouse. Clearly, harshness would result if the noncitizen surviving spouse did the unexpected and remained a resident of the United States until his or her death inasmuch as the property that the surviving spouse received from the decedent would be subject to estate tax at the death of the surviving spouse to the extent that the surviving spouse had not consumed it or disposed of it. Accordingly, a credit is available to the surviving spouse for the estate tax paid at the death of the first spouse to die. I.R.C. § 2056(d)(3).

Also, property passing to a noncitizen surviving spouse free of trust could be placed in a Qualified Domestic Trust by the surviving spouse. I.R.C. § 2056(d)(2)(B). Moreover, nothing prevents a surviving spouse from creating a Qualified Domestic Trust for this purpose (in cases where the deceased spouse had not provided for such a trust). Furthermore, a nonqualifying trust can be reformed to qualify as a Qualified Domestic Trust. I.R.C. § 2056(d)(4).

2.   PART OF GROSS ESTATE

The property given to the surviving spouse for which the marital deduction is claimed must be included in determining the value of the deceased spouse's gross estate. I.R.C. § 2056(a). The marital deduction is not allowed for property not included in the decedent's gross estate. For example, assume that a decedent's mother transfers $1 million to a trust with income payable to the decedent for life. The decedent has the right to designate either the surviving spouse or children to receive the corpus under the decedent's will. The decedent designates the surviving spouse as the recipient of the corpus. Because the decedent does not have a general power of appointment, the $1 million is not included in the decedent's gross estate under section 2041; therefore, the decedent is not entitled to claim the marital deduction.

3.   SURVIVING SPOUSE

a.   Legal Status

The decedent must have left a surviving spouse who takes the property for which the marital deduction is claimed. The term "surviving spouse" has been defined by the IRS as "a legal status that arises from the termination of a lawful marital union by the death of the other mate." Rev. Rul. 76–155, 1976–1 C.B. 286. Status as a surviving spouse is to be determined "from the best evidence available." Thus, the IRS ruled that the marital deduction was not available for payments made to a person claiming to be the surviving spouse of the decedent where the payments were made in compromise of a dispute as to whether a valid common law marriage existed. The alleged spouse claimed a dower interest in the decedent's property. The IRS concluded that "evidence submitted does not support the conclusion that the alleged spouse was decedent's legal surviving spouse" despite the fact that the payments were made as a result of a good faith, arm's-length compromise of the claim.

In United States v. Windsor, 570 U.S. 744 (2013), the Supreme Court held that the Defense of Marriage Act (1 USC Chap. 1, § 7), which had barred recognition of same-sex marriages for federal tax purposes, was unconstitutional. As a result, a decedent spouse in a same-sex marriage is entitled to claim the marital deduction for transfers to the surviving spouse.

b.   Validity of Divorce with Respect to Status as Spouse

It is not uncommon for the availability of the marital deduction to depend on the validity of a divorce decree obtained by either the deceased spouse or the surviving spouse. For example, a marriage of persons who are not validly divorced from their previous spouses is invalid for both tax and nontax purposes. As a result, in such cases, for example, the "true" surviving spouse is the spouse from whom the decedent is invalidly divorced and not the person to whom the decedent is invalidly married. Estate of Goldwater, 539 F.2d 878 (2d Cir.), cert. denied sub nom., Lipkowitz v. Commissioner, 429 U.S. 1023 (1976). Moreover, the validity of the divorce for federal estate tax purposes will be determined by the law applicable in the jurisdiction in which the decedent was domiciled at his or her death. The test was set out in Estate of Steffke, 538 F.2d 730 (7th Cir.), cert. denied sub nom., Wisconsin Valley Trust Co. v. Commissioner, 429 U.S. 1022 (1976), where the court said:

> When there are conflicting judicial decrees regarding the validity of a divorce, the decision should be followed for federal estate tax purposes that would be followed by the state which has primary jurisdiction over the administration of a decedent's estate, i.e., the jurisdiction in which the decedent was domiciled at the time of his death.

Estate of Steffke, 538 F.2d at 735.

In Estate of Grossman v. Commissioner, T.C. Memo. 2021-65, 121 T.C.M (CCH) 1492 (2021), the Internal Revenue Service disallowed the marital deduction for property passing to the decedent's surviving spouse arguing that a purported earlier divorce was invalid in New York, the decedent's domicile. According to the court, New York considers a marriage valid based on the "place of celebration." In this case, the marriage took place in Israel. The Tax Court determined that:

> New York law requires us to look to the law of the place of the marriage celebration to determine the parties' capacity to marry, New York law also requires us to defer to the place of celebration and its determination on whether one of those parties was validly divorced and therefore capable to remarry.

Israel considered the decedent validly divorced. As a result, the court allowed the decedent to claim the marital deduction.

c.   Close Order of Deaths and Presumptions of Survivorship

In cases where two persons both die and it cannot be determined which of them died first, state law will ordinarily supply a presumption as to the order of deaths, which will be recognized for purposes of the marital deduction. See Rev. Rul. 76–303, 1976–2 C.B. 266 (simultaneous death of joint tenants). Many states presume that where there is no sufficient evidence of the order of deaths, each decedent will be presumed to have survived the other decedent.[1] In addition, under section 2–702(c) of the Uniform Probate Code, unless there is clear and convincing evidence that one decedent survived the other decedent by 120 hours, each decedent is presumed to have survived the other.[2] For purposes of the marital deduction, in cases where there is uncertainty as to the order of deaths, a presumption of survivorship included in the will of one of the decedents will be respected (unless a provision of the applicable state law bars such a provision). See Treas. Reg. § 20.2056(c)–2(e). To illustrate, if Tony and Marsha are married and there is uncertainty as to the order of their deaths when they die, a gift to Marsha in Tony's will is eligible for the marital deduction if Tony's will states, for example, that "Marsha shall be deemed to survive me where the order of our deaths cannot be determined without reference to judicial proceedings."

4. PASSING TO SURVIVING SPOUSE

The marital deduction is available only as to property that "passes or has passed" to the surviving spouse from the decedent. I.R.C. § 2056(a). Section 2056(c) lists the types of transfers from the decedent that satisfy the passing requirement. Regulation § 20.2056(c)–2(a) also defines the meaning of passing to surviving spouse, which could be viewed as broadening the scope of passing. As you consider the alternatives presented below that qualify for the marital deduction, remember that an outright and unconditional bequest or devise of property has always been available as a completely secure way of obtaining the marital deduction.

SCHROEDER V. UNITED STATES
United States Court of Appeals, Tenth Circuit, 1991.
924 F.2d 1547.

PER CURIAM.

This is a case of first impression in the area of federal estate tax. A surviving spouse surrendered her survivorship rights to property held in joint tenancy with her husband, and her statutory-election rights to the decedent's property, in settlement of a controversy with decedent's daughters from a previous marriage concerning her entitlement to the property. At issue is whether that property nevertheless "passed" to her within the meaning of the marital deduction statute, § 2056(a), (d). The District Court for the Western District of Oklahoma determined on summary judgment that such property in these circumstances does not pass to the surviving spouse and accordingly disallowed the marital

---

[1]   12 Del. Code Ann. § 701 (2022) (stating generally that where it can't be established whether the deaths were simultaneous, each person's property is disposed of as if each person had survived). Accord Nev. Rev. Stat. Ann. § 135.020 (2021).

[2]   Many states have adopted approaches consistent with the Uniform Probate Code. See, e.g., Mich. Comp. Laws § 700.2702 (2022); Va. Code Ann. § 64.2–2203 (2022); Wis. Stat. § 854.03 (2022).

deduction. Schroeder v. United States, 696 F.Supp. 1426 (W.D.Okla.1988). We agree with the district court and affirm.

I.

Thomas J. Woodmansee (Thomas) was married to Peggy Woodmansee (Peggy) for approximately eighteen years, and had two adult daughters from a previous marriage, Martha Schroeder (Martha) and Lou Ann Waters (Lou). On July 6, 1981, Thomas created a substantial stock account, naming himself and Peggy as joint tenants with a right of survivorship. Neither of his daughters was aware of the creation of this account. On July 16, 1981, Thomas signed a will providing that his property be placed in a trust, the income from which was to be used to provide for Peggy for the remainder of her life. After Peggy's death, the corpus of the trust was to be divided equally between Martha and Lou, or their issue, keeping the property in the family. On the same day, Thomas deeded the family farm over to Martha and Lou. Both of the daughters stated by affidavit that they knew of the provisions of the will and of their father's intent and that both intended to honor their father's wishes. In addition, both daughters stated that Thomas was mentally competent at all times during his life.

Thomas died two months later. At the time of his death, the fair market value of the stock account was approximately $229,843. Later that month, Martha and Lou learned for the first time that Thomas had created the joint stock account, which was wholly and independently owned by Peggy and would not pass through Thomas' will. Relations between Peggy and Thomas' daughters were strained by this revelation. In their affidavits, Martha and Lou stated that they thought Peggy had a "moral duty" to leave the principal of the stock account to them and their children.

The will was admitted to probate and Harry D. Schroeder (Schroeder), Martha's husband, was named executor. Martha and Lou were advised by an attorney to negotiate with Peggy concerning the stock account, and their attorney entered into discussions with Peggy's attorney. In February 1982, in settlement of these discussions, Peggy placed the stock account into a trust account with a neutral trustee. Quarterly income from the trust is divided among the three women, one-fourth to Peggy and three-fourths divided equally between Martha and Lou, or their issue, until Peggy's death. At that time, the principal in the trust account is to be distributed equally to Martha and Lou, or their issue.

In April 1982, Peggy filed her election to take the statutory spousal share of the estate rather than take under the will. At the time of Thomas' death, the spousal election, one-third of the estate, had a fair market value of $77,121. Peggy deposited the spousal share into the trust account, under the conditions for distribution set forth for the stock account.

When Schroeder filed the estate tax return, he included the joint stock account and the spousal election share in the estate, pursuant to §§ 2033,

2040(a). He also claimed them as part of the federal marital deduction, pursuant to § 2056. The IRS issued Schroeder a notice of deficiency after it disallowed the marital deduction with respect to the stock account and Peggy's statutory share of the estate. Schroeder paid the deficiency and claimed a refund, which the IRS denied. Schroeder then brought this action.

* * *

* * * [I]nterpretive regulations provide that property surrendered by a surviving spouse in settlement of a controversy over a decedent's will is constructively deemed not to have "passed" to such spouse. Treas. Reg. § 20.2056(e)–2(d)(1) (will contest regulation). This regulation is consistent with the legislative history of the code section:

> If the surviving spouse takes under the decedent's will, the interest passing to her is determined from the will. In this connection proper regard should be given to interpretations of the will rendered by a court in a bona fide adversary proceeding. If as a result of a controversy involving a bequest or devise to the surviving spouse, such spouse assigns or surrenders an interest in property pursuant to a compromise agreement in settlement of such controversy, the amount so assigned or surrendered is not deductible as an interest passing to such spouse.

S. Rep. No. 1013 Part 2, 80th Cong., 2d Sess. 4 (1948), reprinted in 4 Rabkin & Johnson at 5344.

This statutory and regulatory scheme is built upon the fundamental rule that state law determines what property interest individuals hold, and federal law determines how that property shall be taxed. * * * Thus, federal law controls whether property "passes" from the estate of a deceased individual for the purposes of the federal estate tax.

The IRS and the district court relied heavily on United States Trust Co. v. Commissioner, 321 F.2d 908 (2d Cir.1963), and Citizens & Southern Nat'l Bank v. United States, 451 F.2d 221 (5th Cir.1971). These cases involved situations in which the surviving spouse and a beneficiary reached an agreement modifying the estate which would have otherwise passed to the surviving spouse.

* * *

These two cases invoked policy to expand the reach of Treas. Reg. § 20.2056(e)–2(d)(1) well beyond its plain language. *Citizens & Southern* defined "the decedent's will, or involving any bequest or devise thereunder" to include transfers of property at death under intestacy statutes or spousal election. Both cases expanded the terms "will contest" or "controversy" to include arm's-length negotiations conducted between parties who have potentially adverse positions. Under this view, no litigation is required, much less court adjudication of various parties' rights to the property of the deceased.

Peggy's rights in the present case to a statutory share of the probate estate and to the joint account do not arise under Thomas' will. It is undisputed that Peggy surrendered this property in settlement not of a will contest, but of a more general controversy over the rightful passing of Thomas' property considered as a whole. [The court explained, in a footnote, that Peggy's rights "derive from state law" that gave Peggy a statutorily determined spousal share notwithstanding her husband's will.] By its plain terms, therefore, the will contest regulation is not dispositive here. In the absence of an applicable regulation, we must look directly to the relevant provisions of the Internal Revenue Code.

As previously discussed, section 2056(a) requires that property "pass" from the decedent to his or her surviving spouse to claim the marital deduction. The meaning of this term is dispositive of this appeal. Clearly, transfers of property under spousal election statutes and by survivorship rights concerning joint interests may "pass" within the meaning of the marital deduction provision. See § 2056(d)(3) and (5). The issue in this case is whether the *rationale* for the Secretary's regulatory gloss on the passing requirement in the context of a will contest mandates a similar result based on an analysis of the term "passes" in the marital deduction statute.

In *United States Trust Co.*, the court noted that the statutory "passing" requirement is "crucial in qualifying property for a marital deduction." 321 F.2d at 910. It held that "[w]hen the resolution of a controversy between the beneficiaries regarding the decedent's property culminates in an agreement by which the surviving spouse relinquishes property which qualifies for the marital deduction in return for property which does not so qualify, [the will-contest regulation] is applicable." Id. In essence, the court defined "passing" to mean property to which the surviving spouse retains her rights after resolution of all disputes concerning the decedent's property. The court in *Citizens & Southern* agreed with this definition of passing in concluding that "the medium by which the decedent's property passes * * * is immaterial." 451 F.2d at 227.

Both courts also properly disregarded the significance of the surviving spouse's acquisition of "vested" rights under state law in determining whether the property "passed" for purposes of the marital deduction. See United States Trust, 321 F.2d at 910 (vesting under state law has no bearing on interpretation of federal passing requirement); Citizens & Southern, 451 F.2d at 228 ("acquisition and subsequent relinquishment of 'vested' rights in no way renders the 'will controversy' regulation inapplicable"). Indeed, a contrary view arguably would transgress the Supreme Court's holding in Lyeth v. Hoey, 305 U.S. 188, 193–94 (1938), that federal law controls the incidence of federal taxation of property acquired under state law.

Unlike the district court and the courts in *United States Trust* and *Citizens & Southern*, we believe the will-contest regulation is inapplicable to property passing to a surviving spouse by statutory election or under the law of survivorship because the regulation speaks only in terms of a controversy involving a bequest or devise under decedent's will. Nonetheless, we find the reasons those courts articulated to broaden the reach of the regulation to be persuasive in our own analysis of what Congress intended by the "passing" requirement in the marital deduction statute. To the extent a surviving spouse surrenders her share of the decedent's property to other beneficiaries not entitled to the marital deduction to avoid litigation concerning her rights, it defies common sense to conclude that this property "passed" to the surviving spouse. Not only is the ultimate recipient of the property a person other than the surviving spouse, but the transfer comprising the settlement could altogether escape taxation applying to gratuitous transfers of wealth.

In creating the marital deduction, Congress envisioned a scheme in which interspousal transfers of wealth would not result in a taxable event. See S. Rep. No. 97–144, 97th Cong., 1st Sess. 126, reprinted in 1981 U.S. Code & Cong. Admin. News 105, 228 ("a husband and wife should be treated as one economic unit for purposes of estate and gift taxes, as they generally are for income tax purposes. Accordingly, no tax should be imposed on transfers between a husband and wife."). The marital deduction was designed to eliminate the "double-taxation" that would result when the same property became subject to tax upon the death of each spouse. Once property passes outside of the interspousal unit, however, this exception no longer applies. Under Schroeder's proposed interpretation, property may exit the spousal unit without ever creating a taxable event. Congress clearly did not intend to replace double-taxation with tax avoidance.

Accordingly, we hold that the property comprising Peggy's statutory election and the joint account did not "pass" to her within the meaning of the marital deduction statute. Instead, Peggy surrendered her entitlement to this property in settlement of a bona fide controversy concerning her rights to the property in the decedent's gross estate for federal estate tax purposes. We therefore AFFIRM the district court.

NOTE

The *Schroeder* court noted that Peggy's transfer could "altogether escape taxation applying to transfers of wealth" if she were allowed the marital deduction. In a footnote, the court noted Peggy's claim that she had no gift tax liability for the transfer in settlement of the controversy because the "avoidance of litigation over her rights was appropriate consideration for the transfer." Do you agree? Similarly, the court noted, Peggy claimed that she realized neither gain nor loss on sale "when she transferred the joint tenancy account to the trust even though the premise of [the] * * * argument here is that the property 'passed' to her prior to transfer." *Schroeder*, 924 F.2d at 1554 n.8. Does this position make sense?

5. NONDEDUCTIBLE TERMINABLE INTERESTS

The most troublesome of all the requirements for allowance of the marital deduction is the statutory provision that the interest for which the marital deduction is claimed must not be a nondeductible terminable interest, with its several complex exceptions. In view of the fact that the half interest of the surviving spouse in the community property of the couple is an outright interest, it was the general plan of the Congress to restrict the marital deduction to outright bequests, i.e., nonterminable interests. However, in effectuating this objective, Congress quickly lost sight of this concept of equivalence. Section 2056(b)(1) provides that the interest going to the surviving spouse must not be one which may terminate or fail on the lapse of time or on the occurrence or nonoccurrence of an event or contingency; thus, a life estate, a term for years, or a conditional interest would be terminable and subject to disallowance. However, the statute does not disallow all terminable interests; it disallows only those terminable interests which are coupled with either of the following conditions:

1.   Another interest in the same property, in which the surviving spouse holds his or her interest, is given or has been given to a third party by the decedent, and by reason of such interest, the third party may possess or enjoy the property after the termination or failure of such spouse's interest, or

2.   The terminable interest of the surviving spouse was directed by the decedent to be acquired by the executor or by a trustee.

The first condition would bar all life estates or conditional interests to the spouse in property in which others are given a remainder interest by the decedent that may be enjoyed after the spouse's interest ceases. The second condition strikes down all terminable interests that the decedent directs his or her executor or a trustee to acquire for the surviving spouse, such as the purchase of a life estate or an annuity, without regard to whether interests in the property are held by others.

From an historical standpoint, it is useful to note that the nondeductible terminable interest rule was necessary to accomplish rough equivalence between community property and separate property for transfer tax purposes while allowing persons with separate property to control the disposition of that property while claiming the marital deduction (a privilege not available to person's dying with community property). With the advent, in 1981, of the rule permitting tax-free transfers between spouses, the nondeductible terminable interest rule continues to be of importance in preventing "leakage" by denying the marital deduction in cases where the property will not be included in the estate of the surviving spouse at his or her later death.

a. Spousal Award

Most, if not all, states make provision for the surviving spouse by way of an allowance to be paid from the estate of the decedent before distribution of the decedent's property pursuant to the decedent's will.[3] Normally, this statutory allowance or award is in addition to any provision in favor of the spouse in the decedent's will or provided to the spouse by the intestate laws in cases where the decedent has died intestate. In many states, payment of the spousal award or allowance is conditioned upon the spouse making claim to the award and the court having jurisdiction over the estate entering an order setting the amount of the award. Whether such awards qualify for the marital deduction is an almost never-ending controversy as the litigation marches through the states.

JACKSON V. UNITED STATES
Supreme Court of the United States, 1964.
376 U.S. 503.

MR. JUSTICE WHITE delivered the opinion of the Court.

Since 1948 § 812(e)(1)(A) [1986 Code § 2056(a)] of the Internal Revenue Code of 1939 has allowed a "marital deduction" from a decedent's gross taxable estate for the value of interests in property passing from the decedent to his surviving spouse. Subsection (B) adds the qualification, however, that interests defined therein as "terminable" shall not qualify as an interest in property to which the marital deduction applies. The question raised by this case is whether the allowance provided by California law for the support of a widow during the settlement of her husband's estate is a terminable interest.

Petitioners are the widow-executrix and testamentary trustee under the will of George Richards who died a resident of California on May 27, 1951. Acting under the Probate Code of California, the state court, on June 30, 1952, allowed Mrs. Richards the sum of $3,000 per month from the corpus of the estate for her support and maintenance, beginning as of May

---

[3] See, e.g., Iowa Code § 633.374(1) (2022) (allowing an allowance for the surviving spouse and the decedent's dependents living with the spouse for 12 months); Kan. Stat. Ann. § 59–403 (2022) (allowing a spouse to claim an allowance, either for his/her benefit or for that of the decedent's minor children, provided it is for less than $50,000 money or property); Wash. Rev. Code § 11.54.010 (2022) (permitting a surviving spouse, domestic partner, or minor children to petition the court for an award from the decedent's property); Wis. Stat. § 861.31(1m) (2022) (permitting an allowance initially up to one year which may be extended to surviving spouse, domestic partner, and any minor children).

27, 1951, and continuing for a period of 24 months from that date. Under the terms of the order, an allowance of $42,000 had accrued during the 14 months since her husband's death. This amount, plus an additional $3,000 per month for the remainder of the two-year period, making a total of $72,000, was in fact paid to Mrs. Richards as widow's allowance.

On the federal estate tax return filed on behalf of the estate, the full $72,000 was claimed as a marital deduction under § 812(e) of the Internal Revenue Code of 1939. The deduction was disallowed, as was a claim for refund after payment of the deficiency, and the present suit for refund was then brought in the District Court. The District Court granted summary judgment for the United States, holding * * * that the allowance to the widow was a terminable interest and not deductible under the marital provision * * *. The Court of Appeals affirmed * * *. For the reasons given below, we affirm the decision of the Court of Appeals.

* * * The issue * * * is whether the interest in property passing to Mrs. Richards as widow's allowance would "terminate or fail" upon the "lapse of time, upon the occurrence of an event or contingency, or upon the failure of an event or contingency to occur." [1939 Code § 812(e)(1)(B); 1986 Code § 2056(b)(1)]

We accept the Court of Appeals description of the nature and characteristics of the widow's allowance under California law. In that State, the right to a widow's allowance is not a vested right and nothing accrues before the order granting it. The right to an allowance is lost when the one for whom it is asked has lost the status upon which the right depends. If a widow dies or remarries prior to securing an order for a widow's allowance, the right does not survive such death or remarriage. The amount of the widow's allowance which has accrued and is unpaid at the date of death of the widow is payable to her estate but the right to future payments abates upon her death. The remarriage of a widow subsequent to an order for an allowance likewise abates her right to future payments. 317 F.2d 821, 825.

In light of these characteristics of the California widow's allowance, Mrs. Richards did not have an indefeasible interest in property at the moment of her husband's death since either her death or remarriage would defeat it. If the order for support allowance had been entered on the day of her husband's death, her death or remarriage at any time within two years thereafter would terminate that portion of the interest allocable to the remainder of the two-year period. As of the date of Mr. Richards' death, therefore, the allowance was subject to failure or termination "upon the occurrence of an event or contingency." That the support order was entered in this case 14 months later does not, in our opinion, change the defeasible nature of the interest.

Petitioners ask us to judge the terminability of the widow's interest in property represented by her allowance as of the date of the Probate Court's order rather than as of the date of her husband's death. The court's order, they argue, unconditionally entitled the widow to $42,000 in accrued allowance of which she could not be deprived by either her death or remarriage. It is true that some courts have followed this path, but it is difficult to accept an approach which would allow a deduction of $42,000 on the facts of this case, a deduction of $72,000 if the order had been entered at the end of two years from Mr. Richards' death and none at all if the order had been entered immediately upon his death. Moreover, judging deductibility as of the date of the Probate Court's order ignores the Senate Committee's admonition that in considering terminability of an interest for purposes of a marital deduction "the situation is viewed as at the date of the decedent's death." S.Rep. No. 1013, Part 2, 80th Cong., 2d Sess., p. 10. We prefer the * * * [view which] is in accord with the rule uniformly followed with regard to interests other than the widow's allowance, that qualification for the marital deduction must be determined as of the time of death.

Our conclusion is confirmed by § 812(e)(1)(D) [1986 Code § 2056(b)(3)], which saves from the operation of the terminable interest rule interests which by their terms may (but do not in fact) terminate only upon failure of the widow to survive her husband for a period not in excess of six months. The premise of this provision is that an interest passing to a widow is normally to be judged as of the time of the testator's death rather than at a later time when the condition imposed may be satisfied; hence the necessity to provide an exception to the rule in the case of a six months' survivorship contingency in a will. A gift conditioned upon eight months' survivorship, rather than six, is a nondeductible terminable interest for reasons which also disqualify the statutory widow's allowance in California where the widow must survive and remain unmarried at least to the date of an allowance order to become indefeasibly entitled to any widow's allowance at all.

Petitioners contend, however, that the sole purpose of the terminable interest provisions of the Code is to assure that interests deducted from the estate of the deceased spouse will not also escape taxation in the estate of the survivor. This argument leads to the conclusion that since it is now clear that unless consumed or given away during Mrs. Richard's life, the entire $72,000 will be taxed to her estate, it should not be included in her husband's. But as we have already seen, there is no provision in the Code for deducting all terminable interests which become nonterminable at a later date and therefore taxable in the estate of the surviving spouse if not consumed or transferred. The examples cited in the legislative history make it clear that the determinative factor is not taxability to the surviving spouse but terminability as defined by the statute. Under the view advanced by petitioners all cash allowances actually paid would fall outside § 812(e)(1)(B) [1986 Code § 2056(b)(1)]; on two different occasions the Senate has refused to give its approval to House-passed amendments to the 1954 Code which would have made the terminable interest rule inapplicable to all widows' allowances actually paid within specified periods of time.

We are mindful that the general goal of the marital deduction provisions was to achieve uniformity of federal estate tax impact between those States with community property laws and those without them. But the device of the marital deduction which Congress chose to achieve uniformity was knowingly hedged with limitations, including the terminable interest rule. These provisions may be imperfect devices to achieve the desired end, but they are the means which Congress chose. To the extent it was thought desirable to modify the rigors of the terminable-interest rule, exceptions to the rule were written into the Code. Courts should hesitate to provide still another exception by straying so far from the statutory language as to allow a marital deduction for the widow's allowance provided by the California statute. The achievement of the purposes of the marital deduction is dependent to a great degree upon the careful drafting of wills; we have no fear that our decision today will prevent either the full utilization of the marital deduction or the proper support of widows during the pendency of an estate proceeding.

Affirmed.

NOTES

1. Under *Jackson*, the spousal award or allowance provided by the laws of most states will be disallowed as a marital deduction because of the contingency of remarriage or death. Similarly, where the state statute is designed to provide support to the surviving spouse for the period of administration, as is the usual case, a major change in the circumstances of the surviving spouse, such as subsequent remarriage or death, would affect the amount or the continuance of the payments, thus constituting a terminable interest. However, the marital deduction has been allowed for the spousal allowance in several cases. Estate of Green v. United States, 441 F.2d 303 (6th Cir.1971); Estate of Watson v. Commissioner, 94 T.C. 262 (1990). In both cases, under applicable state law (Michigan and Mississippi, respectively), the spousal allowance could have been lost if the spouse had failed to petition the court for the allowance. Moreover, the amount of the allowance was not fixed, the court having authority to set the amount of the allowance in each case. Both courts rejected the argument that the allowances awarded to the respective spouses were terminable interests. Judge Hamblen of the Tax Court explained in *Watson*:

* * * We agree with the Sixth Circuit that "To hold that an interest is terminable only because legal procedures are invoked to enforce an interest which is otherwise vested at the date of the husband's death, is to hold that all elective rights, such as the widow's allowance and the statutory interest in lieu of dower, are disqualified as marital deductions." Estate of Green v. United States, 441 F.2d at 308. Without a clear expression of intent from Congress that all rights such as the Mississippi widow's allowance should be considered terminable interests, we will not treat the necessity of invoking legal procedures as a condition or contingency making the Mississippi widow's allowance a terminable interest for purposes of section 2056. Accordingly, we hold that the requirement under Mississippi law that the chancellor make a final determination of the amount of the allowance and the possibility that the widow may lose her right to the allowance by failing to take some action to request the allowance are not conditions or contingencies that make the Mississippi widow's allowance a terminable interest. Consequently, we hold that the widow's allowance paid to the decedent's widow qualifies for the marital deduction provided in section 2056(a).[4]

2. Practice varies but states sometimes offer the surviving spouse homestead (perhaps a right to occupy the principal residence for life). Whether the homestead rights qualify for the marital deduction—or are nondeductible terminable interests—is sometimes in dispute. See, e.g., Estate of Kyle v. Commissioner, 94 T.C. 829 (1990) (marital deduction denied for Texas homestead right where homestead will be lost upon abandonment by spouse at any time).

C. EXCEPTIONS TO NONDEDUCTIBLE TERMINABLE INTEREST RULE

Under section 2056, a decedent is not entitled to claim the marital deduction for a bequest to a surviving spouse where the interest will terminate based on a lapse of time or a contingency or a failure of a contingency. Due to the breadth of the rule forbidding nondeductible terminable interests and its serious effect on prior patterns of estate planning, the following important exceptions have been incorporated into the statute.

1. SURVIVORSHIP

A frequently used provision in pre-1948 wills was a clause designed to avoid multiple administration of estates upon the death of the beneficiary "hard upon the heels" of the testator. Thereunder, a beneficiary dying in a

---

[4] *Estate of Watson v. Comm'r*, 94 T.C. at 280–81.

common accident with the testator or within a period of, say, six months of the death of the testator would be considered as having predeceased the testator and thus would not take the gift provided in the will. Inasmuch as such a clause, when applied to the surviving spouse, would result in a nondeductible terminable interest, whether or not the actual deaths occurred as feared, Congress wanted to permit the free use of such a clause. Accordingly, section 2056(b)(3) provides that an interest that will fail if the surviving spouse dies within six months of the decedent's death will not be considered a terminable interest, provided that the deaths do not occur.

However, it should also be noted that a survivorship clause can result in loss of the marital deduction. In Estate of Shepherd v. Commissioner, 58 T.C.M. (CCH) 671 (1989), the marital deduction was denied because the surviving spouse was required to survive until the decedent's will was "admitted to probate." The spouse did, in fact, survive until the will was probated, but the marital deduction was denied for the following reason:

> [T]he possibility existed at the time of the decedent's death that the will might have been admitted to probate beyond the 6-month exception to the terminable interest rule contained in § 2056(b)(3) and that the surviving spouse's interest might have terminated and passed to someone else at a point in time thereafter.

The court said that "the probate of a will has substantive significance and cannot be considered as merely a ministerial act or a method of perfecting title." And, in Rev. Rul. 88–90, 1988–2 C.B. 335, the IRS denied the marital deduction where the spouse was required to survive until a trust provided for in the will was funded. The IRS said that "due to the requirements of local probate law, the possibility exists at the time of the decedent's death that the funding may occur more than 6 months after the decedent's death."

By way of contrast, in Priv. Ltr. Rul. 8809003, the marital deduction was allowed where the surviving spouse was required to survive "for a sufficient length of time to receive" the decedent's property. The IRS explained that the "surviving spouse was competent to serve as Independent Executrix upon the decedent's death, and did in fact assume the position" and for this reason, the surviving spouse "had the unqualified right to initiate and complete probate proceedings immediately under local law without the need for the probate court to respond or take any further action with respect to the acts of the surviving spouse."

Important to the IRS's determination was the freedom from court supervision that an independent executor enjoyed under Texas law after probating the will and filing the inventory and list of claims in cases such as this where the decedent's will specifically states that no further action is needed in the probate court.

Examples of results adverse to taxpayers seeking to have the marital deduction allowed for gifts conditioned on survivorship are numerous.

Witness Tech. Adv. Mem. 8834002 where a clause providing that a decedent's wife was to receive property only if she survived distribution of the estate was ruled to be a contingent interest that did not qualify for the marital deduction. See Treas. Reg. § 20.2056(b)–3(d), Example (4). But cases like Estate of Bond v. Commissioner, 104 T.C. 652 (1995), cause hope to spring eternal in the breast of the creatively assertive taxpayer. There, state property law rules saved the marital deduction despite the will's requirement that the spouse "survive distribution." Looking to Washington law, the Tax Court concluded that, since title to real property vests at death, the words "survive distribution" are, practically speaking, without meaning. To the court, there can be no distribution of that which has already vested. Thus, so long as the testator intended Washington law to apply, in the case of gifts of real property, presence of the words "survive distribution" will not bar the marital deduction. Contrasted, though, is personal property which the Tax Court found did not vest in Washington until actual distribution. Interestingly, the Tax Court found inapplicable a Washington statute—one claimed to be shared with California—that banned application of any survivorship requirement "in excess of six months" for gifts "passing under a marital deduction." Fatal to the statute's application in *Bond* was the absence of any reference to the marital deduction in the decedent's will.

PROBLEMS

1. Consider whether the result reached in Rev. Rul. 88–90, 1988–2 C.B. 335, would have been different had the decedent's will been probated in a state with laws similar to those described in Priv. Ltr. Rul. 8809003.

2. Josh is perplexed. Meeting with Isabel to prepare her will, she tells him (1) she does not want a trust "no how"; (2) she wants to make a substantial cash bequest to her husband, Hobart ("he needs it to live on"), even though she knows that Hobart will give "whatever is left" to his girlfriend when he dies; and (3) Josh is to "make certain that Hobart does not get his hands on my money until everything is wrapped up with the probate" after her death ("maybe he'll die in the meantime and won't need it and *that woman* won't get it"). Suggest how Josh should draft the gift to Hobart.

2. LIFE ESTATE WITH POWER OF APPOINTMENT

Prior to 1948 and the advent of the marital deduction, the common type of provision for a family of some means was a life estate for the surviving spouse with a remainder to the children. Rather than discourage the use of the life estate device, Congress created an exception, sometimes referred to as the "life estate/power of appointment" exception, to the nondeductible terminable interest rule—but only if five basic conditions are met. I.R.C. § 2056(b)(5).

a. The "Income" Requirement

The surviving spouse must be entitled for life to all income from the property or to all income from a specific portion of the property as a condition for allowance of the martial deduction under the life estate/power of appointment exception. I.R.C. § 2056(b)(5). While the property is not required to be held in trust as a condition for allowance of the marital deduction, this is the usual form in which the bequest is found.

WISELY V. UNITED STATES
United States Court of Appeals, Fourth Circuit, 1990.
893 F.2d 660.

JAMES C. FOX, DISTRICT JUDGE:

* * * The principal question for our determination is whether the district court properly granted summary judgment for the government in holding that the deceased's will, as drafted, failed to qualify the marital trust for the marital estate tax deduction under * * * § 2056(b)(5). Having concluded that the district court's disposition was proper, we affirm.

* * *

The decedent, William H. Wisely, died testate on November 9, 1982, leaving his Last Will and Testament which he had executed on April 22, 1982. The will named the decedent's wife, Hazel S. Wisely, as the executor of the Estate.

The will contained provisions for the creation of two trusts, the William H. Wisely Family Trust created under Article V, and the marital trust created under Article VI. The portion of the will which is pertinent to this appeal concerns the payment of income from the marital trust and is found in paragraph 2 of Article VI, which states:

> My trustees shall pay to my said wife so much, or all, of the net income of the said trust as my Trustees shall, in their sole discretion, deem necessary to provide for her care and support in the style and manner of living to which she has been accustomed, and to provide for her medical or other emergency needs. Any income not so used shall be accumulated and added to the corpus. Such payments may also be made from the corpus at any time or times in the event of any illness of my said wife or any other emergency, physical or financial.

The will also granted Mrs. Wisely a general testamentary power of appointment over the marital trust corpus. * * *

On its federal estate tax return, the Estate claimed a marital deduction in the amount of $281,575, representing the full value of the property transferred to the marital trust pursuant to Article VI of the will.

The Internal Revenue Service disallowed the marital deduction on the ground that the marital trust did not fully comply with the requirements of Section 2056(b)(5). * * *

Code Section 2056(a) generally permits a deduction from the gross estate for the value of an interest in property passing to the surviving spouse. Section 2056(b), however, limits marital deductions of "terminable interests." A terminable interest is one "where on the lapse of time, on the occurrence of a contingency, or on the failure of an event or contingency to occur, an interest passing to the surviving spouse will terminate or fail. . . ." Included in such "terminable interests" is property transferred as a life estate to the surviving spouse. § 2056(a), Treas. Reg. § 20.2056(b)–1(b).

An exception to the general rule barring a marital deduction for a terminable interest is contained in Section 2056(b)(5). In order to fall within this exception, the bequest must meet the five separate requirements set forth in Section 20.2056(b)–5(a) * * *.

Under Section 20.2056(b)–5(a)(1), the value of the life estate passing to the surviving spouse with a general power of appointment qualifies for the marital deduction if the surviving spouse is entitled for life either: (1) to all the income from the entire interest; (2) to all the income from a specific portion of the entire interest; or (3) to a specific portion of all the income from the entire interest.

The district court concluded that the terms of the marital trust, as found in Article VI, paragraph 2 of the will, did not meet any of these three requirements because the will failed to expressly state that Mrs. Wisely was entitled to either all the income outright or to some lesser specific portion expressed as a "fractional or percentile share" of the marital trust income. We agree with the district court's conclusion.

Under Article VI paragraph 2 of the will, the trustees may, in their *sole discretion*, decide to accumulate any income they do not deem necessary for Mrs. Wisely's support, medical, or emergency expenses. Moreover, Mrs. Wisely is not entitled, under the terms of the trust, to demand that the trustees distribute income to her. On the contrary, the trustees' affirmative action is required in order for the trust to distribute income to Mrs. Wisely. In short, the consent of persons other than Mrs. Wisely is required as a condition precedent to distribution of the marital trust income. Likewise, it is within the discretion of persons other than Mrs. Wisely to accumulate the trust income rather than to pay it to her, if they should determine that the income is not necessary to maintain her standard of living. We agree with the district court's reasoning that the "sole discretion" language in the trust does not entitle Mrs. Wisely to all of the income from the entire interest for life. Furthermore, we affirm the district court's finding that the language of the trust fails to satisfy the second or third conditions of Section 20.2056(b)–5(a)(1). We rely on the district court's reasoning that the language allowing the trustees to pay Mrs. Wisely income in their "sole discretion" fails to designate either a specific portion of the entire interest or a specific portion of all of the income from the entire interest.

Accordingly, we conclude that the district court did not err in finding that the marital trust failed to meet the requirement of Section 20.2056(b)–5(a)(1).

* * *

The Estate argues that the district court erred in concluding that the marital trust did not qualify for the marital deduction under §§ 20.2056(b)–5(a)(1) & (2) because the district court failed to refer to extrinsic evidence in construing the terms of the will.

The Estate contends that the two-trust structure of the will (i.e., Family Trust and Marital Trust) when juxtaposed with the discretionary income standard used in the marital trust, creates an ambiguity in the will itself requiring reference to extrinsic evidence of the decedent's intent to qualify the marital trust for the marital deduction.

As the district court correctly noted, the property interests bequeathed in the will are to be interpreted pursuant to Virginia law. * * * While the intention of the testator is the "polar star" of construction, intention must be found in the testator's expressed words. The meaning of the words as used by the testator are the equivalent of his legal intention—the intention which the law recognizes as dispositive. A court may not speculate upon what the testator may have intended to do, but rather must give strict effect to the testator's words. Consequently, the true inquiry is not what the testator meant to express, but what the words he has used do actually express. In short, in the construction of a will in Virginia, the intent of the testator rests in the words he uses. The courts may only give the words actually used the meanings and definitions which the testator possibly could have intended. * * *

Here, the Estate's contention that "[t]he decedent's use of a two-trust structure is tantamount to a flat declaration by the decedent that he intended . . . [the Marital Trust to be construed so as to qualify for the marital deduction]" is conjectural. The Estate has not pointed to any language in the will from which it can be concluded that the testator's paramount intention was to qualify the marital trust for a marital deduction, particularly where it requires the court to disregard the decedent's expressed intention that the trustees should use their sole discretion to determine the amount of marital trust income necessary for his wife's support. Because words are not to be rejected unless they manifestly conflict with the plain intention of the testator, * * * there is nothing in the law that would permit reformation of the will to overcome the specific language used in Article VI, paragraph 2, bequeathing marital trust income to decedent's wife in amounts that "the trustees in their sole discretion, deem necessary."

Indeed, the sole discretion vested in decedent's trustees with respect to the marital trust income is likewise vested in the trustees with respect to the Family Trust income, thereby confirming that the decedent intended his words expressed in both Articles V and VI, paragraphs 2. * * *

Here, the decedent did not bequeath the appropriate property interest in the marital trust to his wife to qualify for the marital deduction. Deductions are a matter of legislative grace, and the taxpayer seeking the benefit of a deduction must show that every condition which Congress has seen fit to impose has been fully satisfied. The taxpayer may not haggle with Congress; he either fits squarely within the statute in every particular or the deduction is unavailable. We know of no rule by which the foregoing doctrine is any less applicable to the estate tax than to the income tax. We decline to rewrite Article VI, paragraph 2, to give effect to what the estate contends, based on the will's structure to have been the decedent's intent, when to do so would require ignoring decedent's express intention, stated in two separate places in the will, of granting his trustees sole discretion in determining the amount of income necessary for his wife's support. [Citations omitted.] * * *

NOTES

1. The *Wisely* trust agreement called for distribution to Mrs. Wisely of so much or all of the trust income as the trustees, "in their sole discretion" deemed "necessary to provide for her care and support in the style and manner of living to which she has been accustomed." Suppose that, as a practical matter, there could be no disagreement that the trust income was required to maintain Mrs. Wisely in the specified manner. Should the trust, in these circumstances, thus qualify for the marital deduction? Could the distinction be expressed in terms not of her "need" but of her "right" to the income? Which is it?

2. Creating a trust is a time honored and legislatively permitted technique whereby a spousal gift can qualify for the marital deduction while allowing the donor spouse to establish a measure of control over the trust property by restricting the spouse's enjoyment of the trust property. Most practitioners—but not all—know that the surviving spouse must be entitled to all the income from the trust during life. Despite that knowledge, all too many stumble in fleshing out the trust terms, sometimes including restrictions that inadvertently compromise the spouse's income right. The following IRS memorandum opinion illustrates how an option to purchase property at less than fair market value may disqualify a trust for the marital deduction.

TECHNICAL ADVICE MEMORANDUM 9147065

July 12, 1991.

ISSUE

If a trust for the benefit of the surviving spouse is required to be funded, in part, with closely-held stock subject to specified restrictions and purchase options described below, does that portion of the trust qualify for the marital deduction under section 2056(b)(5)?

FACTS

At the time of his death, the decedent owned 561 shares of stock in the Company, a closely held corporation. The shares owned by the decedent constituted approximately 95 percent of the outstanding shares. The remaining 5 percent were owned by the decedent's family. * * *

The decedent was survived by his spouse and four sons. The decedent's will provides for a preresiduary bequest in trust for the benefit of the surviving spouse. The trust is to be funded with a pecuniary amount equal to the maximum allowable federal estate tax marital deduction, with specified adjustments that would result in no federal estate tax.

During her lifetime, the surviving spouse will be paid all income from the trust at least quarterly and principal, in the trustee's discretion, for her health, maintenance, and best interests. The surviving spouse has the power to appoint by will, to any person including her estate, the trust assets remaining at her death. Any unappointed assets will pass to a residuary trust for the benefit of the decedent's lineal descendants. Unless the surviving spouse directs otherwise in her will, before distribution is made to the residuary trust, trust principal will be used to pay any death taxes attributable to the inclusion of the surviving spouse's trust in her gross estate.

The will states that "[u]nproductive property shall not be held as an asset of the Trust for more than a reasonable time during the lifetime of [the surviving spouse] without her written consent."

The will also specifically provides that the spouse's trust is to be funded with the Company stock only to the extent that other assets are unavailable. One of the decedent's sons is named in the will as trustee of the spouse's trust and the residuary trust. Another son is expressly authorized to manage the corporation, vote the Company stock in the trusts, and determine the price or any other conditions concerning any sale of these shares. The trustee is expressly prohibited from exercising these responsibilities during the life of the authorized son. In addition, the will states, "The Trustee shall sell the securities only as and when [the authorized son] shall direct and shall follow his direction as to price and other terms and conditions of sale."

Thus, although the will contains a general provision to the effect that nonproductive property cannot be held in the spouse's trust for more than a reasonable time, the will specifically precludes the trustee from disposing of the (nonproductive) Company stock at any time unless directed by the son authorized to dispose of the Company stock. Under ordinary rules of construction, subsequent and specific directions prevail over preceding and general directions in a will.

Immediately following the provision prohibiting the trustee from selling the Company stock, the will provides, "[n]otwithstanding anything in the above to the contrary * * * " each of the decedent's sons is granted an option to purchase from the executor or the trustee a specified percentage (totaling 100 percent) of the total Company shares at a specified price of $1,000 per share. Each son must exercise his option within 24 months after the decedent's death. The option price can be paid with a note due not more than 60 months after issuance and bearing interest of 9 percent per year.

On the federal estate tax return, the estate included the 561 shares in the gross estate at a value of approximately $11,000 per share. The return indicates that the spouse's trust was funded, but the residuary trust was not. The return * * * also indicates that, before it was filed, and well before the 24-month period for exercising the options expired, options were exercised on 29.746 of the shares. A marital deduction was claimed for the value of the spouse's trust. The Schedule M indicates that the trust was funded with the proceeds paid to the estate when the options were exercised, the remaining 531.254 shares, and some incidental miscellaneous assets. In computing the marital deduction claimed for the spouse's trust, the estate reported the 531.254 shares at the same $11,000 per share value reported in the gross estate, for a total of more than 5.8 million. This value constituted the major part of the marital deduction claimed. For purposes of the marital deduction, the miscellaneous assets in the spouse's trust were reported at a value of about $1 million.

* * *

Section 20.2056(b)–5(f)(1) of the regulations provides, in part, that if an interest is transferred in trust, the surviving spouse is regarded as "entitled for life to all the income" from the property only if the spouse has that degree of beneficial enjoyment of the property which is accorded to a person who is unqualifiedly designated as a life beneficiary. The requisite degree of enjoyment is given only if it was the decedent's intention, as manifested by the instrument and surrounding circumstances, that the property should produce for the surviving spouse, during life, such an income, or that the spouse should have such use of the property as is consistent with the value of the corpus and with its preservation.

Section 20.2056(b)–5(f)(4) provides, in part, that a trustee's power to retain trust assets which consist substantially of unproductive property will not disqualify the spouse's lifetime income interest if the applicable rules for the trust administration require, or permit the spouse to require, that the trustee either make the property productive or convert it into productive property within a reasonable time.

Section 20.2056(b)–5(f)(5) provides, in part, that the spouse's lifetime income interest will be disqualified if the primary purpose of the trust is to safeguard the property without providing the spouse with the required beneficial enjoyment. Such trusts include those which expressly provide for the accumulation of income and those which indirectly accomplish a similar purpose. The example is given in which the corpus of a trust consists substantially of property unlikely to be income producing during the spouse's life and the spouse cannot compel the trustee to convert or otherwise deal with the property as described in section 20.2056(b)–5(f)(4). Such a trust would not meet the requisite standards for deductibility.

Qualification of an interest for the marital deduction is determined at the time of the decedent's death, based on the facts at that time. Jackson v. United States, 376 U.S. 503 (1964), 1964–2 C.B. 522. See also Rev. Rul. 79–14, 1979–1 C.B. 309.

In the present case, no marital deduction can be allowed with respect to the portion of the spouse's trust that is required to be funded with the Company stock.

First, by giving his sons an option to purchase the Company stock at $1,000 a share, the decedent effectively divided the value of the stock between his sons and the spouse's trust. At the decedent's death, the fair market value of the stock was $11,000 per share. This was nearly 11 times the option price. The fair market value during the 24 months after the decedent's death could be expected to change due to a variety of factors. There was almost no possibility as of the date of decedent's death that the fair market value of the stock would equal the option price when the option was exercised. (Indeed, there must be presumed to be a greater likelihood of exercise where the fair market value exceeds the option price.) Thus, viewed as of the decedent's death, each son held a right, exercisable during the spouse's life, to make a bargain purchase of the Company stock. The effect of the bargain purchase would be to substantially deplete the value of the trust corpus.

Each son's option right is, effectively, a right to appoint to himself the excess of the fair market value of a share on the option exercise date over the option price. The sons' rights to purchase Company stock confers upon them a power to withdraw property with a substantial value from the spouse's trust for less than adequate and full consideration. This right is a "power in any other person to appoint any part of the interest, or such specific portion, to any person other than the surviving spouse" as that phrase is used in section 2056(b)(5). Because of this power, the amount of the marital deduction for the property passing to the spouse's trust must be reduced by the value of the stock passing to the trust.

In this regard, at the decedent's death, it was not certain that the spouse's trust would receive even $1,000 upon the exercise of an option. The will entitled a son to pay the option price with a note bearing annual interest of nine percent. At decedent's death, the date that an option might be exercised certainly could not be predicted nor could the applicable interest rates for most of the 24-month period. If the rate of interest prescribed under section 7872 on the date of exercise is below nine percent, the trust would actually receive value greater than the $1,000 face amount of the nine percent note. (But a son would presumably not borrow from the trust at a rate that was higher than otherwise available from other sources.) Conversely, if the section 7872 rate exceeds nine percent, the trust would receive less than the equivalent of $1,000 on the nine percent note. In view of this financing arrangement prescribed by the will, at the decedent's death no minimum value that the trust would receive upon a son's exercise of his option can be determined. Therefore, for purposes of the marital deduction, we cannot attach even a $1,000 per share minimum value to the stock.

* * *

Under the will, unproductive property generally cannot be held for more than a reasonable time during the spouse's life without her written consent. However, the will expressly prohibits the trustee from selling the Company stock, unless so directed by the son authorized to sell it (except if a son exercises his option). Thus, effectively, neither the spouse nor the trustee have any legal right to establish an adequate income flow for the spouse from the Company stock. Consequently, under section 20.2056(b)–5(f)(4) of the regulations, the spouse is not entitled to "all the income for life" from the stock.

The spouse has a qualifying power of appointment over and income interest in a specific portion of the spouse's trust, the portion funded with miscellaneous assets of about $1 million in value, and this portion qualifies for a marital deduction under section 2056(b)(5). However, we cannot conclude that she has a qualifying income interest in the trust viewed as a whole, because of the relatively large value of the nonproductive portion of the trust funded with the Company stock. * * *

That portion of the spouse's trust that is funded with the Company stock (and the proceeds of Company stock sold pursuant to the exercise of the option) does not qualify for the marital deduction under section 2056(b)(5). Viewed as of the date of the decedent's death, a person other than the spouse has power to appoint trust corpus, the spouse has no right to income from or a power of appointment over that portion of the trust represented by the value of the Company stock. Further, the spouse's income interest attributable to the value of the Company stock fails to satisfy the requisite standard under section 2056(b)(5). Therefore, the marital deduction is allowable only with respect to the specific portion of the spouse's trust that is represented by the trust assets other than the Company stock.

b.   The "Specific Portion" Possibility

A fractional or percentile interest in a property may qualify for the marital deduction. I.R.C. § 2056(b)(10). That is, a partial interest in a property is treated as a "specific portion" within the meaning of section 2056(b)(5) for purposes of allowing the marital deduction for that partial interest so long as the surviving spouse's partial interest in the property constitutes a fractional or percentage share of the entire property interest. That means that the surviving spouse's partial interest must share, proportionally, in "the increase or decrease in the value of the entire property." Treas. Reg. § 20.2056(b)–5(c)(2).

PROBLEM

Zeke's will provided that his widow, Anna, was to receive $300 per month for life from the trust that he provided for her in his will. If the trust income was insufficient, corpus could be invaded to make the trust payments. Consider whether Anna has a qualifying income interest in a specific portion of the property for purposes of section 2056(b)(5). See Treas. Reg. § 20.2056(b)–5(c)(2) through (5). Cf. Northeastern Pa. Nat'l Bank & Trust Co. v. United States, 387 U.S. 213 (1967).

c.   The "Payable Annually" Requirement

The income must be payable at least annually. While the statute specifically requires the income to be payable to the spouse "annually or at more frequent intervals," Regulation § 20.2056(b)–5(e) suggests that silence in the will or trust as to the time for payment is not a failure to meet the statute unless local law permits periodic payments to be delayed more than a year.

d.   The "Power of Appointment" Requirement

A broad power of appointment must be given to the surviving spouse. The surviving spouse must have a power of appointment over the property (or a specific portion thereof) pursuant to which the property can be appointed to the surviving spouse or to the surviving spouse's estate. However, the necessary power is not defined in terms of a general power of appointment taxable under section 2041; rather, section 2056(b)(5) is explicit as to the requirements that will lead to the allowance of the marital deduction. As a result, there are instances where a trust may not qualify for the marital deduction, even though the gross estate of the surviving spouse may include the trust property because the surviving spouse has a general power of appointment over the trust property as described in section 2041. See, e.g., Treas. Reg. § 20.2056(b)–5(g); Estate of Pipe v. Commissioner, 241 F.2d 210 (2d Cir.), cert. denied, 355 U.S. 814 (1957). In *Pipe*, the marital deduction was denied despite the spouse's power during life to use, enjoy, sell or dispose of the trust property "for such purposes or in such manner, as she in her uncontrolled discretion may choose, it being [decedent's] * * * desire to place no restraint on her in any respect concerning the absolute right of full disposition and use * * * [of the trust property] except that she shall have no power over the disposition of such part thereof as remains unexpended at the time of her death." See id. at 211.

e. The "All Events" Requirement

The power of appointment held by the surviving spouse must be exercisable freely by the spouse, and by the spouse alone, and in all events if the marital deduction is to be allowed pursuant to the life estate/power of appointment exception to the nondeductible terminable interest rule. This requirement is strictly applied. For example, in Starrett v. Commissioner, 223 F.2d 163 (1st Cir. 1955), the marital deduction was denied the decedent's estate for property placed in trust by the decedent despite the fact that trust property would be includible in the gross estate of the surviving spouse at the spouse's subsequent death. While the spouse had the unlimited right to withdraw all trust property, her right of withdrawal terminated in the event of her incapacity. As a result, the court concluded that the surviving spouse's right of withdrawal was not exercisable "in all events," as required for the marital deduction. The decedent's estate had argued that the will's prohibition on withdrawals by the spouse (or a guardian for the spouse) during a period of incompetency was no different than the similar limitation imposed by applicable state law. The court distinguished the applicable state law on the ground that state law prohibited withdrawals by the spouse only during the period of incompetency, while the will caused the withdrawal right to terminate if the spouse became incompetent.

Might the *Starrett* court have reached a different result if only the decedent made clearly known his intention to qualify his gift for the marital deduction? Not likely. On similar facts, the marital deduction was disallowed in Estate of Walsh v. Commissioner, 110 T.C. 393 (1998), where the decedent stated "his intention" that the trust "qualify for the marital deduction" and that the trust "provisions shall be so construed and questions pertaining" to the trust "shall be resolved accordingly." The court said the possibility that the "surviving spouse could lose power over the corpus upon the happening of a contingent event; namely incompetency" was the "critical fact," this despite the fact that the spouse had, pursuant to authority given her in the trust, withdrawn the trust corpus shortly after the testator's death—and before any period of incompetency.

Disputes are commonplace when wills are professionally prepared, let alone when a layperson drafts them. Stanley Carpenter did his own trust and created a question as to whether his spouse's broad powers of disposition over the trust property constituted a general power of appointment as contemplated by section 2056(b)(5), warranting the allowance of the marital deduction. Estate of Carpenter v. Commissioner, 52 F.3d 1266 (4th Cir. 1995). Pointing to the decedent's own words, the court denied the marital deduction, concluding that the spouse's powers were not exercisable "alone and in all events." The trust provided:

> My wife is to select the Trust Dept. She is also to take an equal part as an executor with the Trust in all decisions regarding this trust [sic].

> This Trust is to work with my wife + to give her all money necessary to give her a good life and happiness.

> I chose to use a Trust so that no one can dominate or take advantage of her for her entire life.

> I love my wife dearly and she has given me the happiest years of my life and I am concerned that people may try to influence her if she should be depressed or ill.

> The Trust working with my wife may sell any property at anytime if necessary for cash for the Trust in case my wife wants cash for her personal health, needs, trips or anything relating to my wife.

Carpenter, 52 F.3d at 1268.

f.   Forbidden Powers

Qualification for the life estate/power of appointment exception to the nondeductible terminable interest rule depends on the absence of so-called forbidden powers. Forbidden powers are those powers that, if held by a person other than the spouse, could be exercised so as to effectively deny the surviving spouse all the income from the property for which the marital deduction is claimed or in some way limit the exercise of the general power of appointment the surviving spouse must receive. Treas. Reg. § 20.2056(b)–5(f)(8). A prime example is a spendthrift clause. The IRS claims that the marital deduction cannot be allowed where the governing instrument "requires the trustee to accumulate all income of the trust during the period of any attachment, assignment, etc., to or by any creditor rather than pay the income to the surviving spouse." Priv. Ltr. Rul. 8248008. Under these circumstances, the IRS believes, "the surviving spouse is not entitled for life to all the income," as is required for allowance of the marital deduction under the life estate/power of appointment exception.

By way of contrast, purely administrative powers held by a trustee will not disqualify a trust for the marital deduction under the life estate/power of appointment exception. Examples of permitted powers include the ability to apportion items of income and expense between successive beneficial interests where applicable state law requires the trustee's determination to be made fairly so as to balance the interests of the successive beneficiaries; the ability to treat capital gain dividends received from mutual funds as principal; the right to maintain reasonable reserves for depreciation; and the right to charge fiduciary and professional fees to either income or principal, to make distributions in cash or in kind at current values and to make reasonable determinations as to current values. Rev. Rul. 69–56, 1969–1 C.B. 224.

A fairly comprehensive discussion of the permitted discretions appears in Treas. Reg. § 20.2056(b)–5(f)(8).

NOTE

Another exception to the nondeductible terminable interest rule permits the use of certain life insurance settlement options which would otherwise be disallowed as terminable interests. I.R.C. § 2056(b)(6). This exception is hedged with five requirements which are similar in purpose and in structure to the requirements discussed in connection with the life estate/power of appointment exception.

3. QUALIFIED TERMINABLE INTEREST PROPERTY

The most commonly used exception currently is the exception under section 2056(b)(7) for Qualified Terminable Interest Property (sometimes called QTIP). The QTIP exception permits a marital deduction for property that passes from the decedent so long as:

1. All the income generated by the property is payable at least annually to the surviving spouse for life;

2. Distribution of part or all of the property to anyone other than the surviving spouse is barred during the lifetime of the surviving spouse; and

3. The decedent's executor claims the marital deduction on the decedent's estate tax return (i.e., an election is required).

a. The "Income" Requirement

Regulation § 20.2056(b)–7(d)(2) states that all the principles expressed in Regulation § 20.2056(b)–5(f) (as to the life estate/power of appointment exception to the nondeductible terminable interest rule) apply to the QTIP income entitlement requirement.

ESTATE OF NICHOLSON V. COMMISSIONER
United States Tax Court, 1990.
94 T.C. 666.

GERBER, JUDGE:

* * *

The decedent died testate in 1983. His will provided that his share of community property was to be distributed to an existing inter vivos trust. The trustees were directed to pay the income of the trust to the decedent's surviving spouse "as * * * [she] may from time to time require to maintain * * * [her] usual and customary standard of living." Additionally, "in this regard the Trustees may also invade the corpus of the Trust for these purposes." The decedent further granted the trustees "full and complete independent authority to invest, sell, assign, transfer, trade, mortgage, lease or otherwise deal with the property of this Trust as they may deem to be in the best interests of Dorothy Nell Nicholson."

In 1984, the trustees and beneficiary of the trust sought and obtained an "Order of Modification" from a Texas State court. Pursuant to that order, the trust instrument was changed to provide that, at the decedent's death, the trustees were to "pay the net income of the Trust estate to * * * [decedent's wife] in quarterly or more frequent installments."

We must decide whether, at the time of the decedent's death, his wife's interest in the trust qualified for an estate tax marital deduction as * * * "qualified terminable interest property," or "QTIP" interests. QTIP interests are those in which a decedent passes to the surviving spouse a "qualifying income interest for life." Generally, when the surviving spouse has a "qualifying income interest for life" she is entitled to "all the income from the property, payable annually or at more frequent intervals," and, while she is alive, no one else can appoint any part of the property to anyone but her. Sec. 2056(b)(7)(B).

The legislative history underlying the QTIP provisions indicates that a QTIP interest must meet the requirements of section 20.2056(b)–5(f). See H. Rept. 97–201 (1981), 1981–2 C.B. 352, 378. Under that regulation, a surviving spouse is entitled to "all the income from the property" if she has the equivalent "beneficial enjoyment" of the trust estate as one who is "unqualifiedly designated as the life beneficiary." Generally, absent indications to the contrary, the "designation of the spouse as sole income beneficiary for life * * * will be sufficient." Sec. 20.2056(b)–5(f)(1)* * *.

A determination of the nature of the interest which passes to the surviving spouse is made under the law of the jurisdiction under which the interest passes. * * * Here, we look to the law of Texas. Under that law, the issue of whether a beneficiary is entitled to a particular interest in the trust estate depends upon the intention of the settlor. The settlor's intention as it existed at the time the trust was created is determinative. * * *

While we will look to local law in order to determine the nature of the interests provided under a trust document, we are not bound to give effect to a local court order which modifies that document after respondent has acquired rights to tax revenues under its terms.* * * "[N]ot even judicial reformation can operate to change the federal tax consequences of a completed transaction." Van Den Wymelenberg v. United States 397 F.2d 443, 445 (7th Cir.1968), cert. denied 393 U.S. 953 (1968). The reformation of an instrument has retroactive effect as between the parties to the instrument, but not as to third parties who previously acquired rights under the instrument. * * * As the Court of Appeals explained in Van Den Wymelenberg v. United States, supra at 445—

> As to the parties to the reformed instrument the reformation relates back to the date of the original instrument, but it does not affect the rights acquired by non-parties, including the Government. Were the law otherwise there would exist considerable opportunity for "collusive" state court actions having the sole purpose of reducing federal tax liabilities. Furthermore, federal tax liabilities would remain unsettled for years after their assessment if state courts and private persons were empowered to retroactively affect the tax consequences of completed transactions and completed tax years.

Under the terms of the trust at issue, the decedent's wife is not "entitled to all the income from the property, payable annually or at more frequent intervals" as is required by section 2056(b)(7). Instead, the unambiguous language of the trust only allows her "so much of the net income * * * as * * * [she] may from time to time require to maintain * * * [her] usual and customary standard of living." * * *

In the context of the trust instrument at issue, the provision for "so much of the net income * * * as * * * [she] may from time to time require" gives Mrs. Nicholson only such income as she may reasonably *need*, but not necessarily all the income that she may *demand*. The trust instrument reveals clearly the decedent's intention that his children, as trustees, were to determine, and provide, the amounts Mrs. Nicholson required to maintain her "usual and customary" standard of living. As long as they carried out their duties, Mrs. Nicholson had neither the obligation, nor the right, to demand "all the income," or any particular amount of income, from the trust.

* * *

We are aware that respondent's regulations provide a broad scope for interpreting a trust instrument. Those provisions, however, do not permit us to rewrite the trust instrument. The instrument here, as executed by the decedent, and as in existence at the time of his death, fails to establish that Mrs. Nicholson is "unqualifiedly designated as the life beneficiary." Nor does it otherwise designate her as "sole income beneficiary for life." Sec. 20.2056(b)–5(f) * * *. It instead limits Mrs. Nicholson's trust income to amounts she would "require." Any excess would go to the remaindermen. Plainly, then, under the trust instrument at issue, Mrs. Nicholson is not "entitled to all the income" from the property within the meaning of section 2056(b)(7)(B)(ii), and her interest in the trust fails to qualify for the marital deduction.

Petitioner, however, urges that the language of the trust document is ambiguous. It is contended that we must therefore look to the circumstances surrounding the establishment of the trust to determine the decedent's intent. * * *

Even if petitioner were correct, and we were permitted to look at the circumstances surrounding the execution of the trust, those circumstances do not compel a finding that the decedent "entitled" his wife to all the income from the trust. The extrinsic evidence shows instead that the decedent wished only to provide support to his wife in the manner to which she was accustomed. He especially wished to spare her the concerns of providing for herself, because she was not familiar with business operations. A bequest of all the potential trust income would have been inconsistent with this intention.

Additional extrinsic evidence shows that the decedent's grant of "so much of the net income * * * as [she] may from time to time require" was, in effect, a bequest of some $50,000 to $60,000 annually. That bequest, however, does not constitute an automatic entitlement to all the trust income. * * *

Moreover, Mrs. Nicholson was entitled to only so much of the trust's income as she may "from time to time" require to maintain her usual and customary standard of living. The implication of this language is that Mrs. Nicholson's requirements for income from the trust were to be evaluated in light of income from other sources that she might have—such as, perhaps, her share of the community property assets. The availability of income from such other sources would lower the amount of trust income that she might otherwise need, again indicating that she was not "entitled to all the income" from the trust.

The extrinsic evidence further shows that the trustees, consistent with the settlor's intent, might well have managed the trust in a way that would generate more income than the sole beneficiary needed to maintain her standard of living. Reinvestment in income-producing property was a very real possibility. * * *

Accordingly, even a consideration of the extrinsic evidence fails to show that the decedent intended that his wife be "entitled to all the income" from the trust.

The opinion of the Court of Appeals in Estate of Mittleman v. Commissioner, 522 F.2d at 133 n.1, upon which petitioner relies, is not inconsistent with our opinion here. In that case, a decedent left his residuary estate to a trust for the following purposes:

a.   To provide for the proper support, maintenance, welfare and comfort of my beloved wife, HENRIETTA MITTLEMAN, for her entire lifetime.

b.   To invade the corpus of the trust estate from time to time in the sole and exclusive discretion of the Trustees and to use all or any portion of the said corpus for the proper support, maintenance and welfare of my wife, HENRIETTA MITTLEMAN.

Respondent argued that the above language failed to provide that "all of the income" of the trust be payable "annually or at more frequent intervals" to the surviving spouse, for purposes of section 2056(b)(5). Respondent initially prevailed in a Memorandum Opinion, Estate of Mittleman v. Commissioner, T.C. Memo. 1973–112.

In reversing, the Court of Appeals noted that the Mittleman will made no mention of income from the trust. To the court, the will placed no restriction—either "expressly" or "impliedly"—on the amount of income to be spent on behalf of the beneficiary. The only limitation upon trust expenditures were those restricting expenditures from the corpus to those expenditures made in the "sole and exclusive discretion of the [t]rustees." From this, the Court of Appeals concluded that the "compelling inference" was that the decedent intended to make an unqualified disposition of the income to the wife. The court rejected the notion that the decedent's specific provisions for "the proper support, maintenance, welfare and comfort" of his wife established any limit upon the amount of income she would receive. To the Court of Appeals, that language was "a mere declaration of the purpose of the trust." Estate of Mittleman v. Commissioner, 522 F.2d at 138. The court further found the language as to the disposition of income "ambiguous," thus justifying an examination of "surrounding circumstances." The court determined that these surrounding circumstances supported its conclusion that the wife was "entitled to all of the income." It pointed out that the corpus of the trust was "not large" and that the anticipated income, without invasions of the trust, would produce yields "far short of the family income before Mr. Mittleman died." Estate of Mittleman v. Commissioner, 522 F.2d at 139. The court also took into account the decedent's explicit wish that his estate be able to claim the marital deduction.

This case is factually distinguishable. The trust at issue here, unlike the trust in *Mittleman*, contains explicit language limiting the amount of income that would be paid to the surviving wife. Here, the trustees are directed to pay only "so much of the net income" of the trust to the decedent's surviving spouse "as * * * [she] may from time to time require to maintain * * * [her] usual and customary standard of living." That language is not ambiguous, and no examination of "surrounding circumstances" is indicated. Were the situation otherwise, however, this case is still not *Mittleman*. The "surrounding circumstances" here show that the estate was capable of yielding income in excess of that needed to maintain the beneficiary in her accustomed standard of living. Accordingly, she was not necessarily entitled to "all the income." Moreover, here the decedent specifically did not draft his trust with an intention to maximize the marital deduction. There is, accordingly, no reason for us to contort the language he used in order to achieve that result.

Finally, we do not believe that the modification to the trust instrument made in 1984, after the decedent's death, affects the result we have reached. We have not been provided with the evidence presented to the Texas court; we have only the decree allowing the modification. The new language in that modification provides specifically that the trustees "shall pay the net income of the Trust estate to Dorothy Nell Nicholson in quarterly or more frequent installments." The modified trust instrument appears to meet the requirements for the marital deduction set forth in section 2056(b)(7). As indicated above, however, we have found that respondent is entitled to estate taxes on the basis of the trust provisions that existed at the time of the decedent's death. The attempt to claim an estate tax deduction by means of a post-mortem modification to the trust instrument therefore fails. We will not give effect to a local court order or decree that alters or modifies a trust instrument after respondent has acquired rights to tax revenues under its provisions. * * *

Petitioner, in fact, does not now claim that the language of the 1984 modification is controlling. It is instead urged that the 1984 modification is merely a "clarification" of the decedent's original intention that all the trust income be distributed to his wife at least annually. We do not agree that the 1984 modification serves only to clarify the original instrument. * * * The 1984 modification is thus more than a mere clarification; it is instead a substantial change in the trust instrument made after respondent had secured rights under the original instrument. As such, we will not give it effect.

* * *

We are not unsympathetic to the contention that the decedent herein would have wished to establish a QTIP trust, but the fact is that he did not do so. There may well have been an opportunity for him to do so; the QTIP provisions were effective for estates of decedents dying after December 31, 1981, and decedent died in 1983. The evidence, however, does not disclose whether he was informed of the possibility of establishing a QTIP trust. Moreover, the decedent wished to spare his widow concerns about providing for her own support. We cannot dismiss the possibility that he might have preferred to have the trustees determine the amount of trust proceeds she required, rather than to force all income to be paid to her, as his adoption of a QTIP trust would mandate.

It follows that the decedent's desire that the trust "not create a tax problem" does not absolve his failure to take advantage of a possible QTIP marital deduction that Congress made available only in 1981, several years after he established the trust at issue. For estate taxes, as for income taxes, "Deductions are a matter of legislative grace, and a taxpayer seeking the benefit of a deduction must show that every condition which Congress has seen fit to impose has been fully satisfied." * * *

NOTES

1. In Ellingson v. Commissioner, 964 F.2d 959 (9th Cir. 1992), the marital deduction was allowed, based on a QTIP election, in a case where the trustee was expressly allowed to accumulate the trust income if; (1) the trust income exceeded the amount which the trustee deemed to be necessary for the "needs, best interests and welfare" of the surviving spouse, and (2) the trustee deemed such an accumulation "advisable." The court concluded:

> The Commissioner argues that it would make bad law to read a trust agreement as creating an interest which qualifies for a QTIP deduction solely because the settlor expressly declared in the trust that he intended that effect. We agree. However, this case does not implicate the Commissioner's concern. Certainly, the Trust Agreement could have been more clearly drafted. Nevertheless, the choice for this court is between two plausible readings of the agreement, only one of which effectuates the settlors' clearly manifested intent. If the Accumulation Proviso could plausibly be read only as granting the trustee unlimited discretion, the QTIP deduction would be lost. That is not the case here, however.

Id. at 965.

The governing instrument in *Ellingson* was laced with references to the decedent's intention that the spousal gift qualify for the marital deduction. Such references were not present in Estate of Davis v. Commissioner, 394 F.3d 1294 (9th Cir. 2005), where the marital deduction was denied. A significant feature in *Davis* was a California's statute aimed at curing drafting deficiencies. That statute, California Probate Code § 21552, at the time provided as follows:

If an instrument contains a marital deduction gift:

(a) The provisions of the instrument, including any power, duty, or discretionary authority given to a fiduciary, shall be construed to comply with the marital deduction provisions of the Internal Revenue Code.

(b) The fiduciary shall not take any action or have any power that impairs the deduction as applied to the marital deduction gift.

(c) The marital deduction gift may be satisfied only with property that qualifies for the marital deduction.

That statute might well have saved the marital deduction in *Davis*, but the decedent did not expressly state that his gift to his spouse was to qualify for the marital deduction. In fact, the marital deduction was not mentioned. While reference to the marital deduction is not a condition of eligibility, such reference is helpful in cases where the language of the marital gift fails to satisfy the statutory requirements for qualification for the marital deduction. In *Davis*, the disqualifying language was as follows:

[T]he trustee shall pay to or apply for the benefit of the surviving spouse, in quarter annual or more frequent installments, all of the net income from the trust estate as the trustee, in the trustee's reasonable discretion, shall determine to be proper for the health, education, or support, maintenance, comfort and welfare of grantor's surviving spouse in accordance with the surviving spouse's accustomed manner of living.

Id. at 1297. *Davis* is consistent with Estate of Walsh v. Commissioner, 110 T.C. 393 (1998), discussed above where the testator's expressed intent— to qualify for the marital deduction—was said to be insufficient to overcome the words found in the testator's will that limited the surviving spouse's control over the marital deduction property in the event of incompetency, a possibility that ran afoul of the "all events" requirement for allowance of the marital deduction under section 2056(b)(5), the life estate/power of appointment safe harbor.

2.   Estate of Howard v. Commissioner, 910 F.2d 633 (9th Cir. 1990), the so-called stub income case, is a reminder of the careful attention that must be given to statutory requirements when the marital deduction is the object. It also emphasizes the differences between the QTIP exception to the nondeductible terminable interest rule and the life estate/power of appointment exception to that rule. *Howard* presented an unusual fact situation that turned on a particular provision in the trust established in the will of the decedent. The IRS had concluded that the trust qualified

for the marital deduction, but the decedent's estate argued that the trust did not qualify! The provision in question specified that all trust income should be distributed to the surviving spouse at quarterly intervals for life but that any trust income accrued between the date of the death of the surviving spouse and the immediately preceding quarterly payment date was to be distributed not to the spouse's estate but to the remaindermen, i.e., to those who were to enjoy the trust property after the death of the surviving spouse. The dispute related to this "stub income" and presented the question of whether the trust qualified as a QTIP, since the surviving spouse was not entitled to all trust income for life. The court held that the trust was eligible for QTIP treatment, finding congressional intent by looking to legislative history (which was silent as to stub income) and by contrasting the provisions in section 2056(b)(7) relating to QTIPs with those in section 2056(b)(5) applicable to cases where the marital deduction is claimed on the ground that the surviving spouse has a life estate and a general power of appointment over the property for which the marital deduction is claimed. The life estate/power of appointment provision of section 2056(b)(5) is construed as requiring the stub income to be paid to the surviving spouse's estate. Treas. Reg. § 20.2056(b)–5(f)(8). By way of contrast, the court pointed to then-proposed Regulation § 20.2056(b)–7(c)(ii) relating to QTIPs, which specifically concluded that a trust was eligible for the marital deduction as a QTIP even though the surviving spouse was not entitled to the stub income. See Reg. §§ 20.2056(b)–5(f)(8) (life estate/power of appointment) and 20.2056(b)–7(d)(4) (QTIP). It should be noted that Regulation § 20.2044–1(d)(2) provides that the stub income is included in the gross estate of the surviving spouse for estate tax purposes even if not distributed to the spouse or to the spouse's estate.

3.   In Estate of Shelfer v. Commissioner, 86 F.3d 1045 (11th Cir. 1996)—a case that gave rise to the expression *"Shelfer* Shuffle"—Louise Shelfer had been entitled to all but the stub income from a trust established by her husband, Elbert, in his will. Louise Shelfer's executor contended that a trust created by the will of Louise's husband, Elbert, was not included in Louise's estate at her death. The executor's claim became the subject of an IRS challenge when the IRS took note that Elbert's estate had been allowed the marital deduction for the trust property at his earlier death and, as a condition of such allowance, section 2044 required the inclusion of the trust property in Louise's estate at her death. (Recall that the basic premise of the marital deduction is that the marital deduction is allowed where the property for which the deduction is claimed will be included in the estate of the surviving spouse at his or her subsequent death unless consumed or disposed of by that spouse during life). Listening in on the meeting between Louise's executor and the IRS agent examining Louise's estate tax return, Louise's executor might have been heard to retort, "Yes, we acknowledge that the marital deduction was allowed Elbert's estate, but the allowance was improper—because Louise was not entitled to the stub income from the trust! That is, Louise was not entitled to all the trust income for life as required by section 2056(b)(7)(B)(ii)(I) and, therefore,

allowance of the marital deduction at the time of Elbert's death was wrong. Sorry. We'd like to be accommodating but it's out of our hands—and if we volunteer the tax (by including the trust property in Louise's estate for tax purposes) 'to make it right, so-to-speak', we'd have liability to the estate's beneficiaries for paying out money we didn't owe." Interestingly, a bank, Quincy State, was executor of both estates. Perhaps it can be said that "strange bedfellows tax doth make" for it appears that the American Bar Association filed an amicus brief in support of the IRS position. The ABA position was that the statute is satisfied if the surviving spouse has all the income which has been distributed—even if the stub income goes elsewhere. Undertaking the tedious task of statutory construction, the 11th Circuit stepped from word to word and from comma to comma and concluded that it was necessary to look beyond the "plain language" of the statute to its history and purpose—but that, too, was found deficient. The court next turned to policy considerations and said:

> [W]e must decide which interpretation of the statute best comports with the two general goals discussed above: expanding the marital deduction to provide for the spouse while granting the decedent more control over the ultimate disposition of the property, and treating a husband and wife as one economic entity for the purposes of estate taxation.
>
> Under the Commissioner's interpretation of the statute, the decedent would gain the tax benefit, retain control of the trust corpus, and provide the spouse with all of the periodic payments for her personal support. The stub income, which accrues after her death and is thus not used for her maintenance, could be appointed to someone else. This result is consistent with the statutory goals of expanding the deduction while providing for the spouse's support. In contrast, the Tax Court's reading of the statute would condition the tax benefit for the entire trust corpus on ceding control over a much smaller amount that is not needed for the spouse's support.
>
> The statute's second goal, treating a married couple as one economic entity, was effected in a comprehensive statutory scheme. In addition to the QTIP provisions of § 2056(b)(7), Congress added § 2044, which requires the estate of the surviving spouse to include all property for which a marital deduction was previously allowed, and § 2056(b)(7)(B)(v), which states that a QTIP "election, once made, shall be irrevocable." Taken together, these sections * * * provide that assets can pass between spouses without being subject to taxation. Upon the death of the surviving spouse, the spouse's estate will be required to pay tax on all of the previously deducted marital assets. The Commissioner's position comports with the statutory scheme because it compels the surviving spouse to abide by the

irrevocable election of a QTIP trust and to pay taxes on property that had previously been subject to a deduction.

Id. at 1049–1050. The court concluded that the "goals" of the marital deduction favor a "broad interpretation of the statute that would allow the QTIP election" to Elbert's estate and the resulting inclusion of the trust property in Louise's estate as required by section 2044. Notably the court commented that "a broad reading of the marital deduction provisions benefits the federal Treasury and furthers Congressional intent to ensure taxation of all previously deducted property." Here, more than $1 million of taxes and deficiencies were at stake. The windfall that would result from a finding for the taxpayer in this case, the court said, would be a "substantial windfall, encouraging other executors of wills to disclaim previously taken deductions."

While the *Shelfer* outcome might be explained as simple justice, the case speaks volumes about the interpretive issues that routinely develop.

b. The Distribution Limitation

QTIP treatment will be denied if distributions from the trust can be made to a person other than the surviving spouse before the death of the surviving spouse. I.R.C. § 2056(b)(7)(B)(ii)(II). While taxpayer compliance with this requirement so as to ensure the marital deduction would seem relatively easy to accomplish, all too frequently it results in the loss of the marital deduction by the innocent, the uninformed, and the well intentioned. In Estate of Bowling v. Commissioner, 93 T.C. 286 (1989), the marital deduction was denied because the will allowed the trustee to invade the trust "for any emergency needs which effect [sic] the support, maintenance and health needs of any beneficiary" of the trust. The surviving spouse was to receive the income for life and, after the death of the wife, the income was to be distributed to the decedent's son, who was institutionalized because of his mental retardation. The court denied the marital deduction after concluding that, during the lifetime of the spouse, the trustee could make distributions for the emergency needs of the institutionalized child. The court rejected the argument that the "emergency needs" authorization was limited to the needs of the current income beneficiary, namely, the surviving spouse during her lifetime. The court pointed to the severely disabled condition of the child as the reason why it was unlikely that the decedent would have intended to prohibit distributions to the son to meet emergency needs. See also Estate of Manscill v. Commissioner, 98 T.C. 413 (1992) (trustee's power to distribute corpus to the child of the surviving spouse invalidated QTIP election).

The IRS, too, specifically says it will not allow the marital deduction for any part of the trust where the surviving spouse, as sole trustee, holds the power to appoint part of the trust property ("up to $5,000 annually" in the IRS's example) to a minor child for "maintenance and support"—even though all trust income is payable to the surviving spouse for life. Treas. Reg. § 20.2056(b)–7(h), Example 4. Contrast, though, Tech. Adv. Mem. 8943005, which follows—and then note that Example 4 of the regulations was published in 1994 and Tech. Adv. Mem. 8943005 was published in 1989. The clear suggestion is that the IRS, by publishing Example 4, has changed its mind about its conclusion in Tech. Adv. Mem. 8943005. Is the effect to exalt form over substance? What is the IRS afraid of here?

TECHNICAL ADVICE MEMORANDUM 8943005
July 9, 1989.

* * *

Is the Decedent's estate entitled to a marital deduction under § 2056(b)(7) * * * even though the Spouse, in her individual capacity, was given a general power to annually appoint up to $5,000 or 5 percent of the trust corpus annually?

FACTS

The Decedent died testate on December 20, 1985. On the Decedent's estate tax return the estate elected to claim a marital deduction for qualified terminable interest property passing to a residuary trust for the benefit of the surviving spouse.

Paragraph FOURTH: (c) of Decedent's will provides in part:

> My wife, during her lifetime, is hereby given a general power to appoint from the principal of this trust to whomsoever she may designate, including herself, during each taxable year of the trust, an amount or amounts not exceeding Five Thousand Dollars ($5,000.00) in the aggregate, and, in addition, . . . an amount, if any, by which Five Percent (5%) of the then fair market value of the net principal of this trust, . . . exceeds the amount or amounts previously appointed by my wife for such year. . . .

* * *

The issue presented in this case is whether the Spouse's power to appoint property "to whomsoever she may designate" violates section 2056(b)(7)(B)(ii)(II) [which allows a marital deduction for Qualified Terminable Interest Property], in that the Spouse has a power to appoint part of the property to a person other than the surviving spouse.

Since enactment of the marital deduction provisions in 1948, the philosophy behind this deduction has evolved from an attempt to equate community property with noncommunity property states towards recognition of the marital unit as a single taxpayer. Thus, the Code currently provides fewer restrictions on the availability of the deduction for interspousal transfers. However, one aspect of the deduction that has remained constant over the years is that no deduction is available unless a transfer tax will be imposed when the property is transferred outside the marital unit. The restriction imposed by the terminable interest rule of section 2056(b)(1) was enacted in recognition of the fact that many terminable interest arrangements will not be subject to tax when the surviving spouse's interest, in fact, terminates. In general, the exceptions to the terminable interest rule (such as section 2056(b)(7)) are available to taxpayers only in those cases where the nature of the interest passing to the spouse is such that any enjoyment by any person other than the surviving spouse will result in estate or gift tax liability with respect to the surviving spouse.

The legislative history underlying section 2056(b)(7) states, in part:

> "... [T]here must be no power in any person (including the spouse) to appoint any part of the property subject to the qualifying income interest to any person other than the spouse during the spouse's life. This rule will ... insure that the value of the property not consumed by the spouse is subject to tax upon the spouse's death (*or earlier disposition*)." [Emphasis added.]

H.R. Rep. No. 201, 97th Cong., 1st Sess., 161 (1981), 1981–2 C.B. 352 at 378.

While it is true that the first parenthetical phrase in the committee report literally precludes a power in the surviving spouse exercisable in favor of any person other than the surviving spouse, we believe such a reading would be unnecessarily restrictive, and, as a practical matter, meaningless. It is axiomatic that a power to appoint exclusively to oneself includes the power to exercise such dominion and control over the property that one may give it to whomsoever one wishes. Thus, it is reasonable to believe that Congress intended that a spouse would be able to give the property away, especially in view of the second (emphasized) parenthetical.

Consistent with this understanding of legislative history, and recognizing that the philosophy of section 2056 requires the imposition of the transfer tax only once during the lives of a husband and wife, we believe the better reading of the legislative history would preclude a spousal power of appointment only where the exercise of the power would not be subject to transfer taxation; i.e., where the power is not a general power of appointment as defined in section 2514.

An interpretation requiring that a spouse must first take physical possession of the property prior to a transfer to a third party would focus too much attention on the form of the transaction. It is sufficient that the exercise of the power by the spouse in favor of a third party would be subject to transfer taxation.

CONCLUSION

Because the power held by the Spouse in this case is a general power of appointment as defined in section 2514, we conclude that the Decedent's estate is entitled to a marital deduction under section 2056(b)(7) * * *.

PROBLEM

Amy's will created a trust for the benefit of her husband, Sam. Amy appointed Sam as the trustee. The trust's income was to be paid to Sam at least quarterly. Distributions from principal not to exceed $5,000 annually could be made by the trustee to Amy's child, Ned, if needed for his education. The IRS claims that no part of Amy's trust qualifies for the marital deduction. Sam, as executor of Amy's estate, disagrees and claims the marital deduction is available "at least for everything in excess of the $5,000." Who should prevail? See Treas. Reg. § 20.2056(b)–7(h), Ex. 4.

c.   QTIP Election

As a further condition of qualifying the QTIP for the marital deduction, the decedent's executor must make an election on the decedent's estate tax return, and such election is irrevocable. I.R.C. § 2056(b)(7)(B)(v). The election is available for separate properties as well as for specific portions of property. The election is also available to the donor spouse in the case of gifts made to the other spouse while both spouses are living. I.R.C. § 2523(f)(4).

With the availability of the QTIP, the decedent's will need not provide any broad taxable power of appointment in the surviving spouse, so long as no one has the power to appoint the property to anyone else during the spouse's life. This feature, in conjunction with the flexibility of election after death as to the amount of property to be deducted, makes the QTIP an extremely useful tool for the estate planner.

The procedure for making the QTIP election has proved challenging, resulting in litigation. So far as the standard is concerned, one court was moved to say that a "clear manifestation of an affirmative intent to elect qualified terminable interest treatment" is required and "the election must be unequivocally communicated on the estate tax return of the spouse who dies first." Estate of Higgins v. Commissioner, 897 F.2d 856 (6th Cir. 1990). Understandably, then, the marital deduction was appropriately denied where a typewritten "X" appeared in the "No" box on the decedent's federal estate tax return in response to the question "Do you elect to claim a marital deduction for an otherwise nondeductible terminable interest under § 2056(b)(7)?" even though Schedule M, the schedule used to claim the marital deduction on the federal estate tax return, showed property passing to the surviving spouse and an actual deduction was claimed for that property in making the computation of the estate's tax liability in the summary portion of the tax return. Notably, the estate did not designate any of the property listed on Schedule M as QTIP property. The court commented that section 2056(b)(7):

> was not enacted to allow the taxpayer to take a "wait and see" approach. As in the case of other elective provisions, the policy of the section is "furthered by requiring a clear manifestation to the government of taxpayer's election"; any other rule "would leave room for the taxpayer to argue later that it had never intended to make an election."

Higgins, 897 F.2d at 860.

d. Section 2044 and Inclusion of QTIP Property in the Donee Spouse's Gross Estate

Under section 2044, a donee spouse's gross estate includes the value of property where the donor spouse claims the marital deduction under section 2056(b)(7) or section 2523(f). For example, assume that a donor spouse transfers stock worth $6,000,000 to a trust with income payable to the donee spouse annually and makes a valid QTIP election under section 2523(f). Under the terms of the trust, the trust terminates at the donee spouse's death, and the corpus is to be distributed to the donor spouse's children. Assume also that the stock is worth $7,500,000 at the donee spouse's death 10 years later. Per section 2044, the value of the stock ($7,500,000) is included in the donee spouse's gross estate.

If the donee spouse gives away any portion of the QTIP property during life, the donee spouse is considered to have made a gift of the entire property. See I.R.C. § 2519. For example, assume that the fair market value of QTIP property is $10,000,000. Assume also that the donee spouse transfers the income interest of QTIP property worth $500,000 to a child. The donee spouse is considered to not only have made a gift of the $500,000 income interest but also of the entire property worth $10,000,000.

Without section 2044 (or section 2519), the property subject to the QTIP election will escape taxation because the donee/surviving spouse has only a life estate without an includible power (i.e., a general power of appointment). Hence, sections 2044 and 2519 satisfy the premise on which the marital deduction is based that the amount allowed by the marital deduction for one spouse will eventually be taxed by the second spouse once it leaves the marital unit.

Since making the QTIP election will mean that the estate of the donee/surviving spouse will be inflated by the amount of the QTIP property at death, section 2207A provides for recovery of the tax from the QTIP property itself unless the will of the donee/surviving spouse otherwise directs. This rule also applies where the donee spouse is taxed under section 2519.

e.   QTIP Compared to Life Estate/Power of Appointment

Section 2056(b)(7), providing for Qualified Terminable Interest Property (QTIP), is probably the most important exception from a planning perspective to the nondeductible terminable interest rule. The QTIP differs from the life estate/power of appointment exception in two principal respects. First, the decedent's executor has the option whether to elect to claim the marital deduction for the QTIP property or allow the QTIP property to be taxed at the death of the deceased spouse (while the marital deduction is mandatory as to property qualifying for the life estate/power of appointment exception). Second, the marital deduction is available as to the QTIP property even though the surviving spouse has no right to control the disposition of the QTIP property at the subsequent death of the surviving spouse (as contrasted with the life estate/power of appointment exception, the core of which is the general power of appointment which the surviving spouse must have as one of the conditions for qualification for the life estate/power of appointment exception). Thus, as a result of the QTIP exception, a prospective decedent can defer estate taxes until the death of his or her spouse, allow the spouse to enjoy the property during life, while all the while controlling the ultimate disposition of the property.

The QTIP provisions allow the executor to elect to deduct any property passing from the decedent provided: (1) the income is payable to the surviving spouse for life; and (2) no one has any power during the life of the surviving spouse to appoint any part of the property to anyone other than the surviving spouse. Moreover, the election has the added flexibility, comparable to what has been observed with regard to the disclaimer provision under section 2518 (see Chapter 6), of being applicable to all or "a specific portion of property," thus permitting an accurate and careful computation of the tax upon the death of the first to die with a better appraisal of the possible tax upon the estate of the survivor.

The Report of the House Ways and Means Committee, which accompanied the Economic Recovery Tax Act of 1981 (Rep. 97–201, p. 159–160) in its legislative passage, describes the QTIP provision, as follows:

> [T]he committee believes that the present limitations on the nature of interests qualifying for the marital deduction should be liberalized to permit certain transfers of terminable interests to qualify for the marital deduction. Under present law, the marital deduction is available only with respect to property passing outright to the spouse or in specified forms which give the spouse control over the transferred property. Because the surviving spouse must be given control over the property, the decedent cannot insure that the spouse will subsequently pass the property to his children. Because the maximum marital deduction is limited under present law to one-half of the decedent's adjusted

gross estate, a decedent may at least control disposition of one-half of his estate and still maximize current tax benefits. However, unless certain interests which do not grant the spouse total control are eligible for the unlimited marital deduction, a decedent would be forced to choose between surrendering control of the entire estate to avoid imposition of estate tax at his death or reducing his tax benefits at his death to insure inheritance by the children. The committee believes that the tax laws should be neutral and that tax consequences should not control an individual's disposition of property. Accordingly, the committee believes that a deduction should be permitted for certain terminable interests.

f.   Partial QTIP Elections

Partial QTIP elections are often made as part of postmortem estate planning. Fractional or percentile interests can qualify for the marital deduction. See I.R.C. § 2056(b)(10). In the typical case, the decedent's will provides that all the decedent's property is to pass in trust for the benefit of the surviving spouse, that the surviving spouse is to receive all the trust income, and that no one except the spouse is to receive any distribution from the trust so long as the spouse survives. Such a trust obviously meets the requirements for the QTIP election under section 2056(b)(7). However, making the QTIP election for the entire trust causes the entire trust to be included in the estate of the surviving spouse—and will also often mean that the decedent has not utilized the opportunity to shelter from estate tax, at the death of the spouse, the basic exclusion amount available to the decedent under section 2010(c)(3) ($12,920,000 in 2023, but scheduled to reset to $5 million (adjusted for inflation) in 2026 under the Tax Cuts and Jobs Act of 2017. A partial QTIP election can sometimes be utilized to rectify such a development, as can be seen in the following letter ruling.

PRIVATE LETTER RULING 8301050
September 30, 1982.

This is in reference to your letter dated July 13, 1982, requesting rulings concerning the federal estate tax consequences of a proposed election under section 2056(b)(7)(B)(v) * * *. More specifically, you request rulings that: (1) the fractional share of the property subject to the proposed election will constitute qualified terminable property, and (2) the value of the decedent's taxable estate shall be determined, in part, by deducting from the gross estate an amount equal to the value of the fractional share of the property subject to the proposed election.

Your proposed election states as follows: that specific portion, represented by a fractional share up to 100% of all trust property, that is required to reduce the federal estate tax on [the decedent's] estate to zero based on finally determined federal estate tax values, after taking into consideration all other items deducted on the federal estate tax return, the allowable state death tax credit (to the extent it does not increase the amount of death taxes payable to any state) and unified credit.

The submitted information indicates that the decedent died testate after December 31, 1981, survived by a wife and two children. The decedent had previously executed a will in which he bequeathed to his wife an amount equal to 50 percent of his adjusted gross estate as finally determined for federal estate tax purposes, less property which passed to her either by specific bequest or outside the will and which qualifies for the marital deduction. The remainder of his estate passed to an inter vivos family trust of which the decedent was the grantor. * * * The trust provided that, upon the decedent's death, * * * (1) the trustee is to pay all the income of the trust to the wife during her life, at least annually. Any undistributed net income upon the wife's death would be distributed to her estate. (2) The trustee has discretion to pay to the wife all or part of the corpus in order to maintain her in her usual manner and style of living or for illness or other emergency. (3) Upon the death of the wife, the balance of the trust corpus will be divided into separate trusts for the benefit of the decedent's children.

* * *

Section 2056(b)(7)(B) defines qualified terminable interest property as property which passes from the decedent, in which the surviving spouse has a qualifying income interest for life, and as to which an election has been made. In order for the income interest to qualify under section 2056(b)(7)(B), the surviving spouse must be entitled to all the income from the property, payable at least annually, and no person may have the power to appoint any part of the property of any person other than the surviving spouse during the spouse's life. In addition, an irrevocable election must be made by the executor on the estate tax return with respect to such property. Section 2056(b)(7)(B)(iv) provides that a specific portion of property shall be treated as separate property.

The trust * * * provides that all the income is paid solely to the wife for her life, at least annually, and that no person other than the wife has an interest in the trust corpus during her life. You intend to elect for treatment as qualifying terminable interest property, a fractional share of the trust property defined by means of a formula and computed in a manner necessary to reduce the decedent's federal estate tax liability to zero. The temporary regulation under section 2056, section 22.2056–1, provides that such a partial election is valid. The fractional share will be determined in the following manner. The numerator of the fraction will be the smallest amount of the deduction under section 2056(b)(7) that will, after taking into account the allowable unified credit and any other allowable credits and deductions, result in no federal estate tax being imposed on the decedent's estate. The denominator of the fraction will be the value of the trust corpus as finally determined for federal estate tax purposes less any amounts paid out of the trust fund (such as specific bequests, estate taxes, inheritance taxes, any other debts of the estate, decedent, or beneficiaries that are paid out of the trust fund).

The proposed election of the interest of the trust passing to the surviving spouse will result in determination of a specific portion, after final valuation of the decedent's gross estate and taking into account all allowable deductions and credits. Since the surviving spouse has a qualifying income interest in the trust for life, payable at least annually, no other person has an interest in the trust during the spouse's life, and no one has the power to appoint any part of the trust to anyone other than the spouse, the requirements of section 2056(b)(7) are satisfied as to the fractional share subject to the election. Accordingly, the fractional share subject to the election will be treated as qualifying terminable interest property described in section 2056(b)(7) for which a marital deduction will be allowable under section 2056(a).

The value of the decedent's taxable estate shall be determined, in part, by deducting from the value of the gross estate an amount equal to the value of the specific portion (fractional share) of the trust property subject to the election. That same fractional share of the trust will be taxable to the surviving spouse or the surviving spouse's estate under section 2519 or 2044, as the case may be.

If all property included in the decedent's gross estate which does not qualify for the marital deduction, excluding the family trust, does not exceed all allowable credits and other deductions, the fractional share of the trust treated as qualified terminable interest property as described above will reduce the decedent's federal estate tax to zero.

g.   Spousal Gift Contingent on QTIP Election

Consider Mei Ling's will. It provides that all her property is to be placed in trust. Her husband, George, is to receive all the income for life from the trust (and no one other than George is eligible to receive distributions from the trust while George lives). However, these provisions for the benefit of Mei Ling's husband, George, are to apply if, and only if, Mei Ling's executor makes the QTIP election for the trust property. The executor is also authorized to make a partial QTIP election, and the will provides that Mei Ling's sister (not husband, George) is to receive all the income from the portion of the trust for which the QTIP election is not made. (Practically speaking, the executor's refusal to make the QTIP election would mean that Mei Ling's sister is substituted for George as beneficiary of the entire trust.)

Sound pretty straight forward so far? The portion of Mei Ling's estate for which the QTIP election is made will be included in George's estate at his subsequent death. This might not be desirable (for a number of reasons) and allowing Mei Ling's executor discretion to make this election allows for a "last look" at the effectiveness of the tax plan contemplated when the will was drafted.

The IRS's initial reaction—as expressed in Treas. Reg. § 20.2056(b)–7(d)(3)—was negative. Its view was that an income interest that is contingent upon the QTIP election being made does not qualify for the marital deduction. However, the Fifth, Sixth, and Eighth Circuits and the Tax Court, have taken a different approach, concluding that the marital deduction is not lost where the spousal gift is contingent on the QTIP election being made. See, e.g., Estate of Clayton v. Commissioner, 976 F.2d 1486 (5th Cir.1992); Estate of Robertson v. Commissioner, 15 F.3d 779 (8th Cir.1994); Estate of Spencer v. Commissioner, 43 F.3d 226 (6th Cir.1995); Estate of Clack v. Commissioner, 106 T.C. 131 (1996). The *Clayton* court reasoned that the making of the QTIP election is an essential part of the statutory definition of what constitutes the qualified terminable interest property. That is, the court concluded that "property" in the statutory definition means that property which the executor identified by making the QTIP election. The court said that evaluation of whether the interest qualifies for the marital deduction begins only after the QTIP election is made. As for the position of the IRS, the court said to disallow the QTIP election in these cases because of the "circular reasoning advanced by the Commissioner" defies "logic, common sense, and the purpose for which QTIP was designed and implemented." 976 F.2d at 1501.

In 1998, the IRS conceded the issue and promulgated Treas. Reg. § 20.2056(b)–7(d)(3)(ii), which provides that an otherwise qualifying income interest that is contingent on an executor's election will not be precluded from QTIP status under the requirements of section 2056(b)(7).

h.   Spousal Gift Contingent on Tax Payment or Other Election

It goes without saying that drafting a will or trust is a complex undertaking and that it will be uneconomical as well not in the interest of the client for each instrument to be produced from scratch for each client. Boilerplate makes it possible to address myriad issues using techniques that have been refined through repeated use in common situations. Not only do such practices effect economies in the delivery of legal services at prices that clients are willing and able to afford but the client gets the benefit of the draftspersons experience and sophistication. Sometimes, though, the draftsperson is unsuccessful in reconciling custom provisions and boilerplate—or as the draftsperson probably would have explained, "No matter how many times I read it, I would never have foreseen that conflict!" "Good intentions, notwithstanding," the Internal Revenue Service might well have said when it claimed in Patterson v. United States, 181 F.3d 927 (8th Cir. 1999) that the QTIP election was compromised by the tax payment clause that appear in the governing instrument. Fortunately, for the taxpayer, the court believed itself able to provide the needed harmonization by extending what it said was the common sensical rationale of *Clayton* and its progeny. *Query: Was that extension appropriate, i.e., was Patterson really a Clayton-like situation?* Perhaps, too, as an alternative analysis, consider whether *Patterson* might well be more than a failed drafting case; perhaps it represents an IRS testing of some relatively common provisions found in boiler plate documents. Whatever the explanation, it illustrates the perils of boilerplate, a necessary ingredient in the will and trust drafting process.

Mr. Patterson had executed both a will and a trust. The will provided that the residue of his probate estate—the property passing under his will—was to be added to the trust, as is common. The will included a relatively common tax allocation clause, calling on the executor to pay all death taxes from Mr. Patterson's residuary probate estate. But again, as is relatively common, the will also provided that all or part of Mr. Patterson's death taxes could, at the discretion of the trustee, be paid from the trust. For its part, the trust authorized the trustee to pay death taxes from the trust if the trustee believed such payment to be "expedient and in the best interests" of the trust beneficiaries. The death taxes were, in fact, paid from the trust.

The dispute in *Patterson* related to the amount of the marital deduction allowable for estate tax purposes. The trust provided that ten percent of the trust estate "computed before any reduction for . . . death taxes" would be set aside in a separate trust that would qualify for the QTIP election. The executors made the QTIP election. The IRS then did its arithmetic and concluded that payment of the death taxes—more than $4 million—from the probate estate *rather than from the trust estate* would, under the terms of the will and trust taken together, require the payment of additional death taxes. (Why? Using this assumption, the marital deduction would be less than claimed by the taxpayer because the death taxes would be subtracted before applying the ten percent.) The IRS relied on Jackson v. United States, 376 U.S. 503 (1964) (discussed earlier in this chapter) for the proposition that the value of the probate estate must be fixed at the date of death and not when, as in *Patterson*, the trustee exercises his discretion to pay the death taxes or not pay them (thus leaving that task to the executor who would be obligated to pay the death taxes from the probate estate). It was this discretion that the IRS claimed to be an impermissible power of appointment, impermissible in the sense that its exercise could either bring about, postmortem, either an increase or a decrease in the marital deduction. Rejecting the IRS claim, and finding for the taxpayer, the court first looked approvingly to *Clayton* and then borrowed the words "counter-intuitive and against common sense" from *Spencer* and used them inferentially to describe the IRS position in *Patterson*.

i. Postmortem Rehabilitation

Postmortem attempts to rehabilitate gifts to a spouse that do not otherwise qualify for the marital deduction have not generally met with success. There are several illustrations. First consider Estate of Rapp v. Commissioner, 140 F.3d 1211 (9th Cir.1998), where Bert Rapp's will created a discretionary pay trust for the benefit of his surviving spouse. Alleging that Mr. Rapp intended the trust to qualify for the marital deduction, his executor petitioned the probate court to modify the trust so that it would qualify for the marital deduction. The probate court obliged and ordered that the trust income be paid to the surviving spouse. The claimed marital deduction on Mr. Rapp's subsequently filed estate tax return was denied, the Ninth Circuit concluding that the will was unambiguous and therefore the probate court was without authority to modify the trust. Conceding that the probate court's decision to reform the trust was erroneous, the executor nonetheless attached great significance to the fact that the probate court order had become final and was unappealable and argued that, as of the date of the filing of the federal estate tax return, the trust, as reformed, then satisfied the requirements for QTIP property for marital deduction purposes. Relying on Commissioner v. Bosch, 387 U.S. 456 (1967), reprinted in Chapter 1, the Ninth Circuit concluded that the federal court could make an independent determination as to the merits of the case presented to the probate court by Mr. Rapp's executor and was not bound by the state court determination unless that determination had been made by the highest court of the state. That the probate court order had become final and unappealable did not make it a determination of the state's highest court so as to bar the federal court from making an independent determination as to the state property rules that should be applied. From this perspective, the court noted that reference to *Spencer*, *Clayton*, and *Robertson* was misplaced as the issue in *Rapp* was not "the correct measuring date for QTIP election" as it had been in those cases.

The executor used a nonjudicial approach in Estate of Rinaldi v. United States, 38 Fed. Cl. 341 (1997), with a similar lack of success. Again, the marital deduction was claimed for property passing to the surviving spouse which was clearly ineligible for the marital deduction at decedent's death. However, the executor claimed the property became eligible for the marital deduction as a result of postmortem developments initiated by him to remove the taint that precluded the property from qualifying for the marital deduction. Clyde Rinaldi willed stock in his printing company to a trust for his surviving spouse, Nelle, expressly authorizing but not requiring that the QTIP election be made for this gift. However, the company stock was subject to an unusual provision that made it ineligible for the marital deduction. By the trust terms, the company stock was required to be offered to son William Rinaldi at a bargain price if son William ever ceased day-to-day management of the printing company. The stock was, thus, ineligible for the marital deduction because a bargain sale to William—which would diminish the value of the trust—is seen, effectively, as a power to appoint the QTIP property to someone other than the surviving spouse and barred by section 2056(b)(7)(B)(ii)(II). Nonetheless, the executor asserted that the marital deduction was available for the gift to the spouse because the taint of the possible bargain sale was removed from the gift because the shares were redeemed at fair market value by the corporation prior to the filing of the federal estate tax return. Thus, at the time of the filing of the federal estate tax return, son William no longer had the ability to effect the bargain sale (that would result in diminishing the value of the trust). The court explained:

> The initial question for the court, then, is to determine the point at which property must be statutorily eligible for QTIP treatment. If eligibility must be attained at the time of the testator's death, then the court in this case need only look to the terms of the will, and to the right granted thereunder giving the son the opportunity to purchase the Trust's shares at a price below fair market value. Under this approach, the inquiry would end at that point, as the property would clearly fall short of the QTIP non-diminution requirements. If, however, property's QTIP eligibility should not be judged until the estate's executor elects such treatment, then the court's inquiry will expand to include those events occurring subsequent to the testator's death that, according to plaintiff, cured the property's ineligibility.

> A long line of cases echoes the principle that, in general, "qualification for the marital deduction must be determined as of the time of death." Jackson v. United States, 376 U.S. 503, 508, 84 S.Ct. 869, 872, 11 L.Ed.2d 871 (1964). * * * If the trust does not satisfy the statutory requirements at the time of the relevant transaction—usually the death of the decedent—"deductibility of the bequest in controversy cannot hang suspended pending later events." Estate of Weisberger v. Commissioner, 29 T.C. 217, 221–22 (1957).

> Defendant's reliance on this line of cases, though well-founded, does not adequately address the circumstances presented by the QTIP election in this case. Because courts in cases like *Jackson* "ruled on the proper determination date for an interest which is not an exception to the [terminable] interest rule, and not subject to a later election, we do not think [they are]

dispositive of this issue." Estate of Spencer v. Commissioner, 43 F.3d 226, 231 (6th Cir.1995). In most situations in which a marital deduction is sought, the final event of any relevance will be the testator's death. In contrast, when QTIP treatment is sought by a taxpayer's estate, one of the prerequisites is that an election have [sic] been made on the estate tax return—an event which naturally cannot take place until after the testator's death. Several courts have recognized this event as being of significance sufficient to justify postponing the QTIP eligibility determination until its occurrence.

In *Spencer*, the taxpayer's will did not designate specific property to receive QTIP treatment, but rather granted his executor the authority to decide what amount of property would be subject to QTIP treatment when the time came to make the election. The IRS argued that because the executor had the power to decide how much property would go to the QTIP trust, she "possessed an impermissible power to appoint property away from the surviving spouse for the interim period from decedent's death until the date of the QTIP election." Id. at 227.

The court rejected this argument, noting first that "[i]t is often impossible to prudently designate what should be committed as QTIP far in advance of death." Id. at 228. Further, because "no property meets the definition of QTIP until the proper election is made, and no QTIP election can be made until the estate tax form is filed," id. at 231, then logically "no property anywhere can meet the definition of [QTIP] until after the decedent's death." Id. at 228. As such, the court reasoned, it would be "contrary to the policy and meaning of the statute, as well as counter-intuitive and against common sense, to apply the definition before the election can be satisfied." Id. Therefore, the court held that "the date of election is the proper date for deciding if property meets the requirements set out under § 2056(b)(7)." Id.

As to the nature of the QTIP election itself, the court expressed its view as follows:

> The IRS would have us adopt an interpretation that would force property to satisfy every requirement for the QTIP counter-exception on the date of decedent's death except the requirement of election. This would effectively reduce the election requirement to a mere formality, defeat its apparent purpose and its most reasonable interpretation.

Other courts have also refused to invalidate a QTIP election when the subject property is not explicitly defined at the time of the testator's death. In Estate of Clayton v. Commissioner, 976

F.2d 1486, 1490 (5th Cir.1992), the testator's will provided that any property for which a QTIP election was not made would go into a non-QTIP trust. The IRS took the position that this power of the executor to divert part of the estate's property away from a QTIP trust was "'tantamount' to a power of appointment to the testator's children." Id. at 1497. The court disagreed, finding the IRS's argument to be "flawed logic and deliberate disregard of the plain wording of [the statute]," id., and noting "the overarching truism that many acts must be done and many facts must be determined after the death of the testator in order to determine the taxable estate." Id. at 1498. See also Estate of Robertson v. Commissioner, 15 F.3d 779, 781 (8th Cir.1994) ("We believe the [executor's] right to make or refrain from making a QTIP election is not a prohibited 'power to appoint.' ").

The logic of this line of cases is readily apparent in light of the policies underlying the QTIP legislation. Congress enacted § 2056(b)(7) primarily to allow a testator to provide for a surviving spouse while maintaining control over the ultimate disposition of his or her property following the surviving spouse's death. See H.R.Rep. No. 97–201, at 159–60 (1981), U.S. Code Cong. & Admin. News at 105, 258–59. Under prior law, a testator was forced to choose between leaving property outright to his or her surviving spouse, in which case the property would not be included in the taxable estate, and leaving the property to his or her surviving children, in which case it would be taxed at the testator's death. Under the enacted QTIP provision, a testator may give the surviving spouse the benefit of the property for his or her lifetime without also granting the discretion to direct the ultimate disposition of the property away from the testator's intended beneficiaries.

In offering this tax-deferral opportunity, Congress was careful to include several important conditions within the statutory framework. Most important to our inquiry was its requirement that no person have the "power to appoint any part of the property to any person other than the surviving spouse." § 2056(b)(7)(B)(ii)(II). This provision does not reflect a congressional purpose of ensuring the financial stability of the surviving spouse, for "[i]f the intention had been to dangle the carrot of deductibility in front of testators to induce them to ensure the financial well-being of the surviving spouse, Congress would surely have given the power to make the QTIP election to the surviving spouse, not the executor." *Clayton*, supra, at 1498. Rather, the restriction's inclusion is to ensure that QTIP property does not escape taxation in the surviving spouse's estate, apart from that portion of the corpus used in furtherance of the surviving spouse's well-being. Congress was not concerned with that portion of the estate's property that, for whatever reason, is ineligible for QTIP treatment because "that property is taxed right where the Commissioner and Congress want it taxed—in the estate of the first spouse to die." Id.

There is no compelling reason to prohibit QTIP treatment for those assets whose election is left up to the discretion of the executor. If the executor includes a particular asset in the QTIP trust established by the testator's will, then the asset will be taxed in the estate of the surviving spouse. If the executor declines to elect QTIP status for an asset, then it will be taxed in the testator's estate. Congressional objectives thus do not require that the status of a particular asset be determined at the time of the testator's death. As long as property's QTIP eligibility is ascertainable when the executor elects such treatment in the estate tax return, postponing the eligibility determination until that time runs afoul of neither the plain meaning of the statute's language, nor its underlying objectives.

* * * The factual circumstances on which the reasoning of *Spencer* and its progeny were based differ dramatically from the circumstances presented by the case at hand. In *Spencer*, for example, the terms of the testator's will clearly established a valid QTIP trust—the only ambiguity stemmed from the discretion granted to the executor to decide what amount of property to contribute to the trust. See 43 F.3d at 227.

In this case, by contrast, the trust established by the terms of Rinaldi's will was clearly ineligible for QTIP treatment—the will explicitly subjected the trust's value to diminution through the potential sale of its assets at a bargain price to someone other than the surviving spouse. It is only because the terms of the will apparently no longer dictate the make-up of the trust that plaintiff now can assert QTIP eligibility. * * *

The difficulty with accepting plaintiff's characterization stems from the means by which the trust's defect was allegedly remedied. The trust may indeed have rid itself of the troublesome stock in question; what remains unchanged, however, are the terms of the will that rendered the trust ineligible for QTIP treatment in the first place. There exists no legal impediment to the trust's ownership of the printing company's stock. * * * [T]here is nothing to prevent the trust from reacquiring shares of the company. In the event of such a reacquisition, the terms of Rinaldi's will presumably would still govern. Under those terms, the shares potentially would be subject once again to a bargain sale to Rinaldi's son or a third party, thereby diminishing the corpus of the trust. The portion of the trust's corpus lost in the bargain sale would have escaped taxation in both Rinaldi's and his surviving spouse's estates—the very potentiality which the statutory QTIP requirements were implemented to avoid.

* * *

This potential reemergence of the trust's defect reflects an even more fundamental problem with the approach to QTIP eligibility advocated by plaintiff. Plaintiff is asking this court to judge property's QTIP eligibility solely on the basis of the factual circumstances in place at the time of the executor's election, regardless of the specific terms of the testator's will. Under plaintiff's approach, ad hoc measures enacted after the testator's death by the executor would effectively negate the memorialized intent of the testator, no matter how contrary that intent was to the letter and spirit of the QTIP requirements. In *Spencer*, *Clayton*, and *Robertson*, the testators' memorialized intent was to allow their executors to decide whether or not to elect QTIP status as to a particular asset—importantly, however, every aspect of their wills' terms was consistent with QTIP eligibility. Here, in contrast, Rinaldi's explicit intent was to allow his wife's trust to operate in a manner clearly inconsistent with § 2056(b)(7)'s criteria. To say the least, it would take a generous reading of tax law by the court to extract a legally viable QTIP trust from the facially invalid framework set forth by the testator. Such a reading, in this court's view, is not feasible.

* * *

In addition to requiring precision in the crafting of a will's terms, courts interpreting QTIP provisions place an unmistakable emphasis on the expressed intent of the testator. * * *

When measured against these twin strains of judicial analysis—emphasizing the will's language and the testator's intent—Rinaldi's will falls short. The terms of the will are precise, but their precision sets forth a framework directly contradictory to the statutory requirements for QTIP eligibility. And Rinaldi clearly intended to establish the trust with a condition that would render it ineligible for QTIP treatment. Regardless of his motivation, he did not want his wife's trust to be made up of the printing company's stock in the event that his son no longer participated in the company's management. To bring this about, he was willing to arrange a bargain sale of the shares to his son—

an arrangement that violates both the letter and spirit of § 2056(b)(7).

Plaintiff would have us ignore both the terms of the will and the intent of the testator, and focus solely on the factual circumstances as they happened to exist at the time of the QTIP election. The court, however, does not believe that the inquiry into a trust's QTIP eligibility can be divorced from the testamentary framework from which it arose. It is one thing to allow the testator—as the court did in *Spencer*, for example—to defer the identification of particular QTIP assets until after his or her death, when an account of the estate can be made. In those situations, recognizing the validity of the resulting QTIP trust is consistent with the terms and underlying tax policies of § 2056, as well as the intentions and instructions of the testator. It is quite another matter to allow the executor to step in and point to a post-mortem, circumstantial change in the QTIP trust as a remedy for an obvious flaw created by the terms of the trust itself, as set forth in the will.

Id. at 346–350.

Does *Patterson* impact *Rinaldi*? Certainly, the *Patterson* court never mentioned *Rinaldi* despite *Rinaldi* having been decided two years earlier. A possible explanation is that it was only the post mortem rehabilitative steps taken in *Rinaldi* to eliminate the effect of the tainting language in the will that even made it possible for the executor to attempt to claim the marital deduction for the *Rinaldi* gift. In *Patterson*, by way of contrast, paying the death taxes was just one of "many acts [that] must be done and many facts [that] must be determined *after* the death of the testator in order to determine the taxable estate." *Patterson*, 181 F.3d at 930.

PROBLEM

Nick is to receive all of the income from the trust established by his deceased wife, Joanna, in her will. No one else is permitted to receive distributions from the trust while Nick lives. However, if Joanna's executor does not elect QTIP treatment for part or all of Nick's trust, the part for which QTIP is not elected is to be distributed to Sonny, Joanna's son from her first marriage. Is the marital deduction allowed for Nick's entire trust if Joanna's executor makes the QTIP election? Is it allowed for 40 percent of the trust if the executor makes the election for only 40 percent?

D. USE OF THE BYPASS TRUST

With the unlimited marital deduction, all estate tax upon the death of the first spouse can be eliminated merely by leaving all the estate to the surviving spouse. However, it is at the death of second spouse that the aggregate property—that of both spouses—will be taxed and, this time, without benefit of any marital deduction (unless the surviving spouse has remarried and has made a gift to the new spouse) and with only *one* applicable exclusion amount available to shelter the aggregate property. The applicable exclusion amount consists of the $12,920,000 basic exclusion amount available to those dying in 2023 and the deceased spousal unused exclusion amount, if any, under section 2010(c)(2).

In the case of larger estates, so long as there is an estate tax, responsible planning dictates securing the benefits of the basic exclusion amount for the estate of the first spouse to die. Otherwise, the concentration of the family's property in the estate of the surviving spouse will lead to unnecessary estate taxes. A married couple with $26 million in 2023, for example, would want to see that each estate used fully the available basic exclusion amount, without having the property covered by the basic exclusion amount in the first estate added to the second estate to be there taxed. Instead, a trust is typically created that benefits the surviving spouse but "bypasses" the estate of the surviving spouse for tax purposes.

> *Example*: If Hapless and Willful each had estates of $20 million, upon the death of the first (whether it be Hapless or Willful), the deceased spouse's will should give to a so-called "bypass" trust— which is not intended to qualify for the marital deduction—an amount equal to the applicable exclusion amount (then available) with the balance of the decedent's estate being given to the surviving spouse. In this fashion, no tax would be payable upon the death of either spouse (assuming the value of survivor's property remains at or below the applicable exclusion amount available at that person's death).

The bypass trust is sometimes referred to as the "credit shelter trust" or even, less descriptively, as the "family trust." It will provide benefits (income or principal or both) for the surviving spouse or others but will not be taxable in the estate of the surviving spouse unless the surviving spouse is found to have a general power of appointment over the trust—a condition to be scrupulously avoided if the tax sheltering promise of the bypass trust is to be realized. Alternatively, the bypass vehicle could be an outright bequest to persons other than the surviving spouse, thus accomplishing the same tax sheltering effect.

Taxpayers planning to shelter the basic exclusion amount in a bypass trust will normally use a formula to bring about the division of the estate between the bypass trust and the gift to the surviving spouse designed to qualify for the marital deduction. While the following provisions could be further refined, they are examples of what might be found in a so-called tax-planning will:

(a) To my spouse I give the smallest amount necessary to eliminate federal estate tax at my death;

(b) The balance of my estate I give to my trustee to pay the income to my spouse for life and, at the death of my spouse, the trust shall terminate, and the trustee shall distribute the property then constituting the trust estate per stirpes to my then-living lineal descendants.

The basic concept, however, is a rather simple one: to set aside a portion of the estate—the portion that would go free of tax by reason of the unified credit—such portion then being disposed of in such a way as not to fall into the gross estate of the survivor. The balance of the estate then can go to the survivor in a form that will qualify for the marital deduction.

Nontax considerations complicate use of the formula driven bypass trust. The formula commonly employed will, in some cases, cause all the decedent's property to flow to the bypass trust, leaving the surviving spouse with none of the decedent's property *free of trust*. Care will need to be taken to make certain that taxpayers *really* want such a result and, for those who do not, special drafting will be required to make clear the intention of the will maker to give some or all property to the surviving spouse *free of trust* where estate taxes are not thereby increased. Among the possible solutions is a will giving everything to the surviving trust free of trust but, to the extent the surviving spouse disclaims part or all of the gift, the disclaimed share falls back into a bypass trust provided for in the decedent's will. Obviously, this places "control" in the surviving spouse, a situation not welcomed by every testator. Another alternative is to provide a certain "minimum" gift to the surviving spouse free of trust, the minimum gift being determined by making projections as to the likely value of the estate of the surviving spouse at the spouse's later death. Such projections are necessarily fraught with uncertainty and risk disappointing one or more expectant beneficiaries.

In the smaller estates, it might seem that less care would need to be exercised with respect to securing the basic exclusion amount. For example, the section 2010(c) applicable exclusion amount completely shelters estates aggregating $12,920,000. A $12,920,000 exclusion allows a relatively large amount of property to be concentrated in the estate of the surviving spouse free of estate taxes at the death of that spouse.

In past years, some estate planners, who had already seen to it that the spouses' property was divided sufficiently to assure a full use of the credit in each estate, would go further and provide for an equal division between the two spouses at the death of the first of them to die, taking account of values at the death of the first spouse to die. In some cases, such a strategy meant paying estate tax at the death of the first spouse to die (effectively ignoring the right to eliminate all estate taxes at the death of the first to die through use of the marital deduction). Under certain facts such a strategy would result in lower total estate taxes for persons married to each other even though it meant paying estate tax at the death of the first spouse to die. However, with total repeal of the estate tax always a possibility, albeit unlikely, any strategy that contemplates payment of estate tax that is otherwise deferrable is likely flawed. Even without repeal, the strategy is flawed because of the flat rate estate tax of 40 percent. Moreover, the scheduled sunset of the 2017 Act, which will reduce the basic exclusion amount from $10,000,000 to $5,000,000 (both figures adjusted for inflation), complicates tax planning.

Incidentally, while the courts have expressly sanctioned equalization clauses (overcoming IRS challenge), see, e.g., Estate of Smith (C.W.) v. Commissioner, 565 F.2d 455 (7th Cir. 1977), *acq.*, Rev. Rul. 82–23, 1982–1 C.B. 139, it should be noted that equalization clauses vary widely. That suggests that, while unlikely, the IRS might well challenge another equalization clause. The IRS challenge would be expressed in terms of the uncertainty at the date of death as to the amount passing to the spouse for purposes of the marital deduction particularly where the estates are to be equalized, as is common, and the property is to be valued as of the alternate valuation date, a date six months after death.

PROBLEMS

1. Henry's father died in 1990, leaving $100,000 in trust "to pay the income to my son, Henry, for life and upon his death to deliver the entire corpus to such of his blood relatives or to his spouse or to such charity as Henry might by will appoint." Henry died last year, leaving a will in which he exercised the power of appointment by appointing the trust corpus to his wife for her life with the remainder to her estate. Is Henry's estate entitled to a marital deduction with respect to any part of the trust property?

2. Paul created a testamentary trust and transferred $1,000,000 worth of stock to the trust. Under the trust, all income was distributed to his wife, Kelly, for life. Upon Kelly's death, she had the right to appoint the corpus to anyone, including her estate. If Kelly failed to appoint a recipient of the corpus, it would pass equally to Paul's children. Kelly died 10 years later and did not appoint a recipient of the corpus. As a result, it passed to Paul's children. At the time of her death, the stock was worth $2,500,000. What are the estate tax consequences upon Paul's and Kelly's deaths?

3. Assume instead in Problem 2 that Kelly only had the right to appoint the corpus amongst Paul's descendants. Paul's executor made a valid QTIP election. Kelly appointed the corpus to Paul's daughter, Emily. What are the estate tax consequences upon Paul's and Kelly's deaths?

4. Haley by will directed her executor to convert the residue of her estate into cash and distribute it equally between two trusts: Trust A provides for the payment of "all net income to my husband for his life." A further

provision authorizes her husband to withdraw such portion or all of the corpus as he may desire. Upon his death the corpus of Trust A is to go to such beneficiaries as he and the Solid Granite Trust Company, as Trustee, may designate; in default of appointment, the corpus is to be divided among Haley's then-surviving children. Trust B is an accumulation trust for the benefit of Haley's children with distribution to be made upon her husband's death, dividing the accumulated income and corpus equally among her then living children. Is either of the Trusts entitled to marital deduction treatment? To take optimum advantage of the marital deduction and the basic exclusion amount, how should the executor divide the property of Haley's estate between the two trusts in lieu of the "equally" standard? For this purpose, assume that Haley's estate amounts to $20 million and, at the time of her death, her husband's separate property equals $4 million.

5.   Helen owned one-fourth of the outstanding capital stock of General Micro; her three brothers owned the rest of the outstanding stock in equal shares. Helen and her brothers have been employed with General Micro and have been receiving substantial salaries for their services. General Micro has never paid dividends. Helen's will left her shares in General Micro in trust with instructions to pay the trust income to her husband, Horatio, for her life; she also gave Horatio a power to consume the corpus and to appoint any remaining corpus among their children. Will this trust qualify for the marital deduction?

CHAPTER 28

ESTATE TAX CREDITS, RETURNS, PAYMENT, AND APPORTIONMENT

■ ■ ■

A. CREDITS

Several important credits are allowed against the estate tax liability as determined under section 2001. Credits constitute the final step in the tax computation process.

First, the assets to be included in the gross estate are determined in accordance with sections 2031 and 2033–2046, taking into account the exclusion provided by section 2031(c). Those assets are valued in accordance with sections 2031, 2032, 2032A, and 2701–2704 to produce a total value for the gross estate. Then, in accordance with section 2051, the deductions provided by sections 2053–2056 and section 2058 are subtracted to produce the taxable estate amount, and section 2001 is applied to determine the estate tax liability.

At this point the credits provided in sections 2010 and 2012–2015 are applied. The unified credit under section 2010, has the effect of eliminating any tax liability for the vast majority of estates. If liability remains after application of the unified credit, the other credits may significantly reduce the amount actually due.

1. UNIFIED CREDIT

a. In General

As explained in Chapter 7, section 2010 provides a unified credit or an applicable credit amount of a fixed amount that varies with the year of death. The applicable credit amount is defined as the tentative tax computed under section 2001(c) on the applicable exclusion amount. See I.R.C. § 2010(c)(1). The applicable exclusion amount equals the basic exclusion amount plus the "deceased spousal unused exclusion amount." See I.R.C. § 2010(c)(1). The deceased spousal unused exclusion amount is discussed in the next section.

Under the Tax Cuts and Jobs Act of 2017, the "basic exclusion amount" is $10,000,000 (indexed for inflation) from January 1, 2018 through December 31, 2025. See I.R.C. § 2001(a)(3)(C). In 2023, the basic exclusion amount is $12,920,000. Because $5,113,800 is the tax that is imposed on a taxable estate of $12,920,000, the unified credit or basic exclusion amount for 2023 is $5,113,800. The $10,000,000 basic exclusion amount (adjusted by inflation) is subject to a sunset post-2025 when the basic exclusion amount will revert to $5,000,000. The Treasury Department issued "anti-clawback" final regulations to prevent a decedent from being subject to an estate tax if and when the basic exclusion amount reverts to $5,000,000. Under these regulations, to the extent the basic exclusion amount exceeds the allowable amount at the time of the decedent's death, the basic exclusion amount in computing the estate tax equals the sum of the allowable basic exclusion amounts on the decedent's post-1976 gifts. Treas. Reg. § 20.2010–1(c). The regulations apply to decedents dying after November 26, 2019. As noted in chapter 7, the Treasury Department issued proposed regulations to distinguish between lifetime transfers that are included in the computation of the estate tax as "adjusted taxable gifts" per section 2001(b)(1)(B) and transfers that are included in the gross estate for estate tax purposes. See Prop. Treas. Reg. § 20.2010–1(c)(3). Under the proposed regulations, the clawback regulations will not apply to property included in the gross estate, such as retained interests under section 2036. The proposed regulations will apply to decedents dying on or after April 27, 2022.

Under section 2001(b)(1)(B), the decedent's taxable gifts after 1976 are added to the decedent's taxable estate to determine the tax due. Therefore, the credit is consumed by both gifts and transfers at death. For example, assume that the basic exclusion amount is $12,920,000 at the decedent's death. If the decedent made taxable gifts of $8,920,000 (but paid no gift tax) and died with a taxable estate of $6,000,000, the section 2001(b) tax would be determined by the total of all transfers—$14,920,000. The tax on $14,920,000 is $5,913,800. Subtracting the unified credit of $5,113,800 produces a tax due of $800,000. In effect, the first $12,920,000 of all transfers is exempt, and the remaining $2,000,000 is taxed at a 40% rate.

b. Portability of the Unified Credit

Section 2010 allows "portability" of the unified credit between spouses for both gift and estate tax purposes.[1] In essence, this provision permits a surviving spouse to utilize any portion of the unified credit of a previously deceased spouse that went unused. This result is achieved by adding to the "basic exclusion amount" ($12,920,000 in 2023), the "deceased spousal unused exclusion amount" (DSUE). I.R.C. § 2010(c)(2)(B). The portability rule applies only if the first spousal death occurred after December 31, 2010. I.R.C. § 2010(c)(4). The rule was originally subject to a sunset on

---

[1]   Portability applies only to the gift and estate tax unified credit. It does not apply to the generation-skipping transfer tax exemption.

December 31, 2012. However, portability was made permanent under the American Taxpayer Relief Act of 2012.[2]

The DSUE amount is available to the surviving spouse only if the executor files an estate tax return on behalf of the decedent and makes an election on the return that the DSUE may be used by the surviving spouse. I.R.C. § 2010(c)(5)(A). Even if the estate of the first spouse to die is modest and the surviving spouse's property is modest as well, it will be advisable to file a return and make the election if there is any realistic possibility that the surviving spouse's estate may in time exceed $12,920,000. Once the portability election is made, it is irrevocable. The election cannot be made if the estate tax return is filed late. I.R.C. § 2010(c)(5)(A). However, under Treas. Reg. § 20.2010–2(a)(1), the IRS has the discretion to grant an extension under Treas. Reg. § 301.9100–3 where the estate is not required to file an estate tax return, the estate added reasonably and in good faith, and the interest of the government will not be prejudiced.[3] In order for the estate to be granted relief under this regulation, the executor must file the estate tax return within five years of the decedent's death. See Rev. Proc. 2022–32, 2022–30 I.R.B. 101.

To apply the portability rule, assume that a decedent died in 2023 with a taxable estate of $6,920,000. The decedent's $12,920,000 basic exclusion amount produces a section 2010 unified credit that shelters the entire estate from tax, but the decedent has "used" only $6,920,000 of the $12,920,000 basic exclusion amount resulting in an "unused" amount of $6,000,000. If the decedent's executor has so elected, the decedent's $6,000,000 DSUE amount is available for use by the surviving spouse. I.R.C. § 2010(c)(5)(A). The surviving spouse then has a "basic exclusion amount" of $12,920,000 and a DSUE amount of $6,000,000 provided by the decedent. These two produce a total "applicable exclusion amount" of $18,920,000 available to the surviving spouse. I.R.C. § 2010(c)(2). The surviving spouse can use the DSUE amount for either gift or estate tax purposes, or any combination of the two. Hence, in this example, the surviving spouse can make taxable gifts of $8,920,000 and retain an additional $10,000,000 exclusion amount to apply against transfers at death, all without paying either gift or estate tax.

Under the anti-clawback regulations, if a surviving spouse died after 2025 and had a DSUE amount that was higher than the current basic exclusion amount from a deceased spouse who died before 2026, the surviving spouse's applicable exclusion amount would be computed by adding the DSUE amount to the surviving spouse's basic exclusion amount. For example, if the basic exclusion amount was $6 million at the time of the surviving spouse's death, the surviving spouse had not made any

---

[2] Pub. L. No. 112–240, 126 Stat. 2313 (2013).

[3] For examples of where the IRS exercised its discretion in granting the taxpayer's request, see Private Letter Ruling 201710002 and Private Letter Ruling 201850015.

lifetime gifts, and the surviving spouse's DSUE amount was $12,920,000, then the surviving spouse's applicable exclusion amount would be $18,920,000 even though the basic exclusion amount was only $6 million at the surviving spouse's death. See Treas. Reg. § 20.2010–1(c)(2)(iii), Ex. 3.

Only the DSUE amount of the "last" deceased spouse may be used. I.R.C. § 2010(c)(4)(B)(i). In the example above, assume that the surviving spouse remarried before making any gifts, and that the second spouse then dies, using $11,920,000 of his basic exclusion amount. The surviving spouse would then have only $1,000,000 of DSUE amount to apply in conjunction with the surviving spouse's own basic exclusion amount of $12,920,000—a total of $13,920,000. The unused exclusion amount of the first deceased spouse would in effect disappear.

For estate tax purposes there can be only one "last" deceased spouse— the spouse whose death was nearest to the surviving spouse's death. For gift tax purposes, however, a surviving spouse could conceivably exploit the unused exclusion amounts of multiple spouses. Assume for example that Spouse No. 1 dies, leaving a DSUE amount of $2,000,000. The surviving spouse could use the surviving spouse's own exclusion amount of $12,920,000, in conjunction with Spouse No. 1's DSUE amount of $2,000,000, to make $14,920,000 of tax-free gifts. Assume that the surviving spouse later married Spouse No. 2, who then dies, leaving $4,000,000 of basic exclusion amount unused. The surviving spouse's applicable exclusion amount would equal $16,920,000 ($4,000,000 DSUE plus the surviving spouse's $12,920,000 basic exclusion amount). If Spouse No. 2 did not have a DSUE, the surviving spouse's applicable exclusion amount would equal $12,920,000 because the surviving spouse would no longer be able to use Spouse No. 1's DSUE.

As noted, the DSUE amount is available to a surviving spouse only if an election is made on a timely filed estate tax return (including extensions) of the predeceased spouse on which such amount is computed, regardless of whether the estate of the predeceased spouse otherwise is required to file an estate tax return. In addition, notwithstanding the statute of limitations for assessing an estate or a gift tax with respect to a predeceased spouse, the Secretary of the Treasury may examine the return of a predeceased spouse for purposes of determining the DSUE amount available for use by the surviving spouse.

The following case addresses whether the IRS is entitled to examine the deceased spouse's estate tax return where the surviving spouse does not use the DSUE amount against a taxable gift and whether the IRS can adjust the deceased spouse's estate for gifts that preceded the enactment of portability.

ESTATE OF SOWER V. COMMISSIONER

United States Tax Court, 2013.
149 T.C. 279.

BUCH, JUDGE: This is an estate tax deficiency case involving the Estate of Minnie Lynn Sower. Minnie was the surviving spouse of her late husband Frank W. Sower. When Frank's estate filed its estate tax return, the estate did not use all of the basic exclusion amount allowed under section 2010(c)(3). * * * After Minnie passed away, her estate sought to use the deceased spousal unused exclusion (DSUE) as allowed by section 2010(c)(2)(B). As part of examining the return for Minnie's estate, the Commissioner reviewed Frank's estate's tax return and reduced the amount of the DSUE. Minnie's estate raises various arguments as to why the Commissioner should be prohibited from considering the estate tax return of the predeceased spouse for the limited purpose of adjusting the amount of the DSUE allowable to the estate of the surviving spouse. In determining the correct amount of the DSUE allowable to the estate of a surviving spouse, the Commissioner may consider the estate tax return of a predeceased spouse. The period of limitations on assessment for the estate of the predeceased spouse is not implicated because no tax is being assessed against the estate of the predeceased spouse. * * *

Background

* * *At the time of Frank's death, Frank and Minnie were married. During their lifetimes, Frank and Minnie gave $997,920 and $997,921 in taxable gifts, respectively. All of the gifts were given between 2003 and 2005. The Sowers filed a Form 709, United States Gift (and Generation-Skipping Transfer) Tax Return, for each year in which they gave taxable gifts.

Frank died on February 23, 2012. His estate filed a timely return reporting that it had no estate tax liability. The estate also reported zero in taxable gifts but included $945,420 in taxable gifts on the worksheet provided to calculate taxable gifts to be reported on the return. Frank's estate reported a DSUE of $1,256,033 and elected portability of the DSUE to allow the surviving spouse to use it.[3]

* * *

Minnie died on August 7, 2013. Her estate filed a timely return claiming a DSUE of $1,256,033 from Frank's estate. Initially, her estate reported and paid an overall estate tax liability of $369,036. Three months later the estate paid an additional $386,424 in tax and interest to correct a mathematical error on the original return. Like Frank's estate, Minnie's

---

[3] Per the Form 706, United States Estate (and Generation-Skipping Transfer) Tax Return, "A decedent with a surviving spouse elects portability of the deceased spousal unused exclusion (DSUE) amount, if any, by completing and timely-filing this return. An affirmative election is not required.

estate did not include the lifetime taxable gifts on the return, though rather than reporting zero in gifts as on Frank's estate tax return, it left the entry blank on Minnie's estate's tax return.

In February 2015 the Commissioner began an examination of the return filed by Minnie's estate. In connection with that examination, the Commissioner also opened an examination of the return filed by Frank's estate to determine the proper DSUE amount available to Minnie's estate. On March 25, 2015, an attorney assigned to examine the return filed by Frank's estate sent the executors a letter and a draft revised report showing an adjustment to the amount of Frank's lifetime taxable gifts. * * *

As a result of the examination of the return filed by Frank's estate, the Commissioner reduced the DSUE available to Minnie's estate from $1,256,033 to $282,690. The Commissioner also adjusted Minnie's taxable estate by the amount of her lifetime taxable gifts. Finally, the Commissioner reduced Minnie's taxable estate by $850 to account for funeral costs. Together these adjustments increased the estate tax liability for Minnie's estate by $788,165. On December 2, 2015, the Commissioner sent Minnie's estate a notice of deficiency determining a $788,165 estate tax deficiency.

Minnie's estate filed a timely petition for redetermination of that deficiency. The estate disputes the full $788,165 in additional estate tax. At the time of Minnie's death she was a resident of Kentucky, and at the time of the petition the executors were residents of Kentucky.

Discussion

* * *

In its reply brief Minnie's estate argues that the taxable gifts given by Minnie should not be included in the taxable estate for the purpose of determining the estate tax liability. This argument was not properly raised in the petition or the amended petition, and so it has been conceded.[4]

* * *

I.   The Estate Tax, the DSUE, and Applicable Regulations

Section 2001 imposes a tax on the transfer of the taxable estates of U.S. citizens and residents. The tax is based on the sum of the taxable value of the estate and the amount of taxable gifts made by the decedent after 1976. Sec. 2001(b)(1).

---

[4]   Minnie's estate contests the full amount of the deficiency but does not discuss how the Commissioner erred in adjusting the size of the taxable estate to include the taxable gifts given by Minnie during her lifetime. The estate claims in its reply brief that it had argued in its amended opening brief that the taxable gifts should not be included in the estate. The Court does not agree. At no point in the amended petition, the amended opening brief, or the reply brief does Minnie's estate explain why the taxable gifts given by Minnie during her lifetime should be excluded from the value of the taxable estate.

Section 2010 provides a "unified credit against estate tax." This credit effectively reduces the value of the estate for the purpose of calculating the tax. Id. It includes both the basic exclusion amount and "in the case of a surviving spouse, the deceased spousal unused exclusion amount." Sec. 2010(c)(2). At the time of Minnie's death the basic exclusion was $5,250,000. Sec. 2010(c)(3); Rev. Proc. 2013–15, sec 2.13, 2013–5 I.R.B. 444, 448.

The DSUE is the lesser of the basic exclusion amount or "the excess of (i) the applicable exclusion amount of the last such deceased spouse of such surviving spouse, over (ii) the amount with respect to which the tentative tax is determined under section 2001(b)(1) on the estate of such deceased spouse." Sec. 2010(c)(4). If the estate of the predeceased spouse elects portability, the later-deceased spouse's estate can effectively reduce its taxable estate by the amount by which the basic exclusion exceeds the sum of the predeceased spouse's taxable estate and adjusted taxable gifts. Secs. 2010(c)(5)(A), 2001(b)(1).

Section 2010(c)(5)(B) gives the Commissioner the power to examine the estate tax return of the predeceased spouse to determine the DSUE amount, regardless of whether the period of limitations on assessment has expired for the predeceased spouse's estate.

* * *

Here, the Commissioner properly exercised the power conferred by sections 2010(c)(5)(B) and 7602(a)(1). He examined the return filed by the estate of the predeceased spouse. The Commissioner found that the DSUE had been overstated. He adjusted the amount of the DSUE as authorized by section 2010(c)(5)(B) and the regulations, but he did not determine that there was an estate tax deficiency for the predeceased spouse's estate.

* * *

IV. Adjustments Under Section 2010(c)(5)(B) and Applicable Regulations With Respect to Gifts Given Before 2010

Minnie's estate makes two arguments based on its interpretation of the statutory text and regulations governing the DSUE. The estate argues that the Commissioner does not have the power to examine the return of Frank's estate again because the DSUE has not been applied to a taxable gift transfer and that the effective date of section 2010 precludes the Commissioner from adjusting the taxable estate by the gifts made before 2010.

A. Application of the DSUE Regulations

To support the claim that the regulations prohibit the Commissioner's action, the estate cites section 25.250[5]–2(e), Gift Tax Regs., relating to the application of the DSUE to taxable gift transfers. This regulation, and its predecessor temporary regulation, states that the Commissioner's "authority to examine returns of a deceased spouse applies with respect to each transfer by the surviving spouse to which a DSUE amount is or has been applied." [citations omitted]. The estate argues that because the DSUE was not applied to a "taxable gift transfer" the Commissioner is not authorized to examine the return. This is irrelevant.

Under section 2010(c)(5)(B) the Commissioner has the power to examine the return filed by the estate of the predeceased spouse to determine the DSUE amount. The Commissioner's "authority to examine returns of a deceased spouse applies with respect to each transfer by the surviving spouse to which a DSUE amount is or has been applied." Sec. 20.2010–3T(d), Temporary Estate Tax Regs., supra. Although there was no taxable gift transfer to which the DSUE was applied, there is a taxable transfer to which the DSUE has been applied: the transfer of the estate. Consequently, the Commissioner has the power under section 2010(c)(5)(B) to examine the return filed by Frank's estate for the purpose of determining the DSUE available to Minnie's estate.

B.   The Effective Date of Section 2010

The estate argues that because the gifts at the center of this case were given before the effective date of section 2010(c)(5)(B), the Commissioner cannot make adjustments to the DSUE as a result of those gifts.

The Tax Relief, Unemployment Insurance Reauthorization, and Job Creation Act of 2010, Pub. L. No. 111–312, sec. 303, 124 Stat. at 3304, did several things. As is principally relevant here, subsection (a) created section 2010(c)(5)(B). Subsection (b) made amendments to section 2505, a gift tax provision. As for effective dates, subsection (c) provided that "amendments made by this section shall apply to estates of decedents dying and gifts made after December 31, 2010." The estate takes this to mean that the Commissioner cannot adjust the DSUE on the basis of the gifts given before December 31, 2010.

When examining a return, the Commissioner must apply the law in effect for the return that is being examined. Effective dates can vary in their application, sometimes applying for years beginning or ending after a particular date, or for returns filed after a particular date. In context, it is clear that the effective date of section 2010(c)(5)(B), the estate tax amendment, is for decedents dying after December 31, 2010. The effective date for the gift tax provision, which has no relevance here, is for gifts made after December 31, 2010. Because both Frank and Minnie died after December 31, 2010, section 2010(c)(5)(B) applies to both their estates.

V.   Congressional Intent and Due Process Concerns

Finally, the estate argues that section 2010(c)(5)(B) as applied by the Commissioner in this case is contrary to the congressional intent of portability and "unconstitutional for lack of due process" because it overrides the statute of limitations on assessment established in section 6501.

A. Congressional Intent as to Portability

Minnie's estate claims that the Commissioner's application of section 2010(c)(5)(B) in this case is "unfair" and "defeats Congressional intent as to portability." The Supreme Court has held that the statutory text is the most persuasive evidence of congressional intent. United States v. Am. Trucking Ass'ns, Inc., 310 U.S. 534, 542–543, 60 S. Ct. 1059, 84 L. Ed. 1345 (1940). Congress adopted a statute that explicitly gave the Commissioner the power to examine the returns of the predeceased spouse and adjust the amount of the DSUE outside of the period of limitations under section 6501. See sec. 2010(c)(5)(B). This is a clear indication that the Commissioner's exercise of this power is not in violation of congressional intent.

B. Statute of Limitations and Due Process Considerations of Section 2010(c)(5)(B)

Minnie's estate argues that section 2010(c)(5)(B) is "unconstitutional for want of due process of law in that there is no statute of limitations." The statute of limitations on assessment under section 6501 is not subverted by section 2010(c)(5)(B). Under section 2010(c)(5)(B) the Commissioner can examine the return of a predeceased spouse and adjust the DSUE without regard to the statute of limitations in section 6501. Section 2010(c)(5)(B) does not give the Commissioner the power to assess any tax against the estate of the predeceased spouse outside of the period of limitations. Both the temporary and final regulations implicitly make this point, providing that the IRS "may examine returns of each of the surviving spouse's deceased spouses whose DSUE amount is claimed to be included in the surviving spouse's applicable exclusion amount, regardless of whether the period of limitations on assessment has expired for any such return." Sec 20.2010–2(d), Estate Tax Regs.; sec. 20.2010–2T(d), Temporary Estate Tax Regs., 77 Fed. Reg. 36159–36160 (June 18, 2012). And they both go on to provide more explicitly:

> The IRS's authority to examine returns of a deceased spouse applies with respect to each transfer by the surviving spouse to which a DSUE amount is or has been applied. Upon examination, the IRS may adjust or eliminate the DSUE amount reported on such a return [of a deceased spouse]; however, the IRS may assess additional tax on that return only if that tax is assessed within the period of limitations on assessment under section 6501 applicable to the tax shown on that return.

Sec. 20.2010–3(d), Estate Tax Regs.; sec. 20.2010–3T, Temporary Estate Tax Regs., supra (with the bracketed text added to the final regulation). And finally, both the temporary and final regulations cite section 7602 "for the IRS's authority, when ascertaining the correctness of any return, to examine any returns that may be relevant or material to such inquiry."

Section 6501 is a statute of limitations on assessment. It provides that "except as otherwise provided * * * the amount of any tax imposed by this title shall be assessed within 3 years after the return was filed". Sec. 6501(a). Here, the Commissioner did not assess and is not assessing any tax against Frank's estate. Both Estate Tax Closing Documents show "$0" in "Net Estate Tax" for Frank's estate. The Commissioner did not issue a notice of deficiency to Frank's estate. An adjustment of the DSUE of the predeceased spouse, though it may affect the liability for a subsequent estate claiming the exclusion, is not an assessment of tax against the estate of the predeceased spouse. Accordingly, the statute of limitations on assessment under section 6501 is not implicated for the predeceased spouse.

Conclusion

The Commissioner acted within his legal authority when he examined the return filed by Frank's estate and adjusted the DSUE eligible to be claimed by Minnie's estate. And Minnie's estate must include the lifetime taxable gifts in the estate for the purposes of determining the amount of estate tax due under section 2001(b)(1).

To reflect the foregoing,

Decision will be entered for respondent.

PROBLEMS

In these problems, assume that the unified credit (basic exclusion amount) is $12,920,000 for all years.

1. Albert died in 2023, having made taxable transfers of $5,840,000 and having no taxable estate. An election was made on his estate tax return to permit his surviving spouse, Betty, to use his deceased spousal unused exclusion amount. As of Albert's death, Betty had made no taxable gifts. What is Betty's applicable exclusion amount? Can it be used to shelter both lifetime gifts and death time transfers?

2. Assume the same facts as in the prior problem, except that Betty subsequently married Joseph. Joseph predeceased Betty, having made $11,920,000 in taxable transfers during life and having no taxable estate. An election was made on Joseph's estate tax return to permit Betty to use Joseph's deceased spousal unused exclusion amount. What is Betty's applicable exclusion amount?

3. Assume the same facts as in the prior problems, except that Betty predeceased her second husband, Joseph. Betty's taxable estate is $9 million. An election is made on Betty's estate tax return to permit Joseph to use Betty's deceased spousal unused exclusion amount. What was

Betty's applicable exclusion amount? So long as Joseph remains unmarried, what is Joseph's basic exclusion amount? What is his applicable exclusion amount?

4.   Sam, penniless, was living in a trailer with his adult son, Lucky—and Judy, Sam's long-time girlfriend—when Sam learned that he had won $30 million net in the lottery. Later, after meeting with his tax-planning lawyer, Sam had a "chance" congratulatory meeting with equally penniless Rose, the terminally ill mother of Lucky. That meeting led to Sam proposing marriage to Rose. Sam and Rose married, and Rose died in 2022. Rose's will provided "everything to Sam" and named Sam as the executor. Sam, as executor, timely filed a federal estate tax return for Rose—albeit unnecessary except for the opportunity Sam exercised to elect to allow himself, as Rose's surviving spouse, to utilize Rose's deceased spousal unused exclusion amount. Sam then, learning that he, too, had a terminal illness, married penniless Judy, the girlfriend. Sam died in 2022. His will provided that Lucky was to receive "the maximum tax-free amount, free of trust, and the balance of his estate to Judy, free of trust." Judy got $4,160,000 (for which the marital deduction allowed by section 2056 was claimed on Sam's estate tax return) and, Lucky, $25,840,000 of Sam's $30 million. Judy died in 2023 with a will giving "everything to Lucky, Sam's boy." Judy had come to like Lucky during her off-and-on relationship with Sam. As a result, does Lucky take $30 million free of estate tax, $25,840,000 from Sam and $4,160,000 from Judy?

c.   Planning

Is portability a panacea (in the sense that it simplifies planning by eliminating tax as a reason to make use of a so-called bypass or credit shelter trust)? If a combined $25,840,000 estate, gift, and generation-skipping tax exemption is the goal of persons married to each other, portability is clearly no substitute for the credit shelter trust. The credit shelter trust provides credit protection. The credit shelter trust locks in the $12,920,000 exemption in the case where the surviving spouse remarries and is predeceased by the newly acquired spouse, resulting in substitution of the second deceased spouse's unused estate tax exemption—which might well be zero. The only arguments for portability are (1) basis step up at death of second spouse per section 1014; and (2) indexing of exemption for inflation (which would not be available as to property held in the credit shelter trust). See I.R.C. § 2010(c)(3)(B). The stepped-up basis at death for the credit shelter amount would be available for the credit shelter trust where a QTIP election is made. See I.R.C. § 2056(b)(7). However, if a QTIP election is made, there remains the risk that portability will be lost in the event of a subsequent marriage by the surviving spouse, the new spouse predeceases the surviving spouse (resulting in the loss of portability to the surviving spouse from the first marriage).

It should be noted, however, that the portability option, as a planning technique, has practical appeal in at least two cases. The first is the obvious one, that is, the case where the poorer spouse dies first without using fully the exemption available. Prior to the advent of portability, the planning option was for the richer spouse to make a lifetime transfer to the poorer spouse—commonly in the form of a QTIP trust per section 2523(f) to soak up the exemption available to the poorer spouse that otherwise would have gone underutilized. Use of this technique seems not to have become commonplace, richer spouses electing thereby to forego the assured use of the poorer spouse's exemption in anticipation of the poorer spouse dying first. Sometimes, too, the richer spouse will not have had available property readily transferable to the poorer spouse (for purposes of soaking up the poorer spouse's exemption in anticipation of the poorer spouse dying first). Examples include (1) the richer spouse's retirement plan benefits, benefits that will be included in the estate of the richer spouse at the death of the richer spouse but which are not transferable to the poorer spouse while the richer spouse is living; and (2) the situation where the richer spouse holds a testamentary general power of appointment over property, a power that will cause inclusion of the power property in the estate of the richer spouse at death—but a power that, by its terms, is not immediately exercisable, the power being exercisable by will of the richer spouse only at death. See I.R.C. § 2041.

The second case for planned utilization of portability is tax qualified retirement benefits and it is clearly the road more traveled. More particularly, tax deferral for the maximum period is thought the best counsel when planning for tax qualified retirement benefits. That goal is most easily realized, most easily facilitated, most understandable to the client, by selecting the joint and survivor government mandated default option. Dad dies; Mom survives; the tax qualified retirement benefits become Mom's with distribution over Mom's lifetime, all the while income taxation is postponed on the undistributed plan benefits. Taxpayers understand this option readily. Portability enhances its appeal. Passing the plan benefits through the credit shelter trust ensures dead hand control by the first to die spouse; no second spouses or other strangers here coming to receive any plan benefits remaining at Mom's death! However, maintaining income tax deferral for plan benefits until distributed over the lifetime of the surviving spouse requires very careful structuring of the credit shelter trust; otherwise, tax deferral is lost. That coupled with the more complicated arrangement makes the joint and survivor option, for many, the clear choice.

Portability is not available to non-spouses. Thus, from a sociological perspective, it is fair to say that some might find portability a reason to take a spouse while others might find portability a reason not to remarry.

2. CREDIT FOR GIFT TAX

The section 2012 credit for gift tax has very limited importance. It applies only to gift tax paid with respect to a gift made prior to 1977, and then only to a gift that is included in the decedent's gross estate.

For example, assume that in 1970 the decedent made a transfer to a trust but reserved a power to change beneficial enjoyment. Further assume that the power to change beneficial enjoyment could be exercised only with the consent of a person who held a trust interest adverse to exercise. Such a transfer would have been considered a completed gift for gift tax purposes, pursuant to Regulation § 25.2511–2(e), with the result that gift tax might have been paid. Upon the decedent's later death, the trust property would nevertheless be included in the decedent's gross estate pursuant to section 2036. In such a case, the decedent's estate is entitled to a credit for gift tax paid with respect to the 1970 gift, but subject to various limitations described in section 2012(a), (b), and (d).

The section 2012 credit has no application to gifts after 1976 because such gifts are fully addressed under the unified gift and estate tax regime adopted in 1976. Specifically, section 2001(b)(2) reduces the estate tax by the amount of gift tax payable with respect to gifts made after 1976.

3. CREDIT FOR TAX ON PRIOR TRANSFERS

The deaths of members of successive generations within a short period of time could have serious tax consequences for a family. For example, assume that a widowed mother dies with a large estate, almost all of which is subjected to an estate tax burden of 40%. Assume further that the mother bequeaths the entirety of her estate to her unmarried son, who dies a year later, when another 40% tax is imposed on what is left after payment of tax at the mother's death. As a result, the family's resources could be greatly reduced within a single year.

Congress has responded to such circumstances by adopting the section 2013 credit for tax on prior transfers. If the son dies within two years after the mother, the entirety of the estate tax paid by the mother's estate can be credited against the tax that would otherwise be imposed at the son's death, largely preventing double taxation. The credit is subject to important limitations relating to both the mother's estate and the son's estate, as described in section 2013(b) and (c), and fully explored in Regulations §§ 20.2013–2, 20.2013–3, and 20.2013–6.

A credit is available if the son's death occurs at any time up to 10 years after the mother's death, but the credit is progressively limited in amount. If the son dies within two years after the mother's death, a full credit (subject to the section 2013(b) and (c) limitations) is allowed. If the son dies during the third or fourth year after the mother's death, the credit is reduced to 80% of the amount otherwise allowable, and the credit is progressively reduced to 20% if the son's death occurs in the 9th or 10th year. See I.R.C. § 2013(a).

The credit is also available at 100% if the son dies during the two years *before* the mother's death. This rule would apply in circumstances such as these: A mother creates a trust, with income to daughter and a vested remainder to son at daughter's death. The mother retains a power to change beneficial enjoyment that causes the trust to be included in her gross estate under section 2036. The son dies first, and the value of the vested remainder is taxed in his gross estate. One year later the mother dies, and the entire trust is taxed in her gross estate. Under section 2013(a), and subject again to the section 2013(b) and (c) limitations, a credit would be available to the son's estate for a portion of the tax paid at the mother's death.

There is no requirement of family or other relationship between the two decedents. Section 2013 may apply if there is any passage of property from one decedent to another.

B. WHEN A RETURN IS REQUIRED

Form 706, United States Estate Tax Return, must be filed by the executor for the estate of every U.S. citizen or resident whose gross estate exceeds the basic exclusion amount for the year in which the decedent dies. I.R.C. § 6018(a)(1). The basic exclusion amount is specified in section 2010(c)(3). For example, in 2023 the basic exclusion amount was $12,920,000.

If the decedent made taxable gifts after 1976, an estate tax might be payable even if the gross estate is less than the basic exclusion amount. This is so because adjusted taxable gifts are added to the taxable estate for purposes of determining the estate tax under section 2001. I.R.C. § 2001(b)(1)(B). For this reason, section 6018(a)(3)(A) requires that, for purposes of determining whether an estate tax return is required, the basic exclusion amount must be reduced by the decedent's adjusted taxable gifts. For example, assume that the decedent died in 2023, when the basic exclusion amount was $12,920,000. Further assume that the decedent had a gross estate of only $8,000,000 but had made adjusted taxable gifts, as defined in section 2001(b), in the amount of $7,000,000. Although the decedent's gross estate was less than the section 2010(c) basic exclusion amount of $12,920,000, section 6018(a)(3)(A) required that the filing threshold be reduced by the $7,000,000 of adjusted taxable gifts to $5,920,000. Because the $8,000,000 gross estate exceeded this amount, a return was required.

C. WHO MUST PAY AND WHEN

Section 2002 states that the estate tax "shall be paid by the executor." The full import of this brief provision is made clear in the regulations, which describe the extent of the executor's responsibility. The regulations explain that the requirement of payment by the executor pertains to the whole tax without regard to the fact that the gross estate may consist in part of property not included in the probate estate and therefore is not within the possession of the executor. See Treas. Reg. § 20.2002–1. Hence the executor is liable for tax relating to an asset entirely beyond the executor's control. Executors are well advised to make distributions to beneficiaries only after payment of the tax, or at least provision for payment, is complete. However, "if there is no executor or administrator appointed, qualified, and acting within the United States, then any person in actual or constructive possession of any property of the decedent" is considered the "executor" for purposes of section 2002. I.R.C. § 2203.

There are procedures available for securing release from personal liability for the executor. Section 2204 offers the executor and other fiduciaries an opportunity to request early determination of the tax liability and release from personal liability after payment of the stated amount.

Although the executor is personally liable for the estate tax, the executor will not pay the tax out of the executor's own pocket (unless the executor has prematurely distributed the assets to beneficiaries who have left for parts unknown). The estate tax liability is an obligation of the decedent's estate. It is a debt—like any other—to be charged against the decedent's assets.

But several problems complicate the executor's charging of the tax against estate assets. One is the sheer size of the tax obligation. An estate tax rate of 40% can wipe out a substantial portion of the decedent's assets. Another problem is the presence of bequests qualifying for estate tax deductions, such as bequests to a spouse or charity. The spouse or charity may expect to receive the bequest free of any estate tax burden. Furthermore, to the extent the estate tax is actually charged against a marital or charitable bequest, the marital or charitable deduction will be concomitantly reduced, in turn increasing the tax due. I.R.C. §§ 2055(c) and 2056(b)(4)(A). Finally, there may be substantial assets that are beyond the executor's control but nevertheless subject to estate tax, such as life insurance and property in trusts as to which the decedent retained interests or powers. The tax on such nonprobate assets may be large and, if charged against the assets owned outright by the decedent, could wipe out the probate assets, perhaps destroying or dramatically reducing the value of bequests the decedent thought important.

As a result, the question of who will ultimately bear the cost of the United States estate tax (as well as state death tax) should be a central part of any estate plan and must not be left to chance. The prospective decedent should have a well-conceived plan as to who will bear the burden of death taxes, and that plan should be clearly stated in the appropriate documents, especially the will or revocable trust that dictates disposition of the primary assets.

In planning for payment of the estate tax, the planner should take into account these principles:

1. The decedent has the power to dictate where the tax burden will fall, in effect preempting any or all of the rules described below. This is done primarily by including a specific directive in the will or revocable trust that is the decedent's primary dispositive document. Of course, if the tax exceeds the assets designated as the source of funds, the executor will have no choice but to charge the tax against other assets, in accordance with the principles that follow.

2. The Internal Revenue Code empowers the executor to charge an appropriate share of the tax against certain nonprobate assets that are included in the gross estate. In each case the executor's power to charge the nonprobate asset may be negated by the decedent's will.

    (a) If insurance on the life of the decedent is included in the gross estate, the executor may recover the allocable estate tax from the beneficiary of the life insurance. I.R.C. § 2206. The portion of the tax to be recovered is determined by the ratio of the included life insurance to the taxable estate. For example, assume that the estate tax due is $1,050,000, the life insurance included in the gross estate is $2,000,000, and the taxable estate is $8,000,000. The executor would be entitled to recover 2,000,000/8,000,000 × $1,050,000, or $262,500, from the life insurance beneficiary.

    (b) If by reason of section 2041 the gross estate includes a trust over which the decedent had a general power of appointment, the executor can recover the allocable estate tax from the trustee of that trust. I.R.C. § 2207. The allocable tax is determined in the same way as with life insurance.

    (c) If the gross estate includes trust property by reason of section 2036, because of the decedent's retention of a power or interest, the executor can recover the allocable estate tax from the trust. I.R.C. § 2207B. Again, the allocable tax is determined in the same way as with life insurance.

(d) If the gross estate includes property as to which a qualified terminable interest property (QTIP) election under section 2523(f) or section 2056(b)(7) was made, with the result that the property is included in the surviving spouse's gross estate under section 2044, the executor can collect an allocable share of the tax from the QTIP property. I.R.C. § 2207A(a). The tax allocable to the QTIP property is not a pro rata portion, as with life insurance, powers of appointment, and retained life estates. Instead, the tax recoverable by the executor is the incremental tax, i.e., the amount by which the estate tax is increased by reason of inclusion of the QTIP property in the decedent's gross estate. I.R.C. § 2207A(a)(1). Hence the highest applicable tax rates are in effect assigned to the QTIP property, maximizing the amount the executor can recover.

3. If none of the recovery provisions described in Paragraph 2 apply, and the will or revocable trust is silent as to the tax burden, the law of the state governing administration of the estate will determine who bears the tax. The United States Supreme Court has held that for this purpose the estate tax is like any other debt of the decedent, and state (rather than federal) law will determine the assets against which the tax is to be charged. Riggs v. Del Drago, 317 U.S. 95 (1942).

(a) A minority of states apply the "burden-on-the-residue rule," i.e., the tax is charged against the residuary estate until it is exhausted, after which it is charged against specific and pecuniary bequests as determined by local law.[4] This rule can prove very damaging because it may cause the tax to be charged against property going to a spouse or charity, thereby reducing the marital or charitable deduction, which will further increase the tax due, and so on. In some states the courts have created common law exceptions to the residue rule, freeing the marital residue share (and sometimes even a charitable residue share) from tax.

(b) Most states have rejected the residue rule and have adopted "apportionment" statutes that specifically allocate the tax burden in the absence of direction by the

---

4   See, e.g., Fla. Stat. § 733.817(3) (2022); Maierhofer v. Maierhofer, 767 N.E.2d 850, 852 (IL. App. 3d 2002); Estate of Sheppard v. Schleis, 782 N.W.2d 85, 96 (Wis. 2010).

decedent.[5] Typically, such statutes charge the tax only against interests that are not deductible for estate tax purposes; in other words, marital and charitable beneficiaries have no responsibility to pay any of the tax unless other assets are insufficient. The Uniform Estate Tax Apportionment Act (2003) is a typical apportionment statute of this kind.

The presence of a tax burden provision in the will or revocable trust does not guarantee the optimum result unless it clearly resolves all issues. Such a provision should be absolutely clear and take into account the possibility of dispute over interpretation, as occurred in the following case.

FIRST NAT'L BANK OF ATLANTA V. UNITED STATES
United States Court of Appeals, Fifth Circuit, 1981.
634 F.2d 212.

PER CURIAM:

In this will construction case, the district court held that federal estate taxes are to be paid out of the residue of the testator's estate, including the marital trust property. Although plaintiffs vigorously argue on appeal that the testator intended to maximize his marital deduction and thereby minimize estate taxes, that intent is not clear on the face of the document and, absent such a showing, the unambiguous provision of the will that all estate taxes should be paid from the residue of the estate will govern.

Daniel L. McWhorter died testate on June 16, 1972. His will provides for certain specific bequests and then for the residue of his estate to be divided equally between a marital trust and a family trust. Item Three specifically provides:

> If my wife survives me, I direct my Executors (after paying all of the above bequests, and after paying all debts, taxes and expenses other than Estate Taxes) to divide the residue of my estate into two parts, which (after adjusting for the insurance and other property payable to my wife hereinafter mentioned) shall be equal in size. I hereby designate these as Parts A and B. There shall be regarded as a portion of my estate assigned to Part A, for the purpose of this calculation only, the following: (1) any insurance on my life which is so payable to my wife as to be lawfully the subject of a marital deduction for Federal Estate Tax purposes, and (2) the value of any other property passing to my wife either outside this Will or under any other Item of this Will in such manner as to qualify as a part of such marital

---

[5] See, e.g., Kan. Stat. Ann. § 79–15, 126 (2022); Md. Code Ann., Tax-General § 7–308 (2022); N.Y. Estates, Powers and Trusts Law § 2–1.8 (Consol. 2022); S.C. Code Ann. § 62–3–916 (2022); S.D. Codified Laws § 29A–3–916 (2022).

deduction. . . .There shall not be included in Part A any property as to which such a marital deduction would not be allowed.

Regarding payment of estate taxes, Item Seven of the will states that all estate taxes shall be paid from the residue:

> All estate taxes shall be paid from the residue of my estate, and no claim shall be made against any life insurance beneficiaries for payment of any pro rata part of such taxes. Notwithstanding the foregoing, my Executor shall make claim against the appointee, if permitted by law, for any such estate taxes assessed because of any power of appointment which I may have.

An estate tax return was filed which calculated the marital deduction as one-half of the residue before payment of estate taxes. The Internal Revenue Service determined that the deduction should have been calculated after payment of estate taxes and assessed a deficiency. The co-executors of the estate paid the tax and then brought this suit for a refund.

Section 2056 of the Internal Revenue Code allows a deduction from the gross estate for "the value of any interest in property which passes or has passed from the decedent to his surviving spouse," up to fifty percent of the adjusted gross estate [as to decedents dying before 1982]. 26 U.S.C.A. § 2056. The value of any interest passing to the surviving spouse for which a deduction is allowed, however, is the net value of such interest after payment of any estate taxes charged against it under the will. 26 U.S.C.A. § 2056(b)(4). The sole issue on appeal is whether the district court correctly ruled as a matter of law that the McWhorter will requires the estate taxes to be paid out of the residue before division, and thus paid in part out of the marital bequest, or whether the taxes should be paid after division and only out of the non-marital bequest.

Proper construction of a will is determined by reference to state law, Riggs v. Del Drago, 317 U.S. 95, 97–98, 63 S. Ct. 109, 110, 87 L. Ed. 106 (1942), in this case the law of Georgia. * * *

The cardinal rule of will construction under Georgia law is to ascertain the intention of the testator by looking at the document and giving consideration to all of its parts. * * * Plaintiffs argue that the language used by the testator in setting up the marital trust evidences his intent to maximize the marital deduction. They contend that the provision in Item Three that the residue be divided, after payment of taxes other than estate taxes, shows the testator did not intend for the taxes to be paid out of the marital portion. They suggest that the language in Item Seven that all estate taxes be paid from the residue of the estate was mistakenly added as part of a "formbook" provision designed to instruct executors on whether to seek estate taxes from life insurance beneficiaries and appointees of any powers of appointment.

The difficulty with plaintiffs' position is that there is no provision for payment of estate taxes only out of the non-marital portion of the estate, even if the residue were to be divided prior to payment of such taxes. In essence, plaintiffs ask this Court to either eliminate Item Seven, or rewrite it to read "[a]ll estate taxes shall be paid from Part B of the residue of my estate," or otherwise define the word "residue" in Item Three and Item Seven in two different ways.

Item Seven, however, clearly provides that estate taxes are to be paid out of the "residue" of the estate, which includes the marital trust property. Item Three provides that the "residue" will be divided into two parts. Neither part is thereafter referred to any place in the will as the "residue." Nothing in the will suggests that the word "residue" as used in Item Three is to have any different meaning when used in Item Seven. While one of the purposes of the will clearly is to take advantage of the marital deduction, nothing therein suggests the testator's intention to maximize that deduction. Even if plaintiff's interpretation of the will were correct, the marital deduction would not be used to the maximum. To the contrary, the specific bequests to siblings which are to be paid before dividing the residue into the marital and family trusts deprives the arrangement of any maximization of the marital deduction. Finally, even though the parenthetical in Item Three that the residue is to be divided "after paying all debts, taxes and expenses other than Estate Taxes" would indicate that McWhorter might provide that the estate taxes be paid in some manner other than out of the residue, the language of Item Seven is unambiguous, and "if the clause as it stands may have effect, it shall be so construed, however well satisfied the court may be of a different testamentary intention." Ga. Code Ann. § 113–806 (1975). * * *

AFFIRMED.

PROBLEM

Tammy Larson died this year, domiciled in a state that does not impose a death tax. Her husband, Wilmer, had died three years earlier. Tammy's daughter, Linda, was appointed executor of Tammy's estate. Tammy's will bequeaths the entirety of her estate to Linda.

At the time of her death Tammy owned only one asset (other than the Aetna insurance policy described below): Amazon stock worth $6,550,000. The cost of administering Tammy's estate was $50,000, and all of this was paid from Tammy's probate assets. Tammy's administrator elected to deduct the $50,000 for estate rather than income tax purposes.

Tammy was insured under an Aetna Life Insurance Co. policy with a face value of $3,000,000. Tammy owned the policy and all incidents of ownership at the time of her death. The beneficiary was Tammy's nephew, Sam.

Ten years before her death Tammy had transferred $1,000,000 to the Larson Trust. At the time of the transfer Tammy's age was 72. The trust provided that Tammy was to receive all income from the trust until her death, at which time the principal was to be paid to Tammy's uncle, Horatio. On the date of Tammy's death there was no accrued income, and the value of the trust assets was $5,920,000.

Fifteen years before Tammy's death, Tammy's mother, Alice, had created a trust that provided income for life to Tammy, with remainder to Tammy's brother, Wilbur. The trust provided that until Tammy's death Tammy had the power to appoint trust assets to herself to the extent necessary for Tammy's support, health, or comfort. Tammy had never exercised this power. On the date of Tammy's death this trust had a value of $2,500,000.

How much estate tax must be paid as a result of Tammy's death? How much, if any, of the tax will ultimately be borne, respectively, by Linda, Sam, Horatio, and Wilbur?

NOTE

In general, the estate tax shown on the return is due and payable at the time fixed by statute for the filing of the return, without regard to any extension of time obtained for the filing of the return. I.R.C. § 6151(a). Thus, payment of the estate tax must be made within nine months after the date of the decedent's death. See I.R.C. § 6075.

D. EXTENSIONS OF TIME FOR PAYMENT

1. DEFERRAL BY CONSENT

Section 6161(a)(1) authorizes the IRS to extend the time for payment of the tax shown on any return for a period not in excess of six months from the date fixed for payment. This applies to both the estate and gift taxes, except that the period of extension for the estate tax may be as long as 12 months.

In addition, in the case of the estate tax, the IRS may grant an extension not in excess of 10 years from the original due date where reasonable cause is demonstrated. I.R.C. § 6161(a)(2). See Treas. Reg. § 20.6161–1(a)(1) for illustrations of "reasonable cause."

Interestingly, Regulation § 20.6161–1 still includes references to deferral for "undue hardship." However, this is no longer operative, as the "undue hardship" basis for deferral was deleted from the statute in 1976.

2. DEFERRAL BY RIGHT

The executor is entitled to defer payment of the tax allocable to a reversionary or remainder interest included in a decedent's estate for six months after the end of the prior interest.[6] I.R.C. § 6163(a). For example, assume that a mother creates a trust at her death, giving a life estate to a daughter and a vested remainder to a son. Assume further that the son predeceases the daughter, in which case the son's remainder would be taxed in the son's estate, although it will not be possessory until the daughter's death—perhaps many years later. The executor of the son's estate could defer payment of the tax allocable to the son's remainder until six months after the daughter's death, but the Commissioner could require posting of adequate security as a condition of the extension. See I.R.C. §§ 6163(c) and 6165.

A further opportunity for deferral of payment of the estate tax is granted by section 6166 where a substantial portion of the gross estate is represented by a closely held business. The statute provides explicit and detailed rules for determining what constitutes a closely held business. If the estate qualifies under these rules, the estate tax attributable to the interest in the closely held business included in the gross estate may be paid, at the election of the executor, in as many as 10 equal installments beginning five years after the original return due date (nine months after death). Interest must be paid annually until principal payments begin. I.R.C. § 6166(a). Assuming maximum deferral, the payment pattern operates in this fashion:

1. On the return due date (nine months after death) the executor pays the entire estate tax that is not allocable to the qualifying closely held business.

2. On each of the anniversary dates one, two, three, four, and five years after the return due date, the executor pays interest on the deferred tax outstanding during the prior year. On the anniversary date five years after the return due date, the executor also pays one-tenth of the deferred tax. I.R.C. § 6166(a)(3).

3. On each of the anniversary dates six years after the return due date through fourteen years after the return due date, the executor pays one-tenth of the deferred tax. Also, on each of these anniversary dates the executor pays interest on the deferred tax outstanding during the prior year.

This election to pay in installments is limited to estates in which the value of the closely held business exceeds 35 percent of the adjusted gross estate. I.R.C. § 6166(a)(1). For this purpose, the adjusted gross estate is the

---

[6]   The tax originally deferred under section 6166 may become due and payable prior to the end of the elected installment period where substantial portions of the closely held business are sold or distributed or where substantial assets are withdrawn from the business. See I.R.C. § 6166(g) for the detailed rules and exceptions in this regard.

gross estate reduced by deductions under sections 2053 and 2054, such as claims, administration expenses, and losses. I.R.C. § 6166(b)(6).

The term "closely held business" is defined in the statute as a trade or business: (1) carried on by the decedent as a proprietor; (2) carried on by the decedent as a partner in a partnership of which the decedent owned 20 percent or more of the capital interest or in which there were 45 or fewer partners; or (3) operated by a corporation in which the decedent owned 20 percent or more of the voting stock or in which there were 45 or fewer shareholders. I.R.C. § 6166(b)(1). Deferral is not available for "passive assets," and the deferral amount is reduced to the extent an otherwise qualifying business holds "passive assets." I.R.C. § 6166(b)(9). The Tax Court has jurisdiction to render a declaratory judgment as to qualification for deferral under section 6166. I.R.C. § 7479.

Interest is imposed where the tax payment is deferred. In general, the interest rate imposed on the deferred tax is 45% of the underpayment rate established under section 6621(a)(2), which changes quarterly. I.R.C. § 6601(j)(1)(B). A special 2% rate, however, is available for a portion of the deferred tax. The 2% portion is the tax on the applicable exclusion amount for the year of death plus $1,000,000 (indexed after 1998) less the applicable credit amount for the year of death. I.R.C. § 6601(j)(2).

For example, in 2023 the indexed value of the $1,000,000 amount stated in section 6601(j)(2) was $1,750,000. Also, in 2023, the basic exclusion amount was $12,920,000. I.R.C. § 2010(c)(2)(A). The tax before credits on the total of $1,750,000 and $12,920,000, or $14,670,000, was $5,813,800. Subtracting the 2023 applicable credit amount of $5,113,800 from this amount produced the portion of the tax that qualified for the 2% rate: $700,000. Therefore, in the case of a decedent dying during 2023, the first $700,000 of deferred tax qualified for the 2% rate, and the remainder of the deferred tax bore interest at 45% of the section 6621(a)(2) underpayment rate. The $700,000 amount can be reached more directly simply by multiplying the indexed section 6601(j)(2)(A) number ($1,750,000 for 2023) by the tax rate (40%).

The benefits of the favorable interest rates on section 6166 deferred tax are diminished because interest on section 6166 deferral is not deductible for either income or estate tax purposes. See I.R.C. §§ 163(k), 2053(c)(1)(D).

PROBLEM

Norman Wilson, a widower, died on March 20, 2023, with a gross estate of $18,050,000. Funeral and administration expenses deductible under section 2053(a) totaled $50,000. Assume that the total estate tax payable was $2,568,000 after all credits. Further assume that the section 6601(j)(2)(A)(i) indexed dollar amount for 2023 was $1,750,000. A total of $14,500,000 of

Norman's gross estate consisted of shares in a closely held corporation that was actively involved in a manufacturing business. At his death Norman owned 40% of the stock in the corporation, and six unrelated parties owned the remaining 60%. The remaining assets of Norman's estate consisted of readily marketable securities. Norman's executor wished to defer payment of tax as long as possible.

Was deferral available under section 6166? If section 6166 deferral was available, what amounts of taxes and interest would have to be paid on December 20 of each of the years 2023 through 2029, assuming Norman's executor elected to defer payment as long as possible and assuming the section 6621(a)(2) underpayment rate throughout the period 2023 through 2029 was 5% per annum? For purposes of this problem, disregard the daily compounding requirement of section 6622(a).

E. PAYMENT THROUGH STOCK REDEMPTIONS

Even with deferral under section 6166, obtaining cash for payment of estate taxes may be difficult for the decedent's family. That is especially so if the family's assets consist largely of a closely held business in corporate form. If the corporation has not made the election to be taxed as an S Corporation pursuant to section 1361 *et seq.*, the general rule is that withdrawal of funds from the business is treated as a dividend to the extent of the corporation's "earnings and profits"—essentially its retained earnings. See I.R.C. §§ 301(c)(1) and 316. Although there are exceptions to this dividend rule, they are narrow and difficult to satisfy in the case of most closely held businesses.

This problem is greatly alleviated by section 303, which permits withdrawal of an amount sufficient to pay death taxes (including the United States estate tax), as well as funeral and administration expenses, with much more favorable income tax treatment. Under section 303, a redemption of stock for consideration up to this amount is treated as an exchange of the stock by the owner—typically the executor. Therefore, the dividend rule does not apply, and the estate realizes income from the distribution only to the extent the amount received in the redemption exceeds the estate's basis for the stock. Because the estate's basis will be the value of the stock at the date of death (or alternate valuation date) per section 1014(a), and not the decedent's possibly much lower original cost basis, the taxable gain will usually be small.

Section 303 redemption treatment is available only if the stock in the redeeming corporation included in the decedent's gross estate has a value greater than 35% of the decedent's gross estate less sections 2053 and 2054 deductions. I.R.C. § 303(b)(2). In some cases, the stock of multiple corporations may be aggregated to meet the 35% threshold. See I.R.C. § 303(b)(2)(B).

F. NONCOMPLIANCE WITH FILING AND PAYMENT OBLIGATIONS—PENALTIES

1. PENALTIES

a. Failure to File and Failure to Pay Tax

The Treasury has an array of penalties to administer for noncompliance with the filing and payment obligations imposed by the estate, gift, and generation-skipping taxes. First, there is a civil penalty for failure to file estate and gift tax returns imposed under section 6651(a)(1) of five percent of the tax owing added for the first month of delinquency, and an additional five percent for each delinquent month thereafter—but only up to a total penalty of 25 percent. Similar penalties apply in the case of underpayment of tax. I.R.C. § 6651(a)(2). Furthermore, an additional penalty is imposed where the taxpayer fails to pay the tax after notice and demand have been made on the taxpayer by the IRS. I.R.C. § 6651(a)(3).

Whether one is liable for an addition to tax for the untimely filing of a return is essentially a question of fact. Because the decision in each case depends upon its particular circumstances, specific rules capable of easy application are nearly impossible to formulate. However, it is useful to note that the United States Supreme Court has held that a late filing penalty applies even in cases where the executor relies on his attorney to file the estate tax return and the attorney, through no fault of the executor, is delinquent. United States v. Boyle, 469 U.S. 241 (1985). In another case, Estate of Buring v. Commissioner, T.C. Memo, 1985–610, 51 T.C.M. (CCH) 113 (1985), the Tax Court distinguished *Boyle*. In *Buring*, on the advice of an accountant, the donor did not file gift tax returns. When it was later determined that a gift tax return was due, the IRS asserted a late-filing penalty. Holding that no penalty applied, the Tax Court said that reliance on a tax professional in concluding that no tax return is required is "reasonable cause" for not filing the return.

b. Negligence and the Wages of Fraud—Heavier Penalties

1. *Civil Penalties.* Under section 6662, if the underpayment of estate or gift tax is due to negligence or disregard of the rules and regulations, a penalty of 20 percent of the underpayment is imposed unless the taxpayer acted with good faith and for reasonable cause. See I.R.C. § 6664(c). Negligence, for purposes of the 20-percent penalty, means a failure to make a reasonable attempt to comply with the applicable rules and regulations. I.R.C. § 6662(c). If the underpayment is due to fraud, the penalty jumps to 75 percent of the underpayment. I.R.C. § 6663(a). Similarly, the penalty for fraudulent failure to file an estate, gift, or generation-skipping tax return is 15 percent per month of the net tax due (rather than five percent per

month where failure to file is not fraudulent), up to a maximum of 75 percent. I.R.C. § 6651(a)(1) and (f).

2. *Criminal Penalties.* Strong criminal sanctions are in place to chasten persons who willfully or fraudulently endeavor to avoid paying estate and gift taxes. Straightforward and willful refusal to file or pay these taxes is chargeable as a misdemeanor, subject to imprisonment for not more than one year or a fine up to $25,000 or both. I.R.C. § 7203. But, if a person has committed the felony of tax evasion, such as purposeful nondisclosure of taxable assets, section 7201 provides for imprisonment for up to five years and a fine of up to $100,000 or both.

c. Undervaluation

Even if there is no negligence, an "accuracy-related" penalty may be imposed if the value assigned to an asset on the gift or estate tax return is 65% or less of the value finally determined. The penalty is increased if the value reported on the return is 40% or less of the value finally determined. I.R.C. § 6662(g) and (h). This penalty can be avoided if the taxpayer can show that there was "reasonable cause" for the reported value and the taxpayer acted in good faith. I.R.C. § 6664(c)(1).

The penalty for undervaluation is more fully explored above in Chapter 14.

d. Preparer Penalties

1. *Civil Penalties.* Congress has adopted penalties designed to prevent "audit roulette." Very few income tax returns are audited. As a result, a taxpayer might be tempted to take an entirely erroneous (but favorable to the taxpayer) position on the return, thereby reducing tax liability. The odds that the error would be spotted by the IRS might be very low. As a result, Congress has adopted rules designed to penalize tax return preparers who facilitate this practice. Because a high percentage of gift and estate tax returns are subjected to more thorough review than income tax returns, the "audit roulette" potential is much lower with gift and estate tax returns. Nevertheless, the preparer penalties apply to gift and estate tax returns with the same force as income tax returns.

If a preparer prepares a return in which the taxpayer takes a position that is not supported by "substantial authority," the general rule is that the preparer must pay a penalty equal to the greater of $1,000 or 50% of the income derived by the preparer with respect to the return. I.R.C. § 6694(a)(1) and (2)(A). If the unsupported position is adequately disclosed, however, the penalty does not apply if there is a "reasonable basis" for the position. I.R.C. § 6694(a)(2)(B). The regulations describe what constitutes "adequate disclosure." See Treas. Reg. § 1.6694–2(d)(3). The regulations also define "reasonable basis" for this purpose. Treas. Reg. § 1.6694–

2(d)(2). The penalty does not apply if there is a reasonable cause for the understatement and the preparer acted in good faith. I.R.C. § 6694(a)(3).

If the position taken on the return represents a "willful" attempt to understate liability or is attributable to "reckless or intentional disregard of rules or regulations," a more severe penalty is imposed: the greater of $5,000 or 75% of the income to be derived by the preparer with respect to the return (less any penalty under § 6694(a)). I.R.C. § 6694(b).

2. *Criminal Penalties.* The criminal penalties set forth in sections 7201 and 7206 can, in appropriate cases, be imposed on the preparer as well as the taxpayer. A preparer who participates in a false or fraudulent return could be guilty of violating section 7206(2), committing a felony punishable by $100,000 or imprisonment for 3 years, or both. A preparer who participates in willful tax evasion could be guilty of violating section 7201, triggering a penalty of $100,000 or imprisonment for 5 years, or both.

2. INTEREST

Section 6601 imposes interest on tax underpayments, payments under extended time arrangements (such as section 6166), and nonpayments. This interest is imposed on any tax not paid on or before the last date prescribed for payment.

In general, interest on tax underpayments, nonpayments, and extended payments is nondeductible for income tax purposes. I.R.C. § 163(h). However, interest is deductible for income tax purposes if payment of the estate tax is deferred under section 6163 (reversionary interests). I.R.C.§ 163(h)(2)(E).

Interest paid with respect to the estate tax is generally deductible for estate tax purposes under section 2053(a)(2) as an administration expense. Rev. Rul. 80–250, 1980–2 C.B. 278. However, as with other administration expenses, the deduction may not be taken for both income and estate tax purposes. See I.R.C. § 642(g).

Interest on tax deferred under section 6166 is not deductible for either income or estate tax purposes. I.R.C. §§ 163(k), 2053(c)(1)(D).

NOTE

There is a provision in the Internal Revenue Code for a general lien for unpaid federal taxes. See I.R.C. § 6321. There is, in addition to the general lien for unpaid federal taxes under section 6321, a special lien for estate and gift taxes provided by section 6324. The special lien, unlike the general lien, attaches immediately when the tax liability arises and lasts for 10 years.

PART 5

GENERATION-SKIPPING TAX

(Chapter 13 of the Internal Revenue Code)

■ ■ ■

CHAPTER 29

GENERATION-SKIPPING TRANSFER TAX

(SECTIONS 2601–2664)

■ ■ ■

A. INTRODUCTION

After a half-century of experience with gift and estate taxes, it became apparent that taxpayers with substantial resources and astute advisers could dramatically reduce or entirely eliminate the impact of these taxes by "skipping" generations. Typically, this involved use of trusts that provided economic benefits for younger generation family members without causing the trust assets to be included in the gross estates of those younger generation family members.

For example, at her death a mother would create a trust for the benefit of her daughter throughout the daughter's life, with remainder to her granddaughter at the daughter's death. The daughter would be named trustee of the trust, would receive the income from the trust, and she would have a power to invade the trust principal limited by an ascertainable standard. This arrangement would permit the daughter to manage the trust investments, thereby both preserving family control of the trust assets and permitting the daughter to control the amount of income produced. Yet none of the trust assets—other than income or principal actually distributed to the daughter—would be included in the daughter's gross estate for estate tax purposes. Although an estate tax would have been paid at the mother's death, the trust assets would pass to the granddaughter entirely free of gift or estate tax at the daughter's death. For transfer tax purposes, the daughter's generation would be "skipped."

This "generation-skipping" strategy can be extended much further if desired. The mother could provide for the trust to continue not just throughout the daughter's life, but also throughout the life of the granddaughter, and then throughout the life of a great granddaughter, and so on. At each generation the living descendant would manage the property, receive its income, and have a limited opportunity to invade principal—but with no inclusion in her gross estate. Hence, multiple generations could be "skipped" for tax purposes, enabling a family of substantial resources to control its assets (such as a closely held business), enjoy the income from the property, and have access to principal when

773

needed, yet avoid estate tax exposure for many decades subsequent to the mother's death. Such "generation-skipping trusts" became standard practice for families of substantial wealth.

The only limitation on the longevity of these arrangements was the common law Rule Against Perpetuities, which required that the trust property eventually vest in specific individuals, thereby ultimately exposing the property to gift or estate tax. Even so, trusts lasting more than 100 years could readily be devised without running afoul of the Rule Against Perpetuities. Also, as explained later in this chapter, most states have by statute eliminated or relaxed the common law Rule Against Perpetuities.

As a practical matter, generation-skipping trusts were available only to the most prosperous of families—those that could keep their assets locked up in trusts and afford the sophisticated planning and drafting involved. As a result, those who should have been most directly impacted by the gift and estate taxes were often effectively shielded from taxation for several generations.

Congress responded in 1976, adding to the Code Chapter 13, which imposed an entirely new tax on generation-skipping transfers. This early version of the tax proved to be so complex in comprehension and computation that Congress was confronted with two alternatives: repeal it or substantially revise it. With the Tax Reform Act of 1986, Congress took the latter alternative. With the support of the Treasury Congress completely revised Chapter 13, keeping the same objectives but designing provisions intended to be simpler in application and understanding. In the process, Congress repealed the original version of Chapter 13 retroactively and provided for the new version to become effective, generally, with respect to transfers *to* generation-skipping arrangements made after October 22, 1986.

The House Ways and Means Committee Report accompanying the Tax Reform Act of 1986 explained Congress' reasoning:

> The committee believes, as it stated when the generation-skipping transfer tax originally was enacted in 1976, that the purpose of the three transfer taxes (gift, estate, and generation-skipping) is not only to raise revenue, but also to do so in a manner that has as nearly as possible a uniform effect. This policy is best served when transfer tax consequences do not vary widely depending on whether property is transferred outright to immediately succeeding generations or is transferred in ways that skip generations. The committee determined that the present generation-skipping transfer tax is unduly complicated. Therefore, the committee determined that this tax should be replaced with a simplified tax, determined at a flat rate. The bill

accomplishes the committee's goal of simplified administration while ensuring that transfers having a similar substantial effect will be subject to tax in a similar manner.

H.R. Rep. No. 99–426, 99th Cong., 1st Sess. at 824 (1985), reprinted in 1986–3 CB 824 (Vol. 2).

As noted above, the generation-skipping transfer tax applies only to transfers to generation-skipping arrangements made after October 22, 1986. It is important to note that the transfer referred to is the transfer *to* the trust, such as the mother's transfer in trust in the example above. Therefore, the generation-skipping tax has no application to generation-skipping trusts that were irrevocably created and funded before October 23, 1986, regardless of how long those trusts last. As a result, many "old wealth" families who created and funded generation-skipping trusts before October 23, 1986, will be protected from both the estate tax and the generation-skipping transfer tax throughout the existence of the trusts, which may last for many decades. By contrast, "new wealth" entrepreneurs accumulating resources since 1986 do not have this opportunity and will in general see their property fully taxed at each and every generation.

From a reasonably attentive reading of the turgid prose of Chapter 13, it will be clear that of the narrow range of estates actually subject to the estate tax only a small fraction will ever encounter the tax on generation-skipping transfers. However, few lawyers can afford to ignore the generation-skipping tax, because its potential application is universal. For example, as discussed later in this chapter, any gift of more than the section 2503(b) and (e) exclusion amounts to a grandchild will, at a minimum, use up a portion of the donor's generation-skipping transfer tax exemption. While it may not be desirable to attempt to plumb the depths or scale the heights of this subject in the basic course in estate and gift taxation, an acquaintance with the general nature of the generation-skipping transfer tax and especially its plainly marked escape hatches should be assimilated by anyone interested in estate planning.

B. OPERATION OF THE GENERATION-SKIPPING TRANSFER TAX

1. TAXABLE EVENTS

The generation-skipping transfer tax ("GST") is imposed on each of three events: taxable terminations, taxable distributions, and direct skips; all three are considered generation-skipping transfers. I.R.C. §§ 2611 & 2612. Each involves a transfer of income or principal (or a beneficial interest in either) to at least one beneficiary who is two or more generations younger than the transferor. For example, a transfer by a donor to her child is not subject to tax; a transfer by the donor to her grandchildren or descendants of her grandchildren, however, is subject to tax.

A *taxable termination* is the termination of an interest in a trust (whether by reason of death, passage of time, or cessation of a power) under which a "skip person" receives an interest in the trust property. I.R.C. § 2612(a). A skip person is defined as one who is two or more generations younger than the transferor. I.R.C. § 2613(a)(1). An example of such a taxable termination would involve a trust established by a parent to provide life income for a child and then upon the child's death to distribute the principal free of trust to the child's children; the taxable termination occurs upon the child's death.

A *taxable distribution* is a distribution of income or principal from a trust to a skip person, other than a taxable termination or a direct skip. I.R.C. § 2612(b). For example, assume that a parent creates a trust to benefit the parent's children and grandchildren. Generally, any distribution from the trust to a grandchild (other than upon termination of the trust) is a taxable distribution.

The third type of taxable event is the *direct skip*. This is a transfer that is subject to either the estate or gift tax and that gives an interest in the transferred property to a skip person. This would include a transfer in trust, subject to the estate or gift tax, where no one has an interest in the property other than a skip person. I.R.C. §§ 2612(c), 2613(a)(2). For example, a transfer to a trust that can benefit only grandchildren of the grantor is treated as a direct skip. The simplest example of a direct skip, however, would be a transfer of property outright by a grandparent to a grandchild.

The following illustration, taken from the House Ways and Means Committee Report accompanying the Tax Reform Act of 1986, is useful:

> A single trust may provide for transfers to more than one generation of generation-skipping beneficiaries. For example, a trust may provide for income payments to the grantor's child for life, then for such payments to the grantor's grandchild, and finally for distribution of the trust property to the grantor's great-grandchild. Were such property left outright to each such generation, the property would be subject to gift or estate tax a total of three times. Under the bill, the property likewise is subject to transfer tax a total of three times—gift or estate tax on the original transfer and generation-skipping transfer tax on the transfers to the grandchild and the great-grandchild.

H.R. Rep. No. 99–426, 99th Cong., 1st Sess. at 825–26 (1985), reprinted in 1986–3 CB 825–26 (Vol. 2).

2. GENERATION ASSIGNMENT

As indicated above, the GST does not apply unless property goes to a "skip person." Although certain trusts can constitute skip persons under I.R.C. § 2613(a)(2), the most important definition applies to human beings: a skip person is "a natural person assigned to a generation which is 2 or more generations below the generation assignment of the transferor." I.R.C. § 2613(a)(1).

A typical example of a gift to a skip person is a gift from a grandparent to a grandchild. This is an easy case because the grandchild is obviously two generations below the grandparent. The statute provides elaborate mechanisms for determining the generation where relationships are more complex.

Where the recipient is a lineal descendant of a grandparent of the transferor, the relative generation levels are determined by simply counting generations. I.R.C. § 2651(b)(1). For example, assume the following family structure. The transferor is William III, one of whose grandparents was William I. Joseph I is another grandchild of William I, and Joseph's father was Albert, brother of William III's father. Assume further that Joseph I has a child (Joseph II), and that Joseph II has a child (Joseph III). Joseph I is assigned to the same generation as William III; if William III makes a gift to Joseph I, Joseph I is not treated as a skip person. Similarly, Joseph II is only one generation below William III, and if William III makes a gift to Joseph II, Joseph II is not treated as a skip person.

Joseph III, however, is a skip person with respect to William III. Joseph III is four generations below William I, the grandfather of the transferor, William III. William III is only two generations below William I. Hence Joseph III is two generations below William III. A gift from William III to a descendant of Joseph III would likewise be a gift to a skip person.

Note that the tax is imposed only on gifts to younger generations. Under section 2613(a), a skip person must be two or more generations *below* the transferor. A gift by Joseph III to William III is not subject to the tax although Joseph III and William III are two generations apart.

If the gift is to a more distant relative, i.e., a person who does not have a common grandparent with the transferor, or to an unrelated person, arbitrary age ranges are used. I.R.C. § 2651(d). For example, assume that Alice, age 56, gives property to Jackson, age 36, and that the two are not related. Because the difference in their ages is between 12-1/2 and 37-1/2 years, Jackson is assigned to the generation immediately below Alice, and Jackson is not a skip person. By contrast, if Alice gives property to Emily, age 12, the age difference is 44 years, and Emily is treated as being two generations below Alice. Hence Emily is a skip person, and the tax applies.

If the recipient is or has been married to the transferor at any time, the recipient is treated as being in the same generation as the transferor, without regard to their relative ages. I.R.C. § 2651(c)(1).

In some circumstances the generation assignment is modified to reflect the death of a person in an intervening generation. For example, assume that Alan I had a son, Alan II, and that Alan II had a son, Alan III. Ordinarily, a gift from Alan I to Alan III would be a direct skip. If, however, Alan II is deceased when the gift is made, there will be no generation-skipping transfer because Alan III is not treated as a skip person with respect to Alan I. I.R.C. § 2651(e).

3. AMOUNT SUBJECT TO TAX

The taxable amount for a *taxable termination* is the fair market value, at the time of termination, of the property with respect to which the termination occurs, decreased by expenses, debts, and taxes attributable to the property, similar to the deductions allowable under section 2053 of the estate tax. I.R.C. § 2622. One result of this formulation is that the amount taxed will necessarily include the amount used to pay the GST. In this sense, the tax on a taxable termination can be described as "tax-inclusive." In that respect the tax on taxable terminations is analogous to the estate tax, which is likewise "tax-inclusive."

The taxable amount in the case of a *taxable distribution* is the value of the property received by the distributee, less any expense incurred by the distributee in connection with the determination of the generation-skipping tax on the transfer. I.R.C. § 2621. Because the GST is imposed on the distributee, the tax will in effect be paid from the amount received by the distributee. Therefore, the amount subject to tax will include the tax itself—a "tax inclusive" result. In this respect the tax on taxable distributions is analogous to the estate tax. If the tax is paid by the trust, rather than by the distributee, the payment of tax is treated as an additional taxable distribution to the distributee. I.R.C. § 2621(b).

In the case of a *direct skip*, the amount subject to the tax is the amount received by the donee skip person. I.R.C. § 2623. Under section 2603(a)(3), the liability for the tax is imposed on the transferor, and the tax is not included in the taxable amount of the direct skip. In this sense, the tax on a direct skip is "tax-exclusive." In that respect the tax on a direct skip is analogous to the gift tax. But there is a secondary tax on direct skips. Under section 2515, the generation-skipping transfer tax paid by the transferor is treated as an additional gift for *gift tax* purposes, and the amount subject to gift tax is "grossed-up" accordingly. As a result, in the case of a direct skip it is entirely possible for the total tax paid (both GST and gift tax) to equal a large portion of the amount actually received by the donee. Section 2515 applies only to direct skips by gift; it does not apply to direct skips at death.

Distributions of income are fully subject to the GST. Put another way, there is no exemption from tax because the distribution comes from income rather than principal.

4. NONTAXABLE GIFTS

In general, the GST does not apply to an inter vivos direct skip that is exempt from the gift tax by reason of the annual exclusion under section 2503(b) or the exclusion under section 2503(e) for certain educational or medical expenses. I.R.C. § 2642(c).

The exemption of section 2503(b) annual exclusion gifts for GST purposes, however, is available only where the person identified as the donee when the exclusion was claimed is the sole beneficiary of the trust. More specifically, the exclusion is available only in cases where: (1) during the lifetime of the person identified as the donee, distributions from the trust can be made only to that person; and (2) if the person identified as the donee dies before the trust terminates, the property in the trust at that person's death will be included in the gross estate of such person for estate tax purposes. I.R.C. § 2642(c)(2). The most important practical effect of this rule is to deny the exclusion for GST purposes in the case of a *Crummey* withdrawal right if the trust has beneficiaries other than the holder of the withdrawal right. In other words, the *Crummey* withdrawal right will fully qualify for the gift tax section 2503(b) annual exclusion, but it will not qualify for the section 2642(c) GST exclusion. As a result, the transfer to the trust may be treated as a direct skip, or the trust may be treated as subject to the GST when there is a taxable termination or taxable distribution. *Crummey* withdrawal rights are addressed in Chapter 7.

5. GST EXEMPTION

Every transferor is allowed an exemption for purposes of the generation-skipping tax. Under section 2631(c), the GST exemption is equal to the basic exclusion amount under section 2010(c). Because the section 2010(c)(2)(A) basic exclusion amount is to be indexed for inflation in years after 2011, the GST exemption will rise accordingly. I.R.C.§ 2010(c)(3)(B). The significant changes under the Tax Cuts and Jobs Act of 2017 have led to a 2023 exemption amount of $12,920,000.

"Portability" between spouses is not available for purposes of the generation-skipping tax. As explained above in this book, for estate and gift tax purposes a surviving spouse may add the unused portion of the unified credit of a deceased spouse to the surviving spouse's own credit. I.R.C. §§ 2010(c)(2)(B) & 2505(a)(1). For example, assume that the basic exclusion amount is $12,920,000 and that a spouse dies, using only $5,920,000 of the exclusion (leaving $7,000,000 unused). When the surviving spouse dies later, the surviving spouse's applicable exclusion amount is $19,920,000—the surviving spouse's $12,920,000 basic exclusion amount (assuming the surviving spouse has not made any taxable gifts) and the deceased spouse's unused exclusion amount of $7,000,000. This approach is not available for purposes of the GST. Under section 2631(a) the surviving spouse's GST exemption is limited to the surviving spouse's *basic* exclusion amount, and no reference is made to the deceased spouse's exemption. I.R.C. § 2631(c). Therefore, in the above example the GST exemption available to the surviving spouse is $12,920,000.

The exemption may be allocated to any property that is transferred during life or at death; any such allocation is irrevocable. I.R.C. § 2631(b). The House Ways and Means Committee Report provides this example of the practical effect of the exemption:

> Assume a grantor transfers $1 million in trust for the benefit of his or her children and grandchildren. If the grantor allocates $1 million of exemption to the trust, no part of the trust will ever be subject to generation-skipping transfer tax—even if the value of the trust property appreciates in subsequent years to $10 million or more. On the other hand, if the grantor allocates only $500,000 of exemption to the trust, one-half of all distributions to grandchildren will be subject to tax and one-half of the trust property will be subject to tax on termination of the children's interest. If, after creation of the trust, the grantor allocates an additional $250,000 of exemption to the trust, the exempt portion of trust will be redetermined, based upon the values of the trust property at that time. This new inclusion ratio applies to future distributions and terminations, but generally does not change the tax treatment of any past events.

H.R. Rep. No. 99–426, 99th Cong., 1st Sess. at 826 (1985), reprinted in 1986–3 C.B. 826 (Vol. 2).

An allocation of the exemption may be made by the individual (or the individual's executor) at any time before the date prescribed for the filing of the transferor's estate tax return. I.R.C. § 2632(a)(1). If a transferor has made an allocation for the benefit of a same-sex spouse or to a person whose generation is determined based on the generation assignment of the same-sex spouse prior to the Supreme Court's recognition of same-sex marriages in United States v. Windsor, 570 U.S. 744 (2013), the transferor is entitled to recalculate the remaining GST exemption if the generation assignment is changed as a result of the decision. See Notice 2017–15, 2017–6 I.R.B. 783. However, per the notice, the transferor is entitled to claim a refund resulting from the recalculation of the GST exemption only if the statute of limitations under section 6511 has not expired.

If a donor makes a direct skip gift during the donor's life, any unused portion of the donor's exemption is automatically allocated to the direct skip gift unless the donor elects otherwise. I.R.C. § 2632(b). In certain cases, any unused exemption is automatically allocated to an "indirect skip" gift made during the donor's life. In general, an "indirect skip" is a transfer to a trust, later transfers from which might constitute generation-skipping transfers. I.R.C. § 2632(c)(1)–(3). Again, the donor can elect out of such an automatic allocation. I.R.C. § 2632(c)(5).

As noted above, the generation-skipping tax exemption amount is determined by and is equal to the estate tax basic exclusion amount set forth in section 2010(c)(3)(A). I.R.C. § 2631(c). As of this writing, the $12,920,000 basic exclusion amount set forth in section 2010(c)(3)(A) is subject to a sunset. Pursuant to the Tax Cuts and Jobs Act of 2017, on January 1, 2026, the section 2010(c) exclusion amount will revert to the amount dictated by section 2010 as it existed prior to the 2017 Act. That amount is $5,000,000. Therefore, unless legislation to the contrary is enacted, the generation-skipping transfer tax exemption applicable after 2025 will be $5,000,000 (adjusted for inflation).

6. "REVERSE" QTIP ELECTION

A special rule allows a decedent to both: (1) claim the marital deduction for property passing to a trust for the benefit of the decedent's spouse, and (2) allocate part or all of the decedent's GST exemption to that trust. This rule applies only where the trust qualifies for the marital deduction as Qualified Terminable Interest Property (QTIP) under section 2056(b)(7), discussed in Chapter 27.

For example, assume that Hiram dies when the amount of the GST exemption is $12,920,000. Hiram devises his $12,920,000 residuary estate to a trust for the benefit of his wife, Kai, for life, with remainder to Hiram's grandchildren. Hiram's executor could claim the marital deduction by making the QTIP election authorized by section 2056(b)(7)(B)(v). At the same time, on the authority of section 2652(a)(3), Hiram's executor could decline to have the QTIP election be effective for generation-skipping transfer tax purposes. As a result, while section 2044 will cause all of the QTIP property in the trust to be included in Kai's estate for estate tax purposes at her death, the trust property flowing to Hiram's grandchildren will be sheltered by Hiram's $12,920,000 GST exemption. This becomes important in the case where Kai has used her $12,920,000 GST exemption to shield other transfers. From a technical standpoint, this rule, known as the "reverse QTIP election," achieves this result by preventing Kai from being treated as the "transferor" of the QTIP property for generation-skipping tax purposes under section 2652(a)(1)(A) (although she is treated as the "transferor" of the QTIP property for estate tax purposes).

7. SIGNIFICANCE OF THE EXEMPTION

The GST exemption has great importance for estate planning. The reason is that the exemption, although limited in dollar amount when allocated to a transfer, can shelter an unlimited amount of property from later exposure to GST.

Take the case of Fatima, who transfers $12,920,000 to a trust in 2023, paying gift tax on the transfer. The GST exemption for 2023 is $12,920,000, and Fatima allocates the entirety of her $12,920,000 exemption to the trust. The result is that the entire trust—regardless of its later value—is forever free of GST. This occurs because under section 2642, as explained below, the trust has a permanent "inclusion ratio" of zero.

Fatima can also prevent the trust from being subject to estate tax at the deaths of her descendants. For example, she can give each generation only a right to income, accompanied by a right to invade limited by an ascertainable standard. The ascertainable standard prevents inclusion of any of the trust property in the gross estates of the descendants holding the power to invade.

The result is that Fatima can make available to her descendants much of the economic benefit of the property, including a right to invade in case of serious need, while entirely avoiding future exposure to estate tax or GST. Although the trust may be worth only $12,920,000 when Fatima creates it, it may be worth many times that amount at the deaths of Fatima's successive descendants. As a result, allocation of the maximum exemption amount to such a "generation-skipping trust" has become customary estate planning for prosperous families.

The "catch" is that there are property law limits on the period during which property can be held in trust. The most important, of course, is the common law Rule Against Perpetuities, which requires that any interest must vest within 21 years after a life in being at the creation of the interest. Although astute drafting can produce trusts that might well last more than a century without transgressing the Rule, some families want tax protection for an even longer period—preferably forever.

The response has been statutory modification or outright abolition of the common law Rule Against Perpetuities[1] or the adoption of a reform, such as the Statutory Rule Against Perpetuities (the so-called wait-and-see approach) in many states.[2] In such states, a true "dynasty trust" can be

---

[1] See, e.g., Idaho Code § 55–111 (2022); R.I. Gen. Laws § 34–11–38 (2022); S.D. Codified Laws § 55–1–20 (2022); Wis. Stat. § 700.16(5) (2022).

[2] See, e.g., Ark. Code Ann. § 18–3–101(a) (2022); Fla. Stat. Ann. § 689.225(2) (West 2022); Kan. Stat. Ann. § 59–3401(a) (2022); N.C. Gen. Stat. § 41–15(a) (2022); Tenn. Code Ann. § 66–1–

created, protecting the trust assets from estate tax and GST in perpetuity. The number of states repealing the common law Rule Against Perpetuities has expanded rapidly in recent years, encouraged in part by the aggressive sales efforts of banks and trust companies located in the repealing states.

8. COMPUTATION OF THE TAX

The language expressing the procedure for determining the tax is obtuse. We are told that the generation-skipping tax is the taxable amount multiplied by the applicable rate (I.R.C. § 2602), and that the applicable rate is the maximum estate tax rate times the inclusion ratio. I.R.C. § 2641. The inclusion ratio is determined by subtracting the applicable fraction from 1; and in turn the applicable fraction is made up of a numerator consisting of the generation-skipping exemption allocated to the trust or the direct skip and a denominator consisting of the value of the property placed in trust or the property subject to the direct skip, reduced by any estate tax attributable to the property in trust and any charitable gift involved. I.R.C. § 2642. The general purpose of the inclusion ratio is to exempt from GST the portion of the transfer that is covered by the exemption allocated to the transfer.

The computation may be illustrated by a trust established pursuant to the will of a deceased parent. The trust provides income to a child for life, with remainder outright to a grandchild upon the child's death. Assume that the GST exemption at the parent's death is $12,920,000, and that the trust is funded with $17,000,000 from the parent's estate after payment of estate taxes. The child dies 12 years later, when the trust has a value of $20,000,000. The parent did not use any of her GST exemption prior to her death.

At the child's death there is a taxable termination, and the taxable amount will be the $20,000,000 value of the trust property at that time. The trustee must pay the generation-skipping tax out of the trust assets. The parent's $12,920,000 GST exemption was automatically allocated to the trust at the parent's death. See I.R.C. § 2632(e)(1). The inclusion ratio is 1 minus a fraction with a numerator of $12,920,000 (the allocated exemption) and denominator of $17,000,000 (the value of the property placed in trust). The result is an inclusion ratio of 24%.

If the maximum estate tax rate at the child's death is 40%, the generation-skipping tax imposed is 24% × 40% × $20,000,000, or $1,920,000. See I.R.C. §§ 2602 & 2641(a). In effect, 76% of the trust—regardless of its value when the trust terminates—has been sheltered by the exemption. Only the remaining 24% is subject to the 40% tax. The

---

202(a) (2022). Under the Statutory Rule Against Perpetuities, a nonvested interest is valid if it vests within 21 years of the death of someone alive at the time the interest is created, or it vests or terminates within 90 years after the interest was created.

maximum federal estate tax rate is applied to determine the amount of generation-skipping tax that is due. I.R.C. § 2641(a)(1). Currently, that rate is 40%. See I.R.C. § 2001(c).

9. BASIS

Because the GST is intended to approximate the results that would occur if property were held outright rather than in trust, some aspects of the section 1014 stepped-up basis at death are applied to certain generation-skipping transfers. If a taxable termination occurs at the same time and as a result of the death of an individual, the basis of the property subject to the termination is stepped up (or down) to its date of death value. I.R.C. §§ 2654(a)(2) & 1014(a). This rule, however, applies only to the portion of the property subject to GST. For example, if the inclusion ratio is one-fourth, the basis of the property would be increased by only one-fourth of the total step-up or decreased by only one-fourth of the total step-down.

In the case of other generation-skipping transfers, there is an effort to replicate the addition to basis provided for gift tax under section 1015(d). The basis for the property involved in the transfer is increased by the portion of the GST allocable to the excess of the fair market value of the property over its basis immediately prior to the transfer. I.R.C. § 2654(a)(1). For example, if the property has a basis of $400,000 and a fair market value of $1,000,000, and a GST of $300,000 is imposed, the basis increase would be 60% of $300,000, or $180,000.

C. PRACTICAL IMPACT OF THE GENERATION-SKIPPING TRANSFER TAX

The GST can be an expensive trap for the unwary if no unified credit is available. For example, assume that a father created an irrevocable trust in 1990, having exhausted his GST exemption with prior transfers. The result would be an inclusion ratio of 100% for the trust. Assume further that the trust provides income for the father's son throughout the son's life, with a remainder outright to the grandson at the son's death. If the son died in 2023, there would be a taxable termination at that time, and no exemption is available under the GST. If the value of the trust were $12,920,000 at the time of the son's death, the GST would be 40% of $12,920,000, or $5,168,000. The grandson would receive only $7,752,000.

By contrast, if the father had given the property outright to the son in 1990, the son's estate tax applicable credit amount could be used to shelter the property from tax at the son's death. If the son dies in 2023 and has no other property, the $12,920,000 would be entirely sheltered from estate tax at the son's death, and the grandson would receive $12,920,000 tax-free.

The lesson here is that creation of any trust arrangement can be expensive unless there is sufficient GST exemption to shelter the trust from GST. So, the GST should be considered whenever trusts are created.

This bad news is offset by the good news that the GST exemption, although limited in amount at the outset, can shelter an unlimited amount from tax in later years. For example, assume that a mother transferred $12,920,000 to a trust in 2023 and assigned her entire $12,920,000 GST exemption to this trust. The trust provides a life estate for the mother's daughter and then her granddaughter, with the remainder going to the great-granddaughter at the granddaughter's death. The trust has an inclusion ratio of zero throughout its existence, regardless of the later value of the trust property. Although the trust might have a value of $20,000,000 at the daughter's death, the entire $20,000,000 would be sheltered from estate tax and GST tax at that time. Similarly, although the trust might have a value of $25,000,000 at the granddaughter's death, the entire $25,000,000 would be sheltered from both estate tax and GST tax at that time. The entire amount in the trust can remain sheltered from tax for the benefit of future generations, and in perpetuity if the trust is so drafted and the Rule Against Perpetuities has been abrogated in the relevant jurisdiction.

The lesson for prosperous families is clear. There are great advantages in creating generation-skipping trusts that fully utilize the available GST exemption. This can create an important and growing reservoir of family resources that can be protected from both estate tax and GST for several generations—and perhaps forever.

Finally, the section 2642(c) exemption for section 2503(b) annual exclusion gifts and the section 2503(e) tuition and medical expense gifts can be useful. These exemptions can be used to transfer substantial amounts to descendants without exposure to gift tax or GST, and without using any of the donor's GST exemption. The planner must remember, however, that the exemption for section 2503(b) exclusion gifts is very limited when the transfer is in trust. I.R.C. § 2642(c)(2).

PROBLEMS

1. Ray Cook made a cash gift this year of $19,017,000 to his grandson, Conner Cook. Assume that for this year the section 2010(c)(3)(A) basic exclusion amount was $12,920,000 and the section 2503(b) annual exclusion was $17,000. The father of Conner Cook, Jerry Cook, was alive at the time of this gift and was the son of Ray Cook. Ray Cook had not previously made any taxable gifts and had not previously used any of his applicable credit amount. Nor had he used any of his generation-skipping transfer tax (GST) exemption. Ray allocated the entirety of his GST exemption to this gift. Ray was not married.

How much, if any, does Ray owe the United States in gift tax and GST, respectively?

Note: For purposes of the GST, the portion of the transfer that qualifies for the annual exclusion is treated as a separate transfer to which an inclusion ratio of zero is applied, pursuant to section 2642(c)(1).

2.   (a) On March 12, 2006, Dale Hudson, whose wife died in 2002, transferred $8,000,000 to the Hudson Trust, naming the Tenth National Bank as trustee. The trust provides that the income is to be paid to Tony Hudson (son of Dale Hudson) throughout the life of Tony Hudson. Upon the death of Tony Hudson. the trust is to terminate, and the trust property is to be paid outright to Clay Hudson (son of Tony Hudson). Earlier in 2006 Dale Hudson made a $12,000 outright cash gift to Tony Hudson. Assume that the annual exclusion was $12,000 in 2006, and that Dale Hudson applied the entirety of his annual exclusion against this cash gift. Assume that in 2006 the section 2631 GST exemption amount was $2,000,000.

Dale Hudson filed a 2006 gift tax return reporting the $8,012,000 of transfers and electing to allocate the entirety of his GST exemption to the Hudson Trust.

Tony Hudson died in 2018, when the trust property was worth $16,000,000. The entirety of the trust property after payment of taxes was paid to Clay Hudson at this time. Assume that the maximum estate tax rate in 2018 was 40%.

How much GST, if any, was Dale Hudson required to pay with respect to the transfer in 2006?

How much estate tax, gift tax, and GST, if any, was imposed with respect to the 2018 trust termination?

(b) Assume the same facts as in Part (a) except that the Hudson Trust provides that upon the death of Tony Hudson, the property is to remain in trust throughout the life of Clay Hudson, and Clay is to receive all income during this period. Upon Clay's death the trust property is to be distributed outright to Clay's descendants, per stirpes.

Tony Hudson died in 2018, when the trust property was worth $16,000,000. Clay Hudson died in 2023, when the trust property was worth $17,000,000 (after payment of any GST due in 2018). Assume that the maximum estate tax rate was 40% in 2023.

How much GST, if any, was Dale Hudson required to pay with respect to the transfer in 2006? How much GST and estate tax, if any, were due upon the deaths of Tony and Clay?

(c) Assume the same facts as in Part (b), with the following changes:

(i) The Hudson Trust permits the Tenth National Bank to make discretionary distribution of corpus to Clay Hudson at any time.

(ii) In 2014, the Tenth National Bank distributed $2,200,000 from the trust to Clay Hudson.

(iii) Any GST imposed in 2014 was paid by Clay Hudson as distributee.

Assume that the maximum estate tax rate in 2014 was 40%. How much GST and estate tax, if any, were imposed on Clay Hudson in 2014?

3. Antonio White is age 65. His wife, Betty, died ten years ago. Antonio's only child, Maya, is still alive. Maya has three children, Henry, William, and Jordyn, ages 5, 7, and 10.

Antonio made no gifts whatever until 2023. In 2023, he gave $12,937,000 in cash to Sterling, the grandson of Antonio's brother, Samuel. Sterling's father is Arnie, Samuel's son. Arnie is still alive. Antonio allocated the entirety of his GST exemption to this gift. The section 2503(b) annual exclusion for 2023 is $17,000 and the estate tax rate is 40%.

Also, in 2023 Antonio created the White Trust and transferred $51,000 to it, naming the Tenth National Bank as trustee. The White Trust provides that until Henry attains age 30 the trustee has discretionary power to distribute income and principal to Henry according to the best interests of Henry as determined by the trustee. When Henry attains age 30, the entire trust property is to be transferred to Henry. If Henry dies before reaching age 30, the entire trust property is to be transferred outright in equal shares to William and Jordyn.

The White Trust also provides that notice of any contribution to the trust is to be given to Henry, William, Jordyn, and their guardians. Each of Henry, William, and Jordyn, or his or her guardian, has power to withdraw from the trust a maximum of $17,000 of the amount contributed, provided the request for withdrawal is made within 30 days after the notice.

How much gift tax and GST, if any, does Antonio owe as a result of the $51,000 transfer to the White Trust?

4. A father has a substantial estate and has already used the entirety of his GST exemption on prior transfers. He wants to bequeath the remainder of his estate to a trust that will provide income for his son during the son's life. The father does not want to give the son power to dictate the disposition of the property after the son's death. He fears that the son will transfer the property to one or more of the several women in the son's life, with the result that the son's children will get little or nothing. The father wants to require that the trust property be distributed to the son's

children upon the son's death. Will this arrangement have adverse tax consequences at the son's death?

PART 6

TRUST AND ESTATE INCOME AND INCOME FROM DECEDENTS

(Subchapter J of the Internal Revenue Code)

■ ■ ■

CHAPTER 30

INCOME TAXATION OF
ESTATES AND TRUSTS

(SECTIONS 641–667)

■ ■ ■

A. INTRODUCTION

Trusts and estates, like corporations and individuals but unlike partnerships, are income taxpaying entities. Like corporations, which make distributions to their shareholders in the form of dividends, trusts and estates make distributions to the beneficiaries of the trust or estate. However, these distributions will often be tax deductible by the trust or estate, whereas, generally speaking, no deduction can be taken by a corporation for the dividends it pays its noncorporate shareholders.[1]

Subchapter J of the Internal Revenue Code (sections 641 through 691) contains the specialized provisions relating to the income taxation of estates and trusts and related matters. Included are both inter vivos and testamentary trusts and decedents' estates. The rules are designed to minimize or eliminate any income tax advantage to having income received by a trust or estate, i.e., to render the trust and estate income tax neutral so that persons who receive distributions of income from trusts or estates do not enjoy any income tax advantage from having had the income flow through the trust or estate.

The function of the trustee is, by nature, to hold property and manage it for the benefit of the beneficiaries of the trust. The fruit of that management, whether it be income or appreciation realized on the sale of trust property, inures to the benefit of the trust beneficiaries. In the meantime, it may be accumulated by the trustee and added to the other trust property under management by the trustee.

In the case of an estate, the function of the decedent's executor or administrator is to collect the decedent's property and distribute it to the beneficiaries of the decedent's estate. During the course of this collection and distribution process, the estate will normally continue to receive

---

[1] Under section 243(a), dividends received by corporate shareholders are deductible. See I.R.C. § 243(c).

income on the decedent's property, and the decedent's property may well grow in value, pending distribution.

As a means of minimizing or eliminating any income tax advantage to the ultimate recipient of the property that is under management in an estate or trust, Congress has adopted a number of rather specific rules. One rule provides that every distribution from an estate or trust will carry out the income of the estate or trust to the persons who receive that distribution. Thus, the recipient of a distribution from an estate or trust will be taxed on the portion of that distribution that represents the income earned by the estate or trust—and the estate or trust making the distribution will receive an income tax deduction for the amount of that distribution.

It is worth noting that Congress has created a series of descriptive terms to facilitate the implementation of the foregoing rule. For example, "distributable net income" or DNI refers to the amount of income of an estate or trust that is deemed to be available for distribution to the estate or trust's beneficiaries under the rules of Subchapter J. I.R.C. § 643(a). Thus, it can be said, subject to certain limitations, that every distribution from an estate or trust will carry out the income of the estate or trust to the extent of the estate or trust's DNI.

In addition, as discussed later in this chapter, the income tax rates applicable to trusts and estates are described as having been "compressed" relative to those applicable to individuals. Finally, another rule aimed at minimizing the income tax benefits of using trusts requires the consolidation of certain trusts for income tax purposes. I.R.C. § 643(f). However, it is the grantor trust rules that probably supply the most important limitation. See I.R.C. §§ 671–678. These rules identify certain trusts as "grantor trusts" and then stipulate that the person who created the trust (or, in some cases, a person who is deemed to have created the trust)—the grantor—will be taxed on the trust income even though that person does not receive the income. The grantor trust rules are the subject of Chapter 31.

PLANNING NOTE

Despite the efforts to minimize or eliminate any income tax advantages that could result from the use of a trust, oftentimes there are advantages to be realized. For example, generally speaking, unless the trust beneficiary has a general power of appointment over the trust property, the beneficiary will be able to have the benefit of the trust property without having the trust property included in his or her estate for federal estate tax purposes. See Chapter 22. This powerful incentive may well be sufficient to encourage income to be warehoused in the trust—and taxed at the highest marginal income tax rate to the trust rather than be distributed to the beneficiary where it might very well be taxed at a lower marginal rate.

As a means of adding perspective to possible debate on the merits of income tax rate compression as applied to estates and trusts, consider the possible adverse economic consequences to trusts that accumulate income for nontax reasons. For example, in the case where the trust beneficiary is legally disabled and is not competent to manage income distributed from the trust, nontax considerations mandate that the trust accumulate any income not needed by the beneficiary. Yet that accumulated income will be burdened by the compressed income tax rates applicable to trusts.

Not to be ignored, too, is the phenomenon commonly referred to as the "kiddie tax." See I.R.C. § 1(g). The kiddie tax is part of a continuing effort by Congress to limit the ability of taxpayers to shift income within the family unit or family-controlled entities. The effect of the kiddie tax is to tax the unearned income of each child under the age of 18 (and, in some cases, children under 24) to that child but at the marginal income tax rate of the child's parents. Obviously, the kiddie tax, when considered together with income tax rate compression noted above as applied to income warehoused in trusts, can discourage trust creation for beneficiaries under 24 years of age. Why? Because warehoused trust income may be taxed at the highest marginal income tax rates and, if distributed, for example, to an 18-year old beneficiary, the trust income will be taxed to the beneficiary at income tax rates applicable to the beneficiary's parents, possibly also in a high marginal income tax rate bracket. In appraising the need for the kiddie tax—which was adopted in 1986—and the increase in complexity that resulted, it may be useful to note that the Treasury reported that, in 1981, 612,000 persons who filed returns reporting unearned income were claimed as dependents on another taxpayer's return.

B. BASIC CONCEPTS

1. INTRODUCTION

The provisions of Subchapter J reflect Congress's effort to resolve the fundamental questions of taxing What, to Whom, and When in cases where property is held by an estate or trust. The "What" has to do with determinations as to what receipts by a trust or an estate are income in a constitutionally permissible sense. The "to Whom" has to do with determinations as to whether income should be taxed to the trust or estate itself or to some other taxpayer. The "When" relates to the concept of matching revenues and expenses within different tax years so as to avoid distorting income tax liability.

2. WHAT IS INCOME?

Section 641 provides that receipts which constitute gross income when received by an individual will constitute gross income when received by an estate or trust. Thus, the traditional exclusions apply. For example, gratuitous transfers of property to the trust ordinarily will not constitute gross income. I.R.C. § 102(a). But if the subject of a transfer is the right to income from property, the income when earned will be taxable to the recipient, in this case, the trust. See I.R.C. § 102(b)(2); Irwin v. Gavit, 268 U.S. 161 (1925).

> *Example*: A grantor established a trust for his granddaughter by delivering $5,000 to a trustee. Concurrently with the transfer and as a condition of it, the grantor asked the trustee to hold the property in trust for the granddaughter for life and, upon her death, to terminate the trust and distribute the remaining trust property to the granddaughter's then living lineal descendants *per stirpes*. The grantor's transfer is excluded from the trustee's income and from the granddaughter's income because it constituted a gift from the grantor to the trustee for the benefit of the granddaughter and her descendants. See I.R.C. § 102.

In addition, a further distinction is made between income in a trust accounting sense (sometimes referred to as "fiduciary accounting income") and income in a tax accounting sense. The former is determined according to state law and the provisions of the governing instrument. Treas. Reg. § 1.643(b)–1. The latter is as defined by section 641(b), which provides that the taxable income of an estate or trust is to be computed in the same manner as for an individual, subject to certain exceptions. See also I.R.C. § 63(a) and (b) defining taxable income for an individual. For example, state law or the governing instrument may direct that gains from the sale of trust property be allocated to the principal of the trust rather than to the income beneficiary. Such an allocation, however, will not change the federal tax consequences of the sale. To the extent gain is realized on the sale or exchange, the gain will be recognized as gross income except to the extent it qualifies for nonrecognition pursuant to one of several provisions developed by Congress to cover instances where Congress felt that imposition of a tax would contravene social policy. See I.R.C. § 1001; Treas. Reg. § 1.61–6(a) and (b).

3. WHO IS THE TAXPAYER?

a. Trusts Distinguished from Corporations

Trusts, unlike corporations, lack most of the attributes of separate juristic existence. This is because, conceptually, a trust is a relationship rather than an entity. Title to property transferred in trust is held by the trustee (and not the trust), subject, of course, to the trustee's duties to the beneficiary of the trust. Restatement of Trusts (Third) § 2 (2012). For federal tax purposes, however, the trust is treated as a taxpaying entity. I.R.C. § 641(a). It is distinguished from a corporation, however, in the sense that the trust is allowed a deduction in computing its taxable income for amounts of income distributed to its beneficiaries. I.R.C. §§ 651(a), 661(b). Correspondingly, the recipient of the distribution must include the income received in gross income. I.R.C. § 61(a)(14).

A corporation, on the other hand, cannot deduct the dividends it pays to its noncorporate shareholders in computing its taxable income. The obvious incentive to operate a business in trust form, however, is limited by the IRS's power to tax trusts as corporations where the trust has been created for the conduct of a business for profit. See Morrissey v. Commissioner, 296 U.S. 344 (1935). Trust-like tax treatment is limited to arrangements vesting in trustees "responsibility for the protection and conservation of property for beneficiaries. . . ." Treas. Reg. § 301.7701–4(a).

Controversy with respect to when trusts are properly taxed as corporations sometimes arises. In Private Letter Ruling 8552010, the IRS concluded that an irrevocable trust created by a father for the lifetime benefit of his son was an association taxable as a corporation. Ruling that the trustee's powers went beyond merely protecting and conserving trust assets, the IRS pointed to the trustee's broad powers, including the power to engage in such businesses as he deemed prudent; the fact that the trustee had purchased real property from the son and made periodic loans to the son; and the fact that the son acted on behalf of the trust in negotiating sales and other transactions that were coordinated with the son's own real estate activities. However, in Private Letter Ruling 8624015, the IRS concluded that an irrevocable trust for the benefit of the grantor and his family was properly classified as a trust (and not a corporation) for income tax purposes. In reaching this conclusion, the IRS pointed to a provision in the trust agreement specifically prohibiting the trustee from engaging in any business enterprise or operating any business if such activity would constitute the carrying on of a business under Regulation § 301.7701–2.

In Bedell v. Commissioner, 86 T.C. 1207 (1986), the court concluded that a testamentary trust for the benefit of the surviving spouse and children of the decedent was not "an association taxable as a corporation" under Regulation § 301.7701–4 because the beneficiaries were not "associates and their trust is not an association." Bedell is significant, in part, because of three observations made by the court in its opinion:

> [T]he Government regarded this case as a test case in respect of testamentary trusts and trusts engaged in the conduct of a

business, and that high levels in the IRS were active in pressing the matter;

[I]t is difficult to imagine a more unsuitable vehicle than this case [for arguing that the trust was an association taxable as a corporation], and we think it regrettable that extensive misguided efforts were exerted to such a fruitless end in this litigation; and

[T]he case should not be regarded as authority for the conclusion that no testamentary trust can be classified as an association.[2]

b. Governing Principle

The governing principle applied in determining who is to be taxed on the income of trusts and estates can be stated this way: (1) income retained by the trust or estate will be taxed to the trust or estate, and (2) income distributed to a beneficiary will be taxed to the beneficiary. However, to avoid manipulation by the trustee or executor, any distribution from an estate or trust to a beneficiary eligible to receive an income distribution is treated as having carried out income from the trust or estate to the beneficiary to the extent of the trust's or estate's distributable net income (DNI). I.R.C. §§ 651(b) and 661(a).

> *Example*: Ben was a beneficiary of a trust established by his father, Sam. The trustee was authorized "to distribute so much or all of the income and principal of the trust as the trustee determines to be appropriate to Ben's welfare." Although Ben was in a high-income tax bracket this year, he needed cash to make the down payment on a new personal residence. To make it possible for Ben to purchase the house, the trustee distributed $60,000 to Ben. In the same year, the trust had income of $26,000. Ben is required to report the receipt of $26,000 on his personal income tax return this year, and the trustee can deduct the $26,000 on the trust's income tax return.

4. DISTRIBUTABLE NET INCOME (DNI)

A trust is oftentimes merely a conduit insofar as income tax accounting is concerned. That is, to the extent income is retained by the trust, it is taxed to the trust. However, to the extent it is distributed by the trust, it is taxed to the beneficiary.

To limit the role of taxation in motivating distribution decisions, Congress also established the principle that, with certain exceptions, every distribution to a beneficiary would constitute taxable income to the extent of the trust's "distributable net income" (DNI). Mechanically speaking, the trust is entitled to a deduction in computing its taxable income to the

---

[2]   86 T.C. at 1222.

extent of the lesser of the amounts actually distributed or DNI. I.R.C. §§ 651(b) and 661(b). The amount constituting the distribution deduction allowable to the trust will correspondingly constitute gross income to those recipients who receive the distribution. I.R.C. §§ 652(a) and 662(a).

DNI is a legislatively created concept designed to limit the trust's deduction for distributions to beneficiaries and, correspondingly, limit the amount and fix the character of such income to be taxed to the distributee. Practically speaking, the role of DNI is to limit the deduction and inclusion to amounts actually available for distribution by the trust. For example, the governing instrument or state law may mandate that such gains be held in trust as a part of the principal, thus rendering them unavailable for immediate distribution. Nonetheless, the gain continues to be recognized for federal income tax purposes by the trust. See I.R.C. § 61(a)(3); Treas. Reg. § 1.641(a)–2. Moreover, but for the limitation of DNI, the governing principle applied in determining who is to be taxed on the income of the trust would dictate that a distribution to a beneficiary of that trust, which would otherwise be a nontaxable distribution of principal, would constitute taxable income to the beneficiary of that trust. See Treas. Reg. § 1.643(a)–3.

> *Example*: A trust is created to pay the income to LaVonda for life, with a discretionary power in the trustee to invade principal for LaVonda's benefit. In one taxable year the trust had $5,000 of dividend income and realized $10,000 from the sale of securities at a profit. Before year end the trustee distributed $15,000 to LaVonda. No other cash was received or on hand during the taxable year. The trustee allocated the capital gain to the principal. Accordingly, the capital gain will not ordinarily be included in distributable net income. However, if the trustee follows a regular practice of distributing the exact net proceeds of the sale of trust property, capital gains will be included in DNI. Treas. Reg. § 1.643(a)–3(b).

Strictly speaking, the statute approaches DNI from the standpoint of the "taxable income of the estate or trust computed with" certain indicated modifications. I.R.C. § 643(a). The computational scheme is described in the following terms:

> First, the amount of taxable income is increased by (1) all distribution deductions, (2) the deductions allowed of the trust or estate in lieu of the personal exemption, (3) tax-exempt interest, (4) and any excluded interest or dividends. Second, the amount of taxable income is then reduced by certain capital gains, and in the case of simple trusts, stock dividends and extraordinary dividends, which are not distributed to beneficiaries. Finally, additional modifications are required in the case of foreign trusts.

H.R. Rep. No. 99–426, 99th Cong., 1st Sess. at 805 (1985), reprinted in 1986–3 C.B. 805 (Vol. 2).

The statute's approach is confusing in that the trust's taxable income cannot be determined until the trust's distribution deduction is determined. It might be easier to start by developing a conceptual model based on adjusted gross income (even though "adjusted gross income" is computed only for limited purposes in the case of trusts) and then make the appropriate modifications to determine exactly how much is available for distribution. In fact, the Income Tax Return for Estates and Trusts (Form 1041) uses this approach in directing the determination of DNI, using the term "adjusted total income" in place of "adjusted gross income." Thus, it can be said that DNI is determined by adding to what could be called "adjusted gross income" the tax-exempt interest received by the trust and then reducing so-called adjusted gross income by the amount of capital gains, extraordinary dividends, and taxable stock dividends which are allocated to the principal of the trust pursuant to state law or the governing instrument and which accordingly are not available for distribution to the beneficiaries.

The concept of "availability for distribution" is central to the concept of DNI and understanding DNI and how it serves as a limitation on the governing principle is critical to understanding Subchapter J. Equally important is recognizing that the governing principle—every distribution from an estate or trust carries out the income of the estate or trust—is Congress's effort to limit the role of taxation in motivating distribution decisions.

5. FIDUCIARY ACCOUNTING INCOME

a. State Law Deference

Important to understanding distributable net income (DNI) is to recognize, first, that while DNI and "fiduciary accounting income" are not necessarily the same, fiduciary accounting income is the scheme used in the Internal Revenue Code for establishing the competing rights of income beneficiaries and remaindermen. Thus, while fiduciary accounting income is determined by the governing instrument and applicable local law per Regulations § 1.643(b)–1, the concept significantly impacts the trust's adjusted total income, which is the base utilized for computing the trust's DNI.

Moreover, wherever the term "income" appears in Subchapter J and is not preceded by words such as "taxable," "distributable net," "undistributed net," or "gross," it refers to fiduciary accounting income. This is defined by the statute to be the amount of income of the estate or trust for the taxable year determined "under the terms of the governing instrument and applicable local law." I.R.C. § 643(b). This deference to state law is a keystone of federal taxing policy. Thus, exercise of discretion by a fiduciary in allocating between principal and income will be binding if the fiduciary acts in good faith. Thornton v. Commissioner, 5 T.C. 1177 (1945) (acq.), 1946–2 C.B. 4. Where a trustee abused his discretion and allocated ordinary dividends to principal, the IRS refused to be bound. Doty v. Commissioner, 148 F.2d 503 (1st Cir. 1945). The only limitation on this deference to state law and the governing instrument is that the federal courts reserve the right to make an independent determination of what "the state law rule" will be in a particular case in those instances in which the highest court of the state has not yet ruled on the issue. Commissioner v. Estate of Bosch, 387 U.S. 456 (1967); Case v. Commissioner, 8 T.C. 343 (1947).

b. Total Return Trusts, Unitrust Amount, and Equitable Adjustments

Over time widespread agreement has developed as to what generally constitutes "fiduciary accounting income." Recently though changes in the financial markets are forcing a reexamination of these notions. At one level, the situation can be illustrated by reference to the once common provision requiring "all trust income is to be distributed at least annually" to one or more named trust beneficiaries and that "no distributions from principle are to be made." This worked acceptably in an economy where corporations were inclined to distribute corporate profits in the form of dividends. That changed in recent years because of the disparity in the income tax rates applicable to dividends (so-called "ordinary income") and those applicable to appreciation realized when a stock is sold (so called "capital gains"). Until 2003, dividends were taxed as ordinary income at a maximum rate verging on 40 percent (or more, effectively, in some cases) while appreciation—capital gains—were taxed at a maximum rate of 20 percent and not taxed at all until the gain is realized when the property is disposed of. Currently, however, depending on income, a maximum income tax rate of 15 or 20 percent[3] is applicable to both "qualified" dividends and most long-term capital gains.[4] Despite this seeming equality, the enterprise manager, deciding to distribute or not distribute earnings in the form of dividends, may well take into account the income taxation of those earnings first to the corporation at corporate tax rates of 21 percent followed by taxation to shareholders at 15 or 20 percent—and decide against an earnings distribution in the form of a dividend, choosing, instead to reinvest the corporate earnings in the enterprise. As the argument goes, shareholders needing or wanting cash, can sell shares, shares likely to have

---

[3]   During 2023, the rate is 20% for a single taxpayer with income exceeding $492,300 and for married taxpayers filing a joint return with income above $553,850. See Rev. Proc. 2022–38, 2022–45 I.R.B. 445.

[4]   Long-term capital gains from collectibles are taxed at 28 percent, and long-term capital gains from "unrecaptured section 1250 gain" are taxed at 25%. See I.R.C. § 1(h).

appreciated (reflecting the reinvested earnings)—and pay tax on the realized appreciation at a maximum capital gains rate of 15 or 20 percent. I.R.C. §§ 61(a)(3) and 1001(a). And, to encourage share appreciation, corporations not infrequently maintain "stock buyback" programs, i.e., use corporate cash to buy company stock. These buybacks suck out cash that might otherwise go to shareholders in the form of dividends. "Everybody wins," so it might be claimed—except the trust beneficiary limited to receiving distributions of trust income! There does not appear to be an organized lobby of trust beneficiaries and, thus, it is not uncommon to see dividends reduced with the explanation that cash is being conserved to increase the stock price.

Obviously, restrictive dividend policies work a major hardship on shareholders looking only to distributions of trust income for support and to facilitate lifestyle choices. While one rarely hears of trust beneficiaries "living under a bridge" because of dividend cuts (that have led to a reduction in trust income), it is not hard to imagine that trust income in many trusts is lagging trust valuation (or at least it was most profoundly during the bull market of the late 1990s). To address this situation, state legislatures and persons creating new trusts are turning to new concepts of trust income. Talk is of "total return trusts" and making distributions of a "unitrust" amount; trustees fulfilling their duty of impartiality between income and remainder beneficiaries by making "equitable adjustments between income and principal" in cases where the trustee invests and manages the trust property under the state's "prudent investor standard"; or capital gains being allocated to income in a consistent fashion by a trustee exercising discretionary authority pursuant to state law or the governing instrument. Under Regulation § 1.643(b)–1, the IRS will "respect" allocations between income and principal based on these concepts to the extent applicable local law permitted their utilization. Examples are provided in Regulation § 1.643(a)–3.

The effect of the state law changes is to increase the amount distributable to so-called income beneficiaries of the trust. In turn, the effect of the IRS acceptance of these state law changes—sometimes referred to as "ordering" rules—is to cause the tax liability to follow the income to the beneficiary, thereby avoiding an anomalous situation where "income" flows to a beneficiary but tax liability for that income is stuck at the trust level because the IRS based its regulations on an antiquated definition of "fiduciary accounting income."

6.   DISTRIBUTIONS

A trust is entitled to a deduction for amounts distributed to its beneficiaries to the extent of the portion of the trust's distributable net income (DNI) which is not tax exempt, provided such distributions are not merely distributions of specific property or payments of a sum of money (in not more than three installments) which were required by the governing instrument. I.R.C. §§ 651(a), 661(a) and 663(a)(1). Thus, it will not be uncommon for a distribution of corpus to be eligible for the distribution deduction and, thereby, constitute taxable income in the hands of the recipient. That could happen, for instance, where a trustee elects to make a distribution to a beneficiary eligible for distributions of corpus only, makes no other distributions that tax year, and the trust has DNI. Treas. Reg. § 1.661(a)–2(c). Conversely, distributions from whatever source in excess of DNI will not be deductible by the trust or taxable to the distributee.

Example: Mary established a trust for her son, Sean, which provided that:

> The trustee shall distribute so much or all of the trust income to Sean as the trustee determines to be in Sean's best interest. Any income not so distributed is to be accumulated in the trust until Sean reaches maturity at which time the trust is to terminate, and the accumulated income is to be distributed to Sean, but in no event shall the trust terminate before Sean attains 55 years of age.

When Mary established the trust, she thought it unlikely that her daughter, Samantha, a professional basketball player, would ever "come upon hard times." However, in anticipation of the unexpected, Mary included the following provision in the trust:

> The trustee may make distributions of principal for the benefit of my daughter, Samantha, if, in the opinion of the trustee, such distributions would be in the best interests of Samantha.

Samantha was unexpectedly "cut" by her team and found herself destitute. The trustee, recognizing Samantha's plight, distributed $6,000 to Samantha from the trust. No distributions were made to Sean from the trust during that year.

The same year the trust had $4,000 of interest income and $10,000 of capital gain, which it realized from securities transactions. Pursuant to the terms of the trust agreement, the realized capital gain was allocated to principal and was not available for distribution. The trust had no other expenses during this year. Accordingly, the trust had DNI (income available for distribution) of $4,000.

Samantha will be deemed to have received $4,000 of taxable income from the trust this year as well as a $2,000 nontaxable distribution of corpus.

PROBLEM

Under the terms of a trust it is provided that all income, including capital gains, shall be distributed annually to Ben. The trust income for the year includes (1) $10,000 cash dividends on stock of domestic corporations, and (2) $10,000 in long term capital gains realized from the sale of trust property. Trustee's fees totaled $1,200. The trust instrument provides that all expenses are to be charged to income.

1. What is the income of the trust as a matter of fiduciary accounting?

2. What is the taxable income of the trust determined without consideration of distributions to beneficiaries? Note the deduction for the personal exemption in section 642(b) is $300.

3. What is the trust's DNI? Compute DNI by applying the statutory formula. See I.R.C. § 643.

4. How will Ben report his share of the trust income? See § I.R.C. 652.

5. What, if any, income will be taxable to the fiduciary? See I.R.C. § 651.

6. What will be the tax consequences if the trust instrument provides that gains realized on the sale or exchange of trust property will be added to corpus and that all expenses will be charged against principal?

7. SPECIFIC BEQUEST RULE

Section 663 provides that a distribution in satisfaction of a qualified specific bequest will not constitute a distribution deduction to the trust nor will it constitute taxable income to the distributee. I.R.C. § 663(a)(1). To qualify for this specific bequest exclusion, the amount of money or the identity of the specific property must be ascertainable as of the date of the inception of the trust or estate. Treas. Reg. § 1.663(a)–1(b)(1). The following are examples of gifts which qualify for the exclusion: (1) "I give $10,000 to Jane"; (2) "All my stock in Z Corporation. I give to Martin"; (3) a bequest through a testamentary trust of all corporate securities owned by the decedent at death; and (4) a bequest of household items and personal effects, automobiles, and jewelry. Cf. Treas. Reg. § 1.663(a)–1(c)(2), Example (1)(ii) and (c)(2)(i).

On the other hand, a bequest of the residue of a decedent's estate or a stated portion or fraction of the residue does not qualify as specific within the meaning of section 663, because it is not possible to determine the amount of the residue or the property comprising it until the decedent's death. Treas. Reg. § 1.663(a)–1(b)(2)(iii).

In addition, in order to meet the requirements of section 663, the gift or bequest must be payable pursuant to the terms of the trust or estate in not more than three installments. This is an arbitrary rule designed to separate a gift of income (akin to an annuity) from a gift of the property. The will or trust instrument governs, not what the trustee or executor actually does. If the trust or will requires four installment payments, then all flunk the specific bequest rule, and the distribution rules apply. However, the three-installment rule is applied to each beneficiary. Moreover, for this purpose, a trust is a separate beneficiary even though the beneficiary of the three installments from the estate is also a beneficiary of the trust. Thus, three qualified distributions from an estate can be made to a single beneficiary and that same beneficiary can receive three more qualified distributions from each trust into which pour assets from the same estate.

It is irrelevant whether the components of the installment are money or property. However, specific bequests of household items and personal effects, including the family automobile, are not counted in the three-installment test. Treas. Reg. § 1.663(a)–1(c). Also excluded is specifically devised real estate that passes directly from the decedent to the beneficiary under local law.

8.   WHEN TRUST INCOME IS TAXABLE

Trusts and estates are required to report their income on an annual basis like other taxpayers. I.R.C. 441(a). However, estates may elect to report income on a fiscal-year basis (I.R.C. § 441(b)(1)), while trusts generally must report on a calendar-year basis. I.R.C. § 644(a).

An estate's ability to elect a fiscal year for tax purposes provides a distinct income tax planning device for distributions from the estate to a beneficiary. That is, income distributed to a beneficiary will be recognized as such only in the beneficiary's taxable year in which the last month of the estate's taxable year falls. Suppose, for example, the estate elects a January 31st fiscal year (beginning February 1, 2023, and ending January 31, 2024). Assume further that on February 1, 2023, the estate distributes income to a beneficiary. Assuming that the beneficiary is a calendar-year taxpayer, the income will not be taxed to that beneficiary until the beneficiary's taxable year ending December 31, 2024, and, thus, the tax attributable to that income will not be payable until April 15, 2025 (although quarterly estimated payments may be required of the beneficiary during 2024). Thus, the beneficiary has tax-free use of the 2023 distribution for slightly over two years.

This deferral opportunity is permitted because the estate's DNI cannot be calculated until the end of the estate's fiscal year (January 31, 2024);

accordingly, the distribution on February 1, 2023, cannot be characterized as income or principal before January 31, 2024.

C. "SIMPLE" TRUSTS

1. INTRODUCTION

It is commonplace to describe trusts, for income tax purposes, as either "simple" or "complex." While these terms do not appear in the Internal Revenue Code, they are used in the implementing Treasury Regulations.

Simple trusts are those described in sections 651 and 652. Complex trusts are those described in sections 661 and 662.

A trust will be characterized as "simple" if it is required to distribute all of its income "currently," has no charitable beneficiaries, and does not make any distributions of corpus. In those years when the trust makes distributions of corpus, it will be considered a complex trust. Thus, in one year a trust may be a simple trust and, in the next, it may be a complex trust. Crucial to eligibility for classification as a simple trust is that the trust stipulate that all of its income be distributed "currently." The trust does not lose its status as a simple trust merely because the trustee did not, in fact, make the required distribution.

Section 651 describes the tax treatment of simple trusts. These trusts enjoy a tax deduction for the amounts that are "required to be distributed currently." However, the tax deduction is limited by section 651(b) to the trust's DNI.

Section 652 describes the tax consequences to beneficiaries of simple trusts. These beneficiaries will have the trust income "required to be distributed currently" included in their gross income whether or not the income is in fact distributed to the beneficiaries. However, the amount actually included in the beneficiaries' gross income cannot exceed the trust's DNI.

2. PERSONAL EXEMPTION FOR SIMPLE TRUSTS

Trusts that are required to distribute all of the trust's income annually enjoy a $300 exemption for federal income tax purposes. I.R.C. § 642(b)(2)(B). Trusts that are not required to distribute all of the trust's income annually enjoy only a $100 exemption. Estates enjoy a $600 exemption. I.R.C. § 642(b)(1). These exemptions, unchanged in amount since 1954, originally were intended to spare estates and trusts with trivial amounts of income from the burden of filing income tax returns. Spared, too, was the IRS from having to process such returns. See H.R. Rep. No. 1860, 75th Cong., 3d Sess. (1938), reprinted in 1939–1 (Part 2) CB 728, 761. Failure to adjust these exemptions for inflation suggests that, today,

Congress declines to act to increase trust and estate exemptions as part of a plan to limit the tax avoidance incentive that results from being able to warehouse, tax free—or at low tax rates—even small amounts of income in trusts and estates.

There is a tendency to say that trusts entitled to a $300 exemption are "simple" trusts and that trusts not entitled to the $300 exemption are "complex" trusts. Such labels are misleading. A trust required by the governing instrument to distribute all of its income is entitled to the $300 exemption even in years when it is classified as a complex trust because corpus was distributed from the trust in that particular year. See Treas. Reg. § 1.642(b)–1 and I.R.C. § 651. Classification as a complex trust means that the rules set out in sections 661–662 apply to the trust rather than those set out in sections 651–652.

3. WHAT IS INCOME?

A trust is classified as simple if it is required by the terms of its governing instrument to distribute all its "income." For purposes of this classification system, "income" refers to the trust's fiduciary accounting income, i.e., the trust's income determined not for income tax purposes but for trust accounting purposes.

What about the case where the beneficiary has the use of the trust property, i.e., resides rent free in a dwelling house owned by the trust? Is the reasonable value of the use of the dwelling treated as an income distribution to the beneficiary? Consider the following Technical Advice Memorandum and the case which follows.

TECHNICAL ADVICE MEMORANDUM 8341005
June 24, 1983.

[The issue considered in this ruling was whether the rent-free use of trust property by the income beneficiary was taxable income to that beneficiary under § 652. The trust was created by Grantor and funded with shares of stock. All trust income was to be paid to Grantor's Spouse. Using trust property, the trustees purchased residential premises in a resort area ("Resort Home") and Grantor's Spouse occupied Resort Home, rent-free. (The trustees had been given "the power to invest in such property, either real or personal, as may to them, in their absolute and uncontrolled discretion, seem advisable.") Resort Home produced no income. Hence, the trustees used trust income from the trust property to pay the real property taxes on Resort Home and to provide a year-round caretaker. None of the income was used to pay for electricity, heating or the personal expenses of Grantor's Spouse.]

In its income tax return for * * * Trust treated the real property taxes and the cost of the caretaker as its own expenditures. It did not regard those expenditures as distributions to Grantor's Spouse. Instead, Trust deducted the real property taxes. Trust did not deduct the cost of the caretaker but did pay the income tax on the earnings it retained and used for that purpose.

* * *

In Plant v. Commissioner, 30 B.T.A. 133 (1934), acq. 1976–1 C.B. 1, aff'd, 76 F.2d 8 (2d Cir.1935), a settlor created a residuary testamentary trust to pay over specified shares of its net income to his widow and two sons during their lives. The trust instrument provided further that the trustees were to maintain the settlor's elaborate estate in Connecticut so long as Henry, one of the settlor's sons, "may wish to occupy the same as a permanent or summer residence and to charge the expense of such maintenance proportionately against the income of the trusts hereby created for the benefit of my wife and sons before ascertaining the net income from such trusts." 76 F.2d at 9. During [the tax years in question] * * * the trustees expended (exclusive of taxes) $14,754.47 and $37,221.98, respectively, in the maintenance of the Connecticut estate, and charged the amounts against the income of the testamentary trust. The trustees treated the amounts as undistributable income, and paid income taxes thereon. The Commissioner determined that the trustees' expenditures constituted taxable income to Henry.

The Board of Tax Appeals held that the income collected by the trustees and used in maintaining the Connecticut estate did not represent income distributed or distributable to Henry. The Second Circuit agreed with the Board of Tax Appeals and reasoned that the expenditures of the Connecticut estate were not applied to the use of Henry, but were employed in maintaining a capital asset of the testamentary trust. Therefore, in spite of the fact that Henry received some benefit from the expenditures, the income so used was not distributed to him.

[The IRS concluded that the questioned expenditures "were not applied to the use of Grantor's Spouse but were employed in maintaining a capital asset of Trust" and, accordingly, "Grantor's Spouse was not taxable on the income of Trust used to pay the real property taxes and the caretaker."]

DUPONT TESTAMENTARY TRUST V. COMMISSIONER

United States Court of Appeals, Fifth Circuit, 1975.
514 F.2d 917.

CLARK, CIRCUIT JUDGE:

The Commissioner disallowed deductions claimed by the taxpayer, a testamentary trust created under the will of Alfred I. duPont, in the tax years 1966 and 1967 for expenses of maintaining an estate owned by the taxpayer but which was then being used as Mrs. duPont's home. The expense deductions were claimed to be ordinary and necessary expenses under § 212 because the estate was rental property or alternatively because the estate was part of an income producing entity comprised of the estate and securities owned by taxpayer. * * *

About 1910 Alfred I. duPont built a mansion on a 300 acre tract in Brandywine Hundred, New Castle County, Delaware which he named "Nemours." Mr. duPont lived at Nemours with his wife, Jessie Ball duPont * * *

In 1925 Mr. duPont organized Nemours, Inc. (the corporation) and transferred to it full title to the mansion house and grounds in exchange for all of the corporation's stock. Subsequently Mr. and Mrs. duPont leased Nemours for the term of their joint lives plus the life of the survivor. The agreed rental was one dollar a year. The duPonts were required by the lease agreement to pay all taxes and the expense of the upkeep of the buildings and grounds. In January 1929 Mr. duPont transferred to the corporation 20,000 shares of preferred stock of Almour Securities, Inc. valued at 2,000,000 dollars. In exchange for this transfer, the lease agreement was amended to provide that the corporation would pay taxes and expenses of upkeep.

* * *

Mr. duPont died in 1935 survived by his wife. His will vested title to the stock of the corporation in his executors who were instructed by the will to set up a trust to continue the maintenance of the grounds. The stock of the corporation was to comprise the corpus of this testamentary trust along with large blocks of other securities. Mrs. duPont was a trustee and the principal income beneficiary for her life. The trust was to pay her 200,000 dollars plus any income remaining after the payment of specified annuities. The trustees were directed to organize a charitable foundation at the death of Mrs. duPont and to transfer to it the trust assets.

* * *

During 1966 and 1967, the tax years in question, the gross income of the trust was 13,000,000 dollars. Of this sum 11,000,000 dollars was distributed to Mrs. duPont. The trust spent 255,753 dollars in 1966 and 274,451 dollars in 1967 for general maintenance of the Nemours estate. An additional 114,284 dollars was expended during 1967 for repaving existing paved roadways and walkways; paving existing unpaved roadways; rehabilitating various structures such as a classical temple, ornamental balustrades, steps, fountains, terraces, flagstones, and urns; and purchasing a jeep and a dump truck. The Commissioner disallowed all of these deductions. The reasons given were that (1) the property was not held for the production of income; (2) the expenditures did not qualify as administration expenses * * *. Alternatively he contended that the 114,284 dollar outlay represented capital expenditures which were not allowable as deductions.

PREPAID RENT

The taxpayer maintains that the deductions were proper under * * * § 212(1), which provides a deduction for "all the ordinary and necessary expenses paid or incurred during the taxable year . . . for the production or collection of income . . ."

Taxpayer contends that under the 1929 amendment to the 1925 lease to the duPonts, the transfer of the 2,000,000 dollars worth of Almour securities constituted prepaid rent, and therefore that, insofar as the corporation and the trust were concerned, Nemours was income producing rental property.

The attempt to characterize the transfer of the Almour securities as prepaid rent was correctly rejected by the Tax Court both as a matter of form and of substance. No part of these assets or the dividends therefrom were ever reported as taxable rental income on the corporation's income tax returns. The 1929 agreement clearly establishes that Mr. duPont conveyed the Almour securities to the corporation which he continuously owned and controlled until the time of his death, to enable it to pay taxes and maintenance expenses he had previously borne personally. The only payment specified as rent in the initial agreement and in the 1929 amendment was a token 1 dollar a year. The record contains no other indication that the conveyance of Almour stock was intended to constitute prepaid rent. Neither the documentation or the conduct of the parties indicates that the securities were transferred for any purpose other than to relieve the duPonts of the day-to-day burdens of administering the estate.

No attempt was made to show what the anticipated expenses of maintaining the estate might be as compared to the income produced by or the total value of Almour securities. In short, the taxpayer trust simply failed to carry its burden of proving that Nemours was rental property in these tax years. This failure of affirmative proof controls our decision here. * * *

PROPERTY HELD FOR THE PRODUCTION OF INCOME

Alternatively, the taxpayer urges the upkeep and maintenance expense was deductible under § 212(2) which allows a deduction for "all the ordinary and necessary expenses paid or incurred . . . for the management, conservation or maintenance of property held for the production of income. . . ."

To support this argument before us, taxpayer relies principally on Bingham's Trust v. Commissioner of Internal Revenue, 325 U.S. 365, 65

S. Ct. 1232, 89 L. Ed. 1670 (1945) in which the Court held that legal fees incurred to contest an income tax deficiency were deductible since they were funds expended for the conservation of trust property which was held for the production of income. The taxpayer asserts that *Bingham's* rationale covers the expenses incurred in maintaining Nemours even though Nemours was not strictly property held for the production of income.

The thrust of the argument is that the taxpayer trust, an entity for the production of income comparable to a business enterprise, could deduct these expenses as maintenance expenses even though Nemours did not directly produce income, because payment of the maintenance and upkeep expense was a fundamental duty of the trustees in the administration of the trust. This interpretation glosses over the fact that a threshold determination in *Bingham* was that the property which the expenditure protected was held for the production of income. Although it was the duty of the trustees to maintain Nemours, Nemours was not property held for the production of income. * * * In the case at bar, the question which concerned the Court in *Bingham*—whether the expense incurred was connected with, or proximately resulted from, the management of property held for production of income—is never reached.

Despite the lease agreement between the wholly owned corporation and the duPonts and the controlling terms of Mr. duPont's testamentary trust, Nemours remained the duPonts' personal residence. It was the antithesis of income producing property. The expenses incurred in the maintenance and upkeep of this private residence never were deductible expenses relating to property held for the present or future production of income. [The court, in a footnote, commented that the trust itself was not invalid nor was it the result of "sham, fraud, purpose of tax avoidance or other lack of bona fides" and that it had "a real and viable purpose: to hold the property for the benefit of the spouse of testator during her lifetime and for the ultimate disposition to a charitable foundation at her death. This is an entirely proper purpose for the creation and funding of a trust."]

* * *

We agree with the Tax Court that the trustees were entitled to no deduction for the expenses incurred in the maintenance and upkeep of Nemours during Mrs. duPont's life * * *.

Affirmed in part and remanded.

NOTE

On remand, the Tax Court in duPont Testamentary Trust v. Commissioner, 66 T.C. 761 (1976), considered whether the maintenance expenses for the "Nemours" estate were deductible by the trust under sections 651 or 661 as distributions includible in the widow's gross income. On this issue, the court concluded that, since the expenses were incurred by the trust pursuant to a contractual obligation, the expenditures could not be deemed to be distributions to the beneficiary under the terms of the trust.

The court also considered the question as to whether the maintenance expenditures, even if required by the trust, could properly be treated as distributions taxable to the beneficiary. On this point, it is of interest to note that the government argued that the *Plant* decision cited in Tech. Adv. Mem. 8341005 was controlling and that such expenditures were expenses "employed in maintaining a capital asset of the trust estate." Commissioner v. Plant, 76 F.2d 8, 9–10 (2d Cir. 1935), aff'g, 30 B.T.A. 133 (1934). The Tax Court answered by stating that it "did not feel completely comfortable" with the decision in *Plant* and was not relying on that case. Curiously, it was only in 1976 that in 1976–2 C.B. 2 the IRS announced its acquiescence in the decision in *Plant*.

PROBLEM

What is the proper tax treatment of income of a trust that is required to be applied to the maintenance of a residence held in trust for occupancy by a surviving spouse or other designated beneficiary of a trust?

D. COMPLEX TRUSTS

With one exception, the income tax deduction for distributions from complex trusts and estates is mandatory up to the amount of the trust or estate's DNI determined under section 643(a), that is the amount of income available for distribution to the beneficiaries. The exception applies to distributions in satisfaction of a specific bequest. I.R.C. § 663. This is the same rule that applies in the case of simple trusts.

H.R. REP. NO. 99–426
99th Cong., 1st Sess. at 806 (1985), reprinted in 1986–3 C.B. 806 (Vol. 2).

The complex trust rules apply to all trusts that are not simple trusts and all estates. Thus, the complex trust rules apply, for example, if there are distributions of corpus during the year, if the trust has any charitable beneficiaries for the taxable year, if any part of the income of the trust is not distributable that year, or if the trustee has discretion as to whether or not to distribute income that year.

Under the complex trust rules, the trust or estate is allowed a deduction for amounts of income that are required to be distributed that year (whether or not actually distributed during that taxable year) and for all other amounts that are properly paid, credited, or required to be distributed for that taxable year. . . .

E. ESTATES

Estates enjoy a $600 exemption while complex trusts enjoy only a $100 exemption. See I.R.C. § 642(b). However, in other respects for income tax purposes, estates are treated as complex trusts. That means, as a general proposition, that every distribution from the estate carries out the income of the estate unless the distribution is in satisfaction of a specific bequest. See I.R.C. §§ 661(a) & 663(a).

1. SPOUSAL ALLOWANCE

Statutes in most jurisdictions authorize payment or set off of a "spousal allowance" from a decedent's property notwithstanding the absence of any authorization in the decedent's will.[5] This is an amount thought necessary by the court to support the surviving spouse for a short period following the death of the other spouse, usually one year. Tax accounting for this payment is not intuitive. On its face, payment of the spousal allowance would appear to be made out of principal rather than income? Is that to suggest that it is free of income taxes in the hands of the surviving spouse. In Estate of McCoy v. Commissioner, 50 T.C. 562 (1968), the widow was heard to make this claim. The widow received $7,000 in one year and $12,000 the next from her husband's estate as a result of the court's award of a widow's allowance to be paid, as permitted under local law. These amounts were paid out of the estate's principal as ordered by the court—and not out of the estate's income. Despite the widow's claims that the distribution should be free of income tax consequences, the estate was required to deduct the amount of the distribution (to the extent of the estate's DNI) and the widow had taxable income to the extent of the deduction claimed by the estate. The *McCoy* court explained that "a widow's allowance ordered by a Probate Court, whether payable from income or corpus, is an amount properly paid * * * or required to be distributed" as described in section 661(a) and is, as such, a deduction in computing the estate's taxable income. Id. at 566. See also Treas. Regs. §§ 1.661(a)–2(e) and 1.662(a)–3(b).

2. ELECTIVE SHARE

The "spousal allowance" should be compared to the situation where the surviving spouse has claimed his or her "elective share," which gives the surviving spouse the option to reject the will of the deceased spouse and claim a statutorily prescribed share of the property otherwise passing

---

[5]   See, e.g., Iowa Code § 633.374 (2022) (allowing a spouse to submit an application for a 12-month spousal allowance); Miss. Code Ann. § 91–7–135 (2022) (permitting the court to determine amount necessary for "comfortable support" for spouse and/or children for one year); Mo. Rev. Stat. § 474.260 (2022) (permitting the court to consider spouse's standard of living to compute the one-year support allowance and that amount is not chargeable to any amount passing under intestate succession or elective share); N.C. Gen. Stat. § 30–15 (2022) (permitting a $60,000 spousal allowance for one year).

under the will of the deceased spouse. Typically, "elective share" statutes allow the surviving spouse to claim as much as 50 percent of the deceased spouse's property.[6] As a result, this may disappoint the beneficiaries under the will who, as a result of the spouse's election, will receive a corresponding lesser amount. One income tax issue generated by these facts is whether satisfaction of the elective share carries out the income of the estate to the surviving spouse.

The position of the IRS is quite clear. Beginning with decedents who die after 1999, none of the estate's income is carried out to the surviving spouse when the elective share is satisfied. See Treas. Reg. § 1.663(c)–5, Example 7. This conclusion assumes that the surviving spouse, as is quite common under the elective share statutes of the various states, is not entitled to any of the estate's income and does not participate in appreciation or depreciation of the estate's assets.

PROBLEM

Doug died June 1. His will, after providing for the payment of debts, claims, administration expenses and death taxes, devised and bequeathed all the rest, residue and remainder of his estate to Wendy, his surviving spouse. The executor elected the cash method and calendar year for reporting the income of the estate. During the period from June 1 to December 31, the following transactions were consummated:

Receipts

Cash dividends	$15,000
Interest on corporate bonds	15,000
Total receipts	$30,000

Payments and distributions

Debts and funeral expenses	$5,000
Miscellaneous administration expenses	2,500
Distributions to Wendy:	
Cash award to Wendy as surviving spouse by Probate Court	10,000
Family auto (fair market value)	3,000
Total payments and distributions	$20,500

---

[6] See, e.g., Kan. Stat. Ann. § 59–6a202 (2022) (granting an elective share based on the length of time the couple was married up to 50% for those married at least 15 years); Ky. Rev. Stat. Ann. §§ 392.020 & 392.080 (West 2022) (surviving spouse is entitled to 1/3 of any real estate and 1/2 of other property); N.J. Stat. Ann. § 3B:8–1 (West 2022) (providing an elective share of 1/3 as long as the couple had not been living apart); Tenn. Code Ann. § 31–4–101 (West 2022) (granting an elective share ranging from 10%–40% based on the length of the marriage).

What are the income tax consequences of these transactions to Doug's estate and to Wendy?

F. THE TIER SYSTEM

Trusts having more than one beneficiary present additional tax accounting issues relating to the allocation of distributable net income (DNI) among those beneficiaries. Those issues are resolved by the rules provided in sections 652(a) and 662(a), rules typically referred to as the "tier" rules.

> *Example*: Maria Elena was entitled to all of the income from a trust established by her deceased spouse, Luis. The trustee was also authorized to make distributions of principal to Juan, Maria Elena's child, if needed by Juan for his education. This year, at a time when the trust had $12,000 of DNI, the trustee distributed $12,000 to Maria Elena and $4,000 to Juan. As a result of the tier rules, Juan is treated as having received a tax-free distribution of capital and Maria Elena as having received all of the DNI. Treas. Reg. § 1.662(a)–3(d), Example.

The issues are further complicated when distributions of both cash and property are made from the trust in the same year.

1. MANDATORY ALLOCATION OF DNI

Technically speaking, the so-called "tier system" of allocating DNI among multiple distributees from the same trust or estate refers to the mandatory allocation of DNI whenever there are (1) both mandatory and discretionary income recipients, and/or (2) multiple recipients of mandatory payments and/or discretionary payments. Normally, all distributions from estates are "second tier" distributions because usually there is no requirement in the governing instrument that such distributions be made currently.

The "first tier" recipients are those who have a legally enforceable right, using fiduciary accounting rules, to a current distribution of income from the trust. I.R.C. §§ 652(a) and 662(a)(1). The available DNI will be prorated among these beneficiaries, with each beneficiary taking his or her pro rata share of dividends, interest, and tax-exempt income, as well as other income included in the DNI of the trust (even including gains realized from the sale or exchange of property in those few cases where such gains are required to be included in DNI).

The "second tier" distributees are all others who receive distributions but have no legally enforceable right to a distribution of income. I.R.C. § 662(a)(2). Distributions to second tier beneficiaries will constitute taxable income only to the extent that the first tier beneficiaries did not exhaust the available DNI. The DNI remaining after the allocation to the first tier beneficiaries is prorated among the second tier beneficiaries with each one taking his or her proportionate share of dividend income, interest, tax-exempt interest, etc. I.R.C. § 662(a)(2) and (b).

The distribution rules are quite inflexible, the inflexibility resulting from a determination to deny fiduciaries the opportunity to manipulate income tax consequences by allocating income among the distributees of the estate or trust in a fashion designed to minimize income taxes for the estate and beneficiaries as a whole. Instead, as noted above, DNI, to the extent distributed, is annually prorated, first, among "first tier" recipients of distributions from the estate or trust according to the aggregate distribution each receives, and, second, whatever remains of the DNI, to the extent distributed, is prorated among "second tier" recipients of distributions from the estate or trust, here too, according to the aggregate distribution each receives in that tax year.

> *Example*: Ben and Jerry are beneficiaries of their father's trust. Bank, as trustee, is authorized to make distributions to either or both of them "when, Bank, deems it in the proposed distributee's best interest." Last year, Ben needed money and Bank distributed $1,000 to him. No distribution was made to Jerry last year. The trust's DNI last year was $800. In this instance, accordingly, all $800 of the trust's income was taxed to Ben last year (and Ben was deemed to have received a $200 nontaxable distribution from the trust).

PROBLEMS

Sam is trustee of two trusts, the Bigge Family Trust and the Little Family Trust. Each trust has $10,000 of distributable net income this year.

1. The Bigge Family Trust is required to distribute all its income to Mrs. Bigge. In addition, the trustee is authorized to make distributions of principal to Mrs. Bigge and to the Bigge children in such amounts as the trustee "deems appropriate to their respective circumstances." The trustee has distributed $6,000 to the Bigge's son, Thad, this year. Mrs. Bigge received a total of $12,000 from the trust this year. What is the trust's distribution deduction this year? I.R.C. §§ 651 and 661. What are the income tax consequences to Thad and his mother from the trust distributions they received this year? I.R.C. §§ 652 and 662.

2. The trustee of the Little Family Trust is authorized to distribute to Mrs. Little and the Little lineal descendants so much of the income and principal of the trust as the trustee determines to be in the "best interests of the income

beneficiaries" but with "due regard for the interests of the remainderman." This year, the trustee distributed $20,000 to Mrs. Little's son, Fred, and $20,000 to Mrs. Little. I.R.C. §§ 651, 652, 661 and 662. What are the income tax consequences to Mrs. Little and Fred this year?

2. PROPERLY PAID, CREDITED, OR REQUIRED TO BE DISTRIBUTED

Sections 661(a)(2) and 662(a)(2) speak in terms of second-tier distributions being "properly paid, credited, or required to be distributed to all beneficiaries." Each of those words is important in determining whether the trust is entitled to a distribution deduction and whether a distribution constitutes taxable income to the recipients.

For an amount to be determined "paid" or "credited," an actual payment or specific credit to the beneficiary must occur. That is, in determining whether an amount has been "paid," accrual notions are not utilized, nor are ideas of constructive receipt. See McCauley v. United States, 193 F. Supp. 938 (E.D. Ark. 1961) (not considered "paid" where the executor, as sole beneficiary of the estate, deposited estate funds to her own bank account, intending thereby merely to repay herself for advances to the estate). However, there will be a payment, within the meaning of the statute, when the trustee uses trust funds to discharge a legal obligation of the beneficiary. Treas. Reg. § 1.662(a)–4; cf. Old Colony Trust Co. v. Commissioner, 279 U.S. 716 (1929). In such cases, the beneficiary is deemed to have taxable income to the extent that his or her legal obligation is discharged. Rev. Rul. 58–69, 1958–1 C.B. 254. When an amount is "credited" to a beneficiary, actual payment need not be made. However, a mere bookkeeping entry is not sufficient, because the amount must be subject to immediate enjoyment by the beneficiary. This becomes a question of fact for the courts. Harris v. United States, 370 F.2d 887 (4th Cir. 1966).

Determination of whether a payment is "properly" made turns on applicable local law and the governing instrument. See, e.g., Kennedy v. Commissioner, 38 B.T.A. 1307 (1938) (distribution is deductible by the trust in computing its income only if the payment is proper); cf. Bohan v. United States, 456 F.2d 851 (8th Cir.1972) (Nonacq.) and Rev. Rul. 72–396, 1972–2 C.B. 312.

BUCKMASTER V. UNITED STATES

United States Court of Appeals, Tenth Circuit, 1993.
984 F.2d 379.

LOGAN, CIRCUIT JUDGE.

* * *The only issue on appeal is whether the estate is entitled to claim a deduction under I.R.C. § 661 for income it distributed to estate beneficiaries during two of the estate's tax years. The disbursements were made without explicit authority under the will and without any prior order from the state probate court in Oklahoma; but the distributions were approved as part of the final accounting in the probate court's order of final settlement and again later by a nunc pro tunc order specifically referencing the payments.

I

Daisy Murphy died testate on February 9, 1984, leaving a will that gave her entire estate to her niece, Sylvia M. Buckmaster, and to her nephew, Jesse Murphy, in equal shares. Murphy was named as executor. * * * The estate contained valuable mineral interests that earned significant royalties during the course of the estate's administration. Choosing for the estate a tax year ending January 31, 1985, Murphy distributed during that year $437,000 of the estate's income to himself and to Buckmaster in equal shares, and the estate took a deduction for this amount, plus Oklahoma gross production taxes and federal windfall profits taxes relating to that income, on the estate's income tax return. The estate remained open for another year during which it distributed $155,649.51 to the beneficiaries, again claiming similar deductions on the estate's income tax return. In neither year did the estate secure an order from the probate court authorizing the distributions before they were made, but the estate was closed out on February 20, 1986. At that time the probate court issued an order of final settlement in which it approved all actions taken by the personal representative without the order itself referencing the specific disbursements to the beneficiaries. These distributions, however, apparently were shown on the executor's final accounting filed with the petition for final settlement * * * and the probate court's order referenced the final accounting.

When the IRS notified the estate after an August 1987 audit that it was disallowing the deductions taken by the estate, the personal representative obtained from the probate court an order nunc pro tunc to reflect explicit approval of the disbursements. This did not satisfy the IRS, which issued a deficiency assessment disallowing the deductions as unlawful because there was no probate court approval before they were made. * * *

* * *

II

The federal income tax law recognizes the estate of a decedent as a separate tax entity entitled to choose its own tax year ending at the end of any month not exceeding one year after the decedent's death. I.R.C. §§ 441(b), 443(a)(2), 641; Treas. Reg. § 1.443–1(a)(2). It also recognizes the right of the representative of the estate, when acting properly, to spread the income otherwise taxable to the estate between the estate and the beneficiaries. This is accomplished by allowing deductions on the estate's income tax return for income required to be distributed currently or in fact "properly paid" during the tax year to beneficiaries of the estate. I.R.C. § 661(a)(2). It is common practice for personal representatives of decedents' estates to make distributions of income during the estate's tax year either for the support or convenience of the beneficiaries or to obtain the advantages of having the income taxed in the lowest possible rates.

The only question in the instant case is the correctness of the district court's determination that the distributions from the estate were not "properly paid" unless the probate court approved them before they were made. It is acknowledged that the will did not require the payments. The law is that the determination of what is properly paid is a matter governed by local law. See Freuler v. Helvering, 291 U.S. 35, 44–45, 54 S. Ct. 308, 311–312, 78 L. Ed. 634 (1934). * * * We review the district court's determination of local law de novo. * * *

The United States Supreme Court has considered the issue before us in the context of distributions from a trust under California law. In *Freuler*, the Supreme Court found no meaningful distinction between pre-distribution and post-distribution orders: "[I]f the order of the state court does in fact govern the distribution, it is difficult to see why, whether it antedated actual payment or was subsequent to that event, it should not be effective to fix the amount of the taxable income of the beneficiaries." 291 U.S. at 44–45, 54 S. Ct. at 311–312. * * *

A number of state court decisions have upheld post-payment approvals of personal representative's payments to beneficiaries. * * *

The government claims and the district court found that the law in Oklahoma is contrary to these other decisions, * * *.

* * *

Our task is to determine how the Oklahoma Supreme Court, if presented with the issue before us, would rule. * * * The probate laws were not drafted with the income tax laws in mind. Rather, they exist to facilitate resolution of a decedent's affairs and distribution of the estate to the proper beneficiaries. Of course it would be better if the personal representative would secure advance probate court approval of distributions of income from the estate. But these decisions often must be made near the end of the tax year of the estate, when the amount of its income can be estimated reasonably. There may not be time to follow the normal procedures for probate court approval. In such cases the personal representative acts on his own at some peril. Nevertheless, a disbursement that operates to reduce the net tax liability of the estate and the beneficiaries and that does not contravene provisions of the will would almost certainly meet with the approval of the probate court, as it did here.

We hold that the Oklahoma Supreme Court, if presented with the issue, would consider distributions of estate income by an executor or administrator made without prior probate court approval but subsequently ratified by that court to be "properly paid" within the definition of I.R.C. § 661(a)(2). This is the position of every appellate court that has directly considered the question, including the United States Supreme Court. The decision of the district court is therefore reversed, and the cause remanded for further proceedings consistent with this opinion.

3.   SEPARATE SHARE RULE

A single trust or estate may have multiple beneficiaries with differing interests in the trust or estate. Accordingly, section 663(c) provides that distinctly separate shares of a trust or estate will be treated as separate trusts or separate estates for purposes of determining the distributable net income of each separate share when computing the distribution deduction available to each such separate share. The separate share rule applies whenever the trust or estate provides for "substantially separate and independent shares" for different beneficiaries. The rule is mandatory and not elective. Treas. Reg. § 1.663(c)–1(d).

a.   Funding Pecuniary and Fractional Formula Gifts

The separate share rule was extended to estates in 1998. This happy development allowed for Regulation § 1.663(c)–4 in which the IRS takes the position that "pecuniary formula" and "fractional formula" bequests are separate shares. For an illustration of the significant impact of this decision, consider the relief potential in a case like Harkness v. United States, 469 F.2d 310 (Ct. Cl. 1972), a case decided before the separate share rule applied to estates. There, the executors claimed that the surviving spouse should be treated as having received only 50 percent of the estate's 1955 DNI despite having received approximately 76 percent of the total property distributed to all of the beneficiaries of the estate in 1955. In finding for the IRS and concluding that the surviving spouse is taxable on 76 percent of the DNI, the court deemed irrelevant the executors' claim that the disproportionate distribution in favor of the surviving spouse was made purely for reasons of convenience in administering the decedent's estate—and not because of tax considerations.

Noting only the conclusion in *Harkness* illustrates the inflexibility of the distribution rules but it does not say enough about the importance of the case generally or its importance in indicating how application of the separate share rule to estates can be meaningful. The considerations that gave rise to the controversy in *Harkness* are quite commonly encountered. The difficulty in such cases may be said to have stemmed from the provisions of the testator's will, provisions that were undoubtedly carefully crafted (in as much as similar provisions are common in wills). The testator's goal was to minimize estate taxes by taking advantage of the marital deduction available for property passing to his spouse. I.R.C. § 2056. The provision for the spouse was "fractional" rather than "pecuniary", i.e., the testator gave his spouse a gift of a fraction of his estate (e.g., "1/2") rather than a pecuniary amount (e.g., "$300,000"), and in good tax planning fashion he barred his executors from charging any death taxes (that might be paid) to his spouse's gift. Freeing the spouse's gift from death taxes is commonly provided as a means of avoiding a complicated calculation that might otherwise result. So, in *Harkness*, you had a situation where the spouse is to receive 1/2 of the testator's property and all death taxes that become payable are to be paid out of the share passing to beneficiaries other than the surviving spouse.

Enter now the executors engaged in collecting and distributing the testator's property. They are, practically speaking, keeping two accounts, one for the spouse's 1/2 and another for the 1/2 passing to the other beneficiaries. In normal course, death taxes are paid—and charged against the 1/2 not passing to the spouse. At this point, the executors come to a crossroads. Up until now, practically speaking, receipts and disbursements received in the course of administration of the estate had been charged 1/2 to the spouse's account and 1/2 to the other beneficiaries' account. This was all relatively simple—but it was about to change because the 1/2 belonging to the other beneficiaries had been dramatically reduced by the death tax payment—in this case, some $36 million! The executors then came upon a scheme that they believed would facilitate the estate accounting. Rather than adjust the fraction that was to be applied in dividing receipts and disbursements by the estate subsequent to the death tax payment (as would be required to correctly reflect the interests of the spouse relative to those of the other beneficiaries), the executors determined to make a distribution to the surviving spouse of that part of the estate necessary to allow the executors to continue to charge receipts and disbursements 1/2 to the spouse and 1/2 to the other beneficiaries. This resulted in a distribution to the spouse of $27 million in 1955 and, while it may seem hard to feel sorry for the spouse, this decision meant that the spouse received 76 percent of the property distributed to beneficiaries by the executor in 1955—and as a result the IRS claimed that she was taxable on 76 percent of the income earned in 1955 by the estate.

The spouse protested. She said that estate and trust accounting principles entitled her to only 1/2 the estate's income (since she was beneficiary of only 1/2 the testator's estate)—and only 1/2 the income was credited to her account by the executors—and, therefore, it is, as she might have said privately, "plain wrong" that she should be taxed on 76 percent of the income solely because she received 76 percent of the total property distributed in 1955.

The executors, for their part, reiterated that they were only trying to simplify the accounting for the estate. The court's response was unmistakable:

> There can be no doubt but that plaintiff's situation falls squarely within the literal provisions of Section 662(a)(2)(B), and plaintiff is not understood to contend otherwise. The nub of her contention is that the payments here involved should not be treated as being covered by the statute because the executors' actions were not tax motivated. Even so, the section applies. Clear statutory coverage of this kind, based upon a presumption that any distribution is deemed to be a distribution of the estate's income to the extent of its income for the year, does not and cannot be made to depend on such intangible factors as the subjective intent of executors.
>
> Section 662(a)(2)(B) was specifically intended, for the purposes of that section, "to avoid the necessity for tracing of income." [H.R. Rep. No. 1337, 83d Cong., 2d Sess. A199, 3 U.S.C. Cong. & Adm. News 4017, 4339 (1954); S. Rep. No. 1622, 83d Cong., 2d Sess. 349, 3 U.S.C. Cong. & Adm. News 4621, 4990 (1954)]. Such tracing was required by the 1939 Code, which provided that distributions by an estate or trust to its beneficiaries were taxed to the beneficiaries for the taxable year in which they received the distributions only if the distributions were made from the current income of the estate or trust. As shown, this lent itself to various kinds of manipulations by executors in the labeling of estate moneys as "income" or "principal." To eliminate such manipulations and tax consequences based upon such estate tax accounting designations of what was "principal" and "income" and from which source a distribution had been made, the "tracing" requirement was, for such distribution purposes, eliminated.

469 F.2d at 315. Instead, the court, citing 3 U.S.C. Cong. & Adm. News, supra n. 6, at 4340, 4990, noted that " '[t]he beneficiary's proportionate share of the distributable net income * * * is determined by taking the same fractional part of [the] distributable net income as the * * * amounts * * * distributed to him * * * bear to the total of [the] amounts * * * distributed to all beneficiaries.' " Then, taking note, figuratively speaking, that the

executors claimed to be between "the rock and the hard place", the court might have been heard to say "maybe not" when it explained:

> The fact nevertheless remains that, by making the discretionary "balancing" distributions as they did—required neither by the will nor state law—plaintiff received, under their estate accounting, less of the distributable net income than she probably otherwise would have. There is no showing that—either by not making distributions until the estate was wound up finally, or otherwise—the residuary estate could not have been so managed as to produce the same result as the statutory formula. Thus, in that sense (and not in the sense of tax avoidance), the distributions were "manipulated" so that plaintiff, who received over 75 percent of the 1955 payments, is nevertheless said to have received in that year only 50 percent of the taxable distributable net income. On its face and as its purpose is shown by its development and legislative history, the statute was designed to prevent such a result for tax purposes. Indeed, the statutory formula could be considered as providing the more natural and logical result— income earned during the administration of the residuary estate is allocated to the beneficiaries in the same ratio as their interests in the corpus of such estate. Generally, of course, various percentages of corpus will produce like percentages of income. It is thus plain that plaintiff's situation is, by the unambiguous provisions thereof, covered by the statute and although recognizing, of course, the difficulties involved in envisaging every specific situation that could arise under general statutory language, it would nevertheless appear to constitute the type of situation that Congress intended should be covered.

469 F.2d at 316–17.

Applying the separate share rule in cases such as *Harkness* will provide significant relief for those who administer wills and trusts containing complex marital deduction formula clauses. The saga of separate share, however, is more than just formula clauses. Separate share is an issue in the commonest of situations such as distributions in satisfaction of the elective share of a surviving spouse, i.e., where the spouse ignores the decedent's will and exercises an option provided by state law to claim a statutorily determined share of the decedent's estate.

b.   Two-or-More Beneficiaries

The IRS has determined that separate shares are created where the residuary estate passes to several beneficiaries. See Treas. Reg. § 1.663(c)– 1(a). This is an important development because it means that residuary beneficiaries such as, for example, Devon and Jackson will not be at odds over distributions from Dad's estate. Devon needs $5,000; Jackson does not;

the estate's available cash is limited to $5,000; the estate is, at least for a time, otherwise illiquid. Dad's executor distributes the $5,000 to Devon in a year when the estate has $3,000 of taxable income. Prior to the extension of the separate share rule to estates, all $3,000 would be taxable income to Devon. With the separate share rule extended to estates, only $1,500 of the $5,000 distributed to Devon will be taxable income to him; the remaining $1,500 will be taxable income to the estate.

PROBLEMS

Harry's two adult children were the sole beneficiaries under his will. Harry's 19-year old widow elected against the will, claiming her statutory share. Harry's estate was valued at $100,000; the widow's statutory share had a monetary value of $30,000. This year, a year in which the estate had $2,000 of DNI, the executor distributed $30,000 to the widow in satisfaction of her claim. Immediately after the end of the year, on January 1st, the executor distributed the balance of the estate to Harry's children. The children received a total of $72,000, consisting of the $70,000 remaining after the distribution to the widow plus $2,000 earned during administration of Harry's estate.

1. Assuming the widow is in the top income tax bracket and taking into consideration the separate share rule of section 663(c) having been extended to estates, suggest the likely income tax consequences to the widow, and to Harry's two children, the latter two being the estate's beneficiaries in both tax years.

2. What difference would it make, if any, if the elective share in Harry's state of domicile was equal to a (i) fixed dollar amount; or (ii) percentage or fraction of Harry's estate and, if the latter, expressly provided the surviving spouse with a share in the appreciation or depreciation experienced by the estate during the course of administration (and of the income earned by the estate during the course of administration) as is common in certain situations?

G. TAX-EXEMPT INTEREST IN ESTATE OR TRUST

Under section 103, interest on certain state and local government obligations is free from federal income taxation.

Normally, the presence of tax-exempt interest in a trust or an estate means that a portion of the expenses of administration becomes nondeductible. Regulation § 1.265–1(c) requires the allocation of indirect expenses to be made "in the light of all facts and circumstances in each case." The portion that is nondeductible is the portion that is attributed to the tax-exempt interest. Obviously, controversy can arise as to the portion of the expenses that is attributed to the tax-exempt interest and the method of calculation, as can be seen in the following case.

MANUFACTURERS HANOVER TRUST CO. v. UNITED STATES

United States Court of Claims, 1963.
312 F.2d 785.

DAVIS, JUDGE.

* * * [Plaintiff was trustee of a trust required to distribute all of its income to Millicent Rogers during her lifetime. The facts given in the court's opinion suggests that the trustee's accounting might have been presented to the court as follows:

Gross income items allocable to income:

Domestic dividends	$26,245.95	
Foreign dividends	150.00	
Interest	<u>468.75</u>	
Total	$26,864.70	(A)

Gross income items allocable to principal:

Taxable stock dividends	$162.25		
Long term capital gain	71,205.24		
Short term capital loss	<u>(171.10)</u>	$71,196.39	(B)
Tax-exempt interest		<u>8,370.85</u>	(C)
TOTAL		$106,431.94	(D)

In addition, during 1954 the trustee incurred the following expenses:

Trustee fees	$3,350.68		
Legal fees	<u>49,015.25</u>	$52,365.93	(E)
N.Y. Corporate Profits Tax		<u>1,658.88</u>	
Total expenses		$54,024.81	
TENTATIVE TAXABLE INCOME		$52,407.13	

The court was faced with deciding what portion, if not all of the $52,365.93 in the legal and trustee fees was income tax deductible. The dispute arose because the trustee and the IRS differed as to the formula to be used in determining the portion of the legal and trustee fees that should be allocated to tax exempt interest and thereby rendered nondeductible. The litigants used the following formulas, respectively, with the taxpayer determining that $4,121.20 should be nondeductible and the IRS determining that $12,442.14 should be nondeductible:

Trustee:	Internal Revenue Service:
$$\frac{C}{D} \times E = \$4,121.20$$	$$\frac{C}{A+C} \times E = \$12,442.14$$

In broader terms, the dispute raised the question of whether "apples and oranges" were being mixed. The taxpayer claimed that the IRS, in its allocation of indirect expenses between tax exempt interest and taxable income, was inappropriately relying on the rules applied by § 643(a)(5) in determining distributable net income (DNI), DNI being a legislatively created concept meant only as an upper limit to the distribution deduction available to the trust in its determination of taxable income. The taxpayer claimed the true test for the required allocation was found in section 265 and the regulations thereunder.]

* * * [The IRS] allocated the indirect expenses (legal fees and commissions) between tax-exempt interest, on the one hand, and dividends and taxable interest, on the other, but, in so doing, excluded from the allocation base capital gains and taxable stock dividends, both of which, although elements of the trust's taxable income, were allocable to the principal of the trust under local law and the trust indenture. By the exclusion of these elements of taxable income from the base, the portion of the indirect expenses allocable to tax-exempt interest, and hence not deductible, was significantly increased. It is this refusal of the Internal Revenue Service to consider all the elements of the trust's taxable income, in making the allocation, which prompts plaintiff's complaint.

* * *

[The taxpayer, plaintiff in this case, claimed] that, by excluding capital gains and taxable stock dividends from the allocation base used in determining the amount of administration expenses deductible, the Commissioner of Internal Revenue followed Special Instruction 39 of the instructions to Form 1041, the fiduciary income tax return. Instruction 39 applies to the separate schedule on the form to be used for the computation of "distributable net income," and says that for this purpose tax-exempt interest is to be reduced by

> "any amounts which, but for the provisions of Section 265, would be deductible in respect of disbursements, expenses, losses, etc., of the trust or estate, directly or indirectly allocable to such interest. The amount of the indirect disbursements, etc., allocable to tax-exempt interest is that amount which bears the same ratio to the total disbursements, etc., of the trust or estate not directly

attributable to other items of income as the total tax-exempt interest received bears to the total of all the items of gross income (including tax-exempt interest * * *) entering into *distributable net income*" (Emphasis added).

By including only those items of gross income which enter into distributable net income, this instruction excludes capital gains and taxable stock dividends (both allocable to corpus). The plaintiff says that the Commissioner also presumably relied on the examples in [Treas. Reg. § 1.652(c)–4] * * * which similarly determine the amount of administration expenses allocable to tax-exempt interest. The argument is that the instruction and the regulation are unreasonable in arbitrarily ignoring large classes of income, and that this exclusion will result, through the years, in the over-collection of tax. Plaintiff urges that, although the "artificial concept" of distributable net income may be suited to the determination of the maximum amount of income taxable to beneficiaries, "it is peculiarly ill-adapted to answer the far more simple and truly unrelated question of what general administration expenses are allocable to tax-exempt interest."

The [IRS's] reply is that Instruction 39 to Form 1041, and the examples set forth in various regulations under subchapter J, are irrelevant to the question of allocation of deductions by the trust; they relate to the computation of distributable net income, and "although in such computation capital gains and losses are also excluded, this has only an indirect bearing upon the reasonableness of the allocation under Section 265(1) which is here involved." * * *

* * * [W]e cannot agree with the [IRS's] assertion that Instruction 39 and the regulations under subchapter J are irrelevant to the reasonableness of the allocation of trust expenses under Section 265(1). * * * [Reg.] § 1.652(c)–4, to which taxpayer refers, furnishes an example of the application of the rules for trust required to distribute all income currently. Subparagraph (e) of this example consists of a computation of the taxable income of a trust, and the allocation of indirect expenses to the taxable and nontaxable portions of the trust's income is made, without discussion, on a distribution base from which capital gains allocable to corpus have been excluded. This is a plain enough indication, which we cannot ignore, of the specific method the Commissioner has chosen, *by regulation*, for the allocation of the expenses of trusts. Instruction 39, which by its terms purports to operate within the boundaries of Section 265, simply follows suit. More generally, the overall regulation on allocation of expenses between taxable and tax-exempt income (Section 1.265–1(c) * * *) requires that allocation of indirect expenses should be made "in the light of all facts and circumstances in each case." When the income of a trust is involved, the concept of distributable net income, as well as the special system of taxation in subchapter J, is an important component "of all the

facts and circumstances." That concept and system are, as we have said, the primary mechanisms by which the income of a trust is taxed but once, either to the trust or to its beneficiaries; * * * they should not be disregarded in applying the general allocation provisions of Section 265 to the particular problems of trust income. * * *

Since the challenged regulation and instruction are thus applicable, we are controlled by their provisions unless we can agree with plaintiff that they are unreasonable as applied to the case before us. * * * But in the present circumstances—where the deductible expenses fall short of absorbing the distributable net income—the regulation and the instruction do not unfairly ignore large classes of income in making the expense allocation. The income beneficiaries are taxable only to the extent of distributable net income, which excludes gains attributable to corpus. It is not out of key, therefore, to insist that the allocation of expenses between taxable and tax-exempt income should be restricted to the same type of non-corpus gains. This is all the more so since, under Section 652(b), the amounts included in the income beneficiary's gross income have the same character in his hands—e.g., as taxable dividends or tax-exempt interest— as in the hands of the trust. Moreover, under the 1954 Code, as a result of the structure of distributable net income (which has as its starting point the taxable income of the trust), the tax benefit of deductions allocable to corpus is generally shifted to the income beneficiaries. * * * The challenged regulation and instruction allowably balance this incongruity—that the income beneficiary, not the corpus beneficiary, receives the tax benefit of expenses allocable to corpus—by providing that those indirect expenses which are usually chargeable against capital gains must be allocated by the income beneficiary to all the income (both taxable and tax-exempt) required to be distributed to him. All the income required to be distributed currently by the trust and "included" in gross income by the beneficiary (particularly tax-exempt income), rather than just the taxable elements, bears the burden of the expenses attributable to capital gain. The tax benefit of the portion of these expenses assigned to tax-exempt income is lost, but this is not unfair to a taxpayer who has the special advantage of deductions attributable to gains he does not receive. Perhaps there may be other trust situations in which the Commissioner's regulations on allocation are unreasonable, but they are not so in the circumstances we have here. Plaintiff cannot recover the tax computed under those regulations.

* * *

PROBLEMS

1. A trust provides that all income, including capital gains, shall be distributed annually to Ben. The trust income for the year includes (1) $10,000 cash dividends on stock of domestic corporations; (2) $10,000 in

long term capital gains realized from the sale of trust property; and (3) the trust had $10,000 of interest from municipal bonds that was tax exempt under section 103. Trustee's fees totaled $1,200. The trust instrument provides that all expenses are to be charged to income. Consider especially the impact of the tax-exempt interest on the deduction for trustee fees and the increased importance of the personal exemption.

(a)   What is the income of the trust as a matter of fiduciary accounting?

(b)   What is the taxable income of the trust determined without consideration of distributions to beneficiaries? Note the deduction for the personal exemption in section 642(b) is $300.

(c)   What is the "distributable net income" of the trust? Compute DNI by applying the statutory formula. See I.R.C. § 643.

(d)   How will Ben report his share of the trust income? See I.R.C. § 652.

(e)   What, if any, income will be taxable to the fiduciary? See I.R.C. § 651.

(f)   What will be the tax consequences if the trust instrument provided that gains realized on the sale or exchange of trust property should be added to corpus and that all expenses should be charged against principal?

2.   Does the potential loss of a part of the tax deduction for expenses incurred by a trust holding tax-exempt income-producing property suggest that such property should not be included in a trust? Also, when an estate is found to include tax-exempt income-producing property, could the executor do some effective postmortem planning by distributing the tax-exempt income-producing property before the estate incurred any administration expenses? By so doing, could you not avoid prorating administration expenses between taxable and tax-exempt income, thereby rendering such expenses fully deductible?

H. CAPITAL GAINS IN ESTATE OR TRUST

While it is important to note that capital gains enjoy special income tax treatment—in general, a maximum tax rate of 15 or 20 percent—there are also oftentimes questions as to whether such gains are to be taxed to the estate or trust or distributed to the beneficiaries of the estate or trust. Generally, state law or the governing instrument determines whether capital gains are part of DNI and, thus, available for distribution to the beneficiaries, or whether such gains are corpus and retained in the trust (and are not a part of DNI since they are unavailable for distribution). Regulation § 1.643(a)–3(b) sets out standards to be followed in making this determination—and is the subject of the following letter ruling.

PRIVATE LETTER RULING 8324002

February 16, 1983.

* * *

A, a resident of S, died on October 26, 1980. The executors of X, B and C, elected a fiscal year ending on January 31 of each year. B and C filed X's income tax return for the first fiscal year ending January 31, 1981.

A's Will made no specific provision concerning the payment of income earned by the estate. Under the terms of the Will and applicable state law, capital gains are allocated to corpus. During the first fiscal year of the estate, capital gains in the amount of $550,444.42 were realized from the sale of securities, the net proceeds of which amounted to $5,012,758.62. A separate account was maintained for capital gains and losses from all transactions. On January 30, 1981, an amount equal to the net capital gain for the year was segregated for the benefit of two residuary trusts. On the same day this net capital gain was actually distributed equally to the trustees of the two residuary trusts.

In filing the return for the estate, the net capital gain was included in distributable net income. The result was that the residuary trust beneficiaries reported the net capital gain as income. The agent believes the net capital gain should not be included in distributable net income, and thus, is taxable income to the estate.

* * *

Generally, capital gains are excluded from distributable net income unless they are paid, credited or required to be distributed to any beneficiary during the taxable year or are paid, set aside or used for charitable purposes. Section 643(a)(3). * * *

Gains from the sale or exchange of capital assets are not ordinarily considered as paid, credited, or required to be distributed to any beneficiary unless they are (1) allocated to income under the terms of the governing instrument or local law, (2) allocated to corpus and actually distributed to beneficiaries, or (3) utilized (pursuant to the terms of the governing instrument or the practice followed by the fiduciary) in determining the amount which is distributed or required to be distributed. Section 1.643(a)–3(a) * * *.

The first instance, under section 1.643(a)–3(a) [§ 1.643(a)–3(b)], for including capital gains in distributable net income is not satisfied because capital gains are allocated to principal under the terms of the Will and local law.

The second instance, under this regulation, for including capital gains in distributable net income requires that capital gains be allocated to corpus and actually distributed to beneficiaries during the taxable year. As illustrated by Examples (3), (4) and (5) of section 1.643(a)–3(d) [§ 1.643(a)–3(e)], this provision regarding the inclusion of capital gains in distributable net income applies only where there is a distribution required by the terms of the governing instrument upon the happening of a specified event. In the instant case, such a condition for including capital gains in distributable net income is not present. See also Rev. Rul. 68–392, 1968–2 C.B. 284.

The third instance, under this regulation, for including capital gains in distributable net income indicates there are two separate methods that capital gains may be utilized in determining the amount which is distributed or required to be distributed. One is to utilize capital gains pursuant to the terms of the governing instrument to determine the amount distributed or required to be distributed. The second method is to utilize capital gains pursuant to the practice followed by the fiduciary in determining the amount distributed or required to be distributed. In the present case, A's Will contains no instructions as to the treatment of capital gains in determining the amount of any discretionary distribution made by the executors. Thus, capital gains are not utilized pursuant to the terms of the Will. Therefore, capital gains will not be included in distributable net income of the estate under the first method described in section 1.643(a)–3(a)(3).

The second method described in section 1.643(a)–3(a)(3) requires an examination of whether a practice followed by the fiduciary is established in determining the amount which is distributed or required to be distributed. In this regard, Rev. Rul. 68–392 addressed the issue of whether a practice followed by a fiduciary may be established in the first taxable year of a trust, and reasoned that since this is the first taxable year of the trust, capital gains are not utilized pursuant to the practice followed by the fiduciary in determining the amount that is distributed or required to be distributed. Accordingly, since the year involved in the present case is the first taxable year of the estate, capital gains are not utilized pursuant to a practice followed by the fiduciary in determining the amount that is distributed or required to be distributed. Thus, capital gains will not be included in distributable net income of the estate under the second method described in section 1.643(a)–3(a)(3) * * *.

The distributable net income of X does not include the capital gains recognized by X upon the sale of securities held by X.

PLANNING NOTES

1. Taxpayers continually search for techniques by which to manipulate the tax consequences of transactions. In that sense, Private Letter Ruling 8324002 is particularly illustrative. The taxpayer had obviously determined that a tax advantage would be gained if the capital gains could "flow through" to the estate's beneficiaries rather than be taxable to the estate. With that in mind, consider how wills should be drafted to give the

decedent's executor the maximum postmortem planning opportunity. For example, would it be appropriate to provide that "my executor shall have complete discretion in allocating capital gains to income or principal during the administration of my estate"? In reflecting upon this suggestion, consider whether the answer would be different if the estate's beneficiary was also the executor of the estate. In such a case, could it be argued that the beneficiary would be in "constructive" receipt of the capital gains even if they were not distributed to him or her?

Keep in mind that, in Private Letter Ruling 8627043, the IRS took the position that the parties to a trust could not agree that any distributions from a trust would first come from the tax-exempt income of the trust. The IRS concluded that the claimed allocation of the tax-exempt income had no economic effect independent of tax consequences and, therefore, could not be given effect for income tax purposes.

2. Many years ago, H.L. Hunt, the famous oil man, created a trust for the benefit of his daughter, Caroline, the trust to last for her life plus 21 years. On the trust's income tax return for a recent year, the trust claimed that capital gains realized by the trust and distributed to Caroline were a part of DNI. The trust's claim was based on the decision by the trust's auditor to allocate the gains to income rather than corpus for trust accounting purposes. The claim was that trust accounting income is the starting point for determination of DNI and, thus, treating the capital gains as trust accounting income means that the capital gains were part of DNI. The IRS claimed that the auditor's decision was wrong. The dispute, involving millions of dollars in taxes, played out in Crisp v. United States, 34 Fed. Cl. 112 (1995), a case useful to illustrate the interplay of trust accounting determinations based on state law and the governing instrument and tax accounting considerations. The IRS noted that the trust prohibited distributions of corpus to Caroline and, therefore, argued that the auditor's allocation of capital gains to income was manifestly incorrect. The court did not agree. It concluded that the trustee's decision to distribute the capital gains to Caroline was proper and, accordingly, for trust accounting purposes, the capital gains could not be corpus for trust accounting purposes (in as much as the trustee did not have authority to distribute corpus to Caroline). The court reasoned that whether receipts are income or corpus is determined by state law and, according to the state law applicable in this case (Texas), the trust instrument is looked to for this determination. While the trust barred corpus distributions, it permitted distributions of "net profits" and "net earnings" at the discretion of the trustee. (The trust was purely "discretionary" in the sense that it did not require that the trustee make any distributions whatsoever to Caroline.) The capital gains represented the profit realized by the trust as a limited partner in a partnership engaged in active stock market trading. In the court's opinion, the creator of the trust intended these profits to constitute "net profits" or "net earnings." Thus, for trust accounting purposes, the capital gains were income even though the capital gains

were entitled to preferential income tax treatment. The court admitted that had the securities that produced the profits been owned directly by the trust—rather than the limited partnership—the realized profits would be corpus for trust accounting purposes as well as for tax purposes. It rejected the notion, however, that making the distinction meant that taxpayers could manipulate income tax consequences by creating a partnership and generating "profits" rather than capital gains. Instead the court concluded that the creator intended that the trustee have broad discretion in making investments and would in no way have wanted the form of investment to have dictated whether income was available for distribution to the trust beneficiary. And since the trustee thought that the limited partnership investment was the most efficient investment vehicle, that decision should not dictate tax results.

If the *Crisp* capital gains were not part of DNI, these gains would have been taxed to the trust and the amounts distributed to Caroline would have been a nontaxable distribution (to the extent the amount distributed exceeded DNI). By including the capital gains in DNI, DNI was inflated by the amount of the gains, allowing the trust a bigger distribution deduction.

It is possible that the decisions taken by the *Crisp* trustees were part of a tax management scheme perhaps in a year when Caroline, the trust beneficiary, had no other taxable income. Getting the capital gains to her for income tax purposes—and out of the trust—may have resulted in those gains being partially or completely sheltered from income tax because of other losses Caroline had in that tax year.

I.   THE CHARACTER RULES

Sections 652(b) and 662(b) set forth the "character" rules. According to these rules, the amount deemed distributed to beneficiaries of a trust or estate will have the same "character" in the hands of the beneficiaries as it had in the hands of the trust or estate. That is, if the estate's or trust's income was composed of 25-percent dividend income and 75-percent interest income, the beneficiary would be deemed to have received a distribution of dividend income and a distribution of interest income in the same proportions. If there was more than one beneficiary, each of them would be deemed to have received his or her proportionate share of the dividend and interest income. See I.R.C. §§ 652(b) and 662(b). As a result of these "character" rules, the trust's role as merely a "conduit" is readily apparent.

Similarly, tax-exempt interest is included in distributable net income (DNI) and, as such, flows through to the estate or trust beneficiaries. Treas. Reg. § 1.643(a)–5.

The "character" rules also provide principles to be used in allocating, among the items of distributable net income, items of deduction entering into the computation of distributable net income. Expenses such as property taxes on rental properties which can be directly attributed to rental income are to be allocated to the rental income for purposes of determining the character of the distributions made to beneficiaries.

Example: The Smith Trust, which requires all income to be distributed currently to Billy and Clint in equal shares, has the following items of income: $25,000 in rental income; $50,000 in dividend income; $25,000 in tax-exempt interest. The trust has $10,000 in rental expense and $4,000 in trustee's fees. The allocation of taxable income is computed as follows:

Trust Accounting Income:

Rents	$25,000
Rental expense	(10,000)
Dividends	50,000
Tax-exempt interest	25,000
Trustee's fees	(4,000)
	$86,000

Federal Gross Income:

Rent	$25,000
Dividends	50,000
	$75,000

Tentative Taxable Income:

Gross Income	$75,000
Section 642(b) exemption	(300)
Rental expense	(10,000)
Trustee's fees (Because tax-exempt interest constituted one-fourth of total trust income, one-fourth of indirect expense—$4,000 of trustee fees—was allocated to that interest and is disallowed as a deduction.)	(3,000)
	61,700

DNI:

Tentative taxable income	$61,700
Personal exemption	300
Tax-exempt interest	25,000

Trustee's fees allocable to tax-exempt interest (Treas. Reg. § 1.643(a)–5(a))	(1,000)
	$86,000
Distribution Deduction:	
DNI	$86,000
Tax-exempt interest less deduction	(24,000)
	$62,000

Because amounts required to be distributed currently do not exceed DNI, Billy and Clint each receive $43,000 and include that amount in their gross income. The income retains the same character in the hands of the beneficiaries as it had in the trust. Thus, in the above example, Billy and Clint each have received $7,000 in rental income [(25,000−10,000−1,000) ÷ 2]; $24,000 in dividend income [(50,000−2,000) ÷ 2]; and $12,000 in tax-exempt interest income [(25,000−1,000) ÷ 2]. See Treas. Reg. § 1.652(b)–3(b).

J. TRUST AND ESTATE TAXABLE INCOME

1. COMPUTATIONAL SCHEME

Taxable income is computed for estates and trusts in the same manner as for individuals, subject to certain modifications. I.R.C. §§ 67(e) and 641(b). For individuals, gross income is reduced by the cost of producing that income to determine adjusted gross income, and adjusted gross income, in turn, is reduced by certain other deductions specifically authorized by Congress for policy reasons. See I.R.C. § 63. The result is "taxable income," against which is applied the tax table or rate schedule, whichever is appropriate. See I.R.C. § 1. The amount of tax thus determined is further reduced by credits specifically allowed by law. See I.R.C. §§ 21–53.

When these concepts are applied to estate and trust income taxation, receipts that will be gross income to an individual will be gross income to the estate or trust. Treas. Reg. § 1.641(a)–2. Similarly, expenditures that would be deductible by individuals are generally deductible by estates and trusts. Treas. Reg. § 1.641(b)–1. Adjusted gross income, in the case of a trust, is only computed for limited purposes under section 67(e), but, even so, it is determined in the same manner as that prescribed for determining Among the rules peculiar to taxing the income from trusts and estates are the following:

1. Trusts required to distribute all their income currently are entitled to a deduction for a personal exemption of $300. For

all other trusts, the personal deduction is limited to $100. Estates get a $600 exemption. I.R.C. § 642(b).

2. The standard deduction is expressly denied to estates and trusts. I.R.C. § 63(c)(6)(D).

3. Generally, as already discussed, distributions made to beneficiaries are required to be deducted by both trusts and estates in determining taxable income, but only to the extent that the estate has "distributable net income" as determined under section 643(b).

4. While the charitable deduction under section 170 is not available to trusts, amounts "paid" pursuant to the terms of the governing instrument for public charitable purposes are deductible by both estates and trusts, and amounts "permanently set aside" are deductible by estates and certain (not all) trusts. I.R.C. § 642(c). The "permanently set aside" principle is discussed later in this chapter.

2. TWO PERCENT "HAIRCUT"

Prior to the enactment of the Tax Cuts and Jobs Act of 2017, individuals were able to deduct "miscellaneous itemized deductions" to the extent that such deductions exceeded two percent of their adjusted gross income. See I.R.C. § 67(a). However, pursuant to the Act, individuals were not allowed to claim miscellaneous itemized deductions for taxable year beginning after December 31, 2017 and before January 1, 2026. See I.R.C. § 67(g). There is an issue whether section 67(g) applies to trusts and estates. In this regard, the IRS issued Notice 2018–61, 2018–31 I.R.B. 278, to address the effect of section 67(g) on trusts and estates. Notice 2018–61 provides in pertinent part:

Commentators have suggested that new section 67(g) might be read to eliminate the ability of estates and non-grantor trusts to deduct any expenses described in section 67(e)(1) and § 1.67–4 for the taxable years during which the application of section 67(a) is suspended. The Treasury Department and the IRS do not believe that this is a correct reading of section 67(g). For the taxable years during which it is effective, section 67(g) denies a deduction for miscellaneous itemized deductions. Section 67(b) defines miscellaneous itemized deductions as itemized deductions other than those listed therein. Section 63(d) defines itemized deductions by excluding personal exemptions, section § 199A deductions, and deductions used to arrive at adjusted gross income. Therefore, neither the above-the-line deductions used to arrive at adjusted gross income nor the expenses listed in section 67(b)(1)–(12) are miscellaneous itemized deductions. Section

§ 62(a) defines adjusted gross income of an individual, and section § 67(e) provides that the adjusted gross income of a trust or estate is determined in the same way as for an individual, except that expenses described in section 67(e)(1) and deductions pursuant to sections 642(b), 651, and 661 are allowable as deductions in arriving at adjusted gross income. Thus, section 67(e) removes the expenses described in section 67(e)(1) from the category of itemized deductions (and thus necessarily also from the subset of miscellaneous itemized deductions) and instead treats them as above-the-line deductions allowable in determining adjusted gross income under section 62(a). Therefore, the suspension of the deductibility of miscellaneous itemized deductions under section 67(a) does not affect the deductibility of payments described in section 67(e)(1). However, an expense that commonly or customarily would be incurred by an individual (including the appropriate portion of a bundled fee) is affected by section 67(g) and thus is not deductible to the estate or non-grantor trust during the suspension of section 67(a). Nothing in section 67(g) impacts the determination of what expenses are described in section 67(e)(1).

Additionally, nothing in section 67(g) affects the ability of the estate or trust to take a deduction listed under section 67(b). These deductions remain outside of the definition of "miscellaneous itemized deduction." For example, section 691(c) deductions (relating to the deduction for estate tax on income in respect of the decedent), which are identified in section 67(b)(7), remain unaffected by the enactment of section 67(g)). The Treasury Department and the IRS intend to issue regulations clarifying that estates and non-grantor trusts may continue to deduct expenses described in section 67(e)(1) and amounts allowable as deductions under section 642(b), 651 or 661, including the appropriate portion of a bundled fee, in determining the estate or nongrantor trust's adjusted gross income during taxable years, for which the application of section 67(a) is suspended pursuant to section 67(g). Additionally, the regulations will clarify that deductions enumerated in section 67(b) and 67(e) continue to remain outside the definition of "miscellaneous itemized deductions" and thus are unaffected by section 67(g).

The notice also stated that "the regulations will clarify that deductions enumerated in section 67(b) and (e) continue to remain outside the definition of 'miscellaneous itemized deductions' and thus are unaffected by section 67(g)." Under section 67(e), while the adjusted gross income of an estate or trust is "computed in the same manner as in the case of an individual," an estate or trust, in arriving at adjusted gross income, is entitled to a deduction for 100 percent of the "costs which are paid or incurred if the property were not held in such trust or estate."

3. PASSIVE ACTIVITY LOSS LIMITATIONS

Section 469 generally limits deductions and credits derived from passive activities to the amount of income derived from all passive activities. The passive activity loss limitations apply to estates and trusts. However, there are several rules relating to the passive activity loss limitations which are peculiar to estates and trusts.

Generally, an activity is deemed to be passive if it involves the conduct of any trade or business and the taxpayer does not materially participate in the activity. I.R.C. § 469(c)(1). An estate or trust is treated as materially participating in an activity if an executor or fiduciary, in his or her capacity as such, is involved in operations of the activity on a regular, continuous, and substantial basis. I.R.C. § 469(h)(1). However, in the case of a grantor trust, material participation is determined at the grantor level.

Rental activities are considered to be passive activities, whether or not the taxpayer materially participates. In the case of tax years of an estate ending less than two years after the date of death of the decedent, up to $25,000 of the passive activity losses attributable to all rental real estate activities in which the decedent actively participated prior to death are allowed as deductions. I.R.C. § 469(i). The $25,000 offset for rental real estate activities is to be reduced by the amount of the exemption "allowable to the surviving spouse of the decedent for the taxable year ending with or within the taxable year of the estate." I.R.C. § 469(i)(4)(B).

Portfolio income of an estate or trust is not considered to be passive income and may not be offset by losses from passive activities. Portfolio income generally includes interest, dividends, royalties not derived in the ordinary course of business, and income from annuities. I.R.C. § 469(e).

Any unused losses and/or credits are deemed "suspended" passive activity losses for the year and are carried forward indefinitely. If a trust or estate distributes its entire interest in a passive activity to a beneficiary, the basis of the property is increased (no deduction allowed) by the amount of any suspended losses generated by that passive activity. I.R.C. § 469(j)(12). Gain or loss to the trust or estate and the basis of the property to the beneficiary is then determined under the rules set forth in section 643(e).

4. TAX RATE SCHEDULE

To discourage the use of trusts—and estates—as income tax shelters, the income tax rates applied to income that is retained by the trust—or estate—and not distributed to the beneficiaries could be described as "compressed" compared to the tax rates applicable to individuals. For example, for tax years beginning in 2023, adjusted for inflation, the first $44,725 of income received by an unmarried taxpayer (and the first $89,450 of income received by married taxpayers filing jointly) is taxed at a rate of 12 percent or less (the first $11,000 and $22,000 respectively, at 10 percent), I.R.C. § 1(a), (c), and (i); Rev. Proc. 2022–38, 2022–45 I.R.B. 445. By way of contrast, compare the 2022 inflation adjusted income tax rate schedule applicable to trusts and estates (I.R.C. § 1(e) and (i); Rev. Proc. 2022–38, 2022–45 I.R.B. 445):

Not over $2,900	10%
Over $2,900 but not over $10,550	24%
Over $10,550 but not over $14,450	35%
Over $14,450	37%

As a general rule, net long-term capital gains as well as qualified dividends are taxed at a maximum rate of 15 or 20 percent based on an estate's or trust's income. I.R.C. § 1(h). For 2023, the 20 percent rate applies to income above $14,650. Beginning in 2013, an additional 3.8% tax applies to the lesser of undistributed net investment income of estates and trusts or adjusted gross income over the amount taxed in the top bracket, $14,450 for 2023. I.R.C. § 1411(a)(2). Hence, in 2023, the 20% tax on undistributed net investment income, including capital gains and qualified dividends, increases to 23.8% if the surtax applies. This 3.8% tax is the Medicare contributions tax added by the Health Care and Education Reconciliation Act of 2010 (HCERA), P.L. 111–152.

PLANNING NOTE

Possible planning may include accumulating income in a trust rather than distributing it to a beneficiary in those cases where the income will be taxed to the beneficiary at the top rate (if the income is distributed) but taxed to the trust at a lower rate (if not distributed). However, in many such cases, the income savings may well be more than offset by the expenses of trust administration. For that reason, only a few taxpayers will look at the trust as a vehicle to accomplish income tax savings. Instead, trusts will be used either for nontax reasons or because of estate tax and generation-skipping tax considerations. Certainly, from an income tax perspective, the application of the compressed rates constitutes a tax penalty to estates and for the use of trusts, a penalty that will need to be balanced against the nontax benefits of the trust or the estate tax and/or generation-skipping tax savings benefits of the trust.

5. TAX RETURN OBLIGATIONS

An executor must file Form 1041, U.S. Tax Return for Estates and Trusts, for the estate if the estate has gross income for its tax year of $600 or more. I.R.C. § 6012(a)(3).

A trustee must file Form 1041 for the trust for each year in which the trust has "any taxable income" or "gross income of $600 or over, regardless of the amount of taxable income." I.R.C. § 6012(a)(4).

The executor may elect to file the estate's income tax returns on a calendar or fiscal year basis. I.R.C. § 441(b)(1); Treas. Reg. § 1.441–1. However, new and existing trusts (except trusts exempt from tax and charitable trusts) must use a calendar year. I.R.C. § 644.

Certain trusts revocable by the decedent at the time of the decedent's death may elect to be treated and taxed as part of the decedent's estate for income tax purposes for two years after the decedent's death if no federal estate tax return is necessary or for a period ending six months after the conclusion of any proceeding relating to the decedent's federal estate tax return. I.R.C. § 645. Where the decedent has created more than one revocable trust, all can be combined with the decedent's estate. A consolidated income tax return *as an estate* is filed for the combined entities. Both the executor and trustee must indicate that consolidated reporting has been elected. I.R.C. § 645(a). An election to consolidate is irrevocable once made. I.R.C. § 645(c).

6. ALTERNATIVE MINIMUM TAX

The alternative minimum tax applies to trusts and estates. For 2023, the minimum tax rate is 26 percent, and the maximum rate is 28 percent for taxable income above $220,700. I.R.C. § 55(b)(1)(A). Trusts and estates are entitled to a $22,500 exemption. I.R.C. § 55(d)(1)(D). This exemption is adjusted for inflation, and the exemption amount for 2023 is $28,400. The exemption is phased out in cases where the trust or estate has alternative minimum taxable income (AMTI) in excess of $75,000 ($94,600 for 2023). Rev. Proc. 2038–44, 2022–45 I.R.B. 445.

7. ESTIMATED INCOME TAX PAYMENTS

Generally, trusts and estates must make quarterly estimated income tax payments in the same manner as individuals except that estates and revocable trusts are exempt from making such payments during the first two taxable years of the estate. I.R.C. § 6654(*l*). More specifically, estates are required to make quarterly estimated income tax payments for those taxable years "ending before the date 2 years after the date of the decedent's death." I.R.C. § 6654(*l*)(2). This special rule allowing estates an exemption from the burden of making estimated income tax payments extends to revocable trusts in cases where the revocable trust is to receive the grantor's residuary estate under a pour-over will or, if no will is admitted to probate, the special rule extends to the revocable trust primarily responsible for paying the decedent's debts, taxes and administration expenses. I.R.C. § 6654(*l*)(2).

> *Example*: Antonio Lopez died on December 12, 2021. His will, dated April 10, 1996, provided, in pertinent part, as follows: "I give all of my property to the Trustee of the Lopez Family Revocable Living Trust, which I created on April 10, 1996."
>
> The trust reports its income on a calendar year basis, but Antonio's executor elected to report the estate's income on a fiscal year ending November 30th. As far as estimated tax payments are concerned, no estimated income tax payments are required of Antonio's executor for the fiscal years ending on November 30, 2022 and November 30, 2023. As for the trust, estimated income tax payments are not required for the trust tax years ending December 31, 2021 and December 31, 2022, but such payments are required for the trust tax year ending December 31, 2023.

Understandably, the penalties for underpayment of quarterly estimated income tax are applicable to fiduciaries as well as individuals.

In the case of trusts, "the trustee may elect to treat any portion of a payment of estimated tax made by such trust for any taxable year of the trust as a payment made by a beneficiary of such trust." I.R.C. § 643(g)(1)(A). The trustee's election must be made "on or before the 65th day after the close of the taxable year of the trust." I.R.C. § 643(g)(2). Estates may also make this election but only in the "taxable year reasonably expected to be the last taxable year" of the estate. I.R.C. § 643(g)(3). Thus, an estate may find itself in the position of claiming a refund of an overpayment of estimated taxes in a year other than its final year while the estate's beneficiaries will incur an underpayment penalty in the same year as a result of receiving a distribution from the estate during that year and not taking the distribution into account for estimated income tax purposes.

From the standpoint of the beneficiary, in cases where the trust elects to attribute the estimated income tax payment to the trust beneficiary, the payment made by the trust is "treated as a payment of estimated tax made by such beneficiary on January 15 following the taxable year." I.R.C. § 643(g)(1)(C)(ii). In such a case, the amount of tax attributed to the beneficiary is treated as a distribution by the trust (and is deductible by the trust in computing its income tax liability) and as taxable income to the beneficiary. I.R.C. §§ 651 and 661.

K. TERMINATION OF ESTATES AND TRUSTS

1. TIMING

From and after the date on which administration of an estate is deemed completed or a trust is deemed terminated for federal income tax purposes, the income of the estate or trust is taxable to the beneficiaries even though it has not been distributed to those beneficiaries.

In the case of a trust, termination depends on whether the trust property has in fact been distributed to the beneficiaries of the trust—and not on the happening of the event by which the trust's duration is to be measured. Treas. Reg. § 1.641(b)–3(b). However, under the regulations "the winding up of a trust cannot be unduly postponed and if the distribution of the trust corpus is unreasonably delayed, the trust is considered terminated for Federal income tax purposes after the expiration of a reasonable period for the trustee to complete the administration of the trust." Id.

In the case of an estate, for income tax purposes, the period of administration of an estate is the "period actually required * * * to perform the ordinary duties of administration" the duties being principally to collect and distribute the decedent's property while discharging obligations to creditors and taxing authorities. Treas. Reg. § 1.641(b)–3(a). However, under the Treasury approach the "period of administration of an estate cannot be unduly prolonged." Id. On the other hand, as noted in the case that follows, taxpayers have argued that the "period of administration" referred to in section 641(a)(3) is the period actually consumed rather than the Treasury's reasonable time approach.

BROWN v. UNITED STATES
United States Court of Appeals, Fifth Circuit, 1989.
890 F.2d 1329.

KING, CIRCUIT JUDGE:

* * *

[Fourteen years after his mother died, Earl A. Brown Jr., principal beneficiary and executor of her estate had not closed the estate and filed a final income tax return. Brown was also the principal beneficiary and executor of his father's estate and 13 years after the father's death the father's estate remained open. The I.R.S. claimed the income earned by the respective estates was properly reportable on Brown's personal income tax return for at least 5 of the tax years in question (rather than on the income tax returns filed for the estates for those years). In dispute was almost $700,000 in additional income taxes.]

We are concerned in this case with the application of section 641(a)(3) [which imposes the federal income tax on "the taxable income of estates or of any kind of property held in trust, including—* * * income received by estates of deceased persons during the period of administration or settlement of the estate."] The pivotal issue for Taxpayers is the meaning of the term "period of administration." Congress has never provided a statutory definition for this term; therefore, the IRS has long interpreted the broad language of section 641(a)(3) in its regulations. The Treasury Regulations promulgated under the 1939 Internal Revenue Code, interpreting the same statutory language, provided that the period of administration is the time actually required by the executor or administrator to perform the ordinary duties pertaining to administration, "whether longer or shorter than the period specified in the local statute for the settlement of estates." Treas. Reg. § 19.162–1 (1940).

In 1956, the IRS promulgated new regulations under the 1954 Code. The IRS reissued the above-quoted regulation—renumbered to correspond to the 1954 Code—incorporating the substance of the former version, but clarifying the meaning of "period of administration." Two pertinent sentences were added:

> However, the period of administration of an estate cannot be unduly prolonged. If the administration of an estate is unreasonably prolonged, the estate is considered terminated for Federal income tax purposes after the expiration of a reasonable period for the performance by the executor of all the duties of administration.

Treas. Reg. § 1.641(b)–3(a)(1956).

Under the plain language of the amended regulation, the Commissioner has authority to determine whether an estate's administration has been "unduly prolonged" and to deem the estate closed for federal income tax purposes once a reasonable time has elapsed for the administrator to have performed all the ordinary duties of administration. Taxpayers * * * contend that we must interpret the statutory term "period of administration," * * * to mean the period that an administrator actually consumes before closing the estate, regardless of a determination by the Commissioner that a reasonable time has passed for the estate's termination. Taxpayers also argue that, in any event, a 1982 Texas probate court order, authorizing Brown to continue administration of the Estates at his discretion, was conclusive on the issue of whether the period of administration had terminated under section 641(a)(3) * * *.

We construe Taxpayers' arguments as a challenge to the validity of Treasury Regulation § 1.641(b)–3(a) * * *. The Government, in turn, contends that the regulation is a valid and reasonable interpretation of section 641(a)(3) * * *. The Government also asserts that under the teaching of Commissioner v. Estate of Bosch, 387 U.S. 456 (1967), a lower state court ruling cannot be controlling in a federal tax dispute; therefore, the IRS and the district court acted properly in conducting an independent review of whether the Estates had terminated for federal income tax purposes.

* * *

We must determine whether Treasury Regulation § 1.641(b)–3(a), as expanded in 1956, validly vests the Commissioner with authority to deem an estate's administration terminated for purposes of taxing the estate's income to the beneficiaries, even in cases, such as this one, where administration might legally be continued under state law. The broad language of section 641(a)(3) is open to different interpretations, and the legislative history prior to the 1954 Code is unenlightening. However, in the absence of statutory language to the contrary, the Supreme Court has advised that a provision of the Internal Revenue Code should be read "so as to give a uniform application to a nationwide scheme of taxation." * * * Although state probate laws would, of course, be pertinent in the Commissioner's determination of what the ordinary duties of administration entailed in a particular case, the existence of an estate as a *taxable* entity is a question of federal, not state, law. * * * [S]ection 641(a)(3) can be fairly read to require a uniform federal standard by which the Commissioner may deem an estate closed if the reasonable period of time required to perform the ordinary administrative duties has passed, and the administrator is unduly prolonging the estate's termination.

In the committee reports accompanying the enactment of the 1954 Code, both the House and Senate Reports describe the period of administration as

> the period actually required by the administrator or executor to perform the ordinary duties of administration, such as the collection of assets and the payment of debts, legacies, and bequests, whether this period is longer or shorter than the period specified under local law for the settlement of estates.

H.R. Rep. No. 1337, 83d Cong., 2d Sess., reprinted in 1954 U.S. Code Cong. & Ad. News 4017, 4331; S. Rep. No. 1622, 83d Cong., 2d Sess., reprinted in 1954 U.S. Code Cong. & Ad. News 4621, 4980–81. This language adopts the substance of the Treasury Regulation promulgated under the Internal Revenue Code of 1939 interpreting "period of administration," and thus indicates congressional endorsement of the then-existing regulation. Taxpayers do not dispute the validity of the predecessor to Treasury Regulation § 1.641(b)–3(a).

As described above, the IRS added a caveat to the regulation in 1956 that emphasizes the Commissioner's authority to ascertain whether an estate's administration has been unreasonably prolonged for federal income tax purposes. Taxpayers contend that this revision "is not binding on the taxpayer or this Court." However, we find that this change does not contradict the prior regulation, apparently approved by Congress, but merely makes explicit what was formerly implicit. If Congress intended that an estate's period of administration for purposes of section 641(a)(3) should not turn on "local law for the settlement of estates," it appears to us obvious that the period must turn on a federal factual standard, as ascertained by the federal agency charged with enforcement of the Code.

This interpretation of section 641(a)(3) and its accompanying regulation, that the Commissioner is clothed with the authority to deem an estate terminated for income tax purposes if it has been unduly prolonged, has been consistently espoused by the Commissioner—both before and after the amendment to the regulation in 1956—and consistently accepted by the courts. * * * Moreover, the IRS promulgated Treasury Regulation § 1.641(b)–3(a) less than two years after Congress's enactment of the 1954 Code; therefore, the regulation "represents a substantially contemporaneous construction of Subchapter J's conduit principles by those with the expertise to appreciate and define the intent and purposes" of the statute. United States Trust Co. v. IRS, 803 F.2d 1363, 1370 (5th Cir.1986). The amended regulation has now been in effect for over 30 years, yet Congress has left section 641(a)(3) unchanged despite several amendments to the 1954 Code and the enactment of the Internal Revenue Code of 1986. This acquiescence strongly suggests congressional approval of the longstanding interpretation of section 641(a)(3) by the Commissioner. * * *

Taxpayers' position is that "period of administration" should be read to mean the actual period an administrator keeps the estate open, irrespective of whether all ordinary duties actually required for the estate's existence have been completed except for the transfer of the estate's corpus to the legal beneficiaries. We do not believe that Congress intended a rule such as Taxpayers propose that would result both in nonuniform benefits to taxpayers and potential detriment to the Treasury. The increasing popularity of independent estate administrations, for example, in which an administrator operates free of court intervention and under which an estate might legally remain open indefinitely, creates the potential for prolonging an estate to achieve income-splitting and tax avoidance goals, a strategy not available to those estates administered under court supervision. The risk to the Government of lost revenues is most pronounced in cases where the estate fiduciary is also the sole or principal beneficiary of the estate's assets, a not uncommon situation.

Even if we believed Taxpayers' position to be a logical and reasonable interpretation of section 641(a)(3), a conclusion we cannot endorse, Taxpayers could not prevail on that point alone. The issue is whether the

Commissioner's interpretation of the statute is a reasonable one, not whether it is the only, or even the best, one. * * * We conclude, as has every other court faced with this issue, that Treasury Regulation 1.641(b)–3(a) is a reasonable and valid interpretation of section 641(a)(3).

* * *

In March 1982, shortly after the IRS sent deficiency notices to Taxpayers notifying them of the termination of the Estates for income tax purposes, Brown filed petitions in the probate court of Dallas County, Texas, requesting the court to find that the Estates required ongoing management and administration. The United States was not a party to this action. In a nonadversary proceeding in April 1982, the probate court entered an order authorizing Brown to continue to manage the assets of the Estates as independent executor until such time as he determined "in his sole discretion" that it would be in the best interest of the beneficiaries to terminate the Estates. Taxpayers argued below, and maintain on appeal, that this probate court decree was binding on both the IRS and the district court * * *. We reject Taxpayers' argument.

Because the United States was not made a party to the probate court proceeding, the ensuing order was not "binding" on the Commissioner in the sense of res judicata or collateral estoppel; see Commissioner v. Estate of Bosch, 387 U.S. 456, 462–63 (1967). * * * The issue, therefore, is what degree of deference the district court should have accorded this state judgment.

It is axiomatic that federal law controls the interpretation of federal statutes and regulations. In the field of federal taxation, however, federal and state law are tightly intertwined. The Internal Revenue Code does not operate in a vacuum; it attaches tax significance to legal rights and transactions that are created under state law.

When a taxpayer's federal tax liability clearly turns on the characterization under state law of a property interest, a state court's determination of that interest is obviously relevant in a subsequent federal tax controversy. * * * In *Bosch*, * * * the Court held that in such cases, federal authorities are to give "proper regard" to a lower state court's adjudication of the relevant issue, but need not accept such rulings as conclusive. 387 U.S. at 465. Unless the highest court in the state has spoken to the issue, a federal court is to make its own inquiry into state law. Id. When a federal tax law establishes a uniform criterion for taxing certain transactions or situations—irrespective of how state law might label those transactions or situations—the decision of a state probate court as to an underlying issue a fortiori should not be controlling. Thus, regardless of whether section 641(a)(3) creates a uniform federal criterion—as we have concluded in this opinion—or defers to a state's local characterization of the statute's terms, the Supreme Court holds that a federal court must make its own inquiry into relevant issues previously decided by a lower state court.

On the other hand, because state law pervades every tax issue, it would not be accurate to say that a federal court is free to simply ignore a state court's adjudication of relevant underlying facts. The relevance of a state court's judgment to the resolution of a federal tax question will vary, depending on the particular tax statute involved as well as the nature of the state proceeding that produced the judgment. An examination of the state court's judgment will usually be a relevant factor for the federal court's determination of whether "ordinary duties" required under state probate law are "actually required." However, the issue of whether administration has been unduly prolonged for purposes of section 641(a)(3) is ultimately one of federal, not state, law. * * * We next consider the nature of the local proceeding and the resulting decree to evaluate the judgment's relevance to this tax refund case and to determine whether the district court should have accorded it greater weight as an evidentiary factor.

We note first the nonadversary quality of the Texas probate court proceeding instituted by Brown. The United States was not a party. Moreover, Brown and the putative remaindermen agreed that Brown's administration of the Estates should continue, and it was apparently to their economic benefit to do so. Under these circumstances, the court was not presented with all the relevant facts and differing views that would have afforded the basis for a full analysis of the estate administration issue. In addition, the natural tendency of a busy probate court is to accede to a proposed order without great deliberation when all known interested parties are in agreement and when state interests are not adversely affected.

It is evident that Texas state interests were not affected—or even implicated—as a result of the probate court proceeding in question. Not only was there no genuine controversy involved, the probate court's order was unnecessary under the Texas probate Code provisions relating to independent administrations. An independent executor such as Brown has authority to determine when to terminate the administration of an estate free of any court intervention. * * * Absent objection from a person interested in the estate, there is no statutory requirement regarding the period within which independent administration must be closed. The Dallas County Probate Court merely placed official approval on actions that Brown could have legally pursued without the court's direction. Thus, the judgment had no practical consequences apart from this federal tax controversy, and was consequently entitled to little weight in the district court.

* * *

Taxpayers argue in the alternative that, assuming Treasury Regulation § 1.641(b)–3(a) is a valid interpretation of section 641, and one to which this court must defer, the IRS nevertheless acted contrary to the regulation because the Estates were not unduly prolonged. In this case, the IRS determined after its 1981 audit of the Estates that administration had continued for over 12 years and, based on the duties performed and yet to be performed, a reasonable time had passed for terminating the Estates. The district court reviewed that determination and agreed. The court found that by the end of 1976:

> [a]ll papers necessary to probate the wills such as the inventories and appraisals were filed and approved. The inheritance taxes and the federal estate tax returns were filed. All the debts and expenses of the estates were paid. All assets were located and collected. There were no outstanding claims, will contests, or property title disputes. No litigation was pending regarding claims to the assets or claims by the estates. No federal income tax disputes or litigation were pending. . . .

Taxpayers do not dispute that these duties were completed well before December 31, 1976. However, they argue that the IRS should not have deemed the Estates terminated because Brown's continued administration was necessary to * * * disburse legacies to beneficiaries.

* * *

* * * We do not find this argument convincing.

Earl Brown Sr.'s will provided a lifetime income to his secretary, Lucille Cathey, from a $30,000 investment, which was deposited among three savings and loan institutions. The will directed that the savings and loan institutions were to pay the income directly to Ms. Cathey and to return the funds to the estate after her death [in 1979]. We agree with the district court that it is generally unreasonable to continue an estate until the death of a beneficiary. This is particularly true when a bequest is small in relation to the size of the total estate. "The administration of an estate is concerned primarily with the collection of assets and payment of claims, and not with the more or less permanent custody of property for the protection of a legatee." Williams, 16 T.C. at 904. * * *

This reasoning applies with equal force to the purported legacies to Susan Brown Barry—Brown's only child—and her children. Moreover, we agree with the district court that such payments during Brown's lifetime were not specifically mandated by the wills [the court considering such payments, at best, "a moral obligation"].

* * * [T]he question of whether the administration of an estate has been unduly prolonged is one of fact. However, "the facts in a given case may be so clear that reasonable men could not differ on the question of

whether the administration was or was not unduly prolonged, in which case, the question is one of law." [Wylie v. United States, 281 F. Supp. 180, 190 (N.D. Tex. 1968).] We agree with the district court in this case that, as a matter of law, the continuing payments of federal income taxes and of the legacies described above were insufficient reasons to prolong the administration of the Estates for federal tax purposes.

NOTES

1. *Brown* is a case that can be appropriately given close scrutiny because the facts detail some of the practical aspects of estate administration. Apparently, the taxpayer in *Brown*, the executor, had concluded that it was advantageous for income tax purposes to continue the estates as income tax paying entities, the alternative being to conclude the respective estate administrations, whereupon the income would be taxable to the estate's beneficiary, namely himself. Likely only a few taxpayers today would see much practical advantage in warehousing income in an estate because taxing estate income at the estate level (rather than to the beneficiaries) would have yielded what some would say are relatively insignificant tax savings. Nonetheless an aggressive executor might be tempted to keep an estate open as a means of attempting to claim income tax deductions for the expenses incurred in managing the estate property, expenses that would be personal and nondeductible if the property were distributed to the beneficiaries. See, e.g., Hibernia Bank v. United States, 581 F.2d 741 (9th Cir.1978), which is discussed in Chapter 25. And there is always the possibility that a beneficiary's creditors cannot reach property held in an estate during the period of administration, a possibility that might cause a sympathetic executor to postpone distribution to the affected beneficiary.

2. In Turner v. United States, 306 F. Supp. 2d 668 (N.D. Tex. 2004), a charitable deduction had been claimed on the estate tax return for a $10 million pecuniary amount gift. Because the executor was uncertain as to whether the gift qualified for the charitable deduction, payment of the $10 million to the organization was delayed for 2 ½ years pending receipt of the estate tax closing letter—thereby, extending the period of estate administration. As a result of the delayed distribution, the organization was paid more than $1 million interest on its gift (because state law mandated payment of six percent interest on pecuniary amount gifts not satisfied within one year of death). The estate was held able to claim an estate tax administration expense deduction as an administration expense for estate tax purposes under section 2053 because the payment delay was "necessarily incurred" and was not incurred "for a longer period than"

the executor "was reasonably required to retain the property." The court discussed the role of the estate tax closing letter:

> Turner prudently withheld funding the bequest until the estate received an IRS closing letter and resolved any estate tax audit. Receipt of a closing letter prior to distributing estate assets is, in the general practice of estate administration, not an imprudent exercise of an executor's fiduciary duties. *See* IRS Field Service Advisory, 1997 WL 33313776 (Sept. 5, 1997) ("[A] reasonably, prudent person would not make distributions until they were in receipt of an estate tax closing letter . . ."). An estate tax closing letter from the IRS provides assurance to an executrix that issues such as the payment of estate tax and valuation of estate assets have been fully resolved, thus making it safe to distribute the assets of the estate to the beneficiaries. See, e.g., *Estate of Cameron Bommer v. Commissioner of Internal Revenue,* 69 T.C.M. (CCH) 2541 at n. 9, 1995 WL 258415 (U.S. Tax Ct. 1995) ("[C]losing letters are normally issued in estate cases to provide a measure of assurance that the estate's Federal tax liabilities have been satisfied and, thus, to permit the closing of the probate estate at the local level."). Professors Richard Schmalbeck & Jay A. Soled observe the following:
>
> > Many executors choose not to make estate distributions until they receive a closing letter from the Service that verifies the accuracy of the estate tax return. Because estate tax returns are not due until nine months after the death of a taxpayer (fifteen months if the executors file for an extension), and because the IRS usually does not issue an estate tax closing letter until six months after submission of the return, this precautionary stance [taken by executors often means that estates are kept open an extra] fifteen months to two years from the date of the decedent's death.
>
> Richard Schmalbeck & Jay A. Soled, *Many Unhappy Returns: Estate Tax Returns of Married Decedents,* 21 Va. Tax Rev. 361, 366 (2002) (footnotes omitted). Turner prudently followed this practice but promptly paid the * * * bequest two weeks after receiving the IRS closing letter, albeit 2 1/2 years after the decedent's death. * * * In light of these circumstances, the court is satisfied that Turner was properly acting within her fiduciary duty to the beneficiaries of the Will by awaiting the receipt of a closing letter.[7]

---

[7]   *Turner,* 306 F. Supp. 2d at 675–76.

3.   The *Brown* case involved an estate that stayed open too long. For many a fiduciary, the goal is wind up the estate or trust at the earliest possible time, effect distribution—and be released from personal liability (1) to the beneficiaries for his or her stewardship as fiduciary; and (2) income and gift taxes due from the decedent (in the case of an estate) or on account of income taxes owed by the fiduciary *as fiduciary*. Obtaining releases from the beneficiaries for liability for stewardship decisions is beyond the scope of these materials but, suffice it to say, that absent some consideration flowing to the beneficiaries for the release, there is some question as to the effectiveness of such releases. As for tax liability, section 6501(d) provides that the personal representative, upon request, is entitled to receive within 18 months of filing the request, a prompt assessment of any income and gift taxes due from the decedent, including penalties. Section 6905(a) provides that a personal representative, upon request, is entitled to be released or notified of any taxes dues within nine months of making the request. Rare though is the fiduciary who makes either request, it being commonly believed that the making of either request will trigger "an audit or even an arbitrary assessment." Jerry A. Kasner, Post Mortem Tax Planning, 2–46 (3rd ed. 1998).

2.   EXCESS DEDUCTIONS UNDER SECTION 642(h)

The term "excess deductions" refers to the amount by which the tax deductible expenses incurred by an estate or trust in its last tax year exceed the income of the estate or trust in that final year. I.R.C. § 642(h)(2). Under section 642(h)(2), the personal exemption otherwise available to estates and trusts and the charitable deduction is specifically excluded from the definition of these so-called excess deductions. The excess deductions in the final year flow through to the beneficiary or beneficiaries of the estate or trust and are available as deductions on the income tax return of the beneficiaries. However, the excess deductions are available to the beneficiary only as itemized deductions and only in the tax year of the beneficiary in which the estate or trust tax year ended.

PLANNING NOTE

While estate administration expenses are deductible in computing the federal estate tax under section 2053(a)(2) or the estate's income tax, such expenses are not deductible for both purposes. I.R.C. § 642(g). In deciding whether to claim these deductions on the federal estate tax return or on the estate's income tax return, the fiduciary must compare the marginal tax brackets that are applicable for estate tax purposes and income tax purposes to the particular trust or estate. Ordinarily, the deductions will be claimed on the return that provides the greatest dollar amount reduction in tax. Inasmuch as the estate tax rate is 40 percent in 2023 (when the basic exclusion amount is $12,920,000) and the effective income tax rates for the great majority of taxpayers are 32 percent or less (despite higher brackets of 35 percent and 37 percent in 2023, in most instances where an estate has federal estate tax liability, it makes economic sense to claim the deduction for administration expenses on the federal estate tax return rather than on the estate's income tax return. However, because many estates will not have any federal estate tax liability in light of the high basic exclusion amount, the deduction for fiduciary administration expenses should be claimed on the income tax return.

In the case of estates that have little income, tax sensitive planning calls for the executor to postpone payment of estate administration expenses until the final year of the administration. By such postponement, to the extent possible, the expenses are bunched in the final year of the estate administration and will generally exceed the estate's income in that final year, particularly if the final year is a short tax year, as is so often the case. Thus, excess deductions are generated. The pass through of these excess deductions can be economically advantageous. However, whether the beneficiary can actually use the excess deductions will depend on whether the beneficiary itemizes deductions for federal income tax purposes.

Income tax returns should be filed even in small estates where the estate's income is negligible. Filing such returns will give both the IRS and the estate beneficiaries the necessary information concerning the existence and amount of excess deductions.

3. NET OPERATING LOSS AND CAPITAL LOSS CARRYOVER

As in the case of excess deductions, section 642(h) permits an estate or trust to pass on to its beneficiaries any net operating loss carryover and capital loss carryover in the year in which the estate or trust terminates. While the loss need not be generated in the final year of the estate or trust, the loss must have been generated at the estate or trust level. Losses sustained by the decedent prior to death or losses sustained by the creator of the trust cannot be carried into the estate or trust and then out to the beneficiaries. Similarly, the beneficiary can utilize the loss only currently or carry it forward; the loss cannot be carried back to a prior tax year by the beneficiary.

In cases where the terminating year of the estate or trust is the last year for using the operating loss, any amount not utilized by the estate or trust in that last year will qualify as an excess deduction and may be carried out to the beneficiaries under section 642(h)(2). With this exception, neither net operating losses nor capital losses can be considered both a loss carryover and an excess deduction. Treas. Reg. § 1.642(h)–2(b). Moreover, a deductible item used to compute the loss cannot also qualify as a component of "excess deductions" available to the beneficiaries of the estate or trust. Treas. Reg. § 1.642(h)–2(c).

4.   TWO-PERCENT "HAIRCUT"

In the hands of the beneficiary, "excess deductions" in the final year of an estate or trust would appear to be "miscellaneous itemized deductions" as that term is defined in section 67(b) (even though these deductions are not subject to the two-percent haircut in the hands of the estate or trust). Section 67(a) provides that "in the case of an individual, the miscellaneous itemized deductions for any year shall be allowed only to the extent that the aggregate of such deductions exceeds 2 percent of adjusted gross income." Accordingly, it is possible that a beneficiary to whom "excess deductions" are allocated would be required to subject those deductions to the two-percent rule. The IRS issued Notice 2018–61, 2018–31 I.R.B. 278, to address concerns that the enactment of section 67(g) would affect a beneficiary's ability to deduct section 67(e) expenses upon the termination of the trust or estate as provided in section 642(h). The Notice states:

> Section 1.642(h)–1(b) provides, in part, that net operating loss carryovers and capital loss carryovers are taken into account when determining adjusted gross income. Therefore, they are above-the-line deductions and thus are not miscellaneous itemized deductions on the returns of beneficiaries. Conversely, § 1.642(h)–2(a) provides that if, on the termination of an estate or trust, the estate or trust has for its last taxable year deductions (other than the deductions allowed under section 642(b) (relating to personal exemption) or section 642(c) (relating to charitable contributions) in excess of gross income, the excess is allowed under section 642(h)(2) as a deduction (section 642(h)(2) excess deduction) to the beneficiaries. However, the section 642(h)(2) excess deduction is allowed only in computing the taxable income of the beneficiaries and must be taken into account in computing the items of tax preference of the beneficiaries. Therefore, a section 642(h)(2) excess deduction is not used in computing the beneficiaries' adjusted gross income and is treated as a miscellaneous itemized deduction of the beneficiaries. See sections 63(d) and 67(b).

> The section 642(h)(2) excess deduction may include expenses described in section § 67(e). As previously discussed, prior to enactment of section 67(g), miscellaneous itemized deductions were allowed subject to the restrictions contained in section 67(a). For the years in which section 67(g) is effective, miscellaneous itemized deductions are not permitted, and that appears to include the section 642(h)(2) excess deduction. The Treasury Department and the IRS are studying whether section 67(e) deductions, as well as other deductions that would not be subject to the limitations imposed by sections 67(a) and (g) in the hands of the trust or estate, should continue to be treated as

miscellaneous itemized deductions when they are included as a section 642(h)(2) excess deduction. Taxpayers should note that section 67(e) provides that appropriate adjustments shall be made in the application of part I of subchapter J of chapter 1 of the Code to take into account the provisions of section 67.

The Treasury Department and the IRS intend to issue regulations in this area and request comments regarding the effect of section 67(g) on the ability of the beneficiary to deduct amounts comprising the section 642(h)(2) excess deduction upon the termination of a trust or estate in light of sections 642(h) and 1.642(h)–2(a). In particular, the Treasury Department and the IRS request comments concerning whether the separate amounts comprising the section 642(h)(2) excess deduction, such as any amounts that are section 67(e) deductions, should be separately analyzed when applying section 67.

PROBLEM

A trust provided that income should be distributed to Bob until December 31 of the current year. At that time, the trust was to terminate, and the corpus was to be distributed to Chuck. During the year, the trust received dividends of $32,000 and sustained capital losses of $16,000. Capital gains and losses were allocable to corpus under the terms of the trust. The trustee's current fees were $2,000, of which $1,500 was chargeable to income and $500 chargeable to corpus. In addition, there was a trustee's termination fee of $10,000. The trust was duly terminated, and the corpus distributed to Chuck on December 31. How will the various items of income and expense be reported by Bob and Chuck? See I.R.C. §§ 642(h) and 1212.

L. BASIS CONSIDERATIONS

1. INTRODUCTION

When it comes to basis, trusts and estates are treated like any other taxpayer. More specifically, the basis of property purchased by the trustee is its cost. I.R.C. § 1012. Generally, the basis of property acquired by gift is the donor's basis. I.R.C. § 1015(a). However, if the donor's basis exceeds the fair market value of the property at the time of the gift, *for purposes of determining loss,* the donee's basis is the fair market value of the property at the time of the gift. I.R.C. § 1015(a). If the donee disposes of the property for a gain, the general rule applies, and the donee uses the donor's basis instead of the fair market value. And if the property is sold for an amount between the two, neither gain nor loss is recognized. Treas. Reg. § 1.1015–1, Ex.

If there is a testamentary transfer of the property, the basis is its fair market value at date of death or at alternate valuation date. I.R.C. § 1014(a). Technically speaking, property included in the estate of a decedent has, for its basis in the hands of a recipient, its estate tax value at the decedent's date of death or at alternate valuation date, without regard to its basis in the hands of the decedent while the decedent was alive. Thus, while it is common to speak of a "tax free stepped-up basis at death," the rule would be more accurately described as a "new-basis-at-death" rule in as much as property included in the decedent's estate may have lost value since acquisition by the decedent while he or she lived. Such an instance of disappearing basis leads to expressions such as a "stepped-*down* basis at death," normally an undesirable outcome. The rule is inexorable in its application and little or nothing can be done to avoid its application. In practical application, though, in cases where property was transferred to a trust during the decedent's life and is subsequently included in the decedent's gross estate for estate tax purposes, that property will have as its basis in the hands of the trustee its estate tax value at the decedent's death.

2.   ADJUSTMENTS TO BASIS OF TRUST AND ESTATE PROPERTY

Depreciation deductions are allowable to both estates and trusts with respect to income-producing or business property held by the estate or trust. I.R.C. § 167(a)(1) and (2). However, the depreciation deduction will be shared with the beneficiaries in proportion to the income distributed to the beneficiaries and the income retained by the estate or trust. I.R.C. §§ 642(e) and 167(d); Treas. Reg. § 1.167(h)–1. Furthermore, regardless of the allocation of the depreciation deduction, the basis of property in the hands of the fiduciary is required to be adjusted downward to take account of depreciation.

3.   DISTRIBUTIONS RECEIVED BY A BENEFICIARY AFTER DEATH

Section 1014 provides that property "passed" or "acquired" from a decedent receives a basis equal to its fair market value at the decedent's death or on the alternate valuation date. The meaning of the word "acquire" was litigated in Connecticut Nat'l Bank v. United States, 937 F.2d 90 (2d Cir.1991). The husband had died, leaving his wife as beneficiary of the marital trust. The wife received an income interest in and held a general power of appointment (GPOA) over the corpus of the trust. However, at the time of the wife's death, the husband's executor had not distributed to the trust the property to which the trust was entitled. While the trust remained unfunded at the wife's death, the value of the property subject to the GPOA but not yet distributed to the trust was included in her gross estate.

Furthermore, the wife had exercised the GPOA to pass the trust property at her death to an inter vivos trust in favor of her grandchildren. After the wife's death, the husband's estate sold a substantial portion of the trust property, computed a taxable gain based on the fair market value (FMV) of the property at the date of the wife's death and paid the related capital gains tax. The IRS concluded that the estate erroneously computed the income tax payable because the estate was not entitled to use the FMV at the wife's death as the basis of the property sold. It determined that the correct basis for the sold property was the FMV at the date of the husband's death because the property had not been distributed to the trust and therefore the estate did not "acquire" the property at the wife's death. It argued that the correct basis to compute the taxable gain on the fiduciary income tax return was the FMV at the date of the husband's death even though the property would be included in the wife's estate at the FMV at her death for estate tax purposes section 2041.

The Second Circuit, nonetheless, agreed with the estate and held that the correct basis to determine the tax payable on the sale was the FMV of the property at the date of the wife's death, regardless of whether the property was ever distributed to the trust. The court found under section 1014(b)(4) that the trust was entitled to a new basis in computing any capital gains realized on the sale. The Second Circuit, in its holding, denounced the strict interpretation the IRS advanced and invoked a more liberal reading of the terms "acquired" and "passed" in section 1014.

M. DISTRIBUTION IN KIND

1. BASIS

Section 643(e) provides that the basis of property distributed in kind is to be "the adjusted basis of such property in the hands of the estate or trust immediately before the distribution, adjusted for * * * any gain or loss recognized to the estate or trust on the distribution." However, whether gain or loss is recognized by the estate or trust is optional, with the election to be made by the estate or trust. As section 643(e) reads, the estate or trust apparently has the option of treating a distribution in kind "as if such property had been sold to the distributee at its fair market value." This means that the estate or trust recognizes gain if the property has appreciated. Where the property has depreciated in value, section 267(b) bars trusts from deducting such losses. If the estate or trust does not choose—or is unable—to recognize gain or loss on the distribution in kind, the distributee assumes the basis of the property to the estate or trust—essentially "carryover" basis.

Any election made under section 643(e) "shall apply to all distributions made by the estate or trust" during the taxable year and "shall be made on the return of such estate or trust for such taxable year." I.R.C.

§ 643(e)(3)(B). Section 643(e) does not apply in cases where there is no DNI or the cash distributed from the estate or trust "soaks up" the DNI. I.R.C. § 643(e)(4).

> *Example*: Assume that a trust which held appreciated property also provided that all distributions shall be at the sole discretion of the trustee. More specifically, assume that the trust has $500 of distributable net income, that it has an asset with a fair market value of $500 and a basis of $100, and that the trustee plans to exercise his discretion to distribute $500 to the beneficiary. If the trustee distributes $500 in cash, the trust will enjoy a distribution deduction of $500 and the beneficiary will have ordinary income of $500. See I.R.C. §§ 661(a) and 662(a).

If the trustee elects to distribute the appreciated asset to the beneficiary, the trustee will be put to an election. The trustee can elect to claim a distribution deduction of $500. If the trustee does claim a $500 distribution deduction, the beneficiary will have taxable income of $500 and the property will have a basis of $500 in the hands of the beneficiary. In addition, the trust will be required to recognize gain of $400 (fair market value of $500 less basis of $100) on the distribution.

In lieu of claiming the $500 distribution deduction, the trustee could be content with claiming only a $100 distribution deduction. In that case, the beneficiary will be deemed to have received taxable income of only $100 and the beneficiary's basis in the distributed property would only be $100. If the beneficiary then sells the distributed property for $500, he or she would experience a $400 taxable gain.

If the estate includes property that has depreciated in value, i.e., has a fair market value below its basis in the hands of the estate, distribution of that loss property carries out DNI only to the extent of the property's fair market value. However, the distributee will assume the basis of the property in the hands of the estate unless the estate elects to recognize the loss. In the ordinary case, it would seem that loss recognition would be warranted because it has the effect of reducing DNI and providing income tax relief without any immediate tax cost. Of course, if the property is to be sold, the determination of whether the estate or the distributee should claim the loss will depend on the relative tax brackets of the estate and the distributee.

> *Example*: The Jones Estate plans to distribute 100 shares of stock to Ted, the estate beneficiary. The shares had a value of $2,000 at the time of acquisition but have declined in value to $1,200. Both Ted and the estate are in the 37-percent income tax bracket. The estate can elect to recognize the loss on the stock when the stock

is distributed to Ted. His basis in the distributed stock will then be $1,200. If the estate does not elect to recognize the loss, Ted's basis in the distributed stock will be $2,000.

Note that section 643(e) does not apply in cases where there is no DNI. Finally, by way of contrast, remember that section 643(e) does not apply to property distributed in kind in satisfaction of a specific bequest that meets the requirements of section 663(a). I.R.C. § 643(e)(4).

> *Example*: In her will, Allison first provided that all her tangible personal property was to be distributed to her husband, Lennie; next, she provided that the property that she was using for residential purposes at the time of her death was to be distributed to Lennie; and, finally, she provided that "my husband, Lennie, is to receive the rest and residue of my property not otherwise disposed of under this will." Except for Allison's 1987 automobile, nothing was distributed to Lennie in the 12-month period following Allison's death. The automobile had a $3,000 income tax basis in the hands of Allison's executor and a $2,500 fair market value at the date of distribution. The automobile's basis is $3,000 in the hands of the decedent's husband, inasmuch as it was distributed to Lennie pursuant to the specific bequest in Allison's will.

> *Example*: Claire's will provided that "all my property is to be distributed to my husband, Dennie." As in the case of Allison's estate, the only distribution from Claire's estate during the 12-month period following her death was Claire's 1988 automobile, which was distributed to her husband, Dennie. Claire's automobile had a $5,000 income tax basis in the hands of Claire's executor and a $4,500 fair market value at the date of distribution. While Claire's executor has the option of recognizing as a loss the $500 depreciation in the value of Claire's automobile between the date of her death and the date the automobile was distributed (section 643(e)(1)), perhaps the more significant point is that the distribution of Claire's automobile will have the effect of carrying out to Dennie only $4,500 of DNI.

The obvious purpose of the two examples immediately preceding is to demonstrate that distributions from an estate or trust carry out the estate or trust's DNI, often to the surprise of the recipient who thought that he or she was getting a "car" and not "taxable income." The lesson is to draft the document so as to include specific bequests of those items that are likely to be distributed early in the estate administration. See I.R.C. § 663(a)(1). Otherwise, these distributions will "catch" all of the estate's DNI.

PROBLEM

Pedro's will stated that "My friend, Antonio, is to receive all my property at my death." During the year following Pedro's death, Pedro's estate had $5,600 of income. The only distribution from the estate was Pedro's automobile, which was distributed to Antonio. Although the automobile had a value of $3,900 at the time of Pedro's death, its value was $3,000 at the time of distribution to Antonio. What is the income tax basis of the automobile in the hands of Antonio? See I.R.C. § 643(e).

2.   SALE OR EXCHANGE

a.   Pecuniary Bequest

Recognition of loss is denied except when the loss is incurred in connection with a distribution by an estate—but not a trust—in satisfaction of a pecuniary bequest. I.R.C. § 267(a)(1) and (b)(13). Thus, loss recognition is prevented in that all too common situation where the decedent has funded a revocable trust during life and directs that the trustee shall distribute to the surviving spouse a pecuniary bequest intended to qualify for the marital deduction. The alternative, of course, is for the trustee to sell the loss property, realize the loss for income tax purposes, and satisfy the spouse's pecuniary gift with cash.

Recognition of gain is not elective in cases where appreciated property is distributed in satisfaction of a pecuniary bequest. In such cases, the distribution in kind will be treated as a sale or exchange by the trust or estate inasmuch as the trust or estate is satisfying a specific dollar obligation with appreciated property. Treas. Reg. § 1.661(a)–2(f). It is as if the trustee distributed cash and the beneficiary purchased the property with the cash distributed.

KENAN V. COMMISSIONER

United States Court of Appeals, Second Circuit, 1940.
114 F.2d 217.

AUGUSTUS N. HAND, CIRCUIT JUDGE.

The testatrix, Mrs. Bingham, died on July 27, 1917, leaving a will under which she placed her residuary estate in trust and provided in item "Seventh" that her trustees should pay a certain amount annually to her niece, Louise Clisby Wise, until the latter reached the age of forty, "at which time or as soon thereafter as compatible with the interests of my estate they shall pay to her the sum of Five Million ($5,000,000.00) Dollars." The will provided in item "Eleventh" that the trustees, in the case of certain payments including that of the $5,000,000 under item "Seventh", should have the right "to substitute for the payment in money, payment in marketable securities of a value equal to the sum to be paid, the selection of the securities to be substituted in any instance, and the valuation of such securities to be done by the Trustees and their selection and valuation to be final."

Louise Clisby Wise became forty years of age on July 28, 1935. The trustees decided to pay her the $5,000,000 partly in cash and in securities. The greater part of the securities had been owned by the testator and transferred as part of her estate to the trustees; others had been purchased by the trustees. All had appreciated in value during the period for which they were held by the trustees, and the Commissioner determined that the distribution of the securities to the niece resulted in capital gains * * *.

The taxpayers contend that * * * they realized neither gain from the sale or exchange of capital assets nor income of any character by delivering the securities to the legatee pursuant to the permissive terms of the will. The Commissioner contends that gain was realized by the delivery of the securities but that such gain was ordinary income not derived from a sale or exchange and therefore taxable in its entirety.

* * *

In support of their petition the taxpayers contend that the delivery of the securities of the trust estate to the legatee was a donative disposition of property pursuant to the terms of the will, and that no gain was thereby realized. They argue that when they determined that the legacy should be one of securities, it became for all purposes a bequest of property, just as if the cash alternative had not been provided, and not taxable for the reason that no gain is realized on the transfer by a testamentary trustee of specific securities or other property bequeathed by will to a legatee.

We do not think that the situation here is the same as that of a legacy of specific property. The legatee was never in the position occupied by the recipient of specific securities under a will. She had a claim against the estate of $5,000,000, payable either in cash or securities of that value, but had no title or right to the securities, legal or equitable, until they were delivered to her by the trustees after the exercise of their option. She took none of the chances of a legatee of specific securities or of a share of a residue that the securities might appreciate or decline in value between the time of the death of the testator and the transfer to her by the trustees, but instead had at all times a claim for an unvarying amount in money or its equivalent.

If there had merely been a bequest to the legatee of $5,000,000 and she had agreed with the trustees to take securities of that value, the transaction would have been a "sale or other disposition" of the securities * * *.

In the present case, the legatee had a claim which was a charge against the trust estate for $5,000,000 in cash or securities and the trustees had the power to determine whether the claim should be satisfied in one form or the other. The claim, though enforceable only in the alternative, was * * * a charge against the entire trust estate. If it were satisfied by a cash payment securities might have to be sold on which (if those actually delivered in specie were selected) a taxable gain would necessarily have been realized. Instead of making such a sale the trustees delivered the securities and exchanged them pro tanto for the general claim of the legatee, which was thereby satisfied.

It is said that this transaction was not such a "sale or other disposition" as is intended by Section 111(a) [1986 Code § 1001] * * * because it was effectuated only by the will of the trustees and not through a mutual agreement between trustee and legatee. * * * [W]e are not inclined to limit thus the meaning of the words "other disposition" used in Section 111(a), or of "exchange" used in Section 117. The word "exchange" does not necessarily have the connotation of a bilateral agreement which may be said to attach to the word "sale." Thus, should a person set up a trust and reserve to himself the power to substitute for the securities placed in trust other securities of equal value, there would seem no doubt that the exercise of this reserved power would be an "exchange" within the common meaning of the word, even though the settlor consulted no will other than his own, although, of course, we do not here advert to the problems of taxability in such a situation.

* * * Under circumstances like those here, where the legatee did not take securities designated by the will or an interest in the corpus which might be more or less at the time of the transfer than at the time of decedent's death, it seems to us that the trustees realized a gain by using these securities to settle a claim worth $5,000,000 * * *.

It seems reasonably clear that the property was not "transmitted at death" or "acquired by bequest * * * from the decedent." Section 113(a)(5). [1986 Code § 1014(b)]. It follows that the fears of the taxpayers that double taxation of this appreciation will result because the legatee will take the basis of the decedent * * * are groundless. It is true that under Section 113(a)(5) [1986 Code § 1014(a)] the basis for property "acquired by bequest, devise, or inheritance" is "the fair market value of such property at the time of such acquisition" and * * * the date of acquisition has been defined as the date of death of the testator. But the holding of the present case is necessarily a determination that the property here acquired is acquired in an exchange and not "by bequest, devise or inheritance," since Sections § 117 and 113(a)(5) seem to be mutually exclusive. The legatee's basis would seem to be the value of the claim surrendered in exchange for the securities.

* * *

b. Legal Obligation

For tax purposes, distributions in kind in satisfaction of a legal obligation of the trust will be treated as distributions in kind in satisfaction of a pecuniary bequest. A typical example arises where a trust provision calls for distribution of all trust income at least annually. Distributions of appreciated property in satisfaction of the beneficiary's right to income results in recognition of taxable gain to the trust equal to the difference between the basis of the property distributed and the fair market value on the date of distribution. Treas. Reg. § 1.661(a)–2(f).

In a similar factual posture, the IRS has ruled in Revenue Ruling 67–74, 1967–1 C.B. 194 that such a transaction is:

> treated as though the trustee had actually distributed to the beneficiary cash in an amount equal to the trust income required to be distributed currently, and if the beneficiary had purchased the stock from the trustee with cash. The trust is allowed a deduction under § 651(a) limited by the distributable net income of the trust, for the amount of income required to be distributed currently, and the beneficiary must report a like amount in gross income under § 652(a). The instant transfer, involving stock having a fair market value equal to the trust income for the year in question which the trustee was required to distribute to the beneficiary, resulted in a capital gain to the trust equal to the difference between the basis of the stock in the hands of the trustee and the amount of the obligation satisfied by the transfer. Further, the basis of the stock in the hands of the beneficiary is his cost, that is, the price he is deemed to have paid for it.

PROBLEMS

1. Mr. Tweede, a trust officer at Accumulation National Bank, is responsible for a number of accounts that hold shares in Belchfire Automobile, Inc. The shares of Belchfire have risen dramatically in value, but Mr. Tweede wants to "dispose the shares at the top of the market." However, if he sells the shares for his various accounts, the gain to be realized is significant. Instead, he proposes that he distribute the shares to the account beneficiaries and let them decide whether to sell.

    One of his accounts is the Arthur Dawg Estate. Mr. Dawg's will states that his spouse is to receive "the smallest amount necessary to eliminate all federal estate tax" from his estate. That amount, as finally determined, is equal to $50,000. The Belchfire stock in Arthur's estate has a current market value of $50,000, and Mr. Tweede proposes to distribute the stock to Mrs. Dawg in satisfaction of Arthur's gift. The estate's basis in the shares is $10,000. The estate has $80,000 of distributable net income this year.

(a) What are the income tax consequences to the estate if it makes this distribution? See I.R.C. § 661(a) & Treas. Reg. § 1.663(a)–1(b)(1).

(b) What are the tax consequences to Mrs. Dawg upon receipt of the shares? See I.R.C. § 662.

(c) What is her basis if she sells the shares upon receipt? See Treas. Reg. § 1.1014–4(a)(3).

2. In the following situations, Mr. Tweede proposes to distribute Belchfire stock rather than cash. Indicate the income tax consequences to each trust if the stock is distributed in kind. Also indicate the income tax consequences to the beneficiary of each trust. Determine the basis of the shares to each beneficiary. Then consider the tax consequences to the trust if the trustee sold the shares and distributed cash to each beneficiary. In making your analysis, assume each beneficiary is effectively in the top income tax bracket, the trust has $20,000 of DNI for this tax year, and the trustee proposes to distribute either cash or Belchfire stock having a market value of $10,000 and a basis of $2,000.

(a) The Able Trust requires the trustee to distribute all the income of the trust.

(b) The Baker Trust requires the trustee to distribute so much or all of the principal and income of the trust as shall be required for the "maintenance, care, and support" of the trust beneficiary.

(c) The Charlie Trust permits the trustee to make distributions of income and principal whenever the trustee determines such distributions to be in the "best interests" of the beneficiary.

N. INTEGRATED PLANNING FOR ESTATE ADMINISTRATION

1. STATE PROPERTY LAW CONSIDERATIONS

The federal income tax treatment of the income generated by a decedent's property after the decedent's death is complicated not only by the distribution rules of Subchapter J of the Internal Revenue Code but also by questions of title and possession.

In the majority of states, title to real property vests immediately in those persons who are the beneficiaries under the will of the decedent or, if the decedent dies intestate, title vests in the heirs of the decedent.[8] This means that even though the decedent's executor may collect and hold the decedent's property during administration, legal title to that property is in

---

[8] See, e.g., Tenn. Code Ann. § 31–2–103 (2022) (providing that real property vests immediately in the devisees unless the will directs otherwise and vests immediately in the heirs if the decedent dies intestate); In re Estate of Schnur, 485 S.W.2d 682, 688 (Mo. Ct. App. 1972) (stating that whether a decedent dies testate or intestate, title to real property vests immediately in heirs or devisees). Accord In re Estate of Bettis, 340 A.2d 57, 59 (Vt. 1975).

the indicated beneficiary. Conversely, in the majority of states, title to the decedent's personal property vests in the decedent's personal representative.[9]

For income tax purposes, it can be said that, as a general rule, the fruit follows the tree. See Lucas v. Earl, 281 U.S. 111 (1930). Accordingly, income earned by the decedent's property after the decedent's death will be taxable to the person who has title to that property at the time the income is generated. Thus, rental income generated by the decedent's real property will be taxable to the ultimate recipient of that property as determined by the decedent's will or the applicable intestate statute. On the other hand, applying the general rule, income from personal property will be taxable to the decedent's estate.

Some states, particularly those adopting the Uniform Probate Code, stipulate that, while title is in the beneficiaries, the decedent's personal representative is entitled to possession of the decedent's property—both real and personal—during administration of the decedent's estate unless otherwise provided by the decedent's will.[10] In these states, there is some agreement that title is not determinative of income tax liability and the fruit does not follow the tree. In these states, income generated by the decedent's property after the decedent's death is to be taxed to the decedent's estate. See Jones v. Whittington, 194 F.2d 812 (10th Cir.1952).

In addition to these considerations of title, estate administration is often complicated by the receipt after the decedent's death of income that was earned before death. An example would be the decedent's final wages, received after death, for work performed before death. These wages—referred to as income in respect of a decedent (IRD)—are an asset of the decedent's estate for federal estate tax purposes but they are also income. IRD is discussed in Chapter 32.

Another factor in some estates is the presence of community property. Community property refers to the peculiar system of rules that determine the rights of married persons in property acquired by them during marriage. Most of the western states and Wisconsin have adopted the community property system. However, the rules of no two states are exactly alike.

Under the community property system, the term "separate property" refers to property acquired before marriage or property acquired after marriage by gift, devise, bequest or inheritance. By way of contrast,

---

[9]   See, e.g., In re Forfeiture of $234,000, 551 N.W. 2d 444, 446 (Mich. Ct. App. 1996) (stating "legal title to personal property of a decedent, testate or intestate, vests in the personal representative until the estate is fully settled and distributed, or the property is otherwise disposed of"). Accord Wood v. Wingfield, 816 S.W.2d 899, 902 (Ky. Ct. App. (1991); Wood v. Hudson, 823 S.W.2d. 158, 160 (Mo. Ct. App. 1992); Darden v. Boyette, 100 S.E.2d 359, 362 (N.C. Ct. App. 1992).

[10]   See, e.g., Ariz. Rev. Stat. § 14–3709 (2022); Cal. Prob. Code § 9650 (2022); D.C. Code Ann. § 20–702 (2023); Minn. Stat. § 524.3–709 (2022); N.D. Cent. Code § 30.1–18–09 (2021).

community property is property acquired after marriage that is not separate property. In addition, in Texas, Idaho, Louisiana, and Wisconsin, income from separate property is community property.[11] In the five remaining community property states, income from separate property is also separate property, but an increase in the income attributable to community funds is considered community property.[12] Finally, under community property rules generally, each spouse can dispose of his or her 50% of the community property by will at death and any portion of the decedent's one-half that is not effectively disposed of by will passes by intestacy. For example, in California, if a decedent spouse dies intestate, the surviving spouse's intestate share is the decedent's one-half share of the community property.[13] In Texas, a surviving spouse takes the decedent spouse's one-half share; however, if the decedent spouse is survived by a descendant who is not a descendant of the surviving spouse, one-half of the decedent's share passes the descendant and the other half to the surviving spouse.[14]

2. RELATIONSHIP OF ESTATE TAX AND INCOME TAX

Estate administration is complicated by the need to take into account not only provisions of the decedent's will and state property law but also the federal income tax, the federal estate tax, the federal gift tax, and the federal generation-skipping tax as well as state income and death taxes. Of particular importance is the relationship of the requirements imposed by these different elements.

---

[11] See Idaho Code § 32–906 (2022) (providing the income of all property, separate or community, is community property unless otherwise stated in the conveyance document or a written agreement by both spouses); La. Civ. Code Ann. art. 2339 (2022) (providing that unless a spouse reserves by declaration, income derived from separate property is community property); Richardson v. Richardson, 424 S.W. 3d 691, 701) (Tex. App. 2014) (stating "[g]enerally, income produced from separate property is considered community property, regardless of the nature of the separate property generating income, including stock, shares in a corporation, livestock, or other assets"); Wis. Stat. Ann. § 766.31(4) (2022) (providing any income earned by the spouse or attributable to separate property of a spouse is marital property, subject to certain exceptions).

[12] See Reuschenberg v. Reushchenberg, 219 P.3d 852, 857 (Ariz. Ct. App. 2008) (stating that income derived from separate property is generally separate property, but if the income from the separate property is a result of the "toil of the community," the income is community property); Patrick v. Alacer Corp., 136 Cal.Rptr. 3d 669, 679–80 (Cal. 2011) (finding that the general rule is that income derived from separate property remains separate property unless the increase in income is the result of efforts of the community); Cord v. Neuhoff, 573 P.2d 1170, 1173 (1978) (stating that while income from separate property is separate property, Nevada has adopted the apportionment rule to determine whether income from separate property should be classified as separate or community property); Zemke v. Zemke, 860 P.2d 756, 761 (N.M. 1978) (stating "[a]ny increase in the value of separate property is presumed to be also separate unless rebutted by direct and positive evidence that the increase was due to community funds or labor"); Lindemann v. Lindemann, 960 P.2d 966, 969–70 (Wash. App. 1998) (stating that the presumption is that any increase in the value of separate property is also separate property unless there is "direct and positive evidence" that the increase is the result of "community labor").

[13] Cal. Prob. Code § 6401 (2022).

[14] Tex. Estates Code § 201.003 (2021).

In the typical estate, the executor must be concerned about whether items of income are includible on (1) the decedent's final income tax returns because the decedent was in constructive receipt of that item, (2) on the estate's income tax returns, or (3) on the beneficiary's income tax returns because the item was received by the executor as agent for the beneficiary (as can happen in the case of rental income from real property in those states where title to real estate passes to the beneficiary immediately at the death of the decedent). The executor must also be concerned about whether any of these items of income are also subject to state and federal death taxes, i.e., as income in respect of a decedent (which would mean that the recipient of this item of IRD would be entitled to an income tax deduction for the estate tax attributable to the item of IRD). Not to be ignored are the basis rules.

Thus, after death, there are three potential taxpayers and three taxes to be considered. The taxes are the federal estate tax, the federal generation-skipping tax, and the federal income tax. The potential taxpayers are the decedent's estate, which is subject to the estate tax, the generation-skipping tax, and the income tax; the beneficiaries of the decedent's estate, who are also potential income taxpayers; and the decedent, for whom a final federal income tax return may be required. Similarly, in the case of expenditures by the executor, questions arise as to whether the expenditure is a deduction: (1) on the decedent's final income tax return; (2) by the executor on the estate's income tax return; or (3) by the beneficiary on his or her income tax return (because the executor was acting only as agent of the beneficiary in making the expenditure) and whether any of these items are deductions on the decedent's state and federal death tax returns, perhaps even being deductible for both income tax and estate tax purposes. See Treas. Reg. § 1.212–1(i). The matter is complicated because some disbursements are deductible for one tax and not for another. Others are deductible for both taxes but only by certain taxpayers. For example, funeral expenses are deductible for estate tax purposes but not for income tax purposes. See I.R.C. § 2053(a)(1). On the other hand, the medical expenses incurred by the decedent in the final illness and unpaid at the time of death are deductible for estate tax purposes and for income tax purposes but only on the decedent's final income tax return and then only if it is agreed that the estate tax deduction will not be claimed. See I.R.C. § 642(g). An example of a deduction available for both federal income tax and federal estate tax purposes would be real property taxes that become a lien at the beginning of the calendar year but are not paid (nor payable) until the end of the calendar year.[15] By way of further contrast, administration expenses, such as attorney fees, are

---

[15] Property taxes are deductible for federal income tax purposes under section 164(a)(1). However, under the Tax Cuts and Jobs Act, this deduction is limited to a maximum amount of $10,000. See I.R.C. § 164(b)(1)(6)(B). Property taxes that accrued prior to the decedent's death are also deductible from the decedent's gross estate. See Treas. Regs. § 20.2053–6.

deductible on the estate tax return but not by the decedent on the final federal income tax return.

Finally, as noted earlier, generation-skipping taxes paid as the result of the death of the transferor on items of gross income of a trust are deductible for income tax purposes in cases where those items of gross income "were not properly includible in the gross income of the trust for the periods before the date" of the taxable termination or direct skip that gave rise to the imposition of the generation-skipping tax. I.R.C. § 691(c)(3).

a. Final Medical Expenses

REVENUE RULING 77-357
1977–2 C.B. 328.

Advice has been requested whether, under the circumstances described below, a Federal estate tax deduction is allowable under section 2053(a) * * * for the three percent portion of medical expenses that is not deductible for Federal income tax purposes. [Under current law, expenses exceeding 7.5% of adjusted gross income are deductible. § 213(a).]

The decedent died on December 31, 1974, after a six-month illness during which decedent incurred doctor and hospital expenses in the amount of $20,000. These medical expenses were paid by the decedent's representative in 1975. For the 1974 taxable year, the decedent had an adjusted gross income of $100,000. The decedent's representative deducted $5,000 as a claim against the decedent's estate under section 2053 * * *. The necessary statement and the waiver indicating that the balance of the expenses, or $15,000, had not been allowed and would not be allowed at any time as a deduction under section 2053 were filed with the decedent's final income tax return.

* * *

The Senate Finance Committee Report, S. Rep. No. 1983, 85th Cong., 2d Sess., p. 27, 1958–3 C.B. 922, 948, accompanying the Technical Amendments Act of 1958, Pub. L. 85–866, 1958–3 C.B. 254, reads in part as follows:

Present law (sec. § 213(d)) * * * permits the deduction in the last year of a decedent of expenses for his medical care which are paid out of his estate during the 1-year period after his death. These expenses are treated as if they had been paid by the taxpayer at the time they were incurred. This deduction is not available unless a statement is filed that the amount has not been claimed or allowed as a deduction for estate-tax purposes and a waiver of the right to this amount as an estate-tax deduction has been filed. . . .

This provision conforms the language in section 213(d)(2)(a) relating to the deduction of the expenses in the last year of the decedent with the language in section 642(g) which allows other expenses as deductions to the estate. * * *

Section 2053(a)(3) provides that the value of the taxable estate shall be determined by deducting from the value of the gross estate such amounts for claims against the estate as are allowable by the laws of the jurisdiction under which the estate is being administered. [Treas. Reg. § 20.2053–4] * * * states that the amounts that may be deducted as claims against a decedent's estate are such only as represent personal obligations of the decedent existing at the time of decedent's death, whether or not then matured, and interest thereon which has accrued at the time of death.

The medical expenses of a decedent's last illness are a deductible claim against the estate within the meaning of section 2053(a)(3) and, thus, medical expenses are deductible on the estate tax return or on the decedent's final income tax return under section 213(a)(1).

Certain other deductions allowable for income tax purposes are also allowable as deductions for estate tax purposes. For example: section 2053 provides for the deduction, among other things, of administration expenses in determining the value of the taxable estate for estate tax purposes. Such expenses would also constitute allowable deductions as expenses for the production of income under section 212 in determining the net income of the estate for Federal income tax purposes.

However, with respect to the allowance of a deduction in computing the taxable income of the estate, section 642(g) provides [that the deductions allowable under §§ 2053 or 2054 in computing the taxable estate of a decedent are not allowed as a deduction in computing the taxable income of the decedent's estate or that of any other person, unless a written waiver of the right to claim those deductions for estate tax purposes is filed with the IRS] * * *.

The purpose of section 642(g) is to prevent an estate from obtaining a double deduction with respect to the same items of administration expenses. Administration expenses are, therefore, not allowable deductions under section 212 unless there is filed a statement that the items representing such expenses have not been allowed as deductions in the estate tax return, and a waiver of the right to have such items allowed at any time as deductions in the estate tax return. In the event that administration expenses are such that they would be allowable for either income or estate tax purposes, the taxpayer may allocate the expenses to either the estate tax return or the income tax return for the year in which payment is made, provided there is no duplication of deduction and provided the terms of section 642(g) are complied with. See Rev. Rul. 70–361, 1970–2 C.B. 133.

Similarly, with respect to medical expenses, as long as there is no duplication of a deduction and the provisions of section 213(d) are complied with, there is nothing to prevent a decedent's representative from taking a deduction for certain items of the medical expenses of a decedent's last illness in computing the net estate under section 2053 and also taking a deduction for other items of such expenses on the decedent's final income tax return under section 213.

The issue of the deductibility of the three percent portion of medical expenses on the estate tax return pivots on the construction of section 213(d)(2). If the intent of Congress in enacting section 213(d)(2) was simply to prohibit the allowance of a double deduction as might be inferred from its reference to section 642(g) in the 1958 amendment to 213(d)(2)(a), then the three percent portion might arguably be available as an estate tax deduction since such portion is not actually deducted on the decedent's final income tax return but rather is used in computing the allowable amount of the deduction. However, a literal interpretation of section 213(d)(2) requires that section 213(d)(1) not apply if the "amount paid" is allowable under section 2053 as a deduction, unless the requisite waiver and statement are filed to the effect that the "amount paid" has not been nor will be at any time allowed on a 2053 deduction. In the instant case, the "amount paid" for purposes of section 213(d)(2) is $15,000 (total medical expenses of $20,000 less $5,000 deducted as a claim against the decedent's estate). The application of subsection (d)(2) to the portion of medical expenses ($15,000) deemed paid at the time incurred, without consideration of the three percent of adjusted gross income limitation, is clear and unambiguous from the language used by Congress in the enactment of this section.

Accordingly, the three percent portion of medical expenses ($3,000) not allowable as a deduction for income tax purposes is not deductible from the gross estate under section 2053(a). Thus, of the total medical expenses of $20,000 in the instant case, $5,000 is deductible from the decedent's gross estate under section 2053 and $12,000 is deductible on the decedent's final income tax return under section 213.

NOTE

Income received by an estate during administration must be included in the estate's gross income for income tax purposes rather than the gross estate for estate tax purposes. Administration expenses, however, can be taken as a deduction on either the estate's income or estate tax return, but not both. I.R.C. § 642(g).

b. Marital Deduction and Deduction of Administration Expenses

The interplay of the estate tax marital deduction under section 2056 and the availability of an income tax deduction for administration expenses has given rise to a controversy of such significance that it was considered by the Supreme Court in Commissioner v. Estate of Hubert, 520 U.S. 93 (1997), a decision that was followed by a change in course by the IRS. In sum, the issue is whether the estate tax marital deduction otherwise allowable under section 2056 must be reduced by administrative expenses—and interest accruing on federal estate tax and state inheritance tax deficiencies—if a deduction is taken on the estate's income tax return for these items.

Taxpayers see the issue in these terms. Because of the easy availability of the section 2056's unlimited marital deduction for gifts to a surviving spouse, estate taxes can easily be—and *are* routinely—eliminated by the planning expedient of causing the decedent's will to make a gift to the surviving spouse of at least the amount or share necessary to reduce estate taxes to zero. With estate taxes, thus, at zero, practitioners are inclined to claim a deduction on the estate's income tax return for the estate administration expenses—*"where it will do some good."*

Currently—that is post-*Hubert*—the Treasury regulations state that administration expenses are classified as either "estate transmission expenses" or "estate management expenses." See Treas. Reg. § 20.2056(b)–4(d)(1). The regulations then state that the estate tax marital deduction is to be "reduced by the amount of the estate transmission expenses paid from the marital share." Treas. Reg. § 20.2056(b)–4(d)(2). Estate transmission expenses are those expenses that would not have been incurred without the decedent's death and the resulting need for collecting and distributing the decedent's property.[16] Treas. Reg. § 20.2056(b)–4(d)(1)(ii). "Marital share" is defined as the property for which the marital deduction is allowed for estate tax purposes under section 2056(a) and includes the income produced by that property during the period of administration. Treas. Reg. § 20.2056(b)–4(d)(1)(iii).

The Treasury position is illustrated in a series of examples given in Regulation § 20.2056(b)–4(d)(5), the conclusion from which is that the governing instrument—the will or trust—or applicable state law must impose the burden of the estate transmission expenses on the portion of the decedent's property *not* passing to the surviving spouse. This is the crucial point and it bears emphasis. The governing instrument or applicable state law must impose the actual burden of the estate transmission expenses on the share of the decedent's property passing to

---

[16] Examples include attorney fees, court costs, and "any administration expense that is not a management expense." Treas. Reg. § 20.2056(b)–4(d)(1)(ii).

others than the surviving spouse. To the extent that these expenses are imposed on the share passing to the surviving spouse, the marital deduction will be reduced. In the latter case, unless the estate transmission expenses are claimed as a deduction of the estate tax return, the estate will not be "zeroed out" for estate tax purposes—and estate tax may well be payable. Whether estate tax is actually payable depends on whether the section 2010(c)(3) basic exclusion amount ($12,920,000 in 2023) is available to shelter the taxable estate that is thus determined by this process.

As an illustration, consider an example involving spouses Sarah and Lotus. Under the terms of Sarah's will, she devises to Lotus $8 million followed by a devise of the residue to their child, Carol. The will provides that all debts, taxes and administration expenses are to be paid out of the residuary estate. In this case estate transmission expenses can be claimed on the estate's income tax return without impairing the marital deduction for the full $8 million. See Treas. Reg. § 20.2056(b)–4(d)(5), Example 7.

Contrast an example involving spouses Derek and Jane. Under Jane's will, she devised the section 2010(c) basic exclusion amount as of the date of her death (which occurred in 2023) to her child, Sallie. The residue passed to a trust for the benefit of Derek, after payment of debts, taxes, and administration expenses. Jane's estate has a date of death value of $14,920,000; estate transmission expenses are $200,000; the basic exclusion amount is $12,920,000. Sallie gets the $12,920,000. But the IRS insists that only $1.8 million is available for distribution to Derek ($2 million minus $200,000, estate transmission expenses) even if the estate transmission expenses are paid out of income earned during estate administration. See Treas. Reg. § 20.2056(b)–4(d)(4)(2). Hence, Jane's marital deduction is limited to $1.8 million. If the estate transmission expenses are deducted on Jane's estate tax return, the taxable estate is zero ($14,920,000 minus $12,920,000 basic exclusion amount minus $1.8 million marital deduction minus $200,000 estate transmission expenses). However, if the estate transmission expenses are deducted on income tax return for Jane's estate, the net value of the property passing to Derek—and, thus, qualifying for the marital deduction—in the view of the IRS is *not* $2 million. In the opinion of the IRS the marital deduction cannot be greater than $1.8 million (in as much as the marital deduction must be reduced by the $200,000 of estate transmission expenses). And if the marital deduction is only $1.8 million, then $200,000 is subject to estate tax at Jane's death, resulting in a *tentative* estate tax of $80,000 (40% of $200,000). As the IRS reasons, an estate tax of $80,000 payable out of Derek's $1.8 million means that Derek received not $1.8 million but a lesser amount, to wit, $1,720,000 ($1.8 million less $80,000). And if Derek only received $1,720,000, then his marital deduction must be so limited and recomputed—and if it is recomputed, Jane's estate tax bill will be greater. This calculation is circular—but the IRS insists that it be done—because it involves an interdependent variable, i.e., the amount of the marital deduction depends upon the amount of the estate tax and the amount of the estate tax depends upon the amount of the marital deduction. See Treas. Reg. § 20.2056(b)–4(d)(5), Example 6.

Under the regulations, estate management expenses—estate preservation and management expenses such as investment advisory fees—are deductible on the income tax return for the estate without impairing the marital deduction *even if paid from the marital gift*. See Treas. Reg. § 20.2056(b)–4(d)(3).

c.   Income from Community Property

The presence of community property in an estate complicates the tax accounting. The complication results from the fact that both halves of the community are subject to administration at the death of the first spouse to die. Thus, although only one-half of the community property is subject to disposition under the will of the first spouse to die, both halves become subject to the estate administration process in the estate of the first spouse to die. Application of state property law produces this result. For federal tax purposes, however, the decedent's one-half of the community is seen as belonging to his or her estate while the survivor's one-half is treated as belonging to the survivor. Practically speaking, the survivor is taxed on the income generated by the survivor's one-half of the community—even though that income is collected by the decedent's executor and is subject to administration in the decedent's estate—and the income generated by the decedent's one-half of the community is taxed to the decedent's estate. In Grimm v. Commissioner, 894 F.2d 1165 (10th Cir.1990), the taxpayer used a novel approach in an attempt to avoid this result. She claimed that her one-half of the income generated by community property being administered as part of her husband's estate was not taxable to her until distributed to her (in as much as she is restricted in her enjoyment of the her one-half of the community income until the estate administration is completed during which period her half of the community property—and income—could be exhausted by community debts for which she is responsible). The court rejected the taxpayer's claim and explained:

> Grimm's share of the community property accumulated during her marriage and her share of the income from such property is her own. It does not pass to her as part of her husband's estate. * * * [Grimm received her] portion of the community assets and community income as fiduciaries for Grimm herself, not as fiduciaries of the estate; the estate never has title to Grimm's interest in these assets. * * *
>
> The administrative restrictions placed on Grimm's use and disposition of her share of community property during the liquidation procedure do not defeat her ownership interest in that

property and do not effectively negate her receipt of the same. * * * Judge Rives, concurring with the court's opinion [in Sneed v. Commissioner, 220 F.2d 313, 316 (5th Cir.1955)], reasoned: "In every real sense the widow's ownership acquired during the marriage continues uninterruptedly, and the executor has title to that half only of the community property belonging to his decedent. It does not follow from the fact that the executor has control and possession of the community and its income during administration that the income is not taxable to the widow. It is said that the widow may have received no funds with which to pay the tax. I apprehend that under state law it would be the executor's fiduciary duty to provide the widow with such necessary funds."

894 F.2d at 1168–69. Furthermore, the court offered, the community property is "immediately available for the purpose of satisfying community debts" for which the surviving spouse is "personally responsible along with her husband's estate." Id.

d. Community Property and Deduction of Administration Expenses

Taxpayers routinely deduct estate administration expenses, including ordinary and necessary fiduciaries' fees and litigation expenses. Treas. Reg. § 1.212–1(i). Special allocation problems are usually present where the decedent's estate includes community property. While both halves of the community—that of the decedent and that of the surviving spouse— are subject to administration at the death of the first of the spouses to die, only those administration expenses allocable to the decedent's one-half of the community are deductible by the decedent's executor (on his or her estate tax return or, alternatively, on the estate's income tax return). Nonetheless, while it is a perfectly logical to assume that only fifty percent of estate administration fees are thus likely to be deductible (where those fees are attributable to the presence of community property in the decedent's estate), practically speaking, a case for virtually 100 percent deductibility can often be effectively made. For example, in Ray v. United States, 385 F. Supp. 372 (S.D. Tex. 1974), all but five percent of attorney fees were found to be attributable to the decedent's 50 percent of the community. The court based its finding on testimony that 75 percent of the attorney fees were incurred in the process of determining estate and income taxes of the decedent's estate and the court's finding that another 20 percent was attributable to the routine probating of the decedent's will, rather than to the management or division of the community as a whole. Thus, 75% of the fees were deductible, and 100 percent of appraisal fees were deductible. The court found that the appraisal fees were deductible based on the testimony that an appraisal was required only because it was needed in conjunction with preparation of the decedent's estate tax return.

O. CONSOLIDATION OF MULTIPLE TRUSTS

Section 643(f) is an attempt by Congress to further limit the use of multiple trusts as income tax shelters. It provides that trusts having substantially the same grantor or grantors and substantially the same primary beneficiary or beneficiaries are to be consolidated for income tax purposes in cases where the principal purpose of the trusts is the avoidance of income tax. Moreover, for purposes of applying the trust consolidation rule, spouses are to be treated as one person.

The exact text of section 643(f) is important because Congress had the option of copying Regulation § 1.641(a)–0(c) but chose to use other, perhaps more far-reaching, language to accomplish its objective. Regulation § 1.641(a)–0(c) provides that multiple trusts will be consolidated for tax purposes if the trusts have (1) no substantially independent purposes (such as independent dispositive purposes), (2) the same grantor and substantially the same beneficiary, and (3) the avoidance or mitigation of taxes as their principal purpose.

Section 643(f) is obviously broader than Regulation § 1.641(a)–0(c) inasmuch as it dispenses with the "no substantially independent purposes" test of the regulation and provides that it is applicable when "the trusts have substantially the same grantor or grantors." The regulation spoke in the singular and was applicable only if the trusts had "the same grantor." As a result, the IRS has a stronger tool to use in reaching multiple trusts.

The IRS had been less than successful in using Regulation § 1.641(a)–0(c) to consolidate trusts for income tax purposes and ultimately the case law has generally considered trusts with common grantors, terms and beneficiaries to be separate taxpayers if they were administered as separate trusts. See Morris Trusts v. Commissioner, 51 T.C. 20 (1968), aff'd per curiam, 427 F.2d 1361 (9th Cir. 1970). The validity of 20 family trusts created by the same grantors for the same beneficiaries was upheld even though their primary purpose was to avoid tax. They were upheld because they were administered separately. Moreover, in Edward L. Stephenson Trust v. Commissioner, 81 T.C. 283 (1983), the Tax Court held Regulation § 1.641(a)–0(c) unconstitutional.

With the compression of the income tax rates applicable to trusts, fewer trusts will be able to realize any income tax savings as a result of accumulating income within the trust. Accordingly, the trust consolidation rules may be infrequently invoked since it will be easier to show that the nontax purposes of the trust outweighed any possible tax considerations.

Section 643(f) may possibly apply to separate bypass trusts established by spouses for the benefit of their lineal descendants. Clearly, these trusts for the benefit of the same persons would be treated as separate trusts under the consolidation regulation but, according to section 643(f), spouses "shall be treated as 1 person." However, it could be argued that section 643(f) is actually more limiting than the regulation that it replaces. The regulation applied to trusts that had as "their principal purpose" the "avoidance or mitigation of * * * the progressive rates of tax (including mitigation as a result of deferral of tax)." Section 643(f) applies to trusts that have as "a principal purpose" the avoidance of tax. Thus, the question is, must the IRS prove "more" under section 643(f) to bring about consolidation than under the old regulation inasmuch as proving that the grantor had "avoidance" in mind would seem harder to accomplish than merely proving that the grantor wanted to "mitigate" the progressive rates of tax as the regulation contemplated?

Section 643(f) applies only to that portion of a trust that is attributable to contributions to the trust made after March 1, 1984.

P. CHARITABLE BENEFICIARIES

1. INTRODUCTION

Although trusts and estates are generally taxed in the same manner as individuals, one exception provided by section 642(c) is an unlimited deduction for charitable contributions paid or (in certain cases) for amounts permanently set aside for charity out of taxable gross income.

There are several limitations to this general rule. First, to the extent the contribution is paid from tax-exempt income, there is no deduction. Second, in the absence of a specific provision in the trust instrument, charitable contributions are deemed to have been made pro rata from all the several classes of income received by the fiduciary.

Charitable contributions also affect the determination of DNI inasmuch as they are not taken into account in determining DNI for the purpose of ascertaining the amount of income taxable to first-tier beneficiaries. I.R.C. § 662(a)(1). However, to the extent that charitable contributions are made from income, they are deducted in determining the amount of DNI allocable to second-tier beneficiaries. Treas. Reg. § 1.662(b)–2.

2. PAID OR PERMANENTLY SET ASIDE

Two frequent observations are "deductions are a matter of legislative grace" and "deductions are strictly construed." Nothing could be truer when it comes to the charitable deduction. Section 170 provides for deductions for charitable contributions by individuals and corporations; section 170 does not apply to contributions by estates or trusts. Section 642(c) relates to deductions for amounts paid or permanently set aside for charitable purposes by estates or certain trusts specifically described in section 642(c). Sometimes an estate will be entitled to a deduction whereas a trust would be denied a deduction if it were to make the claim. Hence, it matters who is seeking the deduction. The following case is an illustration that in some instances amounts going to charities are not tax deductible. Consider whether there was any way for the taxpayer in the case to have structured the transaction to produce the desired tax deduction. There, prolonging the estate administration proved to be an unsuccessful strategy to qualify for having "permanently set aside" an amount for charity, the statutory requirement imposed by section 642(c) for the charitable deduction where the amount was not "paid" that year.

ESTATE OF BERGER v. COMMISSIONER

United States Tax Court, 1990.
T.C. Memo 1990–554.

CLAPP, JUDGE:

Respondent determined a deficiency in the Federal income tax of the Estate of Helen Barrow Berger in the amount of $15,351.53 for the year 1982. The issues are (1) whether petitioner is an estate or a trust for Federal income tax purposes; and (2) whether petitioner is entitled to a charitable deduction under either § 170 or 642(c) for the portion of a capital gain ultimately designated for charities. * * *

* * *

Decedent was married to Berger, and in her will, which was executed on October 18, 1976, she * * * provided that on Berger's death, the residue was to be liquidated and distributed as follows: 45 percent to various relatives; 20 percent to Catholic Charities of the Roman Catholic Diocese of Joliet, Illinois; 25 percent to Our Lady of Lourdes Roman Catholic Church of Gibson City, Illinois; and 10 percent to the Missionaries of Our Lady of Lasalette of Olivet, Illinois.

The will was admitted to probate on December 7, 1976, and Letters of Office as executor were granted to Berger. Berger filed a probate inventory, which included the second farm. On May 17, 1977, the court granted Berger possession of all realty of the estate. * * * At the time this case was submitted, the probate proceeding in Illinois state court had not been closed.

On February 17, 1982, Berger sold the second farm that was part of the residue of the estate for $354,000. This sale resulted in a capital gain of $140,650.50, which petitioner reported on its 1982 Federal fiduciary income tax return. The return claimed a charitable deduction of

$30,943.11, representing 55 percent of the capital gain (after the gain was reduced by the long-term capital gain deduction). The proceeds from the sale of the second farm were deposited in bank accounts, the income from which has been distributed to Berger.

The basic question for consideration is whether petitioner is entitled to a deduction for the taxable portion of the capital gain realized on the sale of the second farm which is permanently set aside for charities under the terms of decedent's will. * * *

Charitable deductions are allowed under §§ 170 and 642(c). Section 170 provides for deductions for charitable contributions by individuals and corporations, and the provisions of § 170 do not apply to contributions by estates or trusts. § 1.170A–1(h)(1), Income Tax Regs. Section 642(c) relates to deductions for amounts paid or permanently set aside for charitable purposes by estates or certain trusts specifically described in § 642(c). Section 642(c)(1) relates to amounts of gross income actually paid during the taxable year by an estate or trust and specifically provides that a deduction is "in lieu of the deduction allowed by § 170(a)." Section 642(c)(2) allows a deduction for any amount of gross income permanently set aside by an estate or by, generally, a trust created on or before October 9, 1969. If a trust does not meet the requirements of § 642(c)(2), then the trust will receive no deduction under § 642(c) for amounts of gross income permanently set aside for charities. Such a post-October 9, 1969, trust must then look to § 664, and if it qualifies as a charitable remainder annuity trust or a charitable remainder unitrust under § 664(d), it will be exempt from income taxes under § 664(c). If the trust is exempt, gross income is not taxable and, therefore, deductions for any amounts of gross income permanently set aside for charities become academic. In summary, an estate will get a deduction for any amount of gross income paid under § 642(c)(1) or for any such amounts permanently set aside for charities under § 642(c)(2). A trust which is not exempt under § 664 will get a deduction for amounts of gross income paid during the taxable year or, in the limited cases of pre-October 9, 1969 trusts, for amounts permanently set aside. If a trust does not qualify as a pre-October 9, 1969, trust under § 642(c)(2), it will get relief for amounts permanently set aside only if it qualifies for tax exemption under § 664 as an annuity trust or a unitrust. Thus, deductions for amounts of gross income permanently set aside for charity are effectively disallowed except for the limited pre-October 9, 1969 exception.

With that background in mind, we return to the facts before us to see whether there is any basis for a deduction by petitioner for the taxable portion of the capital gain realized on the sale of the second farm, which is permanently set aside for charities.

We first address whether petitioner is an estate or a trust for Federal income tax purposes. Section 1.641(b)–3(a), Income Tax Regs., provides:

The income of an estate * * * is that which is received by the estate during the period of administration * * *. The period of administration * * * is the period actually required by the * * * executor to perform the ordinary duties of administration, such as the collection of assets and the payment of debts, taxes, legacies, and bequests * * * the period of administration * * * cannot be unduly prolonged. If the administration of an estate is unreasonably prolonged, the estate is considered terminated for Federal income tax purposes * * *.

Whether the administration of an estate has been unduly prolonged is a question of fact. If the estate has been essentially fully administered, the residuary bequest, including a bequest in the form of a legal life estate with remainder, will continue as a trust for Federal tax purposes. * * *

Petitioner contends that it is an estate, while respondent asserts petitioner should be treated as a trust. We agree with respondent. On August 1, 1978, an Order Approving First Account and Report for the estate was entered. By such date all assets had been collected, all taxes, debts, and bequests payable by reason of decedent's death had been paid, a Federal estate tax return had been filed, and the estate tax paid. The residue of the estate had not been formally distributed to Berger as trustee by or during 1982, but this is not sufficient to keep the estate open for Federal income tax purposes. The remainder interests did not require estate administration, such as the collection of assets and payment of debts, taxes, and legacies, but rather any administration necessary was in the nature of trust administration. We hold that the estate was terminated for Federal income tax purposes prior to 1982, and that during 1982 petitioner was a trust for Federal income tax purposes.

We will next consider whether petitioner is entitled to a deduction under § 170(a). As already noted above, § 170 provides for deductions for charitable contributions by individuals and corporations and does not apply to contributions by trusts or estates. The Internal Revenue Code deals with deductions for charitable contributions by estates and trusts in § 642(c). * * * Thus, § 170 is inapplicable to the present case without regard to whether petitioner is an estate or a trust, and petitioner is not entitled to a deduction under that section.

We next turn to § 642(c) as it applies to trusts, since we have concluded that petitioner is a trust for tax purposes. Since no amount was paid to a charitable beneficiary during 1982, § 642(c)(1) does not apply, and no deduction is allowable under that section. Section § 642(c)(2) applies only to trusts which were created on or before October 9, 1969, or established by a will executed on or before October 9, 1969. In the instant case, the trust was established by a will executed on October 18, 1976, and decedent died on November 1, 1976. Both dates are well after the cutoff date set forth in § 642(c)(2)(A) and (B), and hence petitioner is not entitled to a deduction under § 642(c)(2) for any amounts of gross income permanently set aside for charitable purposes.

We next look to § 664 to see whether petitioner might be entitled to exempt status, which would allow the capital gain here in question to go untaxed with the same net result as allowing a deduction. Petitioner has not made this argument, nor has either party addressed it on brief. This inattention appears to be with good cause, as the residuary trust here involved would not qualify as either a charitable remainder annuity trust or a charitable remainder unitrust under § 664(d).

Based on the foregoing, we conclude that petitioner is not entitled to a deduction for the taxable portion of the capital gain which is permanently set aside for charitable purposes. * * *

3.   DEDUCTION FOR BOTH ESTATE AND INCOME TAX PURPOSES

UNITED STATES TRUST CO. V. INTERNAL REVENUE SERVICE

United States Court of Appeals, Fifth Circuit, 1986.
803 F.2d 1363.

ROGER MADDEN HILL, CIRCUIT JUDGE:

In this appeal we are asked to determine whether an estate taxpayer which has been allowed a deduction from its federal estate tax return for the amount of a bequest made to a charitable organization is also entitled to a deduction for the amount of the bequest from its income tax return during the taxable year that the bequest was made. * * *

The facts in this case are not in dispute. Alexander F. Chisholm (Chisholm), a resident of Mississippi, died on March 12, 1974, leaving a valid will dated May 17, 1967. * * * In article three of his will, Chisholm made a specific bequest to the Chisholm Foundation (Foundation), a New York-based charity organization. The bequest provided:

> I give to the Chisholm Foundation, a New York membership corporation, a sum equal to ten percent (10%) of the value of my gross testamentary estate as finally determined in the Federal estate tax proceeding relating to my Estate, provided that such bequest is deductible from my gross Estate in determining my taxable Estate for Federal Estate tax purposes.

Ten percent of Chisholm's gross testamentary estate was later calculated to be $2,473,719.

From Chisholm's death in March to December 31, 1974, no part of the specific bequest to the Foundation was paid. During 1975 $1,505,000 in cash and $512,635 in stock was distributed to the Foundation in partial satisfaction of the specific bequest. The cash payments were made in twelve monthly payments from a bank account containing monies derived from the original corpus of Chisholm's estate and the income that had accrued in 1974 and 1975. The remaining balance of the bequest to the Foundation was paid in 1976.

On its 1976 federal estate tax return, the taxpayer claimed an estate tax deduction, as allowed by section 2055(a)(2), for the entire $2,473,719 bequest which had been distributed to the Foundation during 1975 and 1976. The deduction was allowed by the IRS for the full amount of the distributions.

In 1976 the taxpayer also filed an income tax return for the year 1975. On this return the taxpayer claimed an income tax deduction for a part of the cash distributions made to the Foundation. Of the $1,505,000 in cash distributed to the Foundation in 1975, the taxpayer deducted $1,240,467 from its gross income as a deduction for distributions to a beneficiary under section 661(a)(2). These distributions could not qualify for a deduction as distributions to a charitable organization under section 642(c) because Chisholm's will did not direct that the distributions come from gross income. After auditing the 1975 income tax return, the IRS disallowed the deduction.

* * *

The issue as stated before is: May the taxpayer claim an income tax deduction for distributions of present income to a charitable beneficiary under section 661(a)(2) when the distributions did not otherwise qualify as a section 642(c) deduction and the taxpayer had already claimed and received a federal estate tax deduction for the same distributions? In answering this question we decide whether treasury regulation § 1.663(a)–2 is valid.

* * * We recognize that the purpose of tax benefits or deductions arising from charitable distributions is to encourage the making of charitable bequests. Several tax benefits are given to an estate that includes a charitable bequest. * * *

One such benefit is the estate tax deduction embodied in section 2055(a)(2). Section 2055(a)(2) allows an estate to reduce its federal estate tax liability by deducting from the gross value of the estate the amount it pays to satisfy a charitable bequest that is to be funded by property owned by the decedent at death. In this case, the taxpayer was allowed a section 2055(a)(2) deduction for the full amount of its distributions to the Foundation, and the IRS concedes the validity of this deduction.

Another tax benefit conferred upon estates which contain charitable bequests is contained in section 642(c) [which provides an income tax deduction for "any amount of the gross income without limitation, which pursuant to the terms of the governing instrument is, during the taxable year, paid for" a charitable purpose specified in § 170(c)] * * *. Thus, the deduction under section 642(c) is allowed only if the relevant governing instrument provides that the bequest be funded solely from the "gross income" of the estate.

As the plain language of §§ 2055(a)(2) and 642(c) demonstrates, Congress intended that the benefit for a charitable bequest be conferred only once—either as an offset against the gross value of the estate or as an offset against income. This intent is accomplished by limiting section 2055(a)(2) deductions to the value of the property that is included in the gross estate at the time of decedent's death. Thus, no estate tax deduction is available for amounts that are paid to a charitable organization at the direction of the governing instrument from estate income. The tax benefit for income distributions is then bestowed by section 642(c) which allows deductions for amounts payable out of gross income.

In light of these beneficial tax provisions for charitable bequests, the apparent exclusion of charitable distributions from the conduit taxing rules is reflected in [section 663(a) which provides that any "amount paid or permanently set aside or otherwise qualifying for the deduction provided in section 642(c)" shall not be included as an amount "falling within Section 661(a) or 662(a)"] * * *. Therefore, if an estate may take a section 642(c) deduction for a distribution to a charitable organization, it cannot also take a section 661(a)(2) deduction for the same distribution. As one court has noted, the relevant provisions of the Code reflect a "symmetry which insures that all charitable contributions result in a tax benefit, but precludes a double benefit." Pullen v. United States, 45 A.F.T.R.2d 80–381, 80–383 (D. Neb. Nov. 29, 1979), aff'd, No. 80–1034 (8th Cir. Sept. 29, 1980)(mem.).

Furthermore, the committee reports accompanying the enactment of the Code support the conclusion that Congress did not intend the general conduit taxation rules to apply to charitable distributions. * * * Both the House and Senate Reports state:

> Paragraph (3) provides that any amount paid, permanently set aside or to be used for the purposes specified in section 642(c) is excluded from the provisions of section 661 and 662. Since the estate or trust is allowed a deduction under section 642(c) for these amounts, *they are not allowed as an additional deduction for distributions* nor are they treated as amounts distributed for purposes of section 662 in determining the amounts includible in the gross income of beneficiaries.

H.R. Rep. No. 1337, at 4344; S. Rep. No. 1622, at 4995 (emphasis added).

One final fact bolstering our observation that charitable distributions are not considered in the conduit principles of sections 661 and 662 is that Congress has expressly refused to incorporate charitable distributions into the taxing scheme of section 661. In 1960 House Bill 9662 would have amended section 661(a) to encompass all charitable distributions, while eliminating the deduction under section 642(c). See H.R. 9662, 86th Cong., 2d Sess. §§ 102(b), 103(g), 106(a), 107, 108(a) (1960). The House committee report accompanying the bill expressly recognized that deductions for charitable distributions under existing law required tracing and that such distributions therefore fell outside sections 661 and 662 since they did not. H.R. Rep. No. 1231, 86th Cong., 2d Sess. 9–10 (1960). This modification to include all charitable distributions in the conduit taxation scheme was rejected.

* * *

NOTE

In Burke v. United States, 994 F.2d 1576 (Fed.Cir.1993), cert. denied, 510 U.S. 990 (1993), the Federal Circuit upheld the decision of the Court of Federal Claims (previously known as the Claims Court) that an estate cannot effectively increase the amount of a residuary charitable deduction by using postmortem income to pay administrative expenses. The testator's will directed that her entire residuary estate pass to a charitable foundation named after herself, provided that all taxes and administration expenses must first be deducted from the residuary. The executor petitioned the Florida probate court to interpret the testator's will to allow payment of the administrative expenses from income earned by the estate, rather than from the principal of the gross estate. The probate court entered an order allowing payment from the income; subsequently, a fiduciary income tax return was filed, claiming a deduction for administrative expenses of $144,441. The estate tax return was filed thereafter claiming a charitable deduction for the amount actually received by the charity but not diminished by taxes and administration expenses paid out of income earned during administration.

The Federal Circuit Court found that the value of the gross estate was indirectly increased by deducting the administration expenses from the estate's income rather than the gross estate. This accounting method allows the estate "to claim two deductions for the exact same portion of the gross estate as being both an administrative expense deductible under section 2053, which Burke, the executor of the estate, elected to claim on the estate's income tax return, and a charitable donation deductible under section 2055, which Burke claimed on the estate tax return." 994 F.2d, at 1582.

Using a "snapshot" approach, the Burke court said:

In sum, when a decedent dies, a finite amount known as the gross estate is legally created. Any deductions for expenses incurred in administering the estate are theoretically derived from this amount and, regardless of the actual source of payment, must be accounted for within the gross estate. * * *

Burke argues that the only relevant provision of the tax code is § 2055 which allows a deduction from the decedent's gross estate of amounts given to a qualifying charity. Per Burke, for purposes of the § 2055 deduction, the only requirement is that the charity actually receive the amount claimed as the deduction. Burke argues that since the Foundation received more than the amount claimed as a deduction under § 2055 over the probate period, the requirements for claiming a deduction are satisfied.

However, the fact that the charitable deduction taken on Burke's federal estate tax return was less than the actual amount received by the charity over the seven-year probate period is not determinative. The relevant inquiry is the amount received by the charity *under the will*, i.e., the amount of the gross estate that passed to the charity. That the charitable donation was augmented by post-mortem income, resulting in an overall charitable donation of an amount greater than the estate tax deduction claimed, does not increase the amount of the charitable bequest under the will.

Under Williams' will, the Foundation received the residue of the estate. Therefore, the value of the gross estate that passed to the Foundation for which the estate may claim a charitable deduction under section 2055, is the amount remaining in the estate after Burke had accounted for all of the obligations of the estate accruing at the time of death. These obligations included payment of the administrative expenses for which the estate claimed a deduction, albeit on the estate's income tax return. In calculating the residue, the amount of the gross estate passing to charity under the will, Burke failed to take into account the reduction necessitated by administrative expenses. This was error because, for purposes of federal estate taxation, the gross estate is obligated to pay those expenses. In essence, Burke would have us indirectly increase the value of the gross estate by allowing him to use post-mortem income to pay the obligations of the gross estate. While, as we have previously noted, it may be beneficial or convenient to pay such obligations out of post-mortem income, the post-mortem income so used does not itself become part of the gross estate. The result Burke seeks would allow the estate to claim two deductions for the exact same portion of the gross estate as being both an administrative expense deductible under section

2053, which Burke elected to claim on the estate's income tax return, and a charitable donation deductible under section 2055, which Burke claimed on the estate tax return.

The amount of the charitable deduction claimed by Williams' estate was properly reduced by the amount of administrative expenses claimed as a deduction on the estate's fiduciary income tax return because, for federal estate taxation purposes, only this lesser amount was paid to the charity from the gross estate. The additional amount paid to charity over the probation period was post-mortem income for which estate received a deduction on its federal income tax returns.[17]

Subsequent to the decision in *Burke* and the decision in Commissioner v. Estate of Hubert, 520 U.S. 93 (1997), discussed earlier in this chapter, the IRS published new regulations applicable in cases where administration expenses are claimed as a deduction on the estate's income tax return. These regulations, appearing as Regulation § 20.2055–3(b), follow the model of similar regulations applicable when the marital deduction is claimed. They require that estate administration expenses be classified as either estate transmission expenses or estate management expenses. Estate transmission expenses where paid from the charitable share and claimed on the estate's income tax return are viewed by the IRS as reducing the value of the charitable gift and, thus, reduce the estate tax deduction for the gift to charity. Estate management expenses paid from the charitable share do not reduce the charitable gift deduction.

4. INCOME INTERESTS GIVEN TO CHARITY

Special rules apply to charitable gifts of income interests in trust. With respect to such gifts, a charitable contribution deduction is allowed to the grantor only if the grantor is taxable on the trust income under the grantor trust rules set out in sections 671–678 and the income interest of the charity is a guaranteed annuity or a fixed percentage of the value of the trust corpus determined yearly. I.R.C. § 170(f)(2)(B). In this case, however, the grantor is allowed a charitable contribution deduction for the present value of the charitable income interest in the year the trust is established but is taxed each year thereafter on the trust income. Moreover, the trust is not allowed a deduction for the income subsequently distributed to the charity. See I.R.C. § 170(f)(2)(C) and Treas. Reg. § 1.170A–6(d)(1). By way of contrast, though, and as an example of the complex rules that determine the tax deductibility of amounts distributed to charity, consider the following revenue ruling relating to a charitable trust created for a term in excess of ten years.

---

[17] Id. at 1581–82.

By way of contrast, where no income tax deduction is available to the grantor when the trust is established, section 642(c)(1) provides the trust with an income tax deduction, without limitation, for any amount of income that, pursuant to the trust agreement, is paid for any purpose specified in section 170(c).

REVENUE RULING 79–223
1979–2 C.B. 254.

ISSUE

Is a trust allowed a deduction for amounts of gross income paid out to charitable beneficiaries under the circumstances described below?

FACTS

Y, a bank holding company, created an irrevocable trust that will not terminate before ten years and one month after the date of its creation. The governing instrument of the trust provides that no additional property may be contributed to the trust after it is created.

The net income of the trust is to be distributed to organizations described in section 170(c)(1), (2), and (3). All income is to be distributed before the close of the year succeeding the year in which the income is received. Capital gains are to be added to corpus.

Y has reserved the power to designate recipients of income. Such designation is to be made at any time before or after the income is received. If Y fails to designate by the time income is required to be distributed, the trustee is required to select charitable beneficiaries. Distributions are to be made only from income received by the trust.

The trust agreement provides that all powers reserved by Y shall be exercised by Y in a fiduciary capacity and that none of the powers will be construed to permit the trustee to lend any of the principal or income of the trust property, directly or indirectly, to the grantor without adequate interest or security or to borrow directly or indirectly from the grantor at more than adequate interest or other consideration. Except in the case of permitted distributions, Y is prohibited from dealing with or disposing of the principal of the trust property or the income therefrom for less than an adequate consideration. Y is precluded from designating any distribution in satisfaction of its own obligation to a charitable organization.

Upon the termination of the trust, all of the property comprising the principal of the trust will be distributed to Y. All of the then undistributed income of the trust will be distributed to or for the use of the charitable organizations described above.

LAW AND ANALYSIS

Because the terms of the trust require the capital gains of the trust to be accumulated for future distribution by Y, Y will be treated as the owner of the income of the trust with respect to capital gains. See section 677(a). Other items of gross income and deductions and credits attributable to the ordinary income portion of the trust will be subject to the provisions of subparts a through D (section 641 and following), part I, subchapter J, of the Code. See section 1.671–3 of the Income Tax Regulations. Thus, no deduction will be allowed to Y for any amounts of the trust's income paid to charitable organizations. The capital gains allocable to the corpus portion of the trust will be includible in Y's gross income when realized by the trust. See Rev. Rul. 66–161, 1966–1 C.B. 167.

Section 170(a) generally allows a deduction for charitable contributions paid during the taxable year. Section 170(f)(2)(B) provides, with respect to charitable transfers in trusts of income interests, that no deduction under subsection (a) is allowed unless the interest is in the form of a guaranteed annuity or the trust instrument specifies that the interest is a fixed percentage distributed annually, and the grantor is treated as the owner of such interest for purposes of applying section 671.

No income tax deduction was allowable to Y at the time of the creation of the trust since the income interest given to charity did not meet the requirements of section 170(f)(2)(B).

Section 642(c)(1) provides, in part, that in the case of a trust, there shall be allowed as a deduction in computing its taxable income any amount of gross income, without limitation, which pursuant to the terms of the governing instrument is, during the taxable year, paid for a purpose specified in section 170(c). If a charitable contribution is paid after the close of such taxable year and on or before the last day of the year following the close of such taxable year, then the trustee may elect to treat such contribution as paid during such taxable year.

HOLDING

Accordingly, * * * the trust will be allowed a deduction in accordance with section 642(c)(1) for amounts of gross income paid out to charitable beneficiaries described in section 170(c) during its taxable year, or by the close of the following taxable year.

CHAPTER 31

GRANTOR TRUSTS

(SECTIONS 671–678)

■ ■ ■

A. INTRODUCTION

Generally speaking, the income of each trust and estate will be taxed to either the trust or estate or the beneficiaries of the trust or estate who receive distributions from the trust or estate. Much of the discussion in Chapter 30 was concerned with determining, in a particular case, whether the income should be taxed to the estate or trust or to the beneficiaries and, as among the beneficiaries, to which beneficiary the income should be attributed.

This portion of these materials will be devoted to determining under what circumstances the income of a trust will be taxed to either the grantor of the trust or one of the beneficiaries even though the person to whom the income is taxed may not have received it. Sections 671–677 determine the circumstances in which trust income will be taxed to the settlor of the trust.

Example: Mr. Slowe established a trust during his lifetime which provided that all of the income from the trust would be paid to his child, Borne, currently a 20-year old college student. He funded the trust with stock worth $500,000. The trust was to continue for Borne's lifetime and, at Borne's death, the trust corpus was to be distributed to Borne's then living lineal descendants *per stirpes*. Mr. Slowe believed the trust would be a good way to shift income from himself to Borne who was in a much lower income tax bracket than Mr. Slowe. Mr. Slowe was, indeed, proud of his son, but not knowing what kind of a future Borne would have, Mr. Slowe reserved the right to revoke the trust at any time by written notice to the trustee, Accumulation National Bank.

Under these circumstances should Mr. Slowe be permitted to shift the income from the trust property to Borne or to the trust or should it continue to be taxed to Mr. Slowe since he had the power to revoke the trust whenever he determined to do so? See I.R.C. § 676.

The foregoing is an "easy case" but it provides an illustration of the kind of features that can characterize trusts as taxpayers attempt to shift income tax liability to others within the family unit while, at the same time, retaining control, not only of the property that produces the income, but also of the income itself. Sections 671–677 identify those features which, if included in a particular trust, will cause the income of that trust to be taxed to the settlor or "grantor" of the trust.

If it is the grantor to whom the trust income is to be taxed, then, obviously, the grantor trust rules apply only during the lifetime of the settlor (inasmuch as the grantor ceases to be a taxpayer for income tax purposes at death).

However, trust income may be taxed to someone other than the grantor even though that other person did not receive the trust income. That is possible when the nongrantor has such control over the trust income that to allow the nongrantor to avoid income tax liability for that income would—in the opinion of Congress—impair the integrity of the tax system. Section 678 determines the circumstances in which trust income will be taxed to someone other than the settlor even though that other person did not receive the income.

> *Example*: Mr. Quick's will provided that an amount equal to the exemption equivalent to the unified credit for estate tax purposes ($12,920,000 if he died in 2023) be placed in a trust for his wife, Emily. Emily was made the trustee of the trust and, as trustee, she had the power to distribute to herself so much or all of the income of the trust as she "deems appropriate." She also had the power to make distributions of income to Mr. Quick's children in "such amounts as she deems appropriate." Any income not distributed in a particular year was to be added to the principal of the trust. During the last calendar year, Emily made no distributions from the trust to anyone. To whom should the trust income for last year be taxed? Emily says the trust should be taxed on all of the trust income since the income was kept in the trust. Do you agree with her? See I.R.C. § 678.

The concept of "owner" is used as an organizational technique in sections 671–678. The grantor of the trust will be deemed its "owner" if the trust contains any of the features identified in sections 673–677. If the grantor is deemed to be the "owner" of the trust, the income from the trust will be taxed to the grantor as if the trust never existed. I.R.C. § 671.

Procedurally speaking, the trustee of a grantor trust will report the trust's status as a grantor trust to the IRS by filing the normal fiduciary income tax return—U.S. Income Tax Return for Estates and Trusts (Form 1041)—and declaring on that return that the trust is a grantor trust and that all of the income and expenses of the trust are to be reported on the grantor's personal federal income tax return. The trustee will not actually complete the form but will file a blank form to which is attached a schedule reflecting the information that is to be reflected on the grantor's personal income tax return. See Treas. Reg. § 1.671–4(a). As a technical matter, it may be worth noting that not even a Form 1041 is required in the case of a grantor trust in which the grantor is either trustee or co-trustee. In those cases, the grantor may report all the trust income on Form 1040, the grantor's personal income tax return. See Treas. Reg. § 1.671–4(b)(1) and (2).

Finally, there are two special caveats that should be noted. First, the grantor trust rules expressly contemplate that, in some cases, only a portion of the trust's income will be taxed to the grantor, while the remainder of the trust income is taxed to the trust or to the trust beneficiaries. I.R.C. § 671. That is, the rules recognize that only a portion of a trust's income may be subject to one of the features that have been identified as requiring the trust income to be taxed to the grantor of the trust.

Second, section 671 expressly provides that the income of a trust will not be taxed to the grantor of a trust solely because the grantor has "dominion and control over the trust." Section 671 states that the grantor will be taxed on trust income not received only if the trust contains one or more of the features identified in sections 673–677. This is a significant concession by Congress inasmuch as it limits the courts from determining on a case-by-case basis when the grantor of a trust has such substantial dominion and control over the trust to warrant taxing the trust income to the grantor.

The "dominion and control" test was used by the landmark Supreme Court case in Helvering v. Clifford, 309 U.S. 331 (1940). In *Clifford*, the Court established general rules for taxing grantor trusts. These general rules were then endorsed by the IRS in the form of Treasury regulations. Later these regulations were codified as sections 671–678. The grantor trust rules of sections 671–678 are commonly referred to as the *Clifford* rules and, despite the congressional decision to reject the "dominion and control" test, *Clifford* remains a landmark case.

HELVERING V. CLIFFORD

Supreme Court of the United States, 1940.
309 U.S. 331.

MR. JUSTICE DOUGLAS delivered the opinion of the Court:

In 1934 respondent declared himself trustee of certain securities which he owned. All net income from the trust was to be held for the "exclusive benefit" of respondent's wife. The trust was for a term of five years, except that it would terminate earlier on the death of either respondent or his wife. On termination of the trust the entire corpus was to go to respondent, while all "accrued or undistributed net income" and "any proceeds from the investment of such net income" was to be treated as property owned absolutely by the wife. During the continuance of the trust respondent was to pay over to his wife the whole or such part of the net income as he in his "absolute discretion" might determine. And during that period he had full power (a) to exercise all voting powers incident to the trusteed shares of stock; (b) to "sell, exchange, mortgage, or pledge" any of the securities under the declaration of trust "whether as part of the corpus or principal thereof or as investments or proceeds and any income therefrom, upon such terms and for such consideration" as respondent in his "absolute discretion may deem fitting"; (c) to invest "any cash or money in the trust estate or any income therefrom" by loans, secured or unsecured, by deposits in banks, or by purchase of securities or other personal property "without restriction" because of their "speculative character" or "rate of return" or any "laws pertaining to the investment of trust funds"; (d) to collect all income; (e) to compromise, etc., any claims held by him as trustee; (f) to hold any property in the trust estate in the names of "other persons or in my own name as an individual" except as otherwise provided. Extraordinary cash dividends, stock dividends, proceeds from the sale of unexercised subscription rights, or any enhancement, realized or not, in the value of the securities were to be treated as principal, not income. An exculpatory clause purported to protect him from all losses except those occasioned by his "own wilful and deliberate" breach of duties as trustee. And finally it was provided that neither the principal nor any future or accrued income should be liable for the debts of the wife; and that the wife could not transfer, encumber, or anticipate any interest in the trust or any income therefrom prior to actual payment thereof to her.

It was stipulated that while the "tax effects" of this trust were considered by respondent they were not the "sole consideration" involved in his decision to set it up, as by this and other gifts he intended to give "security and economic independence" to his wife and children. It was also stipulated that respondent's wife had substantial income of her own from other sources; that there was no restriction on her use of the trust income, all of which income was placed in her personal checking account, intermingled with her other funds, and expended by her on herself, her children and relatives; that the trust was not designed to relieve respondent from liability for family or household expenses and that after execution of the trust he paid large sums from his personal funds for such purposes.

Respondent paid a federal gift tax on this transfer. During the year 1934 all income from the trust was distributed to the wife who included it in her individual return for that year. The Commissioner, however, determined a deficiency in respondent's return for that year on the theory that income from the trust was taxable to him. The Board of Tax Appeals sustained that redetermination (38 B.T.A. 1532). The Circuit Court of Appeals reversed (105 F. (2d) 586). We granted certiorari because of the importance to the revenue of the use of such short term trusts in the reduction of surtaxes.

Sec. 22(a) of the Revenue Act of 1934 (48 Stat. 680) [1986 Code § 61] includes among "gross income" all "gains, profits, and income derived . . . from professions, vocations, trades, businesses, commerce, or sales, or dealings in property, whether real or personal, growing out of the ownership or use of or interest in such property; also from interest, rent, dividends, securities, or the transaction of any business carried on for gain or profit, or gains or profits and income derived from any source whatever." The broad sweep of this language indicates the purpose of Congress to use the full measure of its taxing power within those definable categories. * * * Hence our construction of the statute should be consonant with that purpose. Technical considerations, niceties of the law of trusts or conveyances, or the legal paraphernalia which inventive genius may construct as a refuge from surtaxes should not obscure the basic issue. That issue is whether the grantor after the trust has been established may still be treated, under this statutory scheme, as the owner of the corpus. * * * In absence of more precise standards or guides supplied by statute or appropriate regulations, the answer to that question must depend on an analysis of the terms of the trust and all the circumstances attendant on its creation and operation. And where the grantor is the trustee and the beneficiaries are members of his family group, special scrutiny of the arrangement is necessary lest what is in reality but one economic unit be multiplied into two or more by devices which, though valid under state law, are not conclusive so far as § 22(a) is concerned.

In this case we cannot conclude as a matter of law that respondent ceased to be the owner of the corpus after the trust was created. Rather, the short duration of the trust, the fact that the wife was the beneficiary, and the retention of control over the corpus by respondent all lead irresistibly to the conclusion that respondent continued to be the owner for purposes of § 22(a).

So far as his dominion and control were concerned it seems clear that the trust did not effect any substantial change. In substance his control over the corpus was in all essential respects the same after the trust was created, as before. The wide powers which he retained included for all practical purposes most of the control which he as an individual would have. There were, we may assume, exceptions, such as his disability to make a gift of the corpus to others during the term of the trust and to make loans to himself. But this dilution in his control would seem to be insignificant and immaterial, since control over investment remained. If it be said that such control is the type of dominion exercised by any trustee, the answer is simple. We have at best a temporary reallocation of income within an intimate family group. Since the income remains in the family and since the husband retains control over the investment, he has rather complete assurance that the trust will not effect any substantial change in his economic position. It is hard to imagine that respondent felt himself the poorer after this trust had been executed or, if he did, that it had any rational foundation in fact. For as a result of the terms of the trust and the intimacy of the familial relationship respondent retained the substance of full enjoyment of all the rights which previously he had in the property. That might not be true if only strictly legal rights were considered. But when the benefits flowing to him indirectly through the wife are added to the legal rights he retained, the aggregate may be said to be a fair equivalent of what he previously had. To exclude from the aggregate those indirect benefits would be to deprive § 22(a) of considerable vitality and to treat as immaterial what may be highly relevant considerations in the creation of such family trusts. For where the head of the household has income in excess of normal needs, it may well make but little difference to him (except income-tax wise) where portions of that income are routed—so long as it stays in the family group. In those circumstances the all-important factor might be retention by him of control over the principal. With that control in his hands he would keep direct command over all that he needed to remain in substantially the same financial situation as before. Our point here is that no one fact is normally decisive but that all considerations and circumstances of the kind we have mentioned are relevant to the question of ownership and are appropriate foundations for findings on that issue. Thus, where, as in this case, the benefits directly or indirectly retained blend so imperceptibly with the normal concepts of full ownership, we cannot say that the triers of fact committed reversible error when they found that the husband was the owner of the corpus for the purposes of § 22(a). To hold otherwise would be to treat the wife as a complete stranger; to let mere formalism obscure the normal consequences of family solidarity; and to force concepts of ownership to be fashioned out of legal niceties which may have little or no significance in such household arrangements.

The bundle of rights which he retained was so substantial that respondent cannot be heard to complain that he is the "victim of despotic power when for the purpose of taxation he is treated as owner altogether." See du Pont v. Commissioner, 289 U.S. 685, 689.

* * *

B. SPOUSAL ATTRIBUTION RULE

All powers and interests of the grantor's spouse are treated as being held by the grantor. I.R.C. § 672(e)(1). Moreover, a spouse's powers and interests are attributed to the grantor even in cases where the parties marry after the power or interest was created. However, people legally separated from each other under a decree of divorce or of separate maintenance are not considered as married. I.R.C. § 672(e)(2).

C. REVOCABLE TRUSTS (SECTION 676)

1. GENERAL RULE

The ability of the grantor of a trust to revoke it is a plain example of a case in which the trust income should be taxed to the grantor even though the income is received by someone other than the grantor. The United States Supreme Court reached this conclusion very early in the history of the income tax and long before the grantor trust rules formally entered the Internal Revenue Code.

CORLISS V. BOWERS
Supreme Court of the United States, 1930.
281 U.S. 376.

MR. JUSTICE HOLMES delivered the opinion of the Court.

* * * In 1922 [petitioner] transferred the fund from which arose the income in respect of which the petitioner was taxed, to trustees, in trust to pay the income to his wife for life with remainder over to their children. By the instrument creating the trust the petitioner reserved power "to modify or alter in any manner, or revoke in whole or in part, this indenture and the trusts then existing, and the estates and interests in property hereby created." It is not necessary to quote more words because there can be no doubt that the petitioner fully reserved the power at any moment to abolish or change the trust at his will. The statute referred to provides that "when the grantor of a trust has, at any time during the taxable year, . . . the power to revest in himself title to any part of the corpus of the trust, then the income of such part of the trust for such taxable year shall be included in computing the net income of the grantor." § 219(g) [currently section 676(a)]. * * * There can be no doubt either that the statute purports to tax the plaintiff in this case. But the net income for 1924 was paid over to the petitioner's wife and the petitioner's argument is that however it might have been in different circumstances the income never was his and he cannot be taxed for it. The legal estate was in the trustee and the equitable interest in the wife.

But taxation is not so much concerned with the refinements of title as it is with actual command over the property taxed—the actual benefit for which the tax is paid. If a man directed his bank to pay over income as received to a servant or friend, until further orders, no one would doubt that he could be taxed upon the amounts so paid. It is answered that in that case he would have a title, whereas here he did not. But from the point of view of taxation there would be no difference. The title would merely mean a right to stop the payment before it took place. The same right existed here although it is not called a title but is called a power. The acquisition by the wife of the income became complete only when the plaintiff failed to exercise the power that he reserved. * * * Still speaking with reference to taxation, if a man disposes of a fund in such a way that another is allowed to enjoy the income which it is in the power of the first to appropriate it does not matter whether the permission is given by assent or by failure to express dissent. The income that is subject to a man's unfettered command and that he is free to enjoy at his own option may be taxed to him as his income, whether he sees fit to enjoy it or not. We consider the case too clear to need help from the local law of New York or from arguments based on the power of Congress to prevent escape from taxes or surtaxes by devices that easily might be applied to that end. Judgment affirmed.

PROBLEMS

1. Aaron, at the time of his divorce, created a trust for the benefit of Henry, an adult son of the marriage. Under the terms of the trust, Aaron may revoke the trust at any time with the consent of his divorced spouse, Henry's mother. Is Aaron taxable on the income of the trust?

2. There are cases where someone other than the grantor has the power to revoke a trust. Or, at least, a grantor (with the assistance of counsel) could conceivably craft an instrument that would give someone who is ostensibly independent of the grantor the power to revoke the grantor's trust and cause the trust property and income to be returned to the grantor. In circumstances like this, should the income be taxable to the grantor prior to the exercise of the power of revocation? Should the answer depend on whether the person holding the power of revocation is truly independent of the grantor?

    (a) What standards should be included in the statute by which true independence could be determined? Are the provisions of section 676(a), which provide that the trust is considered revocable if the power is exercisable by the grantor or "nonadverse party or both," satisfactory? (The terms "adverse party" and "nonadverse party" are defined in section 672(a) and (b)).

    (b) Is a life income beneficiary an adverse party for purposes of section 676(a)?

2. LIMITED POWERS OF REVOCATION

Section 676(b) describes circumstances in which the presence of a power of revocation in the grantor of the trust will not cause the trust income to be taxed to the grantor. These circumstances are limited and are designed to correlate with section 673, which allows the grantor of a trust to retain a reversionary interest in a trust but have the income taxed to the recipient of the income.

D. TRUSTS FOR BENEFIT OF GRANTOR

1. GENERAL RULE

A grantor will be taxed on the trust's income where the income is distributed or accumulated for future distribution to the grantor or to the grantor's spouse or it is used to pay the premiums on policies of life insurance on the life of the grantor or the grantor's spouse. I.R.C. § 677(a).

The rationale for taxing trust income to the grantor where the grantor has the benefit of that income is obvious. Consider a grantor who created an irrevocable trust, funded it with income producing securities, and stipulated in the trust agreement that the trust income was to be used to pay the premiums on insurance on the grantor's life. After the grantor's death, the insurance proceeds were to continue in trust for the benefit of the grantor's son. In Burnet v. Wells, 289 U.S. 670 (1933), the Supreme Court concluded that it was constitutionally permissible to tax the trust income to the trust grantor where it was used to pay premiums on insurance on the grantor's life. In reaching its conclusion, the Court noted that "there has been a progressive endeavor by the Congress and the courts to bring about a correspondence between the legal concept of ownership and the economic realities of enjoyment or fruition."[1] The Court explained further:

> The controversy is one as to the boundaries of legislative power. It must be dealt with in a large way, as questions of due process always are, not narrowly or pedantically, in slavery to forms or phrases. "Taxation is not so much concerned with the refinements of title as it is with the actual command over the property taxed— the actual benefit for which the tax is paid." Corliss v. Bowers, [281 U.S.] 378. * * * Refinements of title have at times supplied the rule when the question has been one of construction and nothing more, a question as to the meaning of a taxing act to be read in favor of the taxpayer. Refinements of title are without controlling force when a statute, unmistakable in meaning, is assailed by a taxpayer as overpassing the bounds of reason, an exercise by the lawmakers of arbitrary power. In such circumstances the question is no longer whether the concept of ownership reflected in the statute is to be squared with the concept embodied, more or less vaguely, in common law traditions. The question is whether it is one that an enlightened legislator

---

[1] Burnet v. Wells, 289 U.S. 670, 677 (1933).

might act upon without affront to justice. Even administrative convenience, the practical necessities of an efficient system of taxation, will have heed and recognition within reasonable limits. * * * Liability does not have to rest upon the enjoyment by the taxpayer of all the privileges and benefits enjoyed by the most favored owner at a given time or place. * * * Government in casting about for proper subjects of taxation is not confined by the traditional classification of interests or estates. It may tax not only ownership, but any right or privilege that is a constituent of ownership. * * * Liability may rest upon the enjoyment by the taxpayer of privileges and benefits so substantial and important as to make it reasonable and just to deal with him as if he were the owner, and to tax him on that basis. A margin must be allowed for the play of legislative judgment. To overcome this statute the taxpayer must show that in attributing to him the ownership of the income of the trusts, or something fairly to be dealt with as equivalent to ownership, the lawmakers have done a wholly arbitrary thing, have found equivalence where there was none nor anything approaching it, and laid a burden unrelated to privilege or benefit. * * * The statute, as we view it, is not subject to that reproach.[2]

The Court explained that many people consider life insurance to be a "pressing social duty" and "a common item in the family budget, kept up very often at the cost of painful sacrifice" and that "[t]rusts for the preservation of policies of insurance involve a continuing exercise by the settlor of a power to direct the application of the income along predetermined channels."[3] Thus, the Court concluded that "Congress does not play the despot in ordaining that trusts for such uses * * * shall be treated for the purpose of taxation as if the income of the trust had been retained by the grantor."[4]

PROBLEMS

1. It should be noted that section 677 was amended by the Tax Reform Act of 1969 to require taxation of the grantor if the trust income may be distributed to or is accumulated for distribution to the grantor's spouse or may be applied to the maintenance of life insurance on the life of the grantor's spouse. Does this change square with the rationale of the *Burnet* decision?

2. From a policy standpoint, would it be consistent to expand section 677 to tax the grantor on the income of a trust created for the benefit of a "family" member (ancestor, descendant, brother, or sister)? See Amabile v.

---

2   Id. at 677–79.

3   Id. at 681–82.

4   Id. at 682.

Commissioner, T.C. Memo. 1986–180, 51 T.C.M. (CCH) 963 (1986) (grantor treated as owner of trust where trustee had discretion to distribute income to grantor's spouse).

3.   Sarah plans to create a substantial irrevocable trust for the benefit of, and ultimate distribution to, her children and grandchildren. It is Sarah's plan to grant broad powers to the independent trustee to apply trust income to the purchase of life insurance contracts on her life. Sarah would, of course, cooperate with the trustee in the acquisition of such contracts as assets of the trust. How would such a power affect the taxability of the trust income to Sarah? Would it make any difference whether the trustee exercised the power?

2. FAMILY TRUSTS

Some taxpayers have undertaken to create trusts for their own benefit that are expressly irrevocable in the hope that the income from the trust will not be taxed to them (and that the trust property will not be included in their gross estates for estate tax purposes despite section 2036(a)(1)). These trusts are referred to as family trusts. Usually, the grantor will transfer all of the property—both real and personal—to the trust, including the "exclusive right" to the grantor's "services and future earnings." While the beneficiaries of the trust are usually the grantor's children, normally the trustee is obligated to pay the living expenses of the grantor. The grantor's spouse is often the trustee, and distributions from the trust beneficiaries are totally discretionary with the trustee.

In Notice 97–24, 1997–1 C.B. 409, the IRS warned taxpayers about abusive trust arrangements and described some of them in detail. The following case addresses these types of trusts.

HOLMAN V. UNITED STATES
United States Court of Appeals, Tenth Circuit, 1984.
728 F.2d 462.

PER CURIAM.

* * *

Plaintiffs, husband and wife, sought to form a trust (the "Bruce Holman Family Estate") which would hold as corpus all personal and real property owned by plaintiffs. In addition, the trust acquired the exclusive right to plaintiff Bruce Holman's services and future earnings. The trust originally named plaintiffs and Bruce Holman's mother, Addie Duncan, as trustees. Approximately five months later, Addie Duncan resigned as trustee leaving plaintiffs as sole trustees. Plaintiffs were also named as officers of the trust for which they were to be paid consulting fees. Plaintiffs, their four children and the "Bruce Holman Educational and Research Trust" were named as beneficiaries. Plaintiffs continued to use their property in the same manner as they had prior to the creation of the trust. The trust was obligated to pay various living expenses for plaintiffs and their family, such as "rent" and maintenance on plaintiffs' home, utilities, automobile expenses such as gas, oil, maintenance, insurance premiums, as well as other miscellaneous expenses.

Under the terms of the trust, the beneficiaries were entitled to receive only what the trustees, in their discretion, decided to distribute. The trustees had the power to fix and pay compensation for themselves in their capacity as trustees. The trustees' powers were "construed as general powers of citizens of the United States of America, to do anything any citizen may do in any state or country," and essentially to take any action that they may "deem advantageous." The duration of the trust was stated as "twenty-five years from date, unless the trustees shall unanimously determine upon an earlier date."

In January 1974 plaintiffs received a letter from the Internal Revenue Service informing them that the Service would not recognize the trust for federal income tax purposes. Nevertheless, the Bruce Holman Family Estate (a Trust) filed a fiduciary income tax return for the tax years 1973 and 1974. Plaintiffs also filed a joint return for those years. The trust included in income the earnings of Dr. Holman and took deductions for various expenses such as payments to the plaintiffs as consultants, officers and trustees of the trust as well as other personal living expenses of plaintiffs.

Upon the filing of the returns in 1973 and 1974, plaintiffs were audited and their income was increased by the amounts reported by the trust. This amount was then decreased by deducting the amounts reported by plaintiffs as consulting fees and distributions from the trust, together with allowable deductions. As a result of the increase in income, plaintiffs were assessed deficiencies for the tax years 1973 and 1974 for taxes, interest, and negligence penalties.

Plaintiffs paid the deficiency and brought the instant action for refund claiming that the trust was valid and that plaintiffs should not have been taxed on the trust's income.

* * *

Although this circuit has not yet considered the tax consequences of this type of "family trust," three circuits and the United States Tax Court have considered the issue and have uniformly applied the assignment of income doctrine and the grantor trust provisions in holding that trusts virtually identical to the one in question are mere shams designed for tax avoidance purposes. [Citations omitted.]

The assignment of income doctrine originated with the Supreme Court decision of Lucas v. Earl, 281 U.S. 111 (1930), which stands for the principle that income is taxed to the one who earned it. The Bruce Holman Family Estate Trust is a transparent attempt to assign the income earned by Dr. Holman. An examination of the terms of the trust reveals that the trust neither supervises Dr. Holman's employment nor determines his compensation. Vnuk, 621 F 2d at 1321. Furthermore, Dr. Holman is under no legal duty to earn money or perform services for the trust. Id. Dr. Holman is no less the earner of the income than he was before simply because he now purports to act as an "employee" or "servant" of the trust.

Under § 671, the grantor of a trust is treated as the owner of that trust if certain conditions specified in §§ 672–679 exist. Critical to the discussion here is § 674(a) which provides that:

> [T]he grantor shall be treated as the owner of any portion of a trust in respect of which the beneficial enjoyment of the corpus or the income therefrom is subject to a power of disposition, exercisable by the grantor or a nonadverse party, or both, without the approval or consent of any adverse party.

"Adverse party" is defined in § 672(a) as "any person having a substantial beneficial interest in the trust which would be adversely affected by the exercise or nonexercise of the power which he possesses respecting the trust." Section 677 * * * provides that the grantor is to be treated as the owner of any portion of a trust whose income could, in the discretion of the grantor or a nonadverse party or both, be distributed to, or accumulated for, the grantor's spouse. The regulations promulgated by the Treasury Department under § 677 specifically exclude the grantor's spouse as an adverse party. * * * § 1.677(a)–1(b)(2). It was on this basis that the district court ruled that the "grantor trust" provisions apply to the Holman Trust.

For the majority of the tax years in question, Bruce Holman and his wife, Audrey, were the sole trustees of the trust. In an attempt to circumvent the grantor trust provisions both Bruce and Audrey held beneficial interests in the trust assets. In this way, plaintiffs sought to be considered as adverse parties to each other thereby avoiding the effects of §§ 671–679. The only way Audrey could be considered adverse would be if she exercised her power as trustee so as to prevent income from being distributed to herself as beneficiary. As pointed out in Vercio, 73 T.C. at 1248–49 and Luman v. Commissioner, 79 T.C. 846 (1982), it is inconceivable that the grantor's spouse would be motivated to prevent income from being distributed for her benefit. Therefore, Audrey cannot be an adverse party as to Bruce. Bruce and Audrey Holman were properly taxed on the income conveyed to the trust under §§ 671–79.

* * *

The Bruce Holman Family Estate (a Trust) is a mere sham, lacking any economic substance. See Hanson, 696 F.2d at 1234. The district court properly applied the assignment of income doctrine and the grantor trust provisions of * * * §§ 671–679 in determining that plaintiffs are not entitled to a refund for overpayment of taxes for the years 1973 and 1974.

* * *

3.   OBLIGATIONS OF SUPPORT

The general rule of section 677 is plainly written and seems to leave little doubt as to its reach. However, section 677(b), while also apparently plainly written, has provoked much controversy. It appears to say that, if trust income is used for the "support or maintenance" of a person that the grantor is "legally obligated to support or maintain," the income "so applied" would be taxable to the grantor. The controversy has arisen over whether the distributions of income from a trust that are used for "support and maintenance" are taxable to the grantor only if the grantor was legally obligated to provide the particular items of support and maintenance for which the trust distributions were applied. A taxpayer's legal obligation may arise out of contract or as a result of a duty imposed by state law.

What is included in the obligation of support is much debated. Is it only the necessaries of life or does it include college education?

WYCHE V. UNITED STATES
United States Court of Claims Trial Judge's Report, 1974.
36 A.F.T.R. 2d (P-H) 75–5816.

WOOD, TRIAL JUDGE: * * *

The first issue is whether or not the income from the corpus of three * * * trusts established by plaintiff for the benefit of his three children is, to the extent used to pay for private school tuition and music and dancing lessons for the children, includible in plaintiff's income for the said years. The facts relating to this issue follow.

Plaintiffs have three children, all of whom were minors throughout the period 1963–67. In 1957, 1960, and 1963, respectively, plaintiff, a successful practicing attorney in Greenville, South Carolina, established three separate trusts, each for the benefit of all of the children, and each extending for more than 10 years, with Mrs. Wyche as trustee. The corpus of each trust consisted of rental real property in Greenville.

Under each trust, the trustee was required, after collecting rentals and paying expenses, to distribute to each of the beneficiaries, in equal shares, all of the current income of each trust, at least annually, on or before April 1 following the preceding calendar year. Under the terms of each trust, the distribution of income could be made directly to the beneficiaries or by "depositing the same in a bank or savings account in the beneficiaries' names, or by purchasing securities in the beneficiaries' names, or the expending of said sums for the education of said beneficiaries."

During each of the years in issue, a portion of the current income of the trusts (administered, at all times here relevant, as a single trust, with all receipts or disbursements processed through a bank account in the name of Mrs. Wyche as trustee) was used to pay for tuition at a private day school, and for certain music and dancing lessons, for plaintiffs' children. The total amount of all such payments, for the years 1963–67, amounted to some $8,500. Plaintiff was financially able to make all such payments from his own funds.

Plaintiffs' children began to attend Christ Church Episcopal School in 1960, at which time plaintiffs' son was in the fourth grade, one daughter was in the first grade, and one daughter was in kindergarten. For two of the children plaintiff, and for one of the children Mrs. Wyche, signed an application form (essentially an information sheet) in connection with their commencement of such attendance. Thereafter, however, plaintiffs did not execute any document with or for the School.

The School had elected as a matter of policy not to enter into contractual arrangements with parents (or others) desirous of having a child attend the School. Instead, tuition charges and enrollment fees (the latter to reserve a place for a current student during the next school year) were payable in advance of school attendance. Tuition charges and enrollment fees for plaintiffs' children were paid from trust funds in advance of any due date. Thus, their accounts were never delinquent, and no bills for tuition were ever sent to plaintiffs, the trustee, or the children.

Payments to the School were made by use of a check printed "Harriet S. Wyche, Trustee." Such checks were made payable to one of plaintiffs' children, and endorsed by the child. Mrs. Wyche then either took the check, or cashed it and took the proceeds, to the School. In the latter event, Mrs. Wyche advised the School representative receiving the money (normally the Church Treasurer or a clerk in that office) that the cash payment was being made from trust funds.

During the years 1963 through 1967, free elementary and secondary public schools, primarily supported by local property taxes, were available in Greenville County, South Carolina, and plaintiffs' children might have attended such public schools at no cost to plaintiffs. Throughout at least most of that period, if not all of it, attendance of a child at any school (public, private, or parochial) was not compulsory under South Carolina law.

During the years 1963–67, a portion of the income of the trusts was also used to pay for music and dancing lessons for one or more of plaintiffs' children. Again, there were no written contracts. Both the music teacher and the ballet teacher were informed by Mrs. Wyche that the trusts were the source of funds for such lessons, and payments, from trust funds, were generally made in essentially the same manner as were payments to the School. On some occasions, however, a check on the trustee account was drawn in favor of the appropriate teacher.

Except for his execution of application forms for two of the children in connection with their commencement of attendance at the School, plaintiff had no contact with either the School or the music and dancing teachers. Plaintiffs' children were not required to attend private school, or to take lessons in music or dancing. One child ultimately decided to, and did, attend public school, and one or more children did not take music or dancing lessons during some of the years in suit.

Under Section 677(a) * * * the grantor "shall be treated as the owner of any portion of a trust * * * whose income without the approval or consent of any adverse party is, or, in the discretion of the grantor or a nonadverse party, or both, may be * * *" distributed to the grantor. Under Section 677(b), however, trust income "shall not be considered taxable to the grantor under subsection (a) * * * merely because such income in the discretion of * * * the trustee * * * may be applied or distributed for the support or maintenance of a beneficiary whom the grantor is legally obligated to support or maintain, except to the extent that such income is so applied or distributed. * * *"

Rev. Rul. 56–484, 1956–2 Cum. Bull. 23, provides, in effect, that trust income "used in the discharge or satisfaction, in whole or in part, of a legal obligation of any person to support or maintain a minor is, to the extent so used, taxable to such person * * *. However, the amount of such income includible in the gross income of a person obligated to support or maintain a minor *is limited by the extent of his obligations under local law.*" (Emphasis supplied.)

The injection into the decisional process of the utilization of state law to determine Federal income tax consequences in a case such as this has rightfully been said to pose difficult problems in terms of tax equity and inequity. * * * It is clear, however, that "local law" is here determinative.

Under South Carolina law, plaintiff had (in broad terms) a statutory obligation to provide for his children "the actual necessaries of life." * * * It is not disputed that obligation extended (notwithstanding the absence of any state statute making school attendance compulsory throughout most if not all of the period here relevant) to education of plaintiff's minor children. * * * Plaintiff's position is, rather, that, under South Carolina law, he had no legal obligation whatever to send his children to private day school, or to provide music and dancing lessons for them, and that, accordingly, the taxing of trust income so used to plaintiff is erroneous and unlawful.

Defendant agrees that the primary issues on this phase of the matter are whether plaintiff was legally obligated under South Carolina law to send his children to private day school, or to afford them such private lessons, but contends that under South Carolina law plaintiff plainly had a legal obligation to do both. Defendant also asserts, alternatively, that plaintiff impliedly obligated himself to pay the amounts in question actually paid from trust income, and that those amounts are accordingly taxable to plaintiff under Section 677 in any event.

In Brooke v. United States, 300 F. Supp. 465 (D.C.Mont.1969), the court, equating a court-administered guardianship with a trust for purposes of Section 677, considered whether payments by the "trustee" from "trust" income for, inter alia, private school tuition and music, swimming, and public speaking lessons for his minor children were in discharge of his legal obligations under Montana law. Under Montana law, a parent must give his child "support and education suitable to his circumstances." Plaintiff in Brooke, in the years there relevant, had income ranging from $26,000 to $30,000.

With plain cognizance of "the result that should happen as a matter of tax equality," the court nonetheless held squarely that the amounts expended for private school tuition and lessons were "not items which plaintiff was legally required to provide for the support and maintenance of the children," and, accordingly, were not includible in the parent's income. Brooke v. United States, supra, 300 F. Supp. at 466–67. That holding was unanimously affirmed on appeal. Brooke v. United States, 468 F.2d 1155 (9th Cir.1972).

Defendant urges that the decision in Brooke reflects a narrow, minority, view of the obligation of a parent to support his minor children, and that, in other jurisdictions (indeed, defendant says, in a majority of the states), a different rule would apply. * * *

These arguments are wide of the mark. The determinative consideration here is South Carolina law, and upon a careful consideration of the record and the briefs and arguments of the parties, together with extensive independent research, it is concluded that, for the years here relevant, plaintiff had no legal obligation under South Carolina law to send his children to private day school or to afford them music and dancing lessons.

* * *

Defendant alternatively contends that plaintiff had an implied contractual obligation to pay the cost of his children's tuition at private day school, and the costs of their music and dancing lessons. Relying on Morrill v. United States, 228 F. Supp. 734 (D.C.Me.1964), defendant asserts that since the amounts here in issue were used to satisfy such an obligation, they are accordingly taxable to plaintiff under Section 677(a).

* * *

Insofar as here relevant, that holding rested on a finding that the schools believed Mr. Morrill responsible for payment of bills incurred on behalf of his children, and the "settled principle of contract law that when one renders services to another at the request, or with the knowledge and consent, of the others, and the surrounding circumstances make it reasonable for him to believe that he will receive payment therefor from the other, and he does so believe, a promise to pay will be inferred, and there is an implied contract." Ibid. Thus, it was held, Mr. Morrill alone was legally liable for payment of the amounts there in issue. On the facts of this cause, however, that "settled principle" is clearly inapplicable.

There being no valid basis for attribution to plaintiff of the trust income in question, plaintiffs are entitled to recover on this issue.

* * *

BRAUN v. COMMISSIONER
United States Tax Court, 1984.
T.C. Memo 1984–285, 48 T.C.M. (CCH) 210.

WHITAKER, JUDGE:

* * * [Dr. Frederick Braun and his wife, Marjorie, jointly established one trust for the benefit of three of their children (Trust I) and another trust for the benefit of their other three children (Trust II). Dr. and Mrs. Braun and "a friend," Mr. Torres, were the trustees. The terms of each trust provided that "the entire net income is to be distributed to the three children for whom the trust was established."]

* * * All of the distributed income was used for educational purposes. In 1976, 1977 and 1978, from Trust I the disbursements were for college tuition, room and board for Cynthia and Fred, two of the three beneficiaries of that trust. Both children were over 18 years of age in 1976. In 1976 the income from Trust II was used for tuition at the private high school attended by two of that trust's beneficiaries, Stephen and Christopher. In 1977 and 1978, a portion of the Trust II income was used for tuition, room and board of Stephen at college and a portion for Christopher at the private high school. During these years, none of the income was used for one beneficiary of each trust. Stephen became 18 in December of 1976, whereas Christopher did not become 18 until 1979.

* * *

Under section 677(b), the income of a trust is taxable to the grantor to the extent that such income is applied or distributed for the support or maintenance of a beneficiary whom the grantor is legally obligated to support or maintain. Petitioners argue that under New Jersey law the petitioners had no obligation to pay college tuition and room and board expenses of an unmarried child over 18 or to pay private school expense for an unmarried child under 18. Petitioners further argue that this issue has come up in New Jersey only in controversies between divorced parents and that such cases are inapplicable to this situation. We do not agree.

The recent decision of Newburgh v. Arrigo, 88 N.J. 529, 443 A.2d 1031 (1982), fully reviews the obligation of parents to continue to provide educational expenses for unmarried children over the age of 18. The Supreme Court of New Jersey held that necessary education is a flexible concept that can vary in different circumstances.

In general, financially capable parents should contribute to the higher education of children who are qualified students. In appropriate circumstances, parental responsibility includes the duty to assure children of a college and even of a post-graduate education such as law school. [Newburgh v. Arrigo, supra at 1038.]

In an adversarial situation, courts in New Jersey consider all relevant factors, which include 12 which were enumerated in Newburgh v. Arrigo, supra. It is obvious that many of these factors would have no bearing except in a controversy between divorced parents or between a child and a noncustodial parent. But the support rule is not limited to such divorced parent context. Sakovits v. Sakovits, 178 N.J.Super. 623, 429 A.2d 1091, 1095 (1981). While many of these factors described by the New Jersey Supreme Court are not directly applicable to the instant facts, the import to our facts is clearly that petitioners retained the obligation to provide their children with a college education. They were both able and willing to do so, a college education was imminently reasonable in the light of the background, values and goals of the parents as well as the children, and petitioners have brought forward no facts or arguments which would militate against the recognition of this obligation on the part of these particular parents. Newburgh v. Arrigo, supra. With respect to private high school education, the law of New Jersey is less clear. There is dictum in the case of Rosenthal v. Rosenthal, 19 N.J. Super, 521, 88 A.2d 655 (1952), to the effect that a father is not required to provide his son with private school, college or professional training, or with any education beyond public schools, but that dictum as to college and professional education is certainly obsolete. Khalaf v. Khalaf, 58 N.J. 63, 275 A.2d 132, 137 (1971), refers with approval to Annot. 56 A.L.R.2d 1207 (1956). While that court's reference to the annotation was with respect to college expenses, the annotation also recognizes the existence of a parental obligation in similar circumstances to provide for private or boarding school education. It would be an anomaly to find a support obligation for college tuition for an emancipated child but none for private high school expense for a younger child in the same family. In view of the recent New Jersey cases cited, we do not think the dictum in Rosenthal v. Rosenthal, supra, represents the current view of the New Jersey courts. We believe that private high school education in appropriate cases would be held by the New Jersey courts to be within the scope of parental obligation. Accordingly, we hold that the income of these two trusts, to the extent actually utilized for tuition, room and board for four of the six children of petitioners was used to discharge Dr. Braun's legal support obligations and is therefore taxable to him under section 677(b).

NOTE

In Stone v. Commissioner, T.C. Memo 1987–454, 54 T.C.M. (CCH) 462 (1987), the court, looking to California divorce cases as precedent, concluded that a parent's affluence rendered "private" high school education furnished his child a part of his legal obligation of support—and, accordingly trust dollars expended for this purpose were taxable to the parent having the obligation rather than to the trust. Furthermore, in *Braun*, the court looked at New Jersey divorce cases as precedent and also concluded that parent's affluence rendered his child's college expenses a part of his legal obligation of support—and, again, trust dollars expended for this purpose were taxable to the parent having the obligation rather than to the trust. Reconciling *Wyche* with *Stone* and *Braun* may well turn on the precedential value of legal obligation of support determinations made in the context of divorce. Despite the *Braun* court's statement, should support and maintenance be relative, i.e., one standard, perhaps taking into account parental affluence, applies when parents are divorcing, and another standard, perhaps one more modest in aspiration, when divorce and division of parental financial responsibility are not at issue? However, *Stone*, like *Braun*, relying on divorce precedents, did not recognize a different standard and, in a footnote, quickly differentiated Brooke v. United States, 468 F.2d 1155 (9th Cir. 1972), a case arising under Montana law, (and cited approvingly in *Wyche*) where the court found that expenditures for private schooling were not legal obligations of the taxpayer. The *Stone* court explained that "few facts were reported" in *Brooke*, and those reported were "markedly different," and that the "similar" Montana statute "was not identical to the California statute." *Stone*, 54 T.C.M. at 466, n.7.

PROBLEMS

Haley transferred property to Granite Trust Co. on trust with the direction that the income shall be distributed annually and applied to the maintenance and support of her grandson, Joel, until Joel attains age 25. At that time, the trust is to terminate and the corpus is to be distributed to Joel. Joel is 15 years old and is attending an exclusive preparatory school. During the current year, the income of the trust was applied to defray all of Joel's expenses. Joel's father is named Michael.

1. Is the income of the trust taxable to Michael? See I.R.C. §§ 662 and 677; Treas. Reg. § 1.662(a)–4.

2. Would the result be different if the trust provided that Joel was to receive all of the trust income during the continuance of the trust? See I.R.C. § 662.

3. What would be the result if Michael were trustee with discretionary power to distribute income to Joel for Joel's support and maintenance? See I.R.C. §§ 674, 677, and 678.

NOTE

All states have adopted the Uniform Transfers to Minors Act (UTMA). South Carolina adopted UTMA in 2022, the last state to do so. The UTMA provides a simplified procedure by which property can be held for the benefit of a person under 18 (or 21 years) of age without the formality of a trust or a formal guardianship proceeding in the state courts. The benefits (and burdens) of UTMA are obtained by titling property as "(name) as custodian under the Uniform Transfers to Minors Act as adopted by (state) for the benefit of (name of child)."

Income earned by property held in a custodianship is taxed directly to the child, the custodianship not being recognized as an income taxpaying entity (unlike a trust, which is an income taxpaying entity). Rev. Rul. 56–484, 1956–2 C.B. 23. However, in cases where custodianship income is used to discharge the legal obligation of support of another person, the custodianship income will be taxable to the person whose legal obligation was so discharged but only to the extent the custodianship income was applied to discharge that obligation. Thus, if the custodianship generated $1,000 of income but only $450 was used to discharge a parent's obligation of support, then only $450 would be taxed to the parent and the balance of the custodianship income that year would be taxed to the child. Rev. Rul. 59–357, 1959–2 C.B. 212, reprinted in Chapter 7.

4. ADVERSE PARTY EXCEPTION

The grantor is taxed on that trust income if it may be used for any of these purposes at the discretion of the grantor or some other person who is not considered an adverse party for these purposes (applying the statutory definition). An adverse party is a person with a "substantial beneficial interest in the trust which would be adversely affected by the exercise or nonexercise of the power" which the person possesses. I.R.C. § 672(a). A trustee is not an adverse party solely because the trustee is a fiduciary with respect to the trust. Treas. Reg. § 1.672(a)–1. However, the holder of a general power of appointment over the trust property is considered an adverse party.

For example, assume that Michael was brain damaged at birth as a result of negligence. A substantial sum of money was awarded to him in the resulting litigation. The damages were ordered to be placed in trust for

Michael's benefit. The trust is not subject to revocation by Michael but is subject to amendment, modification, or revocation at any time by the court. The trust is to terminate when Michael attains 21 or dies. In the meantime, Bank, as trustee, has discretion to distribute income and principal to Michael for his health, education, support and maintenance. To date the trust income has always exceeded the amounts Bank has distributed to Michael. The IRS position is that all the trust income is taxable to Michael under the grantor trust rules in the year it is earned by the trust even though some of that income is warehoused in the trust and not distributed to Michael. See Rev. Rul. 83–25, 1983–1 C.B. 116. While the damages themselves are excluded from Michael's income by section 104(a)(2), as owner of the damages Michael is considered the grantor of the trust. Both the distributed and the undistributed income is taxable to Michael under section 677(a) because it is either distributed to him or held and accumulated for future distribution to him at the discretion of a nonadverse party.

NOTE

Does the IRS position in Rev. Rul. 83–25 suggest that it is impossible to create a trust for your own benefit yet cause the income to be taxed to the trust to the extent that the income is not needed by you? Or can you suggest techniques by which such a trust can be created by taking advantage of the adverse party exception? See I.R.C. § 672.

E. POWER TO CONTROL BENEFICIAL ENJOYMENT

1. GENERAL RULE

Section 674(a) provides that the grantor of a trust will be taxed on the income generated by the trust to the extent that "the beneficial enjoyment of the corpus or the income therefrom is subject to a power of disposition, exercisable by the grantor or a nonadverse party, or both, without the approval or consent of any adverse party." The theory is that a person should not be able to shift income to another while controlling the enjoyment of that income.

BRAUN V. COMMISSIONER
United States Tax Court, 1984.
T.C. Memo 1984–285, 48 T.C.M. (CCH) 210.

[The facts are set forth earlier in this chapter in Part D(3).]

Respondent assumes that Mr. Torres is not an adverse party. The term "adverse party" is defined in § 672 to mean "any person having a substantial beneficial interest in the trust which would be adversely affected by the exercise or nonexercise of the power which he possesses respecting the trust." A nonadverse party means any party who is not an adverse party. We agree with respondent that Mr. Torres is not an adverse party. Thus, under § 674(a), the issue is whether or not the grantors as trustees, along with Mr. Torres, retained the power to sprinkle the income among the three beneficiaries of each of the two trusts.

The trust instrument does not prescribe the shares of each of the three beneficiaries of each trust in the income. While one might tend to assume that each beneficiary was entitled to an equal share, New Jersey follows the rule that extrinsic evidence may be considered to interpret the terms of a trust which is ambiguous. * * * The extrinsic evidence in this case illustrating intent, which under New Jersey law can be looked to, is the contemporaneous action by the parties, that is, the grantor-trustees in making distributions from the two trusts. In each trust, during each of the years, one of the beneficiaries was ignored altogether and income which was distributed was utilized in varying amounts for the benefit of the other two beneficiaries without any apparent pattern. This clearly evidences a sprinkling of the income among the beneficiaries. On the basis of the New Jersey cases cited, we conclude that the trust instrument must be construed as permitting such sprinkling. We agree with respondent that this is not a case such as Bennett v. Commissioner, 79 T.C. 470, 487 (1982), where the grantor-trustees misadministered the express directions of the trust instrument. Based on this interpretation of these trust instruments, we hold that the income of the two trusts is taxable to petitioners under section 674(a).

2. EXCEPTIONS TO GENERAL RULE

There are numerous exceptions to the general rule that the grantor is treated as the owner of a trust, regardless of its duration, where the beneficial enjoyment of the trust property or income is subject to a power of disposition exercisable by the grantor or by a nonadverse party. Whether a power is "excepted" from the reach of the general rule depends on the identity of the holder of that power. For example, some powers are excepted only if they are held by a trustee or trustees other than the grantor or a spouse living with the grantor. And some powers are excepted if they are held by a trustee or trustees who are other than the grantor and at least half of whom are independent. See I.R.C. § 674(c) and Treas. Reg. § 1.674(a)–1(a).

a. Exception: Power to Apply Income of Dependent

A power to apply income to the support or maintenance of the grantor's dependents, exercisable by the grantor as trustee or by another person as trustee or otherwise, will only cause the income of the trust to be taxed to the grantor to the extent that such income is so applied and distributed.

I.R.C. §§ 674(b)(1) and 677(b). In other words, the presence of this power alone will not attract tax to the grantor—it is the exercise of this power that is a taxable event for the grantor.

b.   Exception: Power Exercisable Only by Will

In general, the grantor is not taxable on trust income if the grantor's power to control disposition is exercisable only by will. However, this exception is not applicable where the grantor, or a nonadverse party, or both, also has the power to accumulate trust income for disposition by will, without the approval or consent of any adverse party. I.R.C. § 674(b)(3). For example, if the grantor provides in the trust that the income is to be accumulated during the grantor's life and that the grantor may appoint the accumulated income in the will, the grantor is subject to income tax on the trust income.

c.   Exception: Power to Withhold Income During Minority of Beneficiary

A power to pay or apply income to or for a beneficiary or to accumulate and add the income to the corpus, which is exercisable only while an income beneficiary is under age 21 or under some other legal disability, will not subject the grantor to tax. I.R.C. § 674(b)(7). Such a power is excepted even though the accumulated income will not be paid to the beneficiary from whom it is withheld. Accumulated income may be added to corpus and ultimately be distributed to others. Treas. Reg. § 1.674(b)–1(b)(7).

d.   Exception: Powers Exercisable by Independent Trustees

A broader exception is made for certain powers exercisable solely by independent trustees. I.R.C. § 674(c). Trustees are often given the power to distribute, apportion or accumulate income to or for one or more beneficiaries or within a class of beneficiaries, or to pay out corpus to or for them. Such power will not subject the grantor to tax if it is solely exercisable by a trustee or trustees (without the consent of any other person), none of whom is the grantor, and no more than half of whom are related or subordinate parties who are subservient to the wishes of the grantor. Thus, in the ordinary sprinkling or spray trust, the co-trustees may be a corporate fiduciary and a family member (even the decedent grantor's spouse).

Technically speaking, a "related or subordinate party" means any nonadverse party who is the grantor's spouse, if they are living together; a parent, issue, brother or sister, or employee of the grantor; a corporation or any employee thereof in which the stock holdings of the grantor and the trust are significant from the viewpoint of voting control; or a subordinate employee of a corporation in which the grantor is an executive. There is a rebuttable presumption that a related or subordinate party is subservient to the grantor. I.R.C. § 672(c).

e. Exception: Power to Allocate Income Limited by Standard

A power to distribute, apportion or accumulate income to or for one or more beneficiaries or within a class of beneficiaries, but limited to a standard such as the reasonable needs of the beneficiaries, is excepted from the reach of the general rule. Such a power will not subject the grantor to tax if it is solely exercisable by a trustee or trustees, none of whom is the grantor or a spouse living with the grantor, provided such power is exercisable without the consent of any other person and is limited by a reasonably definite external standard that is set forth in the trust instrument. The exception applies even though the power is held by a related or subordinate trustee (other than the grantor's spouse living with the grantor), who is subservient to the grantor.

This power is not an excepted power, however, if any person has a power to add trust beneficiaries, except where the power is limited to providing for after-born or after-adopted children. I.R.C. § 674(d). Moreover, the power is not an excepted power if the grantor has an unrestricted power to remove the trustee, unless the grantor is under a duty to substitute another independent trustee. Treas. Reg. § 1.674(d)–2(a).

Unlike section 674(b)(6), section 674(d) permits distributions to remaindermen as well as to current income beneficiaries, and it makes no effort to insure that accumulated income will eventually be placed at the disposition of the beneficiary for whom it was withheld.

f. Other Exceptions

There are a number of other exceptions to the general rule that should be noted by reviewing section 674.

F. ADMINISTRATIVE POWERS

All the income of a trust will be taxed to the grantor—rather than to the trust or to the person to whom the income is distributed—if under the terms of the trust the trust is or can be administered for the benefit of the grantor. Section 675 provides specifically for cases in which the grantor or a nonadverse party has the power to deal with or dispose of the trust property for less than adequate and full consideration, to borrow trust funds without adequate interest or adequate security, or to control trust investments or reacquire the trust property by substituting property of an equivalent value (except in cases where these powers of administration are exercisable by the grantor or nonadverse party only when serving in a fiduciary capacity).

REVENUE RULING 85–13

1985–1 C.B. 184.

* * *

In 1980, A, an individual, created an irrevocable trust, T. W., A's spouse, is the trustee of T. The trust instrument of T provides that all income of T is to be paid semiannually to C, A's child, for a term of 15 years. Upon expiration of the trust term, or if C dies before the trust term expires, the corpus of T will be distributed to C's child or to the estate of C's child. Neither A nor any other person has a power over or an interest in T that would cause A to be treated as the owner of T under the grantor trust provisions, section 671 and following.

A funded T with a contribution of 100 shares of stock in Corporation Z. When A funded T, a's basis in the shares was $20x.

On December 27, 1981, when the fair market value of the Corporation Z shares was $40x, W, as trustee, transferred the 100 shares to A. In exchange, A gave W A's unsecured promissory note with a face amount of $40x, bearing an adequate annual rate of interest, payable semiannually, beginning six months following the date on which the shares were transferred to A. Principal payments on the note were scheduled to be paid in 10 equal annual installments, the first installment being due 3 years following the date on which the 100 shares were transferred to A, December 27, 1984.

On January 20, 1984, A sold the 100 shares to an unrelated party for $50x. Corporation Z did not make any distributions with respect to the 100 shares at any time before the sale of those shares to the unrelated party.

LAW AND ANALYSIS

Under section 675(3), a grantor will be treated as the owner of any portion of a trust in respect of which the grantor has directly or indirectly borrowed the trust corpus or income and has not completely repaid the loan, including any interest, before the beginning of the taxable year, unless the loan (1) provides for adequate interest, (2) is adequately secured, and (3) is not made by the grantor or by a related or subordinate trustee who is subservient to the grantor.

* * * [Reg. §]1.675–1 * * * explains that, in effect, section 675 treats the grantor as the owner of a trust if under the terms of the trust instrument, or the circumstances attendant to its operation, administrative control is exercisable primarily for the benefit of the grantor rather than the beneficiaries of the trust. Section 675(3) differs from the other provisions of section 675 which provide rules for determining grantor ownership of a trust, because it requires an affirmative act (borrowing) rather than a retained power, before it applies. Nevertheless, the same theme underlies section 675(3) as underlies the other provisions of section 675 which treat the grantor as owning the trust. In all of these cases the justification for treating the grantor as owner is evidence of substantial grantor dominion and control over the trust.

* * *

In this case, A has acquired control over and use of the entire trust corpus, the 100 shares of Corporation Z stock, in exchange for A's unsecured note. If A, instead of giving W a note in exchange for the 100 shares, had made a cash payment of $40x to W and subsequently borrowed that cash, giving W the unsecured note to evidence the borrowing, section 675(3) * * * would be applicable and a would be the owner of T. Although A did not engage in this kind of direct borrowing, A's acquisition of the entire corpus of T in exchange for an unsecured note was, in substance, the economic equivalent of borrowing trust corpus. Accordingly, under section 675(3), A is treated as the owner of the portion of T represented by A's promissory note. Further, because the promissory note is T's only asset, A is treated as the owner of the entire trust.

Because A is treated as the owner of the entire trust, A is considered to be the owner of the trust assets for federal income tax purposes. [Citations omitted.] In this case, A is considered to be the owner of the promissory note held by the trust. Therefore, the transfer of the Corporation Z shares by T to A is not recognized as a sale for federal income tax purposes because A is both the maker and the owner of the promissory note. A transaction cannot be recognized as a sale for federal income tax purposes if the same person is treated as owning the purported consideration both before and after the transaction. See Dobson v. Commissioner, 1 B.T.A. 1082 (1925).

A's basis in the shares received from T will be equal to A's basis in the shares at the time he funded T because the basis of the shares was not adjusted during the period that T held them. See Rev. Rul. 72–406, 1972–2 C.B. 462, a ruling involving the determination of a grantor's basis in property upon reversion of that property to the grantor at the expiration of a trust's term.

In Rothstein v. United States, 735 F.2d 704 (2d Cir.1984), the court considered a transaction that is in substance identical to the facts described in this ruling. The court held that the grantor was the owner of a trust under section 675(3) because by exchanging an unsecured note for the entire trust corpus, the grantor had indirectly borrowed the trust corpus. The court held further, however, that although the grantor must be treated as the owner of the trust, this means only that the grantor must include items of income, deduction, and credit attributable to the trust in computing the grantor's taxable income and credits, and that the trust must continue to be viewed as a separate taxpayer. The court held, therefore, that the transfer of trust corpus to the grantor in exchange for an unsecured promissory note was a sale and that the taxpayer acquired a cost basis in the assets.

In *Rothstein*, as in this case, section 671 requires that the grantor includes [sic] in computing the grantor's tax liability all items of income, deduction, and credit of the trust as though the trust were not in existence during the period the grantor is treated as the owner. Section 1.671–3(a)(1). It is anomalous to suggest that Congress, in enacting the grantor trust provisions * * *, intended that the existence of a trust would be ignored for purposes of attribution of income, deduction, and credit, and yet, retain its vitality as a separate entity capable of entering into a sales transaction with the grantor. The reason for attributing items of income, deduction, and credit to the grantor under section 671 is that, by exercising dominion and control over a trust, either by retaining a power over or an interest in the trust, or, as in this case, by dealing with the trust property for the grantor's benefit, the grantor has treated the trust property as though it were the grantor's property. The Service position of treating the owner of an entire trust as the owner of the trust's assets is, therefore, consistent with and supported by the rationale for attributing items of income, deduction, and credit to the grantor.

The court's decision in *Rothstein*, insofar as it holds that a trust owned by a grantor must be regarded as a separate taxpayer capable of engaging in sales transactions with the grantor, is not in accord with the views of the Service. Accordingly, the Service will not follow *Rothstein*.

HOLDINGS

(1) A's receipt of the entire corpus of the trust in exchange for A's unsecured promissory note constituted an indirect borrowing of the trust corpus which caused a to be the owner of the entire trust under section 675(3).

(2) At the time A became the owner of the trust, A became the owner of the trust property. As a result, the transfer of trust assets to A was not a sale for federal income tax purposes and A did not acquire a cost basis in those assets. Accordingly, when A sold the shares of Corporation Z stock on January 20, 1984, A recognized gain of $30x (amount realized of $50x less adjusted basis of $20x). Further, this holding would apply even if the trust held other assets in addition to A's promissory note if A, under any of the grantor trust provisions, was treated as the owner of the portion of the trust represented by the promissory note because A would be treated as the owner of the purported consideration (the promissory note) both before and after the transaction. See § 1.671–3(a)(2).

REVENUE RULING 86–82
1986–1 C.B. 253.

ISSUE

If the grantor of a trust borrows the entire trust corpus and makes complete repayment of principal and interest within the same year, is that grantor treated as owner of the trust under section 675(3)?

FACTS

On May 11, 1985, A created an irrevocable trust for the benefit of A's children. The trust instrument names A trustee and gives a power to borrow trust corpus or income at the market rate of interest with adequate security. On June 11, 1985, A borrowed 100x dollars from the trust in compliance with these requirements. The borrowed funds comprised the entire trust corpus. On November 3, 1985, A repaid the loan plus interest. Both A and the trust are calendar year taxpayers.

LAW AND ANALYSIS

Section 671 provides that if any section of subpart E of subchapter J treats the grantor as the owner of any portion of the trust, then the grantor must include in computing taxable income those items of income, deductions, and credits which are attributable to that portion of the trust.

Section 675(3) provides that, generally, the grantor of a trust will be treated as the owner of any portion of a trust in respect to which the grantor has borrowed the corpus or income and has not completely repaid the loan, including any interest, before the beginning of the taxable year.

In Mau v. United States, 355 F. Supp. 909 (D.Haw.1973), the taxpayer established five separate trusts, with the taxpayer designated trustee of each. In 1965, the taxpayer borrowed money from each of the trusts. These amounts were not repaid until 1969. The taxpayer argued that section 675(3) did not cause the taxpayer-grantor to be liable for federal income tax on the trusts' 1965 income because the loans were not outstanding at the beginning of the year. The court rejected this interpretation of the statute, reasoning that section 675(3) was enacted to prevent the shifting of taxable income in situations where a grantor retained control and use of trust properties through borrowing. Therefore, the court held that the borrowing of trust corpus or income by a grantor at any time during a taxable year would result in the grantor being taxed on trust income for that entire year under section 675(3). The court concluded that the taxpayer was taxable on income of the trusts in 1965, the year the borrowing occurred, even though the loans were made after the beginning of the year. If section 675(3) otherwise applies for a given year, its effect is not avoided by making repayment before the year closes. Mau therefore stands for the principle that section 675(3) applies for any year during any part of which a loan by a trust to the grantor-trustee is outstanding.

In the present case, A borrowed the entire trust corpus during calendar 1985. Accordingly, A is treated as the owner of the entire trust under section 675(3) in spite of the fact that A made full payment of principal and interest before the close of 1985. See section 1.671–3(b)(3). Hence, under section 671, A must include in gross income all income earned by the trust in 1985.

* * *

NOTE

In Private Letter Ruling 8802004, a taxpayer, in his capacity as trustee of an irrevocable trust that he had created, failed to enforce the terms of a promissory note held by him as trustee. As a result, the trust was determined to be a grantor trust and the trust income was taxed to the taxpayer personally on the ground that the failure to enforce the repayment terms of the note constituted a borrowing by the taxpayer from the trust under section 675(3). The facts were unusual. The note, secured by real estate, had been given by a partnership in which the taxpayer was a partner. After the taxpayer placed the note in trust, the partnership terminated, and the taxpayer became the sole obligor on the note. Essentially the taxpayer, in his individual capacity, was obligated to himself as trustee. When the cash flow from the encumbered property proved to be less than the obligation on the note, the taxpayer passed through to the trust only the amount of the cash flow despite his obligation under the note to pay a greater amount. The IRS concluded that the taxpayer, in effect, extended credit to himself on terms different from those contained in the mortgage note. This new extension of credit was the economic equivalent of a transaction in which the borrower renegotiates a loan with a lender and substitutes a new note for a preexisting one. In each instance, there is a new borrowing for purposes of section 675(3).

In the ruling, the IRS pointed to the regulations and legislative history and commented that "section 675 was enacted to ensure that ownership of a trust is attributed to a grantor in those situations where a trust is administered in a manner that primarily benefits the grantor."

G. REVERSIONARY INTERESTS

1. INTRODUCTION

Generally, a grantor will be taxed on the income from each trust in which the grantor retains a reversion. More specifically, reversionary trusts—trusts providing benefits to persons other than the grantor but followed by a reversion in the grantor at the death of the nongrantor beneficiary or after a term of years—are effective income-shifting devices. However, they are effective only where the value of the grantor's reversionary interest, at the inception of the trust, is valued at five percent or less of the value of that portion of the trust in which the grantor has the reversionary interest. I.R.C. § 673(a).

Example 1: Larry establishes an irrevocable trust with Accumulation National Bank. Larry funds the trust with $100,000 and provides that the trust is to continue until the first to occur of the following events: (a) the death of his son, Brian, age 20 at the time the trust is created; or (b) the 46th anniversary of the creation of the trust. During the continuance of the trust, all trust income is to be paid to Brian. Upon termination of the trust, the property then constituting the trust is to be paid over to Larry. In this case, the trust income is taxable to Brian and not to Larry since the value of Larry's reversion is only $3,920 (based on the proposed regulations for Table S issued on May 5, 2022 for an applicable interest rate of 6.8 percent). Had the trust been created for only 45 years (and its duration was in no way related to Brian's age), the trust income would be taxable to Larry rather than Brian even though Brian received that income because the value of Larry's reversion (using Table B prescribed in Treas. Reg. § 20.2031–7 and assuming an applicable interest rate of 6.8 percent) would be $5,179.60, which is more than five percent of the value of the trust corpus at the inception of the trust. Similarly, if Brian was 27 at the trust's creation and the trust was to last for his life, the trust income would be taxable to Larry because the value of Larry's reversion (using Table S) would be $5,459, which is more than five percent of the value of the trust corpus at the inception of the trust.

Example 2: Margaret established an irrevocable trust with Rockhard Bank & Trust. Margaret funded the trust with $100,000 and provided that the trust was to continue until the first to occur of the following events: (a) the death of her mother, Abigail, age 60 at the time the trust was created; or (b) the 60th anniversary of the creation of the trust. During the continuance of the trust, all trust income is to be paid to Abigail. Upon termination of the trust, the property then constituting the trust is to be paid over to Margaret. In this case, the trust income is taxable to Margaret and not to Abigail, since the value of Margaret's reversion, $27,303 (determined by applying the proposed regulations for Table S issued on May 5, 2022 for an applicable interest rate of 6.8 percent) is greater than 5 percent of the value of the trust corpus. Note that using Table B would have provided a reversionary value of only $1,930.70, well within the five-percent limit. However, Table S, relating to life expectancy, must be used since it causes a higher value to be placed on Margaret's reversionary interest.

In addition, it should be noted that, in determining the value of any reversionary interest, it is assumed that any discretionary powers over the trust, by whomsoever possessed, will be exercised for the maximum benefit of the grantor. See I.R.C. § 673(c).

2. INTERESTS TAKING EFFECT
AT DEATH OF MINORS

Oftentimes taxpayers make gifts in trust for the benefit of a child, the trust to last only until the child attains 21 years of age, at which time the trust is to terminate and the property then constituting the trust estate is to be distributed to the child. This can be a tax-favored arrangement in the sense that the $17,000 annual exclusion, assuming the gift takes place in 2023, will be available to shelter such a gift if the trust otherwise satisfies the requirements of section 2503(c). Section 673(b) anticipates that the grantor of such a trust may wish to retain, in that trust, a reversion that will be triggered only in the case where the child dies before attaining age 21. If the grantor retains a reversion in such a case, that retention alone will not cause the trust income to be taxed to the grantor (rather than to the child or to the trust itself) even though the value of the retained reversion may be greater than five percent of the trust property in which the grantor has the reversion.

H. MALLINCKRODT TRUSTS (SECTION 678)

Section 678 describes the circumstances in which someone other than the grantor of a trust will be taxed on the income of the trust even though that other person does not receive that income. At first look, this rule appears harsh. However, since the circumstances under which it is applied are limited, it is principally a trap for many taxpayers who are attempting to shelter income in a trust while giving a beneficiary of the trust substantial control over the enjoyment of the trust income.

Section 678 is sometimes referred to as the *Mallinckrodt* rule in deference to the principal case—Mallinckrodt v. Nunan, 146 F.2d 1 (8th Cir.1945), cert. denied, 324 U.S. 871 (1945), reh'g denied, 325 U.S. 892 (1945)—which imposed liability upon a nongrantor nonrecipient. In *Mallinckrodt*, the taxpayer and an independent trust company served as co-trustees of an inter vivos trust created by taxpayer's father. The trust was for the benefit of the taxpayer, his wife, and their descendants, and the taxpayer was given a testamentary power of appointment over the corpus. After payment of $10,000 to his wife, taxpayer had the power to withdraw the balance of the annual trust income. In the absence of such withdrawal, the excess income was added to corpus. At any time, the taxpayer, with the consent of the co-trustee, could terminate the trust and receive the corpus.

Although the taxpayer did not exercise any of these powers, he was held taxable as owner of the annual trust income in excess of $10,000.

PROBLEMS

1. Lotus was the sole trustee of three trusts, each established by the respective wills of her former husbands, who had predeceased Lotus. The trusts were the same in the sense that each trust was to continue for the life of Lotus and, upon her death, to terminate, the property then constituting the respective trusts to be distributed to the children born to Lotus and the spouse who had created that particular trust. The trusts differed, however, as to the distribution provisions during the lifetime of Lotus. Consider whether the trust income should be taxed to Lotus or to the respective trusts in the circumstances presented below. Note that Lotus believed that she had more than adequate resources for her support and, as a result, no distributions had ever been made from any of the trusts to Lotus. See I.R.C. § 678(a)(1).

    (a) Under the terms of the trust established by Lotus's first husband, all trust income was to be distributed to Lotus quarter-annually or more often.

    (b) Under the terms of the trust established by Lotus's second husband, Lotus, as sole trustee, had discretion to distribute to herself "such amounts of income and principal as she, in her sole discretion, shall determine to be essential to her well-being."

    (c) Under the terms of the trust established by Lotus's third husband, Lotus, as sole trustee, had discretion to distribute to herself "such amounts of income and principal as was necessary for health, education, maintenance, and support in her accustomed manner of living."

I. USING INTENTIONALLY DEFECTIVE GRANTOR TRUSTS

The grantor trust rules developed independently and are not in sync with the estate and gift tax rules. Although both are premised on the notion of dominion and control, the grantor trust rules are codified and specifically exclude the notion that the income of a trust is taxed to the grantor solely because he or she has "dominion and control." I.R.C. § 671. The estate and gift rules are much more broadly based, meaning that dominion and control is indicative that a transfer is not complete and thus the retained power or interest causes the transfer to be included in the estate of the transferor even though the transfer is, for example, irrevocable.

The end result is that transferors will structure transfers in trust so that the transferred property is considered a complete gift for gift tax purposes—meaning that it is subject to gift tax but not subject to estate tax at the transferor's later death because, under the estate tax rules, the transferor is not deemed to have retained a tainting power or interest that gives the transferor dominion and control. In structuring that transaction, though, it is possible to include features that will cause the trust be deemed a grantor trust, meaning all the trust income will be taxed to the grantor even though it is retained by the trust of distributed the beneficiary of the trust—someone other than the grantor. In this sense, the trust is described as an intentionally defective grantor trust.

One advantage to creating an intentionally defective grantor trust is that the income is taxed to the grantor (and not to the trust or its beneficiaries). The income tax paid by the grantor on the trust income depletes the grantor's estate (for estate tax purposes) and does not constitute an additional gift to the trust. Rev. Rul. 2004–64, 2004–2 C.B. 7. Moreover, the grantor may well be in a lower income tax bracket than the trust given that trust income is taxed at the top rates once that income exceeds a relatively low threshold. In 2020, for example, the threshold is $12,950.

The estate tax incentive to make the transfer is in the form of shrinking the grantor's estate for estate tax purposes—and getting the amount of any gift tax paid on the transfer out of the grantor's estate for estate tax purposes. The gift tax is tax exclusive while the estate tax is tax inclusive. That is, the amount of gift tax paid is not part of the gift tax computation base but the estate tax paid is part of the estate tax computation base. In that sense the estate tax computational model is like that of the income tax computational model.

Returning to the example, provided at the beginning of this chapter (Part A), of Mr. Slowe and his gift to his son, Borne, the unemployed college graduate, consider the outcome if Mr. Slowe had retained another grantor trust tainting power *other than* the right to revoke the trust. While the power to revoke means the trust is "defective" and thus a grantor trust under section 676, the power to revoke also means that the trust will be included in Mr. Slowe's estate for estate tax purposes under 2038 and that the transfer is not complete for gift tax purposes.

Alternatively, what if the tainting power retained by Mr. Slowe was the power to remove trust assets and substitute property of an equal value? Section 674(c)(4) says that this is a tainting power and, as a result of its inclusion, the trust is a grantor trust. However, this power in no way results in inclusion in the grantor's gross estate for estate tax purposes. See Jordahl v. Commissioner, 65 T.C. 92 (1975); Rev. Rul. 2008–22, 2008–16 I.R.B. 796; Priv. Ltr. Rul. 200603040. Moreover, the transfer to the trust is a completed gift for gift tax purposes. Assuming Mr. Slowe has already used his basic exclusion amount and the annual exclusion for another gift to the son, his gift would result in $40,000 of gift tax with a 40% gift tax rate. Hence, the gift would remove $140,000 from his estate for estate tax purposes.

Assume, too, that his son was surprised by a belated and sizeable offer from a corporation and that Mr. Slowe's only income comes from federally tax-free municipal bonds and dividends taxed at a maximum rate of 15%. The son's income tax bracket may well be greater than that of the dad and, thus, taxing the income *received by the son* to the dad, the grantor (rather than the son), as is required if the grantor trust rules apply may well produce an annual income tax savings; certainly it will result in a shrinkage of the dad's estate for estate tax purposes (because of the income tax he would pay on income received by the son).

CHAPTER 32

INCOME IN RESPECT OF A DECEDENT

(SECTION 691)

■ ■ ■

A. INTRODUCTION

Generally speaking, income in respect of a decedent (IRD) is taxable income received after a taxpayer has died. I.R.C. § 691. More specifically, it is income earned by the taxpayer prior to death but not properly includible on the taxpayer's final income tax return because the taxpayer was not eligible, for one reason or another, to collect the income prior to death. For example, if a salaried employee compensated on a monthly basis, dies on a day other than the last day of the month, she will have earned wages for the period of the month she worked but, in many cases, will be ineligible to receive those wages until the end of the month. Accordingly, if the employee is a cash-basis taxpayer (as distinguished from an accrual-basis taxpayer), the earned but uncollected income is not properly included on the employee's final income tax return. Instead, that income, known as income in respect of a decedent (IRD) for federal income tax purposes, becomes income belonging to the employee's estate. See I.R.C. § 691(a).

Other important illustrations of IRD are accrued vacation and leave pay, billed but uncollected fees, renewal commissions on sales of life insurance policies, lawyer's contingent fees, post death employer provided bonuses, distributions from tax-qualified retirement plans, and accrued interest on Series E and Series EE United States savings bonds.

It is important to note that IRD is subject to two taxes: the federal income tax and the federal estate tax. For example, consider the typical tax-qualified retirement plan. Established by an employer for the benefit of employees, subject to specified limits, the employer will be allowed an income tax deduction for plan contributions on behalf of employees in the year in which contributions are made. During the continuance of the plan, plan property is invested but no income taxes are imposed on the earnings of the plan property. However, distributions from the plan to the plan beneficiaries—usually the employee and the employee's spouse—constitute taxable income to the recipients of the distribution in the year of receipt. In addition, amounts that are included in the plan at the death of a plan beneficiary and become payable to the beneficiary's survivors are subject to federal estate tax at the time of the plan beneficiary's death. When the undistributed plan benefits—IRD—are paid to the survivors of the plan beneficiary, those distributions constitute taxable income to the recipients in the year of receipt.

The situation is similar with respect to accrued interest on widely held Series E, Series EE and Series I United States savings bonds. Interest accrues on each bond while it remains outstanding and, when it is surrendered, the accrued interest constitutes taxable income (unless the owner of the bond has elected to be taxed on the interest as it annually accrues on the bond, even though the interest is not paid until the bond is surrendered). If the bond owner dies before surrendering the bond, the accrued interest is subject to federal estate tax in the bond owner's estate and, when the bond is surrendered by the owner's survivors, the accrued interest—IRD—constitutes taxable income to the recipient.

A distinction should be made between items of income that are earned but not yet payable, which constitute IRD, and items of income that are earned and payable but not collected by the decedent at the time of death. The latter items are deemed to have been constructively received and are included in the decedent's final income tax return. An example would be wages that the employee could have collected before death by simply demanding them from the employer. Assume that an employee failed to pick up his paycheck when he left work—and died later that night. The amount of the paycheck is not IRD but income to be reported on the employee's final income tax return (and as an item of property on his federal estate tax return).

IRD is subject to both income tax and estate tax—but IRD receives no basis as a result of being included in the decedent's estate for federal estate tax purposes. I.R.C. § 1014(c). The recipient of the IRD is, however, entitled to a deduction for the federal estate tax attributed to the IRD as a result of the inclusion of the IRD in the decedent's estate. See I.R.C. § 691(c).

Similarly, items of deductible expense may be incurred prior to death but not be paid until after death. These items are not properly deductible on the decedent's final income tax return. To the extent that they are deductible for federal income tax purposes, they are referred to as deductions in respect of a decedent (DIRD). See I.R.C. § 691(b). An example would be real property taxes that become a lien on January 1st in many states but are not payable until the following January. A decedent's death during the year means that these real property taxes are deductible as a debt of hers for federal estate tax purposes *and* constitute a deduction as DIRD on the income tax return filed for the decedent's estate.

B. TO WHOM IRD IS TAXED AND BY WHOM DIRD MAY BE CLAIMED

Income earned by the decedent that would have been received if the decedent had lived is to be taxed to the actual recipient in the year of actual receipt, provided the recipient is entitled to receive the IRD under applicable state property law principles. The recipient may be the decedent's estate, a legatee, devisee, or next of kin. For example, if the decedent's executor collects renewal commissions due on insurance policies sold by the decedent prior to death but not payable unless the policies are renewed by the buyers in later years, the commissions, when earned and payable, are items of gross income to the decedent's estate. I.R.C. § 691(a)(1). However, where the estate administration has been completed and the decedent's property has been distributed, the proper recipients of the IRD are the decedent's beneficiaries. IRD is never reported on the decedent's final income tax return.

Deductions in respect of a decedent (DIRD) are allowed to whoever actually pays the expense, provided that person is obligated to make the expenditure.

C. WHICH RECEIPTS CONSTITUTE IRD?

1. VOLUNTARY PAYMENTS

ROLLERT RESIDUARY TRUST V. COMMISSIONER
United States Court of Appeals, Sixth Circuit, 1985.
752 F.2d 1128.

WEICK, SENIOR CIRCUIT JUDGE.

[Prior to his death, the decedent's employer, General Motors Corporation, had made a "tentative decision" to award bonuses to a group of employees, including the decedent, who was an executive vice-president. However, it was not until more than three months after the decedent's death that the bonus was formally awarded to the decedent. The taxpayer complained that the decedent had no legal right to the bonus at the time of his death and, therefore, the bonus was not income in respect of a decedent (IRD) "within the meaning of Section 691." In holding that the bonus was IRD, the court said:]

"Income in respect of a decedent" is not defined in the Code. However, the Service's regulations do provide a definition. 26 C.F.R. § 1.691(a)–1(b) states that, in general, "the term refers to those amounts to which a decedent was entitled as gross income but which were not properly includible in computing his taxable income for the taxable year ending with the date of his death or for a previous taxable year. . . ." More specifically, the term includes three categories of income: (1) all accrued income of the decedent who reported his income by use of the cash receipts and disbursements methods; (2) income accrued solely by reason of the decedent's death in case of a decedent who reports his income by use of the accrued method of accounting; and (3) income to which the decedent had a contingent claim at the time of his death. It is not clear from this definition whether the term "entitled" means legally entitled, as appellant contends, or whether it simply means substantial likelihood of receiving the income, as the Commissioner argues.

Our circuit has, on two previous occasions, attempted to clarify this definition. In Keck v. Commissioner, 415 F.2d 531 (6th Cir. 1969), the court held that "entitled", as used in the regulation, contemplated that the decedent was required to have a "right" to the income. However, the court failed to definitively answer whether this "right" had to be legally enforceable or whether the substantial likelihood that the decedent would receive the income would suffice. Twelve years later, in Claiborne v. United States, 648 F.2d 448 (6th Cir. 1981), the court was again faced with this issue. In *Claiborne*, the government asked the court to overrule *Keck* to the extent that it implied that legal enforceability was required. The court, in an opinion written by Judge Edwards, concluded that the decedent had a legally enforceable right to the income at issue in the case and, therefore, it need not address the issue of whether a lesser standard, such as the "economic activities'" test suggested by the government, would be sufficient. This issue is squarely presented in this case, however, because the parties have agreed that the decedent did not have a legally enforceable right to receive the post-mortem bonus.

The Second Circuit held, in O'Daniel's Estate v. Commissioner, 173 F.2d 966 (2d Cir. 1949), a case factually identical to the instant case, that as long as the decedent had provided services from which he had a reasonable expectation that he would be rewarded, any bonuses awarded subsequent to his death for those prior services would constitute income in respect of the decedent, notwithstanding that he did not have a legally enforceable right to the bonus. Other circuits have expressed their approval of this holding.

O'Daniel's Estate should be followed in this case. The key test for determining whether the decedent had a "right" or was "entitled" to the post-mortem bonus should be based on the likelihood, at the time of his death, that he would receive the bonus, not on his legal rights to it. The alternative interpretation "would permit parties to avoid taxation simply by failing to embody obligations incurred by reason of decedent's services into a binding contract even in situations where benefits were otherwise paid to discharge these obligations." Halliday v. United States, 655 F.2d 68, 71 (5th Cir. 1981). If Congress had intended such a result, it could have expressly adopted the legal enforceability test. Similarly, the Service could have done the same, through its regulatory powers, if it had believed that this was Congress' intent. Given their failure to do so, we believe it is unwise for the courts to impose such a requirement.

There was a substantial certainty, at the time of decedent's death, that he would be awarded a bonus for his work for G.M. in 1969. G.M. had consistently awarded bonuses to its executive vice-presidents and it had already made a tentative decision, even prior to his death, to award bonuses to decedent and its other vice-presidents for their 1969 labors. Accordingly, the decedent had a "right" to the post-mortem bonus, within the meaning of § 691, and the bonus, therefore, constituted income in respect of the decedent.

2. EXECUTORY CONTRACTS

Determining whether a sale is completed prior to death can often have significant income tax consequences. If the sale is not deemed completed, the property will assume a new basis equal to its estate tax value. Subsequent sale at a price equal to the new basis will result in no taxable gain. However, if the sale is deemed completed prior to death—because only ministerial acts remain to be performed after the death—taxable gain (or loss) will be determined by the basis of the property in the hands of the decedent during life.[1] Estate tax will be based on the value of the property at death.

In Private Letter Ruling 9023012, the IRS considered the following facts regarding an executory contract:

> A entered into a real estate sales contract containing a clause making the contract cancellable by either party if the buyer did not obtain a mortgage commitment within 45 days. The contract also provided that the contract could be extended in writing. A died before the mortgage commitment was obtained and within the 45-day period. The mortgage commitment was not obtained within the 45-day period, but the buyer and the executor continued to closing without extending the contract in writing.

The IRS concluded that the gain realized on the sale was IRD. In the ruling, the IRS noted that Treas. Reg. § 1.691(a)–1(b) included "income to which the decedent had a contingent claim at the time of his death."

---

[1] In Private Letter Ruling 9319005, prior to the grantor's death, a revocable trust entered into a contract to sell stock short, pledging the trust's own shares in the same company. The grantor died before the trust closed the sale. The IRS said that the proceeds of the short sale did not constitute income in respect of a decedent because "delivery of property is more than a ministerial act." In Private Letter Ruling 9436017, an individual, prior to death, sold stock short, pledging personal shares in the same company. The IRS concluded that, if death occurred prior to the closing of the sale, the proceeds would not constitute income in respect of a decedent, "since the delivery of property to close the short sale is more than a ministerial act."

In Keck v. Commissioner, 415 F.2d 531 (6th Cir. 1969), the court concluded that there was no IRD where, prior to the decedent's death, the decedent's corporation had: (1) contracted to sell its assets—a sale that required approval of the Interstate Commerce Commission; and (2) settled on a plan for liquidating the corporation after the asset sale. The decedent had even delivered his shares to an escrow agent before his death. In rejecting the claim that the gain was IRD the Sixth Circuit approvingly quoted Judge Featherstone who had written the dissenting opinion in the Tax Court's decision in *Keck* that "[t]he proper test for determining whether gain from the sale of property is to be treated as income in respect of a decedent is the status of the transaction at decedent's death, not who carried on the 'economic activity' which brought it to that status. . . ." Id. at 534. The Sixth Circuit further stated:

> It was further pointed out by Judge Featherston that at the time of decedent's death, his stock had not been converted to an item of income 'in respect of a decedent under section 691,' because of the fact that the sale of the stock was subject to a number of contingencies; that it was, at that time, subject to the approval of the Interstate Commerce Commission, a condition precedent which was not met until eighteen months after decedent's death, and that such approval was neither routine or perfunctory; that, at the time of his death, neither the decedent nor the other stockholders were contractually committed to the plan to liquidate the corporation; that . . . the majority stockholder, for reasons of his own, might have decided not to liquidate the corporations. . . .

Keck, 415 F.2d at 534. It should be emphasized that *Keck*, in rejecting use of an "economic activities" test, was joining the Fifth Circuit which had announced its position in Trust Company of Georgia v. Ross, 392 F.2d 694 (5th Cir. 1967), *cert. denied,* 393 U.S. 830 (1968), in these terms:

> Although it is pertinent to inquire whether the income received after death was attributable to activities and economic efforts of the decedent in his lifetime, these activities must give rise to a right to that income. And the right is to be distinguished from the activity which creates the right. Absent such a right, no matter how great the activities or efforts, there would be no taxable income under § 691.

Trust Company of Georgia, 392 F.2d at 695. The *Keck* court added:

> We agree with the United States Court of Appeals for the Fifth Circuit in holding [in *Trust Company of Georgia*] that the right to income, under the provision of the statute here pertinent, is to be distinguished from the economic activities that create that right and that, absent such a right, no matter how great the activities, there is no taxable income under Section 691.

Keck, 415 F.2d at 534–35. By way of contrast, consider Sidles v. Commissioner, 65 T.C. 873, aff'd mem, 553 F.2d 102 (8th Cir. 1977), which also involved the need to adopt a plan of liquidation.

> The *Keck* case is clearly distinguishable on its facts. Unlike *Keck*, the decedent, as Bi-State's sole shareholder, possessed the power to compel payment of the liquidating distribution, as well as the right to that payment, when he died. His right to the liquidation distribution was not subject to the many contingencies involved in *Keck*. The transaction was not subject to the approval of any Government agency; there was no other stockholder who could vote note to liquidate the corporation. The distribution made to the Estate of Harry B. Sidles, was clearly 'income in respect of a decedent' within the meaning of section 691.

Sidles, 65 T.C. at 882–83.

The following case addressed whether sale proceeds received by an estate from performance of a contract that was executory at the decedent's death that constituted income in respect of a decedent.

ESTATE OF PETERSON V. COMMISSIONER
United States Court of Appeals, Eighth Circuit, 1981.
667 F.2d 675.

McMILLIAN, CIRCUIT JUDGE.

This is an appeal from the decision of the Tax Court holding that the sale proceeds received by the estate of Charley W. Peterson from the sale of 2,398 calves did not constitute "income in respect of a decedent" under § 691(a)(1) * * *.

* * * The decedent, Charley W. Peterson, was in the business of raising and selling cattle. On July 11, 1972, he entered into a "livestock sales contract" * * *. Under the terms of this contract, the decedent was to raise and sell to the Max Rosenstock Co. "approximately 3,300 calves" at $0.49 per pound, with the date of delivery to be designated by the decedent upon five days notice. One group of calves (the Brown County calves) was to be delivered no later than November 1, 1972; the other group (the Holt County calves) was to be delivered no later than December 15, 1972. The calves were to be from three to eleven months old and in "merchantable condition" when delivered. * * * The risk of loss was on the decedent until delivery.

The decedent did not designate a delivery date or deliver any calves by the November 1 delivery date. * * * The decedent died on November 9, 1972. The estate (the taxpayer) assumed responsibility for the calves, designated several December delivery dates, and delivered a total of 2,929 calves, 2,398 owned by the estate and 531 owned by the decedent's sons, * * *. As found by the Tax Court, approximately two-thirds of the calves were in a "deliverable" condition as of the date of the decedent's death. The remaining calves were not "deliverable" on that date because they were too young.

The estate reported the sale of the calves on its fiduciary income tax return and computed the gain from the sale by subtracting the fair market value of the calves on the date of the decedent's death from the sale proceeds. The Commissioner, however, determined that the gain from the sale constituted "income in respect of a decedent" under § 691(a)(1) and recomputed the estate's gain on the sale by subtracting the decedent's adjusted basis in the calves from the sale proceeds. See §§ 691(a)(1), 1014(a) (basis of property acquired from decedent is the fair market value at date of decedent's death), 1014(c) (§ 1014(a) does not apply to property which constitutes a right to receive an item of income in respect of a decedent under § 691). The characterization of the sales transaction thus determines whether the estate uses the decedent's adjusted basis or a stepped-up basis (fair market value on date of death) in calculating the gain from the sale. The amount of income tax deficiency at issue is $185,384.10.

The Tax Court decided that the sale proceeds did not constitute "income in respect of a decedent" under § 691(a)(1). 74 T.C. at 641. After noting that § 691 does not itself define "income in respect of a decedent," the Tax Court reviewed the history of the section, referred to the applicable regulations, § 1.691(a)(1)–(3) (1981), examined the case law, and distilled a four-factor test for determining whether sale proceeds constitute "income in respect of a decedent": (1) whether the decedent entered into a legally significant arrangement regarding the subject matter of the sale, (2) whether the decedent performed the substantive (nonministerial) acts required as preconditions to the sale, (3) whether there existed at the time of the decedent's death any economically material contingencies which might have disrupted the sale, and (4) whether the decedent would have eventually received the sale proceeds if he or she had lived. 74 T.C. at 639–41.

The Tax Court concluded that the decedent had entered into a legally significant agreement to sell the calves on the basis of the livestock sales contract. The Tax Court also found that there were no economically material contingencies which could potentially have disrupted the sale; the transaction was not contingent upon the actions or approval of third parties. * * * Further, the decedent, if he had lived, would have received the sale proceeds; the transaction was not effective only at death. * * * The Tax Court, however, concluded that the decedent had not performed the substantive acts required under the livestock sales contract. 74 T.C. at 644. At the date of the decedent's death one-third of the calves were not in "deliverable" condition; all the calves required care and feeding until actually delivered. The estate assumed responsibility for the care and feeding of all the calves until delivery (for approximately one month). The Tax Court concluded that the activities performed by the estate were not perfunctory or ministerial and that these activities were sufficient to remove the sale proceeds from the scope of § 691(a)(1). Id. at 644–45.

On appeal the Commissioner does not disagree with the four-factor test developed by the Tax Court. The Commissioner argues that the Tax Court misapplied the test and that, under a proper application of the test, that portion of the sale proceeds attributable to the calves which were "deliverable" at the date of the decedent's death constitute "income in respect of a decedent" under § 691(a)(1). See 74 T.C. at 646 (Simpson, J., concurring). This argument was not raised below by either party. Ordinarily we do not consider questions of law which were not presented to the court * * *. However, in order to determine whether the Tax Court misapplied its four-factor test, we necessarily reach the Commissioner's apportionment or allocation argument. We think that the apportionment or allocation argument incorrectly emphasizes the condition or character of the subject matter of the sale instead of the status of the transaction itself at the time of the decedent's death. For the reasons discussed below, we affirm the decision of the Tax Court.

Stated in misleadingly simple terms, whether income is considered income in respect of a decedent under § 691 depends upon whether the decedent had a right to receive income at the time of his or her death. The focus is upon the decedent's *right or entitlement to income* at the time of death.

* * *

The leading commentators have proposed the following as a "tentative working definition" of income in respect of a decedent:

> Items of income in respect of a decedent . . . are payments received toward satisfaction of a right or expectancy created almost entirely through the efforts or status of the decedent and which, except for his death and without further action on his part, the decedent would have realized as gross income. Two observations should be made. First, the concept is manifestly broader than the mere accrued earnings of a cash basis decedent. Second, despite the breadth of this tentative definition, § 691 does not reach the income potential in a decedent's appreciated property, even if that appreciation is due to the decedent's own efforts. Further action on the decedent's part (e.g., a sale) would have been required for such appreciation to be realized as income. Within this definition farm produce inventories grown, harvested, and processed for market, but not delivered by the decedent before his death, even though they come very close to representing

ordinary income actually realized, are "property" rather than a bare right to income until they are sold. * * *

M. Ferguson, J. Freeland & R. Stephens, Federal Income Taxation of Estates and Beneficiaries 146 (1970) (footnote omitted). [In a footnote, the court quoted the following from Ferguson, Freeland & Stephens, Id. at 146–8, for purposes of describing the "four salient characteristics" of IRD:

First, the item of income must have been taxable to the decedent had he survived to the time the income was realized. This is to say, the income must have been attributable to his services, his sales, or his income-producing property.

Second, although the decedent must have become "entitled" to the income by his death, his rights must not have matured sufficiently to require inclusion of the income in his final income tax return under the accounting method employed by him. This return, normally filed by the executor, is prepared on the decedent's regular method of accounting without references to any items which might have become accruable solely because of death. . . .

Third, what is transferred at death must be a passive right to receive income, as distinguished from "property" entitled to a fair market value basis under § 1014(a). Although the gross estate for Federal estate tax purposes includes, along with all other kinds of property rights, the value of any rights to future income, §§ 691 and 1014(c) force a differentiation between income rights and other assets for income tax purposes. Here, too, generalization is difficult. . . . Regardless of the nature of the asset, § 691 applies only when the decedent performed all substantial acts within his control necessary to convert prior efforts or property into an intangible right to receive income.

Fourth, the recipient of the right to the income in question must have acquired it solely by reason of the death of the taxpayer who created it. This characteristic subjects income in respect of a decedent to two important limitations, each of which sheds further light upon the basic concept: First, § 691 presupposes a gratuitous transfer from a decedent at death of a right to income. Second, the ultimate proceeds must be received solely because of the taxpayer's passive status as the decedent's transferee of the specific right.]

* * * For example, items of income attributable to the decedent's services are generally income in respect of a decedent. Characterization of items attributable to sales proceeds, as in the present case, however, is less clear, particularly because of the operation of the basis rules of § 1014. Id. at 177–78.

> [I]t may be difficult to determine whether the decedent's steps prior to his death had proceeded sufficiently to treat sales proceeds received after death as income in respect of a decedent. The test here is not quite whether the decedent "closed" the sale or transferred title and possession of an asset before death. Rather, it is whether his successor acquired a right to receive proceeds from an asset's disposition on the one hand, or acquired the asset itself on the other. Depending upon the subject and the terms of a sale, death may interrupt the transaction at a number of stages which do not fall clearly on either side of this murky distinction.

Id. at 178–79.

As noted by Ferguson, Freeland and Stephens, "the definitional problem under § 691(a) is complicated by the general rule of § 1014(a) according to a basis equal to estate tax value to the decedent's 'property' other than such § 691(a) 'rights'." Id. at 180. As illustrated by the present case, the tax consequences of characterizing a particular item of income may be substantial. Ferguson, Freeland and Stephens apparently do not favor characterizing sales proceeds from sales transactions substantially "incomplete" at the time of the decedent's death as income in respect of a decedent:

> [W]here there is a contract of sale which would have been completed during the decedent's life but for his death, the proceeds received upon culmination of the sale by the decedent's transferee will be taxed as income in respect of a decedent if no substantial conditions remained to be performed by the decedent at his death. Thus, if the executor had only a passive or ministerial role to play in completing the sale, the proceeds should be taxed as income in respect of a decedent.
>
> . . . Whenever the decedent negotiates a contract enforceable by his executor after death, the profit may properly be attributed to the decedent's bargaining and other efforts, which would seem to suggest income treatment for a part of the post-death receipts. On the other hand, the basis rules of § 1014(a) suggest that, wherever the risks inherent in ownership remain with the decedent until death, adjustments to the property's basis (and hence variations in the amount of gain or loss under the contract) remain possible until actual disposition by the decedent's successor.

Id. at 183–84 (footnote omitted).

Here, the task remaining to be performed by the estate was performance of the contract. We agree with the conclusion of the Tax Court that performance of the contract, which, under the circumstances, involved care and feeding of livestock and delivery, cannot be characterized as a ministerial or minor act. However, we think that characterization of the tasks which remain after the death of the decedent should not necessarily depend upon the nature of the subject matter of the sales transaction. For example, the subject matter of the sales transaction in the present case was livestock, which obviously required care and feeding. What if the subject matter was not livestock but logs or refrigerators? It would still be the task of the decedent's transferee to deliver or otherwise dispose of the logs or refrigerators, even though that type of property does not require the care that livestock does.

We recognize that the analysis followed by the Tax Court emphasizes delivery or disposal of the subject matter of the sales transaction and, to a certain degree, discounts the significance of the sales contract. * * * After all, the decedent in a sales case does not prearrange his death in order to shift the responsibility for delivering the subject matter of the sale transaction to his executor or to take advantage of the fair market value basis rule of § 1014(a) and thus avoid the reach of § 691.

Accordingly, the decision of the Tax Court is affirmed.

NOTE

Revenue Ruling 64–289, 1964–2 C.B. 173, deals with farm crops. The decedent had leased two parcels of land and was due to receive a percentage of the crops grown on the land as rent. At the decedent's death, the crops had been planted but not yet harvested. Relying on Estate of Davison v. United States, 292 F.2d 937 (Ct. Cl. 1961), cert. denied, 368 U.S. 939 (1961), the IRS concluded that a decedent who used the cash-basis method of accounting and received or had a right to receive livestock or crop shares prior to death is to be deemed to have received income in respect of a decedent. Proceeds attributed to the portion of rent accrued after death to the end of the rental period are ordinary income to the estate. Livestock or crop shares received in kind as rentals and held by the lessor at the decedent's death and later disposed of by the executor are to be allocated between ordinary income and income in respect of a decedent applying the following formulas:

Income in respect of a decedent

$$\text{Proceeds} \times \frac{\text{no. of days in rental period up to death}}{\text{total no. of days in rental period}}$$

Ordinary income

$$\text{Proceeds} \times \frac{\text{no. of days in rental period up to death}}{\text{total no. of days in rental period}}$$

PROBLEM

Tammy sold the assets of three corporations she owned with the intention of subsequently liquidating the corporations. At the time of Tammy's death, the sale of the corporations was subject to a number of contingencies, including the requirements that: (1) federal regulatory approval was given for the sale; and (2) none of the stockholders was contractually committed to the liquidation plan. Before the approval was obtained, Tammy died. Eventually, the liquidations took place and the proceeds were distributed to the stockholders, including Tammy's surviving spouse. Tammy's spouse claims that, at the date of Tammy's death, Tammy was not entitled to receive any proceeds from the contemplated liquidation and, therefore, the amounts eventually received by him after Tammy's death were not income in respect of a decedent. Is Tammy's spouse correct? If so, does that suggest that the IRD test applied in *Rollert* (discussed above) is limited to cases where the payments are made in conjunction with employment?

3. SELF-CANCELING INSTALLMENT NOTES (SCINs)

An "installment sale" refers to a method of property disposition whereby the proceeds of sale are received over a period of more than one year. I.R.C. § 453(b)(1). Installment sale reporting is the default rule for income tax purposes in such cases unless the seller makes a timely election to treat the disposition as a noninstallment sale. I.R.C. § 453(d). One advantage of the installment sale is that the seller is permitted to recognize the gain on the sale as payment is received (rather than in the year of the sale itself). This deferral opportunity is often prized.

A self-canceling installment note (SCIN)—sometimes referred to as "death-terminating installment note" (because the death is the mechanism that triggers cancellation)—is not much different from a regular installment note except that the purchaser's obligation is canceled if the seller dies before the note is fully paid. Often the seller will receive an above market interest rate as a premium for including the self-cancellation feature in the note. Use of the premium is designed to eliminate gift tax on the transfer in as much the SCIN is primarily used for estate planning purposes. For example, where the seller dies before the note is paid, his or her estate is reduced by the amount of the canceled note.

It is obvious from the case that follows that the seller's advisors and the IRS have different views as to the income tax treatment accorded SCINs.

FRANE V. COMMISSIONER

United States Court of Appeals, Eighth Circuit, 1993.
998 F.2d 567.

JOHN R. GIBSON, CIRCUIT JUDGE.

In this case we examine the income tax consequences of an estate planning device known as the "death-terminating installment note." Janet Frane and the estate of Robert Frane, her late husband, appeal from a Tax Court decision holding that they were required to report income resulting from the cancellation of notes from the Franes' children upon Robert Frane's death. On appeal the Franes argue that no one should have to recognize income from the cancellation of the notes or, in the alternative, that if anyone does, it should be the estate and not Mr. Frane himself. We affirm the judgment of the Tax Court in part and reverse in part.

At the age of fifty-three, Robert Frane sold stock in his company, the Sherwood Grove Co., to his four children by four separate stock purchase agreements. Each child signed a note for the appraised value of the stock payable in annual installments over twenty years for a total principal amount of $141,050. Key to this litigation is the self-cancellation clause in the stock purchase agreements, which required the notes to provide "that in the event of [Robert Frane's] death prior to the final payment of principal and interest under said note, the unpaid principal and interest of such note shall be deemed canceled and extinguished as though paid upon the death of [Robert Frane]." * * * The notes so provided, and the Franes contend they also included an above-market interest rate (twelve percent) meant to compensate Robert Frane for assuming the risk that he would die before twenty years passed and thus not receive full payment on the notes. At the time of the sale, Frane's life expectancy (as determined from United States Department of Commerce statistics) exceeded the twenty year term of the promissory notes.

Frane lived to receive two of the installments, recognizing income on each installment according to the ratio between Frane's basis in the stock and the amount he would receive under the contracts if he lived the full twenty years. * * * § 453–1(b)(2). After Frane died in 1984, his children made no further payments. * * * In 1986, Sherwood liquidated its assets. Two of the children reported a capital loss from the transaction, claiming as their basis in the stock only the amount they actually paid for it (rather than the face amount of the note). The two other children did not report a gain or a loss.

Neither Frane's last income tax return nor the estate's income tax return reported any income resulting from the self-cancellation of the notes. The Commissioner issued a notice of deficiency. * * * The Tax Court upheld the Commissioner's position that gain was recognized upon Frane's death and the cancellation of the notes, but concluded that the gain was taxable to Frane himself, rather than to the estate.

The Franes' principal argument is that the automatic cancellation of the note upon Frane's death did not generate taxable income. This is an uphill battle, since the Internal Revenue Code specifically provides that "if any installment obligation is canceled or otherwise becomes unenforceable," and the obligee and obligor are related persons, it shall cause the obligee to recognize income equal to the difference between the basis of the obligation and its face value. § 453B(a), (f). A similar provision applies to estates, requiring "cancellation" of an installment obligation to be treated as a transfer of the obligation, which causes the estate to recognize income in respect of a decedent in the face amount of the obligation less its basis in the hands of the decedent. § 691(a)(2), (4) & (5).

The Franes argue that the automatic self-cancellation of the notes is not the sort of "cancellation" covered by sections 453B and 691(a)(5). The Franes first argue that the word "cancellation" does not, in ordinary usage, cover their death-terminating installment note, and second, they argue that since the code sections were drafted to prevent abuses that occur when an obligation is canceled by an act subsequent and extraneous to the contract, they were not meant to apply to cancellation resulting from an integral term of the contract itself.

The Franes contend that the word "cancellation" describes an action occurring "after the original transaction and independently from it." While we agree with the Franes that there is a distinction to be made between cancellation by act subsequent to the contract and cancellation upon a contingency pursuant to the contract's terms, the term "cancellation" can be used to describe both situations. To establish this we need go no further than point to the commonly used name for the very estate planning device used here: "self-canceling installment notes." * * * Most telling, however, is the use of the words "canceled and extinguished" in the Franes' notes. The Franes' argument is answered by the very words the Franes used.

As for Congressional intent, sections 453B(f) and 691(a)(5) were indeed drafted to prevent an abuse involving after the fact cancellations. In Miller v. Usry, 160 F.Supp. 368 (W.D.La.1958), a father transferred property to his son in exchange for an installment note payable in twenty annual installments. The father had a low basis in the property and the note was for a much higher amount. Id. at 369. The father later canceled the note. Id. The government collected income tax from the father on the difference between his basis and the unpaid balance on the note, but the court held that the father could only be taxed on the amount he actually realized from the sale. Id. at 370–72. The unstated result of the Miller case was that the appreciation of the property could never be taxed at all, since the son's basis in the property was the face amount of the note, even though the son had not had to pay the note. Thus, the father avoided recognizing income on the property and the son obtained a stepped-up basis in the property without paying for it.

To close this loophole, Congress enacted sections 453B(f), which provides that when an installment loan between family members is canceled the obligee recognizes as income the difference between his basis in the obligation and the face amount of the note. The legislative history makes it clear that this is the purpose of section 453B(f):

* * *

Under present law, some have argued that the installment obligation disposition rules can be avoided by making gift cancellations of the obligation or the installments as they come due. In other words, by making an installment sale and then canceling the obligation or a number of installment payments, it is argued that the seller will incur no income tax liability, but possibly some gift taxes, and the buyer will have a cost basis in the property sold although no income tax cost will have been incurred on the transaction. If a direct gift is made, the donee's basis is generally the same as the donor's basis rather than a "cost" basis which reflects future payments which will never be made.

* * *

The committee believes that present law should be clarified to make it clear that the installment obligation disposition rules cannot be circumvented by canceling the obligation.

* * *

The bill makes it clear that the cancellation of an installment obligation is treated as a disposition of the obligation. In the case where the obligor is a related party, the amount taken into account as a disposition triggering recognition of unreported gain attributable (sic) to the obligation is not to be less than the face amount of the installment obligation.

S. Rep. No. 1000, 96th Cong., 2d Sess., at 25–26 (1980), reprinted in 1980 U.S.C.C.A.N. 4696, 4720–21. The legislative history gives a similar explanation for section 691(a)(5). See id. at 26–27.

The Franes argue that sections 453B(f) and 691(a)(5) were not meant to apply to death-terminating installment notes because in such notes the actual price depends on when the obligee dies and the obligor's basis in the property acquired is thus the amount he actually paid on the note, not its face value. The Franes claim that the abuse addressed by the statutes is not possible with death-terminating installment notes, because there is no step-up in the obligor's basis in the property; consequently, there is no reason to adjust the basis on the obligee's side, as there would be in a gratuitous cancellation.

In addressing "Death Terminating Installment Sales," the IRS General Counsel acknowledges that generally a taxpayer may not increase its basis in property "to reflect obligations it assumed in acquiring the property which are contingent or indefinite." Gen. Couns. Mem. 39,503 (May 7, 1986). This reasoning would lead to the conclusion that the Frane childrens' [sic] basis in the property is the principal they actually paid. However, the memorandum concludes that the obligor of a self-canceling installment note has a basis in property purchased with the note equal to the note's face value. Interestingly, the General Counsel's reasoning is that since section 453B will tax the obligee on the amount of appreciation, the obligor should get the benefit of an increased basis. This argument is, of course, circular in our case, for the Franes have tried to establish that section 453B cannot tax the obligee because the obligor will not receive the benefit of an increased basis. The General Counsel's reasoning is nevertheless instructive, because the injustice the Franes complain of only occurs if the treatments accorded the obligor and obligee are inconsistent. The General Counsel's memorandum shows that the plain language of sections 453B and 691(a)(5) can be applied to make the obligee recognize gain, a consistent treatment can be afforded the obligor, and no injustice results.

Therefore, the Franes lose their uphill battle to adopt a specialized meaning for the word "canceled" in sections 453B and 691(a)(5), and we affirm the Tax Court's result.

Next, we must decide whether the income should be taxed to Robert Frane individually or to his estate. The Code provides that income in respect of a decedent which is not properly included in the decedent's last tax return shall be taxed to his estate. § 691(a)(1). "Transfer" of the right to receive such income by the estate would be a taxable event for the estate under section 691(a)(2). Section 691(a)(5)(iii) provides that "any cancellation of [an installment] obligation occurring at the death of the decedent shall be treated as a transfer by the estate of the decedent."

The Tax Court reasoned that the cancellation constituted a "disposition," which 453B(f) provides is taxed to the individual under 453B, rather than a "transmission of installment obligations at death," which section 453B provides is covered under section 691 and thus taxed to the estate. 98 T.C. at 3512.

This reasoning appears to us quite nebulous in comparison with the unambiguous language in section 691(a)(5)(iii) that cancellation occurring at the death of obligee shall be treated as a transfer by the estate, taxable under section 691(a)(2). This language covers the case before us. * * *

We affirm the Tax Court's decision that income was recognized on Robert Frane's death, but reverse the holding that the income was recognizable by Frane himself and hold that instead the estate was responsible for it.

NOTE

1. Has the SCIN lost any of its appeal as a result of *Frane*? And what of taxing the gain to the seller's estate rather than the seller?

2. When speaking of income tax considerations, it is useful to distinguish cases where an installment note is subject to a self-cancellation feature and cases where the installment note, unencumbered by a self-cancellation feature, passes to the maker of the note at the death of the holder of the note either by intestacy or under the holder's will. In the latter cases, while the previously unrecognized gain becomes taxable, the taxable event occurs only when the note is distributed from the estate to the maker. See Priv. Ltr. Rul. 8806048.

PROBLEM

Four years before his death, Doug sold certain farmland to Sam, his son, for $250,000, the fair market value. Doug's basis for the land was $50,000. Under the contract of sale, payment was to be made in 10 equal annual installments of $25,000 each, with interest on the unpaid balance. Prior to Doug's death, Sam made four payments, leaving a balance of $150,000. By a provision in his will, Doug canceled Sam's remaining obligation under the contract. What are the estate and income tax consequences of this transaction? See I.R.C. §§ 691(a)(2), (a)(5), and (c) and 2033.

4. TAX DEFERRED RETIREMENT BENEFITS

Income tax deferred property is the stuff of tax qualified retirement accounts and individual retirement accounts (IRAs). At death of the account owner, the value of the account is part of the owner's estate for estate tax purposes. See I.R.C. § 2039. In addition, the account's value is income in respect of IRD and thus subject to income taxation not later than when distributed to the account's beneficiary (to the extent it exceeds the value of previously taxed property that might be included in the account). See I.R.C. § 72. The amount of the estate tax is deductible for income tax purposes by the recipient of the account balance. I.R.C. § 691(c). In addition, amounts passing to the surviving spouse may well qualify for the marital deduction under section 2056.

REVENUE RULING 92–47

1992–1 C.B. 198.

ISSUE

What are the federal income tax consequences to the non-spouse beneficiary of an individual retirement account (IRA) of a decedent on receipt of a lump sum distribution from the IRA?

FACTS

A died owning an IRA. As of A's death, the IRA held assets that had appreciated since they were acquired by the IRA. Some of the contributions by A to the IRA had been nondeductible contributions. The designated beneficiary of the IRA was A's child, B. The entire balance in the IRA, including appreciation and income accruing before and after a's death, was distributed to B in a lump sum shortly after A's death.

LAW AND ANALYSIS

Section 1.691(a)–1(b) provides that the term "income in respect of a decedent" refers to those amounts to which a decedent was entitled as gross income but that were not properly includible in computing taxable income for the taxable year ending with the date of death or for a previous taxable year under the method of accounting employed by the decedent.

Section 408(d)(1) provides that, except as otherwise provided in section 408(d) (relating to rollover contributions), any amount paid or distributed out of an IRA is included in gross income by the payee or distributee in the manner provided under section 72. Under section 72, nondeductible contributions to an IRA are not included in the gross income of the payee or distributee.

Section 408(e)(1) provides that an IRA is exempt from income taxation.

Section 1.408–4(a)(2) provides that notwithstanding section 1015(d) or any other provision * * *, the basis (or investment in the contract) of any person in an IRA is zero. This regulation has been superseded by changes in the law to the extent that an individual does have basis in his IRA equal to his nondeductible contributions.

Section 691(c)(1)(a) provides that a person who includes an amount in gross income under section 691(a) is allowed, for the same taxable year, as an income tax deduction an amount determined by reference to the estate tax attributable to the amount included in gross income under section 691(a). Section 691(c) and section 1.691(c)–1(a) * * * provide rules for determining the amount of the deduction.

In Rev. Rul. 69–297, 1969–1 C.B. 131, an employee died designating his estate the beneficiary of his interest in a qualified profit-sharing trust. His interest in the trust, which included appreciated securities of the employer corporation, was distributed to his estate within one taxable year of his death. Rev. Rul. 69–297 holds that for the taxable year in which the distribution was made, the estate is required by section 402(a) to include in its gross income an amount equal to the cost or other basis to the trust of the employer securities (thus excluding any net unrealized appreciation in the employer securities), plus an amount equal to the cash and the fair market value of any other property received as part of the distribution, minus the amount of the employee's contributions. Rev. Rul. 69–297 characterizes this income as income in respect of a decedent under section 691(a), and holds that the estate is allowed a deduction under section 691(c) for that portion of the estate tax attributable to the inclusion in the decedent's estate of the distribution from the employee's trust. Rev. Rul. 69–297 further holds that the net unrealized appreciation in the securities of the employer is includible in gross income as income in respect of a decedent in the taxable year of their disposition by either the executor or the residuary legatees in a taxable transaction and that the transferor will be allowed the deduction provided under section 691 for any estate tax paid attributable to the net unrealized appreciation.

In Rev. Rul. 75–125, 1975–1 C.B. 254, a retired employee received from a qualified trust a lump sum distribution consisting entirely of securities of his corporate employer. The securities had a basis to the qualified trust of 5x dollars and a fair market value on the date of distribution of 10x dollars. Under section 402(a)(2), as in effect at the time of the distribution, the 5x dollars net unrealized appreciation in the securities was not taxed to the employee upon distribution. Following the distribution, the employee died leaving the securities to his surviving spouse. Rev. Rul. 75–125 holds that the net unrealized appreciation of 5x dollars attributable to the employer securities constitutes income in respect of a decedent under section 691(a) to be included in gross income by the surviving spouse when she disposes of the securities. Rev. Rul. 75–125 also holds that the surviving spouse is entitled to a deduction under section 691(c) for that portion of the federal estate tax attributable to the amount of the net unrealized appreciation included in the decedent's estate.

Amounts in A's IRA that were not distributed to A prior to A's death are not includible on A's final income tax return. If distributions from the IRA had been made to A prior to A's death, the distributions would have been taxable to A to the extent required under section 72. Upon A's death, the value of the IRA was included in A's estate and the entire balance in the IRA was distributed to B as designated beneficiary.

Under the above facts, the amount of the distribution that equals the balance in the IRA at A's death less A's nondeductible contributions to the IRA constitutes income in respect of a decedent and is includible in B's gross income for the taxable year in which B receives the distribution. The balance of the distribution, which represents appreciation and income accruing between the date of death and the date of distribution, is taxable to B under sections 408(d) and 72. In computing income tax for the taxable year of inclusion of the income in respect of a decedent, B may claim a deduction for any federal estate tax on A's estate attributable to that income in respect of a decedent.

* * *

PLANNING NOTE

Post death income tax deferral opportunities are sometimes available to recipients of tax qualified retirement plan accounts and recipients of IRA balances. For the most part, the complexities of qualifying for tax deferral are beyond the scope of these materials. Suffice it to say that, in specified circumstances, e.g., where the beneficiary is the plan participant's "designated beneficiary" (and not just "any" beneficiary qualifies as a "designated beneficiary," distribution of account balances can be made over the lifetime of the account beneficiary—and, in those cases, the account balance becomes taxable for income tax purposes only upon distribution to the beneficiary. However, using mandated "minimum" required distribution rules (MRD), a certain percentage of the account balance must be distributed annually and taken into income by the beneficiary in that year. I.R.C. § 401(a)(9)(B). A 50 percent penalty applies for failing to take the required minimum distribution. I.R.C. § 4974.

Having the plan benefits payable to the plan participant's estate at death is a likely "worst case" scenario for income tax minimization purposes (where tax deferral is viewed as "tax minimization") because the estate, while a beneficiary does not qualify as a "designated beneficiary," the effect being that all plan benefits, as a general rule, are subject to income tax in the year following death (in cases where death occurs after the plan participant's required beginning date (RBD). Traditionally, the RBD occurred once the participant reached age 70½. However, under the Setting Every Community Up for Retirement Enhancement Act of 2019 (Secure Act), for participants who reach age 70½ after 2019, the RBD is age 72. Moreover, under the Secure Act 2.0 of 2022, the RBD is 73 beginning in 2023 and 75 beginning in 2033. By way of contrast, tax deferral is sometimes possible even if the plan benefits are payable to a trust. Such deferral is possible when the trust beneficiary is recognized as a designated beneficiary, a status not easily obtained. Treas. Reg. § 1.401(a)(9)–4, A–5.

In the case where the beneficiary is the surviving spouse, the spouse can roll the account balance over into his or her own IRA and defer income tax until actual distribution (section 408(d)), distribution being required to begin in the year that the surviving spouse attains 72 (assuming the spouse attains age

70½ after 2019) using prescribed minimum required distribution rules. See I.R.C. § 401(a)(9)(B)(iv).[2]

From the foregoing, it should be clear that naming a qualifying "designated beneficiary" is critical to effective tax planning for plan benefits.

For a complete examination of these extraordinarily complicated rules, see Natalie B. Choate, Life and Death Planning for Retirement Benefits (8th ed. 2019).

5. OTHER EXAMPLES

Some part or all of virtually every annuity received by a beneficiary other than the owner-annuitant will constitute IRD. In Rev. Rul. 2005–30, 2005–20 I.R.B. 1015, the IRS said:

> If the owner-annuitant of a deferred annuity contract dies before the annuity starting date, and the beneficiary receives a death benefit under the annuity contract, the amount received by the beneficiary in a lump sum in excess of the owner-annuitant's investment in the contract is includible in the beneficiary's gross income as IRD within the meaning of § 691. If the death benefit is instead received in the form of a series of periodic payments in accordance with § 72(s), the amounts received are likewise includible in the beneficiary's gross income (in an amount determined under § 72) as IRD within the meaning of § 691.

Furthermore, the IRS said, in accordance with section 1014(c), the beneficiary does not receive a basis adjustment in the contract, and it stated that the beneficiary is entitled to a deduction under section 691(c), if estate tax was due by reason of the owner-annuitant's death. The result would be the same whether the beneficiary receives the death benefit in a lump sum or as periodic payments.

Rent and interest accrued prior to the decedent's death but not properly included in the decedent's final income tax return is also IRD. See Richardson v. United States, 177 F. Supp. 394 (E.D. Mich. 1959), aff'd, 294 F.2d 593 (6th Cir. 1961), cert. denied, 369 U.S. 802 (1962).

D. BASIS OF IRD

Section 1014(c) plainly states that section 1014(a) does not apply to provide a new basis for income in respect of a decedent. Nonetheless, in the following case, the taxpayer creatively invoked—for naught—the rules applicable to distributions from trusts and estates that appear in sections 661 and 662.

---

[2] As of this writing, Congress has not amended this section to account for the RBD of 73 set forth under the Secure Act 2.0.

ROLLERT RESIDUARY TRUST V. COMMISSIONER

United States Tax Court, 1983.
80 T.C. 619, aff'd, 752 F.2d 1128 (6th Cir.1985).

WHITAKER, JUDGE:

[Some of the facts are set forth at Part D(1). In addition, note that the right to receive the bonus installments became part of the residue of the decedent's estate, passing under his will to the Edward D. Rollert Residuary Trust. Both the estate and the legatee treated the distribution of the rights as a distribution of the estate's distributable net income even though the bonus installments would constitute income in respect of a decedent when paid. In the year the rights were distributed, the legatee reported as income under section 662 the date-of-distribution fair market values of the rights, and the estate took a corresponding deduction under section 661(a). Under Treas. Reg. § 1.661(a)–2(f), the legatee took the date-of-distribution values as its basis in the rights, and in the subsequent years when the bonus installments were paid to it, the legatee reported as income only the difference between such basis and the amount received.]

We must determine now whether the estate's distribution to petitioner of the rights to receive bonus installments in subsequent years gave petitioner a basis in these rights equal to their fair market values when distributed and whether such basis could be used by petitioner to reduce the income it received when the bonus installments were actually paid to it. This is a question of first impression.

* * *

In resolving this case, we must analyze the relationship between the rules of section 691 for the taxation of income in respect of a decedent and those of subchapter J, part I, governing the income taxation of estates. In general, the provisions of subchapter J, part I, are designed to allocate between the estate and its beneficiaries taxable income received by the estate, so that income will be taxed at only one level. For an estate that may accumulate income, such as Mr. Rollert's estate, this general allocation scheme is accomplished through the distribution rules of sections 661 through 663. Section 691 serves a totally different purpose. It is designed to deal with the problem of how to tax income that has been earned but not received by an individual as of the date of his or her death. Under section 691, income that has accrued to a decedent prior to death but has not yet been received is not included in the decedent's final income tax return, even though the right to such income may be included on the estate's estate tax return. Instead, the income is reported when received by the person who actually receives the income. * * *

Here, petitioner used the distribution rules of section 662 in an attempt to reduce the income taxed to it under section 691. In effect what petitioner did here was to report part of the payments of income in respect of a decedent as income under section 662, even before the payments were made by General Motors. When the payments were actually made in subsequent years, petitioner excluded the previously reported amounts from its section 691 income. Because the treatment of payments of income in respect of a decedent in this manner would completely undermine the mandate of section 691 that the recipient of such income report it for the year when received, we agree with respondent that petitioner had no right to reduce its income in respect of a decedent in the year it received the bonus payments by the amounts it had previously reported as income under section 662.

Section 691(a)(1) provides that the amount of all items of income in respect of a decedent shall be included in gross income, for the taxable year when received. This rule applies to income in respect of a decedent received by (a) the decedent's estate if it has acquired from the decedent the right to receive such income; (B) a person who has acquired, by reason of the decedent's death, the right to receive such income if the right to receive such income was not acquired by the decedent's estate from decedent; and (c) a person who has acquired the right to receive the amount by bequest, devise or inheritance from the decedent, after a distribution by the decedent's estate of such right. See also section 1.691(a)–2(a), * * *. In this case, subparagraph (a) required Mr. Rollert's estate to include in income amounts received with respect to those rights to bonus installments that it did not distribute to petitioner, and subparagraph (c) required petitioner to include those bonus installments that it received with respect to rights the estate had distributed to it.

Under section 661(a), an estate deducts in computing its taxable income (1) any amount of income required to be distributed currently and (2) "any other amounts properly paid or credited or required to be distributed for such taxable year." However, the total amount of these deductions may not exceed the estate's distributable net income. Under section 662, the beneficiary to whom these distributions are made must include in gross income a corresponding amount. Sections 661(b) and 662(b) are designed to assure that the character of the amounts deducted by the estate and taken into income by the beneficiary is proportionate to the character of items entering into the computation of distributable net income.

Petitioner and the estate applied the distribution rules of sections 661 and 662 to the distribution of the rights to receive subsequent bonus installments. With respect to each bonus right it distributed, the estate deducted the entire fair market value of the right as a distribution of its distributable net income. Petitioner took this same amount into income and used it as its basis in the right to the bonus installment. The character of petitioner's income was determined under sections 661(b) and 662(b) by reference to the character of the estate's distributable net income rather than by reference to the character of the bonus itself.

Petitioner treated section 691 as coming into play only when the actual payments of the bonus installments were made. It treated each bonus payment as income when received but only to the extent, if any, that the amount paid to it exceeded the basis it had previously assigned the bonus right.

Petitioner claims that the distribution to it of the rights to the bonus installments falls squarely within the literal language of sections 661(a)(2) and 662(a)(2) as "amounts properly paid or credited." Since the rights were irrevocably transferred to petitioner and had an acknowledged value to it at the time of distribution, which was taken into income as a distribution from the estate, the distribution appears on its face to fall within the ambit of these provisions. However, the terms "amounts properly paid or credited" would be excessively broad if read literally. Thus, these words must be interpreted in the light of the statutory framework and overall legislative objectives of subchapter J. * * *

In characterizing the distribution of the rights to the bonus installments as amounts properly paid or credited, petitioner placed particular reliance upon sections 1.661(a)–2(c) and (f), * * *. Section 1.661(a)–2(c) specifies that the term "any other amounts properly paid or credited or required to be distributed" includes a distribution of property in kind, which petitioner believes includes the distribution here of the rights to the bonus installments. Section 1.661(a)–2(f)(2) * * * states that, in determining the amount deductible by the estate and includable in gross income of the beneficiary, the property distributed in kind is taken into account at its fair market value at the time it was distributed, credited, or required to be distributed. There is no dispute in this case as to the fair market values of the rights on the dates of distribution. Section 1.661(a)–2(f)(3) provides that to the extent the fair market value of the property is included in a beneficiary's gross income, the beneficiary takes such amount as its basis for the property.

Respondent points out that the assigning of tax basis to the rights to income in respect of a decedent has enabled petitioner to escape income taxation on much of the income payable under those rights. In each year in which the rights to the bonus installments were distributed, the estate had distributable net income consisting primarily of bonus payments actually received by it in that year. The estate retained part of this income, but offset this action by distributing to petitioner rights to bonus installments that had not yet been paid to the estate. Because it treated the transfers of the rights as distributions of distributable net income, the estate's deduction for distributions of distributable net income included the date-of-distribution values of the bonus rights. The estate thereby reduced its taxable income by carrying its distributable net income out to petitioner, even though it retained much of the income it had received. Petitioner increased its income in the years of distribution by taking into income the date-of-distribution values of the bonus rights, in other words the discounted value of the future installments of income. However, by assigning basis under section)1.661(a)–2(f)(3), to these rights, its income was reduced by the same amounts in the later years when the bonus installments were actually paid, except with respect to two installments of stock which had declined in value between the date the rights were awarded and the dates the installments were paid, in which case the reduction in income was limited by the value of the stock when the installments were paid. Thus, for the bonus rights that increased in value between the dates of distribution and receipt, the net effect of the treatment of the bonus rights by petitioner and the estate was to reduce the aggregate taxable income of the estate and petitioner by the fair market values of the bonus rights as of the dates of distribution. For the two stock installments that declined in value during this period, aggregate taxable income was reduced by the values of the stock when paid to petitioner.

We therefore agree with respondent that the approach taken by petitioner and the estate allowed substantial sums of income to escape taxation. Section 691 and its legislative history evince a clear purpose to tax income in respect of a decedent in the same manner as if it had been received by the decedent. Allowing the escape from taxation suggested by petitioner would undermine this purpose. In this respect, we believe the following language from Commissioner v. Linde, 213 F.2d 1, 5–6 (9th Cir.1954), * * * is instructive:

> [T]here is nothing in the legislative history or in the text of Sec. 126 [the 1939 I.R.C. predecessor to section 691] to indicate that it was intended to be anything other than an improved device to accomplish the general purpose of the internal revenue code that all income should pay a tax and that death should not rob the United States of the revenue which otherwise it would have had. * * *

> * * *

> [I]t is our view that section 126 was but an improved method adopted by Congress in aid of its continuing effort to avoid the loss of tax upon income merely because of the death of the decedent who would have paid a tax upon the same economic returns had he lived to receive them.

Petitioner would have us accept its taking into income under section 662(a) the value of the bonus rights when distributed as satisfying the objective of section 691 to tax all income in respect of a decedent to the actual recipient of the income. Petitioner is correct that the overall amount of income reported by it under either section 662(a) or section 691 was similar to the amount it would have reported had it not treated the receipt of the rights to future bonus installments as distributions of the estate's distributable net income. However, as we have explained above, the aggregate amount of income reported by the estate and petitioner was substantially reduced by petitioner's approach since the distributions of the rights to future bonus installments were treated as carrying out to petitioner the estate's distributable net income. The estate thereby reduced its reported income and was able to accumulate funds, which could subsequently be paid out, tax-free, to petitioner, the residuary legatee.

For this reason, we do not believe that petitioner's reporting income under section 662 when it received the rights to subsequent bonus installments should be treated as satisfying the requirement that the recipient report all income in respect of a decedent. Furthermore, even if we were to assume that petitioner's treatment of the bonus rights and installments satisfied the requirement of section 691 that income in respect of a decedent be taxed to the recipient of such income, we see no way that it could also satisfy the timing and characterization rules of that section.

Section 691(a)(1) requires income in respect of a decedent to be included in income "for the taxable year when received." It is designed to defer taxation of these amounts until actual receipt. Were we to accept petitioner's view that its reporting income when the rights to bonus installments were distributed satisfied the objective that it be taxed on the income in respect of a decedent, it would be apparent that the timing rule had been violated. Under petitioner's approach, the only income deferred until actual receipt would be the excess of the amount received over the amount reported in the year the right was distributed.

Section 691(a)(3) requires the character of income in respect of a decedent to be the same as it would have been in the hands of the decedent if the decedent had lived and received such income. Here, however, only that income actually reported in the year of receipt as income in respect of a decedent took its character under section 691(a)(3). The character of the rights to income in respect of a decedent that were distributed was determined under section 662(b) by reference to the character of the estate's distributable net income. Thus, it is apparent that petitioner's approach would also cripple the characterization rule for income in respect of a decedent.

It is a well accepted principle of law that a specific statute controls over a general one even if the latter might otherwise appear to govern. * * * As we have explained, there is an apparent conflict between section 691 and the distribution rules of sections 661 and 662. In view of the nature of section 691 as a specific statutory scheme for the taxation of income in respect of a decedent, which would be largely defeated were rights to income in respect of a decedent allowed to acquire basis under the distribution rules, we believe section 691 must take precedence here.

Although the legislative history of section 691 and the regulations under that section do not specifically address the issue presented in this case, they do tend to support our conclusion that sections 661 and 662 should not be applied to an estate's distribution of rights to income in respect of a decedent. Example 1 of section 1.691(a)–2(b) * * * which illustrates the application of the general principle of taxing income in respect of decedent when received, involves a fact situation quite similar to that now before us. A decedent was entitled to salary payments in five annual installments after his death. The estate collected the first two payments and then distributed to the residuary legatee the right to the remaining three installments. The example states that the estate must include the first two installments in its gross income and the legatee must include the subsequent three installments in his gross income. This example does not even refer to the possibility of the right to the final three installments being treated as distribution governed by sections 661 and 662. If the distribution rules were meant to apply to distributions of rights to income in respect of a decedent, the absence of any reference to this effect in the regulation is incomprehensible.

The current rules in section 691 for the taxation of income in respect of a decedent are derived primarily from section 126 of the 1939 I.R.C. * * * The legislative history of that provision clearly states Congress' intent that amounts of income in respect of a decedent—* * *

> be treated, in the hands of the persons receiving them, as income of the same nature and to the same extent as such amounts would be income if the decedent remained alive and received such amounts. [S. Rept. 1631, 77th Cong., 2d Sess., 1942–2 C.B. 504, 580.]

At several points, the Senate report indicates the provision was designed to place the recipient of the income in respect of a decedent in the same position as the decedent with respect to both the amount and character of income. Nothing in the legislative history of the 1954 I.R.C., which introduced the distribution rules of sections 661 and 662, indicates any congressional desire to change the requirement that income in respect of a decedent be taxed in the same manner as it would have been treated if it had been received by the decedent himself. The decedent would normally report for tax purposes each installment as received, with the full installment being included as income. The provisions of the legislative history cited by petitioner do not indicate otherwise. All that these provisions are concerned with is the general rule of sections 661 and 662 that all distributions are deductible by the estate and includable by the beneficiary when distributed. They do not deal, however, with the question before us now of whether a distribution of rights to income in respect of a decedent is a distribution subject to sections 661 and 662.

Contrary to petitioner's contention, the changes made when the 1954 I.R.C. was enacted actually support respondent. * * * Congress extended section 691(a)(1) so that it applies to rights to income in respect of a prior decedent that are acquired by a beneficiary from a second decedent. As an example of how this provision works, the committee reports mention a widow who was entitled to receive insurance renewal commissions but who died before receiving such commission income. Under the pre-1954 law, the fair market value of the right to receive the commissions had to be included in the widow's final income tax return, even though she left to her son the right to receive the commissions. Congress explained that section 691 was being expanded so that no income would be realized on the transfer to the widow's estate of the right to income from the prior decedent. The commissions earned by the prior decedent should be taxed to the recipient upon receipt and their character determined by reference to the prior decedent. These results outlined in the reports under the post-1954 law could not be obtained if petitioner's theory were accepted, since petitioner would treat the distribution from the estate of the prior decedent to the widow as a distribution of a right to income in respect of a decedent, which would require the widow to recognize income and would create a basis in the right to receive future commissions. The rights to the commission income had necessarily been distributed from the estate of the prior decedent to the widow, and under petitioner's theory the widow would have reported the fair market value of such rights when they were distributed to her and taken such value as her basis in the rights. Nowhere do the committee reports even intimate that this might be the proper treatment.

We address finally petitioner's contention that its treatment of the bonus rights did not defeat the overall scheme of section 691 since section 1.661(a)–2(f) * * * forgives any income tax on the appreciation in value of property in kind distributed by an estate or trust. It is apparent that this regulation does cause the nonrecognition of some unrealized appreciation. However, there are several key distinctions between the nonrecognition sanctioned by this regulation and the situation before us now. First of all, petitioner has assumed that the difference between the value of a right to income in respect of a decedent and its basis can properly be labeled as appreciation. However, the right to income in respect of a decedent is the right to compensation income, which was already earned by the decedent and became nonforfeitable upon his death. This is simply income that has been earned but not yet reported, and thus cannot be seen as constituting appreciation in the value of property. Any increase in the value of bonus rights resulted from the fact that they were initially discounted because of the delay that had to be borne until the recipient could actually enjoy receipt of the income.

More importantly, petitioner's analogy to appreciated property is misplaced because it fails to consider that section 1014(a) generally allows a step-up in basis to the date-of-death valuation for property acquired from a decedent, while section 1014(c) denies a basis step-up for rights to income in respect of a decedent. Petitioner's approach would allow an escape from income taxation for all income in respect of a decedent represented by the value of the right to such income when distributed. This would have the effect of allowing a step-up in basis for increases in value of rights to income in respect of a decedent occurring before the decedent's death, as well as those occurring between the date of death and the date of distribution. Thus, petitioner's interpretation of section 1.661(a)–2(f) * * * sees respondent as having allowed by regulation what was specifically denied by statute under section 1014(c), i.e., a step-up basis to the date-of-death value for rights to income in respect of a decedent.

We hold as a general principle that section 691 overrides sections 661 and 662 and precludes the assignment of a basis to a right to income in respect of a decedent when that right is transferred by an estate to a legatee. Therefore, we find in this case that petitioner improperly offset against its income in respect of a decedent basis previously assigned to the rights to the bonus installments. Because the lifetime bonus installments were included in the gross estate, in computing petitioner's income tax liability relative to the contested bonus installments, a deduction under section 691(c) should be allowed for the Federal estate tax the estate paid with respect to the rights to these installments.

E. RELATIONSHIP OF IRD TO DISTRIBUTION RULES

In *Rollert*, the estate had claimed a distribution deduction for the IRD distributed to the estate's beneficiaries. However, the Tax Court refused to allow the recipients of the IRD to claim that the IRD had a basis for income tax purposes in their hands. Implicit in *Rollert* is the notion that the taxpayer acted improperly in claiming a distribution deduction pursuant to section 661 for the distributed IRD.

Similarly, in Estate of Dean v. Commissioner, 46 T.C.M. (CCH) 184 (1983), the Tax Court refused a distribution deduction under section 661 for the distribution of IRD, in this case, an installment note. In affirming *Rollert*, the Sixth Circuit stated:

> Accordingly, in the absence of § 691, the distribution of the bonus rights would have been governed by §§ 661 and 662 and the regulations thereunder.
>
> However, section 691 does exist and it specifically applies to the transaction at issue here—the distribution of income in respect of a decedent. Sections 661 and 662 apply to a wider range

of property interests, including income which would not qualify under section 691. It is a basic rule of statutory construction that a specific statute controls over a general statute. * * *. If we were to hold that the more general statute controls over the specific one, we would effectively eliminate the specific statute. Congress did not enact section 691 merely to have it subsumed by §§ 661 and 662.

752 F.2d, at 1133.

Thus, with the decision in *Rollert*, IRD joins specific bequests in being disengaged or exempted from the distribution rules of sections 661 and 662. See I.R.C. § 663(a)(1).

F. WHEN IRD IS INCLUDIBLE IN TAXPAYER'S GROSS INCOME

Generally, IRD is included in the gross income of the taxpayer in the taxable year it is received, without regard to the taxpayer's usual method of accounting. See I.R.C. § 691(a)(1). Thus, the decedent's estate or successor in interest is placed on a cash method of accounting with respect to the taxation of IRD amounts. The recipient's tax bracket (not the decedent's) determines the tax liability.

G. CHARACTER OF IRD

The character of the IRD to the estate or successor in interest is considered the same as it would have been to the decedent had the decedent lived and received the income. See I.R.C. § 691(a)(3) and Treas. Reg. § 1.691(a)–3(b). For example, David sold Blackacre on November 15, 2022. The terms of the contract provided that David would receive all cash on or before January 15, 2023. David died on December 15, 2022, however, and the gain from the sale was not properly includible in David's 2022 income tax return. Had the gain been reported, however, it would have been capital gain from the sale or exchange of an asset held for longer than one (1) year (and entitled to preferential income tax treatment under the rules then applicable to capital gains). Thus, to the extent the proceeds are received by David's estate or successor in interest, such income (IRD) would be long-term capital gain, because it is treated in the same manner as if David's estate or successor had held the property for the period David held it and had made the sale.

H. ALLOWANCE OF DEDUCTIONS

Section 691(b) permits certain items of expense that would have been allowed as deductions to the decedent had the decedent lived to pay them to be allowed as deductions to the decedent's estate or to the person who is obliged to pay them and in fact does pay them. These deductions are known as deductions in respect of a decedent (DIRD).

1. DIRD ALLOWED

DIRDs are allowed for expenses, interest and taxes under sections 162, 163, 164, and 212, for the foreign tax paid credit under section 27, and for the section 611 depletion allowance (only to whomever receives income to which the depletion allowance relates).

2. LIMITATIONS ON DIRD

The DIRD is allowed to the estate of the decedent except in those cases where (1) the DIRD is properly allowable to the decedent, or (2) the estate itself is not liable to discharge the obligations to which the deduction or credit relates. In the latter case, the items of DIRD are allowed to the person who, by reason of the death of the decedent, acquires, subject to the obligation, an interest in the property of the decedent, which is liable for these obligations of the decedent.

3. DOUBLE DEDUCTIONS

Section 642(g), which generally disallows deductions on both the federal estate tax return and the fiduciary income tax return, does not apply to DIRD.

Example: At Louise's death on July 30, 2022, the taxes imposed for 2022 on her real property by the city, county, and school district in which she resided had not been paid. Moreover, as of the date of Louise's death, the tax bills were not even required to have been mailed by the respective taxing entities nor, for that matter, was there any requirement that the tax rate for 2022 even be established by the respective taxing districts prior to October 1, 2022. However, under the law applicable in Louise's state—and in many other states—Louise's real property taxes for 2020 became a lien on January 1, 2022, even though payment could be made as late as January 15, 2023, without penalty. Accordingly, the real property taxes, when paid by Louise's executor, would be deductions in respect of a decedent (DIRD)—and would also be deductible on Louise's federal estate tax return as one of Louise's debts. See I.R.C. § 2053(a).

I. RELIEF FROM "DOUBLE" TAXATION

A right to income possessed by a decedent at death (IRD) will be included in the decedent's gross estate and will be subject to the estate tax. In order to avoid what may be perceived as double taxation, i.e., when the item of IRD is later collected by the decedent's estate or successor in interest, the recipient may claim an income tax deduction for the amount of the estate and inheritance taxes that were paid as a result of the inclusion of the IRD item in the decedent's gross estate. I.R.C. § 691(c). Similarly, any generation-skipping tax paid on an item of income may be claimed as an income tax deduction. I.R.C. § 691(c)(3).

The mechanics of the IRD computation are described in Rev. Rul. 67–242, 1967–2 C.B. 227, as follows:

> To determine the deduction allowable, it is first necessary to compute the net value of the items which are to be treated as income in respect of a decedent under the provisions of section 691(a). This net value is the value in the gross estate of all items of income in respect of a decedent, less the claims deductible for Federal estate tax purposes which represent the deductions and credits in respect of the decedent described in section 691(b).

> The estate tax attributable to such net value is an amount equal to the excess of the estate tax over the estate tax computed without including in the gross estate such net value. The recomputation of the estate tax to arrive at the latter figure is effected by excluding from the value of the gross estate the net value of all items of income in respect of the decedent. The difference between the estate tax and the estate tax as so recomputed is the total deduction allowed under section 691(c).

While this general statement of the arithmetic model is easily understood, there is disagreement as to the procedure for determining the section 691(c) amount when either or both the marital and charitable deductions have been claimed on the decedent's federal estate tax return. See Estate of Cherry v. United States, 133 F. Supp. 2d 949 (W.D. Ky. 2001); Estate of Kincaid v. Commissioner, 85 T.C. 25 (1985); Chastain v. Commissioner, 59 T.C. 461 (1972); C. J. Langstraat & A.M Cagle, Deduction Offsets 'Double Tax' on Inherited Income, 67 Prac. Tax Strategies 86 (2001). At issue is whether the marital deduction and/or the charitable deduction need be recalculated once the IRD has been removed from the value of the gross estate as called for by section 691(c).

A more detailed description of the controversy is beyond the scope of these materials, but it is worthy of note that, fortunately, the uncertainty that produces the controversy is eliminated in those instances where the governing instrument—the decedent's will or trust—earmarks the IRD either (1) as part of the property to pass to the spouse (in the case where the marital deduction has been claimed) or to the charity (in the case where the charitable deduction has been claimed), or (2) as part of the property to pass to the other beneficiaries. The ultimate choice of a final destination for the IRD is a function of *other* criteria, i.e., criteria unrelated to the section 691(c) deduction. That is, in earmarking the IRD during the will or trust drafting stage, both tax and nontax factors, for example, affect whether the IRD should be specifically earmarked as part of the gift to the surviving spouse that qualifies for the marital deduction or whether it should be earmarked as part of the share that is to pass to the bypass trust that the decedent has asked to be established after death for the benefit of the children. Identifying these factors, too, is beyond the scope of these materials. Suffice it to say, however, that earmarking, simply put, *should eliminate* the uncertainty—and controversy with the IRS (and possible) litigation that can result—when making the section 691(c) computation. Put another way, directing—or *earmarking*—IRD to a particular beneficiary or beneficiaries can be seen as a will and trust drafting consideration.

J. SERIES E, EE AND I SAVINGS BONDS

1. INTRODUCTION

Series E United States Savings Bonds were bonds sold by the government at a discount from face value. For example, a $25 bond was sold for $18.75. At maturity, the bond was redeemable at face value. Originally, Series E bonds matured on the 10th anniversary of the purchase date. Given the time to maturity, the rate of return on the original investment was not great. Accordingly, as interest rates rose and the American public became more sophisticated, sales of Series E bonds declined. To combat this decline, in recent years the Treasury stopped selling Series E bonds and began the sale of Series EE bonds, Series EE bonds being priced in terms of discount and time to maturity so as to make the rate of return on the investment more competitive. Currently, I bonds are also offered. Interest on I bonds are inflation adjusted. I bonds are sold at face value (without a discount).

The dollar value of outstanding Series E, EE and I bonds is enormous. More importantly, many of the outstanding E and EE bonds have been outstanding for 20–40 years. They were not redeemed because the government offered to extend the maturity date of the outstanding bonds and to continue to credit the bonds with interest. Thus, many of the outstanding bonds can be redeemed for an amount that greatly exceeds the face value of the bonds.

The maturity date on Series E and EE bonds will not, however, be extended beyond 40 years. (I bonds and recently issued EE bonds have maturities limited to 30 years.) For example, a bond purchased in May 1941 did not earn interest after April 30, 1981. More importantly, perhaps, is the fact that any unreported interest on such bonds becomes taxable on the 40th anniversary of the bond's purchase even if the bond is not then redeemed.

For tax purposes the difference between purchase price and the amount received upon redemption is taxable income at ordinary income tax rates. Taxpayers have the option of annually reporting for income tax purposes the interest income as it accrues, or deferring recognition of that income until the bonds are redeemed. Taxpayers also have an intermediate position available to them. They may defer recognition for a number of years and then report for income tax purposes all of the deferred interest in a particular year without redeeming the bonds. Once having elected to report the accrued interest on a Series E, EE or I bond, the taxpayer must thereafter report annually each subsequent year's interest accrual. When a taxpayer dies holding such bonds, important postmortem planning elections should be considered.

2.   SECTION 454(a) ELECTION

If the taxpayer dies holding Series E, EE or I bonds, their full value, including all accrued interest, would be includible in the gross estate. The accrued interest is also IRD. The executor of the estate may elect to report all interest accrued to the date of death as income on the decedent's final income tax return, or on the subsequent estate income tax returns. However, the executor is not obligated to report the accrued income currently (from the date of purchase through the year in which the decedent died). Instead, reporting the accrued interest for income tax purposes can be put off until the bonds are redeemed. I.R.C. § 454(a).

3.   TIMING

Assume a decedent dies this year on October 15. If the executor elects a short calendar year for the estate income tax return rather than a full fiscal year, the estate will have only 2½ months of income to report from sources other than Series EE bonds (e.g., bank accounts, cash dividends). By electing to report all accrued interest from the Series E, EE and I bonds in the short year, the estate can take advantage of what may be lower marginal income tax rates. See Rev. Rul. 68–145, 1968–1 C.B. 203.

a.   Later Recognition of Income

The election of section 454(a), once made, will require annual current income recognition thereafter. Because the tax attributable to such income may be substantial, the costs should be considered by the executor prior to making the election.

b.   Inclusion in Decedent's Final Return

The decedent's executor may elect to include all accrued interest from Series E, EE and I bonds in the decedent's final income tax return. For example, consider Melvin, a person of modest circumstances and modest income, all his income coming from his wages as a stenographer. If Melvin died this year on January 15, income for his final tax year would probably be insubstantial, as would be the tax thereon. Furthermore, increases in income taxes payable as a result of the inclusion of accrued interest on saving bonds in Melvin's return will increase the debt deduction on his estate tax return, if any. The income tax liability shown on Melvin's final income tax return is viewed as Melvin's tax-deductible debt for estate tax purposes. See I.R.C. § 2053(a).

c.   Distribution to Beneficiaries

Series E, EE and I bonds can be distributed to the estate's beneficiaries and reissued in their names. The beneficiaries can then dispose of the bonds and recognize all accrued income at that time. Alternately, the beneficiaries can, at any time before disposition of the bonds, elect to report all accrued interest not previously reported and pay the income tax thereon. I.R.C. § 454(a). In either event, the accrued interest income is not included on the decedent's or fiduciary's income tax return. The executor should determine which of these procedures, or combination of procedures, will result in the least income tax.

APPENDIX

ESTATE TAX RETURN PROBLEM

■ ■ ■

The following information can be used to prepare the United States Estate Tax Return, Form 706 (available at www.irs.gov.) for a hypothetical taxpayer named Melanie L. Rodgers, M.D., who died this year on April 14. Even without completing the estate tax return, you should explain the estate and gift tax consequences of the various transfers.

Melanie, who was born 70 years ago on April 1, had always been a United States citizen and, at the time of her death, was a resident of Massey City in Thorp County. Her address was known for street numbering purposes as 2036 Copulsky Way. Melanie died at the Massey Hospital after an illness of three weeks, her death certificate stating that cancer was the cause of death. Her physician was P.D. Quick, M.D., 2056 Lindblad Street, Massey.

Melanie's social security number was 209-06-1843. The Federal Tax Identification Number issued to her estate is 75-1234567. Her estate is being administered in the Thorp County Probate Court as Case No. P-9113.

Melanie's will was admitted to probate on April 30, and letters testamentary were granted on that day to her son, Cody Murphy (SSN 678-67-8901), age 45, as executor. Cody resides at 2033 Citera Avenue, in Massey City.

In addition to Cody, age 42, Melanie was survived by her daughter, Olivia Lewis (SSN 109-06-1879), age 40; Cody's 10-year-old child, Owen; Olivia's 11 children, ranging in age from 8 to 19; and Melanie's husband, David Rodgers (SSN 456-56-6789), now 84 years old. David and Melanie were married on April 2, three years ago, shortly after the death of Melanie's first husband, William P. "Bill" Murphy. Bill died on January 8, two years ago. On the estate tax return, the executor elected to allow Melanie to use Bill's deceased spousal unused exemption amount of $6,000,000.

In her will, Melanie:

1. Provided for a gift of $2,000,000 to State Ag & Tech Medical School; and

2. Directed her executor to divide the remainder of her estate into two separate funds, one fund to be known as Fund A and

957

the other as Fund B. Her executor was directed to allocate to Fund A "the smallest amount necessary to reduce the federal and state death taxes imposed on my estate to the least possible amount." The balance of her estate was to be placed in Fund B. Under the terms of Melanie's will, Fund A was to be placed in trust for the benefit of her husband, David, for life. During the continuance of the trust, David was to receive all of the income from the trust. Upon termination of the trust, the trust property was to be distributed free of trust to Melanie's grandchildren who were living at that time. As to Fund B, Melanie directed that the property allocated to Fund B was to be distributed free of trust in equal shares "per capita and not per stirpes" to Melanie's grandchildren who were living at the time of her death. Any state or federal death taxes payable as a result of Melanie's death were to be paid from the portion of Melanie's property allocated to Fund B.

At the time of her death, Melanie was a medical doctor under contract with Doc-in-a-Box, Inc., a publicly owned business offering walk-up medical services from kiosks located in shopping malls in a three-state area. The business address of Doc-in-a-Box was 2042 Bank Building, Massey. The taxpayer identification number of Doc-in-a-Box was 75-7654321.

The following additional facts have been developed:

1. *Gifts.* Five years ago, Melanie gave her son and daughter $30,000 each. At that time, the annual exclusion was $14,000.

2. *Investments.* Stocks and bonds, in Melanie's name alone, having a value of $8,990,000 were found in safe deposit box 231 at Granite Bank, Massey. The safe deposit box was jointly owned by Melanie and David. Treas. Reg. § 20.2033–1.

3. *Residence.* Melanie's residence was owned, according to the deed, by "David and Melanie L. Rodgers, husband and wife" which under state law created a joint tenancy with the right of survivorship. Melanie paid $40,000 from her separate property for the property in 1974 and took title in her own name, where it remained until she married David. At that time, Melanie signed a deed placing the property in her name and that of David. The property was valued at $800,000 at Melanie's death. See I.R.C. § 2040(b).

4. *Insurance on Melanie's Life.* Melanie was the insured on two insurance policies, both issued by HMA (Honest Merchants Association). The $1,000,000 proceeds of one, Policy No. 456456, owned by Melanie, were payable in equal shares to

her children, Cody and Olivia. The $1,000,000 proceeds of the other, Policy No. 678678, taken out and owned by her son, Cody (who worked as a merchant), were payable to Cody. See I.R.C. § 2042.

5. *Insurance on Lives of Others.* Melanie also owned $80,000 policies of life insurance on the lives of each of her children. The policy on Cody's life HMA Policy No. 123123, had a cash value at Melanie's death of $43,000 and the policy on Olivia's life, HMA Policy No. 345345, had a surrender value of $37,000. See I.R.C. § 2033.

6. *Claims Owned by Melanie.* After Melanie died, the executor of her estate received $20,626 from the Internal Revenue Service. The payment constituted the refund of Melanie's income tax overpayment for last year. Melanie had filed last year's income tax return prior to her death and claimed the refund at that time.

7. *Retirement Plans.* At her death, Melanie was receiving benefits from a qualified pension plan established by Doc-in-a-Box, Inc., for her benefit (and that of other employees). At the time of her death, the value of Melanie's account in the plan was $1,500,000. Under the terms of the beneficiary designation made by Melanie during her lifetime, the plan benefits continued to be paid to her husband, David, for life. See I.R.C. § 2039.

8. *Kids Trust.* Melanie established an irrevocable trust in 1983 and designated a trust company as the trustee. The trust, known as the Kids Trust, provided that the trustee could distribute income for the best interests, welfare, and happiness of Melanie's children. Melanie had the right to discharge the trustee and appoint herself as trustee at any time for any reason. Kids Trust was to terminate upon the death of the last to die of Melanie's children. Upon termination, the property constituting Kids Trust #2 was to be distributed to those persons selected by Melanie from among her grandchildren and their issue. In default of effective exercise of the power of appointment by Melanie, the trust property was to be distributed to Melanie's issue per stirpes. The trust corpus was valued at $900,000 at Melanie's death. I.R.C. §§ 2036 and 2038.

9. *Bill Trust.* Melanie's first husband, Bill, created a testamentary trust for the benefit of Melanie (which was referred to within the family as the Bill Trust). At Bill's death, his executor claimed the marital deduction for the property

then constituting the Bill Trust which, at the time, had a value of $4,500,000. During her lifetime, all trust income was to be paid to Melanie. At her death, the trust provided that Melanie could appoint the property then constituting the trust estate to one or more of her children (or to the exclusion of one or more of them), as she might designate in her will. Melanie exercised the power by designating her son, Cody, as the recipient of the trust property upon her death. At Melanie's death, the Bill Trust had a value of $5,000,000. See I.R.C. §§ 2041 and 2044; Treas. Regs. §§ 20.2041–3 and 20.2044–1.

10. *Mom's Trust.* Upon her marriage to David, Melanie established a trust to pay the income to herself for life, remainder to such persons, including herself, as she might appoint by her will. This trust was referred to as the Mom's Trust. While Melanie retained the right to revoke the trust at any time, it had not been revoked at the time of her death and had a value of $10,500,000 at that time. Treas. Reg. §§ 20.2036–1(a) and 20.2038–1.

11. *Texas Real Estate.* Melanie's brother, Jackson, owned real estate in Texas. When Jackson died, his will instructed that the real estate go to Melanie as a life estate and Melanie would have the power to appoint the real estate to whomever she wished during her lifetime (including herself or her estate) or through her will. If Melanie did not exercise the power, the real estate would pass to Melanie's children. At the time of Jackson's death, the real estate was valued at $700,000. In 2015, oil was discovered on the real estate, greatly increasing its fair market value. The property was valued at $4,200,000 at Melanie's death. Melanie never exercised her power of appointment. Therefore, the property was distributed equally to her children. See I.R.C. § 2041.

12. *Apartment Complex.* Melanie and her daughter, Olivia Lewis, bought an apartment complex in 2010 as joint tenants with the right of survivorship. When purchasing the property, Melanie paid the entire purchase price of $375,000, and Olivia did not contribute anything toward the purchase price. The apartment complex had a fair market value of $2,100,000 at the time of Melanie's death. See I.R.C. § 2040.

13. *Rozin Trust.* Melanie was a founding member of a closely held corporation named Rozin Inc. and owned 34 shares of the corporate stock with a value of $1,200,000. Melanie created the Rozin Trust and transferred the 34 shares to the trust.

Melanie was the trustee, and she retained the power to vote the shares and the right to pay the trust income to the children as the beneficiaries or accumulate the income and roll it into the principal of the trust. The principal was to be distributed to the grandchildren upon the death of her surviving child, Cody or Olivia. Melanie accumulated the income every year until her death, when the trust had a fair market value of $3,000,000. See I.R.C. § 2036.

14. *Expenses*. Melanie's debts at her death were funeral expenses of $25,000 and administration expenses of $30,000. In addition, the $6,200 real property taxes imposed on Melanie's residence became a lien this year on January 1, even though the taxes will not be billed to Melanie until October and will not be required to be paid under applicable state law until next January 31. Melanie's executor will pay these taxes next year when due. Treas. Reg. § 20.2053.

INDEX

References are to Pages